BRIEF CONTENTS

SEVENTH EDITION

Infants, Children, and Adolescents

Laura E. Berk
Illinois State University

Boston • Columbus • Indianapolis • New York • San Francisco • Upper Saddle River
Amsterdam • Cape Town • Dubai • London • Madrid • Milan • Munich • Paris • Montreal • Toronto
Delhi • Mexico City • Sao Paulo • Sydney • Hong Kong • Seoul • Singapore • Taipei • Tokyo

To Annie and Penny

Editor in Chief: Jessica Mosher
Managing Editor: Tom Pauken
Supplements Editor: Sara Harris
Media Editor: Beth Stoner
Development Editors: Judy Ashkenaz, Lisa McLellan
Editorial Assistants: Paige Clunie, Amelia Benner
Senior Marketing Manager: Wendy Albert
Senior Production Project Manager: Donna Simons
Manufacturing Buyer: Debbie Rossi

Cover Administrator and Designer: Kristina Mose-Libon
Electronic Composition: TexTech, Inc.
Interior Designer: Carol Somberg
Photo Researcher: Sarah Evertson—ImageQuest
Copyeditor: Margaret Pinette
References Editor: William Heckman
Proofreader: Beyond Words Proofreading
Supplements Project Management: LEAP Higher Education

Allyn & Bacon
is an imprint of

ISBN-10:   0-205-00881-X
ISBN-13:   978-0-205-00881-0

Laura E. Berk is a distinguished professor of psychology at Illinois State University, where she has taught child and human development to both undergraduate and graduate students for more than three decades. She received her bachelor's degree in psychology from the University of California, Berkeley, and her master's and doctoral degrees in child development and educational psychology from the University of Chicago. She has been a visiting scholar at Cornell University, UCLA, Stanford University, and the University of South Australia.

Berk has published widely on the effects of school environments on children's development, the development of private speech, and, most recently, the role of make-believe play in development. Her research has been funded by the U.S. Office of Education and the National Institute of Child Health and Human Development. It has appeared in many prominent journals, including *Child Development, Developmental Psychology, Merrill-Palmer Quarterly, Journal of Abnormal Child Psychology, Development and Psychopathology,* and *Early Childhood Research Quarterly.* Her empirical studies have attracted the attention of the general public, leading to contributions to *Psychology Today* and *Scientific American.* She has also been featured on National Public Radio's *Morning Edition* and in *Parents Magazine, Wondertime,* and *Reader's Digest.*

Berk has served as research editor for *Young Children* and consulting editor for *Early Childhood Research Quarterly.* Currently, she is an associate editor for the *Journal of Cognitive Education and Psychology.* She is a frequent contributor to edited volumes on early childhood development, having recently authored chapters on the importance of parenting, on make-believe play and self-regulation, and on the kindergarten child. She has also written the chapter on development for *The Many Faces of Psychological Research in the Twenty-First Century* (Society for the Teaching of Psychology); the article on social development for *The Child: An Encyclopedic Companion;* the article on Vygotsky for the *Encyclopedia of Cognitive Science;* and the chapter on storytelling as a teaching strategy for *Voices of Experience: Memorable Talks from the National Institute on the Teaching of Psychology* (Association for Psychological Science).

Berk's books include *Private Speech: From Social Interaction to Self-Regulation; Scaffolding Children's Learning: Vygotsky and Early Childhood Education; Landscapes of Development: An Anthology of Readings;* and *A Mandate for Playful Learning in Preschool: Presenting the Evidence.* In addition to *Infants, Children, and Adolescents,* she is author of the best-selling texts *Child Development* and *Development Through the Lifespan,* published by Allyn and Bacon. Her book for parents and teachers is *Awakening Children's Minds: How Parents and Teachers Can Make a Difference.*

Berk is active in work for children's causes. In addition to service in her home community, she is a member of the national board of directors and chair of the Chicago advisory board of Jumpstart, a nonprofit organization that provides one-to-one literacy intervention to thousands of low-income preschoolers across the United States, using college and university students as interveners. Berk is a fellow of the American Psychological Association, Division 7: Developmental Psychology.

FEATURES AT A GLANCE

CONTENTS

PART III

INFANCY AND TODDLERHOOD: THE FIRST TWO YEARS

CHAPTER 6

Cognitive Development in Infancy and Toddlerhood 202

CHAPTER 7

Emotional and Social Development in Infancy and Toddlerhood 246

MILESTONES: Development in Infancy and Toddlerhood 286

CHAPTER 16

Emotional and Social Development in Adolescence   598

MILESTONES: Development in Adolescence   640

CHAPTER 17

Emerging Adulthood   642

A PERSONAL NOTE to Students

My more than 30 years of teaching child development have brought me in contact with thousands of students like you—students with diverse college majors, future goals, interests, and needs. Some are affiliated with my own field of psychology, but many come from other related fields—education, sociology, anthropology, family studies, social service, nursing, and biology, to name just a few. Each semester, my students' aspirations have proved to be as varied as their fields of study. Many look toward careers in applied work—teaching, caregiving, nursing, counseling, social work, school psychology, and program administration. Some want to teach, and a few want to do research. Most hope someday to become parents, whereas others are already parents who come with a desire to better understand and rear their children. And almost all arrive with a deep curiosity about how they themselves developed from tiny infants into the complex human beings they are today.

My goal in preparing this seventh edition of *Infants, Children, and Adolescents* is to provide a textbook that meets the instructional goals of your course as well as your personal interests and needs. To achieve these objectives, I have grounded this book in a carefully selected body of classic and current theory and research brought to life with stories and vignettes about children and families, most of whom I have known personally. In addition, the text highlights the joint contributions of biology and environment to the developing child, explains how the research process helps solve real-world problems, illustrates commonalities and differences among ethnic groups and cultures, and pays special attention to policy issues that are crucial for safeguarding children's well-being in today's world. Woven throughout the text is a unique pedagogical program that will assist you in mastering information, integrating the various aspects of development, critically examining controversial issues, applying what you have learned, and relating the information to real life.

I hope that learning about child development will be as rewarding for you as I have found it over the years. I would like to know what you think about both the field of child development and this book. I welcome your comments; please feel free to send them to me at Department of Psychology, Box 4620, Illinois State University, Normal, IL 61790, or in care of the publisher, who will forward them to me.

Laura E. Berk

My decision to write *Infants, Children, and Adolescents* was inspired by a wealth of professional and personal experiences. First and foremost were the interests and concerns of hundreds of students of child development with whom I have worked in more than three decades of college teaching. I aimed for a text that is intellectually stimulating, provides depth as well as breadth of coverage, portrays the complexities of child development with clarity and excitement, and is relevant and useful in building a bridge from theory and research to children's everyday lives. Instructor and student enthusiasm for the book not only has been among my greatest sources of pride and satisfaction but also has inspired me to rethink and improve each edition.

The 18 years since *Infants, Children, and Adolescents* first appeared have been a period of unprecedented expansion and change in theory and research. This seventh edition represents these rapidly transforming aspects of the field, with a wealth of new content and teaching tools:

■ *Diverse pathways of change are highlighted.* Investigators have reached broad consensus that variations in biological makeup, everyday tasks, and the people who support children in mastery of those tasks lead to wide individual differences in children's paths of change and resulting competencies. This edition pays more attention to variability in development and to recent theories—including ecological, sociocultural, and dynamic systems—that attempt to explain it. Multicultural and cross-cultural findings, including international comparisons, are enhanced throughout the text and in revised and expanded Cultural Influences boxes.

■ *The complex, bidirectional relationship between biology and environment is given greater attention.* Accumulating evidence on development of the brain, motor skills, cognitive competencies, temperament, and developmental problems underscores the way biological factors emerge in, are modified by, and share power with experience. The interconnection between biology and environment is revisited throughout the text narrative and in Biology and Environment boxes with new and updated topics.

■ *Inclusion of interdisciplinary research is expanded.* The move toward viewing thoughts, feelings, and behavior as an integrated whole, affected by a wide array of influences in biology, social context, and culture, has motivated developmental researchers to strengthen their ties with other areas of psychology and with other disciplines. Topics and findings included in this edition increasingly reflect the contributions of educational psychology, social psychology, health psychology, clinical psychology, neuropsychology, biology, pediatrics, sociology, anthropology, social service, and other fields.

■ *The links among theory, research, and applications—a theme of this book since its inception—are strengthened.* As researchers intensify their efforts to generate findings that can be applied to real-life situations, I have placed even greater weight on social policy issues and sound theory- and research-based practices. Further applications are provided in the Applying What

We Know tables, which give students concrete ways of building bridges between their learning and the real world.

■ *The educational context of development becomes a stronger focus.* The home, school, and community are featured as vital educational contexts in which the child develops. Research on effective teaching practices appears in many chapters and in new and revised Social Issues: Education boxes.

■ *The role of active student learning is made more explicit.* The *Take a Moment...* feature, built into the chapter narrative, asks students to think deeply and critically as they read. Ask Yourself questions at the end of each major section have been revised and expanded to promote four approaches to engaging actively with the subject matter: *Review, Apply, Connect,* and *Reflect.* This feature assists students in reflecting on what they have read from multiple vantage points. And a new *Look and Listen* feature presents students with opportunities to observe what real children say and do and attend to influences on children in their everyday environments.

■■ Text Philosophy

The basic approach of this book has been shaped by my own professional and personal history as a teacher, researcher, and parent. It consists of seven philosophical ingredients that I regard as essential for students to emerge from a course with a thorough understanding of child development:

1. An understanding of major theories and the strengths and shortcomings of each. The first chapter begins by emphasizing that only knowledge of multiple theories can do justice to the richness of child development. As I take up each age period and domain of development, I present a variety of theoretical perspectives, indicate how each highlights previously overlooked facets of development, and discuss research that evaluates it. Consideration of contrasting theories also serves as the context for an evenhanded analysis of many controversial issues.

2. An appreciation of research strategies for investigating child development. To evaluate theories, students must have a firm grounding in research methods and designs. In addition to a special section in Chapter 1 covering research strategies, throughout the book numerous studies are discussed in sufficient detail for students to use what they have learned to critically assess the findings, conclusions, and implications of research.

3. Knowledge of both the sequence of child development and the processes that underlie it. Students are provided with a description of the organized sequence of development along with processes of change. An understanding of process—how complex interactions of biological and environmental events produce development—has been the focus of most recent research. Accordingly, the text reflects this emphasis. But new information about the timetable of change has also emerged. In many ways, children have proved to be far more competent than they were believed to be in the past. Current evidence on the sequence and timing of development, along with its implications for process, is presented throughout the book.

4. *An appreciation of the impact of context and culture on child development.* A wealth of research indicates that children live in rich physical and social contexts that affect all domains of development. In each chapter, students travel to distant parts of the world as I review a growing body of cross-cultural evidence. The text narrative also discusses many findings on socioeconomically and ethnically diverse children within the United States and on children with varying abilities and disabilities. Besides highlighting the role of immediate settings, such as family, neighborhood, and school, I make a concerted effort to underscore the impact of larger social structures—societal values, laws, and government programs—on children's well-being.

5. *An understanding of the joint contributions of biology and environment to development.* The field recognizes more powerfully than ever before the joint roles of hereditary/constitutional and environmental factors—that these contributions to development combine in complex ways and cannot be separated in a simple manner. Numerous examples of how biological dispositions can be maintained as well as transformed by social contexts are presented throughout the book.

6. *A sense of the interdependency of all domains of development—physical, cognitive, emotional, and social.* Every chapter takes an integrated approach to understanding children. I show how physical, cognitive, emotional, and social development are interwoven. Within the text narrative and in a special series of Ask Yourself *Connect* questions at the end of major sections, students are referred to other sections of the book to deepen their grasp of relationships among various aspects of change.

7. *An appreciation of the interrelatedness of theory, research, and applications.* Throughout this book, I emphasize that theories of child development and the research stimulated by them provide the foundation for sound, effective practices with children. The links among theory, research, and applications are reinforced by an organizational format in which theory and research are presented first, followed by practical implications. In addition, a current focus in the field—harnessing child development knowledge to shape social policies that support children's needs—is reflected in every chapter. The text addresses the current condition of children in the United States and around the world and shows how theory and research have combined with public interest to spark successful interventions.

Text Organization

I have chosen a chronological organization for this text. The chronological approach assists students in thoroughly understanding each age period. It also eases the task of integrating the various domains of development because each is discussed in close proximity. At the same time, a chronologically organized book requires that theories covering several age periods be presented piecemeal. This creates a challenge for students, who must link the various parts together. To assist with this task, I frequently remind students of important earlier achievements before discussing new developments, referring back to related sections with page references. Also, chapters devoted to the same topic (for example, cognitive development) are similarly organized, making it easier for students to draw connections across age periods and construct an overall view of developmental change.

New Coverage in the Seventh Edition

Child development is a fascinating and ever-changing field, with constantly emerging new discoveries and refinements in existing knowledge. The seventh edition represents this burgeoning contemporary literature, with more than 1,500 new citations. Cutting-edge topics throughout the text underscore the book's major themes. Here is a sampling:

■ **CHAPTER 1** ■ Introduction to the concept of plasticity in development • Updated Biology and Environment box on resilience • New, applied examples of the contributions of behaviorism and social learning theory • Revised and updated section on developmental cognitive neuroscience as a new area of investigation • New examples of research using systematic observation, structured interviews, correlational design, and field experimentation • Updated Cultural Influences box on immigrant youths • Expanded discussion of ethics, including informed consent and the use of deception in research with children

■ **CHAPTER 2** ■ Updated Social Issues: Health box on the pros and cons of reproductive technologies • Updated section on development of adopted children • Enhanced attention to the impact of poverty on development • Expanded introduction to family influences on development, including the importance of coparenting • Updated research on neighborhood influences on children's physical and mental health • Updated section on public policies and child development, including current statistics on the condition of children and families in the United States compared with other Western nations • Expanded section and a new Biology and Environment box on epigenesis, including examples of environmental influences on gene expression

■ **CHAPTER 3** ■ New findings on family size and parenting quality • Updated research on fetal sensory and behavioral capacities • Updated Biology and Environment box on the prenatal environment and health in later life • Expanded and updated consideration of a wide range of teratogens • New evidence on the long-term consequences of emotional stress during pregnancy • New findings on older maternal age and prenatal and birth complications • New Biology and Environment box on prenatal iron deficiency, brain development, and memory impairments in infants of diabetic mothers • New Social Issues: Health box on the Nurse–Family Partnership—reducing maternal stress and enhancing child development through social support

■ **CHAPTER 4** ■ Role of placental *corticotrophin-releasing hormone (CRH)* in initiating labor • Updated evidence on the contributions of doula support during childbirth to the birth process and to newborn adjustment • Updated research on the impact of medical interventions on childbirth and on maternal and infant health and postbirth adjustment • New findings on preterm and low-birth-weight infants, including interventions that foster development • Expanded and updated Social Issues box on health care and other policies for parents and newborn babies • New findings on the roles of impaired brain functioning and of maternal smoking and drug abuse in sudden infant death syndrome (SIDS) • New research on the impact of "proximal care"—extensive holding of young babies—in reducing infant crying • Updated research on touch sensitivity in newborns, including techniques for reducing infant stress to painful medical procedures • New research on factors that affect adjustment to new parenthood, including marital quality and partner support • Updated Biology and Environment box on both maternal and paternal depression, including postpartum depression, on child development

■ **CHAPTER 5** ■ Expanded consideration of major methods of assessing brain functioning, including the EEG geodesic sensor net (GSN) and near-infrared spectroscopy (NIRS) • New research on children adopted from Romanian orphanages, including neurophysiological evidence, bearing on the question of whether infancy is a sensitive period of development • Updated Cultural Influences box on cultural variation in infant sleeping arrangements • Updated section on breastfeeding • New section on infants with faltering growth, highlighting the joint contributions of a disturbed parent–infant relationship and feeding difficulties • Expanded and updated section on newborn imitation, including evidence on mirror neurons • New dynamic systems research on development of walking and reaching • Updated evidence on how environmental factors, including caregiving practices and the baby's physical surroundings, contribute to development of motor skills • Enhanced attention to cultural variations in motor development • New research on development of object perception, including the role of object manipulation • Expanded and updated section on intermodal perception, including its contributions to all aspects of psychological development

■ **CHAPTER 6** ■ New evidence on babies' gradual mastery of object permanence, as indicated by object-hiding tasks • Revised and updated section on infant and toddler imitation, revealing toddlers' ability to infer others' intentions • New section on symbolic understanding, including toddlers' developing grasp of words and pictures as symbolic tools • New Social Issues: Education box on baby learning from TV and video, including discussion of the video deficit effect • Updated Cultural Influences box on social origins of make-believe play • Expanded sections on development of attention memory • Revised and updated section on categorization, including various explanations of babies' remarkable categorization skills • Updated section on infant and toddler child care • New findings on the importance of caregiver responsiveness to infant babbling • New evidence on babies' joint attention and preverbal gestures • Updated research on babies' first words

■ **CHAPTER 7** ■ New findings on the early emergence of self-conscious emotions • Updated evidence on parental influences on early development of emotional self-regulation • New research on consequences of effortful control for development • New findings on emergence of an internal working model in the second year • Updated evidence on contextual factors that contribute to changes in attachment pattern over time • Revised and updated section on early caregiving for attachment security, processing of emotion, and adjustment, highlighting studies of children adopted from Eastern European orphanages • New findings on the joint contributions of infant temperament and parenting to disorganized/disoriented attachment • Updated research on extensive early exposure to child care and externalizing behavior problems • New evidence on contributions of fathers' play to attachment security and emotional and social development • Updated survey research on employed fathers' involvement in caregiving • Updated section on grandparents as primary caregivers • New research on contributions of parental sensitivity in toddlerhood to social competence in early childhood • New evidence on development of explicit body self-awareness, including scale errors • New research on cultural influences on early self-development • New findings on active resistance to parents in toddlerhood as a sign of healthy self-assertion and autonomy

■ **CHAPTER 8** ■ Updated consideration of advances in brain development in early childhood, with special attention to the prefrontal cortex and the amygdala • Updated evidence on the health of young U.S. children, including tooth decay, childhood immunizations, and overall health status • New research on development of handedness • Enhanced consideration of hormonal influences on physical growth, including insulin-like growth factor 1 (IGF-1) • New research on ethnic variations in early childhood sleep habits and problems • Expanded attention to the impact of adult mealtime practices on children's eating behavior • New findings on the contribution of child temperament, parenting practices, and societal conditions to unintentional injury in early childhood • Revised and updated Cultural Influences box on child health care in the United States compared with other Western nations, including implications of the U.S. Patient Protection and Affordable Care Act

■ **CHAPTER 9** ■ New evidence on preschoolers' magical beliefs • Updated evidence on preschoolers' grasp of the animate–inanimate distinction • New Social Issues: Education box on children's questions as a catalyst for cognitive development • Updated research on development of attention, highlighting gains in inhibition • New research on Tools of the Mind, a preschool program inspired by Vygotsky's theory • Enhanced discussion of development of autobiographical memory, including cultural variations • New evidence on cognitive attainments and social experiences that contribute to mastery of false belief • Updated Biology and Environment box on "mindblindness" and autism • Enhanced discussion of SES differences in emergent literacy and math knowledge, including interventions that reduce the SES gap in kindergarten readiness • Findings of the Head Start Impact Study, including follow-up at end of first grade • Updated discussion of educational media, including effects of television and computers on academic learning and social experiences • Expanded and updated research on the diverse strategies preschoolers use to figure out word meanings

■ **CHAPTER 10** ■ New evidence on preschoolers' emerging grasp of personality traits • New findings on the contribution of parent–child conversations about the past to early self-concept • New evidence on the contribution of attachment to parent–child narratives about emotions • Updated consideration of emotional self-regulation in early childhood, including the influence of temperament and parenting • Enhanced Cultural Influences box on ethnic differences in the consequences of physical punishment • New section on the role of positive peer relations in school readiness • New evidence on interventions for enhancing preschoolers' social problem solving • New longitudinal findings on the relationship of early corporal punishment to later behavior problems • Updated research on aggression, including proactive and reactive forms • New section on social information-processing deficits of aggressive children • New section on cultural variations in communication within gender-segregated peer groups • New findings on the harmful impact of parental psychological control on children's adjustment • Updated consideration of consequences of child maltreatment, including new evidence on central nervous system damage

■ **CHAPTER 11** ■ Updated coverage of brain development in middle childhood and gains in efficient, flexible, and adaptive information processing • Revised and updated section on overweight and obesity, including contributing factors and consequences • Updated evidence on outcomes of participation in youth sports programs • Updated statistics on physical activity and fitness among U.S. school-age children

■ **CHAPTER 12** ■ Revised and updated Biology and Environment box on children with attention-deficit hyperactivity disorder • Enhanced discussion of school-age children's spatial reasoning, with special attention to map skills • New research on development of planning in middle childhood • Updated evidence on the school-age child's theory of mind • Expanded treatment of cultural influences on mathematical development • Updated Social Issues: Education box on emotional intelligence • Enhanced discussion of dynamic assessment, with implications for ethnic minority children's test performance • New evidence on how culturally acquired knowledge affects reasoning on mental test items • Attention to the educational impact of the U.S. No Child Left Behind Act • Updated research on academic achievement of children with limited English proficiency in U.S. schools • Expanded consideration of the effects of biased teacher judgments on ethnic minority children's academic achievement • New research on the educational consequences of SES and ethnic segregation in American schools • New Social Issues box on magnet schools as a means of attaining equal access to high-quality education • Expanded treatment of the impact of computer and Internet use on academic learning • Revised and updated section on U.S. academic achievement in international perspective

■ **CHAPTER 13** ■ Enhanced attention to cultural variations in school-age children's self-concepts • New research on the impact

of gender-stereotyped expectations on self-esteem • Updated findings on parenting practices and children's achievement-related attributions • Updated research on cultural variations in children's moral judgments of truthfulness and lying • Updated evidence on school-age children's grasp of individual rights • Enhanced section on development of racial and ethnic prejudice and strategies for reducing children's prejudices • Updated findings on development of flexible gender attitudes in middle childhood • Consideration of the contemporary debate over how best to help children who feel gender atypical • Expanded attention to the role of fathers in children's development, with special attention to blended families and dual-career families • New evidence on the impact of self-care and after-school programs on school-age children's adjustment • New findings on children's eyewitness testimony, including factors that contribute to children's suggestibility

■ **CHAPTER 14** ■ Updated evidence on adolescent physical activity and sports participation • New evidence on adolescent brain development, with implications for teenage emotional reactivity, reward seeking, and risk taking • New research on contributions of early family experiences to timing of puberty • Updated findings on adolescent traffic fatalities and the protective role of graduated licensing laws • New research on media exposure to sexual content and teenage sexual activity • Updated evidence on contextual factors affecting long-term adjustment of adolescent parents and their children • New research on teenage parenthood prevention and intervention strategies • New findings on key elements of effective sex education programs, including recent evaluations of U.S. abstinence education

■ **CHAPTER 15** ■ Expanded and updated research on adolescent decision making • Updated evidence on consequences of personal-fable ideation in adolescence • Updated consideration of factors contributing to sex differences in verbal, mathematical, and spatial abilities • New research on the impact of school transitions on adolescent adjustment • New findings on peer influences on adolescents' school achievement • New Social Issues: Education box on the impact of "media multitasking" on attention and learning • Updated Social Issues: Education box on high-stakes testing • Updated discussion of factors contributing to dropping out of school • New evidence on the impact of teachers on vocational choice • Updated consideration of sex differences in career aspirations and attainment

■ **CHAPTER 16** ■ Enhanced section on development of self-esteem in adolescence • Updated Cultural Influences box on identity development among ethnic minority youths • New research on the impact of parenting practices and peer interaction on adolescents' moral reasoning • Expanded evaluation of Kohlberg's stages, including issues raised by a pragmatic approach to moral development • Enhanced consideration of factors that promote moral self-relevance • Updated Social Issues: Education box on development of civic responsibility • New evidence on gender intensification in adolescence • Updated section on parenting and adolescent autonomy • New findings on cultural influences on sibling interactions • New research on characteristics of adolescent friendships, including implications of other-sex friends for adjustment • New findings on Internet friendships, with special attention to teenagers' use of social networking sites • Updated section on dating • New research on cultural variations in adolescent depression, with special attention to China • New evidence on adolescent conformity to peer pressure • Updated findings on adolescent suicide, including the role of cultural disintegration in high suicide rates among Native American youths

■ **CHAPTER 17** ■ New cultural influences box addressing the controversy over whether emerging adulthood really is a distinct period of development • New research on brain development in emerging adulthood • Updated evidence on use of dating websites and other online venues for meeting romantic partners • Current evidence on the debate over whether today's young people forge self-centered worldviews • Updated findings on U.S. college students' community service and political engagement • Enhanced consideration of parenting and adjustment in emerging adulthood, including findings on parental overprotection and psychological control

Pedagogical Features

Maintaining a highly accessible writing style—one that is lucid and engaging without being simplistic—continues to be one of my major goals. I frequently converse with students, encouraging them to relate what they read to their own lives. In doing so, I hope to make the study of child development involving and pleasurable.

CHAPTER INTRODUCTIONS AND VIGNETTES ABOUT CHILDREN To provide a helpful preview of chapter content, I include an outline and overview in each chapter introduction. To help students construct a clear image of development and to enliven the text narrative, each chronological age division is unified by case examples woven throughout that set of chapters. For example, within the infancy and toddlerhood section, we'll look in on three children, observe dramatic changes and striking individual differences, and address the impact of family background, child-rearing practices, and parents' and children's life experiences on development. Besides a set of main characters, many additional vignettes offer vivid examples of development among children and adolescents.

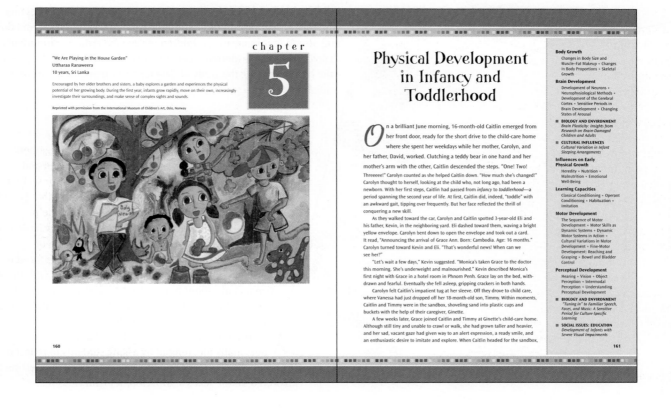

END-OF-CHAPTER SUMMARIES   Comprehensive end-of-chapter summaries, organized according to the major divisions of each chapter and highlighting important terms, remind students of key points in the text discussion. Review questions are included in the summary to encourage active study.

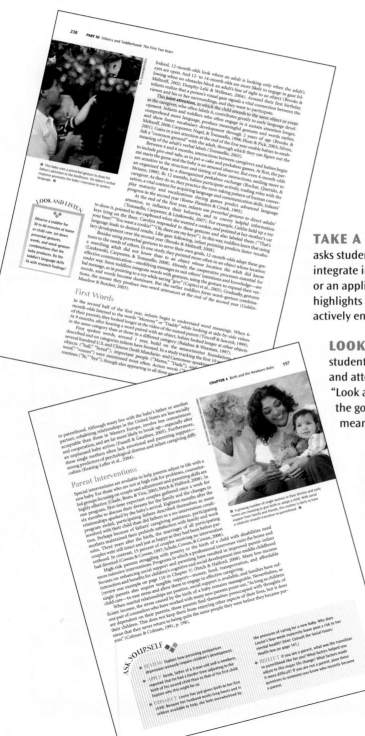

TAKE A MOMENT . . .   Built into the text narrative, this feature asks students to "take a moment" to think about an important point, integrate information on children's development, or engage in an exercise or an application to clarify a challenging concept. **TAKE A MOMENT...** highlights and reinforces the text's strength in conversing with and actively engaging students in learning and in inspiring critical thinking.

LOOK AND LISTEN   This new active-learning feature presents students with opportunities to observe what real children say and do and attend to influences on children in their everyday environments. "Look and Listen" experiences are tied to relevant text sections, with the goal of making the study of development more authentic and meaningful.

ASK YOURSELF QUESTIONS   Active engagement with the subject matter is also supported by revised and expanded study questions at the end of each major section. Four types of questions prompt students to think about child development in diverse ways: Review questions help students recall and comprehend information they have just read. Apply questions encourage the application of knowledge to controversial issues and problems faced by children, parents, and professionals who work with them. Connect questions help students build an image of the whole child by integrating what they have learned across age periods and domains of development. Reflect questions make the study of child development personally meaningful by asking students to reflect on their own development and life experiences. Each question is answered on the text's MyDevelopmentLab website.

THREE TYPES OF THEMATIC BOXES

Thematic boxes accentuate the philosophical themes of this book:

SOCIAL ISSUES boxes discuss the impact of social conditions on children and emphasize the need for sensitive social policies to ensure their well-being. They are divided into two types: **Social Issues: Education** boxes focus on home, school, and community influences on children's learning—for example, *Baby Learning from TV and Video: The Video Deficit Effect; Children's Questions: Catalyst for Cognitive Development; Magnet Schools: Equal Access to High-Quality Education;* and *Media Multitasking Disrupts Attention and Learning.* **Social Issues: Health** boxes address values and practices relevant to children's physical and mental health. Examples include *The Nurse-Family Partnership: Reducing Maternal Stress and Enhancing Child Development Through Social Support; A Cross-National Perspective on Health Care and Other Policies for Parents and Newborn Babies;* and *Like Parent, Like Child: Intergenerational Continuity in Adolescent Parenthood.*

BIOLOGY AND ENVIRONMENT boxes highlight the growing attention to the complex, bidirectional relationship between biology and environment. Examples include *A Case of Epigenesis: Smoking During Pregnancy Alters Gene Expression; Prenatal Iron Deficiency and Memory Impairments in Infants of Diabetic Mothers; Children with Attention-Deficit Hyperactivity Disorder; "Mindblindness" and Autism;* and *Bullies and Their Victims.*

CULTURAL INFLUENCES boxes deepen the attention to culture threaded throughout the text. They highlight both cross-cultural and multicultural variations in child development—for example, *Immigrant Youths: Adapting to a New Land; Cultural Variation in Infant Sleeping Arrangements; Child Health Care in the United States and Other Western Nations;* and *The Impact of Ethnic and Political Violence on Children.*

APPLYING WHAT WE KNOW TABLES In this feature, I summarize research-based applications on many issues, speaking directly to students as parents or future parents and to those pursuing different careers or areas of study, such as teaching, health care, counseling, or social work. They include: *Do's and Don'ts for a Healthy Pregnancy; Keeping Infants and Toddlers Safe; Supporting Emergent Literacy in Early Childhood; Regulating TV and Computer Use;* and *Parenting Practices That Foster Adolescent Competence.*

MILESTONES TABLES A Milestones table appears at the end of each age division of the text. These tables summarize major physical, cognitive, language, emotional, and social attainments, providing a convenient aid for reviewing the chronology of child development.

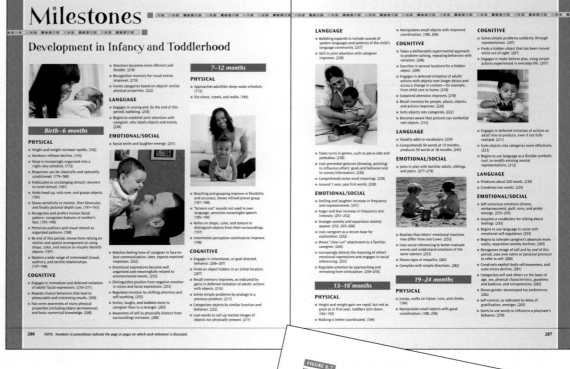

ENHANCED ART AND PHOTO PROGRAM A revised art style presents concepts and research findings with clarity and attractiveness, thereby aiding student understanding and retention. Each photo has been carefully selected to complement the text discussion and to represent the diversity of children around the world.

IN-TEXT KEY TERMS WITH DEFINITIONS, END-OF-CHAPTER TERM LIST, AND END-OF-BOOK GLOSSARY
Mastery of terms that make up the central vocabulary of the field is promoted through in-text highlighting of key terms and definitions, which encourages students to review the terminology of the field in greater depth by rereading related information. Key terms also appear in an end-of-chapter page-referenced term list and an end-of-book glossary.

Acknowledgments

The dedicated contributions of a great many individuals helped make this book a reality and contributed to refinements and improvements in this seventh edition. An impressive cast of reviewers provided many helpful suggestions and constructive criticisms, as well as encouragement and enthusiasm, for the organization and content of the text. I am grateful to each one of them.

Reviewers for the First Through Sixth Editions

Scott Adler, York University
Mark B. Alcorn, University of Northern Colorado
Joseph Allen, University of Virginia
William Aquilino, University of Wisconsin
Armin W. Arndt, Eastern Washington University
Lamia Barakat, Drexel University
Cecelia Benelli, Western Illinois University
Kathleen Bey, Palm Beach Community College
Heather Bouchey, University of Vermont
Donald Bowers, Community College of Philadelphia
Michele Y. Breault, Truman State University
Jerry Bruce, Sam Houston State College
Lanthan D. Camblin, University of Cincinnati
Joseph J. Campos, University of California, Berkeley
Linda A. Camras, DePaul University
Gustavo Carlo, University of Nebraska—Lincoln
Lynn Caruso, Seneca College
Nancy Taylor Coghill, University of Southwest Louisiana
Raymond Collings, SUNY Cortland
Diane Brothers Cook, Gainesville College
Jennifer Cook, Kent State University
Roswell Cox, Berea College
Ronald Craig, Edinboro University of Pennsylvania
Zoe Ann Davidson, Alabama A&M University
Sheridan DeWolf, Grossmont College
Matthew DiCintio, Delaware County Community College
Constance DiMaria-Kross, Union County College
Jacquelynne Eccles, University of Michigan
Bronwyn Fees, Kansas State University
F. Richard Ferraro, University of North Dakota
Kathleen Fite, Southwest Texas State University
Peter Flynn, Northern Essex Community College
Trisha Folds-Bennett, College of Charleston
Nancy Freeman, University of South Carolina
Jayne Gackenbach, MacEwan University
Eugene Geist, Ohio University
Sabine Gerhardt, University of Akron
Kristine Hansen, University of Winnipeg
Vivian Harper, San Joaquin Delta College
Algea Harrison, Oakland University
Janice Hartgrove-Freile, North Harris Community College
Vernon Haynes, Youngstown State University

Bert Hayslip, Jr., University of North Texas
Sandra Hellyer, Butler University
Joan Herwig, Iowa State University
Paula Hillmann, University of Wisconsin, Waukesha
Christie Honeycutt, Stanly Community College
Malia Huchendorf, Normandale Community College
Lisa Huffman, Ball State University
Clementine Hansley Hurt, Radford University
Scott Johnson, New York University
Joline Jones, Worcester State University
Kate Kenney, Howard Community College
Shirin Khosropour, Austin Community College
John S. Klein, Castleton State College
Claire Kopp, Claremont Graduate School
Eugene Krebs, California State University, Fresno
Carole Kremer, Hudson Valley Community College
Gary W. Ladd, University of Illinois, Urbana—Champaign
Deborah Laible, Southern Methodist University
Linda Lavine, State University of New York at Cortland
Sara Lawrence, California State University, Northridge
Gail Lee, Jersey City State College
Judith R. Levine, State University of New York at Farmingdale
David Lockwood, Humber College
Frank Manis, University of Southern California
Martin Marino, Atlantic Cape Community College
Mary Ann McLaughlin, Clarion University of Pennsylvania
Annie McManus, Parkland College
Cloe Merrill, Weber State University
Rich Metzger, University of Tennessee at Chattanooga
Karla Miley, Black Hawk College
Jennifer Trapp Myers, University of Michigan
Virginia Navarro, University of Missouri, St. Louis
Larry Nelson, Brigham Young University
Peggy Norwood, Red Rocks Community College
Peter V. Oliver, University of Hartford
Behnaz Pakizegi, William Patterson University
Virginia Parsons, Carroll College
Julie Poehlmann, University of Wisconsin—Madison
Kavita Prakash, Heritage College
Joe M. Price, San Diego State University
Cathy Proctor-Castillo, Long Beach Community College
Verna Raab, Mount Royal College
Raghu Rao, University of Minnesota
Mary Kay Reed, York College of Pennsylvania
Michael Rodman, Middlesex Community College
Alan Russell, Flinders University
Tizrah Schutzengel, Bergen Community College
Johnna Shapiro, Illinois Wesleyan University
Delores Smith, University of Tennessee
Gregory Smith, Dickinson College
Thomas Spencer, San Francisco State University
Carolyn Spies, Bloomfield College
Kathy Stansbury, University of New Mexico
Connie Steele, University of Tennessee, Knoxville
Janet Strayer, Simon Fraser University
Marcia Summers, Ball State University
Daniel Swingley, University of Pennsylvania

Christy Teranishi, Texas A&M International University
Dennis Thompson, Georgia State University
Tracy Thorndike-Christ, Western Washington University
Connie K. Varnhagen, University of Alberta
Athena Vouloumanos, McGill University
Judith Ward, Central Connecticut State University
Shawn Ward, Le Moyne College
Alida Westman, Eastern Michigan University
Colin William, Columbus State Community College
Belinda Wholeben, Rockford College
Sue Williams, Southwest Texas State University
Deborah Winters, New Mexico State University

Reviewers for the Seventh Edition

Martha Arterberry, Colby College
Kristy Burkholder, University of Wisconsin, Madison
Melissa Burnham, University of Nevada, Reno
Nicole Campione-Barr, University of Missouri, Columbia
Jeff Farrar, University of Florida
William Friedman, Oberlin College
Abi Gewirtz, University of Minnesota
Robert Hiltonsmith, Radford University
Shayla Holub, University of Texas, Dallas
Jennifer Jipson, California Polytechnic State University
Elisa Klein, University of Maryland
Debbie Laible, Lehigh University
Miriam Linver, Montclair State University
Trent Maurer, Georgia Southern University
Megan McLelland, Oregon State University
Daniel Messinger, University of Miami
Joyce Munsch, California State University, Northridge
Karen Peterson, University of Washington, Vancouver
Tom Power, Washington State University
Pamela Schulze, University of Akron
Elizabeth Short, Case Western Reserve University
Laura Sosinsky, Fordham University
Jayne White, Drury University
Ilona Yim, University of California, Irvine
Nicole Zarrett, University of South Carolina, Columbia

An outstanding editorial staff in my home community contributed immeasurably to the entire project. Sara Harris, Supplements Editor and visiting assistant professor of psychology, Bradley University, coordinated the preparation of the teaching ancillaries and wrote major sections of the Instructor's Resource Manual, bringing to these tasks great depth of knowledge, impressive writing skill, enthusiasm, and imagination. Amelia Benner, Editorial Assistant, spent countless hours searching, gathering, and organizing scholarly literature; writing portions of the Study Guide; designing highly creative MyDevelopmentLab simulations; contributing to the Explorations in Child Development video segments and video guide; and expertly handling many additional tasks as they arose.

I have been fortunate to work with a highly capable editorial team at Pearson Education. It has been a great pleasure to work once again with Tom Pauken, Managing Editor, who over-

saw the preparation of the fourth edition of *Infants, Children, and Adolescents* and who returned to edit this seventh edition. His careful review of manuscript, keen organizational skills, responsive day-to-day communication, insightful suggestions, astute problem solving, interest in the subject matter, and thoughtfulness have greatly enhanced the quality of the text and made its preparation especially enjoyable and rewarding. Judy Ashkenaz and Lisa McLellan, Development Editors, carefully reviewed and commented on each chapter, helping to ensure that every thought and concept would be clearly expressed and well-developed. My appreciation, also, to Jessica Mosher, Editor in Chief of Psychology, for reorganizing the management of my projects to enable the focused work that is vital for precise, inspired writing and timely manuscript preparation.

The supplements package benefited from the talents and diligence of several other individuals. Leah Shiro carefully revised the chapter summaries and outlines in the Instructor's Resource Manual. Kimberly Michaud prepared a superb Test Bank along with practice tests for the Study Guide, and Bill Tierney authored the excellent MyDevelopmentLab assessments. Diana Murphy designed and wrote a highly attractive PowerPoint presentation. Maria Henneberry and Phil Vandiver of Contemporary Visuals in Bloomington, IL, prepared an extraordinarily artistic and inspiring set of new video segments covering diverse topics in child development.

Donna Simons, Senior Production Project Manager, coordinated the complex production tasks that resulted in an exquisitely beautiful seventh edition. I am grateful for her keen aesthetic sense, attention to detail, flexibility, efficiency, and thoughtfulness. I thank Sarah Evertson for obtaining the exceptional photographs that so aptly illustrate the text narrative. I am also grateful for Judy Ashkenaz's fine contributions to the photo specifications and captions. Margaret Pinette, Bill Heckman, and Beyond Words Proofreading provided outstanding copyediting and proofreading.

Wendy Albert, Executive Marketing Manager, prepared the beautiful print ads and informative e-mails to the field about *Infants, Children, and Adolescents,* seventh edition. She has also ensured that accurate and clear information reached Pearson Education's sales force and that the needs of prospective and current adopters were met.

A final word of gratitude goes to my family, whose love, patience, and understanding have enabled me to be wife, mother, teacher, researcher, and text author at the same time. My sons, David and Peter, grew up with my texts, passing from childhood to adolescence and then to adulthood as successive editions were written. David has a special connection with the books' subject matter as an elementary school teacher, and Peter is now an experienced attorney and married to his vivacious, talented, and caring Melissa. All three continue to enrich my understanding through reflections on events and progress in their own lives. My husband, Ken, willingly made room for yet another time-consuming endeavor in our life together and communicated his belief in its importance in a great many unspoken, caring ways.

Laura E. Berk

Supplementary Materials

Instructor Supplements

A variety of teaching tools are available for qualified instructors in organizing lectures, planning demonstrations and examinations, and ensuring student comprehension.

MyDevelopmentLab This interactive and instructive multimedia resource can be used as a supplement to a classroom course or to completely administer an online course. Prepared in collaboration with Laura Berk, MyDevelopmentLab includes a variety of assessments that enable continuous evaluation of students' learning. Extensive video footage, multimedia simulations, biographies of major figures in the field, and interactive activities that are unique to *Infants, Children, and Adolescents* are also included. A new MyDevelopmentLab feature, "Careers in Human Development," explains how studying human development is essential for a wide range of career paths. The power of MyDevelopmentLab lies in its design as an all-inclusive teaching and learning tool. For a sampling of its rich content, contact your Pearson representative.

Instructor's Resource Manual (IRM) This thoroughly revised IRM can be used by first-time or experienced instructors to enrich classroom experiences. Each chapter includes a Chapter-at-a-Glance grid, Brief Chapter Summary, Learning Objectives, detailed Lecture Outlines, Lecture Enhancements, Learning Activities, Ask Yourself questions with answers, Suggested Student Readings, a PowerPoint Presentation, and a Media Materials list.

Test Bank The Test Bank contains over 2,000 multiple-choice questions, each of which is page-referenced to chapter content and classified by type (factual, applied, or conceptual). Each chapter also includes a selection of essay questions and sample answers.

Computerized Test Bank This computerized version of the Test Bank, in easy-to-use MyTest format, lets you prepare tests for printing as well as for network and online testing. It has full editing capability. Test items are also available in CourseCompass, Blackboard, and WebCT formats.

PowerPoint Presentation The PowerPoint presentation contains illustrations and outlines of key topics for each chapter from the text, presented in a clear and visually attractive format.

"Explorations in Child Development" DVD and Guide This new DVD is over four hours in length and contains 47 four- to ten-minute narrated segments, designed for effective classroom use, that illustrate the many theories, concepts, and milestones of child development. New additions include *Preterm Birth, Autism, First-Grade Science Education, Childhood Obesity, Civic Engagement in Adolescence,* and *Changing Parent–Adolescent Relationships.* "Explorations in Child Development" DVD and DVD Guide are available to instructors who adopt the text for in-class use and are also available as a student supplement for free when packaged with the text. The DVD Guide helps students use the DVD in conjunction with the textbook, deepening their understanding and applying what they have learned to everyday life.

Student Supplements

Beyond the study aids found in the textbook, Pearson offers a number of supplements for students:

MyDevelopmentLab This interactive and instructive multimedia resource is an all-inclusive learning tool. Prepared in collaboration with Laura Berk, MyDevelopmentLab engages students and reinforces learning through controlled assessments, extensive video footage, multimedia simulations, biographies of major figures in the field, and interactive activities that are unique to *Infants, Children, and Adolescents.* In addition, "Careers in Human Development" explains how knowledge of human development is essential for a wide range of career paths. Easy to use, MyDevelopmentLab meets the individual learning needs of every student. For a sampling of its rich content, visit *www.mydevelopmentlab.com.*

Study Guide with Practice Tests This helpful study guide offers Chapter Summaries, Learning Objectives, Study Questions organized according to major headings in the text, Suggested Readings, Crossword Puzzles for mastering important terms, and two multiple-choice Practice Tests per chapter.

Milestones Study Cards Adapted from the popular Milestones tables featured in the text, these colorfully illustrated study cards outline key developmental attainments. Easy-to-use, they assist students in integrating the various domains of development and constructing a vision of the whole developing child.

About the Chapter Opening Art

I would like to extend grateful acknowledgments to the International Museum of Children's Art, Oslo, Norway; to the International Child Art Foundation, Washington, D.C.; to the World Awareness Children's Museum, Glens Falls, New York; and to the International Collection of Child Art, Milner Library, Illinois State University, for the exceptional cover image and chapter opening art, which depict the talents, concerns, and viewpoints of young artists from around the world. The awe-inspiring collection of children's art gracing this text expresses family, school, and community themes; good times and personal triumphs; profound appreciation for beauty; and great depth of emotion. I am pleased to share with readers this window into children's creativity, insightfulness, sensitivity, and compassion.

INFANTS, CHILDREN, and ADOLESCENTS

"My Vision of the Future"
Bhea Vacio
11 years, Philippines

In this artist's vision of the future, people from around the globe join hands in peace and cooperation, with a rainbow of colors as a backdrop. Chapter 1 will introduce you to a rainbow of theories—a multiplicity of ways to think about and study children's development.

Reprinted with permission from the International Child Art Foundation, Washington, D.C.

History, Theory, and Research Strategies

*N*ot long ago, I left my Midwestern home to live for a year near the small city in northern California where I spent my childhood. One morning, I visited the neighborhood where I grew up—a place I had not seen since I was 12 years old.

I stood at the entrance to my old schoolyard. Buildings and grounds that had looked large to me as a child now seemed strangely small. I peered through the window of my first-grade classroom. The desks were no longer arranged in rows but grouped in intimate clusters. Computers rested against the far wall, near where I once sat. I walked my old route home from school, the distance shrunken by my longer stride. I stopped in front of my best friend Kathryn's house, where we once drew sidewalk pictures, crossed the street to play kickball, and produced plays in the garage. In place of the small shop where I had purchased penny candy stood a child-care center, filled with the voices and vigorous activity of toddlers and preschoolers.

As I walked, I reflected on early experiences that contributed to who and what I am today—weekends helping my father in his downtown clothing shop, the year my mother studied to become a high school teacher, moments of companionship and rivalry with my sister and brother, Sunday outings to museums and the seashore, and visits to my grandmother's house, where I became someone extra special.

As I passed the homes of my childhood friends, I thought of what I knew about their present lives. Kathryn, star student and president of our sixth-grade class—today a successful corporate lawyer and mother of two. Shy, withdrawn Phil, cruelly teased because of his cleft lip—now owner of a thriving chain of hardware stores and member of the city council. Julio, immigrant from Mexico who joined our class in third grade—today director of an elementary school bilingual education program and single parent of an adopted Mexican boy. And finally, my next-door neighbor Rick, who picked fights at recess, struggled with reading, repeated fourth grade, dropped out of high school, and (so I heard) moved from one job to another over the following 10 years.

As you begin this course in child development, perhaps you, too, wonder about some of the same questions that crossed my mind during that nostalgic neighborhood walk:

- In what ways are children's home, school, and neighborhood experiences the same today as they were in generations past, and in what ways are they different?
- How are the infant and young child's perceptions of the world the same as the adult's, and how are they different?
- What determines the features that humans have in common and those that make each of us unique—physically, mentally, and behaviorally?
- How did Julio, transplanted at age 8 to a new culture, master its language and customs and succeed in its society, yet remain strongly identified with his ethnic community?
- Why do some of us, like Kathryn and Rick, retain the same styles of responding that characterized us as children, whereas others, like Phil, change in essential ways?
- How do cultural changes—employed mothers, child care, divorce, smaller families, and new technologies—affect children's characteristics?

These are central questions addressed by **child development,** an area of study devoted to understanding constancy and change from conception through adolescence. Child development is part of a larger, interdisciplinary field known as **developmental science,** which includes all changes we experience throughout the lifespan (Lerner, 2006). Great diversity characterizes the interests and concerns of the thousands of investigators who study child development. But all have a common goal: to describe and identify those factors that influence the consistencies and changes in young people during the first two decades of life.

The Field of Child Development

The questions just listed are not just of scientific interest. Each has *applied,* or practical, importance as well. In fact, scientific curiosity is just one factor that led child development to become the exciting field of study it is today. Research about development has also been stimulated by social pressures to improve the lives of children. For example, the beginning of public education in the early twentieth century led to a demand for knowledge about what and how to teach children of different ages. Pediatricians' interest in improving children's health required an understanding of physical growth and nutrition. The social service profession's desire to treat children's anxieties and behavior problems required information about personality and social development. And parents have continually sought advice about child-rearing practices and experiences that would promote their children's development and well-being.

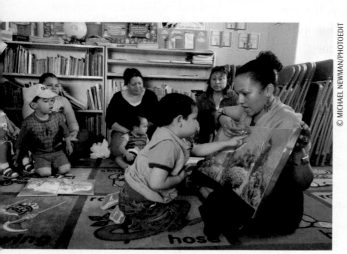

Our large storehouse of information about child development is *interdisciplinary.* It has grown through the combined efforts of people from many fields. Because of the need to solve everyday problems concerning children, researchers from psychology, sociology, anthropology, biology, and neuroscience have joined forces with professionals from education, family studies, medicine, public health, and social service—to name just a few. The field of child development, as it exists today, is a monument to the contributions of these many disciplines. Its body of knowledge is not just scientifically important but also relevant and useful.

■ Theories have practical value in helping us improve the welfare and treatment of children. For example, theories have contributed to new approaches to education that emphasize exploration, discovery, and collaboration. ■

© MICHAEL NEWMAN/PHOTOEDIT

Domains of Development

To make the vast, interdisciplinary study of human constancy and change more orderly and convenient, development is often divided into three broad domains: *physical, cognitive,* and *emotional and social.* Refer to Figure 1.1 for a description and illustration of each. Within each period from infancy through adolescence, we will consider the three domains in the order just mentioned. Yet the domains are not really distinct. Rather, they combine in an integrated, holistic fashion to yield the living, growing child. Furthermore, each domain influences and is influenced by the others. For example, in Chapter 5 you will see that new motor capacities, such as reaching, sitting, crawling, and walking (physical), contribute greatly to infants' understanding of their surroundings (cognitive). When babies think and act more competently, adults stimulate them more with games, language, and expressions of delight at their new achievements (emotional and social). These enriched experiences, in turn, promote all aspects of development.

Although each chapter focuses on a particular domain, you will encounter instances of the interwoven nature of all domains on nearly every page of this book. In the margins of the text you will find occasional *Look and Listen* activities—opportunities for you to see everyday illustrations of development by observing what real children say and do or by attending to everyday influences on children. Through these experiences, I hope to make your study of development more authentic and meaningful.

Also, look for the *Ask Yourself* feature at the end of major sections, designed to deepen your understanding. Within it, I have included *Review* questions, which help you recall and think about information you have just read; *Apply* questions, which encourage you to apply your knowledge to controversial issues and problems faced by parents, teachers, and children; *Connect* questions, which help you form a coherent, unified picture of child development; and *Reflect* questions, which invite you to reflect on your own development and that of people you know well.

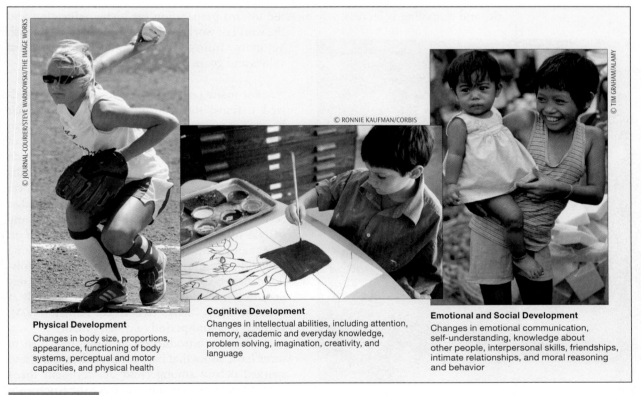

© JOURNAL-COURIER/STEVE WARMOWSKI/THE IMAGE WORKS

© RONNIE KAUFMAN/CORBIS

© TIM GRAHAM/ALAMY

Physical Development

Changes in body size, proportions, appearance, functioning of body systems, perceptual and motor capacities, and physical health

Cognitive Development

Changes in intellectual abilities, including attention, memory, academic and everyday knowledge, problem solving, imagination, creativity, and language

Emotional and Social Development

Changes in emotional communication, self-understanding, knowledge about other people, interpersonal skills, friendships, intimate relationships, and moral reasoning and behavior

FIGURE 1.1

Major domains of development. The three domains are not really distinct. Rather, they overlap and interact.

Periods of Development

Besides distinguishing and integrating the three domains, another dilemma arises in discussing development: how to divide the flow of time into sensible, manageable parts. Researchers usually use the following age periods, according to which I have organized this book. Each brings new capacities and social expectations that serve as important transitions in major theories:

■ *The prenatal period: from conception to birth.* In this nine-month period, the most rapid time of change, a one-celled organism is transformed into a human baby with remarkable capacities for adjusting to life in the surrounding world.

■ *Infancy and toddlerhood: from birth to 2 years.* This period brings dramatic changes in the body and brain that support the emergence of a wide array of motor, perceptual, and intellectual capacities; the beginnings of language; and first intimate ties to others. Infancy spans the first year; toddlerhood spans the second, during which children take their first independent steps, marking a shift to greater autonomy.

■ *Early childhood: from 2 to 6 years.* The body becomes longer and leaner, motor skills are refined, and children become more self-controlled and self-sufficient. Make-believe play blossoms, supporting every aspect of psychological development. Thought and language expand at an astounding pace, a sense of morality becomes evident, and children establish ties with peers.

■ *Middle childhood: from 6 to 11 years.* Children learn about the wider world and master new responsibilities that increasingly resemble those they will perform as adults. Hallmarks of this period are improved athletic abilities; participation in organized games with rules; more logical thought processes; mastery of fundamental reading, writing, math, and other academic knowledge and skills; and advances in understanding the self, morality, and friendship.

■ *Adolescence: from 11 to 18 years.* This period initiates the transition to adulthood. Puberty leads to an adult-sized body and sexual maturity. Thought becomes abstract and idealistic, and schooling is increasingly directed toward preparation for higher education and the world of work. Young people begin to establish autonomy from the family and to define personal values and goals.

For many contemporary youth in industrialized nations, the transition to adult roles has become increasingly prolonged—so much so that some researchers have posited a new period of development called *emerging adulthood,* which spans ages 18 to 25. Although emerging adults have moved beyond adolescence, they have not yet fully assumed adult roles. Rather, during higher education and sometimes beyond, these young people intensify their exploration of options in love, career, and personal values before making enduring commitments. Because emerging adulthood first became apparent during the past few decades, researchers have just begun to study it (Arnett, 2003, 2004; Arnett & Tanner, 2006). Perhaps it is *your* period of development.

With this introduction in mind, let's turn to some basic issues that have captivated, puzzled, and sparked debate among child development theorists. Then our discussion will trace the emergence of the field and survey major theories. We will return to each contemporary theory in greater detail in later chapters.

© UWE OMMER, *1,000 FAMILIES*, TASCHEN

■ Child development is so dramatic that researchers divide it into periods. This large family of the Ivory Coast includes children in infancy, early childhood (boy in front row, girl seated in second row), middle childhood (girl in front row, girl standing in second row), and adolescence (girl standing in center). ■

Basic Issues

Research on child development did not begin until the late nineteenth and early twentieth centuries. But ideas about how children grow and change have a much longer history. As these speculations combined with research, they inspired the construction of *theories* of development. A **theory** is an orderly, integrated set of statements that describes, explains, and predicts behavior. For example, a good theory of infant–caregiver attachment would (1) *describe* the behaviors of babies around 6 to 8 months of age as they seek the affection and comfort of a familiar adult, (2) *explain* how and why infants develop this strong desire to bond with a caregiver, and (3) *predict* the consequences of this emotional bond for future relationships.

Theories are vital tools for two reasons. First, they provide organizing frameworks for our observations of children. In other words, they *guide and give meaning* to what we see. Second, theories that are verified by research often serve as a sound basis for practical action. Once a theory helps us *understand* development, we are in a much better position *to know how to improve* the welfare and treatment of children.

As we will see later, theories are influenced by the cultural values and belief systems of their times. But theories differ in one important way from mere opinion or belief: A theory's continued existence depends on *scientific verification*. This means that the theory must be tested using a fair set of research procedures agreed on by the scientific community, and its findings must endure, or be replicated over time.

Within the field of child development, many theories offer very different ideas about what children are like and how they change. The study of child development provides no ultimate truth because investigators do not always agree on the meaning of what they see. Also, children are complex beings; they change physically, cognitively, emotionally, and socially. No single theory has explained all these aspects. But the existence of many theories helps advance knowledge because researchers are continually trying to support, contradict, and integrate these different points of view.

Although there are many theories, we can easily organize them by looking at the stand they take on three basic issues: (1) Is the course of development continuous or discontinuous? (2) Does one course of development characterize all children, or are there many possible courses? (3) What are the roles of genetic and environmental factors—nature and nurture—in development? Let's look closely at each of these issues.

Continuous or Discontinuous Development?

Recently, the mother of 20-month-old Angelo reported to me with amazement that her young son had pushed a toy car across the living room floor while making a motorlike sound, "Brmmmm, brmmmm," for the first time. When he hit a nearby wall with a bang, Angelo let go of the car, exclaimed, "C'ash!" and laughed heartily.

"How come Angelo can pretend, but he couldn't a few months ago?" queried his mother. "And I wonder what 'Brmmmm, brmmmm' and 'Crash!' mean to Angelo. Does he understand motorlike sounds and collision the same way I do?"

Angelo's mother has raised a puzzling issue about development: How can we best describe the differences in capacities and behavior between small infants, young children, adolescents, and adults? As Figure 1.2 on page 8 illustrates, most major theories recognize two possibilities.

One view holds that infants and preschoolers respond to the world in much the same way as adults do. The difference between the immature and the mature being is simply one of *amount or complexity*. For example, little Angelo's thinking may be just as logical and well-organized as our own. Perhaps (as his mother reports) he can sort objects into simple categories, recognize whether he has more of one kind than of another, and remember where he left his favorite toy at child care the week before. Angelo's only limitation may be that he cannot perform these skills with as much information and precision as we can. If this is so, then Angelo's development is **continuous**—a process of gradually adding more of the same types of skills that were there to begin with.

Is development continuous or discontinuous? (a) Some theorists believe that development is a smooth, continuous process. Children gradually add more of the same types of skills. (b) Other theorists think that development takes place in discontinuous stages. Children change rapidly as they step up to a new level and then change very little for a while. With each step, the child interprets and responds to the world in a qualitatively different way.

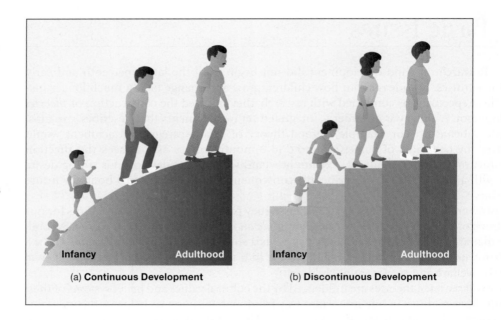

(a) **Continuous Development**   (b) **Discontinuous Development**

According to a second view, Angelo's thoughts, emotions, and behavior differ considerably from those of adults. His development is **discontinuous**—a process in which new ways of understanding and responding to the world emerge at specific times. From this perspective, Angelo is not yet able to organize objects or remember and interpret experiences as we do. Instead, he will move through a series of developmental steps, each with unique features, until he reaches the highest level of functioning.

Theories that accept the discontinuous perspective regard development as taking place in **stages**—*qualitative* changes in thinking, feeling, and behaving that characterize specific periods of development. In stage theories, development is much like climbing a staircase, with each step corresponding to a more mature, reorganized way of functioning. The stage concept also assumes that children undergo periods of rapid transformation as they step up from one stage to the next, alternating with plateaus during which they stand solidly within a stage. In other words, change is fairly sudden rather than gradual and ongoing.

Does development actually occur in a neat, orderly sequence of stages? This ambitious assumption has faced significant challenges. Later in this chapter, we will review some influential stage theories.

One Course of Development or Many?

Stage theorists assume that people everywhere follow the same sequence of development. For example, in the domain of cognition, a stage theorist might try to identify the common influences that lead children to represent their world through language and make-believe play in early childhood, to think more logically and systematically in middle childhood, and to reason more systematically and abstractly in adolescence.

At the same time, the field of child development is becoming increasingly aware that children grow up in distinct **contexts**—unique combinations of personal and environmental circumstances that can result in different paths of change. For example, a shy child who fears social encounters develops in very different contexts from those of an outgoing agemate who readily seeks out other people (Kagan, 2003, 2008). Children in non-Western village societies have experiences in their families and communities that differ sharply from those of children in large Western cities. These different circumstances foster different cognitive capacities, social skills, and feelings about the self and others (Shweder et al., 2006).

As you will see, contemporary theorists regard the contexts that mold development as many-layered and complex. On the personal side, these include heredity and biological makeup. On the environmental side, they include both immediate settings—home, child-care center, school, and neighborhood—and circumstances that are more remote from children's everyday lives: community resources, societal values and priorities, and historical time period. Finally, researchers today are more conscious than ever before of cultural diversity in development.

Relative Influence of Nature and Nurture?

In addition to describing the course of child development, each theory takes a stand on a major question about its underlying causes: Are genetic or environmental factors more important in influencing development? This is the age-old **nature–nurture controversy.** By *nature,* we mean inborn biological givens—the hereditary information we receive from our parents at the moment of conception. By *nurture,* we mean the complex forces of the physical and social world that influence our biological makeup and psychological experiences before and after birth.

Although all theories grant roles to both nature and nurture, they vary in emphasis. Consider the following questions: Is the older child's ability to think in more complex ways largely the result of an inborn timetable of growth, or is it primarily influenced by stimulation from parents and teachers? Do children acquire language because they are genetically predisposed to do so or because parents intensively teach them from an early age? And what accounts for the vast individual differences among children—in height, weight, physical coordination, intelligence, personality, and social skills? Is nature or nurture more responsible?

A theory's position on the roles of nature and nurture affects how it explains individual differences. Some theorists emphasize *stability*—that children who are high or low in a characteristic (such as verbal ability, anxiety, or sociability) will remain so at later ages. These theorists typically stress the importance of *heredity*. If they do regard environment as important, they usually point to *early experiences* as establishing a lifelong pattern of behavior. Powerful negative events in the first few years, they argue, cannot be fully overcome by later, more positive ones (Bowlby, 1980; Johnson, 2000; Sroufe, 2005). Other theorists, taking a more optimistic view, see development as having substantial **plasticity** throughout life—as open to change in response to influential experiences (Baltes, Lindenberger, & Staudinger, 2006; Lerner & Overton, 2008; Lester, Masten, & McEwen, 2006).

Throughout this book, you will see that investigators disagree, often sharply, on the question of *stability versus plasticity*. Their answers have great applied significance. If you believe that development is largely due to nature, then providing experiences aimed at promoting change would seem to be of little value. If, on the other hand, you are convinced of the supreme importance of early experience, then you would intervene as soon as possible, offering high-quality stimulation and support to ensure that children develop at their best. Finally, if you think that environment is profoundly influential throughout development, you would provide assistance any time children or adolescents face difficulties, in the belief that, with the help of favorable life circumstances, they can recover from early negative events.

A Balanced Point of View

So far, we have discussed basic issues of child development in terms of extremes—solutions favoring one side or the other. But as we trace the unfolding of the field in the rest of this chapter, you will see that the positions of many theorists have softened. Today, some theorists believe that both continuous and discontinuous changes occur. Many acknowledge that development has both universal features and features unique to the individual and his or her contexts. And a growing number regard heredity and environment as inseparably interwoven, each affecting the potential of the other to modify the child's traits and capacities (Cole, 2006; Gottlieb, Wahlsten, & Lickliter, 2006; Lerner, 2006; Rutter, 2007b). We will discuss these new ideas about nature and nurture in Chapter 2.

Finally, as you will see later in this book, the relative impact of early and later experiences varies greatly from one domain of development to another and even—as the Biology and Environment box on pages 10–11 indicates—across individuals! Because of the complex network of factors contributing to human change and the challenges of isolating the effects of each, many theoretical points of view have gathered research support. Although debate continues, this circumstance has also sparked more balanced visions of child development.

BIOLOGY AND ENVIRONMENT

Resilient Children

John and his best friend, Gary, grew up in a run-down, crime-ridden inner-city neighborhood. By age 10, each had experienced years of family conflict followed by parental divorce. Reared for the rest of childhood and adolescence in mother-headed households, John and Gary rarely saw their fathers. Both dropped out of high school and were in and out of trouble with the police.

Then their paths diverged. By age 30, John had fathered two children with women he never married, had spent time in prison, was unemployed, and drank alcohol heavily. In contrast, Gary had returned to finish high school, had studied auto mechanics at a community college, and became manager of a gas station and repair shop. Married with two children, he had saved his earnings and bought a home. He was happy, healthy, and well-adapted to life.

A wealth of evidence shows that environmental risks—poverty, negative family interactions and parental divorce, job loss, mental illness, and drug abuse—predispose children to future problems (Masten & Gewirtz, 2006; Sameroff, 2006; Wadsworth & Santiago, 2008). Why did Gary "beat the odds" and come through unscathed?

New evidence on **resilience**—the ability to adapt effectively in the face of threats to development—is receiving increasing attention as investigators look for ways to protect young people from the damaging effects of stressful life conditions (Masten & Powell, 2003). This interest has been inspired by several long-term studies on the relationship of life stressors in childhood to competence and adjustment in adolescence and adulthood (Fergusson & Horwood, 2003; Masten et al., 1995; Werner & Smith, 2001). In each study, some individuals were shielded from negative outcomes, whereas others had lasting problems. Four broad factors seemed to offer protection from the damaging effects of stressful life events.

Personal Characteristics

A child's biologically endowed characteristics can reduce exposure to risk or lead to experiences that compensate for early stressful events. High intelligence and socially valued talents (in music or athletics, for example) increase the chances that a child will have

© ROBERT BRENNER/PHOTOEDIT

■ This boy's close, affectionate relationship with his father helps foster resilience. A strong bond with at least one parent who combines warmth with appropriate expectations for maturity can shield children from the damaging effects of stressful life conditions. ■

ASK YOURSELF

◆ **REVIEW** What is meant by a *stage* of development? Provide your own example of stagewise change. What stand do stage theorists take on the issue of continuous versus discontinuous development?

◆ **APPLY** Anna, a high school counselor, has devised a program that integrates classroom learning with vocational training to help adolescents at risk for school dropout stay in school and transition smoothly to work life. What is Anna's position on *stability versus plasticity* in development? Explain.

◆ **CONNECT** Provide an example of how one domain of development (physical, cognitive, or emotional/social) can affect development in another domain.

◆ **REFLECT** Cite an aspect of your development that differs from a parent's or a grandparent's when he or she was your age. How might *contexts* explain this difference?

rewarding experiences at school and in the community that offset the impact of a stressful home life. Temperament is particularly powerful. Children who have easygoing, sociable dispositions and who can readily inhibit negative emotions and impulses tend to have an optimistic outlook on life and a special capacity to adapt to change—qualities that elicit positive responses from others. In contrast, emotionally reactive and irritable children often tax the patience of people around them (Mathiesen & Prior, 2006; Vanderbilt-Adriance & Shaw, 2008; Wong et al., 2006). For example, both John and Gary moved several times during their childhoods. Each time, John became anxious and angry. Gary looked forward to making new friends and exploring new parts of the neighborhood.

A Warm Parental Relationship

A close relationship with at least one parent who provides warmth, appropriately high expectations, monitoring of the child's activities, and an organized home environment fosters resilience (Masten & Shaffer, 2006). But this factor (as well as the next one) is not independent of children's personal characteristics. Children who are relaxed, socially responsive, and able to deal with change are easier to rear and more likely to enjoy positive relationships with parents and other people. At the same time, some children may develop more attractive dispositions as a result of parental warmth and attention (Conger & Conger, 2002; Gulotta, 2008).

Social Support Outside the Immediate Family

The most consistent asset of resilient children is a strong bond to a competent, caring adult. For children who do not have a close bond with either parent, a grandparent, aunt, uncle, or teacher who forms a special relationship with the child can promote resilience (Masten & Reed, 2002). Gary received support in adolescence from his grandfather, who listened to Gary's concerns and helped him solve problems. Gary's grandfather had a stable marriage and work life and handled stressors skillfully. Consequently, he served as a model of effective coping.

Associations with rule-abiding peers who value school achievement are also linked to resilience. But children who have positive relationships with adults are far more likely to establish these supportive peer ties.

Community Resources and Opportunities

Community supports—good schools, convenient and affordable health care and social services, libraries, and recreation centers—foster both parent's and children's well-being. In addition, opportunities to participate in community life help older children and adolescents overcome adversity. Extracurricular activities at school, religious youth groups, scouting, and other organizations teach important social skills, such as cooperation, leadership, and contributing to others' welfare. As participants acquire these competencies, they gain in self-reliance, self-esteem, and community commitment (Benson et al., 2006). As a college student, Gary volunteered for Habitat for Humanity, joining a team building affordable housing in low-income neighborhoods. Community involvement offered Gary additional opportunities to form meaningful relationships, which further strengthened his resilience.

Research on resilience highlights the complex connections between heredity and environment. Armed with positive characteristics stemming from innate endowment, favorable rearing experiences, or both, children and adolescents can act to reduce stressful situations.

But when many risks pile up, they are increasingly difficult to overcome (Obradović et al., 2009). To inoculate children against the negative effects of risk, interventions must not only reduce risks but also enhance children's protective relationships at home, in school, and in the community. This means attending to both the person and the environment—strengthening children's capacities while also reducing hazardous experiences.

Historical Foundations

Contemporary theories of child development are the result of centuries of change in Western cultural values, philosophical thinking about children, and scientific progress. To understand the field as it exists today, we must return to its early beginnings—to ideas about children that long preceded scientific child study but that linger as important forces in current theory and research.

Medieval Times

Childhood was regarded as a separate period of life as early as medieval Europe—the sixth through the fifteenth centuries. Medieval painters often depicted children wearing loose, comfortable gowns, playing games, and looking up to adults. Written texts contained terms that distinguished children under age 7 or 8 from other people and that recognized even

As early as medieval times, adults viewed childhood as a distinct developmental period. In this sixteenth-century painting, *Children's Games*, by Pieter Bruegel the Elder, boys and girls wearing loose, comfortable clothing play lively outdoor games. *[Children's games (Kinderspiele): Detail of top right hand corner, 1560 (oil on panel) (detail of 68945), Bruegel, Pieter the Elder (c.1525–69).]*

young teenagers as not fully mature. By the fourteenth century, manuals offering advice on many aspects of child care, including health, feeding, clothing, and games, were common (Alexandre-Bidon & Lett, 1997; Lett, 1997). Laws recognized that children needed protection from people who might mistreat them, and courts exercised leniency with lawbreaking youths because of their tender years (Hanawalt, 1993).

In sum, in medieval times, if not before, clear awareness existed of children as vulnerable beings and of childhood as a distinct developmental period. Religious writings, however, contained contradictory depictions of children's basic nature, sometimes portraying them as possessed by the devil and in need of purification, at other times as innocent and close to angels (Hanawalt, 2003). Both ideas foreshadowed later views of childhood.

The Reformation

In the sixteenth century, the Puritan belief in original sin gave rise to the view that children were born evil and stubborn and had to be civilized (Shahar, 1990). Harsh, restrictive child-rearing practices were recommended to tame the depraved child. Children were dressed in stiff, uncomfortable clothing that held them in adultlike postures, and disobedient students were routinely beaten by their schoolmasters. Nevertheless, love and affection for their children prevented most Puritan parents from using extremely repressive measures (Moran & Vinovskis, 1986).

As the Puritans emigrated from England to the American colonies, they brought the belief that child rearing was one of their most important obligations. Although they continued to regard the child's soul as tainted by original sin, they tried to teach their sons and daughters to use reason to tell right from wrong (Clarke-Stewart, 1998). As they trained their children in self-reliance and self-control, Puritan parents gradually adopted a moderate balance between severity and permissiveness.

Philosophies of the Enlightenment

The seventeenth-century Enlightenment brought new philosophies that emphasized ideals of human dignity and respect. Conceptions of childhood were more humane than those of the past.

JOHN LOCKE The writings of British philosopher John Locke (1632–1704) served as the forerunner of a twentieth-century perspective that we will discuss shortly: behaviorism. Locke viewed the child as a *tabula rasa*—Latin for "blank slate." According to this idea, children begin as nothing at all; their characters are shaped entirely by experience. Locke (1690/1892) saw parents as rational tutors who can mold the child in any way they wish through careful instruction, effective example, and rewards for good behavior. He was ahead of his time in recommending child-rearing practices that present-day research supports—for example, the use of praise and approval as rewards, rather than money or sweets. He also opposed physical punishment: "The child repeatedly beaten in school cannot look upon books and teachers without experiencing fear and anger." Locke's philosophy led to a change from harshness toward children to kindness and compassion.

Look carefully at Locke's ideas, and you will see that he regarded development as *continuous*: Adultlike behaviors are gradually built up through the warm, consistent teachings of parents. His view of the child as a tabula rasa led him to champion *nurture*—the power of the environment to shape the child. And his faith in nurture suggests the possibility of *many courses of development* and of *high plasticity at later ages* due to new experiences. Finally, Locke's philosophy characterizes children as doing little to influence their own destiny, which is written on "blank slates" by others. This vision of a passive child has been discarded. All contemporary theories view children as active, purposeful beings who contribute substantially to their own development.

JEAN-JACQUES ROUSSEAU   In the eighteenth century, French philosopher Jean-Jacques Rousseau (1712–1778) introduced a new view of childhood. Children, Rousseau claimed, are not blank slates to be filled by adult instruction. Instead, they are *noble savages,* naturally endowed with a sense of right and wrong and an innate plan for orderly, healthy growth. Unlike Locke, Rousseau believed that children's built-in moral sense and unique ways of thinking and feeling would only be harmed by adult training. His was a child-centered philosophy in which the adult should be receptive to the child's needs at each of four stages: infancy, childhood, late childhood, and adolescence.

Rousseau's philosophy includes two influential concepts. The first is the concept of *stage,* which we discussed earlier. The second is the concept of **maturation,** which refers to a genetically determined, naturally unfolding course of growth. In contrast to Locke, Rousseau saw children as determining their own destinies. And he viewed development as a *discontinuous, stagewise* process that follows a *single, unified course* mapped out by *nature.*

Scientific Beginnings

The study of child development evolved quickly in the late nineteenth and early twentieth centuries. Early observations of children were soon followed by improved methods and theories. Each advance contributed to the firm foundation on which the field rests today.

DARWIN: FOREFATHER OF SCIENTIFIC CHILD STUDY   British naturalist Charles Darwin (1809–1882) joined an expedition to distant parts of the world, where he observed infinite variation among plant and animal species. He also saw that within a species, no two individuals are exactly alike. From these observations, he constructed his famous *theory of evolution.*

The theory emphasized two related principles: *natural selection* and *survival of the fittest.* Darwin explained that certain species survive in particular parts of the world because they have characteristics that fit with, or are adapted to, their surroundings. Other species die off because they are not as well-suited to their environments. Individuals within a species who best meet the environment's survival requirements live long enough to reproduce and pass their more beneficial characteristics to future generations. Darwin's emphasis on the adaptive value of physical characteristics and behavior eventually found its way into important developmental theories.

During his explorations, Darwin discovered that early prenatal growth is strikingly similar in many species. Other scientists concluded from Darwin's observation that the development of the human child followed the same general plan as the evolution of the human species. Although this belief eventually proved inaccurate, efforts to chart parallels between child growth and human evolution prompted researchers to make careful observations of all aspects of children's behavior. Out of these first attempts to document an idea about development, scientific child study was born.

THE NORMATIVE PERIOD   G. Stanley Hall (1844–1924), one of the most influential American psychologists of the early twentieth century, is generally regarded as the founder of the child-study movement (Cairns & Cairns, 2006). Inspired by Darwin's work, Hall and his well-known student Arnold Gesell (1880–1961) devised theories based on evolutionary ideas. These early leaders regarded development as a genetically determined process that unfolds automatically, much like a flower (Gesell, 1933; Hall, 1904).

Hall and Gesell are remembered less for their one-sided theories than for their intensive efforts to describe all aspects of child development. They launched the **normative approach,** in which measures of behavior are taken on large numbers of individuals and age-related averages are computed to represent typical development. Using this procedure, Hall constructed elaborate questionnaires asking children of different ages almost everything they could tell about themselves—interests, fears, imaginary playmates, dreams, friendships, everyday knowledge, and more. Similarly, through observations and parental interviews, Gesell collected detailed normative information on the motor achievements, social behaviors, and personality characteristics of infants and children.

LOOK AND LISTEN

Examine several recent parenting-advice books in your local bookstore or library, and identify the stance each book takes on the three basic issues about child development.

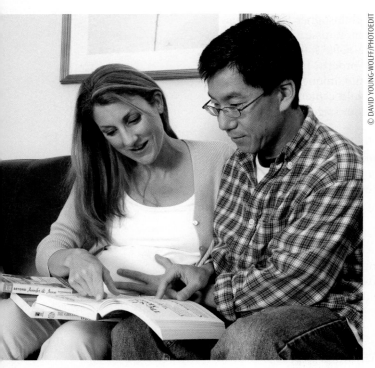

■ Theories of child development have sparked an extensive parenting-advice literature. These expectant parents rely on an array of infant-care manuals to prepare for the challenges of caring for a new baby. ■

Gesell was also among the first to make knowledge about child development meaningful to parents. If, as he believed, the timetable of development is the product of millions of years of evolution, then children are naturally knowledgeable about their needs. His child-rearing advice, in the tradition of Rousseau, recommended sensitivity to children's cues (Thelen & Adolph, 1992). Along with Benjamin Spock's *Baby and Child Care,* Gesell's books became a central part of a rapidly expanding popular literature for parents.

THE MENTAL TESTING MOVEMENT While Hall and Gesell were developing their theories and methods in the United States, French psychologist Alfred Binet (1857–1911) was also taking a normative approach to child development, but for a different reason. In the early 1900s, Binet and his colleague Theodore Simon were asked by Paris school officials to find a way to identify children with learning problems who needed to be placed in special classes. To address these practical educational concerns, Binet and Simon constructed the first successful intelligence test.

Binet began with a well-developed theory of intelligence. Capturing the complexity of children's thinking, he defined intelligence as good judgment, planning, and critical reflection (Sternberg & Jarvin, 2003). Then he created age-graded test items that directly measured these abilities.

In 1916, at Stanford University, Binet's test was adapted for use with English-speaking children. Since then, the English version has been known as the *Stanford-Binet Intelligence Scale.* Besides providing a score that could successfully predict school achievement, the Binet test sparked tremendous interest in individual differences in development. Comparisons of the scores of children who vary in gender, ethnicity, birth order, family background, and other characteristics became a major focus of research. And intelligence tests rose quickly to the forefront of the nature–nurture controversy.

ASK YOURSELF

◆ REVIEW Imagine a debate between John Locke and Jean-Jacques Rousseau on the nature–nurture controversy. Summarize the argument that each historical figure is likely to present.

◆ CONNECT What do the ideas of Rousseau, Darwin, and Hall have in common?

◆ REFLECT Find out whether your parents read any child-rearing advice books when you were growing up. What questions most concerned them? Do you think the concerns of today's parents differ from those of your parents' generation? Explain.

■ ■ Mid-Twentieth-Century Theories
■ ■

In the mid-twentieth century, the field of child development expanded. A variety of theories emerged, each of which continues to have followers today. In these theories, the European concern with the child's inner thoughts and feelings contrasts sharply with the North American academic focus on scientific precision and concrete, observable behavior.

The Psychoanalytic Perspective

By the 1930s and 1940s, parents were increasingly seeking professional help in dealing with children's emotional difficulties. The earlier normative movement had answered the question, What are children like? Now another question had to be addressed: How and why do children become the way they are? To treat psychological problems, psychiatrists and social workers turned to an emerging approach to personality development that emphasized the unique history of each child.

According to the **psychoanalytic perspective,** children move through a series of stages in which they confront conflicts between biological drives and social expectations. How these conflicts are resolved determines the person's ability to learn, to get along with others, and to cope with anxiety. Among the many individuals who contributed to the psychoanalytic perspective, two were especially influential: Sigmund Freud, founder of the psychoanalytic movement, and Erik Erikson.

FREUD'S THEORY   Freud (1856–1939), a Viennese physician, sought a cure for emotionally troubled adults by having them talk freely about painful events of their childhoods. Working with these recollections, Freud examined the unconscious motivations of his patients and constructed his **psychosexual theory,** which emphasizes that how parents manage their child's sexual and aggressive drives in the first few years is crucial for healthy personality development.

In Freud's theory, three parts of the personality—id, ego, and superego—become integrated during a sequence of five stages, summarized in Table 1.1 on page 16. The *id,* the largest portion of the mind, is the source of basic biological needs and desires. The *ego,* the conscious, rational part of personality, emerges in early infancy to redirect the id's impulses so that they are discharged in acceptable ways. Between 3 and 6 years of age, the *superego,* or conscience, develops through interactions with parents, who insist that children conform to the values of society. Now the ego faces the increasingly complex task of reconciling the demands of the id, the external world, and conscience (Freud, 1923/1974)—for example, the id impulse to grab an attractive toy from a playmate, versus the superego's awareness that such behavior is wrong. According to Freud, the relations established between id, ego, and superego during the preschool years determine the individual's basic personality.

Freud (1938/1973) believed that during childhood, sexual impulses shift their focus from the oral to the anal to the genital regions of the body. In each stage, parents walk a fine line between permitting too much or too little gratification of their child's basic needs. If parents strike an appropriate balance, then children grow into well-adjusted adults with the capacity for mature sexual behavior and investment in family life.

Freud's theory was the first to stress the influence of the early parent–child relationship on development—an emphasis that continues to play a role in many contemporary theories. But his perspective was eventually criticized. First, it overemphasized the influence of sexual feelings in development. Second, because it was based on the problems of sexually repressed, well-to-do adults in nineteenth-century Victorian society, it did not apply in other cultures. Finally, Freud had not studied children directly.

ERIKSON'S THEORY   Several of Freud's followers took what was useful from his theory and improved on his vision. The most important of these neo-Freudians is Erik Erikson (1902–1994), who expanded the picture of development at each stage. In his **psychosocial theory,** Erikson emphasized that in addition to mediating between id impulses and superego demands, the ego makes a positive contribution to development, acquiring attitudes and skills that make the individual an active, contributing member of society. A basic psychological conflict, which is resolved along a continuum from positive to negative, determines healthy or maladaptive outcomes at each stage. As Table 1.1 shows, Erikson's first five stages parallel Freud's stages, but Erikson added three adult stages. He was one of the first to recognize the lifespan nature of development.

Unlike Freud, Erikson pointed out that normal development must be understood in relation to each culture's life situation. For example, in the 1940s, he observed that Yurok Indians

TABLE 1.1 Freud's Psychosexual Stages and Erikson's Psychosocial Stages Compared

APPROXIMATE AGE	FREUD'S PSYCHOSEXUAL STAGE	ERIKSON'S PSYCHOSOCIAL STAGE
Birth–1 year	*Oral:* If oral needs are not met through sucking from breast or bottle, the individual may develop such habits as thumb sucking, fingernail biting, overeating, or smoking.	*Basic trust versus mistrust:* From warm, responsive care, infants gain a sense of trust that the world is good. Mistrust occurs if infants are neglected or handled harshly.
1–3 years	*Anal:* Toddlers and preschoolers enjoy holding and releasing urine and feces. If parents toilet train before children are ready or make too few demands, conflicts about anal control may appear in the form of extreme orderliness or disorder.	*Autonomy versus shame and doubt:* Using new mental and motor skills, children want to decide for themselves. Autonomy is fostered when parents permit reasonable free choice and do not force or shame the child.
3–6 years	*Phallic:* As preschoolers take pleasure in genital stimulation, Freud's Oedipus conflict for boys and Electra conflict for girls arise: Children feel a sexual desire for the other-sex parent. To avoid punishment, they give up this desire and adopt the same-sex parent's values. As a result, the superego is formed, and children feel guilty when they violate its standards.	*Initiative versus guilt:* Through make-believe play, children gain insight into the person they can become. Initiative—a sense of ambition and responsibility—develops when parents support their child's sense of purpose. If parents demand too much self-control, children experience excessive guilt.
6–11 years	*Latency:* Sexual instincts die down, and the superego strengthens as the child acquires new social values from adults and same-sex peers.	*Industry versus inferiority:* At school, children learn to work and cooperate with others. Inferiority develops when negative experiences at home or school lead to feelings of incompetence.
Adolescence	*Genital:* With puberty, sexual impulses reappear. Successful development during earlier stages leads to marriage, mature sexuality, and child rearing.	*Identity versus role confusion* By exploring values and vocational goals, the young person forms a personal identity. The negative outcome is confusion about future adult roles.
Early adulthood		*Intimacy versus isolation:* Young adults establish intimate relationships. Because of earlier disappointments, some individuals cannot form close bonds and remain isolated.
Middle adulthood		*Generativity versus stagnation:* Generativity means giving to the next generation through child rearing, caring for others, or productive work. The person who fails in these ways feels an absence of meaningful accomplishment.
Old age		*Integrity versus despair:* Integrity results from feeling that life was worth living as it happened. Older people who are dissatisfied with their lives fear death.

© OLIVE PIERCE/BLACK STAR

Erik Erikson

of the U.S. northwest coast deprived babies of breastfeeding for the first 10 days after birth and instead fed them a thin soup. At age 6 months, infants were abruptly weaned—if necessary, by having the mother leave for a few days. From our cultural vantage point, these practices may seem cruel. But Erikson explained that because the Yurok depended on salmon, which fill the river just once a year, the development of considerable self-restraint was essential for survival. In this way, he showed that child rearing is responsive to the competencies valued and needed by the child's society.

CONTRIBUTIONS AND LIMITATIONS OF PSYCHOANALYTIC THEORY A special strength of the psychoanalytic perspective is its emphasis on the individual's unique life history as worthy of study and understanding. Consistent with this view, psychoanalytic theorists accept the *clinical,* or *case study, method,* which synthesizes information from a variety of sources into a detailed picture of the personality of a single child. (We will discuss this method further at the end of this chapter.) Psychoanalytic theory has also inspired a wealth of research on many aspects of emotional and social development, including infant–caregiver attachment, aggression, sibling relationships, child-rearing practices, morality, gender roles, and adolescent identity.

Despite its extensive contributions, the psychoanalytic perspective is no longer in the mainstream of child development research. Psychoanalytic theorists may have become isolated from the rest of the field because they were so strongly committed to the clinical approach that they failed to consider other methods. In addition, many psychoanalytic ideas, such as psychosexual stages and ego functioning, are too vague to be tested empirically (Crain, 2005; Thomas, 2005). Nevertheless, Erikson's broad outline of psychosocial change captures the essence of personality development during childhood and adolescence. Consequently, we will return to it in later chapters.

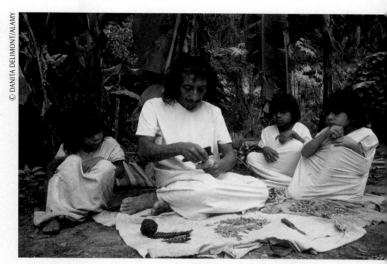

■ Children of the Lacandon Mayan people of southern Mexico learn from their father how to make souvenir arrows similar to those of their hunter-gatherer ancestors. As Erikson recognized, these child-rearing practices can be understood only in relation to the Lacandon's distinct culture. ■

Behaviorism and Social Learning Theory

As the psychoanalytic perspective gained prominence, child study was also influenced by a very different perspective. According to **behaviorism,** directly observable events—stimuli and responses—are the appropriate focus of study. North American behaviorism began in the early twentieth century with the work of psychologist John Watson (1878–1958), who wanted to create an objective science of psychology.

TRADITIONAL BEHAVIORISM   Watson was inspired by Russian physiologist Ivan Pavlov's studies of animal learning. Pavlov knew that dogs release saliva as an innate reflex when they are given food. But he noticed that his dogs started salivating before they tasted any food—when they saw the trainer who usually fed them. The dogs, Pavlov reasoned, must have learned to associate a neutral stimulus (the trainer) with another stimulus (food) that produces a reflexive response (salivation). Because of this association, the neutral stimulus alone could bring about a response resembling the reflex. Eager to test this idea, Pavlov successfully taught dogs to salivate at the sound of a bell by pairing it with the presentation of food. He had discovered *classical conditioning*.

Watson wanted to find out if classical conditioning could be applied to children's behavior. In a historic experiment, he taught Albert, an 11-month-old infant, to fear a neutral stimulus—a soft white rat—by presenting it several times with a sharp, loud sound, which naturally scared the baby. Little Albert, who at first had reached out eagerly to touch the furry rat, began to cry and turn his head away at the sight of it (Watson & Raynor, 1920). In fact, Albert's fear was so intense that researchers eventually challenged the ethics of studies like this one. Consistent with Locke's tabula rasa, Watson concluded that environment is the supreme force in development and that adults can mold children's behavior by carefully controlling stimulus–response associations. He viewed development as continuous—a gradual increase with age in the number and strength of these associations.

Another form of behaviorism was B. F. Skinner's (1904–1990) *operant conditioning theory*. According to Skinner, the frequency of a behavior can be increased by following it with a wide variety of *reinforcers*—food, praise, a friendly smile, or a new toy—or decreased through *punishment*, such as disapproval or withdrawal of privileges. As a result of Skinner's work, operant conditioning became a broadly applied learning principle, which we will consider further when we explore the infant's learning capacities in Chapter 5.

SOCIAL LEARNING THEORY   Psychologists wondered whether behaviorism might offer a more direct and effective explanation of the development of children's social behavior than the less precise concepts of psychoanalytic theory. This sparked approaches that built on the principles of conditioning, offering expanded views of how children and adults acquire new responses.

© BOB DAEMMRICH/THE IMAGE WORKS

■ Social learning theory recognizes that children acquire many skills through modeling. By observing and imitating her mother's behavior, this 19-month-old learns an important skill. ■

Several kinds of **social learning theory** emerged. The most influential, devised by Albert Bandura (1977), emphasizes *modeling,* also known as *imitation* or *observational learning,* as a powerful source of development. The baby who claps her hands after her mother does so, the child who angrily hits a playmate in the same way that he has been punished at home, and the teenager who wears the same clothes and hairstyle as her friends are all displaying observational learning.

Bandura's work continues to influence much research on children's social development. But today, like the field of child development as a whole, his theory stresses the importance of *cognition,* or thinking. Bandura has shown that children's ability to listen, remember, and abstract general rules from complex sets of observed behaviors affects their imitation and learning. In fact, the most recent revision of Bandura's (1992, 2001) theory places such strong emphasis on how children think about themselves and other people that he calls it a *social-cognitive* rather than a social learning approach.

In Bandura's revised view, children gradually become more selective in what they imitate. From watching others engage in self-praise and self-blame and through feedback about the worth of their own actions, children develop *personal standards* for behavior and a *sense of self-efficacy*—the belief that their own abilities and characteristics will help them succeed. These cognitions guide responses in particular situations (Bandura, 1999, 2001). For example, imagine a parent who often remarks, "I'm glad I kept working on that task, even though it was hard," and who encourages persistence by saying, "I know you can do a good job on that homework!" Soon the child starts to view herself as hardworking and high-achieving and selects people with these characteristics as models. In this way, as children acquire attitudes, values, and convictions about themselves, they control their own learning and behavior.

CONTRIBUTIONS AND LIMITATIONS OF BEHAVIORISM AND SOCIAL LEARNING THEORY Behaviorism and social learning theory have had a major impact on practices with children. **Behavior modification** consists of procedures that combine conditioning and modeling to eliminate undesirable behaviors and increase desirable responses. It has been used to relieve a wide range of serious developmental problems, such as persistent aggression, language delays, and extreme fears (Martin & Pear, 2007).

Behavior modification is also effective in dealing with common, everyday difficulties, including poor time management; unwanted habits such as nail biting and smoking; and anxiety over such recurrent events as test-taking, public speaking, and medical and dental treatments. In one study, researchers reduced 4- and 5-year-olds' unruliness in a preschool classroom by reinforcing them with tokens (which they could exchange for treats) when they behaved appropriately and punishing them by taking away tokens when they screamed, threw objects, attacked other children, or refused to comply with a teacher's request (Conyers et al., 2004). In another investigation, children with acute burn injuries played a virtual reality game while nurses engaged in the painful process of changing their bandages. Visual images and sound effects delivered though a headset made the children feel as if they were in a fantasy world. As the game reinforced children's concentration and pleasure, it distracted them from the medical procedure, causing their pain and anxiety to drop sharply compared with dressing changes in which the game was unavailable (Das et al., 2005).

Nevertheless, many theorists believe that behaviorism and social learning theory offer too narrow a view of important environmental influences. These extend beyond immediate reinforcements and modeled behaviors to children's rich physical and social worlds. Behaviorism and social learning theory have also been criticized for underestimating children's

LOOK AND LISTEN

Describe an event you observed in which feedback from a parent or teacher likely strengthened a child's self-efficacy. How might the adult's message have influenced the child's self-perceptions and choice of models?

contributions to their own development. Bandura, with his emphasis on cognition, is unique among theorists whose work grew out of the behaviorist tradition in granting children an active role in their own learning.

Piaget's Cognitive-Developmental Theory

If one individual has influenced the contemporary field of child development more than any other, it is Swiss cognitive theorist Jean Piaget (1896–1980). North American investigators had been aware of Piaget's work since 1930. But they did not grant it much attention until the 1960s, mainly because Piaget's ideas were at odds with behaviorism, which dominated North American psychology in the mid-twentieth century (Cairns & Cairns, 2006). Piaget did not believe that children's learning depends on reinforcers, such as rewards from adults. According to his **cognitive-developmental theory**, children actively construct knowledge as they manipulate and explore their world.

PIAGET'S STAGES Piaget's view of development was greatly influenced by his early training in biology. Central to his theory is the biological concept of *adaptation* (Piaget, 1971). Just as structures of the body are adapted to fit with the environment, so structures of the mind develop to better fit with, or represent, the external world. In infancy and early childhood, Piaget claimed, children's understanding is different from adults'. For example, he believed that young babies do not realize that an object hidden from view—a favorite toy or even the mother—continues to exist. He also concluded that preschoolers' thinking is full of faulty logic. For example, children younger than age 7 commonly say that the amount of a liquid changes when it is poured into a different-shaped container. According to Piaget, children eventually revise these incorrect ideas in their ongoing efforts to achieve an *equilibrium,* or balance, between internal structures and information they encounter in their everyday worlds.

In Piaget's theory, as the brain develops and children's experiences expand, they move through four broad stages, each characterized by qualitatively distinct ways of thinking. Table 1.2 provides a brief description of Piaget's stages. Cognitive development begins in the

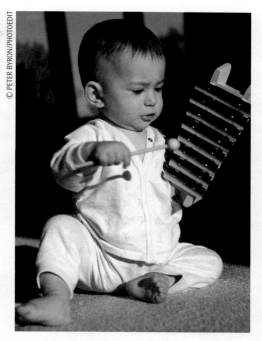

■ In Piaget's sensorimotor stage, babies learn by acting on the world. As this 1-year-old bangs a mallet on a xylophone, he discovers that his movements have predictable effects on objects and that objects influence one another in regular ways. ■

TABLE 1.2 Piaget's Stages of Cognitive Development

STAGE	PERIOD OF DEVELOPMENT	DESCRIPTION
Sensorimotor	Birth–2 years	Infants "think" by acting on the world with their eyes, ears, hands, and mouth. As a result, they invent ways of solving sensorimotor problems, such as pulling a lever to hear the sound of a music box, finding hidden toys, and putting objects in and taking them out of containers.
Preoperational	2–7 years	Preschool children use symbols to represent their earlier sensorimotor discoveries. Development of language and make-believe play takes place. However, thinking lacks the logic of the two remaining stages.
Concrete operational	7–11 years	Children's reasoning becomes logical and better organized. School-age children understand that a certain amount of lemonade or play dough remains the same even after its appearance changes. They also organize objects into hierarchies of classes and subclasses. However, thinking falls short of adult intelligence. It is not yet abstract.
Formal operational	11 years on	The capacity for abstract, systematic thinking enables adolescents, when faced with a problem, to start with a hypothesis, deduce testable inferences, and isolate and combine variables to see which inferences are confirmed. Adolescents can also evaluate the logic of verbal statements without referring to real-world circumstances.

Jean Piaget

sensorimotor stage with the baby's use of the senses and movements to explore the world. These action patterns evolve into the symbolic but illogical thinking of the preschooler in the *preoperational stage*. Then cognition is transformed into the more organized reasoning of the school-age child in the *concrete operational stage*. Finally, in the *formal operational stage*, thought becomes the abstract, systematic reasoning system of the adolescent and adult.

Piaget devised special methods for investigating how children think. Early in his career, he carefully observed his three infant children and also presented them with everyday problems, such as an attractive object that could be grasped, mouthed, kicked, or searched for. From their responses, Piaget derived his ideas about cognitive changes during the first two years. To study childhood and adolescent thought, Piaget adapted the clinical method of psychoanalysis, conducting open-ended *clinical interviews* in which a child's initial response to a task served as the basis for Piaget's next question. We will look more closely at this technique when we discuss research methods later in this chapter.

CONTRIBUTIONS AND LIMITATIONS OF PIAGET'S THEORY

Piaget convinced the field that children are active learners whose minds consist of rich structures of knowledge. Besides investigating children's understanding of the physical world, Piaget explored their reasoning about the social world. His stages have sparked a wealth of research on children's conceptions of themselves, other people, and human relationships. In practical terms, Piaget's theory encouraged the development of educational philosophies and programs that emphasize children's discovery learning and direct contact with the environment.

Despite Piaget's overwhelming contributions, his theory has been challenged. Research indicates that Piaget underestimated the competencies of infants and preschoolers. When young children are given tasks scaled down in difficulty and relevant to their everyday experiences, their understanding appears closer to that of the older child and adult than Piaget assumed. Also, adolescents generally reach their full intellectual potential only in areas of endeavor in which they have had extensive education and experience (Kuhn,

■ In Piaget's preoperational stage, preschoolers represent their earlier sensorimotor discoveries with symbols, and language and make-believe play develop rapidly. These 5-year-olds need only a few props to create an imaginary office scene. ■

■ In Piaget's concrete operational stage, school-age children think in an organized, logical fashion about concrete objects. These 7-year-olds understand that the amount of milk remains the same after being poured into a differently shaped container, even though its appearance changes. ■

■ In Piaget's formal operational stage, adolescents think systematically and abstractly. They solve problems by generating hypotheses about procedures that might work, isolating and combining relevant variables, and conducting systematic tests to observe their real-world consequences. ■

2008). These discoveries have led many researchers to conclude that maturity of thinking depends heavily on the complexity of knowledge sampled and the individual's familiarity with the task. Furthermore, many studies show that children's performance on Piagetian problems can be improved with training—findings that call into question Piaget's assumption that discovery learning rather than adult teaching is the best way to foster development (Klahr & Nigam, 2004; Siegler & Sventina, 2006). Critics also point out that Piaget's stagewise account pays insufficient attention to social and cultural influences—and the resulting wide variation in thinking among children and adolescents of the same age.

Today, the field of child development is divided over its loyalty to Piaget's ideas (Desrochers, 2008). Those who continue to find merit in Piaget's stages often accept a modified view—one in which changes in children's thinking take place more gradually than Piaget believed (Case, 1998; Demetriou et al., 2002; Fischer & Bidell, 2006; Halford & Andrews, 2006). Among those who disagree with Piaget's stage sequence, some have embraced an approach that emphasizes continuous gains in children's cognition: information processing. And still others have been drawn to theories that highlight the role of children's social and cultural contexts. We take up these approaches in the next section.

ASK YOURSELF

◆ REVIEW What aspect of behaviorism made it attractive to critics of psychoanalytic theory? How did Piaget's theory respond to a major limitation of behaviorism?

◆ APPLY A 4-year-old becomes frightened of the dark and refuses to go to sleep at night. How would a psychoanalyst and a behaviorist differ in their views of how this problem developed?

◆ CONNECT Although social learning theory focuses on social development and Piaget's theory on cognitive development, each has enhanced our understanding of other domains. Mention an additional domain addressed by each theory.

Recent Theoretical Perspectives

New ways of understanding the child are constantly emerging—questioning, building on, and enhancing the discoveries of earlier theories. Today, a burst of fresh approaches and research emphases is broadening our understanding of children's development.

Information Processing

In the 1970s and 1980s, researchers turned to the field of cognitive psychology for ways to understand the development of children's thinking. The design of digital computers that use mathematically specified steps to solve problems suggested to psychologists that the human mind might also be viewed as a symbol-manipulating system through which information flows—a perspective called **information processing** (Klahr & MacWhinney, 1998; Munakata, 2006). From the time information is presented to the senses at *input* until it emerges as a behavioral response at *output,* information is actively coded, transformed, and organized.

CONCERN WITH RIGOR AND PRECISION Information-processing researchers often use flowcharts to map the precise steps individuals use to solve problems and complete tasks, much like the plans devised by programmers to get computers to perform a series of "mental operations" (Siegler & Alibali, 2005). To see the usefulness of this approach, let's look at an example.

FIGURE 1.3

Information-processing flowchart showing the steps that a 5-year-old used to solve a bridge-building problem. Her task was to use blocks varying in size, shape, and weight, some of which were planklike, to construct a bridge across a "river" (painted on a floor mat) too wide for any single block to span. The child discovered how to counterweight and balance the bridge. The arrows reveal that even after building a successful counterweight, she returned to earlier, unsuccessful strategies, which seemed to help her understand why the counterweight approach worked. *(Adapted from Thornton, 1999.)*

In a study of problem solving, a researcher provided a pile of blocks varying in size, shape, and weight and asked school-age children to build a bridge across a "river" (painted on a floor mat) that was too wide for any single block to span (Thornton, 1999). Figure 1.3 shows one solution to the problem: Two planklike blocks span the water, each held in place by the counterweight of heavy blocks on the bridge's towers. Whereas older children easily built successful bridges, only one 5-year-old did. Careful tracking of her efforts revealed that she repeatedly tried unsuccessful strategies, such as pushing two planks together and pressing down on their ends to hold them in place. But eventually, her experimentation triggered the idea of using the blocks as counterweights. Her mistaken procedures helped her understand why the counterweight approach worked.

Many information-processing models exist. Some, like the one just considered, track children's mastery of one or a few tasks. Others describe the human cognitive system as a whole (Atkinson & Shiffrin, 1968; Lockhart & Craik, 1990). These general models are used as guides for asking questions about broad age changes in children's thinking: Does a child's ability to solve problems become more organized and "planful" with age? What strategies do younger and older children use to remember new information, and how do those strategies affect children's recall?

The information-processing approach is also being used to clarify the processing of social information. For example, flowcharts exist that track the steps children use to solve social problems (such as how to enter an ongoing play group) and acquire gender-linked preferences and behaviors (Crick & Dodge, 1994; Liben & Bigler, 2002). If we can identify how social problem solving and gender stereotyping arise in childhood, then we can design interventions that promote more favorable social development.

Like Piaget's theory, the information-processing approach regards children as active, sense-making beings who modify their own thinking in response to environmental demands (Halford, 2005; Munakata, 2006). But unlike Piaget's theory, it does not divide development into stages. Rather, the thought processes studied—perception, attention, memory, categorization of information, planning, problem solving, and comprehension of written and spoken prose—are regarded as similar at all ages but present to a lesser or greater extent. Therefore, the view of development is one of continuous change.

A great strength of the information-processing approach is its commitment to rigorous research methods. Because it has provided precise accounts of how children of different ages engage in many aspects of thinking, its findings have led to teaching methods that help children approach academic tasks in more advanced ways (Blumenfeld, Marx, & Harris, 2006). But information processing has fallen short in some respects. It has been better at analyzing thinking into its components than at putting them back together into a comprehensive theory. And it has had little to say about aspects of children's cognition that are not linear and logical, such as imagination and creativity (Birney et al., 2005).

DEVELOPMENTAL COGNITIVE NEUROSCIENCE Over the past three decades, as information-processing research expanded, a new area of investigation arose, called **developmental cognitive neuroscience.** It brings together researchers from psychology, biology, neuroscience, and medicine to study the relationship between changes in the brain and the developing child's cognitive processing and behavior patterns.

Improved methods for analyzing brain activity while children perform various tasks have greatly enhanced knowledge of relationships between brain functioning and behavior (Johnson, 2005; Pennington, Snyder, & Roberts, 2007; Westermann et al., 2007). Armed with these brain-imaging techniques (which we will consider in Chapter 5), neuroscientists are tackling questions like these: How does genetic makeup combine with specific experiences at various ages to influence the growth and organization of the child's brain? How do changes in brain structures support rapid memory development in infancy and toddlerhood? What transformations in brain systems make it harder for adolescents and adults than for children to acquire a second language?

During infancy and early childhood, the brain is highly plastic—especially open to growth and reorganization as a result of experience. But a revolutionary finding of neuroscience research is that the brain retains considerable plasticity throughout life. Neuroscientists are making especially impressive progress in identifying the types of experiences that support or undermine brain development at diverse ages. They are also clarifying the brain bases of many learning and behavior disorders (Durston & Conrad, 2007; Schlaggar & McCandliss, 2007). And they are contributing to effective treatments for children with disabilities by examining the impact of various intervention techniques on both brain functioning and behavior (Luciana, 2007). Although much remains to be discovered, developmental cognitive neuroscience is already transforming our understanding of development and yielding major practical applications.

An advantage of having many theories is that they encourage researchers to attend to previously neglected dimensions of children's lives. The final four perspectives we will discuss focus on *contexts* for development. The first of these views emphasizes that the development of many capacities is influenced by our long evolutionary history.

Ethology and Evolutionary Developmental Psychology

Ethology is concerned with the adaptive, or survival, value of behavior and its evolutionary history. Its roots can be traced to the work of Darwin. Two European zoologists, Konrad Lorenz and Niko Tinbergen, laid its modern foundations. Watching diverse animal species in their natural habitats, Lorenz and Tinbergen observed behavior patterns that promote survival. The best known of these is *imprinting,* the early following behavior of certain baby birds, such as geese, which ensures that the young will stay close to the mother and be fed and protected from danger (Lorenz, 1952). Imprinting takes place during an early, restricted period of development. If the mother goose is absent during this time but an object resembling her in important features is present, young goslings may imprint on it instead.

Observations of imprinting led to a major concept in child development: the *critical period.* It is a limited time span during which the child is biologically prepared to acquire certain adaptive behaviors but needs the support of an appropriately stimulating environment. Many researchers have investigated whether complex cognitive and social behaviors must be learned during certain periods. For example, if children are deprived of adequate food or physical and social stimulation during their early years, will their intelligence be impaired? If language is not mastered in early childhood, is the child's capacity to acquire it reduced?

In later chapters, you will discover that the term *sensitive period* applies better to human development than the strict notion of a critical period (Bornstein, 1989). A **sensitive period** is

AP/WIDE WORLD PHOTOS

■ Ethology focuses on the adaptive, or survival, value of behavior and on similarities between human behavior and that of other species, especially our primate relatives. Observing this mother cuddling her 8-day-old infant helps us understand the human caregiver–infant relationship. ■

a time that is biologically optimal for certain capacities to emerge because the individual is especially responsive to environmental influences. However, its boundaries are less well-defined than are those of a critical period. Development can occur later, but it is harder to induce.

Inspired by observations of imprinting, British psychoanalyst John Bowlby (1969) applied ethological theory to understanding the human caregiver–infant relationship. He argued that infant smiling, babbling, grasping, and crying are built-in social signals that encourage the caregiver to approach, care for, and interact with the baby. By keeping the parent near, these behaviors help ensure that the baby will be fed, protected from danger, and provided with the stimulation and affection necessary for healthy growth. The development of attachment in human infants is a lengthy process involving changes in psychological structures that lead the baby to form a deep affectionate tie with the caregiver (Thompson, 2006). In Chapter 7, we will consider how infant, caregiver, and family context contribute to attachment and how attachment influences later development.

Observations by ethologists have shown that many aspects of children's social behavior, including emotional expressions, aggression, cooperation, and social play, resemble those of our primate relatives. Recently, researchers have extended this effort in a new area of research called **evolutionary developmental psychology.** It seeks to understand the adaptive value of species-wide cognitive, emotional, and social competencies as those competencies change with age (Geary, 2006b). Evolutionary developmental psychologists ask questions like these: What role does the newborn's visual preference for facelike stimuli play in survival? Does it support older infants' capacity to distinguish familiar caregivers from unfamiliar people? Why do children play in gender-segregated groups? What do they learn from such play that might lead to adult gender-typed behaviors, such as male dominance and female investment in caregiving?

As these examples suggest, evolutionary psychologists are not just concerned with the genetic and biological basis of development. They realize that humans' large brain and extended childhood resulted from the need to master an increasingly complex environment, so they are also interested in learning (Grotuss, Bjorklund, & Csinady, 2007). And they realize that today's lifestyles differ so radically from those of our evolutionary ancestors that certain evolved behaviors, such as life-threatening risk taking by adolescents and male-to-male violence, are no longer adaptive (Blasi & Bjorklund, 2003). By clarifying the origins and development of such behaviors, evolutionary developmental psychology may help spark more effective interventions.

In sum, evolutionary psychologists want to understand the entire *organism–environment system.* The next contextual perspective we will discuss, Vygotsky's sociocultural theory, serves as an excellent complement to the evolutionary viewpoint because it highlights the social and cultural dimensions of children's experiences.

Vygotsky's Sociocultural Theory

The field of child development has recently seen a dramatic increase in studies addressing the cultural context of children's lives. Investigations that make comparisons across cultures, and between ethnic groups within cultures, provide insight into whether developmental pathways apply to all children or are limited to particular environmental conditions (Goodnow, 2010).

Today, much research is examining the relationship of *culturally specific beliefs and practices* to development. The contributions of Russian psychologist Lev Vygotsky (1896–1934) have played a major role in this trend. Vygotsky's (1934/1987) perspective, known as **sociocultural theory,** focuses on how *culture*—the values, beliefs, customs, and skills of a social group—is transmitted to the next generation. According to Vygotsky, *social inter-action*—in particular, cooperative dialogues with more knowledgeable members of society—is necessary for children to acquire the ways of thinking and behaving that make up a community's culture. Vygotsky believed that as adults and more expert peers help children master culturally meaningful activities, the communication between them becomes part of children's thinking. As children internalize features of these dialogues, they can use the language within them to guide their own thought and actions and to acquire new skills (Berk & Harris, 2003; Winsler, Fernyhough, & Montero, 2009). The young child instructing herself while working a puzzle or preparing a table for dinner has begun to produce the same kinds of guiding comments that an adult previously used to help her master important tasks.

Vygotsky's theory has been especially influential in the study of children's cognition. Vygotsky agreed with Piaget that children are active, constructive beings. But whereas Piaget emphasized children's independent efforts to make sense of their world, Vygotsky viewed cognitive development as a *socially mediated process,* in which children depend on assistance from adults and more expert peers as they tackle new challenges.

In Vygotsky's theory, children undergo certain stagewise changes. For example, when they acquire language, they gain in ability to participate in dialogues with others, and mastery of culturally valued competencies surges forward. When children enter school, they spend much time discussing language, literacy, and other academic concepts—experiences that encourage them to reflect on their own thinking (Bodrova & Leong, 2007; Kozulin, 2003). As a result, they gain dramatically in reasoning and problem solving.

At the same time, Vygotsky stressed that dialogues with experts lead to continuous changes in thinking that vary greatly from culture to culture. Consistent with this view, a major finding of cross-cultural research is that cultures select different tasks for children's learning (Rogoff, 2003). Social interaction surrounding those tasks leads to competencies essential for success in a particular culture. For example, in industrialized nations, teachers help people learn to read, drive a car, or use a computer. Among the Zinacanteco Indians of southern Mexico, adult experts guide young girls as they master complicated weaving techniques (Greenfield, 2004; Greenfield, Maynard, & Childs, 2000). In Brazil and other developing nations, child candy sellers with little or no schooling develop sophisticated mathematical abilities as the result of buying candy from wholesalers, pricing it in collaboration with adults and experienced peers, and bargaining with customers on city streets (Saxe, 1988).

Research stimulated by Vygotsky's theory reveals that children in every culture develop unique strengths. But Vygotsky's emphasis on culture and social experience led him to neglect the biological side of development. Although he recognized the importance of heredity and brain growth, he said little about their role in cognitive change. Furthermore, Vygotsky's focus on social transmission of knowledge meant that, compared with other theorists, he placed less emphasis on children's capacity to shape their own development. Followers of Vygotsky stress that children strive for social connection, actively participating in the conversations and social activities from which their development springs. From these joint experiences, they not only acquire culturally valued practices but also modify and transform those practices (Nelson, 2007; Rogoff, 2003). Contemporary sociocultural theorists grant the individual and society balanced, mutually influential roles.

Ecological Systems Theory

Urie Bronfenbrenner (1917–2005) is responsible for an approach to child development that has moved to the forefront of the field over the past two decades because it offers the most differentiated and complete account of contextual influences on children's development. **Ecological systems theory** views the child as developing within a complex *system* of relationships affected by multiple levels of

■ According to Lev Vygotsky, shown here with his daughter, many cognitive processes and skills are socially transferred from more knowledgeable members of society to children. Vygotsky's sociocultural theory helps explain the wide cultural variation in cognitive competencies. ■

■ With her mother's guidance, this Navajo child learns to use a vertical weaving loom. She acquires a culturally valued skill through interaction with an older, more experienced weaver. ■

the surrounding environment. Since the child's biologically influenced dispositions join with environmental forces to mold development, Bronfenbrenner characterized his perspective as a *bioecological model* (Bronfenbrenner, 2005; Bronfenbrenner & Morris, 2006).

Bronfenbrenner envisioned the environment as a series of interrelated, nested structures that form a complex functioning whole, or *system*. These include but also extend beyond the home, school, and neighborhood settings in which children spend their everyday lives (see Figure 1.4). Each layer joins with the others to powerfully affect development.

THE MICROSYSTEM   The innermost level of the environment, the **microsystem,** consists of activities and interaction patterns in the child's immediate surroundings. Bronfenbrenner emphasizes that to understand child development at this level, we must keep in mind that all relationships are *bidirectional:* Adults affect children's behavior, but children's biologically and socially influenced characteristics—their physical attributes, personalities, and capacities— also affect adults' behavior. A friendly, attentive child is likely to evoke positive, patient reactions from parents, whereas a distractible child is more likely to receive restriction and punishment. When these reciprocal interactions occur often over time, they have an enduring impact on development (Collins et al., 2000; Crockenberg & Leerkes, 2003b).

Third parties—other individuals in the microsystem—also affect the quality of any two-person relationship. If they are supportive, interaction is enhanced. For example, when parents encourage each other in their child-rearing roles, each engages in more effective parenting. In contrast, marital conflict is associated with inconsistent discipline and hostile reactions toward children. In response, children often react with fear and anxiety or with anger and aggression, and the well-being of both parent and child suffers (Caldera & Lindsey, 2006; Davies & Lindsay, 2004).

THE MESOSYSTEM   The second level of Bronfenbrenner's model, the **mesosystem,** encompasses connections between microsystems, such as home, school, neighborhood, and child-care center. For example, a child's academic progress depends not just on activities that take place in classrooms but also on parent involvement in school life and on the extent

FIGURE 1.4

Structure of the environment in ecological systems theory. The *microsystem* concerns relations between the child and the immediate environment; the *mesosystem,* connections among immediate settings; the *exosystem,* social settings that affect but do not contain the child; and the *macrosystem,* the values, laws, customs, and resources of the culture that affect activities and interactions at all inner layers. The *chronosystem* (not pictured) is not a specific context. Instead, it refers to the dynamic, ever-changing nature of the child's environment.

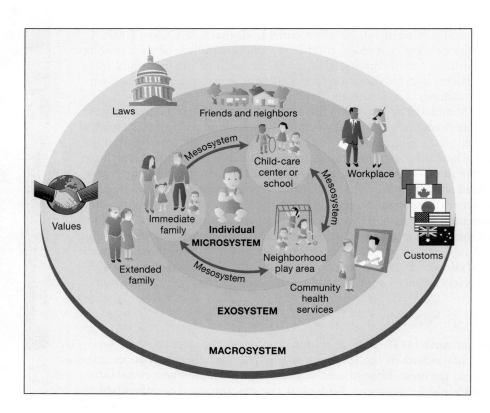

to which academic learning is carried over into the home (Gershoff & Aber, 2006). Similarly, parent–child interaction at home is likely to affect care-giver–child interaction in the child-care setting, and vice versa. Each relationship is more likely to support development when there are links between home and child care, in the form of visits and cooperative exchanges of information.

THE EXOSYSTEM The **exosystem** consists of social settings that do not contain children but that nevertheless affect children's experiences in immediate settings. These can be formal organizations, such as parents' workplaces, their religious institutions, and health and welfare services in the community. For example, parents' work settings can support child rearing and, indirectly, enhance development through flexible work schedules, paid maternity and paternity leave, and sick leave for parents whose children are ill. Exosystem supports also can be informal, such as parents' social networks—friends and extended-family members who provide advice, companionship, and even financial assistance. Research confirms the negative impact of a breakdown in exosystem activities. Families who are affected by unemployment or who are socially isolated, with few personal or community-based ties, show increased rates of conflict and child abuse (Coulton et al., 2007).

■ In ecological systems theory, development occurs within a complex system of relationships affected by multiple levels of the environment. This father says good-bye to his daughter at the start of the school day. The girl's experiences at school (microsystem) and the father's experiences at work (exosystem) affect the father-daughter relationship. ■

THE MACROSYSTEM The outermost level of Bronfenbrenner's model, the **macrosystem**, consists of cultural values, laws, customs, and resources. The priority that the macrosystem gives to children's needs affects the support they receive at inner levels of the environment. For example, in countries that require generous workplace benefits for employed parents and high-quality standards for child care, children are more likely to have favorable experiences in their immediate settings. As you will see in later chapters, such programs are far less available in the United States than in other industrialized nations (Children's Defense Fund, 2008).

AN EVER-CHANGING SYSTEM According to Bronfenbrenner, the environment is not a static force that affects children in a uniform way. Instead, it is ever-changing. Important life events, such as the birth of a sibling, the beginning of school, a move to a new neighborhood, or parents' divorce, modify existing relationships between children and their environments, producing new conditions that affect development. In addition, the timing of environmental change affects its impact. The arrival of a new sibling has very different consequences for a homebound toddler than for a school-age child with many relationships and activities beyond the family.

Bronfenbrenner called the temporal dimension of his model the **chronosystem** (the prefix *chrono-* means "time"). Life changes can be imposed on the child, as in the examples just given. Alternatively, they can arise from within the child, since as children get older they select, modify, and create many of their own settings and experiences. How they do so depends on their physical, intellectual, and personality characteristics and their environmental opportunities. Therefore, in ecological systems theory, development is neither entirely controlled by environmental circumstances nor driven solely by inner dispositions. Rather, children and their environments form a network of interdependent effects. Notice how our discussion of resilient children on pages 10–11 illustrates this idea. You will see many more examples in this book.

LOOK AND LISTEN

❖❖

Ask a parent to explain his or her most worrisome child-rearing challenge. Describe one source of support at each level of Bronfenbrenner's model that could help ease the parent's stress and promote favorable child development.

New Directions: Development as a Dynamic System

Today, researchers recognize both consistency and variability in children's development and want to do a better job of explaining variation. Consequently, a new wave of systems theorists focuses on how children alter their behavior to attain more advanced functioning. According to this **dynamic systems perspective,** the child's mind, body, and physical and social worlds form an *integrated system* that guides mastery of new skills. The system is *dynamic,* or constantly in motion. A change in any part of it—from brain growth to physical or social surroundings—disrupts the current organism–environment relationship. When this happens, the child actively reorganizes his or her behavior so the various components of the system work together again but in a more complex, effective way (Fischer & Bidell, 2006; Spencer & Schöner, 2003; Thelen & Smith, 2006).

Researchers adopting a dynamic systems perspective try to find out just how children attain new levels of organization by studying their behavior while they are in transition (Thelen & Corbetta, 2002). For example, when presented with an attractive toy, how does a 3-month-old baby who engages in many, varied movements discover how to reach for it? On hearing a new word, how does a 2-year-old figure out the category of objects or events to which it refers?

Dynamic systems theorists acknowledge that a common human genetic heritage and basic regularities in children's physical and social worlds yield certain universal, broad outlines of development. But biological makeup, everyday tasks, and the people who support children in mastery of those tasks vary greatly, leading to wide individual differences in specific skills. Even when children master the same skills, such as walking, talking, or adding and subtracting, they often do so in unique ways. And because children build competencies by engaging in real activities in real contexts, different skills vary in maturity within the same child. From this perspective, development cannot be characterized as a single line of change. As Figure 1.5 shows, it is more like a web of fibers branching out in many directions, each representing a different skill area that may undergo both continuous and stagewise transformations (Fischer & Bidell, 2006).

The dynamic systems view has been inspired by other scientific disciplines, especially biology and physics. It also draws on information-processing and contextual theories—evolutionary developmental psychology, sociocultural theory, and ecological systems theory. Dynamic systems research is still in its early stages. The perspective has been applied largely to children's motor and cognitive skills, but some investigators have drawn on it to explain emotional and social development as well (Campos, Frankel, &

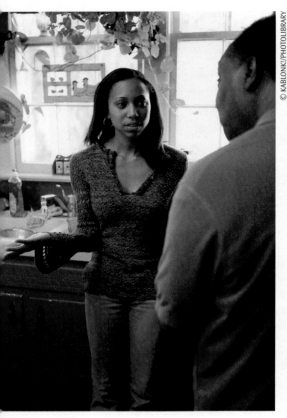

© KABLONK!/PHOTOLIBRARY

■ The dynamic systems perspective views the child's mind, body, and physical and social worlds as a continuously reorganizing, integrated system. A change in any part of the system disrupts the current organism–environment relationship. As this girl experiences the physical, cognitive, and emotional changes of early adolescence, she and her father must devise new, more mature ways of relating to each other. ■

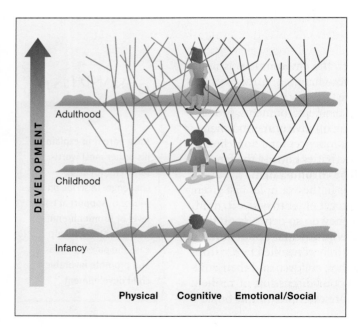

Physical   Cognitive   Emotional/Social

FIGURE 1.5

The dynamic systems view of development. Rather than envisioning a single line of stagewise or continuous change (refer to Figure 1.2 on page 8), dynamic systems theorists conceive of development as a web of fibers branching out in many directions. Each strand in the web represents a skill within the major domains of development—physical, cognitive, and emotional/social. The differing directions of the strands signify possible variations in paths and outcomes as the child masters skills necessary to participate in diverse contexts. The interconnections of the strands at each row of "hills" portray stagelike changes—periods of major transformation in which various skills work together as a functioning whole. As the web expands, skills become more numerous, complex, and effective. *(Adapted from Fischer & Bidell, 2006.)*

Camras, 2004; Fogel & Garvey, 2007; Lewis, 2000). Consider the young teenager, whose body and reasoning powers are changing massively and who also is confronting the challenges of secondary school. Researchers following parent–child interaction over time found that the transition to adolescence disrupted family communication. It became unstable and variable for several years—a mix of positive, neutral, and negative exchanges (Granic et al., 2003). Gradually, as parent and adolescent devised new, more mature ways of relating to one another, the system reorganized and stabilized. Once again, interaction became predictable and mostly positive.

As dynamic systems research illustrates, today investigators are tracking and analyzing development in all its complexity. In doing so, they hope to move closer to an all-encompassing approach to understanding change.

ASK YOURSELF

◆ REVIEW Explain how each recent theoretical perspective regards children as active contributors to their own development.

◆ APPLY Mario wants to find out precisely how children of different ages recall stories. Anna is interested in how adult–child communication in different cultures influences children's storytelling. Which theoretical perspective has Mario probably chosen? How about Anna? Explain.

◆ CONNECT Return to the Biology and Environment box on pages 10–11. How does the story of John and Gary illustrate bidirectional influences within the microsystem, as described in ecological systems theory?

◆ REFLECT To illustrate the chronosystem in ecological systems theory, select an important event from your childhood, such as a move to a new neighborhood or a class with an inspiring teacher. How did the event affect you? How might its impact have differed had you been five years younger? How about five years older?

Comparing Child Development Theories

In the preceding sections, we reviewed theoretical perspectives in child development research. They differ in many respects. First, they focus on different domains of development. Some, such as the psychoanalytic perspective and ethology, emphasize emotional and social development. Others, such as Piaget's cognitive-developmental theory, information processing, and Vygotsky's sociocultural theory, stress changes in thinking. The remaining approaches—behaviorism, social learning theory, evolutionary developmental psychology, ecological systems theory, and the dynamic systems perspective—discuss many aspects of children's functioning. Second, every theory contains a point of view about child development. **TAKE A MOMENT...** As we conclude our review of theoretical perspectives, identify the stand that each theory takes on the controversial issues presented at the beginning of this chapter. Then check your analysis of the theories against Table 1.3 on page 30.

Finally, we have seen that every theory has strengths and limitations. Perhaps you found that you are attracted to some theories, but you have doubts about others. As you read more about child development in later chapters, you may find it useful to keep a notebook in which you test your own theoretical likes and dislikes against the evidence. Don't be surprised if you revise your ideas many times, just as theorists have done throughout the past century. By the end of the course, you will have built your own personal perspective on child development. Very likely, it will be an *eclectic position,* or blend of several theories, since every viewpoint we have considered has contributed to what we know about children.

| TABLE 1.3 | Stances of Major Theories on Basic Issues in Child Development |

THEORY	CONTINUOUS OR DISCONTINUOUS DEVELOPMENT?	ONE COURSE OF DEVELOPMENT OR MANY?	RELATIVE INFLUENCE OF NATURE AND NURTURE?
Psychoanalytic perspective	*Discontinuous*: Psychosexual and psychosocial development takes place in stages.	*One course:* Stages are assumed to be universal.	*Both nature and nurture:* Innate impulses are channeled and controlled through child-rearing experiences. *Early experiences* set the course of later development.
Behaviorism and social learning theory	*Continuous:* Development involves an increase in learned behaviors.	*Many possible courses:* Behaviors reinforced and modeled may vary from child to child.	*Emphasis on nurture:* Development results from conditioning and modeling. *Both early and later experiences* are important.
Piaget's cognitive-developmental theory	*Discontinuous:* Cognitive development takes place in stages.	*One course:* Stages are assumed to be universal.	*Both nature and nurture:* Development occurs as the brain grows and children exercise their innate drive to discover reality in a generally stimulating environment. *Both early and later experiences* are important.
Information processing	*Continuous:* Children gradually improve in perception, attention, memory, and problem-solving skills.	*One course:* Changes studied characterize most or all children.	*Both nature and nurture:* Children are active, sense-making beings who modify their thinking as the brain grows and they confront new environmental demands. *Both early and later experiences* are important.
Ethology and evolutionary developmental psychology	*Both continuous and discontinuous:* Children gradually develop a wider range of adaptive behaviors. Sensitive periods occur, in which qualitatively distinct capacities emerge fairly suddenly.	*One course:* Adaptive behaviors and sensitive periods apply to all members of a species.	*Both nature and nurture:* Evolution and heredity influence behavior, and learning lends greater flexibility and adaptiveness to it. In sensitive periods, *early experiences* set the course of later development.
Vygotsky's sociocultural theory	*Both continuous and discontinuous:* Language acquisition and schooling lead to stagewise changes. Dialogues with more expert members of society also lead to continuous changes that vary from culture to culture.	*Many possible courses:* Socially mediated changes in thought and behavior vary from culture to culture.	*Both nature and nurture:* Heredity, brain growth, and dialogues with more expert members of society jointly contribute to development. *Both early and later experiences* are important.
Ecological systems theory	*Not specified.*	*Many possible courses:* Children's characteristics join with environmental forces at multiple levels to mold development in unique ways.	*Both nature and nurture:* Children's characteristics and the reactions of others affect each other in a bidirectional fashion. Layers of the environment influence child-rearing experiences. *Both early and later experiences* are important.
Dynamic systems perspective	*Both continuous and discontinuous:* Change in the system is always ongoing. Stagelike transformations occur as children reorganize their behavior so components of the system work as a functioning whole.	*Many possible courses:* Biological makeup, everyday tasks, and social experiences vary, yielding wide individual differences in specific skills.	*Both nature and nurture:* The child's mind, body, and physical and social surroundings form an integrated system that guides mastery of new skills. *Both early and later experiences* are important.

■ ■ Studying the Child
■ ■

In every science, research usually begins with a *hypothesis*—a prediction drawn directly from a theory. Theories and hypotheses, however, merely initiate the many activities that result in sound evidence on child development. Conducting research according to scientifically accepted procedures involves many steps and choices. Investigators must decide which participants, and how many, to include. Then they must figure out what the participants will be asked to do and when, where, and how many times each will be seen. Finally, they must examine and draw conclusions from their data.

In the following sections, we look at research strategies commonly used to study children. We begin with common *research methods*—the specific activities of participants, such as taking tests, answering questionnaires, responding to interviews, or being observed. Then we turn to *research designs*—overall plans for research studies that permit the best possible test of the investigator's hypothesis. Finally, we discuss special ethical issues involved in doing research on children.

Why learn about research strategies? Why not leave these matters to research specialists and concentrate on what is already known about the child and how this knowledge can be applied? There are two reasons. First, each of us must be a wise and critical consumer of knowledge. Knowing the strengths and limitations of various research strategies is important in separating dependable information from misleading results. Second, individuals who work directly with children may be in a unique position to build bridges between research and practice by conducting studies, either on their own or in partnership with experienced investigators. Community agencies such as schools, mental health facilities, and parks and recreation programs sometimes collaborate with researchers in designing, implementing, and evaluating interventions aimed at enhancing children's development (Lerner & Overton, 2008). To broaden these efforts, a basic understanding of the research process is essential.

LOOK AND LISTEN

Ask a teacher, counselor, social worker, or nurse to describe a question about development he or she would like researchers to address, as a means of facilitating applied work with children. Recommend research strategies best suited to answering the question, citing their strengths and limitations.

Common Research Methods

How does a researcher choose a basic approach to gathering information about children? Common methods include systematic observation, self-reports (such as questionnaires and interviews), clinical or case studies of a single child, and ethnographies of the life circumstances of a specific group of children. Table 1.4 on page 32 summarizes the strengths and limitations of each of these methods.

SYSTEMATIC OBSERVATION Observations of the behavior of children, and of adults who are important in their lives, can be made in different ways. One approach is to go into the field, or natural environment, and observe the behavior of interest—a method called **naturalistic observation.**

A study of preschoolers' responses to their peers' distress provides a good example of this technique (Farver & Branstetter, 1994). Observing 3- and 4-year-olds in child-care centers, the researchers recorded each instance of a child crying and the reactions of nearby children—whether they ignored, watched curiously, commented on the child's unhappiness, scolded or teased, or shared, helped, or expressed sympathy. Caregiver behaviors—explaining why a child was crying, mediating conflict, or offering comfort—were noted to see if adult sensitivity was related to children's caring responses. A strong relationship emerged. The great strength of naturalistic observation is that investigators can see directly the everyday behaviors they hope to explain.

Naturalistic observation also has a major limitation: Not all individuals have the same opportunity to display a particular behavior in everyday life. In the study just mentioned, some children might have witnessed a child crying more often than others or been exposed to more cues for positive social responses from caregivers. For this reason, they might have displayed more compassion.

Researchers commonly deal with this difficulty by making **structured observations,** in which the investigator sets up a laboratory situation that evokes the behavior of interest

■ In naturalistic observation, the researcher goes into the field and records the behavior of interest. This researcher observes children at a summer camp. She may note their playmate choices, cooperation, helpfulness, or conflicts. ■

TABLE 1.4 Strengths and Limitations of Common Information-Gathering Methods

METHOD	DESCRIPTION	STRENGTHS	LIMITATIONS
Systematic Observation			
Naturalistic observation	Observation of behavior in natural contexts.	Reflects participants' everyday behaviors.	Cannot control conditions under which participants are observed.
Structured observation	Observation of behavior in a laboratory, where conditions are the same for all participants.	Grants each participant an equal opportunity to display the behavior of interest. Permits study of behaviors rarely seen in everyday life.	May not yield observations typical of participants' behavior in everyday life.
Self-Reports			
Clinical interview	Flexible interviewing procedure in which the investigator obtains a complete account of the participant's thoughts.	Comes as close as possible to the way participants think in everyday life. Great breadth and depth of information can be obtained in a short time.	May not result in accurate reporting of information. Flexible procedure makes comparing individuals' responses difficult.
Structured interview, questionnaires, and tests	Self-report instruments in which each participant is asked the same questions in the same way.	Permits comparisons of participants' responses and efficient data collection. Researchers can specify answer alternatives that participants might not think of in an open-ended interview.	Does not yield the same depth of information as a clinical interview. Responses are still subject to inaccurate reporting.
Clinical, or Case Study, Method	A full picture of one individual's psychological functioning, obtained by combining interviews, observations, and sometimes test scores.	Provides rich, descriptive insights into processes of development.	May be biased by researchers' theoretical preferences. Findings cannot be applied to individuals other than the participant.
Ethnography	Participant observation of a culture or distinct social group. By making extensive field notes, the researcher tries to capture the culture's unique values and social processes.	Provides a more complete and accurate description than can be derived from a single observational visit, interview, or questionnaire.	May be biased by researchers' values and theoretical preferences. Findings cannot be applied to individuals and settings other than the ones studied.

so that every participant has an equal opportunity to display the response. In one study, 2-year-olds' emotional reactions to harm that they thought they had caused were observed by asking them to take care of a rag doll that had been modified so its leg would fall off when the child picked it up. To make the child feel at fault, once the leg detached, an adult "talked for" the doll by saying, "Ow!" Researchers recorded children's facial expressions of sadness and concern for the injured doll, efforts to help the doll, and body tension—responses that indicated remorse and a desire to make amends. In addition, mothers were asked to engage in brief conversations about emotions with their children (Garner, 2003). Toddlers whose mothers more often explained the causes and consequences of emotion were more likely to express concern for the injured doll.

Structured observation permits greater control over the research situation than does naturalistic observation. In addition, the method is especially useful for studying behaviors—such as parent–child or friendship interactions—that investigators rarely have an opportunity to see in everyday life. When aggressive and nonaggressive 10-year-old boys were observed playing games with their best friend in a laboratory, the aggressive boys and their friends more often violated game rules, cheated, and encouraged each other to engage in these dishonest acts. In addition, observers rated these boys' interactions as angrier and less cooperative than the interactions of nonaggressive boys (Bagwell & Coie, 2004). The researchers concluded that aggressive boys' close peer ties provide a context in which they practice hostility and other negative behaviors, which may contribute to their antisocial behavior.

The procedures used to collect systematic observations vary, depending on the purpose of the research. Some investigators choose to describe the entire behavior stream—everything said and done over a certain time period. In one study, researchers wanted to find out whether maternal sensitivity in infancy and early childhood contributes to readiness for formal schooling at age 6 (Hirsh-Pasek & Burchinal, 2006). Between age 6 months and 4½ years, the investigators periodically videotaped 15-minute mother–child play sessions. Then they rated each session for maternal positive emotion, support, stimulating play, and respect for the child's autonomy—ingredients of sensitivity that did predict better language and academic progress when the children reached kindergarten.

Researchers have devised ingenious ways of observing difficult-to-capture behaviors. For example, to record instances of bullying, a group of investigators set up video cameras overlooking a classroom and a playground and had fourth to sixth graders wear small, remote microphones and pocket-sized transmitters (Craig, Pepler, & Atlas, 2000). Results revealed that bullying occurred often—at rates of 2.4 episodes per hour in the classroom and 4.5 episodes per hour on the playground. Yet only 15 to 18 percent of the time did teachers take steps to stop the harassment.

Systematic observation provides invaluable information on how children and adults behave, but it tells us little about the reasoning behind their responses. For this kind of information, researchers must turn to self-report techniques.

SELF-REPORTS   Self-reports ask research participants to provide information on their perceptions, thoughts, abilities, feelings, attitudes, beliefs, and past experiences. They range from relatively unstructured interviews to highly structured interviews, questionnaires, and tests.

In a **clinical interview,** a flexible, conversational style is used to probe for the participant's point of view. In the following example, Piaget questioned a 5-year-old child about his understanding of dreams:

> *Where does the dream come from?*—I think you sleep so well that you dream.—*Does it come from us or from outside?*—From outside.—*When you are in bed and you dream, where is the dream?*—In my bed, under the blanket. I don't really know. If it was in my stomach, the bones would be in the way and I shouldn't see it.—*Is the dream there when you sleep?*—Yes, it is in the bed beside me. (Piaget, 1926/1930, pp. 97–98)

The clinical interview has two major strengths. First, it permits people to display their thoughts in terms that are as close as possible to the way they think in everyday life. Second, the clinical interview can provide a large amount of information in a fairly brief period. For example, in an hour-long session, we can obtain a wide range of child-rearing information from a parent—much more than we could capture by observing for the same amount of time.

A major limitation of the clinical interview has to do with the accuracy with which people report their thoughts, feelings, and experiences. Some participants, desiring to please the interviewer, may make up answers. When asked about past events, some may have trouble recalling exactly what happened. And because the clinical interview depends on verbal ability and expressiveness, it may underestimate the capacities of individuals who have difficulty putting their thoughts into words.

The clinical interview has also been criticized because of its flexibility. When questions are phrased differently for each participant, variations in responses may reflect the manner of interviewing rather than real differences in the way people think about a topic. **Structured interviews** (including tests and questionnaires), in which each participant is asked the same questions in the same way, eliminate this problem. These instruments are also much more efficient. Answers are briefer, and researchers can obtain written responses from an entire group at the same time. Furthermore, by listing answer alternatives, researchers can indicate the specific activities and behaviors of interest—ones that participants might not think of in an open-ended clinical interview. For example, when parents were asked what they considered "the most important thing for children to prepare them for life," 62 percent checked "to think for themselves" when this alternative appeared on a list. Yet only 5 percent thought of it during a clinical interview (Schwarz, 1999).

Nevertheless, structured interviews do not yield the same depth of information as a clinical interview. And they can still be affected by inaccurate reporting.

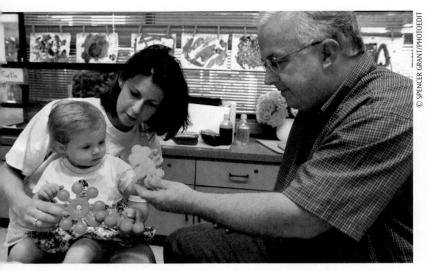

■ Using the clinical, or case study, method, this researcher combines interviews with the mother and observations and testing of the child to construct an in-depth picture of one child's psychological functioning. ■

THE CLINICAL, OR CASE STUDY, METHOD   An outgrowth of psychoanalytic theory, the **clinical, or case study, method** brings together a wide range of information on one child, including interviews, observations, and sometimes test scores. The aim is to obtain as complete a picture as possible of that child's psychological functioning and the experiences that led up to it.

The clinical method is well-suited to studying the development of certain types of individuals who are few in number but vary widely in characteristics. For example, the method has been used to find out what contributes to the accomplishments of *prodigies*—extremely gifted children who attain adult competence in a field before age 10 (Moran & Gardner, 2006). Consider Adam, a boy who read, wrote, and composed musical pieces before he was out of diapers. By age 4, Adam was deeply involved in mastering human symbol systems—French, German, Russian, Sanskrit, Greek, the computer programming language BASIC, ancient hieroglyphs, music, and mathematics. Adam's parents provided a home rich in stimulation and reared him with affection, firmness, and humor. They searched for schools in which he could both develop his abilities and form rewarding social relationships. He graduated from college at age 18 and continued to pursue musical composition. Would Adam have realized his potential without the chance combination of his special gift and nurturing, committed parents? Probably not, researchers concluded (Feldman, 2004).

The clinical method yields richly detailed case narratives that offer valuable insights into the multiplicity of factors affecting development. Nevertheless, like all other methods, it has drawbacks. Because information often is collected unsystematically and subjectively, researchers' theoretical preferences may bias their interpretations. In addition, investigators cannot assume that their conclusions apply, or generalize, to anyone other than the child studied (Stanovich, 2007). Even when patterns emerge across several cases, it is wise to confirm them with other research strategies.

METHODS FOR STUDYING CULTURE   To study the impact of culture on child development, researchers adjust the methods just considered or tap procedures specially devised for cross-cultural and multicultural research (Triandis, 2007). Which approach investigators choose depends on their research goals.

Sometimes researchers are interested in characteristics that are believed to be universal but that vary in degree from one culture to the next: Are parents warmer or more directive in some cultures than in others? How strong are gender stereotypes in different nations? In each instance, several cultural groups will be compared, and all participants must be questioned or observed in the same way. Therefore, researchers draw on the observational and self-report procedures we have already considered, adapting them through translation so they can be understood in each cultural context. For example, to study cultural variation in parenting attitudes, the same questionnaire, asking for ratings on such items as "I often hug and kiss my child" or "I scold my child when his/her behavior does not meet my expectations," is given to all participants (Wu et al., 2002). Still, investigators must be mindful of cultural differences in familiarity with responding to self-report instruments that may bias their findings (Van de Vijver, Hofer, & Chasiotis, 2010).

At other times, researchers want to uncover the *cultural meanings* of children's and adults' behaviors by becoming as familiar as possible with their way of life. To achieve this goal, researchers rely on a method borrowed from the field of anthropology—**ethnography.** Like the clinical method, ethnographic research is a descriptive, qualitative technique. But instead of aiming to understand a single individual, it is directed toward understanding a culture or a distinct social group through *participant observation*. Typically, the researcher spends months and sometimes years in the cultural community, participating in its daily life. Extensive field notes are gathered, consisting of a mix of observations, self-reports from members of the culture, and careful interpretations by the investigator (Miller, Hengst, & Wang, 2003; Shweder et al., 2006). Later, these notes are put together into a description of the community that tries to capture its unique values and social processes.

The ethnographic method assumes that by entering into close contact with a social group, researchers can understand the beliefs and behaviors of its members in a way not possible with an observational visit, interview, or questionnaire. Some ethnographies take in many aspects of children's experience, as one researcher did in describing what it is like to grow up in a small American town. Others focus on one or a few settings, such as home, school, or neighborhood life (Higginbottom, 2006; Peshkin, 1997; Valdés, 1998). And still others are limited to a particular practice, such as uncovering cultural and religious influences on children's make-believe play. For example, ethnographic findings reveal that East Indian Hindu parents encourage preschoolers to communicate with "invisible" characters. They regard this activity as linked to *karma* (the cycle of birth and death) and believe that the child may be remembering a past life. In contrast, Christian fundamentalist parents often discourage children from pretending to be unreal characters, believing that such play promotes dangerous spiritual ideas and deceitful behavior (Taylor & Carlson, 2000). Researchers may supplement traditional self-report and observational methods with ethnography if they suspect that unique meanings underlie cultural differences, as the Cultural Influences box on page 36 reveals.

Ethnographers strive to minimize their influence on the culture they are studying by becoming part of it. Nevertheless, as with clinical research, investigators' cultural values and theoretical commitments sometimes lead them to observe selectively or misinterpret what they see. Finally, the findings of ethnographic studies cannot be assumed to generalize beyond the people and settings in which the research was conducted.

■ This Western ethnographer spent months living among the Efe people of the Republic of Congo. Here he observes young children sharing food. The Efe value and encourage cooperation and generosity at an early age. ■

ASK YOURSELF

◆ REVIEW Why might a researcher choose structured observation over naturalistic observation? How about the reverse? What might lead the researcher to opt for clinical interviewing over systematic observation?

◆ APPLY A researcher wants to study the thoughts and feelings of children who have a parent on active duty in the military. Which method should she use? Why?

◆ CONNECT What strengths and limitations do the clinical, or case study, method and ethnography have in common?

General Research Designs

In deciding on a research design, investigators choose a way of setting up a study that permits them to test their hypotheses with the greatest degree of certainty possible. Two main designs are used in all research on human behavior: *correlational* and *experimental*.

CULTURAL INFLUENCES

Immigrant Youths: Adapting to a New Land

During the past quarter century, a rising tide of immigrants has come to North America, fleeing war and persecution in their homelands or seeking better life chances. Today, nearly one-fourth of U.S. children and adolescents have foreign-born parents, making them the fastest growing sector of the U.S. youth population. About 20 percent of them are foreign-born themselves, mostly from Latin America, the Caribbean, and Asia (Hernandez, Denton, & Macartney, 2008; Suarez-Orozco, Todorova, & Qin, 2006).

How well are immigrant youths adapting to their new country? To find out, researchers use multiple research methods—academic testing, questionnaires assessing psychological adjustment, and in-depth ethnographies.

Academic Achievement and Adjustment

Although educators and laypeople often assume that the transition to a new country has a negative impact on psychological well-being, evidence reveals that many children of immigrant parents from diverse countries adapt amazingly well. Students who are first generation (foreign-born) or second generation (American-born, with immigrant parents) often achieve in school as well as or better than students of native-born parents, graduating from high school at similar or greater overall rates (Fuligni, 2004; Hernandez, Denton, & Macartney, 2008; Saucier et al., 2002). Findings on psychological adjustment are similar. Compared with their agemates, adolescents from immigrant families are less likely to commit delinquent and violent acts, to use drugs and alcohol, or to have early sex. They are also less likely to be obese or to have missed school because of illness. And they tend to report just as favorable, and at times higher, self-esteem as do young people with native-born parents (Fuligni, 1998; Saucier et al., 2002; Supple & Small, 2006).

These outcomes are strongest for Chinese, Filipino, Japanese, Korean, and East Indian youths (Fuligni, 2004; Louie, 2001; Portes & Rumbaut, 2005). Variation in adjustment is greater among Mexican, Central American, and Southeast Asian (Hmong, Cambodian, Laotian, Thai, and Vietnamese) young people, who show elevated rates of school failure and dropout, delinquency, teenage parenthood, and drug use. Disparities in parental economic resources, education, English-language proficiency, and sup-

port of children contribute to these trends (Supple & Small, 2006; Zhou & Xiong, 2005).

Still, many first- and second-generation youths whose parents face considerable financial hardship and who speak little English are successful (Fuligni & Yoshikawa, 2003; Hernandez, Denton, & Macartney, 2008). Factors other than income are responsible—notably, family values and strong ethnic-community ties.

Family and Ethnic-Community Influences

Ethnographies reveal that immigrant parents view education as the surest way to improve life chances (Goldenberg et al., 2001; Lee, 2001; Louie, 2001). Aware of the challenges their children face, they typically emphasize trying hard. They remind their children that, because educational opportunities were not available in their native countries, they themselves are often limited to menial jobs. And while preserving their culture's values, these parents also make certain adaptations—for example, supporting education for daughters even though their culture of origin endorses it only for sons.

Adolescents from these families internalize their parents' valuing of academic achievement, endorsing it more strongly than agemates with native-born parents (Asakawa, 2001; Fuligni, 2004). Because minority ethnicities usually stress allegiance to family and community over individual goals, first- and second-generation young people often feel a strong sense of obligation to their parents. They view school success as an important way of repaying their parents for the hardships they have endured (Bacallao & Smokowski, 2007; Fuligni, Yip, & Tseng, 2002). Both family relationships and school achievement protect these youths from risky behaviors (see the Biology and Environment box on pages 10–11).

Immigrant parents of successful youths typically develop close ties to an ethnic community, which exerts additional control through a high consensus on values and constant monitoring of young people's activities.

⬛ These Hmong boys perform in an ethnic festival in St. Paul, Minnesota, where many Hmong immigrants have settled. Cultural values that engender allegiance to family and community promote high achievement and protect many immigrant youths from involvement in risky behaviors. ⬛

The following comments capture the power of these family and community forces:

- *Elizabeth, age 16, from Vietnam, straight-A student, like her two older sisters:* My parents know pretty much all the kids in the neighborhood. Everybody here knows everybody else. It's hard to get away with much. (Zhou & Bankston, 1998, pp. 93, 130)
- *Juan, teenager from Mexico:* A really big part of the Hispanic population [is] being close to family, and the family being a priority all the time. I hate people who say, "Why do you want to go to a party where your family's at? Don't you want to get away from them?" You know, I don't really get tired of them. I've always been really close to them. That connection to my parents, that trust that you can talk to them, that makes me Mexican. (Bacallao & Smokowski, 2007, p. 62)

The experiences of well-adjusted immigrant youths are not problem-free. Chinese adolescents who had arrived in the United States within the previous year described their adjustment as very difficult because they were not proficient in English and, as a result, found many everyday tasks challenging and felt socially isolated (Yeh et al., 2008). Young immigrants also encounter racial and ethnic prejudices and experience tensions between family values and the new culture. In the long term, however, family and community cohesion, supervision, and high expectations promote favorable outcomes.

© MICHAEL SILUK/THE IMAGE WORKS

CORRELATIONAL DESIGN In a **correlational design,** researchers gather information on individuals, generally in natural life circumstances, and make no effort to alter their experiences. Then they look at relationships between participants' characteristics and their behavior or development. Suppose we want to answer such questions as, Do parents' styles of interacting with their children have any bearing on children's intelligence? Does attending a child-care center promote children's friendliness with peers? How do child abuse and neglect affect children's feelings about themselves and their relationships with peers? In these and many other instances, the conditions of interest are difficult or impossible to arrange and control and must be studied as they currently exist.

Correlational studies have one major limitation: We cannot infer cause and effect. For example, if we find that parental interaction is related to children's intelligence, we would not know whether parents' behavior actually *causes* intellectual differences among children. In fact, the opposite is possible. The behaviors of highly intelligent children may be so attractive that they cause parents to interact more favorably. Or a third variable that we did not even consider, such as amount of noise and distraction in the home, may cause changes in both parental interaction and children's intelligence.

In correlational studies, and in other types of research designs, investigators often examine relationships by using a **correlation coefficient**—a number that describes how two measures, or variables, are associated with one another. We will encounter the correlation coefficient in discussing research findings throughout this book, so let's look at what it is and how it is interpreted. A correlation coefficient can range in value from +1.00 to −1.00. The *magnitude, or size, of the number* shows the *strength of the relationship.* A zero correlation indicates no relationship, but the closer the value is to either +1.00 or −1.00, the stronger the relationship (see Figure 1.6). For instance, a correlation of −.78 is high, −.52 is moderate, and −.18 is low. Note, however that correlations of +.52 and −.52 are equally strong. The *sign of the number* refers to the *direction of the relationship.* A positive sign (+) means that as one variable *increases,* the other also *increases.* A negative sign (−) indicates that as one variable *increases,* the other *decreases.*

Let's look at some examples of how a correlation coefficient works. One researcher reported a +.55 correlation between a measure of maternal language stimulation and the size of children's vocabularies at age 2 years (Hoff, 2003). This is a moderate correlation, which indicates that mothers who spoke more to their infants had children who were more advanced in language development. In two other studies, child-rearing practices were related to toddlers' compliance in consistent ways. First, maternal warmth and sensitivity during play correlated positively (+.34) with 2-year-olds' willingness to comply with their mother's directive to clean up toys (Feldman & Klein, 2003). Second, the extent to which mothers spoke harshly, interrupted, and controlled their 4-year-olds' play correlated negatively (−.31 for boys and −.42 for girls) with children's compliance (Smith et al., 2004).

All these investigations found a relationship between parenting and young children's behavior. **TAKE A MOMENT...** Are you tempted to conclude that parenting influenced children's responses? Although the researchers suspected this was so, they could not be sure of cause and effect. Can you think of other possible explanations? Finding a relationship in a correlational study suggests that tracking down its cause—using a more powerful experimental strategy, if possible—would be worthwhile.

EXPERIMENTAL DESIGN An **experimental design** permits inferences about cause and effect because researchers use an evenhanded procedure to assign people to two or more treatment conditions. In an experiment, the events and behaviors of interest are divided into two types: independent and dependent variables. The **independent variable** is the one the investigator expects to cause changes in another variable. The **dependent variable** is the one the investigator expects to be influenced by the independent variable. Cause-and-effect relationships can be detected because the researcher directly *controls* or *manipulates* changes in the independent variable by exposing participants to the treatment

FIGURE 1.6

The meaning of correlation coefficients. The magnitude of the number indicates the *strength* of the relationship. The sign of the number (+ or −) indicates the *direction* of the relationship.

© BRIAN SUMMERS/GETTY IMAGES/FIRST LIGHT

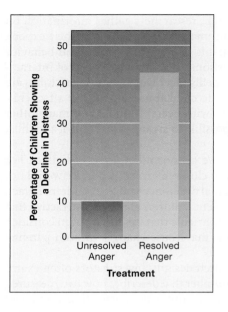

FIGURE 1.7

Does the way adults end their angry encounters affect children's emotional reactions? A laboratory experiment showed that children who had previously witnessed adults resolving their disputes by apologizing and compromising were more likely to decline in distress when witnessing subsequent adult conflicts than were children who witnessed adults leaving their arguments unresolved. Notice in this graph that only 10 percent of children in the unresolved-anger treatment declined in distress (see bar on left), whereas 42 percent of children in the resolved-anger treatment did so (see bar on right). *(Adapted from El-Sheikh, Cummings, & Reiter, 1996.)*

conditions. Then the researcher compares their performance on measures of the dependent variable.

In one *laboratory experiment,* researchers explored the impact of adults' angry interactions on children's adjustment (El-Sheikh, Cummings, & Reiter, 1996). They hypothesized that the way angry encounters end (independent variable) affects children's emotional reactions (dependent variable). Four- and 5-year-olds were brought one at a time to a laboratory, accompanied by their mothers. One group was exposed to an *unresolved-anger treatment,* in which two adult actors entered the room and argued but did not work out their disagreements. The other group witnessed a *resolved-anger treatment,* in which the adults ended their disputes by apologizing and compromising. As Figure 1.7 shows, when they witnessed a follow-up adult conflict, more children in the resolved-anger treatment showed a decline in distress, as measured by fewer anxious facial expressions, less freezing in place, and less seeking of closeness to their mothers. The experiment revealed that anger resolution can reduce the stressful impact of adult conflict on children.

In experimental studies, investigators must take special precautions to control for participants' characteristics that could reduce the accuracy of their findings. For example, in the study just described, if more children from homes high in parental conflict ended up in the unresolved-anger treatment, we could not tell what produced the results—the independent variable or the children's backgrounds. To protect against this problem, researchers engage in **random assignment** of participants to treatment conditions. By using an unbiased procedure, such as drawing numbers out of a hat or flipping a coin, investigators increase the chances that participants' characteristics will be equally distributed across treatment groups.

Sometimes researchers combine random assignment with another technique called *matching.* In this procedure, participants are measured before the experiment on the factor in question—in our example, exposure to parental conflict. Then children from homes high and low in parental conflict are assigned in equal numbers to each treatment condition. In this way, the experimental groups are deliberately matched, or made equivalent, on characteristics that are likely to distort the results.

MODIFIED EXPERIMENTAL DESIGNS: FIELD AND NATURAL EXPERIMENTS Most experiments are conducted in laboratories, where researchers can achieve the maximum possible control over treatment conditions. But as we have already indicated, findings obtained in laboratories may not apply to everyday situations. In *field experiments,* investigators capitalize on rare opportunities to assign participants randomly to treatment conditions in natural settings. In the experiment just described, we can conclude that the emotional climate established by adults affects children's behavior in the laboratory. But does it also do so in daily life?

Another study helps answer this question. Ethnically diverse, poverty-stricken families with a 2-year-old child were scheduled for a home visit, during which researchers assessed family functioning and child problem behaviors by asking parents to respond to questionnaires

■ When researchers cannot randomly assign children to conditions in the real world, they sometimes conduct natural experiments using treatments that already exist. For example, the learning environments of different child-care centers might be compared to explore the impact of storybook reading on preschoolers' language and literacy development. ■

and videotaping parent–child interaction. Then the families were randomly assigned to either an intervention condition, called the Family Check-Up, or a no-intervention control group. The intervention consisted of three home-based sessions in which a consultant gave parents feedback about their child-rearing practices and their child's adjustment, explored parents' willingness to improve, identified community services appropriate to each family's needs, and offered follow-up sessions on parenting practices and other concerns (Dishion et al., 2008). Findings showed that families assigned to the Family Check-Up (but not controls) gained in positive parenting, which predicted a reduction in child problem behaviors—outcomes still evident a year later, when participating children were reassessed at age 3.

Often researchers cannot randomly assign participants and manipulate conditions in the real world, as these investigators were able to do. Sometimes they can compromise by conducting *natural,* or *quasi-, experiments.* Treatments that already exist, such as different family environments, child-care centers, or schools, are compared. These studies differ from correlational research only in that groups of participants are carefully chosen to ensure that their characteristics are as much alike as possible. In this way, investigators do their best to rule out alternative explanations for their treatment effects. But despite these efforts, natural experiments cannot achieve the precision and rigor of true experimental research.

To help you compare correlational and experimental designs, Table 1.5 summarizes their strengths and limitations. It also includes an overview of designs for studying development, to which we turn next.

TABLE 1.5 Strengths and Limitations of Research Designs

DESIGN	DESCRIPTION	STRENGTHS	LIMITATIONS
GENERAL			
Correlational	The investigator obtains information on participants without altering their experiences.	Permits study of relationships between variables.	Does not permit inferences about cause-and-effect relationships.
Experimental	The investigator manipulates an independent variable and examines its effect on a dependent variable. Can be conducted in the laboratory or in the natural environment.	Permits inferences about cause-and-effect relationships.	When conducted in the laboratory, findings may not generalize to the real world. In *field experiments,* control over the treatment is usually weaker than in the laboratory. In *natural,* or *quasi-, experiments,* lack of random assignment substantially reduces the precision of research.
DEVELOPMENTAL			
Longitudinal	The investigator studies the same group of participants repeatedly at different ages.	Permits study of common patterns and individual differences in development and relationships between early and later events and behaviors.	Age-related changes may be distorted because of biased sampling, selective attrition, practice effects, and cohort effects.
Cross-sectional	The investigator studies groups of participants differing in age at the same point in time.	More efficient than the longitudinal design.	Does not permit study of individual developmental trends. Age differences may be distorted because of cohort effects.
Sequential	The investigator follows a sequence of samples (two or more age groups), collecting data on them at the same points in time.	Permits both longitudinal and cross-sectional comparisons. Reveals cohort effects. Permits tracking of age-related changes more efficiently than the longitudinal design.	May have the same problems as longitudinal and cross-sectional strategies, but the design itself helps identify difficulties.
Microgenetic	The investigator presents children with a novel task and follows their mastery over a series of closely spaced sessions.	Offers insights into the process of development.	Requires intensive study of participants' moment-by-moment behaviors. The time required for participants to change is difficult to anticipate. Practice effects may distort developmental trends.

Designs for Studying Development

Scientists interested in child development require information about the way research participants change over time. To answer questions about development, they must extend correlational and experimental approaches to include measurements at different ages. Longitudinal and cross-sectional designs are special *developmental research strategies*. In each, age comparisons form the basis of the research plan.

THE LONGITUDINAL DESIGN In a **longitudinal design,** participants are studied repeatedly, and changes are noted as they get older. The time spanned may be relatively short (a few months to several years) or very long (a decade or even a lifetime). The longitudinal approach has two major strengths. First, because it tracks the performance of each person over time, researchers can identify common patterns as well as individual differences in development. Second, longitudinal studies permit investigators to examine relationships between early and later events and behaviors. Let's illustrate these ideas.

A group of researchers wondered whether children who display extreme personality styles—either angry and explosive or shy and withdrawn—retain the same dispositions when they become adults. In addition, the researchers wanted to know what kinds of experiences promote stability or plasticity in personality and what consequences explosiveness and shyness have for long-term adjustment. To answer these questions, the researchers delved into the archives of the Guidance Study, a well-known longitudinal investigation that was initiated in 1928 at the University of California, Berkeley, and continued for several decades (Caspi, Elder, & Bem, 1987, 1988).

Results revealed that the two personality styles were moderately stable. Between ages 8 and 30, a good number of individuals remained the same, whereas others changed substantially. When stability did occur, it appeared to be due to a "snowballing effect," in which children evoked responses from adults and peers that acted to maintain their dispositions. Explosive youngsters were likely to be treated with anger, whereas shy children were apt to be ignored. As a result, the two types of children came to view their social worlds differently. Explosive children tended to view others as hostile; shy children regarded them as unfriendly (Caspi & Roberts, 2001). Together, these factors led explosive children to sustain or increase their unruliness and shy children to continue to withdraw.

Persistence of extreme personality styles affected many areas of adult adjustment. For men, the results of early explosiveness were most apparent in their work lives, in the form of conflicts with supervisors, frequent job changes, and unemployment. Since few women in this sample of an earlier generation worked after marriage, their family lives were most affected. Explosive girls grew up to be hotheaded wives and parents who were especially prone to divorce. Sex differences in the long-term consequences of shyness were even greater. Men who had been withdrawn in childhood were delayed in marrying, becoming fathers, and developing stable careers. However, because a withdrawn, unassertive style was socially acceptable for females in the mid-twentieth century, women who had shy personalities showed no special adjustment problems.

PROBLEMS IN CONDUCTING LONGITUDINAL RESEARCH Despite their strengths, longitudinal investigations pose a number of problems. For example, *biased sampling*—the failure to enlist participants who adequately represent the population of interest—is a common problem. People who willingly participate in research that requires them to be observed and tested over many years are likely to have distinctive characteristics—perhaps a special appreciation for the scientific value of research, or a unique need or desire for medical, mental health, or educational services provided by the investigators. Furthermore, longitudinal samples generally become more biased as the investigation proceeds because of *selective attrition*. Participants may move away or drop out of the study for other reasons, and the ones who remain are likely to differ in important ways from the ones who continue. Also, from repeated study, people may become "test-wise." Their performance may improve as a result of *practice effects*—better test-taking skills and increased familiarity with the test—not because of factors commonly associated with development.

The most widely discussed threat to the accuracy of longitudinal findings is cultural–historical change, commonly called **cohort effects.** Longitudinal studies examine the development of *cohorts*—children born at the same time, who are influenced by particular cultural and historical conditions. Results based on one cohort may not apply to children developing at other times. For example, look back at the findings on female shyness described in the previous section, which were gathered in the 1950s. Today's shy young women tend to be poorly adjusted—a difference that may be due to changes in gender roles in Western societies. Shy adults, whether male or female, feel more depressed, have fewer social supports, and may do less well in educational and career attainment than their agemates (Caspi, 2000; Caspi et al., 2003; Mounts et al., 2006). Similarly, a longitudinal study of social development would probably result in quite different findings if it were carried out in the second decade of the twenty-first century, around the time of World War II, or during the Great Depression of the 1930s.

Cohort effects don't just operate broadly on an entire generation. They also occur when specific experiences influence some children but not others in the same generation. For example, children who witnessed the terrorist attacks of September 11, 2001 (either because they were near Ground Zero or because they saw injury and death on TV), or who lost a parent in the disaster were far more likely than other children to display persistent emotional problems, including intense fear, anxiety, and depression (Mullett-Hume et al., 2008; Pfeffer et al., 2007). A study of one New York City sample suggested that as many as one-fourth of the city's children were affected (Hoven et al., 2005).

■ These children lost family members, friends, teachers, and other sources of support in the January 2010 earthquake in Haiti. They live and attend school in a refugee camp in Port-au-Prince, where rescue workers try to help them cope with the crisis. This powerfully destructive historical event is a cohort effect, with profound consequences for development. ■

THE CROSS-SECTIONAL DESIGN The length of time it takes for many behaviors to change, even in limited longitudinal studies, has led researchers to turn to a more efficient strategy for studying development. In the **cross-sectional design,** groups of people differing in age are studied at the same point in time. Because participants are measured only once, researchers need not be concerned about such difficulties as participant dropout or practice effects.

An investigation in which students in grades 3, 6, 9, and 12 filled out a questionnaire about their sibling relationships provides a good illustration (Buhrmester & Furman, 1990). Findings revealed that sibling interaction was characterized by greater equality and less power assertion with age. Also, feelings of sibling companionship declined during adolescence. The researchers thought that several factors contributed to these age differences. As later-born children become more competent and independent, they no longer need, and are probably less willing to accept, direction from older siblings. And as adolescents move from psychological dependence on the family to greater involvement with peers, they may have less time and emotional need to invest in siblings. Subsequent research has confirmed these intriguing ideas about the development of sibling relationships.

PROBLEMS IN CONDUCTING CROSS-SECTIONAL RESEARCH Despite its convenience, cross-sectional research does not provide evidence about change at the level at which it actually occurs: the individual. For example, in the cross-sectional study of sibling relationships just discussed, comparisons are limited to age-group averages. We cannot tell if important individual differences exist. Indeed, longitudinal findings reveal that adolescents vary considerably in the changing quality of their sibling relationships. Although many become more distant, others become more supportive and intimate, still others more rivalrous and antagonistic (Branje et al., 2004; Kim et al., 2006; Whiteman & Loken, 2006).

Cross-sectional studies—especially those that cover a wide age span—have another problem. Like longitudinal research, they can be threatened by cohort effects. For example, comparisons of 5-year-old cohorts and 15-year-old cohorts—groups born and reared in different years—may not really represent age-related changes. Instead, they may reflect unique experiences associated with the time period in which the age groups were growing up.

IMPROVING DEVELOPMENTAL DESIGNS Researchers have devised ways of building on the strengths and minimizing the weaknesses of longitudinal and cross-sectional approaches. Several modified developmental designs have resulted.

Sequential Designs. To overcome some of the limitations of traditional developmental designs, investigators sometimes use **sequential designs,** in which they conduct several similar cross-sectional or longitudinal studies (called *sequences*) at varying times. As the illustration in Figure 1.8 reveals, some sequential designs combine longitudinal and cross-sectional strategies, an approach that has three advantages:

- We can find out whether cohort effects are operating by comparing participants of the same age who were born in different years. In Figure 1.8, for example, we can compare the longitudinal samples at seventh, eighth, and ninth grades. If they do not differ, we can rule out cohort effects.
- We can make both longitudinal and cross-sectional comparisons. If outcomes are similar, we can be especially confident about the findings.
- The design is efficient. In our example, we can find out about change over a five-year period by following each cohort for three years.

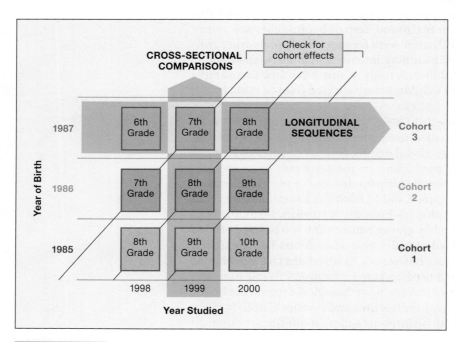

FIGURE 1.8

Example of a sequential design. Three cohorts, born in 1985 (blue), 1986 (orange), and 1987 (pink), respectively, are followed longitudinally for three years. Testing the cohorts in overlapping grades enables researchers to check for cohort effects by comparing participants born in different years when they reach the same grade (see diagonals). In a study using this design, same-grade adolescents who were members of different cohorts scored similarly on a questionnaire assessing family harmony, indicating no cohort effects. By following each cohort for just three years, the investigator could infer a developmental trend across five years, from sixth to tenth grade.

In a study that used the design in Figure 1.8, researchers wanted to find out if family harmony changed as young people experienced the dramatic physical and psychological changes of adolescence (Baer, 2002). A questionnaire assessing emotional bonding among family members was given to three adolescent cohorts, each born a year apart. In longitudinal follow-ups, each cohort again responded to the questionnaire during the following two years.

Findings for the three cohorts converged: All reported (1) a slight decline in family harmony with grade and (2) similar levels of family harmony as they reached the same grade, confirming that there were no cohort effects. Therefore, the researchers concluded that family closeness diminishes steadily from sixth to tenth grade, noting, however, that the change is mild—not enough to threaten supportive family ties. **TAKE A MOMENT...** Turn back to our discussion of parent–adolescent communication as a dynamic system on page 29 and our consideration of adolescent sibling relationships on page 41. How are those results helpful in interpreting the outcomes of the sequential study just described?

Examining Microcosms of Development. In the examples of developmental research we have discussed, observations of children are fairly widely spaced. When we observe once a year or every few years, we can describe development, but we cannot easily capture the processes that produce it. The **microgenetic design,** an adaptation of the longitudinal approach, presents children with a novel task and follows their mastery over a series of closely spaced sessions. Within this "microcosm" of development, researchers observe how change occurs (Flynn & Siegler, 2007; Kuhn, 1995; Siegler & Crowley, 1991). The microgenetic design is especially useful for studying cognitive development—for example, the strategies children use to acquire new knowledge in reading, mathematics, and science (Siegler, 2002, 2006). As you will see in Chapter 5, the microgenetic design has also been used to trace infants' mastery of motor skills.

© BOB DAEMMRICH/THE IMAGE WORKS

■ How will these preschoolers become proficient at building a structure collaboratively? A microgenetic design, which permits researchers to follow children's mastery of a challenging task, is uniquely suited to answering this question. ■

Nevertheless, microgenetic studies are difficult to carry out. Researchers must pore over hours of recorded information, analyzing each participant's behavior many times. In addition, the time required for children to change is hard to anticipate. It depends on a careful match between the child's capabilities and the demands of the task. Finally, as in other longitudinal research, practice effects can distort microgenetic findings. But when researchers overcome these challenges, they reap the benefits of seeing development as it takes place.

Combining Experimental and Developmental Designs. Perhaps you noticed that all the examples of longitudinal and cross-sectional research we have considered permit only correlational, not causal, inferences. Yet causal information is also desirable, both for testing theories and for finding ways to enhance development. Sometimes researchers can explore the causal link between experiences and development by experimentally manipulating the experiences. If, as a result, development improves, then we have strong evidence for a causal association. Today, research that combines an experimental strategy with either a longitudinal or a cross-sectional approach, with the aim of augmenting development, is becoming increasingly common (Lerner & Overton, 2008). For an example, refer to the Social Issues: Education box on page 44.

Ethics in Research on Children

Research into human behavior creates ethical issues because, unfortunately, the quest for scientific knowledge can sometimes exploit people. When children take part in research, the ethical concerns are especially complex. Children are more vulnerable than adults to physical and psychological harm. In addition, immaturity makes it difficult or impossible for children to evaluate for themselves what participation in research will mean. For these reasons, special ethical guidelines for research on children have been developed by the federal government, by funding agencies, and by research-oriented associations such as the American Psychological Association (2002) and the Society for Research in Child Development (2007).

Table 1.6 on page 45 presents a summary of children's basic research rights. **TAKE A MOMENT...** After examining them, read about the following research situations, each of which poses a serious ethical dilemma. What precautions do you think should be taken in each instance? Is either so threatening to children's well-being that it should not be carried out?

■ In a study of moral development, a researcher wants to assess children's ability to resist temptation by videotaping their behavior without their knowledge. She promises 7-year-olds an attractive prize for solving difficult puzzles but tells them not to look at a classmate's correct solutions, which are deliberately placed at the back of the room. Telling

SOCIAL ISSUES: EDUCATION

Can Musical Experiences Enhance Intelligence?

*I*n a 1993 experiment, researchers reported that college students who listened to a Mozart sonata for a few minutes just before taking a test of spatial reasoning abilities did better on the test than students who took the test after listening to relaxation instructions or sitting in silence (Rauscher, Shaw, & Ky, 1993). Strains of Mozart, the investigators concluded, seem to induce changes in the brain that "warm up" neural connections, thereby improving thinking. But the gain in performance, widely publicized as the "Mozart effect," lasted only 15 minutes and proved difficult to replicate. Rather than involving a real change in ability, Mozart seemed to improve arousal and mood, yielding better concentration on the test (Schellenberg et al., 2007).

Despite mounting evidence that the Mozart effect was uncertain at best, the media and politicians were enthralled with the idea that a brief exposure of the brain to classical music in infancy, when neural connections are forming rapidly, might yield lifelong intellectual benefits. For a time, the states of Georgia, Tennessee, and South Dakota provided free classical music CDs for every newborn baby leaving the hospital. Yet no studies of the Mozart effect have ever been conducted on infants! And an experiment with school-age children failed to yield any intellectual gains as a result of simply listening to music (McKelvie & Low, 2002).

Research suggests that to produce lasting gains in mental test scores, interventions must be long-lasting and involve children's active participation. Consequently, Glenn Schellenberg (2004) wondered, Can music lessons enhance intelligence? Children who take music lessons must practice regularly, engage in extended focused attention, read music, memorize lengthy musical passages, understand diverse musical structures, and master technical skills. These experiences might foster cognitive processing, particularly during childhood, when regions of the brain are taking on specialized functions and are highly sensitive to environmental influences.

Schellenberg recruited 132 6-year-olds—children just old enough for formal lessons. First, the children took an intelligence test and were rated on social maturity, permitting the researchers to see whether music lessons would affect some aspects of development but not others. Next, the children were randomly assigned to one of four experimental conditions. Two were music groups; one received piano lessons and the other voice lessons. The third group took drama lessons—a condition that shed light on whether intellectual gains were unique to musical experiences. The fourth group—a no-lessons control—was offered music lessons the following year. All music and drama instruction took place at the prestigious Royal Conservatory of Music in Toronto, where experienced teachers taught the children in small groups. After 36 weeks of lessons, a longitudinal follow-up was conducted: The children's intelligence and social maturity were assessed again.

■ Children who take music lessons over many weeks gain in mental test performance compared to children who take drama lessons or who receive no lessons at all. To make music, children must engage in diverse intellectually challenging activities: reading musical notation, memorizing lengthy passages, analyzing musical structures, and mastering technical skills. ■

All four groups gained in mental test performance, probably because the participants had just entered grade school, which usually leads to an increase in intelligence test scores. But the two music groups consistently gained more than the drama and no-lesson control groups (see Figure 1.9). Their advantage, though just a few points, extended across many mental abilities, including verbal and spatial skills and speed of thinking. At the same time, only the drama group improved in social maturity.

In sum, active, sustained musical experiences can lead to small increases in intelligence among 6-year-olds that do not arise from comparable drama lessons. But other enrichment activities with similar properties, such as reading, science, math, and chess programs, may confer similar benefits. All demand that children invest far more time and effort than they would in listening to a Mozart sonata. Nevertheless—despite absence of evidence to support their claims—music companies persist in selling CDs entitled "Tune Your Brain with Mozart," "Music for Accelerating Learning," and "Mozart for Newborns: A Bright Beginning."

FIGURE 1.9

Music lessons promote gains in intelligence. In a study that combined experimental and longitudinal research strategies, children's mental test performance was tracked longitudinally, before and after they experienced one of four conditions: (1) piano lessons, (2) voice lessons, (3) drama lessons, or (4) no lessons. Children in the two groups receiving music lessons showed greater gains in test scores.

TABLE 1.6 Children's Research Rights

RESEARCH RIGHT	DESCRIPTION
Protection from harm	Children have the right to be protected from physical or psychological harm in research. If in doubt about the harmful effects of research, investigators should seek the opinion of others. When harm seems possible, investigators should find other means for obtaining the desired information or abandon the research.
Informed consent	All research participants, including children, have the right to have explained to them, in language appropriate to their level of understanding, all aspects of the research that may affect their willingness to participate. When children are participants, informed consent of parents as well as others who act on the child's behalf (such as school officials) should be obtained, preferably in writing. Children, and the adults responsible for them, have the right to discontinue participation in the research at any time.
Privacy	Children have the right to concealment of their identity on all information collected in the course of research. They also have this right with respect to written reports and any informal discussions about the research.
Knowledge of results	Children have the right to be informed of the results of research in language that is appropriate to their level of understanding.
Beneficial treatments	If experimental treatments believed to be beneficial are under investigation, children in control groups have the right to alternative beneficial treatments if they are available.

Sources: American Psychological Association, 2002; Society for Research in Child Development, 2007.

children ahead of time that cheating is being studied or that their behavior is being monitored will defeat the purpose of the study.

■ A researcher is interviewing fifth graders about their experiences with bullying. A girl describes frequent name-calling and derogatory comments by her older sister. Although the girl is unhappy, she wants to handle the problem on her own. If the researcher alerts the girl's parents to provide protection and help, he will violate his promise to keep participants' responses private.

Did you find it difficult to evaluate these examples? Virtually every organization that has devised ethical principles for research has concluded that conflicts arising in research situations do not have simple right or wrong answers. The ultimate responsibility for the ethical integrity of research lies with the investigator. But researchers are advised—and often required—to seek advice from others. Committees for this purpose exist in colleges, universities, and other institutions. These *institutional review boards (IRBs)* balance the costs of the research to participants in terms of time, stress, and inconvenience against the study's value for advancing knowledge and improving conditions of life. If any risks to the safety and welfare of participants outweigh the worth of the research, then preference is always given to the interests of the participants.

The ethical principle of *informed consent* requires special interpretation when participants cannot fully appreciate the research goals and activities. Parental consent is meant to protect the safety of children whose ability to decide is not yet mature. In addition, researchers should obtain the agreement of other individuals who act on children's behalf, such as institutional officials when research is conducted in schools, child-care centers, or hospitals. This is especially important when research includes special groups, such as abused children, whose parents may not always represent their best interests (Fisher, 1993; Thompson, 1990).

As soon as children are old enough to appreciate the purpose of the research, and certainly by 7 years of age, their own informed consent should be obtained in addition to parental consent. Around age 7, changes in children's thinking permit them to better understand basic scientific principles and the needs of others. Researchers should respect and enhance these capacities by giving school-age children a full explanation of research activities in language

© STOCKBYTE/GETTY IMAGES

■ Although this 10-year-old responds to the interviewer's questions, she may not know why she is being interviewed, or realize that she has the right to withdraw from the study without negative consequences. Because children have difficulty understanding the research process, extra steps must be taken to protect their research rights. ■

they can understand (Fisher, 1993). Extra care must be taken when telling children that the information they provide will be kept confidential and that they can end their participation at any time. Even adolescents may not understand, and sometimes do not believe, these promises (Bruzzese & Fisher, 2003; Ondrusek et al., 1998). And in certain ethnic minority communities, where deference to authority, maintaining pleasant relationships, and meeting the needs of a guest (the researcher) are highly valued, children and parents may be particularly likely to consent when they would rather not do so (Fisher et al., 2002).

Careful attention to informed consent helps resolve dilemmas about revealing children's responses to parents, teachers, or other authorities when those responses suggest that the child's welfare is in danger. Children can be told in advance that if they report that someone is harming them, the researcher will tell an appropriate adult to take action to ensure the child's safety (Mishna, Antle, & Regehr, 2004).

Finally, young children rely on a basic faith in adults to feel secure in unfamiliar situations. For this reason, they may find some types of research particularly disturbing. All ethical guidelines advise that special precautions be taken in the use of deception and concealment, as occurs when researchers observe children from behind one-way mirrors, give them false feedback about their performance, or do not tell them the truth regarding what the research is about. When these procedures are used with adults, *debriefing,* in which the researcher provides a full account and justification of the activities, occurs after the research session is over. Debriefing should also be done with children, and it sometimes works well. But young children often lack the cognitive skills to understand the reasons for deceptive procedures, and, despite explanations, they may leave the research situation questioning the honesty of adults. Ethical standards permit deception in research with children if investigators satisfy IRBs that such practices are necessary. Nevertheless, because deception may have serious emotional consequences for some youngsters, many child development specialists believe that researchers should use it only if the risk of harm is minimal.

ASK YOURSELF

◆ REVIEW Explain how cohort effects can distort the findings of both longitudinal and cross-sectional studies. How does the sequential design reveal cohort effects?

◆ APPLY A researcher compares children who went to summer leadership camps with children who attended athletic camps. She finds that those who attended leadership camps are friendlier. Should the investigator tell parents that sending children to leadership camps will cause them to be more sociable? Why or why not?

◆ CONNECT Review the experiment on music lessons and intelligence reported in the Social Issues: Education box on page 44. Why was it ethically important for the researchers to offer music lessons to the no-lessons control group during the year after completion of the study? (*Hint:* Refer to Table 1.6. onpage 45)

◆ REFLECT Suppose a researcher asks you to enroll your baby in a 10-year longitudinal study. What factors would lead you to agree and to stay involved? Do your answers shed light on why longitudinal studies often have biased samples? Explain.

Summary

The Field of Child Development

What is the field of child development, and what factors stimulated its expansion?

- **Child development** is an area of study devoted to understanding constancy and change from conception through adolescence. It is part of a larger interdisciplinary field known as **developmental science,** which includes all changes we experience throughout the lifespan. Research on child development has been stimulated both by scientific curiosity and by social pressures to better children's lives.

How can we divide child development into sensible, manageable periods and domains?

- Development is often divided into physical, cognitive, and emotional and social domains. These domains are not really distinct; rather, they combine in an integrated, holistic fashion.

© UWE OMMER, 1,000 FAMILIES, TASCHEN

- Researchers generally divide the flow of time into the following age periods: (1) the prenatal period (conception to birth), (2) infancy and toddlerhood (birth to 2 years), (3) early childhood (2 to 6 years), (4) middle childhood (6 to 11 years), and (5) adolescence (11 to 18 years). To describe the prolonged transition to adulthood typical of contemporary young people in industrialized nations, researchers have posited a new period of development, emerging adulthood, spanning ages 18 to 25.

Basic Issues

Identify three basic issues on which theories of child development take a stand.

- Each **theory** of child development takes a stand on three fundamental issues: (1) Is development a **continuous** process, or is it **discontinuous,** following a series of distinct **stages?** (2) Does one general course of development characterize all children, or are there many possible courses, influenced by the distinct **contexts** in which children grow up? (3) Are genetic or environmental factors more important in influencing development (the **nature–nurture controversy**), and are individual differences stable or characterized by substantial **plasticity?**

- Recent theories take a balanced stand on these issues. And contemporary researchers realize that answers may vary across domains of development and even, as research on **resilience** illustrates, across individuals.

Historical Foundations

Describe major historical influences on modern theories of child development.

- As early as medieval times, the sixth through the fifteenth centuries, childhood was regarded as a separate phase of life.

- In the sixteenth and seventeenth centuries, the Puritan conception of original sin led to a harsh philosophy of child rearing. The seventeenth-century Enlightenment brought a new emphasis on human dignity and respect that led to more humane views of childhood. Locke's notion of the child as a tabula rasa ("blank slate") provided the basis for twentieth-century behaviorism, while Rousseau's idea that children were noble savages foreshadowed the concepts of stage and **maturation.**

- Inspired by Darwin's theory of evolution, efforts to observe the child directly began in the late nineteenth and early twentieth centuries. Soon after, Hall and Gesell introduced the **normative approach,** which produced a large body of descriptive facts about children. Binet and Simon constructed the first successful intelligence test, which sparked interest in individual differences in development and led to a heated controversy over nature versus nurture.

Mid-Twentieth-Century Theories

What theories influenced child development research in the mid-twentieth century?

- In the 1930s and 1940s, psychiatrists and social workers turned to the **psychoanalytic perspective** for help in treating children's emotional problems. In Freud's **psychosexual theory,** children move through five stages, during which three portions of the personality—id, ego, and superego—become integrated.

- Erikson's **psychosocial theory** builds on Freud's theory, emphasizing the development of culturally relevant attitudes and skills and— with the addition of three adult stages—the lifespan nature of development. Despite its extensive contributions, the psychoanalytic perspective is no longer in the mainstream of child development research.

- As the psychoanalytic perspective gained in prominence, **behaviorism** emerged, focusing on directly observable events (stimuli and responses) in an effort to create an objective science of psychology. B. F. Skinner's operant conditioning theory emphasizes the role of reinforcement and punishment in increasing or decreasing the frequency of behaviors.

- A related approach, Albert Bandura's **social learning theory,** focuses on modeling as the major means through which children and adults acquire new responses. Its most recent revision stresses the role of cognition, or thinking, in children's imitation and learning and, therefore, is known as a social-cognitive approach.

© BOB DAEMMRICH/THE IMAGE WORKS

- Behaviorism and social learning theory gave rise to techniques of **behavior modification** to eliminate undesirable behaviors and increase desirable responses.

- Piaget's **cognitive-developmental theory** emphasizes that children actively construct knowledge as they move through four stages, beginning with the baby's sensorimotor action patterns and ending with the abstract, systematic reasoning system of the adolescent and adult. Piaget's work has stimulated a wealth of research on children's thinking and has encouraged educational programs that emphasize children's discovery learning.

Recent Theoretical Perspectives

Describe recent theoretical perspectives on child development.

- **Information processing** views the mind as a complex symbol-manipulating system, much like a computer. This approach helps investigators achieve a detailed understanding of what children of different ages do when faced with tasks and problems.

- Over the past three decades, researchers in **developmental cognitive neuroscience** have begun to study the relationship between changes in the brain and the developing child's cognitive processing and behavior patterns. They have made progress in identifying the types of experiences to which the brain is sensitive at various ages and in clarifying the brain bases of many learning and behavior disorders.

- Four contemporary perspectives emphasize contexts for development. **Ethology,** which stresses the adaptive value and evolutionary history of behavior, inspired the **sensitive period** concept. In a new area of research called **evolutionary developmental psychology,** researchers have extended this emphasis, seeking to understand the adaptiveness of species-wide competencies as they change over time.

- Vygotsky's **sociocultural theory,** which focuses on how culture is transmitted from one generation to the net through social interaction, views cognitive development as a socially mediated process. Through cooperative dialogues with more expert members of society, children come to use language to guide their own thought and actions and acquire culturally relevant knowledge and skills..

- **Ecological systems theory** views the child as developing within a complex system of relationships affected by multiple, nested layers of the surrounding environment—**microsystem, mesosystem, exosystem,** and **macrosystem.** Each of these levels is seen as a major influence on children's well-being. The **chronosystem** represents the dynamic, ever-changing nature of children and their experiences.

- A new wave of theorists has adopted a **dynamic systems perspective** to better understand how children alter their behavior to attain more advanced functioning. According to this view, the mind, body, and physical and social worlds form an integrated system that guides mastery of new skills. A change in any part of the system prompts the child to reorganize her behavior so the various components work together again but in a more complex, effective way.

Comparing Child Development Theories

Identify the stand taken by each major theory on the basic issues of child development.

- Theories that are major forces in child development research vary in their focus on different domains of development, in their view of how development occurs, and in their strengths and weaknesses. (For a full summary, see Table 1.3 on page 30.)

Studying the Child

Describe methods commonly used to gather information on children.

- **Naturalistic observations,** which are gathered in everyday environments, permit researchers to see directly the everyday behaviors they hope to explain. In contrast, **structured observations** take place in laboratories, where every participant has an equal opportunity to display the behaviors of interest.

- Self-report methods can be flexible and open-ended like the **clinical interview,** which permits participants to express their thoughts in ways similar to their thinking in everyday life. Alternatively, **structured interviews,** tests, and questionnaires are more efficient and permit researchers to specify activities and behaviors that participants might not think of in an open-ended interview.

- Investigators use the **clinical,** or **case study, method** to obtain an in-depth understanding of a single child. It involves synthesizing a wide range of information, including interviews, observations, and sometimes test scores.

- Researchers have adapted observational and self-report methods to permit direct comparisons of cultures. To uncover the cultural meanings of behavior, they rely on **ethnography,** engaging in participant observation.

Distinguish between correlational and experimental research designs, noting the strengths and limitations of each.

- The **correlational design** examines relationships between variables, generally as they occur in natural life circumstances, without altering participants' experiences. The **correlation coefficient** describes how two measures, or variables, are associated with one another. Correlational studies do not permit inferences about cause and effect, but they can be helpful in identifying relationships that are worth exploring with a more powerful experimental strategy.

- An **experimental design** permits inferences about cause and effect. Researchers manipulate an **independent variable** by exposing participants to two or more treatment conditions. Then they determine what effect this variable has on a **dependent variable. Random assignment** reduces the chances that characteristics of participants will affect the accuracy of experimental findings.

- Field and natural, or quasi-, experiments compare treatments in natural environments. However, these approaches are less rigorous than laboratory experiments.

Describe designs for studying development, noting the strengths and limitations of each.

- In a **longitudinal design,** participants are studied repeatedly at different ages, revealing common patterns as well as individual differences in development and the relationship between early and later events and behaviors. Longitudinal research poses several problems, including biased sampling, selective attrition, and **cohort effects**—difficulty generalizing to children developing at other historical times, or to children who did not experience a specific event.

- The **cross-sectional design,** in which groups of children differing in age are studied at the same point in time, offers an efficient approach to investigating development. However, it is limited to comparisons of age-group averages. Cross-sectional studies, especially those that cover a wide age span, are also vulnerable to cohort effects.

- By comparing participants of the same age who were born in different years, investigators use **sequential designs** to find out if cohort effects are operating. When sequential designs combine longitudinal and cross-sectional strategies, researchers can see if outcomes are similar, for added confidence in their findings.

- In the **microgenetic design,** researchers track change as it occurs for unique insights into processes of development. However, the time required for children to change is hard to anticipate, and practice effects can bias findings.

- When researchers combine experimental and developmental designs, they can examine causal influences on development. This combined strategy is increasingly common today.

What special ethical concerns arise in doing research on children?

- Because of their immaturity, children are especially vulnerable to harm and often cannot evaluate the risks and benefits of research. Ethical guidelines and institutional review boards that weigh the risks and benefits of research help ensure that children's research rights are protected.

- Besides obtaining consent from parents and others who act on children's behalf, researchers should seek the informed consent of children 7 years and older. The use of deception in research with children is especially risky because it may undermine their basic faith in the honesty of adults.

IMPORTANT TERMS AND CONCEPTS

behaviorism (p. 17)
behavior modification (p. 18)
child development (p. 4)
chronosystem (p. 27)
clinical interview (p. 33)
clinical, or case study, method (p. 34)
cognitive-developmental theory (p. 19)
cohort effects (p. 41)
contexts (p. 8)
continuous development (p. 7)
correlational design (p. 37)
correlation coefficient (p. 37)
cross-sectional design (p. 41)
dependent variable (p. 37)
developmental cognitive neuroscience (p. 23)
developmental science (p. 4)
discontinuous development (p. 8)

dynamic systems perspective (p. 28)
ecological systems theory (p. 25)
ethnography (p. 34)
ethology (p. 23)
evolutionary developmental psychology (p. 24)
exosystem (p. 27)
experimental design (p. 37)
independent variable (p. 37)
information processing (p. 21)
longitudinal design (p. 40)
macrosystem (p. 27)
maturation (p. 13)
mesosystem (p. 26)
microgenetic design (p. 43)
microsystem (p. 26)
naturalistic observation (p. 31)

nature–nurture controversy (p. 9)
normative approach (p. 13)
plasticity (p. 9)
psychoanalytic perspective (p. 15)
psychosexual theory (p. 15)
psychosocial theory (p. 15)
random assignment (p. 38)
resilience (p. 10)
sensitive period (p. 23)
sequential design (p. 42)
social learning theory (p. 18)
sociocultural theory (p. 24)
stage (p. 8)
structured interview (p. 33)
structured observation (p. 31)
theory (p. 7)

Untitled

Mohamed Salahedeen Abd Hamid

11 years, Egypt

A river flows past a city on one shore and a grassy bank on the other. Animals, birds, vehicles, and people are all part of the complexity of our world. Chapter 2 addresses a similarly complex blend of forces—genetic, family, neighborhood, school, and culture—that influence child development.

Genetic and Environmental Foundations

"*I*t's a girl!" announces the doctor, holding up the squalling newborn baby as her parents gaze with amazement at their miraculous creation.

"A girl! We've named her Sarah!" exclaims the proud father to eager relatives waiting for news of their new family member.

As we join these parents in thinking about how this wondrous being came into existence and imagining her future, we are struck by many questions. How could this baby, equipped with everything necessary for life outside the womb, have developed from the union of two tiny cells? What ensures that Sarah will, in due time, roll over, reach for objects, walk, talk, make friends, learn, imagine, and create—just like other typical children born before her? Why is she a girl and not a boy, dark-haired rather than blond, calm and cuddly instead of wiry and energetic? What difference will it make that Sarah is given a name and place in one family, community, nation, and culture rather than another?

To answer these questions, this chapter takes a close look at the foundations of development: heredity and environment. Because nature has prepared us for survival, all humans have features in common. Yet each of us is also unique. TAKE A MOMENT... Think about several children you know well, and jot down the most obvious physical and behavioral similarities between them and their parents. Did you find that one child shows combined features of both parents, another resembles just one parent, whereas a third is not like either parent? These directly observable characteristics are called **phenotypes.** They depend in part on the individual's **genotype**—the complex blend of genetic information that determines our species and influences all our unique characteristics. Yet phenotypes are also affected by each person's lifelong history of experiences.

We begin our discussion at the moment of conception, an event that establishes the hereditary makeup of the new individual. First we review basic genetic principles that help explain similarities and differences among children in appearance and behavior. Then we turn to aspects of the environment that play powerful roles in children's lives. As our discussion proceeds, some findings about the influence of nature and nurture may surprise you. For example, many people believe that when children inherit unfavorable characteristics, not much can be done to help them. Others are convinced that the damage done to a child by a harmful environment can easily be corrected. As we will see, neither of these assumptions is true. In the final section of this chapter, we consider how nature and nurture *work together* to shape the course of development.

Genetic Foundations

Each of us is made up of trillions of units called *cells*. Within every cell (except red blood cells) is a control center, or *nucleus,* that contains rodlike structures called **chromosomes,** which store and transmit genetic information. Human chromosomes come in 23 matching pairs (an exception is the XY pair in males, which we will discuss shortly). Each member of a pair corresponds to the other in size, shape, and genetic functions. One is inherited from the mother and one from the father (see Figure 2.1).

The Genetic Code

Chromosomes are made up of a chemical substance called **deoxyribonucleic acid** or **DNA.** As Figure 2.2 shows, DNA is a long, double-stranded molecule that looks like a twisted ladder. Each rung of the ladder consists of a pair of chemical substances called *bases.* Although the bases always pair up in the same way across the ladder rungs—A with T and C with G—they can occur in any order along its sides. It is this sequence of base pairs that provides genetic instructions. A **gene** is a segment of DNA along the length of the chromosome. Genes can be of different lengths—perhaps 100 to several thousand ladder rungs long. An estimated 20,000 to 25,000 genes lie along the human chromosomes (Human Genome Program, 2008).

We share some of our genetic makeup with even the simplest organisms, such as bacteria and molds, and most of it with other mammals, especially primates. Between 98 and 99 percent of chimpanzee and human DNA is identical. This means that only a small portion of our heredity is responsible for the traits that make us human, from our upright gait to our extraordinary language and cognitive capacities. And the genetic variation from one human to the next is even less! Individuals around the world are about 99.1 percent genetically identical

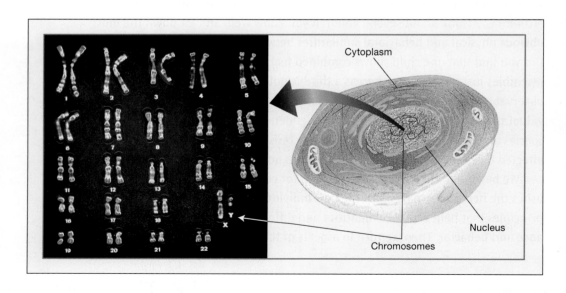

FIGURE 2.1

A karyotype, or photograph, of human chromosomes. The 46 chromosomes shown on the left were isolated from a human cell, stained, greatly magnified, and arranged in pairs according to decreasing size of the upper "arm" of each chromosome. The twenty-third pair, XY, reveals that the cell donor is a male. In a female, this pair would be XX. *(© CNRI/Science Photo Library/Photo Researchers, Inc.)*

Cytoplasm

Nucleus

Chromosomes

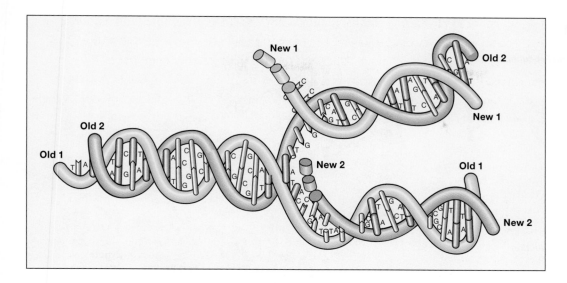

FIGURE 2.2

DNA's ladderlike structure. This figure shows that the pairings of bases across the rungs of the ladder are very specific: Adenine (A) always appears with thymine (T), and cytosine (C) always appears with guanine (G). Here, the DNA ladder duplicates by splitting down the middle of its ladder rungs. Each free base picks up a new complementary partner from the area surrounding the cell nucleus.

(Gibbons, 1998; Gibbons et al., 2004). But it takes a change in only a single base pair to influence human traits. And such tiny changes can combine in unique ways across multiple genes, thereby amplifying variability within the human species.

A unique feature of DNA is that it can duplicate itself through a process called **mitosis.** This special ability permits the one-celled fertilized ovum to develop into a complex human being composed of a great many cells. Refer again to Figure 2.2, and you will see that during mitosis, the chromosomes copy themselves. As a result, each new body cell contains the same number of chromosomes and the identical genetic information.

Genes accomplish their task by sending instructions for making a rich assortment of proteins to the *cytoplasm,* the area surrounding the cell nucleus. Proteins, which trigger chemical reactions throughout the body, are the biological foundation on which our characteristics are built. How do humans, with far fewer genes than scientists once thought (only twice as many as the worm or fly), manage to develop into such complex beings? The answer lies in the proteins our genes make, which break up and reassemble in staggering variety—about 10 to 20 million altogether. Simpler species have far fewer proteins. Furthermore, the communication system between the cell nucleus and cytoplasm, which fine-tunes gene activity, is more intricate in humans than in simpler organisms. Within the cell, a wide range of environmental factors modify gene expression (Lashley, 2007). So even at this microscopic level, biological events are the result of *both* genetic and nongenetic forces.

The Sex Cells

New individuals are created when two special cells called **gametes,** or sex cells—the sperm and ovum—combine. A gamete contains only 23 chromosomes, half as many as a regular body cell. Gametes are formed through a cell division process called **meiosis,** which halves the number of chromosomes normally present in body cells. When sperm and ovum unite at conception, the resulting cell, called a **zygote,** will again have 46 chromosomes. Meiosis ensures that a constant quantity of genetic material is transmitted from one generation to the next.

The steps involved in meiosis are shown in Figure 2.3 on page 54. First, the chromosomes pair up, and each one copies itself. Then a special event called **crossing over** occurs, in which chromosomes next to each other break at one or more points along their length and exchange segments, so that genes from one are replaced by genes from another. This shuffling of genes creates new hereditary combinations. Next, the chromosome pairs separate into different cells, but chance determines which member of each pair will gather with others and end up in the same gamete. Finally, each chromosome leaves its partner and becomes part of a gamete containing only 23 chromosomes instead of the usual 46.

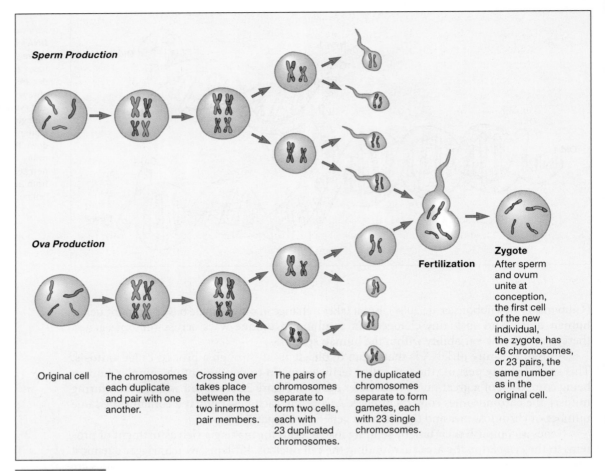

Sperm Production

Ova Production

Fertilization

Zygote
After sperm and ovum unite at conception, the first cell of the new individual, the zygote, has 46 chromosomes, or 23 pairs, the same number as in the original cell.

Original cell

The chromosomes each duplicate and pair with one another.

Crossing over takes place between the two innermost pair members.

The pairs of chromosomes separate to form two cells, each with 23 duplicated chromosomes.

The duplicated chromosomes separate to form gametes, each with 23 single chromosomes.

FIGURE 2.3

The cell division process of meiosis, leading to gamete formation. (Here, original cells are depicted with two rather than the full complement of 23 pairs.) Meiosis creates gametes with only half the usual number of chromosomes. When sperm and ovum unite at conception, the first cell of the new individual (the zygote) has the correct, full number of chromosomes.

These events make the likelihood extremely low—about 1 in 700 trillion—that nontwin siblings will be genetically identical (Gould & Keeton, 1996). The genetic variability produced by meiosis is adaptive: Because it generates offspring that vary in phenotype, it increases the chances that at least some members of a species will cope successfully with ever-changing environments and will survive.

In the male, four sperm are produced when meiosis is complete. Also, the cells from which sperm arise are produced continuously throughout life. For this reason, a healthy man can father a child at any age after sexual maturity. In the female, meiosis results in just one ovum; the remaining genetic material degenerates. In addition, the female is born with all her ova already present in her ovaries, and she can bear children for only three to four decades. Still, there are plenty of female sex cells. About 1 to 2 million are present at birth, 40,000 remain at adolescence, and approximately 350 to 450 will mature during a woman's childbearing years (Moore & Persaud, 2008).

Boy or Girl?

Return to Figure 2.1 on page 52, and note the 22 matching pairs of chromosomes, which geneticists number from longest (1) to shortest (22). These are called **autosomes** (meaning *not* sex chromosomes). The twenty-third pair consists of **sex chromosomes.** In females, this pair is called XX; in males, it is called XY. The X is a relatively large chromosome, whereas the Y is short and carries little genetic material. When gametes form in males, the X and Y chromosomes separate into different sperm cells. The gametes that form in females all carry an X chromosome. Therefore, the sex of the new organism is determined by whether an X-bearing or a Y-bearing sperm fertilizes the ovum. In fact, scientists have isolated a gene on the Y chromosome that initiates the formation of male sex organs during the prenatal period. But they also know that other genes, some yet to be discovered, are involved in the development of sexual characteristics (Bhagavath & Layman, 2007; Sekido & Lovell-Badge, 2009).

Multiple Births

Ruth and Peter, a couple I know well, tried for several years to have a child, without success. When Ruth reached age 33, her doctor prescribed a fertility drug, and Ruth gave birth to twins—Jeannie and Jason. Jeannie and Jason are **fraternal,** or **dizygotic, twins,** the most common type of multiple birth, resulting from the release and fertilization of two ova. Genetically, they are no more alike than ordinary siblings. Table 2.1 summarizes genetic and environmental factors that increase the chances of giving birth to fraternal twins. Older maternal age, fertility drugs, and in vitro fertilization (to be discussed shortly) are major causes of the dramatic rise in fraternal twinning and other multiple births in industrialized nations over the past several decades (Machin, 2005; Russell et al., 2003). Currently, fraternal twins account for 1 in about every 60 births in the United States (U.S. Department of Health and Human Services, 2010c).

Twins can be created in another way. Sometimes a zygote that has started to duplicate separates into two clusters of cells that develop into two individuals. These are called **identical,** or **monozygotic, twins** because they have the same genetic makeup. The frequency of identical twins is the same around the world—about 1 in every 330 births (Hall, 2003). Animal research has uncovered a variety of environmental influences that prompt this type of twinning, including temperature changes, variation in oxygen levels, and late fertilization of the ovum. In a minority of cases, the identical twinning runs in families, suggesting a genetic influence (Lashley, 2007).

During their early years, children of single births often are healthier and develop more rapidly than twins. Jeannie and Jason, like most twins, were born early—three weeks

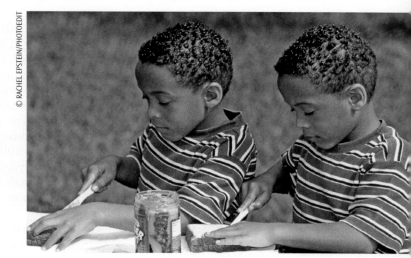

© RACHEL EPSTEIN/PHOTOEDIT

■ These identical, or monozygotic, twins were created when a duplicating zygote separated into two clusters of cells and developed into two individuals with the same genetic makeup. Identical twins look alike, and as we will see later in this chapter, tend to resemble each other in a variety of psychological characteristics. ■

TABLE 2.1	Maternal Factors Linked to Fraternal Twinning

FACTOR	DESCRIPTION
Ethnicity	Occurs in 4 per 1,000 births among Asians, 8 per 1,000 births among whites, 12 to 16 per 1,000 births among blacks[a]
Family history of twinning	Occurs more often among women whose mothers and sisters gave birth to fraternal twins
Age	Rises with maternal age, peaking between 35 and 39 years, and then rapidly falls
Nutrition	Occurs less often among women with poor diets; occurs more often among women who are tall and overweight or of normal weight as opposed to slight body build
Number of births	Is more likely with each additional birth
Fertility drugs and in vitro fertilization	Is more likely with fertility hormones and in vitro fertilization (see pages 66–67), which also increase the chances of bearing triplets, quadruplets, or quintuplets

[a] Worldwide rates, not including multiple births resulting from use of fertility drugs.

Sources: Hall, 2003; Hoekstra et al., 2008; Lashley, 2007.

before Ruth's due date. And, like other premature infants, as you will see in Chapter 4, they required special care after birth. When the twins came home from the hospital, Ruth and Peter had to divide time between them. Perhaps because neither baby got quite as much attention as the average single infant, Jeannie and Jason walked and talked several months later than most other children their age, although both caught up in development by middle childhood (Lytton & Gallagher, 2002). Parental energies are further strained after the birth of triplets, whose early development is slower than that of twins (Feldman, Eidelman, & Rotenberg, 2004).

Patterns of Genetic Inheritance

Jeannie has her parents' dark, straight hair, whereas Jason is curly-haired and blond. Patterns of genetic inheritance—the way genes from each parent interact—explain these outcomes. Recall that except for the XY pair in males, all chromosomes come in corresponding pairs. Two forms of each gene occur at the same place on the chromosomes, one inherited from the mother and one from the father. Each form of a gene is called an **allele.** If the alleles from both parents are alike, the child is **homozygous** and will display the inherited trait. If the alleles are different, the child is **heterozygous,** and relationships between the alleles determine the phenotype.

DOMINANT–RECESSIVE INHERITANCE   In many heterozygous pairings, **dominant–recessive inheritance** occurs: Only one allele affects the child's characteristics. It is called *dominant;* the second allele, which has no effect, is called *recessive.* Hair color is an example. The allele for dark hair is dominant (we can represent it with a capital *D*), whereas the one for blond hair is recessive (symbolized by a lowercase *b*). A child who inherits a homozygous pair of dominant alleles *(DD)* and a child who inherits a heterozygous pair *(Db)* will both be dark-haired, even though their genotypes differ. Blond hair (like Jason's) can result only from having two recessive alleles *(bb)*. Still, heterozygous individuals with just one recessive allele *(Db)* can pass that trait to their children. Therefore, they are called **carriers** of the trait.

Some human characteristics that follow the rules of dominant–recessive inheritance are listed in Table 2.2 and Table 2.3 on page 58. As you can see, many disabilities and diseases are the product of recessive alleles. One of the most frequently occurring recessive disorders is *phenylketonuria,* or *PKU.* It affects the way the body breaks down proteins contained in many foods. Infants born with two recessive alleles lack an enzyme that converts one of the basic amino acids that make up proteins (phenylalanine) into a byproduct essential for body functioning (tyrosine). Without this enzyme, phenylalanine quickly builds to toxic levels that damage the central nervous system. By 1 year, infants with PKU are permanently retarded.

Despite its potentially damaging effects, PKU provides an excellent illustration of the fact that inheriting unfavorable genes does not always lead to an untreatable condition. All U.S. states require that each newborn be given a blood test for PKU. If the disease is found, doctors place the baby on a diet low in phenylalanine. Children who receive this treatment nevertheless show mild deficits in certain cognitive skills, such as memory, planning, decision making, and problem solving, because even small amounts of phenylalanine interfere with brain functioning (Anderson et al., 2007; Christ et al., 2006; DeRoche & Welsh, 2008). But as long as dietary treatment begins early and continues, children with PKU usually attain an average level of intelligence and have a normal lifespan.

TABLE 2.2 Examples of Dominant and Recessive Characteristics

DOMINANT	RECESSIVE
Dark hair	Blond hair
Normal hair	Pattern baldness
Curly hair	Straight hair
Nonred hair	Red hair
Facial dimples	No dimples
Normal hearing	Some forms of deafness
Normal vision	Nearsightedness
Farsightedness	Normal vision
Normal vision	Congenital eye cataracts
Normally pigmented skin	Albinism
Double-jointedness	Normal joints
Type A blood	Type O blood
Type B blood	Type O blood
Rh-positive blood	Rh-negative blood

Note: Many normal characteristics that were previously thought to be due to dominant–recessive inheritance, such as eye color, are now regarded as due to multiple genes. For the characteristics listed here, there still seems to be general agreement that the simple dominant–recessive relationship holds.

Source: McKusick, 2007.

In dominant–recessive inheritance, if we know the genetic makeup of the parents, we can predict the percentage of children in a family who are likely to display or carry a trait. Figure 2.4 illustrates this for PKU. For a child to inherit the condition, each parent must have a recessive allele *(p).* As the figure also illustrates, a single gene can affect more than one trait. Because of their inability to convert phenylalanine into tyrosine (which is responsible for pigmentation), children with PKU usually have light hair and blue eyes. Furthermore, children vary in the degree to which phenylalanine accumulates in their tissues and in the extent to which they respond to treatment. This is due to the action of **modifier genes,** which enhance or dilute the effects of other genes.

Only rarely are serious diseases due to dominant alleles. Think about why this is so. Children who inherit the dominant allele always develop the disorder. They seldom live long enough to reproduce, so the harmful dominant allele is eliminated from the family's heredity in a single generation. Some dominant disorders, however, do persist. One is *Huntington disease,* a condition in which the central nervous system degenerates. Why has this disorder endured? Its symptoms usually do not appear until age 35 or later, after the person has passed the dominant allele to his or her children.

INCOMPLETE DOMINANCE   In some heterozygous circumstances, the dominant–recessive relationship does not hold completely. Instead, we see **incomplete dominance,** a pattern of inheritance in which both alleles are expressed in the phenotype, resulting in a combined trait, or one that is intermediate between the two.

The *sickle cell trait,* a heterozygous condition present in many black Africans, provides an example. *Sickle cell anemia* (see Table 2.3) occurs in full form when a child inherits two recessive alleles. They cause the usually round red blood cells to become sickle (crescent-moon) shaped, especially under low-oxygen conditions. The sickled cells clog the blood vessels and block the flow of blood, causing intense pain, swelling, and tissue damage. Despite medical advances that today allow 85 percent of affected children to survive to adulthood, North Americans with sickle cell anemia have a life expectancy of only 55 years (Driscoll, 2007). Heterozygous individuals are protected from the disease under most circumstances. However, when they experience oxygen deprivation—for example, at high altitudes or after intense physical exercise—the single recessive allele asserts itself, and a temporary, mild form of the illness occurs.

The sickle cell allele is common among black Africans for a special reason. Carriers of it are more resistant to malaria than are individuals with two alleles for normal red blood cells. In Africa, where malaria is common, these carriers have survived and reproduced more frequently than others, leading the gene to be maintained in the black population. But in regions of the world where the risk of malaria is low, the frequency of the gene is declining. For example, only 8 percent of African Americans are carriers, compared with 20 percent of black Africans (National Center for Biotechnology Information, 2007).

X-LINKED INHERITANCE   Males and females have an equal chance of inheriting recessive disorders carried on the autosomes, such as PKU and sickle cell anemia. But when a harmful allele is carried on the X chromosome, **X-linked inheritance** applies. Males are more likely to be affected because their sex chromosomes do not match. In females, any recessive allele on one X chromosome has a good chance of being suppressed by a dominant allele on the other X. But the Y chromosome is only about one-third as long and therefore lacks many corresponding alleles to override those on the X. A well-known example is *hemophilia,* a disorder in which the

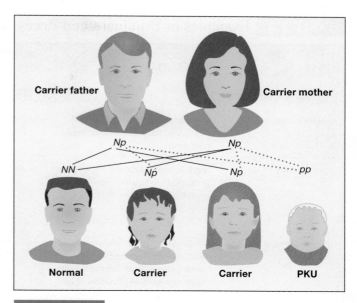

FIGURE 2.4

Dominant–recessive mode of inheritance, as illustrated by PKU. When both parents are heterozygous carriers of the recessive gene *(p),* we can predict that 25 percent of their offspring are likely to be normal *(NN),* 50 percent are likely to be carriers *(Np),* and 25 percent are likely to inherit the disorder *(pp).* Notice that the PKU-affected child, in contrast to his siblings, has light hair. The recessive gene for PKU affects more than one trait. It also leads to fair coloring.

TABLE 2.3 Examples of Dominant and Recessive Diseases

DISEASE	DESCRIPTION	MODE OF INHERITANCE	INCIDENCE	TREATMENT
AUTOSOMAL DISEASES				
Cooley's anemia	Pale appearance, retarded physical growth, and lethargic behavior begin in infancy.	Recessive	1 in 500 births to parents of Mediterranean descent	Frequent blood transfusions. Death from complications usually occurs by adolescence.
Cystic fibrosis	Lungs, liver, and pancreas secrete large amounts of thick mucus, leading to breathing and digestive difficulties.	Recessive	1 in 2,000 to 2,500 Caucasian births; 1 in 16,000 births to North Americans of African descent	Bronchial drainage, prompt treatment of respiratory infection, dietary management. Advances in medical care allow survival with good life quality into adulthood.
Phenylketonuria (PKU)	Inability to metabolize the amino acid phenylalanine, contained in many proteins, causes severe central nervous system damage in the first year of life.	Recessive	1 in 8,000 births	Placing the child on a special diet results in average intelligence and normal lifespan. Subtle difficulties in memory, planning, decision making, and problem solving are often present.
Sickle cell anemia	Abnormal sickling of red blood cells causes oxygen deprivation, pain, swelling, and tissue damage. Anemia and susceptibility to infections, especially pneumonia, occur.	Recessive	1 in 400 to 600 births to North Americans of African descent	Blood transfusions, painkillers, prompt treatment of infection. No known cure; 50 percent die by age 55.
Tay-Sachs disease	Central nervous system degeneration, with onset at about 6 months, leads to poor muscle tone, blindness, deafness, and convulsions.	Recessive	1 in 3,600 births to Jews of European descent and to French Canadians	None. Death occurs by 3 to 4 years of age.
Huntington disease	Central nervous system degeneration leads to muscular coordination difficulties, mental deterioration, and personality changes. Symptoms usually do not appear until age 35 or later.	Dominant	1 in 18,000 to 25,000 births to North Americans	None. Death occurs 10 to 20 years after symptom onset.
Marfan syndrome	Tall, slender build; thin, elongated arms and legs; and heart defects and eye abnormalities, especially of the lens. Excessive lengthening of the body results in a variety of skeletal defects.	Dominant	1 in 5,000 to 10,000 births	Correction of heart and eye defects sometimes possible. Death from heart failure in early adulthood is common.
X-LINKED DISEASES				
Duchenne muscular dystrophy	Degenerative muscle disease. Abnormal gait, loss of ability to walk between ages 7 and 13 years.	Recessive	1 in 3,000 to 5,000 male births	None. Death from respiratory infection or weakening of the heart muscle usually occurs in adolescence.
Hemophilia	Blood fails to clot normally; can lead to severe internal bleeding and tissue damage.	Recessive	1 in 4,000 to 7,000 male births	Blood transfusions. Safety precautions to prevent injury.
Diabetes insipidus	Insufficient production of the hormone vasopressin results in excessive thirst and urination. Dehydration can cause central nervous system damage.	Recessive	1 in 2,500 male births	Hormone replacement.

Note: For recessive disorders, carrier status can be detected in prospective parents through a blood test or genetic analyses. For all disorders listed, prenatal diagnosis is available (see page 63).

Sources: Kliegman et al., 2008; Lashley, 2007; McKusick, 2007.

blood fails to clot normally. Figure 2.5 shows its greater like-lihood of inheritance by male children whose mothers carry the abnormal allele.

Besides X-linked disorders, many sex differences reveal the male to be at a disadvantage. Rates of miscarriage, infant and childhood deaths, birth defects, learning disabilities, behavior disorders, and mental retardation all are higher for boys (Butler & Meaney, 2005). It is possible that these sex differences can be traced to the genetic code. The female, with two X chromosomes, benefits from a greater variety of genes. Nature, however, seems to have adjusted for the male's disadvantage. Worldwide, about 106 boys are born for every 100 girls, and judging from miscarriage and abor-tion statistics, an even greater number of boys are conceived (United Nations, 2006).

Nevertheless, in recent decades the proportion of male births has declined in many industrialized countries, includ-ing the United States, Canada, and European nations (Jongbloet et al., 2001). Some researchers attribute the trend to a rise in stressful living conditions, which heighten spon-taneous abortions, especially of male fetuses. In a test of this hypothesis, male-to-female birth ratios in East Germany were examined between 1946 and 1999. The ratio was low-est in 1991, the year that the country's economy collapsed (Catalano, 2003). Similarly, in a California study spanning the decade of the 1990s, the percentage of male fetal deaths increased in months in which unemployment (a major stressor) also rose above its typical level (Catalano et al., 2005, 2009).

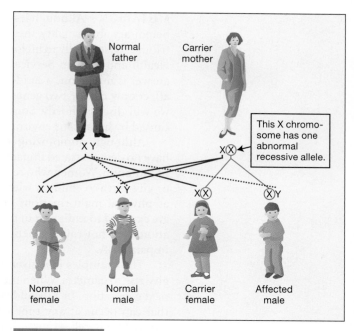

FIGURE 2.5

X-linked inheritance. In the example shown here, the allele on the father's X chromosome is normal. The mother has one normal and one abnormal recessive allele on her X chromosomes. By looking at the possible combinations of the parents' alleles, we can predict that 50 percent of these parents' male children are likely to have the disorder, and 50 percent of their female children are likely to be carriers of it.

GENOMIC IMPRINTING More than 1,000 human characteristics follow the rules of dominant–recessive and incomplete-dominance inheritance (McKusick, 2007). In these cases, whichever parent contributes a gene to the new individual, the gene responds in the same way. Geneticists, however, have identified some exceptions. In **genomic imprinting,** alleles are *imprinted,* or chemically marked, in such a way that one pair member (either the mother's or the father's) is activated, regardless of its makeup. The imprint is often temporary; it may be erased in the next generation, and it may not occur in all individuals (Everman & Cassidy, 2000).

Imprinting helps us understand certain puzzling genetic patterns. For example, children are more likely to develop diabetes if their father, rather than their mother, suffers from it. And people with asthma or hay fever tend to have mothers, not fathers, with the illness. Imprinting is involved in several childhood cancers and in *Prader-Willi syndrome,* a disorder with symp-toms of mental retardation and severe obesity (Benarroch et al., 2007). It may also explain why Huntington disease, when inherited from the father, tends to emerge at an earlier age and to progress more rapidly (Navarrete, Martinez, & Salamanca, 1994).

Genomic imprinting can also operate on the sex chromosomes, as *fragile X syndrome*—the most common inherited cause of mental retardation—reveals. In this disorder, which affects about 1 in 4,000 males and 1 in 6,000 females, an abnormal repetition of a sequence of DNA bases occurs in a special spot on the X chromosome, damaging a particular gene. The defective gene at the fragile site is expressed only when it is passed from mother to child. Because the dis-order is X-linked, males are more severely affected (Hagerman et al., 2009). Females usually have a normally functioning gene on their other X chromosome (inherited from the father) that partially compensates for the abnormal gene. About 25 to 30 percent of individuals with fragile X syndrome also have symptoms of *autism,* a serious disorder usually diagnosed in early childhood that involves impaired social interaction, delayed or absent language and commu-nication, and repetitive motor behavior (Schwarte, 2008).

MUTATION   Although less than 3 percent of pregnancies result in the birth of a baby with a hereditary abnormality, these children account for about 20 percent of infant deaths and contribute substantially to lifelong impaired physical and mental functioning (U.S. Department of Health and Human Services, 2010c). How are harmful genes created in the first place? The answer is **mutation,** a sudden but permanent change in a segment of DNA. A mutation may affect only one or two genes, or it may involve many genes, as in the chromosomal disorders we will discuss shortly. Some mutations occur spontaneously, simply by chance. Others are caused by hazardous environmental agents.

Although nonionizing forms of radiation—electromagnetic waves and microwaves—have no demonstrated impact on DNA, ionizing (high-energy) radiation is an established cause of mutation. Women who receive repeated doses before conception are more likely to miscarry or give birth to children with hereditary defects. The incidence of genetic abnormalities, such as physical malformations and childhood cancer, is also higher in children whose fathers are exposed to radiation in their occupations. However, infrequent and mild exposure to radiation does not cause genetic damage (Jacquet, 2004). Rather, high doses over a long period impair DNA.

The examples just given illustrate *germline mutation,* which takes place in the cells that give rise to gametes. When the affected individual mates, the defective DNA is passed on to the next generation. In a second type, called *somatic mutation,* normal body cells mutate, an event that can occur at any time of life. The DNA defect appears in every cell derived from the affected body cell, eventually becoming widespread enough to cause disease (such as cancer) or disability.

It is easy to see how disorders that run in families can result from germline mutation. But somatic mutation may be involved in these disorders as well. Some people harbor a genetic susceptibility that causes certain body cells to mutate easily in the presence of triggering events (Weiss, 2005). This helps explain why some individuals develop serious illnesses (such as cancer) as a result of smoking, exposure to pollutants, or psychological stress, while others do not.

Although virtually all mutations that have been studied are harmful, some spontaneous ones (such as the sickle cell allele in malaria-ridden regions of the world) are necessary and desirable. By increasing genetic variation, they help individuals adapt to unexpected environmental challenges. Scientists, however, seldom go looking for mutations that underlie favorable traits, such as an exceptional talent or an especially sturdy immune system. They are far more concerned with identifying and eliminating unfavorable genes that threaten health and survival.

POLYGENIC INHERITANCE   So far, we have discussed patterns of inheritance in which people either display a particular trait or do not. These cut-and-dried individual differences are much easier to trace to their genetic origins than are characteristics that vary on a continuum among people, such as height, weight, intelligence, and personality. These traits are due to **polygenic inheritance,** in which many genes affect the characteristic in question. Polygenic inheritance is complex, and much about it is still unknown. In the final section of this chapter, we discuss how researchers infer the influence of heredity on human attributes when they do not know the precise patterns of inheritance.

Chromosomal Abnormalities

Besides harmful recessive alleles, abnormalities of the chromosomes are a major cause of serious developmental problems. Most chromosomal defects result from mistakes during meiosis, when the ovum and sperm are formed. A chromosome pair does not separate properly, or part of a chromosome breaks off. Because these errors involve far more DNA than problems due to single genes, they usually produce many physical and mental symptoms.

DOWN SYNDROME   The most common chromosomal disorder, occurring in 1 out of every 770 live births, is *Down syndrome.* In 95 percent of cases, it results from a failure of the twenty-first pair of chromosomes to separate during meiosis, so the new individual receives three of these chromosomes rather than the normal two. For this reason, Down syndrome is sometimes called *trisomy 21*. In other, less frequent forms, an extra broken piece of a twenty-first chromosome is attached to another chromosome (called *translocation* pattern). Or an error occurs during the early stages of mitosis, causing some but not all body cells to have the defective chromosomal makeup (called *mosaic* pattern) (U.S. Department of Health and Human Services, 2009d). Because the mosaic type involves less genetic material, symptoms may be less extreme.

The consequences of Down syndrome include mental retardation, memory and speech problems, limited vocabulary, and slow motor development. Affected individuals also have distinct physical features—a short, stocky build; a flattened face; a protruding tongue; almond-shaped eyes; and (in 50 percent of cases) an unusual crease running across the palm of the hand. In addition, infants with Down syndrome are often born with eye cataracts, hearing loss, and heart and intestinal defects (Sherman et al., 2007). Because of medical advances, fewer individuals with Down syndrome die early than was the case in the past. Many survive into their fifties and a few into their sixties to eighties. However, more than half of affected individuals who live past age 40 show symptoms of *Alzheimer's disease,* the most common form of dementia (Wiseman et al., 2009). Genes on chromosome 21 are linked to this disorder.

Infants with Down syndrome smile less readily, show poor eye-to-eye contact, have weak muscle tone, and explore objects less persistently (Slonims & McConachie, 2006). But when parents encourage them to engage with their surroundings, children with Down syndrome develop more favorably. They also benefit from infant and preschool intervention programs, although emotional, social, and motor skills improve more than intellectual performance (Carr, 2002). Clearly, environmental factors affect how well children with Down syndrome fare.

As Figure 2.6 shows, the risk of bearing a Down syndrome baby rises dramatically with maternal age (Schonberg & Tifft, 2007). But exactly why older mothers are more likely to release ova with meiotic errors is not yet known (Martin, 2008). In about 5 to 10 percent of cases, the extra genetic material originates with the father. Some studies suggest a role for advanced paternal age, while others show no age effects (De Souza, Alberman, & Morris, 2009; Dzurova & Pikhart, 2005; Sherman et al., 2005).

ABNORMALITIES OF THE SEX CHROMOSOMES Disorders of the autosomes other than Down syndrome usually disrupt development so severely that miscarriage occurs. When such babies are born, they rarely survive beyond early childhood. In contrast, abnormalities of the sex chromosomes usually lead to fewer problems. In fact, sex chromosome disorders often are not recognized until adolescence when, in

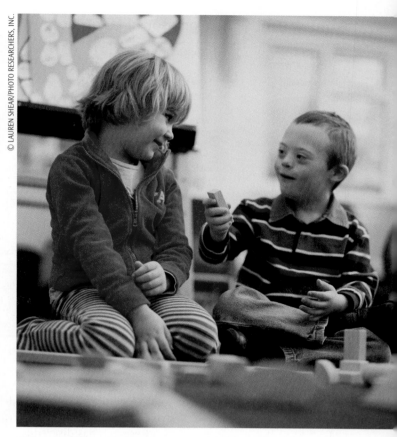

■ A 6-year-old boy with Down syndrome, at right, plays with a typically developing classmate. Despite impaired intellectual development, this boy benefits from exposure to stimulating environments and from opportunities to interact with peers. ■

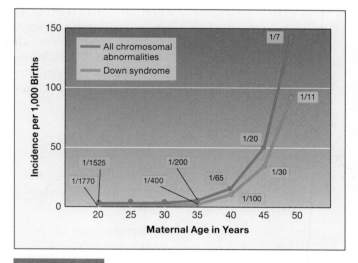

FIGURE 2.6

Risk of Down syndrome and all chromosomal abnormalities by maternal age. Risk rises sharply after age 35. *(Adapted from R. L. Schonberg & C. J. Tifft, 2007, "Birth Defects and Prenatal Diagnosis," from* Children with Disabilities, *6/e, M. L. Matshaw, L. Pellegrino, & N. J. Roizen, eds., p. 85. Baltimore: Paul H. Brookes Publishing Co., Inc. Reprinted by permission.)*

TABLE 2.4	Sex Chromosomal Disorders		
DISORDER	**DESCRIPTION**	**INCIDENCE**	**TREATMENT**
XYY syndrome	Extra Y chromosome. Above-average height, large teeth, and sometimes severe acne. Intelligence, male sexual development, and fertility are normal.	1 in 1,000 male births	No special treatment necessary.
Triple X syndrome (XXX)	Extra X chromosome. Tallness and impaired verbal intelligence. Female sexual development and fertility are normal.	1 in 500 to 1,250 female births	Special education to treat verbal ability problems.
Klinefelter syndrome (XXY)	Extra X chromosome. Tallness, body fat distribution resembling females, incomplete development of sex characteristics at puberty, sterility, and impaired verbal intelligence.	1 in 900 male births	Hormone therapy at puberty to stimulate development of sex characteristics; special education to treat verbal ability problems.
Turner syndrome (XO)	Missing X chromosome. Short stature, webbed neck, incomplete development of sex characteristics at puberty, sterility, and impaired spatial intelligence.	1 in 2,500 to 8,000 female births	Hormone therapy in childhood to stimulate physical growth and at puberty to promote development of sex characteristics; special education to treat spatial ability problems.

Sources: Geerts, Steyaert, & Fryns, 2003; Kesler, 2007; Saitta & Zackai, 2005; Simpson et al., 2003.

some deviations, puberty is delayed. The most common problems involve the presence of an extra chromosome (either X or Y) or the absence of one X in females.

Research has discredited a variety of myths about individuals with sex chromosome disorders. For example, as Table 2.4 reveals, males with *XYY syndrome* are not necessarily more aggressive and antisocial than XY males. And most children with sex chromosome disorders do not suffer from mental retardation. Rather, their intellectual problems are usually very specific. Verbal difficulties—for example, with reading and vocabulary—are common among girls with *triple X syndrome* and boys with *Klinefelter syndrome,* both of whom inherit an extra X chromosome. In contrast, girls with *Turner syndrome,* who are missing an X, have trouble with spatial relationships—for example, drawing pictures, telling right from left, following travel directions, and noticing changes in facial expressions (Kesler, 2007; Lawrence et al., 2003; Simpson et al., 2003). Brain-imaging evidence confirms that adding to or subtracting from the usual number of X chromosomes alters the development of certain brain structures, yielding particular intellectual deficits (Cutter et al., 2006; Itti et al., 2006).

ASK YOURSELF

◆ REVIEW Cite evidence indicating that both heredity and environment contribute to the development of children with PKU and Down syndrome.

◆ REVIEW Using your knowledge of X-linked inheritance, explain why males are more vulnerable than females to miscarriage, infant death, genetic disorders, and other problems.

◆ APPLY Gilbert's genetic makeup is homozygous for dark hair. Jan's is homozygous for blond hair. What color is Gilbert's hair? How about Jan's? What proportion of their children are likely to be dark-haired? Explain.

◆ CONNECT Referring to ecological systems theory (Chapter 1, pages 25–27), explain why parents of children with genetic disorders often experience increased stress. What factors, within and beyond the family, can help these parents support their children's development?

■ ■   Reproductive Choices
■ ■

Two years after they married, Ted and Marianne gave birth to their first child. Kendra appeared to be a healthy infant, but by 4 months her growth had slowed, and she was diagnosed as having Tay-Sachs disease (see Table 2.3). When Kendra died at 2 years of age, Ted and Marianne were devastated. Although they did not want to bring another infant into the world who would endure such suffering, they badly wanted to have a child. They began to avoid family get-togethers, where little nieces and nephews were constant reminders of the void in their lives.

In the past, many couples with genetic disorders in their families chose not to bear a child at all rather than risk the birth of a baby with abnormalities. Today, genetic counseling and prenatal diagnosis help people make informed decisions about conceiving, carrying a pregnancy to term, or adopting a child.

Genetic Counseling

Genetic counseling is a communication process designed to help couples assess their chances of giving birth to a baby with a hereditary disorder and choose the best course of action in view of risks and family goals (Resta et al., 2006). Individuals likely to seek counseling are those who have had difficulties bearing children—for example, repeated miscarriages—or who know that genetic problems exist in their families. In addition, women who delay childbearing past age 35 are often candidates for genetic counseling. After this time, the overall rate of chromosomal abnormalities rises sharply (refer again to Figure 2.6) (Schonberg & Tifft, 2007). But because younger mothers give birth in far higher numbers than older mothers, they still bear the majority of babies with genetic defects. Therefore, some experts argue that maternal needs, not age, should determine referral for genetic counseling (Berkowitz, Roberts, & Minkoff, 2006).

If a family history of mental retardation, psychological disorders, physical defects, or inherited diseases exists, the genetic counselor interviews the couple and prepares a *pedigree,* a picture of the family tree in which affected relatives are identified. The pedigree is used to estimate the likelihood that parents will have an abnormal child, using the genetic principles discussed earlier in this chapter. For many disorders, blood tests or genetic analyses can reveal whether the parent is a carrier of the harmful gene. Carrier detection is possible for all the recessive diseases listed in Table 2.3, as well as others, and for fragile X syndrome.

When all the relevant information is in, the genetic counselor helps people consider appropriate options. These include taking a chance and conceiving, choosing from among a variety of reproductive technologies (see the Social Issues: Health box on pages 66–67), or adopting a child.

Prenatal Diagnosis and Fetal Medicine

If couples who might bear a child with abnormalities decide to conceive, several **prenatal diagnostic methods**—medical procedures that permit detection of developmental problems before birth—are available (see Table 2.5 on page 64). Women of advanced maternal age are prime candidates for *amniocentesis* or *chorionic villus sampling* (see Figure 2.7 on page 65). Except for *maternal blood analysis,* prenatal diagnosis should not be used routinely, since other methods have some chance of injuring the developing organism.

Prenatal diagnosis has led to advances in fetal medicine. For example, by inserting a needle into the uterus, doctors can administer drugs to the fetus. Surgery has been performed to repair such problems as heart, lung, and diaphragm malformations; urinary tract obstructions; and neural defects (Kunisaki & Jennings, 2008). Fetuses with blood disorders have been given blood transfusions. And those with immune deficiencies have received bone marrow transplants that succeeded in creating a normally functioning immune system (Williams, 2006).

TABLE 2.5 Prenatal Diagnostic Methods

METHOD	DESCRIPTION
Amniocentesis	The most widely used technique. A hollow needle is inserted through the abdominal wall to obtain a sample of fluid in the uterus. Cells are examined for genetic defects. Can be performed by the 14th week after conception; 1 to 2 more weeks are required for test results. Small risk of miscarriage.
Chorionic villus sampling	A procedure that can be used if results are desired or needed very early in pregnancy. A thin tube is inserted into the uterus through the vagina, or a hollow needle is inserted through the abdominal wall. A small plug of tissue is removed from the end of one or more chorionic villi, the hairlike projections on the membrane surrounding the developing organism. Cells are examined for genetic defects. Can be performed at 9 weeks after conception; results are available within 24 hours. Entails a slightly greater risk of miscarriage than does amniocentesis. Also associated with a small risk of limb deformities, which increases the earlier the procedure is performed.
Fetoscopy	A small tube with a light source at one end is inserted into the uterus to inspect the fetus for defects of the limbs and face. Also allows a sample of fetal blood to be obtained, permitting diagnosis of such disorders as hemophilia and sickle cell anemia as well as neural defects (see below). Usually performed between 15 and 18 weeks after conception but can be done as early as 5 weeks. Entails some risk of miscarriage.
Ultrasound	High-frequency sound waves are beamed at the uterus; their reflection is translated into a picture on a video screen that reveals the size, shape, and placement of the fetus. By itself, permits assessment of fetal age, detection of multiple pregnancies, and identification of gross physical defects. Also used to guide amniocentesis, chorionic villus sampling, and fetoscopy. When used five or more times, may increase the chances of low birth weight.
Maternal blood analysis	By the second month of pregnancy, some of the developing organism's cells enter the maternal bloodstream. An elevated level of alpha-feto-protein may indicate kidney disease, abnormal closure of the esophagus, or neural tube defects, such as anencephaly (absence of most of the brain) and spina bifida (bulging of the spinal cord from the spinal column). Isolated cells can be examined for genetic defects.
Preimplantation genetic diagnosis	After in vitro fertilization and duplication of the zygote into a cluster of about 8 to 10 cells, 1 or 2 cells are removed and examined for hereditary defects. Only if that sample is free of detectable genetic disorders is the fertilized ovum implanted in the woman's uterus.

Sources: Hahn & Chitty, 2008; Kumar & O'Brien, 2004; Moore & Persaud, 2008; Sermon, Van Steirteghem, & Liebaers, 2004.

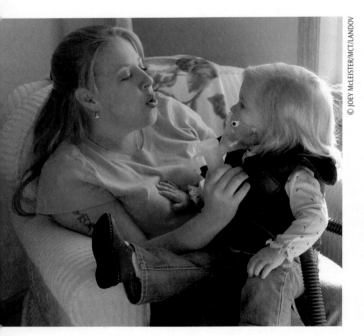

© JOEY McLEISTER/MCT/LANDOV

■ This mother sings while delivering medication through a nebulizer to her 2-year-old daughter, who has cystic fibrosis. The child also wears a vest for a twice-daily treatment that pounds her chest to clear her lungs of thick mucus. In the future, such children may benefit from gene-based treatments for hereditary disorders. ■

These techniques frequently result in complications, the most common being premature labor and miscarriage (Schonberg & Tifft, 2007). Yet parents may be willing to try almost any option, even one with only a slim chance of success. Currently, the medical profession is struggling with how to help parents make informed decisions about fetal surgery.

Advances in *genetic engineering* also offer new hope for correcting hereditary defects. As part of the Human Genome Project—an ambitious international research program aimed at deciphering the chemical makeup of human genetic material (genome)—researchers have mapped the sequence of all human DNA base pairs. Using this information, they are "annotating" the genome—identifying all its genes and their functions, including their protein products and what these products do. A major goal is to understand the estimated 4,000 human disorders, those due to single genes and those resulting from a complex interplay of multiple genes and environmental factors.

Already, thousands of genes have been identified, including those involved in hundreds of diseases, such as cystic fibrosis; Duchenne muscular dystrophy; Huntington disease; Marfan syndrome; heart, digestive, blood, eye, and nervous system abnormalities; and many forms of cancer (National Institutes of Health, 2008). As a result, new treatments are being explored, such as *gene therapy*—correcting genetic abnormalities by delivering DNA carrying a functional gene to the cells. In recent experiments, gene

Amniocentesis and chorionic villus sampling. Today, hundreds of defects and diseases can be detected before birth using these two procedures. (a) In amniocentesis, a hollow needle is inserted through the abdominal wall into the uterus during the fourteenth week after conception or later. Fluid is withdrawn, and fetal cells are cultured, a process that takes one to two weeks. (b) Chorionic villus sampling can be performed much earlier in pregnancy, at nine weeks after conception, and results are available within 24 hours. Two approaches to obtaining a sample of chorionic villus are shown: inserting a thin tube through the vagina into the uterus and inserting a needle through the abdominal wall. In both amniocentesis and chorionic villus sampling, an ultrasound scanner is used for guidance. *(Adapted from* Before We Are Born, *7th ed. By K. L. Moore & T. V. N. Persaud, p. 69. Copyright © 2008, reprinted with permission from Elsevier, Inc.)*

therapy relieved symptoms in hemophilia patients and in patients with severe immune system dysfunction. A few, however, experienced serious side effects (Gillet et al., 2009). In another approach, called *proteomics,* scientists modify gene-specified proteins involved in disease (Van Eyk & Dunn, 2008).

Genetic treatments seem some distance in the future for most single-gene defects, however, and farther off for diseases involving multiple genes that combine in complex ways with each other and the environment. Applying What We Know on page 68 summarizes steps that prospective parents can take before conception to protect the genetic health of their child.

The Alternative of Adoption

Adults who are infertile, who are likely to pass along a genetic disorder, or who are older and single but want a family are turning to adoption in increasing numbers. Those who have children by birth, too, sometimes choose to expand their families through adoption. Adoption agencies try to ensure a good fit by seeking parents of the same ethnic and religious background as the child and, where possible, trying to choose parents who are the same age as typical biological parents. Because the availability of healthy babies has declined (fewer young unwed mothers give up their babies than in the past), more people in North America and Western Europe are adopting from other countries or accepting children who are past infancy or who have known developmental problems (Schweiger & O'Brien, 2005).

Adopted children and adolescents—whether or not they are born in their adoptive parents' country—tend to have more learning and emotional difficulties than other children, a difference that increases with the child's age at time of adoption (Nickman et al., 2005; van IJzendoorn, Juffer, & Poelhuis, 2005; Verhulst, 2008). There are many possible reasons for adoptees' more problematic childhoods. The biological mother may have been unable to care for the child because of problems believed to be partly genetic, such as alcoholism or severe depression, and may have passed this tendency to her offspring. Or perhaps she experienced stress, poor diet, or inadequate medical care during pregnancy—factors that can affect the

SOCIAL ISSUES: HEALTH

The Pros and Cons of Reproductive Technologies

Some couples decide not to risk pregnancy because of a history of genetic disease. Many others—in fact, one-sixth of all couples who try to conceive—discover that they are infertile. And some never-married adults and gay and lesbian partners want to bear children. Today, increasing numbers of individuals are turning to alternative methods of conception—technologies that, although they fulfill the wish for parenthood, have become the subject of heated debate.

Donor Insemination and In Vitro Fertilization

For several decades, *donor insemination*—injection of sperm from an anonymous man into a woman—has been used to overcome male reproductive difficulties. In recent years, it has also permitted women without a male partner to become pregnant. Donor insemination is 70 to 80 percent successful, resulting in about 40,000 deliveries and 52,000 newborn babies in the United States each year (Wright et al., 2008).

In *vitro fertilization* is another reproductive technology that has become increasingly common. Since the first "test tube" baby was born in England in 1978, 1 percent of all children in developed countries—about 40,000 babies in the United States—have been conceived through this technique annually (Jackson, Gibson, & Wu, 2004). With in vitro fertilization, a woman is given hormones that stimulate the ripening of several ova. These are removed surgically and placed in a dish of nutrients, to which sperm are added. Once an ovum is fertilized and begins to duplicate into several cells, it is injected into the mother's uterus.

By mixing and matching gametes, pregnancies can be brought about when either or both partners have a reproductive problem. Usually,

■ Fertility drugs and in vitro fertilization often lead to multiple fetuses. Although these sextuplets are healthy, reproductive technologies can pose grave ethical dilemmas. When three or more fetuses fill the womb, pregnancy complications may be so severe that doctors recommend aborting one or more to save the others. ■

in vitro fertilization is used to treat women whose fallopian tubes are permanently damaged. But a recently developed technique permits a single sperm to be injected directly into an ovum, thereby overcoming most male fertility problems. And a "sex sorter" method helps ensure that couples who carry X-linked diseases (which usually affect males) have a daughter. Fertilized ova and sperm can even be frozen and stored in embryo banks for use at some future time, thereby guaranteeing healthy zygotes should age or illness lead to fertility problems.

The overall success rate of assisted reproductive techniques is about 35 percent. However,

success declines steadily with age, from 40 percent in women younger than age 35 to 8 percent in women age 43 and older (Pauli et al., 2009).

Children conceived through these methods may be genetically unrelated to one or both of their parents. In addition, most parents who have used in vitro fertilization do not tell their children about their origins. Does lack of genetic ties or secrecy surrounding these techniques interfere with parent–child relationships? Perhaps because of a strong desire for parenthood, caregiving is actually somewhat warmer for young children conceived through donor insemination or in vitro fertilization.

child (as we will see in Chapter 3). Furthermore, children adopted after infancy often have a preadoptive history of conflict-ridden family relationships, lack of parental affection, neglect and abuse, or deprived institutional rearing. Finally, adoptive parents and children, who are genetically unrelated, are less alike in intelligence and personality than are biological relatives—differences that may threaten family harmony.

Despite these risks, most adopted children fare well, and those with preexisting problems usually make rapid progress (Arcus & Chambers, 2008; Bimmel et al., 2003). In a study of internationally adopted children in the Netherlands, sensitive maternal care and secure attach-

Also, in vitro infants are as securely attached to their parents, and in vitro children and adolescents as well-adjusted, as their counterparts who were naturally conceived (Golombok et al., 2004; Punamaki, 2006; Wagenaar et al., 2008).

Although reproductive technologies have many benefits, serious questions have arisen about their use. In many countries, including the United States, doctors are not required to keep records of donor characteristics, though information about the child's genetic background might be critical in the case of serious disease (Adamson, 2005). Another concern is that the in vitro "sex sorter" method will lead to parental sex selection, thereby eroding the moral value that boys and girls are equally precious.

Furthermore, about 50 percent of in vitro procedures result in multiple births. Most are twins, but 9 percent are triplets and higher-order multiples. Consequently, among in vitro babies, the rate of low birth weight is nearly three times as high as in the general population (Wright et al., 2008). Risk of major birth defects also doubles because of many factors, including drugs used to induce ripening of ova and delays in fertilizing the ova outside the womb (Machin, 2005; Neri, Takeuchi, & Palermo, 2008). In sum, in vitro fertilization poses greater risks than natural conception to infant survival and healthy development.

Surrogate Motherhood

An even more controversial form of medically assisted conception is *surrogate motherhood*. In this procedure, in vitro fertilization may be used to impregnate a woman (called a surrogate) with a couple's fertilized ovum. Alternatively, sperm from a man whose partner is infertile may be used to inseminate the surrogate, who agrees to turn the baby over to the natural father. The child is then adopted by his partner. In both cases, the surrogate is paid a fee for her child-bearing services.

Although most of these arrangements proceed smoothly, those that end up in court highlight serious risks for all concerned. In one case, both parties rejected the infant with severe disabilities who resulted from the pregnancy. In several others, the surrogate mother wanted to keep the baby, or the couple changed their mind during the pregnancy. These children came into the world in the midst of conflict that threatened to last for years.

Because surrogacy usually involves the wealthy as contractors for infants and the less economically advantaged as surrogates, it may promote exploitation of financially needy women. In addition, most surrogates already have children of their own, who may be deeply affected by the pregnancy. Knowledge that their mother would give away a baby for profit may cause these children to worry about the security of their own family circumstances.

New Reproductive Frontiers

Reproductive technologies are evolving faster than societies can weigh the ethics of these procedures. Doctors have used donor ova from younger women in combination with in vitro fertilization to help postmenopausal women become pregnant. Most recipients are in their forties, but several women in their fifties and sixties have given birth. These cases raise questions about bringing children into the world whose parents may not live to see them reach adulthood. Based on U.S. life expectancy data, 1 in 3 mothers and 1 in 2 fathers having a baby at age 55 will die before their child enters college (U.S. Census Bureau, 2010b).

Currently, experts are debating other reproductive options. At donor banks, customers can select ova or sperm on the basis of physical characteristics and even IQ. And scientists are devising ways to alter the DNA of human ova, sperm, and embryos to protect against hereditary disorders—techniques that could be used to engineer other desired characteristics. Many worry that these practices are dangerous steps toward selective breeding through "designer babies"—controlling offspring traits by manipulating genetic makeup.

Although new reproductive technologies permit many barren couples to rear healthy newborn babies, laws are needed to regulate such practices. In Australia, New Zealand, Sweden, and Switzerland, individuals conceived with donated gametes have a right to information about their genetic origins (Frith, 2001). Pressure from those working in the field of assisted reproduction may soon lead to a similar policy in the United States. Australia, Canada, and the Netherlands prohibit any genetic alteration of human gametes, with other nations following suit (Isasi, Nguyen, & Knoppers, 2006). But some scientists argue that this total ban is too restrictive because it interferes with serving therapeutic needs.

In the case of surrogate motherhood, the ethical problems are so complex that 18 U.S. states have sharply restricted the practice. Australia, Canada, and many European nations have banned it, arguing that the status of a baby should not be a matter of commercial arrangement and that a part of the body should not be rented or sold (Chen, 2003; McGee, 1997). Denmark, France, and Great Britain have prohibited in vitro fertilization for women past menopause (Bioethics Consultative Committee, 2003). At present, nothing is known about the psychological consequences of being a product of these procedures. Research on how such children grow up, including later-appearing medical conditions and knowledge and feelings about their origins, is important for weighing the pros and cons of these techniques.

ment in infancy predicted cognitive and social competence at age 7 (Stams, Juffer, & van IJzendoorn, 2002).

Overall, international adoptees fare much better in development than birth siblings or institutionalized agemates who stay behind. By middle childhood, those who were adopted in infancy have mental test scores resembling those of their nonbiological siblings and school classmates, although they tend to achieve less well in school, to have more learning problems that require special treatment, and to be slightly delayed in language skills (van IJzendoorn, Juffer, & Poelhuis, 2005). Children adopted at older ages develop feelings of trust and affection

Applying What We Know

Steps Prospective Parents Can Take Before Conception to Increase the Chances of a Healthy Baby

RECOMMENDATION	EXPLANATION
Arrange for a physical exam.	A physical exam before conception permits detection of diseases and other medical problems that might reduce fertility, be difficult to treat during pregnancy, or affect the developing organism.
Consider your genetic makeup.	Find out if anyone in your family has had a child with a genetic disease or disability. If so, seek genetic counseling before conception.
Reduce or eliminate toxins under your control.	Because the developing organism is highly sensitive to damaging environmental agents during the early weeks of pregnancy (see Chapter 3), couples trying to conceive should avoid drugs, alcohol, cigarette smoke, radiation, pollution, chemical substances in the home and workplace, and infectious diseases. Furthermore, stay away from ionizing radiation and some industrial chemicals that are known to cause mutations.
Ensure proper nutrition.	A doctor-recommended vitamin–mineral supplement, begun before conception, helps prevent many prenatal problems. It should include folic acid, which reduces the chances of neural tube defects, prematurity, and low birth weight (see Chapter 3, page 114).
Consult a physician after 12 months of unsuccessful efforts at conception.	Long periods of infertility may be due to undiagnosed spontaneous abortions, which can be caused by genetic defects in either partner. If a physical exam reveals a healthy reproductive system, seek genetic counseling.

for their adoptive parents as they come to feel loved and supported in their new families (Verissimo & Salvaterra, 2006). As we will see in Chapter 5, however, later-adopted children—especially those with multiple early-life adversities—are more likely than their agemates to have persistent cognitive, emotional, and social problems.

By adolescence, adoptees' lives are often complicated by unresolved curiosity about their roots. Some have difficulty accepting the possibility that they may never know their birth parents. Others worry about what they would do if their birth parents suddenly reappeared. Nevertheless, the decision to search for birth parents is usually postponed until early adulthood, when marriage and childbirth may trigger it. Despite concerns about their origins, most adoptees appear well-adjusted as adults. And as long as their parents took steps to help them learn about their heritage in childhood, young people adopted into a different ethnic group or culture generally develop identities that are healthy blends of their birth and rearing backgrounds (Nickman et al., 2005; Thomas & Tessler, 2007).

As we conclude our discussion of reproductive choices, perhaps you are wondering how things turned out for Ted and Marianne. Through genetic counseling, Marianne discovered a history of Tay-Sachs disease on her mother's side of the family. Ted had a distant cousin who died of the disorder. The genetic counselor explained that the chances of giving birth to another affected baby were 1 in 4. Ted and Marianne took the risk. Their son Douglas is now 12 years old. Although Douglas is a carrier of the recessive allele, he is a normal, healthy boy. In a few years, Ted and Marianne will tell Douglas about his genetic history and explain the importance of genetic counseling and testing before he has children of his own.

© GOLDEN PIXELS LLC/ALAMY

■ Adoption is one option for adults who are infertile or have a family history of genetic disorders. This couple, who adopted their daughter from China, can promote her successful adjustment by helping her learn about her birth heritage. ■

◆ REVIEW Why is genetic counseling called a *communication process?* Who should seek it?

◆ APPLY Imagine that you must counsel a couple considering in vitro fertilization using the wife's ova and sperm from an anonymous man to overcome the husband's infertility. What medical and ethical risks would you raise?

◆ CONNECT How does research on adoption reveal resilience? Which factor related to resilience (see Chapter 1, pages 10–11) is central in positive outcomes for adoptees?

◆ REFLECT Imagine that you are a woman who is a carrier of fragile X syndrome but who wants to have children. Would you become pregnant, adopt, use a surrogate mother, or give up your desire for parenthood? If you became pregnant, would you opt for prenatal diagnosis? Explain your decisions.

Environmental Contexts for Development

Just as complex as the genetic inheritance is the surrounding environment—a many-layered set of influences that combine to help or hinder physical and psychological well-being. **TAKE A MOMENT...** Think back to your own childhood, and jot down a brief description of people and events that had a significant impact on your development. Do the items on your list resemble those of my students, who mostly mention experiences that involve their families? This emphasis is not surprising, since the family is the first and longest-lasting context for development. Other influences that make most students' top ten are friends, neighbors, school, and community and religious organizations.

Return to Bronfenbrenner's ecological systems theory, discussed in Chapter 1. It emphasizes that environments extending beyond the *microsystem*—the immediate settings just mentioned—powerfully affect development. Indeed, my students rarely mention one important context. Its impact is so pervasive that we seldom stop to think about it in our daily lives. This is the *macrosystem,* or broad social climate of society—its values and programs that support and protect children's development. All families need help in rearing their children—through affordable housing and health care, safe neighborhoods, good schools, well-equipped recreational facilities, and high-quality child care and other services that permit parents to meet both work and family responsibilities. And some families, because of poverty or special tragedies, need considerably more help than others.

In the following sections, we take up these contexts for development. Because they affect every age and aspect of change, we will return to them in later chapters. For now, our discussion emphasizes that environments, as well as heredity, can enhance or create risks for development.

The Family

In power and breadth of influence, no other microsystem context equals the family. The family introduces children to the physical world by providing opportunities for play and exploration of objects. It also creates unique bonds among people. Attachments to parents and siblings are usually lifelong and serve as models for relationships in the wider world. Within the family, children learn the language, skills, and social and moral values of their culture. And people of all ages turn to family members for information, assistance, and pleasurable interaction. Warm, gratifying family ties predict physical and psychological health throughout development. In contrast, isolation or alienation from the family is often associated with developmental problems (Deković & Buist, 2005; Parke & Buriel, 2006).

■ The family is a network of interdependent relationships, in which each person's behavior influences that of others. The positive mealtime atmosphere as these teenagers and their parents gather for breakfast is the result of many forces, including parents who respond to children with warmth and patience and children who, in turn, have developed cooperative dispositions. ■

Contemporary researchers view the family as a network of interdependent relationships (Bronfenbrenner & Morris, 2006; Lerner et al., 2002). Recall from ecological systems theory that *bidirectional influences* exist in which the behaviors of each family member affect those of others. Indeed, the very term *system* implies that the responses of all family members are related. These system influences operate both directly and indirectly.

DIRECT INFLUENCES Recently, as I passed through the checkout counter at the supermarket, I witnessed two episodes, each an example of how parents and children directly influence each other:

■ Four-year-old Danny looked longingly at the tempting rows of candy as his mother lifted groceries from her cart onto the counter. "Pleeeeease, can I have it, Mom?" Danny begged, holding up a large package of bubble gum. "Do you have a dollar? Just one?"

"No, not today," his mother answered. "Remember, we picked out your special cereal. That's what I need the dollar for." Gently taking the bubble gum from his hand, Danny's mother handed him the box of cereal. "Here, let's pay," she said, lifting Danny so he could see the cash register.

■ Three-year-old Meg was sitting in the shopping cart while her mother transferred groceries to the counter. Suddenly Meg turned around, grabbed a bunch of bananas, and started pulling them apart.

"Stop it, Meg!" shouted her mother, snatching the bananas from Meg's hand. But as she turned her attention to swiping her debit card, Meg reached for a chocolate bar from a nearby shelf. "Meg, how many times have I told you, don't touch!" Loosening the candy from Meg's tight little fist, Meg's mother slapped her hand. Meg's face turned red with anger as she began to wail.

These observations fit with a wealth of research on the family system. Studies of families of diverse ethnicities show that when parents are firm but warm, children tend to comply with their requests. And when children willingly cooperate, their parents are likely to be warm and gentle in the future. In contrast, children whose parents discipline harshly and impatiently are more likely to refuse and rebel. And because children's misbehavior is stressful, parents may increase their use of punishment, leading to more unruliness by the child (Stormshak et al., 2000; Whiteside-Mansell et al., 2003). In each case, the behavior of one family member helps sustain a form of interaction in the other that either promotes or undermines children's well-being.

INDIRECT INFLUENCES The impact of family relationships on child development becomes even more complicated when we consider that interaction between any two members is affected by others present in the setting. Bronfenbrenner calls these indirect influences the effect of *third parties* (see Chapter 1, page 26).

Third parties can serve as supports for or barriers to development. For example, when a marital relationship is warm and considerate, mothers and fathers are more likely to engage in effective **coparenting,** mutually supporting each other's parenting behaviors. Such parents are warmer, praise and stimulate children more, and nag and scold them less. In contrast, parents whose marriage is tense and hostile often interfere with one another's child-rearing efforts, are less responsive to children's needs, and are more likely to criticize, express anger, and punish (Caldera & Lindsey, 2006; McHale et al., 2002). Children who are chronically exposed to angry, unresolved parental conflict have serious emotional problems resulting from disrupted emotional security (Cummings & Merrilees, 2010; Schacht, Cummings, & Davies, 2009). These

LOOK AND LISTEN

❖

Observe several parent–young child pairs in a supermarket or department store, where parents are likely to place limits on children's behavior. How does the quality of parent communication seem to influence the child's response? How does the child's response affect the parent's subsequent interaction?

include both *internalizing difficulties* (especially among girls), such as feeling worried and fearful and trying to repair their parents' relationship, and *externalizing difficulties* (especially among boys), including anger and aggression (Cummings, Goeke-Morey, & Papp, 2004). These child problems can further disrupt parents' marital relationship.

Yet even when parental conflict strains children's adjustment, other family members may help restore effective interaction. Grandparents, for example, can promote children's development both directly, by responding warmly to the child, and indirectly, by providing parents with child-rearing advice, models of child-rearing skill, and even financial assistance. Of course, as with any indirect influence, grandparents can sometimes be harmful. When quarrelsome relations exist between parents and grandparents, parent–child communication may suffer.

ADAPTING TO CHANGE   Think back to the *chronosystem* in Bronfenbrenner's theory (see page 27 in Chapter 1). The interplay of forces within the family is dynamic and ever-changing, as each member adapts to the development of other members.

For example, as children acquire new skills, parents adjust the way they treat their more competent youngsters. **TAKE A MOMENT...** The next time you have a chance, notice the way a parent relates to a tiny baby as compared with a walking, talking toddler. During the first few months, parents spend much time feeding, changing, bathing, and cuddling the infant. Within a year, things change dramatically. The 1-year-old points, shows, names objects, and makes his way through the household cupboards. In response, parents devote less time to physical care and more to talking, playing games, and disciplining. These new ways of interacting, in turn, encourage the child's expanding motor, cognitive, and social skills.

Parents' development affects children as well. In Chapter 14, we will see that the rise in parent–child conflict that often occurs in early adolescence is not solely due to teenagers' striving for independence. This is a time when most parents of adolescents have reached middle age and—conscious that their children will soon leave home and establish their own lives—are reconsidering their own commitments (Steinberg & Silk, 2002). Consequently, while the adolescent presses for greater autonomy, the parent presses for more togetherness. This imbalance promotes friction, which parent and teenager gradually resolve by accommodating to changes in each other. Indeed, no social unit other than the family is required to adjust to such vast changes in its members.

Historical time period also contributes to a dynamic family system. In recent decades, a declining birth rate, a high divorce rate, expansion of women's roles, increased acceptance of homosexuality, and postponement of parenthood have led to a smaller family size and a greater number of single parents, remarried parents, gay and lesbian parents, employed mothers, and dual-earner families. Clearly, families in industrialized nations have become more diverse than ever before. In later chapters we will take up these family forms, examining how each affects family relationships and, ultimately, children's development.

Nevertheless, some general patterns in family functioning do exist. In the United States and other industrialized nations, one important source of these consistencies is socioeconomic status.

Socioeconomic Status and Family Functioning

People in industrialized nations are stratified on the basis of what they do at work and how much they earn for doing it—factors that determine their social position and economic well-being. Researchers assess a family's standing on this continuum through an index called **socioeconomic status (SES),** which combines three related, but not completely overlapping, variables: (1) years of education and (2) the prestige of one's job and the skill it requires, both of which measure social status, and (3) income, which measures economic status. As SES rises and falls, parents and children face changing circumstances that profoundly affect family functioning.

SES is linked to timing of parenthood and to family size. People who work in skilled and semiskilled manual occupations (for example, construction workers, truck drivers, and custodians) tend to marry and have children earlier as well as give birth to more children than people in professional and technical occupations. The two groups also differ in child-rearing values and expectations. For example, when asked about personal qualities they desire for their children, lower-SES parents tend to emphasize external characteristics, such as obedience, politeness, neatness, and cleanliness. In contrast, higher-SES parents emphasize psychological traits, such as curiosity, happiness, self-direction, and cognitive and social maturity (Duncan & Magnuson, 2003; Hoff, Laursen, & Tardif, 2002; Tudge et al., 2000).

These differences are reflected in family interaction. Parents higher in SES talk to, read to, and otherwise stimulate their infants and preschoolers more and grant them greater freedom to explore. With older children and adolescents, higher-SES parents use more warmth, explanations, and verbal praise; set higher academic and other developmental goals; and allow their children to make more decisions. Commands ("You do that because I told you to"), criticism, and physical punishment all occur more often in low-SES households (Bush & Peterson, 2008; Mandara et al., 2009).

Education contributes substantially to these variations in child rearing. Higher-SES parents' interest in providing verbal stimulation, nurturing inner traits, and promoting academic achievement is supported by years of schooling, during which they learned to think about abstract, subjective ideas (Mistry et al., 2008; Vernon-Feagans et al., 2008). In diverse cultures around the world, as the Social Issues: Education box on the following page makes clear, education of women in particular fosters patterns of thinking and behaving that greatly improve quality of life, for both parents and children.

Because of limited education and low social status, many lower-SES parents feel a sense of powerlessness and lack of influence in their relationships beyond the home. At work, for example, they must obey rules made by others in positions of power and authority. When they get home, their parent–child interaction seems to duplicate these experiences—but now they are in authority. Higher levels of stress, along with a stronger belief in the value of physical punishment, contribute to low-SES parents' greater use of coercive discipline (Conger & Donnellan, 2007; Pinderhughes et al., 2000). Higher-SES parents, in contrast, typically have more control over their own lives. At work, they are used to making independent decisions and convincing others of their point of view. At home, they teach these skills to their children (Greenberger, O'Neil, & Nagel, 1994).

As early as the second year of life, higher SES is associated with enhanced cognitive and language development and with reduced incidence of emotional and behavior problems. And throughout childhood and adolescence, higher-SES children do better in school (Bradley & Corwyn, 2003; Melby et al., 2008). As a result, they attain higher levels of education, which greatly enhances their opportunities for a prosperous adult life. Researchers believe that differences in family functioning have much to do with these outcomes.

Affluence

Despite their advanced education and great material wealth, affluent parents—those in prestigious and high-paying occupations—too often fail to engage in family interaction and parenting that promote favorable development. In several studies, researchers tracked the adjustment of youths growing up in wealthy suburbs (Luthar & Latendresse, 2005a). By seventh grade, many showed serious problems that worsened in high school. Their school grades were poor, and they were more likely than low-SES youths to engage in alcohol and drug use and to report high levels of anxiety and depression (Luthar & Becker, 2002; Luthar & Goldstein, 2008). Furthermore, among affluent (but not low-SES) teenagers, substance use was correlated with anxiety and depression, suggesting that wealthy youths took drugs to self-medicate—a practice that predicts persistent abuse (Luthar & Sexton, 2004).

© INTI ST. CLAIR/GETTY IMAGES/PHOTODISC

■■ Advanced education and material wealth do not guarantee a healthy family life. When children in affluent families lack parental supervision and emotional closeness, they are at risk for academic and emotional difficulties, including poor grades, alcohol and drug use, and anxiety and depression. ■

SOCIAL ISSUES: EDUCATION

Worldwide Education of Girls: Transforming Current and Future Generations

When a new school opened in the Egyptian village of Beni Shara'an, Ahmen, an illiterate shopkeeper, immediately enrolled his 8-year-old daughter Rawia (Bellamy, 2004, p. 19). Until that day, Rawia had divided her days between back-breaking farming and confinement to her home.

Before long, Rawia's advancing language, literacy, and reasoning skills transformed her family's quality of life. "My store accounts were in a mess, but soon Rawia started straightening out the books," Ahmen recalled. She also began helping her older sister learn to read and write and explaining to her family the instructions on prescription medicines and the news on television. In addition, Rawia began to envision a better life for herself. "When I grow up," she told her father, "I want to be a doctor. Or maybe a teacher."

Over the past century, the percentage of children in the developing world who go to school has increased from a small minority of boys to a majority of all children in most regions. Still, some 73 million children, most of them poverty-stricken girls, do not start elementary school, and more than 200 million, again mostly girls, do not go to secondary school (UNICEF, 2009a).

Although schooling is vital for all children, educating girls has an especially powerful impact on the welfare of families, societies, and future generations. The diverse benefits of girls' schooling largely accrue in two ways: (1) through enhanced verbal skills—reading, writing, and oral communication; and (2) through empowerment—a growing desire to improve their life conditions (LeVine, LeVine, & Schnell, 2001).

Family Health

Education gives people the communicative skills and confidence to seek health services and to benefit from public health information. As a result, years of schooling strongly predicts women's preventive health behavior: prenatal visits, child immunizations, healthy diet, and sanitary practices (LeVine et al., 2004; Peña, Wall, & Person, 2000). In addition, because educated women have more life opportunities, they are more likely to take advantage of family planning services, delay marriage and child-bearing, and have more widely spaced and fewer children (Stromquist, 2007). All these practices are linked to increased maternal and child survival and family health.

Family Relationships and Parenting

In developed and developing nations alike, the empowerment that springs from education is associated with more equitable husband–wife relationships and a reduction in harsh disciplining of children (LeVine et al., 1991; LeVine, LeVine, & Schnell, 2001). Also, educated mothers engage in more verbal stimulation and teaching of literacy skills to their children, which fosters success in school, higher educational attainment, and economic gains in the next generation. Regions of the world that have invested more in girls' education, such as Southeast Asia and Latin America, tend to have higher levels of economic development (King & Mason, 2001).

According to a United Nations report, educating girls is the most effective means of combating the most profound, global threats to human development: poverty, maternal and child mortality, and disease (UNICEF, 2010). Rawia got the chance to go to school because of an Egyptian national initiative, which led to the establishment of several thousand one-classroom schools in rural areas with the poorest record in educating girls. Because of cultural beliefs about gender roles or reluctance to give up a daughter's work at home, parents sometimes resist. But the largest barrier is that many countries continue to charge parents a fee for each child enrolled in school, often amounting to nearly one-third of the income of poverty-stricken families. Under these conditions, parents—if they send any children—tend to send only sons.

In 2003, Kenya eliminated fees for primary school. Immediately, enrollments of both boys and girls surged—by more than 30 percent. Uganda followed suit, increasing its primary school enrollment by 70 percent (Alter, 2008; RESULTS, 2006). When governments abolish enrollment fees, provide information about the benefits of education for girls, and create employment possibilities for women, the overwhelming majority of parents—including the very poor—choose to send their daughters to school, and some make great sacrifices to do so.

For these girls huddling in an open-air class in a village in Pakistan, attending school will dramatically improve their life opportunities and their nation's welfare. In both developed and developing nations, educating girls leads to gains in family income and relationships that carry over to improved health, education, and economic well-being in the next generation. ■

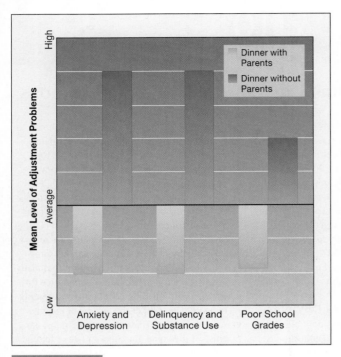

Relationship of regularly eating dinner with parents to affluent youths' adjustment problems. Compared with sixth graders who often ate dinner with their parents, those who rarely did so were far more likely to display anxiety and depression, delinquency and substance use, and poor school grades, even after many other aspects of parenting were controlled. In this study, frequent family mealtimes also protected low-SES youths from delinquency and substance use and from classroom learning problems. *(Adapted from Luthar & Latendresse, 2005b.)*

Why are so many affluent youths troubled? Compared to their better-adjusted counterparts, poorly adjusted affluent young people report less emotional closeness and supervision from their parents, who lead professionally and socially demanding lives. As a group, wealthy parents are nearly as physically and emotionally unavailable to their youngsters as parents coping with serious financial strain. At the same time, these parents often make excessive demands for achievement (Luthar & Becker, 2002). Adolescents whose parents value their accomplishments more than their character are more likely to have academic and emotional problems.

For both affluent and low-SES youths, a simple routine—eating dinner with parents—is associated with a reduction in adjustment difficulties, even after many other aspects of parenting are controlled (see Figure 2.8) (Luthar & Latendresse, 2005b). Interventions that make wealthy parents aware of the high costs of a competitive lifestyle and minimal family time are badly needed.

Poverty

When families slip into poverty, development is seriously threatened. Consider Zinnia Mae, who grew up in a close-knit black neighborhood located in a small southeastern American city (Heath, 1990). As unemployment struck the community and citizens moved away, 16-year-old Zinnia Mae caught a ride to Atlanta. Two years later, she was the mother of a daughter and twin boys, and she had moved into high-rise public housing.

Zinnia Mae worried constantly about scraping together enough money to put food on the table, finding babysitters so she could go to the laundry or grocery, freeing herself from a cycle of rising debt, and finding the twins' father, who had stopped sending money. Her most frequent words were, "I'm so tired." The children had only one set meal—breakfast; otherwise, they ate whenever they were hungry or bored. Their play space was limited to the living room sofa and a mattress on the floor. Toys consisted of scraps of a blanket, spoons and food cartons, a small rubber ball, a few plastic cars, and a roller skate abandoned in the building. At a researcher's request, Zinnia Mae agreed to tape record her interactions with her children. Cut off from family and community ties and overwhelmed by financial strains and feelings of helplessness, she found herself unable to join in activities with her children. In 500 hours of tape, she started a conversation with them only 18 times.

Although poverty rates in the United States declined slightly in the 1990s, in recent years they have risen. Today, about 13 percent—nearly 40 million Americans—are affected. Those hit hardest are parents under age 25 with young children and elderly people who live alone. Poverty is also magnified among ethnic minorities and women. For example, 19 percent of U.S. children are poor, rates that climb to 30 percent for Hispanic children, 32 percent for Native-American children, and 34 percent for African-American children. For single mothers with preschool children, the poverty rate is close to 50 percent (DeNavas-Walt, Proctor, & Smith, 2009).

Joblessness, a high divorce rate, a high rate of adolescent parenthood, and (as we will see later) inadequate government programs to meet family needs are responsible for these disheartening statistics. The poverty rate is higher among children than any other age group. And of all Western nations, the United States has the highest percentage of extremely poor children. Nearly 8 percent of U.S. children live in deep poverty (at less than half the poverty threshold, the income level judged necessary for a minimum living standard). In contrast, in Denmark, Finland, Norway, and Sweden, child poverty rates have remained at 5 percent or less for several decades, and deep child poverty is rare (UNICEF, 2007). The earlier poverty begins, the deeper it is, and the longer it lasts, the more devastating are its effects. Children of poverty are more likely than other children to suffer from lifelong poor physical health, persistent deficits in cognitive development and academic achievement, high school dropout, mental illness, and impulsivity, aggression, and antisocial behavior (Aber, Jones & Raver, 2007; Dearing, 2008; Morgan et al., 2009; Ryan, Fauth, & Brooks-Gunn, 2006).

The constant stressors that accompany poverty gradually weaken the family system. Poor families have many daily hassles—bills to pay, the car breaking down, loss of welfare and unemployment payments, something stolen from the house, to name just a few. When daily crises arise, family members become depressed, irritable, and distracted; hostile interactions increase; and children's development suffers (Conger & Donnellan, 2007; Evans, 2006). Negative outcomes are especially severe in single-parent families and families who must live in poor housing and dangerous neighborhoods—conditions that make everyday existence even more difficult, while reducing social supports that assist in coping with economic hardship (Hart, Atkins, & Matsuba, 2008; Leventhal & Brooks-Gunn, 2003).

■ Homelessness poses enormous challenges for maintaining positive family relationships. This family has spent the last three years living in Chicago-area shelters, a circumstance that can lead to feelings of helplessness and isolation and to weakening of the family system. ■

Besides poverty, another problem—one that has become more common in the past 30 years—has reduced the life chances of many children. On any given night, approximately 350,000 people in the United States have no place to live. An estimated 23 percent of the homeless are families with children (National Coalition for the Homeless, 2008). The rise in homelessness is mostly due to two factors: a decline in the availability of government-supported low-cost housing and the release of large numbers of mentally ill people from hospitals, without an increase in community treatment programs to help them adjust to ordinary life and get better.

Most homeless families consist of women with children under age 5. Besides health problems (which affect the majority of homeless people), many homeless children suffer from developmental delays and chronic emotional stress due to their harsh, insecure daily lives (Bratt, 2002). An estimated 25 to 30 percent of those who are old enough do not go to school. Those who do enroll achieve less well than other poverty-stricken children because of poor attendance and health and emotional difficulties (Obradović et al., 2009; Shinn et al., 2008).

Beyond the Family: Neighborhoods and Schools

As the concepts of *mesosystem* and *exosystem* in ecological systems theory make clear, connections between family and community are vital for children's well-being. From our discussion of poverty, perhaps you can see why: In poverty-stricken urban areas, community life is usually disrupted. Families move often, parks and playgrounds are in disarray, and community centers providing leisure-time activities do not exist. In such neighborhoods, family violence, child abuse and neglect, children's problem behavior, youth antisocial activity, and adult criminal behavior are especially high (Brody et al., 2003; Dunn, Schaefer-McDaniel, & Ramsay, 2010). In contrast, strong family ties to the community—as indicated by frequent contact with friends and relatives, organized youth activities, and regular church, synagogue, or mosque attendance—reduce family stress and adjustment problems (Boardman, 2004; Leventhal & Brooks-Gunn, 2003).

NEIGHBORHOODS Let's look closely at the functions of communities in the lives of children by beginning with the neighborhood. **TAKE A MOMENT...** What were your childhood experiences like in the yards, streets, parks, and community centers surrounding your home?

© TONY AVELAR/AP IMAGES FOR SPRITE

■ These girls enjoy step-dancing lessons at a Boys and Girls Club in their California community. Neighborhood resources are especially important for economically disadvantaged children and families. ■

How did you spend your time, whom did you get to know, and how important were these moments to you?

Neighborhoods offer resources and social ties that play an important part in children's development. In several studies, low-SES families were randomly assigned vouchers to move out of public housing into neighborhoods varying widely in affluence. Compared with their peers who remained in poverty-stricken areas, children and youths who moved into low-poverty neighborhoods showed substantially better physical and mental health and school achievement (Goering, 2003; Leventhal & Brooks-Gunn, 2003).

Neighborhood resources have a greater impact on economically disadvantaged than on well-to-do young people. Higher-SES families are less dependent on their immediate surroundings for social support, education, and leisure pursuits. They can afford to transport their children to lessons and entertainment and, if necessary, to better-quality schools in distant parts of the community. In low-income neighborhoods, in-school and after-school programs that substitute for lack of other resources by providing art, music, sports, scouting, and other enrichment activities are associated with improved school performance and a reduction in emotional and behavior problems in middle childhood (Peters, Petrunka, & Arnold, 2003; Vandell & Posner, 1999; Vandell, Reisner, & Pierce, 2007). Neighborhood organizations, such as religious youth groups and special-interest clubs, contribute to favorable development in adolescence, including increased self-confidence, school achievement, and educational aspirations (Barnes et al., 2007; Gonzales et al., 1996).

Yet in dangerous, disorganized neighborhoods, high-quality activities for children and adolescents are usually scarce. Even when they are available, crime and social disorder limit young people's access, and attendance is low (Dynarski et al., 2004). Furthermore, home and neighborhood obstacles often combine to reduce involvement. Parents overwhelmed by financial and other stressors are less likely to provide the stimulation and encouragement that motivate their children to participate (Kohen et al., 2008). In an investigation of a large sample of elementary school students diverse in SES and neighborhood residence, those living in the least stimulating homes and the most chaotic neighborhoods were least likely to participate in after-school and community-center enrichment activities (Dearing et al., 2009). Thus, the neediest children were especially likely to miss out on these development-enhancing experiences.

Just how do family–neighborhood ties reduce parenting stress and promote child development? One answer lies in their provision of *social support*, which leads to the following benefits:

- *Parental self-worth.* A neighbor or relative who listens and tries to relieve a parent's concern enhances her self-esteem. The parent, in turn, is likely to interact in a more sensitive and involved manner with her children.
- *Parental access to valuable information and services.* A friend who suggests where a parent might find a job, housing, and affordable child care and youth activities helps make the multiple roles of spouse, parent, and provider easier to fulfill.
- *Child-rearing controls and role models.* Friends, relatives, and other community members may encourage and demonstrate effective parenting practices and discourage ineffective practices.
- *Direct assistance with child rearing.* As children and adolescents participate in their parents' social networks and in neighborhood settings, other adults can influence children through warmth, stimulation, and exposure to a wider array of competent models. In this way, family–neighborhood ties can reduce the impact of ineffective parenting (Silk et al., 2004). Nearby adults can also intervene when they see young people skipping school or behaving antisocially.

The Better Beginnings, Better Futures Project of Ontario, Canada, is a government-sponsored set of pilot programs aimed at preventing the dire consequences of home and neighborhood poverty, including child and adolescent externalizing difficulties, antisocial activity, school failure, and high school dropout (Gershoff & Aber, 2006). The most successful of these efforts, using a local elementary school as its base, provided children with in-class and summer enrichment activities. Project staff also visited each child's parents regularly, informed them about community resources, and encouraged their involvement in the child's school and neighborhood life (Peters, 2005; Peters, Petrunka, & Arnold, 2003). An evaluation after four years revealed wide-ranging benefits—gains in neighborhood satisfaction, family functioning, effective parenting, and children's reading skills, along with a reduction in emotional and behavior problems.

SCHOOLS   Unlike the informal worlds of family and neighborhood, school is a formal institution designed to transmit knowledge and skills that children need to become productive members of their society. Children in the developed world spend many hours in school—6 hours a day, 5 days a week, 36 weeks a year—a total of about 14,000 hours, on average, by high school graduation. And today, because many children younger than age 5 attend "school-like" child-care centers or preschools, the impact of schooling begins even earlier and is more powerful than these figures suggest.

Schools are complex social systems that affect many aspects of development. Schools differ in their physical environments—student body size, number of children per class, and space available for work and play. They also vary in their educational philosophies—whether teachers regard children as passive learners to be molded by adult instruction; as active, curious beings who determine their own learning; or as collaborative partners assisted by adult experts, who guide their mastery of new skills. Finally, the social life

■ Schools are complex social systems that powerfully affect development. By encouraging students' active participation, this fifth-grade teacher promotes mastery of new knowledge and skills along with enthusiastic attitudes toward learning. ■

of schools varies—for example, in the degree to which students cooperate or compete; in the extent to which students of different abilities, SES, and ethnic backgrounds learn together; and in whether classrooms, hallways, and play yards are safe, humane settings or are riddled with violence (Evans, 2006). We will discuss each of these aspects of schooling in later chapters.

Regular parent–school contact supports development at all ages. Students whose parents are involved in school activities and attend parent–teacher conferences show better academic achievement. Higher-SES parents, whose backgrounds and values are similar to those of teachers, are more likely to make phone calls and visits to school. In contrast, low-SES and ethnic minority parents often feel uncomfortable about coming to school, and daily stressors reduce the energy they have for school involvement (Grant & Ray, 2010; Jeynes, 2005; Reschly & Christenson, 2009). Parent–teacher contact is also more frequent in small towns, where most citizens know each other and schools serve as centers of community life (Peshkin, 1994). Teachers and administrators must take extra steps with low-SES and ethnic minority families and in urban areas to build supportive family–school ties.

When these efforts lead to cultures of good parenting and teaching, they deliver an extra boost to children's well-being. For example, students attending schools with many highly involved parents achieve especially well (Darling & Steinberg, 1997). And when excellent education becomes a team effort of teachers, administrators, and community members, its effects on learning are stronger and reach many more students (Hauser-Cram et al., 2006).

The Cultural Context

Our discussion in Chapter 1 emphasized that child development can be fully understood only when viewed in its larger cultural context. In the following sections, we expand on this important

LOOK AND LISTEN

Ask a teacher whose classroom has many students from low-SES families what percentage of parents attend parent–teacher conferences. What steps does the teacher take to promote parent–school involvement?

theme by taking up the role of the *macrosystem* in development. First, we discuss ways that cultural values and practices affect environmental contexts for development. Then we consider how healthy development depends on laws and government programs that shield children from harm and foster their well-being.

CULTURAL VALUES AND PRACTICES Cultures shape family interaction, school experiences, and community settings beyond the home—in short, all aspects of daily life. Many of us remain blind to aspects of our own cultural heritage until we see them in relation to the practices of others.

TAKE A MOMENT…Consider the question, Who should be responsible for rearing young children? How would you answer it? Here are some typical responses from my students: "If parents decide to have a baby, then they should be ready to care for it." "Most people are not happy about others intruding into family life." These statements reflect a widely held opinion in the United States—that the care and rearing of young children, and paying for that care, are the duty of parents, and only parents. This view has a long history—one in which independence, self-reliance, and the privacy of family life emerged as central American values (Halfon & McLearn, 2002). It is one reason, among others, that the public has been slow to endorse publicly supported benefits for all families, such as high-quality child care and paid employment leave for meeting family needs. And it has also contributed to the large number of U.S. children who remain poor, even though their parents are gainfully employed (Gruendel & Aber, 2007; Pohl, 2002; UNICEF, 2007).

Although the culture as a whole may value independence and privacy, not all citizens share the same values. Some belong to **subcultures**—groups of people with beliefs and customs that differ from those of the larger culture. Many ethnic minority groups in the United States have cooperative family structures, which help protect their members from the harmful effects of poverty. As the Cultural Influences box on the following page indicates, the African-American tradition of **extended-family households,** in which parent and child live with one or more adult relatives, is a vital feature of black family life that has enabled its members to survive, despite a long history of prejudice and economic deprivation. Within the extended family, grandparents play meaningful roles in guiding younger generations; adults who face employment, marital, or child-rearing difficulties receive assistance and emotional support; and caregiving is enhanced for children and the elderly. Active, involved extended families also characterize other minorities, such as Asian, Native-American, and Hispanic subcultures (Becker et al., 2003; Harwood et al., 2002).

Our discussion so far reflects a broad dimension on which cultures and subcultures differ: the extent to which *collectivism* versus *individualism* is emphasized. In **collectivist societies,** people define themselves as part of a group and stress group over individual goals. In **individualistic societies,** people think of themselves as separate entities and are largely concerned with their own personal needs (Triandis, 1995, 2005). As these definitions suggest, the two cultural patterns are associated with two distinct views of the self. Collectivist societies value an *interdependent self,* which stresses social harmony, obligations and responsibility to others, and collaborative endeavors. In contrast, individualistic societies value an *independent self,* which emphasizes personal exploration, discovery, and achievement and individual choice in relationships. Both interdependence and independence are part of the makeup of every person and occur in varying mixtures (Greenfield et al., 2003; Tamis-LeMonda et al., 2008). But societies vary greatly in the extent to which they emphasize each alternative and—as later chapters will reveal—instill it in their young.

Although individualism tends to increase as cultures become more complex, cross-national differences remain. The United States is strongly individualistic, whereas most Western European countries lean toward collectivism. As we will see next, collectivist versus individualistic values have a powerful impact on a nation's approach to protecting the well-being of its children and families.

PUBLIC POLICIES AND CHILD DEVELOPMENT When widespread social problems arise, such as poverty, homelessness, hunger, and disease, nations attempt to solve them by developing **public policies**—laws and government programs designed to improve current

CULTURAL INFLUENCES

The African-American Extended Family

The African-American extended family can be traced to the African heritage of most black Americans. In many African societies, newly married couples do not start their own households. Instead, they live with a large extended family, which assists its members with all aspects of daily life. This tradition of maintaining a broad network of kinship ties traveled to North America during the period of slavery. Since then, it has served as a protective shield against the destructive impact of poverty and racial prejudice on African-American family life. Today, more black than white adults have relatives other than their own children living in the same household. African-American parents also live closer to kin, often establish family-like relationships with friends and neighbors, see more relatives during the week, and perceive them as more important in their lives (Boyd-Franklin, 2006; Kane, 2000).

By providing emotional support and sharing income and essential resources, the African-American extended family helps reduce the stress of poverty and single parenthood. Extended-family members often help with child rearing, and adolescent mothers living in extended families are more likely to complete high school and get a job and less likely to be on welfare than mothers living on their own—factors that in turn benefit children's well-being (Gordon, Chase-Lansdale, & Brooks-Gunn, 2004; Trent & Harlan, 1994).

For single mothers who were very young at the time of their child's birth, extended-family living continues to be associated with more positive mother–child interaction during the preschool years. Otherwise, establishing an independent household with the help of nearby relatives is related to improved child rearing. Perhaps this arrangement permits the more mature teenage mother who has developed effective parenting skills to implement them (Chase-Lansdale, Brooks-Gunn, & Zamsky, 1994). In families rearing adolescents, kinship support increases the likelihood of effective parenting, which is related to adolescents' self-reliance, emotional well-being, and reduced antisocial behavior (Hamilton, 2005; Simons et al., 2006).

Finally, the extended family plays an important role in transmitting African-American culture. Compared with nuclear-family households (which include only parents and their children), extended-family arrangements place more emphasis on cooperation and on moral and religious values. And older black adults, such as grandparents and great-grandparents, regard educating children about their African heritage as especially important (Mosely-Howard & Evans, 2000; Taylor, 2000). Family reunions—sometimes

■ A grandmother shares a photo album chronicling family history with her son and grandchildren. Strong bonds with extended-family members have helped protect many African-American children against the destructive effects of poverty and racial prejudice. ■

held in grandparents' and great-grandparents' hometowns in the South—are especially common among African Americans, giving young people a strong sense of their roots (Boyd-Franklin, 2006). These influences strengthen family bonds, enhance children's development, and increase the chances that the extended-family lifestyle will carry over to the next generation.

---

conditions. For example, when poverty increases and families become homeless, a country might decide to build more low-cost housing, provide economic aid to homeowners having difficulty making mortgage payments, and increase welfare benefits. When reports indicate that many children are not achieving well in school, federal and state governments might grant more tax money to school districts, strengthen teacher preparation, and make sure that help reaches children who need it most.

Nevertheless, U.S. public policies safeguarding children and youths have lagged behind policies in other developed nations. As Table 2.6 on page 80 reveals, the United States does not rank well on any key measure of children's health and well-being.

The problems of children and youths extend beyond the indicators in Table 2.6. Despite improved health-care provisions signed into law in 2010, the United States remains the only industrialized nation without a universal, publicly funded health-care system. Approximately 10 percent of U.S. children—most in low-income families—have no health insurance (Kenney, Lynch, & Cook, 2010). Furthermore, the United States has been slow to move toward national standards and funding for child care. Affordable care is in short supply, and much of it is sub-standard in quality (Lamb & Ahnert, 2006; Muenchow & Marsland, 2007). In families affected

TABLE 2.6 How Does the United States Compare to Other Nations on Indicators of Children's Health and Well-Being?

INDICATOR	U.S. RANK[a]	SOME COUNTRIES THE UNITED STATES TRAILS
Childhood poverty (among 25 industrialized nations considered)	25th	Canada, Czech Republic, Germany, Norway, Sweden, Poland, Spain[b]
Infant deaths in the first year of life (worldwide)	28th	Canada, Hong Kong, Ireland, Singapore, Spain
Teenage pregnancy rate (among 28 industrialized nations considered)	28th	Australia, Canada, Czech Republic, Denmark, Hungary, Iceland, Poland, Slovak Republic
Public expenditure on education as a percentage of gross domestic product[c] (among 22 industrialized nations considered)	12th	Belgium, France, Iceland, New Zealand, Portugal, Spain, Sweden
Public expenditure on early childhood education and child care as a percentage of gross domestic product (among 14 industrialized nations considered)	9th	Austria, Germany, Italy, Netherlands, France, Sweden
Public expenditure on health as a percentage of total health expenditure, public plus private (among 29 industrialized nations considered)	29th	Austria, Australia, Canada, France, Hungary, Iceland, Switzerland, New Zealand

[a] 1 = highest, or best, rank.

[b] U.S. childhood poverty and, especially, deep poverty rates greatly exceed poverty in these nations. For example, the poverty rate is 9.5 percent in Canada, 6 percent in the Czech Republic, 4 percent in Norway, and 2.5 percent in Sweden. Deep poverty affects just 2.5 percent of children in Canada, and a fraction of 1 percent in the other countries just listed.

[c] Gross domestic product is the value of all goods and services produced by a nation during a specified time period. It provides an overall measure of a nation's wealth.

Sources: Canada Campaign 2000, 2009; OECD, 2006, 2008a, 2008b; UNICEF, 2007; U.S. Census Bureau, 2010b; U.S. Department of Education, 2010.

by divorce, weak enforcement of child support payments heightens poverty in mother-headed households. When they finish high school, many American non-college-bound young people lack the vocational preparation they need to contribute fully to society. And 8 percent of 16- to 24-year olds who dropped out of high school have not returned to earn a diploma (U.S. Department of Education, 2010).

Why have attempts to help children and youths been difficult to realize in the United States? A complex set of political and economic forces is involved. Cultural values of self-reliance and privacy have made government hesitant to become involved in family matters. Furthermore, good social programs are expensive, and they must compete for a fair share of a country's economic resources. Children can easily remain unrecognized in this process because they cannot vote or speak out to protect their own interests (Ripple & Zigler, 2003). Instead, they must rely on the goodwill of others to make them an important government priority.

Without vigilance from child advocates, policies directed at solving a particular social problem can work at cross-purposes with children's well-being, leaving them in dire straits or even worsening their condition. For example, U.S. welfare policy aimed at returning welfare recipients to the workforce—by reducing or terminating their welfare benefits after 24 continuous months—can either help or harm children, depending on whether it lifts a family out of poverty. When welfare-to-work reduces financial strain, it relieves maternal stress, improves quality of parenting, and is associated with cognitive gains and a reduction in child behavior problems (Dunifon, Kalil, & Danziger, 2003; Gennetian & Morris, 2003; Jackson, Bentler, & Franke, 2006). In contrast, former welfare recipients who must take very low-paying jobs that perpetuate poverty often engage in harsh, coercive parenting and have poorly adjusted children (Smith et al., 2001).

LOOKING TOWARD THE FUTURE   Public policies aimed at fostering children's development can be justified on two grounds. The first is that children are the future—the parents, workers, and citizens of tomorrow. Investing in children yields valuable returns to a nation's quality of life (Heckman & Masterov, 2004).

Second, child-oriented policies can be defended on humanitarian grounds—children's basic rights as human beings. In 1989, the U.N. General Assembly, with the assistance of experts from many child-related fields, drew up the *Convention on the Rights of the Child,* a legal agreement among nations that commits each cooperating country to work toward guaranteeing environments that foster children's development, protect them from harm, and enhance their community participation and self-determination. Examples of rights include the highest attainable standard of health; an adequate standard of living; free and compulsory education; a happy, understanding, and loving family life; protection from all forms of abuse and neglect; and freedom of thought, conscience, and religion, subject to appropriate parental guidance and national law.

Although the United States played a key role in drawing up the Convention, it is one of only two countries in the world whose legislature has not yet ratified it. (The other is war-torn Somalia, which currently does not have a recognized national government.) American individualism has stood in the way. Opponents maintain that the Convention's provisions would shift the burden of child rearing from the family to the state (Melton, 2005).

Although the worrisome state of many children and families persists, efforts are being made to improve their condition. Throughout this book, we will discuss many successful programs that could be expanded. Also, growing awareness of the gap between what we know and what we do to better children's lives has led experts in child development to join with concerned citizens as advocates for more effective policies. As a result, several influential interest groups devoted to the well-being of children have emerged.

In the United States, the most vigorous is the Children's Defense Fund—a private, nonprofit organization founded by Marian Wright Edelman in 1973—which engages in research, public education, legal action, drafting of legislation, congressional testimony, and community organizing. It also publishes many reports on U.S. children's condition, government-sponsored programs that serve children and families, and proposals for improving those programs. To learn more about the Children's Defense Fund, visit its website at *www.childrensdefense.org.*

Besides strong advocacy, public policies that enhance child development depend on policy-relevant research that documents needs and evaluates programs to spark improvements. Today, more researchers are collaborating with community and government agencies to enhance the social relevance of their investigations. They are also doing a better job of disseminating their findings to the public in easily understandable, compelling ways, through television documentaries, newspaper stories, magazine articles, websites, and direct reports to government officials. In these ways, they are helping to create the sense of immediacy about the condition of children and families that is necessary to spur a society into action.

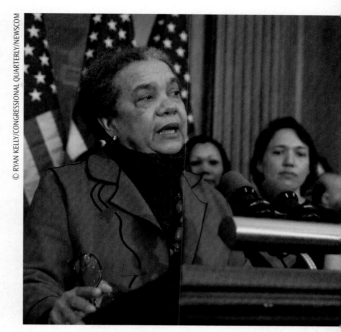

■ Marian Wright Edelman, founder and president of the Children's Defense Fund, speaks in support of U.S. health-care reform legislation in Washington, DC. The bill, signed into law on March 23, 2010, immediately prevented children with pre-existing health conditions from being denied insurance coverage. ■

ASK YOURSELF ◆◆

◆ REVIEW   Links between family and community are essential for children's well-being. Provide examples and research findings from our discussion that support this idea.

◆ APPLY   Check your local newspaper or one or two national news magazines or news websites to see how often articles on the condition of children and families appear. Why is it important for researchers to communicate with the general public about children's needs?

◆ CONNECT   How does poverty affect the functioning of the family system, placing all aspects of development at risk?

◆ REFLECT   Do you agree with the widespread American sentiment that government should not become involved in family life? Explain.

Understanding the Relationship Between Heredity and Environment

Throughout this chapter, we have discussed a wide variety of genetic and environmental influences, each of which has the power to alter the course of development. Yet children who are born into the same family (and who therefore share both genes and environments) are often quite different in characteristics. We also know that some children are affected more than others by their homes, neighborhoods, and communities. In some cases, a child who is given many advantages nevertheless does poorly, while another, though exposed to unfavorable rearing conditions, does well. How do scientists explain the impact of heredity and environment when they seem to work in so many different ways?

Behavioral genetics is a field devoted to uncovering the contributions of nature and nurture to this diversity in human traits and abilities. All contemporary researchers agree that both heredity and environment are involved in every aspect of development. But for polygenic traits (those due to many genes) such as intelligence and personality, scientists are a long way from knowing the precise hereditary influences involved. Although they are making progress in identifying the multiple variations in DNA sequences associated with complex traits, so far these genetic markers explain only a small amount of variation in human behavior, and a minority of cases of most psychological disorders (Plomin, 2005; Plomin & Davis, 2009). For the most part, scientists are still limited to investigating the impact of genes on complex characteristics indirectly.

■ Children vary widely in mental abilities and personality traits. Most contemporary researchers seek to clarify how heredity and environment jointly contribute to individual differences in these complex characteristics. ■

Some believe that it is useful and possible to answer the question of *how much each factor contributes* to differences among children. A growing consensus, however, regards that question as unanswerable. These investigators believe that heredity and environment are inseparable (Gottlieb, Wahlsten, & Lickliter, 2006; Lerner & Overton, 2008). The important question, they maintain, is *how nature and nurture work together*. Let's consider each position in turn.

The Question, "How Much?"

To infer the role of heredity in complex human characteristics, researchers use special methods, the most common being the *heritability estimate*. Let's look closely at the information this procedure yields, along with its limitations.

HERITABILITY   **Heritability estimates** measure the extent to which individual differences in complex traits in a specific population are due to genetic factors. We will take a brief look at heritability findings on intelligence and personality here and will return to them in later chapters, when we consider these topics in greater detail. Heritability estimates are obtained from **kinship studies,** which compare the characteristics of family members. The most common type of kinship study compares identical twins, who share all their genes, with fraternal twins, who share only some. If people who are genetically more alike are also more similar in intelligence and personality, then the researcher assumes that heredity plays an important role.

Kinship studies of intelligence provide some of the most controversial findings in the field of child development. Some experts claim a strong genetic influence, whereas others believe that heredity is barely involved. Currently, most kinship findings support a moderate role for heredity. When many twin studies are examined, correlations between the scores of identical twins are consistently higher than those of fraternal twins. In a summary of more than 10,000 twin pairs, the average correlation was .86 for identical twins and .60 for fraternal twins (Plomin & Spinath, 2004).

Researchers use a complex statistical procedure to compare these correlations, arriving at a heritability estimate ranging from 0 to 1.00. The value for intelligence is about .50 for child and adolescent twin samples in Western industrialized nations. This suggests that differences in genetic makeup explain half the variation in intelligence. Adopted children's mental test scores are more strongly related to their biological parents' scores than to those of their adoptive parents, offering further support for the role of heredity (Petrill & Deater-Deckard, 2004).

Heritability research also reveals that genetic factors are important in personality. For frequently studied traits, such as sociability, anxiety, agreeableness, and activity level, heritability estimates obtained on child and adolescent and young adult twins are moderate, in the .40s and .50s (Caspi & Shiner, 2006; Rothbart & Bates, 2006; Wright et al., 2008).

Twin studies of schizophrenia—a psychological disorder involving delusions and hallucinations, difficulty distinguishing fantasy from reality, and irrational and inappropriate behaviors—consistently yield high heritabilities, around .80. The role of heredity in antisocial behavior and major depression, though still apparent, is less strong, with heritabilities in the .30s and .40s (Faraone, 2008). Again, adoption studies support these results. Biological relatives of schizophrenic and depressed adoptees are more likely than adoptive relatives to share the same disorder (Plomin et al., 2001; Ridenour, 2000; Tienari et al., 2003).

■ Adriana and Tamara, identical twins born in Mexico, were separated at birth and adopted into different homes in the New York City area. They were unaware of each other's existence until age 20, when they met through a mutual acquaintance. The twins found that they had many similarities—academic achievement, a love of dancing, even similar taste in clothing. The study of identical twins reared apart reveals that heredity contributes to many personality characteristics. But generalizing from twin evidence to the population is controversial. ■

LIMITATIONS OF HERITABILITY Serious questions have been raised about the accuracy of heritability estimates, which depends on the extent to which the twin pairs studied reflect genetic and environmental variation in the population. Within a population in which all people have very similar home, school, and community experiences, individual differences in intelligence and personality would be largely genetic, and heritability estimates would be close to 1.00. Conversely, the more environments vary, the more likely they are to account for individual differences, yielding lower heritability estimates. In twin studies, most twin pairs are reared together under highly similar conditions. Even when separated twins are available for study, social service agencies have often placed them in advantaged homes that are alike in many ways (Rutter et al., 2001). Because the environments of most twin pairs are less diverse than those of the general population, heritability estimates are likely to exaggerate the role of heredity.

Heritability estimates are controversial measures because they can easily be misapplied. For example, high heritabilities have been used to suggest that ethnic differences in intelligence, such as the poorer performance of black children compared to white children, have a genetic basis (Jensen, 1969, 1998, 2001; Rushton & Jensen, 2005, 2006). Yet this line of reasoning is widely regarded as incorrect. Heritabilities computed on mostly white twin samples do not tell us what causes test score differences between ethnic groups. We have already seen that large economic and cultural differences are involved. In Chapter 12, we will discuss research indicating that when black children are adopted into economically advantaged homes at an early age, their scores are well above average and substantially higher than those of children growing up in impoverished families.

Perhaps the most serious criticism of heritability estimates has to do with their limited usefulness. Though interesting, these estimates give us no precise information on how intelligence and personality develop or how children might respond to environments designed to help them develop as far as possible (Baltes, Lindenberger, & Staudinger, 2006; Rutter, 2002). Indeed, the heritability of children's intelligence increases as parental education and income increase—that is, as children grow up in conditions that allow them to make the most of their genetic endowment. In impoverished environments, children are prevented from realizing their potential. Consequently, enhancing experiences through interventions—such as parent education and high-quality preschool or child care—has a greater impact on the development of low-SES than higher-SES children (Bronfenbrenner & Morris, 2006; Turkheimer et al., 2003).

According to one group of experts, heritability estimates have too many problems to yield any firm conclusions about the relative strength of nature and nurture (Collins et al., 2000). Although these statistics confirm that heredity contributes to complex traits, they do not tell us how environment can modify genetic influences.

The Question, "How?"

Today, most researchers view development as the result of a dynamic interplay between heredity and environment. How do nature and nurture work together? Several concepts shed light on this question.

REACTION RANGE The first of these ideas is **range of reaction**—each person's unique, genetically determined response to the environment (Gottesman, 1963). Let's explore this idea in Figure 2.9. Reaction range can apply to any characteristic; here it is illustrated for intelligence. Notice that when environments vary from extremely unstimulating to highly enriched, Ben's intelligence increases steadily, Linda's rises sharply and then falls off, and Ron's begins to increase only after the environment becomes modestly stimulating.

Reaction range highlights two important points. First, it shows that because each of us has a unique genetic makeup, we respond differently to the same environment. Note in Figure 2.9 how a poor environment results in similarly low scores for all three individuals. But when the environment provides an intermediate level of stimulation, Linda is by far the best-performing child. And in a highly enriched environment, Ben does best, followed by Ron, both of whom now outperform Linda.

Second, sometimes different genetic–environmental combinations can make two people look the same! For example, if Linda is reared in a minimally stimulating environment, her score will be about 100—average for children in general. Ben and Ron can also obtain this score, but to do so, they must grow up in a fairly enriched home. In sum, range of reaction reveals that unique blends of heredity and environment lead to both similarities and differences in behavior (Gottlieb, Wahlsten, & Lickliter, 2006).

CANALIZATION Another way of understanding how heredity and environment combine comes from the concept of **canalization**—the tendency of heredity to restrict the development of some characteristics to just one or a few outcomes. A behavior that is strongly canalized develops similarly in a wide range of environments; only strong environmental forces can change it (Waddington, 1957). For example, infant perceptual and motor development seems to be strongly canalized because all normal human babies eventually roll over, reach for objects, sit up, crawl, and walk. It takes extreme conditions to modify these behaviors or cause them not to appear. In contrast, intelligence and personality are less strongly canalized; they vary much more with changes in the environment.

When we look at behaviors that are constrained by heredity, we can see that canalization is highly adaptive. Through it, nature ensures that children will develop certain species-typical skills under a wide range of rearing conditions, thereby promoting survival.

GENETIC–ENVIRONMENTAL CORRELATION A major problem in trying to separate heredity and environment is that

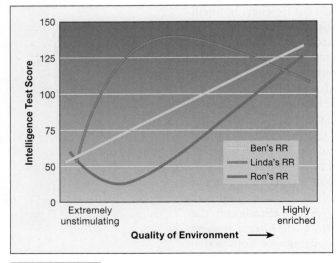

FIGURE 2.9

Intellectual ranges of reaction (RR) for three children in environments that vary from extremely unstimulating to highly enriched. Each child, because of his or her genetic makeup, responds differently to changes in quality of the environment. Ben's intelligence test score increases steadily, Linda's rises sharply and then falls off, and Ron's begins to increase only after the environment becomes modestly stimulating. *(Adapted from Wahlsten, 1994.)*

they are often correlated (Plomin, 2009; Scarr & McCartney, 1983). According to the concept of **genetic–environmental correlation,** our genes influence the environments to which we are exposed. The way this happens changes with age.

Passive and Evocative Correlation. At younger ages, two types of genetic–environmental correlation are common. The first is called *passive* correlation because the child has no control over it. Early on, parents provide environments influenced by their own heredity. For example, parents who are good athletes emphasize outdoor activities and enroll their children in swimming and gymnastics. Besides being exposed to an "athletic environment," the children may have inherited their parents' athletic ability. As a result, they are likely to become good athletes for both genetic and environmental reasons.

The second type of genetic–environmental correlation is *evocative.* The responses children evoke from others are influenced by the child's heredity, and these responses strengthen the child's original style. For example, an active, friendly baby is likely to receive more social stimulation than a passive, quiet infant. And a cooperative, attentive child probably receives more patient and sensitive interactions from parents than an inattentive, distractible child. In support of this idea, the less genetically alike siblings are, the more their parents treat them differently, in both warmth and negativity. Thus, parents' treatment of identical twins is highly similar, whereas their treatment of fraternal twins and nontwin biological siblings is only moderately so. And little resemblance exists in parents' warm and negative interactions with unrelated stepsiblings (see Figure 2.10) (Reiss, 2003).

Active Correlation. At older ages, *active* genetic–environmental correlation becomes common. As children extend their experiences beyond the immediate family and are given the freedom to make more choices, they actively seek environments that fit with their genetic tendencies. The well-coordinated, muscular child spends more time at after-school sports, the musically talented youngster joins the school orchestra and practices his violin, and the intellectually curious child is a familiar patron at her local library.

This tendency to actively choose environments that complement our heredity is called **niche-picking** (Scarr & McCartney, 1983). Infants and young children cannot do much niche-picking because adults select environments for them. In contrast, older children and adolescents are much more in charge of their environments.

The niche-picking idea explains why pairs of identical twins reared apart during childhood and later reunited may find, to their surprise, that they have similar hobbies, food preferences, and vocations—a trend that is especially marked when twins' environmental opportunities are similar (Plomin, 1994). Niche-picking also helps us understand why identical twins become somewhat more alike, and fraternal twins and adopted siblings less alike, in intelligence with age (Bouchard, 2004; Loehlin, Horn, & Willerman, 1997). And niche-picking sheds light on why adolescent identical twin pairs—far more often than same-sex fraternal pairs, ordinary siblings, and adopted siblings—report similar stressful life events influenced by personal decisions and actions, such as failing a course, quitting a job, or getting in trouble for drug-taking (Bemmels et al., 2008).

The influence of heredity and environment is not constant but changes over time. With age,

■ This mother shares her love of the piano with her daughter, who also may have inherited her mother's musical talent. When heredity and environment are correlated, they jointly foster the same capacities, and the influence of one cannot be separated from the influence of the other. ■

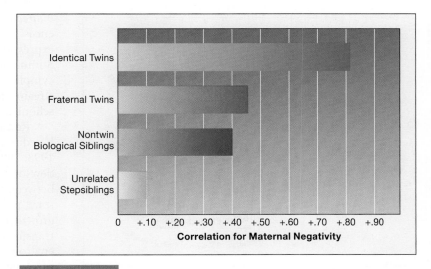

FIGURE 2.10

Similarity in mothers' interactions for pairs of siblings differing in genetic relatedness. The correlations shown are for maternal negativity. The pattern illustrates evocative genetic–environmental correlation. Identical twins evoke similar maternal treatment because of their identical heredity. As genetic resemblance between siblings declines, the strength of the correlation drops. Mothers vary their interactions as they respond to each child's unique genetic makeup. *(Adapted from Reiss, 2003.)*

genetic factors may become more important in influencing the environments we experience and choose for ourselves.

ENVIRONMENTAL INFLUENCES ON GENE EXPRESSION   Notice how, in the concepts just considered, heredity is granted priority. In range of reaction, it *determines* individual responsiveness to varying environments. In canalization, it *restricts* the development of certain behaviors. Similarly, genetic–environmental correlation is viewed as *driven* by genetics, in that children's genetic makeup causes them to receive, evoke, or seek experiences that actualize their inborn tendencies (Plomin, 2009; Rowe, 1994).

A growing number of researchers take issue with the supremacy of heredity, arguing that it does not dictate children's experiences or development in a rigid way. In one study, boys with a genetic tendency toward antisocial behavior (based on the presence of a gene on the X chromosome known to predispose both animals and humans to aggression) were no more aggressive than boys without this gene, *unless* they also had a history of severe child abuse (Caspi et al., 2002). Boys with and without the gene did not differ in their experience of abuse, indicating that the "aggressive genotype" did not increase exposure to abuse. And in a large Finnish adoption study, children whose biological mothers had schizophrenia but who were being reared by healthy adoptive parents showed little mental illness—no more than a control group with healthy biological and adoptive parents. In contrast, schizophrenia and other psychological impairments piled up in adoptees whose biological and adoptive parents were both disturbed (Tienari et al., 2003; Tienari, Wahlberg, & Wynne, 2006).

Furthermore, parents and other caring adults can *uncouple* unfavorable genetic–environmental correlations. They often provide children with positive experiences that modify the expression of heredity, yielding favorable outcomes. For example, in a study that tracked the development of 5-year-old identical twins, pair members tended to resemble each other in level of aggression. And the more aggression they displayed, the more maternal anger and criticism they received (a genetic–environmental correlation). Nevertheless, some mothers treated their twins differently. When followed up at age 7, twins who had been targets of more maternal negativity engaged in even more antisocial behavior. In contrast, their better-treated, genetically identical counterparts showed a reduction in disruptive acts (Caspi et al., 2004). Good parenting protected them from a spiraling, antisocial course of development.

Accumulating evidence reveals that the relationship between heredity and environment is not a one-way street, from genes to environment to behavior. Rather, like other system influences considered in this and the previous chapter, it is *bidirectional:* Genes affect children's behavior and experiences, but their experiences and behavior also affect gene expression (Diamond, 2009; Gottlieb, 2003; Rutter, 2007a). Stimulation—both *internal* to the child (activity within the cytoplasm of the cell, hormones released into the bloodstream) and *external* to the child (home, neighborhood, school, and society)—modifies gene activity.

Researchers call this view of the relationship between heredity and environment the *epigenetic framework* (Gottlieb, 1998, 2007). It is depicted in Figure 2.11. **Epigenesis** means development resulting from ongoing, bidirectional exchanges between heredity and all levels of the environment. To illustrate, providing a baby with a healthy diet promotes brain growth, leading to new connections among nerve cells, which transform gene expression. This opens the door to new gene–environment exchanges—for example, advanced exploration of objects and interaction with caregivers, which further enhance brain growth and gene expression. These ongoing bidirectional influences foster cognitive and social development. In contrast, harmful environments can interfere with gene expression (see the Biology and Environment box on the following page for an example). And at times, the impact

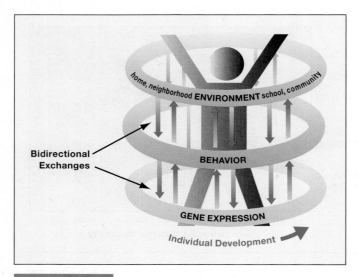

FIGURE 2.11

The epigenetic framework. Development takes place through ongoing, bidirectional exchanges between heredity and all levels of the environment. Genes affect behavior and experiences. Experiences and behavior also affect gene expression. *(Adapted from Gottlieb, 2007.)*

BIOLOGY AND ENVIRONMENT

A Case of Epigenesis: Smoking During Pregnancy Alters Gene Expression

A wealth of experimental research with animals confirms that environment can modify the genome in ways that have no impact on a gene's sequence of base pairs but nevertheless affect the operation of that gene (Zhang & Meaney, 2010). This epigenetic interplay, in which a gene's impact on the individual's phenotype depends on the gene's context, is now being vigorously investigated in humans.

Maternal smoking during pregnancy is among the risk factors for *attention-deficit hyperactivity disorder (ADHD)*—one of the most common disorders of childhood, which we will take up in greater detail in Chapter 12. ADHD symptoms—inattention, impulsivity, and over-activity—typically result in serious academic and social problems. Several studies report that individuals who are homozygous for a chromosome-12 gene (DD) containing a special repeat of base pairs are at increased risk for ADHD. Other research, however, has not confirmed any role for this gene (Fisher et al., 2002; Gill et al., 1997; Waldman et al., 1998).

Animal evidence suggests that one reason for this inconsistency is that environmental influences associated with ADHD—such as prenatal exposure to toxins—modify the gene's activity. To test this possibility, researchers recruited several hundred mothers and their 6-month-old babies, obtaining infant blood samples for genetic analysis and asking mothers whether they smoked regularly during pregnancy (Kahn et al., 2003). At a 5-year follow-up, parents responded to a widely used behavior rating scale that assesses children for ADHD symptoms.

Findings revealed that by itself, the DD genotype was unrelated to impulsivity, overactivity, or oppositional behavior. But children whose mothers had smoked during pregnancy scored higher in these behaviors than children of nonsmoking mothers. Furthermore, as Figure 2.12 illustrates, 5-year-olds with both prenatal nicotine exposure and the DD genetic makeup obtained substantially higher impulsivity, overactivity, and oppositional scores than all other groups—outcomes that persisted even after a variety of other factors (quality of the home environment and maternal ethnicity, marital status, and post-birth smoking) had been controlled.

Another investigation following participants into adolescence obtained similar findings, suggesting that the genotype–prenatal

■ Because his mother smoked during pregnancy, this baby may be at increased risk for developing attention-deficit hyperactivity disorder (ADHD). Prenatal exposure to nicotine seems to alter expression of a chromosome-12 gene in ways that greatly heighten impulsivity, overactivity, and oppositional behavior. ■

environment effect persists (Becker et al., 2008). What processes might account for it? In animal research, tobacco smoke stimulates the DD genotype to release chemicals in the brain that promote impulsivity and overactivity (Ernst, Moolchan, & Robinson, 2001). These behaviors, in turn, often evoke harsh, punitive parenting, which can trigger defiance in children.

The DD genotype is widespread, present in more than 50 percent of people. Thus, the majority of children prenatally exposed to nicotine are at high risk for learning and behavior problems. As we will see in Chapter 3, smoking during pregnancy has additional negative health consequences. And other genes, in epigenetic interplay with as yet unknown environmental factors, contribute to ADHD symptoms (Hudziak & Rettew, 2009).

FIGURE 2.12

Combined influence of maternal prenatal smoking and genotype on impulsivity and overactivity at age 5. In the absence of prenatal smoking, 5-year-olds who were homozygous for a chromosome-12 gene (DD) showed no elevation in impulsivity and overactivity (orange bar) compared with children of other genotypes (Dd or dd) (red bar). Among children of all genotypes, prenatal smoking was associated with an increase in these behaviors (green and purple bars). And the combination of prenatal smoking and the DD genotype greatly magnified impulsivity and overactivity (purple bar). Children's oppositional behavior followed a similar epigenetic pattern. *(Adapted from Kahn et al., 2003.)*

Chart: Mean Impulsivity and Overactivity Score (y-axis, 54 to 70)

	No Prenatal Smoking		Prenatal Smoking	
Genotype	Dd or dd	DD	Dd or dd	DD
Score	~60.7	~59	~61.9	~68.2

is so profound that later experiences can do little to change characteristics (such as intelligence and personality) that originally were flexible.

A major reason that researchers are interested in the nature–nurture issue is that they want to improve environments so that children can develop as far as possible. The concept of epigenesis reminds us that development is best understood as a series of complex exchanges between nature and nurture. Although children cannot be changed in any way we might desire, environments can modify genetic influences. The success of any attempt to improve development depends on the characteristics we want to change, the genetic makeup of the child, and the type and timing of our intervention.

ASK YOURSELF

◆ REVIEW What is epigenesis, and how does it differ from range of reaction and genetic–environmental correlation? Provide an example of epigenesis.

◆ APPLY Bianca's parents are accomplished musicians. At age 4, Bianca began taking piano lessons. By age 10, she was accompanying the school choir. At age 14, she asked if she could attend a special music high school. Explain how genetic–environmental correlation promoted Bianca's talent.

◆ CONNECT Explain how each of the following concepts supports the conclusion that genetic influences on human characteristics are not constant but change over time: somatic mutation (page 60), niche-picking (page 85), and epigenesis (page 86).

◆ REFLECT What aspects of your own development— for example, interests, hobbies, college major, or vocational choice—are probably due to niche-picking? Explain.

Summary

Genetic Foundations

What are genes, and how are they transmitted from one generation to the next?

■ Each individual's **phenotype,** or directly observable characteristics, is a product of both **genotype** and environment. **Chromosomes,** rodlike structures within the cell nucleus, contain our hereditary endowment. Along their length are **genes,** segments of **deoxyribonucleic acid (DNA),** that send instructions for making a rich assortment of proteins to the cytoplasm of the cell—a process that makes us distinctly human and influences our development and characteristics.

■ **Gametes,** or sex cells, are produced through a cell division process called **meiosis. Crossing over** and chance assortment of chromosomes into gametes ensure that each receives a unique set of genes from each parent. Once sperm and ovum unite, the resulting **zygote** starts to develop into a complex human being through cell duplication, or **mitosis.**

■ If the fertilizing sperm carries an X chromosome, the child will be a girl; if it contains a Y chromosome, a boy. **Fraternal,** or **dizygotic, twins** result when two ova are released from the mother's ovaries and each is fertilized. **Identical,** or **monozygotic, twins** develop when a zygote divides in two during the early stages of cell duplication.

© RACHEL EPSTEIN/PHOTOEDIT

Describe various patterns of genetic inheritance.

■ Traits controlled by single genes follow **dominant–recessive** and **incomplete dominance** patterns of inheritance. **Homozygous** individuals have two identical **alleles,** or forms of a gene. **Heterozygous** individuals, with one dominant and one recessive allele, are **carriers** of the recessive trait. In **incomplete dominance,** both alleles are expressed in the phenotype, resulting in a trait that combines aspects of both. **Modifier genes** enhance or dilute the effects of other genes.

■ **X-linked inheritance** applies when recessive disorders are carried on the X chromosome and, therefore, are more likely to affect males. In **genomic imprinting,** one parent's allele is activated, regardless of its makeup.

■ Harmful genes arise from **mutation,** which can occur spontaneously or be caused by hazardous environmental agents. Germline mutation occurs in the cells that give rise to gametes; somatic mutation can occur in body cells at any time of life.

■ Human traits that vary continuously among people, such as intelligence and personality, result from **polygenic inheritance**—the effects of many genes. For such characteristics, scientists must study the influence of heredity indirectly.

Describe major chromosomal abnormalities, and explain how they occur.

- Most chromosomal abnormalities are due to errors in meiosis. The most common is Down syndrome, which results in physical defects and mental retardation. Disorders of the **sex chromosomes**—XYY, triple X, Klinefelter, and Turner syndromes—are milder than defects of the **autosomes.**

Reproductive Choices

What procedures can assist prospective parents in having healthy children?

- **Genetic counseling** helps couples at risk for giving birth to children with genetic abnormalities consider appropriate reproductive options. **Prenatal diagnostic methods** allow early detection of genetic problems.

- Reproductive technologies, such as donor insemination, in vitro fertilization, surrogate motherhood, and postmenopausal-assisted childbirth, permit many individuals to become parents who otherwise would not, but they raise serious legal and ethical concerns.

- Many parents who cannot conceive or who have a high likelihood of transmitting a genetic disorder decide to adopt. Although adopted children tend to have more learning and emotional problems than children in general, most fare well in the long run. Warm, sensitive parenting predicts favorable development.

Environmental Contexts for Development

Describe family functioning from the perspective of ecological systems theory, along with aspects of the environment that support family well-being and children's development.

- The first and foremost context for child development is the family, a dynamic system characterized by bidirectional influences, in which each family member's behaviors affect those of others. Both direct and indirect influences operate within the family system, which must continually adjust to new events and changes in its members.

- **Socioeconomic status (SES)** profoundly affects family functioning. Higher-SES families tend to be smaller, to emphasize psychological traits, and to engage in warm, verbally stimulating interaction with children. Lower-SES families often stress external characteristics and use more commands, criticism, and physical punishment. Many affluent families are physically and emotionally unavailable, thereby impairing their children's adjustment. Poverty and homelessness undermine effective parenting and pose serious threats to children's development.

- Children benefit from supportive ties between the family and the surrounding environment, including stable, socially cohesive neighborhoods that provide constructive leisure and enrichment activities and that offer parents access to social support. High-quality schools with frequent parent–teacher contact are also vital.

- The values and practices of cultures and **subcultures** affect all aspects of children's daily lives. **Extended-family households,** which are common among many ethnic minority groups, help protect children from negative effects of poverty and other stressful conditions.

- **Collectivist societies,** which emphasize group needs and goals, and **individualistic societies,** which emphasize individual well-being, take different approaches to developing **public policies** to address social problems, including those affecting children. Largely because of its strongly individualistic values, the United States lags behind other developed nations in policies safeguarding children and youths.

Understanding the Relationship Between Heredity and Environment

Explain the various ways heredity and environment may combine to influence complex traits.

- **Behavioral genetics** is a field that examines the contributions of nature and nurture to complex traits. Researchers use **kinship studies** to compute **heritability estimates,** which show that genetic factors influence such traits as intelligence and personality. However, the accuracy and usefulness of heritability estimates have been challenged.

- According to the concepts of **range of reaction** and **canalization,** heredity influences children's responsiveness to varying environments. **Genetic–environmental correlation** and **niche-picking** describe how children's genes affect the environments to which they are exposed. **Epigenesis** reminds us that development is best understood as a series of complex exchanges between nature and nurture.

IMPORTANT TERMS AND CONCEPTS

allele (p. 56)
autosomes (p. 54)
behavioral genetics (p. 82)
canalization (p. 84)
carrier (p. 56)
chromosomes (p. 52)
collectivist societies (p. 78)
coparenting (p. 70)
crossing over (p. 53)
deoxyribonucleic acid (DNA) (p. 52)
dominant–recessive inheritance (p. 56)
epigenesis (p. 86)
extended-family household (p. 78)
fraternal, or dizygotic, twins (p. 55)

gametes (p. 53)
gene (p. 52)
genetic counseling (p. 63)
genetic–environmental correlation (p. 85)
genomic imprinting (p. 59)
genotype (p. 51)
heritability estimate (p. 82)
heterozygous (p. 56)
homozygous (p. 56)
identical, or monozygotic, twins (p. 55)
incomplete dominance (p. 57)
individualistic societies (p. 78)
kinship studies (p. 82)
meiosis (p. 53)

mitosis (p. 53)
modifier genes (p. 57)
mutation (p. 60)
niche-picking (p. 85)
phenotype (p. 51)
polygenic inheritance (p. 60)
prenatal diagnostic methods (p. 63)
public policies (p. 78)
range of reaction (p. 84)
sex chromosomes (p. 54)
socioeconomic status (SES) (p. 71)
subculture (p. 78)
X-linked inheritance (p. 57)
zygote (p. 53)

"Pregnant Mummy"
Eliska Kocová
5 years, Czech Republic

In this painting, the rapidly growing fetus claims a central place in the parent's world. How is the one-celled organism transformed into a baby with the capacity to participate in family life? What factors support or undermine this earliest period of development? Chapter 3 provides answers to these questions.

Reprinted with permission from the International Museum of Children's Art, Oslo, Norway

Prenatal Development

When I met Yolanda and Jay one fall in my child development class, Yolanda was just two months pregnant. Approaching age 30, married for several years and their careers well under way, they had decided to have a baby. To prepare for the transition to parenthood, they enrolled in my evening section, arriving once a week after work full of questions: "How does the baby grow before birth?" "When is each organ formed?" "Has its heart begun to beat?" "Can it hear, feel, or sense our presence?"

Most of all, Yolanda and Jay wanted to do everything possible to make sure their baby would be born healthy. At first, they believed that the uterus completely shielded the developing organism from any dangers in the environment. All babies born with problems, they thought, had unfavorable genes. After browsing through several pregnancy books, Yolanda and Jay realized they were wrong. Yolanda wondered about her diet and whether she should keep up her daily aerobics routine. And she asked me whether an aspirin for a headache, a glass of wine at dinner, or a few cups of coffee during the workday might be harmful.

In this chapter, we answer Yolanda and Jay's questions, along with a great many more that scientists have asked about the events before birth. We begin our discussion during the time period before pregnancy with these puzzling questions: Why is it that generation after generation, most couples who fall in love and marry want to become parents? And how do they decide whether to have just one child or more than one?

Then we trace prenatal development, paying special attention to environmental supports for healthy growth, as well as damaging influences that threaten the child's health and survival. Finally, we look at how couples prepare psychologically for the arrival of the baby and start to forge a new sense of self as mother or father.

■■ Motivations for Parenthood
■■

TAKE A MOMENT... What, in your view, are the benefits and drawbacks of having children? How large would your ideal family be, and why? As part of her semester project for my class, Yolanda interviewed her grandmother, asking why she had wanted children and how she had settled on a particular family size. Yolanda's grandmother, whose children were born in the 1950s, replied:

> We didn't think much about whether or not to have children in those days. We just had them—everybody did. It would have seemed odd not to! I was 22 years old when I had the first of my four children, and I had four because—well, I wouldn't have had just one because we all thought children needed brothers and sisters, and only children could end up spoiled and selfish. Life is more interesting with children, you know. And now that we're older, we've got family we can depend on and grandchildren to enjoy.

Why Have Children?

In some ways, the reasons Yolanda's grandmother wanted children are much like those of contemporary parents. In other ways, they are very different. In the past, the issue of whether to have children was, for many adults, a biological given or a compelling social expectation. Today, in Western industrialized nations, it is a matter of true individual choice. Effective birth control techniques enable adults to avoid having children in most instances. And changing cultural values allow people to remain childless with far less fear of social criticism and rejection than a generation or two ago (Scott, 2009). In 1950, 78 percent of U.S. married couples were parents. Today, 70 percent bear children—a choice affected by a complex array of factors including financial circumstances, career goals, personal and religious values, and health conditions (Theil, 2006).

When Americans are asked about their desire to have children, they mention a variety of advantages and disadvantages, which are listed in Table 3.1. Although some ethnic and regional differences exist, reasons for having children that are most important to all groups include the warm, affectionate relationship and the stimulation and fun that children provide. Also frequently mentioned are growth and learning experiences that children bring into the lives of adults, the desire to have someone carry on after one's own death, and feelings of accomplishment and creativity that come from helping children grow (Cowan & Cowan, 2000; Langridge, Connolly, & Sheeran, 2000; O'Laughlin & Anderson, 2001).

Most adults are also aware that having children means years of extra burdens and responsibilities. Among disadvantages of parenthood, they cite "loss of freedom" most often, followed by "financial strain." According to a conservative estimate, new parents in the United States today will spend about $210,000 to rear a child from birth to age 18, and many will incur substantial additional expense for higher education and financial dependency during emerging adulthood—a reality that has contributed to the declining birthrate in industrialized nations (Lino & Carlson, 2009). Finally, many adults worry greatly about family–work conflict—not having enough time to meet both child-rearing and job responsibilities (Jacobs & Gerson, 2004).

Greater freedom to choose whether, when, and how to have children (see the discussion of reproductive choices in Chapter 2) makes contemporary family planning more challenging than it was in Yolanda's grandmother's day. As each partner expects to have equal say, childbearing often becomes a matter of delicate negotiation (Cowan & Cowan, 2000). Yet careful weighing of the pros and cons of having children means that many more couples are making informed and personally meaningful decisions—a trend that increases the chances that they will have children when ready and will find parenting an enriching experience.

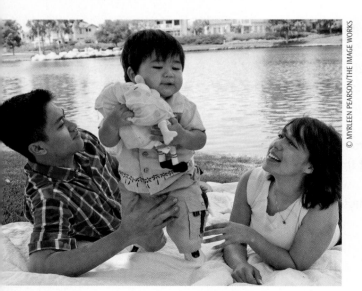

© MYRLEEN PEARSON/THE IMAGE WORKS

■ Individuals from diverse cultures mention many of the same reasons for becoming parents. This young couple takes pleasure in the affectionate, playful relationship they have with their toddler son. ■

TABLE 3.1   Advantages and Disadvantages of Parenthood Mentioned by American Couples

ADVANTAGES	DISADVANTAGES
Giving and receiving warmth and affection	Loss of freedom, being tied down
Experiencing the stimulation and fun that children add to life	Financial strain
Being accepted as a responsible and mature member of the community	Family–work conflict—not enough time to meet both child-rearing and job responsibilities
Experiencing new growth and learning opportunities that add meaning to life	Interference with mother's employment opportunities and career progress
Having someone carry on after one's own death	Worries over children's health, safety, and well-being
Gaining a sense of accomplishment and creativity from helping children grow	Risks of bringing up children in a world plagued by crime, war, and pollution
Having someone to provide care in old age	Reduced time to spend with partner
Learning to become less selfish and to sacrifice	Loss of privacy
Having offspring who help with parents' work or add their own income to the family's resources	Fear that children will turn out badly, through no fault of one's own

Sources: Cowan & Cowan, 2000; O'Laughlin & Anderson, 2001.

How Large a Family?

In contrast to her grandmother, Yolanda plans to have no more than two children. And she and Jay are talking about whether to limit their family to a single child. In 1960, the average number of children per North American couple was 3.1. Currently, it is 2.1 in the United States; 1.9 in the United Kingdom; 1.8 in Australia; 1.7 in Sweden; 1.6 in Canada; 1.4 in Germany; and 1.3 in Italy and Japan (U.S. Census Bureau, 2010a; 2010b). In addition to more effective birth control, a major reason for this decline is that a family size of one or two children is more compatible with a woman's decision to divide her energies between family and career. Marital instability has also contributed to smaller families: More couples today get divorced before their childbearing plans are complete.

Popular advice to prospective parents often recommends limiting family size in the interests of "child quality"—more parental affection, attention, and material resources per child, which enhance children's intellectual development. Do large families make less intelligent children, as prevailing attitudes suggest? Or do less intelligent parents—as a result of heredity, environment, or both—tend to have larger families? To find out researchers turned to a large, two-generation longitudinal study.

Starting in 1972, the U.S. National Longitudinal Survey of Youth (NLSY) followed a nationally representative sample of several thousand U.S. 14- to 22-year-olds; in 1986 the children of the original participants were added to the investigation. Because both cohorts took intelligence tests, the researchers could (1) examine the relationship of sibling birth order within families to mental test scores, to find out whether having more children depresses children's intellectual functioning; and (2) correlate maternal scores with family size, for insight into whether mothers who score poorly are prone to have larger families.

As the horizontal lines in Figure 3.1 reveal, children's mental test performance did not decline with later birth

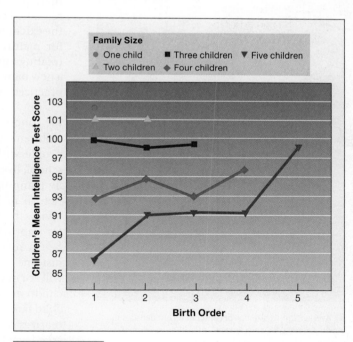

FIGURE 3.1

Relationship of birth order and family size to intelligence. In the U.S. National Longitudinal Survey of Youth, children's intelligence test scores did not decline with later birth order, as would be predicted if large families diluted the quality of children's experiences. To the contrary, in the largest families, the youngest children tended to score higher than their siblings. But note the differences among the lines, which indicate that the larger the family, the lower the scores of all siblings. *(From J. L. Rodgers, H. H. Cleveland, E. van den Oord, & D. C. Rowe, 2000, "Resolving the Debate Over Birth Order, Family Size, and Intelligence," American Psychologist, 55, p. 607. © 2000 by the American Psychological Association. Reprinted with permission.)*

TABLE 3.2 Advantages and Disadvantages of a One-Child Family

ADVANTAGES		DISADVANTAGES	
Mentioned by Parents	*Mentioned by Children*	*Mentioned by Parents*	*Mentioned by Children*
Having time to pursue one's own interests and career	Having no sibling rivalry	Walking a "tightrope" between healthy attention and overindulgence	Not getting to experience the closeness of a sibling relationship
Less financial pressure	Having more privacy	Having only one chance to "make good" as a parent	Feeling too much pressure from parents to succeed
Not having to worry about "playing favorites" among children	Enjoying greater affluence	Being left childless in case of the child's death	Having no one to help care for parents when they get old
	Having a closer parent–child relationship		

Source: Hawke & Knox, 1978.

order—a finding that contradicts the belief that having more children depresses children's intellectual ability. At the same time, the differences among the lines show that the larger the family, the lower the scores of all siblings. The researchers found that the link between family size and children's scores can be explained by the strong trend for mothers who are low in intelligence to give birth to more children (Rodgers et al., 2000). In other NLSY research, among children of bright, economically advantaged mothers, the family size–intelligence correlation disappeared (Guo & VanWey, 1999).

Other evidence confirms that rather than parenting quality declining as new children are born, parents reallocate their energies. In a longitudinal study of Canadian two-parent families, new births led to a decrease in maternal affection toward older siblings, though most mothers probably remained generally warm. At the same time, the consistency of parenting—the extent to which mothers insisted older children meet their expectations for mature behavior, such as completing chores, doing homework, and treating others respectfully—rose over time (Strohschein et al., 2008). After a new baby joined the family, mothers seemed to reorganize their parenting practices to best meet all their children's needs.

In sum, although many good reasons exist for limiting family size, the concern that additional births will reduce parenting quality and, thus, children's intelligence and life chances is not warranted. Rather, young people with lower mental test scores—many of whom dropped out of school, live in poverty, lack hope for their future, and fail to engage in family planning—are most likely to have large families (Amato et al., 2008). Return to the Social Issues: Education box on page 73 in Chapter 2 to review the close link between education and family planning. Both are vital for improving children's quality of life.

Is Yolanda's grandmother right when she says that parents who have just one child are likely to end up with a spoiled, selfish youngster? As we will see in Chapter 13, research also challenges this widely held belief. Only children are just as well-adjusted as children with siblings. Still, the one-child family, like all family lifestyles, has both pros and cons. Table 3.2 summarizes results of a survey in which only children and their parents were asked what they liked and disliked about living in a single-child family. The list is useful for parents to consider when deciding how many children would best fit their life plans.

© PHOTODISC/GETTY IMAGES

■ Average family size has declined in recent decades in North America, Western Europe, and other developed nations. But, contrary to popular belief, having more children does not reduce the intelligence or life chances of later-born children. ■

Is There a Best Time During Adulthood to Have a Child?

Yolanda's grandmother had her first child in her early twenties. Yolanda, at age 29, is pregnant for the first time. Many people believe that women should, ideally, give birth in their twenties, not only because the risk of having a baby with a chromosomal disorder increases with age (see Chapter 2) but also because younger parents have more energy to keep up with active children.

However, as Figure 3.2 reveals, first births to women in their thirties have increased greatly over the past several decades. Many people are delaying childbearing until their education is complete, their careers are established, and they know they can support a child. Older parents may be somewhat less energetic than they once were, but they are financially better off and emotionally more mature. For these reasons, they may be better able to invest in parenting.

Nevertheless, reproductive capacity does decline with age. Fertility problems among women increase from age 15 to 50, with a sharp rise in the mid-thirties. Between ages 25 and 34, nearly 20 percent of women are affected, a figure that climbs to 34 percent for 35- to 39-year-olds and to 43 percent for 40- to 44-year-olds. Age also affects male reproductive capacity. Amount of semen and concentration of sperm in each ejaculation decline gradually after age 35. Consequently, compared to a 25-year-old man, a 45-year-old is 12 times as likely to take more than two years to achieve a conception (Lambert, Masson, & Fisch, 2006; U.S. Department of Health and Human Services, 2009e). Women with demanding careers are especially likely to delay parenthood (Tough et al., 2007). Many believe, incorrectly, that if they have difficulty conceiving, they can rely on reproductive technologies. But recall from Chapter 2 that the success of these procedures drops steadily with age. Although no one time during adulthood is best to begin parenthood, individuals who decide to put off childbirth until well into their thirties or early forties risk having fewer children than they desire or none at all.

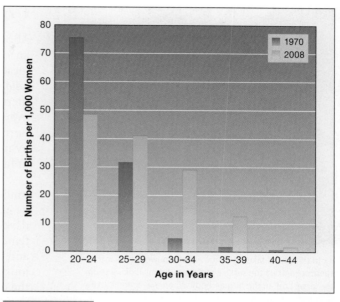

FIGURE 3.2

First births to American women of different ages in 1970 and 2008. The birthrate decreased during this period for women 20 to 24 years of age, whereas it increased for women 25 years of age and older. For women in their thirties, the birthrate more than doubled. Similar trends have occurred in other industrialized nations. *(Adapted from U.S. Census Bureau, 2010b.)*

ASK YOURSELF

◆ REVIEW Using research findings, explain why the common assumption that larger families make less intelligent children is incorrect.

◆ APPLY Rhonda and Mark are career-oriented, 35-year-old parents of an only child. They are thinking about having a second baby. What factors should they keep in mind as they decide whether to add to their family at this time in their lives?

◆ CONNECT Why is it incorrect for couples who postpone childbearing until age 35 or later to conclude that medical advances can overcome fertility problems? (See Chapter 2, pages 66–67.)

◆ REFLECT Ask one of your parents or grandparents to list his or her motivations for having children. How do those motivations compare with your own? What factors—for example, education or cultural changes—might account for any differences?

Prenatal Development

The sperm and ovum that unite to form the new individual are uniquely suited for the task of reproduction. The ovum is a tiny sphere, measuring $1/175$ inch in diameter, that is barely visible to the naked eye as a dot the size of the period at the end of this sentence. But in its microscopic world, it is a giant—the largest cell in the human body. The ovum's size makes it a perfect target for the much smaller sperm, which measure only $1/500$ inch.

In this photo taken with the aid of a powerful microscope, sperm penetrate the surface of the enormous-looking ovum, the largest cell in the human body. When one sperm successfully fertilizes the ovum, the resulting zygote begins to duplicate. ■

Conception

About once every 28 days, in the middle of a woman's menstrual cycle, an ovum bursts from one of her *ovaries,* two walnut-sized organs located deep inside her abdomen, and is drawn into one of two *fallopian tubes*—long, thin structures that lead to the hollow, soft-lined uterus (see Figure 3.3). While the ovum is traveling, the spot on the ovary from which it was released, now called the *corpus luteum,* secretes hormones that prepare the lining of the uterus to receive a fertilized ovum. If pregnancy does not occur, the corpus luteum shrinks, and the lining of the uterus is discarded two weeks later with menstruation.

The male produces sperm in vast numbers—an average of 300 million a day—in the *testes,* two glands located in the *scrotum,* sacs that lie just behind the penis. In the final process of maturation, each sperm develops a tail that permits it to swim long distances upstream in the female reproductive tract, through the *cervix* (opening of the uterus), and into the fallopian tube, where fertilization usually takes place. The journey is difficult, and many sperm die. Only 300 to 500 reach the ovum, if one happens to be present. Sperm live for up to six days and can lie in wait for the ovum, which survives for only one day after being released into the fallopian tube. However, most conceptions result from intercourse during a three-day period—on the day of ovulation or during the two days preceding it (Wilcox, Weinberg, & Baird, 1995).

With conception, the story of prenatal development begins to unfold. The vast changes that take place during the 38 weeks of pregnancy are usually divided into three phases: (1) the period of the zygote, (2) the period of the embryo, and (3) the period of the fetus. As we look at what happens in each, you may find it useful to refer to Table 3.3, which summarizes milestones of prenatal development.

FIGURE 3.3

Female reproductive organs, showing fertilization, early cell duplication, and implantation. *(From* Before We Are Born, *6th ed., by K. L. Moore and T. V. N. Persaud, p. 87. Copyright © 2003, reprinted with permission from Elsevier, Inc.)*

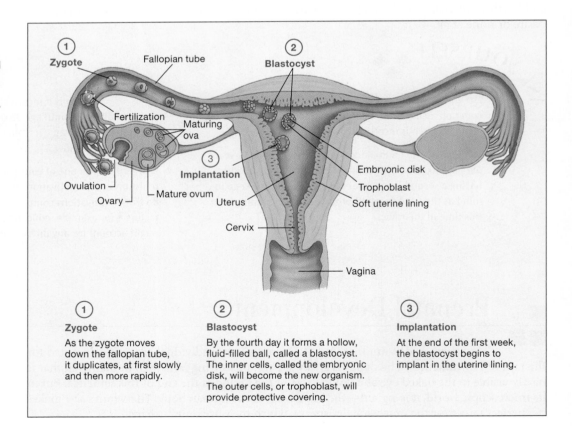

① Zygote

As the zygote moves down the fallopian tube, it duplicates, at first slowly and then more rapidly.

② Blastocyst

By the fourth day it forms a hollow, fluid-filled ball, called a blastocyst. The inner cells, called the embryonic disk, will become the new organism. The outer cells, or trophoblast, will provide protective covering.

③ Implantation

At the end of the first week, the blastocyst begins to implant in the uterine lining.

TABLE 3.3 Milestones of Prenatal Development

TRIMESTER	PERIOD	WEEKS	LENGTH AND WEIGHT	MAJOR EVENTS
First	Zygote	1		The one-celled zygote multiplies and forms a blastocyst.
		2		The blastocyst burrows into the uterine lining. Structures that feed and protect the developing organism begin to form—*amnion, chorion, yolk sac, placenta,* and *umbilical cord*.
	Embryo	3–4	¼ inch (6 mm)	A primitive brain and spinal cord appear. Heart, muscles, ribs, backbone, and digestive tract begin to develop.
		5–8	1 inch (2.5 cm); ¹/₇ ounce (4 g)	Many external body structures (face, arms, legs, toes, fingers) and internal organs form. The sense of touch begins to develop, and the embryo can move.
	Fetus	9–12	3 inches (7.6 cm); less than 1 ounce (28 g)	Rapid increase in size begins. Nervous system, organs, and muscles become organized and connected, and new behavioral capacities (kicking, thumb sucking, mouth opening, and rehearsal of breathing) appear. External genitals are well-formed, and the fetus's sex is evident.
Second		13–24	12 inches (30 cm); 1.8 pounds (820 g)	The fetus continues to enlarge rapidly. In the middle of this period, fetal movements can be felt by the mother. Vernix and lanugo keep the fetus's skin from chapping in the amniotic fluid. Most of the brain's neurons are present by 24 weeks. Eyes are sensitive to light, and the fetus reacts to sound.
Third		25–38	20 inches (50 cm); 7.5 pounds (3,400 g)	The fetus has a good chance of survival if born during this time. Size increases. Lungs mature. Rapid brain development causes sensory and behavioral capacities to expand. In the middle of this period, a layer of fat is added under the skin. Antibodies are transmitted from mother to fetus to protect against disease. Most fetuses rotate into an upside-down position in preparation for birth.

Source: Moore & Persaud, 2008.

Photos (from top to bottom): © Claude Cortier/Photo Researchers, Inc.; © G. Moscoso/Photo Researchers, Inc.; © John Watney/Photo Researchers, Inc.; © James Stevenson/Photo Researchers, Inc.; © Lennart Nilsson, *A Child Is Born*/Scanpix.

Period of the Zygote

The period of the zygote lasts about two weeks, from fertilization until the tiny mass of cells drifts down and out of the fallopian tube and attaches itself to the wall of the uterus. The zygote's first cell duplication is long and drawn out; it is not complete until about 30 hours after conception. Gradually, new cells are added at a faster rate. By the fourth day, 60 to 70 cells exist that form a hollow, fluid-filled ball called a **blastocyst** (refer again to Figure 3.3). The cells on the inside of the blastocyst, called the **embryonic disk,** will become the new organism; the thin outer ring of cells, termed the **trophoblast,** will become the structures that provide protective covering and nourishment.

IMPLANTATION   Between the seventh and ninth days, **implantation** occurs: The blastocyst burrows deep into the uterine lining. Surrounded by the woman's nourishing blood, it starts to grow in earnest. At first, the trophoblast (protective outer layer) multiplies fastest. It forms a membrane, called the **amnion,** that encloses the developing organism in **amniotic fluid,** which helps keep the temperature of the prenatal world constant and provides a cushion against any jolts caused by the woman's movement. A *yolk sac* emerges that produces blood cells until the developing liver, spleen, and bone marrow are mature enough to take over this function (Moore & Persaud, 2008).

The events of these first two weeks are delicate and uncertain. As many as 30 percent of zygotes do not survive this period. In some, the sperm and ovum did not join properly. In others, for some unknown reason, cell duplication never begins. By preventing implantation in these cases, nature eliminates most prenatal abnormalities (Sadler, 2009).

THE PLACENTA AND UMBILICAL CORD   By the end of the second week, cells of the trophoblast form another protective membrane—the **chorion,** which surrounds the amnion. From the chorion, tiny fingerlike *villi,* or blood vessels, emerge.[1] As these villi burrow into the uterine wall, the placenta starts to develop. By bringing the mother's and the embryo's blood close together, the **placenta** permits food and oxygen to reach the developing organism and waste products to be carried away. A membrane forms that allows these substances to be exchanged but prevents the mother's and the embryo's blood from mixing directly (see Figure 3.4).

The placenta is connected to the developing organism by the **umbilical cord,** which first appears as a primitive body stalk and, during the course of pregnancy, grows to a

■ **Period of the zygote: seventh to ninth day.** The fertilized ovum duplicates at an increasingly rapid rate, forming a hollow ball of cells, or blastocyst, by the fourth day after fertilization. Here the blastocyst, magnified thousands of times, burrows into the uterine lining between the seventh and ninth day. ■

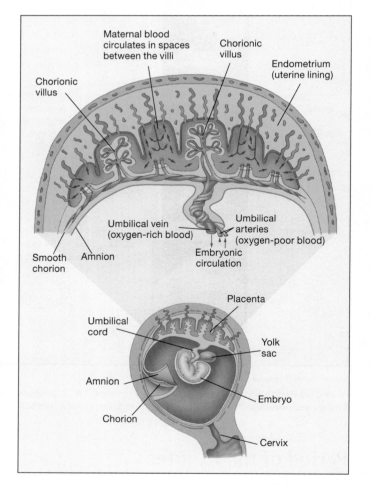

FIGURE 3.4

Cross-section of the uterus, showing detail of the placenta. The embryo's blood flows from the umbilical cord arteries into the chorionic villi and returns via the umbilical cord vein. The mother's blood circulates in spaces surrounding the chorionic villi. A membrane between the two blood supplies permits food and oxygen to be delivered and waste products to be carried away. The two blood supplies do not mix directly. The umbilical arteries carry oxygen-poor blood (shown in blue) to the placenta, and the umbilical vein carries oxygen-rich blood (shown in red) to the fetus. *(From* Before We Are Born, *6th ed., by K. L. Moore and T. V. N. Persaud, p. 95. Copyright © 2003, reprinted with permission from Elsevier, Inc.)*

---

[1]Recall from Chapter 2 that *chorionic villus sampling* is the prenatal diagnostic method that can be performed earliest, at nine weeks after conception. In this procedure, tissues from the ends of the villi are removed and examined for genetic abnormalities.

length of 1 to 3 feet. The umbilical cord contains one large vein that delivers blood loaded with nutrients and two arteries that remove waste products. The force of blood flowing through the cord keeps it firm, much like a garden hose, so it seldom tangles while the embryo, like a space-walking astronaut, floats freely in its fluid-filled chamber (Moore & Persaud, 2008).

By the end of the period of the zygote, the developing organism has found food and shelter. Already, it is a very complex being. These dramatic beginnings take place before most mothers know they are pregnant.

Period of the Embryo

The period of the **embryo** lasts from implantation through the eighth week of pregnancy. During these brief six weeks, the most rapid prenatal changes take place, as the ground-work is laid for all body structures and internal organs. Because all parts of the body are forming, the embryo is especially vulnerable to interference with healthy develop-ment. But the short time span of embryonic growth helps limit opportunities for serious harm.

LAST HALF OF THE FIRST MONTH In the first week of this period, the embryonic disk forms three layers of cells: (1) the *ectoderm,* which will become the nervous system and skin; (2) the *mesoderm,* from which will develop the muscles, skeleton, circulatory system, and other internal organs; and (3) the *endoderm,* which will become the digestive system, lungs, urinary tract, and glands. These three layers give rise to all parts of the body.

At first, the nervous system develops fastest. The ecto-derm folds over to form the **neural tube,** or spinal cord. At 3½ weeks, the top swells to form the brain. Production of *neurons* (nerve cells that store and transmit information) begins deep inside the neural tube at the astounding pace of more than 250,000 per minute. Once formed, neurons travel along tiny threads to their permanent locations, where they will form the major parts of the brain (Nelson, Thomas, & de Haan, 2006).

While the nervous system is developing, the heart begins to pump blood, and muscles, backbone, ribs, and digestive tract start to appear. At the end of the first month, the curled embryo—only ¼ inch long—consists of millions of orga-nized groups of cells with specific functions.

THE SECOND MONTH In the second month, growth continues rapidly. The eyes, ears, nose, jaw, and neck form. Tiny buds become arms, legs, fingers, and toes. Internal organs are more distinct: The intestines grow, the heart de-velops separate chambers, and the liver and spleen take over production of blood cells so that the yolk sac is no longer needed. Changing body proportions cause the embryo's pos-ture to become more upright. Now 1 inch long and ¹/₇ ounce in weight, the embryo can sense its world. It responds to touch, particularly in the mouth area and on the soles of the feet. And it can move, although its tiny flutters are still too light to be felt by the mother (Moore & Persaud, 2008).

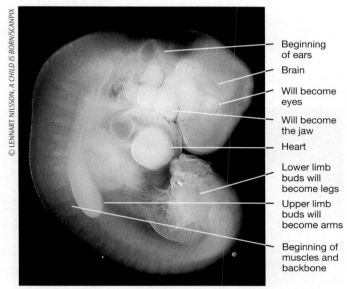

© LENNART NILSSON, *A CHILD IS BORN*/SCANPIX

- Beginning of ears
- Brain
- Will become eyes
- Will become the jaw
- Heart
- Lower limb buds will become legs
- Upper limb buds will become arms
- Beginning of muscles and backbone

■ **Period of the embryo: fourth week.** This 4-week-old embryo is only ¼ inch long, but many body structures have begun to form. ■

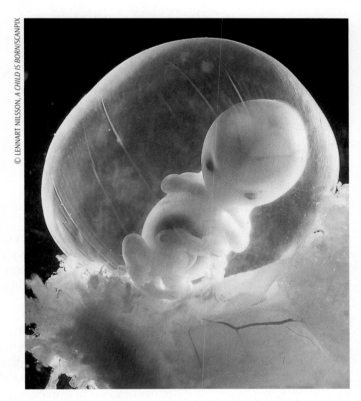

© LENNART NILSSON, *A CHILD IS BORN*/SCANPIX

■ **Period of the embryo: seventh week.** The embryo's posture is more upright. Body structures—eyes, nose, arms, legs, and internal organs—are more distinct. The embryo now responds to touch. It also can move, although at less than one inch long and an ounce in weight, it is still too tiny to be felt by the mother. ■

Period of the Fetus

The period of the **fetus,** from the ninth week to the end of pregnancy, is the longest prenatal period. During this "growth and finishing" phase, the developing organism increases rapidly in size, especially from the ninth to the twentieth week.

THE THIRD MONTH   In the third month, the organs, muscles, and nervous system start to become organized and connected. When the brain signals, the fetus kicks, bends its arms, forms a fist, curls its toes, turns its head, opens its mouth, and even sucks its thumb, stretches, and yawns. Body position changes are frequent, occurring as often as 25 times per hour (Einspieler, Marschik, & Prechtl, 2008). The tiny lungs begin to expand and contract in an early rehearsal of breathing movements. By the twelfth week, the external genitals are well-formed, and the sex of the fetus can be detected with ultrasound (Sadler, 2009). Other finishing touches appear, such as fingernails, toenails, tooth buds, and eyelids that open and close. The heartbeat can now be heard through a stethoscope.

Prenatal development is sometimes divided into **trimesters,** or three equal time periods. At the end of the third month, the *first trimester* is complete.

THE SECOND TRIMESTER   By the middle of the second trimester, between 17 and 20 weeks, the new being has grown large enough that the mother can feel its movements. A white, cheeselike substance called **vernix** protects its skin from chapping during the long months spent bathing in the amniotic fluid. White, downy hair called **lanugo** also appears over the entire body, helping the vernix stick to the skin.

At the end of the second trimester, many organs are well-developed. And most of the brain's billions of neurons are in place; few will be produced after this time. However, *glial cells,* which support and feed the neurons, continue to increase at a rapid rate throughout the remaining months of pregnancy, as well as after birth. Consequently, brain weight increases tenfold from the twentieth week until birth (Roelfsema et al., 2004).

Brain growth means new behavioral capacities. The 20-week-old fetus can be stimulated as well as irritated by sounds. Slow eye movements appear, with rapid eye movements following at 22 weeks. And if a doctor looks inside the uterus using fetoscopy (see Chapter 2, page 64), fetuses try to shield their eyes from the light with their hands, indicating that sight has begun to emerge (Moore & Persaud, 2008). Still, a fetus born at this time cannot survive. Its lungs are immature, and the brain cannot yet control breathing movements or body temperature.

© LENNART NILSSON, *A CHILD IS BORN*/SCANPIX

■ **Period of the fetus: eleventh week.** The organism grows rapidly, and body structures are completed. At 11 weeks, the brain and muscles are better connected. The fetus can kick, bend its arms, open and close its hands and mouth, and suck its thumb. Notice the yolk sac, which shrinks as pregnancy advances. The internal organs have taken over its function of producing blood cells. ■

THE THIRD TRIMESTER   During the final trimester, a fetus born early has a chance for survival. The point at which the baby can first survive, called the **age of viability,** occurs sometime between 22 and 26 weeks (Moore & Persaud, 2008). A baby born between the seventh and eighth month, however, usually needs oxygen assistance to breathe. Although the brain's respiratory center is now mature, tiny air sacs in the lungs are not yet ready to inflate and exchange carbon dioxide for oxygen.

The brain continues to make great strides. The *cerebral cortex,* the seat of human intelligence, enlarges. Convolutions and grooves in its surface appear, permitting a dramatic increase in surface area that allows for maximum prenatal brain growth without the full-term baby's head becoming too large to pass through the birth canal. As neurological organization improves, the fetus spends more time awake. At 20 weeks, fetal heart rate reveals no periods of alertness. But by 28 weeks, fetuses are awake about 11 percent of the time, a figure that rises to 16 percent just before birth (DiPietro et al., 1996). Between 30 and 34 weeks, fetuses show rhythmic alternations between sleep and wakefulness that gradually increase in organization (Rivkees, 2003). Around this time, synchrony between fetal heart rate and motor activity peaks: A rise in heart rate is usually followed within five seconds by a burst of motor activity (DiPietro et al., 2006). These are clear signs that coordinated neural networks are beginning to form in the brain.

By the end of pregnancy, the fetus also takes on the beginnings of a personality. Higher fetal activity in the last weeks of pregnancy predicts a more active infant in the first month of life—a relationship that, for boys, persists into early childhood (Groome et al., 1999). Fetal activity is linked in other ways to infant temperament. In one study, more active fetuses during the third trimester became 1-year-olds who could better handle frustration and 2-year-olds who were less fearful, in that they more readily interacted with toys and with an unfamiliar adult in a laboratory (DiPietro et al., 2002). Perhaps fetal activity level is an indicator of healthy neurological development, which fosters adaptability in childhood. The relationships just described, however, are only modest. As we will see in Chapter 7, sensitive caregiving can modify the temperaments of children who have difficulty adapting to new experiences.

■ **Period of the fetus: twenty-second week.** This fetus is almost a foot long and weighs slightly more than one pound. Its movements can be felt easily by the mother and by other family members who place a hand on her abdomen. The fetus has reached the age of viability; if born, it has a slim chance of surviving. ■

The third trimester also brings greater responsiveness to external stimulation. As we will see later when we discuss newborn capacities, fetuses acquire taste and odor preferences from bathing in and swallowing amniotic fluid (its makeup is influenced by the mother's diet). Between 23 and 30 weeks, connections form between the cerebral cortex and brain regions involved in pain sensitivity. By this time, painkillers should be used in any surgical procedures performed on a fetus (Lee et al., 2005). Around 28 weeks, fetuses blink their eyes in reaction to nearby sounds (Kisilevsky & Low, 1998; Saffran, Werker, & Werner, 2006). And at 30 weeks, fetuses presented with a repeated auditory stimulus against the mother's abdomen initially react with a rise in heart rate and body movements. But over the next 5 to 6 minutes, responsiveness gradually declines, indicating habituation (adaptation) to the sound. If the stimulus is reintroduced after a 10-minute delay, heart rate falls off far more quickly (Dirix et al., 2009). This suggests that fetuses can remember for at least a brief period.

Within the next six weeks, fetuses distinguish the tone and rhythm of different voices and sounds. They show systematic heart rate changes in response to a male versus a female speaker, to the mother's voice versus a stranger's, to a stranger speaking their native language (English) versus a foreign language (Mandarin Chinese), and to a simple familiar melody (descending tones) versus an unfamiliar melody (ascending tones) (Granier-Deferre et al., 2003; Huotilainen et al., 2005; Kisilevsky et al., 2003, 2009; Lecanuet et al., 1993). And in one clever study, mothers read aloud Dr. Seuss's lively book *The Cat in the Hat* each day during the last six weeks of pregnancy. After birth, their infants learned to turn on recordings of the mother's voice by sucking on nipples. They sucked hardest to hear *The Cat in the Hat*—the sound they had come to know while still in the womb (DeCasper & Spence, 1986).

TAKE A MOMENT...On the basis of these findings, would you recommend that expectant mothers provide fetuses with stimulation specially designed to enhance later mental

© LENNART NILSSON, A CHILD IS BORN/SCANPIX

■ **Period of the fetus: thirty-sixth week.** This fetus fills the uterus. To support its need for nourishment, the umbilical cord and placenta have grown large. The vernix (cheeselike substance) on the skin protects it from chapping. The fetus has accumulated a layer of fat to assist with temperature regulation after birth. In two more weeks, it will be full-term. ■

development? Notice how risky it is to draw such conclusions. First, specific forms of fetal stimulation, such as reading aloud or playing classical music, are unlikely to have a long-lasting impact on cognitive development because of the developing child's constantly changing capacities and experiences, which can override the impact of fetal stimulation (Lecanuet, Granier-Deferre, & DeCasper, 2005). Second, although ordinary stimulation contributes to the functioning of sensory systems, excessive input can be dangerous. For example, animal studies indicate that a sensitive period (see pages 23–24 in Chapter 1) exists in which the fetal ear is highly susceptible to injury. During that time, prolonged exposure to sounds that are harmless to the mature ear can permanently damage fetal inner-ear structures (Pierson, 1996).

In the final three months, the fetus gains more than 5 pounds and grows 7 inches. As it fills the uterus, it gradually moves less often. In addition, brain development, which enables the organism to inhibit behavior, contributes to a decline in physical activity (DiPietro et al., 1996). In the eighth month, a layer of fat is added to assist with temperature regulation. The fetus also receives antibodies from the mother's blood to protect against illnesses, since the newborn's own immune system will not work well until several months after birth. In the last weeks, most fetuses assume an upside-down position, partly because of the shape of the uterus and partly because the head is heavier than the feet. Growth slows, and birth is about to take place.

ASK YOURSELF

◆ REVIEW Why is the period of the embryo regarded as the most dramatic prenatal phase? Why is the period of the fetus called the "growth and finishing" phase?

◆ APPLY Amy, two months pregnant, wonders how the embryo is being fed and what parts of the body have formed. "I don't look pregnant yet, so does that mean not much development has taken place?" she asks. How would you respond to Amy?

◆ CONNECT How is brain development related to fetal capacities and behavior? What implications do individual differences in fetal behavior have for infant temperament after birth?

Prenatal Environmental Influences

Although the prenatal environment is far more constant than the world outside the womb, a great many factors can affect the embryo and fetus. Yolanda and Jay learned that parents—and society as a whole—can do a great deal to create a safe environment for development before birth.

Teratogens

The term **teratogen** refers to any environmental agent that causes damage during the prenatal period. Scientists chose this label (from the Greek word *teras,* meaning "malformation" or "monstrosity") because they first learned about harmful prenatal influences from cases in which babies had been profoundly damaged. But the harm done by teratogens is not always simple and straightforward. It depends on the following factors:

- *Dose.* As we discuss particular teratogens, you will see that larger doses over longer time periods usually have more negative effects.
- *Heredity.* The genetic makeup of the mother and the developing organism plays an important role. Some individuals are better able than others to withstand harmful environments.
- *Other negative influences.* The presence of several negative factors at once, such as additional teratogens, poor nutrition, and lack of medical care, can worsen the impact of a single harmful agent.
- *Age.* The effects of teratogens vary with the age of the organism at time of exposure. To understand this last idea, think of the *sensitive period* concept. Recall that a sensitive period is a limited time span in which a part of the body or a behavior is biologically prepared to develop rapidly. During that time, it is especially sensitive to its surroundings. If the environment is harmful, then damage occurs, and recovery is difficult and sometimes impossible.

Figure 3.5 summarizes prenatal sensitive periods. Look at it carefully, and you will see that some parts of the body, such as the brain and eye, have long sensitive periods that extend throughout prenatal development. Other sensitive periods, such as those for the limbs and palate, are much shorter. Figure 3.5 also indicates that we can make some general statements

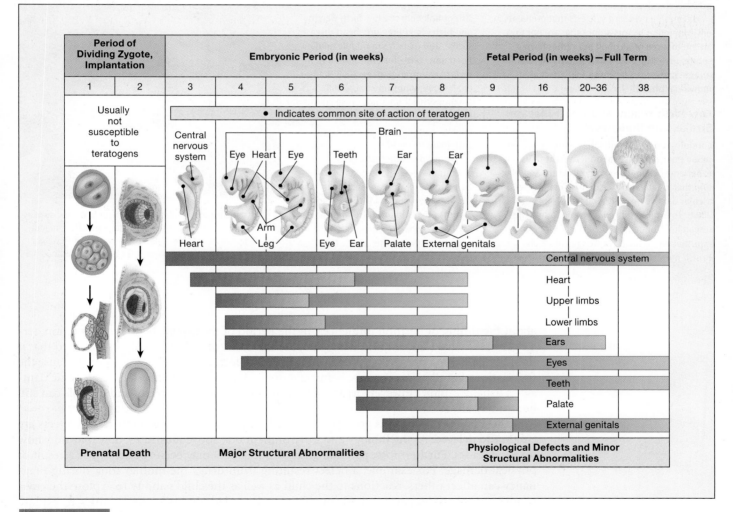

FIGURE 3.5

Sensitive periods in prenatal development. Each organ or structure has a sensitive period, during which its development may be disturbed. Blue horizontal bars indicate highly sensitive periods. Green horizontal bars indicate periods that are somewhat less sensitive to teratogens, although damage can occur. *(Adapted from* Before We Are Born, *7th ed., by K. L. Moore and T. V. N. Persaud, p. 313. Copyright © 2008, reprinted by permission from Elsevier, Inc.)*

BIOLOGY AND ENVIRONMENT

The Prenatal Environment and Health in Later Life

When Michael entered the world 55 years ago, 6 weeks premature and weighing only 4 pounds, the doctor delivering him wasn't sure he would make it. Michael not only survived but enjoyed good health until his mid-forties, when, during a routine medical checkup, he was diagnosed with high blood pressure and type 2 diabetes. Michael had no apparent risk factors for these conditions: He wasn't overweight, didn't smoke, and didn't eat high-fat foods. Nor did the illnesses run in his family. Could the roots of Michael's health problems date back to his prenatal development?

Increasing evidence suggests that prenatal environmental factors—ones that are not toxic (as are tobacco or alcohol) but rather fairly subtle, such as the flow of nutrients and hormones across the placenta—can affect an individual's health decades later.

Low Birth Weight and Heart Disease, Stroke, and Diabetes

Carefully controlled animal experiments reveal that a poorly nourished, underweight fetus experiences changes in body structure and function that greatly increase the risk of cardiovascular disease in adulthood (Franco et al., 2002). To explore this relationship in humans, researchers tapped public records, gathering information on the birth weights of 15,000 British men and women and the occurrence

of disease in middle adulthood. Those weighing less than 5 pounds at birth had a 50 percent greater chance of dying of heart disease and stroke, even after SES and a variety of other health risks were controlled. The connection between birth weight and cardiovascular disease was strongest for people whose weight-to-length ratio at birth was very low—a sign of prenatal growth stunting (Godfrey & Barker, 2000; Martyn, Barker, & Osmond, 1996).

In other large-scale studies, a consistent link between low birth weight and high blood pressure, heart disease, stroke, and diabetes in middle adulthood emerged—for both sexes and in diverse countries (Barker, 2008; Kaijser et al., 2009; Whincup et al., 2008). Smallness itself does not cause later health problems; rather, researchers believe, complex factors associated with it are involved.

Some speculate that a poorly nourished fetus diverts large amounts of blood to the brain, causing organs in the abdomen, such as the liver and kidneys (involved in controlling cholesterol and blood pressure), to be undersized (Hales & Ozanne, 2003). The result is heightened later risk of heart

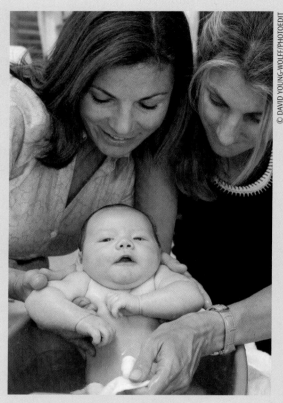

■ Prenatal environmental factors—even subtle ones, such as the flow of nutrients across the placenta—can affect an individual's health in later life. This newborn's high birth weight places her at increased risk for breast cancer in adulthood. ■

about the timing of harmful influences. In the period of the zygote, before implantation, teratogens rarely have any impact. If they do, the tiny mass of cells is usually so damaged that it dies. The *embryonic period* is the time when serious defects are most likely to occur because the foundations for all body parts are being laid down. During the *fetal period,* teratogenic damage is usually minor. However, organs such as the brain, ears, eyes, teeth, and genitals can still be strongly affected.

The effects of teratogens go beyond immediate physical damage. Some health effects are subtle and delayed. As the Biology and Environment box above illustrates, they may not show up for decades. Furthermore, psychological consequences may occur indirectly, as a result of physical damage. For example, a defect resulting from drugs the mother took during pregnancy can affect others' reactions to the child as well as the child's ability to explore the environment. Over time, parent–child interaction, peer relations, and opportunities to explore may suffer. Furthermore, prenatally exposed children may be less resilient in the face of environmental risks, such as single parenthood, parental emotional disturbance, or maladaptive parenting (Yumoto, Jacobson, & Jacobson, 2008). As a result, their long-term adjustment may be compromised.

disease and stroke. In the case of diabetes, inadequate prenatal nutrition may permanently impair functioning of the pancreas, leading glucose intolerance to rise as the person ages (Wu et al., 2004). Yet another hypothesis, supported by both animal and human research, is that the malfunctioning placentas of some expectant mothers permit high levels of stress hormones to reach the fetus, which retards fetal growth, increases fetal blood pressure, and promotes excess blood glucose, predisposing the developing person to later disease (Stocker, Arch, & Cawthorne, 2005).

Finally, prenatally growth-stunted babies often gain excessive weight in childhood, once they have access to plentiful food. This excess weight usually persists, greatly increasing the risk of diabetes (Hyppönen, Power, & Smith, 2003).

High Birth Weight and Breast Cancer

The other prenatal growth extreme—high birth weight—is linked to breast cancer, the most common malignancy in adult women (Ahlgren et al., 2004). In one study of more than 2,000 British women, high birth weight—especially weight above 8.8 pounds—was associated with a greatly increased incidence of breast cancer, even after other cancer risks were controlled (see Figure 3.6) (dos Santos Silva et al., 2004). Researchers suspect that the culprit is excessive maternal estrogen in the overweight expectant mother, which promotes large fetal size and alters the makeup of beginning breast tissue so

that it may respond to estrogen in adulthood by becoming malignant (Barker et al., 2008).

High birth weight is also associated with increases in prostate cancer in men and digestive, blood, and lymphatic cancers in both genders (Caughey & Michels, 2009; Cnattingius et al., 2009; McCormack et al., 2005). As yet, the reasons are unclear.

Prevention

The relationships between prenatal development and later-life illnesses emerging in research do not mean that the illnesses are inevitable. Rather, prenatal environmental conditions *influence* adult health, and the steps we take to protect our health can prevent prenatal risks from becoming reality. Researchers advise individuals who were low-weight or high-weight at birth to get regular medical checkups and screening tests that increase the odds of early disease detection. They also recommend consistent attention to diet, weight, fitness, and stress—controllable factors that contribute to cardiovascular disease, adult-onset diabetes, and cancer.

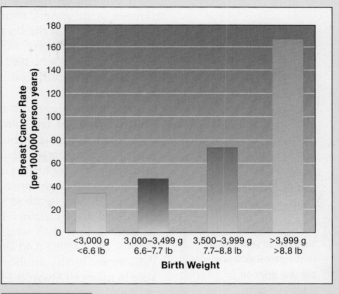

Relationship of birth weight to breast cancer risk in adulthood. In a study of more than 2,000 British births with follow-ups in adulthood, birth weight predicted breast cancer incidence after many other prenatal and postnatal health risks were controlled. The breast cancer risk was especially high for women whose birth weights were greater than 3,999 grams, or 8.8 pounds. *(Adapted from dos Santos Silva et al., 2004.)*

Notice how an important idea about development that we discussed in earlier chapters is at work here: *bidirectional influences* between child and environment. Now let's look at what scientists have discovered about a variety of teratogens.

PRESCRIPTION AND NONPRESCRIPTION DRUGS In the early 1960s, the world learned a tragic lesson about drugs and prenatal development. At that time, a sedative called *thalidomide* was widely available in Canada, Europe, and South America. When taken by mothers four to six weeks after conception, thalidomide produced gross deformities of the embryo's developing arms and legs and, less frequently, damage to the ears, heart, kidneys, and genitals. About 7,000 infants worldwide were affected (Moore & Persaud, 2008). As children exposed to thalidomide grew older, many scored below average in intelligence. Perhaps the drug damaged the central nervous system directly. Or the child-rearing conditions of these severely deformed youngsters may have impaired their intellectual development.

Another medication, a synthetic hormone called *diethylstilbestrol (DES),* was widely prescribed between 1945 and 1970 to prevent miscarriages. As daughters of these mothers reached adolescence and young adulthood, they showed unusually high rates of cancer of the vagina, malformations of the uterus, and infertility. When they tried to have children, their pregnancies more often resulted in prematurity, low birth weight, and miscarriage than those of non-DES-exposed women. Young men showed an increased risk of genital abnormalities and cancer of the testes (Hammes & Laitman, 2003; Palmer et al., 2001).

Currently, the most widely used potent teratogen is a vitamin A derivative called *Accutane* (known by the generic name *isotretinoin),* prescribed to treat severe acne. Hundreds of thousands of women of childbearing age in industrialized nations take it. Exposure during the first trimester results in eye, ear, skull, brain, heart, and immune system abnormalities (Honein, Paulozzi, & Erickson, 2001). Accutane's packaging warns users to avoid pregnancy by using two methods of birth control, but many women do not heed this advice (Garcia-Bournissen et al., 2008).

Indeed, any drug with a molecule small enough to penetrate the placental barrier can enter the embryonic or fetal bloodstream. Yet many pregnant women continue to take over-the-counter medications without consulting their doctors. Aspirin is one of the most common. Several studies suggest that regular aspirin use is linked to low birth weight, infant death around the time of birth, poorer motor development, and lower intelligence test scores in early childhood, although other research fails to confirm these findings (Barr et al., 1990; Kozer et al., 2003; Streissguth et al., 1987). Coffee, tea, cola, and cocoa contain another frequently consumed drug, caffeine. As amounts exceed 100 milligrams per day (equivalent to one cup of coffee), low birth weight and miscarriage increase (CARE Study Group, 2008; Weng, Odouli, & Li, 2008). And antidepressant medications are linked to increased risk of premature delivery and birth complications, including respiratory distress and persistent high blood pressure in infancy (Alwan & Friedman, 2009; Lund, Pedersen, & Henriksen, 2009; Oberlander et al., 2006).

Because children's lives are involved, we must take findings like these seriously. At the same time, we cannot be sure that these frequently used drugs actually cause the problems just mentioned. Often mothers take more than one drug. If the embryo or fetus is injured, it is hard to tell which drug might be responsible or whether other factors correlated with drug taking are really at fault. Until we have more information, the safest course is the one Yolanda took: Avoid these drugs entirely. Unfortunately, many women do not know that they are pregnant during the early weeks of the embryonic period, when exposure to medications (and other teratogens) can be of greatest threat.

ILLEGAL DRUGS The use of highly addictive mood-altering drugs, such as cocaine and heroin, has become more widespread, especially in poverty-stricken inner-city areas, where these drugs provide a temporary escape from a daily life of hopelessness. Nearly 4 percent of U.S. pregnant women take these substances (U.S. Department of Health and Human Services, 2007a).

Babies born to users of cocaine, heroin, or methadone (a less addictive drug used to wean people away from heroin) are at risk for a wide variety of problems, including prematurity, low birth weight, physical defects, breathing difficulties, and death around the time of birth (Behnke et al., 2001; Howell, Coles, & Kable, 2008; Schuetze & Eiden, 2006). In addition, these infants are born drug-addicted. They are often feverish and irritable and have trouble sleeping, and their cries are abnormally shrill and piercing—a common symptom among stressed newborns (Bauer et al., 2005). When mothers with many problems of their own must care for these babies, who are difficult to calm, cuddle, and feed, behavior problems are likely to persist.

Throughout the first year, heroin- and methadone-exposed infants are less attentive to the environment than nonexposed babies, and their motor development is slow. After infancy, some children get better, while others remain jittery and inattentive (Cosden, Peerson, & Elliott, 1997). The kind of parenting they receive may explain why problems persist for some but not for others (Hans & Jeremy, 2001).

Evidence on cocaine suggests that some prenatally exposed babies develop lasting difficulties. Cocaine constricts the blood vessels, causing oxygen delivered to the developing organism to fall for 15 minutes following a high dose. It also can alter the production and functioning of neurons and the chemical balance in the fetus's brain. These effects may contribute to an array of cocaine-associated physical defects, including eye, bone, genital, urinary tract, kidney, and heart deformities; brain hemorrhages and seizures; and severe growth retardation (Covington et al., 2002; Feng, 2005; Mayes, 1999). Some studies report perceptual, motor, attention, memory, language, and impulse-control problems that persist into the preschool years (Dennis et al., 2006; Lester et al., 2003; Linares et al., 2006; Noland et al., 2005; Singer et al., 2004).

But other investigations reveal no major negative effects of prenatal cocaine exposure (Behnke et al., 2006; Frank et al., 2005; Hurt et al., 2005). These contradictory findings indicate how difficult it is to isolate the precise damage caused by illegal drugs. Cocaine users vary greatly in the amount, potency, and purity of the cocaine they ingest. Also, they often take several drugs, display other high-risk behaviors, suffer from poverty and other stresses, and engage in insensitive caregiving—factors that worsen outcomes for children (Jones, 2006). But researchers have yet to determine exactly what accounts for findings of cocaine-related damage in some studies but not in others.

Another illegal drug, marijuana, is used more widely than heroin and cocaine. Studies examining its relationship to low birth weight and prematurity reveal mixed findings (Fried, 1993). Several researchers have linked prenatal marijuana exposure to smaller head size (a measure of brain growth); to sleep, attention, memory, and academic achievement difficulties and to depression in childhood; and to poorer problem-solving performance in adolescence (Dahl et al., 1995; Goldschmidt et al., 2004; Gray et al., 2005; Huizink & Mulder, 2006). As with cocaine, however, lasting consequences are not well-established. Overall, the effects of illegal drugs are far less consistent than the impact of two legal substances to which we now turn: tobacco and alcohol.

■ This 3-day-old infant, who was born many weeks before his due date, breathes with the aid of a respirator. Prematurity and low birth weight can result from a variety of environmental influences during pregnancy, including maternal drug use and cigarette smoking. ■

TOBACCO   Although smoking has declined in Western nations, an estimated 14 percent of U.S. women smoke during their pregnancies (Tong et al., 2009). The best-known effect of smoking during the prenatal period is low birth weight. But the likelihood of other serious consequences, such as miscarriage, prematurity, impaired heart rate and breathing during sleep, infant death, and asthma and cancer later in childhood, is also increased (Howell, Coles, & Kable, 2008; Jaakkola & Gissler, 2004). The more cigarettes a mother smokes, the greater the chances that her baby will be affected. If a pregnant woman decides to stop smoking at any time, even during the last trimester, she reduces the likelihood that her infant will be born underweight and suffer from future problems (Klesges et al., 2001).

Even when a baby of a smoking mother appears to be born in good physical condition, slight behavioral abnormalities may threaten the child's development. Newborns of smoking mothers are less attentive to sounds, display more muscle tension, are more excitable when touched and visually stimulated, and more often have colic (persistent crying). These findings suggest subtle negative effects on brain development (Law et al., 2003; Sondergaard et al., 2002). Consistent with this view, prenatally exposed children and adolescents tend to have shorter attention spans, difficulties with impulsivity and overactivity, poorer memories, lower mental test scores, and more externalizing behavior problems (Fryer, Crocker, & Mattson, 2008; Huizink & Mulder, 2006; Nigg & Breslau, 2007; Rogers, 2009).

Exactly how can smoking harm the fetus? Nicotine, the addictive substance in tobacco, constricts blood vessels, lessens blood flow to the uterus, and causes the placenta to grow abnormally. This reduces the transfer of nutrients, so the fetus gains weight poorly. Also, nicotine raises the concentration of carbon monoxide in the bloodstreams of both mother and fetus. Carbon monoxide displaces oxygen from red blood cells, damaging the central nervous system and slowing body growth in the fetuses of laboratory animals. Similar effects may occur in humans. Also, recall from Chapter 2 that nicotine-exposed fetuses with a certain genotype are at high risk for becoming impulsive, overactive, and oppositional children and adolescents (see page 87).

From one-third to one-half of nonsmoking pregnant women are "passive smokers" because their husbands, relatives, or co-workers use cigarettes. Passive smoking is also related to low birth weight, infant death, childhood respiratory illnesses, and possible long-term attention, learning, and behavior problems (Hanke, Sobala, & Kalinka, 2004; Makin, Fried, & Watkinson, 1991; Pattenden et al., 2006). Clearly, expectant mothers should avoid smoke-filled environments.

ALCOHOL   In his moving book *The Broken Cord*, Michael Dorris (1989), a Dartmouth College anthropology professor, described what it was like to raise his adopted son Abel (called Adam in the book), whose biological mother drank heavily throughout pregnancy and died of alcohol poisoning shortly after his birth. A Sioux Indian, Abel was born with **fetal alcohol spectrum disorder (FASD),** a term that encompasses a range of physical, mental, and behavioral outcomes caused by prenatal alcohol exposure. As Table 3.4 shows, children with FASD are given one of three diagnoses, which vary in severity:

1. **Fetal alcohol syndrome (FAS),** distinguished by (a) slow physical growth, (b) a pattern of three facial abnormalities (short eyelid openings; a thin upper lip; a smooth or flattened philtrum, or indentation running from the bottom of the nose to the center of the upper lip), and (c) brain injury, evident in a small head and impairment in at least three areas of functioning—for example, memory, language and communication, attention span and activity level (overactivity), planning and reasoning, motor coordination, or social skills. Other defects—of the eyes, ears, nose, throat, heart, genitals, urinary tract, or immune system—may also be present. Abel was diagnosed as having FAS. As is typical for this disorder, his mother drank heavily throughout pregnancy.
2. **Partial fetal alcohol syndrome (p-FAS),** characterized by (a) two of the three facial abnormalities just mentioned and (b) brain injury, again evident in at least three areas of impaired functioning. Mothers of children with p-FAS generally drank alcohol in smaller quantities, and children's defects vary with the timing and length of alcohol exposure. Furthermore, recent evidence suggests that paternal alcohol use around the time of conception can alter gene expression (see page 86 in Chapter 2), thereby contributing to symptoms (Ouko et al., 2009).

■ This toddler's mother drank heavily during pregnancy. Her widely spaced eyes, thin upper lip, and short eyelid openings are typical of fetal alcohol syndrome (FAS). ■

■ This 11-year-old girl also has the facial abnormalities of FAS and shows the slow physical growth that accompanies the disorder. ■

| TABLE 3.4 | Fetal Alcohol Spectrum Disorder: Criteria for Diagnosis |

	DIAGNOSTIC CATEGORY		
Criteria	**FAS**	**p-FAS**	**ARND**
Slow physical growth	Yes	No	No
Facial abnormalities: • Short eyelid openings • Thin upper lip • Smooth or flattened philtrum	All three are present	Two of the three are present	None are present
Brain injury	Impairment in a minimum of three areas of functioning	Impairment in a minimum of three areas of functioning	Impairment in a minimum of three areas of functioning

Source: Loock et al., 2005.

3. **Alcohol-related neurodevelopmental disorder (ARND),** in which at least three areas of mental functioning are impaired, despite typical physical growth and absence of facial abnormalities. Again, prenatal alcohol exposure, though confirmed, is less pervasive than in FAS (Chudley et al., 2005; Loock et al., 2005).

Even when provided with enriched diets, FAS babies fail to catch up in physical size during infancy or childhood. Mental impairment associated with all three FASD diagnoses is also permanent: In his teens and twenties, Abel Dorris had trouble concentrating and keeping a routine job, and he suffered from poor judgment. For example, he would buy something and not wait for change or would wander off in the middle of a task. He died in 1991, at age 23, after being hit by a car.

The more alcohol a woman consumes during pregnancy, the poorer the child's motor coordination, speed of information processing, reasoning, and intelligence and achievement test scores during the preschool and school years (Burden, Jacobson, & Jacobson, 2005; Korkman, Kettunen, & Autti-Raemoe, 2003; Mattson, Calarco, & Lang, 2006). In adolescence and early adulthood, FASD is associated with persisting attention and motor-coordination deficits, poor school performance, trouble with the law, inappropriate sexual behavior, alcohol and drug abuse, and lasting mental health problems (Barr et al., 2006; Fryer, Crocker, & Mattson, 2008; Howell et al., 2006; Streissguth et al., 2004).

How does alcohol produce its devastating effects? First, it interferes with production and migration of neurons in the primitive neural tube. Brain-imaging research reveals reduced brain size, damage to many brain structures, and abnormalities in brain functioning, including the electrical and chemical activity involved in transferring messages from one part of the brain to another (Riley, McGee, & Sowell, 2004; Spadoni et al., 2007). Second, the body uses large quantities of oxygen to metabolize alcohol. A pregnant woman's heavy drinking draws away oxygen that the developing organism needs for cell growth.

About 25 percent of U.S. mothers reported drinking at some time during their pregnancies. As with heroin and cocaine, alcohol abuse is higher in poverty-stricken women. On some Native-American reservations, the incidence of FAS is as high as 10 to 20 percent (Szlemko, Wood, & Thurman, 2006; U.S. Department of Health and Human Services, 2007a). Unfortunately, when affected girls later become pregnant, the poor judgment caused by the syndrome often prevents them from understanding why they themselves should avoid alcohol. Thus, the tragic cycle is likely to be repeated in the next generation.

How much alcohol is safe during pregnancy? Even mild drinking, less than one drink per day, is associated with reduced head size and body growth among children followed into adolescence (Jacobson et al., 2004; Martinez-Frias et al., 2004). Recall that other factors—both genetic and environmental—can make some fetuses more vulnerable to teratogens. Therefore, no amount of alcohol is safe. Couples planning a pregnancy and expectant mothers should avoid alcohol entirely.

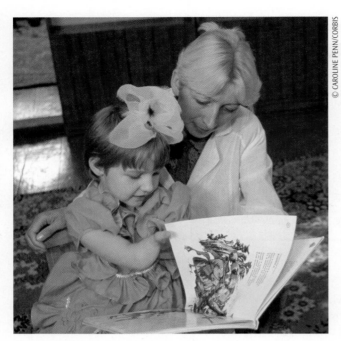

■ This child's deformities are linked to radiation exposure during the Chernobyl nuclear power plant disaster of 1986. Her mother was just a few weeks pregnant at the time. Prenatal radiation exposure also increased the risk of low intelligence and language and emotional disorders. ■

RADIATION   In Chapter 2, we saw that ionizing radiation can cause mutation, damaging DNA in ova and sperm. When mothers are exposed to radiation during pregnancy, the embryo or fetus can suffer additional harm. Defects due to radiation were tragically apparent in children born to pregnant women who survived the bombing of Hiroshima and Nagasaki during World War II. Similar abnormalities surfaced in the nine months following the 1986 Chernobyl, Ukraine, nuclear power plant accident. After each disaster, the incidence of miscarriage and babies born with underdeveloped brains, physical deformities, and slow physical growth rose dramatically (Hoffmann, 2001; Schull, 2003).

Even when a radiation-exposed baby seems normal, problems may appear later. For example, even low-level radiation, as the result of industrial leakage or medical X-rays, can increase the risk of childhood cancer (Fattibene et al., 1999). In middle childhood, prenatally exposed Chernobyl children had abnormal brain-wave activity, lower intelligence test scores, and rates of language and emotional disorders two to three times greater than those of nonexposed Russian children. Furthermore, the more tension parents reported, due to forced evacuation from their homes and worries about living in irradiated areas, the poorer their children's emotional functioning (Loganovskaja & Loganovsky, 1999; Loganovsky et al., 2008). Stressful rearing conditions seemed to combine with the damaging effects of prenatal radiation to impair children's development.

Women should do their best to avoid medical X-rays during pregnancy. If dental, thyroid, chest, or other X-rays are necessary, insisting on the use of an abdominal X-ray shield is a key protective measure.

ENVIRONMENTAL POLLUTION   In industrialized nations, an astounding number of potentially dangerous chemicals are released into the environment. More than 75,000 are in common use in the United States, and many new pollutants are introduced each year. When 10 newborns were randomly selected from U.S. hospitals for analysis of umbilical cord blood, researchers uncovered a startling array of industrial contaminants—287 in all! They concluded that many babies are "born polluted" by chemicals that not only impair prenatal development but also increase the chances of life-threatening diseases and health problems later on (Houlihan et al., 2005).

In the 1950s, an industrial plant released waste containing high levels of *mercury* into a bay providing seafood and water for the town of Minamata, Japan. Many children born at the time displayed physical deformities, mental retardation, abnormal speech, difficulty in chewing and swallowing, and uncoordinated movements. High levels of prenatal mercury exposure disrupt production and migration of neurons, causing widespread brain damage (Clarkson, Magos, & Myers, 2003; Hubbs-Tait et al., 2005). Pregnant women are wise to avoid eating long-lived predatory fish, such as swordfish, albacore tuna, and shark, which are heavily contaminated with mercury.

For many years, *polychlorinated biphenyls (PCBs)* were used to insulate electrical equipment, until research showed that, like mercury, they found their way into waterways and entered the food supply. In Taiwan, prenatal exposure to very high levels of PCBs in rice oil resulted in low birth weight, discolored skin, deformities of the gums and nails, brain-wave abnormalities, and delayed cognitive development (Chen & Hsu, 1994; Chen et al., 1994). Steady, low-level PCB exposure is also harmful. Women who frequently ate PCB-contaminated fish, compared with those who ate little or no fish, had infants with lower birth weights, smaller heads, persisting attention and memory difficulties, and lower intelligence test scores in childhood (Boucher, Muckle, & Bastien, 2009; Jacobson & Jacobson, 2003; Stewart et al., 2008).

Another teratogen, *lead,* is present in paint flaking off the walls of old buildings and in certain materials used in industrial occupations. High levels of prenatal lead exposure are consistently related to prematurity, low birth weight, brain damage, and a wide variety of physical defects. Even low levels may be dangerous. In some studies, affected babies showed slightly poorer mental and motor development (Bellinger, 2005). In one investigation, unfavorable effects—in the form of increased delinquent and antisocial behaviors—were evident in adolescence (Dietrich et al., 2001).

Finally, prenatal exposure to *dioxins*—toxic compounds resulting from incineration—is linked to brain, immune system, and thyroid damage in babies and to an increased incidence of breast and uterine cancers in women, perhaps through altering hormone levels (ten Tusscher & Koppe, 2004). Furthermore, even tiny amounts of dioxin in the paternal bloodstream cause a dramatic change in sex ratio of offspring: Affected men father nearly twice as many girls as boys (Ishihara et al., 2007; Mocarell et al., 2000). Dioxin seems to impair the fertility of Y-bearing sperm prior to conception.

INFECTIOUS DISEASE   During her first prenatal visit, Yolanda's doctor asked her if she and Jay had already had measles, mumps, chickenpox, and several other illnesses. In addition, Yolanda was checked for the presence of several infections—and for good reason. As you can see in Table 3.5, certain diseases are major causes of miscarriage and birth defects.

Viruses. In the mid-1960s, a worldwide epidemic of *rubella* (three-day, or German, measles) led to the birth of more than 20,000 American babies with serious defects and to 13,000 fetal and newborn deaths. Consistent with the sensitive-period concept, the greatest damage occurs when rubella strikes during the embryonic period. More than 50 percent of infants whose mothers become ill during that time show deafness; eye deformities, including cataracts; heart, genital, urinary, intestinal, bone, and dental defects; and mental retardation. Infection during the fetal period is less harmful, but low birth weight, hearing loss, and bone defects may still

TABLE 3.5   Effects of Some Infectious Diseases During Pregnancy

DISEASE	MISCARRIAGE	PHYSICAL MALFORMATIONS	MENTAL RETARDATION	LOW BIRTH WEIGHT AND PREMATURITY
VIRAL				
Acquired immune deficiency syndrome (AIDS)	0	?	+	?
Chickenpox	0	+	+	+
Cytomegalovirus	+	+	+	+
Herpes simplex 2 (genital herpes)	+	+	+	+
Mumps	+	?	0	0
Rubella (German measles)	+	+	+	+
BACTERIAL				
Chlamydia	+	?	0	+
Syphilis	+	+	+	?
Tuberculosis	+	?	+	+
PARASITIC				
Malaria	+	0	0	+
Toxoplasmosis	+	+	+	+

+ = established finding; 0 = no present evidence; ? = possible effect that is not clearly established.

Sources: Jones, Lopez, & Wilson, 2003; Kliegman et al., 2008; Mardh, 2002; O'Rahilly & Müller, 2001.

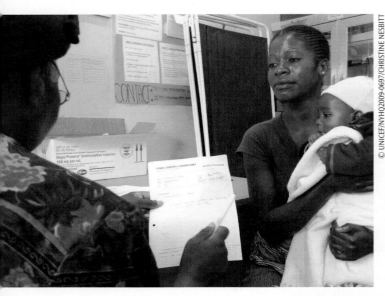

■ In Zambia, Africa, a mother who is HIV-positive learns that her 11-week-old infant tested negative for the virus. The baby benefited from prenatal and post-birth antiviral drug treatment, provided by a UNICEF-sponsored clinic that focuses on preventing HIV transmission from mother to child. ■

occur. The organ damage inflicted by prenatal rubella often leads to lifelong health problems, including severe mental illness, diabetes, cardiovascular disease, and thyroid and immune-system dysfunction in adulthood (Brown, 2006; Duszak, 2009). Routine vaccination in infancy and childhood has made new rubella outbreaks unlikely in industrialized nations. But an estimated 100,000 cases of prenatal infection continue to occur each year, primarily in developing countries in Africa and Asia with weak or absent immunization programs (Robinson et al., 2006).

The *human immunodeficiency virus (HIV)*, which can lead to *acquired immune deficiency syndrome (AIDS)*, a disease that destroys the immune system, has infected increasing numbers of women over the past two decades. Currently, women account for one-fourth of cases in North America, Western Europe, and East Asia. Although the incidence of AIDS has declined in industrialized nations, the disease is rampant in developing countries, where 95 percent of new infections occur, more than half of which affect women. In South Africa, for example, nearly 30 percent of all pregnant women are HIV-positive (Quinn & Overbaugh, 2005; South African Department of Health, 2009). HIV-infected expectant mothers pass the deadly virus to the fetus 20 to 30 percent of the time.

AIDS progresses rapidly in infants. By 6 months, weight loss, diarrhea, and repeated respiratory illnesses are common. The virus also causes brain damage, as indicated by seizures, gradual loss in brain weight, and delayed mental and motor development. Nearly half of prenatal AIDS babies die by 1 year of age and 90 percent by age 3 (Devi et al., 2009). The antiviral drug zidovudine (ZDV) reduces prenatal AIDS transmission by as much as 95 percent, with no harmful consequences of drug treatment for children (Culnane et al., 1999). ZDV has led to a dramatic decline in prenatally acquired AIDS in Western nations. Although distribution is increasing, the drug is still not widely available in impoverished regions of the world (UNICEF, 2009b).

As Table 3.5 reveals, the developing organism is especially sensitive to the family of herpes viruses, for which no vaccine or treatment exists. Among these, *cytomegalovirus* (the most frequent prenatal infection, transmitted through respiratory or sexual contact, often without symptoms) and *herpes simplex 2* (which is sexually transmitted) are especially dangerous. In both, the virus invades the mother's genital tract, infecting babies either during pregnancy or at birth. Both diseases often have no symptoms, very mild symptoms, or symptoms with which people are unfamiliar, thereby increasing the likelihood of contagion. Pregnant women who are not in a mutually monogamous relationship are at greatest risk.

Bacterial and Parasitic Diseases. Table 3.5 also includes several bacterial and parasitic diseases. Among the most common is *toxoplasmosis,* an infection caused by a parasite found in many animals. Pregnant women may become infected from eating raw or undercooked meat or from contact with the feces of infected cats. About 40 percent of women who have the disease transmit it to the developing organism. If it strikes during the first trimester, it is likely to cause eye and brain damage. Infection during the second and third trimesters is linked to mild visual and cognitive impairments. And about 80 percent of affected newborns with no obvious signs of damage develop learning or visual disabilities in later life (Jones, Lopez, & Wilson, 2003). Expectant mothers can avoid toxoplasmosis by making sure that the meat they eat is well-cooked, having pet cats checked for the disease, and turning over the care of litter boxes to other family members.

Other Maternal Factors

Besides avoiding teratogens, expectant parents can support the embryo and fetus in other ways. Regular exercise, good nutrition, and emotional well-being of the mother are essential. Problems that may result from maternal and fetal blood type differences can be prevented.

Finally, many prospective parents wonder how a mother's age affects the course of pregnancy. We examine each of these factors in the following sections.

EXERCISE Yolanda continued her half-hour of aerobics three times a week into the third trimester, although her doctor cautioned against bouncing, jolting, and jogging movements that might subject the fetus to too many shocks and startles. In healthy, physically fit women, regular moderate exercise, such as walking, swimming, biking, or an aerobic workout, is related to increased birth weight and a reduction in risk for certain complications, such as pregnancy-induced maternal diabetes and high blood pressure (Leiferman & Evenson, 2003; Olson et al., 2009). However, frequent, vigorous, extended exercise—working up a sweat for more than 30 minutes, four or five days a week, especially late in pregnancy—results in lower birth weight than in healthy, nonexercising controls (Clapp et al., 2002; Leet & Flick, 2003). Hospital-sponsored childbirth education programs frequently offer exercise classes and suggest appropriate routines that help prepare for labor and delivery.

During the last trimester, when the abdomen grows very large, mothers have difficulty moving freely and often must cut back on exercise. Most women, however, do not engage in sufficient moderate exercise during pregnancy to promote their own and their baby's health (Hausenblas & Downs, 2005). An expectant mother who remains fit experiences fewer physical discomforts, such as back pain, upward pressure on the chest, or difficulty breathing in the final weeks.

Pregnant women with health problems, such as circulatory difficulties or a history of miscarriages, should consult their doctor about a physical fitness routine. For these mothers, exercise (especially the wrong kind) can endanger the pregnancy.

NUTRITION During the prenatal period, when children are growing more rapidly than at any other time, they depend totally on the mother for nutrients. A healthy diet, consisting of a gradual increase in calories—an extra 100 calories a day in the first trimester, 265 in the second, and 430 in the third—resulting in a weight gain of 25 to 30 pounds (10 to 13.5 kilograms), helps ensure the health of mother and baby.

Consequences of Prenatal Malnutrition. During World War II, a severe famine occurred in the Netherlands, giving scientists a rare opportunity to study the impact of nutrition on prenatal development. Findings revealed that the sensitive-period concept operates with nutrition, just as it does with teratogens. Women affected by the famine during the first trimester were more likely to have miscarriages or give birth to babies with physical defects. When women were past the first trimester, fetuses usually survived, but many were born underweight and had small heads (Stein et al., 1975).

Prenatal malnutrition can cause serious damage to the central nervous system. The poorer the mother's diet, the greater the loss in brain weight, especially if malnutrition occurred during the third trimester. During that time, the brain is increasing rapidly in size, and for it to reach its full potential, the mother must have a diet high in all the basic nutrients (Morgane et al., 1993). An inadequate diet during pregnancy can also distort the structure of other organs, including the liver, kidney, and pancreas, resulting in lifelong health problems (refer again to the Biology and Environment box on pages 104–105).

Because poor nutrition suppresses development of the immune system, prenatally malnourished babies frequently catch respiratory illnesses (Chandra, 1991). In addition, they often are irritable and unresponsive to stimulation. Like drug-addicted newborns, they have a high-pitched cry that is particularly distressing to their caregivers. In poverty-stricken families, these effects quickly combine with a stressful home life. With age, low intelligence test scores and serious learning problems become more apparent (Pollitt, 1996).

Prevention and Treatment. Many studies show that providing pregnant women with adequate food has a substantial impact on the health of their

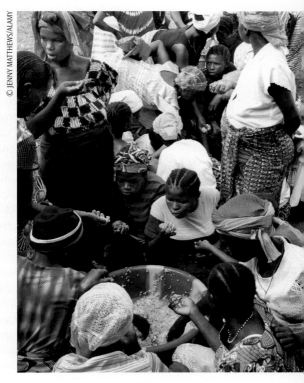

■ These pregnant women of Sierra Leone share a healthy meal they prepared together. They are members of a support group that seeks to improve maternal and infant health by preventing prenatal malnutrition. ■

newborn babies. Yet the growth demands of the prenatal period require more than just increased quantity of food. Vitamin–mineral enrichment is also crucial. For example, taking a folic acid supplement around the time of conception reduces by more than 70 percent abnormalities of the neural tube, such as *anencephaly* and *spina bifida* (see Table 2.5 on page 64). Folic acid supplementation early in pregnancy also reduces the risk of other physical defects, including cleft lip and palate, urinary tract abnormalities, and limb deformities. Furthermore, adequate folic acid intake during the last 10 weeks of pregnancy cuts in half the risk of premature delivery and low birth weight (Goh & Koren, 2008; MCR Vitamin Study Research Group, 1991; Scholl, Hediger, & Belsky, 1996).

Because of these findings, U.S. government guidelines recommend that all women of childbearing age consume 0.4 milligrams of folic acid per day. For women who have previously had a pregnancy affected by neural tube defect, the recommended amount is 4 or 5 milligrams (dosage must be carefully monitored, as excessive intake can be harmful) (American Academy of Pediatrics, 2006). About half of U.S. pregnancies are unplanned, so government regulations mandate that bread, flour, rice, pasta, and other grain products be fortified with folic acid.

Other vitamins and minerals also have established benefits. Enriching women's diets with calcium helps prevent maternal high blood pressure and premature births. Adequate magnesium and zinc reduce the risk of many prenatal and birth complications (Durlach, 2004; Kontic-Vucinic, Sulovic, & Radunovic, 2006). Fortifying table salt with iodine virtually eradicates *cretinism*—a condition of stunted growth and cognitive impairment, caused by prenatal iodine deficiency, that is a common cause of mental retardation in many parts of the world (Williams, 2008). And sufficient vitamin C and iron beginning early in pregnancy promote growth of the placenta and healthy birth weight (Mathews, Yudkin, & Neil, 1999). Nevertheless, a supplement program should complement, not replace, efforts to improve maternal diets during pregnancy. For women who do not get enough food or an adequate variety of foods, multivitamin tablets are a necessary, but not a sufficient, intervention.

When poor nutrition continues throughout pregnancy, infants usually require more than dietary improvement. In response to their tired, restless behavior, parents tend to be less sensitive and stimulating. The babies, in turn, become even more passive and withdrawn. Successful interventions must break this cycle of apathetic caregiver–baby interaction. Some do so by teaching parents how to interact effectively with their infants; others focus on stimulating infants to promote active engagement with their physical and social surroundings (Grantham-McGregor et al., 1994; Grantham-McGregor, Schofield, & Powell, 1987).

Although prenatal malnutrition is highest in poverty-stricken regions of the world, it is not limited to developing countries. The U.S. Special Supplemental Food Program for Women, Infants, and Children (WIC), which provides food packages and nutrition education to low-income pregnant women, reaches about 90 percent of those who qualify because of their extremely low incomes (U.S. Department of Agriculture, 2009). But many U.S. women who need nutrition intervention are not eligible for WIC.

EMOTIONAL STRESS When women experience severe emotional stress during pregnancy, their babies are at risk for a wide variety of difficulties. Intense anxiety—especially during the first two trimesters—is associated with higher rates of miscarriage, prematurity, low birth weight, infant respiratory and digestive illnesses, colic (persistent infant crying), sleep disturbances, and irritability during the child's first three years (Field et al., 2007; Huizink, Mulder, & Buitelaar, 2004; Lazinski, Shea, & Steiner, 2008; van der Wal, van Eijsden, & Bonsel, 2007). Prenatal stress is also related to several commonly occurring physical defects, such as cleft lip and palate, heart deformities, and pyloric stenosis (tightening of the infant's stomach outlet, which often must be treated surgically) (Carmichael & Shaw, 2000).

How can maternal stress affect the developing organism? **TAKE A MOMENT...** To understand this process, list the changes you sensed in your own body the last time you were under stress. When we experience fear and anxiety, stimulant hormones released into our bloodstream cause us to be "poised for action." Large amounts of blood are sent to parts of the body involved in the defensive response—the brain, the heart, and muscles in the arms, legs, and trunk. Blood flow to other organs, including the uterus, is reduced. As a result, the fetus is deprived of a full supply of oxygen and nutrients.

Maternal stress hormones also cross the placenta, causing a dramatic rise in fetal stress hormones (evident in the amniotic fluid) and in fetal heart rate, blood pressure, and activity level (Monk et al., 2000, 2004; Weinstock, 2008). Excessive fetal stress may permanently alter neurological functioning, thereby heightening stress reactivity in later life. In one study, researchers identified mothers who had been directly exposed to the September 11, 2001, World Trade Center collapse during their pregnancies. At age 9 months, their babies were tested for saliva concentrations of *cortisol,* a hormone involved in regulating the stress response. Infants whose mothers had reacted to the disaster with severe anxiety had cortisol levels that were abnormally low—a symptom of reduced physiological capacity to manage stress. Consistent with this finding, these 9-month-olds showed greater distress when confronted with novel stimuli than did other infants (Brand et al., 2006; Yehuda et al., 2005). Maternal emotional stress during pregnancy also predicts anxiety, short attention span, anger, aggression, overactivity, and lower mental test scores among preschool and school-age children, above and beyond the impact of other risks, such as maternal smoking during pregnancy, low birth weight, postnatal maternal anxiety, and low SES (de Weerth & Buitelaar, 2005; Gutteling et al., 2006; Lazinski, Shea, & Steiner, 2008; Van den Bergh, 2004).

But stress-related prenatal complications are greatly reduced when mothers have partners, other family members, and friends who offer social support (Glover, Bergman, & O'Connor, 2008). The relationship of social support to positive pregnancy outcomes and subsequent child development is particularly strong for low-income women, who often lead highly stressful lives (see the Social Issues: Health box on page 116) (Olds et al., 2002, 2004).

BLOOD INCOMPATIBILITY   When the inherited blood types of mother and fetus differ, serious problems sometimes result. The most common cause of these difficulties is **Rh factor incompatibility.** When the mother is Rh-negative (lacks the Rh blood protein) and the father is Rh-positive (has the protein), the baby may inherit the father's Rh-positive blood type. (Recall from Table 2.2 on page 57 that Rh-positive blood is dominant and Rh-negative blood is recessive, so the chances are good that a baby will be Rh-positive.) If even a little of a fetus's Rh-positive blood crosses the placenta into the Rh-negative mother's bloodstream, she begins to form antibodies to the foreign Rh protein. If these enter the fetus's system, they destroy red blood cells, reducing the oxygen supply to organs and tissues. Mental retardation, miscarriage, heart damage, and infant death can occur.

It takes time for the mother to produce Rh antibodies, so firstborn children are rarely affected. The danger increases with each additional pregnancy. Fortunately, Rh incompatibility can be prevented in most cases. After the birth of each Rh-positive baby, Rh-negative mothers are routinely given a vaccine to prevent the buildup of antibodies. In emergency cases, blood transfusions can be performed immediately after delivery or, if necessary, even before birth.

MATERNAL AGE AND PREVIOUS BIRTHS   In Chapter 2, we noted that women who delay childbearing until their thirties or forties face increased risk of infertility, miscarriage, and babies born with chromosomal defects. Are other pregnancy complications also more common for older mothers? Research consistently indicates that healthy women in their thirties have about the same rates as those in their twenties (Bianco et al., 1996; Dildy et al., 1996; Prysak, Lorenz, & Kisly, 1995). Thereafter, as Figure 3.7 reveals, complication rates increase, with a sharp rise among women age 50 to 55—an age at which, because of menopause (end of menstruation) and aging reproductive organs, few women can conceive naturally (Salihu et al., 2003; Usta & Nassar, 2008).

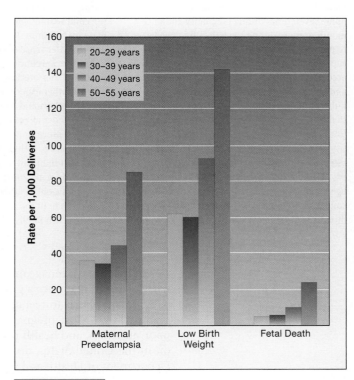

FIGURE 3.7

Relationship of maternal age to prenatal and birth complications. Complications increase after age 40, with a sharp rise between 50 and 55 years. See page 117 for a description of preeclampsia. *(Adapted from Salihu et al., 2003.)*

SOCIAL ISSUES: HEALTH

The Nurse–Family Partnership: Reducing Maternal Stress and Enhancing Child Development Through Social Support

At age 17, Denise—an unemployed high-school dropout living with her disapproving parents—gave birth to Tara. Having no one to turn to for help during pregnancy and beyond, Denise felt overwhelmed and anxious much of the time. Tara was premature and cried uncontrollably, slept erratically, and suffered from frequent minor illnesses throughout her first year. When she reached school age, she had trouble keeping up academically, and her teachers described her as distractible, unable to sit still, angry, and uncooperative.

The Nurse–Family Partnership, currently implemented in hundreds of counties across 29 U.S. states, is a voluntary home visiting program for first-time, low-income expectant mothers like Denise. Its goals are to reduce pregnancy and birth complications, promote competent early caregiving, and improve family conditions, thereby protecting children from lasting adjustment difficulties. A registered nurse visits the home seven times during pregnancy and once a month or more during the baby's first two years to provide the mother with intensive social support—a sympathetic ear; assistance in accessing health and other community services and the help of family members (especially fathers and grandmothers); and encouragement to finish high school, find work, and engage in future family planning.

To evaluate the program's effectiveness, researchers randomly assigned over 1,000 mothers at risk for high prenatal stress (due to teenage pregnancy, poverty, and other negative life conditions) to nurse-visiting or comparison conditions (just prenatal care, or prenatal care plus infant referral for developmental problems). Families were followed through their child's first three years of elementary school (Olds et al., 2004, 2007).

As kindergartners, Nurse–Family Partnership children obtained higher language and intelligence test scores. And at both ages 6 and 9, children of home-visited mothers in the poorest mental health during pregnancy exceeded comparison children in academic achievement and displayed fewer behavior problems. Furthermore, from their baby's birth on, home-visited mothers were on a more favorable life course: They had fewer subsequent births, longer intervals between their first and second births, more frequent contact with the child's father, more stable intimate partnerships, less welfare dependence, and a greater sense of control over their lives— key factors in reducing subsequent prenatal stress and in protecting children's development.

In another experiment involving over 700 at-risk mothers and babies, professional nurses were far more effective than trained paraprofessionals in preventing outcomes associated with prenatal stress, including high infant fearfulness to novel stimuli and delayed mental development (Olds et al., 2002). Nurses were probably more proficient in individualizing program guidelines to fit the strengths and challenges faced by each family. They also might have

■ Through the Nurse–Family Partnership, this 15-year-old first-time mother-to-be receives regular home visits from a registered nurse, which will continue after her baby is born. In follow-up research, the children of home-visited mothers developed more favorably—cognitively, emotionally, and socially—than did comparison children whose mothers did not receive this individualized intervention. ■

had unique legitimacy as experts in the eyes of stressed mothers, more easily convincing them to take steps to reduce pregnancy complications that can trigger persisting developmental problems—such as those Tara displayed.

The Nurse–Family Partnership is highly cost-effective. For $1 spent, it saves more than $5 in public spending on pregnancy complications, preterm births, and child and youth learning and behavior problems (Dawley, Loch, & Bindrich, 2007). To find out more about the Nurse–Family Partnership, visit *www.nursefamilypartnership.org*.

In the case of teenage mothers, does physical immaturity cause prenatal problems? Nature tries to ensure that once a girl can conceive, she is physically ready to carry and give birth to a baby. Infants born to teenagers have a higher rate of problems, but not directly because of maternal age. Most pregnant teenagers come from low-income backgrounds, where stress, poor nutrition, and health problems are common. Also, many are afraid to seek medical care or, in the United States, do not have access to care because they lack health insurance (U.S. Department of Health and Human Services, 2009b).

The Importance of Prenatal Health Care

Yolanda had her first prenatal appointment three weeks after missing her menstrual period. After that, she visited the doctor's office once a month until she was seven months pregnant, then twice during the eighth month. As birth grew near, Yolanda's appointments increased to once a week. The doctor kept track of her general health, her weight gain, and the capacity of her uterus and cervix to support the fetus. The fetus's growth was also carefully monitored.

Yolanda's pregnancy, like most others, was free of complications. But unexpected difficulties can arise, especially if mothers have health problems. For example, women with diabetes need careful monitoring. Extra sugar in the diabetic mother's bloodstream increases the risk of pregnancy and birth problems, as well as brain damage and later learning difficulties (see the Biology and Environment box on page 118). Another complication, experienced by 5 to 10 percent of pregnant women, is *preeclampsia* (sometimes called *toxemia*), in which blood pressure increases sharply and the face, hands, and feet swell in the second half of pregnancy. If untreated, preeclampsia can cause convulsions in the mother and fetal death. Usually, hospitalization, bed rest, and drugs can lower blood pressure to a safe level (Vidaeff, Carroll, & Ramin, 2005). If not, the baby must be delivered at once.

Unfortunately, 8 percent of pregnant women in the United States wait until after the first trimester to seek prenatal care or receive none at all. As Figure 3.8 shows, inadequate care is far more common among adolescent and low-income, ethnic minority mothers. Their infants are three times as likely to be born underweight and five times as likely to die as are babies of mothers who receive early medical attention (Child Trends, 2007). Why do these mothers delay going to the doctor? One reason is that they lack health insurance. Although the very poorest of them are eligible for government-sponsored health services, many low-income women do not qualify. As we will see when we take up birth complications in Chapter 4, in nations where affordable medical care is universally available, such as Australia, Canada, Japan, and European countries, late-care pregnancies and maternal and infant health problems are greatly reduced.

Besides financial hardship, some mothers have other reasons for not seeking early prenatal care. These include both *situational barriers* (difficulty finding a doctor, getting an appointment, and arranging transportation, and insensitive or unsatisfying experiences with clinic staff) and *personal barriers* (psychological stress, the demands of taking care of other young children, family crises, lack of knowledge about signs of pregnancy and benefits of prenatal care, and ambivalence about the pregnancy). Many also engage in high-risk behaviors, such as smoking and drug abuse, which they do not want to reveal to health professionals (Maupin et al., 2004). These women, who receive little or no prenatal care, are among those who need it most!

Clearly, public education about the importance of early and sustained prenatal care for all pregnant women is badly needed. For women who are young, less-educated, low-income, or under stress and therefore at risk for inadequate prenatal care, assistance in making appointments, drop-in child-care centers, and convenient, free, or low-cost transportation are vital.

Culturally sensitive health-care practices are also helpful. Low-SES minority women often report depersonalizing experiences during prenatal appointments, including condescending interactions with medical staff and hurried

© CHAD EHLERS/ALAMY

 During a routine prenatal visit, a doctor uses ultrasound to evaluate the development of this expectant mother's 5-month-old fetus. All pregnant women should receive regular prenatal care to protect their own health as well as the health of their babies. ■

LOOK AND LISTEN

◆◆

List prenatal environmental factors that can compromise later academic performance and social adjustment. Ask several adults who hope someday to be parents to explain what they know about each factor. How great is their need for prenatal education?

FIGURE 3.8

Expectant mothers in the United States with late (after the first trimester) or no prenatal care. More than 10 percent of low-income minority mothers, and nearly 30 percent of adolescent mothers, receive inadequate prenatal care. *(From Hueston, Geesey, & Diaz, 2008; U.S. Department of Health and Human Services, 2009b.)*

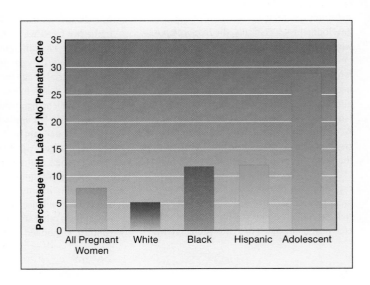

BIOLOGY AND ENVIRONMENT

Prenatal Iron Deficiency and Memory Impairments in Infants of Diabetic Mothers

Diabetes affects nearly 11 percent of Americans age 20 and older—a rate that has risen sharply over the past quarter century as a result of widespread overweight and obesity. Although it is increasingly prevalent among all sectors of the population, diabetes is at least twice as likely to affect low-income ethnic minority as white adults. Today, about 5 percent of pregnant mothers are diabetic—a 50 percent increase over the past decade. Most had the disease before becoming pregnant; others developed it during pregnancy (American Diabetes Association, 2010). In either case, their newborn babies are at risk for long-term developmental problems.

In the early weeks of pregnancy, when organs are forming, a diabetic mother's out-of-control blood glucose increases the risk of birth defects. Later in pregnancy, excess blood glucose causes the fetus to be "overfed" and to grow unusually large, often causing birth complications. Furthermore, to metabolize this flood of maternal glucose, the fetus secretes abnormally high levels of insulin—a circumstance that greatly increases demand for oxygen. To extract extra oxygen from the mother's system, the fetus increases production of oxygen-carrying red blood cells. This expanding red blood-cell mass requires extra iron, which the fetus can obtain only by taxing its own iron stores in the liver, muscles, heart, and brain.

In animal research on maternal diabetes, by late pregnancy iron stores decline sharply in the brain's temporal lobes (located on each side of the brain, just above the ears), which house structures centrally involved in memory development—specifically, the *hippocampus,* which plays a crucial role in the formation of new memories. Prenatal iron depletion interferes with growth of brain cells and their connections, permanently reducing the size and altering the structure of the hippocampus in laboratory rats (deUngria et al., 2000).

In human research, diabetic mothers bear children who, at school age, tend to score lower than their agemates on intelligence tests (Rizzo et al., 1997). Is prenatal iron deficiency and resulting early damage to the brain's memory areas responsible? In a series of studies, Charles Nelson (2007a) and his collaborators recorded electrical brain waves to assess young infants'

memory performance, focusing on a particular slow brain wave in the temporal lobes believed to reflect memory processing.

Typically developing newborns come to recognize their mother's voice through repeated exposure during pregnancy; they suck more on a nipple to hear a recording of it than the voice of an unfamiliar woman (DeCasper & Spence, 1988). In a comparison of newborns of diabetic mothers likely to have a brain iron deficiency (based on a measure of body iron stores) with normal-iron controls, brain waves were recorded as the babies listened to sound clips of their mother's or a stranger's voice (Sidappa et al., 2004). The controls showed a distinctive slow wave to each stimulus, indicating recognition of the mother's voice. The brain iron–deficient babies showed no difference in brain waves to the two stimuli, suggesting memory impairment of prenatal origin.

Do these memory deficits persist beyond the newborn period—evidence that diabetes-linked prenatal brain damage has lasting consequences? At 6 months, the researchers recorded brain waves while infants alternately viewed a videotaped image of their mother's face and that of an unfamiliar woman. Consistent with the newborn findings, control infants responded with distinct slow waves in the temporal lobes to the two faces, while infants of diabetic mothers displayed no difference. Even after months of experience, they could not recognize their mother's facial image (Nelson et al., 2000).

At an 8-month follow-up, babies were given a more challenging memory task. After feeling a novel object (an unusually shaped wooden block) held beneath an apron so they could not see it, the infants were tested visually: They viewed photos of the novel object interspersed with photos of familiar objects (Nelson et al., 2003). Again, infants of diabetic mothers showed no evidence of distinguishing the novel object from other stimuli. The control babies, in contrast, responded to the novel object with a

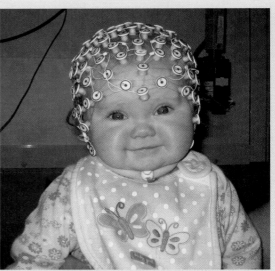

COURTESY OF DR. CHARLES NELSON

■ Prenatal iron supplementation is especially important for pregnant mothers with diabetes, which increases the fetus's risk of iron depletion and resulting memory impairments. To study the impact of prenatal diabetes on early memory development, researchers recorded this 8-month-old's electrical brain waves during a challenging memory task. ■

stronger temporal-lobe slow wave, suggesting an ability to recognize the novel stimulus, even when presented in a different sensory modality.

Nelson and his colleagues have followed their research participants through the preschool years, amassing additional evidence for poorer memory (especially more rapid forgetting) in children born to diabetic mothers than in controls (deRegnier et al., 2007). The findings highlight a previously hidden pregnancy complication: As a result of iron depletion in critical brain areas, a diabetic pregnancy places the fetus at risk for lasting memory deficits and thus for long-term learning and academic problems. The researchers believe that damage to the hippocampus, located deep inside the temporal lobes, is responsible.

Nelson's research underscores the need to find more effective ways of intervening with iron supplementation in diabetic pregnancies, as well as the importance of sufficient dietary iron for every expectant mother and her developing fetus. Diabetes prevention is also vital, through weight control, increased exercise, and improved diet beginning in childhood.

Applying What We Know

Do's and Don'ts for a Healthy Pregnancy

DO	DON'T
Do make sure that you have been vaccinated against infectious diseases dangerous to the embryo and fetus, such as rubella, before you get pregnant. Most vaccinations are not safe during pregnancy.	Don't take any drugs without consulting your doctor.
Do see a doctor as soon as you suspect that you are pregnant, and continue to get regular medical checkups throughout pregnancy.	Don't smoke. If you have already smoked during part of your pregnancy, cut down or, better yet, quit. If other members of your family smoke, ask them to quit or to smoke outside.
Do eat a well-balanced diet and take vitamin–mineral supplements, as prescribed by your doctor, both prior to and during pregnancy. On average, a woman should increase her intake by 100 calories a day in the first trimester, 265 in the second, and 430 in the third. Gain 25 to 30 pounds gradually.	Don't drink alcohol from the time you decide to get pregnant.
	Don't engage in activities that might expose your embryo or fetus to environmental hazards, such as radiation or chemical pollutants. If you work in an occupation that involves these agents, ask for a safer assignment or a leave of absence.
Do obtain literature from your doctor, local library, and bookstore about prenatal development and care, and ask questions about anything that concerns you.	Don't engage in activities that might expose your embryo or fetus to harmful infectious diseases, such as toxoplasmosis.
Do keep physically fit through moderate exercise. If possible, join a special exercise class for expectant mothers.	Don't choose pregnancy as a time to go on a diet.
Do avoid emotional stress. If you are a single expectant mother, find a relative or friend on whom you can count for emotional support.	Don't gain too much weight during pregnancy. A very large weight gain is associated with complications.
Do get plenty of rest. An overtired mother is at risk for pregnancy complications.	
Do enroll in a prenatal and childbirth education class with your partner or other companion. When you know what to expect, the nine months before birth can be one of the most joyful times of life.	

checkups with no opportunity to ask questions. These behaviors are especially disturbing to women whose cultures emphasize warm, personalized interaction styles and a relaxed sense of time—causing many to avoid returning (Daniels, Noe, & Mayberry, 2006; Downe et al., 2009). In a strategy called *group prenatal care,* after each medical checkup, trained leaders provide minority expectant mothers with a group discussion session after each medical checkup, which is conducted in their native language and encourages them to talk about important health issues (Massey, Rising, & Ickovics, 2006). Compared to mothers receiving traditional brief appointments, participants engaged in more health-promoting behaviors and also gave birth to babies with a reduced incidence of prematurity and low birth weight—major predictors of newborn survival and healthy development. Applying What We Know above lists "do's and don'ts" for a healthy pregnancy, based on our discussion of the prenatal environment.

ASK YOURSELF

◆ REVIEW Why is it difficult to determine the prenatal effects of many environmental agents, such as drugs and pollution?

◆ APPLY Nora, pregnant for the first time, believes that a few cigarettes and a glass of wine a day won't be harmful. Provide Nora with research-based reasons for not smoking or drinking.

◆ CONNECT How do teratogens illustrate the notion of epigenesis, presented in Chapter 2, that environments can affect gene expression? (See page 86 to review.)

◆ REFLECT If you had to choose five environmental influences to publicize in a campaign aimed at promoting healthy prenatal development, which ones would you choose, and why?

Preparing for Parenthood

Although we have discussed many ways that development can be thrown off course during the prenatal period, more than 90 percent of pregnancies in industrialized nations result in healthy newborn babies. For most expectant parents, the prenatal period is not a time of medical hazard. Rather, it is a period of major life change accompanied by excitement, anticipation, and looking inward. The nine months before birth not only permit the fetus to grow but also give men and women time to develop a new sense of themselves as mothers and fathers.

This period of psychological preparation is vital. In one study, more than 100 first-time expectant married couples, varying widely in age and SES, were interviewed about their pregnancy experiences. Participants reported a wide range of reactions to learning they were expecting. Nearly two-thirds were positive, about one-third mixed or neutral, and only a handful negative (Feeney et al., 2001). An unplanned pregnancy was especially likely to spark negative or ambivalent feelings. But as the pregnancy moved along, these reactions subsided. By the third trimester, no participants felt negatively, and only about 10 percent remained mixed or neutral. Couples' increasingly upbeat attitudes reflected acceptance of parenthood—a coming to terms with this imminent, radical change in their lives.

How effectively individuals construct a parental identity during pregnancy has important consequences for the parent–child relationship. A great many factors contribute to the personal adjustments that take place.

Seeking Information

We know most about how mothers adapt to the psychological challenges of pregnancy, although some evidence suggests that fathers use many of the same techniques. One common strategy is to seek information, as Yolanda and Jay did when they read books on pregnancy and childbirth and enrolled in my class. In fact, expectant mothers regard books as an extremely valuable source of information, rating them as second in importance only to their doctors. And the more a pregnant woman seeks information—by reading, accessing relevant websites, asking friends, consulting her own mother, or attending a prenatal class—the more confident she tends to feel about her own ability to be a good mother (Cowan & Cowan, 2000; Deutsch et al., 1988).

The Baby Becomes a Reality

At the beginning of pregnancy, the baby seems far in the future. But gradually, the woman's abdomen enlarges, and the baby starts to become a reality. A major turning point occurs when expectant parents have concrete proof that a fetus is, indeed, developing inside the uterus. For Yolanda and Jay, this happened 13 weeks into the pregnancy, when their doctor showed them an ultrasound image. As Jay described the experience, "We saw it, these little hands and feet waving and kicking. It's really a baby in there!" Sensing the fetus's movements for the first time can be just as thrilling. Of course, the mother feels these "kicks" first, but soon after, the partner (and siblings) can participate by touching her abdomen.

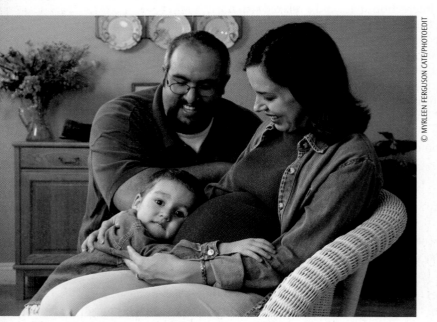

© MYRLEEN FERGUSON CATE/PHOTOEDIT

■ These parents express affection toward their preschooler while preparing him for the birth of a sibling. In this way, they expand their identity as a family to include the new baby while fostering the older child's sense of security. ■

Parents get to know the fetus as an individual through these signs of life. And both are likely to form an emotional attachment to the new being, especially when their relationship is positive, extended family members are supportive, and the mother reports favorable psychological well-being (Alhusen, 2008). In a Swedish study, the stronger mothers' and fathers' attachment to their fetus, the more positively they related to each other and to their baby after birth, and the more upbeat the baby's mood at age 8 months (White et al., 1999).

Models of Effective Parenthood

As pregnancy proceeds, expectant parents think about important models of parenthood in their own lives. When men and women have had good relationships with their own parents, they are more likely to develop positive images of themselves as parents during pregnancy (Deutsch et al., 1988). These images, in turn, predict harmonious marital communication and effective parenting during infancy and early childhood (Curran et al., 2005; Klitzing et al., 1999; McHale et al., 2004).

If their own parental relationships are mixed or negative, expectant mothers and fathers may have trouble building a healthy picture of themselves as parents. Some adults handle this challenge by seeking other examples of effective parenthood. One expectant father named Roger shared these thoughts with his wife and several couples, who met regularly with a counselor to talk about their concerns during pregnancy:

> I rethink past experiences with my father and my family and am aware of how I was raised. I just think I don't want to do that again. . . . I wish there had been more connection and closeness and a lot more respect for who I was. For me, my father-in-law . . . is a mix of empathy and warmth plus stepping back and being objective that I want to be as a father. (Colman & Colman, 1991, p. 148)

Like Roger, many people come to terms with negative experiences in their own childhood, recognize that other options are available to them, and build healthier and happier relationships with their children (Thompson, 2006). Roger achieved this understanding after participating in a special intervention program for expectant mothers and fathers. Couples who take part in such programs feel better about themselves and their marital relationships, communicate more effectively, feel more competent as parents after the baby arrives, and adapt more easily when family problems arise (Glade, Bean, & Vira, 2005; Petch & Halford, 2008).

The Parental Relationship

The most important preparation for parenthood takes place in the context of the parents' relationship. Expectant couples who are unhappy in their marriages and who have difficulty working out their differences continue to be distant, dissatisfied, and poor problem solvers after childbirth (Cowan & Cowan, 2000; Curran et al., 2005). Deciding to have a baby in hopes of improving a troubled relationship is a serious mistake. In a distressed marriage, pregnancy adds to rather than lessens family conflict (Perren et al., 2005).

When a couple's relationship is faring well and both partners want and plan for the baby, the excitement of a first pregnancy may bring husband and wife closer (Feeney et al., 2001). Parents who have forged a solid foundation of love and respect are well-equipped for the challenges of pregnancy. They are also prepared to handle the much more demanding changes that will take place as soon as their baby is born.

■ Couples who have a warm, respectful relationship and who look forward to parenthood often find that pregnancy brings them closer. As a result, they are well-equipped to handle the changes that will come after the baby arrives. ■

◆ REVIEW List psychological factors during pregnancy that predict parenting effectiveness after childbirth.

◆ APPLY Muriel, who is expecting her first child, recalls her own mother as cold and distant. Suggest steps she can take to form a confident, positive picture of herself as a new parent.

◆ REFLECT Ask your parents and/or your grandparents to describe attitudes and experiences that fostered or interfered with their capacity to build a positive parental identity when they were expecting their first child. Do you think building a healthy picture of oneself as a parent is more challenging today than it was in your parents' or grandparents' generation?

Summary

Motivations for Parenthood

How has decision making about childbearing changed over the past half-century, and what are the consequences for child rearing and child development?

■ Today, adults in Western industrialized nations have greater freedom to choose whether, when, and how to have children. In industrialized nations, family size has declined over the past half-century. But no link has been found between later birth order and lower mental test performance. Rather, less intelligent parents—as a result of heredity, environment, or both—tend to have larger families.

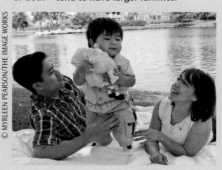

© MYRLEEN PEARSON/THE IMAGE WORKS

■ Although reproductive capacity declines with age, adults who delay childbearing until their education is complete, their careers are established, and they are emotionally more mature may be better able to invest in parenting.

Prenatal Development

List the three phases of prenatal development, and describe the major milestones of each.

■ The first prenatal phase, the period of the zygote, lasts about two weeks, from fertilization through **implantation** of the **blastocyst** in the uterine lining. During this time, structures that will support prenatal growth begin to form, including the **placenta** and the **umbilical cord.**

■ During the period of the **embryo,** from weeks 2 to 8, the foundations for all body structures are laid down. The nervous system develops fastest, starting with the formation of the **neural tube,** the top of which swells to form the brain. Other organs follow and grow rapidly. At the end of this phase, the embryo responds to touch and can move.

■ The period of the **fetus,** lasting until the end of pregnancy, involves a dramatic increase in body size and completion of physical structures. At the end of the second trimester, most of the brain's neurons are in place. At the beginning of the third trimester, between 22 and 26 weeks, the fetus reaches the **age of viability.** The brain continues to develop rapidly, and new sensory and behavioral capacities emerge. Gradually the lungs mature, the fetus fills the uterus, and birth is near.

Prenatal Environmental Influences

What are teratogens, and what factors influence their impact?

■ **Teratogens** are environmental agents that cause damage during the prenatal period. Their impact varies with the amount and length of exposure, the genetic makeup of mother and fetus, the presence or absence of other harmful agents, and the age of the organism at time of exposure. The developing organism is especially vulnerable during the embryonic period. In addition to immediate physical damage, some health outcomes may appear later in development, and physical defects may lead to psychological consequences as well.

List agents known to be or suspected of being teratogens, and discuss evidence supporting their harmful impact.

■ Drugs, cigarettes, alcohol, radiation, environmental pollution, and infectious diseases are teratogens that can endanger the developing organism. Currently, the most widely used potent teratogen is Accutane, a drug used to treat severe acne. The prenatal impact of many other commonly used medications, such as aspirin and caffeine, is hard to separate from other factors correlated with drug taking. Babies born to users of heroin, methadone, or cocaine are at risk for a wide variety of problems, including prematurity, low birth weight, physical defects, and breathing difficulties around the time of birth.

■ Infants whose parents use tobacco are often born underweight and have attention, learning, and behavior problems in early childhood. Maternal alcohol consumption can lead to **fetal alcohol spectrum disorder (FASD). Fetal alcohol syndrome (FAS)** involves slow physical growth, facial abnormalities, and impairment in mental functioning. Milder forms—**partial fetal alcohol syndrome (p-FAS) or alcohol-related neurodevelopmental disorder (ARND)**—affect children whose mothers consumed smaller quantities of alcohol.

■ Prenatal exposure to high levels of radiation, mercury, lead, dioxins, and PCBs leads to physical malformations and severe brain damage. Low-level exposure to these teratogens has also been linked to diverse impairments, including cognitive deficits and emotional and behavior disorders.

■ Among infectious diseases, rubella causes a wide variety of abnormalities. Babies with prenatally transmitted HIV rapidly develop AIDS, leading to brain damage and early death. Cytomegalovirus, herpes simplex 2, and toxoplasmosis can also be devastating to the embryo and fetus.

Describe the impact of other maternal factors on prenatal development.

■ Regular moderate exercise during pregnancy contributes to general health and readiness for childbirth and is related to higher birth weight. However, very vigorous exercise results in lower birth weight.

■ When the mother's diet is inadequate, low birth weight and damage to the brain and other organs are major concerns. Vitamin–mineral supplementation, including folic acid, before conception and continuing during pregnancy can prevent prenatal and birth complications.

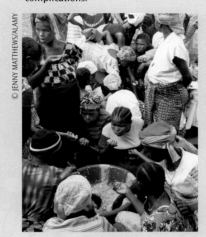

■ Severe emotional stress is linked to many pregnancy complications and may permanently alter fetal neurological functioning, resulting in anxiety, short attention span, behavior problems, and lower mental tests scores in childhood The negative impact of prenatal stress can be reduced by providing the mother with emotional support.

■ **Rh factor incompatibility**—an Rh-positive fetus developing within an Rh-negative mother—can lead to oxygen deprivation, brain and heart damage, and infant death.

■ Aside from the risk of chromosomal abnormalities in older women, maternal age through the early forties is not a major cause of prenatal problems. Poor health and environmental risks associated with poverty are the strongest predictors of pregnancy complications in both teenagers and older women.

Why is early and regular health care vital during the prenatal period?

■ Unexpected difficulties, such as preeclampsia, can arise, especially when pregnant women have health problems to begin with. Prenatal care is especially crucial for those women least likely to seek it—in particular, those who are young or poverty-stricken. Among low-SES ethnic minority mothers, culturally sensitive health-care practices—such as group prenatal care—can lead to more health-promoting behaviors.

Preparing for Parenthood

What factors contribute to preparation for parenthood during the prenatal period?

■ Over the course of pregnancy, reactions to expectant parenthood become increasingly positive. Mothers and fathers prepare for their new role by seeking information from books and other sources. Ultrasound images and fetal movements make the baby a reality, and parents may form an emotional attachment to the new being. They also rely on effective models of parenthood to build positive images of themselves as mothers and fathers.

■ The most important preparation for parenthood takes place in the context of the couple's relationship. During pregnancy, parents adjust their roles and their expectations of each other as they prepare to welcome the baby into the family.

IMPORTANT TERMS AND CONCEPTS

age of viability (p. 100)
alcohol-related neurodevelopmental disorder (ARND) (p. 109)
amnion (p. 98)
amniotic fluid (p. 98)
blastocyst (p. 98)
chorion (p. 98)
embryo (p. 99)

embryonic disk (p. 98)
fetal alcohol spectrum disorder (FASD) (p. 108)
fetal alcohol syndrome (FAS) (p. 108)
fetus (p. 100)
implantation (p. 98)
lanugo (p. 100)
neural tube (p. 99)
partial fetal alcohol syndrome (p-FAS) (p. 108)

placenta (p. 98)
Rh factor incompatibility (p. 115)
teratogen (p. 102)
trimesters (p. 100)
trophoblast (p. 98)
umbilical cord (p. 98)
vernix (p. 100)

"I'll Love Becoming a Mother"
Tina Crnjak
12 years, Slovenia

Safely held and nurtured by his mother and older sister, this baby thrives both physically and emotionally. In Chapter 4, we explore the birth process, the marvelous competencies of the newborn, and the challenges of new parenthood.

Birth and the Newborn Baby

Although Yolanda and Jay completed my course three months before their baby was born, both agreed to return the following spring to share with my next class their reactions to birth and new parenthood. Two-week-old Joshua came along as well. Yolanda and Jay's story revealed that the birth of a baby is one of the most dramatic and emotional events in human experience. Jay was present throughout Yolanda's labor and delivery. Yolanda explained:

> By morning, we knew I was in labor. It was Thursday, so we went in for my usual weekly appointment. The doctor said, yes, the baby was on the way, but it would be a while. He told us to go home and relax, and come to the hospital in 3 or 4 hours. We checked in at 3 in the afternoon; Joshua arrived at 2 o'clock the next morning. When, finally, I was ready to deliver, it went quickly; a half hour or so and some good hard pushes, and there he was! His face was red and puffy, and his head was misshapen, but I thought, "Our son! I can't believe he's really here."

Jay was also elated by Joshua's birth. "I wanted to support Yolanda and to experience as much as I could. It was awesome, indescribable," he said, holding little Joshua over his shoulder and patting and kissing him gently.

In this chapter, we explore the experience of childbirth, from both the parents' and the baby's point of view. As recently as 40 years ago, the birth process was treated more like an illness than a natural part of life. Today, women in industrialized nations have many choices about where and how they give birth, and hospitals go to great lengths to make the arrival of a new baby a rewarding, family-centered event.

Joshua reaped the benefits of Yolanda and Jay's careful attention to his needs during pregnancy. He was strong, alert, and healthy at birth. Nevertheless, the birth process does not always go smoothly. We will consider the pros and cons of medical interventions, such as pain-relieving drugs and surgical deliveries, designed to ease a difficult birth and protect the health of mother and baby. Our discussion also addresses the problems of infants born underweight or too early.

Finally, Yolanda and Jay spoke candidly about how their lives had changed since Joshua's arrival. "It's exciting and wonderful," reflected Yolanda, "but the adjustments are enormous. I wasn't quite prepared for the intensity of Joshua's 24-hour-a-day demands." In the concluding sections of this chapter, we look closely at the remarkable capacities of newborns to adapt to the external world and to communicate their needs. We also consider how parents adjust to the realities of everyday life with a new baby.

The Stages of Childbirth

It is not surprising that childbirth is often referred to as labor. It is the hardest physical work a woman may ever do. A complex series of hormonal changes initiates the process. As pregnancy advances, the placenta releases increasing amounts of *corticotropin-releasing hormone (CRH),* a hormone involved in the stress response. High levels of CRH trigger additional placental hormone adjustments that induce uterine contractions. And as CRH rises in the fetal bloodstream in the final prenatal weeks, it stimulates fetal production of the stress hormone cortisol, which promotes development of the lungs in preparation for breathing (Norwitz, 2009; Smith, 2007). An abnormal increase in maternal CRH in the third trimester of pregnancy is currently being evaluated as an early predictor of premature birth (Smith et al., 2009).

Several signs indicate that labor is near:

- Yolanda occasionally felt the upper part of her uterus contract. These contractions are often called *false labor* or *prelabor* because they remain brief and unpredictable for several weeks.
- About two weeks before birth, an event called *lightening* occurred; Joshua's head dropped low into the uterus. Placental hormone changes had caused Yolanda's cervix to soften, and it no longer supported Joshua's weight so easily.
- A sure sign that labor is only hours or days away is the *bloody show.* As the cervix begins to open, the plug of mucus that sealed it during pregnancy is released, producing a reddish discharge. Soon after, uterine contractions become more frequent, and mother and baby have entered the first of three stages of labor (see Figure 4.1).

Stage 1: Dilation and Effacement of the Cervix

Stage 1 is the longest, lasting an average of 12 to 14 hours with a first birth and 4 to 6 hours with later births. **Dilation and effacement of the cervix** take place—that is, as uterine contractions gradually become more frequent and powerful, they cause the cervix to open (dilate) and thin (efface), forming a clear channel from the uterus into the birth canal, or vagina. The uterine contractions that open the cervix are forceful and regular, starting out 10 to 20 minutes apart and lasting about 15 to 20 seconds. Gradually, they get closer together, occurring every 2 to 3 minutes, and become stronger, persisting for as long as 60 seconds.

During this stage, Yolanda could do nothing to speed up the process. Jay held her hand, provided sips of juice and water, and helped her get comfortable. Throughout the first few hours, Yolanda walked, stood, or sat upright. As the contractions became more intense, she leaned against pillows or lay on her side.

The climax of Stage 1 is a brief phase called **transition,** in which the frequency and strength of contractions are at their peak and the cervix opens completely. Although transition

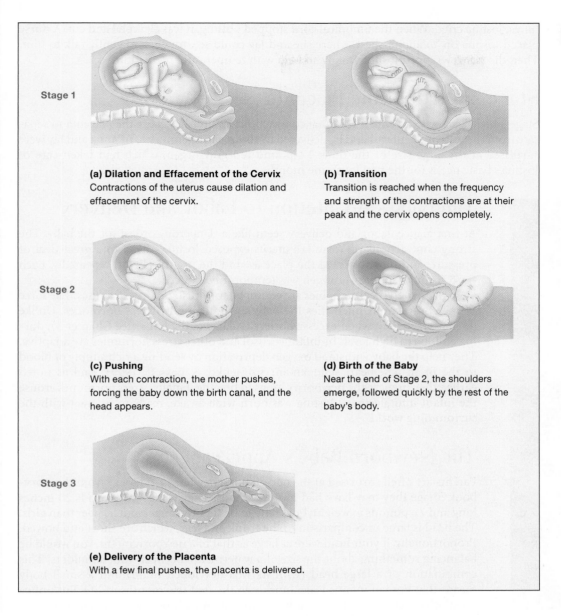

FIGURE 4.1

The three stages of labor.

Stage 1

(a) Dilation and Effacement of the Cervix
Contractions of the uterus cause dilation and effacement of the cervix.

(b) Transition
Transition is reached when the frequency and strength of the contractions are at their peak and the cervix opens completely.

Stage 2

(c) Pushing
With each contraction, the mother pushes, forcing the baby down the birth canal, and the head appears.

(d) Birth of the Baby
Near the end of Stage 2, the shoulders emerge, followed quickly by the rest of the baby's body.

Stage 3

(e) Delivery of the Placenta
With a few final pushes, the placenta is delivered.

is the most uncomfortable part of childbirth, it is especially important that the mother relax. If she tenses or bears down with her muscles before the cervix is completely dilated and effaced, she may bruise the cervix and slow the progress of labor.

Stage 2: Delivery of the Baby

In Stage 2, which lasts about 50 minutes for a first baby and 20 minutes in later births, the infant is born. Strong contractions of the uterus continue, but the mother also feels a natural urge to squeeze and push with her abdominal muscles. As she does so with each contraction, she forces the baby down and out.

Between contractions, Yolanda dozed lightly. When the doctor announced that the baby's head was *crowning*—the vaginal opening had stretched around the entire head—Yolanda felt renewed energy; she knew that soon the baby would arrive. Quickly, with several more pushes, Joshua's forehead, nose, and chin emerged, then his upper body and trunk. The doctor held him up, wet with amniotic fluid and still attached to the umbilical cord. As air rushed into his lungs, Joshua cried. When the umbilical cord stopped pulsing, it was clamped and cut. A nurse placed Joshua on Yolanda's chest, where she and Jay could see, touch, and gently talk to him. Then the nurse wrapped Joshua snugly, to help with temperature regulation.

Stage 3: Birth of the Placenta

Stage 3 brings labor to an end. A few final contractions and pushes cause the placenta to separate from the wall of the uterus and be delivered in about 5 to 10 minutes. Yolanda and Jay were surprised at the large size of the thick 1½-pound red-gray organ, which had taken care of Joshua's basic needs for the previous nine months.

The Baby's Adaptation to Labor and Delivery

At first glance, labor and delivery seem like a dangerous ordeal for the baby. The strong contractions of Yolanda's uterus exposed Joshua's head to a great deal of pressure, and they squeezed the placenta and the umbilical cord repeatedly. Each time, Joshua's supply of oxygen was temporarily reduced.

Fortunately, healthy babies are equipped to withstand these traumas. The force of the contractions intensifies the baby's production of stress hormones. Unlike during pregnancy, when excessive stress endangers the fetus (see Chapter 3), during childbirth high levels of infant cortisol and other stress hormones are adaptive. They help the baby withstand oxygen deprivation by sending a rich supply of blood to the brain and heart (Gluckman, Sizonenko, & Bassett, 1999). And as noted earlier, they prepare the newborn's lungs to breathe. Finally, stress hormones arouse the infant into alertness. Joshua was born wide-awake, ready to interact with the surrounding world.

The Newborn Baby's Appearance

Parents are often surprised at the odd-looking newborn—a far cry from the storybook image they may have had in their minds. The average newborn is 20 inches long and 7½ pounds in weight; boys tend to be slightly longer and heavier than girls. The head is large in comparison to the trunk and legs, which are short and bowed. Proportionally, if your head were as large as that of a newborn infant, you would be balancing something about the size of a watermelon between your shoulders! This combination of a large head (with its well-developed brain) and a small body means that human infants learn quickly in the first few months of life. But unlike most other mammals, they cannot get around on their own until much later.

Even though newborn babies may not match parents' idealized image, some features do make them attractive. Their round faces, chubby cheeks, large foreheads, and big eyes make adults feel like picking them up and cuddling them (Berman, 1980).

■ To accommodate the well-developed brain, a newborn's head is large in relation to the trunk and legs. This newborn's body readily turns pink as he takes his first few breaths. ■

Assessing the Newborn's Physical Condition: The Apgar Scale

Infants who have difficulty making the transition to life outside the uterus must be given special help at once. To assess the newborn's physical condition quickly, doctors and nurses use the **Apgar Scale.** As Table 4.1 shows, a rating of 0, 1, or 2 on each of five characteristics is made at 1 minute and again at 5 minutes after birth. A combined Apgar score of 7 or better indicates that the infant is in good physical condition. If the score is between 4 and 6, the baby requires assistance in establishing breathing and other vital signs. If the score is 3 or below, the infant is in serious danger and requires emergency medical attention. Two Apgar ratings are given because some babies have trouble adjusting at first but do quite well after a few minutes (Apgar, 1953).

TABLE 4.1 The Apgar Scale

| Sign[a] | SCORE | | |
	0	1	2
Heart rate	No heartbeat	Under 100 beats per minute	100 to 140 beats per minute
Respiratory effort	No breathing for 60 seconds	Irregular, shallow breathing	Strong breathing and crying
Reflex irritability (sneezing, coughing, and grimacing)	No response	Weak reflexive response	Strong reflexive response
Muscle tone	Completely limp	Weak movements of arms and legs	Strong movements of arms and legs
Color[b]	Blue body, arms, and legs	Body pink with blue arms and legs	Body, arms, and legs completely pink

[a]To remember these signs, you may find it helpful to use a technique in which the original labels are reordered and renamed as follows: color = **A**ppearance; heart rate = **P**ulse; reflex irritability = **G**rimace; muscle tone = **A**ctivity; and respiratory effort = **R**espiration. Together, the first letters of the new labels spell **Apgar.**

[b]The skin tone of nonwhite babies makes it difficult to apply the "pink" color criterion. However, newborns of all races can be rated for pinkish glow resulting from the flow of oxygen through body tissues.

Source: Apgar, 1953.

ASK YOURSELF

◆ REVIEW Name and briefly describe the three stages of labor.

◆ APPLY On seeing her newborn baby for the first time, Caroline exclaimed, "Why is she so out of proportion?" What observations prompted Caroline to ask this question? Explain why her baby's appearance is adaptive.

◆ CONNECT Contrast the positive impact of the baby's production of stress hormones during childbirth with the negative impact of maternal stress on the fetus, discussed on pages 114–115 in Chapter 3.

■ ■ Approaches to Childbirth
■ ■

Childbirth practices, like other aspects of family life, are molded by the society of which mother and baby are a part. In many village and tribal cultures, expectant mothers are well-acquainted with the childbirth process. For example, the Jarara of South America and the Pukapukans of the Pacific Islands treat birth as a vital part of daily life. The Jarara mother gives birth in full view of the entire community, including small children. The Pukapukan girl is so familiar with the events of labor and delivery that she can frequently be seen playing at it. Using a coconut to represent the baby, she stuffs it inside her dress, imitates the mother's pushing, and lets the nut fall at the proper moment. In most nonindustrialized cultures, women are assisted—though often not by medical personnel—during labor and delivery. Among the Mayans of the Yucatán, the mother leans against the body of a woman called the "head helper," who supports her weight and breathes with her during each contraction. And in Bolivia, a Siriono mother delivers her own baby in a hammock with a crowd of women close by, who keep her company. The father cuts the umbilical cord and joins the mother in tending to the newborn for the first few days (Jordan, 1993; Mead & Newton, 1967; Reed, 2005).

In Western nations, childbirth has changed dramatically over the centuries. Before the late 1800s, birth usually took place at home and was a family-centered event. The industrial revolution brought greater crowding to cities, along with new health problems. As a result, childbirth moved from home to hospital, where the health of mothers and babies could be protected.

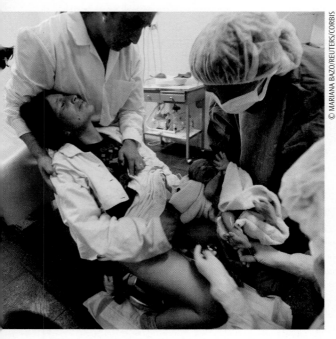

In this Peruvian health clinic, families are encouraged to incorporate practices of their village culture into the birth experience. Here, a familiar attendant supports and soothes a new mother as her baby is delivered. ■

Once doctors assumed responsibility for childbirth, women's knowledge of it declined, and relatives and friends no longer participated (Borst, 1995).

By the 1950s and 1960s, women had begun to question the medical procedures that had come to be used routinely during labor and delivery. Many felt that routine use of strong drugs and delivery instruments had robbed them of a precious experience and was often neither necessary nor safe for the baby. Gradually, a natural childbirth movement arose in Europe and spread to North America. Its purpose was to make hospital birth as comfortable and rewarding for mothers as possible. Today, most hospitals offer birth centers that are family-centered and homelike. *Freestanding birth centers,* which permit greater maternal control over labor and delivery, including choice of delivery positions, presence of family members and friends, and early contact between parents and baby, also exist. And a small number of North American women reject institutional birth entirely and choose to have their babies at home.

Natural, or Prepared, Childbirth

Yolanda and Jay chose **natural,** or **prepared, childbirth**—a group of techniques aimed at reducing pain and medical intervention and making childbirth as rewarding an experience as possible. Most natural childbirth programs draw on methods developed by Grantly Dick-Read (1959) in England and Fernand Lamaze (1958) in France. These physicians recognized that cultural attitudes had taught women to fear the birth experience. An anxious, frightened woman in labor tenses her muscles, heightening the pain that usually accompanies strong contractions.

In a typical natural childbirth program, the expectant mother and a companion (a partner, relative, or friend) participate in three activities:

■ *Classes.* Yolanda and Jay attended a series of classes in which they learned about the anatomy and physiology of labor and delivery. Knowledge about the birth process reduces a mother's fear.
■ *Relaxation and breathing techniques.* During each class, Yolanda was taught relaxation and breathing exercises aimed at counteracting the pain of uterine contractions.
■ *Labor coach.* Jay learned how to help Yolanda during childbirth by reminding her to relax and breathe, massaging her back, supporting her body, and offering encouragement and affection.

Studies reveal many benefits for mothers who experience natural childbirth compared with those who do not. Because mothers feel more in control of labor and delivery, their attitudes toward the childbirth experience are more positive. They also feel less pain. As a result, they require less pain-relieving medication—very little or none at all (Taylor, 2002; Waldenström, 1999).

SOCIAL SUPPORT AND NATURAL CHILDBIRTH   Social support is important to the success of natural childbirth techniques. In Guatemalan and American hospitals that routinely isolated patients during childbirth, some mothers were randomly assigned a *doula*—a Greek word referring to a trained lay attendant—who stayed with them throughout labor and delivery, talking to them, holding their hands, and rubbing their backs to promote relaxation. These mothers had fewer birth complications, and their labors were several hours shorter than those of women who did not have supportive companionship. Guatemalan mothers who received doula support also interacted more positively with their babies after delivery, talking, smiling, and gently stroking (Kennell et al., 1991; Sosa et al., 1980).

LOOK AND LISTEN

❖❖

Talk to several mothers about social supports available to them during labor and delivery. From the mothers' perspectives, how did those supports (or lack of support) affect the birth experience?

© MARIANA BAZO/REUTERS/CORBIS

Other studies indicate that mothers who are supported during labor—either by a lay birth attendant or a relative or friend with doula training—less often have instrument-assisted or cesarean (surgical) deliveries or need medication to control pain. Also, their babies' Apgar scores are higher, and they are more likely to be breastfeeding at a two-month follow-up (Campbell et al., 2006, 2007; Hodnet et al., 2003; McGrath & Kennell, 2008).

The continuous rather than intermittent support of a doula during labor and delivery strengthens these outcomes. It is particularly helpful during a first childbirth, when mothers are more anxious (DiMatteo & Kahn, 1997; Scott, Berkowitz, & Klaus, 1999). And this aspect of natural childbirth makes Western hospital-birth customs more acceptable to women from parts of the world where assistance from family and community members is the norm (Dundek, 2006).

POSITIONS FOR DELIVERY   When natural childbirth is combined with delivery in a birth center or at home, mothers often give birth in an upright, sitting position rather than lying flat on their backs with their feet in stirrups (the traditional hospital delivery room practice). Use of special seats to enable an upright birth has become more common. One type of birthing seat permits the partner to sit behind the mother, providing physical support (see Figure 4.2).

Research findings favor the sitting position. When mothers are upright, labor is shortened because pushing is easier and more effective. The baby benefits from a richer supply of oxygen because blood flow to the placenta is increased. Because the mother can see the delivery, she can track the effectiveness of each contraction in pushing the baby out of the birth canal. This helps her work with the doctor or midwife to ensure that the baby's head and shoulders emerge slowly, which reduces the chances of tearing the mother's tissues and, thus, the need for an *episiotomy* (incision that increases the size of the vaginal opening). Compared with those who give birth lying on their backs, women who choose an upright position are less likely to use pain-relieving medication (Eberhard, Stein, & Geissbuehler, 2005; Romano & Lothian, 2008).

In another increasingly popular method, water birth, the mother sits in a warm tub of water, which supports her weight, relaxes her, and provides her with the freedom to move into any position she finds most comfortable. Recent evidence indicates that water birth is associated with reduced maternal stress, shorter labor, lower episiotomy rate, and a greater likelihood of medication-free delivery than both back-lying and birthing-stool approaches (Cluett & Burns, 2009; Eberhard, Stein, & Geissbuehler, 2005; Ohlsson et al., 2001). As long as water birth is carefully managed by health professionals, it poses no additional risk of infection or safety to mothers or babies (Zanetti-Daellenbach et al., 2007).

Home Delivery

Home birth has always been popular in certain industrialized nations, such as England, the Netherlands, and Sweden. The number of American women choosing to have their babies at home rose during the 1970s and 1980s but remains small, at less than 1 percent (U.S. Department of Health and Human Services, 2009b). Although some home births are attended by doctors, many more are handled by

FIGURE 4.2

A birthing seat. The mother gives birth in an upright posture. Her partner can sit behind, supporting her body.

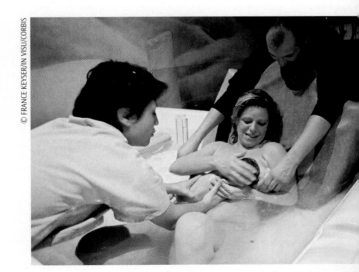

© FRANCE KEYSER/IN VISU/CORBIS

■ This woman has chosen a water birth, an increasingly popular childbirth option. Sitting in a warm tub of water relaxes the mother, supports her weight, and gives her the freedom to move into a comfortable position. ■

certified nurse-midwives, who have degrees in nursing and additional training in childbirth management.

The joys and perils of home delivery are well illustrated by the story I heard from Don, who was painting my house as I worked on this book. "Our first child was delivered in the hospital," he said. "Even though I was present, Kathy and I found the atmosphere to be rigid and insensitive. We wanted a warmer, more personal birth environment." With the coaching of a nurse-midwife, Don delivered their second child, Cindy, at their farmhouse, 3 miles out of town. Three years later, when Kathy went into labor with Marnie, their third child, a heavy snowstorm prevented the midwife from reaching the house on time, so Don delivered the baby alone. The birth was difficult, and Marnie failed to breathe for several minutes. With great effort, Don managed to revive her. The frightening memory of Marnie's limp, blue body convinced Don and Kathy to return to the hospital to have their last child. By then, the hospital's birth practices had changed, and the event was a rewarding one for both parents.

Don and Kathy's experience raises the question: Is it just as safe to give birth at home as in a hospital? For healthy women who are assisted by a well-trained doctor or midwife, it seems so because complications rarely occur (Fullerton, Navarro, & Young, 2007; Johnson & Daviss, 2005). However, if attendants are not carefully trained and prepared to handle emergencies, the rate of infant death is high (Mehlmadrona & Madrona, 1997). When mothers are at risk for any kind of complication, the appropriate place for labor and delivery is the hospital, where life-saving treatment is available.

Medical Interventions

Medical interventions during childbirth occur in both industrialized and non-industrialized cultures. For example, some tribal and village societies have discovered labor-inducing drugs and devised surgical techniques to deliver babies (Jordan, 1993). Yet childbirth in North America, more so than elsewhere in the world, is a medically monitored and controlled event. Use of some medical procedures has reached epic proportions—in part because of rising rates of multiple births and other high-risk deliveries, which are associated with increased maternal age and use of fertility treatments. But births unaffected by these factors are also highly medicalized.

What medical techniques are doctors likely to use during labor and delivery? When are they justified, and what dangers do they pose to mothers and babies?

Fetal Monitoring

Fetal monitors are electronic instruments that track the baby's heart rate during labor. An abnormal heartbeat pattern may indicate that the baby is in distress due to lack of oxygen and needs to be delivered immediately. Continuous fetal monitoring, which is required in most U.S. hospitals, is used in over 80 percent of U.S. births (Natale & Dodman, 2003). The most popular type of monitor is strapped across the mother's abdomen throughout labor. A second, more accurate method involves threading a recording device through the cervix and placing it directly under the baby's scalp.

Fetal monitoring is a safe medical procedure that has saved the lives of many babies in high-risk situations. But in healthy pregnancies, it does not reduce the already low rates of infant brain damage and death (Haws et al., 2009). Furthermore, most infants have some heartbeat irregularities during labor, and critics worry that fetal monitors identify many babies as in danger who, in fact, are not. Monitoring is linked to an increase in the number of instrument and cesarean

■ The fetal monitor strapped across this mother's abdomen uses ultrasound to record fetal heart rate throughout labor. In high-risk situations, fetal monitoring saves many lives. But it also may encourage unnecessary instrument and cesarean deliveries. ■

© JASON EDWARDS/GETTY IMAGES/NATIONAL GEOGRAPHIC

(surgical) deliveries, practices we will discuss shortly (Thacker & Stroup, 2003). In addition, some women complain that the devices are uncomfortable and interfere with the normal course of labor.

Still, fetal monitors will probably continue to be used routinely in the United States, even though they are not necessary in most cases. Doctors fear that they will be sued for malpractice if an infant dies or is born with problems and they cannot show that they did everything possible to protect the baby.

Labor and Delivery Medication

Some form of medication is used in more than 80 percent of U.S. births (Althaus & Wax, 2005). *Analgesics,* drugs used to relieve pain, may be given in mild doses during labor to help a mother relax. *Anesthetics* are a stronger type of painkiller that blocks sensation. Currently, the most common approach to controlling pain during labor is *epidural analgesia,* in which a regional pain-relieving drug is delivered continuously through a catheter into a small space in the lower spine. Unlike older spinal block procedures, which numb the entire lower half of the body, epidural analgesia limits pain reduction to the pelvic region. Because the mother retains the capacity to feel the pressure of the contractions and to move her trunk and legs, she is able to push during the second stage of labor.

Although pain-relieving drugs help women cope with childbirth and enable doctors to perform essential medical interventions, they also can cause problems. Epidural analgesia, for example, weakens uterine contractions. As a result, labor is prolonged, and the chances of cesarean (surgical) delivery increase (Klein, 2006). And because drugs rapidly cross the placenta, exposed newborns tend to have lower Apgar scores, to be sleepy and withdrawn, to suck poorly during feedings, and to be irritable when awake (Caton et al., 2002; Eltzschig, Lieberman, & Camann, 2003; Emory, Schlackman, & Fiano, 1996).

Do heavy doses of childbirth medication have a lasting impact on physical and mental development? Some researchers have claimed so (Brackbill, McManus, & Woodward, 1985), but their findings have been challenged (Riordan et al., 2000). Use of medication may be related to other risk factors that could account for the long-term consequences in some studies. Nevertheless, the negative impact of these drugs on the newborn's adjustment supports the current trend to limit their use.

Instrument Delivery

Forceps, metal clamps placed around the baby's head to pull the infant from the birth canal, have been used since the sixteenth century to speed up delivery (see Figure 4.3). A more recent instrument, the *vacuum extractor,* consists of a plastic cup (placed on the baby's head) attached to a suction tube. Instrument delivery is appropriate if the mother's pushing during the second stage of labor does not move the baby through the birth canal in a reasonable period of time.

Instrument use has declined considerably over the past two decades, partly because doctors more often deliver babies surgically when labor problems arise. Nevertheless, forceps and vacuum extractors continue to be used in about 5 percent of American births (U.S. Department of Health and Human Services, 2009b). These figures suggest that instruments are applied too freely in U.S. hospitals.

Using forceps to pull the baby through most or all of the birth canal greatly increases the risk of brain damage. As a result, forceps are seldom used this way today. Low-forceps delivery (carried out when the baby is most of the way through the vagina) is associated with risk of injury to the baby's head and the mother's tissues. Vacuum extractors, rapidly replacing forceps as the dominant instrument, are less likely to tear the mother's tissues. Cup suction does cause bleeding beneath the baby's skin and on the outside of the skull in about 15 percent of cases and more serious complications, including bleeding within the eye and beneath the skull (which can damage the brain), in 5 percent of cases (Ali &

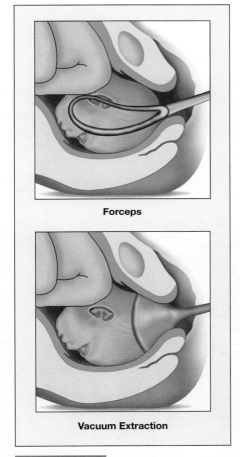

Forceps

Vacuum Extraction

FIGURE 4.3

Instrument delivery. The pressure that must be applied to pull the infant from the birth canal with forceps can injure the baby's head. An alternative method, the vacuum extractor, is less likely than forceps to injure the mother's tissues. Nevertheless, risk of infant scalp injuries and internal bleeding in the eyes and skull remains.

Norwitz, 2009). Consequently, neither method should be used when mothers can be encouraged to deliver normally and there is no special reason to hurry the birth.

Induced Labor

An **induced labor** is one that is started artificially, usually by breaking the amnion, or bag of waters (an event that typically occurs naturally in the first stage of labor), and giving the mother synthetic oxytocin, a hormone that stimulates contractions. About 22 percent of American labors are induced—a figure that has more than doubled over the past two decades (U.S. Department of Health and Human Services, 2009b).

Induced labors are justified when continuing the pregnancy threatens the well-being of mother or baby. Often, though, they are performed for the doctor's or the patient's convenience—a major reason they have increased. An induced labor often proceeds differently from a naturally occurring one. Contractions are longer, harder, and closer together, increasing the possibility of inadequate oxygen supply to the baby. In addition, mothers often find it more difficult to stay in control of an induced labor, even when they have been coached in natural childbirth techniques. As a result, labor and delivery medication is likely to be used in larger amounts, and the chances of instrument delivery are slightly greater (Cammu et al., 2002; Hoffman et al., 2006).

Occasionally, induction is performed before the mother is physically ready to give birth, and the procedure fails. When this happens, a cesarean delivery is necessary. The rate of cesareans is substantially higher in induced than spontaneous labors. Ripening of the cervix—initial dilation and effacement—is the best predictor of the success of labor induction (Clark et al., 2009).

Cesarean Delivery

A **cesarean delivery** is a surgical birth; the doctor makes an incision in the mother's abdomen and lifts the baby out of the uterus. Forty years ago, cesarean delivery was rare. Since then, cesarean rates have climbed internationally, reaching 16 percent in Finland, 20 percent in New Zealand, 22 percent in Australia, 26 percent in Canada, and 31 percent in the United States (Betrán et al., 2007; Society of Obstetricians and Gynaecologists, 2008; U.S. Department of Health and Human Services, 2009b).

Cesareans have always been warranted by medical emergencies, such as Rh incompatibility, premature separation of the placenta from the uterus, or serious maternal illness or infection (for example, the herpes simplex 2 virus, which can infect the baby during a vaginal delivery). Cesareans are also justified when babies are in **breech position,** turned so that the buttocks or feet would be delivered first (about 1 in every 25 births). The breech position increases the chances of squeezing of the umbilical cord as the large head moves through the birth canal, thereby depriving the infant of oxygen. Head injuries are also more likely (Golfier et al., 2001). But the infant's exact position makes a difference. Certain breech babies fare just as well with a normal delivery as with a cesarean (Giuliani et al., 2002). Sometimes the doctor can gently turn the baby into a head-down position during the early part of labor.

Until recently, many women who have had a cesarean have been offered the option of a vaginal birth in subsequent pregnancies. But growing evidence indicates that compared with repeated cesareans, a natural labor after a cesarean is associated with slightly increased rates of rupture of the uterus and infant death (Cahill & Macones, 2007). As a result, the rule "Once a cesarean, always a cesarean" has made a comeback.

Repeated cesareans, however, do not explain the worldwide rise in cesarean deliveries. Instead, medical control over childbirth is largely responsible. Because many needless cesareans are performed, pregnant women should ask questions about the procedure when choosing a doctor. Although the operation itself is safe, mother and baby require more time for recovery. Anesthetic may have crossed the placenta, making cesarean newborns sleepy and unresponsive and putting them at increased risk for breathing difficulties (McDonagh, Osterweil, & Guise, 2005).

© BSIP/PHOTO RESEARCHERS, INC.

■ A nurse shows a mother her newborn following a cesarean delivery. Cesareans have become increasingly common over the past forty years, largely because of medical control over childbirth. ■

◆ REVIEW Describe the features and benefits of natural childbirth. What aspect contributes greatly to favorable outcomes, and why?

◆ APPLY Sharon, a heavy smoker, has just arrived at the hospital in labor. Which one of the medical interventions discussed in the preceding sections is her doctor justified in using? (For help in answering this question, review the prenatal effects of tobacco on page 107 in Chapter 3.)

◆ CONNECT How might use of epidural analgesia negatively affect the parent–newborn relationship? Explain how your answer illustrates bidirectional influences between parent and child, emphasized in ecological systems theory.

◆ REFLECT If you were an expectant parent, would you choose home birth? Why or why not?

Birth Complications

We have seen that some babies—in particular, those whose mothers are in poor health, do not receive good medical care, or have a history of pregnancy problems—are especially likely to experience birth complications. Inadequate oxygen, a pregnancy that ends too early, and a baby who is born underweight are serious risks to development that we have touched on many times. A baby remaining in the uterus too long is yet another risk. Let's look at the impact of each complication on later development.

Oxygen Deprivation

Some years ago, I got to know 4-year-old Melinda and her mother, Judy, both of whom participated in a special program for children with disabilities at our laboratory school. Melinda has *cerebral palsy,* a general term for a variety of impairments in muscle coordination caused by brain damage before, during, or just after birth. The disorder can range from very mild tremors to severe crippling and mental retardation. One out of every 500 American children has cerebral palsy. About 10 percent experienced **anoxia,** or inadequate oxygen supply, along with a buildup of harmful acids and deficiency of vital blood substrates, as a result of decreased maternal blood supply during labor and delivery (Bracci, Perrone, & Buonocore, 2006; Clark, Ghulmiyyah, & Hankins, 2008).

Melinda walks with a halting, lumbering gait and has difficulty keeping her balance. "Some mothers don't know how the palsy happened," confided Judy, "but I do. I got pregnant accidentally, and my boyfriend didn't want to have anything to do with it. I was frightened and alone most of the time. I arrived at the hospital at the last minute. Melinda was breech, and the cord was wrapped around her neck."

Squeezing of the umbilical cord, as in Melinda's case, is one cause of anoxia. Another cause is *placenta abruptio,* or premature separation of the placenta, a life-threatening event with a high rate of infant death. Factors related to it include multiple fetuses and teratogens that cause constriction of blood vessels and abnormal development of the placenta, such as tobacco and cocaine (Ovelese & Ananth, 2006). Just as serious is *placenta previa,* a condition caused by implantation of the blastocyst so low in the uterus that the placenta covers the cervical opening. As the cervix dilates and effaces in the third trimester, part of the placenta may detach. Women who have had previous cesareans or who are carrying multiple fetuses are at increased risk (Ovelese & Smulian, 2006). Although placenta abruptio and placenta previa occur in only 1 to 2 percent of births, they can cause severe hemorrhaging, which requires that an emergency cesarean be performed.

In still other instances, the birth seems to go along all right, but the baby fails to start breathing within a few minutes. Healthy newborns can survive periods of little or no oxygen longer than adults can; they reduce their metabolic rate, thereby conserving the limited oxygen available. Nevertheless, brain damage is likely if a baby is suffering from infection and therefore cannot initiate these protective reactions or if regular breathing is delayed more than 10 minutes (Kendall & Peebles, 2005). **TAKE A MOMENT...** Can you think of other possible causes of oxygen deprivation that you learned about as you studied prenatal development and birth?

PHOTO COURTESY OF SUSAN MERRELL

■ Treatment for this newborn, who experienced oxygen deprivation, combines a cooling head cap with a cooling water blanket to lower the baby's body temperature, which helps prevent brain damage. ■

After initial brain injury from anoxia, another phase of cell death can occur several hours later. Currently, researchers are experimenting with ways to prevent this secondary damage. Compared with routine hospital care, placing anoxic newborns in a head-cooling device shortly after birth for 72 hours substantially reduces brain injury (detected through brain scans) and increases scores on a newborn behavioral assessment (Hoehn et al., 2008; Lin et al., 2006). Another alternative—whole-body cooling by having anoxic newborns lie on a precooled water blanket—leads to an impressive reduction in death and disability rates during the first two years (Shankaran et al., 2005).

How do children who experience anoxia during labor and delivery fare as they get older? Research suggests that the greater the oxygen deprivation, the poorer children's cognitive and language skills in early and middle childhood (Hopkins-Golightly, Raz, & Sander, 2003). Although effects of even mild to moderate anoxia often persist, many children improve over time (Bass et al., 2004; Raz, Shah, & Sander, 1996). In Melinda's case, her physical disability was permanent, but with warm, stimulating intervention services, she was just slightly behind in mental development as a preschooler.

When development is severely impaired, the anoxia was probably extreme. Perhaps it was caused by prenatal insult to the baby's respiratory system, or it may have happened because the infant's lungs were not yet mature enough to breathe. For example, infants born more than six weeks early commonly have *respiratory distress syndrome* (otherwise known as *hyaline membrane disease*). Their tiny lungs are so poorly developed that the air sacs collapse, causing serious breathing difficulties. Today, mechanical respirators keep many such infants alive. In spite of these measures, some babies suffer permanent brain damage from lack of oxygen, and in other cases their delicate lungs are harmed by the treatment itself. Respiratory distress syndrome is only one of many risks for babies born too soon, as we will see in the following section.

Preterm and Low-Birth-Weight Infants

Janet, almost six months pregnant, and her husband, Rick, boarded a flight in Hartford, Connecticut, on their way to a vacation in Hawaii. During a stopover in San Francisco, Janet told Rick she was bleeding. Rushed to a hospital, she gave birth to Keith, who weighed less than 1½ pounds. Delivered 23 weeks after conception, he had barely reached the age of viability (see Chapter 3, page 100).

During Keith's first month, he experienced one crisis after another. Three days after birth, an ultrasound scan suggested that fragile blood vessels feeding Keith's brain had hemorrhaged, a complication that can cause brain damage. Within three weeks, Keith had surgery to close a heart valve that seals automatically in full-term babies. Keith's immature immune system made infections difficult to contain. Repeated illnesses and the drugs used to treat them caused permanent hearing loss. Keith also had respiratory distress syndrome and breathed with the help of a respirator. Soon there was evidence of lung damage. More than three months of hospitalization passed before Keith's rough course of complications and treatment eased.

Babies born three weeks or more before the end of a full 38-week pregnancy or who weigh less than 5½ pounds (2,500 grams) have for many years been referred to as "premature." A wealth of research indicates that premature babies are at risk for many problems. Birth weight is the best available predictor of infant survival and healthy development. Many newborns who weigh less than 3⅓ pounds (1,500 grams) experience difficulties that are not overcome, an effect that becomes stronger as length of pregnancy and birth weight decrease (see Figure 4.4) (Bolisetty et al., 2006; Dombrowski, Noonan, & Martin, 2007). Brain structural abnormalities, frequent illness, inattention, overactivity, sensory impairments, poor motor coordination, language delays, low intelligence test scores, deficits in school learning, and emotional and behavior problems are some of the difficulties that persist through childhood and adolescence and into adulthood (Aarnoudse-Moens, Weisglas-Kuperus, & van Goudoever, 2009; Bayless & Stevenson, 2007; Clark et al., 2008; Delobel-Ayoub et al., 2009).

About 1 in 13 American infants is born underweight. The problem can strike unexpectedly, as it did for Janet and Rick. But it is highest among poverty-stricken women (U.S. Department of Health and Human Services, 2009b). These mothers, as indicated in Chapter 3, are more likely to be undernourished, under stress, and exposed to other harmful environmental influences—factors strongly linked to low birth weight. In addition, they often do not receive the prenatal care necessary to protect their vulnerable babies.

Recall from Chapter 2 that prematurity is also common in multiple births. About 60 percent of twins and more than 90 percent of triplets are born early and low birth weight (U.S. Department of Health and Human Services, 2009b). Because space inside the uterus is restricted, multiples gain less weight than singletons in the second half of pregnancy.

PRETERM VERSUS SMALL-FOR-DATE INFANTS Although low-birth-weight infants face many obstacles to healthy development, most go on to lead normal lives; about half of those born at 23 to 24 weeks gestation and weighing only a couple of pounds at birth have no disability (refer again to Figure 4.4). To better understand why some babies do better than others, researchers divide them into two groups. **Preterm infants** are born several weeks or more before their due date. Although they are small, their weight may still be appropriate, based on time spent in the uterus. **Small-for-date infants** are below their expected weight considering length of the pregnancy. Some small-for-date infants are actually full-term. Others are preterm babies who are especially underweight.

Of the two types of babies, small-for-date infants usually have more serious problems. During the first year, they are more likely to die, catch infections, and show evidence of brain damage. By middle childhood, they are smaller in stature, have lower intelligence test scores, are less attentive, achieve more poorly in school, and are socially immature (Hediger et al., 2002; O'Keefe et al., 2003; Sullivan et al., 2008). Small-for-date infants probably experienced inadequate nutrition before birth. Perhaps their mothers did not eat properly, the placenta did not function normally, or the babies themselves had defects that prevented them from growing as they should. In some of these babies, an abnormally functioning placenta permitted ready transfer of stress hormones from mother to fetus. Consequently, small-for-date infants are especially likely to suffer from prenatal neurological impairments that permanently weaken their capacity to manage stress (Wust et al., 2005).

Even among preterm newborns whose weight is appropriate for length of pregnancy, just seven more days—from 34 to 35 weeks—greatly reduces rates of illness, costly medical procedures, and lengthy hospital stays (although they need greater medical intervention than full-term babies) (Gladstone & Katz, 2004). And despite being relatively low-risk for disabilities, a substantial number of 34-week preterms are below average in physical growth and mildly to moderately delayed in cognitive development in early and middle childhood (Morse et al., 2009; Pietz et al., 2004; Stephens & Vohr, 2009). Yet doctors often induce births several weeks preterm, under the misconception that these babies are developmentally "mature."

CONSEQUENCES FOR CAREGIVING Imagine a scrawny, thin-skinned infant whose body is only a little larger than the size of your hand. You try to play with the baby by stroking and

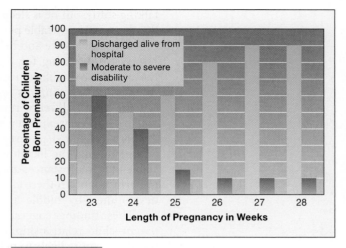

FIGURE 4.4

Rates of infant survival and child disabilities by length of pregnancy. In a follow-up of more than 2,300 babies born between 23 and 28 weeks gestation, the percentage of infants who survived decreased and the percentage who displayed moderate to severe disabilities (assessed during the preschool years) increased with reduced length of pregnancy. Severe disabilities included cerebral palsy (unlikely to ever walk), severely delayed mental development, deafness, and blindness. Moderate disabilities included cerebral palsy (able to walk with assistance), moderately delayed mental development, and hearing impairments partially correctable with a hearing aid. *(Adapted from Bolisetty et al., 2006.)*

talking softly, but he is sleepy and unresponsive. When you feed him, he sucks poorly. During the short, unpredictable periods in which he is awake, he is usually irritable.

The appearance and behavior of preterm babies can lead parents to be less sensitive and responsive in caring for them. Compared to full-term infants, preterm babies—especially those who are very ill at birth—are less often held close, touched, and talked to gently. At times, mothers of these infants resort to interfering pokes and verbal commands, in an effort to obtain a higher level of response from the baby (Barratt, Roach, & Leavitt, 1996; Feldman, 2007b). This may explain why preterm babies as a group are at risk for child abuse. When they are born to isolated, poverty-stricken mothers who cannot provide good nutrition, health care, and parenting, the likelihood of unfavorable outcomes increases. In contrast, parents with stable life circumstances and social supports usually can overcome the stresses of caring for a preterm infant. In these cases, even sick preterm babies have a good chance of catching up in development by middle childhood (Ment et al., 2003).

These findings suggest that how well preterm babies develop has a great deal to do with the parent–child relationship. Consequently, interventions directed at supporting both sides of this tie are more likely to help these infants recover.

■ *Top photo:* New mothers in a hospital ward in the Philippines practice skin-to-skin "kangaroo care," widely used in developing countries to promote the survival and recovery of preterm babies. *Bottom photo:* In Western nations, kangaroo care may be used to supplement hospital intensive care. Here, a U.S. mother engages in the technique with her fragile newborn. ■

INTERVENTIONS FOR PRETERM INFANTS A preterm baby is cared for in a special Plexiglas-enclosed bed called an *isolette*. Temperature is carefully controlled because these infants cannot yet regulate their own body temperature effectively. To help protect the baby from infection, air is filtered before it enters the isolette. When a preterm infant is fed through a stomach tube, breathes with the aid of a respirator, and receives medication through an intravenous needle, the isolette can be very isolating indeed! Physical needs that otherwise would lead to close contact and other human stimulation are met mechanically.

Special Infant Stimulation. At one time doctors believed that stimulating such fragile babies could be harmful. Now we know that in proper doses, certain kinds of stimulation can help preterm infants develop. In some intensive care nurseries, preterm babies can be seen rocking in suspended hammocks or lying on waterbeds designed to replace the gentle motion they would have received while still in the mother's uterus. Other forms of stimulation have also been used—an attractive mobile or a tape recording of a heartbeat, soft music, or the mother's voice. These experiences promote faster weight gain, more predictable sleep patterns, and greater alertness (Arnon et al., 2006; Marshall-Baker, Lickliter, & Cooper, 1998; Standley, 1998).

Touch is an especially important form of stimulation. In baby animals, touching the skin releases certain brain chemicals that support physical growth—effects believed to occur in humans as well. When preterm infants were gently massaged several times each day in the hospital, they gained weight faster and, at the end of the first year, were more advanced in mental and motor development than preterm babies not given this stimulation (Field, 2001; Field, Hernandez-Reif, & Freedman, 2004).

In developing countries where hospitalization is not always possible, skin-to-skin "kangaroo care" is the most readily available intervention for promoting the survival and recovery of preterm babies. It involves placing the infant in a vertical position between the mother's breasts or next to the father's chest (under the parent's clothing) so the parent's body functions as a human incubator. Kangaroo care offers fathers a unique opportunity to increase their involvement in caring for the preterm newborn. Because of its many physical and psychological benefits, the technique is used often in Western nations as a supplement to hospital intensive care.

Kangaroo skin-to-skin contact fosters improved oxygenation of the baby's body, temperature regulation, sleep, breastfeeding, alertness, and infant survival (Feldman, 2007a; Feldman & Eidelman, 2003). In addition, the kangaroo position provides the baby with gentle stimulation of all sensory modalities: hearing (through the parent's voice), smell (through proximity to the parent's body), touch (through skin-to-skin contact), and visual (through the upright position). Mothers and fathers practicing kangaroo care feel more confident about caring for their fragile babies, interact more sensitively and affectionately, and feel more attached to them (Dodd, 2005; Feldman et al., 2002, 2003).

Together, these factors may explain why preterm babies given many hours of kangaroo care in their early weeks, compared to those given little or no such care, are less likely to react negatively to and more likely to explore novel toys and score higher on measures of mental and motor development during the first year (Charpak, Ruiz-Peláez, & Figueroa, 2005; Feldman, 2007a; Tessier et al., 2003). Because of its diverse benefits, more than 80 percent of U.S. hospital nurseries now offer kangaroo care to preterm newborns (Field et al., 2006).

Training Parents in Infant Caregiving Skills. Interventions that support parents of preterm infants generally teach them about the infant's characteristics and promote caregiving skills. For parents with the economic and personal resources to care for a preterm infant, just a few sessions of coaching in recognizing and responding to the baby's needs are linked to enhanced parent–infant interaction, reduced infant crying and improved sleep, more rapid language development in the second year, and steady gains in mental test performance that equal those of full-term children by middle childhood (Achenbach, Howell, & Aoki, 1993; Newnham, Milgrom, & Skouteris, 2009).

When preterm infants live in stressed, low-income households, long-term intensive intervention is necessary. In the Infant Health and Development Project, preterm babies born into poverty received a comprehensive intervention that combined medical follow-up, weekly parent training sessions, and cognitively stimulating child care from 1 to 3 years of age. More than four times as many intervention children as no-intervention controls (39 versus 9 percent) were within normal range at age 3 in intelligence, psychological adjustment, and physical growth (Bradley et al., 1994). In addition, mothers in the intervention group were more affectionate and more often encouraged play and cognitive mastery in their children—one reason their 3-year-olds may have been developing so favorably (McCarton, 1998).

At ages 5 and 8, children who had attended the child-care program regularly—for more than 350 days over the three-year period—continued to show better intellectual functioning. The more they attended, the higher they scored, with greater gains among those whose birth weights were higher—between 4½ and 5½ pounds (2,001 to 2,500 grams) (see Figure 4.5). In contrast, children who attended only sporadically gained little or even lost ground (Hill, Brooks-Gunn, & Waldfogel, 2003). A follow-up at age 18 revealed persisting benefits for the higher-birth-weight participants: They remained advantaged over controls in academic achievement, and they also engaged in fewer risky behaviors (such as unprotected sexual activity and alcohol and drug use) (McCormick et al., 2006).

These findings confirm that babies who are both preterm and economically disadvantaged require *intensive* intervention. And special strategies, such as extra adult–child interaction, may be necessary to achieve lasting changes in children with the lowest birth weights.

VERY LOW BIRTH WEIGHT, ENVIRONMENTAL ADVANTAGES, AND LONG-TERM OUTCOMES

Although very-low-birth-weight individuals often have lasting problems, in a Canadian study, young adults who weighed between 1 and 2.2 pounds (500 to 1,000 grams) at birth were doing well in overall quality of life (Saigal et al., 2006). At 22 to 25 years of age, they resembled normal-birth-weight individuals

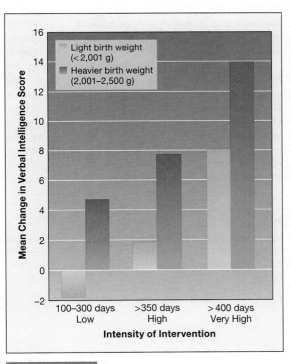

FIGURE 4.5

Influence of intensity of early intervention for low-income, preterm babies on intellectual functioning at age 8. Infants born preterm received cognitively stimulating child care from 1 through 3 years of age. Those who attended the program sporadically gained little in intellectual functioning (heavier-weight babies) or lost ground (lighter-weight babies). The more often children attended, the greater their intellectual gains. Heavier babies consistently gained more than light babies. But boosting the intensity of intervention above 400 days led to a dramatic increase in the performance of the light-weight group. *(Adapted from Hill, Brooks-Gunn, & Waldfogel, 2003.)*

SOCIAL ISSUES: HEALTH

A Cross-National Perspective on Health Care and Other Policies for Parents and Newborn Babies

*I*nfant mortality—the number of deaths in the first year of life per 1,000 live births—is an index used around the world to assess the overall health of a nation's children. The United States has the most up-to-date health-care technology in the world, including a newborn intensive care capacity per number of births far exceeding that of other industrialized nations (Thompson, Goodman, & Little, 2002). Nevertheless, it has made less progress in reducing infant deaths than many other countries. Over the past three decades, it has slipped in the international rankings, from seventh in the 1950s to twenty-eighth in 2009. Members of America's poor ethnic minorities are at greatest risk. African-American and Native-American babies are twice as likely as white infants to die in the first year of life (U.S. Census Bureau, 2010a, 2010b).

Neonatal mortality, the rate of death within the first month of life, accounts for 67 percent of the infant death rate in the United States. Two factors are largely responsible for neonatal mortality. The first is serious physical defects, most of which cannot be prevented. The percentage of babies born with physical defects is about the same in all ethnic and income groups. The second leading cause of neonatal mortality

is low birth weight, which is largely preventable. African-American and Native-American babies are more than twice as likely as white infants to be born early and underweight (U.S. Census Bureau, 2010b).

Widespread poverty and weak health-care programs for mothers and young children are largely responsible for these trends. Each country listed in Figure 4.6 that outranks the United States in infant survival provides all its citizens with government-sponsored health-care benefits. And each takes extra steps to make sure that pregnant mothers and

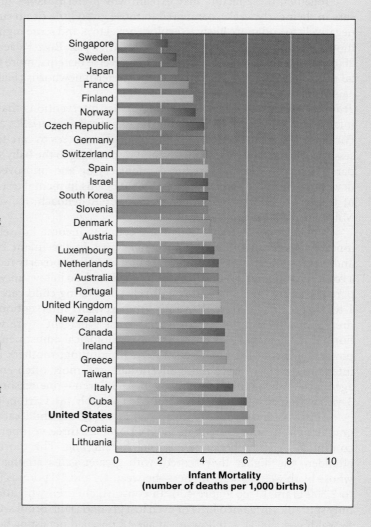

FIGURE 4.6

Infant mortality in 30 nations. Despite its advanced health-care technology, the United States ranks poorly. It is twenty-eighth in the world, with a death rate of 6.1 infants per 1,000 births. *(Adapted from U.S. Census Bureau, 2010a.)*

in educational attainment, rates of marriage and parenthood, and (for those who had no neurological or sensory impairments) employment status. What explains these excellent outcomes? Researchers believe that home, school, and societal advantages are largely responsible (Hack & Klein, 2006). Most participants in this study were reared in two-parent middle-SES homes, attended good schools where they received special services, and benefited from Canada's universal health care system.

Nevertheless, even the best environments cannot "fix" the enormous biological risks associated with very low birth weight. Think back to Keith, the very sick baby you met at the beginning of this section. Despite advanced medical technology and new ways of helping parents, most infants born as early and with as low a birth weight as Keith either die or end up with serious disabilities (Larroque et al., 2008; Mathews & MacDorman, 2006). Six months after he was born, Keith died without ever having left the hospital.

babies have access to good nutrition, high-quality medical care, and social and economic supports that promote effective parenting.

For example, all Western European nations guarantee women a certain number of prenatal visits at very low or no cost. After a baby is born, a health professional routinely visits the home to provide counseling about infant care and to arrange continuing medical services. Home assistance is especially extensive in the Netherlands. For a token fee, each mother is granted a specially trained maternity helper, who assists with infant care, shopping, housekeeping, meal preparation, and the care of other children during the days after delivery (Bradley & Bray, 1996; Zwart, 2007).

Paid, job-protected employment leave is another vital societal intervention for new parents. Canadian mothers are eligible for 15 weeks' maternity leave at 55 percent of prior earnings (up to a maximum of $413 per week), and Canadian mothers or fathers can take an additional 35 weeks of parental leave at the same rate. Paid leave is widely available in other industrialized nations as well. Sweden has the most generous parental leave program in the world. Mothers can begin maternity leave 60 days prior to expected delivery, extending it to six weeks after birth; fathers are granted two weeks of birth leave. In addition, either parent can take full leave for 16 months at 80 percent of prior earnings, followed by an additional three months at a modest flat rate. Each parent is also entitled to another 18 months of unpaid leave. Even less-developed nations provide parental leave benefits. For example, in the People's Republic of China, a new mother is granted three months' leave at regular pay. Furthermore, many countries supplement basic paid leave. In Germany, for example, after a fully paid three-month leave, a parent may take one more year at a flat rate and three additional years at no pay (OECD, 2006; Waldfogel, 2001).

Yet in the United States, the federal government mandates *only 12 weeks of unpaid leave* for employees in companies with at least 50 workers. Most women, however, work in smaller businesses, and even those who work in large enough companies may be unable to afford to take unpaid leave (Hewlett, 2003). And because of financial pressures, many new mothers who are eligible for unpaid work leave take far less than 12 weeks. Similarly, though paternal leave predicts fathers' increased involvement in infant care at the end of first year, many take little or none at all (Nepomnyaschy & Waldfogel, 2007; OECD, 2006). In 2002, California became the first state to guarantee a mother or father paid leave—up to six weeks at half salary, regardless of the size of the company.

Nevertheless, six weeks of childbirth leave (the norm in the United States) is not enough. When a family is stressed by a baby's arrival, leaves of six weeks or less are linked to increased maternal anxiety, depression, marital dissatisfaction, sense of role overload (conflict between work and family responsibilities), and negative interactions with the baby. A longer leave (12 weeks or more) predicts favorable maternal mental health, supportive marital interaction, and sensitive, responsive caregiving (Feldman, Sussman, & Zigler, 2004; Hyde et al., 2001). Single women and their babies are most

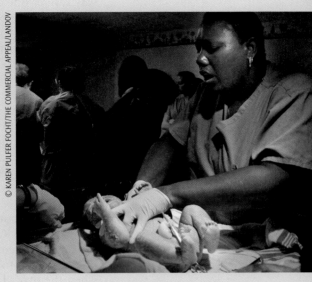

© KAREN PULFER FOCHT/THE COMMERCIAL APPEAL/LANDOV

■ This doctor works with high-risk pregnancies, delivering babies whose poverty-stricken mothers have had little or no prenatal care. Nations that provide government-sponsored health-care benefits for all citizens outrank the United States in infant survival. ■

hurt by the absence of a generous national paid-leave policy. These mothers, who are usually the sole source of support for their families, can least afford to take time from their jobs.

In countries with low infant mortality rates, expectant mothers need not wonder how they will get health care and other resources to support their baby's development. The powerful impact of universal, high-quality health care; generous parental leave; and other social services on maternal and infant well-being provides strong justification for these policies.

Keith's premature birth was unavoidable, but the high rate of underweight babies in the United States—one of the worst in the industrialized world—could be greatly reduced by improving the health and social conditions described in the Social Issues: Health box above. Fortunately, today we can save many preterm babies, but an even better course of action would be to prevent this serious threat to infant survival and development before it happens.

Birth Complications, Parenting, and Resilience

In the preceding sections, we considered a variety of birth complications. Now let's try to put the evidence together. Can any general principles help us understand how infants who survive a traumatic birth are likely to develop? A landmark study carried out in Hawaii provides answers to this question.

In 1955, Emmy Werner began to follow the development of nearly 700 infants on the island of Kauai who experienced either mild, moderate, or severe birth complications. Each was matched, on the basis of SES and ethnicity, with a healthy newborn (Werner & Smith, 1982). Findings showed that the likelihood of long-term difficulties increased if birth trauma was severe. But among mildly to moderately stressed children, those growing up in stable families did almost as well on measures of intelligence and psychological adjustment as those with no birth problems. Those exposed to poverty, family disorganization, and mentally ill parents often developed serious learning difficulties, behavior problems, and emotional disturbance.

The Kauai study tells us that as long as birth injuries are not overwhelming, a supportive home can restore children's growth. But the most intriguing cases in this study were the handful of exceptions. A few children with serious birth complications and troubled family environments grew into competent adults who fared as well as controls in career attainment and psychological adjustment. Werner found that these children relied on factors outside the family and within themselves to overcome stress. Some had attractive personalities that drew positive responses from relatives, neighbors, and peers. In other instances, a grandparent, aunt, uncle, or babysitter provided the needed emotional support (Werner, 1989, 2001; Werner & Smith, 1992).

Do these outcomes remind you of the characteristics of resilient children, discussed in Chapter 1? The Kauai study and other similar investigations reveal that the impact of early biological risks often wanes as children's personal characteristics and social experiences contribute increasingly to their functioning (Laucht, Esser, & Schmidt, 1997; Resnick et al., 1999). In sum, when the overall balance of life events tips toward the favorable side, children with serious birth problems can develop successfully. And when negative factors outweigh positive ones, even a sturdy newborn can become a lifelong casualty.

Ask Yourself

◆ **REVIEW** Sensitive care can help preterm infants recover, but they are less likely than full-term newborns to receive such care. Explain why.

◆ **APPLY** Cecilia and Adena each gave birth to a 3-pound baby seven weeks preterm. Cecilia is single and on welfare. Adena and her husband are happily married and earn a good income. Plan an intervention appropriate for helping each baby develop.

◆ **CONNECT** List factors discussed in this chapter and in Chapter 3 that increase the chances that an infant will be born underweight. How many of these factors could be prevented by better health care for expectant mothers?

◆ **REFLECT** Many people object to the use of extraordinary medical measures to save extremely low-birthweight babies because of their high risk for persistent, serious developmental problems. Do you agree or disagree? Explain.

Precious Moments After Birth

Yolanda and Jay's account of Joshua's birth revealed that the time spent holding and touching him right after delivery was filled with intense emotion. A mother given her infant at this time will usually stroke the baby gently, look into the infant's eyes, and talk softly (Klaus & Kennell, 1982). Fathers respond similarly. Most are overjoyed at their baby's birth; characterize the experience as "awesome," "indescribable," or "unforgettable"; and display intense interest in their newborn child (Bader, 1995; Rose, 2000). Regardless of SES or participation in childbirth classes, fathers touch, look at, talk to, and kiss their newborn infants just as much as mothers do. When they hold the baby, they sometimes exceed mothers in stimulation and affection (Parke & Tinsley, 1981).

Certain parental hormonal changes in the presence of the newborn help foster parents' involvement and sensitivity. Toward the end of pregnancy, mothers begin producing higher levels of the hormone *oxytocin,* which causes the breasts to "let down" milk and heightens responsiveness to the baby (Russell, Douglas, & Ingram, 2001). And in several studies, fathers showed hormonal changes when holding their newborn babies that were compatible with those of mothers—specifically, slight increases in *prolactin* (a hormone that stimulates milk production in females) and *estrogens* (sex hormones produced in larger quantities in females) and a drop in *androgens* (sex hormones produced in larger quantities in males). In animal and human research, these changes are associated with positive emotional reactions to infants and with paternal caregiving (Delahunty et al., 2007; Storey et al., 2000; Wynne-Edwards, 2001).

But do human parents require close physical contact in the hours after birth for **bonding,** or feelings of affection and concern for the infant, to develop—as many animal species do? Current evidence shows that the human parent–infant relationship does not depend on a precise, early period of togetherness. Some parents report sudden, deep feelings of affection on first holding their babies. For others, these emotions emerge gradually (Lamb, 1994). And as successful adoption reveals (see pages 65–68 in Chapter 2), humans can parent effectively without experiencing birth-related hormonal changes. Human bonding is a complex process that depends on many factors, not just on what happens during a short sensitive period.

Still, contact with the baby after birth may be one of several factors that help build a good parent–infant relationship. Research shows that mothers learn to discriminate their newborn baby from other infants on the basis of touch, smell, and sight (a photograph) after as little as one hour of contact (Kaitz et al., 1987, 1988, 1993a). Fathers, as well, can recognize their baby by touch and sight after brief exposure (Bader & Phillips, 2002; Kaitz et al., 1993b). This early recognition probably facilitates responsiveness to the infant.

Clearly, early contact supports parental engagement with the newborn, although it is neither necessary nor a guarantee of it. Realizing this, today hospitals offer **rooming in,** in which the infant stays in the mother's hospital room all or most of the time. If parents do not choose this option or cannot do so for medical reasons, there is no evidence that their competence as caregivers will be compromised or that the baby will suffer emotionally.

■ This father displays great affection for and involvement with his newborn baby. Like mothers, fathers typically express their elation by touching, looking at, talking to, and kissing the infant. ■

The Newborn Baby's Capacities

Newborn infants have a remarkable set of capacities that are crucial for survival and for evoking adult attention and care. In relating to the physical and social world, babies are active from the very start.

Reflexes

A **reflex** is an inborn, automatic response to a particular form of stimulation. Reflexes are the newborn baby's most obvious organized patterns of behavior. As Jay placed Joshua on a table in my classroom, we saw several. When Jay bumped the side of the table, Joshua reacted by flinging his arms wide and bringing them back toward his body. As Yolanda stroked Joshua's cheek, he turned his head in her direction. When she put her finger in Joshua's palm, he grabbed on tightly. TAKE A MOMENT... Look at Table 4.2 on page 144 and see if you can name the newborn reflexes that Joshua displayed. Then let's consider the meaning and purpose of these curious behaviors.

ADAPTIVE VALUE OF REFLEXES   Some reflexes have survival value. The rooting reflex helps a breastfed baby find the mother's nipple. Babies display it only when hungry and touched by another person, not when they touch themselves (Rochat & Hespos, 1997). And if sucking were not automatic, our species would be unlikely to survive for a single generation! At birth, babies adjust their sucking pressure to how easily milk flows from the nipple (Craig & Lee, 1999). The swimming reflex helps a baby who is accidentally dropped into a body of water stay afloat, increasing the chances of retrieval by the caregiver.

TABLE 4.2   Some Newborn Reflexes

REFLEX	STIMULATION	RESPONSE	AGE OF DISAPPEARANCE	FUNCTION
Eye blink	Shine bright light at eyes or clap hand near head	Infant quickly closes eyelids	Permanent	Protects infant from strong stimulation
Rooting	Stroke cheek near corner of mouth	Head turns toward source of stimulation	3 weeks (becomes voluntary head turning at this time)	Helps infant find the nipple
Sucking	Place finger in infant's mouth	Infant sucks finger rhythmically	Replaced by voluntary sucking after 4 months	Permits feeding
Swimming	Place infant face down in pool of water	Baby paddles and kicks in swimming motion	4–6 months	Helps infant survive if dropped into water
Moro	Hold infant horizontally on back and let head drop slightly, or produce a sudden loud sound against surface supporting infant	Infant makes an "embracing" motion by arching back, extending legs, throwing arms outward, and then bringing arms in toward the body	6 months	In human evolutionary past, may have helped infant cling to mother
Palmar grasp	Place finger in infant's hand and press against palm	Spontaneous grasp of finger	3–4 months	Prepares infant for voluntary grasping
Tonic neck	Turn baby's head to one side while infant is lying awake on back	Infant lies in a "fencing position." One arm is extended in front of eyes on side to which head is turned, other arm is flexed	4 months	May prepare infant for voluntary reaching
Stepping	Hold infant under arms and permit bare feet to touch a flat surface	Infant lifts one foot after another in stepping response	2 months in infants who gain weight quickly; sustained in lighter infants	Prepares infant for voluntary walking
Babinski	Stroke sole of foot from toe toward heel	Toes fan out and curl as foot twists in	8–12 months	Unknown

Sources: Knobloch & Pasamanick, 1974; Prechtl & Beintema, 1965; Thelen, Fisher, & Ridley-Johnson, 1984.

© LAURA DWIGHT PHOTOGRAPHY

■ The palmar grasp reflex is so strong during the first week after birth that many infants can use it to support their entire weight. ■

Other reflexes probably helped babies survive during our evolutionary past. For example, the Moro, or "embracing," reflex is believed to have helped infants cling to their mothers when they were carried about all day. If the baby happened to lose support, the reflex caused the infant to embrace and, along with the palmar grasp reflex (so strong during the first week that it can support the baby's entire weight), regain its hold on the mother's body (Kessen, 1967; Prechtl, 1958).

Several reflexes help parents and infants establish gratifying interaction. A baby who searches for and successfully finds the nipple, sucks easily during feedings, and grasps when her hand is touched encourages parents to respond lovingly and feel competent as caregivers. Reflexes can also help parents comfort the baby because they permit infants to control distress and amount of stimulation. For example, on short trips with Joshua to the grocery store, Yolanda brought along a pacifier. If he became fussy, sucking helped quiet him until she could feed, change, or hold and rock him.

REFLEXES AND THE DEVELOPMENT OF MOTOR SKILLS   A few reflexes form the basis for complex motor skills that will develop later. For example, the tonic neck reflex may prepare the baby for voluntary reaching. When infants lie on their backs in this "fencing position," they naturally gaze at the hand in front of their eyes. The reflex may encourage them to combine vision with arm movements and, eventually, reach for objects (Knobloch & Pasamanick, 1974).

Certain reflexes—such as the palmar grasp, swimming, and stepping—drop out early, but the motor functions involved are renewed later. The stepping reflex, for example, looks like a primitive walking response. Unlike other reflexes, it appears in a wide range of situations—

with the newborn's body in a sideways or upside-down position, with feet touching walls or ceilings, and even with legs dangling in the air (Adolph & Berger, 2006). One reason that babies frequently engage in the alternating leg movements of stepping is their ease compared with other movement patterns; repetitive movement of one leg or of both legs at once requires more effort.

In infants who gain weight quickly in the weeks after birth, stepping drops out because thigh and calf muscles are not strong enough to lift the baby's chubby legs. But if the lower part of the infant's body is dipped in water, the reflex reappears because the buoyancy of the water lightens the load on the baby's muscles (Thelen, Fisher, & Ridley-Johnson, 1984). When stepping is exercised regularly, babies display more spontaneous stepping movements and gain muscle strength. Consequently, they tend to walk several weeks earlier than if stepping is not practiced (Zelazo et al., 1993). However, there is no special need for infants to practice the stepping reflex—all normal babies walk in due time.

In the case of the swimming reflex, trying to build on it is risky. Although young babies placed in a swimming pool will paddle and kick, they swallow large amounts of water. This lowers the concentration of salt in the baby's blood, which can cause brain swelling and seizures. Despite this remarkable reflex, swimming lessons are best postponed until at least 3 years of age.

THE IMPORTANCE OF ASSESSING NEWBORN REFLEXES
Look at Table 4.2 again, and you will see that most newborn reflexes disappear during the first six months. Researchers believe that this is due to a gradual increase in voluntary control over behavior as the cerebral cortex develops. Pediatricians test reflexes carefully, especially if a newborn has experienced birth trauma, because reflexes can reveal the health of the baby's nervous system. Weak or absent reflexes, overly rigid or exaggerated reflexes, and reflexes that persist beyond the point in development when they should normally disappear can signal brain damage (Schott & Rossor, 2003; Zafeiriou, 2000). However, individual differences in reflexive responses exist that are not cause for concern. An observer must assess newborn reflexes along with other characteristics to accurately distinguish normal from abnormal central nervous system functioning.

States

Throughout the day and night, newborn infants move in and out of the five **states of arousal,** or degrees of sleep and wakefulness, described in Table 4.3 on page 146. During the first month, these states alternate frequently. The most fleeting is quiet alertness, which usually moves quickly toward fussing and crying. Much to the relief of their fatigued parents, newborns spend the greatest amount of time asleep—about 16 to 18 hours a day. Because the fetus tends to synchronize periods of rest and activity with those of the mother, newborns—even those who are 4 to 6 weeks preterm—sleep more at night than during the day (Heraghty et al., 2008; Rivkees, 2003). Nevertheless, young babies' sleep–wake cycles are affected more by fullness–hunger than by darkness–light (Davis, Parker, & Montgomery, 2004; Goodlin-Jones, Burnham, & Anders, 2000).

However, striking individual differences in daily rhythms exist that affect parents' attitudes toward and interactions with the baby. A few newborns sleep for long periods, increasing the energy their well-rested parents have for sensitive, responsive care. Other babies cry a great deal, and their parents must exert great effort to soothe them. If these parents do not succeed, they may feel less competent and less positive toward their infant. Babies who spend more time alert probably receive more social stimulation and

■ In the Moro reflex, loss of support or a sudden loud sound causes the baby to arch her back, extend her arms outward, and then bring them in toward her body. ■

■ This baby shows the Babinski reflex. When an adult strokes the sole of the foot, the toes fan out. Then they curl as the foot twists in. ■

■ When held upright under the arms, newborn babies show reflexive stepping movements. ■

TABLE 4.3	Infant States of Arousal	

STATE	DESCRIPTION	DAILY DURATION IN NEWBORN
Regular, or NREM, sleep	The infant is at full rest and shows little or no body activity. The eyelids are closed, no eye movements occur, the face is relaxed, and breathing is slow and regular.	8–9 hours
Irregular, or REM, sleep	Gentle limb movements, occasional stirring, and facial grimacing occur. Although the eyelids are closed, occasional rapid eye movements can be seen beneath them. Breathing is irregular.	8–9 hours
Drowsiness	The infant is either falling asleep or waking up. Body is less active than in irregular sleep but more active than in regular sleep. The eyes open and close; when open, they have a glazed look. Breathing is even but somewhat faster than in regular sleep.	Varies
Quiet alertness	The infant's body is relatively inactive, with eyes open and attentive. Breathing is even.	2–3 hours
Waking activity and crying	The infant shows frequent bursts of uncoordinated body activity. Breathing is very irregular. Face may be relaxed or tense and wrinkled. Crying may occur.	1–4 hours

Source: Wolff, 1966.

opportunities to explore and, therefore, may have a slight advantage in mental development (Sadeh et al., 2007; Smart & Hiscock, 2007).

Of the states listed in Table 4.3 the two extremes—sleep and crying—have been of greatest interest to researchers. Each tells us something about normal and abnormal early development.

SLEEP Observing Joshua as he slept, Yolanda and Jay wondered why his eyelids and body twitched and his rate of breathing varied. Sleep is made up of at least two states. During irregular, or **rapid-eye-movement (REM), sleep,** brain-wave activity is remarkably similar to that of the waking state. The eyes dart beneath the lids; heart rate, blood pressure, and breathing are uneven; and slight body movements occur. The expression "sleeping like a baby" was probably not meant to describe this state! In contrast, during regular, or **non-rapid-eye-movement (NREM), sleep,** the body is almost motionless, and heart rate, breathing, and brain-wave activity are slow and even.

Like children and adults, newborns alternate between REM and NREM sleep. However, they spend far more time in the REM state than they ever will again. REM sleep accounts for 50 percent of the newborn baby's sleep time. By 3 to 5 years, it has declined to an adultlike level of 20 percent (Louis et al., 1997).

Why do young infants spend so much time in REM sleep? In older children and adults, the REM state is associated with dreaming. Babies probably do not dream, at least not in the same way we do. But researchers believe that the stimulation of REM sleep is vital for growth of the central nervous system. Young infants seem to have a special need for this stimulation because they spend so little time in an alert state, when they can get input from the environment. In support of this idea, the percentage of REM sleep is especially great in the fetus and in preterm babies, who are even less able than full-term newborns to take advantage of external stimulation (de Weerd & van den Bossche, 2003; Peirano, Algarin, & Uauy, 2003).

Whereas the brain-wave activity of REM sleep safeguards the central nervous system, the rapid eye movements protect the health of the eye. Eye movements cause the vitreous (gelatin-like substance within the eye) to circulate, thereby delivering oxygen to parts of the eye that do not have their own blood supply. During sleep, when the eyes and the vitreous are still, visual structures are at risk for anoxia. As the brain cycles through REM-sleep periods, rapid eye movements stir up the vitreous, ensuring that the eye is fully oxygenated (Blumberg & Lucas, 1996).

Because the normal sleep behavior of the newborn baby is organized and patterned, observations of sleep states can help identify central nervous system abnormalities. In infants who are brain-damaged or who have experienced serious birth trauma, disturbed REM–NREM sleep cycles are often present. Babies with poor sleep organization are likely to be behaviorally disorganized and, therefore, to have difficulty learning and eliciting caregiver interactions that enhance their development. In follow-ups during the preschool years, they show delayed

SOCIAL ISSUES: HEALTH

The Mysterious Tragedy of Sudden Infant Death Syndrome

*M*illie awoke with a start one morning and looked at the clock. It was 7:30, and Sasha had missed both her night waking and her early morning feeding. Wondering if she was all right, Millie and her husband, Stuart, tiptoed into the room. Sasha lay still, curled up under her blanket. She had died silently during her sleep.

Sasha was a victim of **sudden infant death syndrome (SIDS)**, the unexpected death, usually during the night, of an infant younger than 1 year of age that remains unexplained after thorough investigation. In industrialized nations, SIDS is the leading cause of infant mortality between 1 week and 12 months, accounting for about 20 percent of these deaths in the United States (Mathews & MacDorman, 2008).

SIDS victims usually show physical problems from the beginning. Early medical records of SIDS babies reveal higher rates of prematurity and low birth weight, poor Apgar scores, and limp muscle tone. Abnormal heart rate and respiration and disturbances in sleep–wake cycles are also involved (Cornwell & Feigenbaum, 2006; Kato et al., 2003). At the time of death, many SIDS babies have a mild respiratory infection (Samuels, 2003). This seems to increase the chances of respiratory failure in an already vulnerable baby.

Mounting evidence suggests that impaired brain functioning is a major contributor to SIDS. Between 2 and 4 months, when SIDS is most likely to occur, reflexes decline and are replaced by voluntary, learned responses. Neurological weaknesses may prevent SIDS babies from acquiring behaviors that replace defensive reflexes (Lipsitt, 2003). As a result, when breathing difficulties occur during sleep, these infants do not wake up, shift their position, or cry out for help. Instead, they simply give in to oxygen deprivation and death. In support of this

interpretation, autopsies reveal that the brains of SIDS babies contain unusually low levels of serotonin (a brain chemical that assists with arousal when survival is threatened) as well as other abnormalities in centers controlling breathing and arousal (Duncan et al., 2010; Paterson et al., 2006).

Several environmental factors are linked to SIDS. Maternal cigarette smoking, both during and after pregnancy, as well as smoking by other caregivers, doubles risk of the disorder. Babies exposed to cigarette smoke arouse less easily from sleep and have more respiratory infections (Anderson, Johnson, & Batal, 2005; Shah, Sullivan, & Carter, 2006). Prenatal abuse of drugs that depress central nervous system functioning (alcohol, opiates, and barbiturates) increases the risk of SIDS as much as fifteenfold (Hunt & Hauck, 2006). Babies of drug-abusing mothers are especially likely to display SIDS-related brain abnormalities (Kinney, 2009).

SIDS babies are also more likely to sleep on their stomachs than on their backs and often are wrapped very warmly in clothing and blankets. Infants who sleep on their stomachs less often wake when their breathing is disturbed (Richardson, Walker, & Horne, 2008). In other cases, healthy babies sleeping face down in soft bedding may die from continually breathing their own exhaled breath.

Quitting smoking and drug taking, changing an infant's sleeping position, and removing a few bedclothes can reduce the incidence of SIDS. For example, if women refrained from smoking while pregnant, an estimated 30 percent of SIDS cases would be prevented. Public education campaigns that encourage parents to put their infants down on their backs have cut the incidence of SIDS by more than half in many Western nations (Moon, Horne, & Hauck, 2007). Another protective measure is pacifier use: Sleeping babies who suck arouse more

easily in response to breathing and heart-rate irregularities (Li et al., 2006). Nevertheless, compared with white infants, SIDS rates are two to six times higher in poverty-stricken minority groups, where parental stress, substance abuse, reduced access to health care, and lack of knowledge about safe sleep practices are widespread (Pickett, Luo, & Lauderdale, 2005).

When SIDS does occur, surviving family members require a great deal of help to overcome a sudden and unexpected death. As Millie commented six months after Sasha's death, "It's the worst crisis we've ever been through. What's helped us most are the comforting words of others who've experienced the same tragedy."

© BANANASTOCK/GETTY IMAGES/JUPITERIMAGES

■ Public education campaigns encouraging parents to put their infants down on their backs to sleep have helped to reduce the incidence of SIDS, which has dropped by more than half in many Western nations. ■

motor, cognitive, and language development (de Weerd & van den Bossche, 2003; Feldman, 2006; Holditch-Davis, Belyea, & Edwards, 2005). And the brain-functioning problems that underlie newborn sleep irregularities may culminate in sudden infant death syndrome, a major cause of infant mortality (see the Social Issues: Health box above).

CRYING   Crying is the first way that babies communicate, letting parents know that they need food, comfort, and stimulation. During the weeks after birth, all babies seem to have some fussy periods when they are difficult to console. But most of the time, the nature of the cry,

Applying What We Know

Soothing a Crying Baby

TECHNIQUE	EXPLANATION
Lift the baby to the shoulder and rock or walk.	This combination of physical contact, upright posture, and motion is an effective soothing technique, causing young infants to become quietly alert.
Swaddle the baby.	Restricting movement and increasing warmth often soothe a young infant.
Offer a pacifier.	Sucking helps babies control their own level of arousal.
Talk softly or play rhythmic sounds.	Continuous, monotonous, rhythmic sounds (such as a clock ticking, a fan whirring, or peaceful music) are more effective than intermittent sounds.
Take the baby for a short car ride or a walk in a baby carriage; swing the baby in a cradle.	Gentle, rhythmic motion of any kind helps lull the baby to sleep.
Massage the baby's body.	Stroking the baby's torso and limbs with continuous, gentle motions relaxes the baby's muscles.
Combine several of the methods just listed.	Stimulating several of the baby's senses at once is often more effective than stimulating only one.
If these methods do not work, let the baby cry for a short period.	Occasionally, a baby responds well to just being put down and will, after a few minutes, fall asleep.

Sources: Evanoo, 2007; Campos, 1989; Lester, 1985; Reisman, 1987.

combined with the experiences that led up to it, helps guide parents toward its cause. The baby's cry is a complex stimulus that varies in intensity, from a whimper to a message of all-out distress (Gustafson, Wood, & Green, 2000). As early as the first few weeks, infants can be identified by the unique vocal "signature" of their cries, which helps parents locate their baby from a distance (Gustafson, Green, & Cleland, 1994).

Young infants usually cry because of physical needs. Hunger is the most common cause, but babies may also cry in response to temperature change when undressed, a sudden noise, or a painful stimulus. Newborns (as well as older babies) often cry at the sound of another crying baby (Dondi, Simion, & Caltran, 1999). Some researchers believe that this response reflects an inborn capacity to react to the suffering of others. Furthermore, crying typically increases during the early weeks, peaks at about 6 weeks, and then declines. Because this trend appears in many cultures with vastly different infant care practices, researchers believe that normal readjustments of the central nervous system underlie it (Barr, 2001).

TAKE A MOMENT... The next time you hear a baby cry, notice your own reaction. The sound stimulates strong feelings of arousal and discomfort in men and women, parents and nonparents alike (Murray, 1985). This powerful response is probably innately programmed to help ensure that babies receive the care and protection they need to survive.

Soothing Crying Infants. Although parents do not always interpret their baby's cry correctly, their accuracy improves with experience. Fortunately, there are many ways to soothe a crying baby when feeding and diaper changing do not work (see Applying What We Know above). The technique that Western parents usually try first, lifting the baby to the shoulder and rocking or walking, is most effective. Another common soothing method is swaddling—wrapping the baby snugly in a blanket. The Quechua, who live in the cold, high-altitude desert regions of Peru, dress young babies in several layers of clothing and blankets that cover the head and body, a technique that reduces crying and promotes sleep (Tronick, Thomas, & Daltabuit, 1994). It also enables the baby to conserve energy for early growth in the harsh Peruvian highlands.

In many tribal and village societies and in non-Western developed nations, infants spend most of the day and night in close physical contact

■ To soothe his crying infant, this father holds the baby upright against his gently moving body. The combination of physical contact, upright posture, and motion causes infants to stop crying and become quietly alert. ■

© KEVIN DODGE/CORBIS

with their caregivers. Among the !Kung of the desert regions of Botswana, Africa, mothers carry their young babies in grass-lined, animal-skin slings hung on their hips, so the infants can see their surroundings and can nurse at will. Japanese mothers also spend much time holding their babies (Small, 1998). Infants in these cultures show shorter bouts of crying than their American counterparts (Barr, 2001). When Western parents choose to practice "proximal care" by holding their babies extensively, amount of crying in the early months is reduced by about one-third (St James-Roberts et al., 2006).

Abnormal Crying. Like reflexes and sleep patterns, the infant's cry offers a clue to central nervous system distress. The cries of brain-damaged babies and those who have experienced prenatal and birth complications are often shrill, piercing, and shorter in duration than the cries of healthy infants (Boukydis & Lester, 1998; Green, Irwin, & Gustafson, 2000). Even newborns with a fairly common problem—*colic,* or persistent crying—tend to have high-pitched, harsh-sounding cries (Zeskind & Barr, 1997). Although the cause of colic is unknown, certain newborns, who react especially strongly to unpleasant stimuli, are susceptible. Because their crying is intense, they find it harder to calm down than other babies. Colic generally subsides between 3 and 6 months (Barr et al., 2005; St James-Roberts, 2007).

In an intervention aimed at reducing colic, nurses made periodic home visits, providing parents with help in identifying their baby's early warning signs of becoming overly aroused, in using effective soothing techniques, and in modifying light, noise, and activity in the home to promote predictable sleep–wake cycles (Keefe et al., 2005). Colicky infants who received the intervention spent far less time crying than no-intervention controls—1.3 versus 3 hours per day.

Most parents try to respond to a crying baby's call for help with extra care and attention, but sometimes the cry is so unpleasant and the infant so difficult to soothe that parents become frustrated, resentful, and angry. Preterm and ill babies are more likely to be abused by highly stressed parents, who sometimes mention a high-pitched, grating cry as one factor that caused them to lose control and harm the baby (St. James-Roberts, 2007; Zeskind & Lester, 2001). We will discuss a host of additional influences on child abuse in Chapter 10.

■ These Quechua women, who live in the cold, high-altitude desert regions of Peru, dress their young babies in layers of clothing and blankets that cover the head and body. In addition to reducing crying and promoting sleep, swaddling helps babies conserve energy for early growth in the harsh Peruvian highlands. ■

Sensory Capacities

On his visit to my class, Joshua looked wide-eyed at my bright pink blouse and turned to the sound of his mother's voice. During feedings, he lets Yolanda know by the way he sucks that he prefers the taste of breast milk to a bottle of plain water. Clearly, Joshua has some well-developed sensory capacities. In the following sections, we explore the newborn baby's responsiveness to touch, taste, smell, sound, and visual stimulation.

TOUCH   In our discussion of preterm infants, we saw that touch helps stimulate early physical growth. And as we will see in Chapter 7, it is vital for emotional development as well. Therefore, it is not surprising that sensitivity to touch is well-developed at birth.

The reflexes listed in Table 4.2 on page 144 reveal that the newborn baby responds to touch, especially around the mouth, on the palms, and on the soles of the feet. During the prenatal period, these areas, along with the genitals, are the first to become sensitive to touch (Humphrey, 1978; Streri, 2005). Using their palms, newborns can even distinguish the shapes (prism versus cylinder) and textures (smooth versus rough) of small objects, as indicated by their tendency to hold on longer to an object with an unfamiliar shape or texture than to a familiar object (Sann & Streri, 2008; Streri, Lhote, & Dutilleul, 2000).

At birth, infants are quite sensitive to pain. If male newborns are circumcised, anesthetic is sometimes not used because of the risk of giving drugs to a very young infant. Babies often respond with a high-pitched, stressful cry and a dramatic rise in heart rate, blood pressure,

LOOK AND LISTEN

In a public setting, watch several parents soothe their crying babies. What techniques did the parents use, and how successful were they?

palm sweating, pupil dilation, and muscle tension (Lehr et al., 2007; Warnock & Sandrin, 2004). Brain-imaging research suggests that because of central nervous system immaturity, preterm and male babies feel the pain of a medical injection especially intensely (Bartocci et al., 2006).

Recent research establishing the safety of certain local anesthetics for newborns promises to ease the pain of these procedures. Offering a nipple that delivers a sugar solution is also helpful; it quickly reduces crying and discomfort in young babies, preterm and full-term alike. Breast milk may be especially effective: Even the smell of the milk of the baby's mother reduces infant stress to a routine blood-test heelstick more effectively than the odor of another mother's milk or of formula (Nishitani et al., 2009). And combining sweet liquid with gentle holding by the parent lessens pain even more. Research on infant mammals indicates that physical touch releases *endorphins*—painkilling chemicals in the brain (Axelin, Salantera, & Lehtonen, 2006; Gormally et al., 2001).

Allowing a baby to endure severe pain overwhelms the nervous system with stress hormones, which can disrupt the child's developing capacity to handle common, everyday stressors. The result is heightened pain sensitivity, sleep disturbances, feeding problems, and difficulty calming down when upset (Mitchell & Boss, 2002).

TASTE AND SMELL   Facial expressions reveal that newborns can distinguish several basic tastes. Like adults, they relax their facial muscles in response to sweetness, purse their lips when the taste is sour, and show a distinct archlike mouth opening when it is bitter (Steiner, 1979; Steiner et al., 2001). These reactions are important for survival: The food that best supports the infant's early growth is the sweet-tasting milk of the mother's breast. Not until 4 months do babies prefer a salty taste to plain water, a change that may prepare them to accept solid foods (Mennella & Beauchamp, 1998).

(a) Responses by newborns of anise-consuming mothers

(b) Responses by newborns of non-anise-consuming mothers

FIGURE 4.7

Examples of facial expressions of newborns exposed to the odor of anise whose mothers' diets differed in anise-flavored foods during late pregnancy. (a) Babies of anise-consuming mothers spent more time turning toward the odor and sucking, licking, and chewing. (b) Babies of non-anise-consuming mothers more often turned away with a negative facial expression. *(From B. Schaal, L. Marlier, & R. Soussignan, 2000, "Human Foetuses Learn Odours from Their Pregnant Mother's Diet,"* Chemical Senses, *25, p. 731. Reprinted by permission of Benoist Schaal.)*

Nevertheless, newborns can readily learn to like a taste that at first evoked either a neutral or a negative response. For example, babies allergic to cow's milk formula who are given a soy or other vegetable-based substitute (typically very strong and bitter-tasting) soon prefer it to regular formula. A taste previously disliked can come to be preferred when it is paired with relief of hunger (Harris, 1997).

As with taste, certain odor preferences are present at birth. For example, the smell of bananas or chocolate causes a relaxed, pleasant facial expression, whereas the odor of rotten eggs makes the infant frown (Steiner, 1979). During pregnancy, the amniotic fluid is rich in tastes and smells that vary with the mother's diet—early experiences that influence newborns' preferences. In a study carried out in the Alsatian region of France, where anise is frequently used to flavor foods, researchers tested newborns for their reaction to the anise odor (Schaal, Marlier, & Soussignan, 2000). The mothers of some babies had regularly consumed anise during the last two weeks of pregnancy; the other mothers had never consumed it. When presented with the anise odor on the day of birth, the babies of non-anise-consuming mothers were far more likely to turn away with a negative facial expression (see Figure 4.7). These different reactions were still apparent four days later, even though all mothers had refrained from consuming anise during this time.

In many mammals, the sense of smell plays an important role in feeding and in protecting the young from predators by helping mothers and babies identify each other. Although smell is less well-developed in humans, traces of its survival value remain.

Immediately after birth, infants placed face-down between their mother's breasts latch on to a nipple and begin sucking within an hour. If one breast is washed to remove its natural scent, most newborns move toward the unwashed breast, indicating that they are guided by smell (Varendi & Porter, 2001). At 4 days of age, breastfed babies prefer the smell of their own mother's breast to that of an unfamiliar lactating woman (Cernoch & Porter, 1985). And both breast- and bottle-fed 3- to 4-day-olds orient more and display more mouthing to the smell of unfamiliar human milk than to formula milk, indicating that (even without postnatal exposure) the odor of human milk is more attractive to newborns (Marlier & Schaal, 2005). Newborns' dual attraction to the odors of their mother and of breast milk helps them locate an appropriate food source and, in the process, distinguish their caregiver from other people.

HEARING   Although conduction of sound through the structures of the ear and transmission of auditory information to the brain are inefficient at birth, newborn infants can hear a wide variety of sounds—sensitivity that improves greatly over the first few months (Saffran, Werker, & Werner, 2006; Tharpe & Ashmead, 2001). At birth, infants prefer complex sounds, such as noises and voices, to pure tones. And babies only a few days old can tell the difference between a variety of sound patterns: a series of tones arranged in ascending versus descending order; tone sequences with a rhythmic downbeat (as in music) versus those without; utterances with two versus three syllables; the stress patterns of words, such as "*ma*-ma" versus "ma-*ma*"; happy-sounding speech as opposed to speech with negative or neutral emotional qualities; and even two languages spoken by the same bilingual speaker, as long as those languages differ in their rhythmic features—for example, French from Russian (Mastropieri & Turkewitz, 1999; Ramus, 2002; Sansavini, Bertoncini, & Giovanelli, 1997; Trehub, 2001; Winkler et al., 2009).

Young infants listen longer to human speech than to structurally similar nonspeech sounds (Vouloumanos & Werker, 2004). And they can detect the sounds of any human language. Newborns make fine-grained distinctions among many speech sounds. For example, when given a nipple that turns on a recording of the "*ba*" sound, babies suck vigorously for a while and then slow down as the novelty wears off. When the sound switches to "*ga*," sucking picks up, indicating that infants detect this subtle difference. Using this method, researchers have found only a few speech sounds that newborns cannot discriminate. Their ability to perceive sounds not found in their own language is more precise than an adult's (Aldridge, Stillman, & Bower, 2001; Jusczyk & Luce, 2002). These capacities reveal that the baby is marvelously prepared for the awesome task of acquiring language.

Responsiveness to sound also supports the newborn baby's exploration of the environment. Infants as young as 3 days turn their eyes and head in the general direction of a sound. The ability to identify the precise location of a sound improves greatly over the first six months and shows further gains through the preschool years (Litovsky & Ashmead, 1997).

TAKE A MOMENT... Listen carefully to yourself the next time you talk to a young baby. You will probably speak in ways that highlight important parts of the speech stream—use a high-pitched, expressive voice with a rising tone at the ends of phrases and sentences and a pause before continuing. Adults probably communicate this way with infants because they notice that babies are more attentive when they do so. Indeed, newborns prefer speech with these characteristics (Saffran, Werker, & Werner, 2006). They will also suck more on a nipple to hear a recording of their own mother's voice than that of an unfamiliar woman and to hear their native language as opposed to a foreign language (Moon, Cooper, & Fifer, 1993; Spence & DeCasper, 1987). These preferences may have developed from hearing the muffled sounds of the mother's voice before birth.

VISION   Vision is the least developed of the newborn baby's senses. Visual structures in both the eye and the brain are not yet fully formed at birth. For example, cells in the *retina,* the membrane lining the inside of the eye that captures light and transforms it into messages that are sent to the brain, are not as mature or densely packed as they will be in several months. The optic nerve that relays these messages, and visual centers in the brain that receive them, will not be adultlike for several years. And muscles of the *lens,* which permit us to adjust our visual focus to varying distances, are weak (Kellman & Arterberry, 2006).

As a result, newborn babies cannot focus their eyes well, and their **visual acuity,** or fineness of discrimination, is limited. At birth, infants perceive objects at a distance of 20 feet about

FIGURE 4.8

View of the human face by the newborn and the adult. The new-born baby's limited focusing ability and poor visual acuity lead the mother's face, even when viewed from close up, to look much like the fuzzy image in (a) rather than the clear image in (b). Also, newborn infants have some color vision, although they have difficulty discriminating colors. Researchers speculate that colors probably appear similar, but less intense, to newborns than to older infants and adults. *(From Kellman & Arterberry 2006; Slater, 2001.)*

(a) Newborn View   (b) Adult View

as clearly as adults do at 600 feet (Slater, 2001). In addition, unlike adults (who see nearby objects most clearly), newborn babies see unclearly across a wide range of distances (Banks, 1980; Hainline, 1998). As a result, images such as the parent's face, even from close up, look like the blurry image in Figure 4.8. Nevertheless, as we will see in Chapter 5, newborns can detect human faces. And as with their preference for their mother's smell and voice, from repeated exposures they quickly learn to prefer her face to that of an unfamiliar woman, although they are more sensitive to its broad outlines than its fine-grained, internal features (Bartrip, Morton, & de Schonen, 2001; Walton, Armstrong, & Bower, 1998).

Although they cannot yet see well, newborns actively explore their environment by scanning it for interesting sights and tracking moving objects. However, their eye movements are slow and inaccurate (von Hofsten & Rosander, 1998). Joshua's captivation with my pink blouse reveals that he is attracted to bright objects. Nevertheless, once newborns focus on an object, they tend to look only at a single feature—for example, the corner of a triangle instead of the entire shape. And despite their preference for colored over gray stimuli, newborn babies are not yet good at discriminating colors. It will take about four months for color vision to become adultlike (Adams & Courage, 1998; Kellman & Arterberry, 2006).

Neonatal Behavioral Assessment

A variety of instruments permit doctors, nurses, and researchers to assess the behavior of new-born babies. The most widely used of these tests, T. Berry Brazelton's **Neonatal Behavioral Assessment Scale (NBAS),** evaluates the baby's reflexes, muscle tone, state changes, responsiveness to physical and social stimuli, and other reactions (Brazelton & Nugent, 1995). A recently developed instrument consisting of similar items, called the *Neonatal Intensive Care Unit Network Neurobehavioral Scale (NNNS),* is specially designed for use with newborns at risk for developmental problems—because of low birth weight, preterm delivery, prenatal substance exposure, or other conditions (Lester & Tronick, 2004). Scores are used to recommend appropriate interventions and to guide parents in meeting their baby's unique needs.

The NBAS has been given to many infants around the world. As a result, researchers have learned about individual and cultural differences in newborn behavior and how child-rearing practices can maintain or change a baby's reactions. For example, NBAS scores of Asian and Native-American babies reveal that they are less irritable than Caucasian infants. Mothers in these cultures often encourage their babies' calm dispositions through holding and nursing at the first signs of discomfort (Muret-Wagstaff & Moore, 1989; Small, 1998). In contrast, maternal care quickly changes the poor NBAS scores of undernourished infants in Zambia, Africa. The Zambian mother carries her baby about on her hip all day, providing a rich variety of sensory stimulation. As a result, a once unresponsive newborn becomes an alert, contented 1-week-old (Brazelton, Koslowski, & Tronick, 1976).

■ This mother of the El Molo people of northern Kenya carries her baby about all day, providing close physical contact, a rich variety of stimulation, and ready feeding. Many Western parents find similar benefits in using a sling to keep their babies physically close. ■

TAKE A MOMENT... Using these examples, can you explain why a single neonatal assessment score is not a good predictor of later development? Because newborn behavior and parenting styles combine to shape development, *changes in scores* over the first week or two of life (rather than a single score) provide the best estimate of the baby's ability to recover from the stress of birth. NBAS "recovery curves" predict intelligence and absence of emotional and behavior problems with moderate success well into the preschool years (Brazelton, Nugent, & Lester, 1987; Ohgi et al., 2003a, 2003b).

In some hospitals, health professionals use the NBAS or the NNNS to help parents get to know their newborns through discussion or demonstration of the capacities these instruments assess. Parents of both preterm and full-term newborns who participate in these programs interact more effectively with their babies (Browne & Talmi, 2005; Bruschweiler-Stern, 2004). Although lasting effects on development have not been demonstrated, neonatal behavioral assessment interventions are useful in helping the parent–infant relationship get off to a good start.

ASK YOURSELF

◆ REVIEW What functions does REM sleep serve in young infants? Can sleep tell us anything about the health of the newborn's central nervous system? Explain.

◆ APPLY After a difficult delivery, Jackie observes her 2-day-old daughter, Kelly, being given the NBAS. Kelly scores poorly on many items. Seeing this, Jackie wonders if Kelly will develop normally. How would you respond to Jackie's concern?

◆ CONNECT How do the diverse capacities of newborn babies contribute to their first social relationships? Provide as many examples as you can.

◆ REFLECT Are newborns more competent than you thought they were before you read this chapter? Which of their capacities most surprised you?

The Transition to Parenthood

The early weeks after a new baby enters the family are full of profound changes. The mother needs to recover from childbirth and adjust to massive hormone shifts in her body. If she is breastfeeding, energies must be devoted to working out this intimate relationship. The father must become a part of this new threesome while supporting the mother in her recovery. At times, he may feel ambivalent about the baby, who constantly demands and gets the mother's attention.

While all this is going on, the tiny infant is assertive about his urgent physical needs, demanding to be fed, changed, and comforted at odd times of the day and night. The family schedule becomes irregular and uncertain. Yolanda spoke candidly about the changes she and Jay experienced:

> When we brought Joshua home, he seemed so small and helpless, and we worried about whether we would be able to take proper care of him. It took us 20 minutes to change the first diaper. I rarely feel rested because I'm up two to four times every night, and I spend a good part of my waking hours trying to anticipate Joshua's rhythms and needs. If Jay weren't so willing to help by holding and walking Joshua, I think I'd find it much harder.

Changes in the Family System

The demands of new parenthood—constant caregiving, added financial responsibilities, and less time for couples to devote to one another—usually cause the gender roles of husband and wife to become more traditional (Cowan & Cowan, 2000; Salmela-Aro et al., 2000). This is true even for couples like Yolanda and Jay, who are strongly committed to gender equality and are used to sharing household tasks. Yolanda took a leave of absence from work, whereas Jay's career continued as it had before. As a result, Yolanda spent more time at home with the baby, while Jay focused more on his provider role.

For most new parents, however, the arrival of a baby—though often associated with mild declines in relationship satisfaction and communication quality—does not cause significant marital strain. Marriages that are gratifying and supportive tend to remain so (Doss et al., 2009; Feeney et al., 2001; Miller, 2000). But troubled marriages usually become more distressed after a baby is born. In a study of newlyweds who were interviewed annually for six years, the husband's affection, expression of "we-ness" (values and goals similar to his wife's), and awareness of his wife's daily life predicted mothers' stable or increasing marital satisfaction after childbirth. In contrast, the husband's negativity and the couple's out-of-control conflict predicted a drop in mothers' satisfaction (Shapiro, Gottman, & Carrere, 2000). When expectant couples anticipate lack of partner support in parenting, their prediction generally becomes reality, yielding an especially difficult post-birth adjustment (McHale & Rotman, 2007). For some new parents, problems are severe (see the Biology and Environment box on the following page).

Violated expectations about division of labor in the home powerfully affect family well-being. In dual-earner marriages, the larger the difference between men's and women's caregiving responsibilities, the greater the decline in marital satisfaction after childbirth, especially for women—with negative consequences for parent–infant interaction. In contrast, sharing caregiving predicts greater parental happiness and sensitivity to the baby (McHale et al., 2004; Moller, Hwang, & Wickberg, 2008). An exception exists, however, for employed lower-SES women who endorse traditional gender roles. When their husbands help extensively with child care, these mothers tend to report more distress, perhaps because they feel disappointed at being unable to fulfill their desire to do most of the caregiving (Goldberg & Perry-Jenkins, 2003).

Postponing parenthood until the late twenties or thirties, as more couples do today, eases the transition to parenthood. Waiting permits couples to pursue occupational goals and gain life experience. Under these circumstances, men are more enthusiastic about becoming fathers and therefore more willing to participate. And women whose careers are well under way and whose marriages are happy are more likely to encourage their husbands to share housework and child care, which fosters fathers' involvement (Lee & Doherty, 2007; Schoppe-Sullivan et al., 2008).

BIOLOGY AND ENVIRONMENT

Parental Depression and Child Development

About 8 to 10 percent of women experience chronic depression—mild to severe feelings of sadness and withdrawal that continue for months or years. Often, the beginnings of this emotional state cannot be pinpointed. In other instances, depression emerges or strengthens after childbirth but fails to subside as the new mother adjusts to hormonal changes in her body and gains confidence in caring for her baby. This is called *postpartum depression.*

Although it is less recognized and studied, fathers, too, experience chronic depression. About 3 to 5 percent of fathers report symptoms after the birth of a child (Madsen & Juhl, 2007; Spector, 2006). Parental depression can interfere with effective parenting and seriously impair children's development. Genetic makeup increases the risk of depressive illness, but social and cultural factors are also involved.

Maternal Depression

During Julia's pregnancy, her husband, Kyle, showed so little interest in the baby that Julia worried that having a child might be a mistake. Then, shortly after Lucy was born, Julia's mood plunged. She felt anxious and weepy, overwhelmed by Lucy's needs, and angry at loss of control over her own schedule. When Julia approached Kyle about her own fatigue and his unwillingness to help with the baby, he snapped that she was overreacting. Julia's childless friends stopped by just once to see Lucy but did not call again.

Julia's depressed mood quickly affected her baby. In the weeks after birth, infants of depressed mothers sleep poorly, are less attentive to their surroundings, and have elevated levels of the stress hormone cortisol (Field, 1998). The more extreme the depression and the greater the number of stressors in a mother's life (such as marital discord, little or no social support, and poverty), the more the parent–child relationship suffers (Simpson et al., 2003). Julia rarely smiled at, comforted, or talked to Lucy, who responded to her mother's sad, vacant gaze by turning away, crying, and often looking sad or angry herself (Herrera, Reissland, & Shepherd, 2004; Stanley, Murray, & Stein, 2004). Julia, in turn, felt guilty and inadequate, and her depression deepened. By age 6 months, Lucy showed mental and emotional symptoms common in babies of

depressed mothers—delays in development, an irritable mood, and attachment difficulties (Cornish et al., 2005; McMahon et al., 2006).

When maternal depression persists, the parent–child relationship worsens. Depressed parents view their infants more negatively than independent observers do (Forman et al., 2007). And they use inconsistent discipline—sometimes lax, at other times too forceful. As we will see in later chapters, children who experience these maladaptive parenting practices often have serious adjustment problems. Some withdraw into a depressive mood themselves; others become impulsive and aggressive. In one study, infants born to mothers who were depressed during pregnancy were four times as likely as babies of nondepressed mothers to have engaged in violent antisocial behavior (such as fighting, bullying, assault with a weapon, and extreme bodily harm) by age 16, after other stressors in the mother's life that could contribute to youth antisocial conduct had been controlled (Hay et al., 2010).

Paternal Depression

Paternal depression is also linked to dissatisfaction with marriage and family life after childbirth and to other life stressors, including job loss and divorce (Bielawska-Batorowicz & Kossakowska-Petrycka, 2006). In a study of a large representative sample of British parents and babies, researchers assessed depressive symptoms of fathers shortly after birth and again the following year. Then they tracked the children's development into the preschool years. Persistent paternal depression was, like maternal depression, a strong predictor of child behavior problems—especially overactivity, defiance, and aggression in boys (Ramchandani et al., 2008).

Paternal depression is linked to frequent father–child conflict as children grow older (Kane & Garber, 2004). Over time, children subjected to parental negativity develop a pessimistic worldview—one in which they

© RICHARD NEWTON/ALAMY

■ This depressed mother appears completely uninterested in her infant. If her disengagement continues, the baby is likely to become negative and irritable, eventually withdraw, and develop serious emotional and behavior problems. ■

lack self-confidence and perceive their parents and other people as threatening. Children who constantly feel in danger are especially likely to become overly aroused in stressful situations, easily losing control in the face of cognitive and social challenges (Sturge-Apple et al., 2008). Although children of depressed parents may inherit a tendency toward emotional and behavior problems, quality of parenting is a major factor in their adjustment.

Interventions

Early treatment is vital to prevent parental depression from interfering with the parent–child relationship. Julia's doctor referred her to a therapist, who helped Julia and Kyle with their marital problems. At times, antidepressant medication is prescribed.

In addition to alleviating parental depression, therapy that encourages depressed mothers to revise their negative views of their babies and to engage in emotionally positive, responsive caregiving is vital for reducing young children's attachment and other developmental problems (Forman et al., 2007). When a depressed parent does not respond easily to treatment, a warm relationship with the other parent or another caregiver can safeguard children's development (Mezulis, Hyde, & Clark, 2004).

Applying What We Know

How Couples Can Ease the Transition to Parenthood

STRATEGY	DESCRIPTION
Devise a plan for sharing household tasks.	As soon as possible, discuss division of household responsibilities. Decide who does a particular chore based on who has the needed skill and time, not gender. Schedule regular times to reevaluate your plan to fit changing family circumstances.
Begin sharing child care right after the baby's arrival.	For fathers, strive to spend equal time with the baby early. For mothers, refrain from imposing your standards on your partner. Instead, share the role of "child-rearing expert" by discussing parenting values and concerns often. Attend a new-parenthood course together.
Talk over conflicts about decision making and responsibilities.	Face conflict through communication. Clarify your feelings and needs, and express them to your partner. Listen and try to understand your partner's point of view. Then be willing to negotiate and compromise.
Establish a balance between work and parenting.	Critically evaluate the time you devote to work in view of new parenthood. If it is too much, try to cut back.
Press for workplace and public policies that assist parents in rearing children.	Difficulties faced by new parents may be partly due to lack of workplace and societal supports. Encourage your employer to provide benefits that help combine work and family roles, such as paid employment leave, flexible work hours, and on-site high-quality, affordable child care. Communicate with lawmakers and other citizens about improving policies for children and families, including paid, job-protected leave to support the transition to parenthood.

In a study of well-educated mothers, those who had recently given birth to their second child reported just as much stress as first-time mothers (Krieg, 2007). A second birth typically requires that fathers take an even more active role in parenting—by caring for the firstborn while the mother is recuperating and by sharing in the high demands of tending to both a baby and a young child. Consequently, well-functioning families with a newborn second child typically pull back from the traditional division of responsibilities that occurred after the first birth. In a study that tracked parents from the end of pregnancy through the first year after their second child's birth, fathers' willingness to place greater emphasis on the parenting role was strongly linked to mothers' adjustment after the arrival of a second baby (Stewart, 1990). And the support and encouragement of family, friends, and partner are crucial for fathers' well-being.

Finally, both parents must help their firstborn child adjust. Preschool-age siblings understandably may feel displaced and react with jealousy and anger—a topic we will take up in Chapter 7. For strategies couples can use to ease the transition to parenthood, refer to Applying What We Know above.

Single-Mother Families

Nearly 39 percent of babies in the United States are born to single mothers, one-third of whom are teenagers (U.S. Department of Health and Human Services, 2009b). Because of poverty, poor health care, stressful life conditions, high rates of drug and alcohol abuse, and weak parenting skills, adolescent mothers and their newborns are at high risk for developmental problems.

At the other extreme, planned births and adoptions by single 30- to 45-year-old women are increasing. These mothers are generally financially secure, have readily available social support from family members and friends, and adapt to parenthood with relative ease. In fact, older single mothers in well-paid occupations who plan carefully for a new baby may encounter fewer parenting difficulties than married couples, largely because their family structure is simpler: They do not have to coordinate parenting roles with a partner, and they have no unfulfilled expectations for shared caregiving (Ambert, 2006). And because of their psychological maturity, these mothers are likely to cope effectively with parenting challenges.

The majority of nonmarital births are unplanned and to women in their twenties. Most of these single mothers have incomes below the poverty level and experience a stressful transition

LOOK AND LISTEN

Ask a couple or a single mother to describe the challenges of new parenthood, along with factors that aided or impeded this transition.

to parenthood. Although many live with the baby's father or another partner, cohabiting relationships in the United States are less socially acceptable than those in Western Europe, involve less commitment and cooperation, and are far more likely to break up—especially after an unplanned baby arrives (Fussell & Gauthier, 2005). Furthermore, these single mothers often lack emotional and parenting support—strong predictors of psychological distress and infant caregiving difficulties (Keating-Lefler et al., 2004).

Parent Interventions

Special interventions are available to help parents adjust to life with a new baby. For those who are not at high risk for problems, counselor-led groups focusing on couple and adjustment and parenting skills are highly effective (Glade, Bean, & Vira, 2005; Petch & Halford, 2008). In one program, first-time expectant couples gathered once a week for six months to discuss their dreams for the family and the changes in relationships sparked by the baby's arrival. Eighteen months after the program ended, participating fathers described themselves as more involved with their child than did fathers in a no-intervention condition. Perhaps because of fathers' caregiving assistance, participating mothers maintained their prebirth satisfaction with family and work roles. Three years after the birth, the marriages of all participating couples were still intact and just as happy as they had been before parenthood. In contrast, 15 percent of couples receiving no intervention had divorced (Cowan & Cowan, 1997; Schulz, Cowan, & Cowan, 2006).

■ A growing number of single women in their thirties and early forties are choosing to give birth or adopt a child. With social support from family and friends, this mother is likely to have a relatively smooth transition to parenthood. ■

High-risk parents struggling with poverty or the birth of a child with disabilities need more intensive interventions. Programs in which a professional intervener visits the home and focuses on enhancing social support and parenting have resulted in improved parent–infant interaction and benefits for children's cognitive and social development into middle childhood (review one example on page 116 in Chapter 3) (Petch & Halford, 2008). Many low-income single parents also require tangible support—money, food, transportation, and affordable child care—to ease stress and allow them to engage in effective caregiving.

When marital relationships are positive, social support is available, and families have sufficient income, the stress caused by the birth of a baby remains manageable. Nevertheless, as one pair of counselors who have worked with many new parents point out, "As long as children are dependent on their parents, those parents find themselves preoccupied with thoughts of their children. This does not keep them from enjoying other aspects of their lives, but it does mean that they never return to being quite the same people they were before they became parents" (Colman & Colman, 1991, p. 198).

ASK YOURSELF

◆ **REVIEW** Explain how persisting postpartum depression seriously impairs children's development.

◆ **APPLY** Derek, father of a 3-year-old and a newborn, reported that he had a harder time adjusting to the birth of his second child than to that of his first child. Explain why this might be so.

◆ **CONNECT** Louise has just given birth to her first child. Because her husband works long hours and is seldom available to help, she feels overwhelmed by the pressures of caring for a new baby. Why does Louise's four-week maternity leave pose a risk to her mental health? (*Hint:* Consult the Social Issues: Health box on page 141.)

◆ **REFLECT** If you are a parent, what was the transition to parenthood like for you? What factors helped you adjust to this major life change? What factors made it more difficult? If you are not a parent, pose these questions to someone you know who recently became a parent.

Summary

The Stages of Childbirth

Describe the three stages of childbirth, the baby's adaptation to labor and delivery, and the newborn baby's appearance.

- In the first stage of childbirth, **dilation and effacement of the cervix** occur as uterine contractions increase in strength and frequency. This stage culminates in **transition,** a brief period in which contractions are at their peak and the cervix opens completely. In the second stage, the mother feels an urge to bear down with her abdominal muscles, and the baby is born. In the final stage, the placenta is delivered.

- During labor, the force of the contractions causes infants to produce high levels of stress hormones, which help them withstand oxygen deprivation, clear the lungs for breathing, and arouse them into alertness at birth.

- Newborn infants have large heads and small bodies. The **Apgar Scale** is used to assess the baby's physical condition at birth.

Approaches to Childbirth

Describe natural childbirth and home delivery, noting benefits and concerns associated with each.

- In **natural,** or **prepared, childbirth,** the expectant mother and a companion typically attend classes where they learn about labor and delivery, master relaxation and breathing techniques to counteract pain, and prepare for coaching during childbirth. The method reduces pain and use of medication and fosters more positive maternal attitudes toward the birth experience. Social support, from a partner, relative, or doula, reduces the length of labor and the incidence of birth complications.

- Home birth is relatively rare in the United States but is common in some other industrialized nations. It is safe for healthy mothers who are assisted by a well-trained doctor or midwife, but mothers at risk for any kind of complication are safer giving birth in a hospital.

© FRANCE KEYSER/IN VISU/CORBIS

Medical Interventions

List common medical interventions during childbirth, circumstances that justify their use, and any dangers associated with each.

- **Fetal monitors** help save the lives of many babies whose mothers have a history of pregnancy and birth complications. But they also may identify infants as in danger who, in fact, are not, and are linked to an increase in cesarean deliveries.

- Use of analgesics and anesthetics to control pain during childbirth can prolong labor and cause newborns to be withdrawn and irritable. Instrument delivery using *forceps* or a *vacuum extractor* may be appropriate if the mother's pushing does not move the infant through the birth canal in a reasonable period of time. However, because they can cause serious complications, they should be avoided if possible.

- **Induced labor** is more difficult than naturally occurring labor and is more likely to be associated with the use of labor and delivery medication and instrument delivery. Inductions should be scheduled only when continuing the pregnancy threatens the well-being of mother or baby.

- **Cesarean deliveries** are justified in cases of medical emergency or serious maternal illness and when the baby is in **breech position.** A dramatic worldwide rise has occurred in cesarean deliveries, many of which are unnecessary.

Birth Complications

What are the risks of oxygen deprivation, preterm birth, and low birth weight, and what factors can help infants who survive a traumatic birth?

- Squeezing of the umbilical cord during childbirth, placenta abruptio, and placenta previa can cause **anoxia** (oxygen deprivation), with risk of brain damage and infant death. Effects of even mild to moderate anoxia on cognitive and language development are still evident in middle childhood, though many children improve over time. Infants born more than six weeks early commonly have respiratory distress syndrome, which can cause brain damage due to immaturity of the lungs and associated anoxia.

- Low birth weight, a major cause of **neonatal** and **infant mortality** and wide-ranging developmental problems, is most common in infants born to poverty-stricken women. Compared with **preterm** babies, whose weight is appropriate for time spent in the uterus, **small-for-date** infants usually have longer-lasting difficulties.

- Some interventions provide special infant stimulation in the intensive care nursery. Others teach parents how to care for and interact with their babies. Preterm infants in stressed, low-income households need long-term, intensive intervention.

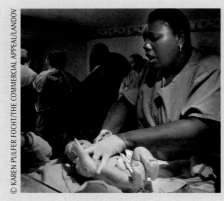

© KAREN PULFER FOCHT/THE COMMERCIAL APPEAL/LANDOV

- When babies experience birth trauma, a supportive family environment or relationships with other caring adults can help restore their growth. Even infants with fairly serious birth complications can recover with the help of positive life events.

© STEVEN WHITE/GETTY IMAGES/RISER

Precious Moments After Birth

Is close parent–infant contact shortly after birth necessary for bonding?

- Human parents do not require close physical contact with the baby immediately after birth for **bonding** and effective parenting to occur. Nevertheless, early contact supports parents' feelings of caring and affection. Hospital practices that promote parent–infant closeness, such as **rooming in,** may help parents build a good relationship with their newborn.

The Newborn Baby's Capacities

Describe the newborn baby's reflexes and states of arousal, including sleep characteristics and ways to soothe a crying baby.

- **Reflexes** are the newborn baby's most obvious organized patterns of behavior. Some have survival value, others help parents and infants establish gratifying interaction, and still others provide the foundation for voluntary motor skills.

- Although newborns move in and out of five **states of arousal,** they spend most of their time asleep. Sleep includes at least two states: **rapid-eye-movement (REM) sleep** and **non-rapid-eye-movement (NREM) sleep.** Newborns spend about 50 percent of their sleep time in REM sleep, far more than they ever will again. REM sleep provides young infants with stimulation essential for central nervous system development. Disturbed REM–NREM cycles are a sign of central nervous system abnormalities, which may lead to **sudden infant death syndrome (SIDS),** a major cause of infant mortality.

- A crying baby stimulates strong feelings of discomfort in nearby adults. The intensity of the cry and the experiences that led up to it help parents identify what is wrong. Once feeding and diaper changing have been tried, lifting the baby to the shoulder and rocking or walking is the most effective soothing technique. Other helpful soothing methods include swaddling, offering a pacifier, and talking softly.

Describe the newborn baby's sensory capacities.

- The senses of touch, taste, smell, and sound are well-developed at birth. Newborns can use their palms to distinguish the shapes of small objects. They are also sensitive to pain, prefer sweet tastes and smells, and orient toward the odor of their own mother's lactating breast and toward human milk rather than formula milk.

- Newborns can distinguish a few sound patterns, as well as nearly all speech sounds. They are especially responsive to human speech, high-pitched expressive voices, their own mother's voice, and speech in their native language.

- Vision is the least developed of the newborn's senses. At birth, focusing ability and **visual acuity** are limited. Nevertheless, newborns can detect human faces and prefer their mother's familiar face to the face of a stranger. In exploring the visual field, they are attracted to bright objects but limit their looking to single features. Newborn babies have difficulty discriminating colors.

Why is neonatal behavioral assessment useful?

- The most widely used instrument for assessing the behavior of the newborn infant, Brazelton's **Neonatal Behavioral Assessment Scale (NBAS),** has helped researchers understand individual and cultural differences in newborn behavior. Sometimes it is used to teach parents about their baby's capacities.

The Transition to Parenthood

Describe typical changes in the family after the birth of a new baby, along with interventions that foster the transition to parenthood.

- In response to the demands of new parenthood, the gender roles of husband and wife usually become more traditional. Parents in gratifying marriages who continue to support each other's needs generally adapt well. But a large difference between a husband's and wife's caregiving responsibilities can strain the marriage and negatively affect parent–infant interaction. Favorable adjustment to a second birth typically requires that fathers take an even more active role in parenting.

- Most nonmarital births are unplanned and to young mothers who have incomes below the poverty level and experience a stressful transition to parenthood. Planned births and adoptions by financially secure single women in their thirties and forties are increasing. These mothers adapt to new parenthood as well as, and sometimes more favorably than, married couples.

- When parents are at low risk for problems, counselor-led parenting groups involving discussion of changing family relationships can ease the transition to parenthood. High-risk parents struggling with poverty or the birth of a baby with disabilities are more likely to benefit from intensive home interventions focusing on enhancing social support and parenting.

IMPORTANT TERMS AND CONCEPTS

"We Are Playing in the House Garden"
Uttharaa Ranaweera
10 years, Sri Lanka

Encouraged by her older brothers and sisters, a baby explores a garden and experiences the physical potential of her growing body. During the first year, infants grow rapidly, move on their own, increasingly investigate their surroundings, and make sense of complex sights and sounds.

Physical Development in Infancy and Toddlerhood

*O*n a brilliant June morning, 16-month-old Caitlin emerged from her front door, ready for the short drive to the child-care home where she spent her weekdays while her mother, Carolyn, and her father, David, worked. Clutching a teddy bear in one hand and her mother's arm with the other, Caitlin descended the steps. "One! Two! Threeeee!" Carolyn counted as she helped Caitlin down. "How much she's changed!" Carolyn thought to herself, looking at the child who, not long ago, had been a newborn. With her first steps, Caitlin had passed from *infancy* to *toddlerhood*—a period spanning the second year of life. At first, Caitlin did, indeed, "toddle" with an awkward gait, tipping over frequently. But her face reflected the thrill of conquering a new skill.

As they walked toward the car, Carolyn and Caitlin spotted 3-year-old Eli and his father, Kevin, in the neighboring yard. Eli dashed toward them, waving a bright yellow envelope. Carolyn bent down to open the envelope and took out a card. It read, "Announcing the arrival of Grace Ann. Born: Cambodia. Age: 16 months." Carolyn turned toward Kevin and Eli. "That's wonderful news! When can we see her?"

"Let's wait a few days," Kevin suggested. "Monica's taken Grace to the doctor this morning. She's underweight and malnourished." Kevin described Monica's first night with Grace in a hotel room in Phnom Penh. Grace lay on the bed, withdrawn and fearful. Eventually she fell asleep, gripping crackers in both hands.

Carolyn felt Caitlin's impatient tug at her sleeve. Off they drove to child care, where Vanessa had just dropped off her 18-month-old son, Timmy. Within moments, Caitlin and Timmy were in the sandbox, shoveling sand into plastic cups and buckets with the help of their caregiver, Ginette.

A few weeks later, Grace joined Caitlin and Timmy at Ginette's child-care home. Although still tiny and unable to crawl or walk, she had grown taller and heavier, and her sad, vacant gaze had given way to an alert expression, a ready smile, and an enthusiastic desire to imitate and explore. When Caitlin headed for the sandbox,

Grace stretched out her arms, asking Ginette to carry her there, too. Soon Grace was pulling herself up at every opportunity. Finally, at age 18 months, she walked!

This chapter traces physical growth during the first two years—one of the most remarkable and busiest times of development. We will see how rapid changes in the infant's body and brain support learning, motor skills, and perceptual capacities. Caitlin, Grace, and Timmy will join us along the way to illustrate individual differences and environmental influences on physical development.

Body Growth

TAKE A MOMENT... The next time you're walking in your neighborhood park or at the mall, note the contrast between infants' and toddlers' physical capabilities. One reason for the vast changes in what children can do over the first two years is that their bodies change enormously—faster than at any other time after birth.

Changes in Body Size and Muscle–Fat Makeup

By the end of the first year a typical infant's height is about 32 inches—more than 50 percent greater than at birth. By 2 years, it is 75 percent greater (36 inches). Similarly, by 5 months of age, birth weight has doubled, to about 15 pounds. At 1 year it has tripled, to 22 pounds, and at 2 years it has quadrupled, to about 30 pounds.

Figure 5.1 illustrates this dramatic increase in body size. But rather than making steady gains, infants and toddlers grow in little spurts. In one study, children who were followed over the first 21 months of life went for periods of 7 to 63 days with no growth, then added as much as half an inch in a 24-hour period! Almost always, parents described their babies as irritable and very hungry on the day before the spurt (Lampl, 1993; Lampl, Veldhuis, & Johnson, 1992).

One of the most obvious changes in infants' appearance is their transformation into round, plump babies by the middle of the first year. This early rise in "baby fat," which peaks at about 9 months, helps the infant maintain a constant body temperature. In the second year, most toddlers slim down, a trend that continues into middle childhood (Fomon & Nelson, 2002). In contrast, muscle tissue increases very slowly during infancy and will not reach a peak until adolescence. Babies are not very muscular; their strength and physical coordination are limited.

In infancy, girls are slightly shorter and lighter than boys, with a higher ratio of fat to muscle. These small sex differences persist throughout early and middle childhood and are greatly magnified at adolescence. Ethnic differences in body size are apparent as well. Grace was below the *growth norms* (height and weight averages for children her age). Early malnutrition played a part, but even after substantial catch-up, Grace—as is typical for Asian children—remained below North American norms. In contrast, Timmy is slightly above average in size, as African-American children tend to be (Bogin, 2001).

Changes in Body Proportions

As the child's overall size increases, parts of the body grow at different rates. Two growth patterns describe these changes. The first is the **cephalocaudal trend**—from the Latin for "head to tail." During the prenatal period, the head develops more rapidly than the lower part of the body. At birth, the head takes up one-fourth of total body length, the legs only one-third. Notice how, in Figure 5.1, the lower portion of the body catches up. By age 2, the head accounts for only one-fifth and the legs for nearly one-half of total body length.

In the second pattern, the **proximodistal trend,** growth proceeds, literally, from "near to far"—from the center of the body outward. In the prenatal period, the head, chest, and trunk grow first, then the arms and legs, and finally the hands and feet. During infancy and childhood, the arms and legs continue to grow somewhat ahead of the hands and feet.

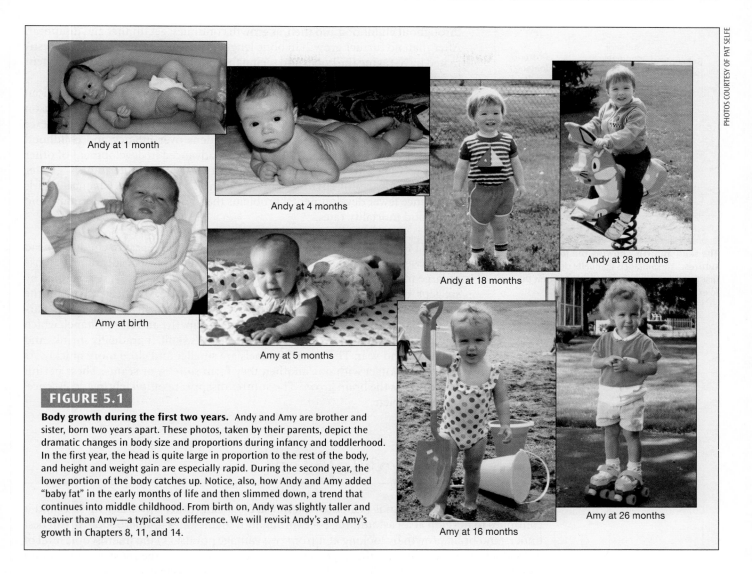

FIGURE 5.1

Body growth during the first two years. Andy and Amy are brother and sister, born two years apart. These photos, taken by their parents, depict the dramatic changes in body size and proportions during infancy and toddlerhood. In the first year, the head is quite large in proportion to the rest of the body, and height and weight gain are especially rapid. During the second year, the lower portion of the body catches up. Notice, also, how Andy and Amy added "baby fat" in the early months of life and then slimmed down, a trend that continues into middle childhood. From birth on, Andy was slightly taller and heavier than Amy—a typical sex difference. We will revisit Andy's and Amy's growth in Chapters 8, 11, and 14.

Andy at 1 month

Andy at 4 months

Amy at birth

Amy at 5 months

Andy at 18 months

Andy at 28 months

Amy at 16 months

Amy at 26 months

Skeletal Growth

Children of the same age differ in *rate* of physical growth; some make faster progress toward a mature body size than others. But current body size is not enough to tell us how quickly a child's physical growth is moving along. Although Timmy is larger and heavier than Caitlin and Grace, he is not physically more mature. In a moment, you will see why.

GENERAL SKELETAL GROWTH The best estimate of a child's physical maturity is **skeletal age,** a measure of development of the bones of the body. The embryonic skeleton is first formed out of soft, pliable tissue called *cartilage.* In the sixth week of pregnancy, cartilage cells begin to harden into bone, a gradual process that continues throughout childhood and adolescence (Moore & Persaud, 2008).

Just before birth, special growth centers, called **epiphyses,** appear at the two extreme ends of each of the long bones of the body (see Figure 5.2). Cartilage cells continue to be produced at the growth plates of these epiphyses, which increase in number

FIGURE 5.2

Diagram of a long bone showing upper and lower epiphyses. Cartilage cells are produced at the growth plates of the epiphyses and gradually harden into bone. *(Adapted and reprinted by permission of the publisher from Fetus into Man: Physical Growth from Conception to Maturity by J. M. Tanner, pp. 16, 32. Cambridge, Mass.: Harvard University Press and Castlemead Publications. Copyright © 1978, 1989 by J. M. Tanner.)*

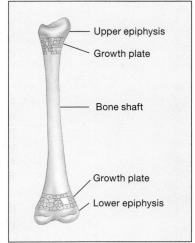

Upper epiphysis

Growth plate

Bone shaft

Growth plate

Lower epiphysis

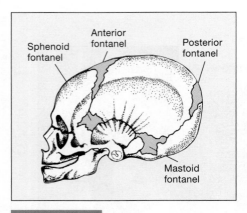

FIGURE 5.3

The skull at birth, showing the fontanels and sutures. The fontanels gradually close during the first two years, forming sutures that permit the skull to expand easily as the brain grows.

throughout childhood and then, as growth continues, get thinner and disappear. After that, no further growth in bone length is possible. Skeletal age can be estimated by X-raying the bones and seeing the number of epiphyses and the extent to which they are fused.

African-American children tend to be slightly ahead of Caucasian-American children in skeletal age. And girls are considerably ahead of boys—the reason Timmy's skeletal age lags behind that of Caitlin and Grace. At birth, the sexes differ by about 4 to 6 weeks, a gap that widens over infancy and childhood (Tanner, Healy, & Cameron, 2001). Girls are advanced in development of other organs as well. This greater physical maturity may contribute to girls' greater resistance to harmful environmental influences. As noted in Chapter 2, girls experience fewer developmental problems than boys and have lower infant and childhood mortality rates.

GROWTH OF THE SKULL Pediatricians routinely measure children's head size between birth and age 2 years, when skull growth is especially rapid because of large increases in brain size. At birth, the bones of the skull are separated by six gaps, or "soft spots," called **fontanels** (see Figure 5.3). The gaps permit the bones to overlap as the large head of the baby passes through the mother's narrow birth canal. You can easily feel the largest gap, the anterior fontanel, which measures slightly more than an inch across at the top of a baby's skull. It gradually shrinks and is filled in during the second year. The other fontanels are smaller and close more quickly. As the skull bones come in contact with one another, they form *sutures,* or seams. These permit the skull to expand easily as the brain grows. The sutures disappear completely in adolescence, when skull growth is complete.

Brain Development

At birth, the brain is nearer to its adult size than any other physical structure, and it continues to develop at an astounding pace throughout infancy and toddlerhood. We can best understand brain growth by looking at it from two vantage points: (1) the microscopic level of individual brain cells and (2) the larger level of the cerebral cortex, the most complex brain structure and the one responsible for the highly developed intelligence of our species.

Development of Neurons

The human brain has 100 to 200 billion **neurons,** or nerve cells, that store and transmit information, many of which have thousands of direct connections with other neurons. Unlike other body cells, neurons are not tightly packed together. Between them are tiny gaps, or **synapses,** where fibers from different neurons come close together but do not touch (see Figure 5.4). Neurons send messages to one another by releasing chemicals called **neurotransmitters,** which cross the synapse.

The basic story of brain growth concerns how neurons develop and form this elaborate communication system. Figure 5.5 summarizes major milestones of brain development. In the prenatal period, neurons are produced in the embryo's primitive neural tube. From there, they migrate to form the major parts of the brain (see Chapter 3, page 99). Once neurons are in place, they differentiate, establishing their unique functions by extending their fibers to form synaptic connections with neighboring cells. During infancy and toddlerhood, neural fibers and synapses increase at an astounding pace (Huttenlocher, 2002; Moore & Persaud, 2008). Because developing neurons require space for these connective structures, a surprising aspect of brain growth is that as synapses form, many surrounding neurons die—20 to 80 percent, depending on the brain region (de Haan & Johnson, 2003; Stiles, 2008). Fortunately, during the prenatal period, the neural tube produces far more neurons than the brain will ever need.

As neurons form connections, *stimulation* becomes vital to their survival. Neurons that are stimulated by input from the surrounding environment continue to establish new synapses, forming increasingly elaborate systems of communication that support more complex abilities. At first, stimulation results in a massive overabundance of synapses, many of which serve identical functions, thereby ensuring that the child will acquire the motor, cognitive, and social skills that our species needs to survive. Neurons that are seldom stimulated soon lose their synapses, in a process called **synaptic pruning** that returns neurons not needed at the moment to an uncommitted state so they can support future development. In all, about 40 percent of synapses are pruned during childhood and adolescence (Webb, Monk, & Nelson, 2001). For this process to go forward, appropriate stimulation of the child's brain is vital during periods in which the formation of synapses is at its peak (Nelson, Thomas, & de Haan, 2006).

If few neurons are produced after the prenatal period, what causes the dramatic increase in brain size during the first two years? About half the brain's volume is made up of **glial cells,** which are responsible for **myelination,** the coating of neural fibers with an insulating fatty sheath (called *myelin*) that improves the efficiency of message transfer. Certain types of glial cells also participate directly in neural communication, by picking up and passing on neuronal signals and releasing neurotransmitters (LoTurco, 2000). Glial cells multiply rapidly from the end of pregnancy through the second year of life—a process that continues at a slower pace through middle childhood and accelerates again in adolescence. Gains in neural fibers and myelination are responsible for the extraordinary gain in overall size of the brain—from nearly 30 percent of its adult weight at birth to 70 percent by age 2 (Johnson, 2005; Knickmeyer et al., 2008).

Brain development can be compared to molding a "living sculpture." After neurons and synapses are overproduced, cell death and synaptic pruning sculpt away excess building material

FIGURE 5.4

Neurons and their connective fibers. This photograph of several neurons, taken with the aid of a powerful microscope, shows the elaborate synaptic connections that form with neighboring cells.

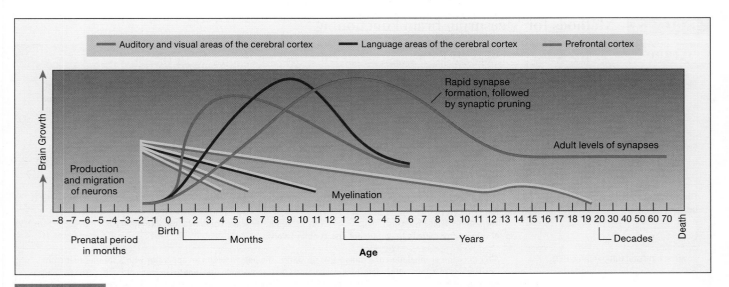

FIGURE 5.5

Major milestones of brain development. Formation of synapses is rapid during the first two years, especially in the auditory, visual, and language areas of the cerebral cortex. The prefrontal cortex undergoes more extended synaptic growth. In each area, overproduction of synapses is followed by synaptic pruning. The prefrontal cortex is among the last regions to attain an adult level of synaptic connections—in mid- to late adolescence. Myelination occurs at a dramatic pace during the first two years and then at a slower pace through childhood, followed by an acceleration at adolescence. The multiple yellow lines indicate that the timing of myelination varies among different brain areas. For example, neural fibers myelinate over a longer period in the language areas, and especially in the prefrontal cortex, than in the visual and auditory areas. *(Adapted from Thompson & Nelson, 2001).*

to form the mature brain—a process jointly influenced by genetically programmed events and the child's experiences. The resulting sculpture is a set of interconnected regions, each with specific functions—much like countries on a globe that communicate with one another (Johnston et al., 2001). This "geography" of the brain permits researchers to study its organization and the activity of its regions using *neurophysiological* techniques.

Neurophysiological Methods

Table 5.1 describes major measures of brain functioning. The first two methods detect changes in *electrical activity* in the cerebral cortex. Researchers can examine *EEG brain-wave patterns* for stability and organization—signs of mature cortical functioning (see Figure 5.6). And as a child processes a particular stimulus, *ERPs* detect the general location of brain-wave activity—a method often used to study preverbal infants' responsiveness to various stimuli, the impact of experience on specialization of specific brain regions, and atypical brain functioning in children at risk for learning and emotional problems (DeBoer, Scott, & Nelson, 2007; deRegnier, 2005).

Neuroimaging techniques, which yield detailed, three-dimensional computerized pictures of the entire brain and its active areas, provide the most precise information about which brain regions are specialized for certain capacities. In *PET,* the child must lie quietly on a scanner bed, and in fMRI, inside a tunnel-like apparatus. But unlike PET, fMRI does not depend on X-ray photography, which requires injection of a radioactive substance. Rather, when a child is exposed to a stimulus, fMRI detects changes in blood flow and oxygen metabolism magnetically; a computer combines frequently recorded images into a colorful, moving picture of parts of the brain used to perform a given activity (see Figure 5.7a and b).

Because PET and fMRI require that the participant to lie as motionless as possible for an extended time, they are not suitable for infants and young children (Nelson, Thomas, & de Haan, 2006). A neuroimaging technique that works well in infancy and early childhood is *near infrared spectroscopy (NIRS),* in which infrared (invisible) light is beamed at regions of the cerebral cortex to measure blood flow and oxygen metabolism while the child attends to a stimulus (refer again to Table 5.1). Because the apparatus consists only of thin, flexible optical

TABLE 5.1 Methods for Measuring Brain Functioning

METHOD	DESCRIPTION
Electroencephalogram (EEG)	Electrodes embedded in a head cap record electrical brain-wave activity in the brain's outer layers—the cerebral cortex. Researchers use an advanced tool called a geodesic sensor net (GSN) to hold interconnected electrodes (up to 128 for infants and 256 for children and adults) in place through a cap that adjusts to each person's head shape, yielding improved brain-wave detection.
Event-related potentials (ERPs)	Using the EEG, the frequency and amplitude of brain waves in response to particular stimuli (such as a picture, music, or speech) are recorded in the cerebral cortex. Enables identification of general regions of stimulus-induced activity.
Functional magnetic resonance imaging (fMRI)	While the person lies inside a tunnel-shaped apparatus that creates a magnetic field, a scanner magnetically detects increased blood flow and oxygen metabolism in areas of the brain as the individual processes particular stimuli. The scanner typically records images every 1 to 4 seconds; these are combined into a computerized moving picture of activity anywhere in the brain (not just its outer layers).
Positron emission tomography (PET)	After injection or inhalation of a radioactive substance, the person lies on an apparatus with a scanner that emits fine streams of X-rays, which detect increased blood flow and oxygen metabolism in areas of the brain as the person processes particular stimuli. As with fMRI, the result is a computerized image of activity anywhere in the brain.
Near-infrared spectroscopy (NIRS)	Using thin, flexible optical fibers attached to the scalp through a head cap, infrared (invisible) light is beamed at the brain; its absorption by areas of the cerebral cortex varies with changes in blood flow and oxygen metabolism as the individual processes particular stimuli. The result is a computerized moving picture of active areas in the cerebral cortex. Unlike fMRI and PET, NIRS is appropriate for infants and young children, who can move within limited range during testing.

fibers attached to the scalp using a head cap, a baby can sit on the parent's lap and move during testing—as Figure 5.7c illustrates (Hespos et al., 2010; Meek, 2002). But unlike PET and fMRI, which map activity changes throughout the brain, NIRS is limited to examining the functioning of the cerebral cortex.

Neurophysiological methods are powerful tools for uncovering relationships between the brain and psychological development. But like all research methods, they have limitations. Even though a stimulus produces a consistent pattern of brain activity, investigators cannot be certain that an individual has processed it in a certain way. And a researcher who takes a change in brain activity as an indicator of information processing must make sure that the change was not due instead to hunger, boredom, fatigue, or body movements. Consequently, other methods must be combined with brain-wave and -imaging findings to clarify their meaning (Nicholson, 2006). Now let's turn to the developing organization of the cerebral cortex.

Development of the Cerebral Cortex

The **cerebral cortex** surrounds the rest of the brain, resembling half of a shelled walnut. It is the largest brain structure—accounting for 85 percent of the brain's weight and containing the greatest number of neurons and synapses. Because the cerebral cortex is the last part of the brain to stop growing, it is sensitive to environmental influences for a much longer period than any other part of the brain.

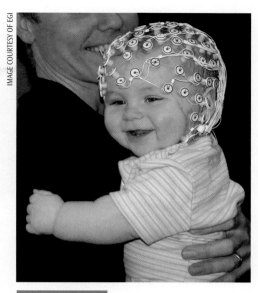

FIGURE 5.6

Electroencephalogram (EEG) using the geodesic sensor net (GSN). Interconnected electrodes embedded in the head cap record electrical brain-wave activity in the cerebral cortex.

REGIONS OF THE CORTEX   Figure 5.8 on page 168 shows specific functions of regions of the cerebral cortex, such as receiving information from the senses, instructing the body to move, and thinking. The order in which cortical regions develop corresponds to the order in which various capacities emerge in the infant and growing child. For example, a burst of synaptic growth occurs in the auditory and visual cortexes and in areas responsible for body movement over the first year—a period of dramatic gains in auditory and visual perception and mastery of motor skills (Johnson, 2005). Language areas are especially active from late infancy through the preschool years, when language development flourishes (Pujol et al., 2006; Thompson et al., 2000).

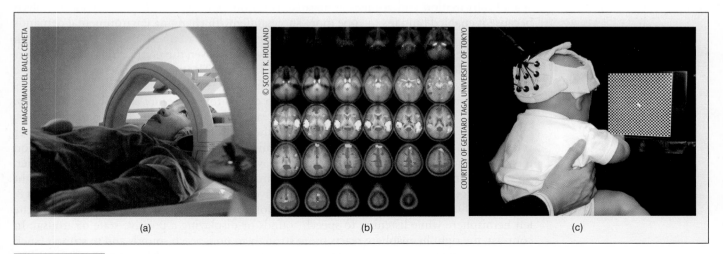

(a)   (b)   (c)

FIGURE 5.7

Functional magnetic resonance imaging (fMRI) and near infrared spectroscopy (NIRS). (a) This 6-year-old is part of a study that uses fMRI to find out how his brain processes light and motion. (b) The fMRI image shows which areas of the boy's brain are active while he views changing visual stimuli. (c) Here, NIRS is used to investigate a 2-month-old's response to a visual stimulus. During testing, the baby can move freely within a limited range. *(Photo (c) From G. Taga, K. Asakawa, A. Maki, Y. Konishi, & H. Koisumi, 2003, "Brain Imaging in Awake Infants by Near-Infrared Optical Topography," Proceedings of the National Academy of Sciences, 100, p. 10723. Reprinted by permission.)*

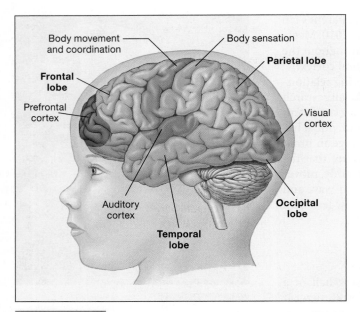

FIGURE 5.8

The left side of the human brain, showing the cerebral cortex. The cortex is divided into different lobes, each of which contains a variety of regions with specific functions. Some major regions are labeled here.

The cortical regions with the most extended period of development are the *frontal lobes*. The **prefrontal cortex,** lying in front of areas controlling body movement, is responsible for thought—in particular, for consciousness, inhibition of impulses, integration of information, and use of memory, reasoning, planning, and problem-solving strategies. From age 2 months on, the prefrontal cortex functions more effectively. But it undergoes especially rapid myelination and formation and pruning of synapses during the preschool and school years, followed by another period of accelerated growth in adolescence, yielding an adult level of synaptic connections around mid- to late adolescence (Nelson, 2002; Nelson, Thomas, & de Haan, 2006; Sowell et al., 2002).

LATERALIZATION AND PLASTICITY OF THE CERE-BRAL CORTEX The cerebral cortex has two *hemispheres,* or sides, that differ in their functions. Some tasks are done mostly by the left hemisphere, others by the right. For example, each hemisphere receives sensory information from the side of the body opposite to it and controls only that side.[1] For most of us, the left hemisphere is largely responsible for verbal abilities (such as spoken and written language) and positive emotion (for example, joy). The right hemisphere handles spatial abilities (judging distances, reading maps, and recognizing geometric shapes) and negative emotion (such as distress) (Banish & Heller, 1998; Nelson & Bosquet, 2000). In left-handed people, this pattern may be reversed or, more commonly, the cerebral cortex may be less clearly specialized than in right-handers.

Why does this specialization of the two hemispheres, called **lateralization,** occur? Studies using fMRI reveal that the left hemisphere is better at processing information in a sequential, analytic (piece-by-piece) way, a good approach for dealing with communicative information—both verbal (language) and emotional (a joyful smile). In contrast, the right hemisphere is specialized for processing information in a holistic, integrative manner, ideal for making sense of spatial information and regulating negative emotion. A lateralized brain may have evolved because it enabled humans to cope more successfully with changing environmental demands (Falk, 2005). It permits a wider array of functions to be carried out effectively than if both sides processed information in exactly the same way. However, the popular notion of a "right-brained" or "left-brained" person is an oversimplification. The two hemispheres communicate and work together, doing so more rapidly and effectively with age.

Researchers study when brain lateralization occurs to learn more about **brain plasticity.** A highly *plastic* cerebral cortex, in which many areas are not yet committed to specific functions, has a high capacity for learning. And if a part of the cortex is damaged, other parts can take over the tasks it would have handled. But once the hemispheres lateralize, damage to a specific region means that the abilities it controls cannot be recovered to the same extent or as easily as earlier.

At birth, the hemispheres have already begun to specialize. Most newborns favor the right side of the body in their head position and reflexive reactions (Grattan et al., 1992; Rönnqvist & Hopkins, 1998). Most also show greater activation (detected either with ERP or NIRS) in the left hemisphere while listening to speech sounds or displaying a positive state of arousal. In contrast, the right hemisphere reacts more strongly to nonspeech sounds and to stimuli (such as a sour-tasting fluid) that evoke a negative reaction (Davidson, 1994; Fox & Davidson, 1986; Hespos et al., 2010).

---

[1]The eyes are an exception. Messages from the right half of each retina go to the right hemisphere; messages from the left half of each retina go to the left hemisphere. Thus, visual information from *both* eyes is received by *both* hemispheres.

Nevertheless, research on brain-damaged children and adults offers dramatic evidence for substantial plasticity in the young brain, summarized in the Biology and Environment box on page 170. Furthermore, early experience greatly influences the organization of the cerebral cortex. For example, deaf adults who, as infants and children, learned sign language (a spatial skill) depend more than hearing individuals on the right hemisphere for language processing (Neville & Bavelier, 2002). And toddlers who are advanced in language development show greater left-hemispheric specialization for language than their more slowly developing age-mates (Casey et al., 2002; Luna et al., 2001; Mills et al., 2005). Apparently, the very process of acquiring language and other skills promotes lateralization.

In sum, the brain is more plastic during the first few years than it will ever be again. An overabundance of synaptic connections supports brain plasticity and, therefore, young children's ability to learn, which is fundamental to their survival. And although the cortex is genetically programmed for hemispheric specialization, experience greatly influences the rate and success of its advancing organization.

Sensitive Periods in Brain Development

Animal studies confirm that early, extreme sensory deprivation results in permanent brain damage and loss of functions—findings that verify the existence of sensitive periods in brain development. For example, early, varied visual experiences must occur for the brain's visual centers to develop normally. If a 1-month-old kitten is deprived of light for just three or four days, these areas of the brain degenerate. If the kitten is kept in the dark during the fourth week of life and beyond, the damage is severe and permanent (Crair, Gillespie, & Stryker, 1998). And the general quality of the early environment affects overall brain growth. When animals reared from birth in physically and socially stimulating surroundings are compared with those reared in isolation, the brains of the stimulated animals show much denser synaptic connections (Greenough & Black, 1992).

HUMAN EVIDENCE: VICTIMS OF DEPRIVED EARLY ENVIRONMENTS For ethical reasons, we cannot deliberately deprive some infants of normal rearing experiences and observe the impact on their brains and competencies. Instead, we must turn to natural experiments, in which children were victims of deprived early environments that were later rectified. Such studies have revealed some parallels with the animal evidence just described.

For example, when babies are born with cataracts in both eyes (clouded lenses, preventing clear visual images), those who have corrective surgery within four to six months show rapid improvement in vision, except for subtle aspects of face perception, which require early visual input to the right hemisphere to develop (Le Grand et al., 2001, 2003). But the longer cataract surgery is postponed beyond infancy, the less complete the recovery in visual skills. And if surgery is delayed until adulthood, vision is severely and permanently impaired (Lewis & Maurer, 2005; Maurer et al., 1999).

Studies of infants placed in orphanages who were later exposed to ordinary family rearing confirm the importance of a generally stimulating environment for psychological development. In one investigation, researchers followed the progress of a large sample of children transferred between birth and 3½ years from extremely deprived Romanian orphanages to adoptive families in Great Britain (Beckett et al., 2006; O'Connor et al., 2000; Rutter et al., 1998, 2004, 2010). On arrival, most were impaired in all domains of development. Cognitive catch-up was impressive for children adopted before 6 months, who consistently attained average mental test scores in childhood and adolescence, performing as well as a comparison group of early-adopted British-born children.

■ These children in an orphanage in Romania receive very little adult contact or stimulation. The longer they remain in this barren environment, the more they will withdraw and wither, displaying profound impairments in all domains of development. ■

BIOLOGY AND ENVIRONMENT

Brain Plasticity: Insights from Research on Brain-Damaged Children and Adults

*I*n the first few years of life, the brain is highly plastic. It can reorganize areas committed to specific functions in a way that the mature brain cannot. Consistently, adults who suffered brain injuries in infancy and early childhood show fewer cognitive impairments than adults with later-occurring injuries (Holland, 2004; Huttenlocher, 2002). Nevertheless, the young brain is not totally plastic. When it is injured, its functioning is compromised. The extent of plasticity depends on several factors, including age at time of injury, site of damage, and skill area.

Brain Plasticity in Infancy and Early Childhood

In a large study of children with injuries to the cerebral cortex that occurred before birth or in the first six months of life, language and spatial skills were assessed repeatedly into adolescence (Akshoomoff et al., 2002; Stiles, 2001a; Stiles et al., 2005, 2008). All the children had experienced early brain seizures or hemorrhages. Brain-imaging techniques (fMRI and PET) revealed the precise site of damage.

Regardless of whether injury occurred in the left or right cerebral hemisphere, the children showed delays in language development that persisted until about 3½ years of age. That damage to either hemisphere affected early language competence indicates that at first, language functioning is broadly distributed in the brain. But by age 5, the children caught up in vocabulary and grammatical skills. Undamaged areas—in either the left or the right hemisphere—had taken over these language functions.

Compared with language, spatial skills were more impaired after early brain injury. When preschool through adolescent-age youngsters were asked to copy designs, those with early right-hemispheric damage had trouble with holistic processing—accurately representing the overall shape. In contrast, children with left-hemispheric damage captured the basic shape but omitted fine-grained details. Nevertheless, the children showed improvements in their drawings with age—gains that did not occur in brain-injured adults (Akshoomoff et al., 2002; Stiles et al., 2003, 2008).

Clearly, recovery after early brain injury is greater for language than for spatial skills. Why is this so? Researchers speculate that spatial processing is the older of the two capacities in our evolutionary history and, therefore, more lateralized at birth (Stiles, 2001b; Stiles et al., 2002, 2008). But early brain injury has far less impact than later injury on both language and spatial skills. In sum, the young brain is remarkably plastic.

The Price of High Plasticity in the Young Brain

Despite impressive recovery of language and (to a lesser extent) spatial skills, children with early brain injuries show deficits in a wide variety of complex mental abilities during the school years. For example, their reading and math progress is slow. And in telling stories, they produce simpler narratives than agemates without early brain injuries (although many catch up in narrative skills by early adolescence) (Reilly, Bates, & Marchman, 1998; Reilly et al., 2004). Furthermore, the more brain tissue destroyed in infancy or early childhood, the poorer children score on intelligence tests (Anderson et al., 2006).

High brain plasticity, researchers explain, comes at a price. When healthy brain regions take over the functions of damaged areas, a "crowding effect" occurs: Multiple tasks must be done by a smaller-than-usual volume of brain tissue. Consequently, the brain processes information less quickly and accurately than it would if it were intact. Complex mental abilities of all kinds suffer into middle childhood, and often longer, because performing them well requires considerable space in the cerebral cortex (Huttenlocher, 2002).

Later Plasticity

Brain plasticity is not restricted to early childhood. Although far more limited, reorganization in the brain can occur later, even in adulthood. For example, adult stroke victims often display considerable recovery, especially in response to stimulation of language and motor skills. Brain-imaging techniques reveal that structures adjacent to the permanently damaged area or in the opposite cerebral hemisphere reorganize to support the impaired ability (Kalra & Ratan, 2007; Murphy & Corbett, 2009).

In infancy and childhood, the goal of brain growth is to form neural connections that ensure mastery of essential skills. Animal research reveals that plasticity is greatest while the brain is forming many new synapses; it declines during synaptic pruning (Murphy & Corbett, 2009). At older ages, specialized brain structures are in place, but after injury they can still reorganize to some degree. The adult brain can produce a small number of new neurons. And when an individual practices relevant tasks, the brain strengthens existing synapses and generates new ones (Nelson, Thomas, & de Haan, 2006). Plasticity seems to be a basic property of the nervous system. Researchers hope to discover how experience and brain plasticity work together throughout life, so they can help people of all ages—with and without brain injuries—develop at their best.

© JIM WEST/THE IMAGE WORKS

■ This preschooler, who experienced brain damage in infancy, has been spared massive impairments because of high plasticity of the brain. Here, a teacher guides his hand in drawing shapes to strengthen spatial skills, which remain more impaired than language after early brain injury. ■

But Romanian children who had been institutionalized for more than the first six months showed serious intellectual deficits (see Figure 5.9). Although they improved in test scores during middle childhood and adolescence, they remained substantially below average. And most displayed at least three serious mental health problems, such as inattention, overactivity, unruly behavior, and autistic-like symptoms (social disinterest, stereotyped behavior) (Kreppner et al., 2007, 2010). A major correlate of both time spent in the institution and poor cognitive and emotional functioning was below-average head size, suggesting that early lack of stimulation permanently damaged the brain (Sonuga-Barke, Schlotz, & Kreppner, 2010).

Neurophysiological findings indicate that early, prolonged institutionalization leads to a generalized reduction in brain-wave and metabolic activity in the cerebral cortex—especially the prefrontal cortex, which governs complex cognition and impulse control. Neural fibers connecting the prefrontal cortex with other brain structures involved in control of emotion are also reduced (Eluvathingal et al., 2006; Nelson, 2007b).

Additional evidence shows that the chronic stress of early, deprived orphanage rearing disrupts the brain's capacity to manage stress. In another investigation, researchers followed the development of children who had spent their first eight months or more in Romanian institutions and were then adopted into Canadian homes (Gunnar et al., 2001; Gunnar & Cheatham, 2003). Compared with agemates adopted shortly after birth, these children showed extreme stress reactivity, as indicated by high concentrations of the stress hormone *cortisol* in their saliva—a physiological response linked to illness, retarded physical growth, and learning and behavior problems, including deficits in attention and control of anger and other impulses. The longer the children spent in orphanage care, the higher their cortisol levels—even 6½ years after adoption. In other research, orphanage children displayed abnormally low cortisol—a blunted physiological stress response that may be the central nervous system's adaptation to earlier, frequent cortisol elevations (Carlson & Earls, 1997; Gunnar & Vasquez, 2001).

Finally, early deprived rearing may also disrupt the brain's typical response to pleasurable social experiences. After sitting on their mother's lap and playing an enjoyable game, preschoolers adopted, on average, at age 1½ years from Romanian orphanages had abnormally low urine levels of *oxytocin*—a hormone released by the brain that evokes calmness and contentment in the presence of familiar, trusted people (Fries et al., 2005). As we will see in Chapter 7, children who spend their infancy in neglectful institutions often display attachment difficulties that even a caring adoptive family cannot completely overcome.

APPROPRIATE STIMULATION   Unlike the orphanage children just described, Grace, whom Monica and Kevin had adopted in Cambodia at 16 months of age, showed favorable progress. Two years earlier, they had adopted Grace's older brother, Eli. When Eli was 2 years old, Monica and Kevin sent a letter and a photo of Eli to his biological mother, describing a bright, happy child. The next day, the Cambodian mother tearfully asked an adoption agency to send her baby daughter to join Eli and his American family.

Although Grace's early environment was very depleted, her biological mother's loving care—holding gently, speaking softly, and breastfeeding—may have prevented irreversible damage to her brain. Besides offering gentle, appropriate stimulation, sensitive adult care helps normalize cortisol production in both typically developing and emotionally traumatized infants and young children (Gunnar & Quevedo, 2007; Tarullo & Gunnar, 2006). Good parenting seems to protect the young brain from the potentially damaging effects of both excessive and inadequate stress-hormone exposure.

FIGURE 5.9

Relationship of age at adoption to mental test scores at ages 6 and 11 among British and Romanian adoptees. Children transferred from Romanian orphanages to British adoptive homes in the first six months of life attained average scores and fared as well as British early-adopted children, suggesting that they had fully recovered from extreme early deprivation. Romanian children adopted after 6 months of age performed well below average. And although those adopted after age 2 improved between ages 6 and 11, they continued to show serious intellectual deficits. *(Adapted from Beckett et al., 2006.)*

■ Experience-expectant brain growth takes place naturally, through ordinary, stimulating experiences. This toddler shoveling pebbles into her bucket engages in the type of activity that best promotes brain development in the early years. ■

© ERIN HOGAN/GETTY IMAGES/PHOTODISC

In addition to impoverished environments, ones that overwhelm children with expectations beyond their current capacities interfere with the brain's potential. In recent years, expensive early learning centers have sprung up, in which infants are trained with letter and number flash cards and slightly older toddlers are given a full curriculum of reading, math, science, art, gym, and more. There is no evidence that these programs yield smarter, better "superbabies" (Hirsh-Pasek & Golinkoff, 2003). To the contrary, trying to prime infants with stimulation for which they are not ready can cause them to withdraw, thereby threatening their interest in learning and creating conditions much like stimulus deprivation!

How, then, can we characterize appropriate stimulation during the early years? To answer this question, researchers distinguish between two types of brain development. The first, **experience-expectant brain growth,** refers to the young brain's rapidly developing organization, which depends on ordinary experiences—opportunities to see and touch objects, to hear language and other sounds, and to move about and explore the environment. As a result of millions of years of evolution, the brains of all infants, toddlers, and young children expect to encounter these experiences and, if they do, grow normally. The second type of brain development—**experience-dependent brain growth**—occurs throughout our lives. It consists of additional growth and the refinement of established brain structures as a result of specific learning experiences that vary widely across individuals and cultures (Greenough & Black, 1992). Reading and writing, playing computer games, weaving an intricate rug, and practicing the violin are examples. The brain of a violinist differs in certain ways from the brain of a poet because each has exercised different brain regions for a long time.

Experience-expectant brain development occurs early and naturally, as caregivers offer babies and preschoolers age-appropriate play materials and engage them in enjoyable daily routines—a shared meal, a game of peekaboo, a bath before bed, a picture book to talk about, or a song to sing. The resulting growth provides the foundation for later-occurring, experience-dependent development (Huttenlocher, 2002; Shonkoff & Phillips, 2001). No evidence exists for a sensitive period in the first few years of life for mastering skills that depend on extensive training, such as reading, musical performance, or gymnastics (Bruer, 1999). To the contrary, rushing early learning also harms the brain by overwhelming its neural circuits, thereby reducing the brain's sensitivity to the everyday experiences it needs for a healthy start in life.

Changing States of Arousal

Rapid brain growth means that the organization of sleep and wakefulness changes substantially between birth and 2 years, and fussiness and crying also decline. The newborn baby takes round-the-clock naps that total about 16 to 18 hours (Davis, Parker, & Montgomery, 2004). Total sleep time declines slowly; the average 2-year-old still needs 12 to 13 hours. But periods of sleep and wakefulness become fewer and longer, and the sleep–wake pattern increasingly conforms to a night–day schedule. Most 6- to 9-month-olds take two daytime naps; by about 18 months, children generally need only one nap. Finally, between ages 3 and 5, napping subsides (Iglowstein et al., 2003).

These changing arousal patterns are due to brain development, but they are also affected by the social environment. In Western nations, many parents try to get their babies to sleep through the night around 4 months of age by feeding them solid foods before bedtime, then putting them down in a separate, quiet room—practices that may be at odds with young infants' neurological development. Not until the middle of the first year is the secretion of *melatonin,* a hormone within the brain that promotes drowsiness, much greater at night than during the day (Sadeh, 1997). Babies of this age, whose caregivers take them out on regular early-afternoon outings and expose them to more bright sunlight, sleep better at night (Harrison, 2004).

As the Cultural Influences box on the following page reveals, isolating infants to promote sleep is rare elsewhere in the world. When babies sleep with their parents, their average sleep period remains constant at three hours from 1 to 8 months of age. Only at the end of the first year, as REM sleep (the state that usually prompts waking) declines, do infants move in the direction of an adultlike sleep–wake schedule (Ficca et al., 1999).

LOOK AND LISTEN

Interview a parent of a baby about sleep challenges. What strategies has the parent tried to ease these difficulties? Are the techniques likely to be effective, in view of evidence on infant sleep development?

CULTURAL INFLUENCES

Cultural Variation in Infant Sleeping Arrangements

While awaiting the birth of a new baby, North American parents typically furnish a room as the infant's sleeping quarters. For decades, child-rearing advice from experts strongly encouraged the nighttime separation of baby from parent. For example, the most recent edition of Benjamin Spock's *Baby and Child Care* recommends that babies sleep in their own room by 3 months of age, explaining, "By 6 months, a child who regularly sleeps in her parents' room may become dependent on this arrangement" (Spock & Needlman, 2004, p. 60). And the American Academy of Pediatrics (2005) has issued a controversial warning that parent–infant bedsharing may increase the risk of sudden infant death syndrome (SIDS).

Yet parent–infant "cosleeping" is the norm for approximately 90 percent of the world's population, in cultures as diverse as the Japanese, the rural Guatemalan Maya, the Inuit of northwestern Canada, and the !Kung of Botswana. Japanese and Korean children usually lie next to their mothers throughout infancy and early childhood, and many continue to sleep with a parent or other family member until adolescence (Takahashi, 1990; Yang & Hahn, 2002). Among the Maya, mother–infant cosleeping is interrupted only by the birth of a new baby, at which time the older child is moved next to the father or to another bed in the same room (Morelli et al., 1992). Cosleeping is also common in U.S. ethnic minority families (McKenna & Volpe, 2007). African-American children, for example, frequently fall asleep with their parents and remain with them for part or all of the night (Buswell & Spatz, 2007).

Cultural values—specifically, collectivism versus individualism (see Chapter 2, page 78)—strongly influence infant sleeping arrangements. In one study, researchers interviewed Guatemalan Mayan mothers and American middle-SES mothers about their sleeping practices. Mayan mothers stressed a collectivist perspective, explaining that cosleeping builds a close parent–child bond, which is necessary for children to learn the ways of people around them. In contrast, American mothers conveyed

an individualistic perspective, mentioning the importance of instilling early independence, preventing bad habits, and protecting their own privacy (Morelli et al., 1992).

Over the past two decades, cosleeping has increased in Western nations. In the United States, an estimated 13 percent of infants routinely bedshare, and an additional 30 to 35 percent sometimes do so (Buswell & Spatz, 2007; Willinger et al., 2003). Proponents of the practice say that it helps infants sleep, makes breastfeeding more convenient, and provides valuable bonding time—especially for employed parents who have limited contact with their baby during the day (McKenna & Volpe, 2007).

During the night, cosleeping babies breastfeed three times longer than infants who sleep alone. Because infants arouse to nurse more often when sleeping next to their mothers, some researchers believe that cosleeping may actually help safeguard babies at risk for SIDS. Consistent with this view, SIDS is rare in Asian cultures where cosleeping is widespread, including Cambodia, China, Japan, Korea, Thailand, and Vietnam (McKenna, 2002; McKenna & McDade, 2005). And contrary to popular belief, cosleeping does not reduce mothers' total sleep time, although they experience more brief awakenings, which permit them to check on their baby (Mao et al., 2004).

Infant sleeping practices affect other aspects of family life. For example, Mayan babies doze off in the midst of ongoing family activities and are carried to bed by their mothers. In contrast, for many North American parents, bedtime often requires a lengthy, elaborate ritual. Perhaps bedtime struggles, so common in Western homes but rare elsewhere in the world, are related to the stress young children feel when they must fall asleep without assistance (Latz, Wolf, & Lozoff, 1999).

Critics of bedsharing warn that cosleeping children will develop emotional problems, especially excessive

dependency. Yet a longitudinal study following children from the end of pregnancy through age 18 showed that young people who had bedshared in the early years were no different from others in any aspect of adjustment (Okami, Weisner, & Olmstead, 2002). Another concern is that infants might become trapped under the parent's body or in soft covers, mattresses, or sofas and suffocate. Parents who are obese or who use alcohol, tobacco, or illegal drugs do pose a serious risk to their sleeping babies, as does the use of quilts and comforters or an overly soft mattress (Willinger et al., 2003).

But with appropriate precautions, parents and infants can cosleep safely (McKenna & Volpe, 2007). In cultures where cosleeping is widespread, parents and infants usually sleep with light covering on hard surfaces, such as firm mattresses, floor mats, and wooden planks, or infants sleep in a cradle or hammock next to the parents' bed (McKenna, 2001, 2002). And when sharing the same bed, infants typically lie on their back or side facing the mother—positions that promote frequent, easy communication between parent and baby and arousal if breathing is threatened.

Finally, breastfeeding mothers usually assume a distinctive sleeping posture. They face the infant, with knees drawn up under the baby's feet and arm above the baby's head. Besides facilitating feeding, the position prevents the infant from sliding down under covers or up under pillows (Ball, 2006). Because this posture is also seen in female great apes while sharing sleeping nests with their infants, researchers believe it may have evolved to enhance infant safety.

■ This Cambodian father and child sleep together, a practice common in their culture and around the globe. The family sleeps on hard wooden surfaces, which protect cosleeping children from entrapment in soft bedding. ■

Even after infants sleep through the night, they continue to wake occasionally. When babies begin to crawl and walk, they often show temporary periods of disrupted sleep (Scher, Epstein, & Tirosh, 2004). And studies carried out in Australia, Great Britain, and Israel revealed that night wakings increased between 1½ and 2 years, then declined (Scher, Epstein, & Tirosh, 2004; Scher et al., 1995). As we will see in Chapter 7, the challenges of the second year—ability to range farther from the familiar caregiver and awareness of the self as separate from others—often prompt anxiety in toddlers, evident in disturbed sleep and clinginess. When parents offer comfort, these behaviors subside.

ASK YOURSELF

◆ REVIEW How do overproduction of synapses and synaptic pruning support infants' and children's ability to learn?

◆ APPLY Which infant enrichment program would you choose: one that emphasizes gentle talking and touching and social games, or one that includes reading and number drills and classical music lessons? Explain.

◆ CONNECT Explain how inappropriate stimulation—either too little or too much—can impair cognitive and emotional development in the early years.

◆ REFLECT What is your attitude toward parent–infant cosleeping? Is it influenced by your cultural background? Explain.

■ ■ Influences on Early Physical Growth
■ ■

Physical growth, like other aspects of development, results from the continuous and complex interplay between genetic and environmental factors. Heredity, nutrition, relative freedom from disease, and emotional well-being all affect early physical growth.

Heredity

Because identical twins are much more alike in body size than fraternal twins, we know that heredity is important in physical growth (Estourgie-van Burk et al., 2006). When diet and health are adequate, height and rate of physical growth are largely determined by heredity. In fact, as long as negative environmental influences such as poor nutrition or illness are not severe, children and adolescents typically show *catch-up growth*—a return to a genetically determined growth path—once conditions improve. After her adoption, Grace grew rapidly until, at age 2, she was nearly average in size by Cambodian standards. Still, the health of many organs may be permanently compromised by inadequate early nutrition.

Twin studies reveal that genetic makeup also contributes considerably to body weight (Kinnunen, Pietilainen, & Rissanen, 2006). At the same time, environment—in particular, nutrition and eating habits—plays a powerful role.

Nutrition

Nutrition is especially crucial for development in the first two years because the baby's brain and body are growing so rapidly. Pound for pound, an infant's energy needs are at least twice those of an adult. Twenty-five percent of infants' total caloric intake is devoted to growth, and babies need extra calories to keep rapidly developing organs functioning properly (Meyer, 2009).

BREASTFEEDING VERSUS BOTTLE-FEEDING   Babies not only need enough food; they also need the right kind of food. In early infancy, breast milk is ideally suited to their needs, and bottled formulas try to imitate it. Applying What We Know on the following page summarizes major nutritional and health advantages of breastfeeding.

◆ Applying What We Know

Reasons to Breastfeed

NUTRITIONAL AND HEALTH ADVANTAGES	EXPLANATION
Provides the correct balance of fat and protein	Compared with the milk of other mammals, human milk is higher in fat and lower in protein. This balance, as well as the unique proteins and fats contained in human milk, is ideal for a rapidly myelinating nervous system.
Ensures nutritional completeness	A mother who breastfeeds need not add other foods to her infant's diet until the baby is 6 months old. The milks of all mammals are low in iron, but the iron contained in breast milk is much more easily absorbed by the baby's system. Consequently, bottle-fed infants need iron-fortified formula.
Helps ensure healthy physical growth	One-year-old breastfed babies are leaner (have a higher percentage of muscle to fat), a growth pattern that persists through the preschool years and that may help prevent later overweight and obesity.
Protects against many diseases	Breastfeeding transfers antibodies and other infection-fighting agents from mother to baby and enhances functioning of the immune system. Compared with bottle-fed infants, breastfed babies have far fewer allergic reactions and respiratory and intestinal illnesses. Breast milk also has anti-inflammatory effects, which reduce the severity of illness symptoms. Breastfeeding in the first four months (especially when exclusive) is linked to lower blood cholesterol levels in adulthood and, thereby, may help prevent cardiovascular disease.
Protects against faulty jaw development and tooth decay	Sucking the mother's nipple instead of an artificial nipple helps avoid malocclusion, a condition in which the upper and lower jaws do not meet properly. It also protects against tooth decay due to sweet liquid remaining in the mouths of infants who fall asleep while sucking on a bottle.
Ensures digestibility	Because breastfed babies have a different kind of bacteria growing in their intestines than do bottle-fed infants, they rarely suffer from constipation or other gastrointestinal problems.
Smooths the transition to solid foods	Breastfed infants accept new solid foods more easily than do bottle-fed infants, perhaps because of their greater experience with a variety of flavors, which pass from the maternal diet into the mother's milk.

Sources: American Academy of Pediatrics, 2005a; Buescher, 2001; Michels et al., 2007; Owen et al., 2008; Rosetta & Baldi, 2008; Weyermann, Rothenbacher, & Brenner, 2006.

Because of these benefits, breastfed babies in poverty-stricken regions of the world are much less likely to be malnourished and 6 to 14 times more likely to survive the first year of life. The World Health Organization recommends breastfeeding until age 2 years, with solid foods added at 6 months. These practices, if widely followed, would save the lives of more than a million infants annually (World Health Organization, 2010b). Even breastfeeding for just a few weeks offers some protection against respiratory and intestinal infections, which are devastating to young children in developing countries. Also, because a nursing mother is less likely to get pregnant, breastfeeding helps increase spacing among siblings, a major factor in reducing infant and childhood deaths in nations with widespread poverty. (Note, however, that breastfeeding is not a reliable method of birth control.)

Yet many mothers in the developing world do not know about these benefits. In Africa, the Middle East, and Latin America, most babies get some breastfeeding, but fewer than 40 percent are exclusively breastfed for the first six months, and one-third are fully weaned from the breast before 1 year (Lauer et al., 2004). In place of breast milk, mothers give their babies commercial formula or low-grade nutrients, such as rice water or highly diluted cow or goat milk. Contamination of these foods as a result of poor sanitation is common and often leads to illness and infant death. The United Nations has encouraged all hospitals and maternity units in developing countries to promote breastfeeding as long as mothers do not have viral or bacterial infections (such as HIV or tuberculosis) that can be transmitted to the baby. Today, most developing countries have banned the practice of giving free or subsidized formula to new mothers.

Partly as a result of the natural childbirth movement, breastfeeding has become more common in industrialized nations, especially among well-educated women. Today, 74 percent of American mothers breastfeed, but half of them stop after a few months (U.S. Centers for Disease Control, 2009). And despite the health benefits of breast milk, only 50 percent of

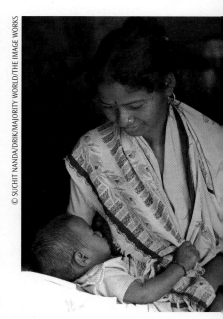

■ Breastfeeding is especially important in developing countries. This breastfed baby from a village in India is likely to grow normally during the first year. ■

© SUCHIT NANDA/DRIK/MAJORITY WORLD/THE IMAGE WORKS

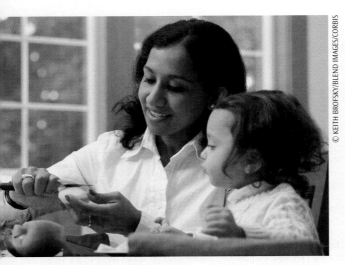

By providing nutritious meals and snacks, this mother supports her toddler's desire to feed herself while also promoting healthy eating habits that protect against overweight and obesity. ■

LOOK AND LISTEN

◆❖◆

Ask several parents of 1- to 2-year-olds to keep a diary of all the foods and drinks they offer their toddler over a weekend. How healthy are the toddlers' diets? Did any of the parents report heightened awareness of family nutrition as a result of the diary exercise?

preterm infants are breastfed at hospital discharge. Breastfeeding a preterm baby presents special challenges, including maintaining a sufficient milk supply with artificial pumping until the baby is mature enough to suck at the breast and providing the infant with enough sucking experience to learn to feed successfully (Callen & Pinelli, 2005). Kangaroo care (see pages 138–139 in Chapter 4) and the support of health professionals are helpful.

Breast milk is so easily digestible that a breastfed infant becomes hungry quite often—every 1½ to 2 hours, compared to every 3 or 4 hours for a bottle-fed baby. This makes breastfeeding inconvenient for many employed women. Not surprisingly, mothers who return to work sooner wean their babies from the breast earlier (Kimbro, 2006). But mothers who cannot be with their babies all the time can still combine breast- and bottle-feeding. The U.S. Department of Health and Human Services (2009a) advises exclusive breastfeeding for the first 6 months and inclusion of breast milk in the baby's diet until at least 1 year.

Women who do not breastfeed sometimes worry that they are depriving their baby of an experience essential for healthy psychological development. Yet breastfed and bottle-fed infants in industrialized nations do not differ in quality of the mother–infant relationship or in later emotional adjustment (Fergusson & Woodward, 1999; Jansen, de Weerth, & Riksen-Walraven, 2008). Some studies report a slight advantage in intelligence test performance for children and adolescents who were breastfed, after controlling for many factors. Most, however, find no cognitive benefits (Der, Batty, & Deary, 2006).

ARE CHUBBY BABIES AT RISK FOR LATER OVERWEIGHT AND OBESITY? From early infancy, Timmy was an enthusiastic eater who nursed vigorously and gained weight quickly. By 5 months, he began reaching for food on his parents' plates. Vanessa wondered: Was she overfeeding Timmy and increasing his chances of being permanently overweight?

Most chubby babies thin out during toddlerhood and the preschool years, as weight gain slows and they become more active. Infants and toddlers can eat nutritious foods freely without risk of becoming overweight. But recent evidence does indicate a strengthening relationship between rapid weight gain in infancy and later obesity (Botton et al., 2008; Chomtho et al., 2008). The trend may be due to the rise in overweight and obesity among adults, who promote unhealthy eating habits in their young children. Interviews with more than 3,000 U.S. parents of 4- to 24-month-olds revealed that many routinely served them french fries, pizza, candy, sugary fruit drinks, and soda. For example, 60 percent of 12-month-olds ate candy at least once a day! On average, infants consumed 20 percent and toddlers 30 percent more calories than they needed. At the same time, one-third ate no fruits or vegetables (Briefel et al., 2004).

How can concerned parents prevent their infants from becoming overweight children and adults? One way is to breastfeed for the first six months, which is associated with slower weight gain over the first year and leaner body build through early childhood (Gunnarsdottir et al., 2010; Sloan et al., 2008). Another is to avoid giving them foods loaded with sugar, salt, and saturated fats. Once toddlers learn to walk, climb, and run, parents can also provide plenty of opportunities for energetic play. Finally, because research shows a correlation between excessive television viewing and overweight in older children, parents should limit the time very young children spend in front of the TV.

Malnutrition

Osita is an Ethiopian 2-year-old whose mother has never had to worry about his gaining too much weight. When she weaned him at 1 year, he had little to eat besides starchy rice flour cakes. Soon his belly enlarged, his feet swelled, his hair fell out, and a rash appeared on his skin. His bright-eyed curiosity vanished, and he became irritable and listless.

In developing countries and war-torn areas where food resources are limited, malnutrition is widespread. Recent evidence indicates that about 27 percent of the world's children suffer

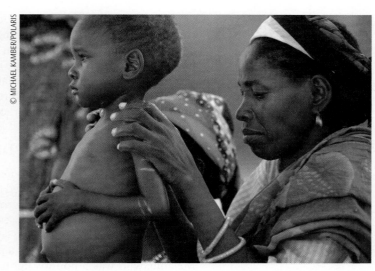

■ The baby on the left, of Niger, Africa, has marasmus, a wasted condition caused by a diet low in all essential nutrients. The swollen abdomen of the toddler on the right, also from Niger, is a symptom of kwashiorkor, which results from a diet very low in protein. If these children survive, they are likely to be growth stunted and to suffer from lasting organ damage as well as serious cognitive and emotional impairments. ■

from malnutrition before age 5 (World Health Organization, 2009b). The 10 percent who are severely affected suffer from two dietary diseases.

Marasmus is a wasted condition of the body caused by a diet low in all essential nutrients. It usually appears in the first year of life when a baby's mother is too malnourished to produce enough breast milk and bottle-feeding is also inadequate. Her starving baby becomes painfully thin and is in danger of dying.

Osita has **kwashiorkor,** caused by an unbalanced diet very low in protein. The disease usually strikes after weaning, between 1 and 3 years of age. It is common in regions where children get just enough calories from starchy foods but little protein. The child's body responds by breaking down its own protein reserves, which causes the swelling and other symptoms that Osita experienced.

Children who survive these extreme forms of malnutrition often grow to be smaller in all body dimensions and suffer from lasting damage to the brain, heart, liver, or other organs (Müller & Krawinkel, 2005). When their diets do improve, they tend to gain excessive weight (Uauy et al., 2008). A malnourished body protects itself by establishing a low basal metabolism rate, which may endure after nutrition improves. Also, malnutrition may disrupt appetite control centers in the brain, causing the child to overeat when food becomes plentiful.

Learning and behavior are also seriously affected. In one long-term study of marasmic children, an improved diet led to some catch-up growth in height, but not in head size (Stoch et al., 1982). The malnutrition probably interfered with growth of neural fibers and myelination, causing a permanent loss in brain weight. And animal evidence reveals that a deficient diet alters the production of neurotransmitters in the brain—an effect that can disrupt all aspects of development (Haller, 2005). These children score low on intelligence tests, show poor fine-motor coordination, and have difficulty paying attention (Galler et al., 1990; Liu et al., 2003). They also display a more intense stress response to fear-arousing situations, perhaps caused by the constant, gnawing pain of hunger (Fernald & Grantham-McGregor, 1998).

Recall from our discussion of prenatal malnutrition in Chapter 3 that the passivity and irritability of malnourished children worsen the impact of poor diet. These behaviors may appear even when protein-calorie deprivation is only mild to moderate. They also accompany *iron-deficiency anemia,* a condition common among poverty-stricken infants and children that interferes with many central nervous system processes. Withdrawal and listlessness reduce the nutritionally deprived child's ability to pay attention, explore, and evoke sensitive caregiving from parents, whose lives are already disrupted by poverty and stressful living conditions (Corapci, Radan, & Lozoff, 2006; Grantham-McGregor & Ani, 2001). For this reason, interventions for malnourished children must improve the family situation as well as the child's nutrition.

Inadequate nutrition is not confined to developing countries. Because government-supported supplementary food programs do not reach all families in need, an estimated 22 percent of U.S. children suffer from *food insecurity*—uncertain access to enough food for a healthy, active life. Food insecurity is especially high among single-parent families (35 percent) and low-income ethnic minority families—for example, Hispanics and African Americans (26 and 27 percent, respectively) (Nord, Andrews, & Carlson, 2009). Although few of these children have marasmus or kwashiorkor, their physical growth and ability to learn are still affected.

Emotional Well-Being

We may not think of affection as necessary for healthy physical growth, but it is as vital as food. **Growth faltering** is a term applied to infants whose weight, height, and head circumference are substantially below age-related growth norms and who are withdrawn and apathetic (Black, 2005). In as many as half such cases, a disturbed parent–infant relationship contributes to this failure to grow normally.

Lana, an observant nurse at a public health clinic, became concerned about 8-month-old Melanie, who was 3 pounds lighter than she had been at her last checkup. Lana noted that Melanie kept her eyes on nearby adults, anxiously watching their every move, and rarely smiled at her mother. During feeding and diaper changing, Melanie's mother sometimes appeared depressed and distant, at other times impatient and hostile. Melanie tried to protect herself by tracking her mother's whereabouts and, when she approached, avoiding her gaze.

Often an unhappy marriage and parental psychological disturbance contribute to these serious caregiving problems. And most of the time, the baby is irritable and displays abnormal feeding behaviors, such as poor sucking or vomiting, that both disrupt growth and lead parents to feel anxious and helpless, which stress the parent–infant relationship further (Batchelor, 2008; Linscheid, Budd, & Rasnake, 2005).

In Melanie's case, her alcoholic father was out of work, and her parents argued constantly. Melanie's mother had little energy to meet Melanie's psychological needs. When treated early, by intervening in infant feeding problems, helping parents with their own life challenges, and encouraging sensitive caregiving, babies show quick catch-up growth. But if the disorder is not corrected in infancy, most of these children remain small and show lasting cognitive and emotional difficulties (Black et al., 2007; Drewett, Corbett, & Wright, 2006).

ASK YOURSELF

◆ REVIEW Explain why breastfeeding can have lifelong consequences for the development of babies born in poverty-stricken regions of the world.

◆ APPLY Eight-month-old Shaun is well below average in height and painfully thin. He cries during feedings and is listless and irritable. Shaun's single mother feels overwhelmed and discouraged. Why do Shaun and his mother need intervention quickly? What should health professionals do?

◆ CONNECT How are bidirectional influences between parent and child involved in the impact of malnutrition on psychological development? After her adoption, how did those influences change for Grace?

◆ REFLECT Imagine that you are the parent of a newborn baby. Describe feeding practices you would use, and ones you would avoid, to prevent overweight and obesity.

Learning Capacities

Learning refers to changes in behavior as the result of experience. Babies come into the world with built-in learning capacities that permit them to profit from experience immediately. Infants are capable of two basic forms of learning, which were introduced in Chapter 1: classical and operant conditioning. They also learn through their natural preference for novel stimulation. Finally, shortly after birth, babies learn by observing others; they can imitate the facial expressions and gestures of adults.

Classical Conditioning

Newborn reflexes, discussed in Chapter 4, make **classical conditioning** possible in the young infant. In this form of learning, a neutral stimulus is paired with a stimulus that leads to a reflexive response. Once the baby's nervous system makes the connection between the two stimuli, the neutral stimulus produces the behavior by itself. Classical conditioning helps infants recognize which events usually occur together in the everyday world, so they can anticipate what is about to happen next. As a result, the environment becomes more orderly and predictable. Let's take a closer look at the steps of classical conditioning.

As Carolyn settled down in the rocking chair to nurse Caitlin, she often stroked Caitlin's forehead. Soon Carolyn noticed that each time she did this, Caitlin made active sucking movements. Caitlin had been classically conditioned. Here is how it happened (see Figure 5.10):

1. Before learning takes place, an **unconditioned stimulus (UCS)** must consistently produce a reflexive, or **unconditioned, response (UCR).** In Caitlin's case, sweet breast milk (UCS) resulted in sucking (UCR).
2. To produce learning, a *neutral stimulus* that does not lead to the reflex is presented just before, or at about the same time as, the UCS. Carolyn stroked Caitlin's forehead as each nursing period began. The stroking (neutral stimulus) was paired with the taste of milk (UCS).
3. If learning has occurred, the neutral stimulus alone produces a response similar to the reflexive response. The neutral stimulus is then called a **conditioned stimulus (CS),** and the response it elicits is called a **conditioned response (CR).** We know that Caitlin has been classically conditioned because stroking her forehead outside the feeding situation (CS) results in sucking (CR).

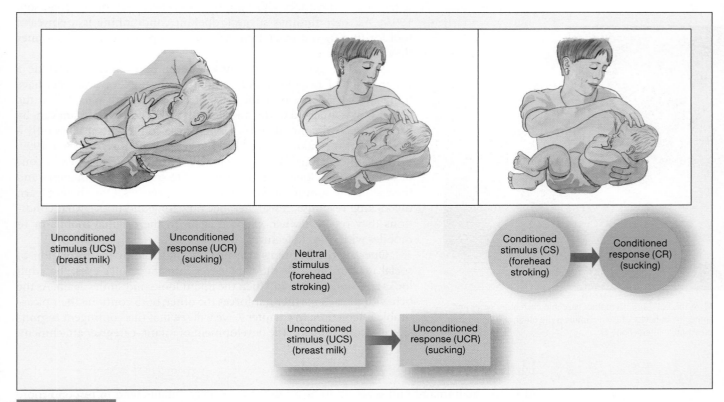

FIGURE 5.10

The steps of classical conditioning. This example shows how Caitlin's mother classically conditioned her to make sucking movements by stroking her forehead at the beginning of feedings.

If the CS is presented alone enough times, without being paired with the UCS, the CR will no longer occur, an outcome called *extinction.* In other words, if Carolyn repeatedly strokes Caitlin's forehead without feeding her, Caitlin will gradually stop sucking in response to stroking.

Young infants can be classically conditioned most easily when the association between two stimuli has survival value. Learning which stimuli regularly accompany feeding improves the infant's ability to get food and survive (Blass, Ganchrow, & Steiner, 1984). In contrast, some responses, such as fear, are very difficult to classically condition in young babies. Until infants have the motor skills to escape unpleasant events, they have no biological need to form these associations. After age 6 months, however, fear is easy to condition. **TAKE A MOMENT...** Return to Chapter 1, page 17, to review John Watson's well-known experiment in which he conditioned Little Albert to withdraw and cry at the sight of a furry white rat. Then test your knowledge of classical conditioning by identifying the UCS, UCR, CS, and CR in Watson's study.

Operant Conditioning

In classical conditioning, babies build expectations about stimulus events in the environment, but they do not influence the stimuli that occur. In **operant conditioning,** infants act, or *operate,* on the environment, and stimuli that follow their behavior change the probability that the behavior will occur again. A stimulus that increases the occurrence of a response is called a **reinforcer.** For example, sweet liquid *reinforces* the sucking response in newborns. Removing a desirable stimulus or presenting an unpleasant one to decrease the occurrence of a response is called **punishment.** A sour-tasting fluid *punishes* newborn babies' sucking response. It causes them to purse their lips and stop sucking entirely.

Many stimuli besides food can serve as reinforcers of infant behavior. For example, newborns will suck faster on a nipple that produces interesting sights and sounds, including visual designs, music, or human voices (Floccia, Christophe, & Bertoncini, 1997). Even preterm babies will seek reinforcing stimulation. In one study, they increased their contact with a soft teddy bear that "breathed" at a rate reflecting the infant's respiration, whereas they decreased their contact with a nonbreathing bear (Thoman & Ingersoll, 1993). As these findings suggest, operant conditioning is a powerful tool for finding out what stimuli babies can perceive and which ones they prefer.

As infants get older, operant conditioning expands to include a wider range of responses and stimuli. For example, researchers have hung special mobiles over the cribs of 2- to 6-month-olds. When the baby's foot is attached to the mobile with a long cord, the infant can, by kicking, make the mobile turn. Under these conditions, it takes only a few minutes for infants to start kicking vigorously (Rovee-Collier, 1999; Rovee-Collier & Barr, 2001). As you will see in Chapter 6, operant conditioning with mobiles is frequently used to study infants' memory and their ability to group similar stimuli into categories. Once babies learn the kicking response, researchers see how long and under what conditions they retain it when exposed again to the original mobile or to mobiles with varying features.

Operant conditioning also plays a vital role in the formation of social relationships. As the baby gazes into the adult's eyes, the adult looks and smiles back, and then the infant looks and smiles again. As the behavior of each partner reinforces the other, both continue their pleasurable interaction. In Chapter 7, we will see that this contingent responsiveness contributes to the development of infant–caregiver attachment.

■ As this baby and his mother gaze into each other's eyes and smile, the behavior of each reinforces the other, sustaining their pleasurable interaction. ■

Habituation

At birth, the human brain is set up to be attracted to novelty. Infants tend to respond more strongly to a new element that has entered their environment, an inclination that ensures that they will continually add to their knowledge base. **Habituation** refers to a gradual reduction in the strength of a response due to repetitive stimulation. Looking, heart rate, and respiration rate may all decline, indicating a loss of interest. Once this has occurred, a new stimulus—a change in the environment—causes responsiveness to return to a high level, an increase called **recovery.** For example, when you walk through a familiar space, you notice things that are new and different—a recently hung picture on the wall or a piece of furniture that has been moved. Habituation and recovery promote learning by focusing our attention on those aspects of the environment we know least about.

Researchers studying infants' understanding of the world rely on habituation and recovery more than any other learning capacity. For example, a baby who first *habituates* to a visual pattern (a photo of a baby) and then *recovers* to a new one (a photo of a bald man) appears to remember the first stimulus and perceive the second one as new and different from it. This method of studying infant perception and cognition, illustrated in Figure 5.11, can be used with newborns, including preterm infants. It has even been used to study the fetus's sensitivity to external stimuli—for example, by measuring changes in fetal heart rate when various repeated sounds are presented (Dirix et al., 2009; Doherty & Hepper, 2000). Habituation to an auditory stimulus is evident in the third trimester of pregnancy.

Recovery to a new stimulus, or *novelty preference*, assesses infants' *recent memory.* **TAKE A MOMENT...** Think about what happens when you return to a place you have not seen for a long time. Instead of attending to novelty, you are likely to focus on aspects that are familiar: "I recognize that—I've been here before!" Like adults, infants shift from a novelty preference to a familiarity preference as more time intervenes between habituation and test phases in research. That is, babies recover to the familiar stimulus rather than to a novel stimulus (see Figure 5.11) (Bahrick, Hernandez-Reif, & Pickens, 1997; Bahrick & Pickens, 1995; Courage & Howe, 1998; Richmond, Colombo, & Hayne, 2007). By focusing on that shift, researchers can also use habituation to assess *remote memory,* or memory for stimuli to which infants were exposed weeks or months earlier.

With age, babies habituate and recover to stimuli more quickly, indicating that they process information more efficiently. Habituation and recovery have been used to assess a wide range of infant perceptual and cognitive capacities—speech perception, musical and visual pattern perception, object perception, categorization, and knowledge of the social world. But despite the strengths of habituation research, its findings are not clear-cut. When looking, sucking, or heart rate declines and recovers, what babies actually know about the stimuli to which they responded is sometimes uncertain. We will return to this difficulty in Chapter 6.

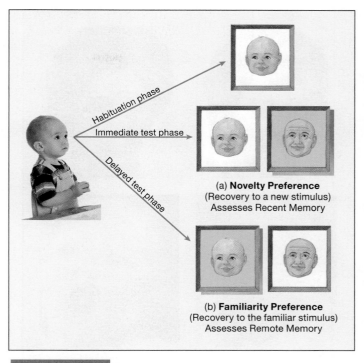

(a) **Novelty Preference**
(Recovery to a new stimulus)
Assesses Recent Memory

(b) **Familiarity Preference**
(Recovery to the familiar stimulus)
Assesses Remote Memory

FIGURE 5.11

Using habituation to study infant perception and cognition. In the habituation phase, infants view a photo of a baby until their looking declines. In the test phase, infants are again shown the baby photo, but this time it appears alongside a photo of a bald-headed man. (a) When the test phase occurs soon after the habituation phase (within minutes, hours, or days, depending on the age of the infants), participants who remember the baby face and distinguish it from the man's face show a *novelty preference;* they recover to (spend more time looking at) the new stimulus. (b) When the test phase is delayed for weeks or months, infants who continue to remember the baby face shift to a *familiarity preference;* they recover to the familiar baby face rather than to the novel man's face.

Imitation

Babies come into the world with a primitive ability to learn through **imitation**—by copying the behavior of another person. For example, Figure 5.12 on page 182 shows a human newborn imitating two adult facial expressions (Meltzoff & Moore, 1977). The newborn's capacity to imitate extends to certain gestures, such as head and index-finger movements, and has been demonstrated in many ethnic groups and cultures (Meltzoff & Kuhl, 1994; Nagy et al., 2005). As the figure reveals, even newborn chimpanzees, our closest evolutionary ancestors, imitate some behaviors (Myowa-Yamakoshi et al., 2004).

FIGURE 5.12

Imitation by human and chimpanzee newborns. The human infants in the middle row imitating (left) tongue protrusion and (right) mouth opening are 2 to 3 weeks old. The chimpanzee imitating both facial expressions is 2 weeks old. *(From A. N. Meltzoff & M. K. Moore, 1977, "Imitation of Facial and Manual Gestures by Human Neonates," Science, 198, p. 75; and M. Myowa-Yamakoshi et al., 2004, "Imitation in Neonatal Chimpanzees [Pan Troglodytes]." Developmental Science, 7, p. 440. Copyright © 1977 by AAAS, copyright 2004 by Blackwell Publishing. Reprinted by permission.)*

Although newborns' capacity to imitate is widely accepted, a few studies have failed to reproduce the human findings (see, for example, Anisfeld et al., 2001). And because newborn mouth and tongue movements occur with increased frequency to almost any arousing change in stimulation (such as lively music or flashing lights), some researchers argue that certain newborn "imitative" responses are actually mouthing—a common early exploratory response to interesting stimuli (Jones, 2006). Furthermore, imitation is harder to induce in babies 2 to 3 months old than just after birth. Therefore, skeptics believe that the newborn imitative response is little more than an automatic response that declines with age, much like a reflex (Heyes, 2005).

Others claim that newborns imitate a variety of facial expressions and head movements with effort and determination, even after short delays—when the adult is no longer demonstrating the behavior (Hayne, 2002; Meltzoff & Moore, 1999). Furthermore, these investigators argue that imitation—unlike reflexes—does not decline. Human babies several months old often do not imitate an adult's behavior right away because they first try to play familiar social games—mutual gazing, cooing, smiling, and waving their arms. But when an adult models a gesture repeatedly, older human infants soon get down to business and imitate (Meltzoff & Moore, 1994). Similarly, imitation declines in baby chimps around 9 weeks of age, when mother–baby mutual gazing and other face-to-face exchanges increase.

According to Andrew Meltzoff, newborns imitate much as older children and adults do—by actively trying to match body movements they *see* with ones they *feel* themselves make (Meltzoff, 2007). Later we will encounter evidence that young babies are remarkably adept at coordinating information across sensory systems.

Indeed, scientists have identified specialized cells in many areas of the cerebral cortex of primates—called **mirror neurons**—that underlie these capacities. Mirror neurons fire identically when a primate hears or sees an action and when it carries out that action on its own (Rizzolatti & Craighero, 2004). Humans have especially elaborate systems of mirror neurons, which enable us to observe another person's behavior (such as smiling or throwing a ball) while simulating the behavior in our own brain. Mirror neurons are believed to be the biological basis of a variety of interrelated, complex social abilities, including imitation, empathic sharing of emotions, and understanding others' intentions (Iocaboni et al., 2005; Schulte-Ruther et al., 2007).

Brain-imaging findings support a functioning mirror-neuron system as early as 6 months of age. Using NIRS, researchers found that the same motor areas of the cerebral cortex were activated in 6-month-olds and in adults when they observed a model engage in a behavior that could be imitated (tapping a box to make a toy pop out) as when they themselves engaged in the motor action (Shimada & Hiraki, 2006). In contrast, when infants and adults observed an object that appeared to move on its own, without human intervention (a ball hanging from the ceiling on a string, swinging like a pendulum), motor areas were not activated.

Still, Meltzoff's view of newborn imitation as a flexible, voluntary capacity remains controversial. Mirror neurons, though possibly functional at birth, undergo an extended period of development (Bertenthal & Longo, 2007; Lepage & Théoret, 2007). Similarly, as we will see in Chapter 6, the capacity to imitate expands greatly over the first two years. But however limited it is at birth, imitation is a powerful means of learning. Using imitation, young infants explore their social world, getting to know people by matching their behavioral states. As babies notice similarities between their own actions and those of others, they learn about themselves. By tapping into infants' ability to imitate, adults can get infants to exhibit desirable behaviors. Finally, caregivers take great pleasure in a baby who imitates their facial gestures and actions, which helps get the infant's relationship with parents off to a good start.

ASK YOURSELF

◆ REVIEW Provide an example of classical conditioning, of operant conditioning, and of habituation/recovery in young infants.

◆ APPLY Nine-month-old Byron has a toy with large, colored push buttons on it. Each time he pushes a button, he hears a nursery tune. Which learning

capacity is the manufacturer of this toy taking advantage of? What can Byron's play with the toy reveal about his perception of sound patterns?

◆ CONNECT Which learning capacities contribute to an infant's first social relationships? Explain, providing examples.

Motor Development

Carolyn, Monica, and Vanessa each kept a baby book, filled with proud notations about when their children held up their heads, reached for objects, sat by themselves, and walked alone. Parents are understandably excited about these new motor skills, which allow babies to master their bodies and the environment in new ways. For example, sitting upright gives infants a new perspective on the world. Reaching permits babies to find out about objects by acting on them. And when infants can move on their own, their opportunities for exploration multiply.

Babies' motor achievements have a powerful effect on their social relationships. When Caitlin crawled at 7½ months, Carolyn and David began to restrict her movements by saying no and expressing mild impatience. When she walked three days after her first birthday, the first "testing of wills" occurred (Biringen et al., 1995). Despite her mother's warnings, she sometimes pulled items from shelves that were off limits. "I said, 'Don't do that!'" Carolyn would repeat firmly, taking Caitlin's hand and redirecting her attention.

At the same time, newly walking babies more actively attend to and initiate social interaction (Clearfield, Osborne, & Mullen, 2008). Caitlin frequently toddled over to her parents to express a greeting, give a hug, or initiate a gleeful game of hide-and-seek. Soon after, she held out a book and then turned its pages as she and her parents named each picture. Carolyn and David, in turn, increased their expressions of affection and playful activities. Caitlin's delight as she worked on new motor skills triggered pleasurable reactions in others, which encouraged her efforts further (Mayes & Zigler, 1992). Motor, social, cognitive, and language competencies developed together and supported one another.

The Sequence of Motor Development

Gross-motor development refers to control over actions that help infants get around in the environment, such as crawling, standing, and walking. *Fine-motor development* has to do with smaller movements, such as reaching and grasping. Table 5.2 on page 184 shows the average ages at which U.S. infants and toddlers achieve a variety of gross- and fine-motor skills. It also presents the age range during which most babies accomplish each skill, indicating large

TABLE 5.2	Gross- and Fine-Motor Development in the First Two Years

MOTOR SKILL	AVERAGE AGE ACHIEVED	AGE RANGE IN WHICH 90 PERCENT OF INFANTS ACHIEVE THE SKILL
When held upright, holds head erect and steady	6 weeks	3 weeks–4 months
When prone, lifts self by arms	2 months	3 weeks–4 months
Rolls from side to back	2 months	3 weeks–5 months
Grasps cube	3 months, 3 weeks	2–7 months
Rolls from back to side	4½ months	2–7 months
Sits alone	7 months	5–9 months
Crawls	7 months	5–11 months
Pulls to stand	8 months	5–12 months
Plays pat-a-cake	9 months, 3 weeks	7–15 months
Stands alone	11 months	9–16 months
Walks alone	11 months, 3 weeks	9–17 months
Builds tower of two cubes	11 months, 3 weeks	10–19 months
Scribbles vigorously	14 months	10–21 months
Walks up stairs with help	16 months	12–23 months
Jumps in place	23 months, 2 weeks	17–30 months
Walks on tiptoe	25 months	16–30 months

Sources: Bayley, 1969, 1993, 2005.

individual differences in *rate* of motor progress. Also, a baby who is a late reacher will not necessarily be a late crawler or walker. We would be concerned about a child's development only if many motor skills were seriously delayed.

Historically, researchers assumed that the motor milestones listed in Table 5.2 are separate, innate abilities that emerge in a fixed sequence governed by a built-in maturational timetable. This view has long been discredited. Rather, motor skills are interrelated: Each is a product of earlier motor attainments and a contributor to new ones. And children acquire motor skills in highly individual ways. For example, before her adoption, Grace spent most of her days lying in a hammock. Because she was rarely placed on her tummy and on firm surfaces that enabled her to move on her own, she did not try to crawl. As a result, she pulled to a stand and walked before she crawled! Even Western babies display such skills as rolling, sitting, crawling, and walking in diverse orders rather than in the sequence implied by motor norms (Adolph, Karasik, & Tamis-LeMonda, 2010).

Many influences—both internal and external to the child—join together to support the vast transformations in motor competencies of the first two years. The *dynamic systems perspective,* introduced in Chapter 1 (see pages 28–29), helps us understand how motor development takes place.

Motor Skills as Dynamic Systems

According to the **dynamic systems theory of motor development,** mastery of motor skills involves acquiring increasingly complex *systems of action.* When motor skills work as a *system,* separate abilities blend together, each cooperating with others to produce more effective ways of exploring and controlling the environment. For example, control of the head and upper chest combine into sitting with support. Kicking, rocking on all fours, and reaching combine to become crawling. Then crawling, standing, and stepping are united into walking (Adolph & Berger, 2006; Thelen, 1989).

Each new skill is a joint product of the following factors: (1) central nervous system development, (2) the body's movement capacities, (3) the goals the child has in mind, and (4) environmental supports for the skill. Change in any element makes the system less stable, and the child starts to explore and select new, more effective motor patterns. The factors that induce change vary with age. In the early weeks of life, brain and body growth are especially important as infants achieve control over the head, shoulders, and upper torso. Later, the baby's goals (getting a toy or crossing the room) and environmental supports (parental encouragement, objects in the infants' everyday setting) play a greater role.

The broader physical environment also profoundly influences motor skills. Infants with stairs in their home learn to crawl up stairs at an earlier age and also more readily master a back-descent strategy—the safest but also the most challenging position because the baby must turn around at the top, give up visual guidance of her goal, and crawl backward (Berger, Theuring, & Adolph, 2007). And if children were reared on the moon with its reduced gravity, they would prefer jumping to walking or running!

When a skill is first acquired, infants must refine it. For example, in trying to crawl, Caitlin often collapsed on her tummy and moved backward. Soon she figured out how to propel herself forward by alternately pulling with her arms and pushing with her feet, "belly-crawling" in various ways for several weeks (Vereijkin & Adolph, 1999). As they attempt a new skill, most babies move back and forth between its presence and absence: An infant might roll over, sit, crawl, or take a few steps on Monday but not do so again until Friday, and then not again until the following week. And related, previously mastered skills often become less secure. As the novice walker experiments with balancing the body vertically over two small moving feet, balance during sitting may become temporarily less stable (Adolph & Berger, 2006; Chen et al., 2007). This variability is evidence of loss of stability in the system—in dynamic systems theory, a necessary transition between a less mature and a more mature stable state.

Furthermore, motor mastery involves intense practice. In learning to walk, for example, toddlers practice six or more hours a day, traveling the length of 29 football fields! Gradually their small, unsteady steps change to a longer stride, their feet move closer together, their toes point to the front, and their legs become symmetrically coordinated (Adolph, Vereijken, & Shrout, 2003). As movements are repeated thousands of times, they promote new synaptic connections in the brain that govern motor patterns.

Dynamic systems theory shows us why motor development cannot be genetically determined. Because it is motivated by exploration and the desire to master new tasks, heredity can map it out only at a general level. Rather than being *hardwired* into the nervous system, behaviors are *softly assembled,* allowing for different paths to the same motor skill (Adolph, 2008; Thelen & Smith, 2006).

Dynamic Motor Systems in Action

To find out how infants acquire motor capacities, researchers conduct microgenetic studies (see Chapter 1, page 43), following babies from their first attempts at a skill until it becomes smooth and effortless. Using this strategy, James Galloway and Esther Thelen (2004) held sounding toys alternately in front of infants' hands and feet, from the time they first showed interest until they engaged in well-coordinated reaching and grasping. As Figure 5.13 illustrates, the infants violated the normative sequence of arm and hand control preceding leg and foot control, shown in Table 5.2. They

LOOK AND LISTEN

Spend an hour observing a newly crawling or walking baby. Note the goals that motivate the baby to move, along with the baby's effort and motor experimentation. Describe parenting behaviors and features of the environment that promote mastery of the skill.

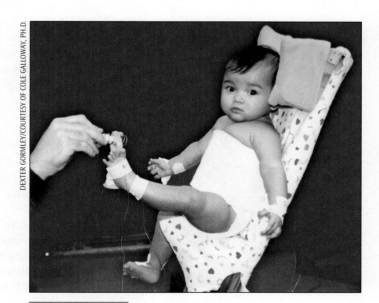

DEXTER GORMLEY/COURTESY OF COLE GALLOWAY, PH.D.

FIGURE 5.13

Reaching "feet first." When sounding toys were held in front of babies' hands and feet, they reached with their feet as early as 8 weeks of age, a month or more before they reached with their hands—a clear violation of the cephalocaudal pattern. Reduced freedom of movement in the hip joint makes leg movements easier to control than arm movements. This 2½-month-old skillfully explores an object with her foot.

■ The West Indians of Jamaica believe that exercise helps infants grow up strong and physically attractive. This mother "walks" her baby up her body—an activity that contributes to earlier mastery of walking. ■

first explored the toys with their feet—as early as 8 weeks of age, at least a month before reaching with their hands!

Why did babies reach "feet first"? Because the hip joint constrains the legs to move less freely than the shoulder joint constrains the arms, infants could more easily control their leg movements. Consequently, foot reaching required far less practice than hand reaching. As these findings confirm, rather than following a strict, predetermined cephalocaudal pattern, the order in which motor skills develop depends on the anatomy of the body part being used, the surrounding environment, and the baby's efforts.

Cultural Variations in Motor Development

Cross-cultural research further illustrates how early movement opportunities and a stimulating environment contribute to motor development. Half a century ago, Wayne Dennis (1960) observed infants in Iranian orphanages who were deprived of the tantalizing surroundings that induce infants to acquire motor skills. These babies spent their days lying on their backs in cribs, without toys to play with—conditions far worse than Grace experienced lying in a hammock in her Cambodian home. As a result, most did not move on their own until after 2 years of age. When they finally did move, the constant experience of lying on their backs led them to scoot in a sitting position rather than crawl on their hands and knees. Because babies who scoot come up against furniture with their feet, not their hands, they are far less likely to pull themselves to a standing position in preparation for walking. Indeed, by 3 to 4 years of age, only 15 percent of the Iranian orphans were walking alone.

Cultural variations in infant-rearing practices also affect motor development. **TAKE A MOMENT...** Take a quick survey of several parents you know: Should sitting, crawling, and walking be deliberately encouraged? Answers vary widely from culture to culture. Japanese mothers, for example, believe such efforts are unnecessary (Seymour, 1999). Among the Zinacanteco Indians of southern Mexico and the Gusii of Kenya, rapid motor progress is actively discouraged. Babies who walk before they know enough to keep away from cooking fires and weaving looms are viewed as dangerous to themselves and disruptive to others (Greenfield, 1992).

In contrast, among the Kipsigis of Kenya and the West Indians of Jamaica, babies hold their heads up, sit alone, and walk considerably earlier than North American infants. Kipsigi parents deliberately teach these motor skills. In the first few months, babies are seated in holes dug in the ground, with rolled blankets to keep them upright. Walking is promoted by frequently standing babies in adults' laps and bouncing them on their feet. Infants respond with stepping movements, often "walking" up the adult's body (Hopkins & Westra, 1988; Super, 1981). And as parents in these cultures support babies in upright postures and rarely put them down on the floor, their infants usually skip crawling—a motor skill regarded as crucial in Western nations!

Finally, because it decreases exposure to "tummy time," the current Western practice of having babies sleep on their backs to protect them from SIDS (see page 147 in Chapter 4) delays gross-motor milestones of rolling, sitting, and crawling (Majnemer & Barr, 2005; Scrutton, 2005). To prevent these delays, caregivers can regularly expose babies to the tummy-lying position during waking hours.

Fine-Motor Development: Reaching and Grasping

Of all motor skills, reaching may play the greatest role in infant cognitive development. By grasping things, turning them over, and seeing what happens when they are released, infants learn a great deal about the sights, sounds, and feel of objects.

FIGURE 5.14

Some milestones of reaching. The average age at which each skill is attained is given. (Ages from Bayley, 1969; Rochat, 1989.)

Reaching and grasping, like many other motor skills, start out as gross, diffuse activity and move toward mastery of fine movements. Figure 5.14 illustrates some milestones of voluntary reaching over the first nine months. Newborns will actively work to bring their hands into their field of vision: In a dimly lit room, they keep their hand within a narrow beam of light, moving the hand when the light beam moves (van der Meer, 1997). Newborns also make poorly coordinated swipes, called **prereaching,** toward an object in front of them, but because of poor arm and hand control they rarely contact the object. Like newborn reflexes, prereaching drops out around 7 weeks of age, when babies improve in eye movements involved in tracking and fixating on objects, which are essential for accurate reaching. Yet these early behaviors suggest that babies are biologically prepared to coordinate hand with eye in the act of exploring (Rosander & von Hofsten, 2002; von Hofsten, 2004).

DEVELOPMENT OF REACHING AND GRASPING   At about 3 to 4 months, as infants develop the necessary eye, head, and shoulder control, reaching appears as purposeful, forward arm movements in the presence of a nearby toy and gradually improves in accuracy (Bhat, Heathcock, & Galloway, 2005; Spencer et al., 2000). By 5 to 6 months, infants reach for an object in a room that has been darkened during the reach by switching off the lights—a skill that improves over the next few months (Clifton et al., 1994; McCarty & Ashmead, 1999). This indicates that the baby does not need to use vision to guide the arms and hands in reaching. Rather, reaching is largely controlled by *proprioception*—our sense of movement and location in space, arising from stimuli within the body. When vision is freed from the basic act of reaching, it can focus on more complex adjustments, such as fine-tuning actions to fit the distance and shape of objects.

Reaching improves as depth perception advances and as infants gain greater control of body posture and arm and hand movements. Four-month-olds aim their reaches ahead of a moving object so they can catch it (von Hofsten, 1993). Around 5 months, babies reduce their efforts when an object is moved beyond their reach (Robin, Berthier, & Clifton, 1996). By 7 months, the arms become more independent: Infants reach for an object by extending one arm rather than both (Fagard & Pezé, 1997). During the next few months, infants become more efficient at reaching for moving objects—ones that spin, change direction, and move sideways, closer, or farther away (Fagard, Spelke, & von Hofsten, 2009; Wentworth, Benson, & Haith, 2000).

Once infants can reach, they modify their grasp. The newborn's grasp reflex is replaced by the **ulnar grasp,** a clumsy motion in which the young infant's fingers close against the palm. Still, even 4-month-olds adjust their grasp to the size and shape of an object—a capacity that improves over the first year as infants orient the hand more precisely and do so in advance of

■ The capacity to sit unsupported contributes to independent movement of the two arms, enabling this 7-month-old to reach for a tantalizing toy with one hand, rather than both. ■

contacting the object (Barrett, Traupman, & Needham, 2008; Witherington, 2005). Around 4 to 5 months, when infants begin to sit up, both hands become coordinated in exploring objects. Babies of this age can hold an object in one hand while the other scans it with the tips of the fingers, and they frequently transfer objects from hand to hand (Rochat & Goubet, 1995). By the end of the first year, infants use the thumb and index finger in a well-coordinated **pincer grasp.** Then the ability to manipulate objects greatly expands. The 1-year-old can pick up raisins and blades of grass, turn knobs, and open and close small boxes.

Between 8 and 11 months, reaching and grasping are well-practiced. As a result, attention is released from the motor skill to events that occur before and after obtaining the object. For example, 10-month-olds easily modify their reach to anticipate their next action. They reach for a ball faster when they intend to throw it than when they intend to drop it carefully through a narrow tube (Claxton, Keen, & McCarty, 2003). Around this time, too, infants begin to solve simple problems that involve reaching, such as searching for and finding a hidden toy.

Finally, the capacity to reach for and manipulate an object increases infants' attention to the way an adult reaches for and plays with that same object (Hauf, Aschersleben, & Prinz, 2007). As babies watch what others do, they broaden their understanding of others' behaviors and of the range of actions that can be performed on various objects, gradually incorporating those possibilities into their own object-related behaviors.

EARLY EXPERIENCE AND REACHING Like other motor milestones, reaching is affected by early experience. In cultures where mothers carry their infants on their hips or in slings for most of the day, babies have rich opportunities to explore with their hands. Among the !Kung of Botswana, infants grasp their mothers' colorful, beaded necklaces to steady themselves while breastfeeding as the mother moves. While riding along, they also frequently swipe at and manipulate their mother's jewelry and other dangling objects (Konner, 1977). As a result, !Kung infants are advanced in development of reaching and grasping. And because babies of Mali and Uganda spend half or more of their day held in sitting or standing positions, which facilitate reaching, they, too, develop manual skills earlier than Western infants, who spend much of their day lying down (Adolph, Karasik, & Tamis-LeMonda, 2010).

Babies' visual surroundings are also influential. In a well-known study, institutionalized infants given a moderate amount of visual stimulation—at first, simple designs and, later, a mobile hung over their crib—reached for objects six weeks earlier than infants given nothing to look at. A third group given massive stimulation—patterned crib bumpers and mobiles at an early age—also reached sooner than unstimulated babies. But this heavy enrichment took its toll. These infants looked away and cried a great deal, and they were less advanced in reaching than the moderately stimulated group (White & Held, 1966). Recall from our discussion of brain development that more stimulation is not necessarily better. Trying to push infants beyond their readiness to handle stimulation can undermine the development of important motor skills.

Bowel and Bladder Control

More than any other aspect of early muscular development, parents wonder about bowel and bladder control. Two or three generations ago, many mothers tried to toilet train infants, but they only caught the baby's reflexive release of urine or a bowel movement at a convenient moment.

Toilet training is best delayed until the months following the second birthday, when children can consistently identify the signals from a full bladder or rectum and wait for the right place to open these muscles—physiological developments essential for the child to cooperate with training. A toddler who stays dry for several hours at a time, stops playing during urination or a bowel movement, and is bothered by a wet or full diaper shows signs of readiness. Children whose parents postpone intensive training until the beginning or middle of the third year are generally fully trained within four months. Starting before 27 months simply prolongs the process (Choby & George, 2008; Brazelton & Sparrow, 2004).

Effective training techniques include establishing regular toileting routines (for example, after getting up, after eating, before going to bed), using gentle encouragement, and praising children for their efforts (Christophersen & Mortweet, 2003). As we will see in Chapter 7, pressuring too much in this area, as in others, can negatively affect the toddler's emotional well-being.

ASK YOURSELF

◆ REVIEW Cite evidence that motor development is a joint product of biological, psychological, and environmental factors.

◆ APPLY List everyday experiences that support mastery of reaching, grasping, sitting, and crawling. Why should caregivers place young infants in a variety of waking-time body positions?

◆ CONNECT Provide several examples of how motor development influences infants' and toddlers' social experiences. How do social experiences, in turn, influence motor development?

◆ REFLECT Do you favor early, systematic training of infants in motor skills such as crawling, walking, running, hopping, and stair climbing? Why or why not?

Perceptual Development

In Chapter 4, you learned that the senses of touch, taste, smell, and hearing—but not vision—are remarkably well-developed at birth. Now let's turn to a related question: How does perception change over the first year? Our discussion will address hearing and vision, the focus of almost all research. Unfortunately, little evidence exists on how touch, taste, and smell develop after birth. Also, in Chapter 4 we used the word *sensation* to talk about these capacities. It suggests a fairly passive process—what the baby's receptors detect when exposed to stimulation. Now we use the word *perception,* which is active: When we perceive, we organize and interpret what we see.

As we review the perceptual achievements of infancy, you may find it hard to tell where perception leaves off and thinking begins. The research we are about to discuss provides an excellent bridge to the topic of Chapter 6—cognitive development during the first two years.

Hearing

On Timmy's first birthday, Vanessa bought several tapes of nursery songs, and she turned one on each afternoon at naptime. Soon Timmy let her know his favorite tune. If she put on "Twinkle, Twinkle," he stood up in his crib and whimpered until she replaced it with "Jack and Jill." Timmy's behavior illustrates the greatest change in hearing over the first year of life: Babies start to organize sounds into complex patterns.

Between 4 and 7 months, infants display a sense of musical phrasing. They prefer Mozart minuets with pauses between phrases to those with awkward breaks (Krumhansl & Jusczyk, 1990). Around 6 to 7 months, they can distinguish musical tunes on the basis of variations in rhythmic patterns, including beat structure (duple or triple) and accent structure (emphasis on the first note of every beat unit or at other positions) (Hannon & Johnson, 2004). And by the end of the first year, infants recognize the same melody when it is played in different keys (Trehub, 2001). As we will see next, 6- to 12-month-olds make comparable discriminations in human speech: They readily detect sound regularities that will facilitate later language learning.

SPEECH PERCEPTION Recall from Chapter 4 that newborns can distinguish nearly all sounds in human languages and that they prefer listening to speech over nonspeech sounds and to their native tongue rather than a rhythmically distinct foreign language. As infants listen to people talking, they learn to focus on meaningful sound variations. ERP brain-wave recordings reveal that around 5 months, infants become sensitive to syllable stress patterns in their own language (Weber et al., 2004). Between 6 and 8 months, they start to "screen out" sounds not

■ This baby already responds to sound regularities in his mother's speech. As he listens, he becomes sensitive to syllable stress patterns and will eventually screen out sounds not used in his own language. ■

used in their own language (Anderson, Morgan, & White, 2003; Polka & Werker, 1994). As the Biology and Environment box on the following page explains, this increased responsiveness to native-language sounds is part of a general "tuning" process in the second half of the first year—a possible sensitive period in which babies acquire a range of perceptual skills for picking up socially important information.

Soon after, infants focus on larger speech units that are critical to figuring out meaning. They recognize familiar words in spoken passages and listen longer to speech with clear clause and phrase boundaries (Johnson & Seidl, 2008; Jusczyk & Hohne, 1997; Soderstrom et al., 2003). Around 7 to 9 months, infants extend this sensitivity to speech structure to individual words: They begin to divide the speech stream into wordlike units (Jusczyk, 2002; Saffran, Werker, & Werner, 2006).

ANALYZING THE SPEECH STREAM How do infants make such rapid progress in perceiving the structure of speech? Research reveals that they have an impressive **statistical learning capacity.** By analyzing the speech stream for patterns—repeatedly occurring sequences of sounds—they acquire a stock of speech structures for which they will later learn meanings, long before they start to talk around age 12 months.

For example, when presented with controlled sequences of nonsense syllables, babies listened for statistical regularities: They locate words by discriminating syllables that often occur together (indicating that they belong to the same word) from syllables that seldom occur together (indicating a word boundary). Consider the English word sequence *pretty#baby.* After listening to the speech stream for just one minute (about 60 words), babies can distinguish a word-internal syllable pair *(pretty)* from a word-external syllable pair *(ty#ba).* They prefer to listen to new speech that preserves the word-internal pattern (Saffran, Aslin, & Newport, 1996; Saffran & Thiessen, 2003).

Once infants locate words, they focus on the words and, around 7 to 8 months, detect regular syllable-stress patterns—for example, in English and Dutch, that the onset of a strong syllable (*hap*-py, *rab*-bit) often signals a new word (Thiessen & Saffran, 2007; Swingley, 2005). By 10 months, infants can detect words that start with weak syllables, such as "sur*prise,*" by listening for sound regularities before and after the words (Jusczyk, 2001; Kooijman, Hagoort, & Cutler, 2009).

Infants also attend to regularities in word sequences. In a study using nonsense words, 7-month-olds distinguished the ABA structure of "ga ti ga" and "li na li" from the ABB structure of "wo fe fe" and "ta la la" (Marcus et al., 1999). They seemed to detect simple word-order rules—a capacity that may eventually help them figure out basic grammar. After extracting these rules, babies generalize them to nonspeech sounds. Seven-month-olds who were exposed to regularities in sequences of nonsense words could identify similar patterns in strings of musical tones and animal sounds. But when presented alone, these stimuli yielded no rule learning (Marcus, Fernandes, & Johnson, 2007). Analyzing speech seems to help babies structure other aspects of their auditory world.

Clearly, babies have a powerful ability to extract patterns from complex, continuous speech. As a result, they acquire a great deal of language-specific knowledge—including a stock of words and other speech structures for which they will later learn meanings—before they start to talk around 12 months of age. As we will see in Chapter 6, adults' style of communicating with infants greatly facilitates analysis of the structure of speech.

Vision

For exploring the environment, humans depend on vision more than any other sense. Although at first a baby's visual world is fragmented, it undergoes extraordinary changes during the first 7 to 8 months of life.

Visual development is supported by rapid maturation of the eye and visual centers in the cerebral cortex. Recall from Chapter 4 that the newborn baby focuses and perceives color poorly. Around 2 months, infants can focus on objects about as well as adults, and their color vision is adultlike by 4 months (Kellman & Arterberry, 2006). Visual acuity (fineness of discrimination) increases steadily throughout the first year, reaching a near-adult level of about

BIOLOGY AND ENVIRONMENT

"Tuning in" to Familiar Speech, Faces, and Music: A Sensitive Period for Culture-Specific Learning

To share experiences with members of their family and community, babies must become skilled at making perceptual discriminations that are meaningful in their culture. As we have seen, at first babies are sensitive to virtually all speech sounds but, around six months, they narrow their focus, limiting the distinctions they make to the language they hear and will soon learn.

The ability to perceive faces shows a similar path of development. After habituating to one member of each pair of faces in Figure 5.15, 6-month-olds were shown the familiar and novel faces side by side. For both pairs, they recovered to (looked longer at) the novel face,

indicating that they could discriminate the individual faces of both humans and monkeys equally well (Pascalis, de Haan, & Nelson, 2002). But at 9 months, infants no longer showed a novelty preference when viewing the monkey pair. Like adults, they could distinguish only the human faces.

This developmental trend appears again in musical rhythm perception. Western adults are accustomed to the even-beat pattern of Western music—repetition of the same rhythmic structure in every measure of a tune—and easily notice rhythmic changes that disrupt this familiar beat. But present them with music that does not follow this typical Western rhythmic form— Baltic folk tunes, for example—and they fail to pick up on rhythmic-pattern deviations. Six-month-olds, however, can detect such disruptions in both Western and non-Western melodies. But by 12 months, after added exposure to Western music, babies

are no longer aware of deviations in foreign musical rhythms, although their sensitivity to Western rhythmic structure remains unchanged (Hannon & Trehub, 2005b).

Several weeks of regular interaction with a foreign-language speaker and of daily opportunities to listen to non-Western music fully restore 12-month-olds' sensitivity to wide-ranging speech sounds and music rhythms (Hannon & Trehub, 2005a; Kuhl, Tsao, & Liu, 2003). Adults given similar extensive experiences, by contrast, show little improvement in perceptual sensitivity.

Taken together, these findings suggest a heightened capacity—or sensitive period—in the second half of the first year, when babies are biologically prepared to "zero in" on socially meaningful perceptual distinctions. Notice how, between 6 and 12 months, learning is especially rapid across several domains (speech, faces, and music) and is easily modified by experience. This suggests a broad neurological change— perhaps a special time of experience-expectant brain growth (see page 172) in which babies analyze everyday stimulation of all kinds similarly, in ways that prepare them to participate in their cultural community.

FIGURE 5.15

Discrimination of human and monkey faces. Which of these pairs is easiest for you to tell apart? After habituating to one of the photos in each pair, infants were shown the familiar and the novel face side-by-side. For both pairs, 6-month-olds recovered to (looked longer at) the novel face, indicating that they could discriminate human and monkey faces equally well. By 12 months, babies lost their ability to distinguish the monkey faces. Like adults, they showed a novelty preference only to human stimuli. *(From O. Pascalis et al., 2002, "Is Face Processing Species-Specific During the First Year of Life?" Science, 296, p. 1322. Reprinted with permission from AAAS.)*

20/20 by 6 months (Slater, 2001). Scanning the environment and tracking moving objects also improve over the first half-year as infants see more clearly and better control their eye movements. In addition, as young infants build an organized perceptual world, they scan more thoroughly and systematically, strategically picking up important information (Johnson, Slemmer, & Amso, 2004; von Hofsten & Rosander, 1998). Consequently, scanning enhances perception, and—in bidirectional fashion—perception also enhances scanning.

As babies explore their visual field, they figure out the characteristics of objects and how they are arranged in space. To understand how they do so, let's examine the development of three aspects of vision: depth, pattern, and object perception.

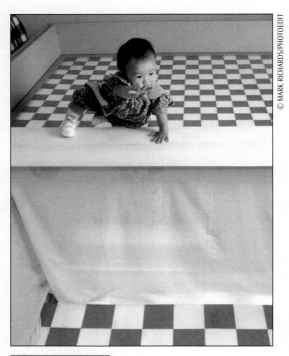

FIGURE 5.16

The visual cliff. Plexiglas covers the deep and shallow sides. By refusing to cross the deep side and showing a preference for the shallow side, this infant demonstrates the ability to perceive depth.

DEPTH PERCEPTION   *Depth perception* is the ability to judge the distance of objects from one another and from ourselves. It is important for understanding the layout of the environment and for guiding motor activity.

Figure 5.16 shows the well-known *visual cliff,* designed by Eleanor Gibson and Richard Walk (1960) and used in the earliest studies of depth perception. It consists of a Plexiglas-covered table with a platform at the center, a "shallow" side with a checkerboard pattern just under the glass, and a "deep" side with a checkerboard several feet below the glass. The researchers found that crawling babies readily crossed the shallow side, but most avoided the deep side. They concluded that around the time infants crawl, most distinguish deep from shallow surfaces and avoid drop-offs.

The visual cliff shows that crawling and avoidance of drop-offs are linked, but not how they are related or when depth perception first appears. Recent research has looked at babies' ability to detect specific depth cues, using methods that do not require that they crawl.

Emergence of Depth Perception.   How do we know when an object is near rather than far away? **TAKE A MOMENT...** Try these exercises to find out. Pick up a small object (such as your cup) and move it toward and away from your face. Did its image grow larger as it approached and smaller as it receded? Next time you take a bike or car ride, notice that nearby objects move past your field of vision more quickly than those far away.

Motion is the first depth cue to which infants are sensitive. Babies 3 to 4 weeks old blink their eyes defensively when an object moves toward their face as though it is going to hit (Nánez & Yonas, 1994). As they are carried about and people and things turn and move before their eyes, infants learn more about depth. By the time they are 3 months old, motion has helped them figure out that objects are not flat but three-dimensional (Arterberry, Craton, & Yonas, 1993).

Binocular depth cues arise because our two eyes have slightly different views of the visual field. The brain blends these two images, resulting in perception of depth. Research in which two overlapping images are projected before the baby, who wears special goggles to ensure that each eye receives only one image, reveals that sensitivity to binocular cues emerges between 2 and 3 months and improves rapidly over the first year (Birch, 1993; Brown & Miracle, 2003). Infants soon make use of binocular cues in their reaching, adjusting arm and hand movements to match the distance of objects from the eyes.

Finally, between 5 and 7 months, infants display sensitivity to *pictorial depth cues*—the ones artists often use to make a painting look three-dimensional. Examples include receding lines that create the illusion of perspective, changes in texture (nearby textures are more detailed than faraway ones), overlapping objects (an object partially hidden by another object is perceived to be more distant), height-in-the-picture-plane (objects closer to the horizon appear further away), and shadows cast on surfaces (indicating a separation in space between the object and the surface) (Arterberry, 2008; Sen, Yonas, & Knill, 2001; Yonas, Elieff, & Arterberry, 2002; Yonas & Granrud, 2006).

Why does perception of depth cues emerge in the order just described? Researchers speculate that motor development is involved. For example, control of the head during the early weeks of life may help babies notice motion and binocular cues. Around 5 to 6 months, the ability to turn, poke, and feel the surface of objects may promote perception of pictorial cues (Bushnell & Boudreau, 1993). And as we will see next, one aspect of motor progress—independent movement—plays a vital role in refinement of depth perception.

Independent Movement and Depth Perception.   At 6 months, Timmy started crawling. "He's fearless!" exclaimed Vanessa. "If I put him down in the middle of the bed, he crawls right over the edge. The same thing happens by the stairs." Will Timmy become wary of the side of the bed and the staircase as he becomes a more experienced crawler? Research suggests that he will. Infants with more crawling experience (regardless of when they started to crawl) are far more likely to refuse to cross the deep side of the visual cliff (Campos et al., 2000).

■ Increased experience at crawling will help this 7-month-old gain in three-dimensional understanding, including how to avoid falling and where objects are in relation to herself and to other objects. ■

From extensive everyday experience, babies gradually figure out how to use depth cues to detect the danger of falling. But because the loss of body control that leads to falling differs greatly for each body position, babies must undergo this learning separately for each posture. In one study, 9-month-olds, who were experienced sitters but novice crawlers, were placed on the edge of a shallow drop-off that could be widened (Adolph, 2002, 2008). While in the familiar sitting position, infants avoided leaning out for an attractive toy at distances likely to result in falling. But in the unfamiliar crawling position, they headed over the edge, even when the distance was extremely wide! And newly walking babies, while avoiding sharp drop-offs, careen down slopes and over uneven surfaces without making the necessary postural adjustments, even when their mothers discourage them from proceeding! Thus, they fall frequently (Adolph et al., 2008; Joh & Adolph, 2006). As infants discover how to avoid falling in different postures and situations, their understanding of depth expands.

Crawling experience promotes other aspects of three-dimensional understanding. For example, seasoned crawlers are better than their inexperienced agemates at remembering object locations and finding hidden objects (Bai & Bertenthal, 1992; Campos et al., 2000). Why does crawling make such a difference? **TAKE A MOMENT...** Compare your own experience of the environment when you are driven from one place to another with what you experience when you walk or drive yourself. When you move on your own, you are much more aware of landmarks and routes of travel, and you take more careful note of what things look like from different points of view. The same is true for infants. In fact, crawling promotes a new level of brain organization, as indicated by more organized EEG brain-wave activity in the cerebral cortex (Bell & Fox, 1996). Perhaps crawling strengthens certain neural connections, especially those involved in vision and understanding of space. As the Social Issues: Education box on page 194 reveals, the link between independent movement and spatial knowledge is also evident in a population with very different perceptual experience: infants with severe visual impairments.

PATTERN PERCEPTION   Even newborns prefer to look at patterned rather than plain stimuli—for example, a drawing of the human face or one with scrambled facial features rather than a black-and-white oval (Fantz, 1961). As they get older, infants prefer more complex patterns. For example, 3-week-olds look longest at black-and-white checkerboards with a few large squares, whereas 8- and 14-week-olds prefer those with many squares (Brennan, Ames, & Moore, 1966).

A general principle, called **contrast sensitivity**, explains early pattern preferences (Banks & Ginsburg, 1985). *Contrast* refers to the difference in the amount of light between adjacent regions in a pattern. If babies are *sensitive to* (can detect) the contrast in two or more patterns, they prefer the one with more contrast. To understand this idea, look at the checkerboards in the top row of Figure 5.17. To us, the one with many small squares has more contrasting elements. Now look at the bottom row, which shows how these checkerboards appear to infants in the first few weeks of life. Because of their poor vision, very young babies cannot resolve the small features in more complex patterns, so they prefer to look at the large, bold checkerboard. Around 2 months, when detection of fine-grained detail has improved, infants become sensitive to the contrast in complex patterns and spend more time looking at them (Gwiazda & Birch, 2001).

■ This 3-month-old's visual acuity has improved greatly since birth. He detects the contrast in complex patterns and spends more time looking at them. ■

© JULIE O'NEIL/INDEX STOCK IMAGERY/PHOTOLIBRARY

Bold checkerboard   Complex checkerboard

Appearance of checkerboards to very young infants

FIGURE 5.17

The way two checkerboards differing in complexity look to infants in the first few weeks of life. Because of their poor vision, very young infants cannot resolve the fine detail in the *complex checkerboard*. It appears blurred, like a gray field. The large, *bold checkerboard* appears to have more contrast, so babies prefer to look at it. *(Adapted from M. S. Banks & P. Salapatek, 1983, "Infant Visual Perception," in M. M. Haith & J. J. Campos (Eds.), Handbook of Child Psychology: Vol. 2. Infancy and Developmental Psychobiology [4th ed.], New York: John Wiley & Sons, p. 504. Reprinted with permission from John Wiley & Sons, Inc.)*

SOCIAL ISSUES: EDUCATION

Development of Infants with Severe Visual Impairments

Research on infants who can see little or nothing at all dramatically illustrates the interdependence of vision, motor exploration, social interaction, and understanding of the world. In a longitudinal study, infants with a visual acuity of 20/800 or worse—that is, they had only dim light perception or were blind—were followed through the preschool years. Compared to agemates with less severe visual impairments, they showed serious delays in all aspects of development. Motor and cognitive functioning suffered the most. With age, performance in both domains became increasingly distant from that of other children (Hatton et al., 1997).

What explains these profound developmental delays? Minimal or absent vision can alter the child's experiences in at least two crucial, interrelated ways.

Impact on Motor Exploration and Spatial Understanding

Infants with severe visual impairments attain gross- and fine-motor milestones many months later than their sighted counterparts (Levtzion-Korach et al., 2000). For example, on average, blind infants do not reach for and manipulate objects until 12 months, crawl until 13 months, or walk until 19 months (compare these averages to the norms in Table 5.2 on page 184). Why is this so?

Infants with severe visual impairments must rely on sound to identify the whereabouts of objects. But sound does not function as a precise clue to object location until much later than vision—around the middle of the first year (Litovsky & Ashmead, 1997). And because infants who cannot see have difficulty engaging their caregivers, adults may not provide them with rich, early exposure to sounding objects. As a result, the baby comes to understand relatively late that there is a world of interesting objects to explore.

Until "reaching on sound" is achieved, infants with severe visual impairments are not motivated to move independently. Because of their own uncertainty and their parents' protectiveness and restraint to prevent injury, blind infants are typically tentative in their movements. These factors delay motor development further.

Motor and cognitive development are closely linked, especially for infants with little or no vision. These babies build an understanding of the location and arrangement of objects in space only after reaching and crawling (Bigelow, 1992). Inability to imitate the motor actions of others presents additional challenges as these children get older, contributing to declines in motor and cognitive progress relative to peers with better vision (Hatton et al., 1997).

Impact on the Caregiver–Infant Relationship

Infants who see poorly have great difficulty evoking stimulating caregiver interaction. They cannot make eye contact, imitate, or pick up nonverbal social cues. Their emotional expressions are muted; for example, their smile is fleeting and unpredictable. And because they cannot gaze in the same direction as a partner, they are greatly delayed in establishing a shared focus of attention on objects as the basis for play (Bigelow, 2003). Consequently, these infants may receive little adult attention and other stimulation vital for all aspects of development.

When a visually impaired child does not learn how to participate in social interaction during infancy, communication is compromised in early childhood. In an observational study of blind children enrolled in preschools with sighted agemates, the blind children seldom initiated contact with peers and teachers. When they did interact, they had trouble interpreting the meaning of others' reactions and responding appropriately (Preisler, 1991, 1993).

Interventions

Parents, teachers, and caregivers can help infants with minimal vision overcome early

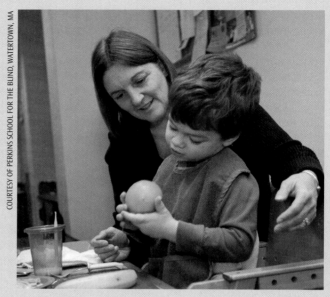

COURTESY OF PERKINS SCHOOL FOR THE BLIND, WATERTOWN, MA

■ This child has no light perception as a result of an optic nerve disorder. His caregiver encourages manipulative play with objects, which enhances awareness of his physical and social surroundings and promotes both motor and cognitive development. ■

developmental delays through stimulating, responsive interaction. Until a close emotional bond with an adult is forged, babies with visual impairments cannot establish vital links with their environments.

Techniques that help infants become aware of their physical and social surroundings include heightened sensory input through combining sound and touch (holding, touching, or bringing the baby's hands to the adult's face while talking or singing), engaging in many repetitions, and consistently reinforcing the infant's efforts to make contact. Manipulative play with objects that make sounds is also vital.

Finally, rich language stimulation can compensate for visual loss (Conti-Ramsden & Pérez-Pereira, 1999). It gives young children a ready means of finding out about objects, events, and behaviors they cannot see. Once language emerges, many children with limited or no vision show impressive rebounds. Some acquire a unique capacity for abstract thinking, and most master social and practical skills that enable them to lead productive, independent lives (Warren, 1994).

FIGURE 5.18

Subjective boundaries in visual patterns. (a) Do you perceive a square in the middle of the figure? By 4 months of age, infants do, too. (b) What does the image, missing two-thirds of its outline, look like to you? By 12 months, infants detect a motorcycle. After habituating to the incomplete motorcycle image, they were shown an intact motorcycle figure paired with a novel form. Twelve-month-olds recovered to (looked longer at) the novel figure, indicating that they recognized the motorcycle pattern on the basis of very little visual information. *(Adapted from Ghim, 1990; Rose, Jankowski, & Senior, 1997.)*

Combining Pattern Elements. In the early weeks of life, infants respond to the separate parts of a pattern. They stare at single high-contrast features, generally on the edges, and have difficulty shifting their gaze away toward other interesting stimuli (Hunnius & Geuze, 2004a, 2004b). At 2 to 3 months, when scanning ability and contrast sensitivity improve, infants thoroughly explore a pattern's internal features, pausing briefly to look at each part (Bronson, 1994).

Once babies can take in all aspects of a pattern, they integrate the parts into a unified whole. Around 4 months, babies are so good at detecting pattern organization that they perceive subjective boundaries that are not really present. For example, they perceive a square in the center of Figure 5.18a, just as you do (Ghim, 1990). And like adults, 3- to 4-month-olds engage in *boundary extension:* When re-exposed to a photo of a natural scene, they remember it as extending beyond its original boundaries. The visual system seems to interpret the photographed scene like a view through a window, which is understood to extend beyond the edges of the window (Quinn & Intraub, 2007).

Older infants carry this sensitivity to subjective form further. For example, 9-month-olds look much longer at an organized series of moving lights that resembles a human being walking than at an upside-down or scrambled version. Three- to 5-month-olds, though able to discriminate the three patterns, do not prefer the walking-human display (Proffitt & Bertenthal, 1990). At 12 months, infants can detect familiar objects represented by incomplete drawings, even when as much as two-thirds of the drawing is missing (see Figure 5.18b) (Rose, Jankowski, & Senior, 1997). As these findings reveal, infants' increasing knowledge of objects and actions supports pattern perception.

Face Perception. Infants' tendency to search for structure in a patterned stimulus applies to face perception. Newborns prefer to look at photos and simplified drawings of faces with features arranged naturally (upright) rather than unnaturally (upside down or sideways) (see Figure 5.19a and b on page 196) (Cassia, Turati, & Simion, 2004; Mondloch et al., 1999). They also track a facelike pattern moving across their visual field farther than they track other stimuli (Johnson, 1999). And although they rely more on outer features (hairline and chin) than inner features to distinguish real faces, newborns prefer photos of faces with eyes open and a direct gaze (Farroni et al., 2002; Turati et al., 2006). Yet another amazing capacity is their tendency to look longer at faces judged by adults as attractive—a preference that may be the origin of the widespread social bias favoring physically attractive people (Slater et al., 2000).

Some researchers claim that these behaviors reflect a built-in capacity to orient toward members of one's own species, just as many newborn animals do (Johnson, 2001a; Slater & Quinn, 2001). In support of this view, the upright face preference occurs only when newborns view stimuli in the periphery of their visual field—an area of the retina governed by primitive brain centers (Cassia, Simion, & Umiltá, 2001). Others assert that newborns simply prefer any stimulus in which the most salient elements are arranged horizontally in the upper part of a pattern—like the "eyes" in Figure 5.19b. Indeed, newborns do prefer patterns with these characteristics over other arrangements (Cassia, Turati, & Simion, 2004; Simion et al., 2001). But a bias favoring the facial pattern possibly promotes such preferences. Still other researchers argue that newborns are exposed to faces more often than to other stimuli—early experiences that could quickly "wire" the brain to detect faces and prefer attractive ones (Nelson, 2001).

Although newborns respond to facelike structures, they cannot discriminate a complex facial pattern from other, equally complex patterns (see Figure 5.19c). But from repeated exposures to their mother's face, they quickly learn to prefer her face to that of an unfamiliar woman, although they mostly attend to its broad outlines.

FIGURE 5.19

Early face perception.
Newborns prefer to look at the
photo of a face (a) and the simple pattern resembling a face (b)
over the upside-down versions.
(c) When the complex drawing of
a face on the left and the equally
complex, scrambled version on the
right are moved across newborns'
visual field, they follow the face
longer. But if the two stimuli are
stationary, infants show no preference for the face until around
2 months of age. *(From Cassia,
Turati, & Simion, 2004; Johnson,
1999; Mondloch et al., 1999.)*

Around 2 months, when they can combine pattern elements into an organized whole, babies prefer a complex drawing of the human face to other equally
complex stimulus arrangements (Dannemiller & Stephens, 1988). And they
clearly prefer their mother's detailed facial features to those of another woman
(Bartrip, Morton, & de Schonen, 2001).

Around 3 months, infants readily make fine distinctions among the features
of different faces—for example, between photographs of two strangers, even
when the faces are moderately similar (Farroni et al., 2007). At 5 months—and
strengthening over the second half-year—infants perceive emotional expressions as meaningful wholes. They treat positive faces (happy and surprised) as
different from negative ones (sad and fearful) (Bornstein & Arterberry, 2003;
Ludemann, 1991).

Experience influences face processing, leading babies to form group biases
at a tender age. As early as 3 months, infants prefer and more easily discriminate
among female faces than among male faces, probably because they typically
spend much more time with female adults (Quinn et al., 2002). Furthermore,
3- to 6-month-olds exposed mostly to members of their own race prefer to look
at the faces of members of that race and more easily detect differences among
those faces—perceptual narrowing that increases in the next few months
(Bar-Haim et al., 2006; Kelly et al., 2007a, 2007b). This own-race preference is
absent in babies who have frequent contact with members of other races, and it
can be reversed through exposure to racial diversity (Sangrigoli et al., 2005).

Clearly, extensive face-to-face interaction with caregivers contributes to
infants' refinement of face perception. And as babies recognize and respond to
the expressive behavior of others, face perception supports their earliest social
relationships.

Object Perception

Research on pattern perception involves only two-dimensional stimuli, but our
environment is made up of stable, three-dimensional objects. Do young infants
perceive a world of independently existing objects—knowledge essential for distinguishing
among the self, other people, and things?

SIZE AND SHAPE CONSTANCY   As we move around the environment, the images that
objects cast on our retina constantly change in size and shape. To perceive objects as stable and
unchanging, we must translate these varying retinal images into a single representation.

Size constancy—perception of an object's size as the same, despite changes in the size of
its retinal image—is evident in the first week of life. To test for it, researchers habituated infants
to a small cube at varying distances from the eye, in an effort to desensitize them to changes in
the cube's retinal image size and direct their attention to the object's actual size. When the small
cube was presented together with a new, large cube—but at different distances so that they cast
retinal images of the same size—all babies recovered to (looked longer at) the novel large cube,
indicating that they distinguished objects on the basis of actual size, not retinal image size
(Slater, 2001).

Perception of an object's shape as stable, despite changes in the shape projected on the
retina, is called **shape constancy.** Habituation research reveals that it, too, is present within the
first week of life, long before babies can actively rotate objects with their hands and view them
from different angles (Slater & Johnson, 1999).

In sum, both size and shape constancy seem to be built-in capacities that assist babies in
detecting a coherent world of objects. Yet they provide only a partial picture of young infants'
object perception.

PERCEPTION OF OBJECT IDENTITY   At first, babies rely heavily on motion and spatial
arrangement to identify objects (Jusczyk et al., 1999; Spelke & Hermer, 1996). When two objects
are touching and either move in unison or stand still, babies younger than 4 months cannot
distinguish them. Infants, of course, are fascinated by moving objects. As they observe objects'

motions, they pick up additional information about objects' boundaries, such as shape, color, and texture.

For example, as Figure 5.20 reveals, around 2 months, babies realize that a moving rod whose center is hidden behind a box is a complete rod rather than two rod pieces. Motion, a patterned background, alignment of the top and bottom of the rod, and a small box (so most of the rod is visible) are necessary for young infants to infer object unity. Because their ability to scan for relevant information is still immature, infants need all these cues to heighten the distinction between the objects in the display (Amso & Johnson, 2006; Johnson, 2009).

As infants become familiar with many types of objects, they rely more on object features, such as shape and surface pattern, and less on motion (Cohen & Cashon, 2001). Babies as young as 4½ months can distinguish two touching objects on the basis of these features in very simple, easy-to-process situations. And prior visual exposure to one of the objects enhances the ability of 4½-month-olds to discern the boundary between two touching objects—a finding that highlights the role of experience (Dueker, Modi, & Needham, 2003; Needham, 2001).

In everyday life, objects frequently move in and out of sight, so infants must keep track of their disappearance and reappearance to perceive their identity. Habituation research, in which a ball moves back and forth behind a screen, reveals that at age 4 months, infants first perceive the ball's path as continuous (Johnson et al., 2003). Between 4 and 5 months, infants can monitor more intricate paths of objects. As indicated by their future-oriented eye movements (looking ahead to where they expect an object to reappear from behind a barrier), 5-month-olds even keep track of an object that travels on a curvilinear course at varying speeds (Rosander & von Hofsten, 2004). From 4 to 11 months, infants increasingly rely on featural information to detect the identity of an object traveling behind a screen—at first, form (size and shape) and later in the first year, surface features (pattern and then color) (Wilcox & Woods, 2009). Again, experience—in particular, physically manipulating the object—enhances older infants' attention to its surface features.

In sum, perception of object identity is mastered gradually over the first year. We will consider a related attainment—infants' understanding of object permanence, awareness that an object still exists when hidden—in Chapter 6.

Intermodal Perception

Our world provides rich, continuous *intermodal stimulation*—simultaneous input from more than one *modality,* or sensory system. In **intermodal perception,** we make sense of these running streams of light, sound, tactile, odor, and taste information, perceiving them as integrated wholes. We know, for example, that an object's shape is the same whether we see it or touch it, that lip movements are closely coordinated with the sound of a voice, and that dropping a rigid object on a hard surface will cause a sharp, banging sound.

Recall that newborns turn in the general direction of a sound and reach for objects in a primitive way. These behaviors suggest that infants expect sight, sound, and touch to go together. Research reveals that babies perceive input from different sensory systems in a unified way by detecting **amodal sensory properties,** information that is not specific to a single modality but that overlaps two or more sensory systems, such as rate, rhythm, duration, intensity, temporal synchrony (for vision and hearing), and texture and shape (for vision and touch). Consider the sight and sound of a bouncing ball or the face and voice of a speaking person. In each event, visual and auditory information are conveyed simultaneously and with the same rate, rhythm, duration, and intensity.

Even newborns are impressive perceivers of amodal properties. After touching an object (such as a cylinder) placed in their palms, they recognize it visually, distinguishing it from a

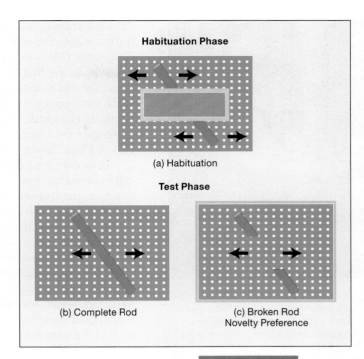

Habituation Phase

(a) Habituation

Test Phase

(b) Complete Rod

(c) Broken Rod Novelty Preference

FIGURE 5.20

Testing infants' ability to perceive object unity. (a) Infants were habituated to a rod moving back and forth behind a box against a textured background. Next, they were shown two test displays in alternation: (b) a complete rod and (c) a broken rod with a gap corresponding to the location of the box. Each stimulus was moved back and forth against the textured background, in the same way as the habituation stimulus. Infants 2 months of age and older recovered to (looked longer at) the broken rod than the complete rod. Their novelty preference suggests that they perceive the rod behind the box in the first display as a single unit. *(Adapted from Johnson, 1997.)*

■ This 10-month-old exploring the surface of a guitar readily picks up amodal information, such as common rate, rhythm, duration, and temporal synchrony, in the visual appearance and sounds of its moving strings. Detection of amodal properties seems to provide the basis for more specific intermodal matches—for example, between the shape of a guitar and its verbal label. ■

LOOK AND LISTEN

While watching a parent and infant playing, list instances of parental intermodal stimulation and communication. What is the baby likely learning about people, objects, or language from each intermodal experience?

different-shaped object (Sann & Streri, 2007). And they require just one exposure to learn the association between the sight and sound of a toy, such as a rhythmically jangling rattle (Morrongiello, Fenwick, & Chance, 1998).

Within the first half-year, infants master a remarkable range of intermodal relationships. Three- to 4-month-olds can match faces with voices on the basis of lip–voice synchrony, emotional expression, and even age and gender of the speaker (Bahrick, Netto, & Hernandez-Reif, 1998). Between 4 and 6 months, infants can perceive and remember the unique face–voice pairings of unfamiliar adults (Bahrick, Hernandez-Reif, & Flom, 2005).

How does intermodal perception develop so quickly? Young infants seem biologically primed to focus on amodal information. Their detection of amodal relations—for example, the common tempo and rhythm in sights and sounds—precedes and seems to provide the basis for detecting more specific intermodal matches, such as the relation between a particular person's face and the sound of her voice or between an object and its verbal label (Bahrick, Hernandez-Reif, & Flom, 2005).

Intermodal sensitivity is crucial for perceptual development. In the first few months, when much stimulation is unfamiliar and confusing, it enables babies to notice meaningful correlations between sensory inputs and rapidly make sense of their surroundings. As a result, inexperienced perceivers notice a unitary event, such as a hammer's tapping, without being distracted by momentarily irrelevant aspects of the situation, such as the hammer's color or orientation (Bahrick, Lickliter, & Flom, 2004).

In addition to easing perception of the physical world, intermodal perception facilitates processing of the social world. For example, as 3- to 4-month-olds gaze at an adult's face, they initially require both vocal and visual input to distinguish positive from negative emotional expressions (Walker-Andrews, 1997). Only later do infants discriminate positive from negative emotion in each sensory modality—first in voices (around 4 to 5 months), later (from 5 months on) in faces (Bahrick, Hernandez-Reif, & Flom, 2005).

Finally, because communication is often intermodal (simultaneously verbal, visual, and tactile), infants receive much support from other senses in detecting units of speech. When parents speak to infants, they often provide temporal synchrony between words, object motions, and touch—for example, saying "doll" while moving a doll and occasionally having the doll touch the infant. In doing so, caregivers greatly increase the chances that babies will remember the association between the word and the object (Gogate & Bahrick, 1998, 2001).

In sum, intermodal stimulation fosters all aspects of psychological development. When caregivers provide many concurrent sights, sounds, and touches, babies process more information and learn faster (Lickliter & Bahrick, 2000). Intermodal perception is yet another fundamental capacity that assists infants in their active efforts to build an orderly, predictable world.

Understanding Perceptual Development

Now that we have reviewed the development of infant perceptual capacities, how can we put together this diverse array of amazing achievements? Widely accepted answers come from the work of Eleanor and James Gibson. According to the Gibsons' **differentiation theory,** infants actively search for *invariant features* of the environment—those that remain stable—in a constantly changing perceptual world. In pattern perception, for example, young babies search for features that stand out and orient toward faces. Soon they explore internal features, noticing *stable relationships* among them. As a result, they detect patterns, such as complex designs and individual faces. Similarly, infants analyze the speech stream for regularities, detecting words, word-order sequences, and—within words—syllable-stress patterns. The development of intermodal perception also reflects this principle. Babies seek out invariant relationships—first, amodal properties, such as common rate and rhythm, in a voice and face, later more detailed associations, such as unique voice–face matches.

The Gibsons described their theory as *differentiation* (where *differentiate* means "analyze" or "break down") because over time the baby detects finer and finer invariant features among stimuli. In addition to pattern perception and intermodal perception, differentiation applies to depth and object perception: Recall how in each, sensitivity to motion precedes detection of fine-grained features. So one way of understanding perceptual development is to think of it as a built-in tendency to seek order and consistency—a capacity that becomes increasingly fine-tuned with age (Gibson, 1970; Gibson, 1979).

Acting on the environment is vital in perceptual differentiation. According to the Gibsons, perception is guided by the discovery of **affordances**—the action possibilities that a situation offers an organism with certain motor capabilities (Gibson, 2000, 2003). By moving about and exploring the environment, babies figure out which objects can be grasped, squeezed, bounced, or stroked and whether a surface is safe to

FIGURE 5.21

Acting on the environment plays a major role in perceptual differentiation. Crawling and walking change the way babies perceive a sloping surface. The newly crawling infant on the left plunges headlong down the slope. He has not yet learned that it affords the possibility of falling. The toddler on the right, who has been walking for more than a month, approaches the slope cautiously. Experience in trying to remain upright but frequently tumbling over has made him more aware of the consequences of his movements. He perceives the incline differently than he did at a younger age. *(Courtesy of Karen Adolph, New York University.)*

cross or presents the possibility of falling. Sensitivity to these affordances means that we spend far less time correcting ineffective actions than we would otherwise: It makes our actions future-oriented and largely successful rather than reactive and blundering.

To illustrate, recall how infants' changing capabilities for independent movement affect their perception. When babies crawl, and again when they walk, they gradually realize that a sloping surface *affords the possibility* of falling (see Figure 5.21). With added weeks of practicing each skill, they hesitate to crawl or walk down a risky incline. Experience in trying to keep their balance on various surfaces makes crawlers and walkers more aware of the consequences of their movements. Crawlers come to detect when surface slant places so much body weight on their arms that they will fall forward, and walkers come to sense when an incline shifts body weight so their legs and feet can no longer hold them upright. Learning is gradual and effortful because newly crawling and walking babies traverse many types of surfaces in their homes each day (Adolph, 2008; Adolph & Joh, 2009). As they experiment with balance and postural adjustments to accommodate each, they perceive surfaces in new ways that guide their movements. As a result, they act more competently.

As we conclude this chapter, it is only fair to note that some researchers believe that babies do more than make sense of experience by searching for invariant features and discovering affordances: They also *impose meaning on* what they perceive, constructing categories of objects and events in the surrounding environment. We have seen the glimmerings of this cognitive point of view in this chapter. For example, older babies *interpret* a familiar face as a source of pleasure and affection and a pattern of blinking lights as a moving human being. This cognitive perspective also offers insight into the achievements of infancy. In fact, many researchers combine these two positions, regarding infant development as proceeding from a perceptual to a cognitive emphasis over the first year of life.

ASK YOURSELF

◆ REVIEW Using examples, explain why intermodal stimulation is vital for infants' developing understanding of their physical and social worlds.

◆ APPLY After several weeks of crawling, Ben learned to avoid going headfirst down a steep incline. Now he has started to walk. Can his mother trust him not to try walking down a steep surface? Explain, using the concept of affordances.

◆ CONNECT According to differentiation theory, perceptual development reflects infants' active search for invariant features. Provide examples from research on hearing, pattern perception, and intermodal perception.

◆ REFLECT Are young infants more competent than you thought they were before you read this chapter? List the capacities that most surprised you.

Summary

Body Growth

Describe major changes in body size, proportions, muscle–fat makeup, and skeletal growth over the first two years.

- Height and weight gains are greater during the first two years than at any other time after birth. Body fat is laid down quickly during the first nine months, whereas muscle development is slow and gradual. Parts of the body grow at different rates, following the **cephalocaudal** and **proximodistal trends,** resulting in changing body proportions.

- **Skeletal age,** a measure based on the number of **epiphyses** and the extent to which they are fused, is the best way to estimate the child's overall physical maturity. At birth, the bones of an infant's skull are separated by six gaps, or **fontanels,** which permit the skull to expand as the brain grows.

Brain Development

Describe brain development during infancy and toddlerhood, current methods of measuring brain functioning, and appropriate stimulation to support the brain's potential.

- Early in development, the brain grows faster than any other organ of the body. Once **neurons** are in place, they rapidly form **synapses** and release **neurotransmitters,** which cross synapses to send messages to other neurons. During the peak period of synaptic growth in any brain area, many surrounding neurons die. Neurons that are seldom stimulated lose their synapses in a process called **synaptic pruning. Glial cells,** responsible for **myelination,** multiply rapidly through the second year, contributing to large gains in brain weight.

- Neurophysiological methods for measuring brain functioning include those that detect changes in electrical activity in the cerebral cortex (EEG, ERPs), neuroimaging techniques (PET, fMRI), and NIRS, which uses infrared light and is suitable for infants and young children.

- The **cerebral cortex** is the largest, most complex brain structure and the last to stop growing. Its regions develop in the general order in which various capacities emerge in the growing child, with the frontal lobes (which contain the **prefrontal cortex**) having the most extended period of development. The hemispheres of the cerebral cortex specialize, a process called **lateralization.** In the first few years of life, there is high **brain plasticity,** with many areas not yet committed to specific functions.

- Both heredity and early experience contribute to brain organization. Stimulation of the brain is essential during sensitive periods—periods in which the brain is developing most rapidly. Prolonged early deprivation, as in some babies reared in orphanages, can disrupt brain growth and interfere with the brain's capacity to manage stress, with long-term physical and psychological consequences.

- Appropriate early stimulation promotes **experience-expectant brain growth,** which depends on ordinary experiences. No evidence exists for a sensitive period in the first few years for **experience-dependent brain growth,** which relies on specific learning experiences. In fact, environments that overwhelm children with inappropriately advanced expectations can undermine the brain's potential.

How does the organization of sleep and wakefulness change over the first two years?

- Infants' changing arousal patterns are primarily affected by brain growth, but the social environment also plays a role. Periods of sleep and wakefulness become fewer but longer over the first two years, conforming to a night–day schedule. Parents in Western nations try to get their babies to sleep through the night much earlier than parents throughout most of the world, who are more likely to sleep with their babies.

Influences on Early Physical Growth

Cite evidence indicating that heredity, nutrition, and parental affection and stimulation contribute to early physical growth.

- Twin and adoption studies reveal that heredity contributes to body size and rate of physical growth.

- Breast milk is ideally suited to infants' growth needs. Breastfeeding protects against disease and prevents malnutrition and infant death in poverty-stricken areas of the world.

- Most infants and toddlers can eat nutritious foods freely without risk of becoming overweight. However, the relationship between rapid weight gain in infancy and obesity at older ages is strengthening, perhaps because of a rise in unhealthy early feeding practices, in which babies are given high-fat foods and sugary drinks.

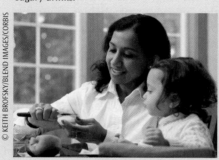

- **Marasmus** and **kwashiorkor** are dietary diseases caused by malnutrition that affect many children in developing countries and, if prolonged, can permanently stunt body growth and brain development. **Growth faltering** illustrates the importance of parental affection for normal physical growth.

Learning Capacities

Describe infant learning capacities, the conditions under which they occur, and the unique value of each.

- **Classical conditioning** is based on the infant's ability to associate events that usually occur together in the everyday world. Infants can be classically conditioned most easily when the pairing of an **unconditioned stimulus (UCS)** and a **conditioned stimulus (CS)** has survival value—for example, learning which stimuli regularly accompany feeding.

- In **operant conditioning,** infants act on their environment and their behavior is followed by either **reinforcers,** which increase the occurrence of a preceding behavior, or **punishment,** which either removes a desirable stimulus or presents an unpleasant one to decrease the occurrence of a response. In young infants, interesting sights and sounds and pleasurable caregiver interaction serve as effective reinforcers.

- **Habituation** and **recovery** reveal that at birth, babies are attracted to novelty. Novelty preference (recovery to a novel stimulus) assesses recent memory, whereas familiarity preference (recovery to the familiar stimulus) assesses remote memory.

- Newborns also have a primitive ability to imitate adults' facial expressions and gestures. **Imitation** is a powerful means of learning, which contributes to the parent–infant bond. Scientists have identified specialized cells called **mirror neurons** that underlie these capacities. However, whether newborn imitation is a voluntary capacity remains controversial.

Motor Development

Describe the general course of motor development during the first two years, along with factors that influence it.

- According to the **dynamic systems theory of motor development,** children acquire new motor skills by combining existing skills into increasingly complex systems of action. Each new skill is a joint product of central nervous system development, the body's movement possibilities, the child's goals, and environmental supports for the skill.

- Movement opportunities and a stimulating environment profoundly affect motor development, as shown by research on infants reared in deprived institutions. Cultural values and child-rearing customs contribute to the emergence and refinement of early motor skills.

- During the first year, infants perfect their reaching and grasping. The poorly coordinated **prereaching** of the newborn period drops out. Gradually, reaching becomes more flexible and accurate, and the clumsy **ulnar grasp** is transformed into a refined **pincer grasp** by the end of the first year.

- Young children are not physically and psychologically ready for toilet training until the months following their second birthday. Effective training techniques include regular toileting routines, gentle encouragement, and praise.

Perceptual Development

What changes in hearing and in depth, pattern, object, and intermodal perception take place during infancy?

- Infants organize sounds into increasingly complex patterns and, in the middle of the first year, become more sensitive to the sounds of their own language. They have an impressive **statistical learning capacity,** which enables them to detect speech regularities for which they will later learn meanings.

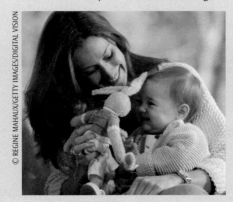

© REGINE MAHAUX/GETTY IMAGES/DIGITAL VISION

- Rapid maturation of the eye and visual centers in the cerebral cortex supports the development of focusing, color discrimination, and visual acuity during the first few months. The ability to scan the environment and track moving objects also improves.

- Research on depth perception reveals that responsiveness to motion develops first, followed by sensitivity to binocular and then to pictorial depth cues. Experience in crawling enhances depth perception and other aspects of three-dimensional understanding, but babies must learn to avoid drop-offs for each body position.

- **Contrast sensitivity** accounts for infants' early pattern preferences. At first, babies stare at single, high-contrast features. At 2 to 3 months, they thoroughly explore internal features of a pattern and start to detect pattern organization. Over time, they discriminate increasingly complex and meaningful patterns.

- Newborns prefer to look at photos and simplified drawings of faces, but whether they have a built-in tendency to orient toward human faces is a matter of dispute. Around 2 months, they recognize and prefer their mother's facial features, and at 3 months, they distinguish the features of different faces. From 5 months on, they perceive emotional expressions as meaningful wholes.

- At birth, **size** and **shape constancy** help babies build a coherent world of objects. At first, infants depend on motion and spatial arrangement to identify objects. After 4 months of age, they rely increasingly on object features, such as distinct shape and surface pattern. Around this time, they first perceive the path of a ball moving back and forth behind a screen as continuous. Soon they can monitor increasingly intricate paths of objects, and they look for featural information to detect the identity of a moving object.

- From the start, infants are capable of **intermodal perception**—combining information across sensory modalities. Detection of **amodal sensory properties,** such as common rate, rhythm, or intensity, may provide the basis for detecting many intermodal matches.

Explain the Gibsons' differentiation theory of perceptual development.

- According to **differentiation theory,** perceptual development is a matter of detecting increasingly fine-grained invariant features in a constantly changing perceptual world. Perceptual differentiation is guided by discovery of **affordances**—the action possibilities that a situation offers the individual.

IMPORTANT TERMS AND CONCEPTS

affordances (p. 199)
amodal sensory properties (p. 197)
brain plasticity (p. 168)
cephalocaudal trend (p. 162)
cerebral cortex (p. 167)
classical conditioning (p. 179)
conditioned response (CR) (p. 179)
conditioned stimulus (CS) (p. 179)
contrast sensitivity (p. 193)
differentiation theory (p. 198)
dynamic systems theory of motor
    development (p. 184)
epiphyses (p. 163)
experience-dependent brain growth (p. 172)
experience-expectant brain growth (p. 172)

fontanels (p. 164)
glial cells (p. 165)
growth faltering (p. 178)
habituation (p. 180)
imitation (p. 181)
intermodal perception (p. 197)
kwashiorkor (p. 177)
lateralization (p. 168)
marasmus (p. 177)
mirror neurons (p. 182)
myelination (p. 165)
neurons (p. 164)
neurotransmitters (p. 164)
operant conditioning (p. 180)
pincer grasp (p. 188)

prefrontal cortex (p. 168)
prereaching (p. 187)
proximodistal trend (p. 162)
punishment (p. 180)
recovery (p. 181)
reinforcer (p. 180)
shape constancy (p. 196)
size constancy (p. 196)
skeletal age (p. 163)
statistical learning capacity (p. 190)
synapses (p. 164)
synaptic pruning (p. 165)
ulnar grasp (p. 187)
unconditioned response (UCR) (p. 179)
unconditioned stimulus (UCS) (p. 179)

"My Family"
Aldo Pablo Fernandez
5 years, Mexico

With a glorious wash of earth and sky as a backdrop, a family accompanies a toddler on an expedition of discovery. In Chapter 6, you will see that a stimulating environment combined with the guidance of more mature members of their culture ensures that young children's cognition will develop at its best.

Reprinted with permission from the International Museum of Children's Art, Oslo, Norway

Cognitive Development in Infancy and Toddlerhood

W hen Caitlin, Grace, and Timmy gathered at Ginette's child-care home, the playroom was alive with activity. The three spirited explorers, each nearly 18 months old, were bent on discovery. Grace dropped shapes through holes in a plastic box that Ginette held and adjusted so the harder ones would fall smoothly into place. Once a few shapes were inside, Grace grabbed the box and shook it, squealing with delight as the lid fell open and the shapes scattered around her. The clatter attracted Timmy, who picked up a shape, carried it to the railing at the top of the basement steps, and dropped it overboard, then followed with a teddy bear, a ball, his shoe, and a spoon. Meanwhile, Caitlin pulled open a drawer, unloaded a set of wooden bowls, stacked them in a pile, knocked it over, and then banged two bowls together. With each action, the children seemed to be asking, "How do things work? What makes interesting events happen? Which ones can I control?"

As the toddlers experimented, I could see the beginnings of spoken language—a whole new way of influencing the world. "All gone baw!" Caitlin exclaimed as Timmy tossed the bright red ball down the basement steps. "Bye-bye," Grace chimed in, waving as the ball disappeared from sight. Later that day, Grace revealed the beginnings of make-believe. "Night-night," she said, putting her head down and closing her eyes, ever so pleased that she could decide for herself when and where to go to bed.

Over the first two years, the small, reflexive newborn baby becomes a self-assertive, purposeful being who solves simple problems and starts to master the most amazing human ability: language. Parents wonder, how does all this happen so quickly? This question has also captivated researchers, yielding a wealth of findings along with vigorous debate over how to explain the astonishing pace of infant and toddler cognition.

In this chapter we take up three perspectives on early cognitive development: Piaget's *cognitive-developmental theory, information processing,* and Vygotsky's *sociocultural theory*. We also consider the usefulness of tests that measure infants' and toddlers' intellectual progress. Finally, we look at the beginnings of language. We will see how toddlers' first words build on early cognitive achievements and how, very soon, new words and expressions greatly increase the speed and flexibility of their thinking. Throughout development, cognition and language mutually support each other.

Piaget's Cognitive-Developmental Theory

Swiss theorist Jean Piaget inspired a vision of children as busy, motivated explorers whose thinking develops as they act directly on the environment. Influenced by his background in biology, Piaget believed that the child's mind forms and modifies psychological structures so they achieve a better fit with external reality. Recall from Chapter 1 that in Piaget's theory, children move through four stages between infancy and adolescence. During these stages, Piaget claimed, all aspects of cognition develop in an integrated fashion, changing in a similar way at about the same time.

Piaget's first stage, the **sensorimotor stage,** spans the first two years of life. Piaget believed that infants and toddlers "think" with their eyes, ears, hands, and other sensorimotor equipment. They cannot yet carry out many activities inside their heads. But by the end of toddlerhood, children can solve everyday practical problems and represent their experiences in speech, gesture, and play. To appreciate Piaget's view of how these vast changes take place, let's consider some important concepts.

© LAURA DWIGHT PHOTOGRAPHY

■ In Piaget's theory, first schemes are sensorimotor action patterns. As this 11-month-old experiments with her dropping scheme, her dropping behavior becomes more deliberate and varied. ■

Piaget's Ideas About Cognitive Change

According to Piaget, specific psychological structures—organized ways of making sense of experience called **schemes**—change with age. At first, schemes are sensorimotor action patterns. For example, at 6 months, Timmy dropped objects in a fairly rigid way, simply by letting go of a rattle or teething ring and watching with interest. By 18 months, his "dropping scheme" had become deliberate and creative. In tossing objects down the basement stairs, he threw some in the air, bounced others off walls, released some gently and others forcefully. Soon, instead of just acting on objects, he will show evidence of thinking before he acts. For Piaget, this change marks the transition from sensorimotor to preoperational thought.

In Piaget's theory, two processes, *adaptation* and *organization,* account for changes in schemes.

ADAPTATION   **TAKE A MOMENT...** The next time you have a chance, notice how infants and toddlers tirelessly repeat actions that lead to interesting effects. **Adaptation** involves building schemes through direct interaction with the environment. It consists of two complementary activities: *assimilation* and *accommodation.* During **assimilation,** we use our current schemes to interpret the external world. For example, when Timmy dropped objects, he was assimilating them all into his sensorimotor "dropping scheme." In **accommodation,** we create new schemes or adjust old ones after noticing that our current ways of thinking do not capture the environment completely. When Timmy dropped objects in different ways, he modified his dropping scheme to take account of the varied properties of objects.

According to Piaget, the balance between assimilation and accommodation varies over time. When children are not changing much, they assimilate more than they accommodate. Piaget called this a state of cognitive *equilibrium,* implying a steady, comfortable condition. During rapid cognitive change, however, children are in a state of *disequilibrium,* or cognitive discomfort. Realizing that new information does not match their current schemes, they shift away from assimilation toward accommodation. After modifying their schemes, they move back toward assimilation, exercising their newly changed structures until they are ready to be modified again.

Each time this back-and-forth movement between equilibrium and disequilibrium occurs, more effective schemes are produced. Because the times of greatest accommodation are the earliest ones, the sensorimotor stage is Piaget's most complex period of development.

ORGANIZATION Schemes also change through **organization,** a process that takes place internally, apart from direct contact with the environment. Once children form new schemes, they rearrange them, linking them with other schemes to create a strongly interconnected cognitive system. For example, eventually Timmy will relate "dropping" to "throwing" and to his developing understanding of "nearness" and "farness." According to Piaget, schemes reach a true state of equilibrium when they become part of a broad network of structures that can be jointly applied to the surrounding world (Piaget, 1936/1952).

In the following sections, we will first describe infant development as Piaget saw it, noting research that supports his observations. Then we will consider evidence demonstrating that in some ways, babies' cognitive competence is more advanced than Piaget believed.

The Sensorimotor Stage

The difference between the newborn baby and the 2-year-old child is so vast that Piaget divided the sensorimotor stage into six substages, summarized in Table 6.1. Piaget based this sequence on observations of his own three children—a very small sample. But he watched his son and two daughters carefully and also presented them with everyday problems (such as hidden objects) that helped reveal their understanding of the world.

According to Piaget, at birth infants know so little about their world that they cannot purposefully explore it. The **circular reaction** provides a special means of adapting their first schemes. It involves stumbling onto a new experience caused by the baby's own motor activity. The reaction is "circular" because, as the infant tries to repeat the event again and again, a sensorimotor response that originally occurred by chance becomes strengthened into a new scheme.

TABLE 6.1 Summary of Piaget's Sensorimotor Stage

SENSORIMOTOR SUBSTAGE	TYPICAL ADAPTIVE BEHAVIORS
1. Reflexive schemes (birth–1 month)	Newborn reflexes (see Chapter 4, page 143)
2. Primary circular reactions (1–4 months)	Simple motor habits centered around the infant's own body; limited anticipation of events
3. Secondary circular reactions (4–8 months)	Actions aimed at repeating interesting effects in the surrounding world; imitation of familiar behaviors
4. Coordination of secondary circular reactions (8–12 months)	Intentional, or goal-directed, behavior; ability to find a hidden object in the first location in which it is hidden (object permanence); improved anticipation of events; imitation of behaviors slightly different from those the infant usually performs
5. Tertiary circular reactions (12–18 months)	Exploration of the properties of objects by acting on them in novel ways; imitation of novel behaviors; ability to search in several locations for a hidden object (accurate A–B search)
6. Mental representation (18 months–2 years)	Internal depictions of objects and events, as indicated by sudden solutions to problems; ability to find an object that has been moved while out of sight (invisible displacement); deferred imitation; and make-believe play

■ This 3-month-old sees his hands touch, open, and close. He tries to repeat these movements, in a primary circular reaction that helps him gain voluntary control over his behavior. ■

■ When this 4-month-old accidentally hits a toy hung in front of her, her action causes it to swing. Using the secondary circular reaction, she tries to recapture this interesting effect. In the process, she forms a new "hitting scheme." ■

Consider Caitlin, who at age 2 months accidentally made a smacking sound after a feeding. Finding this new sound intriguing, she tried to repeat it until, after a few days, she became quite expert at smacking her lips.

The circular reaction initially centers on the infant's own body but later turns outward, toward manipulation of objects. In the second year, it becomes experimental and creative, aimed at producing novel outcomes. Infants' difficulty inhibiting new and interesting behaviors may underlie the circular reaction. This immaturity in inhibition seems to be adaptive, helping to ensure that new skills will not be interrupted before they strengthen (Carey & Markman, 1999). Piaget considered revisions in the circular reaction so important that, as Table 6.1 shows, he named the sensorimotor substages after them.

REPEATING CHANCE BEHAVIORS

Piaget saw newborn reflexes as the building blocks of sensorimotor intelligence. In Substage 1, babies suck, grasp, and look in much the same way, no matter what experiences they encounter. In one amusing example, Carolyn described how 2-week-old Caitlin lay on the bed next to her sleeping father. Suddenly, he awoke with a start. Caitlin had latched on and begun to suck on his back!

Around 1 month, as babies enter Substage 2, they start to gain voluntary control over their actions through the *primary circular reaction,* by repeating chance behaviors largely motivated by basic needs. This leads to some simple motor habits, such as sucking their fists or thumbs. Babies of this substage also begin to vary their behavior in response to environmental demands. For example, they open their mouths differently for a nipple than for a spoon. And they start to anticipate events. At age 3 months, when Timmy awoke from his nap, he cried out with hunger. But as soon as Vanessa entered the room, his crying stopped. He knew that feeding time was near.

During Substage 3, from 4 to 8 months, infants sit up and become skilled at reaching for and manipulating objects. These motor achievements strengthen the *secondary circular reaction,* through which babies try to repeat interesting events in the surrounding environment that are caused by their own actions. For example, 4-month-old Caitlin accidentally knocked a toy hung in front of her, producing a fascinating swinging motion. Over the next three days, Caitlin tried to repeat this effect, gradually forming a new "hitting" scheme. Improved control over their own behavior permits infants to imitate others' behavior more effectively. However, 4- to 8-month-olds cannot adapt flexibly and quickly enough to imitate novel behaviors (Kaye & Marcus, 1981). Therefore, although they enjoy watching an adult demonstrate a game of pat-a-cake, they are not yet able to participate.

INTENTIONAL BEHAVIOR

In Substage 4, 8- to 12-month-olds combine schemes into new, more complex action sequences. As a result, actions that lead to new schemes no longer have a random, hit-or-miss quality—*accidentally* bringing the thumb to the mouth or *happening* to hit the toy. Instead, 8- to 12-month-olds can engage in **intentional, or goal-directed, behavior,** coordinating schemes deliberately to solve simple problems. The clearest example is provided

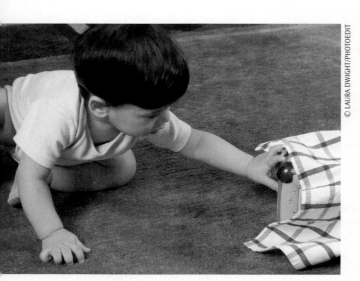

■ The capacity to find a hidden object, a major advance in cognitive development, emerges between 8 and 12 months. To find the toy under the cloth, this 10-month-old engages in intentional, goal-directed behavior—the basis for all problem solving. ■

by Piaget's famous object-hiding task, in which he shows the baby an attractive toy and then hides it behind his hand or under a cover. Infants of this substage can find the object by coordinating two schemes—"pushing" aside the obstacle and "grasping" the toy. Piaget regarded these *means–end action sequences* as the foundation for all problem solving.

Retrieving hidden objects reveals that infants have begun to master **object permanence,** the understanding that objects continue to exist when they are out of sight. But awareness of object permanence is not yet complete. Babies still make the **A-not-B search error:** If they reach several times for an object at a first hiding place (A), then see it moved to a second (B), they still search for it in the first hiding place (A). Consequently, Piaget concluded that they do not have a clear image of the object as persisting when hidden from view.

Infants of Substage 4, who can better anticipate events, sometimes use their capacity for intentional behavior to try to change those events. At 10 months, Timmy crawled after Vanessa when she put on her coat, whimpering to keep her from leaving. Also, babies can now imitate behaviors slightly different from those they usually perform. After watching someone else, they try to stir with a spoon, push a toy car, or drop raisins into a cup. Again, they draw on intentional behavior, purposefully modifying schemes to fit an observed action (Piaget, 1945/1951).

In Substage 5, from 12 to 18 months, the *tertiary circular reaction,* in which toddlers repeat behaviors with variation, emerges. Recall how Timmy dropped objects over the basement steps, trying this action, then that, then another. Because they approach the world in this deliberately exploratory way, 12- to 18-month-olds become better problem solvers. For example, Grace figured out how to fit a shape through a hole in a container by turning and twisting it until it fell through, and she discovered how to use a stick to get toys that were out of reach. According to Piaget, this capacity to experiment leads to a more advanced understanding of object permanence. Toddlers look for a hidden toy in several locations, displaying an accurate A–B search. Their more flexible action patterns also permit them to imitate many more behaviors, such as stacking blocks, scribbling on paper, and making funny faces.

MENTAL REPRESENTATION   Substage 6 brings the ability to create **mental representations**—internal depictions of information that the mind can manipulate. Our most powerful mental representations are of two kinds: (1) *images,* or mental pictures of objects, people, and spaces; and (2) *concepts,* or categories in which similar objects or events are grouped together. We can use a mental image to retrace our steps when we've misplaced something or to imitate someone's behavior long after we've observed it. And by thinking in concepts and labeling them (for example, "ball" for all rounded, movable objects used in play), we become more efficient thinkers, organizing our diverse experiences into meaningful, manageable, and memorable units.

Piaget noted that 18- to 24-month-olds arrive at solutions suddenly rather than through trial-and-error behavior. In doing so, they seem to experiment with actions inside their heads—evidence that they can mentally represent their experiences. For example, at 19 months, Grace—after bumping her new push toy against a wall—paused for a moment as if to "think," and then immediately turned the toy in a new direction.

Representation enables older toddlers to solve advanced object permanence problems involving *invisible displacement*—finding a toy moved while out of sight, such as into a small box while under a cover. It also permits **deferred imitation**—the ability to remember and copy the behavior of models who are not present. And it makes possible **make-believe play,** in which children act out everyday and imaginary activities. Grace's pretending to go to sleep, in the opening to this chapter, illustrates the very simple make-believe of toddlers. Make-believe expands greatly in early childhood, and it is so important for psychological development that we will return to it again. In sum, as the sensorimotor stage draws to a close, mental symbols have become major instruments of thinking.

■ Using a tertiary circular reaction, this baby twists, turns, and pushes until a block fits through its matching hole in her shape sorter. Between 12 and 18 months, toddlers take a deliberately experimental approach to problem solving, repeating behaviors with variation. ■

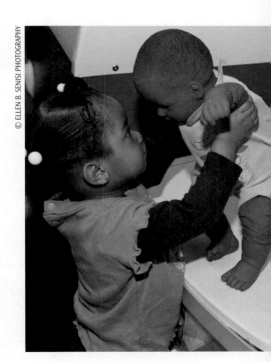

■ The capacity for mental representation enables this 2-year-old to engage in make-believe play. With the expansion of make-believe in early childhood, mental symbols become major instruments of thinking. ■

Follow-Up Research on Infant Cognitive Development

Many studies suggest that infants display a wide array of understandings earlier than Piaget believed. Recall the operant conditioning research reviewed in Chapter 5, in which newborns sucked vigorously on a nipple to gain access to interesting sights and sounds. This behavior, which closely resembles Piaget's secondary circular reaction, shows that babies try to explore and control the external world long before 4 to 8 months. In fact, they do so as soon as they are born.

To discover what infants know about hidden objects and other aspects of physical reality, researchers often use the **violation-of-expectation method.** They may *habituate* babies to a physical event (expose them to the event until their looking declines) to familiarize them with a situation in which their knowledge will be tested. Or they may simply show babies an *expected event* (one that is consistent with reality) or an *unexpected event* (a variation of the first event that violates reality). Heightened attention to the unexpected event suggests that the infant is "surprised" by a deviation from physical reality and, therefore, is aware of that aspect of the physical world.

The violation-of-expectation method is controversial. Some critics believe that it indicates limited awareness of physical events, not the full-blown, conscious understanding that was Piaget's focus in requiring infants to act on their surroundings, as in searching for hidden objects (Munakata, 2001; Thelen & Smith, 1994). Others maintain that the method reveals only babies' perceptual preference for novelty, not their understanding of experience (Bremner & Mareschal, 2004; Hood, 2004; Kagan, 2008). Let's examine this debate in light of recent evidence.

OBJECT PERMANENCE   In a series of studies using the violation-of-expectation method, Renée Baillargeon and her collaborators claimed to have found evidence for object permanence in the first few months of life. One of Baillargeon's studies is illustrated in Figure 6.1 (Aguiar & Baillargeon, 2002; Baillargeon & DeVos, 1991). After habituating to a short and a tall carrot moving behind a screen, infants were given two test events: (1) an *expected event,* in which the short carrot moved behind a screen, could not be seen in its window, and reappeared on the other side, and (2) an *unexpected event,* in which the tall carrot moved behind a screen, could not be seen in its window (although it was taller than the window's lower edge), and reappeared. Infants as young as 2½ to 3½ months looked longer at the unexpected event, suggesting that they had some awareness that an object moved behind a screen would continue to exist.

Additional violation-of-expectation studies yielded similar results (Baillargeon, 2004; Wang, Baillargeon, & Paterson, 2005). But several researchers using similar procedures failed to confirm some of Baillargeon's findings (Bogartz, Shinskey, & Shilling, 2000; Cashon & Cohen, 2000; Cohen & Marks, 2002; Rivera, Wakeley, & Langer, 1999). Baillargeon and others maintain that these opposing investigations did not include crucial controls. And they emphasize that infants look longer at a wide variety of unexpected events involving hidden objects (Newcombe, Sluzenski, & Huttenlocher, 2005; Wang, Baillargeon, & Paterson, 2005). Still, critics question what babies' looking preferences tell us about what they actually know.

But another type of looking behavior suggests that young infants are aware that objects persist when out of view. Four- and 5-month-olds will track a ball's path of movement as it disappears and

FIGURE 6.1

Testing young infants for understanding of object permanence using the violation-of-expectation method. (a) First, infants were habituated to two events: a short carrot and a tall carrot moving behind a yellow screen, on alternate trials. Next, the researchers presented two test events. The color of the screen was changed to help infants notice its window. (b) In the *expected event,* the carrot shorter than the window's lower edge moved behind the blue screen and reappeared on the other side. (c) In the *unexpected event,* the carrot taller than the window's lower edge moved behind the screen and did not appear in the window, but then emerged intact on the other side. Infants as young as 2½ to 3½ months recovered to (looked longer at) the *unexpected event,* suggesting that they had some understanding of object permanence. *(Adapted from R. Baillargeon & J. DeVos, 1991, "Object Permanence in Young Infants: Further Evidence,"* Child Development, 62, p. 1230. © The Society for Research in Child Development. Adapted with permission.)

reappears from behind a barrier, even gazing ahead to where they expect it to emerge (Bertenthal, Longo, & Kenny, 2007; Rosander & von Hofsten, 2004). With age, babies are more likely to fixate on the predicted place of the ball's reappearance and wait for it—evidence of an increasingly secure grasp of object permanence.

In related research, investigators recorded 6-month-olds' ERP brain-wave activity as the babies watched two events on a computer screen. In one event, a black square moved until it covered an object, then moved away to reveal the object (object permanence). In the other event, as a black square started to move across an object, the object disintegrated (object disappearance) (Kaufman, Csibra, & Johnson, 2005). Only while watching the first event did the infants show a particular brain-wave pattern in the right temporal lobe—the same pattern adults exhibit when told to sustain a mental image of an object.

If young infants do have some notion of object permanence, how do we explain Piaget's finding that even infants capable of reaching do not try to search for hidden objects before 8 months of age? Violation-of-expectation tasks require only that the baby react (through looking) to whether a post-object-hiding scene accords with ordinary experience. Searching for a hidden object is far more cognitively demanding: The baby must *predict* where the hidden object is. Consistent with this idea, infants solve some object-hiding tasks before others: Eight- to 10-month-olds remove the cover from a partially hidden object before they are able to do so from a fully covered object (Moore & Meltzoff, 2008). And 10-month-olds search for an object placed on a table and covered by a cloth before they search for an object that a hand deposits under a cloth (Moore & Meltzoff, 1999). In the second, more difficult task, infants seem to expect the object to reappear in the hand because that is where the object initially disappeared. When the hand emerges without the object, they conclude that there is no other place the object could be. Not until 14 months can most babies infer that the hand deposited the object under the cloth.

Around this age, toddlers demonstrate a thorough understanding of hidden objects. Fourteen-month-olds know that objects continue to exist in their hidden locations even after the infants have left the location. After seeing an object hidden in a cupboard, when the toddlers returned the next day, they correctly searched for the specific object in its original location. When exposed to a similar cupboard in a new room, the infants behaved just as adults do: They saw no reason to search (Moore & Meltzoff, 2004).

SEARCHING FOR OBJECTS HIDDEN IN MORE THAN ONE LOCATION   Once 8- to 12-month-olds search for hidden objects, they make the A-not-B search error. Some research suggests that they search at A (where they found the object on previous reaches) instead of B (its most recent location) because they have trouble inhibiting a previously rewarded motor response (Diamond, Cruttenden, & Neiderman, 1994). In support of this view, the more prior reaches to A, the greater the likelihood that the infant will reach again toward A when the object is hidden at B. Another possibility is that after finding the object several times at A, babies do not attend closely when it is hidden at B (Ruffman & Langman, 2002). A more comprehensive explanation is that a complex, dynamic system of factors—having built a habit of reaching toward A, continuing to look at A, having the hiding place at B appear similar to the one at A, and maintaining a constant body posture—increases the chances that the baby will make the A-not-B search error. Research shows that disrupting any one of these factors increases 10-month-olds' accurate searching at B (Thelen et al., 2001).

In sum, mastery of object permanence is a gradual achievement. Babies' understanding becomes increasingly complex with age: They must perceive an object's identity by integrating feature and movement information (see Chapter 5, page 197), distinguish the object from the barrier concealing it and the surface on which it rests, keep track of the object's whereabouts, and use this knowledge to obtain the object (Cohen & Cashon, 2006; Moore & Meltzoff, 2008; Munakata & Stedron, 2002). Success at object search tasks coincides with rapid development of the frontal lobes of the cerebral cortex (Bell, 1998). Also crucial are a wide variety of experiences perceiving, acting on, and remembering objects.

MENTAL REPRESENTATION   In Piaget's theory, infants lead purely sensorimotor lives. They cannot represent experience until about 18 months of age. Yet 8- to 10-month-olds' ability to recall the location of hidden objects after delays of more than a minute, and 14-month-olds' recall after delays of a day or more, clearly indicate that babies construct mental

LOOK AND LISTEN

Using an attractive toy and cloth, try several object-hiding tasks with 8- to 14-month-olds. Is their searching behavior consistent with research findings?

representations of objects and their whereabouts (McDonough, 1999; Moore & Meltzoff, 2004). In studies of deferred imitation and problem solving, representational thought is evident even earlier. And toddlers make impressive strides in symbolic understanding, as their grasp of words and photos reveals.

Deferred and Inferred Imitation. Piaget studied imitation by noting when his three children demonstrated it in their everyday behavior. Under these conditions, a great deal must be known about the infant's daily life to be sure that deferred imitation—which requires infants to represent another's past behavior—has occurred.

Laboratory research reveals that deferred imitation is present at 6 weeks of age! Infants who watched an unfamiliar adult's facial expression imitated it when exposed to the same adult the next day (Meltzoff & Moore, 1994). As motor capacities improve, infants copy actions with objects. In one study, adults showed 6- and 9-month-olds a novel series of actions with a puppet: taking its glove off, shaking the glove to ring a bell inside, and replacing the glove. When tested a day later, infants who had seen the novel actions were far more likely to imitate them (see Figure 6.2). And when researchers paired a second, motionless puppet with the first puppet a day before the demonstration, 6-month-olds generalized the actions to this new, very different-looking puppet (Barr, Marrott, & Rovee-Collier, 2003). Even more impressive, after having seen Puppet A paired with B and Puppet B paired with C on successive days, infants transferred modeled actions from A to C and from C to A, though they had not directly observed this pair together (Townsend & Rovee-Collier, 2007). Already, infants can form flexible mental representations that include chains of relevant associations.

Gains in recall, expressed through deferred imitation, are accompanied by changes in brain-wave activity during memory tasks, as measured by ERPs. This suggests that improvements in memory storage in the cerebral cortex contribute to these advances (Bauer et al., 2006). Between 12 and 18 months, toddlers use deferred imitation skillfully to enrich their range of schemes. They retain modeled behaviors for at least several months, copy the actions of peers as well as adults, and imitate across a change in context—for example, enact at home a behavior seen at child care (Klein & Meltzoff, 1999).

Toddlers even imitate rationally, by *inferring* others' intentions! They are more likely to imitate purposeful than accidental behaviors (Carpenter, Akhtar, & Tomasello, 1998). And they adapt their imitative acts to a model's goals. If 12-month-olds see an adult perform an unusual

(a)　　　　　　　　　　(b)

FIGURE 6.2

Testing infants for deferred imitation. After researchers performed a novel series of actions with a puppet, this 6-month-old imitated the actions a day later—(a) removing the glove; (b) shaking the glove to ring a bell inside. With age, gains in recall are evident in deferred imitation of others' behaviors over longer delays.

action for fun (make a toy dog enter a miniature house by jumping through the chimney, even though its door is wide open), they copy the behavior. But if the adult engages in the odd behavior because she *must* (she makes the dog go through the chimney only after first trying to use the door and finding it locked), 12-month-olds typically imitate the more efficient action (putting the dog through the door) (Schwier et al., 2006).

Between 14 and 18 months, toddlers become increasingly adept at imitating actions an adult *tries* to produce, even if these are not fully realized (Bellagamba, Camaioni, & Colonnesi, 2006; Meltzoff, 1995; Olineck & Poulin-Dubois, 2007). On one occasion, Ginette attempted to pour some raisins into a small bag but missed, spilling them onto the counter. A moment later, Grace began dropping the raisins into the bag, indicating that she had inferred Ginette's goal.

Though advanced in terms of Piaget's predictions, toddlers' ability to represent others' intentions—a cornerstone of social understanding and communication—seems to have roots in earlier sensorimotor activity. In several studies, infants' skill at engaging in goal-directed actions—reaching for objects at 3 to 4 months, pointing to objects at 9 months—predicted their awareness of an adult's similar behavior as goal-directed in a violation-of-expectation task (Gerson & Woodward, 2010; Woodward, 2009). And the better 10-month-olds are at detecting the goals of others' gazes and reaches, the more successful they are four months later at inferring an adult's intention from her incomplete actions in an imitation task (Olineck & Poulin-Dubois, 2009).

Problem Solving. As Piaget indicated, around 7 to 8 months, infants develop intentional means–end action sequences, which they use to solve simple problems, such as pulling on a cloth to obtain a toy resting on its far end (Willatts, 1999). Soon after, infants' representational skills permit more effective problem solving than Piaget's theory suggests.

By 10 to 12 months, infants can *solve problems by analogy*—apply a solution strategy from one problem to other relevant problems. In one study, babies of this age were given three similar problems, each requiring them to overcome a barrier, grasp a string, and pull it to get an attractive toy. The problems differed in many aspects of their superficial features—texture and color of the string, barrier, and floor mat and type of toy (horse, doll, or car). For the first problem, the parent demonstrated the solution and encouraged the infant to imitate. Babies obtained the toy more readily on each additional problem (Chen, Sanchez, & Campbell, 1997). Similarly, 12-month-olds who were repeatedly presented with a spoon in the same orientation (handle to one side) readily adapted their motor actions when the spoon was presented in the opposite orientation (handle to the other side), successfully transporting food to their mouths most of the time (McCarty & Keen, 2005).

These findings suggest that at the end of the first year, infants form flexible mental representations of how to use tools to get objects. They have some ability to move beyond trial-and-error experimentation, represent a solution mentally, and use it in new contexts.

Symbolic Understanding. One of the most momentous advances in early development is the realization that words can be used to cue mental images of things not physically present—a symbolic capacity called **displaced reference** that emerges around the first birthday. It greatly expands toddlers' capacity to learn about the world through communicating with others. Observations of 12-month-olds reveal that they respond to the label of an absent toy by looking at and gesturing toward the spot where it usually rests (Saylor, 2004). And on hearing the name of a parent or sibling who has just left the room, most 13-month-olds turn toward the door (DeLoache & Ganea, 2009). The more experience toddlers have with an object and its verbal label, the more likely they are to call up a mental representation when they hear the object's name. As memory and vocabulary improve, skill at displaced reference expands.

But at first, toddlers have difficulty using language to acquire new information about an absent object—an ability that is essential to learn from symbols. In one study, an adult taught 19- and 22-month-olds a name for a stuffed animal—"Lucy" for a frog. Then, with the frog out of sight, the toddler was told that some water had spilled, so "Lucy's all wet!" Finally, the adult showed the toddler three stuffed animals—a wet frog, a dry frog, and a pig—and said, "Get Lucy!" (Ganea et al., 2007). Although all the children remembered that Lucy was a frog, only the 22-month-olds identified the wet frog as Lucy. Nevertheless, older toddlers' reliance on verbal information is fragile. When a verbal message about a toy's new location conflicts with a previously observed location, most 23-month-olds simply go to the initial location. At

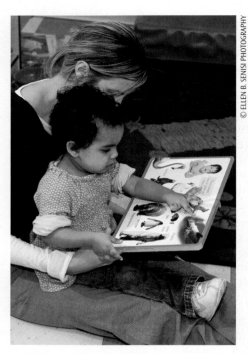

■ A 17-month-old points to a picture in a book, revealing her beginning awareness of the symbolic function of pictures. But pictures must be highly realistic for toddlers to treat them symbolically. ■

30 months, children succeed at finding the toy (Ganea & Harris, 2010). The capacity to use language as a flexible symbolic tool—to modify an existing mental representation—improves from the end of the second into the third year.

Awareness of the symbolic function of pictures also emerges in the second year. Even newborns perceive a relation between a picture and its referent, as indicated by their preference for looking at a photo of their mother's face (see page 195 in Chapter 5). At the same time, infants do not treat pictures as symbols. Rather, they touch, rub, and pat a color photo of an object or pick it up and manipulate it—behaviors that reveal confusion about the picture's true nature. This manual exploration increases from 4 to 9 months and then declines, becoming rare around 18 months (DeLoache et al., 1988; DeLoache & Ganea, 2009).

As long as pictures strongly resemble real objects, by the middle of the second year toddlers treat them symbolically. After hearing a novel label ("blicket") applied to a color photo of an unfamiliar object, most 15- to 24-month-olds—when presented with both the real object and its picture and asked to indicate the "blicket"—gave a symbolic response. They selected either the real object or both the object and its picture, not the picture alone, a tendency that strengthened with age (Ganea et al., 2009). Around this time, toddlers increasingly use pictures as vehicles for communicating with others and acquiring new knowledge. They point to, name, and talk about pictures, and they can apply something learned from a book with realistic-looking pictures to real objects, and vice versa (Ganea, Pickard, & DeLoache, 2008).

But even after coming to appreciate the symbolic nature of pictures, young children continue to have difficulty grasping the distinction between some pictures (such as line drawings) and their referents, as we will see in Chapter 8. How do infants and toddlers interpret another ever-present, pictorial medium—video? Turn to the Social Issues: Education box on the following page to find out.

Evaluation of the Sensorimotor Stage

Table 6.2 summarizes the remarkable cognitive attainments we have just considered. **TAKE A MOMENT...** Compare this table with the description of Piaget's sensorimotor substages in Table 6.1 on page 205. You will see that infants anticipate events, actively search for hidden objects, master the A–B object search, flexibly vary their sensorimotor schemes, engage in make-believe play, and treat pictures and video images symbolically within Piaget's time frame. Yet

TABLE 6.2	Some Cognitive Attainments of Infancy and Toddlerhood

AGE	COGNITIVE ATTAINMENTS
Birth–1 month	Secondary circular reactions using limited motor skills, such as sucking a nipple to gain access to interesting sights and sounds
1–4 months	Awareness of object permanence, object solidity, and gravity, as suggested by violation-of-expectation findings; deferred imitation of an adult's facial expression over a short delay (one day)
4–8 months	Improved knowledge of object properties and basic numerical knowledge, as suggested by violation-of-expectation findings; deferred imitation of an adult's novel actions on objects over a short delay (one to three days)
8–12 months	Ability to search for a hidden object when covered by a cloth; ability to solve simple problems by analogy to a previous problem
12–18 months	Ability to search in several locations for a hidden object when a hand deposits it under a cloth and when it is moved from one location to another (accurate A–B search); deferred imitation of an adult's novel actions on an object over a long delay (at least several months) and across a change in situation (from child care to home); rational imitation, inferring the model's intentions; displaced reference of words
18 months–2 years	Deferred imitation of actions an adult tries to produce, even if these are not fully realized, again indicating a capacity to infer others' intentions; imitation of everyday behaviors in make-believe play; beginning awareness of pictures and video as symbols of reality
TAKE A MOMENT...	Which of the capacities listed in this table indicate that mental representation emerges earlier than Piaget believed?

SOCIAL ISSUES: EDUCATION

Baby Learning from TV and Video: The Video Deficit Effect

Children first become TV and video viewers in early infancy, as they are exposed to programs watched by parents and older siblings. Many parents also turn on TV shows or videos aimed at viewers not yet out of diapers, such as the Baby Einstein products. About 40 percent of U.S. 3-month-olds watch regularly, a figure that rises to 90 percent at age 2, a period during which average viewing time increases from just under an hour to 1½ hours a day (Zimmerman, Christakis, & Meltzoff, 2007). Although parents assume that babies learn from TV and videos, research indicates that they cannot take full advantage of them.

Initially, infants respond to videos of people as if viewing people directly—smiling, moving their arms and legs, and (by 6 months) imitating actions of a televised adult. But they confuse the images with the real thing (Barr, Muentener, & Garcia, 2007; Marian, Neisser, & Rochat, 1996). When 9- to 19-month-olds were shown videos of attractive toys, the 9-month-olds manually explored the screen, as they do with pictures. By 19 months, touching and grabbing had declined in favor of pointing at the images (Pierroutsakos & Troseth, 2003). Nevertheless, toddlers continue to have difficulty applying what they see on video to real situations.

In a series of studies, some 2-year-olds watched through a window while a live adult hid an object in an adjoining room, while others watched the same event on a video screen. Children in the direct viewing condition retrieved the toy easily; those in the video condition had difficulty (Troseth, 2003; Troseth & DeLoache, 1998). This **video deficit effect**—poorer performance after a video than a live demonstration—has also been found for 2-year-olds' deferred imitation, word learning, and means–end problem solving (Deocampo, 2003; Hayne, Herbert, & Simcock, 2003; Krcmar, Grela, & Linn, 2007).

One explanation for the video deficit effect is that 2-year-olds typically do not view a video character as offering socially relevant information.

After an adult on video announced where she hid a toy, few 2-year-olds searched (Schmidt, Crawley-Davis, & Anderson, 2007). In contrast, when the adult stood in front of the child and uttered the same words, 2-year-olds promptly retrieved the object.

Toddlers seem to discount information on video as relevant to their everyday experiences because people do not look at and converse with them directly or establish a shared focus on objects, as their caregivers do. In one study, researchers gave some 2-year-olds an interactive video experience (using a two-way, closed-circuit video system). An adult on video interacted with the child for five minutes—calling the child by name, talking about the child's siblings and pets, waiting for the child to respond, and playing interactive games (Troseth, Saylor, & Archer, 2006). Compared with 2-year-olds who viewed the same adult in a noninteractive video, those in the interactive condition were far more successful in using a verbal cue from a person on video to retrieve a toy.

Around age 2½, the video deficit effect declines. Before this age, the American Academy of Pediatrics (2001) recommends against mass

media exposure, emphasizing that babies require rich responsive exchanges with caregivers and exploration of their physical surroundings for optimal brain growth and psychological development (see Chapter 5, page 169). In support of this advice, amount of TV viewing is negatively related to 8- to 18-month-olds' language progress (Tanimura et al., 2004; Zimmerman, Christakis, & Meltzoff, 2007). And heavy 1- to 3-year-old viewers tend to have attention, memory, and reading difficulties in the early school years (Christakis et al., 2004; Zimmerman & Christakis, 2005).

Toddlers face a complex task in making sense of video. Although they no longer confuse it with reality, they do not know how to mentally represent the relationship between video images and real objects and people. Video for 2-year-olds is likely to work best as a teaching tool when it is rich in social cues—close-ups of characters who look directly at the camera, address questions to viewers, and pause to invite their response. Repetition of video programs also helps children over age 2 make sense of video content (Anderson, 2004).

© NIAMH BALDOCK/ALAMY

■ This baby reaches for the TV screen because she thinks the child she sees there is real. Not until about age 2½ will she understand how onscreen images relate to real people and objects. ■

other capacities—including secondary circular reactions, understanding of object properties, first signs of object permanence, deferred imitation, problem solving by analogy, and displaced reference of words—emerge earlier than Piaget expected. These findings show that the cognitive attainments of infancy and toddlerhood do not develop together in the neat, stepwise fashion Piaget predicted.

Recent research raises questions about Piaget's view of how infant development takes place. Consistent with Piaget's ideas, sensorimotor action helps infants construct some forms of knowledge. For example, in Chapter 5 we saw that crawling enhances depth perception and ability to find hidden objects and that handling objects fosters awareness of object properties. Yet we have also seen evidence that infants comprehend a great deal before they are capable of the motor behaviors that Piaget assumed led to those understandings. How can we account for babies' amazing cognitive accomplishments?

ALTERNATIVE EXPLANATIONS   Unlike Piaget, who thought young babies constructed all mental representations out of sensorimotor activity, most researchers now believe that young babies have some built-in cognitive equipment for making sense of experience. But intense disagreement exists over the extent of this initial understanding. As we have seen, much evidence on young infants' cognition rests on the violation-of-expectation method. Researchers who lack confidence in this method argue that babies' cognitive starting point is limited (Campos et al., 2008; Cohen & Cashon, 2006; Kagan, 2008). For example, some believe that newborns begin life with a set of biases for attending to certain information and with general-purpose learning procedures—such as powerful techniques for analyzing complex perceptual information. Together, these capacities enable infants to construct a wide variety of schemes (Bahrick, Lickliter, & Flom, 2004; Huttenlocher, 2002; Mandler, 2004; Quinn, 2008).

Others, convinced by violation-of-expectation findings, believe that infants start out with impressive understandings. According to this **core knowledge perspective,** babies are born with a set of innate knowledge systems, or *core domains of thought.* Each of these "prewired" understandings permits a ready grasp of new, related information and therefore supports early, rapid development (Carey & Markman, 1999; Leslie, 2004; Spelke, 2004; Spelke & Kinzler, 2007). Core knowledge theorists argue that infants could not make sense of the complex stimulation around them without having been genetically "set up" in the course of evolution to comprehend its crucial aspects.

© STEPHEN MALLABY/ALAMY

■ Did this 3-year-old acquire the physical knowledge necessary to create this structure through repeatedly acting on objects, as Piaget assumed? Or did he begin life with innate knowledge that helps him understand objects and their relationships quickly, with little hands-on exploration? ■

Researchers have conducted many studies of infants' *physical knowledge,* including object permanence, object solidity (that one object cannot move through another), and gravity (that an object will fall without support). Violation-of-expectation findings suggest that in the first few months, infants have some awareness of all these basic object properties and quickly build on this knowledge (Baillargeon, 2004; Hespos & Baillargeon, 2001; Luo & Baillargeon, 2005; Spelke, 2000). Core knowledge theorists also assume that an inherited foundation of *linguistic knowledge* enables swift language acquisition in early childhood—a possibility we will consider later in this chapter. Further, these theorists argue, infants' early orientation toward people initiates swift development of *psychological knowledge*—in particular, understanding of mental states, such as intentions, emotions, desires, and beliefs, which we will address further in Chapter 7.

Researchers have even examined infants' *numerical knowledge!* In the best-known study, 5-month-olds saw a screen raised to hide a single toy animal and then watched a hand place a second toy behind a screen. Finally, the screen was removed to reveal either one or two toys. If infants kept track of the two objects (requiring them to add one object to another), then they should look longer at the unexpected, one-toy display—which is what they did (see Figure 6.3) (Wynn, Bloom, & Chiang, 2002). These findings and others suggest that babies can discriminate quantities up to three and use that knowledge to perform simple arithmetic—both addition and subtraction (in which two objects are covered and one is removed) (Kobayashi et al., 2004; Kobayashi, Hiraki, & Hasegawa, 2005; Wynn, Bloom, & Chiang, 2002). As further support, ERP brain-wave recordings taken while babies view correct and incorrect simple arithmetic solutions reveal a response pattern identical to the pattern adults show when detecting errors (Berger, Tzur, & Posner, 2006).

Further evidence suggests that infants can distinguish among large sets of items, as long as the difference between those sets is great enough. For example,

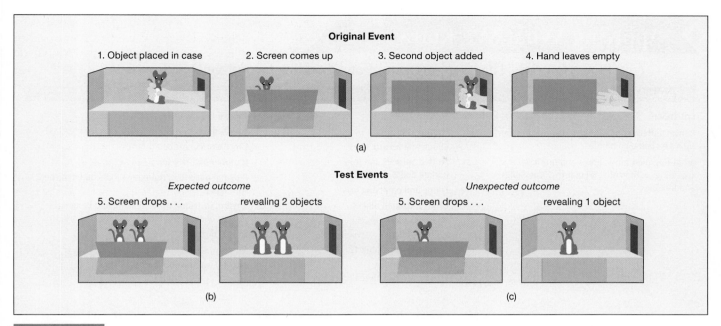

FIGURE 6.3

Testing infants for basic number concepts. (a) First, infants saw a screen raised in front of a toy animal. Then an identical toy was added behind the screen. Next, the researchers presented two outcomes. (b) In the *expected outcome,* the screen dropped to reveal two toy animals. (c) In the *unexpected outcome,* the screen dropped to reveal one toy animal. Five-month-olds shown the unexpected outcome looked longer than 5-month-olds shown the expected outcome. The researchers concluded that infants can discriminate the quantities "one" and "two" and use that knowledge to perform simple addition: 1 + 1 = 2. A variation of this procedure suggested that 5-month-olds could also do simple subtraction: 2 − 1 = 1. *(From K. Wynn, 1992, "Addition and Subtraction by Human Infants,"* Nature, *358, p. 749. © 1992 by Nature Publishing Group. Reprinted by permission of Nature Publishing Group. Adapted by permission of Macmillan Publishers, Ltd.)*

6-month-olds can tell the difference between 8 versus 16 dots but not 8 versus 12, and 9-month-olds can discriminate 8 versus 12 but not 8 versus 10 (Lipton & Spelke, 2003; Xu, Spelke, & Goddard, 2005). As a result, some researchers believe that infants can represent approximate large-number values, in addition to the small-number discriminations evident in Figure 6.3.

These findings—like other violation-of-expectation results—are controversial. In other experiments similar to those just described, looking preferences were inconsistent (Langer, Gillette, & Arriaga, 2003; Wakeley, Rivera, & Langer, 2000). These researchers point out that claims for infants' knowledge of number concepts is surprising, given other research indicating that before 14 to 16 months, toddlers have difficulty with less-than and greater-than relationships between small sets. And, as we will see in Chapter 9, not until the preschool years do children add and subtract small sets correctly.

Even when violation-of-expectation results are consistent, critics take issue with the assumption that infants are endowed with *knowledge.* They argue that young infants' looking behaviors may indicate only a perceptual preference, not the existence of concepts and reasoning (Cohen, 2009; Cohen & Cashon, 2006). Similarly, investigators of brain development add that little evidence exists for prewiring of complex cognitive functions in the brain (Johnson, 2001b; Nelson, Thomas, & de Haan, 2006). Instead, they say, the cerebral cortex is initially highly plastic and gradually specializes, largely as the result of children's experiences (see Chapter 5, pages 167–169).

Finally, although the core knowledge perspective emphasizes native endowment, it acknowledges that experience is essential for children to extend this initial knowledge. But so far, it has said little about which experiences are most important in each core domain of thought and how those experiences advance children's thinking. Despite ongoing challenges from critics, core knowledge research has sharpened the field's focus on clarifying the starting point for human cognition and on carefully tracking the changes that build on it.

Applying What We Know

Play Materials That Support Infant and Toddler Cognitive Development

FROM 2 MONTHS	FROM 6 MONTHS	FROM 1 YEAR
Crib mobile	Squeeze toys	Large dolls, toy dishes, toy telephone
Rattles and other handheld sound-making toys, such as a bell on a handle	Nesting cups	Cars and trucks
	Clutch and texture balls	Large blocks, cardboard boxes
Adult-operated music boxes and music recordings with gentle, regular rhythms, songs, and lullabies	Stuffed animals and soft-bodied dolls	Hammer-and-peg toy
	Filling and emptying toys	Pull and push toys, riding toys that can be pushed with feet
	Large and small blocks	Rhythm instruments for shaking and banging, such as bells, cymbals, and drums
	Pots, pans, and spoons from the kitchen	Simple puzzles
	Simple, floating objects for the bath	Sandbox, shovel, and pail
	Picture books with realistic color images	Shallow wading pool and water toys
		Balls of various sizes

PIAGET'S LEGACY   Follow-up research on Piaget's sensorimotor stage yields broad agreement on two issues. First, many cognitive changes of infancy are gradual and continuous rather than abrupt and stagelike, as Piaget thought (Bjorklund, 2004; Courage & Howe, 2002). Second, rather than developing together, various aspects of infant cognition change unevenly because of the challenges posed by different types of tasks and infants' varying experiences with them. These ideas serve as the basis for another major approach to cognitive development—*information processing*—which we take up next.

Before we turn to this alternative point of view, let's recognize Piaget's enormous contributions. Piaget's work inspired a wealth of research on infant cognition, including studies that challenged his theory. Today, researchers are far from consensus on how to modify or replace his account of infant cognitive development, and some believe that his general approach continues to make sense and fits most of the evidence (Cohen, 2010). Piaget's observations also have been of great practical value. Teachers and caregivers continue to look to the sensorimotor stage for guidelines on how to create developmentally appropriate environments for infants and toddlers.

TAKE A MOMENT... Now that you are familiar with some milestones of the first two years, what play materials do you think would support the development of sensorimotor and early representational schemes? Prepare a list, justifying it by referring to the cognitive attainments described in the previous sections. Then compare your suggestions to the ones given in Applying What We Know above.

ASK YOURSELF

◆ **REVIEW** Using the text discussion on pages 204–212, construct your own table providing an overview of infant and toddler cognitive development. Which entries in your table are consistent with Piaget's sensorimotor stage? Which ones develop earlier than Piaget anticipated?

◆ **APPLY** Several times, after her father hid a teething biscuit under a red cup, 12-month-old Mimi retrieved it easily. Then Mimi's father hid the biscuit under a nearby yellow cup. Why did Mimi persist in searching for it under the red cup?

◆ **CONNECT** Recall from Chapter 5 (page 197) that around the middle of the first year, infants identify objects by their features and by their paths of movement, even when they cannot observe the entire path. How might these attainments contribute to infants' understanding of object permanence?

◆ **REFLECT** Which explanation of infants' cognitive competencies do you prefer, and why?

Information Processing

Information-processing researchers agree with Piaget that children are active, inquiring beings. But instead of providing a single, unified theory of cognitive development, they focus on many aspects of thinking, from attention, memory, and categorization skills to complex problem solving.

Recall from Chapter 1 that the information-processing approach frequently relies on computer-like flowcharts to describe the human cognitive system. Information-processing researchers are not satisfied with general concepts, such as assimilation and accommodation, to describe how children think. Instead, they want to know exactly what individuals of different ages do when faced with a task or problem (Halford, 2002; Miller, 2009). The computer model of human thinking is attractive because it is explicit and precise.

Structure of the Information-Processing System

Most information-processing researchers assume that we hold information in three parts of the mental system for processing: the *sensory register; working,* or *short-term, memory;* and *long-term memory* (see Figure 6.4). As information flows through each, we can use **mental strategies** to operate on and transform it, increasing the chances that we will retain information, use it efficiently, and think flexibly, adapting the information to changing circumstances. To understand this more clearly, let's look at each aspect of the mental system.

First, information enters the **sensory register,** where sights and sounds are represented directly and stored briefly. **TAKE A MOMENT...** Look around you, and then close your eyes. An image of what you saw persists for a few seconds, but then it decays, or disappears, unless you use mental strategies to preserve it. For example, by *attending to* some information more carefully than to other information, you increase the chances that it will transfer to the next step of the information-processing system.

In the second part of the mind, **working,** or **short-term, memory,** we actively apply mental strategies as we "work" on a limited amount of information. For example, if you are studying this book effectively, you are taking notes, repeating information to yourself, or grouping

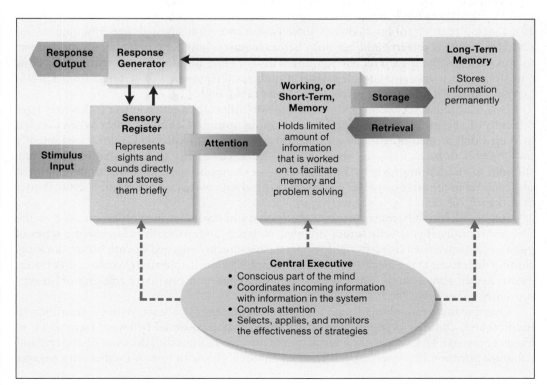

FIGURE 6.4

Model of the human information-processing system. Information flows through three parts of the mental system: the *sensory register; working,* or *short-term, memory;* and *long-term memory.* In each, mental strategies can be used to manipulate information, increasing the efficiency and flexibility of thinking and the chances that information will be retained. The *central executive* is the conscious, reflective part of working memory. It coordinates incoming information already in the system, decides what to attend to, and oversees the use of strategies.

pieces of information together. Why do you apply these strategies? The sensory register, though limited, can take in a wide panorama of information. The capacity of working memory is more restricted. By meaningfully connecting pieces of information into a single representation, we reduce the number of pieces we must attend to, thereby making room in working memory for more. Also, the more thoroughly we learn information, the more *automatically* we use it. Automatic cognitive processing expands working memory by permitting us to focus on other information simultaneously.

To manage its complex activities, a special part of working memory—called the **central executive**—directs the flow of information. It decides what to attend to, coordinates incoming information with information already in the system, and selects, applies, and monitors strategies (Baddeley, 2000; Pressley & Hilden, 2006). The central executive is the conscious, reflective part of our mental system. It works closely with working memory to direct such activities as comprehension, reasoning, and problem solving.

The longer we hold information in working memory, the more likely it will transfer to the third and largest storage area—**long-term memory,** our permanent knowledge base, which is unlimited. In fact, we store so much in long-term memory that *retrieval*—getting information back from the system—can be problematic. To aid retrieval, we apply strategies, just as we do in working memory. Information in long-term memory is *categorized* according to a master plan based on content, much like a library shelving system that allows us to retrieve items by following the same network of associations used to store them in the first place.

Information-processing researchers believe that the basic structure of the human mental system remains similar throughout life. But the *capacity* of the system—the amount of information that can be retained and processed at once—and the speed with which it can be processed increases, making more complex forms of thinking possible with age (Case, 1998; Kail, 2003). Gains in information-processing capacity are due in part to brain development and in part to improvements in strategies—such as attending to information and categorizing it effectively—that are already under way in the first two years of life.

Attention

How does attention develop in early infancy? Recall from our discussion of perceptual development in Chapter 5 that between 1 and 2 months of age, infants shift from focusing on single, high-contrast features of their visual world to exploring objects and patterns more thoroughly. Besides attending to more aspects of the environment, infants gradually become more efficient at managing their attention, taking in information more quickly with age. Habituation research reveals that preterm and newborn babies require a long time to habituate and recover to novel visual stimuli—about 3 or 4 minutes. But by 4 or 5 months, infants require as little as 5 to 10 seconds to take in a complex visual stimulus and recognize that it differs from a previous one (Rose, Feldman, & Janowski, 2001; Slater et al., 1996).

One reason that very young babies' habituation times are so much longer is that they have difficulty disengaging their attention from interesting stimuli (Colombo, 2002). When Carolyn held up a doll dressed in red-and-white checked overalls, 2-month-old Caitlin stared intently until, unable to break her gaze, she burst into tears. The ability to shift attention from one stimulus to another improves by 3 to 4 months—a change believed to be due to development of structures in the cerebral cortex controlling eye movements (Blaga & Colombo, 2006; Posner & Rothbart, 2007a).

Infants' attention becomes increasingly flexible and voluntary in another way: Within the first few months, it is already future-oriented. When 2- and 3-month-olds viewed a series of pictures that alternated in a left–right sequence, they quickly engaged in anticipatory looking, shifting their focus to the location of the next stimulus before it appeared (Wentworth & Haith, 1998). Recall, also, 4- and 5-month-olds' ability to engage in predictive tracking of objects' movements (see page 208).

Over the first year, infants attend to novel and eye-catching events. With the transition to toddlerhood, children become increasingly capable of intentional behavior (refer back to Piaget's Substage 4). Consequently, attraction to novelty declines (but does not disappear) and *sustained attention* improves, especially when children play with toys. A toddler who engages even in simple goal-directed behavior, such as stacking blocks or putting them in a container, must sustain attention to reach the goal (Ruff & Capozzoli, 2003). As plans and activities gradually become more complex, so does the duration of attention.

Adults can foster sustained attention by taking note of an infant or toddler's current interest, encouraging it ("Oh, you like that bell!"), and prompting the child to stay focused ("See, it makes a noise!"). Consistently helping babies focus attention at 10 months predicts higher mental test scores at 18 months (Bono & Stifter, 2003). Also, infants and toddlers gradually become more interested in what others are attending to. Later we will see that this joint attention between caregiver and child is important for language development.

Memory

Operant conditioning and habituation provide windows into early memory. Both methods show that retention of visual events increases dramatically over infancy and toddlerhood.

OPERANT CONDITIONING RESEARCH   Using operant conditioning, researchers study infant memory by teaching 2- to 6-month-olds to move a mobile by kicking a foot tied to it with a long cord. Two-month-olds remember how to activate the mobile for 1 to 2 days after training, and 3-month-olds for one week. By 6 months, memory increases to two weeks (Rovee-Collier, 1999; Rovee-Collier & Bhatt, 1993). Around the middle of the first year, babies can manipulate switches or buttons to control stimulation. When 6- to 18-month-olds pressed a lever to make a toy train move around a track, duration of memory continued to increase with age; 13 weeks after training, 18-month-olds still remembered how to press the lever (Hartshorn et al., 1998b). Figure 6.5 on page 220 shows this dramatic rise in retention of operant responses over the first year and a half.

Even after 2- to 6-month-olds forget an operant response, they need only a brief prompt— an adult who shakes the mobile—to reinstate the memory (Hildreth & Rovee-Collier, 2002). And when 6-month-olds are given a chance to reactivate the response themselves for just a couple of minutes—jiggling the mobile by kicking or moving the train by lever-pressing—their memory not only returns but also extends dramatically, to about 17 weeks (Hildreth, Sweeney, & Rovee-Collier, 2003). Furthermore, with just five widely spaced adult-provided reminders of the train task extending over 1½ years, babies trained at age 6 months still remembered the response after reaching their second birthday (Hartshorn, 2003).

At first, infants' memory for operant responses is highly *context-dependent*. If 2- to 6-month-olds are not tested in the same situation in which they were trained—with the same mobile and crib bumper and in the same room—they remember poorly (Hayne, 2004; Hayne & Rovee-Collier, 1995). After 9 months, the importance of context declines. Older infants and toddlers remember how to make the toy train move even when its features are altered and testing takes place in a different room (Hartshorn et al., 1998a; Hayne, Boniface, & Barr, 2000). As babies move on their own and experience frequent changes in context, they apply learned responses more flexibly, generalizing them to relevant new situations.

HABITUATION RESEARCH   Habituation studies show that infants learn and retain a wide variety of information just by watching objects and events, without being physically active. Sometimes, they do so for much longer time spans than in operant conditioning studies. Babies

■ As toddlers become increasingly capable of goal-directed play, sustained attention improves. Adults can promote the development of sustained attention by encouraging the child's current interest and prompting the child to stay focused. ■

■ Memory for operant responses improves dramatically over the first 18 months. Here, a 12-month-old has learned to press a lever to make a toy train move around a track—a response she is likely to remember when re-exposed to the task after an interval as long as six weeks (see Figure 6.5 on page 220). ■

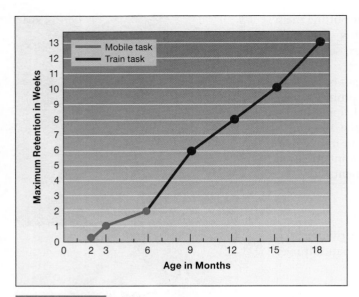

FIGURE 6.5

Increase in retention in two operant conditioning tasks from 2 to 18 months. Two- to 6-month-olds were trained to make a kicking response that turned a mobile. Six- to 18-month-olds were trained to press a lever that made a toy train move around a track. Six-month-olds learned both responses and retained them for an identical length of time, indicating that the tasks are comparable. Consequently, researchers could plot a single line tracking gains in retention of operant responses from 2 to 18 months of age. The line shows that memory improves dramatically. *(From C. Rovee-Collier & R. Barr, 2001, "Infant Learning and Memory," in G. Bremner & A. Fogel, eds., Blackwell Handbook of Infant Development, Oxford, U.K.: Blackwell, p. 150. Reprinted by permission of Blackwell Publishing Ltd.)*

are especially attentive to the movements of objects and people. In one investigation, 5½-month-olds remembered a woman's captivating action (such as blowing bubbles or brushing hair) seven weeks later, as indicated by a *familiarity preference* (see page 181 in Chapter 5) (Bahrick, Gogate, & Ruiz, 2002). The babies were so attentive to the woman's action that they did not remember her face, even when tested one minute later for a *novelty preference.*

In Chapter 4, we saw that 3- to 5-month-olds are excellent at discriminating faces. But their memory for the faces of unfamiliar people and for other visual patterns is short-lived—at 3 months, only about 24 hours; at the end of the first year, several days to a few weeks (Fagan, 1973; Pascalis, de Haan, & Nelson, 1998). By contrast, 3-month-olds' memory for the unusual movements of objects (such as a metal nut swinging on the end of a string) persists for at least three months (Bahrick, Hernandez-Reif, & Pickens, 1997).

By 10 months, infants remember both novel actions and features of objects involved in those actions equally well (Horst, Oakes, & Madole, 2005). Thus, over the second half-year, sensitivity to object appearance increases. This change, as noted earlier, is fostered by infants' increasing ability to manipulate objects, which helps them learn about objects' observable properties.

Habituation research confirms that infants need not be physically active to acquire new information. Nevertheless, as illustrated by research presented in Chapter 5 on the facilitating role of crawling in finding hidden objects (see page 193), motor activity does promote certain aspects of learning and memory.

RECALL MEMORY So far, we have discussed only **recognition**—noticing when a stimulus is identical or similar to one previously experienced. It is the easiest form of memory: All babies have to do is indicate (by kicking, pressing a lever, or looking) whether a new experience is identical or similar to a previous one. **Recall** is more challenging because it involves remembering something without perceptual support. To recall, you must generate a mental image of the past experience. Can infants engage in recall? By the middle of the first year, they can, as indicated by their ability to imitate actions hours or days after observing the behavior.

Recall memory improves steadily with age. In several studies, 1-year-olds who briefly observed an adult's actions on a novel toy imitated those behaviors one month later. Among 2-year-olds, retention persisted for at least three months (Herbert & Hayne, 2000; Klein & Meltzoff, 1999). Other evidence suggests that toddlers' recall endures even longer—three months for short sequences of adult-modeled actions at 1 year and up to 12 months for sequences observed at 1½ years. The ability to recall modeled behaviors in the order in which the actions occurred—evident as early as 6 months—strengthens over the second year (Rovee-Collier & Cuevas, 2009). And when toddlers imitate in correct sequence, processing not just separate actions but relations between actions, they remember more (Knopf, Kraus, & Kressley-Mba, 2006).

Long-term recall depends on connections among multiple regions of the cerebral cortex, especially with the prefrontal cortex. During infancy and toddlerhood, these neural circuits develop rapidly (Nelson, Thomas, & de Haan, 2006). The evidence as a whole indicates that infants' memory processing is remarkably similar to that of older children and adults: Babies acquire information quickly, retain it over time, and apply it flexibly—doing so more effectively with age (Bauer, 2009; Rovee-Collier & Cuevas, 2009). Yet a puzzling finding is that older children and adults no longer recall their earliest experiences! See the Biology and Environment box on the following page for a discussion of *infantile amnesia.*

BIOLOGY AND ENVIRONMENT

Infantile Amnesia

If infants and toddlers recall many aspects of their everyday lives, how do we explain **infantile amnesia**—that most of us cannot retrieve events that happened to us before age 3? The reason cannot be merely the passage of time because we can recall many personally meaningful one-time events from both the recent and the distant past: the day a sibling was born or a move to a new house—recollections known as **autobiographical memory.**

Several explanations of infantile amnesia exist. One theory credits brain development, suggesting that vital changes in the frontal lobes of the cerebral cortex pave the way for an *explicit* memory system—one in which children remember deliberately rather than *implicitly,* without conscious awareness (Boyer & Diamond, 1992). But as we have seen, mounting evidence indicates that even young infants engage in conscious recall (Rovee-Collier & Cuevas, 2009).

Another conjecture is that older children and adults often use verbal means for storing information, whereas infants' and toddlers' memory processing is largely nonverbal—an incompatibility that may prevent long-term retention of early experiences. To test this idea, researchers sent two adults to the homes of 2- to 4-year-olds with an unusual toy that the children were likely to remember: The Magic

Shrinking Machine, shown in Figure 6.6. One adult showed the child how, after inserting an object in an opening on top of the machine and turning a crank that activated flashing lights and musical sounds, the child could retrieve a smaller, identical object (discreetly dropped down a chute by the second adult) from behind a door on the front of the machine.

A day later, the researchers tested the children to see how well they recalled the event. Their nonverbal memory—based on acting out the "shrinking" event and recognizing the "shrunken" objects in photos—was excellent. But even when they had the vocabulary, children younger than age 3 had trouble describing features of the "shrinking" experience. Verbal recall increased sharply between ages 3 and 4—the period during which children "scramble over the amnesia barrier" (Simcock & Hayne, 2003, p. 813). In a second study, preschoolers could not translate their nonverbal memory for the game into language six months to one year later, when their language had improved dramatically. Their verbal reports were "frozen in time," reflecting their limited language skill at the age they played the game (Simcock & Hayne, 2002).

These findings help us reconcile infants' and toddlers' remarkable memory skills with infantile amnesia. During the first few years, children

rely heavily on nonverbal memory techniques, such as visual images and motor actions. But as language develops, their ability to use it to refer to preverbal memories requires strong contextual cues, such as direct exposure to the physical setting of the to-be-recalled experience (Morris & Baker-Ward, 2007). Only after age 3 do children often represent events verbally. As children encode autobiographical events in verbal form, they can use language-based cues to retrieve them, increasing the accessibility of those memories at later ages (Hayne, 2004).

Other findings suggest that the advent of a clear self-image contributes to the end of infantile amnesia. Toddlers who were advanced in development of a sense of self demonstrated better verbal memories a year later while conversing about past events with their mothers (Harley & Reese, 1999). Very likely, both biology and social experience contribute to the decline of infantile amnesia. Brain development and adult–child interaction may jointly foster self-awareness, language, and improved memory, which enable children to talk with adults about significant past experiences (Bauer, 2007; Nelson & Fivush, 2004). As a result, preschoolers begin to construct a long-lasting autobiographical narrative of their lives and enter into the history of their family and community.

(a)

(b)

(c)

FIGURE 6.6

The Magic Shrinking Machine, used to test young children's verbal and nonverbal memory of an unusual event. After being shown how the machine worked, the child participated in selecting objects from a polka-dot bag, dropping them into the top of the machine (a), and turning a crank, which produced a "shrunken" object (b). When tested the next day, 2- to 4-year-olds' nonverbal memory for the event was excellent. But below 36 months, verbal recall was poor, based on the number of features recalled about the game during an open-ended interview (c). Recall improved between 36 and 48 months, the period during which infantile amnesia subsides. *(From G. Simcock & H. Hayne, 2003, "Age-Related Changes in Verbal and Nonverbal Memory During Early Childhood,"* Developmental Psychology, 39, *pp. 807, 809. Copyright © 2003 by the American Psychological Association. Reprinted with permission of the American Psychological Association.)* Photos: *Ross Coombes/Courtesy of Harlene Hayne.*

Categorization

Even young infants can categorize, grouping similar objects and events into a single representation. Categorization helps infants make sense of experience—reduce the enormous amount of new information they encounter every day so they can learn and remember (Cohen, 2003; Oakes & Madole, 2003).

Some creative variations of operant conditioning research with mobiles have been used to find out about infant categorization. One such study, of 3-month-olds, is described and illustrated in Figure 6.7. Similar investigations reveal that in the first few months, babies categorize stimuli on the basis of shape, size, and other physical properties (Wasserman & Rovee-Collier, 2001). By 6 months of age, they can categorize on the basis of two correlated features—for example, the shape and color of an alphabet letter (Bhatt et al., 2004). This ability to categorize using clusters of features prepares babies for acquiring many complex everyday categories.

Habituation has also been used to study infant categorization. Researchers show babies a series of pictures belonging to one category and then see whether they recover to (look longer at) a picture that is not a member of the category (see Figure 6.8). Findings reveal that in the second half of the first year, as long as they have sufficient familiarity with category members, infants group objects into an impressive array of categories—food items, furniture, birds, land animals, air animals, sea animals, plants, vehicles, kitchen utensils, and spatial location ("above" and "below," "on" and "in") (Bornstein, Arterberry, & Mash, 2010; Casasola, Cohen, & Chiarello, 2003; Mandler & McDonough, 1998; Oakes, Coppage, & Dingel, 1997). Besides organizing the physical world, infants of this age categorize their emotional and social worlds. Their looking responses reveal that they sort people and their voices by gender and age, have begun to distinguish emotional expressions, can separate people's natural actions (walking) from other motions, and expect people (but not inanimate objects) to move spontaneously (Spelke, Phillips, & Woodward, 1995; see also Chapter 5, pages 180–181).

Babies' earliest categories are based on similar overall appearance or prominent object parts: legs for animals, wheels for vehicles. But as infants approach their first birthday, more categories appear to be based on subtle sets of features (Cohen, 2003; Mandler, 2004; Quinn, 2008). Older infants can even make categorical distinctions when the perceptual contrast between two categories is minimal (birds versus airplanes).

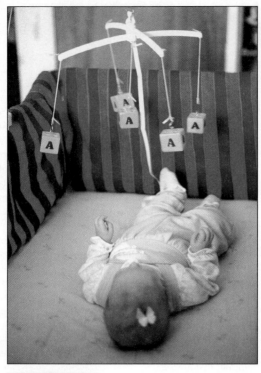

FIGURE 6.7

Investigating infant categorization using operant conditioning. Three-month-olds were taught to kick to move a mobile that was made of small blocks, all with the letter *A* on them. After a delay, kicking returned to a high level only if the babies were shown a mobile whose blocks were labeled with the same form (the letter *A*). If the form was changed (from *A*s to *2*s), infants no longer kicked vigorously. While making the mobile move, the babies had grouped together its features. They associated the kicking response with the category *A* and, at later testing, distinguished it from the category *2* (*Bhatt, Rovee-Collier, & Weiner, 1994; Hayne, Rovee-Collier, & Perris, 1987*).

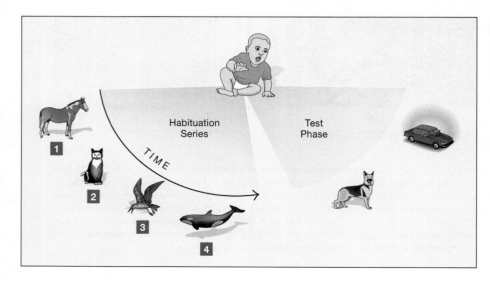

FIGURE 6.8

Using habituation to study infant categorization. After habituating to a series of items belonging to one category (in this example, animals), infants are shown two novel items, one that is a member of the category (dog) and one that is not (car). If infants recover to (look longer at or spend more time manipulating) the out-of-category item (car), this indicates that they distinguish it from the set of within-category items (animals). Habituating another group of infants to a series of vehicles and seeing if, when presented with the two test items above, they recover to the dog confirms that babies can distinguish animals from vehicles. This pattern of responding has been found in many infant categorization studies.

As they gain experience in comparing to-be-categorized items in varied ways and their store of verbal labels expands, toddlers start to categorize flexibly: When 14-month-olds are given four balls and four blocks, some made of soft rubber and some of rigid plastic, their sequence of object touching reveals that after classifying by shape, they can switch to classifying by material (soft versus hard) if an adult calls their attention to the new basis for grouping (Ellis & Oakes, 2006).

In addition to touching and sorting, toddlers' categorization skills are evident in their play behaviors. After watching an adult give a toy dog a drink from a cup, most 14-month-olds shown a rabbit and a motorcycle offered the drink only to the rabbit (Mandler & McDonough, 1998). They clearly understood that certain actions are appropriate for some categories of items (animals) but not for others (vehicles).

By the end of the second year, toddlers' grasp of the animate–inanimate distinction expands. Nonlinear motions are typical of animates (a person or a dog jumping), linear motions of inanimates (a car or a table pushed along a surface). At 18 months, toddlers more often imitate a nonlinear motion with a toy that has animate-like parts (legs), even if it represents an inanimate (a bed). At 22 months, displaying a much fuller understanding, they imitate a nonlinear motion only with toys in the animate category (a cat but not a bed) (Rakison, 2005). They seem to realize that whereas animates are self-propelled and therefore have varied paths of movement, inanimates move only when acted on, in highly restricted ways (Rakison, 2006).

Researchers disagree on how babies arrive at these impressive attainments. One view holds that older infants and toddlers categorize more effectively because they become increasingly sensitive to fine-grained perceptual features and to stable relations among those features—for example, objects with flapping wings and feathers belong to one category; objects with rigid wings, windows, and a smooth surface belong to another category (Cohen & Cashon, 2006; Oakes et al., 2009; Rakison & Lupyan, 2008). An alternative view is that before the end of the first year, babies undergo a fundamental shift from a perceptual to a conceptual basis for constructing categories, increasingly grouping objects by their common function or behavior (birds versus airplanes, cars versus motorcycles, dogs versus cats) (Mandler, 2004). And yet a third view, stemming from the core knowledge perspective, assumes an inherited foundation of conceptual knowledge, which is enlarged and refined with experience (Gelman & Kalish, 2006).

All researchers acknowledge that infants' and toddlers' exploration of objects and expanding knowledge of the world contribute to advances in categorization, eventually enriching conceptual understanding. In addition, adult labeling of a set of objects with a consistently applied word ("Look at the car!" "Do you see the car?") calls babies' attention to commonalities among objects, fostering categorization as early as 3 to 4 months of age. Words are uniquely facilitating, as pairing the same tone with each object is ineffective (Ferry, Hespos, & Waxman, 2010). Toddlers' vocabulary growth, in turn, fosters categorization (Cohen & Brunt, 2009; Waxman, 2003).

Variations among languages lead to cultural differences in development of categories. Korean toddlers, who learn a language in which object names are often omitted from sentences, develop object-sorting skills later than their English-speaking counterparts (Gopnik & Choi, 1990). At the same time, Korean contains a common word, *kkita,* with no English equivalent, referring to a tight fit between objects in contact (a ring on a finger, a cap on a pen), and Korean toddlers are advanced in forming the spatial category "tight-fit" (Choi et al., 1999). After English-speaking 18-month-olds heard the word *tight* while observing several instances of objects fitting together tightly, they readily acquired the tight-fit category (Casasola, Bhagwat, & Burke, 2009). Those who viewed the events without the label did not form this challenging category.

Evaluation of Information-Processing Findings

The information-processing perspective underscores the continuity of human thinking from infancy into adult life. In attending to the environment, remembering everyday events, and categorizing objects, Caitlin, Grace, and Timmy think in ways that are remarkably similar to our own, though their mental processing is far from proficient. Findings on memory and

LOOK AND LISTEN

Observe a toddler playing with a variety of small toys—some representing animals and some representing household objects. What play behaviors reveal the child's ability to categorize?

categorization join with other research in challenging Piaget's view of early cognitive development. Infants' capacity to recall events and to categorize stimuli attests, once again, to their ability to mentally represent their experiences.

Information-processing research has contributed greatly to our view of infants and toddlers as sophisticated cognitive beings. But its central strength—analyzing cognition into its components, such as perception, attention, memory, and categorization—is also its greatest drawback: Information processing has had difficulty putting these components back together into a broad, comprehensive theory.

One approach to overcoming this weakness has been to combine Piaget's theory with the information-processing approach, an effort we will take up in Chapter 12. A more recent trend has been the application of a *dynamic systems view* (see Chapter 1, page 28) to early cognition. In this approach, researchers analyze each cognitive attainment to see how it results from a complex system of prior accomplishments and the child's current goals (Courage & Howe, 2002; Spencer & Perone, 2008; Thelen & Smith, 2006). Once these ideas are fully tested, they may move the field closer to a more powerful view of how the minds of infants and children develop.

The Social Context of Early Cognitive Development

Recall the description at the beginning of this chapter of Grace dropping shapes into a container. Notice that she learns about the toy with Ginette's help. With adult support, Grace will gradually become better at matching shapes to openings and dropping them into the container. Then she will be able to perform the activity (and others like it) on her own.

Vygotsky's sociocultural theory emphasizes that children live in rich social and cultural contexts that affect the way their cognitive world is structured (Bodrova & Leong, 2007; Rogoff, 2003). Vygotsky believed that complex mental activities, such as voluntary attention, deliberate memory, categorization, and problem solving, have their origins in social interaction. Through joint activities with more mature members of their society, children master activities and think in ways that have meaning in their culture.

A special Vygotskian concept explains how this happens. The **zone of proximal** (or potential) **development** refers to a range of tasks that the child cannot yet handle alone but can do with the help of more skilled partners. To understand this idea, think about how a sensitive adult (such as Ginette) introduces a child to a new activity. The adult picks a task that the child can master but that is challenging enough that the child cannot do it by herself. Or the adult capitalizes on an activity that the child has chosen. The adult guides and supports, adjusting the level of support offered to fit the child's current level of performance. As the child joins in the interaction and picks up mental strategies, her competence increases, and the adult steps back, permitting the child to take more responsibility for the task. This form of teaching—known as *scaffolding*—promotes learning at all ages, and we will consider it further in Chapter 9.

Vygotsky's ideas have been applied mostly to preschool and school-age children, who are more skilled in language and social communication. Recently, however, his theory has been extended to infancy and toddlerhood. Recall that babies are equipped with capabilities that ensure that caregivers will interact with them. Then adults adjust the environment and their communication in ways that promote learning adapted to their cultural circumstances.

A study by Barbara Rogoff and her collaborators (1984) illustrates this process. Placing a jack-in-the-box nearby, the researchers watched how several adults played with Rogoff's son and daughter over the first two years. In the early months, adults tried to focus the baby's attention by working the toy and, as the bunny popped out, saying something like "My, what happened?" By the end of the first year, when the baby's cognitive and motor skills had improved, interaction centered on how to use the toy: The adults guided the baby's hand in turning the crank and putting the bunny back in the box. During the second year, adults helped from a distance, using gestures and verbal prompts, such as making a turning motion with the hand near the crank. Research indicates that this fine-tuned support is related to advanced play, language, and problem solving during the second year (Bornstein et al., 1992; Charman et al., 2001; Tamis-LeMonda & Bornstein, 1989).

As early as the first year, cultural variations in social experiences affect mental strategies. In the jack-in-the-box example, adults and children focused their attention on a single activity. This strategy, common in Western families, is well-suited to lessons in which children master skills apart from the everyday situations in which they will later use those skills. In contrast, Guatemalan Mayan adults and babies often attend to several events at once. For example, one 12-month-old skillfully put objects in a jar while watching a passing truck and blowing into a toy whistle his mother had slipped in his mouth (Chavajay & Rogoff, 1999). Processing several competing events simultaneously may be vital in cultures where children largely learn not through lessons but through keen observation of others' ongoing activities at home, at work, and in public life. Children of Guatemalan Mayan, Mexican, and Native-American parents without extensive education continue to display this style of attention well into middle childhood (Chavajay & Rogoff, 2002; Correa-Chavez, Rogoff, & Arauz, 2005; Philips, 1983).

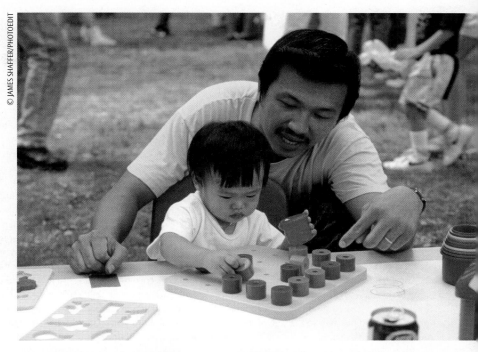

■ With gentle physical support and simple words, this father helps his young son put together a puzzle. By bringing the task within the child's zone of proximal development and adjusting his communication to suit the child's needs, the father transfers mental strategies to the child, promoting his cognitive development. ■

Earlier we saw how infants and toddlers create new schemes by acting on the physical world (Piaget) and how certain skills become better-developed as children represent their experiences more efficiently and meaningfully (information processing). Vygotsky adds a third dimension to our understanding by emphasizing that many aspects of cognitive development are socially prompted and encouraged. The Cultural Influences box on page 226 presents additional evidence for this idea. And we see even more evidence in the next section, where we look at individual differences in mental development during the first two years.

ASK YOURSELF ◆◆

◆ REVIEW What impact does toddlers' more advanced play with toys have on the development of attention?

◆ APPLY When Timmy was 18 months old, his mother stood behind him, helping him throw a large ball into a box. As his skill improved, she stepped back, letting him try on his own. Using Vygotsky's ideas, explain how Timmy's mother is supporting his cognitive development.

◆ CONNECT Review the research on page 211, indicating that by age 10 to 12 months, infants can solve problems by analogy. How might this attainment be related to the development of categorization (less emphasis on similar appearance, more on common function and behavior) over the second half-year?

◆ REFLECT Describe your earliest autobiographical memory. How old were you when the event occurred? Do your responses fit with research on infantile amnesia?

CULTURAL INFLUENCES

Social Origins of Make-Believe Play

One of the activities my husband, Ken, used to do with our two sons when they were young was to bake pineapple upside-down cake, a favorite treat. One Sunday afternoon when a cake was in the making, 21-month-old Peter stood on a chair at the kitchen sink, busily pouring water from one cup to another.

"He's in the way, Dad!" complained 4-year-old David, trying to pull Peter away from the sink.

"Maybe if we let him help, he'll give us some room," Ken suggested. As David stirred the batter, Ken poured some into a small bowl for Peter, moved his chair to the side of the sink, and handed him a spoon.

"Here's how you do it, Petey," instructed David, with an air of superiority. Peter watched as David stirred, then tried to copy his motion. When it was time to pour the batter, Ken helped Peter hold and tip the small bowl.

"Time to bake it," said Ken.

"Bake it, bake it," repeated Peter, watching Ken slip the pan into the oven.

Several hours later, we observed one of Peter's earliest instances of make-believe play. He got his pail from the sandbox and, after filling it with a handful of sand, carried it into the kitchen and put it down on the floor in front of the oven. "Bake it, bake it," Peter called to Ken. Together, father and son placed the pretend cake in the oven.

Piaget and his followers concluded that toddlers discover make-believe independently, once they are capable of representational schemes. Vygotsky's theory has challenged this view. He believed that society provides children with opportunities to represent culturally meaningful activities in play. Make-believe, like other complex mental activities, is first learned under the guidance of experts (Berk, Mann, & Ogan, 2006). In the example just described, Peter extended his capacity to represent daily events when Ken drew him into the baking task and helped him act it out in play.

Current evidence supports the idea that early make-believe is the combined result of children's readiness to engage in it and social experiences that promote it. In one observational study of U.S. middle-SES toddlers, 75 to 80 percent of make-believe involved mother–child interaction (Haight & Miller, 1993). At 12 months, make-believe was fairly one-sided: Almost all play episodes were initiated by mothers. But by the end of the second year, half of pretend episodes were initiated by each.

During make-believe, mothers offer toddlers a rich array of cues that they are pretending—looking and smiling at the child more, making more exaggerated movements, and using more "we" talk (acknowledging that pretending is a joint endeavor) than they do during the same real-life event (Lillard et al., 2007). These maternal cues encourage toddlers to join in and probably facilitate their ability to distinguish pretend from real acts, which strengthens over the second and third years (Lillard & Witherington, 2004; Ma & Lillard, 2006).

Also, when adults participate, toddlers' make-believe is more elaborate (Keren et al., 2005). They are more likely to combine schemes into complex sequences, as Peter did when he put the sand in the bucket ("making the batter"), carried it into the kitchen, and, with Ken's help, put it in the oven ("baking the cake"). The more parents pretend with their toddlers, the more time their children devote to make-believe. In certain collectivist societies, such as Argentina and Japan, mother–toddler other-directed pretending, as in feeding or putting a doll to sleep, is particularly rich in maternal expressions of affection and praise (Bornstein et al., 1999a).

In some cultures, such as those of Indonesia and Mexico, where extended-family households and sibling caregiving are common, make-believe is more frequent and more complex with older siblings than with mothers. As early as age 3 to 4, children provide rich, challenging stimulation to their younger brothers and sisters, take these teaching responsibilities seriously, and, with age, become better at them (Zukow-Goldring, 2002). In a study of Zinacanteco Indian children of southern Mexico, by age 8, sibling teachers were highly skilled at showing 2-year-olds how to play at everyday tasks, such as washing and cooking. They often guided toddlers verbally and physically through the task and provided feedback (Maynard, 2002).

In Western middle-SES families, older siblings less often teach deliberately but still serve as influential models of playful behavior. In a study of New Zealand families of Western European descent, when both a parent and an older sibling were available, toddlers more often imitated the actions of the sibling, especially when siblings engaged in make-believe (Barr & Hayne, 2003).

As Chapters 9 and 10 will reveal, make-believe is a major means through which children extend their cognitive and social skills and learn about important activities in their culture. Vygotsky's theory, and the findings that support it, tell us that providing a stimulating environment is not enough to promote early cognitive development. In addition, toddlers must be invited and encouraged by more skilled members of their culture to participate in the social world around them. Parents and teachers can enhance early make-believe by playing often with toddlers, guiding and elaborating their make-believe themes.

© CAROLINE PENN/PANOS PICTURES

■ In cultures where sibling caregiving is common, make-believe play is more frequent and complex with older siblings than with mothers. These Kenyan brothers pretend with sand and rocks—"toys" that are plentiful in their surroundings. The older boy easily engages his toddler sibling, teaching him how to play. ■

Individual Differences in Early Mental Development

Because of Grace's deprived early environment, Kevin and Monica had a child psychologist give her one of many tests available for assessing mental development in infants and toddlers. Worried about Timmy's progress, Vanessa also arranged for him to be tested. At age 22 months, he had only a handful of words in his vocabulary, played in a less mature way than Caitlin and Grace, and seemed restless and overactive.

The cognitive theories we have just discussed try to explain the *process* of development—how children's thinking changes. Mental tests, in contrast, focus on cognitive *products*. Their goal is to measure behaviors that reflect development and to arrive at scores that *predict* future performance, such as later intelligence, school achievement, and adult vocational success. This concern with prediction arose nearly a century ago, when French psychologist Alfred Binet designed the first successful intelligence test, which predicted school achievement (see Chapter 1). It inspired the design of many new tests, including ones that measure intelligence at very early ages.

Infant Intelligence Tests

Accurately measuring infants' intelligence is a challenge because young babies cannot answer questions or follow directions. All we can do is present them with stimuli, coax them to respond, and observe their behavior. As a result, most infant tests emphasize perceptual and motor responses. But increasingly, new tests are being developed that tap early language, cognition, and social behavior, especially with older infants and toddlers.

One commonly used test, the *Bayley Scales of Infant Development,* is suitable for children between 1 month and 3½ years. The most recent edition, the Bayley-III, has three main subtests: (1) the Cognitive Scale, which includes such items as attention to familiar and unfamiliar objects, looking for a fallen object, and pretend play; (2) the Language Scale, which taps understanding and expressions of language—for example, recognition of objects and people, following simple directions, and naming objects and pictures; and (3) the Motor Scale, which includes gross- and fine-motor skills, such as grasping, sitting, stacking blocks, and climbing stairs (Bayley, 2005).

Two additional Bayley-III scales depend on parental report: (4) the Social-Emotional Scale, which asks caregivers about such behaviors as ease of calming, social responsiveness, and imitation in play; and (5) the Adaptive Behavior Scale, which asks about adaptation to the demands of daily life, including communication, self-control, following rules, and getting along with others.

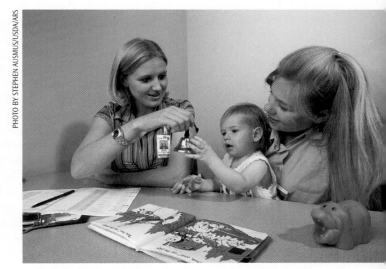

PHOTO BY STEPHEN AUSMUS/USDA/ARS

■ A trained examiner administers a test based on the Bayley Scales of Infant Development to a 1-year-old sitting in her mother's lap. Compared with earlier editions, the Bayley-III Cognitive and Language Scales better predict preschool mental test performance. ■

COMPUTING INTELLIGENCE TEST SCORES   Intelligence tests for infants, children, and adults are scored in much the same way—by computing an **intelligence quotient (IQ),** which indicates the extent to which the raw score (number of items passed) deviates from the typical performance of same-age individuals. To make this comparison possible, test designers engage in **standardization**—giving the test to a large, representative sample and using the results as the *standard* for interpreting scores. The standardization sample for the Bayley-III included 1,700 infants, toddlers, and young preschoolers, reflecting the U.S. population in SES and ethnic diversity.

FIGURE 6.9

Normal distribution of intelligence test scores. To determine what percentage of same-age individuals in the population a person with a certain IQ outperformed, add the figures to the left of that IQ score. For example, an 8-year-old child with an IQ of 115 scored better than 84 percent of the population of 8-year-olds.

Within the standardization sample, performances at each age level form a **normal distribution,** in which most scores cluster around the mean, or average, with progressively fewer falling toward the extremes (see Figure 6.9). This *bell-shaped distribution* results whenever researchers measure individual differences in large samples. When intelligence tests are standardized, the mean IQ is set at 100. An individual's IQ is higher or lower than 100 by an amount that reflects how much his or her test performance deviates from the standardization-sample mean.

The IQ offers a way of finding out whether an individual is ahead, behind, or on time (average) in mental development compared with others of the same age. For example, if Timmy's score is 100, then he did better than 50 percent of his agemates, and his score will be 100. A child with an IQ of 85 did better than only 16 percent, whereas a child with an IQ of 130 outperformed 98 percent. The IQs of 96 percent of individuals fall between 70 and 130; only a few achieve higher or lower scores.

PREDICTING LATER PERFORMANCE FROM INFANT TESTS   Despite careful construction, most infant tests—including previous editions of the Bayley—predict later intelligence poorly. Longitudinal research reveals that the majority of children show substantial fluctuations in IQ between toddlerhood and adolescence—typically 10 to 20 points, and sometimes much more (McCall, 1993; Weinert & Hany, 2003).

Infants and toddlers easily become distracted, fatigued, or bored during testing, so their scores often do not reflect their true abilities. And infant perceptual and motor items differ from the tasks given to older children, which increasingly emphasize verbal, conceptual, and problem-solving skills. In contrast, the Bayley-III Cognitive and Language Scales, which better dovetail with childhood tests, are good predictors of preschool mental test performance (Albers & Grieve, 2007). But because most infant test scores do not tap the same dimensions of intelligence measured at older ages, they are conservatively labeled **developmental quotients (DQs)** rather than IQs.

Infant tests are somewhat better at making long-term predictions for extremely low-scoring babies. Today, they are largely used for *screening*—helping to identify for further observation and intervention babies whose very low scores mean that they are likely to have developmental problems.

As an alternative to infant tests, some researchers have turned to information-processing measures, such as habituation, to assess early mental progress. Their findings show that speed of habituation and recovery to novel visual stimuli are among the best available infant predictors of IQ from early childhood to early adulthood, with correlations ranging from the .30s to the .60s (Fagan, Holland, & Wheeler, 2007; Kavsek, 2004; McCall & Carriger, 1993).

Habituation and recovery seem to be especially effective early indexes of intelligence because they assess memory as well as quickness and flexibility of thinking, which underlie intelligent behavior at all ages (Colombo, 1995; Rose & Feldman, 1997). Piagetian object-permanence tasks are also relatively good predictors of later IQ, perhaps because they, too, reflect a basic intellectual process—problem solving (Rose, Feldman, & Wallace, 1992). The consistency of these findings has prompted designers of the Bayley-III to include items that tap such cognitive skills as habituation, object permanence, and categorization.

Early Environment and Mental Development

In Chapter 2, we indicated that intelligence is a complex blend of hereditary and environmental influences. Many studies have examined the relationship of environmental factors to infant and toddler mental test scores. As we consider this evidence, you will encounter findings that highlight the role of heredity as well.

Applying What We Know

Features of a High-Quality Home Life for Infants and Toddlers: The HOME Infant–Toddler Subscales

HOME SUBSCALE	SAMPLE ITEM
Emotional and verbal responsiveness of the parent	Parent caresses or kisses child at least once during observer's visit.
	Parent spontaneously speaks to child twice or more (excluding scolding) during observer's visit.
Parental acceptance of the child	Parent does not interfere with child's actions or restrict child's movements more than three times during observer's visit.
Organization of the physical environment	Child's play environment appears safe and free of hazards.
Provision of appropriate play materials	Parent provides toys or interesting activities for child during observer's visit.
Parental involvement with the child	Parent tends to keep child within view and to look at child often during observer's visit.
Opportunities for variety in daily stimulation	Child eats at least one meal per day with mother and/or father, according to parental report.
	Child frequently has a chance to get out of house (for example, accompanies parent on trips to grocery store).

Source: Bradley, 1994; Bradley et al., 2001.

HOME ENVIRONMENT   The **Home Observation for Measurement of the Environment (HOME)** is a checklist for gathering information about the quality of children's home lives through observation and parental interview (Caldwell & Bradley, 1994). Applying What We Know above lists the factors measured by HOME during the first three years. Each is positively related to toddlers' mental test performance. Regardless of SES and ethnicity, an organized, stimulating physical setting and parental affection, involvement, and encouragement of new skills repeatedly predict better language and IQ scores in toddlerhood and early childhood (Fuligni, Han, & Brooks-Gunn, 2004; Linver, Martin, & Brooks-Gunn, 2004; Tamis-LeMonda et al., 2004; Tong et al., 2007). The extent to which parents talk to infants and toddlers is particularly important. It contributes strongly to early language progress, which, in turn, predicts intelligence and academic achievement in elementary school (Hart & Risley, 1995).

Yet we must interpret these correlational findings cautiously. In all the studies, children were reared by their biological parents, with whom they share not just a common environment but also a common heredity. Parents who are genetically more intelligent may provide better experiences while also giving birth to genetically brighter children, who evoke more stimulation from their parents. Research supports this hypothesis, which refers to *genetic–environmental correlation* (see Chapter 2, pages 84–85) (Saudino & Plomin, 1997). Still, heredity does not account for the entire association between home environment and mental test scores. Family living conditions—both HOME scores and affluence of the surrounding neighborhood—continue to predict children's IQ beyond the contribution of parental IQ and education (Chase-Lansdale et al., 1997; Klebanov et al., 1998). In one study, infants and children growing up in less crowded homes had parents who were far more verbally responsive to them—a major contributor to language, intellectual, and academic progress (Evans, Maxwell, & Hart, 1999).

How can the research summarized so far help us understand Vanessa's concern about Timmy's development? Ben, the psychologist who tested Timmy, found that he scored only slightly below average. Ben talked with Vanessa about her child-rearing practices and watched her play with Timmy. A single parent who worked long hours, Vanessa had little energy for Timmy at the end of the day. Ben also noticed that Vanessa, anxious about Timmy's progress, tended to pressure him, dampening his active behavior and bombarding him with directions: "That's enough ball play. Stack these blocks."

Ben explained that when parents are intrusive in these ways, infants and toddlers are likely to be distractible, play immaturely, and do poorly on mental tests (Bono & Stifter, 2003;

High-quality child care centers, with small group sizes and well-trained caregivers who provide developmentally appropriate stimulation, can be especially beneficial for children from low-SES homes. ■

Stilson & Harding, 1997). He coached Vanessa in how to interact sensitively with Timmy, while also assuring her that Timmy's current performance need not forecast his future development. Warm, responsive parenting that builds on toddlers' current capacities is a much better indicator than an early mental test score of how children will do later.

INFANT AND TODDLER CHILD CARE Today, more than 60 percent of U.S. mothers with a child under age 2 are employed (U.S. Census Bureau, 2010b). Child care for infants and toddlers has become common, and its quality—though not as influential as parenting—affects mental development. Research consistently shows that young children exposed to long hours of mediocre to poor-quality child care—whether they come from middle-class or from low-SES homes—score lower on measures of cognitive, language, and social skills during the preschool and elementary school years (Belsky et al., 2007; Hausfather et al., 1997; NICHD Early Child Care Research Network, 2000b, 2001, 2003b, 2006).

In contrast, good child care can reduce the negative impact of a stressed, poverty-stricken home life, and it sustains the benefits of growing up in an economically advantaged family (Lamb & Ahnert, 2006; McCartney et al., 2007; NICHD Early Child Care Research Network, 2003b). In Swedish longitudinal research, entering high-quality child care in infancy and toddlerhood was associated with cognitive, emotional, and social competence in middle childhood and adolescence (Andersson, 1989, 1992; Broberg et al., 1997).

In contrast to most European countries and to Australia and New Zealand, where child care is nationally regulated and funded to ensure its quality, reports on U.S. child care raise serious concerns. Standards are set by the individual states and vary widely. In studies of quality, only 20 to 25 percent of child-care centers and family child-care settings provided infants and toddlers with sufficiently positive, stimulating experiences to promote healthy psychological development. Most settings offered substandard care (NICHD Early Child Care Research Network, 2000a, 2004).

Unfortunately, many U.S. children from low-income families experience inadequate child care (Brooks-Gunn, 2004). But U.S. settings providing the very worst care tend to serve middle-SES families. These parents are especially likely to place their children in for-profit centers, where quality tends to be lowest. Low-SES children more often attend publicly subsidized, nonprofit centers, which have smaller group sizes and better teacher–child ratios (Lamb & Ahnert, 2006). Still, child-care quality for low-SES children varies widely. And probably because of greater access to adult stimulation, infants and toddlers in high-quality family child care score higher than those in center care in cognitive and language development (NICHD Early Child Care Research Network, 2000b).

See Applying What We Know on the following page for signs of high-quality child care for infants and toddlers, based on standards for **developmentally appropriate practice.** These standards, devised by the U.S. National Association for the Education of Young Children, specify program characteristics that serve young children's developmental and individual needs, based on both current research and consensus among experts. Caitlin, Grace, and Timmy are fortunate to be in family child care that meets these standards.

Child care in the United States is affected by a macrosystem of individualistic values and weak government regulation and funding. Furthermore, many parents think that their children's child-care experiences are better than they really are. Unable to identify good care, they do not demand it (Helburn, 1995). In recent years, recognizing that child care is in a state of crisis, the U.S. federal government and some states have allocated additional funds to subsidize its cost, especially for low-income families. Though far from meeting the need, this increase in resources has had a positive impact on child-care quality and accessibility (Children's Defense Fund, 2009).

Good child care is a cost-effective means of protecting children's well-being. And much like the programs we are about to consider, it can serve as effective early intervention for children whose development is at risk.

LOOK AND LISTEN

❖❖

Ask several employed parents of infants or toddlers to describe what they sought in a child-care setting, along with challenges they faced in finding child care. Are the parents knowledgeable about the ingredients of high-quality care?

Applying What We Know

Signs of Developmentally Appropriate Infant and Toddler Child Care

PROGRAM CHARACTERISTIC	SIGNS OF QUALITY
Physical setting	Indoor environment is clean, in good repair, well-lighted, and well-ventilated. Fenced outdoor play space is available. Setting does not appear overcrowded when children are present.
Toys and equipment	Play materials are appropriate for infants and toddlers and are stored on low shelves within easy reach. Cribs, highchairs, infant seats, and child-sized tables and chairs are available. Outdoor equipment includes small riding toys, swings, slide, and sandbox.
Caregiver–child ratio	In child-care centers, caregiver–child ratio is no greater than one to three for infants and one to six for toddlers. Group size (number of children in one room) is no greater than six infants with two caregivers and 12 toddlers with two caregivers. In family child care, caregiver is responsible for no more than six children; within this group, no more than two are infants or toddlers. Staffing is consistent, so infants and toddlers can form relationships with particular caregivers.
Daily activities	Daily schedule includes times for active play, quiet play, naps, snacks, and meals. It is flexible rather than rigid, to meet the needs of individual children. Atmosphere is warm and supportive, and children are never left unsupervised.
Interactions among adults and children	Caregivers respond promptly to infants' and toddlers' distress; hold, talk to, sing, and read to them; and interact with them in a manner that respects the individual child's interests and tolerance for stimulation.
Caregiver qualifications	Caregiver has some training in child development, first aid, and safety.
Relationships with parents	Parents are welcome anytime. Caregivers talk frequently with parents about children's behavior and development.
Licensing and accreditation	Child-care setting, whether a center or a home, is licensed by the state or province. Voluntary accreditation by the National Academy of Early Childhood Programs *(www.naeyc.org/accreditation)* or the National Association for Family Child Care *(www.nafcc.org)* is evidence of an especially high-quality program.

Source: Copple & Bredekamp, 2009.

Early Intervention for At-Risk Infants and Toddlers

Children living in poverty are likely to show gradual declines in intelligence test scores and to achieve poorly when they reach school age (Bradley et al., 2001; Gutman, Sameroff, & Cole, 2003). These problems are largely due to stressful home environments that undermine children's ability to learn and increase the likelihood that they will remain poor as adults (McLoyd, Aikens, & Burton, 2006). A variety of intervention programs have been developed to break this tragic cycle of poverty. Although most begin during the preschool years (we will discuss these in Chapter 9), a few start during infancy and continue through early childhood.

In center-based interventions, children attend an organized child-care or preschool program where they receive educational, nutritional, and health services and their parents receive child-rearing and other social service supports. In home-based interventions, a skilled adult visits the home and works with parents, providing social support and teaching them how to stimulate a very young child's development. In most programs of either type, participating children score higher than untreated controls on mental tests by age 2. The earlier intervention begins, the longer it lasts, and the greater its scope and intensity (for example, year-round high-quality child care plus generous support services for parents), the better participants' cognitive and academic performance is throughout childhood and adolescence (Brooks-Gunn, 2004; Ramey, Ramey, & Lanzi, 2006; Sweet & Appelbaum, 2004).

The Carolina Abecedarian Project illustrates these positive outcomes. In the 1970s, more than 100 infants from poverty-stricken families, ranging in age from 3 weeks to 3 months, were randomly assigned to either a treatment group or a control group. Treatment infants were enrolled in full-time, year-round child care through the preschool years. There they received

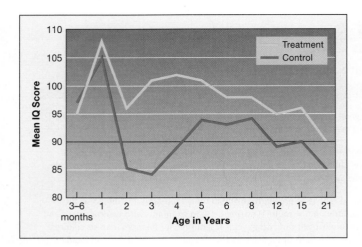

FIGURE 6.10

IQ scores of treatment and control children from infancy to 21 years in the Carolina Abecedarian Project. At 1 year, treatment children outperformed controls, an advantage consistently maintained through age 21. The IQ scores of both groups declined gradually during childhood and adolescence—a trend probably due to the damaging impact of poverty on mental development. *(Adapted from Campbell et al., 2001.)*

stimulation aimed at promoting motor, cognitive, language, and social skills and, after age 3, literacy and math concepts. Special emphasis was placed on rich, responsive adult–child verbal communication. All children received nutrition and health services; the primary difference between treatment and controls was the intensive child-care experience.

As Figure 6.10 shows, by 12 months of age, the IQs of the two groups diverged. Treatment children sustained their advantage until last tested—at age 21. In addition, throughout their years of schooling, treatment youths achieved considerably higher scores in reading and math. These gains translated into more years of schooling completed, higher rates of college enrollment and employment in skilled jobs, and lower rates of drug use and adolescent parenthood (Campbell et al., 2001, 2002; Ramey & Ramey, 1999).

Without early intervention, many children born into economically disadvantaged families will not reach their potential. Recognition of this reality led the U.S. Congress to provide limited funding for intervention services directed at infants and toddlers who already have serious developmental problems or who are at risk for problems because of poverty. Early Head Start, begun in 1995, currently has 700 sites serving 65,000 low-income families. It offers an array of coordinated services—child care, educational experiences for infants and toddlers, parenting education, family social support, and health care—delivered through a center-based, home-based, or mixed approach, depending on community needs. A recent evaluation, conducted when children reached age 3, showed that intervention led to warmer, more stimulating parenting, a reduction in harsh discipline, gains in cognitive and language development, and lessening of child aggression. The strongest effects occurred at sites offering a mix of center- and home-based services (Love et al., 2005; Love, Chazan-Cohen, & Raikes, 2007). Though not yet plentiful enough to meet the need, such programs are a promising beginning.

© MICHAEL NEWMAN/PHOTOEDIT

■ Interventions like Early Head Start show parents how to create a stimulating home environment for their young children. Here, mothers and toddlers gather for a session devoted to picture-book reading, an activity that promotes cognitive and language development. ■

ASK YOURSELF

◆ **REVIEW** What probably accounts for the finding that speed of habituation and recovery to visual stimuli predicts later IQ better than an infant mental test score?

◆ **APPLY** Fifteen-month-old Joey's developmental quotient (DQ) is 115. His mother wants to know exactly what this means and what she should do to support his mental development. How would you respond?

◆ **CONNECT** Using what you learned about brain development in Chapter 5, explain why it is best to initiate intervention for poverty-stricken children in the first two years rather than later.

◆ **REFLECT** Suppose you were seeking a child-care setting for your baby. What would you want it to be like, and why?

Language Development

Improvements in perception and cognition during infancy pave the way for an extraordinary human achievement—language. In Chapter 5, we saw that by the second half of the first year, infants make dramatic progress in distinguishing the basic sounds of their language and in segmenting the flow of speech into word and phrase units. They also start to comprehend some word meanings and, around 12 months of age, say their first word. Sometime between 1½ and 2 years, toddlers combine two words (Gleason, 2009). By age 6, children have a vocabulary of about 10,000 words, speak in elaborate sentences, and are skilled conversationalists.

To appreciate this awesome task, think about the many abilities involved in your own flexible use of language. When you speak, you must select words that match the underlying concepts you want to convey. To be understood, you must pronounce words correctly. Then you must combine them into phrases and sentences using a complex set of grammatical rules. Finally, you must follow the rules of everyday conversation—taking turns, making comments relevant to what your partner just said, and using an appropriate tone of voice.

How do infants and toddlers make such remarkable progress in launching these skills? To address this question, let's examine several prominent theories of language development.

■ Infants communicate from the very beginning of life, as seen in this interchange between a father and his baby. How will this child become a fluent speaker of his native language within just a few years? Theorists disagree sharply. ■

Three Theories of Language Development

In the 1950s, researchers did not take seriously the idea that very young children might be able to figure out important properties of language. As a result, the first two theories of how children acquire language were extreme views. One, *behaviorism*, regards language development as entirely due to environmental influences. The second, *nativism*, assumes that children are "prewired" to master the intricate rules of their language.

THE BEHAVIORIST PERSPECTIVE   Behaviorist B. F. Skinner (1957) proposed that language, like any other behavior, is acquired through *operant conditioning*. As the baby makes sounds, parents reinforce those that are most like words with smiles, hugs, and speech in return. For example, at 12 months, my older son, David, often babbled something like "book-a-book-a-dook-a-dook-a-book-a-nook-a-book-aaa." One day as he babbled away, I held up his picture book and said, "Book!" Soon David was saying "book-aaa" in the presence of books.

Some behaviorists believe that children rely on *imitation* to rapidly acquire complex utterances, such as whole phrases and sentences (Moerk, 2000). Imitation can combine with reinforcement to promote language, as when a parent coaxes, "Say 'I want a cookie,'" and delivers praise and a treat after the toddler responds, "Wanna cookie!"

Although reinforcement and imitation contribute to early language development, they are best viewed as supporting rather than fully explaining it. "It's amazing how creative Caitlin is with language," Carolyn remarked one day. "She combines words in ways she's never heard before, like 'needle it' when she wants me to sew up her teddy bear and 'allgone outside' when she has to come in."

Carolyn's observations are accurate: Young children create many novel utterances that are not reinforced by or copied from others. And when they do imitate others' language, they do so selectively, focusing mainly on building their vocabularies and on refining aspects of language that they are working on at the moment (Owens, 2008).

THE NATIVIST PERSPECTIVE   Linguist Noam Chomsky (1957) proposed a *nativist* account that regards the young child's amazing language skill as a uniquely human accomplishment, etched into the structure of the brain. Focusing on grammar, Chomsky reasoned that the rules for sentence organization are much too complex to be directly taught to or discovered by even a cognitively adept young child. Rather, he argued, all children have a **language acquisition device (LAD),** an innate system that contains a *universal grammar,* or set of rules common to all languages. It enables children, no matter which language they hear, to understand and speak in a rule-oriented fashion as soon as they pick up enough words. In sharp contrast to the behaviorist view, nativists regard deliberate training by parents as unnecessary (Pinker, 1999).

Are children biologically primed to acquire language? Recall from Chapter 4 that newborn babies are remarkably sensitive to speech sounds. And children everywhere reach major language milestones in a similar sequence (Gleitman & Newport, 1996). Also, the ability to master a grammatically complex language system seems to be unique to humans, as efforts to teach language to nonhuman primates—using either specially devised artificial symbol systems or American Sign Language (ASL), a gestural language used by the deaf—have met with limited success. Even after extensive training, chimpanzees (who are closest to humans in terms of evolution) master only a basic vocabulary and short word combinations, and they produce these far less consistently than human preschoolers (Tomasello, Call, & Hare, 2003).

Evidence for specialized language areas in the brain and a sensitive period for language development have also been interpreted as supporting Chomsky's theory. Let's take a closer look at these findings.

Language Areas in the Brain. Recall from Chapter 5 that for most individuals, language is housed in the left hemisphere of the cerebral cortex. Within it are two important language-related structures (see Figure 6.11). To clarify their functions, researchers have, for several decades, studied adults who experienced damage to these structures and display *aphasias,* or communication disorders. *Broca's area,* located in the left frontal lobe, supports grammatical processing and language production. *Wernicke's area,* located in the left temporal lobe, plays a role in comprehending word meaning.

But recent brain-imaging research suggests more complicated relationships between language functions and brain structures. The impaired pronunciation and grammar of patients with Broca's aphasia and the meaningless speech streams of patients with Wernicke's aphasia involve the spread of injury to nearby cortical areas and widespread abnormal activity in the left cerebral hemisphere, triggered by the brain damage (Bates et al., 2003; Keller et al., 2009). Contrary to long-held belief, then, Broca's and Wernicke's areas are not solely or even mainly responsible for specific language functions. Nevertheless, depending on the site of injury to the adult left hemisphere, language deficits do vary predictably. Damage to frontal-lobe areas usually yields language production problems, whereas damage to areas in the other lobes yields comprehension problems (Dick et al., 2004).

The broad association of language functions with left-hemispheric regions is consistent with Chomsky's notion of a brain prepared to process language. But critics point out that at birth, the brain is not fully lateralized; it is highly plastic. Language areas in the cerebral cortex *develop* as children acquire language (Mills & Conboy, 2005). Although the left hemisphere is biased for language processing, if it is injured in the first few years, other regions take over language functions, and most such children eventually attain normal language competence. Thus, left-hemispheric localization, though typical, is not necessary for effective language processing. Additional research reveals that many regions of the cerebral cortex participate in language activities to different degrees, depending on the language skill and the individual's mastery of that skill (Shafer & Garrido-Nag, 2007).

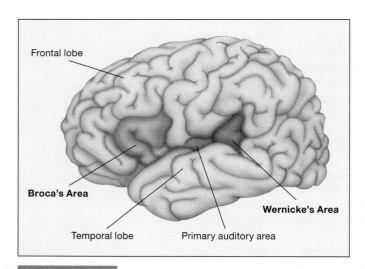

Frontal lobe

Broca's Area

Wernicke's Area

Temporal lobe   Primary auditory area

FIGURE 6.11

Broca's and Wernicke's areas, in the left hemisphere of the cerebral cortex. Broca's area, located in the frontal lobe, supports grammatical processing and language production. Wernicke's area, located in the temporal lobe, is involved in comprehending word meaning. Contrary to what was once believed, however, neither area is solely or even mainly responsible for these functions.

Nevertheless, when the young brain allocates language to the right hemisphere—as a result of left-hemispheric damage or learning of sign language (see page 169 in Chapter 5)—it localizes it in roughly the same regions that typically support language in the left hemisphere (Newman et al., 2002; Rosenberger et al., 2009). This suggests that those brain structures are uniquely disposed for language processing.

A Sensitive Period for Language Development. Must language be acquired early in life, during an age span in which the brain is particularly responsive to language stimulation? Evidence for a sensitive period that coincides with brain lateralization would support the view that language development has unique biological properties.

To test this idea, researchers have examined the language competence of deaf adults who acquired their first language—American Sign Language (ASL)—at different ages. The later learners, whose parents chose to educate them through the oral method, which relies on speech and lip-reading, did not acquire spoken language because of their profound deafness. And consistent with the sensitive-period notion, those who learned ASL in adolescence or adulthood never became as proficient as those who learned in childhood (Mayberry, 1994; Newport, 1991; Singleton & Newport, 2004). However, a precise age cutoff for a decline in first-language competence has not been established.

Is acquiring a second language also harder after a sensitive period has passed? In one study, researchers examined U.S. census data, selecting immigrants from non-English-speaking countries who had resided in the United States for at least ten years. The census form had asked the immigrants to rate how competently they spoke English, from "not at all" to "very well"—self-reports that correlate strongly with objective language measures. As age of immigration increased from infancy and early childhood into adulthood, English proficiency declined (Hakuta, Bialystok, & Wiley, 2003). Furthermore, ERP and fMRI measures of brain activity indicate that second-language processing is less lateralized in older than in younger learners (Neville & Bruer, 2001). But second-language competence does not drop sharply at a certain age. Rather, a continuous, age-related decrease occurs.

In sum, research on both first- and second-language learning reveals a biologically based timeframe for optimum language development. However, the boundaries of this sensitive period remain unclear.

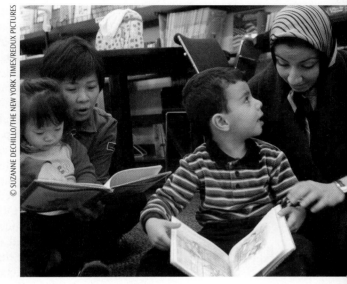

Immigrant mothers read English with their children as part of a literacy program at a library in Queens, New York. Although the capacity to learn a second language does not drop sharply at a certain age, childhood seems to be a sensitive period for optimum language development. As a result, these mothers may never become as proficient in English as their children. ■

LIMITATIONS OF THE NATIVIST PERSPECTIVE Chomsky's theory has had a major impact on current views of language development. It is now widely accepted that humans have a unique, biologically based capacity to acquire language. Still, Chomsky's account of development has been challenged on several grounds.

First, researchers have had great difficulty specifying Chomsky's universal grammar. A major problem is the absence of a complete description of these abstract grammatical structures or even an agreed-on list of how many exist or the best examples of them. Chomsky's critics doubt that one set of rules can account for the extraordinary variation in grammatical forms among the world's languages (Christiansen & Chater, 2008; Tomasello, 2003, 2005). How children manage to link such rules with the strings of words they hear is also unclear.

Second, Chomsky's assumption that grammatical knowledge is innately determined does not fit with certain observations of language development. Once children begin to use an innate grammatical structure, we would expect them to apply it to all relevant instances in their language. But children refine and generalize many grammatical forms gradually, engaging in much piecemeal learning and making errors along the way. For example, one 3-year-old, in grappling with prepositions, initially added *with t* to the verb *open* ("You open with scissors") but not to the word *hit* ("He hit me stick") (Tomasello, 2000, 2003, 2006). As we will see in Chapter 12, complete mastery of some grammatical forms, such as the passive voice, is not achieved until well into middle childhood (Tager-Flusberg & Zukowski, 2009). This suggests that more experimentation and learning are involved than Chomsky assumed.

THE INTERACTIONIST PERSPECTIVE Recent ideas about language development emphasize *interactions* between inner capacities and environmental influences. One type of interactionist theory applies the information-processing perspective to language development. A second type emphasizes social interaction.

Some information-processing theorists assume that children make sense of their complex language environments by applying powerful cognitive capacities of a general kind (Bates, 2004; Elman, 2001; Munakata, 2006; Saffran, 2009). These theorists note that regions of the brain housing language also govern similar perceptual, motor, and cognitive abilities. For example, damage to parts of the left hemisphere, including Wernicke's area, results in difficulty comprehending both language and other patterned stimuli, such as music and a series of moving lights that depict familiar shapes (Koelsch et al., 2002; Saygin et al., 2004).

Other theorists blend this information-processing view with Chomsky's nativist perspective. They agree that infants are amazing statistical analyzers of speech and other information (see Chapter 5). But, they argue, these capacities probably are not sufficient to account for mastery of higher-level aspects of language, such as intricate grammatical structures (Aslin & Newport, 2009; Newport & Aslin, 2000). They also point out that grammatical competence may depend more on specific brain structures than other components of language. When 2- to 2½-year-olds and adults listened to short sentences—some grammatically correct, others with phrase-structure violations—both groups showed similarly distinct ERP brain-wave patterns for each sentence type in the left frontal and temporal lobes of the cerebral cortex (Oberecker & Friederici, 2006; Oberecker, Friedrich, & Friederici, 2005). This suggests that 2-year-olds process sentence structures using the same neural system as adults do. Furthermore, in studies of older children and adults with left-hemispheric brain damage, grammar is more impaired than other language functions (Baynes & Gazzaniga, 1988; Stromswold, 2000).

Still other interactionists emphasize that children's social skills and language experiences are centrally involved in language development. In this social-interactionist view, an active child, well-endowed for making sense of language, strives to communicate. In doing so, she cues her caregivers to provide appropriate language experiences, which help her relate content and structure of language to its social meanings (Bohannon & Bonvillian, 2009; Chapman, 2000, 2006).

Among social interactionists, disagreement continues over whether or not children are equipped with specialized language structures (Lidz, 2007; Shatz, 2007; Tomasello, 2003, 2006). Nevertheless, as we chart the course of language development, we will encounter much support for their central premise—that children's social competencies and language experiences greatly affect their language progress. In reality, native endowment, cognitive-processing strategies, and social experience probably operate in different balances with respect to each aspect of language: pronunciation, vocabulary, grammar, and communication skills. Table 6.3 provides an overview of early language milestones that we will examine in the next few sections.

Getting Ready to Talk

Before babies say their first word, they make impressive progress toward understanding and speaking their native tongue. They listen attentively to human speech, and they make speechlike sounds. As adults, we can hardly help but respond.

COOING AND BABBLING Around 2 months, babies begin to make vowel-like noises, called **cooing** because of their pleasant "oo" quality. Gradually, consonants are added, and around 6 months **babbling** appears, in which infants repeat consonant–vowel combinations, often in long strings, such as "babababababa" or "nanananana."

Babies everywhere (even those who are deaf) start babbling at about the same age and produce a similar range of early sounds. But for babbling to develop further, infants must be able to hear human speech. In hearing-impaired babies, these speechlike sounds are greatly delayed. And a deaf infant not exposed to sign language will stop babbling entirely (Oller, 2000).

TABLE 6.3	Milestones of Language Development During the First Two Years

APPROXIMATE AGE	MILESTONE
2 months	Infants coo, making pleasant vowel sounds.
4 months on	Infants observe with interest as the caregiver plays turn-taking games, such as pat-a-cake and peekaboo.
6 months on	Infants babble, adding consonants to their cooing sounds and repeating syllables. By 7 months, babbling starts to include many sounds of spoken languages. Infants comprehend commonly heard words.
8–12 months	Infants become more accurate at establishing joint attention with the caregiver, who often verbally labels what the baby is looking at. Infants actively participate in turn-taking games, trading roles with the caregiver. Infants use preverbal gestures, such as showing and pointing, to influence others' goals and behavior and to convey information.
12 months	Babbling includes sound and intonation patterns of the child's language community. Speed and accuracy of word comprehension increase rapidly. Toddlers say their first recognizable word.
18–24 months	Spoken vocabulary expands from about 50 to 200 words. Toddlers combine two words.

In one case, a deaf-born 5-month-old received a *cochlear implant*—an electronic device surgically inserted into the ear that converts external sounds into a signal to stimulate the auditory nerve. She showed typical babbling in infancy and resembled her hearing agemates in language development at 3 to 4 years (Schauwers et al., 2004). But if auditory input is not restored until after age 2 (the usual time for cochlear implant surgery), children remain behind in language development. And if implantation occurs after age 4, language delays are severe and persistent (Govaerts et al., 2002; Svirsky, Teoh, & Neuburger, 2004). These outcomes suggest an early sensitive period for the brain to develop the necessary organization for normal speech processing.

TAKE A MOMENT... When a baby coos or babbles and gazes at you, how do you respond? One day, as I stood in line at the post office behind a mother and her 7-month-old, the baby babbled, and three adults—myself and two people standing beside me—started to talk to the infant. We cooed and babbled in return, and we also said things like "Oooo, really?" "My, you're a big girl! Out to help Mommy mail letters today?" The baby smiled and babbled all the more. As infants listen to spoken language, babbling increases. Around 7 months, it starts to include many sounds of spoken languages. And as caregivers respond contingently to infant babbles, older infants modify their babbling to include sound patterns like those in the adult's speech (Goldstein & Schwade, 2008). By 8 to 10 months, babbling reflects the sound and intonation patterns of children's language community, some of which are transferred to their first words (Boysson-Bardies & Vihman, 1991).

Deaf infants exposed to sign language from birth babble with their hands much as hearing infants do through speech (Petitto & Marentette, 1991). Furthermore, hearing babies of deaf, signing parents produce babblelike hand motions with the rhythmic patterns of natural sign languages (Petitto et al., 2001, 2004). This sensitivity to language rhythm, evident not just in perception of speech but also in babbling, whether spoken or signed, supports both discovery and production of meaningful language units.

BECOMING A COMMUNICATOR   At birth, infants are prepared for some aspects of conversational behavior. For example, they initiate interaction through eye contact and terminate it by looking away. By 3 to 4 months, infants start to gaze in the same general direction adults are looking—a skill that becomes more accurate at 10 to 11 months, as babies realize that others' focus offers information about their communicative intentions (to talk about an object) or other goals (to obtain an object) (Brooks & Meltzoff, 2005; Senju, Csibra, & Johnson, 2008).

© S. FELD/ROBERTSTOCK

■ This baby uses a preverbal gesture to draw his father's attention to the birdhouse. His father's verbal response promotes the baby's transition to spoken language. ■

LOOK AND LISTEN

Observe a toddler for 30 to 60 minutes at home or child care. Jot down preverbal gestures, words, and word–gesture combinations that the baby produces. Do the toddler's language skills fit with research findings?

Indeed, 12-month-olds look where an adult is looking only when the adult's eyes are open. And 12- to 14-month olds are more likely to engage in gaze following when no obstacles block an adult's line of sight to an object (Brooks & Meltzoff, 2002; Dunphy-Lelii & Wellman, 2004). Around their first birthday, infants realize that a person's visual gaze signals a vital connection between the viewer and his or her surroundings, and they want to participate.

This **joint attention,** in which the child attends to the same object or event as the caregiver, who often labels it, contributes greatly to early language development. Infants and toddlers who often engage in it sustain attention longer, comprehend more language, produce meaningful gestures and words earlier, and show faster vocabulary development through 2 years of age (Brooks & Meltzoff, 2008; Carpenter, Nagel, & Tomasello, 1998; Flom & Pick, 2003; Silvén, 2001). Gains in joint attention at the end of the first year enable babies to establish a "common ground" with the adult, through which they can figure out the meaning of the adult's verbal labels (Tomasello, 2003).

Between 4 and 6 months, interactions between caregivers and babies begin to include *give-and-take,* as in pat-a-cake and peekaboo games. At first, the parent starts the game and the baby is an amused observer. But even 4-month-olds are sensitive to the structure and timing of these interactions, smiling more to an organized than to a disorganized peekaboo exchange (Rochat, Querido, & Striano, 1999). By 12 months, babies participate actively, trading roles with the caregiver. As they do so, they practice the turn-taking pattern of human conversation, a vital context for acquiring language and communication skills. Infants' play maturity and vocalizations during games predict advanced language progress in the second year (Rome-Flanders & Cronk, 1995).

At the end of the first year, infants use *preverbal gestures* to direct adults' attention, to influence their behavior, and to convey helpful information (Tomasello, Carpenter, & Liszkowski, 2007). For example, Caitlin held up a toy to show it, pointed to the cupboard when she wanted a cookie, and pointed at her mother's car keys lying on the floor. Carolyn responded to these gestures and also labeled them ("That's your bear!" "You want a cookie!" "Oh, there are my keys!"). In this way, toddlers learn that using language leads to desired results. Like gaze following, infant pointing predicts faster vocabulary development over the second year (Brooks & Meltzoff, 2008).

Besides using preverbal gestures to serve their own goals, 12-month-olds adapt these gestures to the needs of others. In one study, they pointed more often to an object whose location a searching adult did not know than to an object whose location the adult did know (Liszkowski, Carpenter, & Tomasello, 2008). Already, the cooperative processes essential for effective communication—modifying messages to suit others' intentions and knowledge—are under way. Soon toddlers integrate words with gestures, using the gesture to expand their verbal message, as in pointing to a toy while saying "give" (Capirci et al., 2005). Gradually, gestures recede, and words become dominant. But the earlier toddlers form word–gesture combinations, the sooner they produce two-word utterances at the end of the second year (Goldin-Meadow & Butcher, 2003).

First Words

In the second half of the first year, infants begin to understand word meanings. When 6-month-olds listened to the words "Mommy" or "Daddy" while looking at side-by-side videos of their parents, they looked longer at the video of the named parent (Tincoff & Jusczyk, 1999). At 9 months, after hearing a word paired with an object, babies looked longer at other objects in the same category than at those in a different category (Balaban & Waxman, 1997).

First spoken words, around 1 year, build on the sensorimotor foundations Piaget described and on categories infants have formed. In a study tracking the first 10 words used by several hundred U.S. and Chinese (both Mandarin- and Cantonese-speaking) babies, common objects ("ball," "bread"), important people ("Mama," "Dada"), and sound effects ("woof-woof," "vroom") were mentioned most often. Action words ("hit," "grab," "hug") and social routines ("hi," "bye"), though also appearing in all three groups, were more often produced by

Chinese than U.S. babies—differences we will consider shortly (Tardif et al., 2008). Other investigations concur that earliest words usually include people, objects that move, foods, animals (in families with pets), familiar actions, outcomes of such actions ("hot," "wet"), and social terms (Hart, 2004; Nelson, 1973). In their first 50 words, toddlers rarely name things that just *sit there*, like "table" or "vase."

When young children first learn words, they sometimes apply them too narrowly, an error called **underextension.** At 16 months, Caitlin used "bear" only to refer to the worn and tattered teddy bear she carried nearly constantly. As vocabulary expands, a more common error is **overextension**—applying a word to a wider collection of objects and events than is appropriate. For example, Grace used "car" for buses, trains, trucks, and fire engines. Toddlers' overextensions reflect their sensitivity to categories (MacWhinney, 2005). They apply a new word to a group of similar experiences: "car" to wheeled objects, "open" to opening a door, peeling fruit, and untying shoelaces. This suggests that children often overextend deliberately because they have difficulty recalling or have not acquired a suitable word. And when a word is hard to pronounce, toddlers are likely to substitute a related one they can say (Bloom, 2000). As vocabulary and pronunciation improve, overextensions disappear.

The Two-Word Utterance Phase

Young toddlers add to their spoken vocabularies at a rate of one to three words a week. Because gains in word production between 18 and 24 months are so impressive (one or two words per day), many researchers concluded that toddlers undergo a *spurt in vocabulary*—a transition from a slower to a faster learning phase. But recent evidence indicates that most children show a steady, continuous increase in rate of word learning that extends through the preschool years (Ganger & Brent, 2004).

How do toddlers build their vocabularies so quickly? Over the second year, they improve in ability to categorize experience, recall words, and grasp others' social cues to meaning, such as eye gaze, pointing, and handling objects (Dapretto & Bjork, 2000; Golinkoff & Hirsh-Pasek, 2006; Liszkowski, Carpenter, & Tomasello, 2007). Furthermore, as toddlers' experiences broaden, they have a wider range of interesting objects and events to label. For example, children approaching age 2 more often mention places to go ("park," "store"). And as they construct a clearer self-image, they add more words that refer to themselves ("me," "mine," "Katy") and to their own and others' bodies and clothing ("eyes," "mouth," "jacket" (Hart, 2004). In Chapter 9, we will consider young children's specific strategies for word learning.

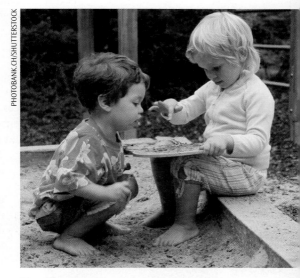

■ Toddlers typically utter their first word around 1 year. As their experiences broaden, they label more objects and events, first with single words and then with two-word utterances known as telegraphic speech. ■

Once toddlers produce about 200 words, they start to combine two words: "Mommy shoe," "go car," "more cookie." These two-word utterances are called **telegraphic speech** because, like a telegram, they focus on high-content words, omitting smaller, less important ones ("can," "the," "to"). Children the world over use them to express an impressive variety of meanings.

Two-word speech consists largely of simple formulas ("more + X," "eat + X"), with different words inserted in the "X" position. Toddlers rarely make gross grammatical errors, such as saying "chair my" instead of "my chair." But their word-order regularities are usually copies of adult word pairings, as when Carolyn remarked to Caitlin, "How about *more sandwich?*" or "Let's see if you can *eat the berries?*" (Tomasello, 2003; Tomasello & Brandt, 2009). When 18- to 23-month-olds were taught noun and verb nonsense words (for example, "meek" for a doll and "gop" for a snapping action), they easily combined the new nouns with words they knew well ("more meek"). But they seldom formed word combinations with the new verbs (Tomasello, 2000; Tomasello et al., 1997). This suggests that they did not yet grasp subject–verb and verb–object relations, which are the foundation of grammar.

In sum, toddlers are absorbed in figuring out word meanings and using their limited vocabularies in whatever way possible to get their thoughts across. They first acquire "concrete pieces of language," gradually generalizing from those pieces to construct the word-order and other grammatical rules of their native tongue (Tomasello, 2006). As we will see in Chapter 7, they make steady progress over the preschool years.

Comprehension versus Production

So far, we have focused on language **production**—the words and word combinations children use. What about **comprehension**—the language they understand? At all ages, comprehension develops ahead of production. A five-month lag exists between the time toddlers comprehend 50 words (around 13 months) and the time they produce that many (around 18 months) (Menyuk, Liebergott, & Schultz, 1995).

Think back to the distinction made earlier in this chapter between two types of memory—recognition and recall. Comprehension requires only that children *recognize* the meaning of a word. But for production, children must *recall*, or actively retrieve from their memories, not only the word but also the concept for which it stands. Still, the two capacities are related. The speed and accuracy of toddlers' comprehension of spoken language increase dramatically over the second year. And toddlers who are faster and more accurate in comprehension tend to show more rapid growth in words understood and produced as they approach age 2 (Fernald, Perfors, & Marchman, 2006). Quick comprehension frees space in working memory for picking up new words and for the more demanding task of using them to communicate.

Individual and Cultural Differences

Although, on average, children produce their first word around their first birthday, the range is large, from 8 to 18 months—variation due to a complex blend of genetic and environmental influences. Earlier we saw that Timmy's spoken language was delayed, in part because of Vanessa's tense, directive communication with him. But Timmy is also a boy, and many studies show that girls are slightly ahead of boys in early vocabulary growth (Fenson et al., 1994). The most common explanation is girls' faster rate of physical maturation, which is believed to promote earlier development of the left cerebral hemisphere.

Temperament matters, too. Shy toddlers often wait until they understand a great deal before trying to speak. Once they do speak, their vocabularies increase rapidly, although they remain slightly behind their agemates (Spere et al., 2004). Temperamentally negative toddlers also acquire language more slowly because their high emotional reactivity diverts them from processing linguistic information (Salley & Dixon, 2007).

The surrounding environment also plays a role: The more words caregivers use, the more children learn (Weizman & Snow, 2001). Mothers talk much more to toddler-age girls than to boys, and parents converse less often with shy than with sociable children (Leaper, Anderson, & Sanders, 1998; Patterson & Fisher, 2002). Low-SES children, who receive less verbal stimulation in their homes than higher-SES children, usually have smaller vocabularies (Hoff, 2006). Limited parent–child book reading is a major factor. On average, a middle-SES child is read to for 1,000 hours between 1 and 5 years, a low-SES child for only 25 hours (Neuman, 2003). As a result, low-SES kindergartners have vocabularies only one-fourth as large as those of their higher-SES agemates (Lee & Burkam, 2002).

Young children have distinct styles of early language learning. Caitlin and Grace, like most toddlers, used a **referential style;** their vocabularies consisted mainly of words that referred to objects. A smaller number of toddlers use an **expressive style;** compared to referential children, they produce many more social formulas and pronouns ("thank you," "done," "I want it") uttered as compressed phrases that sound like single words ("Iwannit"). These styles reflect early ideas about the functions of language. Grace, for example, thought words were for naming things. In the week after her adoption, she uttered only a single word in Khmer, her native language. But after two months of listening to English conversation, Grace added words quickly: "Eli," then "doggie," "kitty," "Mama," "Dada," "book," "ball," "car," "cup," "clock," and "chicken"—all within one week. In contrast, expressive-style children believe words are for talking about people's feelings and needs. The vocabularies of referential-style toddlers grow faster because all languages contain many more object labels than social terms (Bates et al., 1994).

■ This Chinese mother's communication with her toddler probably includes many words for actions and social routines. Her child—like other Chinese children—is likely to display an expressive style, focused on strengthening social relationships. ■

© TINA MANLEY/ASIA/ALAMY

What accounts for a toddler's language style? Rapidly developing referential-style children often have an especially active interest in exploring objects. They also eagerly imitate their parents' frequent naming of objects, and their parents imitate back—a strategy that supports swift vocabulary growth by helping children remember new labels (Masur & Rodemaker, 1999). Expressive-style children tend to be highly sociable, and their parents more often use verbal routines ("How are you?" "It's no trouble") that support social relationships (Goldfield, 1987).

The two language styles are also linked to culture. Object words (nouns) are particularly common in the vocabularies of English-speaking toddlers, but Chinese, Japanese, and Korean toddlers have more words for actions (verbs) and social routines. When mothers' speech is examined in each culture, it reflects this difference (Choi & Gopnik, 1995; Fernald & Morikawa, 1993; Tardif, Gelman, & Xu, 1999). American mothers frequently label objects when interacting with their babies. Asian mothers, perhaps because of a cultural emphasis on the importance of group membership, emphasize actions and social routines as soon as their babies begin to speak.

At what point should parents become concerned if their child talks very little or not at all? If a toddler's development is greatly delayed when compared with the norms in Table 6.3, then parents should consult the child's doctor or a speech and language therapist. Late babbling may be a sign of slow language development that can be prevented with early intervention (Fasolo, Majorano, & D'Odorico, 2008). Some toddlers who do not follow simple directions or who, after age 2, have difficulty putting their thoughts into words may suffer from a hearing impairment or a language disorder that requires immediate treatment.

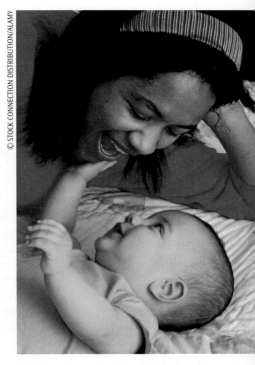

■ This mother speaks to her baby in short, clearly pronounced sentences with high-pitched, exaggerated intonation. This form of communication, called child-directed speech, eases language learning for infants and toddlers. ■

Supporting Early Language Development

Consistent with the interactionist view, a rich social environment builds on young children's natural readiness to speak their native tongue. For a summary of how caregivers can consciously support early language learning, see Applying What We Know below. Caregivers also do so unconsciously—through a special style of speech.

Adults in many countries speak to young children in **child-directed speech (CDS),** a form of communication made up of short sentences with high-pitched, exaggerated expression, clear pronunciation, distinct pauses between speech segments, clear gestures to support verbal meaning, and repetition of new words in a variety of contexts ("See the ball." "The ball bounced!") (Fernald et al., 1989; O'Neill et al., 2005). Deaf parents use a similar style of communication when signing to their deaf babies (Masataka, 1996). From birth on, infants prefer CDS over other kinds of adult talk, and by 5 months they are more emotionally responsive to it (Aslin, Jusczyk, & Pisoni, 1998).

◆ Applying What We Know

Supporting Early Language Learning

STRATEGY	CONSEQUENCE
Respond to coos and babbles with speech sounds and words.	Encourages experimentation with sounds that can later be blended into first words
	Provides experience with the turn-taking pattern of human conversation
Establish joint attention and comment on what child sees.	Predicts earlier onset of language and faster vocabulary development
Play social games, such as pat-a-cake and peekaboo.	Provides experience with the turn-taking pattern of human conversation
Engage toddlers in joint make-believe play.	Promotes all aspects of conversational dialogue
Engage toddlers in frequent conversations.	Predicts faster early language development and academic success during the school years
Read to toddlers often, engaging them in dialogues about picture books.	Provides exposure to many aspects of language, including vocabulary, grammar, communication skills, and information about written symbols and story structures

CDS builds on several communicative strategies we have already considered: joint attention, turn-taking, and caregivers' sensitivity to toddlers' preverbal gestures. Here is an example of Carolyn using CDS with 18-month-old Caitlin as she picks her up from child care:

Caitlin: "Go car."
Carolyn: "Yes, time to go in the car. Where's your jacket?"
Caitlin: [looks around, walks to the closet] "Dacket!" [*Points to her jacket.*]
Carolyn: "There's that jacket! [*She helps Caitlin into the jacket.*] On it goes! Let's zip up. [*Zips up the jacket.*] Now, say bye-bye to Grace and Timmy."
Caitlin: "Bye-bye, G-ace. Bye-bye, Te-te."
Carolyn: "Where's your bear?"
Caitlin: [*Looks around.*]
Carolyn: [*Pointing*] "See? By the sofa." [*Caitlin gets the bear.*]

LOOK AND LISTEN

While observing a parent and toddler playing, describe how the parent adapts his or her language to the child's needs. Did the parent use child-directed speech?

Notice how Carolyn kept her utterance length just ahead of Caitlin's, creating a sensitive match between language stimulation and Caitlin's current capacities. Parents constantly fine-tune the length and content of their utterances in CDS to fit children's needs—adjustments that enable toddlers to join in and that foster both language comprehension and production (Cameron-Faulkner, Lieven, & Tomasello, 2003; Rowe, 2008). As the Social Issues: Education box on the following page makes clear, when a child's disability makes it difficult for parents to engage in the sensitive communication of CDS, language and cognitive development are drastically delayed.

As we saw earlier, parent–toddler conversation strongly predicts language development and later academic success. It provides many examples of speech just ahead of the child's current level and a sympathetic environment in which children can try out new skills. Dialogues about picture books are particularly effective. They expose children to great breadth of language and literacy knowledge, from vocabulary, grammar, and communication skills to information about written symbols and story structures. From the end of the first year through early childhood, children who experience regular adult–child book reading are substantially ahead of their agemates in language skills (Karrass & Braungart-Rieker, 2005; Whitehurst & Lonigan, 1998).

Do social experiences that promote language development remind you of those that strengthen cognitive development in general? CDS and parent–child conversation create a *zone of proximal development* in which children's language expands. In contrast, impatience with and rejection of children's efforts to talk lead them to stop trying and result in immature language skills (Baumwell, Tamis-LeMonda, & Bornstein, 1997; Cabrera, Shannon, & Tamis-LeMonda, 2007). In the next chapter, we will see that sensitivity to children's needs and capacities supports their emotional and social development as well.

ASK YOURSELF

◆ REVIEW Why is the social-interactionist perspective attractive to many investigators of language development? Cite evidence that supports it.

◆ APPLY Fran frequently corrects her 17-month-old son Jeremy's attempts to talk and—fearing that he won't use words—refuses to respond to his gestures. How might Fran be contributing to Jeremy's slow language progress?

◆ CONNECT Cognition and language are interrelated. List examples of how cognition fosters language development. Next, list examples of how language fosters cognitive development.

◆ REFLECT Find an opportunity to speak to an infant or toddler. How did your manner of speaking differ from the way you typically speak to an adult? What features of your speech are likely to promote early language development, and why?

SOCIAL ISSUES: EDUCATION

Parent–Child Interaction: Impact on Language and Cognitive Development of Deaf Children

About 2 to 3 out of every 1,000 American infants is born profoundly or fully deaf (Deafness Research Foundation, 2010). When a deaf child cannot participate fully in communication with caregivers, development is severely compromised. Yet the consequences of deafness for children's language and cognition vary with social context, as comparisons of deaf children of hearing parents with deaf children of deaf parents reveal.

Over 90 percent of deaf children have hearing parents who are not fluent in sign language. In toddlerhood and early childhood, these children often are delayed in development of language and make-believe play. In middle childhood, many achieve poorly in school, are deficient in social skills, and display impulse-control problems (Arnold, 1999; Edmondson, 2006). Yet deaf children of deaf parents escape these difficulties! Their language (use of sign) and play maturity are on a par with hearing children's. After school entry, deaf children of deaf parents learn easily and get along well with adults and peers (Bornstein et al., 1999b; Spencer & Lederberg, 1997).

These differences can be traced to early parent–child communication. Beginning in infancy, hearing parents of deaf children are less positive, less responsive to their child's efforts to communicate, less effective at achieving joint attention and turn-taking, less involved in play, and more directive and intrusive (Spencer, 2000;

Spencer & Meadow-Orlans, 1996). In contrast, the quality of interaction between deaf children and deaf parents resembles that of hearing children and hearing parents.

Hearing parents are not to blame for their deaf child's problems. Rather, they lack experience with visual communication, which enables deaf parents to respond readily to a deaf child's needs. Deaf parents know they must wait for the child to turn toward them before interacting (Loots & Devise, 2003). Hearing parents tend to speak or gesture while the child's attention is directed elsewhere—a strategy that works with a hearing but not with a deaf partner. When the child is confused or unresponsive, hearing parents often feel overwhelmed and become overly controlling (Jamieson, 1995).

The impact of deafness on language and cognitive development can best be understood by considering how it affects parents and other significant people in the child's life. Deaf children need access to language models—deaf adults and peers—to experience natural language learning. And their hearing parents benefit from social support along with training in how to interact sensitively with a nonhearing partner.

Screening techniques can identify deaf babies at birth. Many U.S. states and an increasing number of Western nations require that every newborn be tested, enabling immediate enrollment in programs aimed at fostering

effective parent–child interaction. When children with profound hearing loss start to receive intervention within the first year of life, they show much better language, cognitive, and social development (Vohr et al., 2008; Yoshinaga-Itano, 2003).

© CHRISTINA KENNEDY/PHOTOEDIT

■ As this mother signs words to her toddler, who is deaf, the child responds with babblelike hand motions, similar to the vocal babbling of hearing infants. Babbling, whether spoken or signed, supports production of meaningful language. ■

Summary

Piaget's Cognitive-Developmental Theory

According to Piaget, how do schemes change over the course of development?

■ By acting directly on the environment, children move through four stages in which psychological structures, or **schemes,** achieve a better fit with external reality.

■ Schemes change in two ways: through **adaptation,** which is made up of two complementary activities—**assimilation** and **accommodation;** and through **organization,** the internal rearrangement of schemes into a strongly interconnected cognitive system.

Describe the major cognitive achievements of the sensorimotor stage.

■ In the **sensorimotor stage,** the **circular reaction** provides a means of adapting first schemes, and the newborn baby's reflexes gradually transform into the more flexible action patterns of the older infant. Around 8 months, infants develop **intentional,** or **goal-directed, behavior** and begin to understand **object permanence.**

■ Twelve- to 18-month-olds engage in more deliberate, varied exploration and no longer make the **A-not-B search error.** Between 18 and 24 months, **mental representation** is evident in sudden solutions to sensorimotor problems, mastery of object-permanence problems involving invisible displacement, **deferred imitation,** and **make-believe play.**

What does follow-up research say about the accuracy of Piaget's sensorimotor stage?

■ Many studies suggest that infants display a variety of understandings earlier than Piaget believed. Some awareness of object permanence, as revealed by the **violation-of-expectation method** and object-tracking research, may be evident in the first few months, although searching for hidden objects is a true cognitive advance, as Piaget suggested.

■ Furthermore, young infants display deferred imitation, and by 10 to 12 months, they engage in analogical problem solving—attainments that that require mental representation. Toddlers even imitate rationally, by inferring others' intentions.

■ A major advance in symbolic understanding, occurring around the first birthday, is **displaced reference**—the realization that words can be used to cue mental images of things not physically present. The capacity to use language to modify mental representations improves from the end of the second into the third year. By the middle of the second year, toddlers treat realistic-looking pictures symbolically. At about 2½ years, children grasp the symbolic meaning of video.

■ Today, researchers believe that newborns have more built-in equipment for making sense of their world than Piaget assumed, although they disagree on how much initial understanding infants have. According to the **core knowledge perspective,** infants are born with core domains of thought that support rapid cognitive development.

■ Although findings on early, ready-made knowledge are mixed, broad agreement exists on two issues. First, many cognitive changes of infancy are continuous rather than stagelike. Second, various aspects of cognition develop unevenly, rather than in an integrated fashion.

Information Processing

Describe the information-processing view of cognitive development and the general structure of the information- processing system.

■ Information-processing researchers want to know precisely what individuals of different ages do when faced with a task or problem. Most assume that we hold information in three parts of the mental system: the **sensory register; working,** or **short-term, memory;** and **long-term memory.** As information flows through the system, **mental strategies** operate on it so that it can be retained and used efficiently. To manage the complex activities of working memory, the **central executive** directs the flow of information.

What changes in attention, memory, and categorization take place over the first two years?

■ With age, infants attend to more aspects of the environment, take information in more quickly, anticipate future events, and flexibly shift their attention from one stimulus to another. In the second year, attention to novelty declines and sustained attention improves, especially during play with toys.

■ Young infants are capable of **recognition** memory. By the middle of the first year, they also engage in **recall** and can even retain modeled behaviors in the order in which they occurred. Both recognition and recall improve steadily with age.

■ Infants group stimuli into increasingly complex categories, shifting from categorical distinctions based on similar overall appearance to ones based on subtle sets of features. In the second year, toddlers begin to categorize flexibly, switching their basis of object sorting, and their grasp of the animate–inanimate distinction expands. Babies' exploration of objects, expanding knowledge of the world, and advancing language skills foster categorization.

Describe the contributions and limitations of the information-processing approach to our understanding of early cognitive development.

■ Information-processing findings challenge Piaget's view of infants as purely sensorimotor beings who cannot mentally represent experiences. But information processing has not yet provided a broad, comprehensive theory of children's thinking.

The Social Context of Early Cognitive Development

How does Vygotsky's concept of the zone of proximal development expand our understanding of early cognitive development?

■ Vygotsky believed that children master tasks within the **zone of proximal development**—ones just ahead of their current capacities—through the support and guidance of more skilled partners. As early as the first year, cultural variations in social experiences affect mental strategies.

Individual Differences in Early Mental Development

Describe the mental testing approach, the meaning of intelligence test scores, and the extent to which infant tests predict later performance.

■ The mental testing approach measures intellectual development in an effort to predict future performance. Scores are arrived at by computing an **intelligence quotient,** or **IQ,** which compares an individual's performance with that of a **standardization** sample of same-age individuals, whose performances form a **normal distribution.**

■ Infant tests, which consist largely of perceptual and motor responses, predict later intelligence poorly. As a result, scores on infant tests are called **developmental quotients,** or **DQs,** rather than IQs. Speed of habituation and recovery to visual stimuli and object permanence are better predictors of future performance.

Discuss environmental influences on early mental development, including home, child care, and early intervention for at-risk infants and toddlers.

■ Research with the **Home Observation for Measurement of the Environment (HOME)** shows that an organized, stimulating home environment and parental affection, involvement, and encouragement of new skills repeatedly predict higher mental test scores. Although the HOME–IQ relationship is partly due to heredity, family living conditions also affect mental development.

- Quality of infant and toddler child care influences cognitive, language, and social skills. Standards for **developmentally appropriate practice** specify program characteristics that meet young children's developmental needs.

- Intensive early intervention beginning in infancy and extending through early childhood can prevent the gradual declines in intelligence and the poor academic performance evident in many poverty-stricken children.

Language Development

Describe three theories of language development, and indicate the emphasis each places on innate abilities and environmental influences.

- According to the *behaviorist* perspective, parents train children in language skills through operant conditioning and imitation. Behaviorism has difficulty accounting for children's novel utterances.

- In contrast, Chomsky's *nativist* theory regards children as naturally endowed with a **language acquisition device (LAD).** Consistent with this perspective, a complex language system is unique to humans.

- Although language-related structures—Broca's and Wernicke's areas—exist in the left hemisphere of the cerebral cortex, their roles are more complex than previously assumed. But the broad association of language functions with left-hemispheric regions is consistent with Chomsky's notion of a brain prepared to process language. Evidence for a sensitive period for language development also supports this view.

- Difficulty specifying the universal grammar that underlies the vast diversity among languages challenges the nativist perspective. Children's gradual, piecemeal learning of many constructions is also inconsistent with Chomsky's theory.

- Recent theories suggest that language development results from *interactions* between inner capacities and environmental influences. Some interactionists apply the information-processing perspective to language development. Others emphasize the importance of children's social skills and language experiences.

Describe major milestones of language development in the first two years, individual differences, and ways adults can support infants' and toddlers' emerging capacities.

- Infants begin **cooing** at 2 months and **babbling** around 6 months. At 10 to 11 months, babies' skill at establishing **joint attention** improves, and by 12 months they actively engage in turn-taking games and use preverbal gestures. Adults can encourage language progress by responding to infants' coos and babbles, playing turn-taking games, establishing joint attention and labeling what babies see, and responding verbally to their preverbal gestures.

- Around 12 months, toddlers say their first word. Young children often make errors of **underextension** and **overextension.** Rate of word learning increases steadily, and once vocabulary reaches about 200 words, two-word utterances called **telegraphic speech** appear. At all ages, language **comprehension** develops ahead of **production.**

- Individual differences in early language development exist. Girls show faster progress than boys, and reserved, cautious toddlers may wait before trying to speak. Low-SES children, who receive less verbal stimulation than higher- SES children, usually have smaller vocabularies.

- Most toddlers use a **referential style** of language learning, in which early words consist largely of names for objects. A few use an **expressive style,** in which social formulas and pronouns are common and vocabulary grows more slowly.

- Adults in many cultures speak to young children in **child-directed speech (CDS),** a simplified form of language that is well-suited to their learning needs. Parent–toddler conversation is one of the best predictors of early language development and academic competence during the school years.

IMPORTANT TERMS AND CONCEPTS

accommodation (p. 204)
adaptation (p. 204)
A-not-B search error (p. 207)
assimilation (p. 204)
autobiographical memory (p. 221)
babbling (p. 236)
central executive (p. 218)
child-directed speech (CDS) (p. 241)
circular reaction (p. 205)
comprehension (p. 240)
cooing (p. 236)
core knowledge perspective (p. 214)
deferred imitation (p. 207)
developmentally appropriate
    practice (p. 230)
developmental quotient (DQ) (p. 228)

displaced reference (p. 211)
expressive style (p. 240)
Home Observation for Measurement of the
    Environment (HOME) (p. 229)
infantile amnesia (p. 221)
intelligence quotient (IQ) (p. 227)
intentional, or goal-directed, behavior
    (p. 206)
joint attention (p. 238)
language acquisition device (LAD) (p. 234)
long-term memory (p. 218)
make-believe play (p. 207)
mental representation (p. 207)
mental strategies (p. 217)
normal distribution (p. 228)
object permanence (p. 207)

organization (p. 205)
overextension (p. 239)
production (p. 240)
recall (p. 220)
recognition (p. 220)
referential style (p. 240)
scheme (p. 204)
sensorimotor stage (p. 204)
sensory register (p. 217)
standardization (p. 227)
telegraphic speech (p. 239)
underextension (p. 239)
video deficit effect (p. 213)
violation-of-expectation method (p. 208)
working, or short-term, memory (p. 217)
zone of proximal development (p. 224)

"Our Baby Sister"
Marna
Age 13, Kentucky

A mother provides a soft, intimate shelter, protecting the baby from danger while supporting her mastery of the environment. Chapter 7 considers the importance of parental love and sensitivity for infants' and toddlers' feelings of security and competence.

Reprinted with permission from the International Collection of Child Art, Milner Library, Illinois State University, Normal, Illinois

Emotional and Social Development in Infancy and Toddlerhood

As Caitlin reached 8 months of age, her parents noticed that she had become more fearful. One evening, when Carolyn and David left her with a babysitter, she wailed as they headed for the door—an experience she had accepted easily a few weeks earlier. Caitlin and Timmy's caregiver Ginette also observed an increasing wariness of strangers. When she turned to go to another room, both babies dropped their play to crawl after her. At the mail carrier's knock at the door, they clung to Ginette's legs, reaching out to be picked up.

At the same time, each baby seemed more willful. Removing an object from the hand produced little response at 5 months. But at 8 months, when Timmy's mother, Vanessa, took away a table knife he had managed to reach, Timmy burst into angry screams and could not be consoled or distracted.

All Monica and Kevin knew about Grace's first year was that she had been deeply loved by her destitute, homeless mother. Separation from her, followed by a long journey to an unfamiliar home, had left Grace in shock. At first she was extremely sad, turning away when Monica or Kevin picked her up. She did not smile for over a week. But as Grace's new parents held her close, spoke gently, and satisfied her craving for food, Grace returned their affection. Two weeks after her arrival, her despondency gave way to a sunny, easygoing disposition. She burst into a wide grin, reached out at the sight of Monica and Kevin, and laughed at her brother Eli's funny faces. Among her first words were the names of family members—"Eli," "Mama," and "Dada." As her second birthday approached, she pointed to herself, exclaiming "Gwace!" and laid claim to treasured possessions. "Gwace's chicken!" she would announce at mealtimes, sucking the marrow from the drumstick, a practice she had brought with her from Cambodia.

Taken together, the children's reactions reflect two related aspects of personality that develop during the first two years: close ties to others and a sense of self.

We begin with Erikson's psychosocial theory, which provides an overview of personality development during infancy and toddlerhood. Then, as we chart the course of emotional development, we will discover why fear and anger became more apparent in Caitlin's and Timmy's range of emotions by the end of the first year. Our attention then turns to individual differences in temperament. We will examine biological and environmental contributions to these differences and their consequences for future development.

Next, we take up attachment to the caregiver, the child's first affectionate tie. We will see how the feelings of security that grow out of this important bond support the child's exploration, sense of independence, and expanding social relationships.

Finally, we focus on early self-development. By the end of toddlerhood, Grace recognized herself in mirrors and photographs, labeled herself as a girl, and showed the beginnings of self-control. "Don't touch!" she instructed herself one day as she resisted the desire to pull a lamp cord out of its socket. Cognitive advances combine with social experiences to produce these changes during the second year.

Erikson's Theory of Infant and Toddler Personality

Our discussion of major theories in Chapter 1 revealed that psychoanalytic theory is no longer in the mainstream of child development research. But one of its lasting contributions is its ability to capture the essence of personality development during each period of development. Recall that Sigmund Freud, founder of the psychoanalytic movement, believed that psychological health and maladjustment could be traced to the early years—in particular, to the child's relationships with parents. Although Freud's preoccupation with the channeling of biological drives and his neglect of important experiences beyond infancy and early childhood came to be heavily criticized, the basic outlines of his theory were accepted and elaborated in several subsequent theories. The most influential is Erik Erikson's *psychosocial theory,* also introduced in Chapter 1.

Basic Trust versus Mistrust

Erikson accepted Freud's emphasis on the importance of the parent–infant relationship during feeding, but he expanded and enriched Freud's view. A healthy outcome during infancy, Erikson believed, does not depend on the *amount* of food or oral stimulation offered but rather on the *quality* of caregiving: relieving discomfort promptly and sensitively, holding the infant gently, waiting patiently until the baby has had enough milk, and weaning when the infant shows less interest in breast or bottle.

Erikson recognized that no parent can be perfectly in tune with the baby's needs. Many factors affect parental responsiveness—feelings of personal happiness, current life conditions (for example, additional young children in the family), and culturally valued child-rearing practices. But when the *balance of care* is sympathetic and loving, the psychological conflict of the first year—**basic trust versus mistrust**—is resolved on the positive side. The trusting infant expects the world to be good and gratifying. As a result, he feels confident about venturing out and exploring it, and he emerges from this stage well-prepared for the challenges of toddlerhood. The mistrustful baby cannot count on the kindness and compassion of others, so she protects herself by withdrawing from people and things around her.

Autonomy versus Shame and Doubt

With the transition to toddlerhood, Freud viewed the parent's manner of toilet training as decisive for psychological health. In Erikson's view, toilet training is only one of many influential experiences. The familiar refrains of newly walking, talking toddlers—"No!" "Do it myself!"—reveal that they have entered a new period of budding selfhood. They want to decide for themselves, not just in toileting but also in other situations. The conflict of toddlerhood, **autonomy versus shame and doubt,** is resolved favorably when parents provide young children with suitable guidance and reasonable choices. A self-confident, secure 2-year-old has parents who do not criticize or attack him when he fails at new skills—using the toilet, eating with a spoon, or putting away toys. And they meet his assertions of independence with tolerance and understanding—for example, by giving him an extra five minutes to finish his play before leaving for the grocery store. In contrast, when parents are over- or undercontrolling, the outcome is a child who feels forced and shamed and who doubts his ability to control his impulses and act competently on his own.

In sum, basic trust and autonomy grow out of warm, sensitive parenting and reasonable expectations for impulse control starting in the second year. If children emerge from the first few years without sufficient trust in caregivers and without a healthy sense of individuality, the seeds are sown for adjustment problems. Adults who have difficulty establishing intimate ties, who are overly dependent on a loved one, or who continually doubt their own ability to meet new challenges may not have fully mastered the tasks of trust and autonomy during infancy and toddlerhood.

■ Toddlers who are given appropriate opportunities to try new skills without criticism develop a sense of autonomy—a feeling of being able to act competently on their own. ■

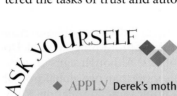

◆ APPLY Derek's mother fed him in a warm and loving manner during the first year. But when he became a toddler, she kept him in a playpen for many hours because he got into too much mischief while exploring freely. Use Erikson's theory to evaluate Derek's early experiences.

◆ CONNECT Do Erikson's recommendations for fostering autonomy in toddlerhood fit with Vygotsky's concept of the zone of proximal development, described on page 224 in Chapter 6? Explain.

■ ■ Emotional Development

TAKE A MOMENT... Observe several infants and toddlers, noting the emotions each displays, the cues you rely on to interpret the baby's emotional state, and how caregivers respond. Researchers have conducted many such observations to find out how babies convey their emotions and interpret those of others. They have discovered that emotions play powerful roles in organizing the attainments that Erikson regarded as so important: social relationships, exploration of the environment, and discovery of the self (Halle, 2003; Saarni et al., 2006).

Think back to the *dynamic systems perspective* introduced in Chapters 1 and 5. As you read about early emotional development in the sections that follow, notice how emotions are an integral part of young children's dynamic systems of action. Emotions energize development. At the same time, they are an aspect of the system that develops, becoming more varied and complex as children reorganize their behavior to attain new goals (Campos, Frankel, & Camras, 2004; Witherington, Campos, & Hertenstein, 2001).

Because infants cannot describe their feelings, determining exactly which emotions they are experiencing is a challenge. Although vocalizations and body movements provide some information, facial expressions offer the most reliable cues. Cross-cultural evidence reveals that people around the world associate photographs of different facial expressions with emotions in the same way (Ekman, 2003; Ekman & Friesen, 1972). These findings inspired researchers to analyze infants' facial patterns to determine the range of emotions they display at different ages.

Nevertheless, assuming a close correspondence between a pattern of behavior and an underlying emotional state can lead to error. Infants, children, and adults use diverse responses to express a particular emotion. For example, babies on the visual cliff (see page 192 in Chapter 5) generally do not display a fearful facial expression, though they do show other signs of fear—drawing back and refusing to crawl over the deep side. Recall, also, from Chapter 5 that the emotional expressions of blind babies, who cannot make eye contact, are muted, prompting parents to withdraw (see page 194). When therapists show parents how blind infants express emotions through finger movements, parents become more interactive (Saarni et al., 2006; Fraiberg, 1971). Furthermore, the same general response can express several emotions. Depending on the situation, a smile might convey joy, embarrassment, contempt, or a social greeting.

In line with the dynamic systems view, emotional expressions vary with the person's developing capacities, goals, and context. To infer babies' emotions more accurately, researchers must attend to multiple interacting expressive cues—vocal, facial, and gestural—and see how they vary across situations believed to elicit different emotions (Lewis, 2000, 2008). With these ideas in mind, let's chart the course of early emotional development.

Development of Basic Emotions

Basic emotions—happiness, interest, surprise, fear, anger, sadness, and disgust—are universal in humans and other primates and have a long evolutionary history of promoting survival. Do infants come into the world with the ability to express basic emotions? Although signs of some emotions are present, babies' earliest emotional life consists of little more than two global arousal states: attraction to pleasant stimulation and withdrawal from unpleasant stimulation. Only gradually do emotions become clear, well-organized signals (Camras et al., 2003; Fox, 1991).

The dynamic systems perspective helps us understand how this happens: Children coordinate separate skills into more effective, emotionally expressive systems as the central nervous system develops and the child's goals and experiences change. Videotaping the facial expressions of her daughter from 6 to 14 weeks, Linda Camras (1992) found that in the early weeks, the baby displayed a fleeting angry face as she was about to cry and a sad face as her crying waned. These expressions first appeared on the way to or away from full-blown distress and were not clearly linked to the baby's experiences and desires. With age, she was better able to sustain an angry signal when she encountered a blocked goal and a sad signal when she could not overcome an obstacle.

According to one view, sensitive, contingent caregiver communication, in which parents selectively mirror aspects of the baby's diffuse emotional behavior, helps infants construct emotional expressions that more closely resemble those of adults (Gergely & Watson, 1999). Around 6 months, face, gaze, voice, and posture form organized patterns that vary meaningfully with environmental events. For example, Caitlin typically responded to her parents' playful interaction with a joyful face, pleasant babbling, and a relaxed posture, as if to say, "This is fun!" In contrast, an unresponsive parent often evokes a sad face, fussy sounds, and a drooping body (sending the message, "I'm despondent") or an angry face, crying, and "pick-me-up" gestures (as if to say, "Change this unpleasant event!") (Weinberg & Tronick, 1994; Yale et al., 1999). By the middle of the first year, emotional expressions are well-organized and specific—and therefore able to tell us a great deal about the infant's internal state.

We will begin by looking at four basic emotions—happiness, anger, sadness, and fear—that have received the most research attention. Later in the chapter, we will examine other emotions that develop in the first two years.

HAPPINESS Happiness—expressed first in blissful smiles, later through exuberant laughter—contributes to many aspects of development. When infants achieve new skills, they smile and laugh, displaying delight in motor and cognitive mastery. As the smile encourages caregivers to be affectionate and stimulating, the baby smiles even more (Aksan & Kochanska, 2004). Happiness binds parent and baby into a warm, supportive relationship that fosters the infant's developing competencies.

During the early weeks, newborn babies smile when full, during REM sleep, and in response to gentle touches and sounds, such as stroking of the skin, rocking, and the mother's soft, high-pitched voice. By the end of the first month, infants smile at dynamic, eye-catching sights, such as a bright object jumping suddenly across their field of vision. And as infants attend to the parent's face, and the parent talks and smiles, babies knit their brows, open their mouths to coo, and move their arms and legs excitedly, gradually becoming more emotionally positive until, between 6 and 10 weeks, the parent's communication evokes a broad grin called the **social smile** (Lavelli & Fogel, 2005; Sroufe & Waters, 1976). These changes parallel the development of infant perceptual capacities—in particular, sensitivity to visual patterns, including the human face (see Chapter 5). And social smiling becomes better-organized and stable as babies learn to use it to evoke and sustain pleasurable face-to-face interaction with the parent.

Laughter, which appears around 3 to 4 months, reflects faster processing of information than smiling. But, as with smiling, the first laughs occur in response to very active stimuli, such as the parent saying playfully, "I'm gonna get you!" and kissing the baby's tummy. As infants understand more about their world, they laugh at events with subtler elements of surprise, such as a silent game of peekaboo (Sroufe & Wunsch, 1972).

■ This baby's laughter encourages his mother to respond in kind, binding them together in a warm, affectionate relationship that promotes all aspects of development. ■

Around the middle of the first year, babies smile and laugh more often when interacting with familiar people, a preference that strengthens the parent–child bond. Between 8 and 10 months, infants more often interrupt their play with an interesting toy to relay their delight to an attentive adult (Venezia et al., 2004). And like adults, 10- to 12-month-olds have several smiles, which vary with context—a broad, "cheek-raised" smile in response to a parent's greeting; a reserved, muted smile for a friendly stranger; and a "mouth-open" smile during stimulating play (Bolzani et al., 2002; Dickson, Fogel, & Messinger, 1998). By the end of the first year, the smile has become a deliberate social signal.

ANGER AND SADNESS Newborn babies respond with generalized distress to a variety of unpleasant experiences, including hunger, painful medical procedures, changes in body temperature, and too much or too little stimulation (see Chapter 4). From 4 to 6 months into the second year, angry expressions increase in frequency and intensity. Older infants react with anger in a wider range of situations—when an object is taken away, an expected pleasant event does not occur, their arms are restrained, the caregiver leaves for a brief time, or they are put down for a nap (Camras et al., 1992; Stenberg & Campos, 1990; Sullivan & Lewis, 2003).

Why do angry reactions increase with age? As infants become capable of intentional behavior (see Chapter 6), they want to control their own actions and the effects they produce. They are also more persistent about obtaining desired objects (Mascolo & Fischer, 2007). Furthermore, older infants are better at identifying who caused them pain or removed a toy. Their anger is particularly intense when a caregiver from whom they have come to expect warm behavior causes discomfort. The rise in anger is also adaptive. New motor capacities enable an angry infant to defend herself or overcome an obstacle (Izard & Ackerman, 2000). Finally, anger motivates caregivers to relieve the infant's distress and, in the case of separation, may discourage them from leaving again soon.

Although expressions of sadness also occur in response to pain, removal of an object, and brief separations, they are less common than anger. In contrast, sadness occurs often when infants are deprived of a familiar, loving caregiver (as illustrated by Grace's despondency in the weeks after her adoption) and when parent–infant interaction is seriously disrupted. In several studies, researchers had parents assume either a still-faced, unreactive pose or a depressed emotional state. Their 2- to 7-month-olds tried facial expressions, vocalizations, and body

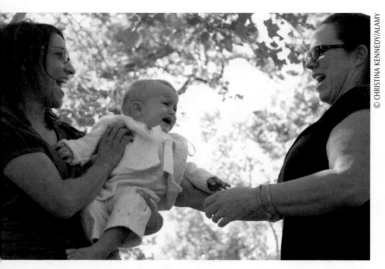

When an unfamiliar adult attempts to hold her, this 8-month-old makes it clear that she prefers her mother! Fear rises during the second half of the first year. Its most frequent expression is stranger anxiety. ■

movements to get their mother or father to respond again. When these efforts failed, they turned away, frowned, and cried (Moore, Cohn, & Campbell, 2001; Papoušek, 2007). The still-face reaction is identical among American, Canadian, and Chinese babies, suggesting that it is a built-in withdrawal response to caregivers' lack of communication (Kisilevsky et al., 1998). Return to Chapter 4, page 155, and note that infants of depressed parents respond this way. When allowed to persist, a sad, vacant outlook disrupts all aspects of early development.

FEAR　Like anger, fear rises during the second half of the first year. Older infants hesitate before playing with a new toy, and newly crawling infants soon back away from heights (see Chapter 5). But the most frequent expression of fear is to unfamiliar adults, a response called **stranger anxiety.** Many infants and toddlers are quite wary of strangers, although the reaction does not always occur. It depends on several factors: temperament (some babies are generally more fearful), past experiences with strangers, and the current situation. When an unfamiliar adult picks up the infant in a new situation, stranger anxiety is likely. But if the adult sits still while the baby moves around and a parent is nearby, infants often show positive and curious behavior (Horner, 1980). The stranger's style of interaction—expressing warmth, holding out an attractive toy, playing a familiar game, and approaching slowly rather than abruptly—reduces the baby's fear.

Cross-cultural research reveals that infant-rearing practices can modify stranger anxiety. Among the Efe hunters and gatherers of the Republic of Congo, where the maternal death rate is high, infant survival is safeguarded by a collective caregiving system in which, starting at birth, Efe babies are passed from one adult to another. Consequently, Efe infants show little stranger anxiety (Tronick, Morelli, & Ivey, 1992). In contrast, among infants in Israeli kibbutzim (cooperative agricultural settlements), who live in isolated communities vulnerable to terrorist attacks, wariness of strangers is widespread. By the end of the first year, when infants look to others for cues about how to respond emotionally, kibbutz babies display far greater stranger anxiety than their city-reared counterparts (Saarni et al., 2006).

The rise in fear after 6 months of age keeps newly mobile babies' enthusiasm for exploration in check. Once wariness develops, infants use the familiar caregiver as a **secure base,** or point from which to explore, venturing into the environment and then returning for emotional support. As part of this adaptive system, encounters with strangers lead to two conflicting tendencies: approach (indicated by interest and friendliness) and avoidance (indicated by fear). The infant's behavior is a balance between the two.

As cognitive development permits toddlers to discriminate more effectively between threatening and nonthreatening people and situations, stranger anxiety and other fears of the first two years decline. Fear also wanes as children acquire a wider array of strategies for coping with it, as you will see when we discuss emotional self-regulation.

LOOK AND LISTEN

❖❖

While observing an 8- to 18-month-old with his or her parent, gently approach the baby, offering a toy. Does the baby respond with stranger anxiety? To better understand the baby's behavior, ask the parent to describe his or her temperament and past experiences with strangers.

Understanding and Responding to the Emotions of Others

Infants' emotional expressions are closely tied to their ability to interpret the emotional cues of others. We have seen that in the first few months, babies match the feeling tone of the caregiver in face-to-face communication. Some researchers claim that young babies respond in kind to others' emotions through a built-in, automatic process of *emotional contagion* (Stern, 1985). Others, however, believe that infants acquire these emotional contingencies through operant conditioning—for example, learning that a smile generally triggers caregiver responsiveness and that distress prompts a comforting response (Saarni et al., 2006).

Around 3 to 4 months, infants become sensitive to the structure and timing of face-to-face interactions (see Chapter 6, page 238). When they gaze, smile, or vocalize, they now expect their social partner to respond in kind, and they reply with positive vocal and emotional reactions (Markova & Legerstee, 2006; Rochat, Striano, & Blatt, 2002). Within these exchanges, babies become increasingly aware of the range of emotional expressions (Montague & Walker-Andrews, 2001). According to some researchers, out of this early imitative communication, infants start to view others as "like me"—an awareness believed to lay the foundation for understanding others' thoughts and feelings (Gergeley & Watson, 1996; Meltzoff, 2007).

By 4 to 5 months, infants distinguish positive from negative emotion in voices, and soon after, they do so in facial expressions (see Chapter 5). Gradually, they become better at matching specific facial and vocal displays of emotion. By 7 months, they look longer at an appropriate face–voice pairing (such as a happy face with a happy voice) than at an inappropriate one (a happy face with an angry voice) (de Haan & Matheson, 2009). Responding to emotional expressions as organized wholes suggests that these signals are becoming meaningful to babies. Between 7 and 12 months, ERPs recorded while babies attend to facial expressions reveal reorganized brain-wave patterns resembling those of adults, suggesting enhanced processing of emotional cues (Grossmann, Striano, & Friederici, 2007). As skill at establishing joint attention improves (see Chapter 6), infants realize that an emotional expression not only has meaning but is also a meaningful reaction to a specific object or event (Moses et al., 2001; Tomasello, 1999).

Once these understandings are in place, infants engage in **social referencing**—actively seeking emotional information from a trusted person in an uncertain situation (Mumme et al., 2007). Many studies show that a caregiver's emotional expression (happy, angry, or fearful) influences whether a 1-year-old will be wary of strangers, play with an unfamiliar toy, or cross the deep side of the visual cliff (Repacholi, 1998; Stenberg, 2003; Striano & Rochat, 2000). The adult's voice—either alone or combined with a facial expression—is more effective than a facial expression alone (Vaish & Striano, 2004). The voice conveys both emotional and verbal information, and the baby need not turn toward the adult but, instead, can focus on evaluating the novel event.

As recall memory and language skills improve, and as parents' warnings to their newly walking youngsters become more frequent and intense, babies retain these emotional messages over longer time intervals. At 11 months, they respond appropriately after a delay of a few minutes, at 14 months after a delay of an hour or more (Hertenstein & Campos, 2004). By the middle of the second year, social referencing expands to include indirect emotional signals. After observing an adult react angrily to a second adult's play with a toy, 18-month-olds increased their monitoring of the angry adult's facial expression and reduced their touching of the object (Repacholi & Meltzoff, 2007).

As toddlers begin to appreciate that others' emotional reactions may differ from their own, social referencing allows them to compare their own and others' assessments of events. In one study, an adult showed 14- and 18-month-olds broccoli and crackers. In one condition, she acted delighted with the taste of broccoli but disgusted with the taste of crackers. In the other condition, she showed the reverse preference. When asked to share the food, 14-month-olds offered only the type of food they themselves preferred—usually crackers. In contrast, 18-month-olds gave the adult whichever food she appeared to like, regardless of their own preferences (Repacholi & Gopnik, 1997).

In sum, in social referencing, toddlers move beyond simply reacting to others' emotional messages. They use those signals to evaluate the safety and security of their surroundings, to guide their own actions, and to gather information about others' intentions and preferences. These experiences, along with cognitive and language development, probably help toddlers refine the meanings of emotions of the same valence—for example, happiness versus surprise, anger versus fear—during the second year (Gendler, Witherington, & Edwards, 2008; Saarni et al., 2006).

Emergence of Self-Conscious Emotions

Besides basic emotions, humans are capable of a second, higher-order set of feelings, including guilt, shame, embarrassment, envy, and pride. These are called **self-conscious emotions** because each involves injury to or enhancement of our sense of self. We feel guilt when we

> ### LOOK AND LISTEN
>
> ❖❖
>
> Observe a toddler and parent at a playground, park, or shopping mall, noting circumstances that trigger social referencing. How does the parent convey emotional information? How does the toddler respond?

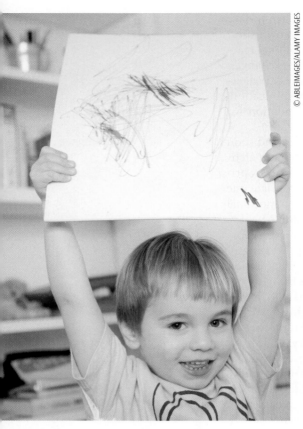

© ABLEIMAGES/ALAMY IMAGES

■ This 2-year-old proudly displays his artistic accomplishment. Pride and other self-conscious emotions appear in the middle of the second year as children become firmly aware of the self as a separate, unique individual. ■

know that we have harmed someone and want to correct the wrongdoing. When we are ashamed or embarrassed, we have negative feelings about our behavior, and we want to retreat so others will no longer notice our failings. In contrast, pride reflects delight in the self's achievements, and we are inclined to tell others what we have accomplished and to take on further challenges (Saarni et al., 2006).

Self-conscious emotions appear in the middle of the second year, as 18- to 24-month-olds become firmly aware of the self as a separate, unique individual. Toddlers show shame and embarrassment by lowering their eyes, hanging their heads, and hiding their faces with their hands. They show guilt-like reactions, too. After noticing Grace's unhappiness, 22-month-old Caitlin returned a toy she had grabbed and patted her upset playmate. Pride also emerges around this time, and envy by age 3 (Barrett, 2005; Garner, 2003; Lewis et al., 1989).

Besides self-awareness, self-conscious emotions require an additional ingredient: adult instruction in *when* to feel proud, ashamed, or guilty. Parents begin this tutoring early when they say, "Look how far you can throw that ball!" or "You should feel ashamed for grabbing that toy!" Self-conscious emotions play important roles in children's achievement-related and moral behaviors. The situations in which adults encourage these feelings vary from culture to culture. In Western individualistic nations, most children are taught to feel pride over personal achievement—throwing a ball the farthest, winning a game, and (later on) getting good grades. In collectivist cultures such as China and Japan, calling attention to individual success evokes embarrassment and self-effacement. And violating cultural standards by failing to show concern for others—a parent, a teacher, or an employer—sparks intense shame (Akimoto & Sanbinmatsu, 1999; Lewis, 1992).

Beginnings of Emotional Self-Regulation

Besides expressing a wider range of emotions, infants and toddlers begin to manage their emotional experiences. **Emotional self-regulation** refers to the strategies we use to adjust our emotional state to a comfortable level of intensity so we can accomplish our goals (Eisenberg & Spinrad, 2004; Thompson & Goodvin, 2007). When you remind yourself that an anxiety-provoking event will be over soon, suppress your anger at a friend's behavior, or decide not to see a scary horror film, you are engaging in emotional self-regulation.

Emotional self-regulation requires voluntary, effortful management of emotions. This capacity for *effortful control* improves gradually, as the result of development of the prefrontal cortex and the assistance of caregivers, who help children manage intense emotion and teach them strategies for doing so (Fox & Calkins, 2003; Rothbart, Posner, & Kieras, 2006). Individual differences in control of emotion are evident in infancy and, by early childhood, play such a vital role in children's adjustment that—as we will see later—effortful control is regarded as a major dimension of temperament. A good start in regulating emotion during the first two years contributes greatly to autonomy and mastery of cognitive and social skills. Poorly regulated toddlers, by contrast, are likely to be delayed in mental development and to have behavior problems in the preschool years and are at risk for long-lasting problems (Eisenberg et al., 2004b; Lawson & Ruff, 2004).

In the early months, infants have only a limited capacity to regulate their emotional states. When their feelings get too intense, they are easily overwhelmed. They depend on the soothing interventions of caregivers for distraction and reorienting of attention—being lifted to the shoulder, rocked, gently stroked, and talked to softly.

More effective functioning of the prefrontal cortex increases the baby's tolerance for stimulation. Between 2 and 4 months, caregivers build on this capacity by initiating face-to-face play and attention to objects. In these interactions, parents arouse pleasure in the baby while adjusting the pace of their own behavior so the infant does not become overwhelmed and distressed. As a result, the baby's tolerance for stimulation increases further (Kopp & Neufeld, 2003).

By 4 to 6 months, the ability to shift attention and to engage in self-soothing helps infants control emotion. Babies who more readily turn away from unpleasant events or engage in self-soothing are less prone to distress (Crockenberg & Leerkes, 2003a). At the end of the first year, crawling and walking enable infants to regulate emotion more effectively by approaching or retreating from various situations. And further gains in attention permit toddlers to sustain interest in their surroundings and in play activities for a longer time (Rothbart & Bates, 2006).

As caregivers help infants regulate their emotional states, they contribute to the child's style of emotional self-regulation. Infants whose parents "read" and respond contingently and sympathetically to their emotional cues tend to be less fussy, to express more pleasurable emotion, to be more interested in exploration, and to be easier to soothe (Crockenberg & Leerkes, 2004; Volling et al., 2002). In contrast, parents who respond impatiently or angrily or who wait to intervene until the infant has become extremely agitated reinforce the baby's rapid rise to intense distress. This makes it harder for parents to soothe the baby in the future—and for the baby to learn to calm herself. When caregivers fail to regulate stressful experiences for infants who cannot yet regulate them for themselves, brain structures that buffer stress may fail to develop properly, resulting in an anxious, reactive child who has a reduced capacity for regulating emotion (Crockenberg & Leerkes, 2000; Feldman, 2007b; Little & Carter, 2005).

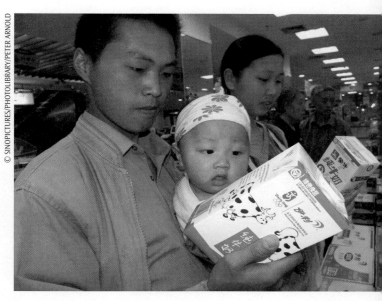

■ Chinese and Japanese adults discourage the expression of strong emotion in infants. This baby's calm demeanor is typical of Chinese infants, who tend to smile and cry less than American babies. ■

Caregivers also provide lessons in socially approved ways of expressing feelings. Beginning in the first few months, parents encourage infants to suppress negative emotion by imitating their expressions of interest, happiness, and surprise more often than their expressions of anger and sadness. Boys get more of this training than infant girls, in part because boys have a harder time regulating negative emotion (Else-Quest et al., 2006; Malatesta et al., 1986). As a result, the well-known sex difference—females as emotionally expressive and males as emotionally controlled—is promoted at a tender age. Collectivist cultures place particular emphasis on socially appropriate emotional behavior. Compared with North Americans, Japanese and Chinese adults discourage the expression of strong emotion in babies (Fogel, 1993; Kuchner, 1989). By the end of the first year, Chinese and Japanese infants smile and cry less than American babies (Camras et al., 1998).

In the second year, growth in representation and language leads to new ways of regulating emotions. A vocabulary for talking about feelings—"happy," "love," "surprised," "scary," "yucky," "mad"—develops rapidly after 18 months, but toddlers are not yet good at using language to manage their emotions. Temper tantrums tend to occur because toddlers cannot control the intense anger that often arises when an adult rejects their demands, particularly when they are fatigued or hungry (Mascolo & Fischer, 2007). Toddlers whose parents are emotionally sympathetic but set limits (by not giving in to tantrums), who distract the child by offering acceptable alternatives, and who later suggest better ways to handle adult refusals display more effective anger-regulation strategies and social skills during the preschool years (Lecuyer & Houck, 2006).

Patient, sensitive parents also encourage toddlers to describe their internal states. Then, when 2-year-olds feel distressed, they can guide caregivers in helping them (Cole, Armstrong, & Pemberton, 2010). For example, while listening to a story about monsters, Grace whimpered, "Mommy, scary." Monica put the book down and gave Grace a comforting hug.

Older toddlers' use of words to label emotions shows that they have a remarkable understanding of themselves and others as emotional beings. The more parents label and talk about mental states in the second year, the greater their 2-year-olds' emotion vocabulary and ability to identify how others feel from situational cues—for example, a cartoon of a child being chased by a lion (Taumoepeau & Ruffman, 2006). As we will see in later chapters, with the ability to think about feelings, emotional self-regulation improves greatly in early and middle childhood.

ASK YOURSELF

◆ REVIEW Why do many infants show stranger anxiety in the second half of the first year? What factors can increase or decrease wariness of strangers?

◆ APPLY At 14 months, Reggie built a block tower and gleefully knocked it down. But at age 2, he called to his mother and pointed proudly at his tall block tower. What explains this change in Reggie's emotional behavior?

◆ CONNECT Why do children of depressed parents have difficulty regulating emotion (see page 155 in Chapter 4)? What implications do their weak self-regulatory skills have for their response to cognitive and social challenges?

◆ REFLECT How do you typically manage negative emotion? Describe several recent examples. How might your early experiences, gender, and cultural background have influenced your style of emotional self-regulation?

Temperament and Development

From early infancy, Caitlin's sociability was unmistakable. She smiled and laughed while interacting with adults and, in her second year, readily approached other children. Meanwhile, Monica marveled at Grace's calm, relaxed disposition. At 19 months, she sat contentedly in a highchair through a two-hour family celebration at a restaurant. In contrast, Timmy was active and distractible. Vanessa found herself chasing him as he dropped one toy, moved on to the next, and climbed on chairs and tables.

When we describe one person as cheerful and "upbeat," another as active and energetic, and still others as calm, cautious, or prone to angry outbursts, we are referring to **temperament**— early-appearing, stable individual differences in reactivity and self-regulation. *Reactivity* refers to quickness and intensity of emotional arousal, attention, and motor activity. *Self-regulation,* as we have seen, refers to strategies that modify that reactivity (Rothbart & Bates, 2006). The psychological traits that make up temperament are believed to form the cornerstone of the adult personality.

In 1956, Alexander Thomas and Stella Chess initiated the New York Longitudinal Study, a groundbreaking investigation of the development of temperament that followed 141 children from early infancy well into adulthood. Results showed that temperament can increase a child's chances of experiencing psychological problems or, alternatively, protect a child from the negative effects of a highly stressful home life. At the same time, Thomas and Chess (1977) discovered that parenting practices can modify children's emotional styles considerably.

These findings stimulated a growing body of research on temperament, including its stability, biological roots, and interaction with child-rearing experiences. Let's begin to explore these issues by looking at the structure, or makeup, of temperament and how it is measured.

The Structure of Temperament

Thomas and Chess's model of temperament inspired all others that followed. When detailed descriptions of infants' and children's behavior obtained from parental interviews were rated on nine dimensions of temperament, certain characteristics clustered together, yielding three types of children:

- The **easy child** (40 percent of the sample) quickly establishes regular routines in infancy, is generally cheerful, and adapts easily to new experiences.
- The **difficult child** (10 percent of the sample) is irregular in daily routines, is slow to accept new experiences, and tends to react negatively and intensely.

■ The **slow-to-warm-up child** (15 percent of the sample) is inactive, shows mild, low-key reactions to environmental stimuli, is negative in mood, and adjusts slowly to new experiences.

Note that 35 percent of the children did not fit any of these categories. Instead, they showed unique blends of temperamental characteristics.

The "difficult" pattern has sparked the most interest because it places children at high risk for adjustment problems—both anxious withdrawal and aggressive behavior in early and middle childhood (Bates, Wachs, & Emde, 1994; Ramos et al., 2005; Thomas, Chess, & Birch, 1968). Compared with difficult children, slow-to-warm-up children present fewer problems in the early years. However, they tend to show excessive fearfulness and slow, constricted behavior in the late preschool and school years, when they are expected to respond actively and quickly in classrooms and peer groups (Chess & Thomas, 1984; Schmitz et al., 1999).

Today, the most influential model of temperament is Mary Rothbart's, described in Table 7.1. It combines related traits proposed by Thomas and Chess and other researchers, yielding a concise list of just six dimensions. For example, distractibility and persistence are considered opposite ends of the same dimension, which is labeled "attention span/persistence." A unique feature of Rothbart's model is inclusion of both "fearful distress" and "irritable distress," which distinguish between reactivity triggered by fear and reactivity due to frustration. And the model deletes overly broad dimensions such as regularity of body functions and intensity of reaction (Rothbart, Ahadi, & Evans, 2000; Rothbart & Mauro, 1990). A child who is regular in sleeping is not necessarily regular in eating or bowel habits. And a child who smiles and laughs intensely is not necessarily intense in fear, irritability, or motor activity.

Rothbart's dimensions represent the three underlying components included in the definition of temperament: (1) emotion ("fearful distress," "irritable distress," "positive affect," and "soothability"), (2) attention ("attention span/persistence"), and (3) action ("activity level"). According to Rothbart, individuals differ not just in their reactivity on each dimension but also in the self-regulatory dimension of temperament, **effortful control**—the capacity to

© FELICIA MARTINEZ/PHOTOEDIT

■ Despite his older brother's comforting offer of a stuffed animal, this toddler reacts with distress to a new situation. Patient, supportive parenting can help him modify his biologically based temperament and better manage his reactivity. ■

TABLE 7.1   Rothbart's Model of Temperament

DIMENSION	DESCRIPTION
REACTIVITY	
Activity level	Level of gross-motor activity
Attention span/persistence	Duration of orienting or interest
Fearful distress	Wariness and distress in response to intense or novel stimuli, including time to adjust to new situations
Irritable distress	Extent of fussing, crying, and distress when desires are frustrated
Positive affect	Frequency of expression of happiness and pleasure
SELF-REGULATION	
Effortful control	Capacity to voluntarily suppress a dominant, reactive response in order to plan and execute a more adaptive response

voluntarily suppress a dominant response in order to plan and execute a more adaptive response (Rothbart, 2003; Rothbart & Bates, 2006). Variations in effortful control are evident in how effectively a child can focus and shift attention, inhibit impulses, and manage negative emotion. Beginning in early childhood, capacity for effortful control predicts favorable development and adjustment in cultures as diverse as China and the United States (Zhou, Lengua, & Wang, 2009). Positive outcomes include persistence, task mastery, academic achievement, cooperation, moral maturity (such as concern about wrongdoing and willingness to apologize), and positive social behaviors of sharing and helpfulness (Eisenberg, 2010; Harris et al., 2007; Kochanska & Aksan, 2006; Posner & Rothbart, 2007b).

Measuring Temperament

Temperament is often assessed through interviews or questionnaires given to parents. Behavior ratings by pediatricians, teachers, and others familiar with the child and laboratory observations by researchers have also been used. Parental reports are convenient and take advantage of parents' depth of knowledge about their child across many situations (Gartstein & Rothbart, 2003). Although information from parents has been criticized as being biased, parental reports are moderately related to researchers' observations of children's behavior (Majdandžić & van den Boom, 2007; Mangelsdorf, Schoppe, & Buur, 2000). And parent perceptions are vital for understanding how parents view and respond to their child.

Observations by researchers in the home or laboratory avoid the subjectivity of parent reports but can lead to other inaccuracies. In homes, observers find it hard to capture all relevant information, especially events that are rare but important, such as infants' response to frustration. And in the unfamiliar lab setting, fearful children who calmly avoid certain experiences at home may become too upset to complete the session (Wachs & Bates, 2001). Still, researchers can better control children's experiences in the lab. And they can conveniently combine observations of behavior with physiological measures to gain insight into the biological basis of temperament.

Most neurophysiological research has focused on children who fall at opposite extremes of the positive-affect and fearful-distress dimensions of temperament: **inhibited, or shy, children,** who react negatively to and withdraw from novel stimuli, and **uninhibited, or sociable, children,** who display positive emotion and approach novel stimuli. As the Biology and Environment box on the following page reveals, biologically based reactivity—evident in heart rate, hormone levels, and EEG brain waves in the frontal region of the cerebral cortex—differentiates children with inhibited and uninhibited temperaments.

Stability of Temperament

Young children who score low or high on attention span, irritability, sociability, shyness, or effortful control tend to respond similarly when assessed again several months to a few years later and, occasionally, even into the adult years (Caspi et al., 2003; Kochanska & Knaack, 2003; Komsi et al., 2006; Majdandžić & van den Boom, 2007; Rothbart, Ahadi, & Evans, 2000; Ruff & Rothbart, 1996). However, the overall stability of temperament is low in infancy and toddlerhood and only moderate from the preschool years on (Putnam, Samson, & Rothbart, 2000). Some children remain the same, but many others change.

Why isn't temperament more stable? A major reason is that temperament itself develops with age. To illustrate, let's look at irritability and activity level. Recall from Chapter 4 that the early months are a period of fussing and crying for most babies. As infants better regulate their attention and emotions, many who initially seemed irritable become calm and content. In the case of activity level, the meaning of the behavior changes. At first, an active, wriggling infant tends to be highly aroused and uncomfortable, whereas an inactive baby is often alert and attentive. Once infants move on their own, the reverse is so! An active crawler is usually alert and interested in exploration, whereas an inactive baby may be fearful and withdrawn.

These discrepancies help us understand why long-term prediction from early temperament is best achieved after age 3, when children's styles of responding are better established (Roberts & DelVecchio, 2000). In line with this idea, between 2½ and 3, children improve substantially and also perform more consistently across a wide range of tasks requiring effortful

BIOLOGY AND ENVIRONMENT

Development of Shyness and Sociability

wo 4-month-old babies, Larry and Mitch, visited the laboratory of Jerome Kagan, who observed their reactions to a variety of unfamiliar experiences. When exposed to new sights and sounds, such as a moving mobile decorated with colorful toys, Larry tensed his muscles, moved his arms and legs with agitation, and began to cry. In contrast, Mitch remained relaxed and quiet, smiling and cooing at the excitement around him.

As toddlers, Larry and Mitch returned to the laboratory, where they experienced a variety of procedures designed to induce uncertainty. Electrodes were placed on their bodies and blood pressure cuffs on their arms to measure heart rate; toy robots, animals, and puppets moved before their eyes; and unfamiliar people entered and behaved in unexpected ways or wore novel costumes. While Larry whimpered and quickly withdrew, Mitch watched with interest, laughed at the strange sights, and approached the toys and strangers.

On a third visit, at age 4½, Larry barely talked or smiled during an interview with an unfamiliar adult. In contrast, Mitch asked questions and communicated his pleasure at each new activity. In a playroom with two unfamiliar peers, Larry pulled back and watched, while Mitch made friends quickly.

In longitudinal research on several hundred Caucasian infants followed into adolescence, Kagan found that about 20 percent of 4-month-olds were, like Larry, easily upset by novelty; another 40 percent, like Mitch, were comfortable, even delighted, with new experiences. About 20 to 30 percent of these extreme groups retained their temperamental styles as they grew older (Kagan, 2003; Kagan & Saudino, 2001; Kagan et al., 2007). But most children's dispositions became less extreme over time. Genetic makeup and child-rearing experiences jointly influenced stability and change in temperament.

Neurophysiological Correlates of Shyness and Sociability

Individual differences in arousal of the *amygdala,* an inner brain structure that controls avoidance reactions, contribute to these contrasting temperaments. In shy, inhibited children, novel stimuli easily excite the amygdala and its connections to the cerebral cortex and sympathetic nervous system, which prepares the body to act in the face of threat. In sociable,

uninhibited children, the same level of stimulation evokes minimal neural excitation (Kagan & Fox, 2006). In support of this theory, while viewing photos of unfamiliar faces, adults who had been classified as inhibited in the second year of life showed greater fMRI activity in the amygdala than adults who had been uninhibited as toddlers (Schwartz et al., 2003). And additional neurophysiological responses known to be mediated by the amygdala distinguish these two emotional styles:

- *Heart rate.* From the first few weeks of life, the heart rates of shy children are consistently higher than those of sociable children, and they speed up further in response to unfamiliar events (Schmidt et al., 2007; Snidman et al., 1995).
- *Cortisol.* Saliva concentrations of the stress hormone cortisol tend to be higher, and to rise more in response to a stressful event, in shy than in sociable children (Schmidt et al., 1997, 1999; Zimmermann & Stansbury, 2004).
- *Pupil dilation, blood pressure, and skin surface temperature.* Compared with sociable children, shy children show greater pupil dilation, rise in blood pressure, and cooling of the fingertips when faced with novelty (Kagan et al., 1999, 2007).

Another physiological correlate of approach–withdrawal to people and objects is the pattern of brain waves in the frontal lobes of the cerebral cortex. Shy infants and preschoolers show greater EEG activity in the right frontal lobe, which is associated with negative emotional reactivity; sociable children show the opposite pattern (Kagan & Snidman, 2004; Kagan et al., 2007). Neural activity in the amygdala, which is transmitted to the frontal lobes, probably contributes to these differences. Inhibited children also show greater generalized activation of the cerebral cortex, an indicator of high emotional arousal and monitoring of new situations for potential threats (Henderson et al., 2004).

Child-Rearing Practices

According to Kagan, extremely shy or sociable children inherit a physiology that biases them toward a particular temperamental style. Yet heritability research indicates that genes contribute only modestly to shyness and sociability

■ A strong physiological response to uncertain situations prompts this child to cling to her mother. With patient, insistent encouragement, her parents can help her overcome the urge to retreat from unfamiliar events. ■

(Kagan & Fox, 2006). Experience has a profound impact.

Child-rearing practices affect the chances that an emotionally reactive baby will become a fearful child. Warm, supportive parenting reduces shy infants' and preschoolers' intense physiological reaction to novelty, whereas cold, intrusive parenting heightens anxiety (Hane et al., 2008; Rubin, Burgess, & Hastings, 2002). And if parents overprotect infants and young children who dislike novelty, they make it harder for the child to overcome an urge to retreat. Parents who make appropriate demands for their child to approach new experiences help shy youngsters overcome fear (Rubin & Burgess, 2002).

When inhibition persists, it leads to excessive cautiousness, low self-esteem, and loneliness (Fordham & Stevenson-Hinde, 1999; Rubin, Stewart, & Coplan, 1995). In adolescence, persistent shyness increases the risk of severe anxiety, especially social phobia—intense fear of being humiliated in social situations (Kagan & Fox, 2006). For inhibited children to acquire effective social skills, parenting must be tailored to their temperaments—a theme we will encounter again in this and later chapters.

control, such as waiting for a reward, lowering their voice to a whisper, succeeding at games like "Simon Says," and selectively attending to one stimulus while ignoring competing stimuli (Kochanska, Murray, & Harlan, 2000; Li-Grining, 2007). Researchers believe that around this time, areas in the prefrontal cortex involved in suppressing impulses develop rapidly (Gerardi-Caulton, 2000; Rothbart & Bates, 2006).

Nevertheless, the ease with which children manage their reactivity in early childhood depends on the type and strength of the reactive emotion involved. Preschoolers who were highly fearful as toddlers score slightly better than their agemates in effortful control. In contrast, angry, irritable toddlers tend to be less effective at effortful control at later ages (Bridgett et al., 2009; Kochanska & Knaack, 2003; Kochanska, Murray, & Harlan, 2000). Other evidence confirms that child rearing plays an important role in modifying biologically based temperamental traits. Toddlers and young preschoolers who have fearful or negative, irritable temperaments but experience patient, supportive parenting are better at managing their reactivity and are especially likely to decline in difficultness (Warren & Simmens, 2005).

In sum, many factors affect the extent to which a child's temperament remains stable, including development of the biological systems on which temperament is based, the child's capacity for effortful control, and the success of her efforts, which depend on the quality and intensity of her emotional reactivity. When we consider the evidence as a whole, the low to moderate stability of temperament makes sense. It also confirms that experience can modify biologically based temperamental traits considerably, although children rarely change from one extreme to the other—that is, a shy toddler practically never becomes highly sociable, and irritable toddlers seldom become easy-going. With these ideas in mind, let's turn to genetic and environmental contributions to temperament and personality.

Genetic Influences

The word *temperament* implies a genetic foundation for individual differences in personality. Research indicates that identical twins are more similar than fraternal twins across a wide range of temperamental traits (activity level, attention span, shyness/sociability, irritability, and effortful control) and personality measures (introversion/extroversion, anxiety, agreeableness, curiosity and imaginativeness, and impulsivity) (Bouchard, 2004; Bouchard & Loehlin, 2001; Caspi & Shiner, 2006; Roisman & Fraley, 2006; Saudino & Cherny, 2001). In Chapter 2, we noted that heritability estimates derived from twin studies suggest a moderate role for genetic factors in temperament and personality: About half of individual differences have been attributed to differences in genetic makeup.

Consistent ethnic and sex differences in early temperament exist, again implying a role for heredity. Compared with Caucasian-American infants, Chinese and Japanese babies tend to be less active, irritable, and vocal, more easily soothed when upset, and better at quieting them-

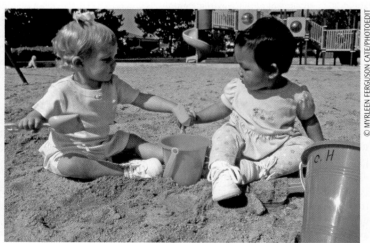

■ Sex differences in temperament are evident in children's play styles. Boys tend to engage in more active, high-intensity play. And girls' large advantage in effortful control helps explain their greater cooperativeness. ■

selves (Kagan et al., 1994; Lewis, Ramsay, & Kawakami, 1993). Grace's capacity to remain contentedly seated in her high chair through a long family dinner certainly fits with this evidence.

Timmy's high rate of activity illustrates a typical sex difference (Gartstein & Rothbart, 2003). From an early age, boys are more active and daring, more irritable when frustrated, more likely to express high-intensity pleasure in play, and slightly more impulsive than girls—factors that contribute to boys' higher injury rates throughout childhood and adolescence. Girls, in contrast, tend to be more anxious and timid. And girls' large advantage in effortful control undoubtedly contributes to their greater cooperativeness, better school performance, and lower incidence of behavior problems (Eisenberg et al., 2004a; Else-Quest et al., 2006).

Nevertheless, genetic influences vary with the temperamental trait and with the age of individuals being studied. For example, heritability estimates are higher for expressions of negative emotion than for positive emotion. And the role of heredity is considerably smaller in infancy than in childhood and later years, when temperament becomes more stable (Wachs & Bates, 2001).

Environmental Influences

Environment also has a powerful influence on temperament. For example, persistent nutritional and emotional deprivation profoundly alters temperament, resulting in maladaptive emotional reactivity. Recall from Chapter 5 that children exposed to severe malnutrition in infancy remain more distractible and fearful than their agemates, even after dietary improvement. And infants reared in deprived orphanages are easily overwhelmed by stressful events. Their poor regulation of emotion results in inattention and weak impulse control, including frequent expressions of anger (see pages 171 and 177).

GENETIC–ENVIRONMENTAL CORRELATION Other evidence confirms that heredity and environment often jointly contribute to temperament, since a child's approach to the world affects the experiences to which she is exposed—an instance of genetic–environmental correlation (see page 85 in Chapter 2). To illustrate how this works, let's take a second look at ethnic and sex differences in temperament.

Japanese mothers usually say that babies come into the world as independent beings who must learn to rely on their parents through close physical contact. American mothers typically believe just the opposite—that they must wean babies away from dependency toward autonomy. And while Asian cultures tend to view calmness as an ideal emotional state, Americans highly value the arousal and excitement generated by new places and activities (Kagan, 2010). Consistent with these beliefs, Asian mothers interact gently, soothingly, and gesturally with their babies, whereas Caucasian mothers use a more active, stimulating, verbal approach (Rothbaum et al., 2000a). Also, recall from our discussion of emotional self-regulation that Chinese and Japanese adults discourage babies from expressing strong emotion, which contributes further to their infants' tranquility.

A similar process seems to contribute to sex differences in temperament. Within 24 hours after birth (before they have had much experience with the baby), parents already perceive male and female newborns differently. Sons are rated as larger, better coordinated, more alert, and stronger; daughters as softer, weaker, and more delicate and awkward (Stern & Karraker, 1989; Vogel et al., 1991). In line with these gender-stereotyped beliefs, parents more often encourage their young sons to be physically active and assertive and their daughters to seek help and physical closeness—through the toys they provide (trucks and footballs for boys, dolls and tea sets for girls) and through more positive reactions when their child exhibits temperamental traits consistent with gender stereotypes (Bryan & Dix, 2009; Ruble, Martin, & Berenbaum, 2006).

CHILDREN'S UNIQUE EXPERIENCES In families with several children, an additional influence on temperament is at work. Parents often look for differences between siblings: "She's a lot more active." "He's more sociable." "She's far more persistent." As a result, parents often regard siblings as more distinct than other observers do. In a large study of 1- to 3-year-old twin pairs, parents rated identical twins as resembling each other less in temperament than researchers' ratings indicated. And whereas researchers rated fraternal twins as moderately

LOOK AND LISTEN

❖❖

Ask several parents of siblings to describe their children's personalities, along with child-rearing practices they use with each. Do the parents tend to emphasize differences? Are their child-rearing practices responsive to their views of each child's unique qualities?

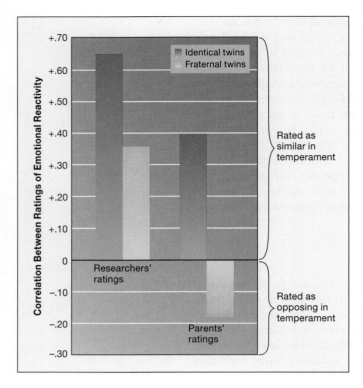

FIGURE 7.1

Temperament correlations for identical and fraternal twin pairs, as rated by researchers and parents. Parents rated 1- to 3-year-old identical twins as resembling each other less in temperament than researchers did. And whereas researchers rated fraternal twins as moderately similar, parents rated them as somewhat opposing in temperament. The correlations depicted here are for emotional reactivity. Activity level, shyness, and attention span/persistence yielded similar findings. *(Adapted from Saudino, 2003.)*

similar, parents viewed them as somewhat opposite in temperamental style (see Figure 7.1) (Saudino, 2003).

Parents' tendency to emphasize each child's unique qualities affects their child-rearing practices. In an investigation of identical-twin toddlers, mothers' differential treatment predicted differences in psychological adjustment. The twin who received more warmth and less harshness was more positive in mood and social behavior (Deater-Deckard et al., 2001). Each child, in turn, evokes responses from caregivers that are consistent with parental beliefs and the child's developing temperament.

Besides different experiences within the family, siblings have distinct experiences with teachers, peers, and others in their community that affect development. And in middle childhood and adolescence, they often seek ways to differ from one another. For all these reasons, both identical and fraternal twins tend to become increasingly dissimilar in personality with age (Loehlin & Martin, 2001; McCartney, Harris, & Bernieri, 1990). In sum, temperament and personality can be understood only in terms of complex interdependencies between genetic and environmental factors.

Temperament and Child Rearing: The Goodness-of-Fit Model

If a child's disposition interferes with learning or getting along with others, adults must gently but consistently counteract the child's maladaptive style. Thomas and Chess (1977) proposed a **goodness-of-fit model** to explain how temperament and environment can together produce favorable outcomes. Goodness of fit involves creating child-rearing environments that recognize each child's temperament while simultaneously encouraging more adaptive functioning.

Goodness of fit helps explain why difficult children (who withdraw from new experiences and react negatively and intensely) frequently experience parenting that fits poorly with their dispositions, putting them at high risk for later adjustment problems. As infants, they are less likely to receive sensitive caregiving (van den Boom & Hoeksma, 1994). By the second year, their parents tend to resort to angry, punitive discipline, which undermines the development of effortful control. As the child reacts with defiance and disobedience, parents become increasingly stressed (Bridgett et al., 2009; Paulussen-Hoogeboom et al., 2007). As a result, they continue their coercive tactics and also discipline inconsistently, sometimes rewarding the child's noncompliance by giving in to it. These practices sustain and even increase the child's irritable, conflict-ridden style (van Aken et al., 2007; Pesonen et al., 2008). In contrast, when parents are positive and sensitive, which helps infants and toddlers regulate emotion, difficultness declines by age 2 or 3 (Feldman, Greenbaum, & Yirmiya, 1999; Raikes et al., 2007).

Effective parenting, however, also depends on life conditions—good parental mental health, marital happiness, and favorable economic conditions (Schoppe-Sullivan et al., 2007). In a comparison of the temperaments of Russian and U.S. babies, Russian infants were more emotionally negative, fearful, and upset when frustrated (Gartstein, Slobodskaya, & Kinsht, 2003). At the time of the study, Russian parents faced a severely depressed national economy. Because of financial worries and longer work hours, Russian parents may have lacked time and energy for the patient parenting that protects against difficultness.

Cultural values also affect the fit between parenting and child temperament, as research in China illustrates. In the past, collectivist values, which discourage self-assertion, led Chinese adults to evaluate shy children positively. Several studies showed that shy Chinese children of a decade or two ago appeared well-adjusted, both academically and socially (Chen, Rubin, & Li, 1995; Chen et al., 1998). But rapid expansion of a market economy in China, which requires assertiveness and sociability for success, may be responsible for a recent change in Chinese parents' and teachers' attitudes toward childhood shyness (Chen, Wang, & DeSouza, 2006; Yu, 2002). Among Shanghai fourth graders, the association between shyness and adjustment also changed over time. Whereas shyness was positively correlated with teacher-rated competence, peer acceptance, leadership, and academic achievement in 1990, these relationships weakened in 1998 and reversed in 2002, when they mirrored findings of Western research (see Figure 7.2) (Chen et al., 2005). Cultural context makes a difference in whether shy children receive support or disapproval and whether they adjust well or poorly.

An effective match between rearing conditions and child temperament is best accomplished early, before unfavorable temperament–environment relationships produce maladjustment. Both difficult and shy children benefit from warm, accepting parenting that makes firm but reasonable demands for mastering new experiences. With reserved, inactive toddlers, highly stimulating parental behavior—encouraging, questioning, and pointing out objects—fosters exploration. Yet for highly active babies, this approach is too directive, dampening their play and curiosity (Miceli et al., 1998). Recall from Chapter 6 that Vanessa often behaved in a harsh, directive way with Timmy. A poor fit between her parenting and Timmy's active temperament may have contributed to his tendency to move from one activity to the next with little involvement.

The goodness-of-fit model reminds us that babies have unique dispositions that adults must accept. Parents can neither take full credit for their children's virtues nor be blamed for all their faults. But parents can turn an environment that exaggerates a child's problems into one that builds on the child's strengths. As we will see, goodness of fit is also at the heart of infant–caregiver attachment. This first intimate relationship grows out of interaction between parent and baby, to which the emotional styles of both partners contribute.

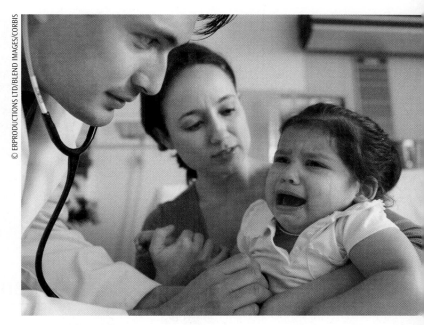

■ "Goodness of fit" describes the interaction between a child's temperament and the child-rearing environment. This mother's calm, soothing manner will help her child learn to regulate intense emotional reactions. ■

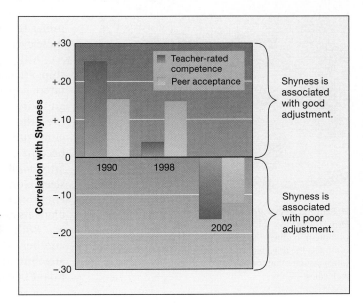

FIGURE 7.2

Changes over time in correlations between shyness and adjustment among Chinese fourth graders. In 1990, shy Chinese children appeared well-adjusted. But as China's market economy expanded and valuing of self-assertion and sociability increased, the direction of the correlations shifted. In 2002, shyness was negatively associated with adjustment. These findings are for teacher-rated competence and peer acceptance. Those for leadership (holding offices in student organizations) and academic achievement changed similarly. *(Adapted from Chen et al., 2005.)*

ASK YOURSELF

◆ REVIEW How do genetic and environmental factors work together to influence temperament? Cite several examples from research.

◆ APPLY Mandy and Jeff are parents of 2-year-old inhibited Sam and 3-year-old difficult Maria. Explain the importance of effortful control to Mandy and Jeff, and suggest ways they can strengthen it in each of their children.

◆ CONNECT Do findings on ethnic and sex differences in temperament illustrate genetic–environmental correlation, discussed on page 86 in Chapter 2? Explain.

◆ REFLECT How would you describe your temperament as a young child? Do you think your temperament has remained stable, or has it changed? What factors might be involved?

Development of Attachment

Attachment is the strong affectionate tie we have for special people in our lives that leads us to experience pleasure and joy when we interact with them and to be comforted by their nearness in times of stress. By the second half of the first year, infants have become attached to familiar people who have responded to their needs. **TAKE A MOMENT...** Watch how babies of this age single out their parents for special attention: When the parent enters the room, the baby breaks into a broad, friendly smile. When she picks him up, he pats her face, explores her hair, and snuggles against her. When he feels anxious or afraid, he crawls into her lap and clings closely.

Freud first suggested that the infant's emotional tie to the mother is the foundation for all later relationships. Contemporary research indicates that—although the infant–parent bond is vitally important—later development is influenced not just by early attachment experiences but also by the continuing quality of the parent–child relationship.

Attachment has also been the subject of intense theoretical debate. Recall that the *psychoanalytic perspective* regards feeding as the central context in which caregivers and babies build this close emotional bond. *Behaviorism,* too, emphasizes the importance of feeding, but for different reasons. According to a well-known behaviorist account, infants learn to prefer the mother's soft caresses, warm smiles, and tender words because these events are paired with tension relief as she satisfies the baby's hunger.

Although feeding is an important context for building a close relationship, attachment does not depend on hunger satisfaction. In the 1950s, a famous experiment showed that rhesus monkeys reared with terry-cloth and wire-mesh "surrogate mothers" clung to the soft terry-cloth substitute, even though the wire-mesh "mother" held the bottle and infants had to climb onto it to be fed (Harlow & Zimmerman, 1959). Human infants, too, become attached to family members who seldom feed them, including fathers, siblings, and grandparents. And toddlers in Western cultures who sleep alone and experience frequent daytime separations from their parents sometimes develop strong emotional ties to cuddly objects, such as blankets and teddy bears, that play no role in infant feeding!

Both psychoanalytic and behaviorist accounts of attachment have another problem: They emphasize the caregiver's contribution to the attachment relationship but pay little attention to the importance of the infant's characteristics.

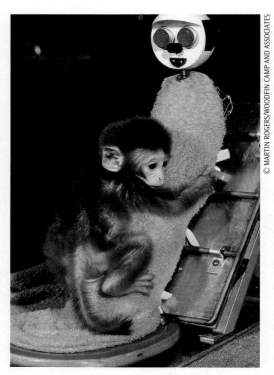

© MARTIN ROGERS/WOODFIN CAMP AND ASSOCIATES

■ Baby monkeys reared with "surrogate mothers" preferred to cling to a soft terry-cloth "mother" instead of a wire-mesh "mother" that held a bottle. These findings contradict the drive-reduction explanation of attachment, which assumes that the parent–infant relationship is based on feeding. ■

Bowlby's Ethological Theory

Today, **ethological theory of attachment,** which recognizes the infant's emotional tie to the caregiver as an evolved response that promotes survival, is the most widely accepted view. John Bowlby (1969), who first applied this idea to the infant–caregiver bond, retained the psychoanalytic idea that quality of attachment to the caregiver has profound implications for the child's feelings of security and capacity to form trusting relationships.

At the same time, Bowlby was inspired by Konrad Lorenz's studies of imprinting in baby geese (see Chapter 1). Bowlby believed that the human infant, like the young of other animal species, is endowed with a set of built-in behaviors that keep the parent nearby to protect the infant from danger and to provide support for exploring and mastering the environment (Waters & Cummings, 2000). Contact with the parent also ensures that the baby will be fed, but Bowlby was careful to point out that feeding is not the basis for attachment. Rather, attachment can best be understood in an evolutionary context in which survival of the species—through ensuring both safety and competence—is of utmost importance.

According to Bowlby, the infant's relationship with the parent begins as a set of innate signals that call the adult to the baby's side. Over time, a true affectionate bond forms, supported by new cognitive and emotional capacities as well as by a history of warm, sensitive care. Attachment develops in four phases:

■ Separation anxiety increases as clear-cut attachment develops. But this child's distress at his mother's departure will probably be brief because his caregiver is supportive and sensitive. ■

1. *Preattachment phase* (birth to 6 weeks). Built-in signals—grasping, smiling, crying, and gazing into the adult's eyes—help bring newborn babies into close contact with other humans, who comfort them. Babies of this age recognize their own mother's smell, voice, and face (see Chapter 4). But they are not yet attached to her, since they do not mind being left with an unfamiliar adult.

2. *"Attachment in the making" phase* (6 weeks to 6 to 8 months). During this phase, infants respond differently to a familiar caregiver than to a stranger. For example, at 4 months, Timmy smiled, laughed, and babbled more freely when interacting with his mother and quieted more quickly when she picked him up. As infants learn that their own actions affect the behavior of those around them, they begin to develop a *sense of trust*—the expectation that the caregiver will respond when signaled—but they still do not protest when separated from her.

3. *"Clear-cut" attachment phase* (6 to 8 months to 18 months to 2 years). Now attachment to the familiar caregiver is evident. Babies display **separation anxiety,** becoming upset when their trusted caregiver leaves. Like stranger anxiety (see page 252), separation anxiety does not always occur; it depends on infant temperament and the current situation. But in many cultures, separation anxiety increases between 6 and 15 months, suggesting that infants have developed a clear understanding that the caregiver continues to exist when not in view. Besides protesting the parent's departure, older infants and toddlers try hard to maintain her presence. They approach, follow, and climb on her in preference to others. And they use the familiar caregiver as a secure base from which to explore.

4. *Formation of a reciprocal relationship* (18 months to 2 years and on). By the end of the second year, rapid growth in representation and language enables toddlers to understand some of the factors that influence the parent's coming and going and to predict her return. As a result, separation protest declines. Now children negotiate with the caregiver, using requests and persuasion to alter her goals. For example, at age 2, Caitlin asked Carolyn and David to read her a story before leaving her with a babysitter. The extra time with her parents, along with a better understanding of where they were going ("to have dinner with Uncle Sean") and when they would be back ("right after you go to sleep"), helped Caitlin withstand her parents' absence.

LOOK AND LISTEN

Watch an 8- to 18-month-old at play for 20 to 30 minutes. Describe the baby's use of the parent or other familiar caregiver as a secure base from which to explore.

FIGURE 7.3

Testing toddlers for internal working models of attachment. (a) First, 12- to 16-month-olds were habituated to a video of two animated shapes, one large (the "caregiver") and one small (the "child"). The caregiver traveled halfway up an incline to a plateau, and the child began to "cry," depicted by pulsing and bouncing accompanied by an infant cry. Next the researchers presented two test events: (b) In the *responsive caregiver outcome,* the caregiver returned to the child. (c) In the *unresponsive caregiver outcome,* the caregiver continued up the slope away from the child. Securely attached toddlers looked longer at the unresponsive outcome, depicting caregiver behavior inconsistent with their expectations. Insecurely attached toddlers did not differentiate between the two test events. *(Adapted from Johnson, Dweck, & Chen, 2007.)*

According to Bowlby (1980), out of their experiences during these four phases, children construct an enduring affectionate tie to the caregiver that they can use as a secure base in the parent's absence. This image serves as an **internal working model,** or set of expectations about the availability of attachment figures, their likelihood of providing support during times of stress, and the self's interaction with those figures. The internal working model becomes a vital part of personality, serving as a guide for all future close relationships (Bretherton & Munholland, 1999).

Consistent with these ideas, as early as the second year, toddlers form attachment-related expectations about parental comfort and support. In one study, securely attached 12- to 16-month-olds looked longer at a video of an unresponsive caregiver (inconsistent with their expectations) than a video of a responsive caregiver. Insecurely attached toddlers, in contrast, did not distinguish between the two (see Figure 7.3) (Johnson, Dweck, & Chen, 2007).

With cognitive development and continuing experiences in close relationships, this budding internal working model expands into a broader, more complex representation. Children continue to revise it as they interact with parents and form other bonds with adults, siblings, and friends.

Measuring the Security of Attachment

Although all family-reared babies become attached to a familiar caregiver by the second year, the quality of this relationship differs from child to child. Some infants appear relaxed and secure in the presence of the caregiver; they know they can count on her for protection and support. Others seem anxious and uncertain.

A widely used laboratory technique for assessing the quality of attachment between 1 and 2 years of age is the **Strange Situation.** In designing it, Mary Ainsworth and her colleagues reasoned that securely attached infants and toddlers should use the parent as a secure base from which to explore in an unfamiliar playroom. In addition, when the parent leaves, an unfamiliar adult should be less comforting than the parent. The Strange Situation takes the baby through eight short episodes in which brief separations from and reunions with the parent occur (see Table 7.2).

Observing infants' responses to these episodes, researchers identified a secure attachment pattern and three patterns of insecurity; a few babies cannot be classified (Ainsworth et al., 1978; Barnett & Vondra, 1999; Main & Solomon, 1990; Thompson, 2006). Although separation anxiety varies among the groups, the baby's reunion responses largely define attachment quality. **TAKE A MOMENT...** From the description at the beginning of this chapter, which pattern do you think Grace displayed after adjusting to her adoptive family?

■ **Secure attachment.** These infants use the parent as a secure base. When separated, they may or may not cry, but if they do, it is because the parent is absent and they prefer her to the stranger. When the parent returns, they actively seek contact, and their crying is reduced immediately. About 60 percent of North American infants in middle-SES families show this pattern. (In low-SES families, a smaller proportion of babies show the secure pattern, with higher proportions falling into the insecure patterns.)

TABLE 7.2 Episodes in the Strange Situation

EPISODE	EVENTS	ATTACHMENT BEHAVIOR OBSERVED
1	Researcher introduces parent and baby to playroom and then leaves.	
2	Parent is seated while baby plays with toys.	Parent as a secure base
3	Stranger enters, is seated, and talks to parent.	Reaction to unfamiliar adult
4	Parent leaves room. Stranger responds to baby and offers comfort if baby is upset.	Separation anxiety
5	Parent returns, greets baby, and offers comfort if necessary. Stranger leaves room.	Reaction to reunion
6	Parent leaves room.	Separation anxiety
7	Stranger enters room and offers comfort.	Ability to be soothed by stranger
8	Parent returns, greets baby, offers comfort if necessary, and tries to reinterest baby in toys.	Reaction to reunion

Note: Episode 1 lasts about 30 seconds; each of the remaining episodes lasts about 3 minutes. Separation episodes are cut short if the baby becomes very upset. Reunion episodes are extended if the baby needs more time to calm down and return to play.

Source: Ainsworth et al., 1978.

■ **Avoidant attachment.** These infants seem unresponsive to the parent when she is present. When she leaves, they usually are not distressed, and they react to the stranger in much the same way as to the parent. During reunion, they avoid or are slow to greet the parent, and when picked up, they often fail to cling. About 15 percent of North American infants in middle-SES families show this pattern.

■ **Resistant attachment.** Before separation, these infants seek closeness to the parent and often fail to explore. When the parent leaves, they are usually distressed, and on her return they combine clinginess with angry, resistive behavior, struggling when held and sometimes hitting and pushing. Many continue to cry after being picked up and cannot be comforted easily. About 10 percent of North American infants in middle-SES families show this pattern.

■ **Disorganized/disoriented attachment.** This pattern reflects the greatest insecurity. At reunion, these infants show confused, contradictory behaviors—for example, looking away while the parent is holding them or approaching the parent with flat, depressed emotion. Most display a dazed facial expression, and a few cry out unexpectedly after having calmed down or display odd, frozen postures. About 15 percent of North American infants in middle-SES families show this pattern.

An alternative method, the **Attachment Q-Sort,** suitable for children between 1 and 4 years, depends on home observations (Waters et al., 1995). Either the parent or a highly trained observer sorts 90 behaviors—such as "Child greets mother with a big smile when she enters the room," "If mother moves very far, child follows along," and "Child uses mother's facial expressions as a good source of information when something looks risky or threatening"—into nine categories ranging from "highly descriptive" to "not at all descriptive" of the child. Then a score, ranging from high to low in security, is computed.

Because the Q-Sort taps a wider array of attachment-related behaviors than the Strange Situation, it may better reflect the parent–infant relationship in everyday life. However, the Q-sort method is time-consuming, requiring a nonparent informant to spend several hours observing the child before sorting the descriptors, and it does not differentiate between types of insecurity. The Q-Sort responses of expert observers correspond well with babies' secure-base behavior in the Strange Situation, but parents' Q-Sorts do not (van IJzendoorn et al., 2004). Parents of insecure children, especially, may have difficulty accurately reporting their child's attachment behaviors.

Stability of Attachment

Research on the stability of attachment patterns between 1 and 2 years of age yields a wide range of findings. In some studies, as many as 70 to 90 percent of children remain the same in their reactions to parents; in others, only 30 to 40 percent do (Thompson, 2000, 2006). A close look at which babies stay the same and which ones change yields a more consistent picture. Quality of attachment is usually secure and stable for middle-SES babies experiencing favorable life conditions. And infants who move from insecurity to security typically have well-adjusted mothers with positive family and friendship ties. Perhaps many became parents before they were psychologically ready but, with social support, grew into the role.

In contrast, in low-SES families with many daily stresses and little social support, attachment generally moves away from security or changes from one insecure pattern to another (Belsky et al., 1996; Fish, 2004; Vondra, Hommerding, & Shaw, 1999; Vondra et al., 2001). In one long-term follow-up of a poverty-stricken sample, many securely attached infants ended up insecure when reassessed in early adulthood. Child maltreatment, maternal depression, and poor family functioning in adolescence distinguished these young people from the few who stayed securely attached (Weinfield, Sroufe, & Egeland, 2000; Weinfield, Whaley, & Egeland, 2004).

These findings indicate that securely attached babies more often maintain their attachment status than insecure babies, whose relationship with the caregiver is, by definition, fragile and uncertain. The exception is disorganized/disoriented attachment—an insecure pattern that is as stable as attachment security: Nearly 70 percent retain this classification over time (Hesse & Main, 2000; Weinfield, Whaley, & Egeland, 2004). As you will soon see, many disorganized/disoriented infants experience extremely negative caregiving, which may disrupt emotional self-regulation so severely that confused, ambivalent feelings toward parents persist.

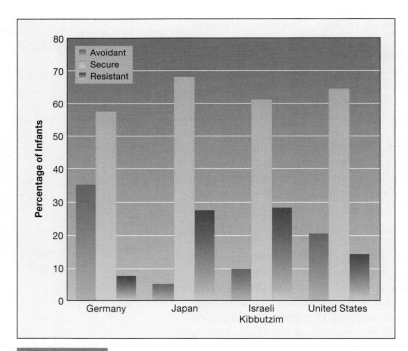

FIGURE 7.4

A cross-cultural comparison of infants' reactions in the Strange Situation. A high percentage of German babies seem avoidantly attached, whereas a substantial number of Japanese and Israeli kibbutz infants appear resistantly attached. Note that these responses may not reflect true insecurity. Instead, they are probably due to cultural differences in child-rearing practices. *(Adapted from Sagi et al., 1995; van IJzendoorn & Kroonenberg, 1988.)*

Cultural Variations

Cross-cultural evidence indicates that attachment patterns may have to be interpreted differently in certain cultures. For example, as Figure 7.4 reveals, German infants show considerably more avoidant attachment than American babies do. But German parents value independence and encourage their infants to be nonclingy, so the baby's behavior may be an intended outcome of cultural beliefs and practices (Grossmann et al., 1985). In contrast, a study of infants of the Dogon people of Mali, Africa, revealed that none showed avoidant attachment to their mothers (True, Pisani, & Oumar, 2001). Even when grandmothers are primary caregivers (as they are with firstborn sons), Dogon mothers remain available to their babies, holding them close and nursing them promptly in response to hunger and distress.

Japanese infants, as well, rarely show avoidant attachment (refer again to Figure 7.4). Rather, many are resistantly attached, but this reaction may not represent true insecurity. Japanese mothers rarely leave their babies in others' care, so the Strange Situation probably induces greater stress in them than in infants who frequently experience maternal separations (Takahashi, 1990). Also, many Japanese mothers expect their babies to be quite upset during reunion in the Strange Situation. They view the attention-seeking that is part of resistant attachment as a normal indicator of infants' efforts to satisfy dependency and security needs (Rothbaum et al., 2000b, 2007). Likewise, infants in Israeli kibbutzim frequently show resistant attachment. For these babies, who can sense the fear of unfamiliar people that is pervasive in their communities (see page 252), the Strange Situation probably induces unusual distress (van IJzendoorn & Sagi, 1999). Despite these and other cultural variations, the secure pattern is still the most common attachment quality in all societies studied to date.

Factors That Affect Attachment Security

What factors might influence attachment security? Researchers have looked closely at four important influences: (1) early availability of a consistent caregiver, (2) quality of caregiving, (3) the baby's characteristics, and (4) family context, including parents' internal working models.

EARLY AVAILABILITY OF A CONSISTENT CAREGIVER   What happens when a baby does not have the opportunity to establish a close tie to a caregiver? In a series of studies, René Spitz (1946) observed institutionalized infants whose mothers had given them up between 3 and 12 months of age. After being placed in a large ward where each shared a nurse with at least seven others, the babies lost weight, wept, withdrew from their surroundings, and had difficulty sleeping. If a consistent caregiver did not replace the mother, the depression deepened rapidly. These institutionalized babies had emotional problems because they were prevented from forming a bond with one or a few adults (Rutter, 1996).

Another study supports this conclusion. Researchers followed the development of infants in an institution with a good caregiver–child ratio and a rich selection of books and toys. However, staff turnover was so rapid that the average child had 50 caregivers by age 4½. Many of these children became "late adoptees" who were placed in homes after age 4. Most developed deep ties with their adoptive parents, indicating that a first attachment can develop as late as 4 to 6 years of age (Hodges & Tizard, 1989; Tizard & Rees, 1975). But these children were more likely to display attachment difficulties, including an excessive desire for adult attention, "overfriendliness" to unfamiliar adults and peers, failure to check back with the parent in anxiety-arousing situations, and few friendships.

Adopted children who spent their first year or more in deprived Eastern European orphanages—though also able to bond with their adoptive parents—show elevated rates of attachment insecurity (van den Dries et al., 2009). And they, too, are at high risk for emotional and social difficulties. Whereas many are indiscriminately friendly, others are sad, anxious, and withdrawn (Chisholm, 1998; Fisher et al., 1997; O'Connor et al., 2003). These symptoms typically persist and are associated with wide-ranging mental health problems in middle childhood and adolescence, including cognitive impairments, inattention and hyperactivity, depression, and either social avoidance or aggressive behavior (O'Connor et al., 2003; Rutter et al., 2007, 2010; Zeanah, 2000).

Furthermore, as early as 7 months, Eastern European orphanage children show reduced ERP brain waves in response to facial expressions of emotion and have trouble discriminating such expressions—outcomes that suggest disrupted formation of neural structures involved in "reading" emotions (Parker et al., 2005). These problems are still evident in preschoolers adopted during the second year, who find it hard to match appropriate facial expressions with situations in stories (Fries & Pollak, 2004). The longer the institutional stay, the worse adopted children perform on these emotion-processing tasks—deficits believed to contribute to their social-relationship and adjustment problems. Taken together, the evidence indicates that fully normal emotional development depends on establishing a close tie with a caregiver early in life.

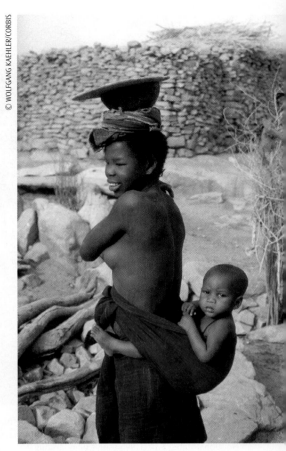

© WOLFGANG KAEHLER/CORBIS

◼ Among the Dogon people of Mali, Africa, mothers stay close to their babies and respond promptly to infant distress. Unlike German infants, whose mothers discourage clinginess, no Dogon babies show avoidant attachment. ◼

This father and baby engage in a sensitively tuned form of communication called interactional synchrony, in which they match emotional states, especially positive ones. Among Western babies, interactional synchrony supports secure attachment. But it does not characterize parent–infant attachment in all cultures. ■

QUALITY OF CAREGIVING Dozens of studies report that **sensitive caregiving**—responding promptly, consistently, and appropriately to infants and holding them tenderly and carefully—is moderately related to attachment security in both biological and adoptive mother–infant pairs and in diverse cultures and SES groups (De Wolff & van IJzendoorn, 1997; Posada et al., 2002, 2004; van IJzendoorn et al., 2004). In contrast, insecurely attached infants tend to have mothers who engage in less physical contact, handle them awkwardly or in a "routine" manner, and are sometimes resentful and rejecting, particularly in response to infant distress (Ainsworth et al., 1978; Isabella, 1993; McElwain & Booth-LaForce, 2006; Pederson & Moran, 1996).

Also, in studies of Western babies, a special form of communication called **interactional synchrony** separated the experiences of secure from insecure babies. It is best described as a sensitively tuned "emotional dance," in which the caregiver responds to infant signals in a well-timed, rhythmic, appropriate fashion. In addition, both partners match emotional states, especially the positive ones (Bigelow et al., 2010; Isabella & Belsky, 1991; Nievar & Becker, 2008). For example, when Caitlin excitedly shook a rattle, Carolyn responded with a broad smile and an enthusiastic "That-a-girl!" In return, Caitlin smiled and cooed. And when Caitlin fussed and cried, Carolyn soothed with gentle touches and soft, sympathetic words.

Earlier we saw that sensitive face-to-face play, in which interactional synchrony occurs, increases babies' sensitivity to others' emotional messages and helps them regulate emotion. But moderate adult–infant coordination is a better predictor of attachment security than "tight" coordination, in which the adult responds to most infant cues (Jaffee et al., 2001). Perhaps warm, sensitive caregivers use a relaxed, flexible style of communication in which they comfortably accept and repair emotional mismatches, returning to a synchronous state.

Cultures vary in their view of sensitivity toward infants. Among the Gusii people of Kenya, mothers rarely cuddle, hug, or interact playfully with their babies, although they are very responsive to their babies' needs. Yet most Gusii infants appear securely attached (LeVine et al., 1994). This suggests that security depends on attentive caregiving, not necessarily on moment-by-moment contingent interaction. Puerto Rican mothers, who highly value obedience and socially appropriate behavior, often physically direct and limit their babies' actions—a caregiving style linked to attachment security in Puerto Rican culture (Carlson & Harwood, 2003). Yet in many Western cultures, such physical control predicts insecurity.

Compared with securely attached infants, avoidant babies tend to receive overstimulating, intrusive care. Their mothers might, for example, talk energetically to them while they are looking away or falling asleep. By avoiding the mother, these infants appear to be escaping from overwhelming interaction. Resistant infants often experience inconsistent care. Their mothers are unresponsive to infant signals. Yet when the baby begins to explore, these mothers interfere, shifting the infant's attention back to themselves. As a result, the baby is overly dependent as well as angry at the mother's lack of involvement (Cassidy & Berlin, 1994; Isabella & Belsky, 1991).

Highly inadequate caregiving is a powerful predictor of disruptions in attachment. Child abuse and neglect (topics we will consider in Chapter 10) are associated with all three forms of attachment insecurity. Among maltreated infants, disorganized/disoriented attachment is especially high (van IJzendoorn, Schuengel, & Bakermans-Kranenburg, 1999). Persistently depressed mothers, mothers with very low marital satisfaction, and parents suffering from a traumatic event, such as serious illness or loss of a loved one, also tend to promote the uncertain behaviors of this pattern (Campbell et al., 2004; Moss et al., 2005; van IJzendoorn, 1995).

And some mothers of disorganized/disoriented infants engage in frightening, contradictory, and unpleasant behaviors, such as looking scared, teasing the baby, holding the baby stiffly at a distance, roughly pulling the baby by the arm, or seeking reassurance from the upset child (Lyons-Ruth, Bronfman, & Parsons, 1999; Madigan, Moran, & Pederson, 2006; Moran et al., 2008). Perhaps the baby's disorganized behavior reflects a conflicted reaction to the parent, who sometimes comforts but at other times arouses fear.

INFANT CHARACTERISTICS   Because attachment is the result of a *relationship* between two partners, infant characteristics should affect how easily it is established. In Chapters 3 and 4 we saw that prematurity, birth complications, and newborn illness make caregiving more taxing. In families under stress, these difficulties are linked to attachment insecurity. In one study, the *combination* of preterm birth and maternal depression—but not preterm birth alone—increased the likelihood of insecure attachment at 12 months (Poehlmann & Fiese, 2001). Infants with special needs probably require greater parental sensitivity, which stressed parents often cannot provide. But at-risk newborns whose parents have adequate time and patience to care for them fare quite well in attachment security (Cox, Hopkins, & Hans, 2000).

The role of infant temperament in attachment security has been intensely debated. Some researchers believe that infants who are irritable and fearful may simply react to brief separations with intense anxiety, regardless of the parent's sensitivity to the baby (Kagan, 1998; Kagan & Fox, 2006). Consistent with this view, emotionally reactive, difficult babies are more likely to develop later insecure attachments (van IJzendoorn et al., 2004; Vaughn & Bost, 1999). And disorganized newborn behavior, evident in scores on the Neonatal Behavioral Assessment Scale (NBAS, see Chapter 4), increases the risk of disorganized/disoriented attachment at the end of the first year (Spangler, Fremmer-Bomik, & Grossmann, 1996).

Again, however, other evidence suggests that parental mental health and caregiving are involved. In a study extending from birth to age 2, difficult infants more often had highly anxious mothers—a combination that, by the second year, frequently resulted in a "disharmonious relationship" characterized by both maternal insensitivity and attachment insecurity (Symons, 2001). Infant difficultness and maternal anxiety seemed to perpetuate each other, impairing caregiving and the security of the parent–infant bond. Similarly, in another study, mothers' experience of traumatic events was associated with disorganized/disoriented attachment only in infants with a chromosome-11 gene having a certain repetition of DNA base pairs (called DRD4 7-repeat), which is linked to deficient self-regulation (van IJzendoorn & Bakermans-Kranenburg, 2006). Babies with this genetic marker, who face special challenges in managing intense emotion, were more susceptible to the negative impact of maternal adjustment problems.

If children's temperaments alone determined attachment quality, we would expect attachment, like temperament, to be at least moderately heritable. Yet the heritability of attachment is virtually nil (O'Connor & Croft, 2001). In fact, about two-thirds of siblings establish similar attachment patterns with their parents, although the siblings often differ in temperament (Cole, 2006; Dozier et al., 2001). This suggests that most parents try to adjust their caregiving to each child's individual needs.

Why don't infant characteristics show strong relationships with attachment quality? Their influence probably depends on goodness of fit. From this perspective, *many* child attributes can lead to secure attachment as long as caregivers sensitively adjust their behavior to fit the baby's needs (Seifer & Schiller, 1995).

Interventions that teach parents to interact sensitively with difficult-to-care-for infants and toddlers are highly successful in enhancing both sensitive care and attachment security (Velderman et al., 2006). One program that focused on both maternal sensitivity and effective discipline was particularly effective in reducing stress reactivity (as indicated by lower cortisol levels) and disruptive behavior among toddlers with the DRD4 7-repeat gene, who are at risk for later attention-deficit hyperactivity disorder and externalizing behavior problems (Bakermans-Kranenburg et al., 2008a, 2008b). But when parents' capacity for sensitivity is strained—by their own personalities or by stressful living conditions—then infants with illnesses, disabilities, and difficult temperaments are at risk for attachment problems.

FAMILY CIRCUMSTANCES Shortly after Timmy's birth, his parents divorced, and his father moved to a distant city. Anxious and distracted, Vanessa placed 1-month-old Timmy in Ginette's child-care home and began working 50-hour weeks to make ends meet. On days Vanessa stayed late at the office, a babysitter picked Timmy up, gave him dinner, and put him to bed. Once or twice a week, Vanessa went to get Timmy from child care. As he neared his first birthday, Vanessa noticed that, unlike the other children, who reached out, crawled, or ran to their parents, Timmy ignored her.

Timmy's behavior reflects a repeated finding: Job loss, a failing marriage, and financial difficulties can undermine attachment indirectly by interfering with parental sensitivity. These stressors can also affect babies' sense of security directly by altering the emotional climate of the family (for example, exposing them to angry adult interactions) or by disrupting familiar daily routines (Finger et al., 2009; Raikes & Thompson, 2005). Parents who manage to sustain a favorable relationship with their baby despite environmental stressors protect the child's development. Social support fosters attachment security by reducing parental stress and improving the quality of parent–child communication (Belsky & Fearon, 2002b; Moss et al., 2005). Ginette's sensitivity toward Timmy was helpful, as was the parenting advice Vanessa received from Ben, a psychologist. As Timmy turned 2, his relationship with his mother seemed warmer.

PARENTS' INTERNAL WORKING MODELS Parents bring to the family context their own history of attachment experiences, from which they construct internal working models that they apply to the bonds they establish with their babies. Monica, who recalled her mother as tense and preoccupied, expressed regret that they had not had a closer relationship. Is her image of parenthood likely to affect Grace's attachment security?

■ Family circumstances are linked to attachment quality. Observing her parents' heated quarrels may undermine this child's sense of emotional security. ■

To assess parents' internal working models, researchers have asked them to evaluate childhood memories of attachment experiences (Main & Goldwyn, 1998). Parents who discuss their childhoods with objectivity and balance, regardless of whether their experiences were positive or negative, tend to have securely attached infants and to behave sensitively toward them. In contrast, parents who dismiss the importance of early relationships or describe them in angry, confused ways usually have insecurely attached babies and engage in less sensitive caregiving (Slade et al., 1999; van IJzendoorn, 1995).

But we must not assume any direct transfer of parents' childhood experiences to quality of attachment with their own children. Internal working models are *reconstructed memories* affected by many factors, including relationship experiences over the life course, personality, and current life satisfaction. Longitudinal research reveals that negative life events can weaken the link between an individual's own attachment security in infancy and a secure internal working model in adulthood. And insecurely attached babies who become adults with insecure internal working models often have lives that, based on self-reports in adulthood, are filled with family crises (Waters et al., 2000; Weinfield, Sroufe, & Egeland, 2000).

In sum, our early rearing experiences do not destine us to become either sensitive or insensitive parents. Rather, the way we *view* our childhoods—our ability to come to terms with negative events, to integrate new information into our working models, and to look back on our own parents in an understanding, forgiving way—appears to be much more influential in how we rear our children than the actual history of care we received (Main, 2000).

ATTACHMENT IN CONTEXT Carolyn and Vanessa returned to work when their babies were 2 to 3 months old. Monica did the same a few weeks after Grace's adoption. When parents divide their time between work and parenting and place their infants and toddlers in child care, is quality of attachment and child adjustment affected? See the Social Issues: Health box on the following page for research that addresses this issue.

SOCIAL ISSUES: HEALTH

Does Child Care in Infancy Threaten Attachment Security and Later Adjustment?

esearch suggests that infants placed in full-time child care before 12 months of age are more likely than infants who remain at home to display insecure attachment—especially avoidance—in the Strange Situation (Belsky, 2001, 2005). Does this mean that infants who experience daily separations from their employed parents and early placement in child care are at risk for developmental problems? Let's look closely at the evidence.

Attachment Quality

In U.S. studies reporting an association between child care and attachment quality, the rate of insecurity among child-care infants is somewhat higher than among non-child-care infants—about 36 versus 29 percent (Lamb, Sternberg, & Prodromidis, 1992). But not all investigations report that babies in child care differ in attachment quality from those cared for solely by parents (NICHD Early Child Care Research Network, 1997; Roggman et al., 1994). Rather, the relationship between child care and emotional well-being depends on both family and child-care experiences.

Family Circumstances

We have seen that family conditions affect attachment security. For employed parents, balancing work and child care can be stressful. Mothers who are fatigued and anxious because they feel overloaded by work and family pressures may respond less sensitively to their babies, thereby risking the infant's security. And as paternal involvement in caregiving has risen (see page 274), many more U.S. fathers in dual-earner families also report work–family life conflict (Galinsky, Aumann, & Bond, 2009). Other employed parents may value and encourage their infant's independence. Or their babies may be unfazed by the Strange Situation because they are used to separating from their parents. In these cases, avoidance in the Strange Situation may represent healthy autonomy, not insecurity (Clarke-Stewart, Allhusen, & Goosens, 2001).

Quality and Extent of Child Care

Long periods spent in poor-quality child care may contribute to a higher rate of insecure attachment. In the U.S. National Institute of Child Health and Development (NICHD) Study of Early Child Care—the largest longitudinal study to date, including more than 1,300 infants and their families—child care alone did not contribute to attachment inse-

curity. But when babies were exposed to combined home and child-care risk factors—insensitive caregiving at home along with insensitive caregiving in child care, long hours in child care, or more than one child-care arrangement—the rate of insecurity increased. Overall, mother–child interaction was more favorable when children attended higher-quality child care and also spent fewer hours in child care (NICHD Early Child Care Research Network, 1997, 1999).

Furthermore, when these children reached age 3, a history of higher-quality child care predicted better social skills (NICHD Early Child Care Research Network, 2002b). However, at age 4½ to 5, children averaging more than 30 child-care hours per week displayed more behavior problems, especially defiance, disobedience, and aggression, an outcome that—for those who had been in child-care centers as opposed to family child-care homes—persisted through elementary school (Belsky et al., 2007; NICHD Early Child Care Research Network, 2003a, 2006). And in kindergarten, children with limited child-care experience but who had many classmates with extensive child-care exposure were rated by their teachers as slightly more aggressive and disobedient (Dmitrieva, Steinberg, & Belsky, 2007). This suggests that externalizing difficulties can spread to peers who interact regularly with child-care exposed children.

These findings do not necessarily mean that child care causes behavior problems. Rather, heavy exposure to substandard care, which is widespread in the United States, may promote these difficulties. In Australia, infants enrolled full-time in government-funded, high-quality child-care centers have a higher rate of secure attachment than infants informally cared for by relatives, friends, or babysitters. And amount of time spent in child care is unrelated to Australian children's behavior problems (Love et al., 2003).

Still, some children may be particularly stressed by long child-care hours. Many infants, toddlers, and preschoolers attending child-care centers for full days show a mild increase in saliva concentrations of the stress hormone cortisol across the day—a pattern that does not occur on days they spend at home. In one study, children rated as highly fearful by their caregivers experienced an especially sharp increase in cortisol levels (Watamura et al., 2003). Inhibited children may find the constant company of large numbers of peers particularly stressful.

Conclusions

Taken together, research suggests that some infants may be at risk for attachment insecurity and adjustment problems due to inadequate child care, long hours in child care, and the joint pressures their parents experience from full-time employment and parenthood. But it is inappropriate to use these findings to justify a reduction in infant child-care services. Instead, it makes sense to increase the availability of high-quality child care, to provide paid employment leave so parents can limit the hours their children spend in child care (see page 141 in Chapter 4), and to educate parents about the vital role of sensitive caregiving and child-care quality in early emotional development.

For child care to foster attachment security, the professional caregiver's relationship with the baby is vital. When caregiver–child ratios are generous, group sizes are small, and caregivers are educated about child development and child rearing, caregivers' interactions are more positive and children develop more favorably (McCartney et al., 2007; NICHD Early Child Care Research Network, 2000b, 2002a, 2006). Child care with these characteristics can become part of an ecological system that relieves rather than intensifies parental and child stress, thereby promoting healthy attachment and development.

■ At the end of his day in child care, this 10-month-old is happy to see his mother. High-quality child care and fewer hours in child care are associated with favorable mother–child interaction, which contributes to attachment security. ■

After reading the box, consider each factor that influences the development of attachment—infant and parent characteristics, the parents' relationship with each other, outside-the-family stressors, the availability of social supports, parents' views of their attachment history, and child-care arrangements. Although attachment builds within the warmth and intimacy of caregiver–infant interaction, it can be fully understood only from an ecological systems perspective (Bornstein, 2002). Return to Chapter 1, pages 25–27, to review Bronfenbrenner's ecological systems theory. Notice how research confirms the importance of each level of the environment for attachment security.

Multiple Attachments

As we have indicated, babies develop attachments to a variety of familiar people—not just mothers, but also fathers, grandparents, siblings, and professional caregivers. Although Bowlby (1969) believed that infants are predisposed to direct their attachment behaviors to a single special person, especially when they are distressed, his theory allowed for these multiple attachments.

FATHERS An anxious, unhappy 1-year-old who is permitted to choose between the mother and the father as a source of comfort and security will usually choose the mother. But this preference typically declines over the second year. And when babies are not distressed, they approach, vocalize to, and smile equally often at both parents, who in turn are equally responsive to their infant's social bids (Bornstein, 2006; Parke, 2002).

Fathers' sensitive caregiving and interactional synchrony with infants, like mothers', predict attachment security (Lundy, 2003; van IJzendoorn et al., 2004). And fathers of 1- to 5-year-olds enrolled in full-time child care report feeling just as much anxiety as mothers about separating from their child and just as much concern about the impact of these daily separations on the child's well-being (Deater-Deckard et al., 1994). But as infancy progresses, mothers and fathers in many cultures, including Australia, Canada, Germany, India, Israel, Italy, Japan, and the United States, tend to interact differently with their babies: Mothers devote more time to physical care and expressing affection, fathers to playful interaction (Freeman & Newland, 2010; Roopnarine et al., 1990).

Mothers and fathers also play differently. Mothers more often provide toys, talk to infants, and gently play conventional games like pat-a-cake and peekaboo. In contrast, fathers—especially with their infant sons—tend to engage in highly stimulating physical play with bursts of excitement and surprise that increase as play progresses (Feldman, 2003). As long as fathers are also sensitive, this stimulating, startling play style helps babies regulate emotion in intensely arousing situations and may prepare them to venture confidently into active, unpredictable contexts, including novel physical environments and play with peers (Cabrera et al., 2007; Hazen et al., 2010; Paquette, 2004). In a German study, fathers' sensitive, challenging play with preschoolers predicted favorable emotional and social adjustment from kindergarten to early adulthood (Grossman et al, 2008).

Play is a vital context in which fathers build secure attachments (Newland, Coyl, & Freeman, 2008). It may be especially influential in cultures where long work hours prevent most fathers from sharing in infant caregiving, such as Japan (Hewlett, 2004; Shwalb et al., 2004). In many Western nations, however, a strict division of parental roles—mother as caregiver, father as playmate—has changed over the past several decades in response to women's workforce participation and to cultural valuing of gender equality.

A recent U.S. national survey of several thousand employed workers indicated that U.S. fathers under age 29 devote about 85 percent as much time as mothers do to children—on average, just over 4 hours per workday, nearly double the hours young fathers reported three decades ago. Although fathers age 29 to 42 spend somewhat less time with children, their involvement has also increased substantially (see Figure 7.5). Today, nearly one-third of U.S. employed women say that their spouse or partner shares equally in or takes most responsibility for child-care tasks (Galinsky, Aumann, & Bond, 2009). Paternal availability to children is fairly similar across SES and ethnic groups, with one exception: Hispanic fathers spend more time engaged, probably because of the particularly high value that Hispanic cultures place on family involvement (Cabrera & García Coll, 2004; Parke et al., 2004).

LOOK AND LISTEN

❖

Observe parents at play with infants at home or a family gathering, describing both similarities and differences in mothers' and fathers' behaviors. Are your observations consistent with research findings?

Mothers in dual-earner families tend to engage in more playful stimulation of their babies than mothers who are at home full-time (Cox et al., 1992). But fathers who are primary caregivers retain their arousing play style (Lamb & Oppenheim, 1989). These highly involved fathers are less gender-stereotyped in their beliefs, have sympathetic, friendly personalities, often had fathers who were more involved in rearing them, and regard parenthood as an especially enriching experience (Cabrera et al., 2000; Levy-Shiff & Israelashvili, 1988).

Fathers' involvement with babies occurs within a complex system of family attitudes and relationships. When both mothers and fathers believe that men are capable of nurturing infants, fathers devote more time to caregiving (Beitel & Parke, 1998). A warm marital bond and supportive coparenting (see page 70 in Chapter 2) promote both parents' sensitivity and involvement and children's attachment security, but it is especially important for fathers (Brown et al., 2010; Lamb & Lewis, 2004; Laurent, Kim, & Capaldi, 2008). See the Cultural Influences box on page 276 for cross-cultural evidence documenting this conclusion—and also highlighting the powerful role of paternal warmth in children's development.

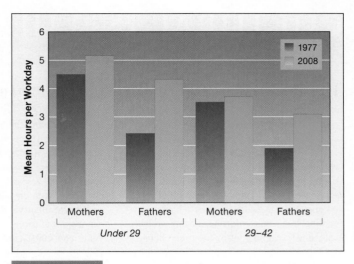

FIGURE 7.5

Average amount of time per workday U.S. employed mothers and fathers reported spending with their children (age 12 and younger) in 1977 and 2008. In national surveys of several thousand employed parents, mothers' time with children remained fairly stable from 1977 to 2008; fathers' time increased substantially. *(Adapted from Galinsky, Aumann, & Bond, 2009.)*

GRANDPARENT PRIMARY CAREGIVERS   Nearly 2.4 million U.S. children—4 to 5 percent of the child population—live with their grandparents but apart from parents, in so-called *skipped-generation families* (U.S. Census Bureau, 2010b). The number of grandparents rearing grandchildren has increased over the past two decades. The arrangement occurs in all ethnic groups, though more often in African-American, Hispanic, and Native-American families than in Caucasian families. Although grandparent caregivers are more likely to be women than men, many grandfathers participate. Grandparents generally step in when parents' troubled lives—as a result of substance abuse, child abuse and neglect, mental illness, or adolescent parenthood—threaten children's well-being (Fuller-Thomson & Minkler, 2005, 2007; Minkler & Fuller-Thomson, 2005). Often these families take in two or more children.

As a result, grandparents tend to assume the parenting role under highly stressful life circumstances. Unfavorable child-rearing experiences have left their mark on children, who show high rates of learning difficulties, depression, and antisocial behavior. Absent parents' adjustment difficulties strain family relationships. Parents may interfere by violating the grandparents' behavioral limits, taking grandchildren away without permission, or making promises to children that they do not keep. These youngsters also introduce financial burdens into households that often are already low-income (Mills, Gomez-Smith, & De Leon, 2005; Williamson, Softas-Nall, & Miller, 2003). And grandparent caregivers, at a time when they anticipated having more time for spouses, friends, and leisure, instead have less. Many report feeling emotionally drained, depressed, and worried about what will happen to the children if their own health fails (Hayslip et al., 2002; Kolomer & McCallion, 2005).

Nevertheless, because they provide physical and emotional care for an extended time and are invested in the child's well-being, grandparent caregivers forge significant attachment relationships with their grandchildren (Poehlmann, 2003). Warm grandparent–grandchild bonds help protect children from worsening adjustment problems,

■ This woman's daughter, a drug addict, dropped each of her sons on her mother's doorstep shortly after they were born. Though she undertook the parenting role under highly stressful conditions, this grandmother has forged deep attachments with her grandsons. ■

CULTURAL INFLUENCES

The Powerful Role of Paternal Warmth in Development

Research in diverse cultures demonstrates that fathers' warmth contributes greatly to children's long-term favorable development. In studies of many societies and ethnic groups around the world, researchers coded paternal expressions of love and nurturance—evident in such behaviors as cuddling, hugging, comforting, playing, verbally expressing love, and praising the child's behavior. Fathers' sustained affectionate involvement predicted later cognitive, emotional, and social competence as strongly as did mothers' warmth—and occasionally more strongly (Rohner & Veneziano, 2001; Veneziano, 2003). And in Western cultures, paternal warmth and secure attachment is associated with children's mature social behavior and protects them against a wide range of difficulties, including childhood emotional and behavior problems and adolescent substance abuse and delinquency (Grant et al., 2000; Michiels et al., 2010; Nelson & Coyne, 2009; Tacon & Caldera, 2001).

Fathers who devote little time to physical caregiving express warmth through play. In a German study, fathers' play sensitivity—accepting toddlers' play initiatives, adapting play behaviors to toddlers' capacities, and responding appropriately to toddlers' expressions of emotion—predicted children's secure internal working models of attachment during middle childhood and adolescence (Grossmann et al., 2002). Through play, fathers seemed to transfer to young children a sense of confidence about parental support, which may strengthen their capacity to master many later challenges.

What factors promote paternal warmth? Cross-cultural research reveals a consistent association between the amount of time fathers spend near infants and toddlers and their expressions of caring and affection (Rohner & Veneziano, 2001). Consider the Aka hunters and gatherers of Central Africa, where fathers spend more time in physical proximity to their babies than in any other known society. Observations reveal that Aka fathers are within arm's reach of infants more than half the day. They pick up, cuddle, and play with their babies at least five times as often as fathers in other hunting-and-gathering societies. Why are Aka fathers so involved? The bond between Aka husband and wife is unusually cooperative and intimate. Throughout the day, couples share hunting, food preparation, and social and leisure activities. The more Aka parents are together, the greater the father's loving interaction with his baby (Hewlett, 1992).

In Western cultures as well, fathers in gratifying marriages feel more confident about their parenting skills and spend more time with and interact more effectively with their infants. In contrast, marital dissatisfaction is associated with insensitive paternal care (Grych & Clark, 1999; Lundy, 2002; Sevigny & Loutzenhiser, 2010). Clearly, mothers' and fathers' warm

■ In both Western and non-Western nations, paternal warmth predicts long-term favorable cognitive, emotional, and social development. ■

interactions with each other and with their babies are closely linked. But paternal warmth promotes long-term favorable development, beyond the influence of maternal warmth (Rohner & Veneziano, 2001). Evidence for the power of fathers' affection, reported in virtually every culture and ethnic group studied, is reason to encourage more men to engage in nurturing care of young children.

---

even under conditions of great hardship (Hicks & Goedereis, 2009). Still, grandparent caregivers have a tremendous need for social and financial support and intervention services for their at-risk grandchildren.

SIBLINGS　Despite declines in family size, 80 percent of North American and European children grow up with at least one sibling (Dunn, 2004). The arrival of a new baby is a difficult experience for most preschoolers, who—realizing that they must now share their parents' attention and affection—often become demanding, clingy, and deliberately naughty for a time. Attachment security also typically declines, especially for children over age 2 (old enough to feel threatened and displaced) and for those with mothers under stress (Baydar, Greek, & Brooks-Gunn, 1997; Teti et al., 1995).

Yet resentment is only one feature of the rich emotional relationship that starts to build between siblings after a baby's birth. Older children also show affection and concern—kissing and patting the baby and calling out, "Mom, he needs you," when the infant cries. By the end of the first year, babies typically spend much time with older siblings and are comforted by the presence of a preschool-age brother or sister during short parental absences. Throughout

Applying What We Know

Encouraging Affectionate Ties Between Infants and Their Preschool Siblings

SUGGESTION	DESCRIPTION
Spend extra time with the older child.	To minimize the older child's feelings of being deprived of affection and attention, set aside time to spend with her. Fathers can be especially helpful, planning special outings with the preschooler and taking over care of the baby so the mother can be with the older child.
Handle sibling misbehavior with patience.	Respond patiently to the older sibling's misbehavior and demands for attention, recognizing that these reactions are temporary. Give the preschooler opportunities to feel proud of being more grown-up than the baby. For example, encourage the older child to assist with feeding, bathing, dressing, and offering toys, and show appreciation for these efforts.
Discuss the baby's wants and needs.	By helping the older sibling understand the baby's point of view, parents can promote friendly, considerate behavior. Say, for example, "He's so little that he just can't wait to be fed" or "He's trying to reach his rattle, and he can't."
Express positive emotion toward your partner and engage in joint problem solving.	When parents model effective problem solving, their good communication helps the older sibling cope adaptively with jealousy and conflict. Also, when family life is happy, children have less reason to feel jealous.

childhood, children continue to treat older siblings as attachment figures, turning to them for comfort in stressful situations when parents are unavailable (Seibert & Kerns, 2009). And in the second year, as toddlers imitate and join in play with their brothers and sisters, siblings start to become gratifying sources of companionship (Barr & Hayne, 2003).

Nevertheless, individual differences in sibling relationships emerge soon after the new baby's arrival. Temperament plays an important role. For example, conflict is greater when one sibling is emotionally intense or highly active (Brody, Stoneman, & McCoy, 1994; Dunn, 1994). And maternal warmth toward both children is related to positive sibling interaction and to preschoolers' support of a distressed younger sibling (Volling, 2001; Volling & Belsky, 1992). Mothers who frequently play with their children and explain the toddler's wants and needs to the preschool sibling foster sibling cooperation. In contrast, maternal harshness and lack of involvement are linked to antagonistic sibling relationships (Howe, Aquan-Assee, & Bukowski, 2001). Finally, a good marriage is correlated with older preschool siblings' capacity to cope adaptively with jealousy and conflict (Volling, McElwain, & Miller, 2002). Perhaps good communication between parents serves as a model of effective problem solving. It may also foster a generally happy family environment, giving children less reason to feel jealous.

Refer to Applying What We Know above for ways to promote positive relationships between babies and their preschool siblings. Siblings offer a rich social context in which children learn and practice a wide range of skills, including affectionate caring, conflict resolution, and control of hostile and envious feelings.

From Attachment to Peer Sociability

In cultures where agemates have regular contact during the first year of life, peer sociability begins early. By age 6 months, Caitlin and Timmy occasionally looked, reached, smiled, and babbled when they saw each other. These isolated social acts increased until, by the end of the first year, an occasional reciprocal exchange occurred in which the children grinned, gestured, or otherwise imitated a playmate's behavior (Vandell & Mueller, 1995).

© LAURA DWIGHT PHOTOGRAPHY

■ The arrival of a baby brother or sister is a difficult experience for most preschoolers. Maternal warmth toward both children assures the older sibling of continuing parental love, models affectionate caring, and is related to positive sibling interaction. ■

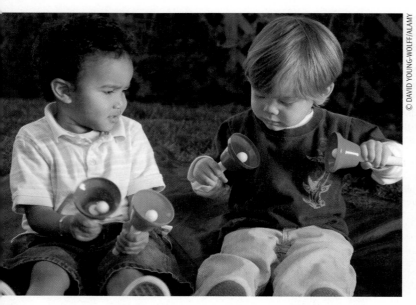

■ Peer sociability among babies can be seen in touches, smiles, and babbles that gradually develop into coordinated interaction—mostly in the form of mutual imitation—during the second year. ■

Between 1 and 2 years, as toddlers appreciate that others have intentions, desires, and emotions distinct from their own, they increasingly view one another as playmates (Brownell & Kopp, 2007). As a result, coordinated interaction occurs more often, largely in the form of mutual imitation involving jumping, chasing, or banging a toy. These imitative, turn-taking games create joint understandings that aid verbal communication. Around age 2, toddlers use words to talk about and influence a peer's behavior, as when Caitlin said to Grace, "Let's play chase," and after the game got going, "Hey, good running!" (Eckerman & Peterman, 2001; Eckerman & Whitehead, 1999). Reciprocal play and positive emotion are especially frequent in toddlers' interactions with familiar agemates, suggesting that they are building true peer relationships (Ross et al., 1992).

Though quite limited, peer sociability is present in the first two years and is promoted by the early caregiver–child bond. From interacting with sensitive adults, babies learn how to send and interpret emotional signals in their first peer associations (Trevarthen, 2003). Toddlers who have a warm parental relationship or who attend high-quality child care with a small group size and a generous caregiver–child ratio—features that promote warm, stimulating caregiving and secure attachment to professional caregivers—engage in more positive and extended peer exchanges. These children, in turn, display more socially competent behavior as preschoolers (Deynoot-Schaub & Riksen-Walraven, 2006a, 2006b; Howes & Matheson, 1992).

Attachment and Later Development

According to psychoanalytic and ethological theories, the inner feelings of affection and security that result from a healthy attachment relationship support all aspects of psychological development. Consistent with this view, an extensive longitudinal study by Alan Sroufe and his collaborators found that preschoolers who had been securely attached as babies were rated by their teachers as higher in self-esteem, social skills, and empathy than were their insecurely attached counterparts, who displayed more behavior problems. When studied again at age 11 in summer camp, children who had been secure infants had more favorable relationships with peers, closer friendships, and better social skills, as judged by camp counselors. And as these well-functioning school-age children became adolescents and young adults, they continued to benefit from more supportive social networks, formed more stable and gratifying romantic relationships, and attained higher levels of education (Elicker, Englund, & Sroufe, 1992; Sroufe, 2002; Sroufe et al., 2005).

For some researchers, these findings seem to indicate that secure attachment in infancy causes improved cognitive, emotional, and social competence in later years. Yet contrary evidence exists. In other longitudinal studies, secure infants generally fared better than insecure infants, but not always (Fearon et al., 2010; McCartney et al., 2004; Schneider, Atkinson, & Tardif, 2001; Stams, Juffer, & van IJzendoorn, 2002). Disorganized/disoriented attachment, however, is an exception: It is consistently related to internalizing problems (fear and anxiety) and externalizing problems (anger and aggression) during the preschool and school years. Disorganized children also show inappropriate role reversals: In an apparent effort to compensate for their parent's confused communication, they use either exaggerated comforting or hostility to try to control the parent's behavior (Lyons-Ruth, 1996; Lyons-Ruth, Easterbrooks, & Cibelli, 1997; Moss et al., 2004, 2006; Moss, Cyr, & Dubois-Comtois, 2004).

What accounts for unevenness in research findings on the consequences of early attachment quality? Mounting evidence indicates that *continuity of caregiving* determines whether attachment security is linked to later development (Lamb et al., 1985; Thompson, 2006).

Children whose parents respond sensitively not just in infancy but also in later years are likely to develop favorably. In contrast, children whose parents react insensitively or who, over a long period, are exposed to a negative family climate tend to establish lasting patterns of avoidant, resistant, or disorganized behavior and are at greater risk for developmental difficulties.

A close look at the relationship between parenting and children's adjustment in the first few years supports this emphasis on continuity of caregiving. Recall that parents of disorganized/disoriented infants tend to have serious psychological problems or engage in highly maladaptive caregiving—conditions that usually persist and that are strongly linked to poor adjustment in children (Lyons-Ruth, Bronfman, & Parsons, 1999). And when more than 1,000 children were tracked from age 1 to 3 years, those with histories of secure attachment followed by sensitive parenting scored highest in cognitive, emotional, and social outcomes. Those with histories of insecure attachment followed by insensitive parenting scored lowest, while those with mixed histories of attachment and maternal sensitivity scored in between (Belsky & Fearon, 2002a). Specifically, insecurely attached infants whose mothers became more positive and supportive in early childhood showed signs of developmental recovery.

Does this trend remind you of our discussion of *resilience* in Chapter 1? A child whose parental caregiving improves or who has other compensating affectionate ties can bounce back from adversity. In contrast, a child who experiences tender care in infancy but lacks sympathetic ties later on is at risk for problems.

Although a secure attachment in infancy does not guarantee continued good parenting, it does launch the parent–child relationship on a positive path that is likely to continue. Much research shows that an early warm, positive parent–child tie, sustained over time, promotes many aspects of children's development: a more confident and complex self-concept, more advanced emotional understanding, more favorable relationships with teachers and peers, more effective social skills, a stronger sense of moral responsibility, and higher motivation to achieve in school (Thompson, 2006; Thompson, Easterbrooks, & Padilla-Walker, 2003). But the effects of early attachment security are *conditional*—dependent on the quality of the baby's future relationships. Finally, as you will see again in future chapters, attachment is just one of the complex influences on children's psychological development.

ASK YOURSELF

◆ REVIEW What factors explain stability in attachment pattern for some children and change for others? Are these factors also involved in the link between attachment in infancy and later development? Explain.

◆ APPLY What attachment pattern did Timmy display when Vanessa arrived home from work, and what factors probably contributed to it?

◆ CONNECT Review research on emotional self-regulation on pages 254–255. How do the caregiving experiences of securely attached infants promote the development of emotional self-regulation?

◆ REFLECT How would you characterize your internal working model? What factors, in addition to your early relationship with your parents, might have influenced it?

Self-Development

Infancy is a rich formative period for the development of physical and social understanding. In Chapter 6, you learned that infants develop an appreciation of the permanence of objects. And in this chapter, we have seen that over the first year, infants recognize and respond appropriately to others' emotions and distinguish familiar from unfamiliar people. That both objects and people achieve an independent, stable existence for the infant implies that knowledge of the self as a separate, permanent entity is also emerging.

Baby's View   Observer's View

(a)

Left   Right   Right   Left

Normal View   **Reversed View**

(b)

FIGURE 7.6

Three-month-olds' emerging self-awareness, as indicated by reactions to video images.
(a) When shown two side-by-side views of their kicking legs, babies looked longer at the novel, observer's view than at their own view. (b) When shown a normal view of their leg positions alongside a reversed view, infants looked longer at the novel, reversed view. *(Adapted from Rochat, 1998.)*

© LAURA DWIGHT PHOTOGRAPHY

■ This 18-month-old's response to her reflection indicates that she recognizes her unique physical features and is aware of herself as a separate being, distinct from other people and objects. ■

Self-Awareness

After Caitlin's bath, Carolyn often held her in front of the bathroom mirror. As early as the first few months, Caitlin smiled and returned friendly behaviors to her image. At what age did she realize that the charming baby gazing and grinning back was herself?

BEGINNINGS OF SELF-AWARENESS   At birth, infants sense that they are physically distinct from their surroundings. For example, newborns display a stronger rooting reflex in response to external stimulation (an adult's finger touching their cheek) than to self-stimulation (their own hand contacting their cheek) (Rochat & Hespos, 1997). Newborns' remarkable capacity for intermodal perception (see pages 197–198 in Chapter 5) supports the beginnings of self-awareness (Rochat, 2003). As they feel their own touch, feel and watch their limbs move, and feel and hear themselves cry, babies experience intermodal matches that differentiate their own body from surrounding bodies and objects.

Over the first few months, infants distinguish their own visual image from other stimuli, but their self-awareness is limited—expressed only in perception and action. When shown two side-by-side video images of their kicking legs, one from their own perspective (camera behind the baby) and one from an observer's perspective (camera in front of the baby), 3-month-olds looked longer at the observer's view (see Figure 7.6a). In another video-image comparison, they looked longer at a reversal of their leg positions than at a normal view (see Figure 7.6b) (Rochat, 1998). This suggests that young babies have a sense of their own body as a distinct entity, since they have habituated to it, as indicated by their interest in novel views of the body. By 4 months, infants look and smile more at video images of others than video images of themselves, indicating that they distinguish between the two and treat another person (as opposed to the self) as a potential social partner (Rochat & Striano, 2002).

This discrimination of one's own limb and facial movements from those of others in real-time video presentations reflects an *implicit sense of self–world differentiation.* It serves as the foundation for the development of *explicit self-awareness:* an objective understanding that the self is a unique object in a world of objects, which includes representations of one's own physical features and body dimensions.

EXPLICIT SELF-AWARENESS   During the second year, toddlers become consciously aware of the self's physical features. In several studies, 9- to 28-month-olds were placed in front of a mirror. Then, under the pretext of wiping the baby's face, each mother rubbed red dye on her child's nose or forehead. Younger babies touched the mirror as if the red mark had nothing to do with them. But those older than 20 months touched or rubbed their strange-looking noses or foreheads, a response indicating clear awareness of their unique facial appearance (Bard et al., 2006; Lewis & Brooks-Gunn, 1979). And some toddlers act silly or coy in front of the mirror, playfully experimenting with the way the self looks (Bullock & Lutkenhaus, 1990).

Around age 2, *self-recognition*—identification of the self as a physically unique being—is well under way. Children point to themselves in photos and refer to themselves by name or with a personal pronoun ("I" or "me") (Lewis & Ramsay, 2004). And soon they will identify themselves in images with less detail and fidelity than mirrors. Around age 2½, most reach for a sticker surreptitiously placed on top of their heads when shown themselves in a live video, and around age 3 most recognize their own shadow (Cameron & Gallup, 1988; Suddendorf, Simcock, & Nielsen, 2007).

As self-recognition takes shape, older toddlers also construct an explicit *body self-awareness*. At the end of the second year, they realize that their own body can serve as an obstacle. When asked to push a shopping cart while standing on a mat attached to its rear axle, most 18- to 21-month-olds (but not younger children) figured out how to remove themselves from the mat so the cart would move—an ability that improved with age (Moore et al., 2007).

Nevertheless, toddlers lack an objective understanding of their own body dimensions. They make **scale errors,** attempting to do things that their body size makes impossible. For example, they will try to put on dolls' clothes, fit themselves into a doll-sized chair, or walk through a doorway too narrow for them to pass through (Brownell, Zerwas, & Ramani, 2007; DeLoache, Uttal, & Rosengren, 2004). They are amazingly persistent, even seeking an adult's help after they repeatedly do not succeed! Scale errors decline around age 2, but many 2½-year-olds still make them. Young preschoolers are still learning to process physical information about their own bodies in the same way they do for other objects.

INFLUENCES ON SELF-AWARENESS What experiences contribute to gains in self-awareness? During the first year, as infants act on the environment, they probably notice effects that help them sort out self, other people, and objects (Nadel, Prepin, & Okanda, 2005; Rochat, 2001). For example, batting a mobile and seeing it swing in a pattern different from the infant's own actions gives the baby information about the relation between self and physical world. Smiling and vocalizing at a caregiver who smiles and vocalizes back helps specify the relation between self and social world. And watching the movements of one's own hands and feet provides still another kind of feedback—one under much more direct control than the movements of other people or objects. The contrast between these experiences helps infants sense that they are separate from external reality.

Researchers do not yet know exactly how toddlers acquire the various aspects of explicit self-awareness. But sensitive caregiving seems to play a role. Compared to their insecurely attached agemates, securely attached toddlers display more complex self-related actions during play, such as making a doll labeled as the self take a drink or kiss a teddy bear. They also show greater knowledge of their own physical features—for example, in labeling body parts (Pipp, Easterbrooks, & Brown, 1993; Pipp, Easterbrooks, & Harmon, 1992). And 18-month-olds who often establish joint attention with their caregivers are advanced in mirror self-recognition (Nichols, Fox, & Mundy, 2005). Joint attention offers toddlers many opportunities to engage in social referencing—to compare their own and others' reactions to objects and events—which may enhance toddlers' awareness of their own physical uniqueness.

Cultural variations exist in early self-development. Urban German and Greek toddlers attain mirror self-recognition earlier than toddlers of the Nso people of Cameroon, a collectivist rural farming society that highly values social harmony and responsibility to others (Keller et al., 2004, 2005). Compared to their German and Greek counterparts, Nso mothers engage in less face-to-face communication and object stimulation and more body contact and physical stimulation of their babies. German and Greek practices reflect a distal parenting style common in cultures that emphasize *independence,* the Nso practice a proximal parenting style typical in cultures that promote *interdependence.* In line with these differences, Nso proximal parenting is associated with later attainment of self-recognition but earlier emergence of toddlers' compliance with adult requests (see Figure 7.7).

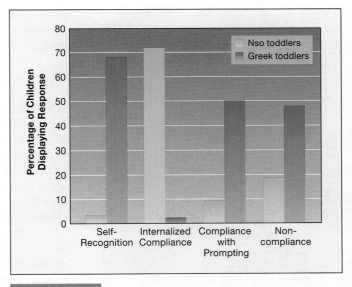

FIGURE 7.7

Self-recognition and compliance among Nso and Greek toddlers.
At 10 and 20 months, toddlers were tested for mirror self-recognition and for compliance (they were told not to open a transparent container with an attractive food). Among Greek toddlers, whose culture values independence, many more had attained self-recognition. But Nso toddlers, reared in an interdependent culture, were greatly advanced in compliance (following directions without prompting), whereas Greek toddlers either needed reminders or did not comply. *(Adapted from Keller et al., 2004.)*

SELF-AWARENESS AND EARLY EMOTIONAL AND SOCIAL DEVELOPMENT Self-awareness quickly becomes a central part of children's emotional and social lives. Recall that self-conscious emotions depend on a strengthening sense of self. Self-awareness also leads to first efforts to understand another's perspective. We have seen that toddlers increasingly appreciate others' intentions, feelings, and desires. Older toddlers who have experienced sensitive caregiving and emotionally available parents draw on their advancing cognitive, language, and social skills to express first signs of **empathy**—the ability to understand another's emotional state and *feel with* that person, or respond emotionally in a similar way. For example, they communicate concern when others are distressed and may offer what they themselves find comforting—a hug, a reassuring comment, or a favorite doll or blanket (Hoffman, 2000; Moreno, Klute, & Robinson, 2008).

At the same time, toddlers demonstrate clearer awareness of how to upset others. One 18-month-old heard her mother talking to another adult about an older sibling: "Anny is really frightened of spiders. In fact, there's a particular toy spider that we've got that she just hates" (Dunn, 1989, p. 107). The innocent-looking toddler ran to the bedroom, returned with the toy spider, and pushed it in front of Anny's face!

Categorizing the Self

By the end of the second year, language becomes a powerful tool in self-development. Between 18 and 30 months, children can categorize themselves and others on the basis of age ("baby," "boy," or "man"), sex ("boy" or "girl"), physical characteristics ("big," "strong"), and even goodness and badness ("I good girl." "Tommy mean!"). They also start to refer to the self's competencies ("Did it!" "I can't") (Stipek, Gralinski, & Kopp, 1990).

Toddlers' use their limited understanding of these social categories to organize their own behavior. As early as 17 months, children select and play in a more involved way with toys that are stereotyped for their own gender—dolls and tea sets for girls, trucks and cars for boys. Their ability to label their own gender predicts a sharp rise in these play preferences over the next few months (Zosuls et al., 2009). Then parents encourage gender-typed behavior by responding more positively when toddlers display it (Ruble, Martin, & Berenbaum, 2006). As we will see in Chapter 10, gender-typing increases dramatically during early childhood.

Self-Control

Self-awareness also contributes to *effortful control*, the extent to which children can inhibit impulses, manage negative emotion, and behave in socially acceptable ways. Indeed, a firmer sense of self may underlie the increasing stability and organization of effortful control in the third year (see pages 258 and 260). To behave in a self-controlled fashion, children must think of themselves as separate, autonomous beings who can direct their own actions. And they must have the representational and memory capacities to recall a caregiver's directive ("Caitlin, don't touch that light socket!") and apply it to their own behavior.

As these capacities emerge between 12 and 18 months, toddlers first become capable of **compliance:** They show clear awareness of caregivers' wishes and expectations and can obey simple requests and commands. And, as every parent knows, they can also decide to do just the opposite! Although defiance in preschoolers is associated with negative parent–child relationships and poor adjustment, toddlers who sometimes strongly resist parental demands tend to have sensitive, supportive parents with whom they interact positively. These parents recognize the young child's need for self-assertion and autonomy (Dix et al., 2007). Indeed, active resistance in toddlerhood does not predict later, persisting defiance. Rather, for most toddlers, assertiveness and opposition occur alongside compliance with an eager, willing spirit, which suggests that the child is beginning to adopt the adult's directives as his own (Kochanska, Murray, & Harlan, 2000). Compliance quickly

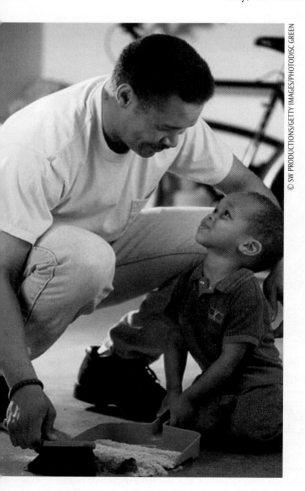

© SW PRODUCTIONS/GETTY IMAGES/PHOTODISC GREEN

■ This father encourages compliance and the beginnings of self-control. The toddler joins in the task with an eager, willing spirit, which suggests he is adopting the adult's directive as his own. ■

◆ Applying What We Know

Helping Toddlers Develop Compliance and Self-Control

SUGGESTION	RATIONALE
Respond to the toddler with sensitivity and encouragement.	Toddlers whose parents are sensitive and supportive at times actively resist, but they are also are more compliant and self-controlled.
Provide advance notice when the toddler must stop an enjoyable activity.	Toddlers find it more difficult to stop a pleasant activity that is already under way to wait before engaging in a desired action.
Offer many prompts and reminders.	Toddlers' ability to remember and comply with rules is limited; they need continuous adult oversight and patient assistance.
Respond to self-controlled behavior with verbal and physical approval.	Praise and hugs reinforce appropriate behavior, increasing the likelihood that it will occur again.
Encourage selective and sustained attention (see Chapter 6, pages 218–219).	Development of attention is related to self-control. Children who can shift attention from a captivating stimulus and focus on a less attractive alternative are better at controlling their impulses.
Support language development (see Chapter 6, pages 241–242).	Early language development is related to self-control. In the second year, children begin to use language to remind themselves of adult expectations and to delay gratification.
Gradually increase rules in a manner consistent with the toddler's developing capacities.	As cognition and language improve, toddlers can follow more rules related to safety, respect for people and property, family routines, manners, and simple chores.

leads to toddlers' first consciencelike verbalizations—for example, correcting the self by saying "No, can't" before reaching for a treat or jumping on the sofa.

Researchers often study the early emergence of self-control by giving children tasks that, like the situations just mentioned, require **delay of gratification**—waiting for an appropriate time and place to engage in a tempting act. Between ages 1½ and 3, children show an increasing capacity to wait before eating a treat, opening a present, or playing with a toy (Vaughn, Kopp, & Krakow, 1984). Children who are advanced in development of attention and language tend to be better at delaying gratification—findings that help explain why girls are typically more self-controlled than boys (Else-Quest et al., 2006). Some toddlers already use verbal and other attention-diverting techniques—talking to themselves, singing, or looking away—to keep from engaging in prohibited acts.

Like effortful control in general, young children's capacity to delay gratification is influenced by both temperament and quality of caregiving (Kochanska & Aksan, 2006; Kochanska & Knaack, 2003). Inhibited children find it easier to wait than angry, irritable children do. But toddlers who experience parental warmth and gentle encouragement are more likely to be cooperative and to resist temptation. Such parenting—which encourages and models patient, nonimpulsive behavior—is particularly important for temperamentally reactive babies. In one study, anger-prone 7-month-olds with gentle, responsive mothers became eagerly compliant 15-month-olds. Angry infants with insensitive mothers, by contrast, developed into strikingly uncooperative toddlers (Kochanska, Aksan, & Carlson, 2005). **TAKE A MOMENT...** Turn back to page 262, and note how these findings provide yet another example of the importance of goodness-of-fit between temperament and child rearing.

As self-control improves, parents gradually expand the rules they expect toddlers to follow, from safety and respect for property and people to family routines, manners, and simple chores (Gralinski & Kopp, 1993). Still, toddlers' control over their own actions depends on constant parental oversight and reminders. Several prompts ("Remember, we're going to go in just a minute") and gentle insistence were usually necessary to get Caitlin to stop playing so that she and her parents could go on an errand. Applying What We Know above summarizes ways to help toddlers develop compliance and self-control.

As the second year of life drew to a close, Carolyn, Monica, and Vanessa were delighted at their children's readiness to learn the rules of social life. As we will see in Chapter 10, advances in cognition and language, along with parental warmth and reasonable demands for maturity, lead preschoolers to make tremendous strides in this area.

◆ REVIEW Why is insisting that infants comply with parental directives inappropriate? What competencies are necessary for the emergence of compliance and self-control?

◆ REFLECT In view of research on toddlers' compliance, active resistance, and budding capacity to delay gratification, do you think that "the terrible twos," a commonly used expression to characterize typical toddler behavior, is an apt description? Explain.

◆ APPLY Len, a caregiver of 1- and 2-year-olds, wonders whether toddlers recognize themselves. List signs of self-recognition in the second year that Len can observe. What behaviors reveal that toddlers are still forming objective representations of their own physical features?

◆ CONNECT What type of early parenting fosters the development of emotional self-regulation, secure attachment, and self-control? Why, in each instance, is it effective?

Summary

Erikson's Theory of Infant and Toddler Personality

What personality changes take place during Erikson's stages of basic trust versus mistrust and autonomy versus shame and doubt?

■ Warm, responsive caregiving leads infants to resolve Erikson's psychological conflict of **basic trust versus mistrust** on the positive side. During toddlerhood, **autonomy versus shame and doubt** is resolved favorably when parents provide appropriate guidance and reasonable choices. If children emerge from the first few years without sufficient trust and autonomy, the seeds are sown for adjustment problems.

Emotional Development

Describe the development of basic emotions over the first year, noting the adaptive function of each.

■ During the first half-year, **basic emotions** gradually become clear, well-organized signals. The **social smile** appears between 6 and 10 weeks, laughter around 3 to 4 months. Happiness strengthens the parent–child bond and reflects as well as supports physical and cognitive mastery.

■ Anger and fear, especially in the form of **stranger anxiety,** increase in the second half of the first year as infants' cognitive and motor capacities improve. Newly mobile babies use the familiar caregiver as a **secure base** from which to explore.

Summarize changes that occur during the first two years in understanding others' emotions, expression of self-conscious emotions, and emotional self-regulation.

■ The ability to understand others' feelings expands over the first year. From 5 months on, babies perceive facial expressions as organized patterns. Between 8 and 10 months, infants engage in **social referencing,** actively seeking emotional information from caregivers in uncertain situations. By the middle of the second year, infants become aware that others' emotional reactions may differ from their own.

■ During toddlerhood, self-awareness and adult instruction provide the foundation for **self-conscious emotions:** shame, embarrassment, guilt, envy, and pride. **Emotional self-regulation** emerges as the prefrontal cortex functions more effectively and as caregivers sensitively assist infants in adjusting their emotional reactions. In the second year, growth in representation and language leads to more effective ways of regulating emotion.

© ABLEIMAGES/ALAMY IMAGES

Temperament and Development

What is temperament, and how is it measured?

■ Children differ greatly in **temperament**—early appearing, stable individual differences in reactivity and self-regulation. The New York Longitudinal Study identified three patterns: the **easy child,** the **difficult child,** and the **slow-to-warm-up child.** The most influential model of temperament, devised by Mary Rothbart, includes dimensions representing emotion, attention, and action, along with **effortful control,** the ability to regulate one's reactivity.

■ Temperament is assessed through parental reports, behavior ratings by others familiar with the child, and laboratory observations. Most neurophysiological research has focused on distinguishing **inhibited,** or **shy, children** from **uninhibited,** or **sociable, children.**

Discuss the roles of heredity and environment in the stability of temperament, including the goodness-of-fit model.

■ Temperament has low to moderate stability: It develops with age and can be modified by experience. Long-term prediction from early temperament is best achieved after age 3.

■ Temperament has a genetic foundation, but child rearing and cultural beliefs and practices have much to do with maintaining or changing it.

■ The **goodness-of-fit model** describes how temperament and environment work together to affect later development. Parenting practices that fit well with the child's temperament help children achieve more adaptive functioning.

Development of Attachment

What are the unique features of ethological theory of attachment?

■ The most widely accepted perspective on development of **attachment**—our strong, affectionate tie with special people in our lives—is **ethological theory,** which recognizes the infant's emotional tie to the caregiver as an evolved response that promotes survival. In early infancy, a set of built-in behaviors encourages the parent to remain close to the baby.

■ Around 6 to 8 months, **separation anxiety** and use of the parent as a secure base indicate the existence of a true attachment bond. Separation anxiety declines as representation and language develop, letting toddlers understand the parent's coming and going. From early caregiving experiences, children construct an **internal working model** that guides all future close relationships.

Cite the four attachment patterns assessed by the Strange Situation and the Attachment Q-Sort, and discuss factors that affect attachment security.

■ Using the **Strange Situation,** a common technique for measuring the quality of attachment between 1 and 2 years of age, researchers have identified four attachment patterns: **secure, avoidant, resistant,** and **disorganized/ disoriented attachment.** The **Attachment Q-Sort,** based on home observations of children between ages 1 and 5, yields a score ranging from low to high security.

■ Securely attached babies in middle-SES families under favorable life conditions more often maintain their attachment pattern than insecure babies. However, the disorganized/ disoriented pattern is highly stable. Cultural conditions must be considered in interpreting the meaning of attachment patterns.

■ Attachment security is influenced by early availability of a consistent caregiver, quality of caregiving, the fit between the baby's temperament and parenting practices, and family circumstances. **Sensitive caregiving** is moderately related to secure attachment.

■ In some cultures, **interactional synchrony** characterizes the experiences of securely attached babies. Parents' internal working models are good predictors of infant attachment patterns, but parents' childhood experiences do not transfer directly to quality of attachment with their own children.

Discuss infants' formation of multiple attachments, and indicate how attachment paves the way for early peer sociability.

■ Infants develop strong affectionate ties to fathers, who tend to engage in more exciting, physical play with babies than do mothers. Especially in cultures where fathers devote little time to infant care, play is a vital context in which fathers and babies build secure attachments, predicting favorable emotional and social adjustment.

■ Grandparents who serve as primary caregivers for grandchildren in skipped-generation families forge significant attachment ties that help protect children with troubled family lives from adjustment problems.

■ Early in the first year, infants start to form rich emotional relationships with siblings that combine rivalry and resentment with affection and sympathetic concern. Individual differences in these relationships are influenced by temperament, parenting practices, and marital quality.

■ Peer sociability begins in infancy with isolated social acts, followed by reciprocal exchanges (largely in the form of mutual imitation) in the second year of life. A warm caregiver–child bond promotes peer sociability.

Describe and interpret the relationship between secure attachment in infancy and psychological development in childhood.

■ A secure attachment in infancy launches the parent–child relationship on a positive path. But continuity of caregiving determines whether attachment security is linked to later development. If caregiving improves, children can recover from an insecure attachment history.

Self-Development

Describe the development of self-awareness in infancy and toddlerhood, along with the emotional and social capacities it supports.

■ Self-awareness begins at birth, when infants implicitly sense that they are physically distinct from their surroundings, and expands over the early months. At the end of the second year, self-recognition emerges as toddlers become explicitly aware of the self's physical features. However, toddlers lack an objective understanding of their own body size, as indicated by their **scale errors.**

■ Self-awareness sets the stage for social referencing and, in the second year, self-conscious emotions. It also leads to toddlers' first efforts to appreciate others' perspectives, including early signs of **empathy.** Between 18 and 30 months, as language develops, children categorize themselves and others on the basis of age, sex, physical characteristics, and competencies.

■ Self-awareness also contributes to effortful control and, between 12 and 18 months, to the emergence of **compliance.** Between ages 1½ and 3, **delay of gratification** strengthens. Toddlers who experience parental warmth and gentle encouragement are likely to be advanced in self-control.

IMPORTANT TERMS AND CONCEPTS

attachment (p. 264)
Attachment Q-Sort (p. 267)
autonomy versus shame and doubt (p. 249)
avoidant attachment (p. 267)
basic emotions (p. 250)
basic trust versus mistrust (p. 248)
compliance (p. 282)
delay of gratification (p. 283)
difficult child (p. 256)
disorganized/disoriented attachment (p. 267)
easy child (p. 256)

effortful control (p. 257)
emotional self-regulation (p. 254)
empathy (p. 282)
ethological theory of attachment (p. 265)
goodness-of-fit model (p. 262)
inhibited, or shy, child (p. 258)
interactional synchrony (p. 270)
internal working model (p. 266)
resistant attachment (p. 267)
scale errors (p. 281)
secure attachment (p. 266)

secure base (p. 252)
self-conscious emotions (p. 253)
sensitive caregiving (p. 270)
separation anxiety (p. 265)
slow-to-warm-up child (p. 257)
social referencing (p. 253)
social smile (p. 251)
stranger anxiety (p. 252)
Strange Situation (p. 266)
temperament (p. 256)
uninhibited, or sociable, child (p. 258)

Milestones

Development in Infancy and Toddlerhood

Birth–6 months

PHYSICAL

- Height and weight increase rapidly. (162)
- Newborn reflexes decline. (145)
- Sleep is increasingly organized into a night–day schedule. (172)
- Responses can be classically and operantly conditioned. (179–180)
- Habituates to unchanging stimuli; recovers to novel stimuli. (181)
- Holds head up, rolls over, and grasps objects. (184)
- Shows sensitivity to motion, then binocular, and finally pictorial depth cues. (191–193)
- Recognizes and prefers human facial pattern; recognizes features of mother's face. (195–196)
- Perceives auditory and visual stimuli as organized patterns. (198)
- By end of this period, moves from relying on motion and spatial arrangement to using shape, color, and texture to visually identify objects. (197)
- Masters a wide range of intermodal (visual, auditory, and tactile) relationships. (197–198)

COGNITIVE

- Engages in immediate and deferred imitation of adults' facial expressions. (210–211)
- Repeats chance behaviors that lead to pleasurable and interesting results. (206)
- Has some awareness of many physical properties (including object permanence) and basic numerical knowledge. (208)

- Attention becomes more efficient and flexible. (218)
- Recognition memory for visual events improves. (219)
- Forms categories based on objects' similar physical properties. (222)

LANGUAGE

- Engages in cooing and, by the end of this period, babbling. (236)
- Begins to establish joint attention with caregiver, who labels objects and events. (238)

EMOTIONAL/SOCIAL

- Social smile and laughter emerge. (251)

- Matches feeling tone of caregiver in face-to-face communication; later, expects matched responses. (252)
- Emotional expressions become well organized and meaningfully related to environmental events. (253)
- Distinguishes positive from negative emotion in voices and facial expressions. (253)
- Regulates emotion by shifting attention and self-soothing. (255)
- Smiles, laughs, and babbles more to caregiver than to a stranger. (265)
- Awareness of self as physically distinct from surroundings increases. (280)

7–12 months

PHYSICAL

- Approaches adultlike sleep–wake schedule. (172)
- Sits alone, crawls, and walks. (184)

- Reaching and grasping improve in flexibility and accuracy; shows refined pincer grasp. (187–188)
- "Screens out" sounds not used in own language; perceives meaningful speech. (189–190)
- Relies on shape, color, and texture to distinguish objects from their surroundings. (197)
- Intermodal perception continues to improve. (198)

COGNITIVE

- Engages in intentional, or goal-directed, behavior. (206–207)
- Finds an object hidden in an initial location. (207)
- Recall memory improves, as indicated by gains in deferred imitation of adults' actions with objects. (210)
- Solves simple problems by analogy to a previous problem. (211)
- Categorizes objects by similar function and behavior. (222)
- Uses words to call up mental images of objects not physically present. (211)

NOTE: Numbers in parentheses indicate the page or pages on which each milestone is discussed.

LANGUAGE

- Babbling expands to include sounds of spoken languages and patterns of the child's language community. (237)
- Skill in joint attention with caregiver improves. (238)

- Takes turns in games, such as pat-a-cake and peekaboo. (238)
- Uses preverbal gestures (showing, pointing) to influence others' goals and behavior and to convey information. (238)
- Comprehends some word meanings. (238)
- Around 1 year, says first words. (238)

EMOTIONAL/SOCIAL

- Smiling and laughter increase in frequency and expressiveness. (251)
- Anger and fear increase in frequency and intensity. (251–252)
- Stranger anxiety and separation anxiety appear. (252, 265–266)
- Uses caregiver as a secure base for exploration. (252)
- Shows "clear-cut" attachment to a familiar caregiver. (265)
- Increasingly detects the meaning of others' emotional expressions and engages in social referencing. (253)
- Regulates emotion by approaching and retreating from stimulation. (254–255)

13–18 months

PHYSICAL

- Height and weight gain are rapid, but not as great as in first year; toddlers slim down. (162–163)
- Walking is better coordinated. (184)

- Manipulates small objects with improved coordination. (188, 206)

COGNITIVE

- Takes a deliberately experimental approach to problem solving, repeating behaviors with variation. (206)
- Searches in several locations for a hidden object. (209)
- Engages in deferred imitation of adults' actions with objects over longer delays and across a change in context—for example, from child care to home. (210)
- Sustained attention improves. (218)
- Recall memory for people, places, objects, and actions improves. (220)
- Sorts objects into categories. (222)
- Becomes aware that pictures can symbolize real objects. (212)

LANGUAGE

- Steadily adds to vocabulary. (239)
- Comprehends 50 words at 13 months; produces 50 words at 18 months. (240)

EMOTIONAL/SOCIAL

- Joins in play with familiar adults, siblings, and peers. (277–278)

- Realizes that others' emotional reactions may differ from one's own. (253)
- Uses social referencing to better evaluate events and understand emotions of the same valence. (253)
- Shows signs of empathy. (282)
- Complies with simple directives. (282)

19–24 months

PHYSICAL

- Jumps, walks on tiptoe, runs, and climbs. (184)
- Manipulates small objects with good coordination. (188, 206)

COGNITIVE

- Solves simple problems suddenly, through representation. (207)
- Finds a hidden object that has been moved while out of sight. (207)
- Engages in make-believe play, using simple actions experienced in everyday life. (207)

- Engages in deferred imitation of actions an adult tries to produce, even if not fully realized. (211)
- Sorts objects into categories more effectively. (223)
- Begins to use language as a flexible symbolic tool, to modify existing mental representations. (212)

LANGUAGE

- Produces about 200 words. (239)
- Combines two words. (239)

EMOTIONAL/SOCIAL

- Self-conscious emotions (shame, embarrassment, guilt, envy, and pride) emerge. (253–254)
- Acquires a vocabulary for talking about feelings. (255)
- Begins to use language to assist with emotional self-regulation. (255)
- Begins to tolerate caregiver's absences more easily; separation anxiety declines. (265)
- Recognizes image of self and by end of this period, uses own name or personal pronoun to refer to self. (280)
- Constructs explicit body self-awareness, and scale errors decline. (281)
- Categorizes self and others on the basis of age, sex, physical characteristics, goodness and badness, and competencies. (282)
- Shows gender-stereotyped toy preferences. (282)
- Self-control, as indicated by delay of gratification, emerges. (283)
- Starts to use words to influence a playmate's behavior. (278)

"On the Slope"
Natasha
6 years, Russia

These young skiers express pride in mastery of new motor skills. Chapter 8 highlights the close link between physical growth and other aspects of development in early childhood.

Physical Development in Early Childhood

*F*or more than a decade, my fourth-floor office window over-looked the preschool and kindergarten play yard of our university laboratory school. On mild fall and spring mornings, the doors of classrooms swung open, and sand table, easels, and large blocks spilled out into a small courtyard. Alongside the building was a grassy area with jungle gyms, swings, a playhouse, and a flower garden planted by the children; beyond it, a circular path lined with tricycles and wagons. Each day, the setting was alive with activity.

Even from my distant vantage point, the physical changes of early childhood were evident. Children's bodies were longer and leaner than they had been a year or two earlier. The awkward gait of toddlerhood had disappeared in favor of more refined movements that included running, climbing, jumping, galloping, and skipping. Children scaled the jungle gym, raced across the lawn, turned somersaults, and vigorously pedaled tricycles. Just as impressive as these gross-motor achievements were gains in fine-motor skills. At the sand table, children built hills, valleys, caves, and roads and prepared trays of pretend cookies and cupcakes. And as they grew older, their paintings at the outdoor easels took on greater structure and detail as family members, houses, trees, birds, sky, monsters, and letterlike forms appeared in the colorful creations.

The years from 2 to 6 are often called "the play years"—aptly so, since play blossoms during this time and supports every aspect of development. Our discussion of early childhood opens with the physical achievements of this period—growth in body size, improvements in motor coordination, and refinements in perception. We pay special attention to genetic and environmental factors that support these changes, as well as to their intimate connection with other domains of development. The children I came to know well, first by watching from my office window and later by observing at close range in their classrooms, will provide many examples of developmental trends and individual differences.

Body Growth

In early childhood, the rapid increase in body size of the first two years tapers off into a slower growth pattern. On average, children add 2 to 3 inches in height and about 5 pounds in weight each year. Boys continue to be slightly larger than girls. As the "baby fat" that began to decline in toddlerhood drops off further, children gradually become thinner, although girls retain somewhat more body fat than boys, who are slightly more muscular. As the torso lengthens and widens, internal organs tuck neatly inside, and the spine straightens. As Figure 8.1 shows, by age 5 the top-heavy, bowlegged, potbellied toddler has become a more streamlined, flat-tummied, longer-legged child with body proportions similar to those of adults. Consequently, posture and balance improve—changes that foster gains in motor coordination.

Individual differences in body size are even more apparent during early childhood than in infancy and toddlerhood. Speeding around the bike path in the play yard, 5-year-old Darryl— at 48 inches tall and 55 pounds—towered over his kindergarten classmates. (The average North American 5-year-old boy is 43 inches tall and weighs 42 pounds.) Priti, an Asian-Indian child, was unusually small because of genetic factors linked to her cultural ancestry. And Lynette and Hal, two Caucasian children with impoverished home lives, were well below average for reasons we will discuss shortly.

The existence of these variations in body size reminds us that growth norms for one population are not good standards for children elsewhere in the world. Consider the Efe of the Republic of Congo, whose typical adult height is less than 5 feet. For genetic reasons, the impact of hormones controlling body size is reduced in Efe children (Bailey, 1991). By age 5, the average Efe child is shorter than more than 97 percent of North American 5-year-olds. The Efe's small size probably evolved because it reduces their caloric requirements in the face of food scarcity in the rain forests of Central Africa and enables them to move easily through the dense forest underbrush (Perry & Dominy, 2009). Efe children's short stature does not indicate growth or health problems. But for other children, such as Lynette and Hal, extremely slow growth is cause for concern.

Skeletal Growth

The skeletal changes of infancy continue throughout early childhood. Between ages 2 and 6, approximately 45 new *epiphyses,* or growth centers in which cartilage hardens into bone, emerge in various parts of the skeleton. Other epiphyses will appear in middle childhood. X-rays of these growth centers enable doctors to estimate children's *skeletal age,* or progress toward physical maturity (see page 163 in Chapter 5)—information helpful in diagnosing growth disorders.

By the end of the preschool years, children start to lose their primary, or "baby," teeth. The age at which they do so is heavily influenced by genetic factors. For example, girls, who are ahead of boys in physical development, lose their primary teeth sooner. Cultural ancestry also makes a difference. North American children typically get their first secondary (permanent) tooth at 6½ years, children in Ghana at just over 5 years, and children in Hong Kong around the sixth birthday (Burns, 2000). But nutritional factors also influence dental development. Prolonged malnutrition delays the appearance of permanent teeth, whereas overweight and obesity accelerate it (Hilgers et al., 2006).

Diseased baby teeth can affect the health of permanent teeth, so preventing decay in primary teeth is essential—by brushing consistently, avoiding sugary foods, drinking fluoridated water, and getting topical fluoride treatments and sealants (plastic coatings that protect tooth surfaces). Another factor is exposure to tobacco smoke, which suppresses children's immune system, including the ability to fight bacteria responsible for tooth decay. The risk associated with this suppression is greatest in infancy and early childhood, when the immune system is not yet fully

© BOB DAEMMRICH/STOCK BOSTON, LLC

■ During early childhood, body fat declines, the torso enlarges to better accommodate the internal organs, and the spine straightens. Compared to her younger brother, this girl looks more streamlined. ■

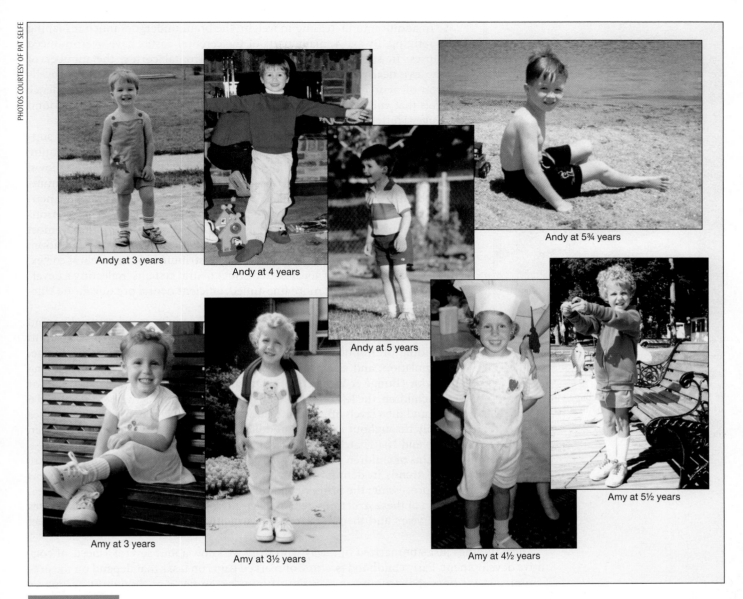

Andy at 3 years

Andy at 4 years

Andy at 5¾ years

Andy at 5 years

Amy at 3 years

Amy at 3½ years

Amy at 4½ years

Amy at 5½ years

FIGURE 8.1

Body growth during early childhood. Andy and Amy grew more slowly during the preschool years than in infancy and toddlerhood (see Chapter 5, page 163). By age 5, their bodies became flat-tummied and longer-legged. Boys continue to be slightly taller and heavier and more muscular than girls. But generally, the two sexes are similar in body proportions and physical capacities.

mature (Aligne et al., 2003). Young children in homes with regular smokers are three times as likely as their agemates to have decayed teeth, even after other factors influencing dental health have been controlled (Shenkin et al., 2004).

Unfortunately, an estimated 30 percent of U.S. preschoolers have tooth decay, a figure that rises to 60 percent by age 18. Causes include poor diet and inadequate health care—factors that are more likely to affect low-SES children. About 12 percent of U.S. children living in poverty have untreated tooth decay (U.S. Department of Health and Human Services, 2007c).

Brain Development

Between ages 2 and 6, the brain increases from 70 percent of its adult weight to 90 percent. At the same time, preschoolers improve in a wide variety of skills—physical coordination, perception, attention, memory, language, logical thinking, and imagination.

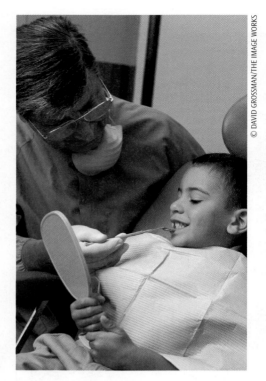

■ Regular dental checkups are important for preschoolers. Diseased baby teeth can affect the long-term health of permanent teeth, which start to appear at the end of the preschool years. ■

In addition to increasing in weight, the brain undergoes much reshaping and refining. By age 4, many parts of the cerebral cortex have overproduced synapses. In some regions, such as the prefrontal cortex, the number of synapses is nearly double the adult value. Together, synaptic growth and myelination of neural fibers result in a high energy need. In fact, fMRI evidence reveals that energy metabolism in the cerebral cortex reaches a peak around this age (Huttenlocher, 2002; Nelson, Thomas, & de Haan, 2006).

Recall from Chapter 5 that overabundance of synaptic connections supports *plasticity* of the young brain, helping to ensure that the child will acquire certain abilities even if some areas are damaged. *Synaptic pruning* follows: Neurons that are seldom stimulated lose their connective fibers, and the number of synapses is reduced (see page 165). As the structures of stimulated neurons become more elaborate and require more space, surrounding neurons die, and brain plasticity declines. By age 8 to 10, energy consumption of most cortical regions diminishes to near-adult levels (Nelson, 2002). In addition, cognitive functions are no longer as widely distributed in the cerebral cortex. Rather, they increasingly localize in distinct neural systems, reflecting a developmental shift toward a more fine-tuned, efficient neural organization (Durston & Casey, 2006; Tsujimoto, 2008).

EEG, NIRS, and fMRI measures of neural activity reveal especially rapid growth from early to middle childhood in prefrontal-cortical areas devoted to inhibition of impulses, attention, working memory (temporary storage, manipulation, and selection of information), and planning and organizing behavior (Bunge & Wright, 2007; Durston & Casey, 2006). Furthermore, for most children, the left cerebral hemisphere is especially active between 3 and 6 years and then levels off. In contrast, activity in the right hemisphere increases steadily throughout early and middle childhood, with a slight spurt between ages 8 and 10 (Thatcher, Walker, & Giudice, 1987; Thompson et al., 2000).

Studies of the brains of children who have died confirm these trends. For example, Figure 8.2 shows age-related trends in density of synapses in three left-hemispheric cortical areas involved in language processing: the primary auditory area, Broca's area, and Wernicke's area. (To review the location of these structures, refer to page 234.) Notice how synaptic density rises during the first three years and then, as a result of synaptic pruning, falls to an adult level around age 10.

The findings just summarized fit nicely with what we know about several aspects of cognitive development. Early childhood is a time of marked gains on tasks that depend on the prefrontal cortex—ones that require suppression of impulses in favor of thoughtful responses

(see page 165).

FIGURE 8.2

Age-related changes in synaptic density of three areas of the cerebral cortex involved in language processing. Density of synapses in all three areas rises sharply during the first three years—the same period in which children rapidly develop language skills. As a result of pruning, density of synapses falls during the late preschool and school years. During this time, plasticity of the cerebral cortex is reduced. *(Adapted from P. Huttenlocher, 1999, "Synaptogenesis in Human Cerebral Cortex and the Concept of Critical Periods," in N. A. Fox, L. A. Leavitt, & J. G. Warhol, Eds., The Role of Early Experience in Development, pp. 15–28. Calverton, NY: Johnson & Johnson Pediatric Institute, L.L.C. Reprinted with permission.)*

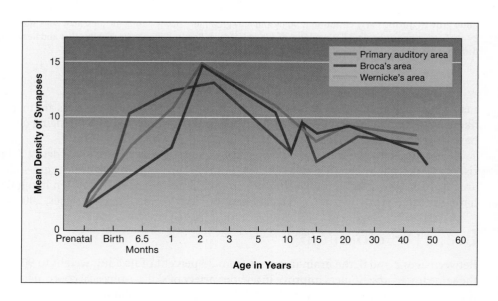

(Rothbart & Bates, 2006). Further, language skills (typically housed in the left hemisphere) increase at an astonishing pace in early childhood, and they support children's increasing control over behavior, also mediated by the prefrontal cortex. In contrast, spatial skills (usually located in the right hemisphere), such as giving directions, drawing pictures, and recognizing geometric shapes, develop gradually over childhood and adolescence.

Differences in rate of development between the two hemispheres suggest that they are continuing to *lateralize* (specialize in functions). Let's take a closer look at brain lateralization during early childhood by focusing on handedness.

HANDEDNESS   On a visit to the preschool, I watched 3-year-old Moira as she drew pictures, worked puzzles, ate a snack, and played outside. Unlike most of her classmates, Moira does most things—drawing, eating, and zipping her jacket—with her left hand. But she uses her right hand for a few activities, such as throwing a ball. Research on handedness, along with other evidence covered in Chapter 5, supports the joint contribution of nature and nurture to brain lateralization.

As early as the tenth prenatal week, most fetuses show a right-hand preference during thumb-sucking (Hepper, McCartney, & Shannon, 1998). And by age 6 months, infants typically display a smoother, more efficient movement when reaching with their right than their left arm. These early tendencies may contribute to the right-handed bias of most children by the end of the first year (Hinojosa, Sheu, & Michael, 2003; Ronnqvist & Domellof, 2006). During toddlerhood and early childhood, handedness gradually extends to a wider range of skills.

Handedness reflects the greater capacity of one side of the brain—the individual's **dominant cerebral hemisphere**—to carry out skilled motor action. Other important abilities are generally located on the dominant side as well. For right-handed people—in Western nations, 90 percent of the population—language is housed in the left hemisphere with hand control. For the left-handed 10 percent, language is occasionally located in the right hemisphere or, more often, shared between the hemispheres (Perelle & Ehrman, 2009). This indicates that the brains of left-handers tend to be less strongly lateralized than those of right-handers. Consistent with this idea, many left-handed individuals (like Moira) are also *ambidextrous*. Although they prefer their left hand, they sometimes use their right hand skillfully as well (McManus et al., 1988).

Left-handed parents show only a weak tendency to have left-handed children (Vuoksimaa et al., 2009). One genetic theory proposes that most children inherit a gene that *biases* them for right-handedness and a left-dominant cerebral hemisphere. But that bias is not strong enough to overcome experiences that might sway children toward a left-hand preference (Annett, 2002). Even prenatal events may profoundly affect handedness. Both identical and fraternal twins are more likely than ordinary siblings to differ in hand preference, probably because twins usually lie in opposite orientations in the uterus (Derom et al., 1996). The orientation of most singleton fetuses—facing toward the left—is believed to promote greater control over movements on the body's right side (Previc, 1991).

Handedness also involves practice. Newborns' bias in head position causes them to spend more time looking at and using one hand, which contributes to greater skillfulness of that hand (Hinojosa, Sheu, & Michael, 2003). Handedness is strongest for complex skills requiring extensive training, such as eating with utensils, writing, and engaging in athletic activities. Also, wide cultural differences exist in rates of left-handedness. In Tanzania, Africa, where children are physically restrained and punished for favoring the left hand, less than 1 percent of adults are left-handed (Provins, 1997).

Although left-handedness occurs more often in people with mental retardation and mental illness than in the general population, atypical brain lateralization

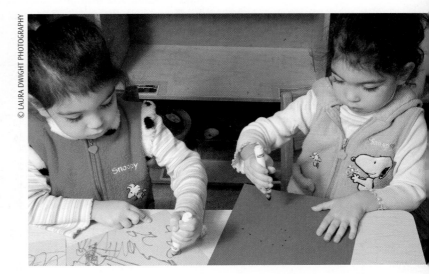

■ Twins are more likely than ordinary siblings to differ in hand preference, perhaps because twins usually lie in opposite orientations in the uterus. ■

is probably not responsible for these individuals' problems. Rather, early damage to the left hemisphere may have caused their disabilities while also leading to a shift in handedness. In support of this idea, left-handedness is associated with prenatal and birth difficulties that can result in brain damage, including maternal stress, prolonged labor, prematurity, Rh incompatibility, and breech delivery (O'Callaghan et al., 1993; Powls et al., 1996; Rodriguez & Waldenström, 2008).

Most left-handers, however, have no developmental problems—in fact, unusual lateralization may have certain advantages. Left- and mixed-handed young people are slightly advantaged in speed and flexibility of thinking, and they are more likely than their right-handed agemates to develop outstanding verbal and mathematical talents (Flannery & Liederman, 1995; Gunstad et al., 2007). More even distribution of cognitive functions across both hemispheres may be responsible.

OTHER ADVANCES IN BRAIN DEVELOPMENT   Besides the cerebral cortex, several other areas of the brain make strides during early childhood (see Figure 8.3). All of these changes involve establishing links between parts of the brain, increasing the coordinated functioning of the central nervous system.

At the rear and base of the brain is the **cerebellum,** a structure that aids in balance and control of body movement. Fibers linking the cerebellum to the cerebral cortex grow and myelinate from birth through the preschool years. This change contributes to dramatic gains in motor coordination: By the end of the preschool years, children can play hopscotch, throw a ball with well-coordinated movements, and print letters of the alphabet. Connections between the cerebellum and the cerebral cortex also support thinking (Diamond, 2000). Children with damage to the cerebellum usually display both motor and cognitive deficits, including problems with memory, planning, and language (Noterdaeme et al., 2002; Riva & Giorgi, 2000).

The **reticular formation,** a structure in the brain stem that maintains alertness and consciousness, generates synapses and myelinates throughout early childhood and into adolescence. Neurons in the reticular formation send out fibers to other areas of the brain. Many go to the prefrontal cortex, contributing to improvements in sustained, controlled attention.

An inner-brain structure called the **hippocampus,** which plays a vital role in memory and in images of space that help us find our way, undergoes rapid synapse formation and myelination in the second half of the first year, when recall memory and independent movement emerge. Over the preschool and elementary school years, the hippocampus and surrounding areas of the cerebral cortex continue to develop swiftly, establishing connections with one another and with the prefrontal cortex (Nelson, Thomas, & de Haan, 2006). These changes make possible the dramatic gains in memory and spatial understanding of early and middle childhood—ability to use strategies to store and retrieve information, expansion of autobio-

FIGURE 8.3

Cross-section of the human brain, showing the location of the cerebellum, the reticular formation, the hippocampus, the amygdala, and the corpus callosum. These structures undergo considerable development during early childhood. Also shown is the pituitary gland, which secretes hormones that control body growth (see page 297).

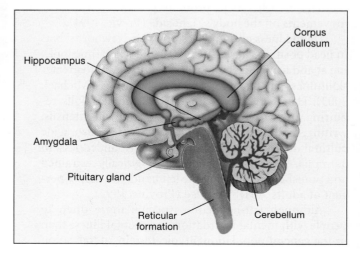

graphical memory (which brings an end to infantile amnesia), and drawing and reading of maps (which we will take up in Chapter 9).

Also located in the inner brain, adjacent to the hippocampus, is the **amygdala,** a structure that plays a central role in processing emotional information. The amygdala is sensitive to facial emotional expressions, especially fear (Whalen et al., 2009). It also enhances memory for emotionally salient events, thereby ensuring that information relevant for survival—stimuli that evoke fear or signify safety—will be retrieved on future occasions. This capacity for emotional learning seems to emerge in early childhood: Damage to the amygdala in the first few years leads to loss of ability to learn about fear and safety signals and typically results in wide-ranging socially inappropriate behaviors (Shaw, Brierley, & David, 2005). Throughout childhood and adolescence, connections between the amygdala and the prefrontal cortex, which governs regulation of emotion, form and myelinate (Tottenham, Hare, & Casey, 2009). Recall from Chapter 7 that in socially anxious children, the amygdala is overly reactive to threatening situations (see page 259).

The **corpus callosum** is a large bundle of fibers connecting the two cerebral hemispheres. Production of synapses and myelination of the corpus callosum increase at 1 year, peak between 3 and 6 years, then continue at a slower pace through middle childhood and adolescence (Thompson et al., 2000). The corpus callosum supports smooth coordination of movements on both sides of the body and integration of many aspects of thinking, including perception, attention, memory, language, and problem solving. The more complex the task, the more essential is communication between the hemispheres.

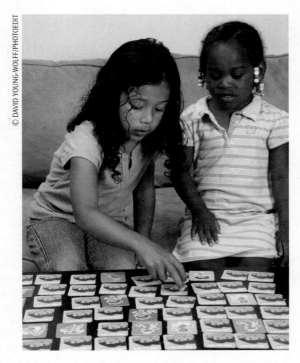

■ In early childhood, the hippocampus develops rapidly, forming connections with surrounding areas of the cerebral cortex and with the prefrontal cortex—changes that enable 4-year-olds to play this complex memory game. ■

ASK YOURSELF

◆ REVIEW What aspects of brain development support the tremendous gains in language, thinking, and motor control of early childhood?

◆ APPLY Dental checkups revealed a high incidence of untreated tooth decay in a U.S. preschool program serving low-income children. Using findings presented in this and previous chapters, list possible contributing factors.

◆ CONNECT What stand on the nature–nurture issue do findings on development of handedness support? Explain, using research findings.

◆ REFLECT How early, and to what extent, did you experience tooth decay in childhood? What factors might have been responsible?

Influences on Physical Growth and Health

As we consider factors affecting growth and health in early childhood, you will encounter some familiar themes. Heredity remains important, but environmental factors—including emotional well-being, good nutrition, relative freedom from disease, and physical safety—are also essential. And as the Biology and Environment box on page 296 illustrates, environmental pollutants can threaten children's healthy development. The extent to which low-level lead—one of the most common—undermines children's mental and emotional functioning is the focus of intensive research.

BIOLOGY AND ENVIRONMENT

Low-Level Lead Exposure and Children's Development

Lead is a highly toxic element that, at blood levels exceeding 60 µg/dL (micrograms per deciliter), causes brain swelling and hemorrhaging. Risk of death rises as blood-lead level exceeds 100 µg/dL. Before 1980, lead exposure resulted from use of lead-based paints in residences (infants and young children often ate paint flakes) and from use of leaded gasoline (car exhaust resulted in a highly breathable form of lead). Laws limiting the lead content of paint and mandating lead-free gasoline led to a sharp decline in children's lead levels, from an average of 15 µg/dL in 1980 to 1.8 µg/dL today (Jones et al., 2009; Meyer et al., 2003).

But in neighborhoods near industries that use lead production processes, or where lead-based paint remains in older homes, children's blood levels are still markedly elevated. About 15 percent of low-income children living in large central cities, and 19 percent of African-American children, have blood-lead levels exceeding 10 µg/dL (the official "level of concern"), warranting immediate efforts to reduce exposure (Jones et al., 2009).

How much lead exposure is too much? Does lead contamination impair children's mental functioning even in small quantities? Until recently, answers were unclear. Studies reporting a negative relationship between children's current lead levels and cognitive performance had serious limitations. Researchers knew nothing about children's history of lead exposure and

often failed to control for factors associated with both blood-lead levels and mental test scores (such as SES, home environmental quality, and nutrition) that might account for the findings.

Over the past two decades, seven longitudinal studies of the developmental consequences of lead have been conducted—three in the United States, two in Australia, one in Mexico City, and one in Yugoslavia. Some focused on inner-city, low-SES minority children, others on middle- and upper-middle SES suburban children, and one on children living close to a lead smelter. Each tracked children's lead exposure over an extended time and included relevant controls.

Five sites reported negative relationships between lead exposure and children's IQs (Hubbs-Tait et al., 2005). Higher blood levels were also associated with deficits in verbal and visual-motor skills and with distractibility, overactivity, poor organization, and behavior problems. And an array of findings suggested that persistent childhood lead exposure contributes to antisocial behavior in adolescence (Dietrich et al., 2001; Needleman et al., 2002; Nevin, 2000; Stretesky & Lynch, 2001).

The investigations did not agree on an age period of greatest vulnerability. In some, relationships were strongest in toddlerhood and early childhood; in others, at the most recently studied age—suggesting cumulative effects over time. Still other studies reported similar lead-related cognitive deficits from infancy through adolescence. Overall, poorer mental test scores associated with lead exposure persisted over time and seemed to be permanent. Children given drugs to induce excretion of lead (chelation) did not improve in

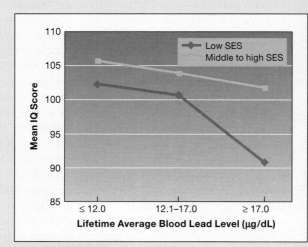

FIGURE 8.4

Relationship of lifetime average lead exposure to 11-to-13-year-old IQ by SES. In this study, conducted in the lead-smelting city of Port Pirie, Australia, blood-lead levels of 375 children were measured repeatedly from birth to age 11 to 13. The lead-exposure-related drop in IQ was much greater for low-SES than higher-SES children. *(Adapted from Tong, McMichael, & Baghurst, 2000.)*

long-term outcomes (Dietrich et al., 2004; Rogan et al., 2001). And negative cognitive consequences were evident at all levels of lead exposure—even below 10 µg/dL (Lamphear et al., 2005).

Although the overall impact of low-level lead exposure on all outcomes is modest, in three longitudinal investigations, cognitive consequences were much greater for low-SES than higher-SES children (see, for example, Figure 8.4) (Bellinger, Leviton, & Sloman, 1990; Ris et al., 2004; Tong, McMichael, & Baghurst, 2000). A stressed, disorganized home life seems to heighten lead-induced damage. Dietary factors can also magnify lead's toxic effects. Iron and zinc deficiencies, especially common in low-SES children, increase lead concentration in the blood (Noonan et al., 2003; Wolf, Jimenez, & Lozoff, 2003; Wright et al., 2003).

In sum, lead impairs learning and contributes to behavior problems. Low-SES children are more likely both to live in lead-contaminated areas and to experience additional risks that magnify lead-induced damage. Because lead is a stable element, its release into the air and soil is difficult to reverse. Therefore, in addition to laws that control lead pollution, interventions that reduce the negative impact of lead—through involved parenting, better schools, and dietary enrichment—are vital.

■ Children play near a factory in Cairo, Egypt, one of the world's most polluted cities in levels of lead and other toxins. Studies consistently show lasting negative effects of lead exposure, including learning and behavior problems. ■

Heredity and Hormones

The impact of heredity on physical growth is evident throughout childhood. Children's physical size and rate of growth are related to those of their parents (Bogin, 2001). Genes influence growth by controlling the body's production of hormones. Figure 8.3 on page 294 shows the **pituitary gland,** located at the base of the brain, which plays a critical role by releasing two hormones that induce growth.

The first, **growth hormone (GH),** is necessary from birth on for development of almost all body tissues. GH acts directly but also accomplishes its task with the help of an intermediary. It stimulates the liver and epiphyses of the skeleton to release another hormone called *insulin-like growth factor 1 (IGF-1),* which triggers cell duplication throughout the body, especially the skeleton, muscles, nerves, bone marrow (origin of blood cells), liver, kidney, skin, and lungs.

About 2 percent of children suffer from inherited conditions that cause either GH deficiency or IGF-1 deficiency (in which GH fails to stimulate IGF-1). Without medical intervention, such children reach an average mature height of only 4 to 4½ feet. When treated early with injections of GH or IGF-1 (depending on the disorder), such children show catch-up growth and then grow at a normal rate, becoming much taller than they would have without treatment (Bright, Mendoza, & Rosenfeld, 2009; Saenger, 2003).

The availability of synthetic GH has also made it possible to treat short, normal-GH children with hormone injections, in hopes of increasing their final height. Thousands of parents, concerned that their children will suffer social stigma because of their shortness, have sought this GH therapy. But most normal-GH children given GH treatment grow only slightly taller than their previously predicted mature height (Rosenbloom, 2009). And contrary to popular belief, normal-GH short children are not deficient in self-esteem or other aspects of psychological adjustment (Sandberg & Voss, 2002). So despite the existence of "heightism" in Western cultures, little justification exists for medically intervening in short stature that is merely the result of biologically normal human diversity.

■ When a child is extremely short because of growth hormone (GH) deficiency, early treatment with injections of GH leads to substantial gains in height. But little justification exists for medical intervention with normal-GH children whose short stature simply reflects human diversity. ■

A second pituitary hormone, **thyroid-stimulating hormone (TSH),** prompts the thyroid gland in the neck to release *thyroxine,* which is necessary for brain development and for GH to have its full impact on body size. Infants born with a deficiency of thyroxine must receive it at once, or they will be mentally retarded. Once the most rapid period of brain development is complete, children with too little thyroxine grow at a below-average rate, but the central nervous system is no longer affected. With prompt treatment, such children catch up in body growth and eventually reach normal size (Salerno et al., 2001).

Emotional Well-Being

In childhood as in infancy, emotional well-being can profoundly affect growth and health. Preschoolers with very stressful home lives (due to divorce, financial difficulties, or parental job loss) suffer more respiratory and intestinal illnesses and more unintentional injuries than others (Cohen & Herbert, 1996; Kemeny, 2003).

In addition, high stress suppresses the release of GH (Deltondo et al., 2008). Consequently, extreme emotional deprivation can lead to **psychosocial dwarfism,** a growth disorder that appears between ages 2 and 15. Typical characteristics include decreased GH secretion, very short stature, immature skeletal age, and serious adjustment problems, which help distinguish psychosocial dwarfism from normal shortness (Tarren-Sweeney, 2006). Lynette, the 4-year-old mentioned earlier in this chapter, was diagnosed with this condition. She was placed in foster care after child welfare authorities discovered that she spent most of the day at home alone, unsupervised, and also might have been physically abused. When children like Lynette are removed from their emotionally inadequate environments, their GH levels quickly return to normal, and they grow rapidly. But if treatment is delayed, the dwarfism can be permanent.

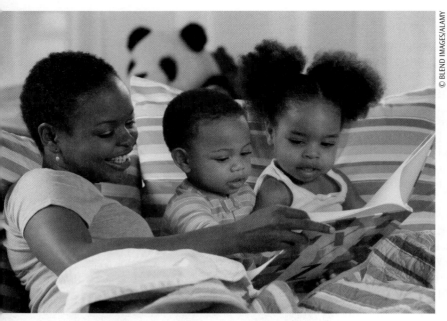

■ Compared with their Caucasian peers, African-American preschoolers are more likely to share a bedroom with siblings or cosleep with parents. As a result, they less often depend on a security object to reduce the discomfort of being left alone in a darkened room. ■

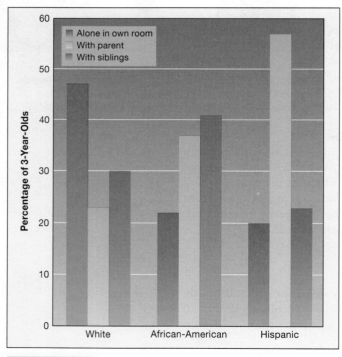

FIGURE 8.5

Sleeping arrangements of U.S. 3-year-olds by ethnicity. A survey of several thousand mothers who were asked about their 3-year-old's typical sleep location revealed that white preschoolers were far more likely to sleep alone in their own bedroom than African-American and Hispanic preschoolers. Among minority children, more Hispanic preschoolers slept with a parent, more African-American preschoolers with siblings. *(Adapted from Milan, Snow, & Belay, 2007.)*

Sleep Habits and Problems

Sleep contributes to body growth, since GH is released during the child's sleeping hours. A well-rested child is better able to play, learn, and contribute positively to family functioning. Many studies confirm that sleep difficulties are associated with impaired cognitive performance, including decreased attention, speed of thinking, working memory, and intelligence and achievement test scores. The impact of disrupted sleep on cognitive functioning is more pronounced for low-SES children. Perhaps insufficient sleep heightens the impact of other environmental stressors prevalent in their daily lives (Buckhalt et al., 2009; Sadeh, 2007). Also, children who sleep poorly disturb their parents' sleep, which can generate significant family stress—a major reason that sleep difficulties are among the most frequent concerns parents raise with their preschooler's doctor (Mindell, 2005).

Total sleep declines in early childhood; on average, 2- and 3-year-olds sleep 11 to 12 hours, 4- to 6-year-olds 10 to 11 hours. But substantial variability exists, with lesser- or greater-than-average sleep remaining fairly stable over time (Jenni et al., 2007). Younger preschoolers typically take a 1- to 2-hour nap in the early afternoon, although daytime sleep need also varies widely. Some continue to take two naps, as they did in toddlerhood; others give up napping entirely. Most Caucasian-American children stop napping between ages 3 and 4, although a quiet play period or rest after lunch helps them rejuvenate for the rest of the day (Howard & Wong, 2001). Perhaps because of greater cultural acceptance, napping remains common among African-American and Hispanic children throughout the preschool years, balanced by a tendency to sleep less at night (Crosby, LeBourgeois, & Harsh, 2005; Lavigne et al., 1999).

The majority of Western parents engage in bedtime routines with their preschoolers, though in the United States this is slightly more common among white than African-American and Hispanic parents. As Figure 8.5 shows, Caucasian preschoolers are less likely to cosleep with their parents or to share a room with siblings than their African-American agemates. White children more often go to bed with a security object, which may help them adjust to feelings of uneasiness at being left by themselves in a darkened room (Milan, Snow, & Belay, 2007). In most cases, cosleeping is not associated with problems during the preschool years, other than more frequent night wakings by parents due to children's movements during sleep (Gaylor et al., 2005; Thiedke, 2001). Western cosleeping children generally ask to sleep in their own bed by age 6 or 7.

Difficulty falling asleep—calling to the parent or asking for another drink of water—is common in early childhood, occurring in about one-third of preschoolers. But Caucasian parents more often express concern about their child falling asleep at a regular time than do African-American parents (Milan, Snow, & Belay, 2007). Perhaps Caucasian parents more highly value a scheduled bedtime and tend to view falling asleep without protest as a sign of maturity—expectations likely to be unmet at least occasionally.

Sometimes, sleep problems stem from a mismatch between parental demands and children's biology. The parent may step up pressure on the child, who vigorously resists because of a lower-than-average need for sleep. Consequently, sleep interventions should include parent education about individual differences in young children's sleep requirements (Jenni & O'Connor, 2005). Intense bedtime struggles sometimes result from family turmoil, as children worry about how their parents may get along when they are asleep and not available to distract them. In these cases, addressing family stress and conflict is the key to improving children's sleep.

Finally, most children waken during the night from time to time, and those who cannot return to sleep on their own may suffer from a sleep disorder. Because young children have vivid imaginations and difficulty separating fantasy from reality, *nightmares* are common; half of 3- to 6-year-olds experience them from time to time. And about 4 percent of children are frequent *sleepwalkers,* who are unaware of their wanderings during the night. Gently awakening and returning the child to bed helps avoid self-injury. *Sleep terrors,* which affect 3 percent of young children, are perhaps the most upsetting sleep problem to parents. In these panic-stricken arousals from deep sleep, the child may scream, thrash, speak incoherently, show a sharp rise in heart rate and breathing, and initially be unresponsive to parents' attempts to comfort. Sleepwalking and sleep terrors tend to run in families, suggesting a genetic influence (Guilleminault et al., 2003; Thorpy & Yager, 2001). But they can also be triggered by stress or extreme fatigue.

Fortunately, sleep disorders of early childhood usually subside without treatment. In the few cases that persist, children require a medical and psychological evaluation (Gregory et al., 2004). Their disturbed sleep may be a sign of neurological or emotional difficulties.

Nutrition

With the transition to early childhood, many children become unpredictable, picky eaters. One father I know wistfully recalled how his son, as a toddler, eagerly sampled Chinese food: "He ate rice, chicken chow mein, egg rolls—and now, at age 3, the only thing he'll try is the ice cream!"

Preschoolers' appetites decline because their growth has slowed. Their wariness of new foods is also adaptive: If they stick to familiar foods, they are less likely to swallow dangerous substances when adults are not around to protect them (Birch & Fisher, 1995). Parents need not worry about variations in amount eaten from meal to meal. Over the course of a day, preschoolers compensate for eating little at one meal by eating more at a later one (Hursti, 1999).

Though they eat less, preschoolers need a high-quality diet, including the same foods adults need, but in smaller amounts. Milk and milk products, meat or meat alternatives (such as eggs, dried peas or beans, and peanut butter), vegetables and fruits, and breads and cereals should be included. Fats, oils, and salt should be

■ As this child's grandmother shows him how to eat with chopsticks, he also acquires a taste for foods commonly served in his culture. ■

kept to a minimum because of their link to high blood pressure and heart disease in adulthood. And foods high in sugar should be eaten only in small amounts to prevent tooth decay and protect against overweight and obesity—a topic we will take up in Chapter 11.

The social environment powerfully influences young children's food preferences. Children tend to imitate the food choices and eating practices of people they admire, both adults and peers. For example, mothers who drink milk or soft drinks tend to have 5-year-old daughters with a similar beverage preference (Fisher et al., 2001). In Mexico, where children see family members delighting in the taste of peppery foods, preschoolers enthusiastically eat chili peppers, whereas most American children reject them (Birch, Zimmerman, & Hind, 1980).

Repeated, unpressured exposure to a new food also increases acceptance (Fuller et al., 2005). In one study, preschoolers were given one of three versions of a food they had never eaten before (sweet, salty, or plain tofu). After 8 to 15 exposures, they readily ate the food. But they preferred the version they had already tasted. For example, children in the "sweet" condition liked sweet tofu best, and those in the "plain" condition liked plain tofu best (Sullivan & Birch, 1990). These findings reveal that adding sugar or salt in hopes of increasing a young child's willingness to eat healthy foods simply strengthens the child's desire for a sugary or salty taste. Similarly, offering children sweet fruit or soft drinks promotes "milk avoidance." Compared to their milk-drinking agemates, milk-avoiders are shorter in stature and have a lower bone density—a condition that leads to a lifelong reduction in strength and to increased risk of bone fractures (Black et al., 2002).

The emotional climate at mealtimes has a powerful impact on children's eating habits. When parents are worried about how well their preschoolers are eating, meals can become unpleasant and stressful. Offering bribes ("Finish your vegetables, and you can have an extra cookie"), as some parents do, causes children to like the healthy food less and the treat more (Birch, Fisher, & Davison, 2003).

Similarly, restricting access to tasty foods focuses children's attention on those foods and increases their desire to eat them. After caregivers in a child-care center prevented 3- to 6-year-olds from selecting apple-bar cookies at snack time by enclosing them in a transparent jar but gave them free access to peach-bar cookies (which they liked just as well), the children more often talked about and requested the apple-bar cookies and otherwise attempted to obtain them (see Figure 8.6) (Fisher & Birch, 1999). And when given access, they ate more apple-bar cookies than they had during previous, unrestricted snack times.

Children's healthy eating depends on a healthy food environment, but too much adult control limits their opportunities to develop self-control, thereby promoting overeating. For ways to encourage healthy, varied eating in young children, refer to Applying What We Know on the following page.

Finally, as indicated in earlier chapters, many children in North America and in developing countries lack access to sufficient high-quality food to support healthy growth. Five-year-old Hal rode a bus from a poor neighborhood to our laboratory preschool. His mother's paycheck barely covered her rent, let alone food. Hal's diet was deficient in protein and in essential vitamins and minerals—iron (to prevent anemia), calcium (to support development of bones and teeth), zinc (to support immune system functioning, neural communication, and cell duplication), vitamin A (to help maintain eyes, skin, and a variety of internal organs), and vitamin C (to facilitate iron absorption and wound healing). These are the most common dietary deficiencies of the preschool years (Ganji, Hampl, & Betts, 2003).

Hal was small for his age, pale, inattentive, and unruly at preschool. By the school years, low-SES U.S. children are, on average, about ½ to 1 inch shorter than their economically advantaged counterparts (Cecil et al., 2005; Yip, Scanlon, & Trowbridge, 1993). And throughout childhood and adolescence, a nutritionally deficient diet is associated with

LOOK AND LISTEN

❖ ❖

Arrange to join a family with at least one preschooler for a meal, and closely observe parental mealtime practices. Are they likely to promote healthy eating habits? Explain.

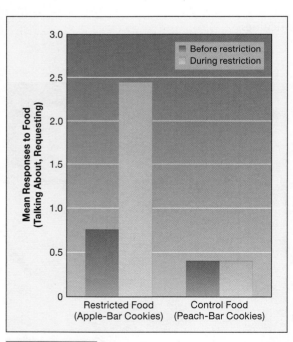

FIGURE 8.6

Children's spontaneous behavioral responses to a tasty food before and during restriction at snack times. Three- to 6-year-olds talked about, requested, and otherwise attempted to obtain a tasty food (apple-bar cookies) three times more often after they were restricted from eating it. They rarely responded this way to an equally tasty control food (peach-bar cookies) that remained unrestricted throughout the study. *(Adapted from Fisher & Birch, 1999.)*

Applying What We Know

Encouraging Good Nutrition in Early Childhood

SUGGESTION	DESCRIPTION
Offer a varied, healthy diet.	Provide a well-balanced variety of nutritious foods that are colorful and attractively served. Avoid including sweets and "junk" foods in the child's regular food environment.
Offer predictable meals as well as several snacks each day.	Preschoolers' stomachs are small, and they may not be able to eat enough in three meals to satisfy their energy requirements. They benefit from extra opportunities to eat.
Offer small portions, and permit the child to serve him- or herself and to ask for seconds.	When too much food is put on the plate, preschoolers (like adults) often overeat, increasing the risk of obesity. On average, preschoolers consume 25 percent less at a meal when permitted to serve themselves.
Offer healthy new foods early in a meal and repeatedly at subsequent meals, and respond with patience if the child rejects the food.	Introduce healthy new foods before the child's appetite is satisfied. Let children see you eat and enjoy the new food. If the child rejects it, accept the refusal and serve it again at another meal. As foods become more familiar, they are more readily accepted.
Keep mealtimes pleasant, and include the child in mealtime conversations.	A pleasant, relaxed eating environment helps children develop positive attitudes about food. Refrain from constantly offering food and prompting eating; these practices are associated with excessively fast eating and overeating. Avoid confrontations over disliked foods and table manners, which may lead to refusal to eat.
Avoid using food as a reward and forbidding access to certain foods.	Saying "No dessert until you clean your plate" tells children that they must eat even if they are not hungry and that dessert is the best part of the meal. Restricting access to a food increases children's valuing of that food and efforts to obtain it.

Sources: Birch, 1999; Fisher, Rolls, & Birch, 2003; Spruijt-Metz et al., 2002.

attention and memory difficulties, poorer intelligence and achievement test scores, and behavior problems—especially hyperactivity and aggression—even after family factors that might account for these relationships (such as stressors, parental psychological health, education, warmth, and stimulation of the child) are controlled (Liu et al., 2004; Pollitt, 2001; Slack & Yoo, 2005).

Infectious Disease

One day, I noticed that Hal had been absent from the play yard for several weeks, so I asked Leslie, his preschool teacher, what was wrong. "Hal's been hospitalized with the measles," she explained. "He's had difficulty recovering—lost weight when there wasn't much to lose in the first place." In well-nourished children, ordinary childhood illnesses have no effect on physical growth. But when children are undernourished, disease interacts with malnutrition in a vicious spiral, with potentially severe consequences.

INFECTIOUS DISEASE AND MALNUTRITION Hal's reaction to the measles is commonplace in developing nations, where a large proportion of the population lives in poverty and children do not receive routine immunizations. Illnesses such as measles and chicken pox, which typically do not appear until after age 3 in industrialized nations, occur much earlier. Poor diet depresses the body's immune system, making children far more susceptible to disease. Of the 10 million annual deaths of children under age 5 worldwide, 98 percent are in developing countries, and 70 percent are due to infectious diseases (World Health Organization, 2008a).

Disease, in turn, is a major contributor to malnutrition, hindering both physical growth and cognitive development. Illness reduces appetite and limits the body's ability to absorb foods, especially in children with intestinal infections. In developing countries, widespread diarrhea,

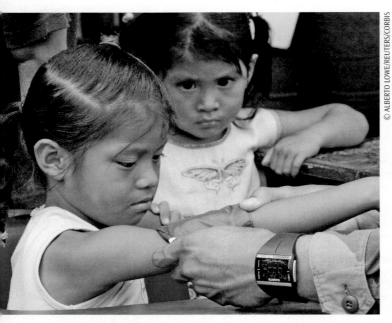

■ A health care worker examines a child of the Ngobe people of Panama. The Ngobes are subsistence farmers whose homes lack basic amenities, including clean water. As a result, diarrhea is widespread, placing Ngobe children at risk for growth stunting and impaired mental development. ■

resulting from unsafe water and contaminated foods, leads to growth stunting and nearly two million childhood deaths each year (World Health Organization, 2008a). Studies carried out in the slums and shantytowns of Brazil and Peru reveal that the more persistent diarrhea is in early childhood, the shorter children are in height and the lower they score on mental tests during the school years (Checkley et al., 2003; Niehaus et al., 2002).

Most developmental impairments and deaths due to diarrhea can be prevented with nearly cost-free *oral rehydration therapy (ORT)*, in which sick children are given a glucose, salt, and water solution that quickly replaces fluids the body loses. Since 1990, public health workers have taught nearly half the families in the developing world how to administer ORT. Also, supplements of zinc (essential for immune system functioning), which cost only 30 cents for a month's supply, substantially reduce the incidence of severe and prolonged diarrhea (Aggarwal, Sentz, & Miller, 2007). Through these interventions, the lives of millions of children are saved each year.

IMMUNIZATION   In industrialized nations, childhood diseases have declined dramatically during the past half-century, largely as a result of widespread immunization of infants and young children. Hal got the measles because, unlike his classmates from more advantaged homes, he did not receive a full program of immunizations.

About 20 percent of U.S. infants and toddlers are not fully immunized. Of the 80 percent who receive a complete schedule of vaccinations in the first two years, some do not receive the immunizations they need later, in early childhood. Overall, 24 percent of U.S. preschoolers lack essential immunizations. The rate rises to 28 percent for poverty-stricken children, many of whom do not receive full protection until age 5 or 6, when it is required for school entry (U.S. Department of Health and Human Services, 2008b). In contrast, fewer than 10 percent of preschoolers lack immunizations in Denmark and Norway, and fewer than 7 percent in Great Britain, Canada, the Netherlands, and Sweden (United Nations, 2002; UNICEF, 2008).

Why does the United States lag behind these other countries in immunization? As noted in earlier chapters, many U.S. children do not have access to the health care they need. The Cultural Influences box on the following page compares child health care in the United States with that in other Western nations.

In 1994, all medically uninsured children in the United States were guaranteed free immunizations, a program that has led to gains in immunization rates. Still, the cost of the doctor's visit to obtain the immunization may not be covered. Inability to pay for vaccines is only one cause of inadequate immunization. Parents with stressful daily lives often fail to schedule vaccination appointments, and those without a primary care physician do not want to endure long waits in crowded U.S. public health clinics. Some parents have been influenced by media reports suggesting a link between a mercury-based preservative used for decades in vaccines and a rise in the number of children diagnosed with autism. But large-scale studies show no association with autism and no consistent effects on cognitive performance (Dales, Hammer, & Smith, 2001; Richler et al., 2006; Stehr-Green et al., 2003; Thompson et al., 2007). Still, as a precautionary measure, mercury-free versions of childhood vaccinations are now available. In areas where many parents refuse to immunize their children, disease outbreaks of whooping cough and rubella have occurred, with life-threatening consequences (Kennedy & Gust, 2008; Tuyen & Bisgard, 2003). Public education programs directed at increasing parental knowledge about the importance of timely immunizations are badly needed.

A final point regarding communicable disease in early childhood deserves mention. Childhood illness rises with child-care attendance. On average, an infant or toddler in child

CULTURAL INFLUENCES

Child Health Care in the United States and Other Western Nations

The U.S. Patient Protection and Affordable Care Act, signed into law in March 2010, will expand health-insurance coverage to millions of Americans who are currently uninsured, requiring every citizen to purchase health insurance by 2014 while improving its affordability through industry regulation and subsidies for low-income families. The law's greatest immediate benefits for children include a prohibition on denial of coverage by insurance companies because of preexisting conditions and expansion of Medicaid—government-sponsored health insurance for very-low-income families.

Still, health insurance in the United States will remain an optional employment-related fringe benefit. Larger companies will suffer penalties for not providing affordable coverage to full-time workers and their families, but many parents who work part-time or for small businesses may face continued challenges in obtaining high-quality, reasonably priced insurance.

At the time of the Affordable Care Act's passage, about 7.3 million children (10 percent of the child population), many with working parents, were uninsured (U.S. Census Bureau, 2010b). In the United States, uninsured children are three times as likely as insured children to go without needed doctor visits (Newachek et al., 2002). Partly because of weak health-care services, an estimated one-fifth of U.S. children younger than age 5 who come from economically disadvantaged families are in less than very good health. And 12 percent of children living in poverty have activity limitations due to chronic illnesses—a rate nearly double the national average (U.S. Department of Health and Human Services, 2009f).

U.S. child health-care policies contrast with services provided in Australia, Canada, New Zealand, Western Europe, and other industrialized nations, where government-sponsored health insurance is regarded as a fundamental human right and is made available to all citizens at low or no cost. Let's look at two examples.

In the Netherlands, every child receives free medical examinations from birth through adolescence. Children's health care also includes parental counseling in nutrition, disease prevention, and child development (de Winter, Balledux, & de Mare, 1997). The Netherlands achieves its extraordinarily high childhood immunization rate by giving parents of every newborn baby a written schedule that shows exactly when and where the child should be immunized. If a parent does not bring the child at the specified time, a public health nurse calls the family. When appointments are missed repeatedly, the nurse goes to the home to ensure that the child receives the recommended immunizations (de Pree-Geerlings, de Pree, & Bulk-Bunschoten, 2001).

In Norway, federal law requires that all communities establish well-baby and child clinics and that health check-ups occur three times in the first year, then at ages 2 and 4. On other occasions, children are seen by specialized nurses who monitor their development, provide immunizations, and counsel parents on physical and mental health (AWC Oslo, 2005). Although citizens pay a small fee for routine medical visits, hospital services are free.

Currently, many government officials, organizations, and concerned citizens are working to guarantee every American child basic health care. Under the Children's Health Insurance Program (CHIP), launched in 1997, the states receive federal matching funds for upgrading children's health insurance. State control over program implementation enables each state to adapt insurance coverage to meet its unique needs. In 2009, CHIP federal funding was greatly expanded. By 2013, it is expected to provide coverage to 4 million additional children whose families are low-income but not eligible for Medicaid (Kaiser Commission on Medicaid and the Uninsured, 2009).

But even many insured U.S. children do not see a doctor regularly. Parents with no health benefits of their own are less inclined to make appointments for their children—circumstances likely to improve with activation of

■ Parents bring their three children to a rural Colorado public clinic offering low-cost medical checkups. Although the father works full-time, his job offers no health insurance. Recent expansion of the Children's Health Insurance Program (CHIP) and provisions of the U.S. Patient Protection and Affordable Care Act of 2010 aim to guarantee affordable health care to families like this one. ■

the Affordable Care law's provisions. Still, because of low insurance-reimbursement rates, many doctors refuse to take public-aid patients. As a result, children with public insurance frequently do not have a primary care physician. Instead, they endure long waits in crowded public health clinics, and their parents often say they cannot gain access to needed services (Dombrowski, Lantz, & Freed, 2004; Hughes & Ng, 2003).

Finally, millions of eligible children are not enrolled in CHIP because their parents either do not understand the eligibility requirements or find the application process confusing. The 2009 CHIP reauthorization simplified enrollment procedures, further augmenting gains in the health-care arena for American children. Still, the United States has some distance to go before all its children have access to excellent health care.

SOCIAL ISSUES: HEALTH

Otitis Media and Development

During his first year in child care, 2-year-old Alex caught five colds, had the flu on two occasions, and experienced repeated *otitis media* (middle ear infection). Alex is not unusual. By age 3, 75 percent of U.S. children have had respiratory illnesses that resulted in at least one bout of otitis media; nearly half of these have had three or more bouts (Aronson & Henderson, 2006). Although antibiotics eliminate the bacteria responsible for otitis media, they do not reduce fluid buildup in the middle ear, which causes mild to moderate hearing loss that can last for weeks or months.

The incidence of otitis media is greatest between 6 months and 3 years, when children are first acquiring language. Frequent infections predict delayed language progress in early childhood and poorer academic performance after school entry that, in one study, was still evident in adolescence (Bennett et al., 2001; Casby, 2001; Miccio et al., 2002).

How might otitis media disrupt language and academic progress? Difficulties in perceiving and processing speech sounds, particularly in noisy settings, may be responsible (Polka & Rvachew, 2005). Children with many bouts are less attentive to others' speech and less persistent at tasks (Asbjornsen et al., 2005; Petinou et al., 2001). Their distractibility may result from an inability to make out what people around them are saying—which, in turn, may reduce the quality of others' interactions with them.

Because otitis media is so widespread, current evidence argues strongly in favor of early prevention. Crowded living conditions and exposure to cigarette smoke and other pollutants are linked to the disease, probably accounting for its high incidence among low-SES children. And rates of otitis media are greatly elevated in children who attend child-care centers, where severe, antibacterial-resistant strains of respiratory infections can easily develop and spread (Greenberg et al., 2008).

Early otitis media can be prevented in the following ways:

- *Frequent screening for the disease, followed by prompt medical intervention.* Plastic tubes that drain the narrow Eustachian tubes of the middle ear often are used to treat chronic otitis media in children, although their effectiveness has been disputed.
- *Child-care settings that control infection.* Because infants and young children often put toys in their mouths, these objects should be rinsed frequently with a disinfectant. Pacifier use has also been linked to a greater risk of otitis media (Rovers et al., 2008). Spacious, well-ventilated rooms and small group sizes help limit spread of the disease.
- *Verbally stimulating adult–child interaction.* Developmental problems associated with otitis media are reduced or eliminated in high-quality child-care centers. When caregivers are verbally stimulating and keep noise to a minimum, children have more opportunities to hear, and benefit from, spoken language (Roberts et al., 1998; Vernon-Feagans, Hurley, & Yont, 2002).
- *Vaccines.* Researchers have developed several vaccines that seem to prevent otitis media. But more evidence is needed before they can be made widely available (O'Brien et al., 2009).

■ Otitis media is widespread among children who attend child-care centers, where close contact leads to rapid spread of respiratory infection. ■

care becomes sick 9 to 10 times a year, a preschooler 6 to 7 times. The diseases that spread most rapidly are those most frequently suffered by young children—diarrhea and respiratory infections. The risk that a respiratory infection will result in *otitis media,* or middle ear infection, is almost double that for children remaining at home (Nafstad et al., 1999). To learn about the consequences of otitis media and how to prevent it, consult the Social Issues: Health box above.

Childhood Injuries

More than any other child in the preschool classroom, 3-year-old Tommy had trouble sitting still and paying attention. Instead, he darted from one place and activity to another. One day, he narrowly escaped serious injury when he put his mother's car in gear while she was outside scraping ice from its windows. The vehicle rolled through a guardrail and over the side of a 10-foot concrete underpass, where it hung until rescue workers arrived. Police charged Tommy's mother with failing to use a restraint seat for a child younger than age 8.

FIGURE 8.7

International death rates due to unintentional injury among 1- to 14-year-olds. Compared with other industrialized nations, the United States has a high injury death rate, largely because of widespread childhood poverty and shortages of high-quality child care. Injury death rates are many times higher in developing nations, where poverty, rapid population growth, overcrowding in cities, and inadequate safety measures endanger children's lives. *(Adapted from World Health Organization, 2008b.)*

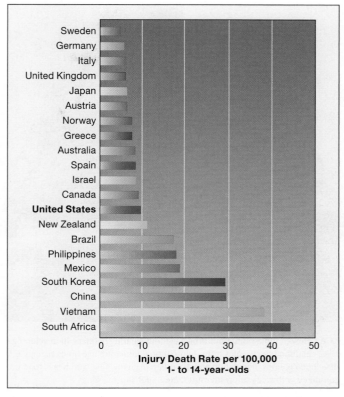

Injury Death Rate per 100,000
1- to 14-year-olds

Unintentional injuries are the leading cause of childhood mortality in industrialized nations. Although U.S. childhood injury fatalities have declined steadily over the past 35 years due to state laws and community policies aimed at improving child safety, as Figure 8.7 reveals, the United States continues to rank poorly in these largely preventable events. Nearly 35 percent of childhood deaths and 50 percent of adolescent deaths are due to injury (Children's Defense Fund, 2008; Safe Kids USA, 2008). And among injured children and youths who survive, thousands suffer pain, brain damage, and permanent physical disabilities.

Auto and traffic accidents, drownings, and burns are the most common childhood injuries (Safe Kids USA, 2008). Motor vehicle collisions are by far the most frequent source of injury across all ages, ranking as the leading cause of death among children more than 1 year old.

FACTORS RELATED TO CHILDHOOD INJURIES　　The common view of childhood injuries as "accidental" suggests that they are due to chance and cannot be prevented (Sleet & Mercy, 2003). In fact, these injuries occur within a complex *ecological system* of individual, family, community, and societal influences—and we can do something about them.

As Tommy's case suggests, individual differences exist in the safety of children's behaviors. Because of their higher activity level and greater impulsivity and risk taking, boys are 1.5 times more likely to be injured than girls, and their injuries are more severe (Safe Kids USA, 2009). Parents realize that they need to take more steps to protect their young sons than daughters from injury, and most do so. Still, mothers judge the chances of preventing injury in sons to be lower—a belief that may keep them from exercising sufficient oversight and control over the most injury-prone boys (Morrongiello & Kiriakou, 2004; Morrongiello, Ondejko, & Littlejohn, 2004).

Children with certain temperamental characteristics—inattentiveness, overactivity, irritability, defiance, and aggression—are also at greater risk for injury (Ordonana, Caspi, & Moffitt, 2008; Schwebel & Gaines, 2007). As we saw in Chapter 7, these children present child-rearing challenges. They are likely to protest when placed in auto seat restraints, to refuse to take a companion's hand when crossing the street, and to disobey after repeated instruction and discipline.

Poverty, single parenthood, and low parental education are also strongly associated with injury (Schwebel & Brezausek, 2007; World Health Organization, 2008b). Parents who must cope with many daily stresses often have little time or energy to monitor the safety of their children. And their homes and neighborhoods are likely to be noisy, crowded, and run-down, posing further risks (Dal Santo et al., 2004).

Broad societal conditions also affect childhood injury. In developing countries, the rate of death from injury before age 15 is five times as high as

■ Boys' higher activity level and greater impulsivity and risk taking explain why they are more likely to be injured and to suffer severe injuries than girls. ■

© DAVID PEARSON/ALAMY

■ A family in India rides a motorbike without wearing helmets. In developing countries, childhood death rates from unintentional injury are five times as high as in developed nations. Population growth, urban overcrowding, and heavy road traffic, combined with weak safety measures, are major causes. ■

in developed nations and soon may exceed disease as the leading cause of childhood mortality (World Health Organization, 2008b). Rapid population growth, overcrowding in cities, and heavy road traffic combined with weak safety measures are major causes. Safety devices, such as car safety seats and bicycle helmets, are neither readily available nor affordable.

Childhood injury rates are high in the United States because of extensive poverty, shortages of high-quality child care (to supervise children in their parents' absence), and a high rate of births to teenagers, who are neither psychologically nor financially ready for parenthood (Ekeus, Christensson, & Hjern, 2003; Safe Kids USA, 2008). But U.S. children from advantaged families are also at considerably greater risk for injury than children in Western Europe (World Health Organization, 2008b). This indicates that besides reducing poverty and teenage pregnancy and upgrading the status of child care, additional steps are needed to ensure children's safety.

PREVENTING CHILDHOOD INJURIES Childhood injuries have many causes, so a variety of approaches are needed to control them. Laws prevent many injuries by requiring car safety seats, child-resistant caps on medicine bottles, flameproof clothing, and fencing around backyard swimming pools (the site of 50 percent of early childhood drownings) (Brenner & Committee on Injury, Violence, and Poison Prevention, 2003). Communities can help by modifying their physical environments. Providing inexpensive and widely available public transportation can reduce the amount of time that children spend in cars. Playgrounds, a common site of injury, can be covered with protective surfaces (Safe Kids USA, 2009). Free, easily installed window guards can be given to families in high-rise apartment buildings to prevent falls. And media campaigns can inform parents and children about safety issues.

But even though they know better, many parents and children behave in ways that compromise safety. During the past three decades, parents have changed very little in the amount they do to protect their children, citing such reasons as "the chances of serious injury are slim," taking necessary steps "is a hassle," and (among low-income families) safety devices (such as home fire extinguishers and bicycle helmets) "cost too much" (Safe Kids USA, 2008). For example, 27 percent of U.S. parents (like Tommy's mother) fail to place their children in car safety seats, and 84 percent of infant seats and 41 percent of child booster seats are improperly used. Yet research confirms that young children properly restrained in car safety seats have an 80 percent reduced risk of fatal injury (Safe Kids USA, 2007). American parents, especially, seem willing to ignore familiar safety practices, perhaps because of the high value they place on individual rights and personal freedom (Damashek & Peterson, 2002).

Furthermore, many parents begin relying on children's knowledge of safety rules, rather than monitoring and controlling access to hazards, as early as 2 or 3 years of age—a premature transition associated with a rise in home injuries (Morrongiello, Ondejko, & Littlejohn, 2004). But even older preschoolers spontaneously recall only about half the safety rules their parents teach them. And even with well-learned rules, they need supervision to ensure that they comply (Morrongiello, Midgett, & Shields, 2001).

Parent interventions that highlight risk factors and that model and reinforce safety practices are effective in reducing home hazards and childhood injuries (Kendrick et al., 2008). But attention must also be paid to family conditions that can prevent childhood injury: relieving crowd-

Applying What We Know

Reducing Unintentional Injuries in Early Childhood

SUGGESTION	DESCRIPTION
Provide age-appropriate supervision and safety instruction.	Despite increasing understanding and self-control, preschoolers need nearly constant supervision. Establish and enforce safety rules, explain the reasons behind them, and praise children for following them, thereby encouraging the child to remember and obey.
Know the child's temperament.	Children who are unusually active, distractible, negative, or curious have more than their share of injuries and need extra monitoring.
Eliminate the most serious dangers from the home.	Examine all spaces for safety. For example, in the kitchen, store dangerous products in high cabinets out of sight, and keep sharp implements in a latched drawer. Remove guns; if that is impossible, store them unloaded in a locked cabinet. Always accompany young preschoolers to the bathroom, and keep all medicines in containers with safety caps.
During automobile travel, always restrain the child properly in the back seat of the car.	Use an age-appropriate, properly installed car safety seat or booster seat up to age 8 or until the child is 4 feet 9 inches tall, and strap the child in correctly every time. Children should always ride in the back seat; passenger-side air bags in the front seat deploy so forcefully that they can cause injury or death to a child. Never leave a child alone in a car, even on a cool, sunny day; a child's core body temperature increases 3 to 5 times faster than an adult's, with risk of permanent injury or death.
Select safe playground equipment and sites.	Make sure sand, wood chips, or rubberized matting has been placed under swings, see-saws, and jungle gyms. Check yards for dangerous plants. Always supervise outdoor play.
Be extra cautious around water.	Constantly observe children during water play; even shallow, inflatable pools are frequent sites of drownings. While they are swimming, young children's heads should not be immersed in water; they may swallow so much that they develop water intoxication, which can lead to convulsions and death.
Practice safety around animals.	Wait to get a pet until the child is mature enough to handle and care for it—usually around age 5 or 6. Never leave a young child alone with an animal; bites often occur during playful roughhousing. Model and teach humane pet treatment.

Source: Damashek & Peterson, 2002; Safe Kids USA, 2008.

ing in the home, providing social supports to ease parental stress, and teaching parents to use effective discipline—a topic we will take up in Chapter 10. Positive parenting—an affectionate, supportive relationship with the child; consistent, reasonable expectations for maturity; and oversight—substantially reduces injury rates, especially in overactive and temperamentally difficult children (Schwebel et al., 2004). But to implement these strategies, parents must have ample time and emotional resources as well as relevant knowledge and skills. Refer to Applying What We Know above for ways to minimize unintentional injuries in early childhood.

ASK YOURSELF

◆ **REVIEW** Describe ethnic variations in sleep problems during the preschool years. What factors likely contribute to those differences?

◆ **APPLY** One day, Leslie prepared a new snack to serve at preschool: celery stuffed with ricotta cheese and pineapple. The first time she served it, few children touched it. How can Leslie encourage her students to accept the snack? What tactics should she avoid?

◆ **CONNECT** Using research on malnutrition or on unintentional injuries, show how physical growth and health in early childhood result from a continuous, complex interplay between heredity and environment.

◆ **REFLECT** Ask a parent or other family member whether, as a preschooler, you were a picky eater, suffered from many infectious diseases, or sustained any serious injuries. In each instance, what factors might have been responsible?

■ ■ Motor Development
■ ■

TAKE A MOMENT... Observe several 2- to 6-year-olds at play in a neighborhood park, preschool, or child-care center. You will see that an explosion of new motor skills occurs in early childhood, each of which builds on the simpler movement patterns of toddlerhood.

During the preschool years, children continue to integrate previously acquired skills into more complex, *dynamic systems*. Then they revise each new skill as their bodies grow larger and stronger, their central nervous systems develop, their environments present new challenges, and they set new goals, aided by gains in perceptual and cognitive capacities.

Gross-Motor Development

As children's bodies become more streamlined and less top-heavy, their center of gravity shifts downward, toward the trunk. As a result, balance improves greatly, paving the way for new motor skills involving large muscles of the body. By age 2, preschoolers' gaits become smooth and rhythmic—secure enough that soon they leave the ground, at first by running and later by jumping, hopping, galloping, and skipping.

As children become steadier on their feet, their arms and torsos are freed to experiment with new skills—throwing and catching balls, steering tricycles, and swinging on horizontal bars and rings. Then upper- and lower-body skills combine into more refined actions. Five- and 6-year-olds simultaneously steer and pedal a tricycle and flexibly move their whole body when throwing, catching, hopping, and jumping. By the end of the preschool years, all skills are performed with greater speed and endurance. Table 8.1 provides a closer look at gross-motor development in early childhood.

Changes in ball skills provide an excellent illustration of preschoolers' gross-motor progress. Young preschoolers stand still, facing the target, throwing with their arm thrust forward. Catching is equally awkward. Two-year-olds extend their arms and hands rigidly, using them as a single unit to trap the ball. By age 3, children flex their elbows enough to trap the ball against the chest. But if the ball arrives too quickly, they cannot adapt, and it may bounce off the body (Haywood & Getchell, 2005).

Gradually, children call on the shoulders, torso, trunk, and legs to support throwing and catching. By age 4, the body rotates as the child throws, and at 5 years, preschoolers shift their weight forward, stepping as they release the ball. As a result, the ball travels faster and farther. When the ball is returned, older preschoolers predict its place of landing by moving forward, backward, or sideways (see Figure 8.8). Soon, they will catch it with their hands and fingers, "giving" with arms and body to absorb the force of the ball.

Play a game of catch with a 2- to 3-year-old, then with a 4- to 6-year-old. What differences in movement and coordination are evident?

FIGURE 8.8

Changes in catching during early childhood. At age 2, children extend their arms rigidly, and the ball tends to bounce off the body. At age 3, they flex their elbows in preparation for catching, trapping the ball against the chest. By ages 5 and 6, children involve the entire body. Instead of pressing the ball against the chest, they catch it with only the hands and fingers.

Age 2   Age 3   Age 5–6

TABLE 8.1	Changes in Gross- and Fine-Motor Skills During Early Childhood	

AGE	GROSS-MOTOR SKILLS	FINE-MOTOR SKILLS
2–3 years	Walks more rhythmically; hurried walk changes to run Jumps, hops, throws, and catches with rigid upper body Pushes riding toy with feet; little steering	Puts on and removes simple items of clothing Zips and unzips large zippers Uses spoon effectively

3–4 years	Walks up stairs, alternating feet, and down stairs,
	    leading with one foot
	Jumps and hops, flexing upper body
	Throws and catches with slight involvement of upper body; still
	    catches by trapping ball against chest
	Pedals and steers tricycle
		Fastens and unfastens large buttons
		Serves self food without assistance
		Uses scissors
		Copies vertical line and circle
		Draws first picture of person, using tadpole image

4–5 years	Walks down stairs, alternating feet Runs more smoothly Gallops and skips with one foot Throws ball with increased body rotation and transfer of weight on feet; catches ball with hands Rides tricycle rapidly, steers smoothly	Uses fork effectively Cuts with scissors following line Copies triangle, cross, and some letters
5–6 years	Increases running speed Gallops more smoothly; engages in true skipping Displays mature throwing and catching pattern Rides bicycle with training wheels	Uses knife to cut soft food Ties shoes Draws person with six parts Copies some numbers and simple words

Sources: Cratty, 1986; Haywood & Getchell, 2005; Malina & Bouchard, 1991.

Fine-Motor Development

Like gross-motor development, fine-motor skills take a giant leap forward in the preschool years. As control of the hands and fingers improves, young children put puzzles together, build with small blocks, cut and paste, and string beads. To parents, fine-motor progress is most apparent in two areas: (1) children's care of their own bodies, and (2) the drawings and paintings that fill the walls at home, child care, and preschool.

SELF-HELP SKILLS   As Table 8.1 shows, young children gradually become self-sufficient at dressing and feeding. Two-year-olds put on and take off simple items of clothing. By age 3, children can dress and undress well enough to take care of toileting needs by themselves. Between ages 4 and 5, children can dress and undress without supervision. At mealtimes, young preschoolers use a spoon well, and they can serve themselves. By age 4 they are adept with a fork, and around 5 to 6 years they can use a knife to cut soft foods. Roomy clothing with large buttons and zippers and child-sized eating utensils help children master these skills.

Preschoolers get great satisfaction from managing their own bodies. They are proud of their independence, and their new skills also make life easier for adults. But parents must be patient about these abilities: When tired and in a hurry, young children often revert to eating with their fingers. And the 3-year-old who dresses himself in the morning sometimes ends up with his shirt on inside out, his pants on backward, and his left snow boot on his right foot! Perhaps the most complex self-help skill of early childhood is shoe tying, mastered around age 6. Success requires a longer attention span, memory for an intricate series of hand movements, and the dexterity to perform them. Shoe tying illustrates the close connection between motor and cognitive development, as do two other skills: drawing and writing.

DRAWING   When given crayon and paper, even toddlers scribble in imitation of others. As the young child's ability to mentally represent the world expands, marks on the page take on meaning. A variety of factors combine with fine-motor control in

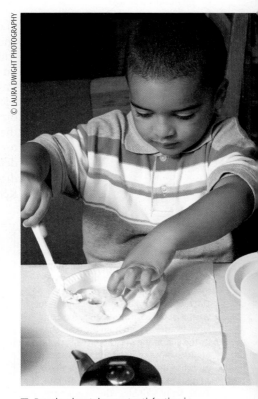

© LAURA DWIGHT PHOTOGRAPHY

■ Preschoolers take great satisfaction in their growing independence. For this child, using a knife to spread cream cheese on a bagel is a challenging but rewarding task. ■

the development of children's artful representations (Golomb, 2004). These include the realization that pictures can serve as symbols, improved planning and spatial understanding, and the emphasis that the child's culture places on artistic expression.

Typically, drawing progresses through the following sequence:

1. *Scribbles.* Western children begin to draw during the second year. At first, the intended representation is contained in gestures rather than in the resulting marks on the page. For example, one 18-month-old made her crayon hop and, as it produced a series of dots, explained, "Rabbit goes hop-hop" (Winner, 1986).

   Recall from Chapter 6 that 2-year-olds treat realistic-looking pictures symbolically, but they have difficulty interpreting line drawings. When an adult held up a drawing indicating which of two objects preschoolers should drop down a chute, 3-year-olds used the drawing as a symbol to guide their behavior but 2-year-olds did not (Callaghan, 1999).

2. *First representational forms.* Around age 3, children's scribbles start to become pictures. Often children make a gesture with the crayon, notice that they have drawn a recognizable shape, and then label it. In one case, a 2-year-old made some random marks on a page and then, realizing the resemblance between his scribbles and noodles, named the creation "chicken pie and noodles" (Winner, 1986).

   Few 3-year-olds spontaneously draw so others can tell what their picture represents. However, after an adult demonstrated how drawings can be used to stand for objects in a game, more 3-year-olds drew recognizable forms (Callaghan & Rankin, 2002). Western parents and teachers spend much time promoting 2- and 3-year-olds' language and make-believe play but relatively little time showing them how they can use drawings to represent their world. When adults draw with children and point out resemblances between drawings and objects, preschoolers' pictures become more comprehensible and detailed (Braswell & Callanan, 2003).

   A major milestone in drawing occurs when children use lines to represent the boundaries of objects. This enables 3- and 4-year-olds to draw their first picture of a person. Fine-motor and cognitive limitations lead the preschooler to reduce the figure to the simplest form that still looks human—the universal "tadpole" image, a circular shape with lines attached, shown on the left in Figure 8.9. Four-year-olds add features, such as eyes, nose, mouth, hair, fingers, and feet, as the tadpole drawings illustrate.

3. *More realistic drawings.* Five- and 6-year-olds create more complex drawings, like the one on the right in Figure 8.9, containing more conventional human and animal figures, with the head and body differentiated. Older preschoolers' drawings still contain perceptual distortions because they have just begun to represent depth (Cox & Littlejohn, 1995). Use of depth cues, such as overlapping objects, smaller size for distant than for near objects, diagonal placement, and converging lines, increases during middle childhood (Nicholls & Kennedy, 1992).

LOOK AND LISTEN

❖❖

Visit a preschool or child-care center where artwork by 3- to 5-year-olds is plentiful. Note age differences in rendering of human and animal figures and in the complexity of children's drawings.

FIGURE 8.9

Examples of young children's drawings. The universal tadpole-like shape that children use to draw their first picture of a person is shown on the left. The tadpole soon becomes an anchor for greater detail as arms, fingers, toes, and facial features sprout from the basic shape. By the end of the preschool years, children produce more complex, differentiated pictures like the one on the right, drawn by a 6-year-old child. *(Left: From H. Gardner, 1980, Artful Scribbles: The Significance of Children's Drawings, New York: Basic Books, p. 64. Reprinted by permission of Basic Books, a member of Perseus Books Group. Right: From E. Winner, August 1986, "Where Pelicans Kiss Seals," Psychology Today, 20[8], p. 35. Reprinted by permission from the collection of Ellen Winner.)*

FIGURE 8.10

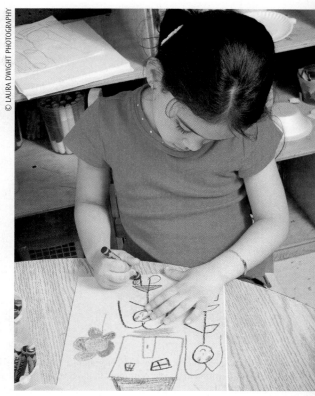

Drawing Category and Approximate Age Range	Cube	Cylinder
Single Units (3 to 7 years)		
Object Parts (4 to 13 years)		
Integrated Whole (8 years and older)		

Development of children's drawings of geometric objects—a cube and a cylinder. As these examples show, drawings change from single units to representation of object parts. Then the parts are integrated into a realistic whole. *(Adapted from Toomela, 1999.)*

■ As cognitive and fine-motor skills advance, children's drawings increase in detail and realism. This 5-year-old depicts a house with door and windows, a flower with petals, and people with an array of distinctive features—eyes, nose, mouth, hair, and hands. ■

Realism in drawings appears gradually, as perception, language (ability to describe visual details), memory, and fine-motor capacities improve (Toomela, 2002). Drawing of geometric objects follows the steps illustrated in Figure 8.10. (1) Three- to 7-year olds draw a single unit to stand for an object. To represent a cube, they draw a square; to represent a cylinder, they draw a circle, an oval, or a rectangle. (2) During the late preschool and school years, children represent salient object parts. They draw several squares to stand for a cube's sides and draw two circles and some lines to represent a cylinder. However, the parts are not joined properly. (3) Older school-age children and adolescents integrate object parts into a realistic whole (Toomela, 1999).

Preschoolers' free depiction of reality makes their artwork look fanciful and inventive. Accomplished artists often must work hard to achieve what they did effortlessly as 5- and 6-year-olds.

CULTURAL VARIATIONS IN DEVELOPMENT OF DRAW-ING In cultures with rich artistic traditions, children create elaborate drawings that reflect the conventions of their culture. Adults encourage young children by offering suggestions, modeling ways to draw, and asking children to label their pictures. Peers, as well, discuss one another's drawings and copy from one another's work (Boyatzis, 2000; Braswell, 2006). All of these practices enhance young children's drawing progress.

But in cultures with little interest in art, even older children and adolescents produce simple forms. In the Jimi Valley, a remote region of Papua New Guinea with no indigenous pictorial art, many children do not go to school and therefore have little opportunity to develop drawing skills. When a Western researcher asked nonschooled Jimi 10- to 15-year-olds to draw a human figure for the first time, most produced nonrepresentational scribbles and shapes or simple "stick" or "contour" images (see Figure 8.11) (Martlew & Connolly, 1996). These forms, which resemble those of preschoolers, seem to be a universal beginning in drawing. Once children realize that lines must evoke human features, they find solutions to figure drawing that vary somewhat from culture to culture but, overall, follow the sequence described earlier.

(a)   (b)   (c)

FIGURE 8.11

Drawings produced by nonschooled 10- to 15-year-old children of the Jimi Valley of Papua New Guinea when asked to draw a human figure for the first time. Many produced nonrepresentational scribbles and shapes (a), "stick" figures (b), or "contour" figures (c). Compared with the Western tadpole form, the Jimi "stick" and "contour" figures emphasize the hands and feet. Otherwise, the drawings of these older children resemble those of young preschoolers. *(From M. Martlew & K. J. Connolly, 1996, "Human Figure Drawings by Schooled and Unschooled Children in Papua New Guinea," Child Development, 67, pp. 2750–2751. © The Society for Research in Child Development. Adapted by permission.)*

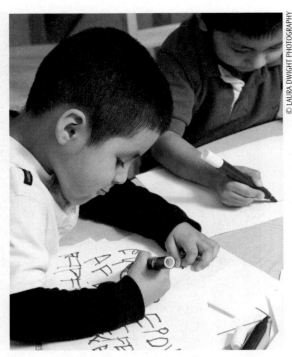

■ Gains in fine-motor control and perception, along with experience with written materials, contribute to this 5-year-old's skill at printing. ■

Adult Grips

FIGURE 8.12

Variations in 3-year-olds' pencil grip. Through experimenting with different grips, preschoolers gradually discover an adult grip with one or two fingers on top of the pencil, which maximizes writing stability and efficiency. *(Adapted from Greer & Lockman, 1998.)*

EARLY PRINTING   When preschoolers first try to write, they scribble, making no distinction between writing and drawing. As they experiment with lines and shapes, notice print in storybooks, and observe people writing, they attempt to print letters and, later, words. Around age 4, children's writing shows some distinctive features of print, such as separate forms arranged in a line on the page. But children often include picturelike devices. For example, they might use a circular shape to write "sun." Or they might call a large scribble the word *lion,* a small scribble the word *caterpillar,* and a red scribble the word *apple* (Ehri & Roberts, 2006; Levin & Bus, 2003). Applying their understanding of the symbolic function of drawings, 4-year-olds asked to write typically make a "drawing of print." Only gradually, as they learn to name the letters of the alphabet and to link them with language sounds, do preschoolers realize that writing stands for language.

Preschoolers' first attempts to print often involve their name, generally using a single letter. "How do you make a *D?*" my older son, David, asked at age 3½. When I printed a large uppercase *D,* he tried to copy. "*D* for David," he proclaimed, quite satisfied with his backward, imperfect creation. A year later, David added several letters, and around age 5, he printed his name clearly enough that others could read it.

Between ages 3 and 5, children acquire skill in gripping a pencil. As Figure 8.12 shows, 3-year-olds display diverse grip patterns and pencil angles, varying their grip depending on the direction and location of the marks they want to make. By trying out different forms of pencil-holding, they discover the grip and angle that maximize stability and writing efficiency. By age 5, most children use an adult grip pattern and a fairly constant pencil angle across a range of drawing and writing conditions (Greer & Lockman, 1998).

In addition to gains in fine-motor control, advances in perception contribute to the ability to print. Like many children, David continued to reverse letters until well into second grade. Once preschoolers distinguish writing from nonwriting around age 4, they make progress in identifying individual letters. Many preschoolers confuse letter pairs that are alike in shape with subtle distinctive features, such as *C* and *G, E* and *F,* and *M* and *W* (Bornstein & Arterberry, 1999). Mirror-image letter pairs (*b* and *d, p* and *q*) are especially hard to discriminate. Until children start to read, they do not find it especially useful to notice the difference between these forms.

The ability to tune in to mirror images and to scan a printed line from left to right improves as children gain experience with written materials (Casey, 1986). The more parents and teachers assist preschoolers in their efforts to print, the more advanced children are in writing and other aspects of literacy development (Aram & Levin, 2001, 2002). We will consider early childhood literacy in greater detail in Chapter 9.

Individual Differences in Motor Skills

Wide individual differences exist in the ages at which children reach motor milestones. A child with a tall, muscular body tends to move more quickly and to acquire certain skills earlier than a short, stocky youngster. And as in other domains, parents and teachers probably provide more encouragement to children with biologically based motor-skill advantages.

Sex differences in motor skills are evident in early childhood. Boys are ahead of girls in skills that emphasize force and power. By age 5, they can jump slightly farther, run slightly faster, and throw a ball about 5 feet farther. Girls have an edge in fine-motor skills and in certain gross-motor skills that require a combination of good balance and foot movement, such as hopping and skipping (Fischman, Moore, & Steele, 1992; Haywood & Getchell, 2005). Boys' greater muscle mass and, in the case of throwing, slightly longer forearms contribute to their skill advantages. And girls' greater overall physical maturity may be partly responsible for their better balance and precision of movement.

From an early age, boys and girls are usually channeled into different physical activities. For example, fathers are more likely to play catch with their sons than with their daughters. Baseballs and footballs are purchased for boys, jump ropes and sewing materials for girls. Sex differences in motor skills increase with age, but they remain small throughout childhood. This suggests that social pressures for boys to be active and physically skilled and for girls to play quietly at fine-motor activities exaggerate small genetically based sex differences (Greendorfer, Lewko, & Rosengren, 1996). In support of this view, boys can throw a ball much farther than girls only when using their dominant hand. When they use their nondominant hand, the sex difference is minimal (Williams, Haywood, & Painter, 1996). Boys' superior throwing largely results from practice.

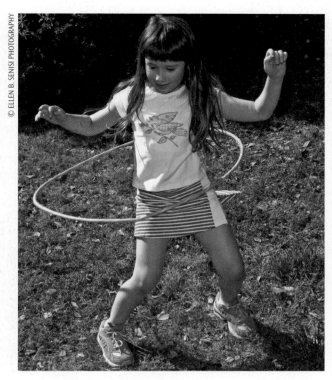

■ Sex differences in motor development are already apparent in early childhood. Girls have an edge in skills that require balance and precision of movement. But in throwing, catching, and running, boys benefit from greater encouragement to improve their skill level. ■

Enhancing Early Childhood Motor Development

Many Western parents provide preschoolers with early training in gymnastics, tumbling, and other physical activities. These experiences offer excellent opportunities for exercise and social interaction. But aside from throwing (where direct instruction is helpful), formal lessons during the preschool years have little impact on motor development. Rather, children master the motor skills of early childhood naturally, as part of their everyday play.

Nevertheless, the physical environment in which informal play takes place can affect mastery of complex motor skills. The National Association for Sport and Physical Education (2009) recommends that preschoolers engage in at least 60 minutes, and up to several hours, of unstructured physical activity every day. When children have play spaces and equipment appropriate for running, climbing, jumping, and throwing and are encouraged to use them, they respond eagerly to these challenges. But if balls are too large and heavy to be properly grasped and thrown, or jungle gyms, ladders, and horizontal bars are suitable for only the largest and strongest children, then preschoolers cannot easily acquire new motor skills. Playgrounds must offer a range of equipment to meet the diverse needs of individual children.

■ When play spaces are properly designed and equipped, young children respond eagerly to motor challenges and develop new skills through informal play. ■

Similarly, development of fine-motor skills can be supported through daily routines, such as dressing and pouring juice, and through play that involves puzzles, construction sets, drawing, painting, sculpting, cutting, and pasting. Exposure to artwork of their own and others' cultures enhances children's awareness of the creative possibilities of artistic media. And opportunities to represent their own ideas and feelings, rather than coloring in predrawn forms, foster artistic development.

Finally, the social climate created by adults can enhance or dampen preschoolers' motor development. When parents and teachers criticize a child's performance, push specific motor skills, or promote a competitive attitude, they risk undermining children's self-confidence and, in turn, their motor progress (Berk, 2006). Adult involvement in young children's motor activities should focus on fun rather than on winning or perfecting the "correct" technique.

ASK YOURSELF

◆ **REVIEW** Describe typical changes in children's drawings in early childhood, along with factors that contribute to those changes.

◆ **APPLY** Mabel and Chad want to do everything they can to support their 3-year-old daughter's athletic development. What advice would you give them?

◆ **CONNECT** How are experiences that best support preschoolers' motor development consistent with experience-expectant brain growth of the early years? (Return to page 172 in Chapter 5 to review.)

Summary

Body Growth

Describe changes in body size, proportions, and skeletal maturity during early childhood.

■ Gains in body size taper off in early childhood as children become longer and leaner, and individual differences in body size and rate of growth are more apparent. In various parts of the skeleton, new epiphyses emerge, where cartilage hardens into bone.

■ By the end of the preschool years, children start to lose their primary teeth. Care of primary teeth is essential because diseased baby teeth can affect the health of permanent teeth. Childhood tooth decay remains common, especially among low-SES children.

Describe brain development in early childhood.

■ Neural fibers in the brain continue to form synapses and myelinate. By this time, many parts of the cerebral cortex have overproduced synapses, and *synaptic pruning* occurs. To make room for the connective structures of active neurons, many surrounding neurons die, leading to reduced brain plasticity.

■ Prefrontal-cortical areas devoted to inhibition, attention, working memory, and planning show rapid growth from early to middle childhood. In addition, for most children, the left cerebral hemisphere develops ahead of the right, supporting rapidly expanding language skills.

© LAURA DWIGHT PHOTOGRAPHY

■ Hand preference, which reflects an individual's **dominant cerebral hemisphere,** strengthens during early childhood. Research on handedness supports the joint contribution of nature and nurture to brain lateralization.

■ During early childhood, connections are established between brain structures. Fibers linking the **cerebellum** to the cerebral cortex grow and myelinate, enhancing motor coordination. The **reticular formation,** responsible for alertness and consciousness; the **hippocampus,** which plays a vital role in memory; the **amygdala,** which plays a central role in processing emotional information; and the **corpus callosum,** which connects the two cortical hemispheres, also form synapses and myelinate.

Influences on Physical Growth and Health

Explain how heredity influences physical growth.

■ Heredity influences physical growth by controlling production and release of two vital hormones from the **pituitary gland: growth hormone (GH),** which affects the development of almost all body tissues, and **thyroid-stimulating hormone (TSH),** which affects brain growth and body size.

Describe the effects of emotional well-being, restful sleep, nutrition, and infectious disease on physical growth and health in early childhood.

■ Emotional well-being continues to influence body growth and health. Extreme emotional deprivation can lead to **psychosocial dwarfism.**

■ Restful sleep contributes to body growth, since GH is released during the child's sleeping hours. Sleep difficulties impair cognitive functioning, especially for low-SES children. Although total sleep need declines, substantial variability exists.

■ Sleep problems sometimes stem from a mismatch between parental demands and children's sleep needs. Many preschoolers have difficulty falling asleep, and most awaken occasionally at night. A few children suffer from sleep disorders, such as sleepwalking or sleep terrors, which run in families, suggesting a genetic influence. These problems can also be triggered by stress or extreme fatigue.

■ As growth rate slows, preschoolers' appetites decline, and they often become wary of new foods. Young children's social environments powerfully influence their food preferences. Modeling by others, repeated exposure to new foods, and a positive emotional climate at mealtimes can promote healthy, varied eating in young children.

■ Dietary deficiencies—most commonly in protein, vitamins, and minerals—are associated with attention and memory difficulties, academic and behavior problems, and greater susceptibility to infectious diseases. Disease also contributes to malnutrition, especially when intestinal infections cause persistent diarrhea. In developing countries, inexpensive oral rehydration therapy (ORT) and supplements of zinc can prevent most developmental impairments and deaths due to diarrhea.

■ Immunization rates are lower in the United States than in other industrialized nations because many economically disadvantaged children lack access to necessary health care. Parental stress and misconceptions about vaccine safety also contribute.

What factors increase the risk of unintentional injuries, and how can childhood injuries be prevented?

■ Unintentional injuries are the leading cause of childhood mortality in industrialized nations. Injury victims are more likely to be boys; to be temperamentally irritable, inattentive, overactive, and defiant; and to live in stressed, poverty-stricken, crowded family environments.

■ Effective injury prevention includes passing laws that promote child safety; creating safer home, travel, and play environments; relieving sources of family stress; improving public education; and changing parent and child behaviors.

Motor Development

Cite major milestones of gross- and fine-motor development in early childhood.

■ As the child's center of gravity shifts toward the trunk, balance improves, paving the way for new gross-motor achievements. Preschoolers' gaits become smooth and rhythmic; they run, jump, hop, gallop; eventually skip, throw, and catch; and generally become better coordinated.

■ Increasing control of the hands and fingers leads to dramatic improvements in fine-motor skills. Preschoolers gradually dress themselves and use a fork and knife.

■ By age 3, children's scribbles become pictures. As perceptual, cognitive, and fine-motor capacities improve, children's drawings increase in complexity and realism. Children's drawings are also influenced by their culture's artistic traditions.

■ Between 3 and 5 years, children experiment with pencil grip; by age 5, most use an adult-like grip that maximizes stability and writing efficiency.

■ Advances in perception and exposure to written materials contribute to progress in discriminating and accurately printing individual letters. When parents and teachers support children's efforts to print, preschoolers are more advanced in writing and other aspects of literacy development.

Describe individual differences in preschoolers' motor skills and ways to enhance motor development in early childhood.

■ Body build and opportunity for physical play affect early childhood motor development. Sex differences that favor boys in skills requiring force and power and girls in skills requiring good balance and fine movements are partly genetic, but social pressures exaggerate them.

■ Children master the motor skills of early childhood through informal play experiences, with little benefit from exposure to formal training. Richly equipped play environments that accommodate a wide range of physical abilities are important. Emphasizing pleasure in motor activities is the best way to foster motor development during the preschool years.

IMPORTANT TERMS AND CONCEPTS

amygdala (p. 295)
cerebellum (p. 294)
corpus callosum (p. 295)
dominant cerebral hemisphere (p. 293)

growth hormone (GH) (p. 297)
hippocampus (p. 294)
pituitary gland (p. 297)

psychosocial dwarfism (p. 297)
reticular formation (p. 294)
thyroid-stimulating hormone (TSH) (p. 297)

"My Weekend"
Jingyi Liu
6 years, China

This avid painter's creations reflect her rapidly expanding knowledge of the wider world. Mental representation blossoms in early childhood, contributing greatly to cognitive and language development.

Reprinted with permission from the International Museum of Children's Art, Oslo, Norway

Cognitive Development in Early Childhood

One rainy morning, as I observed in our laboratory preschool, Leslie, the children's teacher, joined me at the back of the room for a moment. "Preschoolers' minds are such a curious blend of logic, fantasy, and faulty reasoning," Leslie reflected. "Every day, I'm startled by the maturity and originality of what they say and do. Yet at other times, their thinking seems limited and inflexible."

Leslie's comments sum up the puzzling contradictions of early childhood cognition. That day, for example, 3-year-old Sammy looked up, startled, after a loud crash of thunder outside. "A magic man turned on the thunder!" he pronounced. Even when Leslie patiently explained that thunder is caused by lightning, not by a person turning it on or off, Sammy persisted: "Then a magic lady did it."

In other respects, Sammy's thinking was surprisingly advanced. At snack time, he accurately counted, "One, two, three, four!" and then got four cartons of milk, one for each child at his table. Sammy's keen memory and ability to categorize were also evident. He could recite by heart *The Very Hungry Caterpillar,* a story he had heard many times. And he could name and classify dozens of animals.

But when his snack group included more than four children, Sammy's counting broke down. And some of his notions about quantity seemed as fantastic as his understanding of thunder. After Priti dumped out her raisins, scattering them in front of her, Sammy asked, "How come you got lots, and I only got this little bit?" He didn't realize that he had just as many raisins; his were simply all bunched up in a tiny red box. While Priti was washing her hands after snack, Sammy put her remaining raisins in her cubby. When Priti returned and looked for her raisins, Sammy pronounced, "You know where they are!" He failed to grasp that Priti, who hadn't seen him move the raisins, would expect them to be where she had left them.

In this chapter, we explore early childhood cognition, drawing on three theories with which you are already familiar. To understand Sammy's reasoning, we turn first to Piaget's and Vygotsky's theories along with evidence highlighting the strengths and limitations of each. Then we examine additional research on young children's cognition inspired by the information-processing perspective. Next, we address factors that contribute to individual differences in mental development—the home environment, the quality of preschool and child care, and the many hours young children spend watching television and using computers. Our chapter concludes with the dramatic expansion of language in early childhood.

Piaget's Theory: The Preoperational Stage

As children move from the sensorimotor to the **preoperational stage,** which spans the years 2 to 7, the most obvious change is an extraordinary increase in representational, or symbolic, activity. Recall that infants and toddlers have considerable ability to mentally represent their world. In early childhood, this capacity blossoms.

Advances in Mental Representation

Piaget acknowledged that language is our most flexible means of mental representation. By detaching thought from action, it permits far more efficient thinking than was possible earlier. When we think in words, we overcome the limits of our momentary experiences. We can deal with past, present, and future at once and combine concepts in unique ways, as when we imagine a hungry caterpillar eating bananas or monsters flying through the forest at night.

But Piaget did not regard language as a primary ingredient in childhood cognitive change. Instead, he believed that sensorimotor activity leads to internal images of experience, which children then label with words (Piaget, 1936/1952). In support of Piaget's view, recall from Chapter 6 that children's first words have a strong sensorimotor basis. And toddlers acquire an impressive range of categories long before they use words to label them (see pages 222–223). But as we will see, other theorists regard Piaget's account of the link between language and thought as incomplete.

Make-Believe Play

Make-believe play is another excellent example of the development of representation in early childhood. Piaget believed that through pretending, young children practice and strengthen newly acquired representational schemes. Drawing on his ideas, several investigators have traced changes in make-believe play during the preschool years.

DEVELOPMENT OF MAKE-BELIEVE   One day, Sammy's 20-month-old brother, Dwayne, visited the classroom. Dwayne wandered around, picked up a toy telephone receiver, eyed his mother, said, "Hi, Mommy," and then dropped it. Next, he found an empty cup, pretended to drink, and then toddled off again. Meanwhile, Sammy joined Vance and Lynette in the block area for a space shuttle launch.

"That can be our control tower," Sammy suggested, pointing to a corner by a bookshelf. "Countdown!" he announced, speaking into his "walkie-talkie"—a small wooden block. "Five, six, two, four, one, blastoff!" Lynette made a doll push a pretend button, and the rocket was off!

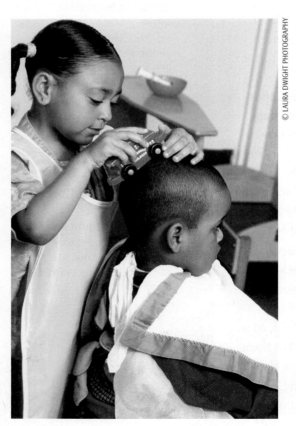
© LAURA DWIGHT PHOTOGRAPHY

■ Make-believe play increases in sophistication during the preschool years. Children increasingly coordinate make-believe roles and pretend with less realistic toys, so a toy truck can stand for an electric hair clipper. ■

Comparing Dwayne's pretend play with Sammy's, we see three important changes that reflect the preschool child's growing symbolic mastery:

■ *Play detaches from the real-life conditions associated with it.* In early pretending, toddlers use only realistic objects—a toy telephone to talk into or a cup to drink from. Their earliest pretend acts usually imitate adults' actions and are not yet flexible. Children younger than age 2, for example, will pretend to drink from a cup but refuse to pretend a cup is a hat (Rakoczy, Tomasello, & Striano, 2005). They have trouble using an object (cup) that already has an obvious use as a symbol of another object (hat).

   After age 2, children pretend with less realistic toys—for example, a block for a telephone receiver. Gradually, they can flexibly imagine objects and events without support from the real world, as Sammy's imaginary control tower illustrates (O'Reilly, 1995; Striano, Tomasello, & Rochat, 2001).

■ *Play becomes less self-centered.* At first, make-believe is directed toward the self. For example, Dwayne pretends to feed only himself. Soon, children begin to direct pretend actions toward objects, as when a child feeds a doll. Early in the third year, they become detached participants, making a doll feed itself or pushing a button to launch a rocket. Make-believe becomes less self-centered as children realize that agents and recipients of pretend actions can be independent of themselves (McCune, 1993).

■ *Play includes more complex combinations of schemes.* Dwayne can pretend to drink from a cup, but he does not yet combine drinking with pouring. Later, children combine schemes with those of peers in **sociodramatic play,** the make-believe with others that is under way by the end of the second year and that increases rapidly in complexity during early childhood (Kavanaugh, 2006a). Already, Sammy and his classmates can create and coordinate several roles in an elaborate plot. By the end of the preschool years, children have a sophisticated understanding of role relationships and story lines.

Children as young as age 2 display awareness that make-believe is a representational activity. They distinguish make-believe from real experiences and grasp that pretending is a deliberate effort to act out imaginary ideas—an understanding that strengthens over early childhood (Lillard, 2003; Rakoczy, Tomasello, & Striano, 2004; Sobel, 2006). **TAKE A MOMENT...** Listen closely to preschoolers as they assign roles and negotiate plans in sociodramatic play: "*You pretend to be* the astronaut, *I'll act like* I'm operating the control tower!" "Wait, *I gotta set up* the spaceship." In communicating about pretend, children think about their own and others' fanciful representations—evidence that they have begun to reason about people's mental activities, a topic we will return to later in this chapter.

BENEFITS OF MAKE-BELIEVE   Today, Piaget's view of make-believe as mere practice of representational schemes is regarded as too limited. Play not only reflects but also contributes to children's cognitive and social skills. Sociodramatic play has been studied most thoroughly. Compared with social nonpretend activities (such as drawing or putting puzzles together), during sociodramatic play preschoolers' interactions last longer, show more involvement, draw more children into the activity, and are more cooperative (Creasey, Jarvis, & Berk, 1998).

It is not surprising, then, that preschoolers who spend more time in sociodramatic play are seen as more socially competent by their teachers (Connolly & Doyle, 1984). And many studies reveal that make-believe strengthens a wide variety of mental abilities, including sustained attention, memory, logical reasoning, language and literacy, imagination, creativity, and the ability to reflect on one's own thinking, regulate one's own emotions and behavior, and take another's perspective (Bergen & Mauer, 2000; Berk, Mann, & Ogan, 2006; Elias & Berk, 2002; Hirsh-Pasek et al., 2009; Lindsey & Colwell, 2003; Ogan & Berk, 2009; Ruff & Capozzoli, 2003).

Between 25 and 45 percent of preschoolers and young school-age children spend much time in solitary make-believe, creating *imaginary companions*—special fantasized friends endowed with humanlike qualities. For example, one preschooler created Nutsy and Nutsy, a pair of boisterous birds who lived outside her bedroom window and often went along on family outings (Gleason, Sebanc, & Hartup, 2000; Taylor et al., 2004). Imaginary companions were once viewed as a sign of maladjustment, but research challenges this assumption. Children with an

LOOK AND LISTEN

❖❖

Observe the make-believe play of several 2- to 4-year-olds at home or in a preschool or child-care center. Describe pretend acts that exemplify important developmental changes.

Applying What We Know

Enhancing Make-Believe Play in Early Childhood

STRATEGY	DESCRIPTION
Provide sufficient space and play materials.	Generous space and materials allow for many play options and reduce conflict.
Encourage children's play without controlling it.	Model, guide, and build on young preschoolers' play themes. Provide open-ended suggestions (for example, "Would the animals like a train ride?"), and talk with the child about the thoughts, motivations, and emotions of play characters. These forms of adult support lead to more elaborate pretending. Refrain from directing the child's play; excessive adult control destroys the creativity and pleasure of make-believe.
Offer a variety of both realistic materials and materials without clear functions.	Children use realistic materials, such as trucks, dolls, tea sets, dress-up clothes, and toy scenes (house, farm, garage, airport) to act out everyday roles in their culture. Materials without clear functions (such as blocks, cardboard cylinders, paper bags, and sand) inspire fantastic role play, such as "pirate" and "creature from outer space."
Ensure that children have many rich, real-world experiences to inspire positive fantasy play.	Opportunities to participate in real-world activities with adults and to observe adult roles in the community provide children with rich social knowledge to integrate into make-believe. Restricting television viewing, especially programs with violent content, limits the degree to which violent themes and aggressive behavior become part of children's play. (See Chapter 10, pages 387–389.)
Help children solve social conflicts constructively.	Cooperation is essential for sociodramatic play. Guide children toward positive relationships with agemates by helping them resolve disagreements constructively. For example, ask, "What could you do if you want a turn?" If the child cannot think of possibilities, suggest options, and assist the child in implementing them.

Sources: Berk, Mann, & Ogan, 2006; Nielsen & Christie, 2008; Ogan & Berk, 2009.

invisible playmate typically treat it with care and affection and say it offers caring, comfort, and good company, just as their real friendships do (Gleason & Hohmann, 2006; Hoff, 2005). Such children also display more complex and imaginative pretend play, are advanced in understanding others' viewpoints and emotions, and are more sociable with peers (Bouldin, 2006; Gleason, 2002; Taylor & Carlson, 1997).

Applying What We Know above lists ways to enhance preschoolers' make-believe. Later we will return to the origins and consequences of make-believe from an alternative perspective—that of Vygotsky.

■ Children who experience a variety of symbols come to understand dual representation—for example, that this dollhouse is both an object in its own right and can stand for another, a full-sized house that people live in. ■

Symbol–Real-World Relations

In a corner of the classroom, Leslie set up a dollhouse, replete with tiny furnishings. Sammy liked to arrange the furniture to match his real-world living room, kitchen, and bedroom. Representations of reality, like Sammy's, are powerful cognitive tools. When we understand that a picture, model, or map corresponds to something specific in everyday life, we can use these tools to find out about objects and places we have not experienced.

In Chapter 6, we saw that by the middle of the second year, children grasp the symbolic function of realistic-looking pictures (such as photos). When do children comprehend scale models as symbols for real-world spaces? In one study, 2½- and 3-year-olds watched an adult hide a small toy (Little Snoopy) in a scale model of a room and then were asked to retrieve it. Next, they had to find a larger toy (Big Snoopy) hidden in the room that the model represented. Not until age 3 could most children use the model as a guide to finding Big Snoopy in the real room (DeLoache, 1987). The 2½-year-olds did not realize that the model could be both *a toy room* and *a symbol of another room.* They had trouble with **dual representation**—viewing a symbolic object as both an object in its own right and a symbol. In support of this interpretation, when researchers made the model room less prominent as an object, by placing it behind a window and preventing children from touching it, more 2½-year-olds succeeded at the search task (DeLoache, 2000, 2002).

Recall that in make-believe play, 1½- to 2-year-olds cannot use an object that has an obvious use (cup) to stand for another object (hat). Likewise, 2-year-olds do not yet grasp that a line drawing—an object in its own right—also represents real-world objects (see page 310 in Chapter 8). Difficulty with dual representation may contribute to 2-year-olds' scale errors—for example, attempts to put on dolls' clothes or sit in a doll-sized chair (see page 281 in Chapter 7).

How do children grasp the dual representation of symbolic objects? When adults point out similarities between models and real-world spaces, 2½-year-olds perform better on the find-Snoopy task (Peralta de Mendoza & Salsa, 2003). Also, insight into one type of symbol–real-world relation helps preschoolers master others. For example, children regard realistic-looking pictures as symbols early, around 1½ to 2 years, because a picture's primary purpose is to stand for something; it is not an interesting object in its own right (Preissler & Carey, 2004; Simcock & DeLoache, 2006). And 3-year-olds who can use a model of a room to locate Big Snoopy readily transfer their understanding to a simple map (Marzolf & DeLoache, 1994).

In sum, exposing young children to diverse symbols—picture books, photographs, drawings, make-believe, and maps—helps them appreciate that one object can stand for another. With age, children come to understand a wide range of symbols that have little physical similarity to what they represent (Liben, 2009). As a result, doors open to vast realms of knowledge.

Limitations of Preoperational Thought

Aside from gains in representation, Piaget described preschoolers in terms of what they *cannot* understand (Beilin, 1992). As the term *preoperational* suggests, he compared them to older, more competent children who have reached the concrete operational stage. According to Piaget, young children are not capable of *operations*—mental actions that obey logical rules. Rather, their thinking is rigid, limited to one aspect of a situation at a time, and strongly influenced by the way things appear at the moment.

EGOCENTRISM   For Piaget, the most fundamental deficiency of preoperational thinking is **egocentrism**—failure to distinguish the symbolic viewpoints of others from one's own. He believed that when children first mentally represent the world, they tend to focus on their own viewpoint and assume that others perceive, think, and feel the same way they do.

Piaget's most convincing demonstration of egocentrism involves his *three-mountains problem,* described in Figure 9.1. He also regarded egocentrism as responsible for preoperational children's **animistic thinking**—the belief that inanimate objects have lifelike qualities, such as thoughts, wishes, feelings, and intentions (Piaget, 1926/1930). Recall Sammy's insistence that someone must have turned on the thunder. According to Piaget, because young children egocentrically assign human purposes to physical events, magical thinking is common during the preschool years.

Piaget argued that preschoolers' egocentric bias prevents them from *accommodating,* or reflecting on and revising their faulty reasoning in response to their physical and social worlds. To understand this shortcoming, let's consider some additional tasks that Piaget gave to children.

INABILITY TO CONSERVE   Piaget's famous conservation tasks reveal several deficiencies of preoperational thinking. **Conservation** refers to the idea that certain physical characteristics of objects remain the same, even when their outward appearance changes. At snack time, Sammy and Priti had identical boxes of raisins, but when Priti spread her raisins out on the table, Sammy was convinced that she had more.

FIGURE 9.1

Piaget's three-mountains problem. Each mountain is distinguished by its color and by its summit. One has a red cross, another a small house, and the third a snow-capped peak. Children at the preoperational stage respond egocentrically. They cannot select a picture that shows the mountains from the doll's perspective. Instead, they simply choose the photo that reflects their own vantage point.

Some Piagetian conservation tasks. Children at the preoperational stage cannot yet conserve. These tasks are mastered gradually over the concrete operational stage. Children in Western nations typically acquire conservation of number, mass, and liquid sometime between 6 and 7 years and of weight between 8 and 10 years.

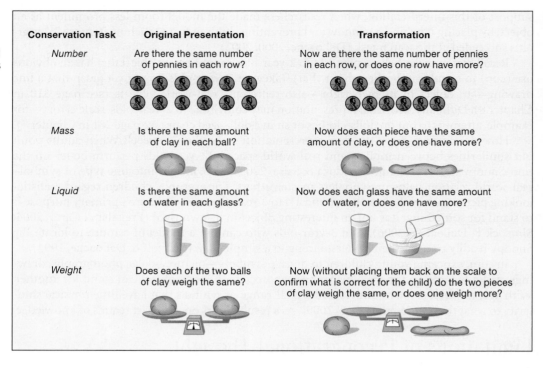

In another conservation task involving liquid, the child is shown two identical tall glasses of water and asked if they contain equal amounts. Once the child agrees, the water in one glass is poured into a short, wide container, changing its appearance but not its amount. Then the child is asked whether the amount of water is the same or has changed. Preoperational children think the quantity has changed. They explain, "There is less now because the water is way down here" (that is, its level is so low) or, "There is more now because it is all spread out." Figure 9.2 illustrates other conservation tasks that you can try with children.

The inability to conserve highlights several related aspects of preoperational children's thinking. First, their understanding is *centered,* or characterized by **centration.** They focus on one aspect of a situation, neglecting other important features. In conservation of liquid, the child *centers* on the height of the water, failing to realize that changes in width compensate for the changes in height. Second, children are easily distracted by the *perceptual appearance* of objects. Third, children treat the initial and final *states* of the water as unrelated events, ignoring the *dynamic transformation* (pouring of water) between them.

The most important illogical feature of preoperational thought is its **irreversibility**—an inability to mentally go through a series of steps in a problem and then reverse direction, returning to the starting point. *Reversibility* is part of every logical operation. After Priti spills her raisins, Sammy cannot reverse by thinking, "I know Priti doesn't have more raisins than I do. If we put them back in that little box, her raisins and mine would look just the same."

LACK OF HIERARCHICAL CLASSIFICATION Preoperational children have difficulty with **hierarchical classification**—the organization of objects into classes and subclasses on the basis of similarities and differences. Piaget's famous *class inclusion problem,* illustrated in Figure 9.3, demonstrates this limitation. Preoperational children *center* on the overriding feature, red. They do not think reversibly, moving from the whole class (flowers) to the parts (red and blue) and back again.

A Piagetian class inclusion problem. Children are shown 16 flowers, 4 of which are blue and 12 of which are red. Asked, "Are there more red flowers or flowers?" the preoperational child responds, "More red flowers," failing to realize that both red and blue flowers are included in the category "flowers."

Follow-Up Research on Preoperational Thought

Over the past three decades, researchers have challenged Piaget's view of preschoolers as cognitively deficient. Because many Piagetian problems contain unfamiliar elements or too many pieces of information for young children to handle at once, preschoolers' responses often do not reflect their true abilities. Piaget also missed many naturally occurring instances of effective reasoning by preschoolers. Let's look at some examples.

EGOCENTRIC, ANIMISTIC, AND MAGICAL THINKING　Do young children really believe that a person standing elsewhere in a room sees exactly what they see? When researchers change the nature of Piaget's three-mountains problem to include familiar objects and use methods other than picture selection (which is difficult even for 10-year-olds), 4-year-olds show clear awareness of others' vantage points (Borke, 1975; Newcombe & Huttenlocher, 1992). Even 2-year-olds realize that what they see sometimes differs from what another person sees. When asked to help an adult look for a lost object, 24-month-olds—but not 18-month-olds—handed her a toy resting behind a bucket that was within their line of sight but not the adult's (Moll & Tomasello, 2006).

Nonegocentric responses also appear in young children's conversations. For example, preschoolers adapt their speech to fit the needs of their listeners. Four-year-olds use shorter, simpler expressions when talking to 2-year-olds than to agemates or adults (Gelman & Shatz, 1978). And in describing objects, children do not use such words as "big" and "little" in a rigid, egocentric fashion. Instead, they *adjust* their descriptions to allow for context. By age 3, children judge a 2-inch shoe as small when seen by itself (because it is much smaller than most shoes) but as big for a tiny 5-inch-tall doll (Ebeling & Gelman, 1994).

In previous chapters, we saw that toddlers have already begun to infer others' intentions and perspectives. And in his later writings, Piaget (1945/1951) did describe preschoolers' egocentrism as a tendency rather than an inability. As we revisit the topic of perspective taking, we will see that it develops gradually throughout childhood and adolescence.

Piaget also overestimated preschoolers' animistic beliefs. Even infants have begun to distinguish animate from inanimate, as indicated by their remarkable categorical distinctions among living and nonliving things (see Chapter 6, pages 222–223). By age 2½, children give psychological explanations ("he likes to" or "she wants to") for people and other animals but rarely for objects (Hickling & Wellman, 2001). And 3- to 5-year-olds asked whether a variety of animals and objects can eat, grow, talk, think, remember, see, or feel mostly attribute these capacities to animals, not objects. In addition, they rarely attribute biological properties (like eating and growing) to robots, indicting that they are well aware that even a self-moving object with lifelike features is not alive. But unlike adults, preschoolers often say that robots have perceptual and psychological capacities—for example, seeing, thinking, and remembering (Jipson & Gelman, 2007; Subrahmanyam, Gelman, & Lafosse, 2002). These responses result from incomplete knowledge about certain objects, and they decline with age.

Similarly, preschoolers think that magic accounts for events they otherwise cannot explain, as in Sammy's magical explanation of thunder in the opening to this chapter. Consequently, most 3- and 4-year-olds believe in the supernatural powers of fairies, goblins, and other enchanted creatures (Rosengren & Hickling, 2000). But their notions of magic are flexible and appropriate. For example, older

© TATSUYUKI TAYAMA/FUJIFOTOS/THE IMAGE WORKS

■ Most 3- to 5-year-olds have a well-developed understanding of the distinction between animate and inanimate. For example, they realize that a robot with lifelike features is really not alive and cannot eat or grow. But because of incomplete knowledge, they often claim that robots have perceptual and psychological capacities, such as seeing, thinking, and remembering. ■

3-year-olds and 4-year-olds think that violations of physical laws (walking through a wall) require magic more than violations of social conventions (taking a bath with shoes on) (Browne & Woolley, 2004). And they are more likely to say that a magical process—wishing—caused an event (an object to appear in a box) when a person made the wish before the event occurred, the event was consistent with the wish (the wished-for object rather than another object appeared in the box), and no alternative causes were apparent (Woolley, Browne, & Boerger, 2006). These features of causality are the same ones preschoolers rely on in ordinary situations.

Between ages 4 and 8, as children gain familiarity with physical events and principles, their magical beliefs decline. They figure out who is really behind Santa Claus and the Tooth Fairy, and they realize that the antics of magicians are due to trickery (Subbotsky, 2004). And increasingly, they say that events in fantastical stories couldn't really happen and that characters in such stories aren't real (Wooley & Cox, 2007). Still, because children entertain the possibility that something they imagine might materialize, they may react with anxiety to scary stories, TV shows, and nightmares. In one study, researchers had 4- to 6-year-olds imagine that a monster was inside one empty box and a puppy inside another. Almost all the children approached the "puppy" box, but many avoided putting their finger in the "monster" box, even though they knew that imagination cannot create reality (Harris et al., 1991).

Religion and culture play a role in how quickly children give up certain fantastic ideas. For example, Jewish children are more likely than their Christian agemates to express disbelief in Santa Claus and the Tooth Fairy. Having heard at home that Santa is imaginary, they seem to generalize this attitude to other magical figures (Woolley, 1997). And cultural myths about wishing—for example, the custom of making a wish before blowing out birthday candles—probably underlie the conviction of most 3- to 6-year-olds that by wishing, you can sometimes make your desires come true (Woolley, 2000).

LOGICAL THOUGHT Many studies show that when preschoolers are given tasks that are simplified and made relevant to their everyday lives, they do not display the illogical characteristics that Piaget saw in the preoperational stage. For example, when a conservation-of-number task is scaled down to include only three items instead of six or seven, 3-year-olds perform well (Gelman, 1972). And when preschoolers are asked carefully worded questions about what happens to substances (such as sugar) after they are dissolved in water, they give accurate explanations. Most 3- to 5-year-olds know that the substance is conserved—that it continues to exist, can be tasted, and makes the liquid heavier, even though it is invisible in the water (Au, Sidle, & Rollins, 1993; Rosen & Rozin, 1993).

Preschoolers' ability to reason about transformations is evident on other problems. They can engage in impressive *reasoning by analogy* about physical changes. When presented with the picture-matching problem "Play dough is to cut-up play dough as apple is to . . . ?," even 3-year-olds choose the correct answer (a cut-up apple) from a set of alternatives, several of which (a bitten apple, a cut-up loaf of bread) share physical features with the right choice (Goswami, 1996). These findings indicate that in familiar contexts, preschoolers can overcome appearances and think logically about cause and effect.

Finally, even without detailed biological or mechanical knowledge, preschoolers realize that the insides of animals are responsible for certain cause–effect sequences (such as willing oneself to move) that are impossible for nonliving things, such as machines (Gelman, 2003; Keil & Lockhart, 1999). Preschoolers seem to use illogical reasoning only when they must grapple with unfamiliar topics, too much information, or contradictory facts that they cannot reconcile (Ruffman, 1999).

CATEGORIZATION Despite their difficulty with Piagetian class inclusion tasks, preschoolers organize their everyday knowledge into nested categories at an early age. By the beginning of early childhood, children's categories include objects that go together because of their common function, behavior, or natural kind (animate versus inanimate), challenging Piaget's assumption that preschoolers' thinking is wholly governed by appearances.

Indeed, 2- to 5-year-olds readily draw appropriate inferences about nonobservable characteristics shared by category members. For example, after being told that a bird has warm blood and that a stegosaurus (dinosaur) has cold blood, preschoolers infer that a pterodactyl (labeled a dinosaur) has cold blood, even though it closely resembles a bird (Gopnik & Nazzi, 2003).

LOOK AND LISTEN

❖❖

Try the conservation of number and mass tasks in Figure 9.2 with a 3- or 4-year-old. Next, simplify conservation of number by reducing the number of pennies, and relate conservation of mass to the child's experience by pretending the clay is baking dough and transforming it into cupcakes. Did the child perform more competently?

And when shown a set of three characters—two of whom look different but share an inner trait ("outgoing") and two of whom look similar but have different inner traits (one "shy," one "outgoing")—preschoolers rely on the trait category, not physical appearance, to predict similar preferred activities (Heyman & Gelman, 2000).

During the second and third years, and perhaps earlier, children's categories differentiate. They form many *basic-level categories*—ones at an intermediate level of generality, such as "chairs," "tables," and "beds." By the third year, children easily move back and forth between basic-level categories and *general categories,* such as "furniture." And they break down the basic-level categories into *subcategories,* such as "rocking chairs" and "desk chairs." In fact, a case study of a highly verbal toddler with a strong interest in birds revealed that by age 2, he had constructed a hierarchical understanding of the bird domain that included such basic-level categories and subcategories as "waterbirds" ("ducks" and "swans"),

■ Preschoolers form many categories based on nonobservable characteristics. These 4-year-olds clearly understand which of a wide array of animals are prone to fight. ■

"landbirds" ("roosters" and "turkeys"), and "other birds" ("bluebirds," "cardinals," and "seagulls") (Mervis, Pani, & Pani, 2003). The boy's category structure was not quite the same as that of many adults, but it was, indeed, hierarchical. And he used that knowledge to make many correct inferences about category membership—for example, that baby birds and their parents must be members of the same species (both "robins") even though they look strikingly different.

Preschoolers' rapidly expanding vocabularies and general knowledge support their impressive skill at categorizing (Gelman & Koenig, 2003). As they learn more about their world, they devise theories about underlying characteristics that category members share, which help them identify new instances (Gelman & Kalish, 2006; Gelman & Koenig, 2003). For example, they realize that animals have an inborn potential for certain physical characteristics and behaviors that determine their identity. In categorizing, they look for causal links among these features. In one study, researchers invented two categories of animals—one with horns, armor, and a spiky tail; the other with wings, large ears, long toes, and a monkeylike tail (see Figure 9.4). Four-year-olds who were given a theory that identified an inner cause for the coexistence of the animals' features—animals in the first category "like to fight"; those in the second category "like to hide in trees"—easily classified new examples of animals. But 4-year-olds for whom animal features were merely pointed out or who were given a separate function for each feature could not remember the categories (Krascum & Andrews, 1998).

Finally, adult–child conversations are major sources of categorical learning. Adults frequently label and explain categories to young children. When they use the word *bird* for hummingbirds, turkeys, and swans, they signal to children that something other than physical

---

FIGURE 9.4

Categories of imaginary animals shown to preschoolers. When an adult provided a theory about the coexistence of animals' features—"likes to fight" and "likes to hide in trees"—4-year-olds easily classified new examples of animals with only one or two features. Without the theory, preschoolers could not remember the categories. Theories about underlying characteristics support the formation of many categories in early childhood. *(From R. M. Krascum & S. Andrews, 1998, "The Effects of Theories on Children's Acquisition of Family-Resemblance Categories,"* Child Development, 69, *p. 336. © The Society for Research in Child Development, Inc. Reprinted by permission.)*

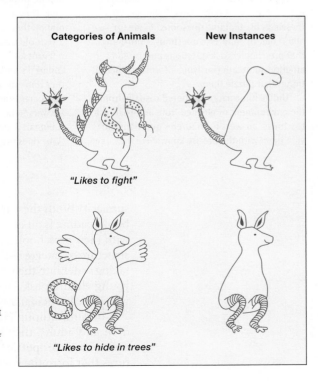

Categories of Animals   New Instances

"Likes to fight"

"Likes to hide in trees"

SOCIAL ISSUES: EDUCATION

Children's Questions: Catalyst for Cognitive Development

"Dad, what's that?" asked 4-year-old Emily as her father chopped vegetables for dinner.

"It's an onion," her father said.

"Is an onion a fruit?" Emily asked.

"It's a vegetable," her father replied. "A root vegetable because it grows underground."

Emily wrinkled her nose. "Why does it smell yucky?"

"I don't know," her father admitted. "But after dinner we can look it up online and find out."

When young children converse with adults, they ask, on average, more than one question per minute! Do inquisitive children like Emily really want answers to their many questions? Or are they—as their parents sometimes conclude—merely clamoring for attention?

An analysis of diaries that parents diverse in SES and ethnicity kept of their children's questions and of audio recordings of parent–child interactions revealed that at every age between 1 and 5 years, 70 to 90 percent of children's questions were information-seeking ("What's that [pointing to a crawfish]?") as opposed to non-information-seeking ("Can I have a cookie?") (Chouinard, 2007). And from age 2 on, children increasingly built on their fact-oriented questions with follow-up questions that asked for causes and explanations ("What do crawfish eat?" "Why does it have claws?"). By age 3½, these sets of "building questions" made up about half of children's questions, confirming that preschoolers ask questions purposefully, in an effort to obtain clarifying information about things that puzzle them.

Unlike information gathered casually from the environment or gleaned from adults' direct teachings, answers to children's questions provide them with the precise knowledge they need

at the precise moment they need it. Even before children can talk, they ask questions by gesturing at objects in their environment. A pointing gesture, for example, might lead a parent to say, "That's a ball. See, it bounces!" And the content of children's questions is related to their cognitive development. At a time when vocabulary is advancing rapidly, about 60 percent of 1½- to 2-year-olds' questions ask for names of objects. With age, preschoolers increasingly ask about function ("What's it do?"), activity ("What's he doing?"), state ("Is she hungry?"), and theory of mind ("How does the pilot *know* where to fly?").

Context also makes a difference. Compared with everyday situations, a visit to a zoo elicits many more questions about biological information from 2- to 4-year-olds: "Why is the lion sleeping?" "Is he dead?" "What do bats eat?" "Will the baby lion grow bigger?" Biological questions calling for explanations increased with age as 3- and 4-year-olds tried to make sense of such processes as growth, life, illness, and death—concepts they are currently grappling with and that will soon advance (see page 426 in Chapter 11).

The usefulness of children's questions depends on adults' answers. Most of the time, parents respond informatively. If they do not, preschoolers are amazingly persistent: They ask again until they get the information they wanted. Especially for 1- and 2-year-olds, parents often include additional relevant knowledge aimed at enhancing children's understanding and guiding further thinking. An earlier study also revealed that parents adjust the complexity of their answers to fit their children's maturity (Callanan & Oakes, 1992). To a question like "Why does the light come on?" 3-year-olds

typically get simpler, "prior cause" explanations ("I turned on the switch"). Slightly older children frequently get "mechanism" explanations ("The switch allows electricity to reach the light bulb").

Clearly, asking questions is a major means through which children expand their knowledge and reorganize their conceptual structures as they strive to attain adultlike understandings. Children's questions offer parents and teachers a fascinating window into their factual and conceptual knowledge, along with a wealth of opportunities to help them learn.

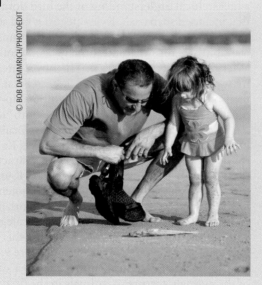

© BOB DAEMMRICH/PHOTOEDIT

■ A high percentage of preschoolers' questions are purposeful efforts to understand things that puzzle them. Adults' answers provide the precise knowledge children need at the precise moment they need it, making question-asking a powerful source of cognitive development. ■

similarity binds these instances together (Gelman, 2003, 2006; Gelman & Kalish, 2006). Picture-book reading is an especially rich context for understanding categories. While looking at books with their preschoolers, parents provide information that guides children's inferences about the structure of categories: "Penguins live at the South Pole, swim, and catch fish" or "Fish breathe by taking water into their mouths." Furthermore, as the Social Issues: Education box above indicates, young children ask many questions about their world and generally get informative answers, which are particularly well-suited to advancing their conceptual understanding.

In sum, although preschoolers' category systems are less complex than those of older children and adults, they already have the capacity to classify hierarchically and on the basis of nonobvious properties. And they use logical, causal reasoning to identify the interrelated features that form the basis of a category and to classify new members.

APPEARANCE VERSUS REALITY As we have seen, when presented with familiar situations and simplified problems, preschoolers show remarkably advanced reasoning—including the capacity to overcome perceptual appearances. But what happens when preschoolers encounter objects that have two identities—an apparent one and a real one? Can they distinguish appearance from reality? In a series of studies, John Flavell and his colleagues presented children with objects that were disguised in various ways and asked what each "looks like" and what each "is really and truly." Preschoolers had difficulty. For example, when asked whether a candle that looks like a crayon "is really and truly" a crayon or whether a stone painted to look like an egg "is really and truly" an egg, they often responded, "Yes!" Not until age 6 or 7 did children do well on these tasks (Flavell, Green, & Flavell, 1987).

Younger children's poor performance, however, is not due to a general difficulty in distinguishing appearance from reality, as Piaget suggested. Rather, they have trouble with the language of these tasks (Deák, Ray, & Brenneman, 2003). When permitted to solve appearance–reality problems nonverbally, by selecting from an array of objects the one that "really" has a particular identity, most 3-year-olds perform well (Sapp, Lee, & Muir, 2000).

These findings suggest that preschoolers begin to grasp the appearance–reality distinction sometime during the third year. Note how it involves an attainment we discussed earlier: *dual representation*—the realization that an object can be one thing (a candle) while symbolizing another (a crayon). At first, however, children's understanding is fragile. After putting on a Halloween mask, young preschoolers may be frightened when they see themselves in a mirror. Performing well on verbal appearance–reality tasks signifies a more secure understanding and is related to further progress in representational ability (Bialystok & Senman, 2004).

■ This 3-year-old has begun to grasp the distinction between appearance and reality—that this object, which looks like a pig, is really and truly a bank. Around age 6 to 7, his knowledge will be solid and secure. ■

Evaluation of the Preoperational Stage

Table 9.1 on page 328 provides an overview of the cognitive attainments of early childhood just considered. **TAKE A MOMENT...** Compare them with Piaget's description of the preoperational child on pages 321–322. The evidence as a whole indicates that Piaget was partly wrong and partly right about young children's cognitive capacities. When given simplified tasks based on familiar experiences, preschoolers show the beginnings of logical thinking. How can we make sense of the contradictions between Piaget's conclusions and the findings of recent research?

That preschoolers have some logical understandings that strengthen with age indicates that they attain logical operations gradually. Over time, children rely on increasingly effective mental (as opposed to perceptual) approaches to solving problems. For example, children who cannot use counting to compare two sets of items do not conserve number. Rather, they rely on perceptual cues to compare the amounts in two sets of items (Rouselle, Palmers, & Noël, 2004; Sophian, 1995). Once preschoolers can count, they apply this skill to conservation-of-number tasks involving just a few items. As counting improves, they extend the strategy to problems with more items. By age 6, they understand that number remains the same after a transformation in the length and spacing of a set of items as long as nothing is added or taken away (Halford & Andrews, 2006). Consequently, they no longer need to count to verify their answer.

Evidence that preschool children can be trained to perform well on Piagetian problems also supports the idea that operational thought is not absent at one point in time and present at another (Ping & Goldin-Meadow, 2008; Siegler & Svetina, 2006). Children who possess some understanding would naturally benefit from training, unlike those with no understanding at all. The gradual development of logical operations poses a serious challenge to Piaget's assumption of abrupt change toward logical reasoning around age 6 or 7. Does a preoperational stage really exist? Some no longer think so. Recall from Chapter 6 that according to the

TABLE 9.1	Some Cognitive Attainments of Early Childhood

APPROXIMATE AGE		COGNITIVE ATTAINMENTS
2–4 years		Shows a dramatic increase in representational activity, as reflected in the development of language, make-believe play, understanding of dual representation, and categorization
		Takes the perspective of others in simplified, familiar situations and in everyday, face-to-face communication
		Distinguishes animate beings from inanimate objects; denies that magic can alter everyday experiences
		Grasps conservation, notices transformations, reverses thinking, and understands many cause-and-effect relationships in familiar contexts
		Categorizes objects on the basis of common function, behavior, and natural kind. Devises ideas about underlying characteristics that category members share and uses inner causal features to categorize objects varying widely in external appearance.
		Sorts familiar objects into hierarchically organized categories
		Distinguishes appearance from reality
4–7 years		Becomes increasingly aware that make-believe (and other thought processes) are representational activities
		Replaces magical beliefs about fairies, goblins, and events that violate expectations with plausible explanations
		Solves verbal appearance–reality problems, signifying a more secure understanding

information-processing perspective, children work out their understanding of each type of task separately, and their thought processes are basically the same at all ages—just present to a greater or lesser extent.

Other experts think that the stage concept is still valid, with modifications. For example, some *neo-Piagetian theorists* combine Piaget's stage approach with the information-processing emphasis on task-specific change (Case, 1998; Halford & Andrews, 2006). They believe that Piaget's strict stage definition must be transformed into a less tightly knit concept, one in which a related set of competencies develops over an extended period, depending on brain development and specific experiences. These investigators point to findings indicating that as long as the complexity of tasks and children's exposure to them are carefully controlled, children approach those tasks in similar, stage-consistent ways (Andrews & Halford, 2002; Case & Okamoto, 1996). For example, in drawing pictures, preschoolers depict objects separately, ignoring their spatial arrangement (return to the drawing on page 310 in Chapter 8 for an example). In understanding stories, they grasp a single story line but have trouble with a main plot plus one or more subplots.

This flexible stage notion recognizes the unique qualities of early childhood thinking. At the same time, it provides a better account of why, as Leslie put it, "Preschoolers' minds are such a blend of logic, fantasy, and faulty reasoning."

Piaget and Education

Three educational principles derived from Piaget's theory continue to influence teacher training and classroom practices, especially during early childhood:

■ *Discovery learning.* In a Piagetian classroom, children are encouraged to discover for themselves through spontaneous interaction with the environment. Instead of presenting ready-made knowledge verbally, teachers provide a rich variety of activities designed to promote exploration and discovery, including art, puzzles, table games, dress-up clothing, building blocks, books, measuring tools, musical instruments.

■ *Sensitivity to children's readiness to learn.* In a Piagetian classroom, teachers introduce activities that build on children's current thinking, challenging their incorrect ways of viewing the world. But they do not try to speed up development by imposing new skills before children indicate they are interested and ready.

■ *Acceptance of individual differences.* Piaget's theory assumes that all children go through the same sequence of development, but at different rates. Therefore, teachers must plan activities for individual children and small groups, not just for the whole class. In addition, teachers evaluate each child's educational progress in relation to the child's previous development, rather than on the basis of normative standards, or average performance of same-age peers.

Like his stages, educational applications of Piaget's theory have met with criticism. Perhaps the greatest challenge has to do with his insistence that young children learn primarily through acting on the environment (Brainerd, 2003). As we have already seen, children also use language-based routes to knowledge—a point emphasized by Vygotsky's sociocultural theory, to which we now turn. Nevertheless, Piaget's influence on education has been powerful. He gave teachers new ways to observe, understand, and enhance young children's development and offered strong theoretical justification for child-oriented approaches to classroom teaching and learning.

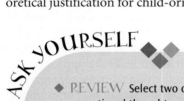

◆ REVIEW Select two of the following features of pre-operational thought: egocentrism, a focus on perceptual appearances, difficulty reasoning about transformations, and lack of hierarchical classification. Present evidence indicating that preschoolers are more capable thinkers than Piaget assumed.

◆ APPLY Three-year-old Will understands that his tricycle isn't alive and can't feel or move on its own. But at the beach, while watching the sun dip below the horizon, Will exclaimed, "The sun is tired. It's going to sleep!" What explains this apparent contradiction in Will's reasoning?

◆ CONNECT Make-believe play promotes both cognitive and social development (see page 319). Explain why this is so.

◆ REFLECT Did you have an imaginary companion as a young child? If so, what was your companion like, and why did you create it? Were your parents aware of your companion? What was their attitude toward it?

Vygotsky's Sociocultural Theory

Piaget's deemphasis on language as a source of cognitive development brought on yet another challenge, this time from Vygotsky's sociocultural theory, which stresses the social context of cognitive development. In Vygotsky's view, the child and the social environment collaborate to mold cognition in culturally adaptive ways. During early childhood, rapid growth of language broadens preschoolers' participation in social dialogues with more knowledgeable individuals, who encourage them to master culturally important tasks. Soon children start to communicate with themselves in much the same way they converse with others. This greatly enhances the complexity of their thinking and their ability to control their own behavior. Let's see how this happens.

Private Speech

TAKE A MOMENT... Watch preschoolers as they play and explore the environment, and you will see that they frequently talk out loud to themselves. For example, as Sammy worked a puzzle, he said, "Where's the red piece? I need the red one. Now, a blue one. No, it doesn't fit. Try it here."

A preschooler explores the possibilities in a handful of soap bubbles with the aid of private speech. Research supports Vygotsky's theory that children use private speech to guide their own thinking and behavior. ■

Piaget (1923/1926) called these utterances *egocentric speech,* reflecting his belief that young children have difficulty taking the perspectives of others. Their talk, he said, is often "talk for self" in which they express thoughts in whatever form they happen to occur, regardless of whether a listener can understand. Piaget believed that cognitive development and certain social experiences eventually bring an end to egocentric speech. Specifically, through disagreements with peers, children see that others hold viewpoints different from their own. As a result, egocentric speech declines in favor of social speech, in which children adapt what they say to their listeners.

Vygotsky (1934/1987) disagreed strongly with Piaget's conclusions. Because language helps children think about their mental activities and behavior and select courses of action, Vygotsky viewed it as the foundation for all higher cognitive processes, including controlled attention, deliberate memorization and recall, categorization, planning, problem solving, and self-reflection. In Vygotsky's view, children speak to themselves for self-guidance. As they get older and find tasks easier, their self-directed speech is internalized as silent, *inner speech*—the internal verbal dialogues we carry on while thinking and acting in everyday situations.

Over the past three decades, almost all studies have supported Vygotsky's perspective (Berk & Harris, 2003; Winsler, 2009). As a result, children's self-directed speech is now called **private speech** instead of egocentric speech. Research shows that children use more of it when tasks are appropriately challenging—neither too easy nor too hard but within their *zone of proximal development,* or range of mastery (see page 224 in Chapter 6). For example, Figure 9.5 shows how 5- and 6-year-olds' private speech increased as researchers made a problem-solving task moderately difficult, then decreased as the task became very difficult (Fernyhough & Fradley, 2005).

With age, as Vygotsky predicted, private speech goes underground, changing into whispers and silent lip movements. Furthermore, children who freely use private speech during a challenging activity are more attentive and involved and show better task performance than their less talkative agemates (Al-Namlah, Fernyhough, & Meins, 2006; Fernyhough & Fradley, 2005; Winsler, Naglieri, & Manfra, 2006).

Finally, compared with their agemates, children with learning and behavior problems engage in private speech over a longer period of development (Berk, 2001b; Ostad & Sorensen, 2007; Paladino, 2006; Winsler et al., 2007). They seem to use private speech to help compensate for impairments in attention and cognitive processing that make many tasks more difficult for them.

Social Origins of Early Childhood Cognition

Where does private speech come from? Recall from Chapter 6 that Vygotsky believed children's learning takes place within the *zone of proximal development*—a range of tasks too difficult for the child to do alone but possible with the help of others. Consider the joint activity of Sammy and his mother, who helps him put together a difficult puzzle:

Sammy: I can't get this one in. [*Tries to insert a piece in the wrong place.*]

Mother: Which piece might go down here? [*Points to the bottom of the puzzle.*]

Sammy: His shoes. [*Looks for a piece resembling the clown's shoes but tries the wrong one.*]

FIGURE 9.5

Relationship of private speech to task difficulty among 5- and 6-year-olds. Researchers increased the difficulty of a problem-solving task. Private speech rose as the task became moderately difficult, then declined as it became highly difficult. Children are more likely to use private speech for self-guidance when tasks are within their zone of proximal development, or range of mastery. *(Adapted from Fernyhough & Fradley, 2005.)*

Mother: Well, what piece looks like this shape? [*Pointing again to the bottom of the puzzle.*]

Sammy: The brown one. [*Tries it, and it fits; then attempts another piece and looks at his mother.*]

Mother: Try turning it just a little. [*Gestures to show him.*]

Sammy: There! [*Puts in several more pieces while his mother watches.*]

Sammy's mother keeps the puzzle within his zone of proximal development, at a manageable level of difficulty, by questioning, prompting, and suggesting strategies.

EFFECTIVE SOCIAL INTERACTION   To promote cognitive development, social interaction must have two vital features. The first is **intersubjectivity,** the process by which two participants who begin a task with different understandings arrive at a shared understanding (Newson & Newson, 1975). Intersubjectivity creates a common ground for communication, as each partner adjusts to the other's perspective. Adults try to promote it when they translate their own insights in ways that are within the child's grasp. As the child stretches to understand the adult, she is drawn into a more mature approach to the situation (Rogoff, 1998).

The capacity for intersubjectivity is present early, in parent–infant mutual gaze, exchange of emotional signals, and imitation. Later, language facilitates it. As conversational skills improve, preschoolers increasingly seek others' help and direct that assistance to ensure that it is beneficial (Whitington & Ward, 1999). Between ages 3 and 5, children strive for intersubjectivity in dialogues with peers, as when they affirm a playmate's message, add new ideas, and make contributions to ongoing play to sustain it. They can also be heard saying, "I think [this way]. What do you think?"—evidence of a willingness to share viewpoints (Berk, 2001b). In these ways, children create zones of proximal development for one another.

A second important feature of social experience is **scaffolding**—adjusting the support offered during a teaching session to fit the child's current level of performance. When the child has little notion of how to proceed, the adult uses direct instruction, breaking the task into manageable units, suggesting strategies, and offering rationales for using them. As the child's competence increases, effective scaffolders—like Sammy's mother—gradually and sensitively withdraw support, turning over responsibility to the child. Then children take the language of these dialogues, make it part of their private speech, and use this speech to organize their independent efforts.

■ A father engages in scaffolding by breaking the task of preparing rice balls into manageable units, suggesting strategies, and gradually turning over responsibility to the child. ■

Scaffolding captures the form of teaching interaction that occurs as children work on school or school-like tasks, such as puzzles, model building, picture matching, and (later) academic assignments. It may not apply to other contexts that are equally vital for cognitive development—for example, play or everyday activities, during which adults usually support children's efforts without deliberately teaching. To encompass children's diverse opportunities to learn through involvement with others, Barbara Rogoff (1998, 2003) suggests the term **guided participation,** a broader concept than scaffolding. It refers to shared endeavors between more expert and less expert participants, without specifying the precise features of communication. Consequently, it allows for variations across situations and cultures.

RESEARCH ON SOCIAL INTERACTION AND COGNITIVE DEVELOPMENT   What evidence supports Vygotsky's ideas on the social origins of cognitive development? In previous chapters, we reviewed evidence indicating that when adults establish intersubjectivity by being stimulating, responsive, and supportive, they foster many competencies—attention, language, complex play, and understanding of others' perspectives. In several studies, children whose parents

LOOK AND LISTEN

Ask a preschooler to join you in working a difficult puzzle or other challenging task. How did you scaffold the child's progress? Did the child display any self-guiding private speech?

were effective scaffolders used more private speech, were more successful when attempting difficult tasks on their own, and were advanced in overall cognitive development (Berk & Spuhl, 1995; Conner & Cross, 2003; Mulvaney et al., 2006). Adult cognitive support—teaching in small steps and offering strategies—predicts children's mature thinking. And adult emotional support—offering encouragement and transferring responsibility to the child—predicts children's effort (Neitzel & Stright, 2003). The result is a winning combination for school success.

Other research shows that although young children benefit from working on tasks with same-age peers, their planning and problem solving improve more when their partner is either an "expert" peer (especially capable at the task) or an adult (Radziszewska & Rogoff, 1988). And peer disagreement (emphasized by Piaget) seems to be less important for cognitive development than the extent to which children achieve intersubjectivity—resolve differences of opinion and cooperate (Kobayashi, 1994; Tudge, 1992).

Vygotsky and Early Childhood Education

Both Piagetian and Vygotskian classrooms emphasize active participation and acceptance of individual differences. But a Vygotskian classroom goes beyond independent discovery to promote *assisted discovery.* Teachers guide children's learning with explanations, demonstrations, and verbal prompts, tailoring their interventions to each child's zone of proximal development. Assisted discovery is aided by *peer collaboration,* as children with varying abilities work in groups, teaching and helping one another.

© ELLEN B. SENISI PHOTOGRAPHY

■ In this Vygotksy-inspired classroom, 4- and 5-year-olds benefit from peer collaboration. As they jointly make music, their conductor ensures that each player stays on beat. ■

Vygotsky (1935/1978) saw make-believe play as the ideal social context for fostering cognitive development in early childhood. As children create imaginary situations, they learn to follow internal ideas and social rules rather than their immediate impulses. For example, a child pretending to go to sleep follows the rules of bedtime behavior. A child imagining himself as a father and a doll as a child conforms to the rules of parental behavior. According to Vygotsky, make-believe play is a unique, broadly influential zone of proximal development in which children try out a wide variety of challenging activities and acquire many new competencies.

Turn back to page 319 to review findings that make-believe play enhances a diverse array of cognitive and social skills. Pretending is also rich in private speech—a finding that supports its role in helping children bring action under the control of thought (Krafft & Berk, 1998). And preschoolers who spend more time engaged in sociodramatic play are better at taking personal responsibility for following classroom rules and at regulating emotion (Berk, Mann, & Ogan, 2006; Lemche et al., 2003). These findings support the role of make-believe in children's increasing self-control.

Evaluation of Vygotsky's Theory

In granting social experience a fundamental role in cognitive development, Vygotsky's theory underscores the vital role of teaching and helps us understand the wide cultural variation in children's cognitive skills. Nevertheless, it has not gone unchallenged. Verbal communication may not be the only means through which children's thinking develops—or even, in some cultures, the most important means. When Western parents scaffold their young children's mastery of challenging tasks, they assume much responsibility for children's motivation by frequently

CULTURAL INFLUENCES

Children in Village and Tribal Cultures Observe and Participate in Adult Work

*I*n Western societies, children are largely excluded from participating in adult work, which generally takes place outside the home. The role of equipping children with the skills they need to become competent workers is assigned to school. In early childhood, middle-SES parents' interactions with children dwell on preparing children to succeed in school through child-focused activities—especially adult–child conversations and play that enhance language, literacy, and other school-related knowledge. In village and tribal cultures, children receive little or no schooling, spend their days in contact with or participating in adult work, and start to assume mature responsibilities in early childhood (Rogoff et al., 2003). Consequently, parents have little need to rely on conversation and play to teach children.

A study comparing 2- and 3-year-olds' daily lives in four cultures—two U.S. middle-SES suburbs, the Efe hunters and gatherers of the Republic of Congo, and a Mayan agricultural town in Guatemala—documented these differences (Morelli, Rogoff, & Angelillo, 2003). In the U.S. communities, young children had little access to adult work and spent much time conversing and playing with adults. In contrast, the Efe and Mayan children rarely engaged in these child-focused activities. Instead, they spent their days close to—and frequently observing—adult work, which often took place in or near the Efe campsite or the Mayan family home.

An ethnography of a remote Mayan village in Yucatán, Mexico, shows that when young children are legitimate onlookers and participants in a daily life structured around adult work, their competencies differ from those of Western preschoolers (Gaskins, 1999; Gaskins, Haight, & Lancy, 2007). Yucatec Mayan adults are subsis-

tence farmers. Men tend cornfields, aided by sons age 8 and older. Women oversee the household and yard; they prepare meals, wash clothes, and care for the livestock and garden, assisted by daughters and by sons not yet old enough to work in the fields. Children join in these activities from the second year on. When not participating, they are expected to be self-sufficient. Young children make many nonwork decisions for themselves—how much to sleep and eat, what to wear, when to take their daily bath, and even when to start school. As a result, Yucatec Mayan preschoolers are highly competent at self-care. In contrast, their make-believe play is limited; when it occurs, they usually imitate adult work. Otherwise, they watch others—for hours each day.

Yucatec Mayan parents rarely converse or play with preschoolers or scaffold their learning. Rather, when children imitate adult tasks, parents conclude that they are ready for more responsibility. Then they assign chores, selecting tasks the child can do with little help so that adult work is not disturbed. If a child cannot do a task, the adult takes over and the child observes, reengaging when able to contribute.

Expected to be autonomous and helpful, Yucatec Mayan children seldom display attention-getting behaviors or ask others for something interesting to do. From an early age, they can sit quietly for long periods—through a long

religious service or a three-hour truck ride. And when an adult interrupts their activity and directs them to do a chore, they respond eagerly to a command that Western children frequently avoid or resent. By age 5, Yucatec Mayan children spontaneously take responsibility for tasks beyond those assigned.

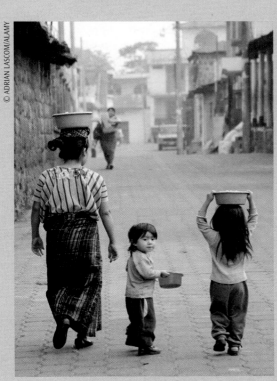

© ADRIAN LASCOM/ALAMY

■ A Mayan 3-year-old imitates her mother in balancing a basin of water on her head, while her younger sibling prepares to attempt the skill. From an early age, children in Yucatec Mayan culture spend many hours observing adults and join in the work of their community. ■

instructing and conversing with the child. Their communication resembles the teaching that takes place in school, where their children will spend years preparing for adult life. But in cultures that place less emphasis on schooling and literacy, parents often expect children to take greater responsibility for acquiring new skills through keen observation and participation in community activities (Paradise & Rogoff, 2009; Rogoff, 2003). See the Cultural Influences box above for research illustrating this difference.

Vygotsky's theory has also been criticized for saying little about how basic motor, perceptual, attention, memory, and problem-solving skills, discussed in Chapters 5 and 6, contribute to socially transmitted higher cognitive processes. For example, his theory does not address how these elementary capacities spark changes in children's social experiences, from which more advanced cognition springs (Miller, 2009; Moll, 1994). Piaget paid far more attention than Vygotsky to the development of basic cognitive processes. It is intriguing to speculate about the broader theory that might exist today had Piaget and Vygotsky—the two twentieth-century giants of cognitive development—had had a chance to meet and weave together their extraordinary accomplishments.

ASK YOURSELF

◆ **REVIEW** Describe features of social interaction that support children's cognitive development. How does such interaction create a zone of proximal development?

◆ **APPLY** Tanisha sees her 5-year-old son Toby talking aloud to himself as he plays. She wonders whether she should discourage this behavior. Use Vygotsky's theory to explain why Toby talks to himself. How would you advise Tanisha?

◆ **CONNECT** Explain how Piaget's and Vygotsky's theories complement each other. How would classroom practices inspired by these theories be similar? How would they differ?

◆ **REFLECT** When do you use private speech? Does it serve a self-guiding function for you, as it does for children? Explain.

Information Processing

Return to the model of information processing discussed on pages 217–218 in Chapter 6. Recall that information processing focuses on *mental strategies* that children use to transform stimuli flowing into their mental systems. During early childhood, advances in representation and in children's ability to guide their own behavior lead to more efficient and flexible ways of attending, manipulating information, and solving problems. Preschoolers also become more aware of their own mental life and begin to acquire academically relevant knowledge important for school success.

Attention

As parents and teachers know, preschoolers—compared with school-age children—spend shorter times involved in tasks and are more easily distracted. But recall from Chapter 5 that sustained attention improves in toddlerhood, a trend that continues during early childhood.

INHIBITION A major reason is a steady gain in children's ability to inhibit impulses and keep their mind on a competing goal. Consider a task in which the child must tap once when the adult taps twice and tap twice when the adult taps once, or must say "night" to a picture of the sun and "day" to a picture of the moon with stars. As Figure 9.6 shows, 3- and 4-year-olds make many errors. But by age 6 to 7, children find such tasks easy (Johnson, Im-Bolter, & Pascual-Leone, 2003; Kirkham, Cruess, & Diamond, 2003; Zelazo et al., 2003). They can resist the "pull" of their attention toward a dominant stimulus—a skill that, as early as age 3 to 5, predicts social maturity as well as subsequent reading and math achievement from kindergarten through high school (Blair & Razza, 2007; Duncan et al., 2007; Rhoades, Greenberg, & Domitrovich,

FIGURE 9.6

Gains between ages 3 and 7 in performance on tasks requiring children to inhibit an impulse and focus on a competing goal. In the tapping task, children had to tap once when the adult tapped twice and tap twice when the adult tapped once. In the day–night task, children had to say "night" to a picture of the sun and "day" to a picture of the moon with stars. *(From A. Diamond, 2004, "Normal Development of Prefrontal Cortex from Birth to Young Adulthood: Cognitive Functions, Anatomy, and Biochemistry,"* as appeared in D. T. Stuss & R. T. Knight, (Eds.), Principles of Frontal Lobe Function, *New York: Oxford University Press, p. 474. Reprinted by permission of Adele Diamond.)*

2009). Simultaneously, ERP and fMRI measures reveal a steady age-related increase in activation of the prefrontal cortex while children engage in activities requiring suppression of inappropriate responses (Bartgis, Lilly, & Thomas, 2003; Luna et al., 2001).

The capacity to generate increasingly complex play goals (requiring concentration) and adult scaffolding of attention also contribute to development of attention (Ruff & Cappozoli, 2003). Preschoolers whose parents help them maintain a focus, by offering suggestions, questions, and comments about the child's current interest, are more mature, cognitively and socially, when reassessed a year or two later (Bono & Stifter, 2003; Landry et al., 2000).

High-quality preschool education also makes a difference. In *Tools of the Mind*—a preschool curriculum inspired by Vygotsky's theory—scaffolding of attention skills is woven into virtually all classroom activities. For example, teachers provide external aids to support attention: A child might hold a drawing of an ear as a reminder to listen and refrain from interrupting a classmate who is telling a story. Teachers also lead games requiring frequent inhibition and memory for instructions. And they encourage make-believe play, which helps children follow rules and use thought to guide behavior (Bodrova & Leong, 2007).

When preschoolers from low-income families were randomly assigned to either Tools of the Mind or comparison classrooms, Tools children performed substantially better on end-of-year tasks assessing inhibition and other attentional capacities (Diamond et al., 2007). Nurturing attention through the Tools curriculum may prove powerful in early prevention of academic, emotional, and behavior problems. Many capacities, including language, exploration, problem solving, social interaction, and cooperation, benefit from an improved ability to concentrate.

■ In Tools of the Mind preschool classrooms, scaffolding of attention skills is woven into virtually all activities. Here, during "buddy reading," one child holds a drawing of an ear as a reminder to listen and not interrupt her classmate's storytelling. ■

PLANNING   During early childhood, children also become better at **planning**—thinking out a sequence of acts ahead of time and allocating attention accordingly to reach a goal. As long as tasks are familiar and not too complex, preschoolers can generate and follow a plan. For example, 4-year-olds can search for a lost object in a play area systematically if possible locations are few (McColgan & McCormack, 2008). But when asked to compare detailed pictures, preschoolers fail to search thoroughly. And on tasks with several steps, they often fail to decide what to do first and what to do next in an orderly fashion (Baughman & Cooper, 2006; Friedman & Scholnick, 1997; Kaller et al., 2008). They seem to have difficulty postponing action in favor of mapping out a sequence of moves and evaluating the consequences of each—procedures that require inhibition and increased working-memory capacity in addition to planning skill.

Children learn much from cultural tools that support planning—directions for playing games, patterns for construction, recipes for cooking—especially when they collaborate with more expert planners. When 4- to 7-year-olds were observed jointly constructing a toy with their mothers, the mothers provided basic information about the usefulness of plans and how to implement specific steps: "Do you want to look at the picture and see what goes where? What piece do you need first?" After working with their mothers, younger children more often referred to the plan when building on their own (Gauvain, 2004; Gauvain, de la Ossa, & Hurtado-Ortiz, 2001). When parents encourage planning in everyday activities, from loading the dishwasher to packing for a vacation, they help children plan more effectively.

Memory

Unlike infants and toddlers, preschoolers have the language skills to describe what they remember, and they can follow directions on simple memory tasks. As a result, memory becomes easier to study in early childhood.

RECOGNITION AND RECALL TAKE A MOMENT... Show a young child a set of 10 pictures or toys. Then mix them up with some unfamiliar items, and ask the child to point to the ones in the original set. You will find that preschoolers' *recognition* memory—ability to tell whether a stimulus is the same as or similar to one they have seen before—is remarkably good. It becomes even more accurate by the end of early childhood. In fact, 4- and 5-year-olds perform nearly perfectly.

Now keep the items out of view, and ask the child to name the ones she saw. This more demanding task requires *recall*—generating a mental image of an absent stimulus. Young children's recall is much poorer than their recognition. At age 2, they can recall no more than one or two items, at age 4 only about three or four (Perlmutter, 1984).

Of course, recognition is much easier than recall for adults as well, but in comparison to adults, children's recall is quite deficient. Better recall in early childhood is strongly associated with language development, which greatly enhances long-lasting representations of past experiences (Simcock & Hayne, 2003). But even preschoolers with good language skills recall poorly because they are not skilled at using **memory strategies,** deliberate mental activities that improve our chances of remembering. For example, to retain information, you may *rehearse,* repeating the items over and over, or *organize,* intentionally grouping items that are alike so that you can easily retrieve them by thinking of their similar characteristics.

Preschoolers do show the beginnings of memory strategies. When circumstances permit, they arrange items in space to aid their memories. In one study, an adult placed either an M&M or a wooden peg in each of 12 identical containers and handed them one by one to preschoolers, asking them to remember where the candy was hidden. By age 4, children put the candy containers in one place and the peg containers in another, a strategy that almost always led to perfect recall (DeLoache & Todd, 1988). But preschoolers do not yet rehearse or organize items (for example, all the vehicles together, all the animals together) to aid recall, even when they are trained to do so (Gathercole, Adams, & Hitch, 1994).

Why do young children seldom use memory strategies? One reason is that strategies tax their limited working memories. *Digit span* tasks, in which children try to repeat an adult-provided string of numbers, assess the capacity of working memory, which improves slowly, from an average of two digits at age 2½ to five digits at age 7 (Kail, 2003). With such limits, preschoolers have difficulty holding on to pieces of information while simultaneously applying a strategy.

MEMORY FOR EVERYDAY EXPERIENCES Think about the difference between your recall of listlike information and your memory for everyday experiences—what researchers call **episodic memory.** In remembering lists, you recall isolated bits, reproducing them exactly as you originally learned them. In remembering everyday experiences, you recall complex, meaningful information. Between 3 and 6 years, children improve sharply in memory for relations among stimuli. For example, in a set of photos, they remember not just the animals they saw but the contexts in which they saw them—a bear emerging from a tunnel, a zebra tied to a tree on a city street (Sluzenski, Newcombe, & Kovacs, 2006). The capacity to *bind together stimuli* when encoding and retrieving them supports the development of an increasingly rich event memory during early childhood.

■ Like adults, preschoolers remember everyday experiences, like brushing teeth, in terms of scripts—general descriptions of what occurs and when it occurs. Over time, children construct more elaborate scripts: "You squeeze out the toothpaste and brush your teeth. You rinse your mouth and then your toothbrush." ■

Memory for Familiar Events. Like adults, preschoolers remember familiar, repeated events—what you do when you go to child care or have dinner—in terms of **scripts,** general descriptions of what occurs and when it occurs in a particular situation. Young children's scripts begin as a structure of main acts. For example, when asked to tell what happens at a restaurant, a 3-year-old might say, "You go in, get the food, eat, and then pay." Although children's first scripts contain only a few acts, as long as events in a situation take place in logical order, they are almost always recalled in correct sequence (Bauer, 2002, 2006). With age, scripts become more spontaneous and elaborate, as in this 5-year-old's account of going to a restaurant: "You go in. You can sit in a booth or at a table. Then you tell the waitress what you want. You eat. If you want dessert, you can have some. Then you pay and go home" (Hudson, Fivush, & Kuebli, 1992).

Scripts help children organize, interpret, and predict everyday experiences. Once formed, they can be used to predict what will happen on similar occasions in the future. Children rely on scripts to assist recall when listening to and telling stories. They also act out scripts in make-believe play as they pretend to put the baby to bed, go on a trip, or play school. And scripts support children's earliest efforts at planning by helping them represent sequences of actions that lead to desired goals (Hudson, Sosa, & Shapiro, 1997).

Memory for One-Time Events.   In Chapter 6, we considered a second type of episodic memory—*autobiographical memory,* or representations of personally meaningful, one-time events. As 3- to 6-year-olds' cognitive and conversational skills improve, their descriptions of special events become better organized in time, more detailed, enriched with a personal perspective, and related to the larger context of their lives (Fivush, 2001). A young preschooler simply reports, "I went camping." Older preschoolers include specifics: where and when the event happened and who was present. And with age, preschoolers increasingly include subjective information—why, for example, an event was exciting, funny, sad, or made them feel proud or embarrassed ("I loved sleeping all night in the tent!")—that explains the event's personal significance (Fivush, 2001).

Adults use two styles to elicit children's autobiographical narratives. In the *elaborative style,* they follow the child's lead, ask varied questions, add information to the child's statements, and volunteer their own recollections and evaluations of events. For example, after a field trip to the zoo, Leslie asked, "What was the first thing we did? Why weren't the parrots in their cages? I thought the roaring lion was scary. What did you think?" In this way, she helped the children reestablish and reorganize their memory of the field trip. In contrast, adults who use the *repetitive style* provide little information and keep repeating the same questions, regardless of the child's interest: "Do you remember the zoo? What did we do at the zoo? Which animals did you see at the zoo?"

Preschoolers who experience the elaborative style recall more information about past events and also produce more organized and detailed personal stories when followed up one to two years later (Cleveland & Reese, 2005; Farrant & Reese, 2000). Parents can be trained to use an elaborative style, which also enhances the richness of preschoolers' event memories (Reese & Newcombe, 2007).

As children converse with adults about the past, they not only improve their autobiographical memory but also create a shared history that strengthens close relationships and self-understanding. Parents and preschoolers with secure attachment bonds engage in more elaborate reminiscing (Bost et al., 2006; Reese, Newcombe, & Bird, 2006). And 5- and 6-year-olds of elaborative-style parents describe themselves in clearer, more consistent ways (Bird & Reese, 2006).

Girls produce more organized and detailed narratives about past events than boys. And Western children typically include more comments about their own thoughts, emotions, and preferences than do Asian children. These differences fit with variations in parent–child conversations. Parents reminisce in more detail with daughters (Bruce, Dolan, & Phillips-Grant, 2000). And collectivist cultural values lead many Asian parents to discourage children from talking about themselves. Chinese parents, for example, engage in less detailed and evaluative past-event dialogues with their preschoolers (Fivush & Wang, 2005; Wang, 2006a). Consistent with these early experiences, women report an earlier age of first memory and more vivid early memories than men. And Western adults' autobiographical memories include earlier, more detailed events that focus more on their own roles than do the memories of Asians, who tend to highlight the roles of others (Wang, 2006b).

■ As she converses with her father about past experiences, this young child in Shanghai builds an autobiographical memory. Perhaps because Asian parents tend to discourage children from talking about themselves, Asian adults' autobiographical memories focus less on their own roles than on those of others. ■

Problem Solving

How do preschoolers use their cognitive competencies to discover new problem-solving strategies? To find out, let's look in on 5-year-old Darryl as he adds marbles tucked into pairs of small bags that Leslie set out on a table.

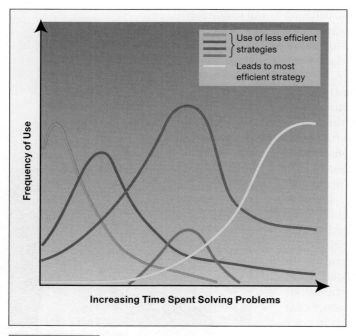

Overlapping-waves pattern of strategy use in problem solving. When given challenging problems, a child generates a variety of strategies, each represented by a wave. The waves overlap because the child tries several different strategies at the same time. Use of each strategy, depicted by the height of the wave, is constantly changing. As the child observes which strategies work best, which work less well, and which are ineffective, the one that results in the most rapid, accurate solutions wins out. *(From R. S. Siegler,* Emerging Minds: The Process of Change in Children's Thinking. *Copyright © 1996 by Oxford University Press, Inc. Used by permission of Oxford University Press, Inc.)*

As Darryl deals with adding each pair, his strategies vary. Sometimes he guesses, without applying any strategy. At other times, he counts from one on his fingers. For example, for bags containing 2 + 4 marbles, his fingers pop up one by one as he exclaims, "One, two, three, four, five, six!" On still other occasions, he starts with the lower digit, 2, and "counts on" ("two, three, four, five, six"). Or he begins with the higher digit, 4, and "counts on" ("four, five, six")—a strategy called *min* because it minimizes the work. Sometimes, he simply retrieves the answer from memory.

To study children's problem solving, Robert Siegler (1996, 2006) used the microgenetic research design (see Chapter 1, page 43), presenting children with many problems over an extended time. He found that children experiment with diverse strategies on many types of problems—basic math facts, numerical estimation, conservation, memory for lists of items, reading first words, spelling, even tic-tac-toe. And their strategy use follows the overlapping-waves pattern shown in Figure 9.7. According to **overlapping-waves theory,** when given challenging problems, children try out various strategies and observe which work best, which work less well, and which are ineffective. Gradually, they select strategies on the basis of two criteria: *accuracy* and *speed*—for basic addition, the *min* strategy. As children home in on effective strategies for solving the problems at hand, correct solutions become more strongly associated with problems, and children display the most efficient strategy—automatic retrieval of the answer.

How do children move from less to more efficient strategies? Often they discover a faster procedure by using a more time-consuming technique. For example, by repeatedly counting on fingers, Darryl began to recognize the number of fingers he held up (Siegler & Jenkins, 1989). Also, certain problems dramatize the need for a better strategy. When Darryl opened a pair of bags, one containing ten marbles and the other with only two, he realized that *min* would be best. Teaching children to reason logically with concepts relevant to the problems is also helpful (Alibali, Phillips, & Fischer, 2009; Siegler & Svetina, 2006). Once Darryl understood that he got the same result regardless of the order in which he combined two sets (3 + 6 = 9 and 6 + 3 = 9), he more often used *min* and arrived at correct answers. Finally, a large improvement in the accuracy of a newly discovered strategy over previous strategies generally leads to rapid adoption of the new approach (Siegler, 2006; Siegler & Booth, 2004).

Many factors, including practice, reasoning, tasks with new challenges, and adult assistance, contribute to improved problem solving. And experimenting with less mature strategies lets children see the limitations of those techniques. In sum, overlapping-waves theory emphasizes that trying many strategies is vital for developing new, more effective solution techniques. Even 2-year-olds use an overlapping-waves pattern to solve problems, such as how to use a tool to obtain an out-of-reach toy (Chen & Siegler, 2000). The pattern characterizes problem solving across a wide range of ages. And in the tradition of the information-processing approach, the theory views development as occurring gradually, rather than in discontinuous stages.

The Young Child's Theory of Mind

As representation of the world, memory, and problem solving improve, children start to reflect on their own thought processes. They begin to construct a *theory of mind,* or coherent set of ideas about mental activities. This understanding is also called **metacognition,** or "thinking about thought" (the prefix *meta-* means "beyond" or "higher"). As adults, we have a complex appreciation of our inner mental worlds, which we use to interpret our own and others' behavior and to improve our performance on various tasks. How early are children aware of their mental lives, and how complete and accurate is their knowledge?

AWARENESS OF MENTAL LIFE   At the end of the first year, babies view people as intentional beings who can share and influence one another's mental states, a milestone that opens the door to new forms of communication—joint attention, social referencing, preverbal gestures, and spoken language. These early milestones serve as the foundation for later mental understandings. In longitudinal research, 10-month-olds' ability to discern others' intentions predicted theory-of-mind competence at age 4 (Wellman et al., 2008).

As they approach age 2, children display a clearer grasp of others' emotions and desires, evident in their realization that people often differ from one another and from themselves in likes, dislikes, wants, needs, and wishes ("Mommy like broccoli. Daddy like carrots. I no like carrots."). As 2-year-olds' vocabularies expand, their first verbs include such words as *think, remember,* and *pretend* (Wellman, 2002).

By age 3, children realize that thinking takes place inside their heads and that a person can think about something without seeing, touching, or talking about it (Flavell, Green, & Flavell, 1995). But 2- to 3-year-olds' verbal responses indicate that they think people always behave in ways consistent with their *desires* and that they do not understand less obvious, more interpretive mental states, such as *beliefs,* also affect behavior.

Between ages 3 and 4, children use *think* and *know* to refer to their own and others' thoughts and beliefs (Wellman, 2002). And from age 4 on, they realize that both *beliefs* and *desires* determine behavior. Dramatic evidence for this advance comes from games that test whether preschoolers realize that *false beliefs*—ones that do not represent reality accurately— can guide people's behavior. **TAKE A MOMENT...** For example, show a child two small closed boxes—a familiar Band-Aid box and a plain, unmarked box (see Figure 9.8). Then say, "Pick the box you think has the Band-Aids in it." Children usually pick the marked container. Next, open the boxes and show the child that, contrary to her own belief, the marked one is empty, and the unmarked one contains the Band-Aids. Finally, introduce the child to a hand puppet and explain, "Here's Pam. She has a cut, see? Where do you think she'll look for Band-Aids? Why would she look in there? Before you looked inside, did you think that the plain box contained the Band-Aids? Why?" (Bartsch & Wellman, 1995). Only a handful of 3-year-olds can explain Pam's—and their own—false beliefs, but many 4-year-olds can.

Some researchers claim that the procedures just described, which require verbal responses, grossly underestimate younger children's ability to attribute false beliefs to others. Relying on the violation-of-expectation method (which depends on looking behavior), these investigators assert that children comprehend others' false beliefs by age 15 months (Baillargeon, Scott, & He, 2010). But like other violation-of-expectation evidence, this conclusion is controversial (see page 208 in Chapter 6) (Ruffman & Perner, 2005; Sirios & Jackson, 2007). In another study using an active behavioral measure (helping), most 18-month-olds—after witnessing an object moved from one box to another while an adult was not looking—helped the adult, when he tried to open the original box, locate the object in the new box (Buttelmann, Carpenter, & Tomasello, 2009). Still, much more evidence is needed to confirm that toddlers implicitly grasp mental states as complex as false belief (Poulin-Dubois, Brooker, & Chow, 2009).

FIGURE 9.8

Example of a false-belief task. (a) An adult shows a child the contents of a Band-Aid box and of an unmarked box. The Band-Aids are in the unmarked container. (b) The adult introduces the child to a hand puppet named Pam and asks the child to predict where Pam would look for the Band-Aids and to explain Pam's behavior. The task reveals whether children understand that without having seen that the Band-Aids are in the unmarked container, Pam will hold a false belief.

(a)   (b)

Among children of diverse cultural and SES backgrounds, false-belief understanding assessed in verbal tasks strengthens after age 3½, becoming more secure between ages 4 and 6 (Amsterlaw & Wellman, 2006; Callaghan et al., 2005; Flynn, 2006). During that time, it becomes a powerful tool for reflecting on the thoughts and emotions of oneself and others and a good predictor of social skills (Harwood & Farrar, 2006; Watson et al., 1999). Understanding of false belief also is also associated with early reading ability, probably because it helps children comprehend story narratives (Astington & Pelletier, 2005). To follow a story line, children generally must link plot actions with characters' motives and beliefs.

FACTORS CONTRIBUTING TO PRESCHOOLERS' THEORY OF MIND   How do children develop a theory of mind at such a young age? Language, cognitive abilities, make-believe play, and social interaction all contribute.

Language and Verbal Reasoning.   The prefrontal cortex seems to play a crucial role in theory-of-mind development. ERP brain-wave recordings obtained while 4- to 6-year-olds reasoned about others' beliefs revealed that children who pass false-belief tasks (as opposed to those who fail) display a pattern of activity in the left prefrontal cortex similar to that of adults engaged in the same tasks (Liu et al., 2009). This left-prefrontal ERP pattern typically appears when adults reason verbally about mental concepts.

Indeed, understanding the mind requires the ability to reflect on thoughts, which is greatly aided by language. Many studies indicate that language ability strongly predicts preschoolers' grasp of false belief (Milligan, Astington, & Dack, 2007). Children who spontaneously use, or who are trained to use, complex sentences with mental-state words are especially likely to pass false-belief tasks (de Villiers & de Villiers, 2000; Hale & Tager-Flusberg, 2003). The Quechua people of the Peruvian highlands refer to mental states such as "think" and "believe" indirectly, because their language lacks mental-state terms. Quechua children have difficulty with false-belief tasks for years after children in industrialized nations have mastered them (Vinden, 1996). In contrast, Chinese languages have verb markers that can label the word *believe* as decidedly false. When adults use those markers in false-belief tasks, Chinese preschoolers perform better (Tardif, Wellman, & Cheung, 2004).

Cognitive Abilities.   The ability to inhibit inappropriate responses, think flexibly, and plan fosters mastery of false belief (Hughes, 1998; Sabbagh et al., 2006). Gains in inhibition are strongly related to mastery of false belief, perhaps because to do well on false-belief tasks, children must suppress an irrelevant response—the tendency to assume that others' knowledge and beliefs are the same as their own (Birch & Bloom, 2003; Carlson, Moses, & Claxton, 2004).

Make-Believe Play.   Make-believe offers a rich context for thinking about the mind. As children act out roles, they often express the thoughts and emotions of the characters they portray and then reason about their implications (Kavanaugh, 2006b). These experiences may increase children's awareness that belief influences behavior. In support of this idea, preschoolers who engage in extensive fantasy play or who have imaginary companions—and, thus, are deeply absorbed in creating make-believe characters—are advanced in understanding false belief and other aspects of the mind (Astington & Jenkins, 1995; Lalonde & Chandler, 1995). And the better 3- and 4-year-olds can reason about situations that contradict a real-world state of affairs, the more likely they are to pass false-belief tasks (Riggs & Peterson, 2000).

Social Interaction.   Social experience also promotes understanding of the mind. In longitudinal research, mothers of securely attached babies were more likely to comment appropriately on their infants' mental states: "Do you *remember* Grandma?" "You really *like* that swing!" These mothers continued to describe their children, when they reached preschool age, in terms of mental characteristics: "She's got *a mind of her own!*" This maternal "mind-mindedness" was positively associated with later performance on false-belief and other theory-of-mind tasks (Meins et al., 1998, 2003; Ruffman et al., 2006). As we saw earlier, secure attachment is related to more elaborative parent–child narratives, which often include discussions of mental states—conversations that expose preschoolers to concepts and language that help them think about their own and others' mental lives (Ontai & Thompson, 2008; Taumoepeau & Ruffman, 2006).

Also, preschoolers with siblings who are children (but not infants)—especially older siblings or two or more siblings—tend to be more aware of false belief because they experience more family talk about others' perspectives (Jenkins et al., 2003; McAlister & Peterson, 2006, 2007). Similarly, preschool friends who often engage in mental-state talk are ahead in false-belief understanding (de Rosnay & Hughes, 2006). Interacting with more mature members of society contributes, too. In a study of Greek preschoolers, daily contact with many adults and older children predicted mastery of false belief (Lewis et al., 1996). All these encounters offer extra opportunities to observe different viewpoints and talk about inner states.

Core knowledge theorists (see Chapter 6, page 214) believe that to profit from the social experiences just described, children must be biologically prepared to develop a theory of mind. They claim that children with *autism*, for whom mastery of false belief is either greatly delayed or absent, are deficient in the brain mechanism that enables humans to detect mental states. See the Biology and Environment box on page 342 to find out more about the biological basis of reasoning about the mind.

■ Interaction with siblings, especially older siblings, contributes to preschoolers' awareness of others' perspectives and, therefore, promotes understanding of false belief. ■

LIMITATIONS OF THE YOUNG CHILD'S THEORY OF MIND Though surprisingly advanced, preschoolers' awareness of mental activities is far from complete. For example, 3- and 4-year-olds are unaware that people continue to think while they wait, look at pictures, listen to stories, or read books—that is, when there are no obvious cues that they are thinking. Preschoolers also do not realize that when two people view the same object, their trains of thought will differ because of variations in their knowledge and other characteristics (Eisbach, 2004; Flavell, Green, & Flavell, 1993, 1995; Flavell et al., 1997).

A major reason for these findings is that children younger than age 5 pay little attention to the *process* of thinking. When asked about subtle distinctions between mental states, such as *know* and *forget,* they express confusion (Lyon & Flavell, 1994). And they often say they have always known information they just learned (Taylor, Esbenson, & Bennett, 1994). Finally, they believe that all events must be directly observed to be known. They do not understand that *mental inferences* can be a source of knowledge (Miller, Hardin, & Montgomery, 2003).

These findings suggest that preschoolers view the mind as a passive container of information. Consequently, they greatly underestimate the amount of mental activity that people engage in and are poor at inferring what people know or are thinking about (Flavell, 2000; Wellman, 2002). In contrast, older children view the mind as an active, constructive agent that selects and interprets information—a change we will consider in Chapter 12.

Early Literacy and Mathematical Development

Researchers have begun to study how children's information-processing capacities affect the development of basic reading, writing, and mathematical skills that prepare them for school. The study of how preschoolers start to master these complex activities gives us additional information about their cognitive strengths and limitations—knowledge we can use to foster early literacy and mathematical development.

LITERACY One week, Leslie's students created a make-believe grocery store. They brought empty food boxes from home, placed them on shelves in the classroom, labeled items with prices, made shopping lists, and wrote checks at the cash register. A sign at the entrance announced the daily specials: "APLS BNS 5¢" ("apples bananas 5¢").

As such play reveals, preschoolers understand a great deal about written language long before they learn to read or write in conventional ways. This is not surprising: Children in industrialized nations live in a world filled with written symbols. Each day, they observe

BIOLOGY AND ENVIRONMENT

"Mindblindness" and Autism

Michael stood at the water table in Leslie's classroom, repeatedly filling a plastic cup and dumping out its contents—dip-splash, dip-splash—until Leslie came over and redirected his actions. Without looking at Leslie's face, Michael moved to a new repetitive pursuit: pouring water from one cup into another and back again. As other children entered the play space and conversed, Michael hardly noticed. He rarely spoke, and when he did, he usually used words to get things he wanted, not to exchange ideas.

Michael has *autism* (a term that means "absorbed in the self"), the most severe behavior disorder of childhood. Like other children with autism, by age 3 he displayed deficits in three core areas of functioning. First, he had only limited ability to engage in nonverbal behaviors required for successful social interaction, such as eye gaze, facial expressions, gestures, imitation, and give-and-take. Second, his language was delayed and stereotyped. He used words to echo what others said and to get things he wanted, not to exchange ideas. Third, he engaged in much less make-believe play than other children (Frith, 2003; Walenski, Tager-Flusberg, & Ullman, 2006). And Michael showed another typical feature of autism: His interests were narrow and overly intense. For example, one day he sat for more than an hour spinning a toy Ferris wheel.

Researchers agree that autism stems from abnormal brain functioning, usually due to genetic or prenatal environmental causes. Beginning in the first year, children with the disorder have larger-than-average brains, perhaps due to massive overgrowth of synapses and lack of synaptic pruning, which accompanies normal development of cognitive, language, and communication skills (Courchesne, Carper, & Akshoomoff, 2003).

The amygdala, especially, grows abnormally large in childhood, followed by a greater than average reduction in size in adolescence and adulthood. This deviant growth pattern is believed to contribute to deficits in emotion processing and social interaction involved in the disorder (Schumann et al., 2009; Schumann & Amaral, 2010). The larger the amygdala compared with typically developing preschoolers, the more severe the child's social and communication impairments. Furthermore, fMRI studies reveal that autism is associated with reduced activity in areas of the cerebral cortex involved in emotional and social responsiveness and

with weaker connections between the amygdala and the temporal lobes (important for processing facial expressions) (Monk et al., 2010; Théoret et al., 2005).

Growing evidence reveals that children with autism have a deficient theory of mind. Long after they reach the intellectual level of an average 4-year-old, they have great difficulty with false belief. Most find it hard to attribute mental states to themselves or others (Steele, Joseph, & Tager-Flusberg, 2003). They rarely use mental-state words such as *believe, think, know, feel,* and *pretend.*

As early as the second year, children with autism show emotional and social deficits believed to contribute to an understanding of mental life. Compared with other children, they less often establish eye contact and joint attention, have difficulty distinguishing facial expressions, and seldom engage in social referencing or imitate an adult's novel behaviors (Chawarska & Shic, 2009; Mundy & Stella, 2000; Vivanti et al., 2008). And because children with autism are relatively insensitive to eye gaze as a cue to what a speaker is talking about, they often assume that another person's language refers to what they themselves are looking at—a possible reason for their frequent nonsensical expressions (Baron-Cohen, Baldwin, & Crowson, 1997).

Do these findings indicate that autism is due to impairment in an innate, core brain function, which leaves the child "mindblind" and therefore deficient in human sociability? Some researchers think so (Baron-Cohen & Belmonte, 2005; Scholl & Leslie, 2000). But others point out that individuals with mental retardation but not autism also do poorly on tasks assessing mental understanding (Yirmiya et al., 1998). This suggests that some kind of general intellectual impairment may be involved.

One conjecture is that children with autism are impaired in *executive processing* (refer to the *central executive* in the information-processing

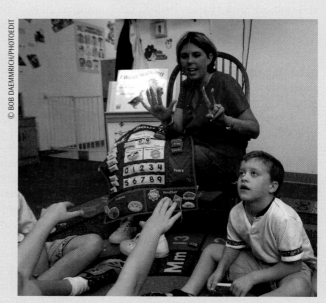

■ This child, who has autism, is barely aware of his teacher and classmates. Researchers disagree on whether the "mindblindness" accompanying autism results from a specific deficit in social understanding, a general impairment in executive processing, or a style of information processing that focuses on parts rather than patterns and coherent wholes. ■

model on page 217 in Chapter 6). This leaves them deficient in skills involved in flexible, goal-oriented thinking, including shifting attention to address relevant aspects of a situation, inhibiting irrelevant responses, applying strategies to hold information in working memory, and generating plans (Joseph & Tager-Flusberg, 2004; Robinson et al., 2009).

Another possibility is that children with autism display a peculiar style of information processing, preferring to process the parts of stimuli over patterns and coherent wholes (Happé & Frith, 2006). Deficits in thinking flexibly and in holistic processing of stimuli would each interfere with understanding the social world because social interaction requires quick integration of information from various sources and evaluation of alternative possibilities.

It is not clear which of these hypotheses is correct. Some research suggests that impairments in social awareness, flexible thinking, processing coherent wholes, and verbal ability contribute independently to autism (Morgan, Maybery, & Durkin, 2003; Pellicano et al., 2006). Perhaps several biologically based cognitive deficits underlie the tragic social isolation of children like Michael.

and participate in activities involving storybooks, calendars, lists, and signs. Children's active efforts to construct literacy knowledge through informal experiences are called **emergent literacy.**

Young preschoolers search for units of written language as they "read" memorized versions of stories and recognize familiar signs ("PIZZA"). But they do not yet understand the symbolic function of the elements of print (Bialystok & Martin, 2003). Many preschoolers think that a single letter stands for a whole word or that each letter in a person's signature represents a separate name. Initially, as we noted in Chapter 8, preschoolers do not distinguish between drawing and writing but often believe that letters (like pictures) resemble the meanings they represent. For example, one child explained that the word *sun* begins with the letter *O* because that letter is shaped like the sun; to demonstrate, he drew an *O* surrounded with rays to produce a picture of the sun.

Children revise these ideas as their perceptual and cognitive capacities improve, as they encounter writing in many contexts, and as adults help them with written communication. Gradually preschoolers notice more features of written language and depict writing that varies in function, as in the "story" and "grocery list" in Figure 9.9.

Eventually children figure out that letters are parts of words and are linked to sounds in systematic ways, as seen in the invented spellings that are typical between ages 5 and 7. At first, children rely on sounds in the names of letters: "ADE LAFWTS KRMD NTU A LAVATR" ("eighty elephants crammed into a[n] elevator"). Soon they grasp sound–letter correspondences and learn that some letters have more than one common sound and that context affects their use ("*a*" is pronounced differently in "cat" than in "table") (McGee & Richgels, 2008).

Literacy development builds on a broad foundation of spoken language and knowledge about the world. Over time, children's language and literacy progress facilitate each other. **Phonological awareness**—the ability to reflect on and manipulate the sound structure of spoken language, as indicated by sensitivity to changes in sounds within words, to rhyming, and to incorrect pronunciation—is a strong predictor of emergent literacy and later reading and spelling achievement (Dickinson et al., 2003; Paris & Paris, 2006). When combined with sound–letter knowledge, it enables children to isolate speech segments and link them with their written symbols. Vocabulary and grammatical knowledge are also influential. And adult–child narrative conversations enhance diverse language skills essential for literacy progress.

The more informal literacy experiences young children have, the better their language and emergent literacy development and their later reading skills (Dickinson & McCabe, 2001; Speece et al., 2004). Pointing out letter–sound correspondences and playing language-sound games enhance children's awareness of the sound structure of language and how it is represented in print (Ehri & Roberts, 2006; Foy & Mann, 2003). *Interactive* reading, in which adults discuss storybook content with preschoolers, promotes many aspects of language and literacy development. And adult-supported writing activities that focus on narrative, such as preparing a letter or a story, also have wide-ranging benefits (Purcell-Gates, 1996; Wasik & Bond, 2001). In longitudinal research, each of these literacy experiences is linked to improved reading achievement in middle childhood (Hood, Conlon, & Andrews, 2008; Senechal & LeFevre, 2002; Storch & Whitehurst, 2001).

Preschoolers from low-SES families have fewer home and preschool language and literacy learning opportunities—a major reason that they are behind in emergent literacy skills and in reading achievement throughout the school years (Foster et al., 2005; Foster & Miller, 2007; Turnbull et al., 2009). Age-appropriate books, for example, are scarce in their environments. In one survey of four middle- and

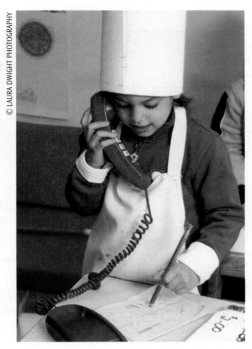

■ Preschoolers acquire literacy knowledge informally by participating in everyday activities involving written symbols. This young chef "jots down" a phone order for a take-out meal. ■

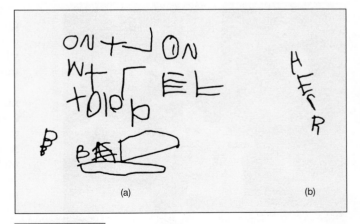

(a)   (b)

FIGURE 9.9

A story (a) and a grocery list (b) written by a 4-year-old child. This child's writing has many features of real print. It also reveals an awareness of different kinds of written expression. *(From McGee & Richgels,* Literacy's Beginnings, *Figure 3.10 "A Story and a Grocery List" p. 76. © 2004. Reproduced by permission of Pearson Education.)*

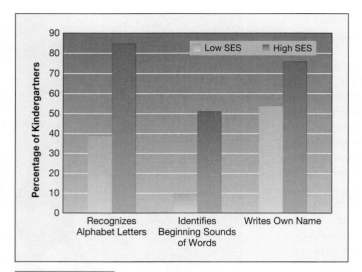

Some reading readiness skills at kindergarten entry by SES. The SES gap in emergent literacy development is large. *(Adapted from Lee & Burkham, 2002.)*

low-income communities, the middle-income neighborhoods averaged 13 books per child, the low-income neighborhoods just 1 book for every 300 children (Neuman & Celano, 2001).

On average, a low SES child is read to for a total of 25 hours during the preschool years, a higher-SES child for 1,000 hours. The SES gap in early literacy experiences translates into large differences in knowledge and skills vital for reading readiness at kindergarten entry (see Figure 9.10). Kindergartners who are behind in emergent literacy development tend to remain behind, performing poorly in reading in the early grades (National Early Literacy Panel, 2008). Over time, skilled readers acquire wide-ranging knowledge more efficiently, progressing more rapidly than poor readers in all achievement areas (Neuman, 2006). In this way, literacy deficiencies at the start of school contribute to widening achievement disparities between economically advantaged and disadvantaged children that often persist into high school.

High-quality intervention can reduce the SES gap in early literacy development substantially. Providing low-SES parents with children's books, along with guidance in how to stimulate emergent literacy, greatly enhances literacy activities in the home (High et al., 2000). And in a program that "flooded" child-care centers with children's books and provided caregivers with training on how to get 3- and 4-year-olds to spend time with books, low-SES children showed far greater gains in emergent literacy than a no-intervention control group (Neuman, 1999). Teachers who were given a tuition-free college course on effective early childhood literacy instruction readily applied what they learned, offering many more literacy activities in their classrooms (Dickinson & Sprague, 2001). For ways to support early childhood literacy development, refer to Applying What We Know on the following page.

MATHEMATICAL REASONING Mathematical reasoning, like literacy, builds on informal knowledge. Between 14 and 16 months, toddlers display a beginning grasp of **ordinality,** or order relationships between quantities—for example, that 3 is more than 2, and 2 is more than 1. In the early preschool years, children attach verbal labels *(lots, little, big, small)* to amounts and sizes. Sometime in the third year, they begin to count. By the time children turn 3, most can count rows of about five objects, although they do not yet know what the words mean. For example, when asked for *one,* they give one item, but when asked for *two, three, four,* or *five,* they usually give a larger, but incorrect, amount. Nevertheless, 2½- to 3½-year-olds realize that a number word refers to a unique quantity—that when a number label changes (for example, from *five* to *six*), the number of items should also change (Sarnecka & Gelman, 2004).

By age 3½ to 4, most children have mastered the meaning of numbers up to ten, count correctly, and grasp the vital principle of **cardinality**—that the last number in a counting sequence indicates the quantity of items in the set (Geary, 2006a). In the preschool scene described in the opening of this chapter, Sammy showed an understanding of cardinality when he counted four children at his snack table and then retrieved four milk cartons. Mastery of cardinality increases the efficiency of counting. By age 4, children use counting to solve simple arithmetic problems. At first, their strategies are tied to the order of numbers presented; when given 2 + 4, they count on from 2 (Bryant & Nunes, 2002). But soon they experiment with other strategies and master the *min* strategy, a more efficient approach (see page 338). Around this time, children realize that subtraction cancels out addition. Knowing, for example, that 4 + 3 = 7, they infer without counting that 7 − 3 = 4

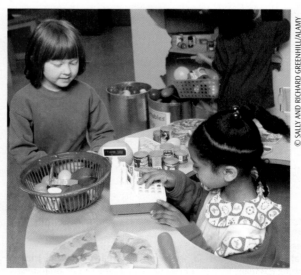

■ Preschoolers understand basic arithmetic sooner when they have many opportunities to count, compare quantities, and talk about number concepts. ■

◆ Applying What We Know

Supporting Emergent Literacy in Early Childhood

STRATEGY	EXPLANATION
Provide literacy-rich home and preschool environments.	Homes and preschools with abundant reading and writing materials—including a wide variety of children's storybooks, some relevant to children's ethnic backgrounds—open the door to a wealth of language and literacy experiences. Make-believe play, in which children have many opportunities to use newly acquired literacy skills in meaningful ways, spurs literacy development.
Engage in interactive book reading.	When adults discuss story content, ask open-ended questions about story events, explain the meaning of words, and point out features of print, they promote language development, comprehension of story content, knowledge of story structure, and awareness of units of written language.
Provide outings to libraries, museums, parks, zoos, and other community settings.	Visits to child-oriented community settings enhance children's general knowledge and offer many opportunities to see how written language is used in everyday life. They also provide personally meaningful topics for narrative conversation, which promote many language skills essential for literacy development.
Point out letter–sound correspondences, play rhyming and other language-sound games, and read rhyming poems and stories.	Experiences that help children isolate the sounds in words foster *phonological awareness*—a powerful predictor of early childhood literacy knowledge and later reading and spelling achievement.
Support children's efforts at writing, especially narrative products.	Assisting children in their efforts to write—especially letters, stories, and other narratives—fosters many language and literacy skills.
Model literacy activities.	When children see adults engaged in reading and writing activities, they better understand the diverse everyday functions of literacy skills and the knowledge and pleasure that literacy brings. As a result, children's motivation to become literate is strengthened.

Sources: McGee & Richgels, 2008; Neuman, 2006.

(Rasmussen, Ho, & Bisanz, 2003). Grasping basic arithmetic rules greatly facilitates rapid, accurate computation.

Understanding of basic arithmetic makes possible beginning *estimation*—the ability to generate approximate answers, which are useful for evaluating the accuracy of exact answers. After watching several doughnuts being added to or removed from a plate of four to ten doughnuts, 3- and 4-year-olds make sensible predictions about how many are on the plate (Zur & Gelman, 2004). Still, children can estimate only just beyond their calculation competence (Dowker, 2003). For example, preschoolers who can solve addition problems with sums up to 10 can estimate answers with sums up to about 20. And as with arithmetic operations, children try out diverse estimation strategies, gradually moving to more efficient, accurate techniques.

The arithmetic knowledge just described emerges universally around the world. But when adults provide many occasions for counting, comparing quantities, and talking about number concepts, children acquire these understandings sooner (Ginsburg, Lee, & Boyd, 2008; Klibanoff et al., 2006). Math proficiency at kindergarten entry strongly predicts math achievement years later, in elementary and secondary school (Duncan et al., 2007; Geary, 2006a).

As with emergent literacy, children from low-SES families begin kindergarten with considerably less math knowledge than their higher-SES agemates—a gap due to differences in environmental supports. Just a few sessions devoted to playing a number board game with an adult (see Figure 9.11) led to a dramatic improvement in low-SES 4-year-olds' number concepts and proficiency at counting from 1 to 10 (Siegler,

FIGURE 9.11

A number board game. An adult and child took turns using a spinner with a "1" section and a "2" section, which indicated how far to move a token on each turn. Children were asked to say the number spun and the numbers on the spaces as they moved. For example, a child on 5 who spun 2 would say "6, 7." Compared with agemates who played a color version of the game (it had only colored spaces on the board and a spinner with matching color sections), low-SES 4-year-olds who played the number board game showed large gains in number concepts and counting proficiency from 1 to 10. *(From R. S. Siegler, 2009, "Improving Preschoolers' Number Sense Using Information-Processing Theory," in O. A. Barbarin & B. H. Wasik, eds.,* Handbook of Child Development and Early Education. *New York: Guilford, p. 438. Reprinted by permission of Guilford Publications, Inc.)*

2009). And in an early childhood math curriculum called *Building Blocks,* materials that promote math concepts and skills through three types of media—computers, manipulatives, and print—enable teachers to weave math into many preschool daily activities, from building blocks to art and stories (Clements & Sarama, 2008). Compared with agemates randomly assigned to other preschool programs, low-SES preschoolers experiencing Building Blocks showed substantially greater year-end gains in math concepts and skills, including counting, sequencing, arithmetic computation, and geometric shapes.

ASK YOURSELF

◆ REVIEW Describe a typical 4-year-old's understanding of mental activities, noting both strengths and limitations.

◆ APPLY Lena, mother of 4-year-old Gregor, wonders why his preschool teacher provides extensive playtime in learning centers instead of formal lessons in literacy and math skills. Explain to Lena why adult-supported play is the best way for preschoolers to develop academically.

◆ CONNECT Cite evidence on the development of preschoolers' memory, theory of mind, and literacy and mathematical understanding that is consistent with Vygotsky's sociocultural theory.

◆ REFLECT Describe informal experiences important for literacy and math development that you experienced while growing up. How do you think those experiences contributed to your academic progress in school?

Individual Differences in Mental Development

Psychologists and educators typically measure how well preschoolers are developing mentally by giving them intelligence tests. Scores are computed in the same way as they are for infants and toddlers (return to Chapter 6, pages 227–228, to review). But instead of emphasizing perceptual and motor responses, tests for preschoolers sample a wide range of mental abilities. Understanding the link between early childhood experiences and mental test performance highlights ways to intervene in support of children's cognitive development.

Early Childhood Intelligence Tests

Five-year-old Hal sat in a small, unfamiliar testing room while Sarah gave him an intelligence test. Some of Sarah's questions were *verbal.* For example, she showed Hal a picture of a shovel and said, "Tell me what this is"—an item measuring vocabulary. She tested Hal's memory by asking him to repeat sentences and lists of numbers back to her. She probed his quantitative knowledge and problem solving by seeing if he could count and solve simple addition and subtraction problems. Finally, to assess Hal's spatial reasoning, Sarah used *nonverbal* tasks: Hal copied designs with special blocks, figured out the pattern in a series of shapes, and indicated what a piece of paper folded and cut would look like when unfolded (Roid, 2003; Wechsler, 2002).

Sarah knew that Hal came from an economically disadvantaged family. When low-SES and certain ethnic minority preschoolers are bombarded with questions by an unfamiliar adult, they sometimes react with anxiety. Also, such children may not define the testing situation in achievement terms. Instead, they may look for attention and approval from the adult and may settle for lower performance than their abilities allow. Sarah spent time playing with Hal before she began testing and encouraged him while the test was in progress. Under these conditions, low-SES preschoolers improve in performance (Bracken, 2000).

The questions Sarah asked Hal tap knowledge and skills that not all children have had an equal opportunity to learn. In Chapter 12, we will take up the hotly debated issue of *cultural bias* in mental testing. For now, keep in mind that intelligence tests do not sample all human abilities, and performance is affected by cultural and situational factors (Sternberg, 2005). Nevertheless, test scores remain important: By age 6 to 7, they are good predictors of later IQ and academic achievement, which are related to vocational success in industrialized societies. Let's see how the environments in which children spend their days—home, preschool, and child care—affect mental test performance.

Home Environment and Mental Development

A special version of the *Home Observation for Measurement of the Environment (HOME),* covered in Chapter 6, assesses aspects of 3- to 6-year-olds' home lives that foster intellectual growth (see Applying What We Know below). Preschoolers who develop well intellectually have homes rich in educational toys and books. Their parents are warm and affectionate, stimulate language and academic knowledge, and arrange interesting outings. They also make reasonable demands for socially mature behavior—for example, that the child perform simple chores and behave courteously toward others. And these parents resolve conflicts with reason instead of physical force and punishment (Bradley & Caldwell, 1982; Espy, Molfese, & DiLalla, 2001; Roberts, Burchinal, & Durham, 1999).

As we saw in Chapter 2, these characteristics are less often seen in low-SES families. When parents manage, despite low education and income, to obtain high HOME scores, their preschoolers do substantially better on intelligence tests and measures of language and emergent literacy skills (Berger, Paxson, & Waldfogel, 2009; Foster et al., 2005; Mistry et al., 2008). And in a study of African-American 3- and 4-year-olds in low-income families, HOME cognitive stimulation and emotional support subscales predicted reading achievement four years later (Zaslow et al., 2006). These findings (along with others we will discuss in Chapter 12) indicate that the home plays a major role in the generally poorer intellectual performance of low-SES children compared to their higher-SES peers.

◆ Applying What We Know

Features of a High-Quality Home Life for Preschoolers: The HOME Early Childhood Subscales

HOME SUBSCALE	SAMPLE ITEMS
Cognitive stimulation through toys, games, and reading material	Home includes toys to learn colors, sizes, and shapes.
Language stimulation	Parent teaches child about animals through books, games, and puzzles.
	Parent converses with child at least twice during observer's visit.
Organization of the physical environment	All visible rooms are reasonably clean and minimally cluttered.
Emotional support	Parent spontaneously praises child's qualities or behavior twice during observer's visit.
	Parent caresses, kisses, or hugs child at least once during observer's visit.
Stimulation of academic behavior	Child is encouraged to learn colors.
Modeling and encouragement of social maturity	Parent introduces interviewer to child.
Opportunities for variety in daily stimulation	Family member takes child on one outing at least every other week (picnic, shopping).
Avoidance of physical punishment	Parent neither slaps nor spanks child during observer's visit.

Sources: Bradley, 1994; Bradley et al., 2001.

Preschool, Kindergarten, and Child Care

Children between ages 2 and 6 spend even more time away from their homes and parents than infants and toddlers do. Largely because of the rise in maternal employment, over the past several decades the number of young children enrolled in preschool or child care has steadily increased to more than 60 percent in the United States (U.S. Census Bureau, 2010b).

A *preschool* is a program with planned educational experiences aimed at enhancing the development of 2- to 5-year-olds. In contrast, *child care* includes a variety of arrangements for supervising children of employed parents, ranging from care in the caregiver's or the child's home to some type of center-based program. The line between preschool and child care is fuzzy. Parents often select a preschool as a child-care option. And in response to the needs of employed parents, many U.S. preschools, as well as most public school kindergartens, have increased their hours from half to full days (U.S. Department of Education, 2010).

With age, preschoolers tend to shift from home-based to center programs. But many children experience several types of arrangements at once. In the United States, children of higher-income parents and children of very low-income parents are especially likely to be in preschools or child-care centers (Federal Interagency Forum on Child and Family Statistics, 2009). Many low-income working parents rely on care by relatives because they are not eligible for public preschool or government-subsidized center child care.

Good child care means more than simply keeping children safe and adequately fed. It should provide the same high-quality educational experiences that an effective preschool does, the only difference being that children attend for an extended day.

TYPES OF PRESCHOOL AND KINDERGARTEN Preschool and kindergarten programs range along a continuum from child-centered to teacher-directed. In **child-centered programs,** teachers provide activities from which children select, and much learning takes place through play. In contrast, in **academic programs,** teachers structure children's learning, teaching letters, numbers, colors, shapes, and other academic skills through formal lessons, often using repetition and drill.

Despite evidence that formal academic training undermines young children's motivation and emotional well-being, early childhood teachers have felt increased pressure to take this approach. Preschoolers and kindergartners who spend much time passively sitting and completing worksheets, as opposed to being actively engaged in learning centers, display more stress behaviors (such as wiggling and rocking), have less confidence in their abilities, prefer less challenging tasks, and are less advanced in motor, academic, language, and social skills at the end of the school year (Marcon, 1999a; Stipek et al., 1995). Follow-ups reveal lasting effects through elementary school in poorer study habits and lower achievement test scores (Burts et al., 1992; Hart et al., 1998, 2003). These outcomes are strongest for low-SES children, with whom teachers more often use an academic approach—a disturbing trend in view of its negative impact on motivation and learning (Stipek, 2004; Stipek & Byler, 1997). Yet another concern is that public preschool programs serving low-SES children are more likely to be staffed by teachers who lack a bachelor's degree and who therefore tend to communicate in less stimulating and encouraging ways (Clifford et al., 2005; Pianta et al., 2005).

A special type of child-centered approach is *Montessori education,* devised more than a century ago by Italian physician and child development researcher Maria Montessori, who originally applied her method to poverty-stricken children. Features of Montessori schooling include multiage classrooms, teaching materials specially designed to promote exploration and discovery, long time periods for individual and small-group learning in child-chosen activities, and equal emphasis on academic and social development (Lillard, 2007). In an evaluation of Montessori public preschools serving mostly urban minority children in Milwaukee, researchers compared students randomly assigned to either Montessori or other classrooms (Lillard & Else-Quest, 2006). Five-year-olds who had completed two years of Montessori education outperformed controls in literacy and math skills, cognitive flexibility, false-belief understanding, concern with fairness in solving conflicts with peers, and cooperative play with agemates.

EARLY INTERVENTION FOR AT-RISK PRESCHOOLERS   In the 1960s, as part of the "War on Poverty" in the United States, many intervention programs for low-SES preschoolers were initiated in an effort to address learning problems before formal schooling begins. The most extensive of these federal programs, **Project Head Start,** began in 1965. A typical Head Start center provides children with a year or two of preschool, along with nutritional and health services. Parent involvement is central to the Head Start philosophy. Parents serve on policy councils, contribute to program planning, work directly with children in classrooms, attend special programs on parenting and child development, and receive services directed at their own emotional, social, and vocational needs. Currently, more than 18,000 U.S. Head Start centers serve about 908,000 children (Head Start Bureau, 2008).

Benefits of Preschool Intervention.   More than two decades of research have established the long-term benefits of preschool intervention. The most extensive of these studies combined data from seven interventions implemented by universities or research foundations. Results showed that poverty-stricken children who attended programs scored higher in IQ and achievement than controls during the first two to three years of elementary school. After that, differences declined (Lazar & Darlington, 1982). But on real-life measures of school adjustment, children and adolescents who had received intervention remained ahead. They were less likely to be placed in special education or retained in grade, and a greater number graduated from high school.

A separate report on one program—the High/Scope Perry Preschool Project—revealed benefits lasting well into adulthood. Two years' exposure to cognitively enriching preschool was associated with increased employment and reduced pregnancy and delinquency rates in adolescence. At age 27, those who had attended preschool were more likely than no-preschool counterparts to have graduated from high school and college, have higher earnings, be married, and own their own home—and less likely to have been involved with the criminal justice system (see Figure 9.12) (Weikart, 1998). In the most recent follow-up, at age 40, the intervention group sustained its advantage on all measures of life success, including education, income, family life, and law-abiding behavior (Schweinhart et al., 2005).

Do the effects on school adjustment of these well-designed and well-delivered programs generalize to Head Start and other community-based preschool interventions? Gains are similar, though not as strong. Head Start preschoolers, who are more economically disadvantaged than children in university-based programs, have more severe learning and behavior problems. And quality of services is more variable across community programs (Barnett, 2004; U.S. Department of Health and Human Services, 2010b). But interventions of documented high quality are associated with diverse, long-lasting favorable outcomes, including higher rates of high school graduation and college enrollment and lower rates of adolescent drug use and delinquency (Garces, Thomas, & Currie, 2002; Love et al., 2006; Mashburn, 2008).

A consistent finding is that gains in IQ and achievement test scores from attending Head Start and other interventions quickly dissolve. In the Head Start Impact Study, a nationally representative sample of 5,000 Head Start–eligible 3- and 4-year-olds was randomly assigned to one year of Head Start or to a control group that could attend other types of preschool programs (U.S. Department of Health and Human Services, 2010b). By year's end, Head Start 3-year-olds had gained relative to controls in vocabulary, emergent

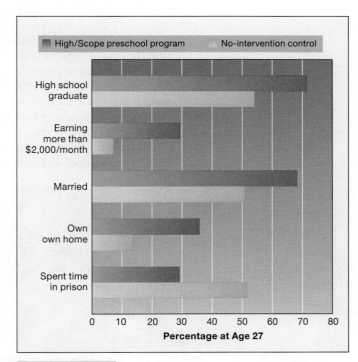

FIGURE 9.12

Some outcomes of the High/Scope Perry Preschool Project on follow-up at age 27. Although two years of a cognitively enriching preschool program did not eradicate the effects of growing up in poverty, children who received intervention were advantaged over no-intervention controls on all measures of life success when they reached adulthood. *(Adapted from Schweinhart et al., 2005.)*

■ Project Head Start provides children from poverty-stricken families with preschool education and nutritional and health services. High-quality early educational intervention has benefits lasting into adulthood. ■

literacy, and math skills; 4-year-olds in vocabulary, emergent literacy, and color identification. Head Start 3-year-olds also benefitted socially, displaying declines in overactivity and withdrawn behavior. But except for language skills, academic advantages were no longer evident by the end of first grade.

What explains these disappointing outcomes? Head Start children typically enter inferior public schools in poverty-stricken neighborhoods, which undermine the benefits of preschool education (Brooks-Gunn, 2003; Ramey, Ramey, & Lanzi, 2006). Among children who attended the Chicago Child–Parent Centers, a program emphasizing literacy intervention and parent involvement that began at age 3 and continued through third grade, gains in academic achievement were still evident in junior high school (Reynolds & Temple, 1998). And recall from Chapter 6 that when intensive intervention persists from infancy through early childhood and children enter good-quality schools, IQ gains endure into adulthood (see page 232).

Still, the improved school adjustment that results from attending a one- or two-year Head Start program is impressive. Program effects on parents may contribute: The more involved parents are in Head Start, the better their child-rearing practices and the more stimulating their home learning environments—factors positively related to preschoolers' independence, task persistence in the classroom, and year-end academic, language, and social skills (Marcon, 1999b; McLoyd, Aidens, & Burton, 2006; Parker et al., 1999).

Strengthening Preschool Intervention. Head Start is highly cost-effective when compared with the cost of providing special education, treating criminal behavior, and supporting unemployed adults. Economists estimate a lifetime return to society of more than $250,000 on an investment of $15,000 per preschool child—a potential savings of many billions of dollars if every poverty-stricken preschooler in the United States were enrolled (Heckman & Masterov, 2004; Temple & Reynolds, 2006). Because of funding shortages, however, many eligible children do not receive services.

A few supplementary programs have responded to this shortage—and to the need to intensify preschool intervention to strengthen its impact—by delivering extra educational enrichment to children in Head Start and other preschool classrooms serving low-income children. The largest of these programs is Jumpstart for Young Children. Two or three times a week, Jumpstart corps members (college students and older adults) go to an early childhood center, where they read to and converse with 1 to 3 designated 3-to 5-year-olds, engage in additional individualized learning activities, and play collaborative games in small groups.

Currently, Jumpstart reaches more than 13,000 children in over 60 communities. Evaluations indicate that preschoolers who experience Jumpstart show greater end-of-year gains in language, literacy, task persistence, and social skills than non-Jumpstart comparison children in the same Head Start or other centers (Harris & Berk, 2011; Jumpstart Evaluation Team, 2008).

■ A Jumpstart corps member reads to and converses with a 4-year-old in a Head Start classroom. By delivering extra educational enrichment, this supplementary intervention program yields gains in language, literacy, task persistence, and social skills for participating children. ■

CHILD CARE We have seen that high-quality early intervention can enhance the development of economically disadvantaged children. As noted in Chapter 6, however, much U.S. child care lacks quality. Preschoolers exposed to substandard child care, particularly for long hours, score lower in cognitive and social skills and display more behavior problems (Belsky, 2006; Lamb & Ahnert, 2006; NICHD Early Child Care Research Network, 2003b, 2006). Externalizing difficulties are especially likely to endure into the school years after extensive exposure to mediocre center-based (as opposed to home-based) care (Belsky et al., 2007). Psychological well-being also declines when children experience the instability of several child-care settings. The emotional problems of temperamentally difficult preschoolers worsen considerably (De Schipper, van IJzendoorn, & Tavecchio, 2004; De Schipper et al., 2004).

In contrast, good child care enhances cognitive, language, and social development, especially for low-SES children—effects that persist into elementary school (Belsky et al., 2007; Lamb & Ahnert, 2006; NICHD Early Child Care Research Network, 2006). In a study that followed 400 very-low-income children over the preschool years, center-based care was more strongly associated with cognitive gains than were other child-care arrangements, probably because good-quality child-care centers are more likely than family child-care homes to provide a systematic educational program (Loeb et al., 2004).

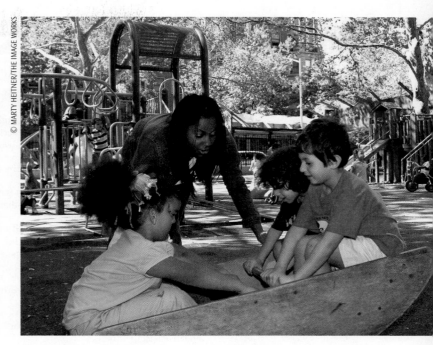

■ Ingredients of high-quality child care include small group size, generous caregiver–child ratios, richly equipped activity areas, and well-educated caregivers. Child care that meets these criteria enhances development, especially for low-SES preschoolers. ■

What are the ingredients of high-quality child care for preschoolers? Large-scale studies identify several important factors: group size (number of children in a single space), caregiver–child ratio, caregivers' educational preparation, and caregivers' personal commitment to learning about and caring for children. When these characteristics are favorable, adults are more verbally stimulating and sensitive to children's needs (Lamb & Ahnert, 2006). Applying What We Know on page 352 summarizes characteristics of high-quality early childhood programs, based on standards for developmentally appropriate practice devised by the U.S. National Association for the Education of Young Children. These standards offer a set of worthy goals as the United States strives to upgrade child-care and educational services for young children.

Educational Media

Besides home and preschool, young children spend much time in another learning environment: electronic media, including both television and computers. In the United States and other industrialized nations, nearly all homes have at least one television set, and most have two or more. About 85 percent of U.S. children live in homes with one or more computers, two-thirds of which have an Internet connection (Roberts, Foehr, & Rideout, 2005; U.S. Census Bureau, 2010b).

EDUCATIONAL TELEVISION   Sammy's favorite TV program, *Sesame Street,* uses lively visual and sound effects to stress basic literacy and number concepts and presents engaging puppet and human characters to teach general knowledge, emotional and social understanding, and social skills. Today, *Sesame Street* is broadcast in more than 120 countries, making it the most widely viewed children's program in the world (Sesame Workshop, 2008).

Time devoted to watching children's educational programs is associated with gains in early literacy and math skills and academic progress in elementary school (Ennemoser & Schneider, 2007; Linebarger et al., 2004; Wright et al., 2001). Consistent with these findings, one study reported a link between preschool viewing of *Sesame Street* and other similar educational programs and getting higher grades, reading more books, and placing more value on achievement

LOOK AND LISTEN

Arrange to observe at a child-care center and to talk to its director. Jot down signs of quality, referring to Applying What We Know on page 352. How would you rate the center's overall quality?

Applying What We Know

Signs of Developmentally Appropriate Early Childhood Programs

PROGRAM CHARACTERISTIC	SIGNS OF QUALITY
Physical setting	Indoor environment is clean, in good repair, and well-ventilated. Classroom space is divided into richly equipped activity areas, including make-believe play, blocks, science, math, games and puzzles, books, art, and music. Fenced outdoor play space is equipped with swings, climbing equipment, tricycles, and sandbox.
Group size	In preschools and child-care centers, group size is no greater than 18 to 20 children with two teachers.
Caregiver–child ratio	In preschools and child-care centers, teacher is responsible for no more than 8 to 10 children. In family child-care homes, caregiver is responsible for no more than 6 children.
Daily activities	Children mainly work individually or in small groups, selecting many of their own activities and learning through experiences relevant to their own lives. Teachers facilitate children's involvement, accept individual differences, and adjust expectations to children's developing capacities.
Interactions between adults and children	Teachers move among groups and individuals, asking questions, offering suggestions, and adding more complex ideas. Teachers use positive guidance techniques, such as modeling and encouraging expected behavior and redirecting children to more acceptable activities.
Teacher qualifications	Teachers have college-level specialized preparation in early childhood development, early childhood education, or a related field.
Relationships with parents	Parents are encouraged to observe and participate. Teachers talk frequently with parents about children's behavior and development.
Licensing and accreditation	Child-care setting, whether a center or a home, is licensed by the state. Voluntary accreditation by the National Academy of Early Childhood Programs *(www.naeyc.org/accreditation)* or the National Association for Family Child Care *(www.nafcc.org)* is evidence of an especially high-quality program.

Sources: Copple & Bredekamp, 2009.

in high school (Anderson et al., 2001). In recent years, *Sesame Street* has modified its rapid-paced format in favor of more leisurely episodes with a clear story line. Watching children's programs with slow-paced action and easy-to-follow narratives, such as *Barney and Friends,* leads to more elaborate make-believe play than viewing programs that present quick, disconnected bits of information (Singer & Singer, 2005).

Despite the spread of computers, television remains the dominant form of youth media, with children first becoming viewers in early infancy. About 40 percent of U.S. 3-month-olds regularly watch either TV or videos, a figure that rises to 90 percent by age 2 (Zimmerman, Christakis, & Meltzoff, 2007). The average U.S. 2- to 6-year-old watches TV programs and videos from 1½ to 2½ hours a day. In middle childhood, viewing time increases to an average of 3½ hours a day, then declines slightly in adolescence (Rideout & Hamel, 2006; Scharrer & Comstock, 2003).

Low-SES children are more frequent TV viewers, perhaps because few alternative forms of entertainment are available in their neighborhoods or affordable for their parents. On the positive side, preschoolers in low-SES families watch as much educational television as their economically advantaged agemates (Vandewater & Bickham, 2004). But parents with limited education are more likely to engage in practices that heighten TV viewing of all kinds, including eating family meals in front of the set and failing to limit children's TV access (Hesketh et al., 2007). About one-third of U.S. preschoolers and two-thirds of school-age children and adolescents have a TV set in their bedroom. These children spend from 40 to 90 minutes more per day watching TV, usually without any parental restrictions on what they view (Rideout & Hamel, 2006).

Does extensive TV viewing take children away from worthwhile activities? The more preschool and school-age children watch prime-time television and cartoons, the less time they spend reading and interacting with others and the poorer their academic skills (Ennemoser & Schneider, 2007; Huston et al., 1999; Wright et al., 2001). Educational programs, as noted above, are beneficial, but watching entertainment TV—especially heavy viewing—detracts from children's school success and social experiences. More than one-third of U.S. children live in homes where the TV is on constantly, or nearly so. Kindergartners and first graders in such families, regardless of SES, are far less likely than their agemates to have acquired beginning reading skills (Vandewater et al., 2005).

LEARNING WITH COMPUTERS　According to a survey of 1,000 U.S. parents, 70 percent of 4- to 6-year-olds have used a computer at one time or another, and more than one-fourth use one regularly, spending on average just over an hour a day at the keyboard. Preschoolers of higher-SES parents have greater computer access (Calvert et al., 2005; Rideout, Vandewater, & Wartella, 2003). Children as young as age 3 can type simple keyboard commands, use a mouse to point and click, and load a CD or DVD on their own.

Because computers can have rich educational benefits, many early childhood classrooms include computer-learning centers. Computer storybooks and other literacy programs expand children's general knowledge and encourage diverse language and emergent literacy skills (Hutinger et al., 1998). When adults turn over control of the mouse to preschoolers, allowing them to interact directly with computer stories, children's sustained attention and interest increase (Calvert, Strong, & Gallagher, 2005). Kindergartners who use computers to draw or write produce more elaborate pictures and text, make fewer writing errors, and edit their work much as older children do. And combining everyday and computer experiences with math manipulatives is especially effective in promoting math concepts and skills (Clements & Sarama, 2003).

Simplified computer languages that children can use to make designs or build structures introduce them to programming skills. As long as adults support children's efforts, computer programming promotes improved problem solving and metacognition (awareness of thought processes) because children must plan and reflect on their thinking to get their programs to work. Furthermore, while programming, children are especially likely to help one another and to persist in the face of challenge (Nastasi & Clements, 1994; Resnick & Silverman, 2005). Small groups often gather around classroom computers, and children more often collaborate than in other pursuits (Svensson, 2000).

As with television, children spend much time using computers for entertainment, especially game playing. Although parental reports suggest that only 3 percent of preschoolers play video games on a daily basis, that figure rises to 35 percent in middle childhood and adolescence, when—as we will see in Chapter 12—a large sex difference favoring boys emerges. Nevertheless, game consoles are among the bedroom furnishings of 10 percent of children age 6 and younger (Rideout, Vandewater, & Wartella, 2003; Roberts, Foehr, & Rideout, 2005).

Video games designed for young children generally have specific educational goals, including literacy, math, science, colors, and other concepts (Garrison & Christakis, 2005). But on the whole, TV and computer-game media are rife with gender stereotypes and violence. We will consider the impact of media on emotional and social development in the next chapter.

ASK YOURSELF

◆ REVIEW　What findings indicate that child-centered rather than academic preschools and kindergartens are better suited to fostering academic development?

◆ APPLY　Your senator has heard that IQ gains resulting from Head Start do not last, so he plans to vote against additional funding. Write a letter explaining why he should support Head Start.

◆ CONNECT　Compare outcomes resulting from preschool intervention programs with those from interventions beginning in infancy (see pages 231–232 in Chapter 6). Which are more likely to lead to lasting cognitive gains? Explain.

◆ REFLECT　How much and what kinds of TV viewing and computer use did you engage in as a child? How do you think your home media environment influenced your development?

Language Development

Language is intimately related to virtually all the cognitive changes discussed in this chapter. Between ages 2 and 6, children make momentous advances in language. Their remarkable achievements, as well as their mistakes along the way, reveal their active, rule-oriented approach to mastering their native tongue.

Vocabulary

At age 2, Sammy had a spoken vocabulary of 200 words. By age 6, he will have acquired around 10,000 words (Bloom, 1998). To accomplish this feat, Sammy will learn about five new words each day. How do children build their vocabularies so quickly? Research shows that they can connect new words with their underlying concepts after only a brief encounter, a process called **fast mapping.** Even toddlers comprehend new labels remarkably quickly, but they need more repetitions of the word's use across several situations than preschoolers, who process speech-based information faster and are better able to categorize and recall it (Akhtar & Montague, 1999; Fernald, Perfors, & Marchman, 2006). During the preschool years, children become increasingly adept at fast-mapping two or more new words encountered in the same situation (Wilkinson, Ross, & Diamond, 2003).

TYPES OF WORDS One day, Leslie announced to the children that they would soon take a field trip. That night, Sammy excitedly told his mother, "We're going on a field trip!" When she asked where the class would go, Sammy responded matter-of-factly, "To a field!" Sammy's error suggests that young children fast-map some words more easily than others.

Children in many Western and non-Western language communities fast-map labels for objects especially rapidly because these refer to concepts that are easy to perceive (Gentner & Namy, 2004; Kern, 2007). When adults point to, label, and talk about an object, they help the child figure out the word's meaning (Gershoff-Stowe & Hahn, 2007). Soon children add verbs *(go, run, broke),* which require understandings of relationships between objects and actions. Because learning verbs is more cognitively challenging, preschoolers speaking quite different languages take longer to extend a new verb ("*push* the bike") to other instances of the same action ("*push* the box") than they do to extend a novel noun to other objects in the same category (Imai et al., 2008). In mastering verb meanings, they benefit from many examples of the same verb used in different contexts.

Nevertheless, young children learning Chinese, Japanese, and Korean—languages in which nouns are often omitted from adults' sentences, while verbs are stressed—acquire verbs more readily than their English-speaking agemates (Kim, McGregor, & Thompson, 2000; Tardif, 2006). Besides increased exposure to verbs, Chinese-speaking children hear a greater variety of verbs denoting physical actions, which are easiest to master—for example, several verbs for *carry,* each referring to a different way of carrying, such as on one's back, in one's arms, or with one's hands (Ma et al., 2009).

Gradually, preschoolers add modifiers *(red, round, sad).* First they make general distinctions *(big–small),* then more specific ones *(tall–short, high–low, wide–narrow)* (Stevenson & Pollitt, 1987).

STRATEGIES FOR WORD LEARNING Children figure out the meanings of words by contrasting them with words they already know and assigning the new label to a gap in their vocabulary (Clark, 1990). On hearing a new word in conversation, 2-year-olds repeat the word or acknowledge it with "yeah" or "uh-huh" in their next verbalization 60 percent of the time (Clark, 2007). This suggests that they assign the word a preliminary meaning and start to use it right away. Over time, they refine its meaning, striving to match its conventional use in their language community.

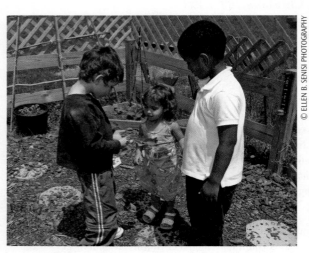

© ELLEN B. SENISI PHOTOGRAPHY

■ To engage in effective verbal communication, preschoolers must master and combine principles of word meaning, grammar, and everyday conversation. How they accomplish this feat so rapidly is the focus of intensive research and debate. ■

When learning a new noun, toddlers and preschoolers acquiring diverse languages tend to assume it refers to an object category at the basic level—an intermediate level of generality (see page 325). This preference helps young children narrow the range of possible meanings. Once they acquire a basic-level name *(dog)*, they add names at other hierarchical levels, both more general *(animal)* and more specific *(beagle, greyhound)* (Imai & Haryu, 2004; Waxman & Lidz, 2006).

How do children discover which concept each word picks out? This process is not yet fully understood. One speculation is that early in vocabulary growth, children adopt a **mutual exclusivity bias**—the assumption that words refer to entirely separate (nonoverlapping) categories (Markman, 1992). Two-year-olds seem to rely on mutual exclusivity when the objects named are perceptually distinct—for example, differ clearly in shape. After hearing the labels for two distinct novel objects (for example, *clip* and *horn*), they assign each word correctly, to the whole object, not just a part of it (Waxman & Senghas, 1992).

Indeed, children's first several hundred nouns refer mostly to objects well-organized by shape. In a study in which toddlers repeatedly played with and heard names for novel objects of different shapes ("That's a *wif*") over a nine-week period, they soon formed the generalization that only similar-shaped objects have the same name (Smith et al., 2002; Yoshida & Smith, 2003). Toddlers with this training added more than three times as many object names to their vocabularies outside the laboratory as did untrained controls. Because shape is a perceptual property relevant to most object categories for which they have already learned names, this *shape bias* helps preschoolers master additional names of objects, and vocabulary accelerates.

Once the name of a whole object is familiar, on hearing a new name for the object, 2- and 3-year-olds set aside the mutual exclusivity assumption. For example, if the object *(bottle)* has a part that stands out *(spout)*, children readily apply the new label to it (Hansen & Markman, 2009). In these instances, mutual exclusivity helps limit the possibilities the child must consider. Still, mutual exclusivity and object shape cannot account for preschoolers' remarkably flexible responses when objects have more than one name.

By age 3, preschoolers' memory, categorization, and language skills have expanded, and they assign multiple labels to many objects (Deák, Yen, & Pettit, 2001). For example, they refer to a sticker of a gray goose as "sticker," "goose," and "gray." In these instances, children often call on other aspects of language. According to one proposal, preschoolers discover many word meanings by observing how words are used in *syntax,* or the structure of sentences—a hypothesis called **syntactic bootstrapping** (Gleitman et al., 2005; Naigles & Swenson, 2007). Consider an adult who says, "This is a *citron* one," while showing the child a yellow car. Two- and 3-year-olds conclude that a new word used as an adjective for a familiar object (car) refers to a property of that object (Hall & Graham, 1999; Imai & Haryu, 2004). As preschoolers hear the word in various sentence structures ("That lemon is bright *citron*"), they use syntactic information to refine the word's meaning and generalize it to other categories.

Young children also take advantage of the rich social information that adults frequently provide when they introduce new words. In one study, an adult performed an action on an object and then used a new label while looking back and forth between the child and the object, as if inviting the child to play. Two-year-olds concluded that the label referred to the action, not the object (Tomasello & Akhtar, 1995). And when an adult first designates the whole object ("The bird has something . . .") and then points to a part of it ("in its beak"), 3-year-olds realize that *beak* is a certain part, not the whole bird (Saylor, Sabbagh, & Baldwin, 2002).

Adults also inform children directly about word meanings. Parents commonly highlight the meaning of adjectives by using the new label with several objects (a "red car," a "red truck")—information that helps children infer that the word refers to an object property (Hall, Burns, & Pawluski, 2003). And adults often explain which of two or more words to use, by saying, for example, "You can call it a sea creature, but it's better to say *dolphin*" (Callanan & Sabbagh, 2004). In these situations, preschoolers often call on their expanding theory of mind to facilitate word learning. For example, by age 3 they can use a speaker's recently expressed desire ("I really want to play with the *riff*") to figure out the label belonging to one of two novel

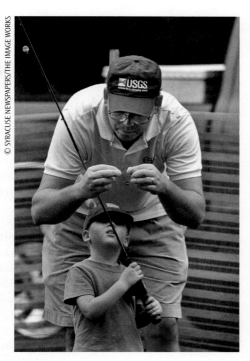

■ Young children rely on any useful information available to add to their vocabulary. This 3-year-old attends to a variety of perceptual, social, and linguistic cues to grasp the meanings of unfamiliar fishing words, such as *bait, line, bobber,* and *sinker.* ■

objects (Saylor & Troseth, 2006). And when an adult expresses certainty about a word's meaning, 3- and 4-year-olds are far more likely to accept her referent than when she expresses uncertainty ("I'm not sure that's a *beluga*") (Sabbagh & Baldwin, 2001).

Furthermore, to fill in for words they have not yet learned, children as young as age 3 coin new words using ones they already know—for example, "plant-man" for a gardener or "crayoner" for a child using crayons. Preschoolers also extend language meanings through metaphor—like the 3-year-old who described a stomachache as a "fire engine in my tummy" (Winner, 1988). Young preschoolers' metaphors involve concrete sensory comparisons: "Clouds are pillows," "Leaves are dancers." As their vocabulary and general knowledge expand, they appreciate nonsensory comparisons: "Friends are like magnets," "Time flies by" (Keil, 1986; Ozçaliskan & Goldin-Meadow, 2005). Metaphors permit young children to communicate in amazingly vivid and memorable ways.

EXPLAINING VOCABULARY DEVELOPMENT   Children acquire vocabulary so efficiently and accurately that some theorists believe that they are innately biased to induce word meanings using certain principles, such as mutual exclusivity and syntactic bootstrapping (Lidz, Gleitman, & Gleitman, 2004; Woodward & Markman, 1998). But critics observe that a small set of built-in, fixed principles cannot account for the varied, flexible manner in which children master vocabulary (Deák, 2000). And many word-learning strategies cannot be innate because children acquiring different languages use different approaches to mastering the same meanings.

An alternative view is that vocabulary growth is governed by the same cognitive strategies that children apply to nonlinguistic information. According to one account, children draw on a *coalition* of cues—perceptual, social, and linguistic—which shift in importance with age (Golinkoff & Hirsh-Pasek, 2006, 2008). Infants rely solely on perceptual features. Toddlers and young preschoolers, while still sensitive to perceptual features (such as object shape and physical action), increasingly attend to social cues—the speaker's direction of gaze, gestures, expressions of intention and desire, and soon the speaker's knowledge (Hollich, Hirsh-Pasek, & Golinkoff, 2000; Pruden et al., 2006). And as language develops further, linguistic cues—sentence structure and intonation (stress, pitch, and loudness)—play larger roles.

Preschoolers are most successful at figuring out new word meanings when several kinds of information are available (Saylor, Baldwin, & Sabbagh, 2005). Researchers have just begun to study the multiple cues that children use for different kinds of words and how their combined strategies change with development.

Grammar

Grammar refers to the way we combine words into meaningful phrases and sentences. Between ages 2 and 3, English-speaking children use simple sentences that follow a subject–verb–object word order. Children learning other languages adopt the word orders of the adult speech to which they are exposed.

BASIC RULES   Studies of children acquiring diverse languages indicate that their first use of grammatical rules is piecemeal—limited to just a few verbs. As children listen for familiar verbs in adults' speech, they expand their own utterances containing those verbs, relying on adult speech as their model (Gathercole, Sebastián, & Soto, 1999; Lieven, Pine, & Baldwin, 1997). Sammy, for example, added the preposition *with* to the verb *open* ("You open with scissors") but not to the word *hit* ("He hit me stick").

To test preschoolers' ability to generate novel sentences that conform to basic English grammar, researchers had them use a new verb in the subject–verb–object form after hearing it in a different construction, such as passive: "Ernie is getting *gorped* by the dog." When children were asked what the dog was doing, the percentage who could respond, "He's *gorping* Ernie," rose steadily with age. But as Figure 9.13 shows, not until age 3½ to 4 could the majority of children apply the fundamental subject–verb–object structure broadly, to newly acquired verbs (Tomasello, 2000, 2003, 2006).

As these examples suggest, once children form three-word sentences, they also make small additions and changes in words that enable speakers to express meanings flexibly and efficiently. For example, they add *-s* for plural *(cats)*, use prepositions *(in* and *on)*, and form various tenses of the verb *to be (is, are, were, has been, will)*. All English-speaking children master these grammatical markers in a regular sequence, starting with those that involve the simplest meanings and structures (Brown, 1973; de Villiers & de Villiers, 1973). For example, children master the plural form *-s* before they learn tenses of the verb *to be*.

Once children acquire these markers, they sometimes overextend the rules to words that are exceptions, a type of error called **overregularization.** "We each got two *foots*" and "My toy car *breaked*" are expressions that appear between ages 2 and 3 and persist into middle childhood (Maratsos, 2000; Marcus, 1995). Children less often make this error on frequently used irregular verbs, such as the past tense of *go (went)* and *say (said)*, which they hear often enough to learn by rote. For rarely used verbs such as *grow* and *sing,* children alternate for months—or even several years—between overregularized forms *(growed, singed)* and correct forms, until the irregular form eventually wins out. Since children do not hear mature speakers use these forms, overregularization provides evidence that children apply grammatical rules creatively.

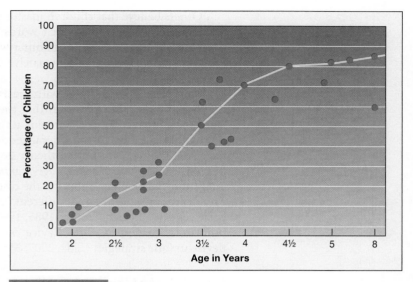

FIGURE 9.13

Percentage of children in different studies who could use a new verb in the subject–verb–object form after hearing it in another construction. Each dot in the graph represents the findings of one study. The ability to use the new verb—an indicator of the child's capacity to apply the subject–verb–object structure broadly—rose steadily with age. Children mastered this fundamental grammatical construction gradually. *(From M. Tomasello, 2000, "Do Young Children Have Adult Syntactic Competence?" Cognition, 74, p. 223. Reprinted with permission from Elsevier.)*

COMPLEX STRUCTURES   Gradually, preschoolers master more complex grammatical structures, although they make errors along the way. In first creating questions, 2- and 3-year-olds use many formulas: "Where's *X?*" "Can I *X?*" (Dabrowska, 2000; Tomasello, 1992, 2003). Question asking remains variable for the next couple of years. An analysis of one child's questions revealed that he inverted the subject and verb when asking certain questions but not others ("What she will do?" "Why he can go?"). The correct expressions were the ones he heard most often in his mother's speech (Rowland & Pine, 2000). And sometimes children produce errors in subject–verb agreement ("Where does the dogs play?") and subject case ("Where can me sit?") (Rowland, 2007).

Similarly, children have trouble with some passive sentences. When told, "The car was pushed by the truck," young preschoolers often make a toy car push a truck. By age 5, they understand such expressions, but full mastery of the passive form is not complete until the end of middle childhood (Horgan, 1978; Lempert, 1990).

Nevertheless, preschoolers' grasp of grammar is remarkable. By age 4 to 5, they form embedded sentences ("I think *he will come*"), tag questions ("Dad's going to be home soon, *isn't he?*"), and indirect objects ("He showed *his friend* the present"). As the preschool years draw to a close, children use most of the grammatical constructions of their language competently (Tager-Flusberg & Zukowski, 2009).

EXPLAINING GRAMMATICAL DEVELOPMENT   Evidence that grammatical development is an extended process has raised questions about Chomsky's *language acquisition device (LAD),* which assumes that children have innate knowledge of grammatical rules (see Chapter 6, page 234). Some experts believe that grammar is a product of general cognitive development—children's tendency to search the environment for consistencies and patterns of all sorts (Bloom, 1999; Chang, Dell, & Bock, 2006; Tomasello, 2003). Yet among these theorists, debate continues over just how children master grammar.

According to one view, young children rely on *semantics,* or word meanings, to figure out grammatical rules—an approach called **semantic bootstrapping.** For example, children might begin by grouping together words with "agent qualities" (things that cause actions) as *subjects* and words with "action qualities" as *verbs.* Then they merge these categories with observations of how words are used in sentences (Bates & MacWhinney, 1987; Braine, 1994).

Others believe that children master grammar through direct observation of the structure of language: They notice which words appear in the same positions in sentences and are combined in the same way with other words. Over time, they group words into grammatical categories and use them appropriately in sentences (Bloom, 1999; Chang, Dell, & Bock, 2006; Tomasello, 2003).

Still other theorists agree with the essence of Chomsky's theory. One idea accepts semantic bootstrapping but proposes that the grammatical categories into which children group word meanings are innate—present at the outset (Pinker, 1989, 1999). Critics, however, point out that toddlers' two-word utterances do not show a grasp of grammar (return to Chapter 6, page 239, to review). Another theory holds that children do not start with innate knowledge but, rather, have a *special language-making capacity*—a set of procedures for analyzing the language they hear, which supports the discovery of grammatical regularities. Research on children learning more than 40 different languages reveals common patterns, consistent with a basic set of strategies (Slobin, 1985, 1997). Yet controversy persists over whether a universal, built-in language-processing device exists or whether children who hear different languages devise unique strategies (Lidz, 2007; Marchman & Thal, 2005).

Conversation

Besides acquiring vocabulary and grammar, children must learn to engage in effective and appropriate communication—by taking turns, staying on the same topic, stating their messages clearly, and conforming to cultural rules for social interaction. This practical, social side of language is called **pragmatics,** and preschoolers make considerable headway in mastering it.

As early as age 2, children are skilled conversationalists. In face-to-face interaction, they take turns and respond appropriately to their partner's remarks (Pan & Snow, 1999). With age, the number of turns over which children can sustain interaction and their ability to maintain a topic over time increase, but even 2-year-olds converse effectively (Snow et al., 1996). These surprisingly advanced abilities probably grow out of early interactive experiences (see Chapter 6).

Indeed, the presence of a sibling seems to be especially conducive to acquiring the pragmatics of language. Preschoolers closely monitor conversations between their twin or older siblings and parents, and they often try to join in. When they do, these verbal exchanges last longer, with each participant taking more turns (Barton & Strosberg, 1997; Barton & Tomasello, 1991). As they listen to these conversations, young language learners pick up important skills, such as use of personal pronouns (*I* versus *you*), which are more common in the early vocabularies of later-born than of firstborn siblings (Pine, 1995). Furthermore, older siblings' remarks to a younger brother or sister often focus on regulating interaction: "Do you like Kermit?" "OK, your turn" (Oshima-Takane & Robbins, 2003). This emphasis probably contributes to younger siblings' conversational skills.

By age 4, children adapt their language to social expectations. For example, in acting out roles with hand puppets, they show that they understand the stereotypic features of different social positions. They use more commands when playing socially dominant and male roles (teacher, doctor, father) but speak more politely and use more indirect requests when playing less dominant and female roles (student, patient, mother) (Andersen, 2000).

Preschoolers' conversational skills occasionally do break down—for example, when talking on the phone. Here is an excerpt from one 4-year-old's phone conversation with his grandfather:

> *Grandfather:* "How old will you be?"
>
> *John:* "Dis many." [*Holding up four fingers*]
>
> *Grandfather:* "Huh?"
>
> *John:* "Dis many." [*Again holding up four fingers*] (Warren & Tate, 1992, pp. 259–260)

Young children's conversations appear less mature in highly demanding situations in which they cannot see their listeners' reactions or rely on typical conversational aids, such as gestures and objects to talk about. But when asked to tell a listener how to solve a simple puzzle, 3- to 6-year-olds give more specific directions over the phone than in person, indicating that they realize that more verbal description is necessary on the phone (Cameron & Lee, 1997).

Between ages 4 and 8, both conversing and giving directions over the phone improve greatly. Telephone talk provides yet another example of how preschoolers' competencies depend on the demands of the situation.

Supporting Language Learning in Early Childhood

How can adults foster preschoolers' language development? As in toddlerhood, interaction with more skilled speakers remains vital in early childhood. Conversational give-and-take with adults, either at home or in preschool, is consistently related to language progress (Hart & Risley, 1995; NICHD Early Child Care Research Network, 2000b). Furthermore, recall that language learning and literacy development are closely linked. Return to Applying What We Know on page 345, and notice how each strategy for supporting emergent literacy also fosters language progress.

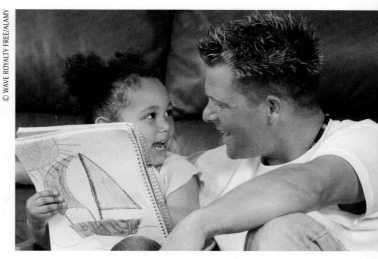

■ Adults can support preschoolers' grammatical learning through indirect feedback, including recasts and expansions. However, exposure to a rich language environment may be more important than these strategies, which are not used in all cultures. ■

Sensitive, caring adults use additional techniques that promote language skills. When children use words incorrectly or communicate unclearly, they give helpful, explicit feedback: "I can't tell which ball you want. Do you mean a large or small one or a red or green one?" But they do not overcorrect, especially when children make grammatical mistakes. Criticism discourages children from freely using language in ways that lead to new skills.

Instead, adults often provide indirect feedback about grammar by using two strategies, often in combination: **recasts**—restructuring inaccurate speech into correct form, and **expansions**—elaborating on children's speech, increasing its complexity (Bohannon & Stanowicz, 1988; Chouinard & Clark, 2003). For example, if a child says, "I gotted new red shoes," the parent might respond, "Yes, you got a pair of new red shoes." In one study, after such corrective input, 2- to 4-year-olds often shifted to correct forms—improvements still evident several months later (Saxton, Backley, & Galloway, 2005). However, the impact of such feedback has been challenged. The techniques are not used in all cultures and, in a few investigations, had no impact on children's grammar (Strapp & Federico, 2000; Valian, 1999). Rather than eliminating errors, perhaps expansions and recasts model grammatical alternatives and encourage children to experiment with them.

Do the findings just described remind you once again of Vygotsky's theory? In language, as in other aspects of intellectual growth, parents and teachers gently prompt young children to take the next developmental step forward. Children strive to master language because they want to connect with other people. Adults, in turn, respond to children's desire to become competent speakers by listening attentively, elaborating on what children say, modeling correct usage, and stimulating children to talk further. In the next chapter, we will see that this combination of warmth and encouragement of mature behavior is at the heart of early childhood emotional and social development as well.

◆ REVIEW Provide a list of recommendations for supporting language development in early childhood, noting research that supports each.

◆ APPLY Sammy's mother explained to him that the family would take a vacation in Miami. The next morning, Sammy announced, "I gotted my bags packed. When are we going to Your-ami?" What explains Sammy's errors?

◆ CONNECT Explain how children's strategies for word learning support the interactionist perspective on language development, described on page 236 in Chapter 6.

Summary

Piaget's Theory: The Preoperational Stage

Describe advances in mental representation, and limitations of thinking, during the preoperational stage.

- Rapid advances in mental representation, notably language and make-believe play, mark the beginning of Piaget's **preoperational stage.** With age, make-believe becomes increasingly complex, evident in **sociodramatic play** with peers. Make-believe supports many aspects of cognitive and social development. **Dual representation** improves rapidly over the third year of life as children realize that models, drawings, and simple maps correspond to circumstances in the real world.

- Aside from representation, Piaget described preschoolers in terms of deficits rather than strengths. Because **egocentrism** prevents them from reflecting on their own thinking and accommodating, it contributes to **animistic thinking, centration,** and **irreversibility.** These difficulties cause preschoolers to fail **conservation** and **hierarchical classification** tasks.

What does follow-up research imply about the accuracy of Piaget's preoperational stage?

- When young children are given familiar and simplified problems, their performance appears more mature than Piaget assumed. Preschoolers recognize differing perspectives, distinguish animate from inanimate objects, have flexible and appropriate notions of magic, and notice and reason about transformations and cause-and-effect relations. They also show impressive skill at categorizing on the basis of nonobservable characteristics and notice distinctions between appearance and reality, revealing that their thinking is not dominated by perceptual appearances.

- These findings challenge Piaget's concept of stage. Rather than being absent in the preschool years, operational thinking develops gradually.

What educational principles can be derived from Piaget's theory?

- A Piagetian classroom promotes discovery learning, sensitivity to children's readiness to learn, and acceptance of individual differences.

Vygotsky's Sociocultural Theory

Describe Vygotsky's perspective on the social origins and significance of children's private speech.

- In contrast to Piaget, Vygotsky regarded language as the foundation for all higher cognitive processes. According to Vygotsky, **private speech,** or language used for self-guidance, emerges out of social communication as adults and more skilled peers help children master challenging tasks within the zone of proximal development. Eventually, private speech is internalized as inner, verbal thought.

- **Intersubjectivity** and **scaffolding** are two features of social interaction that promote transfer of cognitive processes to children. **Guided participation** recognizes situational and cultural variations in adult support of children's efforts.

Describe applications of Vygotsky's theory to education, and evaluate his major ideas.

- A Vygotskian classroom emphasizes assisted discovery, in which both teacher guidance and peer collaboration are vitally important. Make-believe play is a unique, broadly influential zone of proximal development in early childhood.

- Vygotsky's theory helps us understand the wide cultural variation in cognitive skills. In some cultures, verbal communication is not the only means—or even the most important means—through which children learn. Vygotsky said little about how basic cognitive and motor capacities, which develop in infancy, contribute to socially transmitted higher cognitive processes.

Information Processing

How do attention, memory, and problem solving change during early childhood?

- Sustained attention increases sharply between ages 2½ and 3, due to increased activation of the prefrontal cortex, the capacity to generate complex play goals, adult scaffolding, and high-quality preschool education. **Planning** also improves, though on tasks with several steps, they are often unsystematic.

- Young children's recognition memory is remarkably accurate. But their recall of listlike information is poor because they use **memory strategies** less effectively than older children.

- **Episodic memory,** or memory for everyday experiences, improves greatly in early childhood. Like adults, preschoolers remember recurring events as **scripts,** which become more elaborate with age.

- As cognitive and conversational skills improve, children's autobiographical memories become better organized, detailed, and related to the larger context of their lives, especially when adults use an elaborative style to talk about the past.

- According to **overlapping-waves theory,** children try out various strategies to solve challenging problems, gradually selecting those that result in rapid, accurate solutions. Practice with strategies, reasoning, tasks with new challenges, and adult assistance contribute to improved problem solving.

Describe the young child's theory of mind.

- Preschoolers begin to construct a theory of mind, indicating that they are capable of **metacognition,** or thinking about thought. From age 4 on, they realize that both beliefs and desires can influence behavior, in that they pass verbal false-belief tasks.

- Language and cognitive skills, make-believe play, and mental-state talk with older siblings, friends, and adults all contribute to young children's awareness of false belief.

- Preschoolers regard the mind as a passive container of information. As a result, they have difficulty inferring what people know or are thinking about.

Summarize children's literacy and mathematical knowledge during early childhood.

- Young children's **emergent literacy** reveals that they understand a great deal about written language before they read and write in conventional ways. Preschoolers gradually revise incorrect ideas about the meaning of written symbols as their perceptual and cognitive capacities improve, as they encounter writing in many contexts, and as adults help them make sense of written information.

- Literacy development builds on a foundation of spoken language and knowledge about the world. **Phonological awareness** strongly predicts emergent literacy and later reading and spelling achievement. Adult–child narrative conversations and informal literacy experiences, such as interactive storybook reading, foster literacy development.

- Mathematical reasoning also builds on informal knowledge. Toddlers' beginning grasp of **ordinality** serves as the basis for more complex understandings. By age 3½ to 4, they grasp the principle of **cardinality,** which increases the efficiency of counting. Soon children experiment with diverse strategies to solve simple arithmetic problems. When adults provide many occasions for counting and comparing quantities, children construct basic numerical concepts sooner.

Individual Differences in Mental Development

Describe the content of early childhood intelligence tests and the impact of home, preschool and kindergarten programs, child care, and educational media on mental development.

- Intelligence tests in early childhood sample a range of verbal and nonverbal skills, including vocabulary, memory, quantitative knowledge, problem solving, and spatial reasoning. By age 6 to 7, scores are good predictors of later IQ and academic achievement.

- Children growing up in warm, stimulating homes with parents who make reasonable demands for mature behavior score higher on mental tests. Home environment plays a major role in the poorer intellectual performance of low-SES children in comparison to their higher-SES peers.

- Preschools and kindergartens range along a continuum from **child-centered programs,** in which much learning occurs through play, to **academic programs,** in which teachers structure children's learning, often using repetition and drill. Emphasizing formal academic training undermines children's motivation and negatively influences later achievement.

- **Project Head Start** is the most extensive federally funded preschool program for low-income children in the United States. High-quality preschool intervention results in immediate IQ and achievement gains and long-term improvements in school adjustment, educational attainment, and life success. The more parents are involved in Head Start, the higher their children's year-end academic, language, and social skills.

© ELLEN B. SENISI PHOTOGRAPHY

- Poor-quality child care undermines preschoolers' cognitive and social skills. In contrast, good child care enhances cognitive, language, and social development, especially for low-SES children.

- Children pick up academic knowledge from educational television and computer software. TV shows with slow-paced action and easy-to-follow story lines help preschoolers comprehend program content. Heavy exposure to entertainment TV, cartoons, and inappropriate computer games reduces time spent reading and interacting with others and is associated with poorer academic skills.

Language Development

Trace the development of vocabulary, grammar, and conversational skills in early childhood.

- Supported by **fast mapping,** preschoolers' vocabularies increase dramatically. According to one view, children are innately biased to induce word meanings using a **mutual exclusivity bias** and **syntactic bootstrapping.** An alternative perspective is that children use the same cognitive strategies they apply to nonlinguistic information. According to one account, preschoolers figure out word meanings from a coalition of cues—perceptual, social, and linguistic—which shift in importance with age.

- Between ages 2 and 3, children adopt the word order of their language. As they master grammatical constructions, they occasionally **overregularize,** applying the rules to words that are exceptions. By the end of the preschool years, children have acquired a wide variety of complex grammatical forms.

- Some experts believe that grammar is a product of general cognitive development. According to one view, children engage in **semantic bootstrapping,** relying on word meanings to figure out grammatical rules. Others agree with the essence of Chomsky's theory that children's brains are innately tuned for acquiring grammar.

- **Pragmatics** refers to the practical, social side of language. In face-to-face interaction with peers, young preschoolers are already skilled conversationalists. By age 4, they adapt their language to social expectations.

Cite factors that support language learning in early childhood.

- Conversational give-and-take with more skilled speakers fosters preschoolers' language skills. Adults provide both explicit feedback on the clarity of children's utterances and indirect feedback about grammar through **recasts** and **expansions.** However, these strategies, which are not used in all cultures, may be less important than mere exposure to a rich language environment.

IMPORTANT TERMS AND CONCEPTS

academic programs (p. 348)
animistic thinking (p. 321)
cardinality (p. 344)
centration (p. 322)
child-centered programs (p. 348)
conservation (p. 321)
dual representation (p. 320)
egocentrism (p. 321)
emergent literacy (p. 343)
episodic memory (p. 336)
expansions (p. 359)
fast mapping (p. 354)

guided participation (p. 331)
hierarchical classification (p. 322)
intersubjectivity (p. 331)
irreversibility (p. 322)
memory strategies (p. 336)
metacognition (p. 338)
mutual exclusivity bias (p. 355)
ordinality (p. 344)
overlapping-waves theory (p. 338)
overregularization (p. 357)
phonological awareness (p. 343)

planning (p. 335)
pragmatics (p. 358)
preoperational stage (p. 318)
private speech (p. 330)
Project Head Start (p. 349)
recasts (p. 359)
scaffolding (p. 331)
scripts (p. 336)
semantic bootstrapping (p. 357)
sociodramatic play (p. 319)
syntactic bootstrapping (p. 355)

"I Am Walking with Mama"
Tanya
4 years, Russia

A young child accompanies her mother on a winter walk. Warm, suppportive parenting provides a firm foundation for many facets of emotional and social development in early childhood, including self-concept and self-esteem, emotional understanding, peer relations, and morality.

Reprinted with permission from the International Collection of Child Art, Milner Library, Illinois State University, Normal, Illinois

Emotional and Social Development in Early Childhood

*A*s the children in Leslie's classroom moved through the preschool years, their personalities took on clearer definition. By age 3, they voiced firm likes and dislikes as well as new ideas about themselves. "Stop bothering me," Sammy said to Mark, who was reaching for Sammy's beanbag as Sammy aimed it toward the mouth of a large clown face. "See, I'm great at this game," Sammy announced with confidence, an attitude that kept him trying, even though he missed most of the throws.

The children's conversations also revealed their first notions about morality. Often they combined statements about right and wrong with forceful attempts to defend their own desires. "You're 'posed to share," stated Mark, grabbing the beanbag out of Sammy's hand.

"I was here first! Gimme it back," demanded Sammy, pushing Mark. The two boys struggled for the beanbag until Leslie intervened, provided an extra set of beanbags, and showed them how they could both play.

As the interaction between Sammy and Mark reveals, preschoolers have become complex social beings. Young children argue, grab, and push, but cooperative exchanges are far more frequent. Between ages 2 and 6, first friendships form, in which children converse, act out complementary roles, and learn that their own desires for companionship and toys are best met when they consider others' needs and interests.

The children's developing understanding of their social world was especially apparent in their growing attention to the dividing line between male and female. While Lynette and Karen cared for a sick baby doll in the housekeeping area, Sammy, Vance, and Mark transformed the block corner into a busy intersection. "Green light, go!" shouted police officer Sammy as Vance and Mark pushed large wooden cars and trucks across the floor. Already, the children preferred same-sex peers, and their play themes mirrored their culture's gender stereotypes.

This chapter is devoted to the many facets of early childhood emotional and social development. We begin with Erik Erikson's theory, which provides an overview of personality change in the preschool years. Then we consider children's concepts of themselves, their insights into their social and moral worlds, their gender typing, and their increasing ability to manage their emotional and social behaviors. Finally, we ask, What is effective child rearing? And we consider the complex conditions that support good parenting or lead it to break down, including the serious and widespread problems of child abuse and neglect.

Erikson's Theory: Initiative versus Guilt

Erikson (1950) described early childhood as a period of "vigorous unfolding." Once children have a sense of autonomy, they become less contrary than they were as toddlers. Their energies are freed for tackling the psychological conflict of the preschool years: **initiative versus guilt.** As the word *initiative* suggests, young children have a new sense of purposefulness. They are eager to tackle new tasks, join in activities with peers, and discover what they can do with the help of adults. They also make strides in conscience development.

Erikson regarded play as a means through which young children learn about themselves and their social world. Play permits preschoolers to try new skills with little risk of criticism and failure. It also creates a small social organization of children who must cooperate to achieve common goals. Around the world, children act out family scenes and highly visible occupations—police officer, doctor, and nurse in Western societies, rabbit hunter and potter among the Hopi Indians, hut builder and spear maker among the Baka of West Africa (Göncü, Patt, & Kouba, 2004).

Recall that Erikson's theory builds on Freud's psychosexual stages (see Chapter 1, page 16). In Freud's Oedipus and Electra conflicts, to avoid punishment and maintain the affection of parents, children form a *superego*, or conscience, by *identifying* with the same-sex parent. As a result, they adopt the moral and gender-role standards of their society. For Erikson, the negative outcome of early childhood is an overly strict superego that causes children to feel too much guilt because they have been threatened, criticized, and punished excessively by adults. When this happens, preschoolers' exuberant play and bold efforts to master new tasks break down.

Although Freud's ideas are no longer accepted as satisfactory explanations of conscience development, Erikson's image of initiative captures the diverse changes in young children's emotional and social lives. Early childhood is, indeed, a time when children develop a confident self-image, more effective control over their emotions, new social skills, the foundations of morality, and a clear sense of themselves as boy or girl. Now let's look closely at each of these aspects of development.

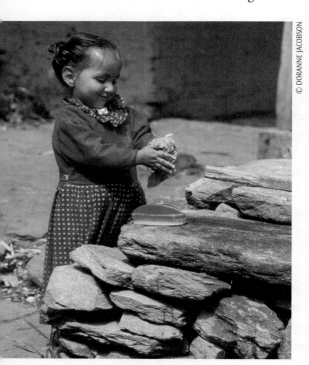

© DORANNE JACOBSON

■ This 3-year-old in India pretends to do laundry on the washing stone outside her family's home. Young children around the world act out family scenes and adult occupations, developing a sense of initiative as they gain insight into what they can do. ■

Self-Understanding

The development of language enables children to talk about their own subjective experience of being. In Chapter 9, we noted that preschoolers acquire a vocabulary for talking about their inner mental lives and refine their understanding of mental states. As self-awareness strengthens, children focus more intently on qualities that make the self unique. They begin to develop a **self-concept,** the set of attributes, abilities, attitudes, and values that an individual believes defines who he or she is. This mental representation of the self has profound implications for children's emotional and social lives, influencing their preferences for activities and social partners and their vulnerability to stress.

Foundations of Self-Concept

Ask a 3- to 5-year-old to tell you about him- or herself, and you are likely to hear something like this: "I'm Tommy. See, I got this new red T-shirt. I'm 4 years old. I can brush my teeth, and I can wash my hair all by myself. I have a new Tinkertoy set, and I made this big, big tower." Preschoolers' self-concepts largely consist of observable characteristics, such as their name, physical appearance, possessions, and everyday behaviors (Harter, 2006; Watson, 1990).

By age 3½, children also describe themselves in terms of typical emotions and attitudes ("I'm happy when I play with my friends"; "I don't like scary TV programs"; "I usually do what Mommy says"), suggesting a beginning understanding of their unique psychological characteristics (Eder & Mangelsdorf, 1997). And by age 5, children's degree of agreement with a battery of such statements coincides with maternal reports of their personality traits, indicating that older preschoolers have a sense of their own timidity, agreeableness, and positive or negative affect (Brown et al., 2008). As further support for this emerging grasp of personality, when given a trait label ("shy," "mean"), 4-year-olds infer appropriate motives and feelings. For example, they know that a shy person doesn't like to be with unfamiliar people (Heyman & Gelman, 1999). But preschoolers do not yet say "I'm helpful" or "I'm shy." Direct references to personality traits must wait for greater cognitive maturity.

A warm, sensitive parent–child relationship seems to foster a more positive, coherent early self-concept. In one study, 4-year-olds with a secure attachment to their mothers were more likely than their insecurely attached agemates to describe themselves in favorable terms at age 5—with statements that reflect agreeableness and positive affect (Goodvin et al., 2008). Also, recall from Chapter 9 that securely attached preschoolers participate in more elaborative parent–child conversations about personally experienced events, which help them understand themselves. Elaborative reminiscing is associated with a more organized, detailed autobiographical memory and with greater consistency in 5- and 6-year-olds' reports of their personal characteristics (see page 337). When, in past-event conversations, a child discovers that she finds swimming, getting together with friends, and going to the zoo fun, she can begin to connect these specific experiences into a general understanding of "what I enjoy," yielding a clearer image of herself (Farrant & Reese, 2000).

As early as age 2, parents use narratives of past events to impart rules, standards for behavior, and evaluative information about the child: "You added the milk when we made the mashed potatoes. That's a very important job!" (Nelson, 2003). As the Cultural Influences box on page 366 reveals, these self-evaluative narratives are a major means through which caregivers imbue the young child's self-concept with cultural values.

As they talk about personally significant events and as their cognitive skills advance, preschoolers gradually come to view themselves as persisting over time. Around age 4, children first become certain that a video image of themselves replayed shortly after it was filmed is still "me" (Povinelli, 2001). Similarly, when researchers asked 3- to 5-year-olds to imagine a future event (walking next to a waterfall) and to envision a future personal state by choosing from three items (a raincoat, money, a blanket) the one they would need to bring with them, performance—along with future-state justifications ("I'm gonna get wet")—increased sharply from age 3 to 4 (Atance & Meltzoff, 2005).

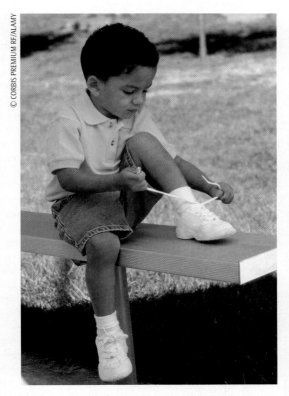

■ When asked to tell about themselves, preschoolers typically mention observable characteristics—physical appearance, possessions, and everyday behaviors and skills, such as "I can tie my own shoes." They also have an emerging grasp of their unique psychological characteristics—for this 5-year-old, persistence and determination! ■

CULTURAL INFLUENCES

Cultural Variations in Personal Storytelling: Implications for Early Self-Concept

*P*reschoolers of many cultural backgrounds participate in personal storytelling with their parents. Striking cultural differences exist in parents' selection and interpretation of events in these narratives, affecting the way children view themselves.

In one study, researchers spent hundreds of hours over a two-year period studying the storytelling practices of six middle-SES Irish-American families in Chicago and six middle-SES Chinese families in Taiwan. From extensive videotapes of adults' conversations with 2½-year-olds, the investigators identified personal stories and coded them for content, quality of their endings, and evaluation of the child (Miller, Fung, & Mintz, 1996; Miller et al., 1997).

Parents in both cultures discussed pleasurable holidays and family excursions in similar ways and with similar frequency. But Chinese parents more often told long stories about the child's misdeeds—using impolite language, writing on the wall, or playing in an overly rowdy way. These narratives were conveyed with warmth and caring, stressed the impact of misbehavior on others ("You made Mama lose face"), and often ended with direct teaching of proper behavior ("Saying dirty words is not good"). By contrast, in the few instances in which Irish-American stories referred to transgressions, parents downplayed their seriousness, attributing them to the child's spunk and assertiveness.

Early narratives about the child seem to launch preschoolers' self-concepts on culturally distinct paths (Miller, Fung, & Koven, 2007). Influenced by Confucian traditions of strict discipline and social obligations, Chinese parents integrated these values into their stories, affirming the importance of not disgracing the family and explicitly conveying expectations in the story's conclusion. Although Irish-American parents disciplined their children, they rarely dwelt on misdeeds in storytelling. Rather, they cast the child's shortcomings in a positive light, perhaps to promote self-esteem.

Whereas most Americans believe that favorable self-esteem is crucial for healthy development, Chinese adults generally see it as unimportant or even negative—as impeding the child's willingness to listen and to be corrected (Miller et al., 2002). Consistent with this view, the Chinese parents did little to cultivate their child's individuality. Instead, they used storytelling to guide the child toward socially responsible behavior. Hence, by the end of the preschool years, the Chinese child's self-image emphasizes membership in the collective and obligations to others ("I belong to the Lee family"; "I like to help my mom wash dishes"), whereas the American child's is more autonomous, consisting largely of personal descriptions ("I do lots of puzzles"; "I like hockey") (Wang, 2004).

■ A Chinese mother speaks gently to her children about proper behavior. Chinese parents often point out how their child's misdeeds affect others. The Chinese child's self-concept, in turn, emphasizes social obligations. ■

Emergence of Self-Esteem

Another aspect of self-concept emerges in early childhood: **self-esteem,** the judgments we make about our own worth and the feelings associated with those judgments. **TAKE A MOMENT...** Make a list of your own self-judgments. Notice that, besides a global appraisal of your worth as a person, you have a variety of separate self-evaluations concerning different activities. These evaluations are among the most important aspects of self-development because they affect our emotional experiences, future behavior, and long-term psychological adjustment.

By age 4, preschoolers have several self-judgments—for example, about learning things well in school, making friends, getting along with parents, and treating others kindly (Marsh, Ellis, & Craven, 2002). But because they have difficulty distinguishing between their desired and their actual competence, they usually rate their own ability as extremely high and often underestimate task difficulty, as Sammy did when he asserted, despite his many misses, that he was great at beanbag throwing (Harter, 2003, 2006).

High self-esteem contributes greatly to preschoolers' initiative during a period in which they must master many new skills. By age 3, children whose parents patiently encourage while offering information about how to succeed are enthusiastic and highly motivated. In contrast, children with a history of parental criticism of their worth and performance give up easily when faced with a challenge and express shame and despondency after failing (Kelley, Brownell, & Campbell, 2000). When preschool nonpersisters use dolls to act out an adult's reaction to failure, they anticipate disapproval—saying, for example, "He's punished because he can't do the puzzle" (Burhans & Dweck, 1995). They are also likely to report that their parents berate them for making small mistakes (Heyman, Dweck, & Cain, 1992). Adults can avoid promoting these self-defeating reactions by adjusting their expectations to children's capacities, scaffolding children's attempts at difficult tasks (see Chapter 9, page 331), and pointing out effort and improvement in children's work or behavior.

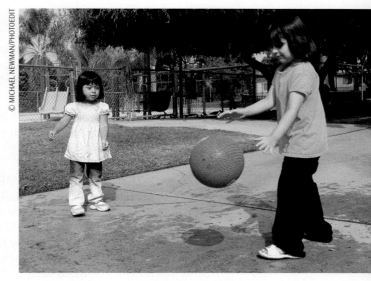

■ This 4-year-old probably overestimates how adept she is at playing catch with her older sister. But her high self-esteem contributes to her enthusiasm and motivation to master new skills. ■

ASK YOURSELF

◆ REVIEW Why is self-esteem typically extremely high in early childhood?

◆ APPLY Reread the description of Sammy and Mark's argument at the beginning of this chapter. On the basis of what you know about self-development, why was it a good idea for Leslie to resolve the dispute by providing an extra set of beanbags?

◆ REFLECT When you were a child, did your parents actively promote your self-esteem? How did their efforts reflect your family's cultural background? Explain.

Emotional Development

Gains in representation, language, and self-concept support emotional development in early childhood. Between ages 2 and 6, children make strides in the emotional abilities that, collectively, researchers refer to as *emotional competence* (Halberstadt, Denham, & Dunsmore, 2001; Saarni et al., 2006). First, preschoolers gain in emotional understanding, becoming better able to talk about feelings and to respond appropriately to others' emotional signals. Second, they become better at emotional self-regulation—in particular, at coping with intense negative emotion. Finally, preschoolers more often experience *self-conscious emotions* and *empathy*, which contribute to their developing sense of morality.

Parenting strongly influences preschoolers' emotional competence. Emotional competence, in turn, is vital for successful peer relationships and overall emotional health.

Understanding Emotion

Preschoolers' vocabulary for talking about emotion expands rapidly, and they use it skillfully to reflect on their own and others' behavior. Here are some excerpts from conversations in which 2-year-olds and 6-year-olds commented on emotionally charged experiences:

Two-year-old: [*After father shouted at child, she became angry, shouting back*] "I'm mad at you, Daddy. I'm going away. Good-bye."

Two-year-old: [*Commenting on another child who refused to nap and cried*] "Mom, Annie cry. Annie sad."

Six-year-old: [*In response to mother's comment, "It's hard to hear the baby crying"*] "Well, it's not as hard for me as it is for you." [*When mother asked why*] "Well, you like Johnny better than I do! I like him a little, and you like him a lot, so I think it's harder for you to hear him cry."

Six-year-old: [*Trying to comfort a small boy in church whose mother had gone up to communion*] "Aw, that's all right. She'll be right back. Don't be afraid. I'm here." (Bretherton et al., 1986, pp. 536, 540, 541)

COGNITIVE DEVELOPMENT AND EMOTIONAL UNDERSTANDING As these examples show, early in the preschool years, children refer to causes, consequences, and behavioral signs of emotion, and over time their understanding becomes more accurate and complex (Stein & Levine, 1999). By age 4 to 5, they correctly judge the causes of many basic emotions ("He's happy because he's swinging very high"; "He's sad because he misses his mother"). Preschoolers' explanations tend to emphasize external factors over internal states, a balance that changes with age (Levine, 1995). In Chapter 9, we saw that after age 4, children appreciate that both desires and beliefs motivate behavior. Once these understandings are secure, children's grasp of how internal factors can trigger emotion expands.

Preschoolers can also predict what a playmate expressing a certain emotion might do next. Four-year-olds know that an angry child might hit someone and that a happy child is more likely to share (Russell, 1990). And they realize that thinking and feeling are interconnected—that a person reminded of a previous sad experience is likely to feel sad (Lagattuta, Wellman, & Flavell, 1997). Furthermore, they come up with effective ways to relieve others' negative feelings, such as hugging to reduce sadness (Fabes et al., 1988). Overall, preschoolers have an impressive ability to interpret, predict, and change others' feelings.

At the same time, preschoolers have difficulty interpreting situations that offer conflicting cues about how a person is feeling. When shown a picture of a happy-faced child with a broken bicycle, 4- and 5-year-olds tended to rely only on the emotional expression: "He's happy because he likes to ride his bike." Older children more often reconciled the two cues: "He's happy because his father promised to help fix his broken bike" (Gnepp, 1983; Hoffner & Badzinski, 1989). As in their approach to Piagetian tasks, young children focus on the most obvious aspect of a complex emotional situation to the neglect of other relevant information.

SOCIAL EXPERIENCE AND EMOTIONAL UNDERSTANDING The more mothers label emotions, explain them, and express warmth and enthusiasm when conversing with preschoolers, the more "emotion words" children use and the better developed their emotional understanding (Fivush & Haden, 2005; Laible & Song, 2006). Maternal prompting of emotional thoughts ("What makes him afraid?") is a good predictor of 2-year-olds' emotion language. For older preschoolers, explanations ("He's sad because his dog ran away") are more important (Cervantes & Callanan, 1998). Does this remind you of the concept of *scaffolding*—that to be effective, adult teaching must adjust to children's increasing competence?

Preschoolers whose parents frequently acknowledge their children's emotional reactions and talk about diverse emotions are better able to judge others' emotions when tested at later ages (Denham & Kochanoff, 2002). Discussions in which family members disagree are particularly helpful. In one study, when mothers explained feelings and negotiated and compromised during conflicts with their 2½-year-olds, their children, at age 3, were advanced in emotional understanding and used similar strategies to resolve disagreements (Laible & Thompson, 2002). Such dialogues seem to help children reflect on the causes and consequences of emotion while also modeling mature communication skills. Furthermore, preschoolers who are securely attached to their mothers better understand emotion. Attachment security, as we have seen, is related to more elaborative parent–child narratives, including discussions of feelings that highlight the emotional significance of past events (Laible, 2004; Laible & Song, 2006; Raikes & Thompson, 2006).

As preschoolers learn more about emotion from interacting with adults, they engage in more emotion talk with siblings and friends, especially during make-believe play (Brown,

Donelan-McCall, & Dunn, 1996; Hughes & Dunn, 1998). Make-believe, in turn, contributes to emotional understanding, especially when children play with siblings (Youngblade & Dunn, 1995). The intense nature of the sibling relationship, combined with frequent acting out of feelings, makes pretending an excellent context for early learning about emotions. And when parents intervene in sibling disputes by reasoning and negotiating, preschoolers gain in sensitivity to their siblings' feelings (Perlman & Ross, 1997). They more often refer to their sibling's emotional perspective ("You get mad when I don't share") and engage in less fighting.

Knowledge about emotions helps children greatly in their efforts to get along with others. As early as 3 to 5 years of age, it is related to friendly, considerate behavior, willingness to make amends after harming another, and constructive responses to disputes with agemates (Brown & Dunn, 1996; Dunn, Brown, & Maguire, 1995; Garner & Estep, 2001). Also, the more preschoolers refer to feelings when interacting with playmates, the better liked they are by their peers (Fabes et al., 2001). Children seem to recognize that acknowledging others' emotions and explaining their own enhance the quality of relationships.

■ During the preschool years, children's understanding of the causes, consequences, and behavioral signs of emotion expands rapidly. Children whose mothers label and explain emotions use more "emotion words" and have better developed emotional understanding. ■

Emotional Self-Regulation

Language also contributes to preschoolers' improved *emotional self-regulation,* or ability to control the expression of emotion. By age 3 to 4, children verbalize a variety of strategies for adjusting their emotional arousal to a more comfortable level. For example, they know they can blunt emotions by restricting sensory input (covering their eyes or ears to block out a scary sight or sound), talking to themselves ("Mommy said she'll be back soon"), or changing their goals (deciding that they don't want to play anyway after being excluded from a game) (Thompson & Goodvin, 2007).

As children use these strategies, emotional outbursts decline. *Effortful control*—in particular, inhibiting impulses and shifting attention—also continues to be vital in managing emotion in early childhood. Three-year-olds who can distract themselves when frustrated tend to become cooperative school-age children with few problem behaviors (Gilliom et al., 2002). By age 3, effortful control predicts children's skill at portraying an emotion they do not feel—for example, reacting cheerfully after receiving an undesirable gift (Kieras et al., 2005). These emotional "masks" are largely limited to the positive feelings of happiness and surprise. Children of all ages (and adults as well) find it harder to act sad, angry, or disgusted than pleased (Denham, 1998). To promote good social relations, most cultures teach children to communicate positive feelings and inhibit unpleasant ones.

Temperament affects the development of emotional self-regulation. Children who experience negative emotion intensely find it harder to inhibit feelings and shift attention away from disturbing events. They are more likely to be anxious and fearful, respond with irritation to others' distress, react angrily or aggressively when frustrated, and get along poorly with teachers and peers (Chang et al., 2003; Eisenberg et al., 2005; Raikes et al., 2007).

To avoid social difficulties, emotionally reactive children must develop effective emotion-regulation strategies (Rothbart & Bates, 2006). By watching parents manage their feelings, children learn strategies for regulating their own. Warm, sensitive parents who use verbal guidance, including suggesting and explaining emotion-regulation strategies, strengthen children's capacity to handle stress (Colman et al., 2006). In contrast, when parents rarely express positive emotion, dismiss children's feelings as unimportant, and have difficulty controlling their own anger, children have continuing problems in managing emotion that seriously interfere with psychological adjustment (Hill et al., 2006; Katz & Windecker-Nelson, 2004; Thompson & Meyer, 2007). And because emotionally reactive children become increasingly difficult to rear, they are often targets of ineffective parenting, which compounds their poor self-regulation.

Applying What We Know

Helping Children Manage Common Fears of Early Childhood

FEAR	SUGGESTION
Monsters, ghosts, and darkness	Reduce exposure to frightening stories in books and on TV until the child is better able to distinguish between appearance and reality. Make a thorough "search" of the child's room for monsters, showing him that none are there. Leave a night-light burning, sit by the child's bed until he falls asleep, and tuck in a favorite toy for protection.
Preschool or child care	If the child resists going to preschool but seems content once there, the fear is probably separation. Provide a sense of warmth and caring while gently encouraging independence. If the child fears being at preschool, try to find out what is frightening—the teacher, the children, or a crowded, noisy environment. Provide extra support by accompanying the child and gradually lessening the amount of time you are present.
Animals	Do not force the child to approach a dog, cat, or other animal that arouses fear. Let the child move at her own pace. Demonstrate how to hold and pet the animal, showing the child that when treated gently, the animal is friendly. If the child is larger than the animal, emphasize this: "You're so big. That kitty is probably afraid of *you*!"
Intense fears	If a child's fear is intense, persists for a long time, interferes with daily activities, and cannot be reduced in any of the ways just suggested, it has reached the level of a *phobia*. Sometimes phobias are linked to family problems, and counseling is needed to reduce them. At other times, phobias diminish without treatment as the child's capacity for emotional self-regulation improves.

Adults' conversations with children also foster emotional self-regulation (Thompson, 2006). Parents who prepare children for difficult experiences by describing what to expect and ways to handle anxiety offer coping strategies that children can apply. Preschoolers' vivid imaginations and incomplete grasp of the distinction between appearance and reality make fears common in early childhood. Consult Applying What We Know above for ways adults can help young children manage fears.

Self-Conscious Emotions

One morning in Leslie's classroom, a group of children crowded around for a bread-baking activity. Leslie asked them to wait patiently while she got a baking pan. But Sammy reached over to feel the dough, and the bowl tumbled off the table. When Leslie returned, Sammy looked at her, then covered his eyes with his hands, and said, "I did something bad." He felt ashamed and guilty.

As their self-concepts develop, preschoolers become increasingly sensitive to praise and blame or (as Sammy did) to the possibility of such feedback. As a result, they more often experience *self-conscious emotions*—feelings that involve injury to or enhancement of their sense of self (see Chapter 7). By age 3, self-conscious emotions are clearly linked to self-evaluation (Lewis, 1995). But because preschoolers are still developing standards of excellence and conduct, they depend on the messages of parents, teachers, and others who matter to them to know *when* to feel proud, ashamed, or guilty, often viewing adult expectations as obligatory rules ("Dad said you're 'posed to take turns") (Thompson, Meyer, & McGinley, 2006).

When parents repeatedly comment on the worth of the child and her performance ("That's a bad job! I thought you were a good girl"), children experience self-conscious emotions intensely—more shame after failure, more pride after success. In contrast, when parents focus on how to improve performance ("You did it this way; now try doing it that way"), they induce moderate, more adaptive levels of shame and pride and greater persistence on difficult tasks (Kelley, Brownell, & Campbell, 2000; Lewis, 1998).

Beginning in early childhood, intense shame is associated with feelings of personal inadequacy ("I'm stupid"; "I'm a terrible person") and with maladjustment—withdrawal and depression as well as intense anger and aggression toward those who participated in the shame-evoking situation (Lindsay-Hartz, de Rivera, & Mascolo, 1995; Mills, 2005). In contrast, guilt—when it occurs in appropriate circumstances and is neither excessive nor accompanied by shame—is related to good adjustment. Guilt helps children resist harmful impulses, and it motivates a misbehaving child to repair the damage and behave more considerately (Mascolo

& Fischer, 2007; Tangney, Stuewig, & Mashek, 2007). But overwhelming guilt—involving such high emotional distress that the child cannot make amends—is linked to depressive symptoms as early as age 3 (Luby et al., 2009).

Finally, the consequences of shame for children's adjustment may vary across cultures. As illustrated in the Cultural Influences box on page 366, people in Asian collectivist societies, who define themselves in relation to their social group, view shame as an adaptive reminder of an interdependent self and of the importance of others' judgments (Bedford, 2004).

Empathy and Sympathy

Another emotional capacity that becomes more common in early childhood is *empathy,* which serves as an important motivator of **prosocial,** or **altruistic, behavior**—actions that benefit another person without any expected reward for the self (Eisenberg, Fabes, & Spinrad, 2006). Compared with toddlers, preschoolers rely more on words to communicate empathic feelings, a change that indicates a more reflective level of empathy. When a 4-year-old received a Christmas gift that she hadn't included on her list for Santa, she assumed it belonged to another little girl and pleaded with her parents, "We've got to give it back—Santa's made a big mistake. I think the girl's crying 'cause she didn't get her present!" As the ability to take the perspective of others improves, empathic responding increases.

Yet empathy—*feeling with* another person and responding emotionally in a similar way—does not always yield acts of kindness and helpfulness. For some children, empathizing with an upset adult or peer escalates into *personal distress.* In trying to reduce these feelings, the child focuses on his own anxiety rather than on the person in need. As a result, empathy does not lead to **sympathy**—feelings of concern or sorrow for another's plight.

Temperament plays a role in whether empathy prompts sympathetic, prosocial behavior or a personally distressed, self-focused response. Children who are sociable, assertive, and good at regulating emotion are more likely to help, share, and comfort others in distress. But poor emotion regulators less often display sympathetic concern and prosocial behavior (Bengston, 2005; Eisenberg et al., 1998; Valiente et al., 2004). When faced with someone in need, they react with facial and physiological distress—frowning, lip biting, a rise in heart rate, and a sharp increase in EEG brain-wave activity in the right cerebral hemisphere, which houses negative emotion—indications that they are overwhelmed by their feelings (Jones, Field, & Davalos, 2000; Pickens, Field, & Nawrocki, 2001).

As with other aspects of emotional development, parenting affects empathy and sympathy. When parents are warm, encourage emotional expressiveness, and show sensitive, empathic concern for their preschoolers' feelings, their children are likely to react in a concerned way to the distress of others—relationships that persist into adolescence and young adulthood (Koestner, Franz, & Weinberger, 1990; Michalik et al., 2007; Strayer & Roberts, 2004). Besides modeling sympathy, parents can teach children the importance of kindness and can intervene when they display inappropriate emotion—strategies that predict high levels of sympathetic responding (Eisenberg, 2003).

In contrast, angry, punitive parenting disrupts the development of empathy at an early age—particularly among children who are poor emotion regulators and who therefore respond to parental hostility with especially high personal distress (Valiente et al., 2004). In one study, physically abused preschoolers at a child-care center rarely expressed concern at a peer's unhappiness but, rather, reacted with fear, anger, and physical attacks (Klimes-Dougan & Kistner, 1990). The children's behavior resembled their parents' insensitive responses to the suffering of others.

© ELLEN B. SENISI PHOTOGRAPHY

■ As children's language skills and ability to take the perspective of others improve, empathy also increases, motivating prosocial, or altruistic, behavior. ■

◆ REVIEW What do preschoolers understand about emotion, and how do cognition and social experience contribute to their understanding?

◆ APPLY Four-year-old Tia had her face painted at a carnival. As she walked around with her mother, the heat of the afternoon caused her balloon to pop. When Tia started to cry, her mother said, "Oh, Tia, balloons aren't such a good idea when it's hot outside. We'll get another on a cooler day. If you cry, you'll mess up your beautiful face painting." What aspect of emotional development is Tia's mother trying to promote, and why is her intervention likely to help Tia?

◆ CONNECT Cite ways that parenting contributes to preschoolers' self-concept, self-esteem, emotional understanding, emotional self-regulation, self-conscious emotions, and empathy and sympathy. Do you see any patterns? Explain.

■■ Peer Relations
■■

As children become increasingly self-aware and better at communicating and understanding the thoughts and feelings of others, their skill at interacting with peers improves rapidly. Peers provide young children with learning experiences they can get in no other way. Because peers interact on an equal footing, they must keep a conversation going, cooperate, and set goals in play. With peers, children form friendships—special relationships marked by attachment and common interests. Let's look at how peer interaction changes over the preschool years.

Advances in Peer Sociability

Mildred Parten (1932), one of the first to study peer sociability among 2- to 5-year-olds, noticed a dramatic rise with age in joint, interactive play. She concluded that social development proceeds in a three-step sequence. It begins with **nonsocial activity**—unoccupied, onlooker behavior and solitary play. Then it shifts to **parallel play,** a limited form of social participation in which a child plays near other children with similar materials but does not try to influence their behavior. At the highest level are two forms of true social interaction. In **associative play,** children engage in separate activities but exchange toys and comment on one another's behavior. Finally, in **cooperative play,** a more advanced type of interaction, children orient toward a common goal, such as acting out a make-believe theme.

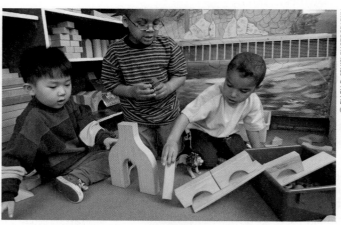

■ These 4-year-olds *(left)* engage in parallel play. Cooperative play *(right)* develops later than parallel play, but preschool children continue to move back and forth between the two types of sociability, often using parallel play as a respite from the complex demands of cooperation. ■

FOLLOW-UP RESEARCH ON PEER SOCIABILITY   Longitudinal evidence indicates that these play forms emerge in the order Parten suggested but that later-appearing ones do not replace earlier ones in a developmental sequence (Rubin, Bukowski, & Parker, 2006). Rather, all types coexist during early childhood.

TAKE A MOMENT... Watch preschool children move from one type of play to another in a play group or classroom, and you will see that they often transition from onlooker to parallel to cooperative play and back again (Robinson et al., 2003). Preschoolers seem to use parallel play as a way station. To successfully join the ongoing play of peers, they often first engage in parallel play nearby, easing into the group's activities—a strategy that increases the likelihood of being accepted. Later, they may return to parallel play as a respite from the high demands of complex social interaction and as a crossroad to new activities. And although nonsocial activity declines with age, it is still the most frequent form among 3- to 4-year-olds. Even among kindergartners it continues to occupy about one-third of children's free-play time. Both solitary and parallel play remain fairly stable from 3 to 6 years, accounting for as much of the young child's play as highly social, cooperative interaction (Rubin, Fein, & Vandenberg, 1983).

We now understand that it is the *type,* not the amount, of solitary and parallel play that changes during early childhood. In studies of preschoolers' play in Taiwan and the United States, researchers rated the *cognitive maturity* of nonsocial, parallel, and cooperative play by applying the categories shown in Table 10.1. Within each play type, older children displayed more cognitively mature behavior than younger children (Pan, 1994; Rubin, Watson, & Jambor, 1978).

Often parents wonder whether a preschooler who spends large amounts of time playing alone is developing normally. But only *certain types* of nonsocial activity—aimless wandering, hovering near peers, and functional play involving immature, repetitive motor action—are cause for concern. Children who behave reticently, by watching peers without playing, are usually temperamentally inhibited—high in social fearfulness. Their parents frequently overprotect them, criticize their social awkwardness, and unnecessarily control their play activities instead of patiently encouraging them to approach other children and helping them form at least one rewarding friendship, which protects against persisting adjustment problems (Coplan et al., 2004; Rubin, Bukowski, & Parker, 2006; Rubin, Burgess, & Hastings, 2002). And preschoolers who engage in solitary, repetitive behavior (banging blocks, making a doll jump up and down) tend to be immature, impulsive children who find it difficult to regulate anger and aggression (Coplan et al., 2001). In the classroom, both reticent and impulsive children experience peer ostracism, with boys at greater risk for rejection than girls (Coplan & Arbeau, 2008).

But other preschoolers with low rates of peer interaction are not socially anxious or impulsive. They simply prefer to play alone, and their solitary activities are positive and constructive. Teachers encourage such play by setting out art materials, books, puzzles, and building toys. Children who spend much time at these activities are usually well-adjusted youngsters who, when they do play with peers, show socially skilled behavior (Coplan & Armer, 2007). Still, a few preschoolers who engage in such age-appropriate solitary play—again, more often boys— are rebuffed by peers. Perhaps because quiet play is inconsistent with the "masculine" gender role, boys who engage in it are at risk for negative reactions from both parents and peers and, eventually, for adjustment problems (Coplan et al., 2001, 2004).

LOOK AND LISTEN

◆◆

Observe several 3- to 5-year-olds during a free-play period in a preschool or child-care program. How much time does each child devote to nonsocial activity, parallel play, and socially interactive play? Do children seem to use parallel play as a way station between activities?

TABLE 10.1   Developmental Sequence of Cognitive Play Categories

PLAY CATEGORY	DESCRIPTION	EXAMPLES
Functional play	Simple, repetitive motor movements with or without objects, especially common during the first two years	Running around a room, rolling a car back and forth, kneading clay with no intent to make something
Constructive play	Creating or constructing something, especially common between 3 and 6 years	Making a house out of toy blocks, drawing a picture, putting together a puzzle
Make-believe play	Acting out everyday and imaginary roles, especially common between 2 and 6 years	Playing house, school, or police officer; acting out storybook or television characters

Source: Rubin, Fein, & Vandenberg, 1983.

■ These village children in India play a "circle tapping" game requiring high levels of cooperation. The child in the center recites a poem, the alphabet, or numbers, then walks around the circle saying, "Whomever I tap, it will be their turn." The tapped child moves to the center to recite. ■

As noted in Chapter 9, *sociodramatic play*—an advanced form of cooperative play—becomes especially common over the preschool years and supports cognitive, emotional, and social development (Göncü, Patt, & Kouba, 2004). In joint make-believe, preschoolers act out and respond to one another's pretend feelings. They also explore and gain control of fear-arousing experiences when they play doctor or pretend to search for monsters in a magical forest. As a result, they can better understand others' feelings and regulate their own (Smith, 2003). Finally, preschoolers spend much time negotiating roles and rules in play. To create and manage complex plots, they must resolve their disputes through negotiation and compromise. With age, preschoolers' conflicts center less on toys and other resources and more on differences of opinion—an indication of their expanding capacity to consider others' attitudes and ideas (Chen, Fein, & Tam, 2001; Hay, Payne, & Chadwick, 2004).

CULTURAL VARIATIONS   Peer sociability in collectivist societies, which stress group harmony, takes different forms than in individualistic cultures (Chen & French, 2008). For example, children in India generally play in large groups. Much of their behavior is imitative, occurs in unison, and involves close physical contact—a play style requiring high levels of cooperation. In a game called Bhatto Bhatto, children act out a script about a trip to the market, touching one another's elbows and hands as they pretend to cut and share a tasty vegetable (Roopnarine et al., 1994).

As another example, Chinese preschoolers—unlike North American preschoolers, who tend to reject reticent classmates—are typically willing to include a quiet, reserved child in play (Chen et al., 2006). In Chapter 7, we saw that until recently collectivist values, which discourage self-assertion, led to positive evaluations of shyness in China (see page 263). Apparently, this benevolent attitude is still evident in the play behaviors of young Chinese children.

Cultural beliefs about the importance of play also affect early peer associations. Caregivers who view play as mere entertainment are less likely to provide props or to encourage pretend than those who value its cognitive and social benefits (Farver & Wimbarti, 1995). Preschool children of Korean-American parents, who emphasize task persistence as vital for learning, spend less time than Caucasian-American children in joint make-believe and more time unoccupied and in parallel play (Farver, Kim, & Lee, 1995).

Recall the description of children's daily lives in village and tribal cultures, described on page 333 in Chapter 9. Mayan parents, for example, do not promote children's play—yet Mayan children are socially competent (Gaskins, 2000). Perhaps Western-style sociodramatic play, with its elaborate materials and wide-ranging themes, is particularly important for social development in societies where the worlds of adults and children are distinct. It may be less crucial in village cultures where children participate in adult activities from an early age.

First Friendships

As preschoolers interact, first friendships form that serve as important contexts for emotional and social development. **TAKE A MOMENT...** Jot down a description of what *friendship* means to you. You probably pictured a mutual relationship involving companionship, sharing, understanding of thoughts and feelings, and caring for and comforting one another in times of need. In addition, mature friendships endure over time and survive occasional conflicts.

Preschoolers understand something about the uniqueness of friendship. They say that a friend is someone "who likes you" and with whom you spend a lot of time playing. Yet their ideas about friendship are far from mature. Four- to 7-year-olds regard friendship as pleasurable play and sharing of toys. But friendship does not yet have a long-term, enduring quality based on mutual trust (Damon, 1988; Hartup, 2006). "Mark's my best friend," Sammy would declare on days when the boys got along well. But when a dispute arose, he would reverse himself: "Mark, you're not my friend!"

Nevertheless, interactions between young friends are unique. Preschoolers give twice as much reinforcement—greetings, praise, and compliance—to children they identify as friends, and they also receive more from them. Friends play together in more complex ways and are more cooperative and emotionally expressive—talking, laughing, and looking at each other more often than nonfriends do (Hartup, 2006; Vaughn et al., 2001). And early childhood friendships offer social support: Children who begin kindergarten with friends in their class or readily make new friends adjust to school more favorably (Ladd, Birch, & Buhs, 1999; Ladd & Price, 1987). Perhaps the company of friends serves as a secure base from which to develop new relationships, enhancing children's feelings of comfort in the new classroom.

Peer Relations and School Readiness

The ease with which kindergartners make new friends and are accepted by their classmates predicts cooperative participation in classroom activities and self-directed completion of learning tasks. These behaviors, in turn, are related to gains in achievement over the kindergarten year (Ladd, Birch, & Buhs, 1999; Ladd, Buhs, & Seid, 2000). Of course, kindergartners with friendly, prosocial behavioral styles make new friends easily, whereas those with weak emotional self-regulation skills and argumentative, aggressive, or peer-avoidant styles establish poor-quality relationships and make few friends. These negative social outcomes impair children's liking for school, classroom participation, and academic learning (Birch & Ladd, 1998).

The capacity to form mutually rewarding friendships, cooperate with peers, and build positive relationships with teachers enables kindergartners to integrate themselves into classroom environments in ways that foster both academic and social competence. In a longitudinal follow-up of more than 900 4-year-olds, children of average intelligence but with above-average social skills fared better in academic achievement in first grade than children of equal mental ability who were socially below average (Konold & Pianta, 2005). Because social maturity in early childhood contributes to later academic performance, a growing number of experts propose that readiness for kindergarten be assessed in terms of not just academic skills but also social skills, including capacity to form supportive bonds with teachers and peers, to participate actively and positively in interactions with classmates, and to behave prosocially (Ladd, Herald, & Kochel, 2006; Thompson & Raikes, 2007).

■ In evaluating readiness for school, children's capacity for friendly, cooperative interaction is just as important as their academic skills. ■

Preschool programs, too, should attend to these vital social prerequisites. Warm, responsive teacher–child interaction is vital, especially for temperamentally shy, impulsive, and emotionally negative children, who are at high risk for social difficulties (McClelland et al., 2007). In studies involving several thousand 4-year-olds in public preschools in six states, teacher sensitivity and emotional support were especially potent predictors of children's social competence during preschool and in a follow-up after kindergarten entry (Curby et al., 2009; Mashburn et al., 2008). Along with excellent teacher preparation, other indicators of program quality—small group sizes, generous teacher–child ratios, and developmentally appropriate daily activities (see page 352)—create classroom conditions that make positive teacher–child relationships more likely.

Social Problem Solving

As noted earlier, children, even those who are best friends, come into conflict—events that provide invaluable learning experiences in resolving disputes constructively. Preschoolers' disagreements only rarely result in hostile encounters. Although friends argue more than other peers do, they are also more likely to work out their differences through negotiation and to continue interacting (Hartup, 1999).

TAKE A MOMENT... At your next opportunity, observe preschoolers' play, noting disputes over objects ("That's mine!" "I had it first!"), entry into and control over play activities ("I'm on your team, Jerry." "No, you're not!"), and disagreements over facts, ideas, and beliefs ("I'm taller than he is." "No, you aren't!"). Children take these matters quite seriously. In Chapter 9, we noted that resolution of conflict, rather than conflict per se, promotes development. Social conflicts provide repeated occasions for **social problem solving**—generating and applying strategies that prevent or resolve disagreements, resulting in outcomes that are both acceptable to others and beneficial to the self. To engage in social problem solving, children must bring together diverse social understandings.

An information-processing model of social problem solving. The model is circular because children often engage in several information-processing activities at once—for example, interpreting information as they notice it and continuing to consider the meaning of another's behavior while they generate and evaluate problem-solving strategies. The model also takes into account the impact of mental state on social information processing—in particular, children's knowledge of social rules, their representations of past social experiences, and their expectations for future experiences. Peer evaluations and responses to enacted strategies are also important factors in social problem solving. *(Adapted from N. R. Crick & K. A. Dodge, 1994, "A Review and Reformulation of Social Information-Processing Mechanisms in Children's Social Adjustment," Psychological Bulletin, 115, 74–101, Figure 2 [adapted], p. 76. Copyright © 1994 by the American Psychological Association. Reprinted with permission of the American Psychological Association and Nicki Crick.)*

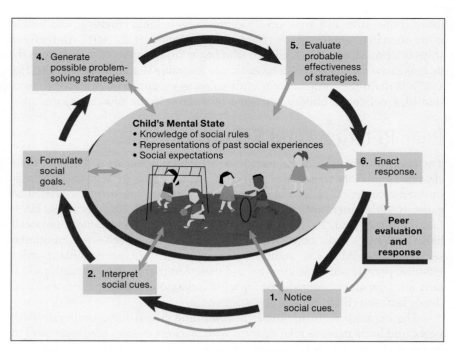

THE SOCIAL PROBLEM-SOLVING PROCESS Nicki Crick and Kenneth Dodge (1994) organize the steps of social problem solving into the circular model shown in Figure 10.1. Notice how this flowchart takes an *information-processing approach,* clarifying exactly what a child must do to grapple with and solve a social problem. It enables identification of processing deficits, so intervention can be tailored to meet individual needs.

Social problem solving profoundly affects peer relations. Children who get along well with agemates interpret social cues accurately, formulate goals (being helpful to peers) that enhance relationships, and have a repertoire of effective problem-solving strategies—for example, politely asking to play, requesting an explanation when they do not understand a peer's behavior, and working out a compromise when faced with peer disagreement. In contrast, children with peer difficulties often hold biased social expectations. Consequently, they attend selectively to social cues (such as hostile acts) and misinterpret others' behavior (view an unintentional jostle as hostile). Their social goals (satisfying an impulse, getting even with or avoiding a peer) often lead to strategies that damage relationships (Dodge, Coie, & Lynam, 2006; Youngstrom et al., 2000). They might barge into a play group without asking, use threats and physical force, or fearfully hover around peers' activities.

Children improve greatly in social problem solving over the preschool and early school years. Instead of grabbing, hitting, or insisting that another child obey, 5- to 7-year-olds tend to rely on friendly persuasion and compromise, to think of alternative strategies when an initial one does not work, and to resolve disagreements without adult intervention (Chen et al., 2001; Mayeiux & Cillessen, 2003). Sometimes they suggest creating new, mutual goals, reflecting awareness that how they solve current problems will influence the future of the relationship (Yeates, Schultz, & Selman, 1991). By kindergarten, the accuracy and effectiveness of each component of social problem solving are related to socially competent behavior (Dodge et al., 1986).

ENHANCING SOCIAL PROBLEM SOLVING Intervening with children who have weak social problem-solving skills can foster development in several ways. Besides improving peer relations, effective social problem solving offers children a sense of mastery in the face of stressful life events. It reduces the risk of adjustment difficulties in children from low-SES and troubled families (Goodman, Gravitt, & Kaslow, 1995).

In one intervention—the Promoting Alternative Thinking Strategies (PATHS) curriculum for preschool children—teachers provide children with weekly lessons in the ingredients of social problem solving. Using stories, puppet characters, discussion, and role-play demonstrations, they teach such skills as detecting others' feelings, planning sequences of action, generating effective strategies, and anticipating probable outcomes. In evaluations of PATHS, preschoolers who had completed 30 lessons in their Head Start classrooms scored higher than no-intervention controls in accurately "reading" others' emotions, inferring how others are likely to feel based on situational cues, selecting competent solutions to social conflicts, and teacher-rated peer cooperation and verbal communication (Bierman et al., 2008; Domitrovich, Cortes, & Greenberg, 2007).

Often preschoolers know how to solve a social problem effectively but do not apply their knowledge (Rudolph & Heller, 1997). And children who have repeatedly enacted maladaptive responses may need to rehearse alternatives to overcome their habitual behaviors and to spark more adaptive social information processing. A unique feature of PATHS is the inclusion of "extension activities" following each lesson—cooperative projects and games through which children practice targeted skills with teacher support. In addition, PATHS provides teachers with mentoring in effective classroom management and use of inductive discipline. These program elements likely strengthened its power to foster children's social competence.

Parental Influences on Early Peer Relations

Children first acquire skills for interacting with peers within the family. Parents influence children's peer sociability both *directly,* through attempts to influence children's peer relations, and *indirectly,* through their child-rearing practices and play behaviors (Ladd & Pettit, 2002; Rubin et al., 2005).

DIRECT PARENTAL INFLUENCES   Outside preschool, child care, and kindergarten, young children depend on parents to help them establish rewarding peer associations. Preschoolers whose parents frequently arrange informal peer play activities tend to have larger peer networks and to be more socially skilled (Ladd, LeSieur, & Profilet, 1993). In providing play opportunities, parents show children how to initiate peer contacts and encourage them to be good "hosts" who consider their playmates' needs.

Parents also influence their children's peer interaction skills by offering guidance on how to act toward others. Their skillful suggestions for managing conflict, discouraging teasing, and entering a play group are associated with preschoolers' social competence and peer acceptance (Laird et al., 1994; Mize & Pettit, 1997; Parke et al., 2004).

INDIRECT PARENTAL INFLUENCES   Many parenting behaviors not directly aimed at promoting peer sociability nevertheless influence it. For example, secure attachments to parents are linked to more responsive, harmonious peer interactions; larger peer networks; and warmer, more supportive friendships throughout childhood and adolescence (Laible, 2007; Lucas-Thompson & Clarke-Stewart, 2007; Wood, Emmerson, & Cowan, 2004). The sensitive, emotionally expressive communication that contributes to attachment security may be responsible. In several studies, highly involved, emotionally positive parent–child conversations and play predicted prosocial behavior and positive peer relations in preschool children (Clark & Ladd, 2000; Lindsey & Mize, 2000).

Parent–child play seems particularly effective for promoting peer interaction skills. During play, parents interact with their child on a "level playing field," much as peers do. And perhaps because parents play more with children of their own sex, mothers' play is more strongly linked to daughters' competence, fathers' play to sons' competence (Lindsey & Mize, 2000; Pettit et al., 1998).

As we have seen, some preschoolers already have great difficulty with peer relations. In Leslie's classroom, Robbie was one of them. Wherever he happened to be, comments like "Robbie ruined our block tower" and "Robbie hit me for no reason" could be heard. As we take up moral development in the next section, you will learn more about how parenting contributed to Robbie's peer problems.

© CULTURA/CORBIS

■ Parents' play with young children, especially same-sex children, is linked to social competence. By playing with his father as he would with a peer, this child acquires social skills that facilitate peer interaction. ■

ASK YOURSELF

◆ REVIEW Among children who spend much time playing alone, what factors distinguish those who are likely to have adjustment difficulties from those who are well-adjusted and socially skilled?

◆ APPLY Three-year-old Ben lives in the country, with no other preschoolers nearby. His parents wonder whether it is worth driving Ben into town once a week to participate in a peer play group. What advice would you give Ben's parents, and why?

◆ CONNECT Illustrate the influence of temperament on social problem solving by explaining how an impulsive child and a shy child might respond at each social problem-solving step in Figure 10.1 on page 376.

◆ REFLECT Think back to your first friendship. How old were you? Describe the quality of your relationship. What did your parents do, directly and indirectly, that might have influenced your earliest peer associations?

Foundations of Morality

Young children's behavior provides many examples of their budding moral sense. In Chapter 4, we noted that newborn (and older) infants often cry in response to the cries of other babies, a possible precursor of empathy. And after watching scenes in which one puppet helps a climber up a hill while a second pushes a climber down a hill, babies as young as 6 months overwhelming reached for the helpful character over a hinderer (Hamlin, Wynn, & Bloom, 2007). They seem implicitly drawn to the "nice" guy and repelled by the "mean" guy.

By age 2, children use words to evaluate their own and others' actions: "I naughty. I wrote on the wall" or (after being hit by another child) "Connie not nice." They also react with distress to aggressive or potentially harmful behaviors (Kochanska, Casey, & Fukumoto, 1995). And we have seen that children of this age share toys, help others, and cooperate in games—early indicators of considerate, responsible, prosocial attitudes.

Adults everywhere take note of this developing capacity to distinguish right from wrong and to accommodate the needs of others. Some cultures have special terms for it. The Utku Indians of Hudson Bay say the child develops *ihuma* (reason). The Fijians believe that *vakayalo* (sense) appears. In response, parents hold children more responsible for their behavior (Dunn, 2005). By the end of early childhood, children can state many moral rules: "Don't take someone's things without asking." "Tell the truth!" In addition, they argue over matters of justice: "You sat there last time, so it's my turn." "It's not fair. He got more!"

All theories of moral development recognize that conscience begins to take shape in early childhood. And most agree that at first, the child's morality is *externally controlled* by adults. Gradually, it becomes regulated by *inner standards*. Truly moral individuals do not do the right thing just to conform to others' expectations. Rather, they have developed compassionate concerns and principles of good conduct, which they follow in many situations.

Each major theory of development emphasizes a different aspect of morality. Psychoanalytic theory stresses the *emotional side* of conscience development—in particular, identification and guilt as motivators of good conduct. Social learning theory focuses on how *moral behavior* is learned through reinforcement and modeling. Finally, the cognitive-developmental perspective emphasizes *thinking*—children's ability to reason about justice and fairness.

The Psychoanalytic Perspective

Recall that according to Freud, young children form a *superego,* or conscience, by *identifying* with the same-sex parent, whose moral standards they adopt. Children obey the superego to avoid *guilt,* a painful emotion that arises each time they are tempted to misbehave. Moral development, Freud believed, is largely complete by 5 to 6 years of age.

Today, most researchers disagree with Freud's view of conscience development. In his theory (see page 16 in Chapter 1), fear of punishment and loss of parental love motivate conscience formation and moral behavior (Tellings, 1999). Yet children whose parents frequently use threats, commands, or physical force tend to violate standards often and feel little guilt, whereas parental warmth and responsiveness predict greater guilt following transgressions (Kochanska et al., 2002, 2005, 2008). And if a parent withdraws love after misbehavior—for example, refuses to speak to or states a dislike for the child—children often respond with high levels of self-blame, thinking, "I'm no good," or "Nobody loves me." Eventually, to protect themselves from overwhelming guilt, these children may deny the emotion and, as a result, also develop a weak conscience (Kochanska, 1991; Zahn-Waxler et al., 1990).

INDUCTIVE DISCIPLINE   In contrast, conscience formation is promoted by a type of discipline called **induction,** in which an adult helps make the child aware of feelings by pointing out the effects of the child's misbehavior on others, especially noting their distress and making clear that the child caused it. For example, a parent might say, "If you keep pushing him, he'll fall down and cry" or "She's crying because you won't give back her doll" (Hoffman,

■ This teacher uses inductive discipline to explain to a child how his misbehavior affects others. She indicates how the child should behave, encouraging empathy and sympathetic concern. ■

2000). When generally warm parents provide explanations that match the child's capacity to understand, while firmly insisting that the child listen and comply, induction is effective as early as age 2. Preschoolers whose parents use it are more likely to refrain from wrongdoing, confess and repair damages after misdeeds, and display prosocial behavior (Kerr et al., 2004; Volling, Mahoney, & Rauer, 2009; Zahn-Waxler, Radke-Yarrow, & King, 1979).

The success of induction may lie in its power to motivate children's active commitment to moral standards, in the following ways:

■ Induction gives children information about how to behave that they can use in future situations.
■ By emphasizing the impact of the child's actions on others, induction encourages empathy and sympathetic concern, which motivate prosocial behavior (Krevans & Gibbs, 1996).
■ Giving children reasons for changing their behavior encourages them to adopt moral standards because those standards make sense.
■ Children who consistently experience induction may form a *script* for the negative emotional consequences of harming others: Child causes harm, inductive message points out harm, child feels empathy for victim, child makes amends (Hoffman, 2000). The script deters future transgressions.

In contrast, discipline that relies too heavily on threats of punishment or withdrawal of love makes children so anxious and frightened that they cannot think clearly enough to figure out what they should do. As a result, these practices do not get children to internalize moral rules and—as noted earlier—also interfere with empathy and prosocial responding (Eisenberg, Fabes, & Spinrad, 2006). Nevertheless, warnings, disapproval, and commands are sometimes necessary to get an unruly child to listen to an inductive message (Grusec, 2006).

THE CHILD'S CONTRIBUTION   Although good discipline is crucial, children's characteristics also affect the success of parenting techniques. Twin studies suggest a modest genetic contribution to empathy and prosocial behavior (Knafo & Plomin, 2006; Zahn-Waxler et al., 2001). More empathic children require less power assertion and are more responsive to induction.

Temperament is also influential. Mild, patient tactics—requests, suggestions, and explanations—are sufficient to prompt guilt reactions and conscience development in anxious, fearful preschoolers (Kochanska et al., 2002). But with fearless, impulsive children, gentle discipline has little impact. Power assertion also works poorly. It undermines the child's capacity for effortful control, which strongly predicts good conduct, empathy, sympathy, and prosocial

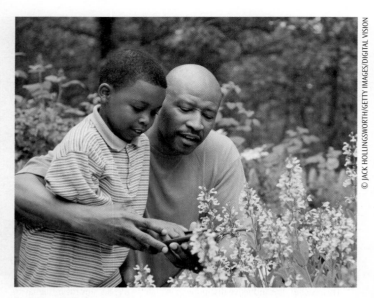

When children are impulsive and low in anxiety, a secure attachment relationship motivates conscience development. This preschooler wants to follow parental rules to preserve an affectionate, supportive relationship with his father. ■

behavior (Kochanska & Aksan, 2006; Kochanska & Knaack, 2003). Parents of impulsive children can foster conscience development by ensuring a secure attachment relationship and combining firm correction of misbehavior with induction (Kochanska, Aksan, & Joy, 2007). When children are so low in anxiety that parental disapproval causes them little discomfort, a close parent–child bond provides an alternative foundation for morality. It motivates children to listen to parents as a means of preserving an affectionate, supportive relationship.

In sum, to foster early moral development, parents must tailor their disciplinary strategies to their child's personality. Does this remind you of *goodness of fit,* discussed in Chapter 7? Return to page 262 to review this idea.

THE ROLE OF GUILT Although little support exists for Freudian ideas about conscience development, Freud was correct that guilt is an important motivator of moral action. By the end of toddlerhood, guilt reactions are evident, and preschoolers' assertions reveal that they have internalized the parent's moral voice: "Didn't you hear my mommy? We'd better not play with these toys" (Thompson, 2009).

Inducing *empathy-based* guilt (expressions of personal responsibility and regret, such as "I'm sorry I hurt him") by explaining that the child is causing someone distress and has disappointed the parent is a means of influencing children without using coercion. Empathy-based guilt reactions are associated with stopping harmful actions, repairing damage caused by misdeeds, and engaging in future prosocial behavior (Baumeister, 1998). At the same time, parents must help children deal with guilt feelings constructively—by guiding them to make up for immoral behavior rather than minimizing or excusing it (Bybee, Merisca, & Velasco, 1998).

But contrary to what Freud believed, guilt is not the only force that compels us to act morally. Nor is moral development complete by the end of early childhood. Rather, it is a gradual process, extending into adulthood.

Social Learning Theory

According to social learning theory, morality does not have a unique course of development. Rather, moral behavior is acquired just like any other set of responses: through reinforcement and modeling.

IMPORTANCE OF MODELING *Operant conditioning*—reinforcement for good behavior, in the form of approval, affection, and other rewards—is not enough for children to acquire moral responses. For a behavior to be reinforced, it must first occur spontaneously. Yet many prosocial acts—sharing, helping, comforting an unhappy playmate—occur so rarely at first that reinforcement cannot explain their rapid development in early childhood. Rather, social learning theorists believe that children learn to behave morally largely through *modeling*—by observing and imitating people who demonstrate appropriate behavior (Bandura, 1977; Grusec, 1988). Once children acquire a moral response, such as sharing or telling the truth, reinforcement in the form of praise for the act ("That was a very nice thing to do") and for the child's character ("You're a very kind and considerate boy") increases its frequency (Mills & Grusec, 1989).

Many studies show that having helpful or generous models increases young children's prosocial responses. And certain characteristics of the model affect children's willingness to imitate:

■ *Warmth and responsiveness.* Preschoolers are more likely to copy the prosocial actions of an adult who is warm and responsive than those of a cold, distant adult (Yarrow, Scott, & Waxler, 1973). Warmth seems to make children more attentive and receptive to the model and is itself an example of a prosocial response.

- *Competence and power.* Children admire and therefore tend to imitate competent, powerful models—especially older peers and adults (Bandura, 1977).
- *Consistency between assertions and behavior.* When models say one thing and do another—for example, announce that "it's important to help others" but rarely engage in helpful acts—children generally choose the most lenient standard of behavior that adults demonstrate (Mischel & Liebert, 1966).

Models are most influential in the early years. In one study, toddlers' eager, willing imitation of their mothers' behavior predicted moral conduct (not cheating in a game) and guilt following transgressions at age 3 (Forman, Aksan, & Kochanska, 2004). At the end of the preschool years, children who have had consistent exposure to caring adults tend to behave prosocially whether or not a model is present: They have internalized prosocial rules from repeated observations and encouragement by others (Mussen & Eisenberg-Berg, 1977).

EFFECTS OF PUNISHMENT   Many parents are aware that angrily yelling at, slapping, and spanking children are ineffective disciplinary tactics. A sharp reprimand or physical force to restrain or move a child is justified when immediate obedience is necessary—for example, when a 3-year-old is about to run into the street. In fact, parents are most likely to use forceful methods under these conditions. But to foster long-term goals, such as acting kindly toward others, they tend to rely on warmth and reasoning (Kuczynski, 1984). And in response to serious transgressions, such as lying or stealing, they often combine power assertion with reasoning (Grusec, 2006; Grusec & Goodnow, 1994).

Frequent punishment, however, promotes only immediate compliance, not lasting changes in behavior. For example, Robbie's parents often punished by hitting, shouting, and criticizing. But as soon as they were out of sight, Robbie usually engaged in the unacceptable behavior again. The more harsh threats, angry physical control, and physical punishment children experience, the more likely they are to develop serious, lasting mental health problems. These include weak internalization of moral rules; depression, aggression, antisocial behavior, and poor academic performance in childhood and adolescence; and depression, alcohol abuse, criminality, and partner and child abuse in adulthood (Afifi et al., 2006; Bender et al., 2007; Gershoff, 2002; Kochanska, Aksan, & Nichols, 2003; Lynch et al., 2006).

Harsh punishment has several undesirable side effects:

- Parents often spank in response to children's aggression (Holden, Coleman, & Schmidt, 1995). Yet the punishment itself models aggression!
- Harshly treated children react with anger, resentment, and a chronic sense of being personally threatened, which prompts a focus on the self's distress rather than a sympathetic orientation to others' needs.
- Children who are frequently punished develop a more conflict-ridden and less supportive parent–child relationship and also learn to avoid the punitive parent (McLoyd & Smith, 2002; Shaw, Lacourse, & Nagin, 2005). Consequently, the parent's effectiveness at teaching desirable behaviors is substantially reduced.
- By stopping children's misbehavior temporarily, harsh punishment gives adults immediate relief, reinforcing them for using coercive discipline. For this reason, a punitive adult is likely to punish with greater frequency over time, a course of action that can spiral into serious abuse.
- Children, adolescents, and adults whose parents used *corporal punishment*—the use of physical force to inflict pain but not injury—are more accepting of such discipline (Bower-Russa, Knutson, & Winebarger, 2001; Deater-Deckard et al., 2003). In this way, use of physical punishment may transfer to the next generation.

Although corporal punishment spans the SES spectrum, its frequency and harshness are elevated among less educated, economically disadvantaged parents (Giles-Sims, Strauss, & Sugarman, 1995; Lansford et al., 2004b, 2009). And consistently, parents with conflict-ridden marriages and with mental health problems (who are emotionally reactive, depressed, or aggressive) are more likely to be punitive and also to have hard-to-manage children, whose disobedience evokes more parental harshness (Berlin et al., 2009; Erath et al., 2006; Knafo &

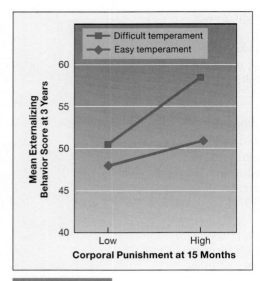

FIGURE 10.2

Relationship of parental corporal punishment at age 15 months to externalizing behavior, by child temperament. Corporal punishment was associated with increased externalizing behavior (anger and aggression) for both easy and difficult children, even after controlling for family and parenting characteristics. The rise in externalizing behavior was greater for difficulty children—a difference also evident in a follow-up during first grade. *(From M. K. Mulvaney & C. J. Mebert, 2007, "Parental Corporal Punishment Predicts Behavior Problems in Early Childhood," Journal of Family Psychology, 21, p. 394. Copyright © 2007 by the American Psychological Association. Reprinted with permission of the American Psychological Association.)*

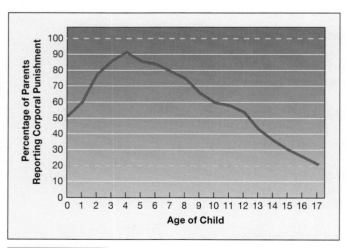

FIGURE 10.3

Prevalence of corporal punishment by child's age. Estimates are based on the percentage of parents in a nationally representative U.S. sample of nearly 1,000 reporting one or more instances of spanking, slapping, pinching, shaking, or hitting with a hard object in the past year. Physical punishment increases sharply during early childhood and then declines, but it is high at all ages. *(From M. A. Straus & J. H. Stewart, 1999, "Corporal Punishment by American Parents: National Data on Prevalence, Chronicity, Severity, and Duration in Relation to Child and Family Characteristics," Clinical Child and Family Psychology Review, 2, p. 59. Adapted with kind permission from Springer Science and Business Media and the author.)*

Plomin, 2006; Taylor et al., 2010). These parent–child similarities suggest that heredity contributes to the link between punitive discipline and children's adjustment difficulties. But heredity is not a complete explanation. **TAKE A MOMENT...** Return to page 86 in Chapter 2 to review findings indicating that good parenting can shield children genetically at risk for aggression and antisocial activity from developing those behaviors.

Furthermore, in a longitudinal study extending from 15 months to 3 years, early corporal punishment predicted externalizing behavior problems in preschoolers of diverse temperaments (see Figure 10.2) (Mulvaney & Mebert, 2007). Negative outcomes were simply more pronounced among temperamentally difficult children. Other longitudinal findings reveal a similar link between physical punishment and later child and adolescent aggression, even after child, parenting, and family characteristics that might otherwise account for the relationship were controlled (Berlin et al., 2009; Lansford et al., 2009; Taylor et al., 2010).

In view of these outcomes, the widespread use of corporal punishment by American parents is cause for concern. A survey of a nationally representative sample of U.S. households revealed that although corporal punishment increases from infancy to age 5 and then declines, it is high at all ages (see Figure 10.3) (Straus & Stewart, 1999). Repeated use of physical punishment is more common with toddlers and preschoolers. And more than one-fourth of physically punishing U.S. parents report having used a hard object, such as a brush or a belt (Gershoff, 2002).

A prevailing American belief is that corporal punishment, if implemented by caring parents, is harmless, perhaps even beneficial. In a recent U.S. opinion poll, 72 percent of adults agreed that it is "OK to spank a child" (Survey USA, 2005). But as the Cultural Influences box on the following page reveals, this assumption is valid only under conditions of limited use in certain social contexts.

ALTERNATIVES TO HARSH PUNISHMENT Alternatives to criticism, slaps, and spankings can reduce the side effects of punishment. A technique called **time out** involves removing children from the immediate setting—for example, by sending them to their rooms—until they are ready to act appropriately. When a child is out of control, a few minutes in time out can be enough to change behavior while also giving angry parents a cooling-off period. Another approach is *withdrawal of privileges*, such as playing outside or watching a favorite TV program. Like time out, removing privileges allows parents to avoid using harsh techniques that can easily intensify into violence.

When parents do decide to use punishment, they can increase its effectiveness in three ways:

- *Consistency.* Permitting children to act inappropriately on some occasions but scolding them on others confuses children, and the unacceptable act persists (Acker & O'Leary, 1996).
- *A warm parent–child relationship.* Children of involved, caring parents find the interruption in parental affection that accompanies punishment especially unpleasant. They want to regain parental warmth and approval as quickly as possible.
- *Explanations.* Providing reasons for mild punishment helps children relate the misdeed to expectations for future behavior. This approach leads to far greater reduction in misbehavior than using punishment alone (Larzelere et al., 1996).

CULTURAL INFLUENCES

Ethnic Differences in the Consequences of Physical Punishment

*I*n an African-American community, six elders, all of whom had volunteered to serve as mentors for parents facing child-rearing challenges, met to discuss parenting issues at a social service agency. Their attitudes toward discipline were strikingly different from those of the white social workers who had brought them together. Each elder argued that successful child rearing required the use of appropriate physical tactics. At the same time, they voiced strong disapproval of screaming or cursing at children, calling such out-of-control parental behavior "abusive." Ruth, the oldest and most respected member of the group, characterized good parenting as a complex combination of warmth, teaching, talking nicely, and disciplining physically. She related how an older neighbor advised her to handle her own children when she was a young parent:

> She said to me says, don't scream . . . you talk to them real nice and sweet and when they do something ugly . . . she say you get a nice little switch and you won't have any trouble with them and from that day that's the way I raised 'em. (Mosby et al., 1999, pp. 511–512)

Use of physical punishment is highest among low-SES ethnic minority parents, who are more likely than middle-SES white parents to advocate slaps and spankings (Pinderhughes et al., 2000; Straus & Stewart, 1999; Taylor et al., 2010). And although corporal punishment is linked to a wide array of negative child outcomes, exceptions do exist.

In one longitudinal study, researchers followed several hundred families for 12 years, collecting information from mothers on disciplinary strategies in early and middle childhood and from both mothers and their children on youth problem behaviors in adolescence. Even after many child and family characteristics were controlled, the findings were striking: In Caucasian-American families, physical punishment was positively associated with adolescent aggression and antisocial behavior. In African-American families, by contrast, the more mothers had disciplined physically in childhood, the less their teenagers displayed angry, acting-out behavior and got in trouble at school and with the police (Lansford et al., 2004a).

African-American and Caucasian-American parents seem to mete out physical punishment differently. In black families, such discipline is culturally approved, generally mild, delivered in a context of parental warmth, and aimed at helping children become responsible adults. White parents, in contrast, typically consider physical punishment to be wrong, so when they resort to it, they are often highly agitated and rejecting of the child (Dodge, McLoyd, & Lansford, 2006). As a result, most black children may view spanking as a practice carried out with their best interests in mind, whereas white children may regard it as an "act of personal aggression" (Gunnoe & Mariner, 1997, p. 768).

In support of this view, when several thousand ethnically diverse children were followed from the preschool through the early school years, spanking was associated with a rise in behavior problems if parents were cold and rejecting but not if they were warm and supportive (McLoyd & Smith, 2002). In another study, spanking predicted depressive symptoms only among a minority of African-American children whose mothers disapproved of the practice and, as a result, tended to use it when they were highly angry and frustrated (McLoyd et al., 2007).

These findings are not an endorsement of physical punishment. Other forms of discipline, including time out, withdrawal of privileges, and the positive strategies listed on page 384, are far more effective. But it is noteworthy that the meaning and impact of physical discipline vary sharply with cultural context.

© JOSE LUIS PELAEZ INC./BLEND IMAGES/PHOTOLIBRARY

■ In African-American families, physical discipline is often culturally approved, generally mild, and delivered in a context of parental warmth. As a result, most African-American children may view spanking as a practice carried out with their best interests in mind, not as an act of aggression. ■

POSITIVE RELATIONSHIPS, POSITIVE DISCIPLINE The most effective forms of discipline encourage good conduct—by building a mutually respectful bond with the child, letting the child know ahead of time how to act, and praising mature behavior (Zahn-Waxler & Robinson, 1995). When sensitivity, cooperation, and shared positive emotion are evident in joint activities between parents and preschoolers, children show firmer conscience development—expressing empathy after transgressions, behaving responsibly, playing fairly in games, and considering others' welfare (Kochanska et al., 2005, 2008). Parent–child closeness leads children to heed parental demands because children feel a sense of commitment to the relationship.

Consult Applying What We Know on page 384 for ways to discipline positively. Parents who use these strategies focus on long-term social and life skills—cooperation, problem solving, and consideration for others. As a result, they greatly reduce the need for punishment.

Applying What We Know

Using Positive Discipline

STRATEGY	EXPLANATION
Use transgressions as opportunities to teach.	When a child engages in harmful or unsafe behavior, intervene firmly, and then use induction, which motivates children to make amends and behave prosocially.
Reduce opportunities for misbehavior.	On long car trips, bring back-seat activities that relieve children's restlessness. At the supermarket, converse with children, and let them help with shopping. As a result, children learn to occupy themselves constructively when options are limited.
Provide reasons for rules.	When children appreciate that rules are fair to all concerned, not arbitrary, they strive to follow the rules because they are reasonable and rational.
Arrange for children to participate in family routines and duties.	By joining with adults in preparing a meal, washing dishes, or raking leaves, children develop a sense of responsible participation in family and community life and acquire many practical skills.
When children are obstinate, try compromising and problem solving.	When a child refuses to obey, express understanding of the child's feelings ("I know it's not fun to clean up"), suggest a compromise ("You put those away, I'll take care of these"), and help the child think of ways to avoid the problem in the future. Responding firmly but kindly and respectfully increases the likelihood of willing cooperation.
Encourage mature behavior.	Express confidence in children's capacity to learn and appreciation for effort and cooperation, as in "You gave that your best!" "Thanks for helping!" Adult encouragement fosters pride and satisfaction in succeeding, thereby inspiring children to improve further.
Be sensitive to children's physical and emotional resources.	When children are tired, ill, or bored, they are likely to engage in attention-getting, disorganized, or otherwise improper behavior as a reaction to discomfort. In these instances, meeting the child's needs makes more sense than disciplining.

Sources: Berk, 2001a; Grusec, 2006; Nelson, 1996.

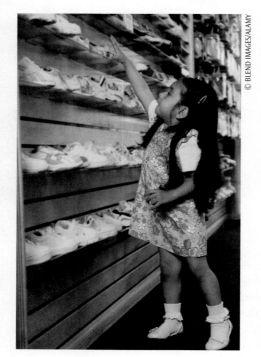

© BLEND IMAGES/ALAMY

■ This 3-year-old understands that the style and color of her new shoes are matters of personal choice, distinct from moral imperatives and social conventions. ■

The Cognitive-Developmental Perspective

The psychoanalytic and behaviorist approaches to morality focus on how children acquire ready-made standards of good conduct from adults. In contrast, the cognitive-developmental perspective regards children as *active thinkers* about social rules. As early as the preschool years, children make moral judgments, deciding what is right or wrong on the basis of concepts they construct about justice and fairness (Gibbs, 2010; Turiel, 2006).

PRESCHOOLERS' MORAL UNDERSTANDING   Young children have some well-developed ideas about morality. As long as researchers emphasize people's intentions, 3-year-olds say that a person with bad intentions—someone who deliberately frightens, embarrasses, or otherwise hurts another—is more deserving of punishment than a well-intentioned person (Helwig, Zelazo, & Wilson, 2001; Jones & Thompson, 2001). Around age 4, children know that a person who expresses an insincere intention—says, "I'll come over and help you rake leaves" but doesn't intend to do so—is lying. And 4-year-olds approve of telling the truth and disapprove of lying, even when a lie remains undetected (Bussey, 1992).

Furthermore, preschoolers in diverse cultures distinguish **moral imperatives,** which protect people's rights and welfare, from two other types of rules and expectations: **social conventions,** customs determined solely by consensus, such as table manners and politeness rituals (saying "please" and "thank you"); and **matters of personal choice,** such as choice of friends, hairstyle, and leisure activities, which do not violate rights and are up to the individual (Killen, Margie, & Sinno, 2006; Nucci, 1996; Smetana, 2006). Interviews with 3- and 4-year-olds reveal that they consider moral violations (unprovoked hitting, stealing an apple) as more wrong than violations of social conventions (eating ice cream with your fingers). They also say that moral violations would still be wrong even if an adult did not see them and no rules existed to prohibit them because they harm others. And preschoolers' concern with personal choice, conveyed through statements like "I'm gonna wear *this* shirt," serves as the springboard for moral concepts of individual rights, which will expand greatly in middle childhood and adolescence (Nucci, 2005).

Within the moral domain, however, preschool and young school-age children tend to reason *rigidly*, making judgments based on salient features and consequences while neglecting other important information. For example, they are more likely than older children to claim that stealing and lying are always wrong, even when a person has a morally sound reason for engaging in these acts (Lourenco, 2003). They view inflicting physical damage (breaking a peer's toy) as a more serious transgression than treating others unfairly (not sharing) (Nucci, 2002). And their focus on outcomes means that they fail to realize that a promise is still a promise, even if it is unfulfilled (Maas, 2008; Maas & Abbeduto, 2001).

Still, preschoolers' ability to distinguish moral imperatives from social conventions is impressive. How do they do so? According to cognitive-developmental theorists, they *actively make sense* of their experiences (Turiel, 2006). They observe that after a moral offense, peers respond with strong negative emotion, describe their own injury or loss, tell another child to stop, or retaliate. And an adult who intervenes is likely to call attention to the rights and feelings of the victim. In contrast, violations of social convention elicit less intense peer reactions. And in these situations, adults usually demand obedience without explanation or point to the importance of keeping order.

SOCIAL EXPERIENCE AND MORAL UNDERSTANDING   Cognition and language support preschoolers' moral understanding, but social experiences are vital. Disputes with siblings and peers over rights, possessions, and property allow preschoolers to negotiate, compromise, and work out their first ideas about justice and fairness. Children also learn from warm, sensitive parental communication and from observing the way adults handle rule violations to care about the welfare of others (Turiel & Killen, 2010). And they benefit greatly from adult–child discussions of moral issues. Children who are advanced in moral thinking tend to have parents who adapt their communications about fighting, honesty, and ownership to what their children can understand, tell stories with moral implications, encourage prosocial behavior, and gently stimulate the child to think further, without being hostile or critical (Janssens & Deković, 1997; Walker & Taylor, 1991).

Preschoolers who verbally and physically assault others, often with little or no provocation, are already delayed in moral reasoning (Helwig & Turiel, 2004; Sanderson & Siegal, 1988). Without special help, such children show long-term disruptions in moral development, deficits in self-control, and ultimately an antisocial lifestyle.

The Other Side of Morality: Development of Aggression

Beginning in late infancy, all children display aggression from time to time, and as opportunities to interact with siblings and peers increase, aggressive outbursts occur more often (Tremblay, 2004). By the second year, aggressive acts with two distinct purposes emerge. Initially, the most common is **proactive** (or *instrumental*) **aggression,** in which children act to fulfill a need or desire—to obtain an object, privilege, space, or social reward, such as adult or peer attention—and unemotionally attack a person to achieve their goal. The other type, **reactive** (or *hostile*) **aggression,** is an angry, defensive response to provocation or a blocked goal and is meant to hurt another person (Dodge, Cole, & Lynam, 2006; Little et al., 2005).

Proactive and reactive aggression come in three varieties, which are the focus of most research:

- **Physical aggression** harms others through physical injury—pushing, hitting, kicking, or punching others, or destroying another's property.
- **Verbal aggression** harms others through threats of physical aggression, name-calling, or hostile teasing.

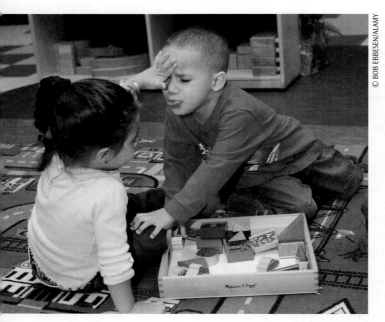

■ These preschoolers display proactive aggression, pushing and grabbing as they argue over a game. Proactive aggression declines with age as children learn to compromise and share, and as their capacity to delay gratification improves. ■

- **Relational aggression** damages another's peer relationships through social exclusion, malicious gossip, or friendship manipulation.

Although verbal aggression is always direct, physical and relational aggression can be either *direct* or *indirect*. For example, hitting injures a person directly, whereas destroying property indirectly inflicts physical harm. Similarly, saying, "Do what I say, or I won't be your friend," conveys relational aggression directly, while spreading rumors, refusing to talk to a peer, or manipulating friendship by saying behind someone's back, "Don't play with her; she's a nerd," does so indirectly.

In early childhood, verbal aggression gradually replaces physical aggression as language develops and adults and peers react negatively and strongly to physical attacks (Alink et al., 2006; Tremblay et al., 1999). And proactive aggression declines as preschoolers' improved capacity to delay gratification enables them to resist grabbing others' possessions. But reactive aggression in verbal and relational forms tends to rise over early and middle childhood (Côté et al., 2007; Tremblay, 2000). Older children are better able to recognize malicious intentions and, as a result, more often retaliate in hostile ways.

By age 17 months, boys are more physically aggressive than girls—a difference found throughout childhood in many cultures (Baillargeon et al., 2007; Card et al., 2008). The sex difference is due in part to biology—in particular, to male sex hormones (androgens) and temperamental traits (activity level, irritability, impulsivity) on which boys score higher. Gender-role conformity is also important. As soon as preschoolers are aware of gender stereotypes—that males and females are expected to behave differently—physical aggression drops off more sharply for girls than for boys (Fagot & Leinbach, 1989). Parents also respond far more negatively to physical fighting in girls (Arnold, McWilliams, & Harvey-Arnold, 1998).

Although girls have a reputation for being both verbally and relationally more aggressive than boys, the sex difference is small (Crick et al., 2004, 2006; Crick, Ostrov, & Werner, 2006). Beginning in the preschool years, girls concentrate most of their aggressive acts in the relational category. Boys inflict harm in more variable ways. Physically and verbally aggressive boys also tend to be relationally aggressive (Card et al., 2008). Therefore, boys display overall rates of aggression that are much higher than girls'.

At the same time, girls more often use indirect relational tactics that—in disrupting intimate bonds especially important to girls—can be particularly mean. Whereas physical attacks are usually brief, acts of indirect relational aggression may extend for hours, weeks, or even months (Nelson, Robinson, & Hart, 2005; Underwood, 2003). In one instance, a 6-year-old girl formed a "pretty-girls club" and—for nearly an entire school year—convinced its members to exclude several classmates by saying they were "dirty and smelly."

An occasional aggressive exchange between preschoolers is normal. Children sometimes assert their sense of self through these encounters, which become important learning experiences as adults intervene and teach social problem solving (Vaughn et al., 2003). But some children—especially those who are emotionally negative, impulsive, and disobedient—are prone to early, high rates of physical or relational aggression (or both) that often persist. These aggressive children are at risk for later internalizing and externalizing difficulties and social skills deficits, including loneliness, anxiety, depression, poor-quality friendships, and antisocial activity in middle childhood and adolescence (Campbell et al., 2006; Côté et al., 2007; Crick, Ostrov, & Werner, 2006).

THE FAMILY AS TRAINING GROUND FOR AGGRESSIVE BEHAVIOR   "I can't control him; he's impossible," Robbie's mother, Nadine, complained to Leslie one day. When Leslie asked if Robbie might be troubled by something happening at home, she discovered that his parents fought constantly and resorted to harsh, inconsistent discipline. The same child-rearing practices that undermine moral internalization—love withdrawal, power assertion, physical punishment, negative comments and emotions, and inconsistency—are linked to aggression from early childhood through adolescence in children of both sexes and in many cultures, with most of these practices predicting both physical and relational forms (Bradford et al., 2003; Côté et al., 2007; Nelson et al., 2006; Rubin et al., 2003; Yang et al., 2003).

In families like Robbie's, anger and punitiveness quickly create a conflict-ridden family atmosphere and an "out-of-control" child. The pattern begins with forceful discipline, which occurs more often with stressful life experiences (such as economic hardship or an unhappy marriage), a parent with an unstable personality, or a temperamentally difficult child (Dodge, Coie, & Lynam, 2006). Typically, the parent threatens, criticizes, and punishes, and the child whines, yells, and refuses until the parent "gives in." At the end of each exchange, both parent and child get relief from stopping the unpleasant behavior of the other, so the behaviors repeat and escalate.

As these cycles become more frequent, they generate anxiety and irritability among other family members, who soon join in the hostile interactions. Compared with siblings in typical families, preschool siblings who have critical, punitive parents are more aggressive toward one another. Physically, verbally, and relationally destructive sibling conflict, in turn, quickly spreads to peer relationships, contributing to poor impulse control and antisocial behavior by the early school years (Garcia et al., 2000; Ostrov, Crick, & Stauffacher, 2006).

Boys are more likely than girls to be targets of harsh, inconsistent discipline because they are more active and impulsive and therefore harder to control. When children who are extreme in these characteristics are exposed to emotionally negative, inept parenting, their capacity for emotional self-regulation, empathic responding, and guilt after transgressions is severely disrupted (Eisenberg, Eggum, & Edwards, 2010). Consequently, they lash out when disappointed, frustrated, or faced with a sad or fearful victim.

SOCIAL INFORMATION-PROCESSING DEFICITS Children who are products of these family processes soon acquire a distorted view of the social world. Those who are high in reactive aggression often see hostile intent where it does not exist—in situations where peers' intentions are unclear, where harm is accidental, and even where peers are trying to be helpful (Lochman & Dodge, 1998; Orobio de Castro et al., 2002). When such children feel threatened (for example, a researcher tells them that a peer partner is in a bad mood and might pick a fight), they are especially likely to interpret accidental mishaps as hostile (Williams et al., 2003). As a result, they make many unprovoked attacks, which trigger aggressive retaliations.

Children high in proactive aggression have different deficits in social information processing. Compared with their agemates, they believe there are more benefits and fewer costs for engaging in destructive acts (Arsenio, 2010; Dodge et al., 1997). And they are more likely to think that aggression "works," producing material rewards and reducing others' unpleasant behaviors (Arsenio & Lemerise, 2001; Goldstein & Tisak, 2004). Thus, they callously use aggression to advance their own goals and are relatively unconcerned about causing suffering in others—an aggressive style associated with later, more severe conduct problems, violent behavior, and delinquency (Marsee & Frick, 2010).

TAKE A MOMENT... Return to the information-processing model of social problem solving on page 376. Notice how reactive aggression is linked to deficiencies in noticing and interpreting social cues. In contrast, proactive aggression is associated with deficiencies in formulating social goals (caring more about satisfying one's own needs than getting along with others) and generating and evaluating strategies (engaging in aggression and evaluating it favorably) (Arsenio, 2010). A substantial number of aggressive children engage in both reactive and proactive acts, while others largely display one type (Fite et al., 2008; Little et al., 2003; Polman et al., 2007).

Highly aggressive children tend to be rejected by peers, to fail in school, and (by adolescence) to seek out deviant peers. Together, these factors contribute to the long-term stability of aggression.

VIOLENT MEDIA AND AGGRESSION In the United States, 57 percent of American TV programs between 6 A.M. and 11 P.M. contain violent scenes, often portraying repeated aggressive acts that go unpunished. TV victims of violence are rarely shown experiencing serious harm, and few programs condemn violence or depict other ways of solving problems. Violent

■ TV violence increases the likelihood of hostile thoughts and emotions and tolerance of real-world aggression. Playing violent video and computer games has similar effects. ■

content is 9 percent above average in children's programming, and cartoons are the most violent (Center for Communication and Social Policy, 1998).

Reviewers of thousands of studies—using a wide variety of research designs, methods, and participants from diverse cultures—have concluded that TV violence increases the likelihood of hostile thoughts and emotions and of verbally, physically, and relationally aggressive behavior (Comstock & Scharrer, 2006; Ostrov, Gentile, & Crick, 2006). And a growing number of studies show that playing violent video and computer games has similar effects (Anderson, 2004; Anderson et al., 2008). Although young people of all ages are susceptible, preschool and young school-age children are especially likely to imitate TV violence because they believe that much TV fiction is real and accept what they see uncritically.

Violent programming not only creates short-term difficulties in parent and peer relations but also has lasting negative consequences. In several longitudinal studies, time spent watching TV in childhood and adolescence predicted aggressive behavior in early adulthood, after other factors linked to TV viewing (such as prior child and parent aggression, IQ, parental education, family income, and neighborhood crime) were controlled (see Figure 10.4) (Graber et al., 2006; Huesmann, 1986; Huesmann et al., 2003; Johnson et al., 2002). Aggressive children and adolescents have a greater appetite for violent TV and computer games. And boys devote more time to violent media than girls, in part because of male-oriented themes of conquest and adventure and use of males as lead characters. But even in nonaggressive children, violent TV sparks hostile thoughts and behavior; its impact is simply less intense (Bushman & Huesmann, 2001).

Furthermore, media violence "hardens" children to aggression, making them more willing to tolerate it in others. Viewers quickly habituate, responding with reduced arousal to real-world instances and tolerating more aggression in others (Anderson et al., 2003). Heavy viewers believe that there is much more violence in society than there actually is—an effect that is especially strong for children who perceive media violence to be relevant to their own lives (Donnerstein, Slaby, & Eron, 1994). As these responses indicate, exposure to violent media images modifies children's attitudes toward social reality so they increasingly match media images.

The ease with which television and computer games can manipulate children's beliefs and behavior has led to strong public pressure to improve its content. In the United States, the First Amendment right to free speech has hampered efforts to regulate TV broadcasting. Instead, all programs must be rated for violent and sexual content, and all new TV sets are required to contain the V-chip, which allows parents to block undesired material. In contrast, Canada's nationwide broadcasting code bans from children's shows realistic scenes of violence that minimize consequences and cartoons with violence as the central theme. Further, violent programming intended for adults cannot be shown on Canadian channels before 9 P.M. (Canadian children, however, have access to violent TV fare on U.S. channels.)

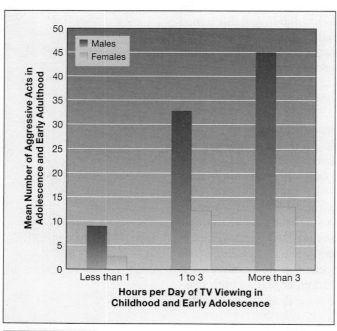

FIGURE 10.4

Relationship of television viewing in childhood and early adolescence to aggressive acts in adolescence and early adulthood. Interviews with more than 700 parents and youths revealed that the more TV watched in childhood and early adolescence, the greater the annual number of aggressive acts committed by the young person, as reported in follow-up interviews at ages 16 and 22. *(Adapted from Johnson et al., 2002.)*

◆ Applying What We Know

Regulating TV and Computer Use

STRATEGY	EXPLANATION
Limit TV viewing and computer use.	Provide clear rules limiting what children can view on TV and do on the computer, and stick to them. Avoid using the TV or the computer as a babysitter. Do not place a TV or a computer in a child's bedroom; doing so substantially increases use and makes the child's activity hard to monitor.
Avoid using TV or computer time as a reward.	When TV or computer access is used as a reward or withheld as punishment, children become increasingly attracted to it.
When possible, watch TV with children, helping them understand what they see.	When adults raise questions about realism in TV depictions, express disapproval of on-screen behavior, and encourage discussion, they help children understand and critically evaluate TV content.
Link TV content to everyday learning experiences.	Parents can extend TV learning in ways that encourage children to engage actively with their surroundings. For example, a program on animals might spark a trip to the zoo, a visit to the library for books about animals, or new ways of observing and caring for the family pet.
Model good TV and computer practices.	Parents' media behavior influences children's behavior. Avoid excessive TV and computer use, and limit your own exposure to violent media content.
Use a warm, rational approach to child rearing.	Children of warm parents who make reasonable demands for mature behavior prefer TV and computer experiences with educational and prosocial content and are less attracted to violent media fare.

At present, parents bear most responsibility for regulating their children's exposure to media violence and other inappropriate content. Besides TV and computer games, the Internet poses risks. As with the V-chip for TV, parents can control children's Internet access by using filters or programs that monitor website visits. Yet surveys of U.S. parents indicate that 20 to 30 percent of preschoolers and 40 percent of school-age children experience no limits on TV or computer use at home. Some children begin visiting websites without parental supervision as early as age 4 (Rideout & Hamel, 2006; Roberts, Foehr, & Rideout, 2005; Varnhagen, 2007). Applying What We Know above lists strategies parents can use to protect children from undesirable TV and computer fare.

HELPING CHILDREN AND PARENTS CONTROL AGGRESSION   Treatment for aggressive children must begin early, before their antisocial behavior becomes well-practiced and difficult to change. Breaking the cycle of hostilities between family members and promoting effective ways of relating to others is crucial. The coercive cycles of punitive parents and aggressive children are so persistent that these children often are punished when they do behave appropriately!

Leslie suggested that Robbie's parents see a family therapist, who observed their inept practices and coached them in alternatives. They learned not to give in to Robbie, to pair commands with reasons, and to replace verbal insults and spankings with more effective punishments, such as time out and withdrawal of privileges. After several weeks of such training, children's aggression declines, and parents view their children more positively—benefits still evident one to four years later (Kazdin, 2003; Patterson & Fisher, 2002). The therapist also encouraged Robbie's parents to be warmer and to give him attention and approval for prosocial acts. Finally, she helped them with their marital problems. This, in addition to their improved ability to manage Robbie's behavior, greatly reduced tension and conflict in the household.

At the same time, Leslie began teaching Robbie more successful ways of relating to peers, had him practice these skills, and praised him whenever she noticed him using them. And as opportunities arose, she encouraged Robbie to talk about a playmate's feelings and to express his own. As Robbie practiced taking the perspective of others, empathizing, and feeling sympathetic concern, his lashing out at peers declined (Izard et al., 2004). Robbie participated in a social problem-solving intervention as well (return to pages 376–377 to review).

LOOK AND LISTEN

◆◆

Watch a half-hour of Saturday morning cartoons and a prime-time movie on TV, and tally the number of violent acts, including those that go unpunished. How often did violence occur in each type of program? What do young viewers learn about the consequences of violence?

Finally, relieving stressors that stem from poverty and neighborhood disorganization and providing families with social supports help prevent childhood aggression (Boyle & Lipman, 2002). When parents better cope with difficulties in their own lives, interventions aimed at reducing children's aggression are even more effective (Kazdin & Whitley, 2003).

ASK YOURSELF

◆ REVIEW What experiences help preschoolers differentiate moral imperatives, social conventions, and matters of personal choice?

◆ APPLY Alice and Wayne want their two young children to become morally mature, caring individuals. List some parenting practices they should use and some they should avoid.

◆ CONNECT What must parents do to foster conscience development in fearless, impulsive children? How does this illustrate goodness of fit (see page 262 in Chapter 7)? Explain.

◆ REFLECT Which types of punishment for a misbehaving preschooler do you endorse, and which types do you reject? Why?

■ ■ Gender Typing
■ ■

Gender typing refers to any association of objects, activities, roles, or traits with one sex or the other in ways that conform to cultural stereotypes (Liben & Bigler, 2002). In Leslie's classroom, girls spent more time in the housekeeping, art, and reading corners, while boys gathered more often in spaces devoted to blocks, woodworking, and active play. Already, the children had acquired many gender-linked beliefs and preferences and tended to play with peers of their own sex.

The same theories that provide accounts of morality have been used to explain children's gender typing: *social learning theory,* with its emphasis on modeling and reinforcement, and *cognitive-developmental theory,* with its focus on children as active thinkers about their social world. As we will see, neither is adequate by itself. *Gender schema theory,* a third perspective that combines elements of both, has gained favor. In the following sections, we consider the early development of gender typing.

Gender-Stereotyped Beliefs and Behaviors

Even before children can label their own sex consistently, they have begun to acquire subtle associations with gender that most of us hold—men as rough and sharp, women as soft and round. In one study, 18-month-olds linked such items as fir trees and hammers with males, although they had not yet learned comparable feminine associations (Eichstedt et al., 2002). Recall from Chapter 7 that around age 2, children use such words as "boy," "girl," "lady," and "man" appropriately. As soon as gender categories are established, children sort out what they mean in terms of activities and behaviors.

Preschoolers associate toys, articles of clothing, tools, household items, games, occupations, colors (pink and blue), and behaviors (physical and relational aggression) with one sex or the other (Giles & Heyman, 2005; Poulin-Dubois et al., 2002; Ruble, Martin, & Berenbaum, 2006). And their actions reflect their beliefs, not only in play preferences but in personality traits as well. As we have seen, boys tend to be more active, impulsive, assertive, and physically aggressive. Girls tend to be more fearful, dependent, emotionally sensitive, compliant, advanced in effortful control, and skilled at understanding self-conscious emotions and at inflicting indirect relational aggression (Bosacki & Moore, 2004; Else-Quest et al., 2006; Underwood, 2003).

During early childhood, children's gender-stereotyped beliefs strengthen—so much so that many children apply them as blanket rules than as flexible guidelines. When children were asked whether gender stereotypes could be violated, half or more of 3- and 4-year-olds answered "no" to clothing, hairstyle, certain play styles (girls playing roughly), and play with certain toys (Barbie dolls and GI Joes) (Blakemore, 2003). Furthermore, most 3- to 6-year-olds are firm about not wanting to be friends with a child who violates a gender stereotype (a boy who wears nail polish, a girl who plays with trucks) or to attend a school where such violations are allowed (Ruble et al., 2007).

The rigidity of preschoolers' gender stereotypes helps us understand some commonly observed everyday behaviors. When Leslie showed her class a picture of a Scottish bagpiper wearing a kilt, the children insisted, "Men don't wear skirts!" During free play, they often exclaimed that girls can't be police officers and boys don't take care of babies. These one-sided judgments are a joint product of gender stereotyping in the environment and young children's cognitive limitations—in particular, their difficulty coordinating conflicting sources of information (Trautner et al., 2005). Most preschoolers do not yet realize that characteristics *associated with* one's sex—activities, toys, occupations, hairstyle, and clothing—do not *determine* whether a person is male or female. They have trouble understanding that males and females can be different in terms of their bodies but similar in many other ways.

■ Gender typing is well under way in the preschool years. Girls tend to play with girls and are drawn to toys and activities that emphasize nurturance, cooperation, and physical attractiveness. ■

Biological Influences on Gender Typing

The sex differences in play and personality traits just described appear in many cultures around the world (Munroe & Romney, 2006; Whiting & Edwards, 1988). Certain ones—male activity level and physical aggression, female emotional sensitivity, and a preference for same-sex playmates—are widespread among mammalian species (de Waal, 1993, 2001). According to an evolutionary perspective, the adult life of our male ancestors was oriented toward competing for mates, that of our female ancestors toward rearing children. Therefore, males became genetically primed for dominance and females for intimacy, responsiveness, and cooperativeness. Evolutionary theorists claim that family and cultural forces can influence the intensity of genetically based sex differences, leading some individuals to be more gender-typed than others. But experience cannot eradicate those aspects of gender typing that served adaptive functions in human history (Geary, 1999; Maccoby, 2002).

Experiments with animals reveal that prenatally administered androgens increase active play and suppress maternal caregiving in both male and female mammals (Sato et al., 2004). Eleanor Maccoby (1998) argues that sex hormones also affect human play styles, leading to rough, noisy movements among boys and calm, gentle actions among girls. Then, as children interact with peers, they choose partners whose interests and behaviors are compatible with their own. Preschool girls increasingly seek out other girls and like to play in pairs because they share a preference for quieter activities involving cooperative roles. Boys come to prefer larger-group play with other boys, who share a desire to run, climb, play-fight, compete, and build up and knock down (Fabes, Martin, & Hanish, 2003). At age 4, children spend three times as much time with same-sex as with other-sex playmates. By age 6, this ratio has climbed to 11 to 1 (Martin & Fabes, 2001).

Even stronger support for the role of biology in human gender typing comes from research on girls exposed prenatally to high levels of androgens due either to normal variation in hormone levels or to a genetic defect. In both instances, these girls showed more "masculine"

BIOLOGY AND ENVIRONMENT

David: A Boy Who Was Reared as a Girl

As a married man and father in his mid-thirties, David Reimer talked freely about his everyday life—his problems at work and the challenges of child rearing. But when asked about his first 15 years, he distanced himself, speaking as if the child of his early life were another person. In essence, she was.

David—named Bruce at birth—underwent the first infant sex reassignment ever reported on a genetically and hormonally normal child. To find out about David's development, researchers interviewed him intensively and studied his medical and psychotherapy records (Colapinto, 2001; Diamond & Sigmundson, 1999).

When Bruce was 8 months old, his penis was accidentally severed during circumcision. Soon afterward, his desperate parents heard about psychologist John Money's success in assigning a sex to children born with ambiguous genitals. They traveled from their home in Canada to Johns Hopkins University in Baltimore, where, under Money's oversight, 22-month-old Bruce had surgery to remove his testicles and sculpt his genitals to look like those of a girl. The operation complete, Bruce's parents named their daughter Brenda.

Brenda's upbringing was tragic. From the outset, she resisted her parents' efforts to steer her in a "feminine" direction. A dominant, rough-and-tumble child, Brenda picked fights with other children and usually won. Brian (Brenda's identical twin brother) recalled that Brenda looked like a delicate, pretty girl—until she moved or spoke. "She walked like a guy. She talked about guy things. . . . She played with my toys: Tinkertoys, dump trucks" (Colapinto, 2001, p. 57).

At school, Brenda's boyish behavior led classmates to taunt and tease her. When she played with girls, she tried organizing large-group, active games, but they weren't interested. Friendless and uncomfortable as a girl, Brenda increasingly displayed behavior problems. During periodic medical follow-ups, she drew pictures of herself as a boy and refused additional surgery to create a vagina.

As adolescence approached, Brenda's parents moved her from school to school and therapist to therapist in an effort to help her fit in socially and accept a female identity—pressures that increased Brenda's anxiety and conflict with her parents. At puberty, when Brenda's shoulders broadened and her body added muscle, her parents insisted that she begin estrogen therapy to feminize her appearance. Soon she grew breasts and added fat around her waist and hips. Repelled by her feminizing shape, Brenda began overeating to hide it. Her classmates reacted to her confused appearance with stepped-up brutality.

At last, Brenda was transferred to a therapist who recognized her despair and encouraged her parents to tell her about her infancy. When Brenda was 14, her father explained the circumcision accident. David recalled reacting with relief. Deciding to return to his biological sex immediately, he chose for himself the name David, after the biblical lad who slew a giant and overcame adversity. David soon started injections of the androgen hormone testosterone to masculinize his body, and he underwent surgery to remove his breasts and to construct a penis. Although his adolescence continued to be troubled, in his twenties he fell in love with Jane, a single mother of three children, and married her.

David's case confirms the impact of genetic sex and prenatal hormones on a person's sense of self as male or female. His gender reassignment failed because his male biology overwhelmingly

COURTESY OF DAVID REIMER

■ Because of a medical accident when he was a baby, David Reimer underwent the first sex reassignment on a genetically and hormonally normal child: He was reared as a girl. David's story shows the overwhelming impact of biology on gender identity. At age 36, as shown here, he was a married man and father. But two years later, the troubled life that sprang from David's childhood ended tragically, in suicide. ■

demanded a consistent sexual identity. At the same time, his childhood highlights the importance of experience. David expressed outrage at adult encouragement of dependency in girls—after all, he had experienced it firsthand.

Although David tried to surmount his tragic childhood, the troubled life that sprang from it persisted. When David was in his mid-thirties, his twin brother, Brian, committed suicide. Then, after David had lost his job and had been swindled out of his life savings in a shady investment deal, his wife left him, taking the children with her. Grief-stricken, David sank into a deep depression. On May 4, 2004, at age 38, he shot himself.

behaviors—a preference for trucks and blocks over dolls, for active over quiet play, and for boys as playmates—even when their parents encouraged them to engage in gender-typical play (Cohen-Bendahan, van de Beek, & Berenbaum, 2005; Pasterski et al., 2005). Similarly, boys with reduced prenatal androgen exposure due to hereditary defects tended to engage in "feminine" behaviors, including toy choices, play behaviors, and preference for girl playmates (Jürgensen et al., 2007).

Additional evidence comes from a case study of a boy who experienced serious sexual-identity and adjustment problems because his biological makeup and sex of rearing were at odds. Refer to the Biology and Environment box above to find out about David's development.

Environmental Influences on Gender Typing

In a study following almost 14,000 British children from ages 2½ to 8, gender-typed behavior rose steadily over early childhood, with the most gender-typed young preschoolers showing the sharpest increase (Golombok et al., 2008). A wealth of evidence reveals that environmental forces—at home, at school, and in the community—build on genetic influences to promote vigorous gender typing in early childhood.

THE FAMILY   Beginning at birth, parents have different expectations of sons than of daughters (see Chapter 7). Many parents prefer that their children play with "gender-appropriate" toys. And they tend to describe achievement, competition, and control of emotion as important for sons and warmth, "ladylike" behavior, and closely supervised activities as important for daughters (Brody, 1999; Turner & Gervai, 1995).

Actual parenting practices reflect these beliefs. Parents give their sons toys that stress action and competition (guns, cars, tools, and footballs) and their daughters toys that emphasize nurturance, cooperation, and physical attractiveness (dolls, tea sets, and jewelry) (Leaper, 1994; Leaper & Friedman, 2007). Parents also actively reinforce independence in boys and closeness and dependency in girls. For example, parents react more positively when a son plays with cars and trucks, demands attention, runs and climbs, or tries to take toys from others. When interacting with daughters, they more often direct play activities, provide help, encourage participation in household tasks, make supportive statements (approval, praise, and agreement), and refer to emotions (Clearfield & Nelson, 2006; Fagot & Hagan, 1991; Kuebli, Butler, & Fivush, 1995; Leaper et al., 1995). Gender-typed play contexts amplify these communication differences. For example, when playing housekeeping, mothers engage in high rates of supportive emotion talk with girls (Leaper, 2000).

Furthermore, parents provide children with indirect cues about gender categories and stereotypes through the language they use. In one study, researchers observed mothers talking about picture books with their 2- to 6-year-olds (Gelman, Taylor, & Nguyen, 2004). Mothers often labeled gender, even when they did not have to do so ("That's a boy." "Is that a she?"). And they frequently expressed *generic utterances*, which referred to many, or nearly all, males and females as alike, ignoring exceptions: "Boys can be sailors." "Most girls don't like trucks." As Figure 10.5 shows, with age, both mothers and children produced more of these generic statements, which—even when they denied a stereotype ("Boys can be ballet dancers, too")—viewed individuals of the same gender as alike and ignored exceptions. At age 2, mothers introduced these sweeping generalizations nearly three times as often as children. By age 6, children were producing generics more often than mothers, suggesting that children picked up many of these expressions from parental speech. And 4- to 6-year-olds frequently made stereotyped generic statements, which their mothers often affirmed (*Child:* "Only boys can drive trucks." *Mother:* "OK.").

Of the two sexes, boys are more gender-typed. Fathers, especially, are more insistent that boys conform to gender roles. They place more pressure to achieve on sons than on daughters and are less tolerant of "cross-gender" behavior in sons—more concerned when a boy acts like a "sissy" than when a girl acts like a "tomboy" (Sandnabba & Ahlberg, 1999; Wood, Desmarais, & Gugula, 2002). Parents who hold nonstereotyped values and consciously avoid behaving in these ways have children who are less gender-typed (Tenenbaum & Leaper, 2002; Weisner & Wilson-Mitchell, 1990). Other family members may also reduce gender typing. For example, children with older, other-sex siblings have many more opportunities to imitate and participate

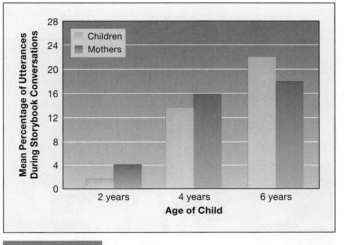

FIGURE 10.5

Mothers' and children's use of generic references to gender during storybook conversations. Generic utterances were broad in scope, in that they referred to many, or nearly all, males and females. Mothers' and children's use of generics increased dramatically between ages 2 and 6. At age 2, mothers produced more generics than children. By age 6, children produced more generics than mothers. *(From S. A. Gelman, M. G. Taylor, & S. P. Nguyen, "Mother–Child Conversations About Gender,"* Monographs of the Society for Research in Child Development, 69[1, Serial No. 275], p. 46. Reprinted by permission of Wiley-Blackwell Publishers.)*

LOOK AND LISTEN

Observe a parent discussing a picture book with a 3- to 6-year-old. How many times did the parent make generic statements about gender? How about the child? Did the parent accept or correct the child's generic utterances?

in "cross-gender" activities and, as a result, are less gender-typed in play preferences, attitudes, and personality traits (McHale et al., 2001; Rust et al., 2000).

TEACHERS Teachers often act in ways that extend gender-role learning. Several times, Leslie caught herself emphasizing gender distinctions when she called out, "Will the girls line up on one side and the boys on the other?" or pleaded "Boys, I wish you'd quiet down like the girls!"

Like parents, preschool teachers give girls more encouragement to participate in adult-structured activities. Girls frequently cluster around the teacher, following directions, while boys are attracted to play areas where adults are minimally involved (Campbell, Shirley, & Candy, 2004; Powlishta, Serbin, & Moller, 1993). As a result, boys and girls engage in different social behaviors. Compliance and bids for help occur more often in adult-structured contexts; assertiveness, leadership, and creative use of materials in unstructured pursuits.

Teachers also use more disapproval and controlling discipline with boys. When girls misbehave, teachers tend to negotiate, coming up with a joint plan to improve behavior (Erden & Wolfgang, 2004). Teachers seem to expect boys to misbehave more often—a belief based partly on boys' actual behavior and partly on gender stereotypes.

PEERS Children's same-sex peer associations make the peer context an especially potent source of gender-role learning. The more preschoolers play with same-sex partners, the more their behavior becomes gender-typed—in toy choices, activity level, aggression, and adult involvement (Martin & Fabes, 2001).

Gender-Role Learning in Gender-Segregated Peer Groups. By age 3, same-sex peers positively reinforce one another for gender-typed play by praising, imitating, or joining in. In contrast, when preschoolers engage in "cross-gender" activities—for example, when boys play with dolls or girls with cars and trucks—peers criticize them. Boys are especially intolerant of cross-gender play in other boys (Fagot, 1984). A boy who frequently crosses gender lines is likely to be ignored by other boys, even when he does engage in "masculine" activities!

Children also develop different styles of social influence in gender-segregated peer groups. To get their way in large-group play, boys often rely on commands, threats, and physical force. Girls' preference for playing in pairs leads to greater concern with a partner's needs, evident in girls' use of polite requests, persuasion, and acceptance. Girls soon find that these gentle tactics succeed with other girls but not with boys, who ignore their courteous overtures (Leaper, 1994; Leaper, Tenenbaum, & Shaffer, 1999). Boys' unresponsiveness gives girls another reason to stop interacting with them.

Over time, children come to believe in the "correctness" of gender-segregated play, which further strengthens gender segregation and gender-stereotyped activities (Martin et al., 1999). As boys and girls separate, *in-group favoritism*—more positive evaluations of members of one's own gender—becomes another factor that sustains the separate social worlds of boys and girls, resulting in "two distinct subcultures" of shared knowledge, beliefs, interests, and behaviors (Maccoby, 2002; Ruble, Martin, & Berenbaum, 2006).

Cultural Variations. Although gender segregation is pervasive, cultures and subcultures differ in the extent of gender-typed communication within those groups. African-American and Hispanic lower-SES girls, for example, are generally more assertive and independent in their interactions with one another and with boys than are Caucasian-American girls (Goodwin, 1998). A comparison of Chinese and U.S. preschoolers' play revealed similar differences.

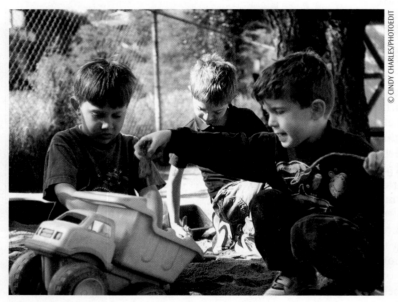

© CINDY CHARLES/PHOTOEDIT

■ These boys positively reinforce one another's gender-typed behavior. Preschoolers, especially boys, tend to be critical of peers who play with "cross-gender" toys or enjoy activities associated with the other sex. ■

LOOK AND LISTEN

While observing 3- to 5-year-olds during a free-play period in a preschool or child-care program, note the extent of gender segregation and gender-typed play. Did styles of social influence differ in boys' and girls' gender-segregated groups? Jot down examples.

Chinese 5-year-old girls used more direct commands, complaints, and critical statements when interacting with both same- and other-sex peers than their American counterparts. And Chinese boys frequently combined commands with warning, appeasing, and justifying statements, which reduced expressions of dominance in boys' playgroups: "Better not open that. You'll spill it." "I'll do it! I'm here to help you" (Kyratis & Guo, 2001).

In collectivist societies where group cohesion is highly valued, children may not feel a need to work as hard at maintaining same-sex peer relations through traditional interaction patterns. In addition to their other benefits, ethnically diverse classrooms might reduce gender-typed peer communication as the "cross-gender" influence attempts of some children rub off on others.

THE BROADER SOCIAL ENVIRONMENT   Although children's everyday environments have changed to some degree, they continue to present many examples of gender typing—in occupations, leisure activities, media portrayals, and achievements of men and women. For example, although today's TV programs include more career-oriented women than in the past, female characters continue to be young, attractive, caring, emotional, and victimized and to be seen in romantic and family contexts. In contrast, male characters are usually dominant and powerful (Signorielli, 2001). Gender stereotypes even pervade preschool educational software, which emphasize male characters exhibiting "masculine" traits (Sheldon, 2004). And stereotypes are especially prevalent in cartoons, computer games, and other entertainment media for children and youths.

As we will see next, children do more than imitate the many gender-linked responses they observe. They soon come to view themselves and their social surroundings through a "gender-biased lens"—a perspective that can seriously restrict their interests and learning opportunities.

Gender Identity

As adults, each of us has a **gender identity**—an image of oneself as relatively masculine or feminine in characteristics. By middle childhood, researchers can measure gender identity by asking children to rate themselves on personality traits. A child or adult with a "masculine" identity scores high on traditionally masculine items (such as *ambitious, competitive,* and *self-sufficient*) and low on traditionally feminine items (such as *affectionate, cheerful,* and *soft-spoken*). Someone with a "feminine" identity does the reverse. And a substantial minority (especially females) have a gender identity called **androgyny,** scoring high on *both* masculine and feminine personality characteristics.

Gender identity is a good predictor of psychological adjustment. "Masculine" and androgynous children and adults have higher self-esteem than "feminine" individuals, perhaps because many typically feminine traits are not highly valued by society (Boldizar, 1991; Bronstein, 2006; Harter, 2006). Also, androgynous individuals are more adaptable—able to show masculine independence or feminine sensitivity, depending on the situation (Huyck, 1996; Taylor & Hall, 1982). The existence of an androgynous identity demonstrates that children can acquire a mixture of positive qualities traditionally associated with each gender—an orientation that may best help them realize their potential.

EMERGENCE OF GENDER IDENTITY   How do children develop a gender identity? According to *social learning theory,* behavior comes before self-perceptions. Preschoolers first acquire gender-typed responses through modeling and reinforcement and only later organize these behaviors into gender-linked ideas about themselves. In contrast, *cognitive-developmental theory* maintains that self-perceptions come before behavior. Over the preschool years, children acquire a cognitive appreciation of the permanence of their sex, or **gender constancy**—a full understanding of the biologically based permanence of their gender, including the realization that sex remains the same over time, even if clothing, hairstyle, and play activities change. Then children use this knowledge to guide their behavior (Kohlberg, 1966).

When 3- to 5-year-olds are asked such questions as "When you (a girl) grow up, could you ever be a daddy?" or "Could you be a boy if you wanted to?" they freely answer yes. And children younger than age 6 who watch an adult dressing a doll in "other-gender" clothing typically insist that the doll's sex has also changed (Chauhan, Shastri, & Mohite, 2005; Fagot, 1985). Mastery of gender constancy occurs in a three-step sequence: *gender labeling* (correct naming of one's own and others' sex), *gender stability* (understanding that gender remains the same over time), and *gender consistency* (realization that gender is not altered by superficial changes in clothing or activities). Full attainment of gender constancy is strongly related to ability to pass Piagetian conservation and verbal appearance–reality tasks (see page 327 in Chapter 9) (De Lisi & Gallagher, 1991; Trautner, Gervai, & Nemeth, 2003). Indeed, gender constancy tasks can be considered a type of appearance–reality problem, in that children must distinguish what a person looks like from who he or she really is.

In many cultures, young children do not have access to basic biological knowledge about gender because they rarely see members of the other sex naked. But giving preschoolers information about genital differences does not result in gender constancy. Preschoolers who have such knowledge usually say that changing a doll's clothing will not change its sex, but when asked to justify their response, they do not refer to sex as an innate, unchanging quality of people (Szkrybalo & Ruble, 1999). This suggests that cognitive immaturity, not social experience, is responsible for preschoolers' difficulty grasping the permanence of sex.

Is cognitive-developmental theory correct that gender constancy is responsible for children's gender-typed behavior? Evidence for this assumption is weak. "Gender-appropriate" behavior appears so early in the preschool years that its initial appearance must result from modeling and reinforcement, as social learning theory suggests. Although outcomes are not entirely consistent, some evidence suggests that gender constancy actually contributes to the emergence of more flexible gender-role attitudes during the school years (Ruble et al., 2007). But overall, the impact of gender constancy on gender typing is not great. As research in the following section reveals, gender-role adoption is more powerfully affected by children's beliefs about how close the connection must be between their own gender and their behavior.

GENDER SCHEMA THEORY **Gender schema theory** is an information-processing approach to gender typing that combines social learning and cognitive-developmental features. It explains how environmental pressures and children's cognitions work together to shape gender-role development (Martin & Halverson, 1987; Martin, Ruble, & Szkrybalo, 2002). At an early age, children pick up gender-stereotyped preferences and behaviors from others. At the same time, they organize their experiences into *gender schemas,* or masculine and feminine categories, that they use to interpret their world. As soon as preschoolers can label their own gender, they select gender schemas consistent with it ("Only boys can be doctors" or "Cooking is a girl's job") and apply those categories to themselves. Their self-perceptions then become gender-typed and serve as additional schemas that children use to process information and guide their own behavior.

We have seen that individual differences exist in the extent to which children endorse gender-typed views. Figure 10.6 shows different cognitive pathways for children who often apply gender schemas to their experiences and those who rarely do (Liben & Bigler, 2002). Consider Billy, who encounters a doll. If Billy is a *gender-schematic child,* his *gender-salience filter* immediately makes gender highly relevant. Drawing on his prior learning, he asks himself, "Should boys play with dolls?" If he answers "yes" and the toy interests him, he will approach it, explore it, and learn more about it. If he answers "no," he will respond by avoiding the "gender-inappropriate" toy. But if Billy is a *gender-aschematic child*—one who seldom views the world in gender-linked terms—he simply asks himself, "Do I like this toy?" and responds on the basis of his interests.

To examine the consequences of gender-schematic processing, researchers showed 4- and 5-year-olds toys that were gender-neutral and that varied in attractiveness. An adult labeled some as boys' toys and others as girls' toys, leaving a third group unlabeled. Most children engaged in gender-schematic reasoning, preferring toys labeled for their gender and predicting that same-sex peers would also like those toys (Martin, Eisenbud, & Rose, 1995). Highly attractive toys, especially, lost their appeal when they were labeled as for the other gender. And because gender-schematic preschoolers typically conclude, "What I like, children of my own sex will also like," they often use their own preferences to add to their gender biases! For example, a girl who dislikes oysters may declare, "Only boys like oysters!" even though she has never actually been given information supporting such a stereotype (Liben & Bigler, 2002).

Gender-schematic thinking is so powerful that when children see others behaving in "gender-inconsistent" ways, they often cannot remember the behavior or they distort their memory to

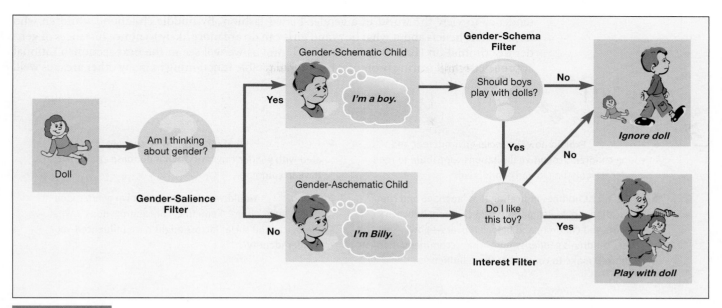

FIGURE 10.6

Cognitive pathways for gender-schematic and gender-aschematic children. In *gender-schematic children,* the gender-salience filter immediately makes gender highly relevant: Billy sees a doll and thinks, "I'm a boy. Should boys play with dolls?" Drawing on his experiences, he answers "yes" or "no." If he answers "yes" and the doll interests him, he plays with the doll. If he answers "no," he avoids the "gender-inappropriate" toy. *Gender-aschematic children* rarely view the world in gender-linked terms. Billy simply asks, "Do I like this toy?" and responds on the basis of his interests. *(Reprinted by permission of Rebecca Bigler, University of Texas, Austin.)*

make it "gender-consistent"—for example, when shown a picture of a male nurse, remembering him as a doctor (Liben & Signorella, 1993; Marin & Ruble, 2004). Over time, children learn much more about people, objects, and events that fit with their gender schemas than they do about "cross-gender" activities and behaviors. Of course, gender-schematic processing could not operate if society did not teach a wide variety of gender-linked associations.

Reducing Gender Stereotyping in Young Children

How can we help young children avoid rigid gender schemas that restrict their behavior and learning opportunities? No easy recipe exists. Biology clearly affects children's gender typing, channeling boys, on average, toward active, competitive play and girls toward quieter, more intimate interaction. But most aspects of gender typing are not built into human nature (Ruble, Martin, & Berenbaum, 2006).

Because young children's cognitive limitations lead them to assume that cultural practices determine gender, parents and teachers are wise to try to delay preschoolers' exposure to gender-stereotyped messages. Adults can begin by limiting traditional gender roles in their own behavior and by providing children with nontraditional alternatives. For example, parents can take turns making dinner, bathing children, and driving the family car, and they can give their sons and daughters both trucks and dolls and both pink and blue clothing. Teachers can make sure that all children spend time in mixed-gender play activities and in both adult-structured and unstructured pursuits. Finally, adults can avoid language that conveys gender stereotypes and can shield children from media presentations that do the same.

Once children notice the vast array of gender stereotypes in their society, parents and teachers can point out exceptions. For example, they can arrange for children to see men and women pursuing nontraditional careers and can explain that interests and skills, not sex, should determine a person's occupation. Research shows that such reasoning is highly effective in reducing children's

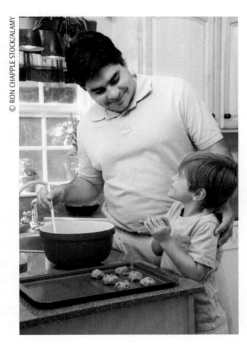

■ Parents and teachers can reduce preschoolers' gender stereotyping by modeling nonstereotyped behaviors and providing nontraditional alternatives. For this boy, making cookies is not "for girls." It's an activity he and his father enjoy together. ■

tendency to view the world in a gender-biased fashion. By middle childhood, children who hold flexible beliefs about what boys and girls can do are more likely to notice instances of gender discrimination (Brown & Bigler, 2004). And as we will see in the next section, a rational approach to child rearing promotes healthy, adaptable functioning in many other areas as well.

ASK YOURSELF

◆ REVIEW Explain how the social environment and young children's cognitive limitations contribute to rigid gender stereotyping in early childhood.

◆ APPLY List findings indicating that language and communication—between parents and children, between teachers and children, and between peers—powerfully affects children's gender typing. What recommendations would you make to counteract these influences?

◆ CONNECT What other cognitive changes are associated with gender constancy? What do these attainments have in common?

◆ REFLECT Would you describe your own gender identity as "masculine," "feminine," or "androgynous"? What biological and social factors might have influenced your gender identity?

Child Rearing and Emotional and Social Development

In this and previous chapters, we have seen how parents can foster children's competence—by building a parent–child relationship based on affection and cooperation, by serving as models and reinforcers of mature behavior, by using reasoning and inductive discipline, and by guiding and encouraging mastery of new skills. Now let's put these practices together into an overall view of effective parenting.

Styles of Child Rearing

Child-rearing styles are combinations of parenting behaviors that occur over a wide range of situations, creating an enduring child-rearing climate. In a landmark series of studies, Diana Baumrind gathered information on child rearing by watching parents interact with their preschoolers (Baumrind, 1971). Her findings, and those of others who have extended her work, reveal three features that consistently differentiate an effective style from less effective ones: (1) acceptance and involvement, (2) control, and (3) autonomy granting (Gray & Steinberg, 1999; Hart, Newell, & Olsen, 2003). Table 10.2 shows how child-rearing styles differ in these features. Let's discuss each style in turn.

AUTHORITATIVE CHILD REARING The **authoritative child-rearing style**—the most successful approach—involves high acceptance and involvement, adaptive control techniques, and appropriate autonomy granting. Authoritative parents are warm, attentive, and sensitive to their child's needs. They establish an enjoyable, emotionally fulfilling parent–child relationship that draws the child into close connection. At the same time, authoritative parents exercise firm, reasonable control: They insist on mature behavior, give reasons for their expectations, and use disciplinary encounters as "teaching moments" to promote the child's self-regulation. Finally, authoritative parents engage in gradual, appropriate autonomy granting, allowing the child to make decisions in areas where he is ready to do so (Kuczynski & Lollis, 2002; Russell, Mize, & Bissaker, 2004).

Throughout childhood and adolescence, authoritative parenting is linked to many aspects of competence—an upbeat mood, self-control, task persistence, cooperativeness, high self-esteem, social and moral maturity, and favorable school performance (Amato & Fowler, 2002; Aunola, Stattin, & Nurmi, 2000; Gonzalez & Wolters, 2006; Mackey, Arnold, & Pratt, 2001; Milevsky et al., 2007; Steinberg, Darling, & Fletcher, 1995).

| TABLE 10.2 | Features of Child-Rearing Styles | | |

CHILD-REARING STYLE	ACCEPTANCE AND INVOLVEMENT	CONTROL	AUTONOMY GRANTING
Authoritative	Is warm, responsive, attentive, and sensitive to the child's needs	Makes reasonable demands for maturity and consistently enforces and explains them	Permits the child to make decisions in accord with readiness

Encourages the child to express thoughts, feelings, and desires

When parent and child disagree, engages in joint decision making when possible |
| Authoritarian | Is cold and rejecting and frequently degrades the child | Makes many demands coercively, using force and punishment; often uses psychological control, withdrawing love and intruding on the child's individuality | Makes decisions for the child

Rarely listens to the child's point of view |
| Permissive | Is warm but overindulgent or inattentive | Makes few or no demands | Permits the child to make many decisions before the child is ready |
| Uninvolved | Is emotionally detached and withdrawn | Makes few or no demands | Is indifferent to the child's decision making and point of view |

AUTHORITARIAN CHILD REARING   The **authoritarian child-rearing style** is low in acceptance and involvement, high in coercive control, and low in autonomy granting. Authoritarian parents appear cold and rejecting. To exert control, they yell, command, criticize, and threaten. "Do it because I said so!" is their attitude. They make decisions for their child and expect their child to accept their word unquestioningly. If the child resists, authoritarian parents resort to force and punishment.

Children of authoritarian parents are anxious, unhappy, and low in self-esteem and self-reliance. When frustrated, they tend to react with hostility and, like their parents, resort to force when they do not get their way. Boys, especially, show high rates of defiance and aggression. Although girls also engage in acting-out behavior, they are more likely to be dependent, lacking interest in exploration, and overwhelmed by challenging tasks (Hart, Newell, & Olsen, 2003; Nix et al., 1999; Thompson, Hollis, & Richards, 2003). Children and adolescents exposed to the authoritarian style typically do poorly in school. However, because of their parents' concern with control, they tend to achieve better and to commit fewer antisocial acts than peers with undemanding parents—that is, whose parents use one of the parenting styles we will consider next (Steinberg, Blatt-Eisengart, & Cauffman, 2006).

In addition to unwarranted direct control, authoritarian parents engage in a more subtle type called **psychological control,** in which they intrude on and manipulate children's verbal expression, individuality, and attachments to parents. In an attempt to decide virtually everything for the child, these parents frequently interrupt or put down the child's ideas, decisions, and choice of friends. When they are dissatisfied, they withdraw love, making their affection contingent on the child's compliance. They also hold excessively high expectations that do not fit the child's developing capacities. Children subjected to psychological control exhibit adjustment problems involving both anxious, withdrawn behavior and defiance and aggression—especially the relational form, which (like parental psychological control) damages relationships through manipulation and exclusion (Barber et al., 2005; Kuppens et al., 2009; Nelson et al., 2006; Silk et al., 2003).

PERMISSIVE CHILD REARING   The **permissive child-rearing style** is warm and accepting but uninvolved. Permissive parents are either overindulgent or inattentive and, thus, engage in little control. Instead of gradually granting autonomy, they allow children to make many of their own decisions at an age when they are not yet capable of doing so. Their children can eat meals and go to bed when they feel like it and watch as much television as they want. They do not have to learn good manners or do household chores. Although some permissive parents truly believe in this approach, many others simply lack confidence in their ability to influence their child's behavior (Oyserman et al., 2005).

Children of permissive parents are impulsive, disobedient, and rebellious. Compared with children whose parents exert more control, they are also overly demanding and dependent on adults, and they show less persistence on tasks, poorer school achievement, and more antisocial behavior. The link between permissive parenting and dependent, nonachieving, rebellious behavior is especially strong for boys (Barber & Olsen, 1997; Baumrind, 1971; Steinberg, Blatt-Eisengart, & Cauffman, 2006).

UNINVOLVED CHILD REARING The **uninvolved child-rearing style** combines low acceptance and involvement with little control and general indifference to issues of autonomy. Often these parents are emotionally detached and depressed and so overwhelmed by life stress that they have little time and energy for children. At its extreme, uninvolved parenting is a form of child maltreatment called *neglect*. Especially when it begins early, it disrupts virtually all aspects of development (see Chapter 4, page 155). Even with less extreme parental disengagement, children and adolescents display many problems—poor emotional self-regulation, school achievement difficulties, and antisocial behavior (Aunola, Stattin, & Nurmi, 2000; Kurdek & Fine, 1994).

What Makes Authoritative Child Rearing Effective?

Like other correlational findings, relationships between parenting styles and children's competence are open to interpretation. Perhaps parents of well-adjusted children are authoritative because their youngsters have especially cooperative dispositions. Children's characteristics do contribute to the ease with which parents can apply the authoritative style. An impulsive, noncompliant child makes it hard for parents to be warm, firm, and rational. But longitudinal research reveals that authoritative child rearing promotes maturity in children of diverse temperaments (Hart, Newell, & Olson, 2003; Olson et al., 2000; Rubin, Burgess, & Coplan, 2002). It seems to create a positive emotional context for parental influence in the following ways:

- Warm, involved parents who are secure in the standards they hold for their children provide models of caring concern as well as confident, self-controlled behavior.
- Children are far more likely to comply with and internalize control that appears fair and reasonable, not arbitrary.
- By making demands and engaging in autonomy granting that matches children's ability to take responsibility for their own behavior, authoritative parents let children know that they are competent individuals who can do things successfully for themselves. In this way, parents foster favorable self-esteem and cognitive and social maturity.
- Supportive aspects of the authoritative style, including parental acceptance, involvement, and rational control, are a powerful source of *resilience*, protecting children from the negative effects of family stress and poverty (Beyers et al., 2003).

Over time, the relationship between parenting and children's attributes becomes increasingly bidirectional (Kuczynski, 2003). When parents intervene patiently but firmly, they promote favorable adjustment, setting the stage for a positive parent–child relationship.

Cultural Variations

Although authoritative parenting is broadly advantageous, ethnic minority parents often have distinct child-rearing beliefs and practices reflecting cultural values. Let's look at some examples.

Compared with Western parents, Chinese parents describe their parenting as more controlling. They are more directive in teaching and scheduling their children's time, as a way of fostering self-control and high achievement. Chinese parents may appear less warm than Western parents because they withhold praise, which they believe results in self-satisfied, poorly motivated children (Chao, 1994; Chen et al., 2001). High control reflects the Confucian belief in strict discipline, respect for elders, and socially desirable behavior, taught by deeply involved parents. Chinese parents report expressing affection and concern and using induction and other reasoning-oriented discipline as much as American parents do, but they more often shame a misbehaving child, withdraw love, and use physical punishment (Cheah et al., 2009; Shwalb et al., 2004; Wu et al., 2002). When these practices become excessive, resulting in an authoritarian style high in psychological or coercive control, Chinese children display the same negative outcomes seen in Western children: poor academic achievement, anxiety, depression, and aggressive behavior (Bradford et al., 2003; Nelson et al., 2005, 2006; Pong, Johnston, & Chen, 2010; Wang, Pomerantz, & Chen, 2007).

In Hispanic families, Asian Pacific Island families, and Caribbean families of African and East Indian origin, firm insistence on respect for parental authority is paired with high parental warmth—a combination suited to promoting competence and strong feelings of family loyalty (Harrison et al., 1994; Roopnarine & Evans, 2007). Hispanic fathers typically spend much time with their children and are warm and sensitive (Cabrera & García Coll, 2004; Jambunathan, Burts, & Pierce, 2000). In Caribbean families that have immigrated to the United States, fathers' authoritativeness—but not mothers'—predicted preschoolers' literacy and math skills, probably because Caribbean fathers take a larger role in guiding their children's academic progress (Roopnarine et al., 2006).

Although wide variation exists, low-SES African-American parents tend to expect immediate obedience, regarding strictness as fostering self-control and a watchful attitude in risky surroundings. Consistent with these beliefs, African-American parents who use more controlling strategies tend to have more cognitively and socially competent children (Brody & Flor, 1998). Recall, also, that a history of mild physical punishment is associated with a reduction in antisocial behavior among African-American youths but with an increase among Caucasian Americans (refer to the Cultural Influences box on page 383). Most African-American parents who use strict, "no-nonsense" discipline use physical punishment sparingly and combine it with warmth and reasoning.

These cultural variations remind us that child-rearing styles must be viewed in their larger context. As we have seen, many factors contribute to good parenting: personal characteristics of the child and parent, SES, access to extended family and community supports, cultural values and practices, and public policies.

As we turn to the topic of child maltreatment, our discussion will underscore, once again, that effective child rearing is sustained not just by the desire of mothers and fathers to be good parents. Almost all want to be. Unfortunately, when vital supports for parenting break down, children—as well as parents—can suffer terribly.

■ In many Caribbean families, parents combine warmth with firm insistence on respect for parental authority, and fathers devote much time to guiding children's academic progress. ■

Child Maltreatment

Child maltreatment is as old as human history, but only recently has the problem been widely acknowledged and research aimed at understanding it. Perhaps public concern has increased because child maltreatment is especially common in large industrialized nations. In the most recently reported year, 770,000 U.S. children (10 out of every 1,000) were identified as victims (U.S. Department of Health and Human Services, 2010a). Most cases go unreported, so the true figures are much higher.

Child maltreatment takes the following forms:

■ *Physical abuse:* Assaults, such as shaking, kicking, biting, punching, or stabbing, that inflict physical injury

- *Sexual abuse:* Fondling, intercourse, exhibitionism, commercial exploitation through prostitution or production of pornography, and other forms of sexual exploitation
- *Neglect:* Failure to meet a child's basic needs for food, clothing, medical attention, education, or supervision
- *Emotional abuse:* Acts that could cause serious mental or behavior disorders, including social isolation, repeated unreasonable demands, ridicule, humiliation, intimidation, or terrorizing

Neglect accounts for about 60 percent of reported cases, physical abuse for 20 percent, emotional abuse for 10 percent, and sexual abuse for 10 percent (U.S. Department of Health and Human Services, 2008b, 2010a). But these figures are only approximate, as many children experience more than one form.

Parents commit more than 80 percent of abusive incidents. Other relatives account for about 7 percent. The remainder are perpetrated by parents' unmarried partners, school officials, camp counselors, and other adults. Mothers engage in neglect more often than fathers, whereas fathers engage in sexual abuse more often than mothers. Maternal and paternal rates of physical and emotional abuse are fairly similar. Infants and young preschoolers are at greatest risk for neglect; preschool and school-age children for physical, emotional, and sexual abuse. But each type occurs at every age (Trocmé & Wolfe, 2002; U.S. Department of Health and Human Services, 2010). Because most sexual abuse victims are identified in middle childhood, we will pay special attention to this form of maltreatment in Chapter 13.

ORIGINS OF CHILD MALTREATMENT   Early findings suggested that child maltreatment was rooted in adult psychological disturbance (Kempe et al., 1962). But although child maltreatment is more common among disturbed parents, it soon became clear that a single "abusive personality type" does not exist. Parents who were abused as children do not necessarily become abusers (Buchanan, 1996; Simons et al., 1991). And sometimes even "normal" parents harm their children!

For help in understanding child maltreatment, researchers turned to *ecological systems theory* (see Chapters 1 and 2). They discovered that many interacting variables—at the family, community, and cultural levels—contribute. The more risks present, the greater the likelihood that abuse or neglect will occur. Table 10.3 summarizes factors associated with child maltreatment.

The Family.   Within the family, children whose characteristics make them more challenging to rear are more likely to become targets of abuse. These include premature or very sick babies and children who are temperamentally difficult, are inattentive and overactive, or have other developmental problems. Child factors, however, only slightly increase the risk of abuse (Jaudes & Mackey-Bilaver, 2008; Sidebotham et al., 2003). Whether such children are maltreated largely depends on parents' characteristics.

TABLE 10.3   Factors Related to Child Maltreatment

FACTOR	DESCRIPTION
Parent characteristics	Psychological disturbance; alcohol and drug abuse; history of abuse as a child; belief in harsh, physical discipline; desire to satisfy unmet emotional needs through the child; unreasonable expectations for child behavior; low educational level
Child characteristics	Premature or very sick baby; difficult temperament; inattentiveness and overactivity; other developmental problems
Family characteristics	Low income or poverty; homelessness; marital instability; social isolation; partner abuse; frequent moves; large families with closely spaced children; overcrowded living conditions; disorganized household; lack of steady employment; other signs of high life stress
Community	Characterized by social isolation; few parks, child-care centers, preschool programs, recreation centers, or churches to serve as family supports
Culture	Approval of physical force and violence as ways to solve problems

Sources: U.S. Department of Health and Human Services, 2010a; Wekerle & Wolfe, 2003; Whipple, 2006.

Maltreating parents are less skillful than other parents in handling discipline confrontations and getting children to cooperate in working toward common goals. They also suffer from biased thinking about their child. For example, they often attribute their baby's crying or their child's misdeeds to a stubborn or bad disposition, evaluate children's transgressions as worse than they are, and feel powerless in parenting—perspectives that lead them to move quickly toward physical force (Bugental & Happaney, 2004; Crouch et al., 2008).

Once abuse begins, it quickly becomes part of a self-sustaining relationship. The small irritations to which abusive parents react—a fussy baby, a preschooler who knocks over her milk, or a child who will not mind immediately—soon become bigger ones. Then the harshness increases. By the preschool years, abusive and neglectful parents seldom interact with their children. When they do, they rarely express pleasure and affection; the communication is almost always negative (Wolfe, 2005).

Most parents have enough self-control not to respond to their children's misbehavior or developmental problems with abuse. Other factors combine with these conditions to prompt an extreme response. Unmanageable parental stress is strongly associated with maltreatment. Abusive parents respond to stressful situations with high emotional arousal. And low income, low education (less than a high school diploma), unemployment, alcohol and drug use, marital conflict, overcrowded living conditions, frequent moves, and extreme household disorganization are common in abusive homes (Wekerle et al., 2007; Wulczyn, 2009). These conditions increase the chances that parents will be too overwhelmed to meet basic child-rearing responsibilities or will vent their frustrations by lashing out at their children.

The Community.   The majority of abusive and neglectful parents are isolated from both formal and informal social supports. Because of their life histories, many have learned to mistrust and avoid others and are poorly skilled at establishing and maintaining positive relationships. Also, maltreating parents are more likely to live in unstable, rundown neighborhoods that provide few links between family and community, such as parks, child-care centers, preschool programs, recreation centers, and religious institutions (Coulton et al., 2007; Zielinski & Bradshaw, 2006). They lack "lifelines" to others and have no one to turn to for help during stressful times.

The Larger Culture.   Cultural values, laws, and customs profoundly affect the chances that child maltreatment will occur when parents feel overburdened. Societies that view violence as an appropriate way to solve problems set the stage for child abuse.

Although the United States has laws to protect children from maltreatment, widespread support exists for use of physical force with children (refer back to page 382). Many countries—including Austria, Croatia, Cyprus, Denmark, Finland, Germany, Israel, Italy, Latvia, Norway, and Sweden—have outlawed physical punishment, a measure that dampens both physical discipline and abuse (Bugental & Grusec, 2006). Furthermore, every industrialized nation except the United States and Canada now prohibits corporal punishment in schools (Center for Effective Discipline, 2005). The U.S. Supreme Court has twice upheld the right of school officials to use corporal punishment. Fortunately, some U.S. states and Canadian provinces have passed laws that ban it.

CONSEQUENCES OF CHILD MALTREATMENT   The family circumstances of maltreated children impair the development of emotional self-regulation, empathy and sympathy, self-concept, social skills, and academic motivation. Over time, these youngsters show serious adjustment problems, including severe depression, aggressive behavior, peer difficulties, substance abuse, and delinquency, including violent crime (Cicchetti & Toth, 2006; Sanchez & Pollak, 2009; Wolfe et al., 2001).

How do these damaging consequences occur? Recall our earlier discussion of hostile cycles of parent–child interaction. For abused children, these are especially severe. Also, a family characteristic strongly associated with child abuse is partner abuse, which predicts similar internalizing and externalizing difficulties (Gewirtz & Edleson, 2004; Kitzmann et al., 2003). Clearly, the home lives of abused children overflow with adult conduct that leads to profound distress, including emotional insecurity (see pages 70–71 in Chapter 2), and to aggression as a way of solving problems.

Furthermore, demeaning parental messages, in which children are ridiculed, humiliated, rejected, or terrorized, result in low self-esteem, high anxiety, self-blame, and efforts to escape from extreme psychological pain—at times severe enough to lead to attempted suicide in adolescence (Wolfe, 2005). At school, maltreated children present serious discipline problems. Their noncompliance, poor motivation, and cognitive immaturity interfere with academic achievement, further undermining their chances for life success (Wekerle & Wolfe, 2003).

Finally, repeated abuse is associated with central nervous system damage, including abnormal EEG brain-wave activity, fMRI-detected reduced size and impaired functioning of the cerebral cortex and corpus callosum, and atypical production of the stress hormone cortisol—initially too high, but after months of abuse, often too low. Over time, the massive trauma of persistent abuse seems to blunt children's normal physiological response to stress (Cicchetti, 2007; Teicher et al., 2004; Watts-English et al., 2006). These effects increase the chances that cognitive and emotional problems will endure.

PREVENTING CHILD MALTREATMENT   Because child maltreatment is embedded in families, communities, and society as a whole, efforts to prevent it must be directed at each of these levels. Many approaches have been suggested, including teaching high-risk parents effective child-rearing strategies, providing direct experience with children in high school child development courses, and developing broad social programs aimed at improving economic and neighborhood conditions and community services for at-risk families.

We have seen that providing social supports to families is effective in easing parental stress. This approach sharply reduces child maltreatment as well (Azar & Wolfe, 1998). A trusting relationship with another person is the most important factor in preventing mothers with childhood histories of abuse from repeating the cycle with their own children (Egeland, Jacobvitz, & Sroufe, 1988). Parents Anonymous, a U.S. organization with affiliate programs around the world, helps child-abusing parents learn constructive parenting practices, largely through social supports. Its local chapters offer self-help group meetings, daily phone calls, and regular home visits to relieve social isolation and teach responsible child-rearing skills.

Early intervention aimed at strengthening both child and parent competencies can improve parenting practices, thereby preventing child maltreatment (Howard & Brooks-Gunn, 2009). Healthy Families America, a program that began in Hawaii and has spread to 440 sites across the United States and Canada, identifies families at risk for maltreatment during pregnancy or at birth. Each receives three years of home visitation, in which a trained worker helps parents manage crises, encourages effective child rearing, and puts parents in touch with community services to meet their own and their children's needs (PCA America, 2009). In an evaluation in which over 600 families were randomly assigned to intervention and control groups, Healthy Families home visitation alone reduced only neglect, not abuse (Duggan et al., 2004). But adding a *cognitive component* dramatically increased its impact. When home visitors helped parents change negative appraisals of their children—by countering inaccurate interpretations (for example, that the baby is behaving with malicious intent) and by working on solving child-rearing problems—physical punishment and abuse dropped sharply after one year of intervention (see Figure 10.7) (Bugental et al., 2002).

■ Each year, fourth to sixth graders across Los Angeles County enter a poster contest to celebrate Child Abuse Prevention Month. This recent winner appeals to parents to treat children with warmth and caring. *(Lisa Valicente and Madeline Zauss, 6th Grade, Jefferson Elementary School, Redondo Beach, CA. Courtesy ICAN Associates, Los Angeles County InterAgency Council on Child Abuse & Neglect, ican4kids.org.)* ■

FIGURE 10.7

Impact of a home visitation program with a cognitive component on preventing physical abuse of young children. In an enhanced home visitation condition, home visitors not only provided social support, encouraged effective child rearing, and connected families with community resources but also helped at-risk parents change their negative appraisals of their babies and solve child-rearing problems. After one year of intervention, this cognitive component sharply reduced physical abuse of babies (hitting, shaking, beating, kicking, biting) compared with an unenhanced home visitation condition and a no-intervention control. *(Adapted from Bugental et al., 2002.)*

Still, many experts believe that child maltreatment cannot be eliminated as long as violence is widespread and harsh physical punishment is regarded as acceptable. In addition, combating poverty and its diverse correlates—family stress and disorganization, inadequate food and medical care, teenage parenthood, low-birth-weight babies, and parental hopelessness—would protect many children.

Although more cases reach the courts than in decades past, child maltreatment remains a crime that is difficult to prove. Usually, the only witnesses are the child victims or other loyal family members. And even when the evidence is strong, judges hesitate to impose the ultimate safeguard against further harm: permanently removing the child from the family. There are several reasons for their reluctance. First, in the United States, government intervention into family life is viewed as a last resort. Second, despite destructive family relationships, maltreated children and their parents usually are attached to one another. Usually, neither desires separation. Finally, the U.S. legal system tends to regard children as parental property rather than as human beings in their own right, and this also has stood in the way of court-ordered protection.

Even with intensive treatment, some adults persist in their abusive acts. An estimated 1,700 U.S. children, most of them infants and preschoolers, die from maltreatment each year. About two-thirds suffered from beatings, drownings, suffocation, or *shaken baby syndrome,* in which shaking an infant or young child inflicts brain and neck injuries. And about one-third were severely neglected (Trocmé & Wolfe, 2002; U.S. Department of Health and Human Services, 2010a). When parents are unlikely to change their behavior, the drastic step of separating parent from child and legally terminating parental rights is the only justifiable course of action.

Child maltreatment is a sad note on which to end our discussion of a period of childhood that is so full of excitement, awakening, and discovery. But there is reason to be optimistic. Great strides have been made over the past several decades in understanding and preventing child maltreatment.

ASK YOURSELF

◆ **REVIEW** Summarize findings on ethnic variations in child-rearing styles. Is the concept of authoritative parenting useful for understanding effective parenting across cultures? Explain.

◆ **APPLY** Chandra heard a news report about 10 severely neglected children, living in squalor in an inner-city tenement. She wondered, "Why would parents so mistreat their children?" How would you answer Chandra?

◆ **CONNECT** Which child-rearing style is most likely to be associated with inductive discipline, and why?

◆ **REFLECT** How would you classify your parents' child-rearing styles? What factors might have influenced their approach to parenting?

Summary

Erikson's Theory: Initiative versus Guilt

What personality changes take place during Erikson's stage of initiative versus guilt?

- Preschoolers develop a new sense of purposefulness as they grapple with Erikson's psychological conflict of **initiative versus guilt.** A healthy sense of initiative depends on exploring the social world through play and experiencing supportive child rearing that fosters a secure (but not overly strict) conscience.

Self-Understanding

Describe preschoolers' self-concepts and the development of autobiographical memory and self-esteem.

- As preschoolers think more intently about themselves, they construct a **self-concept** that consists largely of observable characteristics and typical emotions and attitudes. Older preschoolers also have an emerging grasp of their own personalities.

- Securely attached preschoolers have a more positive, coherent self-concept. They experience more elaborate parent–child conversations about past events, which contribute to a clearer, self-image.

- Preschoolers' **self-esteem** consists of several self-judgments. Their high self-esteem contributes to a mastery-oriented approach to the environment.

Emotional Development

Identify changes in understanding and expressing emotion during early childhood, citing factors that influence those changes.

- Preschoolers have an impressive understanding of the causes, consequences, and behavioral signs of basic emotions, which is supported by cognitive development, secure attachment, and conversations about feelings. By age 3 to 4, children are aware of various strategies for emotional self-regulation. Temperament, parental modeling, and parental communication about coping strategies influence preschoolers' capacity to handle negative emotion.

- As their self-concepts become better developed, preschoolers experience self-conscious emotions more often. However, they depend on parental feedback to know when to feel pride, shame, or guilt.

- Empathy also becomes more common in early childhood. The extent to which empathy leads to **sympathy** and results in **prosocial,** or **altruistic, behavior** depends on temperament and parenting.

Peer Relations

Describe peer sociability, friendship, and social problem solving in early childhood, along with cultural and parental influences on early peer relations.

- During early childhood, peer interaction increases as children move from **nonsocial activity** to **parallel play** and then to **associative** and **cooperative play.** Nevertheless, both solitary and parallel play remain common.

- Sociodramatic play seems especially important in societies where child and adult worlds are distinct. In collectivist cultures, play generally occurs in large groups and is highly cooperative.

- Preschoolers view friendship in concrete, activity-based terms. Their interactions with friends are especially positive and contribute to academic and social adjustment in kindergarten.

- Social conflicts offer occasions for **social problem solving,** which improves over the preschool and early school years. By kindergarten, each of its information-processing components is related to socially competent behavior.

- Parents influence early peer relations both directly, through attempts to influence their child's peer relations, and indirectly, through their child-rearing practices.

Foundations of Morality

What are the central features of psychoanalytic, social learning, and cognitive-developmental approaches to moral development?

- The psychoanalytic perspective emphasizes the emotional side of moral development. Although guilt is an important motivator of moral action, contrary to Freud's theory, discipline promoting fear of punishment and loss of parental love does not foster conscience development. **Induction** is far more effective.

- Social learning theory focuses on how moral behavior is learned through reinforcement and modeling. Effective adult models of morality are warm and powerful, and they practice what they preach.

- Alternatives such as **time out** and withdrawal of privileges can help parents avoid the undesirable side effects of harsh punishment. When parents use punishment, they can increase its effectiveness by being consistent, maintaining a warm parent–child relationship, and offering explanations. The most effective discipline encourages good conduct by building a mutually respectful bond with the child.

- The cognitive-developmental perspective views children as active thinkers about social rules. By age 4, children consider intentions in making moral judgments and distinguish truthfulness from lying. Preschoolers also distinguish **moral imperatives** from **social conventions** and **matters of personal choice,** but they tend to reason rigidly about morality.

- Through sibling and peer interaction, children work out their first ideas about justice and fairness. Parents who discuss moral issues with their children help them reason about morality.

Describe the development of aggression in early childhood, including family and media influences.

- During early childhood, **proactive aggression** declines while **reactive aggression** increases. Proactive and reactive aggression come in three forms: **physical aggression** (more common in boys), **verbal aggression,** and **relational aggression.**

- Ineffective discipline and a conflict-ridden family atmosphere promote children's aggression. Children high in reactive aggression see hostility where it does not exist, making many unprovoked attacks. Those high in proactive aggression callously use it to advance their own goals—a style that predicts severe conduct problems. Media violence also triggers aggression.

- Teaching parents effective child-rearing practices, intervening to enhance children's emotional and social skills, relieving family stress through social supports, and shielding children from violent media reduce aggressive behavior.

Gender Typing

Discuss genetic and environmental influences on preschoolers' gender-stereotyped beliefs and behavior.

- **Gender typing** is well under way in early childhood. Preschoolers acquire a wide range of gender-stereotyped beliefs, which operate as blanket rules rather than flexible guidelines for behavior.

- Prenatal hormones contribute to boys' higher activity level and rowdier play and to children's preference for same-sex playmates. But parents, same-sex older siblings, teachers, peers, and the broader social environment encourage many gender-typed responses. Parents apply more pressure for gender-role conformity to sons, and boys are more gender-typed than girls.

Describe and evaluate major theories that explain the emergence of gender identity.

- Although most people have a traditional **gender identity,** some are **androgynous,** combining both masculine and feminine characteristics. Masculine and androgynous identities are linked to better psychological adjustment.

- According to social learning theory, preschoolers first acquire gender-typed responses through modeling and reinforcement, then organize these into gender-linked ideas about themselves. Cognitive-developmental theory suggests that **gender constancy** must be mastered before children develop gender-typed behavior. However, gender-role behavior is acquired long before gender constancy.

- **Gender schema theory** combines features of social learning and cognitive-developmental perspectives. As children acquire gender-stereotyped preferences and behaviors, they form masculine and feminine categories, or gender schemas, that they apply to themselves and their world.

Child Rearing and Emotional and Social Development

Describe the impact of child-rearing styles on children's development, and explain why authoritative parenting is effective.

- Three features distinguish the major **child-rearing styles:** (1) acceptance and involvement, (2) control, and (3) autonomy granting. Compared with the **authoritarian, permissive, and uninvolved styles,** the **authoritative style** promotes cognitive, emotional, and social competence. Warmth, explanations, and reasonable demands for mature behavior account for the effectiveness of the authoritative style. **Psychological control** is associated with authoritarian parenting and contributes to adjustment problems.

- Certain ethnic groups, including Chinese, Hispanic, Asian Pacific Island, and African-American, combine parental warmth with high levels of control. But when control becomes harsh and excessive, it impairs academic and social competence.

Discuss the multiple origins of child maltreatment, its consequences for development, and prevention strategies.

- Child maltreatment is related to factors within the family, community, and larger culture. Maltreating parents use ineffective discipline and hold a negatively biased view of their child. Unmanageable parental stress and social isolation greatly increase the chances that abuse and neglect will occur. When a society approves of force and violence as a means for solving problems, child abuse is promoted.

- Maltreated children are impaired in emotional self-regulation, empathy and sympathy, self-concept, social skills, and academic motivation. They are also likely to suffer central nervous system damage. Successful prevention of child maltreatment requires efforts at the family, community, and societal levels.

IMPORTANT TERMS AND CONCEPTS

androgyny (p. 395)
associative play (p. 372)
authoritarian child-rearing style (p. 399)
authoritative child-rearing style (p. 398)
child-rearing styles (p. 398)
cooperative play (p. 372)
gender constancy (p. 395)
gender identity (p. 395)
gender schema theory (p. 396)
gender typing (p. 390)
induction (p. 379)

initiative versus guilt (p. 364)
matters of personal choice (p. 384)
moral imperatives (p. 384)
nonsocial activity (p. 372)
parallel play (p. 372)
permissive child-rearing style (p. 399)
physical aggression (p. 385)
proactive aggression (p. 385)
prosocial, or altruistic, behavior (p. 371)
psychological control (p. 399)
reactive aggression (p. 385)

relational aggression (p. 386)
self-concept (p. 365)
self-esteem (p. 366)
social conventions (p. 384)
social problem solving (p. 375)
sympathy (p. 371)
time out (p. 382)
uninvolved child-rearing style (p. 400)
verbal aggression (p. 385)

Milestones

Development in Early Childhood

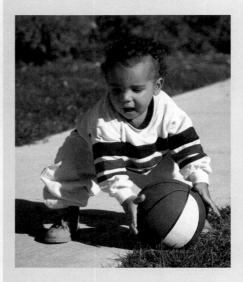

2 years

PHYSICAL

- Throughout early childhood, height and weight increase more slowly than in toddlerhood. (290)
- Balance improves; walking becomes smooth and rhythmic; running emerges. (308)
- Jumps, hops, throws, and catches with rigid upper body. (308)
- Puts on and removes simple items of clothing. (309)
- Uses spoon effectively. (309)
- First drawings are gestural scribbles. (309–310)

COGNITIVE

- Increasingly uses language as a flexible symbolic tool, to modify existing mental representations. (318)
- Make-believe becomes less dependent on realistic objects, less self-centered, and more complex; sociodramatic play increases. (319)
- Takes the perspective of others in simplified, familiar situations and in face-to-face communication. (328)
- Recognition memory is well developed. (336)

- Shows awareness of the difference between inner mental and outer physical events. (339)
- Begins to count. (344)

LANGUAGE

- Vocabulary increases rapidly. (354)
- Uses a coalition of cues—perceptual and, increasingly, social and linguistic—to figure out word meanings. (356)
- Speaks in simple sentences that follow basic word order of native language. (356)
- Adds grammatical markers. (356–357)
- Displays effective conversational skills. (358–359)

EMOTIONAL/SOCIAL

- Understands causes, consequences, and behavioral signs of basic emotions. (368)
- Begins to develop self-concept and self-esteem. (365, 366)
- Shows early signs of developing moral sense—verbal evaluations of own and others' actions and distress at harmful behaviors. (378)
- May display proactive (or instrumental) aggression. (385)
- Gender-stereotyped beliefs and behavior increase. (391)

3–4 years

PHYSICAL

- May no longer need a daytime nap. (298)

- Running, jumping, hopping, throwing, and catching become more refined, with flexible upper body. (308)

- Galloping and one-foot skipping appear. (308)
- Pedals and steers tricycle. (308)
- Uses scissors. (309)
- Uses fork adeptly. (310)
- Draws first picture of a person, using tadpole image. (310)
- Distinguishes writing from nonwriting. (312)

COGNITIVE

- Understands the symbolic function of drawings and of models of real-world spaces. (320)
- Grasps conservation, reasons about transformations, reverses thinking, and understands cause-and-effect relationships in familiar contexts. (324–326)
- Sorts familiar objects into hierarchically organized categories. (324–326)
- Distinguishes appearance from reality. (327)
- Uses private speech to guide behavior during challenging tasks. (330)
- Sustained attention and planning improve. (334–335)
- Uses scripts to recall familiar experiences. (336)
- Understands that both beliefs and desires determine behavior. (339)
- Knows meaning of numbers up to ten, counts correctly, and grasps cardinality. (344)

LANGUAGE

- Aware of some meaningful features of written language. (343)

- Coins new words based on known words; extends language meanings through metaphor. (356)
- Masters increasingly complex grammatical structures. (357)
- Sometimes overextends grammatical rules to exceptions. (357)
- Adjusts speech to fit the age, sex, and social status of listeners. (323)

EMOTIONAL/SOCIAL

- Describes self in terms of observable characteristics and typical emotions and attitudes. (365)
- Has several self-esteems, such as learning things in school, making friends, and getting along with parents. (366)
- Emotional self-regulation improves. (367)
- Experiences self-conscious emotions more often. (367)
- Relies more on language to express empathy. (371)
- Engages in associative and cooperative play with peers, in addition to parallel play. (372–373)
- Proactive aggression declines, while reactive aggression (verbal and relational) increases. (386)
- Forms first friendships, based on pleasurable play and sharing of toys. (374)

- Distinguishes moral imperatives from social conventions and matters of personal choices. (384)
- Preference for same-sex playmates strengthens. (391–392)

5–6 years

PHYSICAL

- Starts to lose primary teeth. (290)
- Increases running speed, gallops more smoothly, and engages in true skipping. (309)
- Displays mature, flexible throwing and catching patterns. (308)
- Uses knife to cut soft foods. (309)
- Ties shoes. (309)

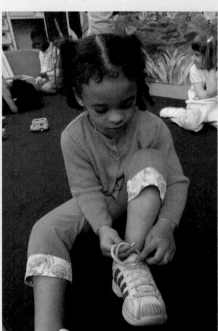

- Draws more complex pictures. (310)
- Uses an adult pencil grip, writes name, copies some numbers and simple words, and discriminates letters of the alphabet. (312)

COGNITIVE

- Magical beliefs decline. (324)
- Ability to distinguish appearance from reality improves. (327)

- Attention and planning continue to improve. (334–335)

- Recognition, recall, scripted memory, and autobiographical memory improve. (336–337)
- Understanding of false belief strengthens. (339)

LANGUAGE

- Understands that letters and sounds are linked in systematic ways. (343)
- Uses invented spellings. (343)
- By age 6, vocabulary reaches about 10,000 words. (354)
- Uses most grammatical constructions competently. (357)

EMOTIONAL/SOCIAL

- Emotional understanding (ability to interpret, predict, and influence others' emotional reactions) improves. (367–368)
- Becomes better at social problem solving. (376)
- Has acquired many morally relevant rules and behaviors. (378–379)
- Gender-stereotyped beliefs and behavior and preference for same-sex playmates continue to strengthen. (394)

- Understands gender constancy. (395)

"Fun with Wooden Cars"
Gabriel Sambo
10 years, Gabon

Through child-organized games, children develop physically, cognitively, and socially. Chapter 11 takes up the diverse physical attainments of middle childhood and their close connection with other domains of development.

Reprinted with permission from the World Awareness Children's Museum, Glens Falls, New York

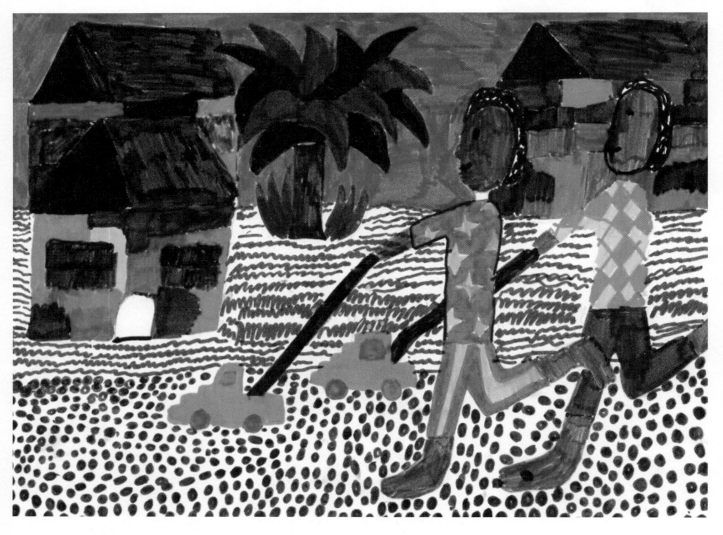

Physical Development in Middle Childhood

"I'm on my way, Mom!" hollered 10-year-old Joey as he stuffed the last bite of toast into his mouth, slung his book bag over his shoulder, dashed out the door, jumped on his bike, and headed down the street for school. Joey's 8-year-old sister Lizzie followed, kissing her mother goodbye and pedaling furiously until she caught up with Joey. Rena, the children's mother and one of my colleagues at the university, watched from the front porch as her son and daughter disappeared in the distance.

"They're branching out," Rena told me over lunch that day, as she described the children's expanding activities and relationships. Homework, household chores, soccer teams, music lessons, scouting, friends at school and in the neighborhood, and Joey's new paper route were all part of the children's routine. "It seems as if the basics are all there; I don't have to monitor Joey and Lizzie so constantly anymore. Being a parent is still very challenging, but it's more a matter of refinements—helping them become independent, competent, and productive individuals."

Joey and Lizzie have entered middle childhood—the years from 6 to 11. Around the world, children of this age are assigned new responsibilities. For children in industrialized nations, like Joey and Lizzie, middle childhood is often called the "school years" because its onset is marked by the start of formal schooling. In village and tribal cultures, the school may be a field or a jungle. But universally, mature members of society guide children of this age period toward real-world tasks that increasingly resemble those they will perform as adults.

This chapter focuses on physical growth in middle childhood—changes less spectacular than those seen in earlier years. By age 6, the brain has reached 90 percent of its adult weight, and the body continues to grow slowly. In this way, nature gives school-age children the mental powers to master challenging tasks as well as added time—before reaching physical maturity—to acquire the knowledge and skills essential for life in a complex social world.

We begin by reviewing typical growth trends and special health concerns. Then we turn to rapid gains in motor abilities, which support practical everyday activities, athletic skills, and participation in organized games. We will see that each of these achievements is affected by and also contributes to cognitive, emotional, and social development. Our discussion will echo a familiar theme—that all domains are interrelated.

Body Growth

Physical growth during the school years continues at the slow, regular pace of early childhood. At age 6, the average North American child weighs about 45 pounds and is 3½ feet tall. Over the next few years, children will add about 2 to 3 inches in height and 5 pounds in weight each year (see Figure 11.1). Between ages 6 and 8, girls are slightly shorter and lighter than boys. By age 9, this trend reverses. Already, Rena noticed, Lizzie was starting to catch up with Joey in physical size as she approached the dramatic adolescent growth spurt, which occurs two years earlier in girls than in boys.

Because the lower portion of the body is growing fastest, Joey and Lizzie appeared longer-legged than they had in early childhood. They grew out of their jeans more quickly than their

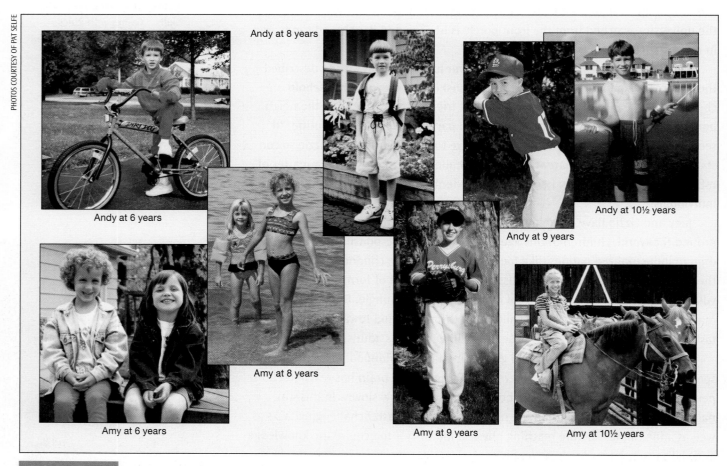

PHOTOS COURTESY OF PAT SELFE

Andy at 8 years

Andy at 6 years

Andy at 10½ years

Amy at 8 years

Andy at 9 years

Amy at 6 years

Amy at 9 years

Amy at 10½ years

FIGURE 11.1

Body growth during middle childhood. Andy and Amy continued the slow, regular pattern of growth that they showed in early childhood (see Chapter 8, page 291). But around age 9, Amy began to grow at a faster rate than Andy. At age 10½, she was taller, heavier, and more mature-looking.

jackets and frequently needed larger shoes. As in early childhood, girls have slightly more body fat and boys more muscle. After age 8, girls begin accumulating fat at a faster rate, and they will add even more during adolescence (Siervogel et al., 2000).

Worldwide Variations in Body Size

TAKE A MOMENT... Glance into any elementary school classroom, and you will see wide individual differences in body growth. Diversity in physical size is especially apparent when we travel to different nations. Worldwide, a 9-inch gap exists between the smallest and the largest 8-year-olds. The shortest children, found in South America, Asia, the Pacific Islands, and parts of Africa, include such ethnic groups as Colombian, Burmese, Thai, Vietnamese, Ethiopian, and Bantu. The tallest children—living in Australia, northern and central Europe, Canada, and the United States—come from Czech, Dutch, Latvian, Norwegian, Swiss, and African populations (Meredith, 1978; Ruff, 2002). These findings remind us that *growth norms* (age-related averages for height and weight) must be applied cautiously, especially in countries with high immigration rates and many ethnic minorities.

What accounts for these vast differences in physical size? Both heredity and environment are involved. Body size sometimes reflects evolutionary adaptations to a particular climate. Long, lean physiques are typical in hot, tropical regions and short, stocky ones in cold, Arctic areas (Katzmarzyk & Leonard, 1998). Also, children who grow tallest usually live in developed countries, where food is plentiful and infectious diseases are largely controlled. Physically small children tend to live in less developed regions, where poverty, hunger, and disease are common (Bogin, 2001). When families move from poor to wealthy nations, their children not only grow taller but also change to a longer-legged body shape. (Recall that during childhood, the legs are growing fastest.) For example, U.S.-born school-age children of immigrant Guatemalan Mayan parents are, on average, 4½ inches taller, with legs nearly 3 inches longer, than their agemates in Guatemalan Mayan villages (Bogin et al., 2002; Varela-Silva et al., 2007).

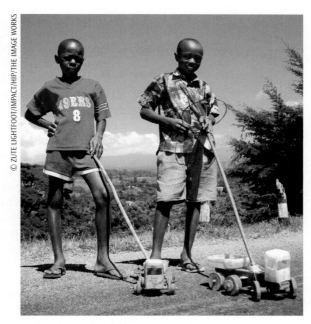

■ Body size is sometimes the result of evolutionary adaptations to a particular climate. These boys of Tanzania, who gather often to play with homemade cars, live on the hot African plains. They have long, lean physiques, which permit their bodies to cool easily. ■

Secular Trends in Physical Growth

Over the past 150 years, **secular trends in physical growth**—changes in body size from one generation to the next—have occurred in industrialized nations. Joey and Lizzie are taller and heavier than their parents and grandparents were as children. These trends have been found in Australia, Canada, Japan, New Zealand, the United States, and nearly all European countries (Ong, Ahmed, & Dunger, 2006). The secular gain appears early in life, increases over childhood and early adolescence, then declines as mature body size is reached. This pattern suggests that the larger size of today's children is mostly due to a faster rate of physical development.

Once again, improved health and nutrition are largely responsible for these growth gains. Secular trends are smaller for low-income children, who have poorer diets and are more likely to suffer from growth-stunting illnesses. And in regions with widespread poverty, famine, and disease, either no secular change or a secular decrease in body size has occurred (Barnes-Josiah & Augustin, 1995; Cole, 2000). In most industrialized nations, the secular gain in height has slowed in recent decades. Weight gain, however, is continuing. As we will see later, overweight and obesity have reached epic proportions.

■ Although they vary greatly in physical size, these 9-year-olds are generally taller and heavier than previous generations were at the same age. Improved health and nutrition account for this secular trend in physical growth throughout the industrialized world. ■

Skeletal Growth

During middle childhood, the bones of the body lengthen and broaden. However, ligaments are not yet firmly attached to bones. This, combined with increasing muscle strength, gives children unusual flexibility of movement. School-age children often seem like "physical contortionists," turning cartwheels and doing splits and handstands. As their bodies become stronger, many children experience a greater desire for physical exercise. Nighttime "growing pains"—stiffness and aches in the legs—are common as muscles adapt to an enlarging skeleton (Evans, 2008).

Between ages 6 and 12, all 20 primary teeth are lost and replaced by permanent ones, with girls losing their teeth slightly earlier than boys. The first teeth to go are the lower and then upper front teeth, giving many first and second graders a "toothless" smile. For a while, the permanent teeth seem much too large. Gradually, growth of the facial bones, especially those of the jaw and chin, causes the child's face to lengthen and the mouth to widen, accommodating the newly erupting teeth.

Care of the teeth is essential during the school years because dental health affects the child's appearance, speech, and ability to chew properly. Parents need to remind children to brush their teeth thoroughly, and most children need help with flossing until about 9 years of age. More than 50 percent of U.S. school-age children have at least some tooth decay. Low-SES children have especially high levels, with nearly 30 percent untreated (U.S. Department of Health and Human Services, 2007c). Children without health insurance are three times as likely to have unmet dental needs. As decay progresses, they experience pain, embarrassment at damaged teeth, distraction from play and learning, and school absences due to dental-related illnesses.

Malocclusion, a condition in which the upper and lower teeth do not meet properly, occurs in one-third of school-age children. In about 14 percent of cases, serious difficulties in biting and chewing result. Malocclusion can be caused by thumb and finger sucking after permanent teeth erupt. Children who were eager thumb suckers during infancy and early childhood may require gentle but persistent encouragement to give up the habit by school entry (Charchut, Allred, & Needleman, 2003). Another cause of malocclusion is crowding of permanent teeth. In some children, this problem clears up as the jaw grows. Others need braces, a common sight by the end of elementary school.

Brain Development

The weight of the brain increases by only 10 percent during middle childhood and adolescence. Nevertheless, considerable growth occurs in certain brain structures. Using fMRI, researchers can detect the volume of two general types of brain tissue: *white matter,* consisting largely of myelinated nerve fibers, and *gray matter,* consisting mostly of neurons and supportive material. White matter increases steadily throughout childhood and adolescence, especially in the prefrontal cortex (responsible for consciousness, impulse control, integration of information, and strategic thinking), in the parietal lobes (supporting spatial abilities), and in the corpus callosum (leading to improved communication between the two cortical hemispheres) (Barnea-Goraly et al., 2005; Nelson, Thomas, & de Haan, 2006). Because interconnectivity among distant regions of the cerebral cortex increases, the prefrontal cortex becomes a more effective "executive"—coordinating integrated functioning of various areas, yielding more complex, flexible, and adaptive behavior.

As children acquire more complex abilities, stimulated neurons increase in synaptic connections, and their neural fibers become more elaborate and myelinated. As a result, gray matter peaks in middle childhood and then declines as synaptic pruning (reduction of unused synapses) and death of surrounding neurons proceed

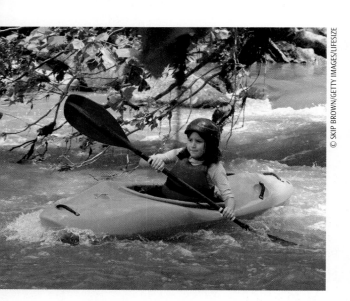

■ In middle childhood, the prefrontal cortex becomes a more effective "executive," coordinating integrated functioning of various brain regions. These changes support more complex, flexible abilities, such as this kayaker's deft maneuvering. ■

© SKIP BROWN/GETTY IMAGES/LIFESIZE

(Giedd et al., 1999; Sowell et al., 2002). Recall from Chapter 5 that about 40 percent of synapses are pruned over childhood and adolescence. Pruning and accompanying reorganization and selection of brain circuits contribute greatly to more efficient information processing, including gains in sustained attention, inhibition, response preparation, and working memory capacity (Nelson, Thomas, & de Haan, 2006). These changes yield more optimized functioning of specific brain regions.

Little information is available on how the brain develops in other ways. One idea is that much development takes place at the level of neurotransmitters, chemicals that permit neurons to communicate across synapses (see Chapter 5, page 164). Over time, neurons become increasingly selective, responding only to certain chemical messages. This change may add to school-age children's more efficient and flexible thinking and behavior. Secretions of particular neurotransmitters are related to cognitive performance, social and emotional adjustment, and ability to withstand stress. When neurotransmitters are not present in appropriate balances, children may suffer serious developmental problems, such as inattention and overactivity, emotional disturbance, and epilepsy (an illness involving brain seizures and loss of motor control) (Brooks et al., 2006; Pearl et al., 2005; Weller, Kloos, & Weller, 2006).

Researchers also believe that brain functioning may change in middle childhood because of the influence of hormones. Around age 7 to 8, an increase in androgens (male sex hormones), secreted by the adrenal glands (located on top of the kidneys), occurs in children of both sexes. Androgens will rise further among boys at puberty, when the testes release them in large amounts. Androgens affect brain organization and behavior in many animal species, including humans. Recall from Chapter 10 that androgens contribute to boys' higher activity level. They may also promote social dominance and play-fighting, topics we will take up at the end of this chapter (Azurmendi et al., 2006).

ASK YOURSELF

◆ **REVIEW** What aspects of physical growth account for the long-legged appearance of many 8- to 12-year-olds?

◆ **APPLY** Joey complained to his mother that it wasn't fair that his younger sister Lizzie was almost as tall as he was. He worried that he wasn't growing fast enough. How should Rena respond to Joey's concern?

◆ **CONNECT** Relate secular trends in physical growth to the concept of cohort effects, discussed on page 41 in Chapter 1.

◆ **REFLECT** In your family, how do members of your generation compare with members of your parents' generation in height and weight? How about your grandparents' generation? Do your observations illustrate secular trends?

Common Health Problems

Children from economically advantaged homes, like Joey and Lizzie, are at their healthiest in middle childhood, full of energy and play. The cumulative effects of good nutrition, combined with rapid development of the body's immune system, offer greater protection against disease. At the same time, growth in lung size permits more air to be exchanged with each breath, so children are better able to exercise vigorously without tiring.

Not surprisingly, poverty continues to be a powerful predictor of poor health during middle childhood. Because economically disadvantaged U.S. children often lack health insurance and, if they are publicly insured, generally receive a lower standard of care (see Chapter 8, page 303), many do not have regular access to a doctor. A substantial number also lack such basic necessities as a comfortable home and regular meals.

Nutrition

Children need a well-balanced, plentiful diet to provide energy for successful learning in school and increased physical activity. With their increasing focus on play, friendships, and new activities, many children spend little time at the table. Joey's hurried breakfast, described at the beginning of this chapter, is a common event in middle childhood. The percentage of children who eat meals with their families drops sharply between ages 9 and 14. Family dinnertimes have waned in general over the past quarter century. Yet eating an evening meal with parents leads to a diet higher in fruits and vegetables and lower in fried foods and soft drinks (Fiese & Schwartz, 2008; Neumark-Sztainer et al., 2003).

School-age children report that they "feel better" and "focus better" after eating healthy foods and that they feel sluggish, "like a blob," after eating junk foods. Even mild nutritional deficits can affect cognitive functioning. Among school-age children from middle- to high-SES families, insufficient dietary iron and folate predicted slightly lower mental test performance (Arija et al., 2006). Children say that a major barrier to healthy eating is the ready availability of unhealthy options, even in their homes. As one sixth grader commented, "When I get home from school, I think, 'I should eat some fruit,' but then I see the chips" (O'Dea, 2003, p. 498). Recall from Chapter 8 that food familiarity and food preferences are strongly linked: Children like best foods they have eaten repeatedly in the past. Readily available, healthy between-meal snacks—such as cheese, fruit, raw vegetables, and peanut butter—can help meet school-age children's nutritional needs and increase their liking for healthy foods.

As we have seen in earlier chapters, many poverty-stricken children in developing countries and in North America suffer from serious, prolonged malnutrition. By middle childhood, the effects are apparent in retarded physical growth, low IQ, poor motor coordination, and inattention. The negative impact of malnutrition on learning and behavior may intensify as children encounter new academic and social challenges at school. First, as in earlier years, growth-stunted school-age children respond with greater fear to stressful situations, as indicated by a sharper rise in heart rate and in saliva levels of the stress hormone cortisol (Fernald & Grantham-McGregor, 1998). Second, animal evidence reveals that a deficient diet alters the production of neurotransmitters in the brain—an effect that can disrupt all aspects of psychological functioning (Haller, 2005).

Unfortunately, malnutrition that persists from infancy or early childhood into the school years usually leads to permanent physical and mental damage (Grantham-McGregor, Walker, & Chang, 2000; Liu et al., 2003). Government-sponsored supplementary food programs from the early years through adolescence can prevent these effects. In studies carried out in Egypt, Kenya, and Mexico, quality of food (protein, vitamin, and mineral content) strongly predicted favorable cognitive development in middle childhood (Sigman, 1995; Watkins & Pollitt, 1998).

IMAGINECHINA VIA AP IMAGES

■ Chinese boys attending a weight-loss summer camp get ready for a swim. Lifestyle changes and a culture that equates excess body fat with prosperity have caused a rapid increase in overweight and obesity in China, especially among boys. ■

Overweight and Obesity

Mona, a very heavy child in Lizzie's class, often watched from the sidelines during recess. When she did join in games, she was slow and clumsy, the target of unkind comments: "Move it, Tubs!" Although Mona was a good student, the other children rejected her in the classroom as well. When they chose partners for special activities, Mona was among the last to be selected. Most afternoons, she walked home alone while her schoolmates gathered in groups, talking, laughing, and chasing. At home, Mona sought comfort in high-calorie snacks.

Mona suffers from **obesity,** a greater-than-20-percent increase over healthy weight, based on *body mass index (BMI)*—a ratio of weight to height associated with body fat. A BMI above the 85th percentile for a child's age and sex is considered *overweight,* a BMI above the 95th percentile *obese.* During the past several decades, a rise in overweight and obesity has occurred in many Western nations (see Figure 11.2), with large increases in Canada, Germany, Israel, Greece, Ireland, New Zealand, United Kingdom, and the United States. Today, 32 percent of U.S. children and adolescents are overweight, more than half extremely so: 17 percent are obese (Ogden et al., 2010; World Health Organization, 2009a, 2010a). Smaller increases have occurred in other industrialized nations, including Australia, Finland, the Netherlands, Norway, and Sweden.

Obesity rates are also increasing rapidly in developing countries, as urbanization shifts the population toward sedentary lifestyles and diets high in meats and energy-dense refined foods (World Health Organization, 2009a, 2010a). In China, for example, where obesity was nearly nonexistent a generation ago, today 20 percent of children are overweight, with 7 percent obese—a nearly fivefold increase over the past twenty-five years, with boys affected more than girls) (Ding, 2008). Childhood obesity in China is especially high in cities, where it has reached 10 percent (Ji & Chen, 2008). In addition to lifestyle changes, a prevailing belief in Chinese culture that excess body fat represents prosperity and health—carried over from a half-century ago, when famine caused millions of deaths—has contributed to this alarming upsurge. High valuing of sons may induce Chinese parents to offer boys especially generous portions of meat, dairy products, and other energy-dense foods that were once scarce but now are widely available.

Overweight rises with age, from 21 percent among U.S. preschoolers to 35 percent among school-age children and adolescents (Ogden et al., 2010). In a longitudinal study of more than 1,000 U.S. children, overweight preschoolers were five times more likely than their normal-weight peers to be overweight at age 12 (Nader et al., 2006). And an estimated 70 percent of affected teenagers become overweight adults (U.S. Department of Health and Human Services, 2007b).

Besides serious emotional and social difficulties, obese children are at risk for lifelong health problems. Symptoms that begin to appear in the early school years—high blood pressure, high cholesterol levels, respiratory abnormalities, and insulin resistance—are powerful predictors of heart disease, circulatory difficulties, type 2 diabetes, gallbladder disease, sleep and digestive disorders, many forms of cancer, and early death (Krishnamoorthy, Hart, & Jelalian, 2006; World Cancer Research Fund, 2007). Furthermore, obesity has caused a dramatic rise in cases of diabetes in children, sometimes leading to early, severe complications, including stroke, kidney failure, and circulatory problems that heighten the risk of eventual blindness and leg amputation (Hannon, Rao, & Arslanian, 2005). As you can see from Table 11.1 on page 418, childhood obesity is a complex physical disorder with multiple causes.

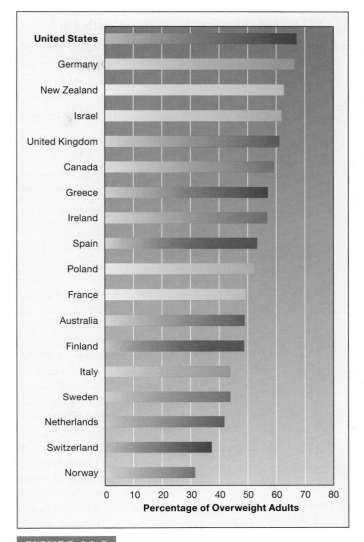

FIGURE 11.2

Overweight adults in eighteen industrialized nations. The United States outranks all other developed nations in pervasiveness of overweight in the adult population, defined here according to the widely accepted adult standard of a BMI greater than 25. *(From World Health Organization, 2010a.)*

CAUSES OF OBESITY Not all children are equally at risk for excessive weight gain. Overweight children tend to have overweight parents, and identical twins are more likely to share the disorder than fraternal twins. But heredity accounts for only a *tendency* to gain weight (Salbe et al., 2002). The importance of environment is seen in the consistent relationship of low SES to overweight and obesity in industrialized nations, especially among ethnic minorities—in the United States, African-American, Hispanic, and Native-American children and adults (Anand et al., 2001; Ogden et al., 2010). Factors responsible include lack of knowledge about healthy diet; a tendency to buy high-fat, low-cost foods; neighborhoods that lack

TABLE 11.1	Factors Associated with Childhood Obesity
FACTOR	**DESCRIPTION**
Heredity	Obese children are likely to have at least one obese parent, and concordance for obesity is greater in identical than in fraternal twins.
Socioeconomic status	Obesity is more common in low-SES families.
Early growth pattern	Infants who gain weight rapidly are at greater risk for obesity, probably because their parents promote unhealthy eating habits (see Chapter 5).
Family eating habits	When parents purchase high-calorie fast foods, treats, and junk food; use them as rewards; anxiously overfeed; or control their children's intake, their children are more likely to be obese.
Responsiveness to food cues	Obese children often decide when to eat on the basis of external cues, such as taste, smell, sight, time of day, and food-related words, rather than hunger.
Physical activity	Obese children are less physically active than their normal-weight peers.
Television viewing	Children who spend many hours watching television are more likely to become obese.
Early malnutrition	Early, severe malnutrition that results in growth stunting increases the risk of later obesity.

convenient access to affordable, healthy foods in grocery stores and restaurants; and family stress, which can prompt overeating.

Furthermore, children who were undernourished in their early years are at risk for later excessive weight gain. Studies in many poverty-stricken regions of the world reveal that growth-stunted children are more likely to be overweight than their nonstunted agemates (Branca & Ferrari, 2002). In industrialized nations, many studies confirm that children whose mothers smoked during pregnancy and who therefore are often born underweight (see Chapter 3) are at elevated risk for later overweight and obesity (Rogers, 2009). A malnourished body protects itself by establishing a low basal metabolism rate, which may endure after nutrition improves. Also, malnutrition may disrupt appetite control centers in the brain, causing the child to overeat when food becomes plentiful.

Parental feeding practices also contribute to childhood obesity. Overweight children are more likely to eat larger quantities of high-calorie sugary and fatty foods, perhaps because these foods are prominent in the diets offered by their parents, who also tend to be overweight. Some parents anxiously overfeed, interpreting almost all their child's discomforts as a desire for food. Others pressure their children to eat, a practice common among immigrant parents and grandparents who, as children themselves, survived deadly famines or periods of food deprivation due to poverty. Still other parents are overly controlling, restricting when, what, and how much their child eats and worrying about weight gain (Moens, Braet, & Soetens, 2007). In each case, parents undermine children's ability to regulate their own food intake. Also, parents of overweight children often use high-fat, sugary foods to reinforce other behaviors, leading children to attach great value to treats (Sherry et al., 2004).

Because of these experiences, obese children soon develop maladaptive eating habits. They are more responsive than normal-weight individuals to external stimuli associated with food—taste, sight, smell, time of day, and food-related words—and less responsive to internal hunger cues (Jansen et al., 2003; Temple et al., 2007). They also eat faster and chew their food less thoroughly, a behavior pattern that appears as early as 18 months of age (Drabman et al., 1979).

Another factor implicated in weight gain is insufficient sleep. A follow-up of more than 2,000 U.S. 3- to 12-year-olds revealed that children who got less nightly sleep were more likely to be overweight five years later (Snell, Adam, & Duncan, 2007). Reduced sleep may increase time available for eating, leave children too fatigued for physical activity, or disrupt the brain's regulation of hunger and metabolism.

Overweight children are less physically active than their normal-weight peers. Inactivity is both cause and consequence of excessive weight gain. Research reveals that the rise in childhood obesity is due in part to the many hours U.S. children spend watching television. In a

LOOK AND LISTEN

❖❖

Observe in the check-out area of a supermarket for an hour on a weekend, recording the percentage of families with children whose carts contain large quantities of high-calorie processed foods and soft drinks. In how many of these families are parents and children overweight?

FIGURE 11.3

Relationship of television viewing to gains in body fat from ages 4 to 11.
Researchers followed more than 100 children from ages 4 to 11, collecting
information on hours per day of television viewing and on body fat, measured
in millimeters of skinfold thickness at five body sites (upper arms, shoulders,
abdomen, trunk, and thighs). The more TV children watched, the greater the
gain in body fat. At ages 10 to 11, the difference between children watching
fewer than 1¾ hours and those watching more than 3 hours had become large.
*(Adapted from M. H. Proctor et al., 2003, "Television Viewing and Change in Body
Fat from Preschool to Early Adolescence: The Framingham Children's Study,"
International Journal of Obesity, 27, p. 831. Reprinted by permission from
Macmillan Publishers Ltd.)*

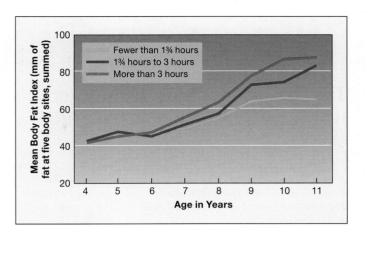

study that tracked children's TV viewing from ages 4 to 11,
the more TV children watched, the more body fat they
added. Children who devoted more than 3 hours per day to
TV accumulated 40 percent more fat than those devoting
less than 1¾ hours (see Figure 11.3) (Proctor et al., 2003). Watching TV reduces time devoted
to physical exercise, and TV ads encourage children to eat fattening, unhealthy snacks.
Children permitted to have a TV in their bedroom—a practice linked to especially high TV
viewing—are at even further risk for overweight (Adachi-Mejia et al., 2007).

Finally, the broader food environment affects the incidence of obesity. The Pima Indians
of Arizona, who two decades ago changed from a traditional diet of plant foods to a high-fat,
typically American diet, have one of the world's highest obesity rates. Compared with descen-
dants of their ancestors living in the remote Sierra Madre region of Mexico, the Arizona Pima
have body weights 50 percent greater. Half the population has diabetes (8 times the national
average), with many in their twenties and thirties already disabled by the disease—blind, in
wheelchairs, and on kidney dialysis. The Pima have a genetic susceptibility to overweight, but
it emerges only under Western dietary conditions (Gladwell, 1998; Traurig et al., 2009). Other
ethnic groups with a hereditary tendency to gain weight include Pacific Islanders, including
native Hawaiians and Samoans (Furusawa et al., 2010). Many now eat an Americanized diet of
high-calorie processed and fast foods, and over 80 percent are overweight. Turn to the Social
Issues: Health box on pages 420–421 for societal changes that have led Americans to become
the heaviest people in the world.

CONSEQUENCES OF OBESITY Unfortunately, physical attractiveness is a
powerful predictor of social acceptance. In Western societies, both children and
adults rate obese youngsters as unlikable, stereotyping them as lazy, sloppy, dirty,
ugly, stupid, and deceitful (Kilpatrick & Sanders, 1978; Penny & Haddock, 2007;
Tiggemann & Anesbury, 2000). In school, obese children and adolescents are often
socially isolated. They report more emotional, social, and school difficulties, including peer teasing and consequent low self-esteem, depression, and (among obese
teenagers) suicidal thoughts and suicide attempts. Because unhappiness and
overeating contribute to each other, the child remains overweight (Puhl & Latner,
2007; Zeller & Modi, 2006). Persistent obesity from childhood into adolescence also
predicts serious behavior problems, including defiance and aggression (Schwimmer,
Burwinkle, & Varni, 2003; Young-Hyman et al., 2006). And overweight girls are more
likely to reach puberty early, increasing their risk for early sexual activity and other
adjustment problems (Kaplowitz, 2007; Rubin et al., 2009).

The psychological consequences of obesity combine with continuing discrimination to result in reduced life chances. Overweight adults are less likely
than their normal-weight agemates to be given financial aid for college, to be
rented apartments, to find mates, and to be offered jobs. And they report frequent
mistreatment by family members, peers, co-workers, and health-care professionals (Carr & Friedman, 2005; Rogge, Greenwald, & Golden, 2004).

TREATING OBESITY Childhood obesity is difficult to treat because it is a
family disorder. In Mona's case, the school nurse suggested that Mona and her

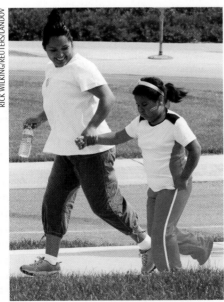

■ This mother and daughter reinforce each
other's efforts to lose weight and get in shape. The
most effective interventions for childhood obesity
focus on changing the whole family's behaviors,
emphasizing fitness and healthy eating. ■

SOCIAL ISSUES: HEALTH

The Obesity Epidemic: How Americans Became the Heaviest People in the World

*I*n the late 1980s, obesity in the United States stared to soar. The maps in Figure 11.4 show how quickly it engulfed the nation. Today more than one-third of U.S. school-age children and adolescents and more than two-thirds of adults are overweight or obese (Flegal et al., 2010). No other country matches the United States in prevalence of this life-threatening condition.

A Changing Food Environment and Lifestyle

Several societal factors have encouraged widespread rapid weight gain:

- *Availability of cheap commercial fat and sugar.* The 1970s saw two massive changes in the U.S. food economy: (1) the discovery and mass production of high-fructose corn syrup, a sweetener six times as sweet as ordinary sugar, and therefore far less expensive; and (2) the importing from Malaysia of large quantities of palm oil, which is lower in cost than other vegetable oils and also tastier, because of its high saturated fat content. As food manufacturers relied on corn syrup and palm oil to make soft drinks and calorie-dense convenience foods, the production costs of these items dropped and their variety expanded, launching a new era of "cheap, abundant, and tasty calories" (Critser, 2003). The rise in U.S. fructose consumption (mostly in beverages) closely paralleled population weight gain (Bray, Nielsen, & Popkin, 2004). Currently, fructose constitutes one-sixth of the caloric intake of the average American age 2 and older.

- *Portion supersizing.* Fast-food chains discovered a successful strategy for attracting customers: increasing portion sizes substantially and prices just a little for foods that had become inexpensive to produce. Customers thronged to buy "value meals," jumbo burgers and burritos, pizza "by the foot," and 20-ounce Cokes (Critser, 2003). And they began to view these huge portions as normal and appropriate. Research reveals that when presented with larger portions, individuals 2 years and older increase their intake, on average, by 25 to 30 percent (Fisher, Rolls, & Birch, 2003; Steenhuis & Vermeer, 2009).

- *Increasingly busy lives.* Between the 1970s and the 1990s, women entered the labor force in record numbers, and the average amount of time Americans worked increased by 15 percent, or about 350 hours per year (Higgins & Duxbury, 2002; Schor, 2002). Number of hours employed mothers work increases risk of childhood obesity because as time for meal preparation shrinks, eating out increases (Midlin, Jenkins, & Law, 2009). In addition, Americans have become frequent snackers, tempted by a growing assortment of high-calorie snack foods on supermarket shelves. During this period, the number of calories Americans consumed away from home nearly doubled, and dietary fat increased from 19 to 38 percent. Overall, average daily food intake rose by almost 200 calories—enough to add an extra pound every 20 days (Nielsen & Popkin, 2003).

- *Declining rates of physical activity.* As Americans spent more time working in sedentary jobs, they—and their

© ALEX SEGRE/ALAMY

■ As busy families eat fewer meals at home, fast food has become a regular part of many children's diets. Portion supersizing promotes increased consumption of inexpensive, tasty, high-calorie foods, putting children at risk for excessive weight gain. ■

obese mother enter a weight-loss program together. But Mona's mother, unhappily married for many years, had her own reasons for overeating. She rejected this idea, claiming that Mona would eventually decide to lose weight on her own. In one study, only one-fourth of overweight parents judged their overweight children to have a weight problem (Jeffrey, 2004). Consistent with these findings, fewer than 20 percent of obese children get any treatment. Although many try to slim down in adolescence, they often go on crash diets that make matters worse. Temporary starvation leads to physical stress, discomfort, and fatigue. Soon the child returns to old eating patterns, and weight rebounds to a higher level. Then, to protect itself, the body burns calories more slowly and becomes more resistant to future weight loss.

The most effective interventions are family-based and focus on changing behaviors (Oude et al., 2009). In one program, both parent and child revised eating patterns, exercised daily, and reinforced each other with praise and points for progress, which they exchanged for special activities and times together. The more weight parents lost, the more their children lost

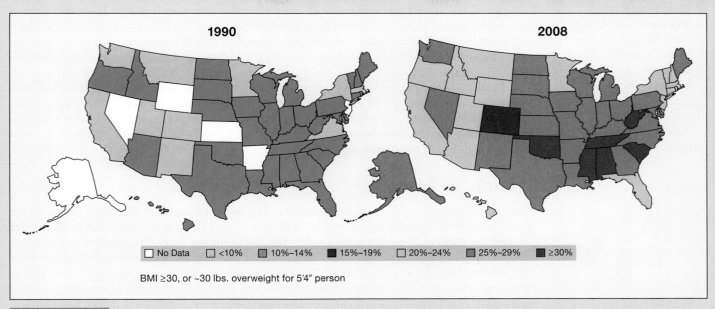

FIGURE 11.4

Obesity trends among Americans, 1990 and 2008. The maps show that obesity has increased sharply. In 2008, only one state (Colorado) had an obesity rate less than 20 percent. Six states (Alabama, Mississippi, Oklahoma, South Carolina, Tennessee, and West Virginia) had rates equal to or greater than 30 percent. *(From U.S. Department of Health and Human Services, 2009g.)*

children—exercised less. At home, TV had become their major leisure pursuit—consuming, on average, about 4 hours per day and linked to weight gain in adults and children alike (Foster, Gore, & West, 2006).

Combating the Obesity Epidemic

Obesity's toll on society is immense. It is responsible for $150 billion in health expenditures and nearly 200,000 premature deaths per year in the United States alone (Finkelstein et al.,

2009; Flegal et al., 2007). Besides individual treatment, societal efforts are needed to combat obesity. These include:

- Government funding to support massive public education about healthy eating and physical activity
- A high priority placed on building parks and recreation centers and expanding access to healthy, affordable foods in low-income neighborhoods, where overweight and obesity are highest

- Laws that mandate prominent posting of the calorie, sugar, and fat content of foods sold in restaurants, movie theaters, and convenience stores
- A special tax on foods high in calories, sugar, or fat
- Incentives to schools and workplaces for promoting healthy eating and daily exercise and for offering weight-management programs
- Increased obesity-related medical coverage in government-sponsored health insurance programs for low-income families

(Wrotniak et al., 2004). Follow-ups after five and ten years showed that children maintained their weight loss more effectively than adults—a finding that underscores the importance of intervening at an early age (Epstein, Roemmich, & Raynor, 2001). Treatment programs that focus on both diet and lifestyle can yield substantial, long-lasting weight reduction among children and adolescents. But these interventions work best when parents' and children's weight problems are not severe (Eliakim et al., 2004; Nemet et al., 2005).

Getting obese children to exercise is challenging because they find being sedentary pleasurable. One successful technique is to reinforce them for spending less time inactive. Providing rewards (such as tickets to the zoo or a baseball game) for reducing sedentary time led to greater liking for physical activity and more weight loss among obese children than reinforcing them directly for exercising or punishing them (by loss of privileges) for remaining inactive (Epstein, Saelens, & O'Brien, 1995; Epstein et al., 1997). Rewarding children for giving up inactivity seems to increase their sense of personal control over exercising—a factor linked to sustained physical activity.

LOOK AND LISTEN

❖❖

Contact your state government to find out about its childhood obesity prevention legislation. Can its policies be improved?

Children consume one-third of their daily energy intake at school. Therefore, schools can help reduce obesity by serving healthier meals and ensuring regular physical activity. Because obesity is expected to rise further without broad prevention strategies, many U.S. states and cities have passed obesity-reduction legislation (Levi et al., 2009). Among measures taken are weight-related school screenings for all children, improved nutrition standards and limited vending machine access in schools, additional recess time in the elementary grades and physical education time in all grades, obesity awareness and weight-reduction programs as part of school curricula, and menu nutrition labeling (including calorie counts) in chain and fast-food restaurants.

Finally, obesity prevention and reduction are becoming U.S. national priorities. The *Let's Move* campaign, launched by First Lady Michelle Obama in 2010, aims to create partnerships among federal and state governments, communities, businesses, schools, and health organizations to solve the childhood obesity problem within a generation. To find out about its goals and strategies, visit *www.letsmove.gov*.

Vision and Hearing

The most common vision problem in middle childhood is *myopia,* or nearsightedness. By the end of the school years, it affects nearly 25 percent of children—a rate that rises to 60 percent by early adulthood. Heredity plays a role: Identical twins are more likely than fraternal twins to share the condition (Pacella et al., 1999). And compared to children with no myopic parents, those with one myopic parent have twice the risk, and those with two myopic parents two to five times the risk, of becoming myopic themselves. Worldwide, myopia occurs far more frequently in Asian than in Caucasian populations (Feldkámper & Schaeffel, 2003). Early biological trauma can also induce myopia. School-age children with low birth weights show an especially high rate, believed to result from immaturity of visual structures, slower eye growth, and a greater incidence of eye disease (O'Connor et al., 2002).

When parents warn their children not to read in dim light or sit too close to the TV or computer screen, their concern ("You'll ruin your eyes!") is well-founded. In diverse cultures, the more time children spend reading, writing, using the computer, and doing other close work, the more likely they are to be myopic (Mutti et al., 2002; Saw et al., 2002). Consequently, myopia is one of the few health conditions to increase with SES, and it has also increased in recent generations. Fortunately, myopia can be overcome easily with corrective lenses.

During middle childhood, the Eustachian tube (canal that runs from the inner ear to the throat) becomes longer, narrower, and more slanted, preventing fluid and bacteria from traveling so easily from the mouth to the ear. As a result, *otitis media* (middle ear infection), common in infancy and early childhood (see Chapter 8), becomes less frequent. Still, about 3 to 4 percent of the school-age population, and as many as 20 percent of low-SES children, develop some hearing loss as a result of repeated infections (Ryding et al., 2002). With regular screening for both vision and hearing, defects can be corrected before they lead to serious learning difficulties.

Bedwetting

One Friday afternoon, Terry called Joey to see if he could sleep over, but Joey refused. "I can't," said Joey anxiously, without offering an explanation.

"Why not? We can take our sleeping bags out in the backyard. Come on, it'll be cool!"

"My mom won't let me," Joey responded, unconvincingly. "I mean, well, I think we're busy. We're doing something tonight."

"Gosh, Joey, this is the third time you've said no. See if I'll ask you again!" snapped Terry as he hung up the phone.

Joey is one of 10 percent of U.S. school-age children who suffer from **nocturnal enuresis,** or bedwetting during the night (Thiedke, 2003). In the overwhelming majority of cases, the problem has biological roots. Heredity is a major contributing factor: Parents with a history of bedwetting are far more likely to have a child with the problem, and identical twins are more likely than fraternal twins to share it (Weaver & Dobson, 2007). Most often, enuresis is caused by a failure of muscular responses that inhibit urination or by a hormonal imbalance that permits too much urine to accumulate during the night. Some children also have difficulty awakening to the sensation of a full bladder (Hjälmäs, 1998). Punishing a school-age child for wetting is only likely to make matters worse.

To treat enuresis, doctors often prescribe antidepressant drugs, which reduce the amount of urine produced. Although medication is a short-term solution for children attending camp or visiting a friend's house, once children stop taking it, they typically begin wetting again. Also, a small number show side effects, such as anxiety, loss of sleep, and personality changes (Diehr, 2003; Harari & Moulden, 2000). The most effective treatment is a urine alarm that wakes the child at the first sign of dampness and works according to conditioning principles. Success rates of about 60 to 70 percent occur after four to six months of treatment. Most children who relapse achieve dryness after trying the alarm a second time (Houts, 2003).

In a study of more than 3,300 U.S. school-age children with nocturnal enuresis, fewer than one-third had seen a health professional about the problem (Butler, Golding, & Heron, 2005). Yet treatment in middle childhood has immediate positive psychological consequences. It leads to gains in parents' evaluation of their child's behavior and in children's self-esteem (Longstaffe, Moffatt, & Whalen, 2000). Although many children outgrow enuresis without intervention, this generally takes years.

Illnesses

Children experience a somewhat higher rate of illness during the first two years of elementary school than later, because of exposure to sick children and an immune system that is still developing. On average, illness causes children to miss about 11 days of school per year, but most absences can be traced to a few students with chronic health problems (Moonie et al., 2006).

About 15 to 20 percent of U.S. children living at home have chronic diseases and conditions (including physical disabilities) (Van Cleave, Gortmaker, & Perrin, 2010). By far the most common—accounting for about one-third of childhood chronic illness and the most frequent cause of school absence and childhood hospitalization—is *asthma,* in which the bronchial tubes (passages that connect the throat and lungs) are highly sensitive (Bonilla et al., 2005). In response to a variety of stimuli, such as cold weather, infection, exercise, allergies, and emotional stress, they fill with mucus and contract, leading to coughing, wheezing, and serious breathing difficulties.

From 1980 to 1997, the prevalence of asthma among U.S. children more than doubled, then stabilized at 9 percent (Akinbami et al., 2009). Although heredity contributes to asthma, researchers believe that environmental factors are necessary to spark the illness. Boys, African-American children, and children who were born underweight, whose parents smoke, and who live in poverty are at greatest risk (Federico & Liu, 2003; Pearlman et al., 2006). The higher rate and greater severity of asthma among African-American and poverty-stricken children may be the result of pollution in inner-city areas (which triggers allergic reactions), stressful home lives, and lack of access to good health care. Childhood obesity is also related to asthma in middle childhood, possibly due to high levels of blood-circulating inflammatory substances associated with body fat and the pressure of excess weight on the chest wall (Story, 2007).

About 2 percent of U.S. children have more severe chronic illnesses, such as sickle cell anemia, cystic fibrosis, diabetes, arthritis, cancer, and acquired immune deficiency syndrome (AIDS). Painful medical treatments, physical discomfort, and changes in appearance often disrupt the sick child's daily life, making it difficult to concentrate in school and separating the child from peers. As the illness worsens, family stress increases (LeBlanc, Goldsmith, & Patel, 2003). For these reasons, chronically ill children are at risk for academic, emotional, and social difficulties. In adolescence, they are more likely than their agemates to suffer from low self-esteem and depression and report more often smoking cigarettes, using illegal drugs, and thinking about and attempting suicide (Erickson et al., 2005).

■ Although heredity contributes to asthma, environmental factors trigger the illness. Pollution may account for higher rates and greater severity of the condition among children living in poverty-stricken, inner-city neighborhoods. ■

A strong link exists between good family functioning and child well-being for chronically ill children, just as it does for physically healthy children (Drotar et al., 2006). Interventions that foster positive family relationships help parent and child cope with the disease and improve adjustment. These include:

- Health education, in which parents and children learn about the illness and get training in how to manage it
- Home visits by health professionals, who offer counseling and social support to enhance parents' and children's strategies for handling the stress of chronic illness
- Schools that accommodate children's special health and education needs
- Disease-specific summer camps, which teach children self-help skills and give parents time off from the demands of caring for an ill youngster
- Parent and peer support groups

Unintentional Injuries

As we conclude our discussion of threats to school-age children's health, let's return to the topic of unintentional injuries (discussed in detail in Chapter 8). As Figure 11.5 shows, injury fatalities increase from middle childhood into adolescence, with rates for boys rising considerably above those for girls. Poverty and either rural or inner-city residence—factors associated with dangerous environments and reduced parental monitoring of children—are also linked to high injury rates (Birken et al., 2006; Schwebel et al., 2004).

Motor vehicle accidents, involving children as passengers or pedestrians, continue to be the leading cause of injury, followed by bicycle accidents (U.S. Department of Health and Human Services, 2008a). Pedestrian injuries most often result from midblock dart-outs, bicycle accidents from disobeying traffic signals and rules. When many stimuli impinge on them at once, young school-age children often fail to think before they act (Tuchfarber, Zins, & Jason, 1997). They need frequent reminders, supervision, and prohibitions against venturing into busy traffic on their own.

As children range farther from home, safety education becomes especially important. Effective school-based prevention programs use extensive modeling and rehearsal of safety practices, give children feedback about their performance along with praise and tangible rewards for acquiring safety skills, and provide occasional booster sessions (Zins et al., 1994).

Parents, who often overestimate their child's safety knowledge and physical abilities, must be educated about children's age-related safety capacities (Schwebel & Bounds, 2003).

One vital safety measure is insisting that children wear protective helmets while bicycling, in-line skating, skateboarding, or using scooters. This simple precaution leads to a 25 percent reduction in head injury, a leading cause of permanent physical disability and death in school-age children (Macpherson & Spinks, 2007; Wesson et al., 2008). Combining helmet use with other prevention strategies is especially effective. In the Harlem Hospital Injury Prevention Program, inner-city children received safety education in classrooms and in a simulated traffic environment. They also attended bicycle safety clinics, during which helmets were distributed. In addition, existing playgrounds were improved and new ones constructed to provide expanded off-street play areas. Finally, more community-sponsored, supervised recreational activities were offered. As a result, motor vehicle and bicycle injuries declined by 36 percent among school-age children (Durkin et al., 1999).

Not all children respond to efforts to increase their safety. By middle childhood, the greatest risk-takers tend to be those whose parents do not act as safety-conscious models, rarely

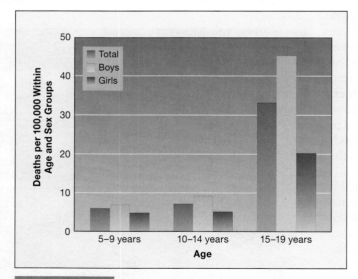

FIGURE 11.5

U.S. rates of injury mortality from middle childhood to adolescence. Injury fatalities increase with age, and the gap between boys and girls expands. Motor vehicle (passenger and pedestrian) accidents are the leading cause, with bicycle injuries next in line. *(From U.S. Department of Health and Human Services, 2008a.)*

supervise their children's activities, or use punitive or inconsistent discipline to enforce rules (Tuchfarber, Zins, & Jason, 1997). These child-rearing tactics, as we saw in Chapter 10, spark children's defiance, reduce their willingness to comply, and actually promote high-risk behavior (Rowe, Maughan, & Goodman, 2004).

Highly active, impulsive children, many of whom are boys, remain particularly susceptible to injury in middle childhood. Although they have just as much safety knowledge as their peers, they are far less likely to implement it. Parents tend to be particularly lax in intervening in the dangerous behaviors of such children (Mori & Peterson, 1995; Schwebel, Hodgens, & Sterling, 2006). Furthermore, compared with girls, boys judge risky play activities as less likely to result in injury, and they pay less attention to injury risk cues, such as a peer who looks hesitant or fearful (Morrongiello & Rennie, 1998). The greatest challenge for injury-control programs is reaching these children, altering high-risk factors in their families, and reducing the dangers to which they are exposed.

■ Unfortunately, parents of these in-line skaters failed to insist that they wear a helmet and use arm and knee protection, placing the children at risk for serious injury. Head injuries are a leading cause of permanent disability and death in school-age children. ■

Health Education

Psychologists, educators, and pediatricians are intensely interested in finding ways to help school-age children understand their bodies, acquire mature conceptions of health and illness, and develop behaviors that foster good health throughout life. Successful health intervention requires information about children's current health-related knowledge. What can they understand? What reasoning processes do they use? What factors influence what they know? The Social Issues: Education box on page 426 summarizes findings on children's concepts of health and illness in middle childhood.

The school-age period may be especially important for fostering healthy lifestyles because of the child's growing independence, increasing cognitive capacities, and rapidly developing self-concept, which includes a sense of physical well-being (Harter, 2006). During middle childhood, children can acquire a wide range of health information—about the structure and functioning of their bodies, about good nutrition, and about the causes and consequences of physical injuries and diseases. Yet most efforts to impart health concepts to school-age children have little impact on behavior (Tinsley, 2003). Several related reasons underlie this gap between knowledge and practice:

- Health is seldom an important goal for children, who feel good most of the time. They are far more concerned about schoolwork, friends, and play.
- Children do not yet have an adultlike time perspective that relates past, present, and future. They cannot see the connection between engaging in preventive behaviors now and experiencing later health consequences.
- Much health information given to children is contradicted by other sources, such as television advertising, and the examples of adults and peers.

Teaching school-age children health-related facts, though important, must be supplemented by other efforts. As we have seen, a powerful means of fostering children's health is to reduce hazards, such as pollution, inadequate medical and dental care, and unhealthy diet. At the same time, because environments will never be totally free of health risks, parents and teachers must coach children in good health practices and must model and reinforce these behaviors. Refer to Applying What We Know on page 427 for ways to foster healthy lifestyles in school-age children.

SOCIAL ISSUES: EDUCATION

Children's Understanding of Health and Illness

*L*izzie lay on the living room sofa with a stuffy nose and sore throat, disappointed that she was missing her soccer team's final game and pizza party. "How'd I get this dumb cold anyhow?" she wondered aloud to Joey. "I probably got it by playing outside when it was freezing cold."

"No, no," Joey contradicted. "Viruses get into your blood and attack, just like an army."

"Gross. I didn't eat any viruses," responded Lizzie.

"You don't eat them, silly, you breathe them in. Somebody probably sneezed them all over you at school. That's how you got sick!"

Lizzie and Joey are at different developmental levels in their understanding of health and illness—due to cognitive development and exposure to biological knowledge. Researchers have asked preschool through high school students questions about the causes of health and of certain illnesses, such as colds, AIDS, and cancer.

During the preschool and early school years, children do not have much biological knowledge to bring to bear on their understanding of health and illness. In research carried out in both the United States and China, 3- to 8-year-olds, who know little about how their internal organs work, generally fell back on their rich knowledge of people's behavior to account for health and illness (Carey, 1995, 1999; Zhu & Liu, 2007). Children of this age regard health as a matter of engaging in specific practices (eating the right foods, getting enough sleep and exercise, wearing warm clothing on cold days), and they regard illness as a matter of failing to follow these rules or coming too close to a sick person.

By age 9 or 10, when children can name many internal organs and view them as an interconnected system, they almost always explain health and illness biologically (Carey, 1999). Joey understands that illness can be caused by contagion—breathing in a harmful substance (a virus), which affects the operation of the body. He also realizes that we eat not just because food tastes good or to stay alive (younger children's explanations) but to build flesh, blood, muscle, and bone (Myant & Williams, 2005; Toyamo, 2000). In early adolescence, explanations become more elaborate and precise, and notions of illness involve clearly

stated ideas about interference in normal biological processes: "You get a cold when your sinuses fill with mucus. Sometimes your lungs do, too, and you get a cough. Colds come from viruses. They get into the bloodstream and make your platelet count go down" (Bibace & Walsh, 1980; Myant & Williams, 2005).

Young school-age children can grasp basic biological ideas that are important for understanding disease. But whether or not they do so depends on information in their environments. When given relevant facts and biological concepts, such as "gene," "germ," and "virus," even 5- and 6-year-olds use the concepts to organize the facts, and their understanding advances (Solomon & Johnson, 2000).

Without such knowledge, children readily generalize from their knowledge of familiar diseases to less familiar ones. As a result, they may conclude that risk factors for colds (sharing a Coke, sneezing on someone) can cause AIDS or that cancer (again, like a cold) is communicable through casual contact (Gonzales-Rivera & Bauermeister, 2007). These incorrect ideas can lead to unnecessary anxiety about getting a serious disease.

Once biological explanations of illness become well-grounded, school-age children (like many adults) seem to combine them with other cultural ideas. For example, children in India, like those in the United States, favor biological explanations of illness. But Indian children tend to suggest moral causes ("Maybe he's being punished by God for his bad behavior") influenced by Hindu notions of karma and retribution—that positive, caring actions lead to positive results, while negative, hurtful actions bring suffering (Raman & Gelman, 2004).

Unfortunately, when certain diseases take on powerfully negative cultural meanings—for example, cancer as a destructive evil or AIDS as a sign of moral

decay—even adults with accurate biological knowledge expect bad things to happen from associating with affected people, and children quickly pick up these attitudes (Bhana, 2008; Gonzales-Rivera & Bauermeister, 2007). This helps explain the severe social rejection experienced by some youngsters with chronic diseases.

Education about the causes of various illnesses leads to an increasingly accurate appreciation of disease transmission and prevention during middle childhood and adolescence. To combat irrational fears and prejudices and foster compassion, teachers can give AIDS, cancer, and other debilitating and deadly illnesses "a human face" by bringing chronically ill people into the classroom or talking about the experiences of people who died of an illness.

© ELLEN B. SENISI PHOTOGRAPHY

■ When school-age children are taught basic biological concepts, such as "germ" and "virus," their understanding of health and disease advances. As a result, they are less likely to harbor incorrect ideas about the causes of illness, which can lead to unnecessary anxiety about getting a serious disease. ■

Applying What We Know

Strategies for Fostering Healthy Lifestyles in School-Age Children

STRATEGY	DESCRIPTION
Increase health-related knowledge and encourage healthy behaviors.	Provide health education that imparts knowledge about healthy lifestyles (including the health risks of overweight and obesity) and that includes modeling, role playing, rehearsal, and reinforcement of good health practices.
Involve parents in supporting health education.	Communicate with parents about health education goals in school, encouraging them to extend these efforts at home. Teach parents about unhealthy feeding practices and how to create healthy food environments at home. Promote proper parental supervision by providing information on children's age-related safety capacities.
Provide healthy environments in schools.	Ask school administrators to ensure that school breakfasts and lunches follow widely accepted dietary guidelines. Limit access to vending machines with junk food. Work for daily recess periods in elementary school and mandatory daily physical education at all grade levels.
Make voluntary screening for risk factors available as part of health education.	Offer periodic measures of height, weight, body mass, blood pressure, and adequacy of diet. Educate children about the meaning of each index, and encourage improvement.
Promote pleasurable physical activity.	Provide opportunities for regular, vigorous physical exercise through activities that de-emphasize competition and stress skill building and personal and social enjoyment.
Teach children to be critical of media advertising.	Besides teaching children to be skeptical of TV ads for unhealthy foods, reduce advertising for such foods in schools.
Work for safer, healthier community environments for children.	Form community action groups to improve child safety, school nutrition, and play environments, and initiate community programs that foster healthy physical activity.

ASK YOURSELF

◆ REVIEW Select one of the following health problems of middle childhood: obesity, myopia, bedwetting, asthma, or unintentional injuries. Explain how both genetic and environmental factors contribute to it.

◆ APPLY Nine-year-old Talia is afraid to hug and kiss her grandmother, who has cancer. What explains Talia's mistaken belief that the same behaviors that cause colds to spread might lead her to catch cancer? What would you do to change her thinking?

◆ CONNECT Children who were undernourished in the early years are more likely to become overweight when their food environments improve. Explain how this finding illustrates epigenesis, described on pages 86–87 in Chapter 2.

◆ REFLECT List unintentional injuries that you experienced as a child. Were you injury-prone? Why or why not?

Motor Development and Play

TAKE A MOMENT... Visit a park on a pleasant weekend afternoon, and watch several preschool and school-age children at play. You will see that gains in body size and muscle strength support improved motor coordination during middle childhood. And greater cognitive and social maturity enables older children to use their new motor skills in more complex ways. A major change in children's play takes place at this time.

Gross-Motor Development

During the school years, running, jumping, hopping, and ball skills become more refined. At Joey and Lizzie's school, I watched during the third to sixth graders' recess. Children burst into sprints as they raced across the playground, jumped quickly over rotating ropes, engaged in

TABLE 11.2   Changes in Gross-Motor Skills During Middle Childhood

SKILL	DEVELOPMENTAL CHANGE
Running	Running speed increases from 12 feet per second at age 6 to over 18 feet per second at age 12.
Other gait variations	Skipping improves. Sideways stepping appears around age 6 and becomes more continuous and fluid with age.
Vertical jump	Height jumped increases from 4 inches at age 6 to 12 inches at age 12.
Standing broad jump	Distance jumped increases from 3 feet at age 6 to over 5 feet at age 12.
Precision jumping and hopping (on a mat divided into squares)	By age 7 children can accurately jump and hop from square to square, a performance that improves until age 9 and then levels off.
Throwing	Throwing speed, distance, and accuracy increase for both sexes, but much more for boys than for girls. At age 6, a ball thrown by a boy travels 39 feet per second, one by a girl 29 feet per second. At age 12, a ball thrown by a boy travels 78 feet per second, one by a girl 56 feet per second.
Catching	Ability to catch small balls thrown over greater distances improves with age.
Kicking	Kicking speed and accuracy improve, with boys considerably ahead of girls. At age 6, a ball kicked by a boy travels 21 feet per second, one by a girl 13 feet per second. At age 12, a ball kicked by a boy travels 34 feet per second, one by a girl 26 feet per second.
Batting	Batting motions become more effective with age, increasing in speed and accuracy and involving the entire body.
Dribbling	Style of hand dribbling gradually changes, from awkward slapping of the ball to continuous, relaxed, even stroking.

Sources: Haywood & Getchell, 2005; Malina & Bouchard, 1991.

© BOB DAEMMRICH/PHOTOEDIT

© LYNN HARTY PHOTOGRAPHY/ALAMY

© MICHAEL NEWMAN/PHOTOEDIT

■ A fancy twist of the rope following each revolution complicates this game of jump rope. Improved physical flexibility, balance, agility, and force, along with more efficient information processing, promote gains in school-age children's gross-motor skills. ■

intricate hopscotch patterns, kicked and dribbled soccer balls, batted at balls pitched by their classmates, and balanced adeptly as they walked heel-to-toe across narrow ledges. Table 11.2 summarizes gross-motor achievements between 6 and 12 years of age. These diverse skills reflect gains in four basic motor capacities:

■ *Flexibility.* Compared with preschoolers, school-age children are physically more pliable and elastic, a difference that is evident as they swing bats, kick balls, jump over hurdles, and execute tumbling routines.
■ *Balance.* Improved balance supports many athletic skills, including running, hopping, skipping, throwing, kicking, and the rapid changes of direction required in many team sports.
■ *Agility.* Quicker and more accurate movements are evident in the fancy footwork of dance and cheerleading and in the forward, backward, and sideways motions used to dodge opponents in tag and soccer.
■ *Force.* Older children can throw and kick a ball harder and propel themselves farther off the ground when running and jumping than they could at earlier ages (Haywood & Getchell, 2005).

Along with body growth, more efficient information processing plays a vital role in improved motor performance. Younger children often have difficulty with skills that require rapid responding, such as dribbling and batting. During middle childhood, the capacity to react only to relevant information increases. And steady gains in reaction time occur, with 11-year-olds responding twice as quickly as 5-year-olds (Band et al., 2000; Kail, 2003; Largo et al., 2001). These differences in speed of reaction have practical implications for physical education. Because 6- and 7-year-olds are seldom successful at batting a thrown ball, T-ball is more appropriate for them than baseball. Similarly, handball, four-square, and kickball should precede instruction in tennis, basketball, and football.

Fine-Motor Development

Fine-motor development also improves over the school years. On rainy afternoons, Joey and Lizzie experimented with yo-yos, built model airplanes, and wove potholders on small looms. Like many children, they took up musical instruments, which demand considerable fine-motor control. And gains in fine-motor skill are especially evident in children's writing and drawing.

By age 6, most children can print the alphabet, their first and last names, and the numbers from 1 to 10 with reasonable clarity. Their writing is large, however, because they make strokes using the entire arm rather than just the wrist and fingers. Children usually master uppercase letters first because their horizontal and vertical motions are easier to control than the small curves of the lowercase alphabet. Legibility of writing gradually increases as children produce more accurate letters with uniform height and spacing. These improvements prepare children for mastering cursive writing by third grade.

Children's drawings show dramatic gains in organization, detail, and representation of depth during middle childhood. By the end of the preschool years, children can accurately copy many two-dimensional shapes, and they integrate these into their drawings. Some depth cues have also begun to appear, such as making distant objects smaller than near ones (Braine et al., 1993). Yet recall from Chapter 8 that before age 8, children have trouble accurately copying a three-dimensional form, such as a cube or cylinder (see page 311). Around 9 to 10 years, the third dimension is clearly evident through overlapping objects, diagonal placement, and converging lines. Furthermore, as Figure 11.6 shows, school-age children not only depict objects in considerable detail but also relate them to one another as part of an organized whole (Case, 1998; Case & Okamoto, 1996).

© LAURA DWIGHT PHOTOGRAPHY

© INTERNATIONAL MUSEUM OF CHILDREN'S ART

FIGURE 11.6

Increase in organization, detail, and depth cues in school-age children's drawings. TAKE A MOMENT... Compare both drawings to the one by a 6-year-old on page 310. In the drawing on the left, an 8-year-old depicts her family at the dinner table. Notice how all parts are depicted in relation to one another and with greater detail. Integration of depth cues increases dramatically over the school years, as shown in the drawing on the right, by a 10-year-old artist from Singapore. Here, depth is indicated by overlapping objects, diagonal placement, and converging lines, as well as by making distant objects smaller than near ones.

Individual Differences in Motor Skills

As at younger ages, school-age children show marked individual differences in motor capacities that are influenced by both heredity and environment. Body build is one factor: Taller, more muscular children excel at many motor tasks. And children whose parents encourage physical exercise tend to enjoy it more and also to be more skilled.

Family income affects children's access to lessons needed to develop abilities in areas such as ballet, tennis, gymnastics, and instrumental music. For low-SES children, school and community provisions for nurturing athletics and other motor skills by making lessons, equipment, and opportunities for regular practice available and affordable are crucial. When these experiences combine with parental encouragement, many low-SES children become highly skilled.

Sex differences in motor skills that appeared during the preschool years extend into middle childhood and, in some instances, become more pronounced. Girls have an edge in fine-motor skills of handwriting and drawing and in gross-motor capacities that depend on balance and agility, such as hopping and skipping. But boys outperform girls on all other skills listed in Table 11.2, especially throwing and kicking (Cratty, 1986; Haywood & Getchell, 2005).

School-age boys' genetic advantage in muscle mass is not large enough to account for their gross-motor superiority. Rather, the social environment plays a larger role. Research confirms that parents hold higher expectations for boys' athletic performance, and children readily absorb these messages. From first through twelfth grades, girls are less positive than boys about the value of sports and their own sports ability—differences explained in part by parental beliefs (Fredricks & Eccles, 2002). But girls and older school-age children regard boys' advantage in sports as unjust. They indicate, for example, that coaches should spend equal time with children of each sex and that female sports should command just as much media attention as male sports (Solomon & Bredemeier, 1999).

Educating parents about the minimal differences between school-age boys' and girls' physical capacities and sensitizing them to unfair biases against promotion of girls' athletic ability may help increase girls' self-confidence and participation in athletics. Greater emphasis on skill training for girls, along with increased attention to their athletic achievements, is also likely to help. As a positive sign, compared with a generation ago, many more girls now participate in individual and team sports such as gymnastics and soccer (National Council of Youth Sports, 2008). Middle childhood is a crucial time to encourage girls' sports participation because during this period, children start to discover what they are good at and make some definite skill commitments.

Games with Rules

The physical activities of school-age children reflect an important advance in quality of play: Games with rules become common. Children around the world engage in an enormous variety of informally organized games, including variants on popular sports such as soccer, baseball, and basketball. In addition to the best-known childhood games, such as tag, jacks, and hopscotch, children have also invented hundreds of other games, including red rover, statues, leapfrog, kick the can, and prisoner's base (Kirchner, 2000).

Gains in perspective taking—in particular, the ability to understand the roles of several players in a game—permit this transition to rule-oriented games. These play experiences, in turn, contribute greatly to emotional and social development. Child-invented games usually rely on simple physical skills and a sizable element of luck. As a result, they rarely become contests of individual ability. Instead, they permit children to try out different styles of cooperating, competing, winning, and losing with little personal risk. Also, in their efforts to organize a game, children discover why rules are necessary and which ones work well. In fact, they often spend as much time working out the details of how a game should proceed as they do playing the game! As we will see in Chapter 13, these experiences help children form more mature concepts of fairness and justice.

© EITAN SIMANOR/ALAMY

■ Two children in Myanmar play a traditional game with marbles. In middle childhood, child-organized games with rules grow increasingly complex. Through them, children explore different ways of cooperating, competing, winning, and losing. ■

Adult-Organized Youth Sports

Compared with past generations, school-age children today spend less time gathering informally on sidewalks and in playgrounds. In part, this change reflects parental concern about neighborhood safety, as well as competition for children's time from TV, video games, and the Internet. Another factor is the rise in adult-organized sports, such as Little League baseball and soccer and hockey leagues, which fill many hours that children used to devote to spontaneous play. About half of U.S. children—60 percent of boys and 37 percent of girls—participate in organized sports outside of school hours at some time between ages 5 and 18 (National Council of Youth Sports, 2008).

For most children, joining community athletic teams is associated with increased self-esteem and social skills (Daniels & Leaper, 2006; Fletcher, Nickerson, & Wright, 2003). Among shy children, sports participation seems to play a protective role, fostering self-confidence and a decline in social anxiety, perhaps because it provides a sense of group belonging and a basis for communicating with peers (Findlay & Coplan, 2008). And children who view themselves as good at sports are more likely to continue playing on teams in adolescence, which predicts greater participation in sports and other physical fitness activities in early adulthood (Marsh et al., 2007; McHale et al., 2005).

In some cases, though, the arguments of critics—that youth sports overemphasize competition and substitute adult control for children's natural experimentation with rules and strategies—are valid. Children who join teams so early that the necessary skills are beyond their abilities soon lose interest. Coaches and parents who criticize rather than encourage can prompt intense anxiety in some children. And especially among boys—for whom competence at sports is linked to peer admiration—weaker performers generally experience social ostracism when coaches make winning the paramount goal (Stryer, Tofler, & Lapchick, 1998).

Parents, even more than coaches, influence children's athletic attitudes and abilities. At the extreme are parents who value sports so highly that they punish their child for making mistakes, insist that the child keep playing after injury, hold the child back in school to ensure a physical advantage, or even seek medical interventions to improve the child's performance. High parental pressure sets the stage for emotional difficulties and early athletic dropout, not elite performance (Tofler, Knapp, & Drell, 1998; Wall & Côté, 2007).

In most organized youth sports, health and safety rules help ensure that injuries are infrequent and mild. The exception is football, which has a high rate of serious injury (Radelet et al., 2002). But frequent, intense practice in any sport can lead to painful "overuse" injuries and, in extreme cases, to stress-related fractures resulting in premature closure of the epiphyses of the long bones (Frank et al., 2007). When parents and coaches emphasize effort, improvement, participation, and teamwork, young athletes enjoy sports more, exert greater effort to improve their skills, and perceive themselves as more competent at their chosen sport (Ullrich-French & Smith, 2006). See Applying What We Know on page 432 for ways to ensure that athletic leagues provide children with positive learning experiences.

Shadows of Our Evolutionary Past

TAKE A MOMENT... While watching children in your neighborhood park, notice how they occasionally wrestle, roll, hit, and run after one another, alternating roles while smiling and laughing. This friendly chasing and play-fighting is called **rough-and-tumble play.** It emerges in the preschool years and peaks in middle childhood, and children in many cultures engage in it with peers whom they like especially well (Pellegrini, 2004). After a rough-and-tumble episode, children continue interacting rather than separating, as they do after an aggressive encounter.

Children's rough-and-tumble play resembles the social behavior of many other young mammals. It seems to originate in parents' physical play with babies, especially fathers' play with sons (see page 274 in Chapter 7). And it is more common among boys, probably because prenatal exposure

LOOK AND LISTEN

Observe a youth athletic-league game, such as soccer, baseball, or hockey. Do coaches and parents encourage children's effort and skill gains, or are they overly focused on winning? Cite examples of adult and child behaviors.

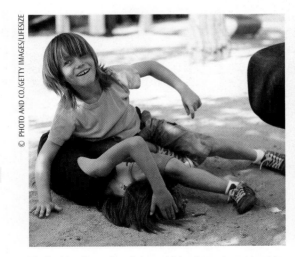

■ The friendly quality of these children's rough-and-tumble play distinguishes it from aggression. In our evolutionary past, rough-and-tumble may have been important for developing fighting skill and establishing dominance hierarchies. ■

© PHOTO AND CO./GETTY IMAGES/LIFESIZE

◆ Applying What We Know

Providing Developmentally Appropriate Organized Sports in Middle Childhood

STRATEGY	DESCRIPTION
Build on children's interests.	Permit children to select from among appropriate activities the ones that suit them best. Do not push children into sports they do not enjoy.
Teach age-appropriate skills.	For children younger than age 9, emphasize basic skills, such as kicking, throwing, and batting, and simplified games that grant all participants adequate playing time.
Emphasize enjoyment.	Permit children to progress at their own pace and to play for the fun of it, whether or not they become expert athletes.
Limit the frequency and length of practices.	Adjust practice time to children's attention spans and need for unstructured time with peers, with family, and for homework. Two practices a week, each no longer than 30 minutes for younger school-age children and 60 minutes for older school-age children, are sufficient.
Focus on personal and team improvement.	Emphasize effort, skill gains, and teamwork rather than winning. Avoid criticism for errors and defeat, which promotes anxiety and avoidance of athletics.
Discourage unhealthy competition.	Avoid all-star games and championship ceremonies that recognize individuals. Instead, acknowledge all participants.
Permit children to contribute to rules and strategies.	Involve children in decisions aimed at ensuring fair play and teamwork. To strengthen desirable responses, reinforce compliance rather than punishing noncompliance.

to androgens predisposes boys toward active play (see Chapter 10, page 386). Boys' rough-and-tumble largely consists of playful wrestling, restraining, and hitting, whereas girls tend to engage in running and chasing, with only brief physical contact (Boulton, 1996).

In middle childhood, rough-and-tumble accounts for as much as 10 percent of free-play behavior, before declining in adolescence. In our evolutionary past, it may have been important for the development of fighting skill (Power, 2000). It also helps children form a **dominance hierarchy**—a stable ordering of group members that predicts who will win when conflict arises. Observations of arguments, threats, and physical attacks between children reveal a consistent lineup of winners and losers that becomes increasingly stable in middle childhood and adolescence, especially among boys. Once school-age children establish a dominance hierarchy, hostility is rare (Pellegrini & Smith, 1998; Roseth et al., 2007). Children seem to use play-fighting as a safe context to assess the strength of a peer before challenging that peer's dominance.

As children reach puberty, individual differences in strength become apparent, and rough-and-tumble play declines. When it does occur, its meaning changes: Adolescent boys' rough-and-tumble is linked to aggression (Pellegrini, 2003). Unlike children, teenage rough-and-tumble players "cheat," hurting their opponent. In explanation, boys often say that they are retaliating, apparently to reestablish dominance. Thus, a play behavior that limits aggression in childhood becomes a context for hostility in adolescence.

Physical Education

Physical activity supports many aspects of children's development—their health, their sense of self-worth as physically active and capable beings, and the cognitive and social skills necessary for getting along with others. Yet to devote more time to academic instruction, U.S. elementary schools have cut back on recess, despite its contribution all domains of development (see the Social Issues: Education box on the following page). Similarly, only 15 percent of U.S. elementary and middle

© MICHAEL NEWMAN/PHOTOEDIT

■ Cheered by their teacher, fourth through sixth graders participate in an enjoyable ball-carrying race. Many experts believe that physical education classes should emphasize informal games, individual exercise, and personal progress rather than competitive sports. ■

SOCIAL ISSUES: EDUCATION

School Recess—A Time to Play, a Time to Learn

When 7-year-old Whitney's family moved to a new city, she left a school with three daily recess periods for one with just a single 15-minute break per day, which her second-grade teacher cancelled if any child misbehaved. Whitney, who had previously enjoyed school, complained daily of headaches and an upset stomach. Her mother, Jill, thought, "My child is stressing out because she can't move all day!" After Jill and other parents successfully appealed to the school board to add a second recess period, Whitney's symptoms vanished (Rauber, 2006).

In recent years, recess—along with its rich opportunities for child-organized play and peer interaction—has diminished or disappeared in many U.S. elementary schools (Pellegrini, 2005; Pellegrini & Holmes, 2006). Under the assumption that extra time for academics will translate into achievement gains, 7 percent of U.S. schools no longer provide recess to students as young as second grade. And over half of schools that do have recess now schedule it just once a day (U.S. Department of Education, 2010).

Yet rather than subtracting from classroom learning, recess periods boost it! Research dating back more than 100 years confirms that distributing cognitively demanding tasks over a longer time by introducing regular breaks, rather than consolidating intensive effort within one period, enhances attention and performance at all ages. Such breaks are particularly important for young children. In a series of studies, school-age children were more attentive in the classroom after recess than before it—an effect that was greater for second than fourth graders (Pellegrini, Huberty, & Jones, 1995).

Teacher ratings of classroom disruptive behavior also decline for children who have more than 15 minutes of recess a day (Barros, Silver, & Stein, 2009).

In another investigation, kindergartners' and first graders' engagement in peer conversation and games during recess positively predicted later academic achievement, even after other factors that might explain the relationship (such as previous achievement) were controlled (Pellegrini, 1992; Pellegrini et al., 2002). Recall from Chapter 10 that children's social maturity contributes substantially to early academic competence. Recess is one of the few remaining contexts devoted to child-organized games that provide practice in vital social skills—cooperation, leadership, followership, and inhibition of aggression—under adult supervision rather than direction. As children transfer these skills to the classroom, they may participate in discussions, collaborate, follow rules, and enjoy academic pursuits more—factors that enhance motivation and achievement.

Finally, children are even more physically active during recess than in gym class (U.S. Department of Education, 2006). School-age girls, especially, engage in more moderate-to-vigorous exercise during recess than at other times of the day (Mota et al., 2005). In sum, regular, unstructured recess fosters children's health and competence—physically, academically, and socially.

TORONTO STAR/FIRSTLIGHT

■ School-age children, especially girls, are even more physically active during recess than in gym class. By providing regular opportunities for unstructured play and games, recess promotes physical, academic, and social competence. ■

---

schools provide students with physical education at least three days a week, a figure that drops to 3 percent in high school (Lee et al., 2007). Not surprisingly, physical inactivity among school-age children is pervasive. Only 49 percent of boys and 35 percent of girls are active enough for good health—that is, engage in at least moderate-intensity exercise for one hour or more per day. As children move into adolescence, these rates drop sharply, to just 10 percent of boys and 4 percent of girls (Troiano et al., 2007).

Many experts believe that schools should not only offer more frequent physical education classes but also change the content of these programs. Training in competitive sports, often a high priority, is unlikely to reach the least physically fit youngsters, who avoid activities demanding a high level of skill. Instead, programs should emphasize enjoyable, informal games and individual exercise (walking, running, jumping, tumbling, and climbing)—pursuits most likely to endure. Furthermore, children of varying skill levels are more likely to sustain physical activity when teachers focus on each child's personal progress and contribution to team accomplishment (Connor, 2003). Then physical education fosters a healthy sense of self while satisfying school-age children's need to participate with others.

Physically fit children take great pleasure in their rapidly developing motor skills. As a result, they develop rewarding interests in physical activity and sports and are more likely to become active adolescents and adults who reap many benefits (Janz, Dawson, & Mahoney, 2000; Kjønniksen, Torsheim, & Wold, 2008; Tammelin et al., 2003). These include greater physical strength, resistance to many illnesses (from colds and flu to cancer, diabetes, and heart disease), enhanced psychological well-being, and a longer life.

ASK YOURSELF

◆ REVIEW Explain the adaptive value of rough-and-tumble play and dominance hierarchies.

◆ APPLY Nine-year-old Allison thinks she isn't good at sports, and she doesn't like physical education class. Suggest some strategies her teacher can use to improve her pleasure and involvement in physical activity.

◆ CONNECT On Saturdays, 10-year-old Billy gathers with friends on the driveway of his house to play basketball. Besides improved ball skills, what else is he learning?

◆ REFLECT Did you participate in adult-organized sports as a child? If so, what kind of climate for learning did coaches and parents create? What impact do you think your experiences had on your development?

Summary

Body Growth

Describe changes in body size, proportions, and skeletal maturity during middle childhood.

■ School-age children's growth is slow and regular, though large individual and ethnic variations exist in physical growth. On average, they add about 2 to 3 inches in height and 5 pounds in weight each year. By age 9, girls overtake boys in physical size.

■ **Secular trends in physical growth** have occurred in industrialized nations. Because of improved health and nutrition, many children are growing larger and reaching physical maturity earlier than their ancestors.

■ Bones continue to lengthen and broaden, and permanent teeth replace primary teeth. Tooth decay affects over half of U.S. school-age children, with especially high levels among low-SES children. One-third of school-age children suffer from **malocclusion,** making braces common by the end of elementary school.

Describe brain development in middle childhood.

■ Only a small gain in brain size occurs during middle childhood. White matter (myelinated nerve fibers) increases steadily. As interconnectivity among distant areas of the cerebral cortex increases, the prefrontal cortex becomes a more effective "executive," yielding more flexible, adaptive behavior. At the same time, gray matter (neurons and supportive material) peaks and then declines as a result of synaptic pruning, and accompanying reorganization and selection of brain circuits result in more efficient information processing.

© SKIP BROWN/GETTY IMAGES/LIFESIZE

Common Health Problems

Describe the causes and consequences of serious nutritional problems in middle childhood, giving special attention to obesity.

■ Poverty-stricken children in developing countries and in North America continue to suffer from serious and prolonged malnutrition, which can permanently impair physical and mental development.

■ Overweight and **obesity** have increased dramatically in both industrialized and developing nations, especially in the United States. Although heredity contributes to obesity, parental feeding practices, maladaptive eating habits, reduced sleep, lack of exercise, and Western high-fat diets are more powerful influences. Obese children are often socially rejected, are more likely to report feeling depressed, and display more behavior problems than their normal-weight peers.

- Family-based interventions aimed at changing parents' and children's eating patterns and lifestyles are the most effective approaches to treating childhood obesity. Rewarding obese children for reducing sedentary time is effective in getting them to enjoy and engage in more physical activity. Schools can help by ensuring regular physical activity and serving healthier meals.

What factors contribute to myopia, otitis media, nocturnal enuresis, and asthma, and how can these health problems be reduced?

- The most common vision problem, myopia, is influenced by heredity, early biological trauma, and time spent reading and doing other close work. It is one of the few health conditions that increases with family education and income. Although ear infections decline during the school years, many low-SES children experience some hearing loss because of chronic, untreated otitis media.

- Heredity is responsible for most cases of **nocturnal enuresis,** through a failure of muscular responses that inhibit urination or a hormonal imbalance that permits too much urine to accumulate. The most effective treatment is a urine alarm that works according to conditioning principles.

- Asthma is the most frequent cause of school absence and childhood hospitalization. It occurs more often among African-American and poverty-stricken children, perhaps because of inner-city pollution, stressful home lives, and lack of access to good health care. Childhood obesity is also a factor.

- Children with severe chronic illnesses are at risk for academic, emotional, and social difficulties, but positive family interactions improve adjustment.

Describe changes in the occurrence of unintentional injuries during middle childhood, and cite effective interventions.

- Unintentional injuries increase over middle childhood and adolescence, especially for boys, with motor vehicle and bicycle accidents accounting for most of the rise.

- Effective school-based safety education programs use modeling and rehearsal of safety practices and reward children for good performance. Parents also must be educated about children's age-related safety capacities. One vital safety measure is insisting that children wear protective bicycle helmets, which dramatically reduces the risk of serious head injury.

Health Education

What can parents and teachers do to encourage good health practices in school-age children?

- Besides providing health-related information, adults must reduce health hazards in children's environments, coach children in good health practices, and model and reinforce these behaviors.

Motor Development and Play

Cite major changes in gross- and fine-motor development during middle childhood.

- Gross-motor improvements in flexibility, balance, agility, and force occur, and gains in responding only to relevant information and in reaction time also contribute to athletic performance.

- Fine-motor development also improves. Handwriting becomes more legible, and children's drawings show dramatic increases in organization, detail, and representation of depth.

Describe individual differences in motor performance during middle childhood.

- Wide individual differences in children's motor capacities are influenced by both heredity and environment, including such factors as body build, parental encouragement, and opportunities to take lessons.

- Gender stereotypes, which affect parental expectations for children's athletic performance, largely account for school-age boys' superiority on a wide range of gross-motor skills. Greater emphasis on skill training for girls and attention to their athletic achievements can help increase their involvement and performance.

What qualities of children's play are evident in middle childhood?

- Games with rules become common during the school years, contributing to emotional and social development. Expansion of adult-organized youth sports programs is associated with increased self-esteem and social competence in most players, but for some children, adult overemphasis on competition promotes undue anxiety and avoidance of sports. Encouraging effort, improvement, participation, and teamwork makes organized sports enjoyable and beneficial for self-esteem.

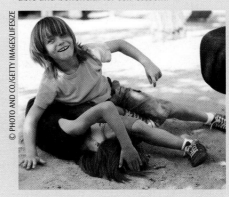

- Some features of children's physical activity reflect our evolutionary past. **Rough-and-tumble play** may once have been important for the development of fighting skill and may help children establish a **dominance hierarchy.** In middle childhood, dominance hierarchies become increasingly stable, especially among boys, and serve the adaptive function of limiting aggression among group members.

What steps can schools take to promote physical fitness in middle childhood?

- In addition to providing an opportunity for physical activity, school recess is a rich context for child-organized games and social interaction.

- Despite cutbacks in U.S. elementary schools, regular physical education classes help ensure that all children have access to the physical, cognitive, and social benefits of exercise and play, which translate into lifelong psychological and physical health benefits.

IMPORTANT TERMS AND CONCEPTS

dominance hierarchy (p. 432)
malocclusion (p. 414)

nocturnal enuresis (p. 422)
obesity (p. 416)

rough-and-tumble play (p. 431)
secular trends in physical growth (p. 413)

"My Favorite Game"
Pabasara Desanjani Wijayawansa
9 years, Sri Lanka

Middle childhood brings dramatic gains in attention, memory, categorization, reasoning, and problem solving. These children use their advancing cognitive skills to play a complex board game.

c h a p t e r

12

Cognitive Development in Middle Childhood

"*F*inally!" 6-year-old Lizzie exclaimed the day she entered first grade. "Now I get to go to real school just like Joey!" Lizzie walked into her classroom confidently, pencils, crayons, and writing pad in hand, ready for a more disciplined approach to learning than she had experienced in early childhood. As a preschooler, Lizzie had loved playing school, giving assignments as the "teacher" and pretending to read and write as the "student." Now she was eager to master the tasks that had sparked her imagination as a 4- and 5-year-old.

Lizzie had entered a whole new world of challenging mental activities. In a single morning, she and her classmates wrote in journals, met in reading groups, worked on addition and subtraction, and sorted leaves gathered for a science project. As Lizzie and Joey moved through the elementary school grades, they tackled increasingly complex tasks and became more accomplished at reading, writing, math skills, and general knowledge of the world.

To understand the cognitive attainments of middle childhood, we turn to research inspired by Piaget's theory and the information-processing approach. And we look at expanding definitions of intelligence that help us appreciate individual differences in mental development. We also examine the genetic and environmental roots of IQ scores, which often influence important educational decisions. Our discussion continues with language, which blossoms further in these years. Finally, we consider the role of schools in children's development.

Piaget's Theory: The Concrete Operational Stage

■ ■

When Lizzie visited my child development class as a 4-year-old, Piaget's conservation problems confused her (see Chapter 9, page 322). For example, when water was poured from a tall, narrow container into a short, wide one, she insisted that the amount of water had changed. But when Lizzie returned at age 8, she found these tasks easy. "Of course it's the same!" she exclaimed. "The water's shorter, but it's also wider. Pour it back," she instructed the college student who was interviewing her. "You'll see, it's the same amount!"

Achievements of the Concrete Operational Stage

Lizzie has entered Piaget's **concrete operational stage,** which extends from about 7 to 11 years. Thought is now more logical, flexible, and organized than it was during early childhood.

CONSERVATION   The ability to pass *conservation tasks* provides clear evidence of *operations*—mental actions that obey logical rules. Notice how Lizzie is capable of *decentration,* focusing on several aspects of a problem and relating them, rather than centering on just one. She also demonstrates **reversibility,** the capacity to think through a series of steps and then mentally reverse direction, returning to the starting point. Recall from Chapter 9 (page 322) that reversibility is part of every logical operation. It is solidly achieved in middle childhood.

CLASSIFICATION   Between ages 7 and 10, children pass Piaget's *class inclusion problem* (see page 322). This indicates that they are more aware of classification hierarchies and can focus on relations between a general category and two specific categories at the same time—that is, on three relations at once (Hodges & French, 1988; Ni, 1998). Collections—stamps, coins, baseball cards, rocks, bottle caps—become common in middle childhood. At age 10, Joey spent hours sorting and resorting his baseball cards, grouping them first by league and team, then by playing position and batting average. He could separate the players into a variety of classes and subclasses and easily rearrange them.

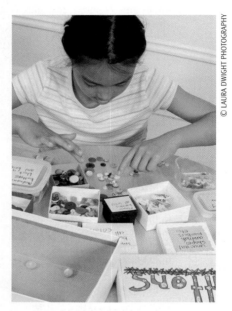

■ An improved ability to categorize underlies children's interest in collecting objects during middle childhood. Here, an 8-year-old sorts and organizes buttons in her extensive collection. ■

SERIATION   The ability to order items along a quantitative dimension, such as length or weight, is called **seriation.** To test for it, Piaget asked children to arrange sticks of different lengths from shortest to longest. Older preschoolers can put the sticks in a row to create the series, but they do so haphazardly, making many errors. In contrast, 6- to 7-year-olds create the series efficiently, moving in an orderly sequence from the smallest stick, to the next largest, and so on.

The concrete operational child can also seriate mentally, an ability called **transitive inference.** In a well-known transitive inference problem, Piaget showed children pairings of sticks of different colors. From observing that stick *A* is longer than stick *B* and that stick *B* is longer than stick *C,* children must infer that *A* is longer than *C.* Like Piaget's class inclusion task, transitive inference requires children to integrate three relations at once—in this instance, *A–B, B–C,* and *A–C.* When researchers take steps to ensure that children remember the premises (*A–B* and *B–C*), 7- to 8-year-olds can grasp transitive inference (Andrews & Halford, 1998; Wright, 2006).

LOOK AND LISTEN

Ask a 7- to 11-year-old to describe, or show you, how he or she organizes a favorite collection of objects. Does the child's sorting reveal a clear classification hierarchy?

SPATIAL REASONING   Piaget found that school-age children's understanding of space is more accurate than that of preschoolers. Let's consider children's **cognitive maps**—their mental representations of familiar large-scale spaces, such as their neighborhood or school. Drawing a map of a large-scale space requires considerable perspective-taking skill. Because the entire space cannot be seen at once, children must infer its overall layout by relating its separate parts.

Preschoolers and young school-age children include *landmarks* on the maps they draw, but their arrangement is not always accurate. They do better when asked to place stickers showing the location of desks and people on a map of a single room, such as their classroom. But if the map is rotated to a position other than the orientation of the classroom, they have difficulty (Liben & Downs, 1993). And prior to age 9 to 10, most children have trouble placing stickers on a map to indicate the location of colored flags within a large-scale outdoor environment (Kasten & Liben, 2007). Furthermore, not until the late elementary school years do children fully appreciate that in interpreting map symbols, a mapmaker's assigned meaning supersedes physical resemblance—for example, that green dots (not red dots) may indicate where red fire trucks are hidden in a room (Myers & Liben, 2008).

Around age 8 to 10, children's maps become better organized, showing landmarks along an *organized route of travel.* At the same time, children are able to give clear, well-organized instructions for getting from one place to another by using a "mental walk" strategy—imagining another person's movements along a route (Gauvain & Rogoff, 1989b). At the end of middle childhood, children form an *overall view of a large-scale space.* And they readily draw and read maps, even when the orientation of the map and the space it represents do not match (Liben, 2009). Ten- to 12-year-olds also grasp the notion of *scale*—the proportional relation between a space and its map representation (Liben, 2006).

Map-related experiences greatly improve children's map skills. When teachers asked fourth graders to write down the clues they used to decide where stickers (signifying landmark locations) should go on a map of an outdoor space, the accuracy of children's performance improved greatly (Kastens & Liben, 2007). Such self-generated explanations seem to induce learners to reflect on and revise their own thinking, sparking gains in many types of problem solving among students from elementary school through college. And a computer-based curriculum called *Where Are We,* consisting of 12 map-reading and map-making lessons, led to substantial improvements in second to fourth graders' performance on diverse mapping tasks (Liben, Kastens, & Stevenson, 2001).

Cultural frameworks influence children's map making. In many non-Western communities, people rarely use maps for way finding but rely on information from neighbors, street vendors, and shopkeepers. Also, compared to their Western agemates, non-Western children less often ride in cars and more often walk, which results in intimate neighborhood knowledge. When a researcher had older school-age children in small cities in India and in the United States draw maps of their neighborhoods, the Indian children represented a rich array of landmarks and aspects of social life, such as people and vehicles, in a small area surrounding their home. The U.S. children, in contrast, drew a more formal, extended space, highlighting main streets and key directions (north–south, east–west) but including few landmarks (see Figure 12.1)

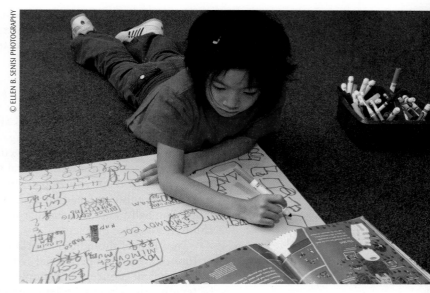

© ELLEN B. SENISI PHOTOGRAPHY

■ This 6-year-old's drawing of a neighborhood map depicts familiar buildings and other landmarks along an organized route of travel. ■

(a)   (b)

FIGURE 12.1

Maps drawn by older school-age children from India and the United States. (a) The Indian child depicted many landmarks and features of social life in a small area near her home. (b) The U.S. child drew a more extended space and highlighted main streets and key directions but included few landmarks and people. *(From G. Parameswaran, 2003, "Experimenter Instructions as a Mediator in the Effects of Culture on Mapping One's Neighborhood,"* Journal of Environmental Psychology, 23, *pp. 415–416. Copyright © 2003, reprinted with permission from Elsevier.)*

(Parameswaran, 2003). Although the U.S. children's maps scored higher in cognitive maturity, this difference reflected cultural interpretations of the task: When asked to create a map to "help people find their way," the Indian children drew spaces as far-reaching and organized as the U.S. children's.

Limitations of Concrete Operational Thought

As the name of this stage suggests, concrete operational thinking suffers from one important limitation: Children think in an organized, logical fashion only when dealing with concrete information they can perceive directly. Their mental operations work poorly with abstract ideas—ones not apparent in the real world. Consider children's solutions to transitive inference problems. When shown pairs of sticks of unequal length, Lizzie easily engaged in transitive inference. But she had great difficulty with a hypothetical version of this task: "Susan is taller than Sally, and Sally is taller than Mary. Who is the tallest?" Not until age 11 or 12 can children solve this problem.

That logical thought is at first tied to immediate situations helps account for a special feature of concrete operational reasoning. Children master concrete operational tasks step by step, not all at once. For example, they usually grasp conservation of number first, followed by length, liquid, and mass, and then weight. This *continuum of acquisition* (or gradual mastery) of logical concepts is another indication of the limitations of concrete operational thinking (Fischer & Bidell, 1991). Rather than coming up with general logical principles that they apply to all relevant situations, children seem to work out the logic of each problem separately.

Follow-Up Research on Concrete Operational Thought

According to Piaget, brain development combined with experience in a rich and varied external world should lead children everywhere to reach the concrete operational stage. Yet recent evidence indicates that specific cultural and school practices have much to do with mastery of Piagetian tasks (Rogoff, 2003). And information-processing research helps explain the gradual mastery of logical concepts in middle childhood.

THE IMPACT OF CULTURE AND SCHOOLING   In tribal and village societies, conservation is often delayed. For example, among the Hausa of Nigeria, who live in small agricultural settlements and rarely send their children to school, even basic conservation tasks—number, length, and liquid—are not understood until age 11 or later (Fahrmeier, 1978). This suggests that taking part in relevant everyday activities helps children master conservation and other Piagetian problems. Joey and Lizzie, for example, think of fairness in terms of equal distribution—a value emphasized in their culture. They frequently divide materials, such as Halloween treats or lemonade, equally among their friends. Because they often see the same quantity arranged in different ways, they grasp conservation early.

The very experience of going to school seems to promote mastery of Piagetian tasks. When children of the same age are tested, those who have been in school longer do better on transitive inference problems (Artman & Cahan, 1993). Opportunities to seriate objects, to learn about order relations, and to remember the parts of complex problems are probably responsible. Yet certain informal, nonschool experiences can also foster operational thought. Brazilian 6- to 9-year-old street vendors, who seldom attend school, do poorly on Piagetian class inclusion tasks. But they perform much better than economically advantaged schoolchildren on versions relevant to street vending—for example, "If you have 4 units of mint chewing gum and 2 units of grape chewing gum, is it better to sell me the mint gum or [all] the gum?" (Ceci & Roazzi, 1994). Similarly, around age 7 to 8, Zinacanteco Indian girls of southern Mexico, who learn to weave elaborately designed fabrics as an alternative to schooling, engage in mental transformations to figure out how a warp strung on will turn out as woven cloth—reasoning expected at the concrete operational stage. North American children of the same age, who do much better than Zinacanteco children on Piagetian tasks, have great difficulty with these weaving problems (Maynard & Greenfield, 2003).

On the basis of such findings, some investigators have concluded that the forms of logic required by Piagetian tasks do not emerge spontaneously in children but, rather, are heavily

■ This Brazilian street vendor might not perform well on Piagetian class inclusion tasks, but he is likely to understand versions relevant to street vending—for example, that "all the chewing gum" represents a larger quantity than the amount of any one flavor. ■

influenced by training, context, and cultural conditions. Does this view remind you of Vygotsky's sociocultural theory, which we discussed in earlier chapters?

AN INFORMATION-PROCESSING VIEW OF CONCRETE OPERATIONAL THOUGHT

As we saw in Chapter 9, preschoolers show the beginnings of logical thinking on simplified and familiar tasks. The gradual mastery of logical concepts in middle childhood raises a familiar question about Piaget's theory: Is an abrupt stagewise transition to logical thought the best way to describe cognitive development in middle childhood?

Some *neo-Piagetian theorists* argue that the development of operational thinking can best be understood in terms of gains in information-processing speed rather than a sudden shift to a new stage (Halford & Andrews, 2006). For example, Robbie Case (1996, 1998) proposed that, with practice, cognitive schemes demand less attention and become more automatic. This frees up space in *working memory* (see Chapter 6, page 217) so children can focus on combining old schemes and generating new ones. For instance, the child who sees water poured from one container to another recognizes that the height of the liquid changes. As this understanding becomes routine, the child notices that the width of the water changes as well. Soon children coordinate these observations, and they grasp conservation of liquid. Then, as this logical idea becomes well-practiced, the child transfers it to more demanding situations, such as weight.

Once the schemes of a Piagetian stage are sufficiently automatic, enough working memory is available to integrate them into an improved representation. As a result, children acquire *central conceptual structures*—networks of concepts and relations that permit them to think more effectively in a wide range of situations (Case, 1996, 1998). The central conceptual structures that emerge from integrating concrete operational schemes are broadly applicable principles that result in increasingly complex, systematic reasoning, signifying the transition to formal operational thought.

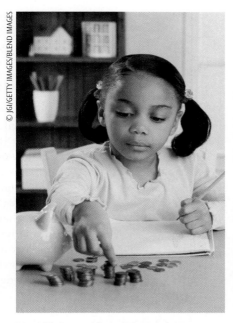

■ As this 6-year-old practices counting money, she will become a more efficient and effective information processor. Eventually she will coordinate an increasing number of task dimensions into a central conceptual structure—a general representation that she can apply in many situations. ■

Case and his colleagues—along with other information processing researchers—have examined children's performance on a wide variety of tasks, including solving arithmetic word problems, understanding stories, drawing pictures, sight-reading music, handling money, and interpreting social situations. In each task, preschoolers typically focus on only one dimension. In understanding stories, for example, they grasp only a single story line. In drawing pictures, they depict objects separately. By the early school years, children coordinate two dimensions—two story lines in a single plot and drawings that show both the features of objects and their relationships. Around 9 to 11 years, children integrate multiple dimensions (Case, 1998; Halford & Andrews, 2006). They tell coherent stories with a main plot and several subplots. And their drawings follow a set of rules for representing perspective and, therefore, include several points of reference, such as near, midway, and far.

Case's theory helps explain why many understandings appear in specific situations at different times rather than being mastered all at once. First, different forms of the same logical insight, such as the various conservation tasks, vary in their processing demands, with those acquired later requiring more space in working memory. Second, children's experiences vary widely. A child who often listens to and tells stories but rarely draws pictures displays more advanced central conceptual structures in storytelling. Compared with Piaget's, Case's theory better accounts for unevenness in cognitive development. When tasks make similar processing demands, such as Piaget's class inclusion and transitive inference problems (each of which requires children to consider three relations at once), children with relevant experiences master those tasks at about the same time (Halford, Wilson, & Phillips, 1998).

As noted in Chapter 9, young children can be trained to solve many Piagetian problems. Many such tasks can be solved either empirically or logically. In the class inclusion problem shown on page 322 in Chapter 9, children can count the yellow flowers and all the flowers (yellow plus blue) to see that there are more *flowers* than *yellow flowers*—an empirical approach. Or they can take a logical approach, reasoning, "There are more flowers than yellow flowers because yellow flowers are just a type of flower." Younger children, in contrast to older children and adults, often rely on cumbersome empirical strategies, perhaps because they do not realize that certain problems can be solved logically. When 5-year-olds were given logical explanations after failing at class-inclusion tasks, they improved rapidly in performance (Siegler & Svetina, 2006). Relying on logical strategies enhances both accuracy and speed of thinking.

Evaluation of the Concrete Operational Stage

Piaget was correct that school-age children approach many problems in more organized, rational ways than preschoolers. But disagreement continues over whether this difference occurs because of *continuous* improvement in logical skills or *discontinuous* restructuring of children's thinking (as Piaget's stage idea assumes). Many researchers think that both types of change may be involved (Carey, 1999; Case, 1998; Demetriou et al., 2002; Fischer & Bidell, 2006; Halford & Andrews, 2006).

During the school years, children apply logical schemes to many more tasks. In the process, their thought seems to change qualitatively—toward a more comprehensive grasp of the underlying principles of logical thought. Piaget himself seems to have recognized this possibility in evidence for gradual mastery of conservation and other tasks. So perhaps some blend of Piagetian and information-processing ideas holds the greatest promise for explaining cognitive development in middle childhood.

ASK YOURSELF

◆ **REVIEW** Children's performance on conservation tasks illustrates a continuum of acquisition of logical concepts. Review the preceding sections, and list additional examples of gradual development of operational reasoning.

◆ **APPLY** Nine-year-old Adrienne spends many hours helping her father build furniture in his woodworking shop. How might this experience facilitate Adrienne's advanced performance on Piagetian seriation problems?

◆ **CONNECT** Explain how advances in perspective taking contribute to school-age children's improved ability to draw and use maps.

◆ **REFLECT** Which aspects of Piaget's description of the concrete operational child do you accept? Which do you doubt? Explain, citing research evidence.

■ ■ Information Processing
■ ■

In contrast to Piaget's focus on overall cognitive change, the information-processing perspective examines separate aspects of thinking. Attention and memory, which underlie every act of cognition, are central concerns in middle childhood, just as they were during infancy and the preschool years. Advances in metacognition and opportunities for self-regulation aid development. Also, increased understanding of how school-age children process information is being applied to their academic learning—in particular, to reading and mathematics.

Researchers believe that brain development contributes to the following basic changes in information processing that facilitate the diverse aspects of thinking we are about to consider:

■ *Increases in information-processing speed and capacity.* Time needed to process information on a wide variety of cognitive tasks declines rapidly between ages 6 and 12 (Kail & Park, 1992, 1994). This suggests a biologically based, age-related gain in speed of thinking, possibly due to myelination and synaptic pruning in the brain. Some researchers believe this greater efficiency contributes to more complex, effective thinking because a faster thinker can hold on to and operate on more information in working memory (Halford & Andrews, 2006; Luna et al., 2004; Nettelbeck & Burns, 2010). Indeed, *digit span,* which assesses the basic capacity of working memory, increases from about five digits at age 7 to seven digits at age 12 (Kail, 2003).

■ *Gains in inhibition.* As indicated in earlier chapters, inhibition—the ability to control internal and external distracting stimuli—improves from infancy on. But additional strides occur in middle childhood as the prefrontal cortex develops further (Luna et al., 2004; Nelson, Thomas, & de Haan, 2006). EEG brain-wave and fMRI measures reveal a steady, age-related increase in activation of diverse cortical regions, especially the prefrontal cortex, in children and adolescents working on tasks that require suppression of inappropriate responses (Bartgis, Lilly, & Thomas, 2003; Luna et al., 2001). Individuals skilled at inhibition can prevent their minds from straying to irrelevant thoughts, an ability that supports many information-processing skills by preserving space in working memory for the task at hand (Dempster & Corkill, 1999; Klenberg, Korkman, & Lahti-Nuuttila, 2001).

Besides brain development, strategy use contributes to more effective information processing. As we have already seen, school-age children think far more strategically than preschoolers. At the same time, neurological change supports gains in strategy use.

■ Gains in processing speed and capacity and in inhibition contribute to the cognitive changes of middle childhood—for example, ability to carry out this complex classroom project, in which third graders study erosion by sprinkling water onto soil and observing the effects of the runoff. ■

Attention

During middle childhood, gains in sustained attention continue. In addition, attention becomes more selective, adaptable, and planful.

SELECTIVITY AND ADAPTABILITY   As Joey and Lizzie moved through elementary school, they became better at deliberately attending to just those aspects of a situation that were relevant to their task goals. Researchers study this increasing selectivity of attention by introducing irrelevant stimuli into a task and seeing how well children attend to its central elements. For example, they might present a stream of numbers on a computer screen and ask children to press a button whenever a particular two-digit sequence (such as "1" followed by "9") appears. Findings show that selective attention improves sharply between ages 6 and 10, with gains continuing through adolescence (Gomez-Perez & Ostrosky-Solis, 2006; Vakil et al., 2009; Tabibi & Pfeffer, 2007).

Older children also flexibly adapt their attention to situational requirements. For example, when asked to sort cards with pictures that vary in both color and shape, children age 5 and older readily switch their basis of sorting from color to shape when asked to do so; younger children have difficulty (Brooks et al., 2003; Zelazo, Frye, & Rapus, 1996). And when studying for a spelling test, 10-year-old Joey was much more likely than Lizzie to devote most attention to the words he knew least well (Masur, McIntyre, & Flavell, 1973).

How do children acquire selective, adaptable attentional strategies? Children's performance on many tasks reveals a predictable, four-step sequence:

1. **Production deficiency.** Preschoolers rarely engage in attentional strategies. In other words, they fail to *produce* strategies when they could be helpful.
2. **Control deficiency.** Young elementary school children sometimes produce strategies, but not consistently. They fail to *control,* or execute, strategies effectively.
3. **Utilization deficiency.** Slightly later, children execute strategies consistently, but their performance either does not improve or improves less than that of older children.
4. **Effective strategy use.** By the mid-elementary school years, children use strategies consistently, and performance improves (Miller, 2000).

As we will soon see, these phases also characterize children's use of memory strategies. Why, when children first use a strategy, does it not work well? A likely reason is that applying a

BIOLOGY AND ENVIRONMENT

Children with Attention-Deficit Hyperactivity Disorder

While the other fifth graders worked quietly at their desks, Calvin squirmed, dropped his pencil, looked out the window, fiddled with his shoelaces, and talked aloud. "Hey Joey," he yelled across the room, "wanna play ball after school?" But the other children weren't eager to play with Calvin, who was physically awkward and failed to follow the rules of the game. He had trouble taking turns at bat. In the outfield, he tossed his mitt up in the air and looked elsewhere when the ball came his way. Calvin's desk was a chaotic mess. He often lost pencils, books, and other school materials, and he had difficulty remembering assignments and due dates.

Symptoms of ADHD

Calvin is one of about 5 percent of U.S. school-age children with **attention-deficit hyperactivity disorder (ADHD),** which involves inattention, impulsivity, and excessive motor activity resulting in academic and social problems (American Psychiatric Association, 2000; Barkley, 2006). Boys are diagnosed about four times as often as girls. However, many girls with ADHD seem to be overlooked, either because their symptoms are less flagrant or because of a gender bias: A difficult, disruptive boy is more likely to be referred for treatment (Abikoff et al., 2002; Biederman et al., 2005).

Children with ADHD cannot stay focused on a task that requires mental effort for more than a few minutes. They often act impulsively, ignoring social rules and lashing out with hostility when frustrated. Many, though not all, are *hyperactive,* exhausting parents and teachers and irritating other children with their excessive motor activity. For a child to be diagnosed with ADHD, these symptoms must have appeared before age 7 as a persistent problem.

Because of their difficulty concentrating, ADHD children score 7 to 15 points lower than other children on intelligence tests (Barkley, 2002b). Researchers agree that deficient executive processing (see page 218 in Chapter 6) underlies ADHD symptoms. According to one view, children with ADHD are impaired in capacity to inhibit action in favor of thought—a basic difficulty that results in wide-ranging inadequacies in strategic thinking and, therefore, in poor self-regulation (Barkley, 2001). Another hypothesis is that ADHD results from a cluster of executive processing problems that interfere with ability to guide one's own behavior (Brown, 2005, 2006). Research confirms that children with ADHD do poorly on tasks requiring sustained attention; find it hard to ignore irrelevant information; have difficulty with memory, planning, reasoning, and problem solving in academic and social situations; and often fail to

manage frustration and intense emotion (Barkley, 2003, 2006).

Origins of ADHD

ADHD runs in families and is highly heritable. Identical twins share it more often than fraternal twins (Freitag et al., 2010; Rasmussen et al., 2004). Children with ADHD show abnormal brain functioning, including reduced electrical and blood-flow activity in the prefrontal cortex and in other areas involved in attention, inhibition of behavior, and other aspects of motor control (Mackie et al., 2007; Sowell et al., 2003). Also, the brains of children with ADHD grow more slowly and are about 3 percent smaller in overall volume, with a thinner cerebral cortex, than the brains of unaffected agemates (Narr et al., 2009; Shaw et al., 2007). Several genes that affect neural communication have been implicated in the disorder (Faraone & Mick, 2010).

At the same time, ADHD is associated with environmental factors. Prenatal teratogens—such as tobacco, alcohol, illegal drugs, and environmental pollutants—are linked to inattention and hyperactivity (see Chapter 3). And they can combine with certain genotypes to greatly increase risk of the disorder (see page 87 in Chapter 2). Furthermore, children with ADHD are more likely to come from homes in which

---

new strategy requires so much effort and attention that little remains to perform other parts of the task well (Woody-Dorning & Miller, 2001). Another reason a new strategy may not lead to performance gains is that younger children are not good at monitoring their task performance (Schneider & Bjorklund, 2003). Because they fail to keep track of how well a strategy is working, they do not apply it consistently or refine it in other ways.

PLANNING   School-age children's attentional strategies also become increasingly planful. They scan detailed pictures and written materials for similarities and differences more thoroughly than preschoolers (Vurpillot, 1968). And on tasks with many parts, they make decisions about what to do first and what to do next in an orderly fashion. In one study, 5- to 9-year-olds were given lists of items to obtain from a play grocery store. Older children more often took time to scan the store before shopping. They also paused more often to look for each item before moving to get it. Consequently, they followed shorter routes through the aisles (Gauvain & Rogoff, 1989a; Szepkouski, Gauvain, & Carberry, 1994).

The development of planning illustrates how attention becomes coordinated with other cognitive processes. To solve problems involving multiple steps, children must postpone action in favor of weighing alternatives, organizing task materials (such as items on a grocery list), and remembering the steps of their plan so they can attend to each one in sequence. Along the way, marriages are unhappy and family stress is high (Bernier & Siegel, 1994). But a stressful home life rarely causes ADHD. Rather, these children's behaviors can contribute to family problems, which intensify the child's preexisting difficulties.

Treating ADHD

Calvin's doctor eventually prescribed stimulant medication, the most common treatment for ADHD. As long as dosage is carefully regulated, these drugs reduce symptoms in 70 percent of children who take them (Greenhill, Halperin, & Abikoff, 1999). Stimulant medication seems to increase activity in the prefrontal cortex, thereby improving the child's capacity to sustain attention and to inhibit off-task behavior.

In 2006, an advisory panel convened by the U.S. Food and Drug Administration warned that stimulants might impair heart functioning, even causing sudden death in a few individuals, and advocated warning labels describing these potential risks. Debate over the safety of medication for ADHD is likely to intensify. In any case, medication is not enough. Drugs cannot teach children to compensate for inattention and impulsivity. The most effective treatment approach combines medication with interventions that model and reinforce appropriate academic and social behavior (American Academy of Pediatrics, 2005b; Smith, Barkley, & Shapiro, 2006).

Family intervention is also important. Inattentive, overactive children strain the patience of parents, who are likely to react punitively and inconsistently—a child-rearing style that strengthens defiant, aggressive behavior. In fact, in 45 to 65 percent of cases, these two sets of behavior problems occur together (Barkley, 2002a).

Some media reports suggest that the number of U.S. children diagnosed with ADHD has increased greatly. But large surveys yielded similar overall prevalence rates 25 years ago and today. Nevertheless, the incidence of ADHD is much higher in some communities than others. At times, children are overdiagnosed and unnecessarily medicated because their parents and teachers are impatient with inattentive, active behavior that is within normal range (Mayes, Bagwell, & Erkulwater, 2008). In Hong Kong, where academic success is particularly prized, children are diagnosed at more than twice the rate in the United States. But in Great Britain, where doctors are hesitant to label a child with ADHD or to prescribe medication, children are underdiagnosed and often do not receive the treatment they need (Taylor, 2004).

ADHD is usually a lifelong disorder. Affected individuals are at risk for persistent antisocial behavior, depression, alcohol and drug abuse, and other problems (Kessler et al., 2005, 2006). Adults with ADHD continue to need help in

© ELLEN B. SENISI/THE IMAGE WORKS

■ For this 7-year-old with ADHD, a classroom offering many opportunities for active learning and peer collaboration may help her sustain attention and improve in social skills. ■

structuring their environments, regulating negative emotion, selecting appropriate careers, and understanding their condition as a biological deficit rather than a character flaw.

they must monitor how well the plan works and revise it if necessary. Clearly, planning places heavy demands on working-memory capacity.

As Chapter 9 revealed, children learn much about planning by collaborating with more expert planners. With age, children take on more responsibility in these joint endeavors, such as organizing task materials and suggesting planning strategies. The demands of school tasks—and teachers' explanations of how to plan—also contribute to gains in planning.

But adult-controlled activities may rob children of opportunities to plan. In one study, researchers videotaped small groups of first and second graders devising plays that they would perform for their class (Baker-Sennett, Matusov, & Rogoff, 2008). Some groups were child-led; others were led by adult volunteers. Child-led groups engaged in extensive planning—brainstorming themes and working out the details of their improvisations. But when adults planned the play in advance, the children spent most of their time in nonplanning pursuits, such as rehearsing lines and making play props. The adults missed a rich opportunity to scaffold learning (see page 331 in Chapter 9) by turning over responsibility for play planning to the children and guiding and supporting, as needed.

The attentional strategies just considered are crucial for success in school. Unfortunately, some children have great difficulty paying attention. See the Biology and Environment box above for a discussion of the serious learning and behavior problems of children with attention-deficit hyperactivity disorder.

Memory Strategies

As attention improves, so do *memory strategies,* the deliberate mental activities we use to store and retain information. During the school years, these techniques for holding information in working memory and transferring it to our long-term knowledge base take a giant leap forward.

REHEARSAL AND ORGANIZATION When Lizzie had a list of things to learn, such as a phone number, the capitals of the United States, or the names of geometric shapes, she immediately used **rehearsal**—repeating the information to herself. This memory strategy first appears in the early grade school years. Soon after, a second strategy becomes common: **organization**—grouping related items together (for example, all state capitals in the same part of the country), an approach that improves recall dramatically (Schneider, 2002).

Perfecting memory strategies requires time and effort. For example, 8-year-old Lizzie rehearsed in a piecemeal fashion. After being given the word *cat* in a list of items, she said, "Cat, cat, cat." But 10-year-old Joey combined previous words with each new item, saying, "Desk, man, yard, cat, cat"—an approach that greatly increases retention (Kunzinger, 1985). In longitudinal research, younger children organized inconsistently (a *control deficiency*) and, when they did organize, showed little or no memory benefit (a *utilization deficiency*). In contrast, between ages 8 and 10, after realizing how effective organization is, many children suddenly began using it consistently, and their recall improved immediately (Schlagmüller & Schneider, 2002; Weinert & Schneider, 1999). With experience, children organize more skillfully, grouping items into fewer categories. And they apply the strategy to a wider range of memory tasks, including ones with less clearly related materials (Bjorklund et al., 1994).

Furthermore, as children gain in processing capacity and familiarity with strategies, they are more likely to use several memory strategies at once—rehearsing, organizing, and stating category names. And the more strategies they apply simultaneously, the better they remember (Coyle & Bjorklund, 1997; DeMarie et al., 2004). Although younger children's use of multiple strategies has little impact on performance (a *utilization deficiency*), their tendency to experiment is adaptive. By generating a variety of strategies, they discover which ones work best and how to combine them effectively. For example, second to fourth graders know that organizing the items first, next rehearsing category names, and finally rehearsing individual items is a good way to study lists (Hock, Park, & Bjorklund, 1998). Recall from *overlapping-waves theory,* discussed in Chapter 9, that children experiment with strategies when faced with many cognitive challenges—an approach that enables them to gradually "home in" on the most effective techniques (Siegler, 1996, 2007).

ELABORATION By the end of middle childhood, children start to use **elaboration**—creating a relationship, or shared meaning, between two or more pieces of information that are not members of the same category. For example, if two of the words you must learn are *fish* and *pipe,* you might generate the verbal statement or mental image, "The fish is smoking a pipe." This highly effective memory technique, which requires considerable effort and space in working memory, becomes increasingly common in adolescence and early adulthood (Schneider & Pressley, 1997).

Because organization and elaboration combine items into *meaningful chunks,* they permit children to hold onto much more information and, as a result, further expand working memory. In addition, when children link a new item to information they already know, they can *retrieve* it easily by thinking of other items associated with it. As we will see, this also contributes to improved memory during the school years.

The Knowledge Base and Memory Performance

During middle childhood, the long-term knowledge base grows larger and becomes organized into increasingly elaborate, hierarchically structured networks. This rapid growth of knowledge helps children use strategies and remember (Schneider, 2002). In other words, knowing more about a topic makes new information more meaningful and familiar, so it is easier to store and retrieve.

To test this idea, researchers classified fourth graders as either experts or novices in knowledge of soccer and then gave both groups lists of soccer and nonsoccer items to learn. Experts remembered far more items on the soccer list (but not on the nonsoccer list) than novices. And during recall, the experts' listing of items was better organized, as indicated by clustering of items into categories (Schneider & Bjorklund, 1992). This superior organization at retrieval suggests that highly knowledgeable children organize information in their area of expertise with little or no effort—by rapidly associating new items with the large number they already know. Consequently, experts can devote more working-memory resources to using recalled information to reason and solve problems (Bjorklund & Douglas, 1997).

But knowledge is not the only important factor in children's strategic memory processing. Children who are expert in an area are usually highly motivated. As a result, they not only acquire knowledge more quickly but also *actively use what they know* to add more. In contrast, academically unsuccessful children often fail to ask how previously stored information can clarify new material. This, in turn, interferes with the development of a broad knowledge base (Schneider & Bjorklund, 1998). By the end of the school years, then, extensive knowledge and use of memory strategies support one another.

Culture, Schooling, and Memory Strategies

Rehearsal, organization, and elaboration are techniques that people usually use when they need to remember information for its own sake. On many other occasions, memory occurs as a natural byproduct of participation in daily activities (Rogoff, 2003). For example, Joey can spout a wealth of facts about baseball teams and players—information he picked up from watching ball games, discussing the game, and trading baseball cards with his friends. And without prior rehearsal, he can recount the story line of an exciting movie or novel—narrative material that is already meaningfully organized.

A repeated finding is that people in non-Western cultures who have no formal schooling do not use or benefit from instruction in memory strategies because they see no practical reason to use these techniques (Rogoff & Chavajay, 1995). Tasks that require children to recall isolated bits of information, which are common in classrooms, strongly motivate use of memory strategies. In fact, Western children get so much practice with this type of learning that they do not refine techniques that rely on cues available in everyday life, such as spatial location and arrangement of objects. For example, Guatemalan Mayan 9-year-olds do slightly better than their U.S. agemates when told to remember the placement of 40 familiar objects in a play scene. U.S. children often rehearse object names when it would be more effective to keep track of spatial relations (Rogoff & Wadell, 1982). The development of memory strategies, then, is not just a product of a more competent information-processing system. It also depends on task demands and cultural circumstances.

■ A mother and daughter of the Colombian U'wa people, who have no written tradition, make "cocara" leaf hats, which girls wear from puberty until marriage. Although the child demonstrates keen memory for how to select, cut, and assemble the leaves, she might have difficulty recalling the isolated bits of information that school tasks often require. ■

The School-Age Child's Theory of Mind

During middle childhood, children's *theory of mind,* or set of beliefs about mental activities, becomes much more elaborate and refined. Recall from Chapter 9 that this awareness of thought is often called *metacognition.* School-age children's improved ability to reflect on their own mental life is another reason that their thinking and problem solving advance.

KNOWLEDGE OF COGNITIVE CAPACITIES   Unlike preschoolers, who view the mind as a passive container of information, older children regard it as an active, constructive agent that selects and transforms information (Kuhn, 2000). Consequently, they have a much better understanding of cognitive processes and the impact of psychological factors on performance.

(a)

Jason has a letter from a friend. Lisa wants to read the letter, but Jason doesn't want her to. Jason puts the letter under his pillow.

(b)

Jason leaves the room to help his mother.

(c)

While Jason is gone, Lisa takes the letter and reads it. Jason returns and watches Lisa, but Lisa doesn't see Jason. Then Lisa puts the letter in Jason's desk.

FIGURE 12.2

A second-order false belief task. After relating the story in the sequence of pictures, the researcher asks a second-order false-belief question: "Where does Lisa think Jason will look for the letter? Why?" Around age 7, children answer correctly—that Lisa thinks Jason will look under his pillow because Lisa doesn't know that Jason saw her put the letter in the desk. *(Adapted from Astington, Pelletier, & Homer, 2002.)*

School-age children, for example, know that doing well on a task depends on focusing attention—concentrating and exerting effort (Miller & Bigi, 1979). With age, they also become increasingly aware of effective memory strategies and why they work (Alexander et al., 2003). And they gradually grasp relationships between mental activities—for example, that remembering is crucial for understanding and that understanding strengthens memory (Schwanenflugel, Henderson, & Fabricius, 1998).

Furthermore, school-age children's understanding of sources of knowledge expands. They realize that when two people view the same object, their trains of thought will differ because of variations in their knowledge, experiences, and other characteristics (Eisbach, 2004). And they are aware that people can extend their knowledge not only by directly observing events and talking to others but also by making *mental inferences* (Miller, Hardin, & Montgomery, 2003).

This grasp of inference enables knowledge of false belief to expand. In several studies, researchers told children complex stories involving one character's belief about a second character's belief. Then the children answered questions about what the first character thought the second character would do (see Figure 12.2). By age 6 to 7, children were aware that people form beliefs about other people's beliefs and that these *second-order beliefs* can be wrong! Appreciation of *second-order false belief* enables children to pinpoint the reasons that another person arrived at a certain belief (Astington, Pelletier, & Homer, 2002; Miller, 2009; Naito & Seki, 2009). This assists them greatly in understanding others' perspectives.

fMRI research reveals that from age 6 to 11, children become increasingly selective in the brain regions they recruit when thinking about a character's thoughts. In addition to the prefrontal cortex, they activate an area connecting the right temporal and parietal lobes (known to play a crucial role in theory-of-mind processes), just as adults do (Saxe et al., 2009).

Besides more complex thinking and language, experiences that foster awareness of mental activities contribute to school-age children's more reflective, process-oriented view of the mind. In a study of rural children of Cameroon, Africa, those who attended school performed much better on theory-of-mind tasks (Vinden, 2002). In school, teachers often call attention to the workings of the mind when they remind children to pay attention, remember mental steps, share points of view with peers, and evaluate their own and others' reasoning.

KNOWLEDGE OF STRATEGIES   Consistent with their more active view of the mind, school-age children are far more conscious of mental strategies than preschoolers. When shown video clips depicting two children using different recall strategies and asked which one is likely to produce better memory, kindergarten and young elementary school children knew that

LOOK AND LISTEN

❖❖

Watch a teacher—in a public school, religious school, recreation center, or other setting—explain a learning activity to 6- to 8-year-olds. How often did the teacher call attention to the workings of the mind?

rehearsing or organizing is better than looking or naming. Older children were aware of more subtle differences—that organizing is better than rehearsing (Justice, 1986; Schneider, 1986).

Between third and fifth grade, children develop a much better appreciation of how and why strategies work (Alexander et al., 2003). Consequently, fifth graders are considerably better than younger children at discriminating good from bad reasoning. When given examples varying in quality, fifth graders consistently rated "good" reasoning as based on weighing of possibilities (rather than jumping to conclusions) and gathering of evidence (rather than ignoring important facts), even if such reasoning led to an unfavorable result (Amsterlaw, 2006).

Once children become conscious of the many factors that influence mental activity, they combine them into a more effective understanding. By the end of middle childhood, children take account of how *interactions* among multiple variables—age and motivation of the learner, effective use of strategies, and nature and difficulty of the task—affect cognitive performance (Wellman, 1990). In this way, metacognition broadens into a more complex theory.

Cognitive Self-Regulation

Although metacognition expands, school-age children often have difficulty putting what they know about thinking into action. They are not yet good at **cognitive self-regulation,** the process of continuously monitoring progress toward a goal, checking outcomes, and redirecting unsuccessful efforts. For example, Lizzie is aware that she should attend closely to her teacher's directions, group items when memorizing, reread a complicated paragraph to make sure she understands it, and relate new information to what she already knows. But she does not always engage in these activities.

To study cognitive self-regulation, researchers sometimes look at the impact of children's awareness of memory strategies on how well they remember. By second grade, the more children know about memory strategies, the more they recall—a relationship that strengthens over middle childhood (Pierce & Lange, 2000). And when children apply a strategy consistently, their knowledge of strategies strengthens, resulting in a bidirectional relationship between metacognition and strategic processing that enhances self-regulation (Schlagmüller & Schneider, 2002).

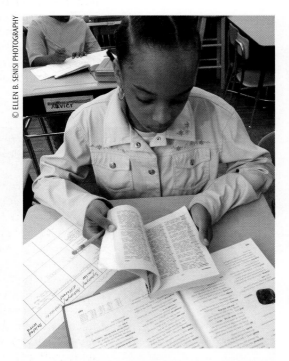

Why does cognitive self-regulation develop gradually? Monitoring learning outcomes is cognitively demanding, requiring constant evaluation of effort and progress. Throughout elementary and secondary school, self-regulation predicts academic success (Valiente et al., 2008; Zimmerman & Cleary, 2009). Students who do well in school know when their learning is going well and when it is not. If they encounter obstacles, they take steps to address them—for example, organize the learning environment, review confusing material, or seek support from more expert adults or peers (Zimmerman & Cleary, 2009). This active, purposeful approach contrasts sharply with the passive orientation of students who achieve poorly.

Parents and teachers can foster self-regulation. In one study, researchers observed parents instructing their children on a problem-solving task during the summer before third grade. Parents who patiently pointed out important features of the task and suggested strategies had children who, in the classroom, more often discussed ways to approach problems and monitored their own performance (Stright et al., 2002). Explaining the effectiveness of strategies is particularly helpful because it provides a rationale for future action.

Children who acquire effective self-regulatory skills develop a sense of *academic self-efficacy*—confidence in their own ability, which supports future self-regulation (Schunk & Pajares, 2005). Unfortunately, some children receive messages from parents and teachers that seriously undermine their academic self-esteem and self-regulatory skills. We will consider these *learned-helpless* youngsters, along with ways to help them, in Chapter 13.

■ This fifth grader's capacity for cognitive self-regulation is evident in the convenient way she organizes materials, making sure her textbook glossary and dictionary are handy. When she encounters an unfamiliar word while working on a language arts assignment, she swiftly looks up its definition. ■

Applications of Information Processing to Academic Learning

When Joey entered first grade, he recognized only a handful of written words. By fifth grade, he was a proficient reader. Similarly, at age 6, Joey had an informally acquired knowledge of number concepts. By age 10, he could add, subtract, multiply, and divide with ease and had begun to master fractions and percentages. Fundamental discoveries about the development of information processing have been applied to children's learning of reading and mathematics. Researchers are identifying the cognitive ingredients of skilled performance, tracing their development, and distinguishing good from poor learners by pinpointing differences in cognitive skills. They hope, as a result, to design teaching methods that will improve children's learning.

READING   Reading makes use of many skills at once, taxing all aspects of our information-processing systems. We must perceive single letters and letter combinations, translate them into speech sounds, recognize the visual appearance of many common words, hold chunks of text in working memory while interpreting their meaning, and combine the meanings of various parts of a text passage into an understandable whole. And because reading is so demanding, most or all of these skills must be done automatically. If one or more are poorly developed, they will compete for resources in our limited working memories, and reading performance will decline.

As children make the transition from emergent literacy to conventional reading, *phonological awareness*—the ability to reflect on and manipulate the sound structure of spoken language—continues to facilitate their progress (see page 343 in Chapter 9). Other information-processing skills also contribute. Gains in processing speed foster children's rapid conversion of visual symbols into sounds (McBride-Chang & Kail, 2002). Visual scanning and discrimination play important roles and improve with reading experience (Rayner, Pollatsek, & Starr, 2003). Performing all these skills efficiently releases working memory for higher-level activities involved in comprehending the text's meaning.

Until recently, researchers were involved in an intense debate over how to teach beginning reading. Those who took a **whole-language approach** argued that from the beginning, children should be exposed to text in its complete form—stories, poems, letters, posters, and lists—so that they can appreciate the communicative function of written language. According to this view, as long as reading is kept meaningful, children will be motivated to discover the specific skills they need (Watson, 1989). Other experts advocated a **phonics approach,** believing that children should first be coached on *phonics*—the basic rules for translating written symbols into sounds. Only after mastering these skills should they get complex reading material (Rayner & Pollatsek, 1989).

Many studies show that children learn best with a mixture of both approaches. In kindergarten, first, and second grades, teaching that includes phonics boosts reading scores, especially for children who lag behind in reading progress (Stahl & Miller, 2006; Xue & Meisels, 2004). And when teachers combine real reading and writing with teaching of phonics and engage in other excellent teaching practices—encouraging children to tackle reading challenges and integrating reading into all school subjects—first graders show far greater literacy progress (Pressley et al., 2002).

Why might combining phonics with whole language work best? Learning the relationships between letters and sounds enables children to *decode,* or decipher, words they have never seen before. Children who enter school low in phonological awareness make far better reading

■ In this first-grade classroom, teaching of phonics is embedded in captivating stories and challenging writing tasks. Combining instruction in basic skills with whole-language teaching is more effective in promoting children's reading progress than either approach alone. ■

© ELLEN B. SENISI PHOTOGRAPHY

TABLE 12.1	Sequence of Reading Development		
GRADE/AGE	**DEVELOPMENT**		**METHOD OF LEARNING**
Preschool and kindergarten 2–6 years	"Pretends" to read; recognizes some familiar signs ("ON," "OFF," "PIZZA"); "pretends" to write; prints own name and other words		Informal literacy experiences through literacy-rich physical environments, literacy-related play, and storybook reading (see Chapter 9, page 343)
Grades 1 and 2 6–7 years	Masters letter–sound correspondences; sounds out one-syllable words; reads simple stories; reads about 600 words		Direct teaching, through exposure to many types of texts and the basic rules of decoding written symbols into sounds
Grades 2 and 3 7–8 years	Reads simple stories more fluently; masters basic decoding rules; reads about 3,000 words		Same as above
Grades 4 to 9 9–14 years	Reads to learn new knowledge, usually without questioning the reading material		Reading and studying; participating in classroom discussion; completing written assignments
Grades 10 to 12 15–17 years	Reads more widely, tapping materials with diverse viewpoints		Reading more widely; writing papers
College 18 years and older	Reads with a self-defined purpose; decoding and comprehension skills reach a high level of efficiency		Reading even more widely; writing more sophisticated papers

Source: Chall, 1983.

progress when given training in phonics (Casalis & Cole, 2009). Soon they detect new letter–sound relations while reading on their own, and as their fluency in decoding words increases, they are freer to attend to text meaning. Without early phonics training, such children (many of whom come from poverty-stricken families) are substantially behind their age-mates in text comprehension skills by third grade (Foster & Miller, 2007).

Yet too much emphasis on basic skills may cause children to lose sight of the goal of reading: understanding. Children who read aloud fluently without registering meaning know little about effective reading strategies—for example, that they must read more carefully if they will be tested than if they are reading for pleasure, or that explaining a passage in their own words is a good way to assess comprehension. Providing instruction aimed at increasing knowledge and use of reading strategies enhances reading performance from third grade on (Paris & Paris, 2006; Van Keer, 2004).

Table 12.1 charts the general sequence of reading development. Notice the major shift, around age 7 to 8, from "learning to read" to "reading to learn" (Melzi & Ely, 2009). As decoding and comprehension skills reach a high level of efficiency, older readers become actively engaged with the text. They adjust the way they read to fit their current purpose—sometimes seeking new facts and ideas, sometimes questioning, agreeing with, or disagreeing with the writer's viewpoint.

MATHEMATICS   Mathematics teaching in elementary school builds on and greatly enriches children's informal knowledge of number concepts and counting. Written notation systems and formal computational techniques enhance children's ability to represent numbers and compute. Over the early elementary school years, children acquire basic math facts through a combination of frequent practice, experimentation with diverse computational procedures (through which they discover faster, more accurate techniques), reasoning about number concepts, and teaching that conveys effective strategies. (Return to Chapter 9, page 345, for research supporting the importance of both extended practice and a grasp of concepts.) Eventually children retrieve answers automatically and apply this basic knowledge to more complex problems.

Arguments about how to teach mathematics resemble those about reading, pitting drill in computing against "number sense," or understanding. Again, a blend of both approaches is most beneficial (Fuson, 2009). In learning basic math, poorly performing students use cumbersome techniques or try to retrieve answers from memory too soon. They have not sufficiently experimented with strategies to see which are most effective and to reorganize their observations in logical, efficient ways—for example, noticing that multiplication problems involving 2 (2 × 8) are equivalent to addition doubles (8 + 8). On tasks assessing their grasp of math concepts, their performance is weak (Canobi, 2004; Canobi, Reeve, & Pattison, 2003). This suggests that encouraging students to apply strategies and making sure they know why certain strategies work well are essential for solid mastery of basic math.

A similar picture emerges for more complex skills, such as carrying in addition, borrowing in subtraction, and operating with decimals and fractions. Children taught by rote cannot apply the procedure to new problems. Instead, they persistently make mistakes, following a "math rule" that they recall incorrectly because they do not understand it (Carpenter et al., 1999). Look at the following subtraction errors:

$$
\begin{array}{r}
427 \\
-138 \\
\hline
311
\end{array}
\qquad
\begin{array}{r}
7002 \\
-5445 \\
\hline
1447
\end{array}
$$

In the first problem, the child consistently subtracts a smaller from a larger digit, regardless of which is on top. In the second, the child skips columns with zeros in a borrowing operation and, whenever there is a zero on top, writes the bottom digit as the answer.

Children who are given rich opportunities to experiment with problem solving, to appreciate the reasons behind strategies, and to evaluate solution techniques seldom make such errors. In one study, second graders who were taught in these ways not only mastered correct procedures but even invented their own successful strategies, some of which were superior to standard, school-taught methods! Consider this solution:

$$
\begin{array}{cccc}
3 & 15 & 14 & 12 \\
\cancel{4} & \cancel{6} & \cancel{5} & \cancel{2} \\
-1 & 9 & 6 & 8 \\
\hline
2 & 6 & 8 & 4
\end{array}
$$

In subtracting, the child performed all trades first, flexibly moving either from right to left or from left to right, and then subtracted all four columns—a highly efficient, accurate approach (Fuson & Burghard, 2003).

In a German study, the more teachers emphasized conceptual knowledge, by having children actively construct meanings in word problems before practicing computation and memorizing math facts, the more children gained in math achievement from second to third grade (Staub & Stern, 2002). Children taught in this way draw on their solid knowledge of relationships between operations (for example, that the inverse of division is multiplication) to generate efficient, flexible procedures: To solve the division problem 360/9, they might multiply 9 × 40 = 360. And because such children have been encouraged to estimate answers, if they go down the wrong track in computation, they are usually self-correcting. Furthermore, they appreciate connections between math operations and problem contexts. They can solve a word problem ("Jesse spent $3.45 for bananas, $2.62 for bread, and $3.55 for peanut butter. Can he pay for it all with a $10 bill?") quickly through estimation instead of exact calculation (De Corte & Verschaffel, 2006).

In Asian countries, students receive a variety of supports for acquiring mathematical knowledge and often excel at math computation and reasoning. Use of the metric system helps Asian children grasp place value. The consistent structure of number words in Asian languages (*ten-two* for 12, *ten-three* for 13) also makes this idea clear (Miura & Okamoto, 2003). And because Asian number words are shorter and more quickly pronounced, more digits can be held in working memory at once, increasing speed of thinking. Furthermore, Chinese parents provide their children with extensive everyday practice in counting

■ Children develop math skills through a combination of frequent practice and reasoning about number concepts. The most effective teaching combines both approaches. ■

and computation—experiences that contribute to the superiority of Chinese over U.S. children's math knowledge, even before school entry (Siegler & Mu, 2008; Zhou et al., 2006). Finally, as we will see later in this chapter, compared with lessons in the United States, those in Asian classrooms devote more time to exploring math concepts and less to drill and repetition.

ASK YOURSELF

- ◆ REVIEW Cite evidence indicating that school-age children view the mind as an active, constructive agent.

- ◆ APPLY After viewing a slide show on endangered species, second and fifth graders in Lizzie and Joey's school were asked to remember as many animals as they could. Explain why fifth graders recalled much more than second graders.

- ◆ APPLY Lizzie knows that if you have difficulty learning part of a task, you should devote extra attention to that part. But she plays each of her piano pieces from beginning to end instead of practicing the hard parts. Explain why Lizzie does not engage in cognitive self-regulation.

- ◆ REFLECT In your elementary school math education, how much emphasis was placed on computational drill and how much on understanding concepts? How do you think that balance affected your interest and performance in math?

Individual Differences in Mental Development

Around age 6, IQ becomes more stable than it was at earlier ages, and it correlates moderately well with academic achievement, typically around .50 to .60. And children with higher IQs are more likely when they grow up to attain higher levels of education and enter more prestigious occupations (Brody, 1997; Deary et al., 2007). Because IQ predicts school performance and educational attainment, it often enters into educational decisions. Do intelligence tests accurately assess the school-age child's ability to profit from academic instruction? Let's look closely at this controversial issue.

Defining and Measuring Intelligence

Virtually all intelligence tests provide an overall score (the IQ), which represents *general intelligence* or reasoning ability, along with an array of separate scores measuring specific mental abilities. But intelligence is a collection of many capacities, not all of which are included on currently available tests (Carroll, 2005; Sternberg, 2005). Test designers use a complicated statistical technique called *factor analysis* to identify the various abilities that intelligence tests measure. It identifies which sets of test items cluster together, meaning that test-takers who do well on one item in the cluster tend to do well on the others. Distinct clusters are called *factors,* each of which represents an ability. See Figure 12.3 on page 454 for items typically included in intelligence tests for children.

The intelligence tests given from time to time in classrooms are *group-administered tests.* They permit large numbers of students to be tested at once and are useful for instructional planning and for identifying children who require more extensive evaluation with *individually administered tests.* Unlike group tests, which teachers can give with minimal training, individually administered tests demand considerable training and experience to give well. The examiner not only considers the child's answers but also observes the child's behavior, noting such reactions as attention to and interest in the tasks and wariness of the adult. These observations provide insight into whether the test score accurately reflects the child's abilities. Two individual tests—the Stanford-Binet and the Wechsler—are often used to identify highly intelligent children and to diagnose children with learning problems.

TYPICAL VERBAL ITEMS

Vocabulary   Tell me what *carpet* means.

General Information   What day of the week comes right after Thursday?

Verbal Comprehension   Why do we need police officers?

Similarities   How are a ship and a train alike?

Arithmetic   If a $60 jacket is 25% off, how much does it cost?

TYPICAL PERCEPTUAL- AND SPATIAL-REASONING ITEMS

Block Design   Make these blocks look just like the picture.

Picture Concepts   Choose one object from each row to make a group of objects that goes together.

Spatial Visualization   Which of the boxes on the right can be made from the pattern on the left?

a   b   c   d   e

TYPICAL WORKING-MEMORY ITEMS

Digit Span   Repeat these digits in the same order. Now repeat these digits (a similar series) backward.
2, 6, 4, 7, 1, 8

Letter–Number Sequencing   Repeat these numbers and letters, first giving the numbers, then the letters, each in correct sequence.
8 G 4 B 5 N 2

TYPICAL PROCESSING-SPEED ITEM

Symbol Search   If the shape on the left is the same as any of those on the right, mark YES. If the shape is not the same, mark NO. Work as quickly as you can without making mistakes.

YES   NO

FIGURE 12.3

Test items like those on commonly used intelligence tests for children. The verbal items emphasize culturally loaded, fact-oriented information. The perceptual- and spatial-reasoning, working-memory, and processing-speed items emphasize aspects of information processing and are assumed to assess more biologically based skills.

The contemporary descendent of Alfred Binet's first successful intelligence test is the *Stanford-Binet Intelligence Scales,* Fifth Edition, for individuals from age 2 to adulthood. In addition to general intelligence, it assesses five intellectual factors: general knowledge, quantitative reasoning, visual–spatial processing, working memory, and basic information processing (such as speed of analyzing information). Each factor includes both a verbal mode and a nonverbal mode of testing, yielding 10 subtests in all (Roid, 2003). The nonverbal subtests, which do not require spoken language, are especially useful when assessing individuals with limited English, hearing impairments, or communication disorders. The knowledge and quantitative reasoning factors emphasize culturally loaded, fact-oriented information, such as vocabulary and arithmetic problems. In contrast, the visual–spatial processing, working-memory, and basic information-processing factors are assumed to be less culturally biased because they require little specific information (see the spatial visualization item in Figure 12.3).

The *Wechsler Intelligence Scale for Children–IV (WISC–IV)* is the fourth edition of a widely used test for 6- through 16-year-olds. A downward extension of it, the *Wechsler Preschool and Primary Scale of Intelligence–Revised (WPPSI–III),* is appropriate for children 2 years 6 months through 7 years 3 months (Wechsler, 2002, 2003). The Wechsler tests offered both a measure of general intelligence and a variety of factor scores long before the Stanford-Binet. As a result, many psychologists and educators came to prefer them. The WISC–IV has four broad intellectual factors: verbal reasoning, perceptual (or visual–spatial) reasoning, working memory, and processing speed. Each factor is made up of two or three subtests, yielding 10 separate scores in all. The WISC-IV was designed to downplay culture-dependent information, which is emphasized on only one factor (verbal reasoning). According to the test designers, the result is the most "culture-fair" intelligence test available (Williams, Weis, & Rolfhus, 2003). The WISC was also the first test to be standardized on children representing the total population of the United States, including ethnic minorities.

Recent Efforts to Define Intelligence

As we have seen, intelligence tests now tap important aspects of information processing. In line with this trend, some researchers are combining the mental-testing approach to defining intelligence with the information-processing approach. They believe that once we identify the processing skills that separate individuals who test well from those who test poorly, we will know more about how to intervene to improve performance. These investigators conduct *componential analyses* of children's test scores. This means that they look for relationships between aspects (or components) of information processing and children's intelligence test scores.

Processing speed, measured in terms of reaction time on diverse cognitive tasks, is moderately related to IQ (Deary, 2001; Li et al., 2004). Individuals whose nervous systems function more efficiently, permitting them to take in more information and manipulate it quickly, appear to have an edge in intellectual skills. In support of this interpretation, fast, strong ERPs (EEG brain waves in response to stimulation) predict both speedy cognitive processing and higher mental test scores (Rijsdijk & Boomsma, 1997; Schmid, Tirsch, & Scherb, 2002). And measures of working-memory capacity (such as digit span) correlate well with IQ (de Ribaupierre & Lecerf, 2006).

But other factors, including flexible attention, memory, and reasoning strategies, are as important as efficient thinking in predicting IQ, and they explain some of the association between response speed and good test performance (Lohman, 2000; Miller & Vernon, 1992). Children who apply strategies effectively acquire more knowledge and can retrieve it rapidly—advantages that carry over to test performance. Similarly, recall from page 443 that available space in working memory depends in part on effective inhibition—keeping irrelevant information from intruding on the task at hand. Inhibition and sustained and selective attention are among a wide array of attentional skills that are good predictors of IQ (Schweizer, Moosbrugger, & Goldhammer, 2006).

The componential approach has one major shortcoming: It regards intelligence as entirely due to causes within the child. Throughout this book, we have seen how cultural and situational factors also affect children's thinking. Robert Sternberg has expanded the componential approach into a comprehensive theory that regards intelligence as a product of inner and outer forces.

STERNBERG'S TRIARCHIC THEORY   As Figure 12.4 shows, Sternberg's (2001, 2005, 2008) **triarchic theory of successful intelligence** is made up of three broad, interacting intelligences: (1) *analytical intelligence,* or information-processing skills; (2) *creative intelligence,* the capacity to solve novel problems; and (3) *practical intelligence,* application of intellectual skills in everyday situations. Intelligent behavior involves balancing all three intelligences to achieve success in life according to one's personal goals and the requirements of one's cultural community.

Analytical Intelligence. *Analytical intelligence* consists of the information-processing components that underlie all intelligent acts: applying strategies, acquiring task-relevant and metacognitive knowledge, and engaging in self-regulation. But on mental tests, processing skills are used in only a few of their potential ways, resulting in far too narrow a view of intelligent behavior. As we have seen, children in tribal and village societies do not necessarily perform well on measures of "school" knowledge but thrive when processing information in out-of-school situations that most Westerners would find highly challenging.

Creative Intelligence. In any context, success depends not only on processing familiar information but also on generating useful solutions to new problems. People who are *creative* think more skillfully than others when faced with novelty. Given a new task, they apply their information-processing skills in exceptionally effective ways, rapidly making these skills automatic so that working memory is freed for more complex aspects of the situation. Consequently, they quickly move to high-level performance. Although all of us are capable of some creativity, only a few individuals excel at generating novel solutions.

Practical Intelligence. Finally, intelligence is a *practical,* goal-oriented activity aimed at *adapting to, shaping,* or *selecting environments.* Intelligent people skillfully *adapt* their thinking to fit with both their desires and the demands

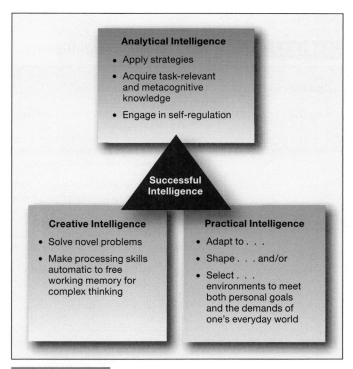

FIGURE 12.4

Sternberg's triarchic theory of successful intelligence. People who behave intelligently balance three interrelated intelligences—analytical, creative, and practical—to achieve success in life, defined by their personal goals and the requirements of their cultural communities.

of their everyday worlds. When they cannot adapt to a situation, they try to *shape,* or change, it to meet their needs. If they cannot shape it, they *select* new contexts that better match their skills, values, or goals. Practical intelligence reminds us that intelligent behavior is never culture-free. Children with certain life histories do well at the behaviors required for success on intelligence tests and adapt easily to the testing conditions and tasks. Others, with different backgrounds, may misinterpret or reject the testing context. Yet such children often display sophisticated abilities in daily life—for example, telling stories, engaging in complex artistic activities, or interacting skillfully with other people.

The triarchic theory emphasizes the complexity of intelligent behavior and the limitations of current intelligence tests in assessing that complexity. For example, out-of-school, practical forms of intelligence are vital for life success and help explain why cultures vary widely in the behaviors they regard as intelligent (Sternberg et al., 2000). When researchers asked ethnically diverse parents for their idea of an intelligent first grader, Caucasian Americans mentioned cognitive traits. In contrast, ethnic minorities (Cambodian, Filipino, Vietnamese, and Mexican immigrants) saw noncognitive capacities—motivation, self-management, and social skills—as particularly important (Okagaki & Sternberg, 1993). According to Sternberg, mental tests can easily underestimate, and even overlook, the intellectual strengths of some children, especially ethnic minorities.

GARDNER'S THEORY OF MULTIPLE INTELLIGENCES In yet another view of how information-processing skills underlie intelligence behavior, Howard Gardner's (1983, 1993, 2000) **theory of multiple intelligences** defines intelligence in terms of distinct sets of processing operations that permit individuals to engage in a wide range of culturally valued activities. Dismissing the idea of general intelligence, Gardner proposes at least eight independent intelligences (see Table 12.2).

Gardner believes that each intelligence has a unique biological basis, a distinct course of development, and different expert, or "end-state," performances. At the same time, he emphasizes that a lengthy process of education is required to trans-

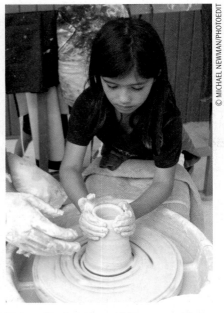

■ According to Gardner, children are capable of at least eight distinct intelligences. As this child learns pottery skills under the guidance of an expert potter, she enriches her spatial intelligence. ■

TABLE 12.2 Gardner's Multiple Intelligences

INTELLIGENCE	PROCESSING OPERATIONS	END-STATE PERFORMANCE POSSIBILITIES
Linguistic	Sensitivity to the sounds, rhythms, and meaning of words and the functions of language	Poet, journalist
Logico-mathematical	Sensitivity to, and capacity to detect, logical or numerical patterns; ability to handle long chains of logical reasoning	Mathematician
Musical	Ability to produce and appreciate pitch, rhythm (or melody), and aesthetic quality of the forms of musical expressiveness	Instrumentalist, composer
Spatial	Ability to perceive the visual-spatial world accurately, to perform transformations on those perceptions, and to re-create aspects of visual experience in the absence of relevant stimuli	Sculptor, navigator
Bodily-kinesthetic	Ability to use the body skillfully for expressive as well as goal-directed purposes; ability to handle objects skillfully	Dancer, athlete
Naturalist	Ability to recognize and classify all varieties of animals, minerals, and plants	Biologist
Interpersonal	Ability to detect and respond appropriately to the moods, temperaments, motivations, and intentions of others	Therapist, salesperson
Intrapersonal	Ability to discriminate complex inner feelings and to use them to guide one's own behavior; knowledge of one's own strengths, weaknesses, desires, and intelligences	Person with detailed, accurate self-knowledge

Sources: Gardner, 1983, 1993, 2000.

SOCIAL ISSUES: EDUCATION

Emotional Intelligence

During recess, Muriel handed birthday party invitations to every fifth-grade girl except Claire, who looked on sadly as her classmates chattered about the party. But one of Muriel's friends, Jessica, looked troubled. Pulling Muriel aside, she exclaimed, "Why'd you do that? You hurt Claire's feelings—you embarrassed her! If you bring invitations to school, you've got to give everybody one!" And after school, Jessica comforted Claire, saying, "If you aren't invited, I'm not going, either!"

Jessica's IQ is only slightly above average, but she excels at *emotional intelligence*—a term that has captured public attention because of popular books suggesting that it is an overlooked set of skills that can greatly improve life success (Goleman, 1995, 1998). According to one influential definition, **emotional intelligence** refers to a set of emotional abilities that enable individuals to process and adapt to emotional information (Salovey & Pizzaro, 2003). To measure it, researchers have devised items tapping emotional skills that enable people to manage their own emotions and interact competently with others. One test requires people to identify and rate the strength of emotions expressed in photographs of faces (emotional perception), to reason about emotions in social situations (emotional understanding), to identify which emotions promote certain thoughts and activities (emotional facilitation), and to evaluate the effectiveness of strategies for controlling negative emotions (emotion regulation). Factor analyses of the scores of hundreds of test-takers

identified several emotional capacities as well as a higher-order general factor (Mayer, Salovey, & Caruso, 2003).

Emotional intelligence is modestly related to IQ. And in school-age children, adolescents, and adults, it is positively associated with self-esteem, empathy, prosocial behavior, cooperation, leadership skills, and life satisfaction and negatively related to drug and alcohol use, dependency, depression, and aggressive behavior (Brackett, Mayer, & Warner, 2004; Mavroveli et al., 2007; Petrides et al., 2006). In adulthood, emotional intelligence predicts many aspects of workplace success, including managerial effectiveness, productive co-worker relationships, and job performance (Mayer, Roberts, & Barsade, 2008; Mayer, Salovey, & Caruso, 2008).

Only a few assessments of emotional intelligence are available for children. These require careful training of teachers in observing and recording children's emotional skills during everyday activities, gathering information from parents, and taking ethnic backgrounds into account (Denham, 2005; Denham & Burton, 2003). As more and better measures are devised, they may help identify children with weak emotional and

social competencies who would profit from intervention (Denham, 2006; Stewart-Brown & Edmonds, 2007).

The concept of emotional intelligence has increased teachers' awareness that providing experiences that meet students' emotional and social needs can improve their adjustment. Lessons that teach emotional understanding, respect and caring for others, strategies for regulating emotion, and resistance to unfavorable peer pressure—using active learning techniques that provide skill practice both in and out of the classroom—are becoming more common (Goetz et al., 2005).

© ELLEN B. SENISI PHOTOGRAPHY

■ The 7-year-old on the right displays high emotional intelligence as she accurately interprets her friend's sadness and offers comfort. ■

---

form any raw potential into a mature social role (Connell, Sheridan, & Gardner, 2003). Cultural values and learning opportunities affect the extent to which a child's intellectual strengths are realized and the way they are expressed.

Gardner's list of abilities has yet to be firmly grounded in research. Neurological evidence for the independence of his abilities is weak. Some exceptionally gifted individuals have abilities that are broad rather than limited to a particular domain (Piirto, 2007). And research with mental tests suggests that several of Gardner's intelligences (linguistic, logico-mathematical, and spatial) have at least some features in common. Nevertheless, Gardner calls attention to several intelligences not tapped by IQ scores. For example, his interpersonal and intrapersonal intelligences include a set of capacities for dealing with people and understanding oneself that has become known as *emotional intelligence*. As the Social Issues: Education box above indicates, researchers are attempting to define, measure, and foster the abilities that make up emotional intelligence, which is vital for a satisfying, successful life.

TAKE A MOMENT... Review the *core knowledge perspective,* discussed on page 214 in Chapter 6, and compare it with Gardner's view. Gardner also accepts the existence of innately specified, core domains of thought, present at birth or emerging early in life. Then, as children respond to the demands of their culture, they transform those intelligences to fit the activities they are called on to perform. Gardner's multiple intelligences have been helpful in efforts to understand and nurture children's special talents, a topic we will take up at the end of this chapter.

Explaining Individual and Group Differences in IQ

When we compare individuals in terms of academic achievement, years of education, and occupational status, it is clear that certain sectors of the population are advantaged over others. In trying to explain these differences, researchers have compared the IQ scores of ethnic and SES groups. American black children and adolescents score, on average, 10 to 12 IQ points below American white children. Although the difference has been shrinking over the past several decades, a substantial gap remains (Flynn, 2007; Edwards & Oakland, 2006; Nisbett, 2009). Hispanic children fall midway between black and white children (Ceci, Rosenblum, & Kumpf, 1998).

The IQ gap between middle-SES and low-SES children—about 9 points—accounts for some of the ethnic differences in IQ, but not all. When black children and white children are matched on parental education and income, the black–white IQ gap is reduced by a third to a half (Brooks-Gunn et al., 2003). Of course, considerable IQ variation exists *within* each ethnic and SES group. Still, these group differences are large enough and of serious enough consequence that they cannot be ignored.

In the 1970s, the IQ nature–nurture controversy escalated after psychologist Arthur Jensen (1969) published a controversial monograph entitled, "How Much Can We Boost IQ and Scholastic Achievement?" Jensen's answer was "not much." He claimed—and still maintains—that heredity is largely responsible for individual, ethnic, and SES variations in intelligence (Jensen, 1998, 2001; Rushton & Jensen, 2006, 2010). Jensen's work prompted an outpouring of research studies and responses, including ethical challenges reflecting deep concern that his conclusions would fuel social prejudices. Richard Herrnstein and Charles Murray rekindled the controversy with *The Bell Curve* (1994). Like Jensen, they argued that heredity contributes substantially to individual and SES differences in IQ, and they implied that heredity plays a sizable role in the black–white IQ gap. Let's look closely at some important evidence.

■ Among these second graders at an urban elementary school, differences in IQ scores may correlate with ethnicity and SES. Research aimed at explaining these associations has generated heated controversy. ■

NATURE VERSUS NURTURE   In Chapter 2 we introduced the *heritability estimate*. Recall that heritabilities are obtained from *kinship studies,* which compare family members. The most powerful evidence on the role of heredity in IQ involves twin comparisons. The IQ scores of identical twins (who share all their genes) are more similar than those of fraternal twins (who are genetically no more alike than ordinary siblings). On the basis of this and other kinship evidence, researchers estimate that about half the differences in IQ among children can be traced to their genetic makeup.

Recall, however, that heritabilities risk overestimating genetic influences and underestimating environmental influences. Although these measures offer convincing evidence that genes contribute to IQ, disagreement persists over how large a role heredity plays (Grigorenko, 2000; Plomin, 2003). As we saw in Chapter 2, the heritability of children's intelligence rises with parental education and income—conditions that enable children to realize their genetic potential. And heritability estimates do not reveal the complex processes through which genes and experiences influence intelligence as children develop.

Compared with heritabilities, adoption studies offer a wider range of information. Findings consistently reveal that when young children are adopted into caring, stimulating homes, their IQs rise substantially compared with the IQs of nonadopted children who remain in economically deprived families (van IJzendoorn, Juffer, & Poelhuis, 2005). But adopted children benefit to varying degrees. In one investigation, children of two extreme groups of biological mothers—those with IQs below 95 and those with IQs above 120—were adopted at birth by parents who were well above average in income and education. During the school years, the children of the low-IQ biological mothers scored above average in IQ, indicating that test performance can be greatly improved by an advantaged home life. But they did not do as well as children of high-IQ biological mothers placed in similar adoptive families (Loehlin, Horn, & Willerman, 1997). Adoption research confirms that heredity and environment contribute jointly to IQ.

Adoption research also sheds light on the black–white IQ gap. In two studies, African-American children adopted into economically well-off white homes during the first year of life scored high on intelligence tests, attaining mean IQs of 110 and 117 by middle childhood—20 to 30 points higher than the typical scores of children growing up in low-income black communities (Moore, 1986; Scarr & Weinberg, 1983). In one investigation, the IQs of black adoptees declined in adolescence, perhaps because of the challenges faced by minority teenagers in forming an ethnic identity that blends birth and adoptive backgrounds (DeBerry, Scarr, & Weinberg, 1996). When this process is filled with emotional turmoil, it can dampen motivation on tests and in school. Still, the black adoptees remained above the IQ average for low-SES African Americans. The IQ gains of black children "reared in the culture of the tests and schools" are consistent with a wealth of evidence that poverty severely depresses the intelligence of ethnic minority children (Nisbett, 2009).

Furthermore, a dramatic *secular trend* in mental test performance—a generational rise in average IQ in both industrialized nations and the developing world—supports the role of environmental factors, such as improved nutrition and education, technological advances, and an increase in cognitively demanding leisure activities (Flynn, 1999, 2003; Rodgers & Wänström, 2007). The greatest gains have occurred on tests of spatial reasoning—tasks often assumed to be "culture fair" and, therefore, more genetically based. These show, on average, an increase of 18 points per generation (30 years). The existence of a large, environmentally induced secular trend that exceeds the black–white IQ gap presents another major challenge to the assumption that black–white and other ethnic variations in IQ are mostly genetic (Flynn, 2007; Nisbett, 2009).

CULTURAL INFLUENCES A controversial question raised about ethnic differences in IQ has to do with whether they result from *test bias*. If a test samples knowledge and skills that not all groups of children have had equal opportunity to learn, or if the testing situation impairs the performance of some groups but not others, the resulting score is a biased, or unfair, measure.

Some experts reject the idea that intelligence tests are biased, claiming that they are intended to represent success in the common culture. According to this view, because IQ predicts academic achievement equally well for majority and minority children, IQ tests are fair to both groups (Edwards & Oakland, 2006; Jensen, 2002). Others believe that lack of exposure to certain communication styles and knowledge, along with negative stereotypes about the test-taker's ethnic group, can undermine children's performance (Ceci & Williams, 1997; Sternberg, 2005). Let's look at the evidence.

Communication Styles. Ethnic minority families often foster unique language skills that do not match the expectations of most classrooms and testing situations. In one study, a researcher spent many hours observing in low-SES black homes in a southeastern U.S. city (Heath, 1990). She found that African-American parents rarely asked their children the types of knowledge-training questions typical of middle-SES white parents ("What color is it?" "What's this story about?"), which resemble the questioning style of tests and classrooms. Instead, the black parents asked only "real" questions, ones that they themselves could not answer. Often these were analogy questions ("What's that like?") or story-starter questions ("Didja hear Miss Sally this morning?") that called for elaborate responses about personal experiences and had no "right" answer.

These experiences led the black children to develop complex verbal skills at home, such as storytelling and exchanging quick-witted remarks. But their language emphasized emotional and social concerns rather than facts about the world. Not surprisingly, when the black children started school, many were unfamiliar with and confused by the "objective" questions they encountered on tests and in classrooms.

■ This Canadian Inuit grandmother and granddaughter communicate collaboratively, smoothly coordinating actions in cleaning freshly caught fish. Many children from ethnic minority families with little education are unfamiliar with the hierarchical communication style typical of classrooms—a reason they may do poorly on tests and assignments. ■

Furthermore, many ethnic minority parents without extensive schooling prefer a *collaborative style of communication* when completing tasks with children. They work together in a coordinated, fluid way, each focused on the same aspect of the problem. This pattern of adult–child engagement has been observed in Native-American, Canadian Inuit, Hispanic, and Guatemalan Mayan cultures (Chavajay & Rogoff, 2002; Crago, Annahatak, & Ningiuruvik, 1993; Delgado-Gaitan, 1994; Paradise & Rogoff, 2009). With increasing education, parents establish a *hierarchical style of communication,* like that of classrooms and tests. The parent directs each child to carry out an aspect of the task, and children work independently (Greenfield, Suzuki, & Rothstein-Fish, 2006). This sharp discontinuity between home and school communication practices may contribute to low-SES minority children's lower IQ and school performance.

Knowledge. Many researchers argue that IQ scores are affected by specific information acquired as part of majority-culture upbringing. Consistent with this view, low-SES African-American children often miss vocabulary words on mental tests that have alternative meanings in their cultural community—for example, interpreting the word *frame* to mean "physique" or *wrapping* as "rapping," referring to the style of music (Champion, 2003a).

Knowledge affects ability to reason effectively. When researchers assessed black and white community college students' familiarity with vocabulary taken from items on an intelligence test, the whites had considerably more knowledge (Fagan & Holland, 2007). But the black students were just as capable as the white students at learning new words, either from dictionary definitions or from their use in sentences. When verbal comprehension, similarities, and analogies test items depended on words and concepts that the white students knew better, the whites scored higher than the blacks. But when the same types of items involved words and concepts that the two groups knew equally well, the two groups did not differ. Prior knowledge, not reasoning ability, fully explained ethnic differences in performance.

Even nonverbal test items, such as spatial reasoning, depend on learning opportunities. For example, using small blocks to duplicate designs and playing video games that require fast responding and mental rotation of visual images increase success on spatial test items (Dirks, 1982; Maynard, Subrahmanyam, & Greenfield, 2005). Low-income minority children, who often grow up in more "people-oriented" than "object-oriented" homes, may lack opportunities to use games and objects that promote certain intellectual skills.

Furthermore, the sheer amount of time a child spends in school predicts IQ. When children of the same age who are in different grades are compared, those who have been in school longer score higher on intelligence tests. Similarly, the earlier young people leave school, the greater their loss of IQ points (Ceci, 1991, 1999). Taken together, these findings indicate that children's exposure to the knowledge and ways of thinking valued in classrooms has a sizable impact on their intelligence test performance.

Stereotypes. TAKE A MOMENT... Imagine trying to succeed at an activity when the prevailing attitude is that members of your group are incompetent. What might you be feeling? **Stereotype threat**—the fear of being judged on the basis of a negative stereotype—can trigger anxiety that interferes with performance. Mounting evidence confirms that stereotype threat undermines test taking in children and adults (Steele, 1997; McKown & Strambler, 2009). For

■ School-age children become increasingly conscious of ethnic stereotypes, and those from stigmatized groups are especially mindful of them. Fear of being judged on the basis of a negative stereotype may be behind this child's hands-off attitude toward his schoolwork. ■

FIGURE 12.5

FIGURE 12.5

Effect of stereotype threat on performance.
Among African-American and Hispanic-American children who were aware of ethnic stereotypes, being told that verbal tasks were a "test of how good children are at school problems" led to far worse performance than being told that tasks "were not a test." These statements had little impact on the performance of Caucasian-American children. *(Adapted from McKown & Weinstein, 2003.)*

example, researchers gave African-American, Hispanic-American, and Caucasian-American 6- to 10-year-olds verbal tasks. Some children were told that the tasks were "not a test." Others were told that they were "a test of how good children are at school problems"—a statement designed to induce stereotype threat in the ethnic minority children. Among children who were aware of ethnic stereotypes (such as "black people aren't smart"), African Americans and Hispanics performed far worse in the "test" condition than in the "not a test" condition. Caucasian children, in contrast, performed similarly in both conditions (see Figure 12.5) (McKown & Weinstein, 2003).

Over middle childhood, children become increasingly conscious of ethnic stereotypes, and those from stigmatized groups are especially mindful of them. By early adolescence, many low-SES, minority students start to devalue doing well in school, saying it is not important to them (Cooper & Huh, 2008; Major et al., 1998). Self-protective disengagement, sparked by stereotype threat, may be responsible. This weakening of motivation can have serious long-term consequences. Research shows that self-discipline—effort and delay of gratification—predicts academic achievement at least as well as IQ does—and sometimes better (Duckworth & Seligman, 2005).

Reducing Cultural Bias in Testing

Although not all experts agree, many acknowledge that IQ scores can underestimate the intelligence of children from ethnic minority groups. A special concern exists about incorrectly labeling minority children as slow learners and assigning them to remedial classes, which are far less stimulating than regular school experiences. Because of this danger, test scores need to be combined with assessments of children's adaptive behavior—their ability to cope with the demands of their everyday environments. The child who does poorly on an IQ test yet plays a complex game on the playground or figures out how to rewire a broken TV is unlikely to be mentally deficient.

In addition, culturally relevant testing procedures enhance minority children's performance. In an approach called **dynamic assessment,** an innovation consistent with Vygotsky's zone of proximal development, the adult introduces purposeful teaching into the testing situation to find out what the child can attain with social support (Lidz, 2001; Sternberg & Grigorenko, 2002). Dynamic assessment often follows a pretest–intervene–retest procedure. While intervening, the adult seeks the teaching style best suited to the child and communicates strategies that the child can apply in new situations.

Research consistently shows that "static" assessments, such as IQ scores, frequently underestimate how well children do on test items after adult assistance. Children's receptivity to teaching and their capacity to transfer what they have learned to novel problems add considerably to the prediction of future performance (Haywood & Lidz, 2007; Sternberg & Grigorenko, 2002; Tzuriel, 2001). In one study, Ethiopian 6- and 7-year-olds who had recently immigrated to Israel scored well below their Israeli-born agemates on spatial reasoning tasks. The Ethiopian children had little experience with this type of thinking. After several dynamic assessment sessions in which the adult suggested effective strategies, the Ethiopian children's scores rose sharply, nearly equaling those of Israeli-born children (see Figure 12.6 on page 462). They also transferred their learning to new test items (Tzuriel & Kaufman, 1999).

Dynamic assessment is time-consuming and requires extensive knowledge of minority children's cultural values and practices. As yet the approach has not been more effective than traditional tests in predicting academic achievement (Grigorenko & Sternberg, 1998). Better correspondence may emerge in classrooms where teaching interactions resemble the dynamic

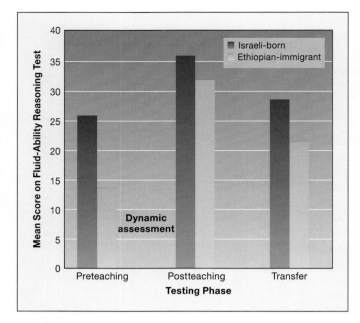

Influence of dynamic assessment on mental test scores of Ethiopian-immigrant and Israeli-born 6- and 7-year-olds. Each child completed test items in a preteaching phase, a postteaching phase, and a transfer phase, in which they had to generalize their learning to new problems. After dynamic assessment, Ethiopian and Israeli children's scores were nearly equal. Ethiopian children also transferred their learning to new test items, performing much better in the transfer phase than in the preteaching phase. *(Adapted from Tzuriel & Kaufman, 1999.)*

assessment approach—namely, individualized assistance on tasks carefully selected to help the child move beyond her current level of development.

In view of its many problems, should intelligence testing in schools be suspended? Most experts regard this solution as unacceptable. Without testing, important educational decisions would be based only on subjective impressions, perhaps increasing discriminatory placement of minority children. Intelligence tests are useful when interpreted carefully by examiners who are sensitive to cultural influences on test performance. And despite their limitations, IQ scores continue to be valid measures of school learning potential for the majority of Western children.

ASK YOURSELF

◆ REVIEW Using Sternberg's triarchic theory and Gardner's theory of multiple intelligences, explain the limitations of current mental tests in assessing the diversity of human intelligence.

◆ APPLY Josefina, a Hispanic fourth grader, does well on homework assignments. But when her teacher announces, "It's time for a test to see how much you've learned," Josefina usually does poorly. How might stereotype threat explain this inconsistency?

◆ CONNECT Explain how dynamic assessment is consistent with Vygotsky's zone of proximal development and with scaffolding (see Chapter 9, pages 330–331).

◆ REFLECT Do you think that intelligence tests are culturally biased? What observations and evidence influenced your conclusion?

Language Development

Vocabulary, grammar, and pragmatics continue to develop in middle childhood, though less obviously than at earlier ages. In addition, children's attitude toward language undergoes a fundamental shift. They develop **metalinguistic awareness,** the ability to think about language as a system.

Schooling contributes greatly to these language competencies. Reflecting on language is extremely common during reading instruction. And fluent reading is a major new source of language learning (Ravid & Tolchinsky, 2002). As we will see, an improved ability to reflect on language grows out of literacy and supports many complex language skills.

Vocabulary

During the elementary school years, vocabulary increases fourfold, eventually exceeding 40,000 words. On average, children learn about 20 new words each day—a rate of growth greater than in early childhood. In addition to the word-learning strategies discussed in

Chapter 9, school-age children enlarge their vocabularies by analyzing the structure of complex words. From *happy* and *decide,* they quickly derive the meanings of *happiness* and *decision* (Larsen & Nippold, 2007). They also figure out many more word meanings from context (Nagy & Scott, 2000).

As at earlier ages, children benefit from conversations with more expert speakers, especially when their partners use and explain complex words (Weizman & Snow, 2001). But because written language contains a far more diverse and complex vocabulary than spoken language, reading contributes enormously to vocabulary growth. Children who engage in as little as 21 minutes of independent reading per day are exposed to nearly 2 million words per year (Cunningham & Stanovich, 1998).

As their knowledge becomes better organized, older school-age children think about and use words more precisely: In addition to the verb *fall,* for example, they also use *topple, tumble,* and *plummet* (Berman, 2007). Word definitions also illustrate this change. Five- and 6-year-olds offer concrete descriptions referring to functions or appearance—*knife:* "when you're cutting carrots"; *bicycle:* "it's got wheels, a chain, and handlebars." By the end of elementary school, synonyms and explanations of categorical relationships appear—for example, *knife:* "something you could cut with. A saw is like a knife. It could also be a weapon" (Wehren, De Lisi, & Arnold, 1981). This advance reflects older children's ability to deal with word meanings on an entirely verbal plane. They can add new words to their vocabulary simply by being given a definition.

School-age children's more reflective and analytical approach to language permits them to appreciate the multiple meanings of words—to recognize, for example, that many words, such as *cool* or *neat,* have psychological as well as physical meanings: "Cool shirt!" or "That movie was really neat!" This grasp of double meanings permits 8- to 10-year-olds to comprehend subtle metaphors, such as "sharp as a tack" and "spilling the beans" (Nippold, Taylor, & Baker, 1996; Wellman & Hickling, 1994). It also leads to a change in children's humor. Riddles and puns that alternate between different meanings of a key word are common: "Hey, did you take a bath?" "Why, is one missing?"

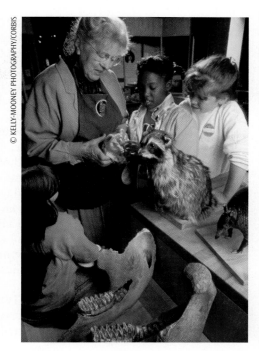

■ As part of a fourth-grade field trip, a staff member at a natural history museum discusses features of the teeth and jaws of several animal species. During middle childhood, children can add new words to their vocabulary simply by being given a definition. ■

Grammar

During the school years, mastery of complex grammatical constructions improves. For example, English-speaking children use the passive voice more frequently, and they more often extend it from an abbreviated structure ("It broke") into full statements ("The glass was broken by Mary") (Israel, Johnson, & Brooks, 2000; Tomasello, 2006). Older children also apply their grasp of the passive voice to a wider range of nouns and verbs. Preschoolers comprehend the passive best when the subject of the sentence is an animate being and the verb is an action word: "The boy is *kissed* by the girl." School-age children extend the passive to inanimate subjects *(drum, hat)* and include experiential verbs *(like, know)* (Lempert, 1989; Pinker, Johnson, & Frost, 1987). Although the passive form is challenging, language input makes a difference. When adults speak a language that emphasizes full passives, such as Inuktitut (spoken by the Inuit people of Arctic Canada), children produce them earlier (Allen & Crago, 1996).

Another grammatical achievement of middle childhood is advanced understanding of infinitive phrases—the difference between "John is eager to please" and "John is easy to please" (Chomsky, 1969). Like gains in vocabulary, appreciation of these subtle grammatical distinctions is supported by improved ability to analyze and reflect on language.

Pragmatics

The school years also bring dramatic gains in *pragmatics,* the communicative side of language. Opportunities to communicate in many situations with a variety of people help children refine these skills.

LOOK AND LISTEN

Record examples of 8- to 10-year-olds' humor, or examine storybooks for humor aimed at second through fourth graders. Does it require a grasp of the multiple meanings of words?

COMMUNICATING CLEARLY   In middle childhood, children can adapt to the needs of listeners in challenging communicative situations, such as describing one object among a group of very similar objects. Whereas preschoolers tend to give ambiguous descriptions ("the red one"), school-age children are precise: "the round red one with stripes on it" (Deutsch & Pechmann, 1982). Because peers challenge unclear messages that adults accept, peer interaction probably contributes greatly to this aspect of conversational competence.

Gains in the ability to evaluate the clarity of others' messages occur as well, and children become better at resolving inconsistencies. Consider the instruction, "Put the frog on the book in the box." Preschoolers cannot make sense of the ambiguity, even though they use similar embedded phrases in their own speech. They respond by attending only to the first prepositional phrase ("on the book") and place a toy frog on a book. School-age children, in contrast, can attend to and integrate two competing representations ("on the book" and "in the box"). They quickly figure out the speaker's meaning and pick up a toy frog resting on a book and place it in a box (Hurewitz et al., 2000).

School-age children are also more sensitive to distinctions between what people say and what they mean (Lee, Torrance, & Olson, 2001). Lizzie, for example, knew that when her mother said, "The garbage is beginning to smell," she really meant, "Take that garbage out!"

NARRATIVES   As a result of improved memory, ability to take the perspective of listeners, and conversations with adults about past experiences, children's narratives increase in organization, detail, and expressiveness. A typical 4- or 5-year-old's narrative states what happened: "We went to the lake. We fished and waited. Paul caught a huge catfish!" Six- and 7-year-olds add orienting information (time, place, participants) and connectives ("next," "then," "so," "finally") that lend coherence to the story. Gradually, narratives lengthen into a *classic form* in which events not only build to a high point but resolve: "After Paul reeled in the catfish, Dad cleaned and cooked it. Then we ate it all up!" And evaluative comments rise dramatically, becoming common by age 8 to 9: "The catfish tasted great. Paul was so proud!" (Melzi & Ely, 2009; Ukrainetz et al., 2005).

Because children pick up the narrative styles of significant adults in their lives, their narratives vary widely across cultures. For example, instead of the *topic-focused style* of most American school-age children, who describe an experience from beginning to end, African-American children often use a *topic-associating style* in which they blend several similar experiences. One 9-year-old related having a tooth pulled, then described seeing her sister's tooth pulled, next told how she had removed one of her baby teeth, and concluded, "I'm a pullin-teeth expert . . . call me, and I'll be over" (McCabe, 1997, p. 164). As a result, African-American children's narratives are usually longer and more complex than those of white children (Champion, 2003b).

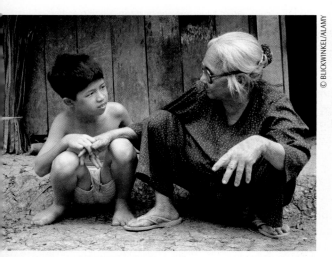

© BLICKWINKEL/ALAMY

■ A Vietnamese 8-year-old tells a story to his grandmother, who listens intently. Children's narratives vary widely across cultures, reflecting the styles of significant adults in their lives. ■

The ability to generate clear oral narratives enhances reading comprehension and prepares children for producing longer, more explicit written narratives. In families who regularly eat meals together, children are advanced in language and literacy development, perhaps because mealtimes offer many opportunities to relate personal stories (Snow & Beals, 2006).

Learning Two Languages

Joey and Lizzie speak only one language—English, their native tongue. Yet throughout the world, many children grow up *bilingual,* learning two languages and sometimes more than two. An estimated 20 percent of U.S. children—10 million in all—speak a language other than English at home (U.S. Census Bureau, 2010b).

BILINGUAL DEVELOPMENT   Children can become bilingual in two ways: (1) by acquiring both languages at the same time in early childhood or (2) by learning a second language after mastering the first. Children of bilingual parents who teach them both languages in infancy and early childhood separate the language systems from the start, distinguishing their sounds, mastering equivalent words in each, and attaining early language milestones according to a typical timetable (Conboy & Thal, 2006; Genesee & Nicoladis, 2007; Holowka, Brosseau-Lapré, & Petitto, 2002). Preschoolers acquire normal native ability in the language of their surrounding community and good-to-native ability in the second language, depending on their exposure to it (Genesee, 2001). When school-age children acquire a second language, they generally take 5 to 7 years to attain speaking and writing skills on a par with those of native-speaking agemates (Paradis, 2007).

Like many bilingual adults, bilingual children sometimes engage in *code switching*—producing an utterance in one language that contains one or more "guest" words from the other—without violating the grammar of either language. Children may engage in code switching because they lack the vocabulary to convey a particular thought in one language, so they use the other. But children who code-switch the most are those whose parents often do so. Bilingual adults frequently code-switch to express cultural identity, and children may follow suit—as when a Korean child speaking English switches to Korean on mentioning her piano teacher, as a sign of respect for authority (Chung, 2006). Opportunities to listen to code switching may facilitate bilingual development (Gawlitzek-Maiwald & Tracy, 1996). For example, a child accustomed to hearing French sentences with English guest words may rely on sentence-level cues to figure out English word meanings.

Recall from Chapter 6 that, just as with first-language development, a *sensitive period* for second-language development exists. Although mastery must begin sometime in childhood for full development to occur, a precise age cutoff for a decline in second-language learning has not been established (see page 235).

A large body of research shows that bilingualism has positive consequences for development. Children who become fluent in two languages develop denser gray matter (neurons and connective fibers) in areas of the left hemisphere devoted to language (Mechelli et al., 2004). Bilingual children outperform others on tests of selective attention, analytical reasoning, concept formation, and cognitive flexibility (Bialystok, 2001; Bialystok & Martin, 2004). They are also advanced in certain aspects of metalinguistic awareness, such as detection of errors in grammar, meaning, and conventions of conversation (responding politely, relevantly, and informatively). And children transfer their phonological awareness skills in one language to the other, especially if the two languages share phonological features and letter–sound correspondences, as Spanish and English do (Bialystok, McBride-Chang, & Luk, 2005; Siegal, Iozzi, & Surian, 2009; Snow & Kang, 2006). These capacities, as noted earlier, enhance reading achievement.

BILINGUAL EDUCATION   The advantages of bilingualism provide strong justification for bilingual education programs in schools. In Canada, about 7 percent of elementary school students are enrolled in *language immersion programs,* in which English-speaking children are taught entirely in French for several years. This strategy succeeds in developing children who are proficient in both languages and who, by grade 6, achieve as well in reading, writing, and math as their counterparts in the regular English program (Harley & Jean, 1999; Holobow, Genesee, & Lambert, 1991; Turnbull, Hart, & Lapkin, 2003).

In the United States, fierce disagreement exists over the question of how best to educate ethnic minority children with limited English proficiency. Some believe that time spent communicating in the child's native tongue detracts from English-language achievement, which is crucial for success in the worlds of school and work. Other educators, committed to developing minority children's native language while fostering mastery of English, note that providing instruction in the native tongue lets minority children know that their heritage is respected. It also prevents inadequate proficiency in both languages. Minority children who gradually lose their first language as a result of being taught the second end up limited in both languages for a time (Ovando & Collier, 1998). This circumstance leads to serious academic difficulties

ROBIN SACHS/PHOTOEDIT

■ In this English–Spanish bilingual classroom, children are more involved in learning, participate more actively in class discussions, and acquire the second language more easily than they would in an English-only classroom. ■

and is believed to contribute to the high rates of school failure and dropout among low-SES Hispanic youngsters, who make up nearly 50 percent of the U.S. language-minority population.

At present, public opinion and educational practice favor English-only instruction. Many U.S. states have passed laws declaring English to be their official language, creating conditions in which schools have no obligation to teach minority students in languages other than English. Yet in classrooms where both languages are integrated into the curriculum, minority children are more involved in learning, participate more actively in class discussions, and acquire the second language more easily. In contrast, when teachers speak only in a language that children can barely understand, minority children display frustration, boredom, and withdrawal. Under these conditions, U.S. kindergartners with limited English proficiency quickly fall behind their English-proficient counterparts in reading skills and are likely to struggle academically throughout their elementary school years (Kieffer, 2008). This downward spiral in achievement is greatest in high-poverty schools, where resources to support the needs of language-minority children are especially scarce.

Supporters of U.S. English-only education often point to the success of Canadian language immersion programs, in which classroom lessons are conducted in the second language. But Canadian parents enroll their children in immersion classrooms voluntarily, and both French and English are majority languages that are equally valued in Canada. Furthermore, teaching in the child's native language is merely delayed, not ruled out. For U.S. non-English-speaking minority children, whose native languages are not valued by the larger society, a different strategy seems necessary: one that promotes children's native-language and literacy skills while they learn English.

ASK YOURSELF

◆ REVIEW Cite examples of how language awareness fosters school-age children's language progress.

◆ APPLY Ten-year-old Shana arrived home from soccer practice and remarked, "I'm wiped out!" Megan, her 5-year-old sister, looked puzzled and asked, "What did'ya wipe out, Shana?" Explain Shana's and Megan's different understandings of this expression.

◆ CONNECT How can bilingual education promote ethnic minority children's cognitive and academic development?

◆ REFLECT Did you acquire a second language at home or study one in school? If so, when did you begin, and how proficient are you in the second language? Considering research on bilingualism, what changes would you make in your second-language learning, and why?

Children's Learning in School

Evidence cited throughout this chapter indicates that schools are vital forces in children's cognitive development. How do schools exert such a powerful influence? Research looking at schools as complex social systems—class size, educational philosophies, teacher–student relationships, and larger cultural context—provides important insights. As you read about these topics, refer to Applying What We Know on the following page, which summarizes characteristics of high-quality education in elementary school.

Class Size

As each school year began, Rena telephoned the principal's office to ask, "How large will Joey's and Lizzie's classes be?" Her concern is well-founded. In a large field experiment, more than 6,000 Tennessee kindergartners were randomly assigned to three class types: "small" (13 to 17 students), "regular" (22 to 25 students) with only a teacher, and regular with a teacher plus a full-time teacher's aide. These arrangements continued into third grade. Small-class students—especially ethnic minority children—scored higher in reading and math achievement each year (Mosteller, 1995). Placing teacher's aides in regular-size classes had no impact.

Applying What We Know

Signs of High-Quality Education in Elementary School

CLASSROOM CHARACTERISTICS	SIGNS OF QUALITY
Class size	Optimum class size is no larger than 18 children.
Physical setting	Space is divided into richly equipped activity centers—for reading, writing, playing math or language games, exploring science, working on construction projects, using computers, and engaging in other academic pursuits. Spaces are used flexibly for individual and small-group activities and whole-class gatherings.
Curriculum	The curriculum helps children both achieve academic standards and make sense of their learning in all subjects, including literacy, mathematics, social studies, art, music, health, and physical education. Subjects are integrated so that children apply knowledge in one area to others. The curriculum is implemented through activities responsive to children's interests, ideas, and everyday lives, including their cultural backgrounds.
Daily activities	Teachers provide challenging activities that include opportunities for small-group and independent work. Groupings vary in size and makeup of children, depending on the activity and on children's learning needs. Teachers encourage cooperative learning and guide children in attaining it.
Interactions between teachers and children	Teachers foster each child's progress and use intellectually engaging strategies, including posing problems, asking thought-provoking questions, discussing ideas, and adding complexity to tasks. They also demonstrate, explain, coach, and assist in other ways, depending on each child's learning needs.
Evaluations of progress	Teachers regularly evaluate children's progress through written observations and work samples, which they use to enhance and individualize teaching. They help children reflect on their work and decide how to improve it. They also seek information and perspectives from parents on how well children are learning and include parents' views in evaluations.
Relationship with parents	Teachers forge partnerships with parents. They hold periodic conferences and encourage parents to visit the classroom anytime, to observe and volunteer.

Source: Copple & Bredekamp, 2009.

Rather, experiencing small classes from kindergarten through third grade predicted substantially higher achievement from fourth through ninth grades, after children had returned to regular-size classes. It also predicted greater likelihood of graduating from high school, particularly for low-income students (Finn, Gerber, & Boyd-Zaharias, 2005; Nye, Hedges, & Konstantopoulos, 2001).

Why is small class size beneficial? With fewer children, teachers spend less time disciplining and more time teaching and giving individual attention. Also, children who learn in smaller groups show better concentration, higher-quality class participation, and more favorable attitudes toward school (Blatchford et al., 2003, 2007; Blatchford, Bassett, & Brown, 2005).

Educational Philosophies

Each teacher brings to the classroom an educational philosophy that plays a major role in children's learning. Two philosophical approaches have received the most research attention. They differ in what children are taught, in the way they are believed to learn, and in how their progress is evaluated.

TRADITIONAL VERSUS CONSTRUCTIVIST CLASSROOMS   In a **traditional classroom,** the teacher is the sole authority for knowledge, rules, and decision making and does most of the talking. Students are relatively passive—listening, responding when called on, and completing teacher-assigned tasks. Their progress is evaluated by how well they keep pace with a uniform set of standards for their grade.

A **constructivist classroom,** in contrast, encourages students to *construct* their own knowledge. Although constructivist approaches vary, many are grounded in Piaget's theory, which views children as active agents who reflect on and coordinate their own thoughts, rather than absorbing those of others. A glance inside a constructivist classroom reveals richly equipped learning centers, small groups and individuals solving self-chosen problems, and a teacher who guides and supports in response to children's needs. Students are evaluated by considering their progress in relation to their own prior development.

In the United States, the pendulum has swung back and forth between these two views. In the 1960s and early 1970s, constructivist classrooms gained in popularity. Then, as concern arose over the academic progress of children and youths, a "back-to-basics" movement arose, and classrooms returned to traditional instruction. This style, still prevalent today, has become increasingly pronounced as a result of the U.S. No Child Left Behind Act, signed into law in 2001 (Darling-Hammond, 2010; Ravitch, 2010). Because it places heavy pressure on teachers and school administrators to improve achievement test scores, it has narrowed the curricular focus in many schools to preparing students to take such tests.

Although older elementary school children in traditional classrooms have a slight edge in achievement test scores, constructivist settings are associated with many other benefits—gains in critical thinking, greater social and moral maturity, and more positive attitudes toward school (DeVries, 2001; Rathunde & Csikszentmihalyi, 2005; Walberg, 1986). And as noted in Chapter 9, when teacher-directed instruction is emphasized in preschool and kindergarten, it actually undermines academic motivation and achievement, especially in low-SES children.

The emphasis on knowledge absorption in many kindergarten and primary classrooms has contributed to a growing trend among parents to delay their child's school entry—especially if the child is a boy with a birth date close to the cutoff for kindergarten enrollment. But research reveals no long-term academic or social benefits (Lincove & Painter, 2006; Stipek, 2002). To the contrary, younger first graders reap achievement gains from on-time enrollment, outperforming same-age children a year behind them (Stipek & Byler, 2001). An alternative perspective is that school readiness can be cultivated through classroom experiences that foster children's individual progress.

NEW PHILOSOPHICAL DIRECTIONS New approaches to education, grounded in Vygotsky's sociocultural theory, capitalize on the rich social context of the classroom to spur children's learning. In these **social-constructivist classrooms,** children participate in a wide range of challenging activities with teachers and peers, with whom they jointly construct understandings. As children *appropriate* (take for themselves) the knowledge and strategies generated through working together, they become competent, contributing members of their classroom community and advance in cognitive and social development (Bodrova & Leong, 2007; Palincsar, 2003). Vygotsky's emphasis on the social origins of complex mental activities has inspired the following educational themes:

- *Teachers and children as partners in learning.* A classroom rich in both teacher–child and child–child collaboration transfers culturally valued ways of thinking to children.
- *Experience with many types of symbolic communication in meaningful activities.* As children master reading, writing, and mathematics, they become aware of their culture's communication systems, reflect on their own thinking, and bring it under voluntary control. **TAKE A MOMENT...** Can you identify research presented earlier in this chapter that supports this theme?
- *Teaching adapted to each child's zone of proximal development.* Assistance that both responds to current understandings and encourages children to take the next step helps ensure that each child makes the best progress possible.

Let's look at two examples of a growing number of programs that have translated these ideas into action.

Reciprocal Teaching. Originally designed to improve reading comprehension in poorly achieving students, this Vygotsky-inspired teaching method has been extended to other subjects and all schoolchildren (Palincsar & Herrenkohl, 1999). In **reciprocal teaching,** a teacher and two to four students form a cooperative group and take turns leading dialogues on the content of a text passage. Within the dialogues, group members apply four cognitive strategies: questioning, summarizing, clarifying, and predicting.

LOOK AND LISTEN

Ask an elementary school teacher to sum up his or her educational philosophy. Is it closest to a traditional, constructivist, or social-constructivist view? Has the teacher encountered any obstacles to implementing that philosophy? Explain.

The dialogue leader (at first a teacher, later a student) begins by *asking questions* about the content of the text passage. Students offer answers, raise additional questions, and, in case of disagreement, reread the original text. Next, the leader *summarizes* the passage, and children discuss the summary and *clarify* unfamiliar ideas. Finally, the leader encourages students to *predict* upcoming content based on clues in the passage.

Elementary and middle school students exposed to reciprocal teaching show impressive gains in reading comprehension compared to controls taught in other ways (Rosenshine & Meister, 1994; Sporer, Brunstein, & Kieschke, 2009; Takala, 2006). Notice how reciprocal teaching creates a zone of proximal development in which children learn to scaffold one another's progress and assume more responsibility for comprehending text passages (Gillies, 2003). Also, by collaborating with others, children forge group expectations for high-level thinking, more often apply their metacognitive knowledge, and acquire skills vital for learning and success in everyday life.

Communities of Learners. Recognizing that collaboration requires a supportive context to be most effective, another Vygotsky-based innovation makes it a schoolwide value. Classrooms become **communities of learners** where teachers guide the overall process of learning but no other distinction is made between adult and child contributors: All participate in joint endeavors and have the authority to define and resolve problems. This approach is based on the assumption that different people have different expertises that can benefit the community and that students, too, may become experts (Sullivan & Glanz, 2006). Classroom activities are often long-term projects addressing complex, real-world problems. In working toward project goals, children and teachers draw on the expertises of one another and of others within and outside the school.

In one classroom, students studied animal–habitat relationships in order to design an animal of the future, suited to environmental changes. The class formed small research groups, each of which selected a subtopic—for example, defense against predators, protection from the elements, reproduction, or food getting. Each group member assumed responsibility for part of the subtopic, consulting diverse experts and preparing teaching materials. Then group members taught one another, assembled their contributions, and brought them to the community as a whole so the knowledge gathered could be used to solve the problem (Brown, 1997; Stone, 2005). The result was a multifaceted understanding of the topic that would have been too difficult and time-consuming for any learner to accomplish alone.

In communities of learners, collaboration is created from within by teachers and children and supported from without by the culture of the school (Sullivan & Glanz, 2006). As a result, the approach broadens Vygotsky's concept of the zone of proximal development, from a child in collaboration with a more expert partner (adult or peer) to multiple, interrelated zones.

■ A teacher and students form a community of learners to plan, plant, and track the growth of a vegetable garden. During this complex, long-term project, all participants—adults as well as children—may become experts who share knowledge, teaching one another. ■

Teacher–Student Interaction

Elementary and secondary school students describe good teachers as caring, helpful, and stimulating—behaviors associated with gains in motivation, achievement, and positive peer relations (Hughes & Kwok, 2006, 2007; Hughes, Zhang, & Hill, 2006; O'Connor & McCartney, 2007). But too many U.S. teachers emphasize repetitive drill over higher-level thinking, such as grappling with ideas and applying knowledge to new situations (Sacks, 2005). In a longitudinal investigation of a large sample of middle school students, those in more academically demanding classrooms showed better attendance and larger gains in math achievement over the following two years (Phillips, 1997).

Of course, teachers do not interact in the same way with all children. Well-behaved, high-achieving students typically get more support and praise, whereas unruly students have more conflicts with teachers and receive more criticism from them (Henricsson & Rydell, 2004). Caring teacher–student relationships have an especially strong impact on the achievement and social behavior of low-SES minority students and other children at risk for learning difficulties (Baker, 2006; Crosno, Kirkpatrick, & Elder, 2004). But overall, higher-SES students—who tend to be higher-achieving and to have fewer learning and behavior problems—have more sensitive and supportive relationships with teachers (Jerome, Hamre, & Pianta, 2008; Pianta, Hamre, & Stuhlman, 2003).

Unfortunately, once teachers' attitudes toward students are established, they can become more extreme than is warranted by children's behavior. Of special concern are **educational self-fulfilling prophecies:** Children may adopt teachers' positive or negative views and start to live up to them. This effect is particularly strong when teachers emphasize competition and publicly compare children, regularly favoring the best students (Kuklinski & Weinstein, 2001; Weinstein, 2002).

Teacher expectations have a greater impact on low-achieving than high-achieving students (Madom, Jussim, & Eccles, 1997). When a teacher is critical, high achievers can fall back on their history of success. Low-achieving students' sensitivity to self-fulfilling prophecies can be beneficial when teachers believe in them. But biased teacher judgments are usually slanted in a negative direction. In one study, African-American and Hispanic elementary school students taught by high-bias teachers (who expected them to do poorly) showed substantially lower end-of-year achievement than their counterparts taught by low-bias teachers (McKown & Weinstein, 2008). Recall our discussion of *stereotype threat*. A child in the position of confirming a negative stereotype may respond with especially intense anxiety and reduced motivation, amplifying a negative self-fulfilling prophecy.

Grouping Practices

In many schools, students are assigned to *homogeneous* groups or classes, in which children of similar ability levels are taught together. Homogeneous grouping can be a potent source of self-fulfilling prophecies. Low-group students—who as early as first grade are more likely to be low-SES, minority, and male—get more drill on basic facts and skills, engage in less discussion, and progress at a slower pace. Gradually, they decline in self-esteem and motivation and fall further behind in achievement (Chorzempa & Graham, 2006; Condron, 2007; Trautwein et al., 2006). Unfortunately, widespread SES and ethnic segregation in U.S. schools consigns large numbers of low-SES, minority students to a form of school-wide, deleterious homogeneous grouping. Refer to the Social Issues: Education box on the following page to find out how magnet schools foster heterogeneous learning contexts, thereby reducing achievement disparities between SES and ethnic minority groups.

Another way schools can increase the *heterogeneity* of student groups is to combine two or three adjacent grades. In *multigrade classrooms*, academic achievement, self-esteem, and attitudes toward school are usually more favorable than in the single-grade arrangement, perhaps because multigrade classrooms often decrease competition and increase harmony (Lloyd, 1999; Ong, Allison, & Haladyna, 2000). The opportunity that mixed-grade grouping affords for peer tutoring may also contribute to its favorable outcomes. When older or more expert students teach younger or less expert students, both tutors and tutees benefit in achievement and self-esteem, with stronger effects for low-income, minority students and students in grades 1 to 3 than grades 4 to 6 (Ginsburg-Block, Rohrbeck, & Fantuzzo, 2006; Renninger, 1998).

However, small, heterogeneous groups of students working together often engage in poorer-quality inter-

■ These first through third graders collaborate on a variety of tasks. Compared to children in single-grade classrooms, those in multigrade classrooms are usually advantaged in academic achievement, self-esteem, and attitudes toward school. ■

© MARY KATE DENNY/PHOTOEDIT

SOCIAL ISSUES: EDUCATION

Magnet Schools: Equal Access to High-Quality Education

Each school-day morning, Emma leaves her affluent suburban neighborhood, riding a school bus 20 miles to a magnet school in an impoverished, mostly Hispanic inner-city neighborhood. In her sixth-grade class, she settles into a science project with her friend, Maricela, who lives in the local neighborhood. For the first hour of the day, the girls use a thermometer, ice water, and a stopwatch to determine which of several materials is the best insulator, recording and graphing their data. Throughout the school, which specializes in innovative math and science teaching, students diverse in SES and ethnicity learn side-by-side.

Despite the 1954 U.S. Supreme Court *Brown v. Board of Education* decision ordering schools to desegregate, school integration has receded since the late 1980s, as federal courts canceled their integration orders and returned this authority to states and cities. Today, the racial divide in American education is deepening. African-American children are just as likely to attend a school that serves a mostly black population as they were in the 1960s; Hispanic children are even more segregated. And when minority students attend ethnically mixed schools, they typically do so with other minorities (Frankenburg & Orfield, 2007).

U.S. schools in inner-city, low-income neighborhoods are vastly disadvantaged in funding and therefore in educational opportunities, largely because public education is primarily supported by local property taxes. Federal and state grants-in-aid are not sufficient to close this funding gap between rich and poor districts (Darling-Hammond, 2010). Consequently, in inner-city segregated neighborhoods, dilapidated school buildings; inexperienced teachers; out-

dated, poor-quality educational resources; and school cultures that fail to encourage strong teaching are widespread (Kozol, 2005). The negative impact on student achievement is severe.

A promising solution is the establishment of magnet schools. In addition to the usual curriculum, they emphasize a specific area of interest—such as performing arts, math and science, or technology. Families outside the school neighborhood are attracted to magnet schools (hence the name) by their rich academic offerings. Often magnets are located in low-income, minority areas, where they serve the neighborhood student population. Other students, who apply and are admitted by lottery, are bussed in—many from well-to-do city and suburban neighborhoods. In another model, all students—including those in the surrounding neighborhood—must apply. In either case, magnet schools are voluntarily desegregated.

Research confirms that less segregated education enhances minority student achievement (Linn & Welner, 2007). Is this so for magnet schools? A Connecticut study comparing seventh- to tenth-grade students enrolled in magnet schools with those whose lottery numbers were not drawn and who therefore attended other city schools confirmed that the magnets served a far more diverse student population. Although

magnet-school enrollees and nonadmitted applicants were similar in ethnicity, SES, and prior academic achievement, magnet students showed greater gains in reading and math achievement over a two-year period—outcomes especially pronounced for low-SES, ethnic minority students (Bifulco, Cobb, & Bell, 2009).

By high school, the higher-achieving peer environments of ethnically diverse schools encourage more students to pursue higher education (Frankenburg & Orfield, 2007). And as we will see in Chapter 13, a diverse student body also provides opportunities for social learning that can combat racial prejudice. In sum, magnet schools are a promising approach for overcoming the negative forces of SES and ethnic isolation in American schools.

© ELLEN B. SENISI/THE IMAGE WORKS

■ Third graders at a fine arts magnet school jointly create a painting. The ethnically diverse learning environments of many magnet schools enhance academic achievement, especially among low-SES minority students. ■

---

action (less accurate explanations and answers) than homogeneous groups of above-average students (Webb, Nemer, & Chizhik, 1998). For collaboration between heterogeneous peers to succeed, children need extensive training and guidance in **cooperative learning,** in which small groups of classmates work toward common goals—by resolving differences of opinion, sharing responsibilities, considering one another's ideas, and providing one another with sufficient explanations to correct misunderstandings. When teachers prompt, explain, model, and have children role-play how to work together effectively, cooperative learning among heterogeneous peers results in clearer explanations, greater enjoyment of learning, and achievement gains across a wide range of school subjects (Gillies, 2003; Terwel et al., 2001; Webb et al., 2008). And children readily cooperate in future group activities, building on others' ideas and offering assistance (Gillies, 2002).

Computers and Academic Learning

Virtually all public schools in industrialized nations have integrated computers into their instructional programs and can access the Internet. And, as noted in Chapter 9, most U.S. children have access to a home computer, usually with an Internet connection. Although higher-SES homes are more likely to have computers and Internet access, over 70 percent of U.S. lower-SES families with school-age children and adolescents now have them (Judge, Puckett, & Bell, 2006; Nielsen Company, 2008).

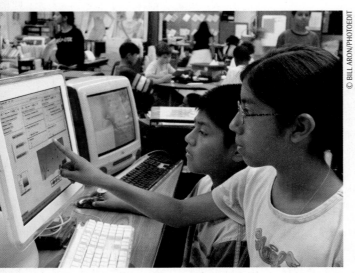

Nongame computer use is associated with academic progress (Calvert et al., 2005). Using the computer for word processing enables children to write freely, experimenting with letters and words without having to struggle with handwriting. Because they can revise their text's meaning and style and also check their spelling, they worry less about making mistakes. As a result, their written products tend to be longer and of higher quality. Often children jointly plan, compose, and revise text, learning from one another (Clements & Sarama, 2003). And as in early childhood, computer programming projects promote problem solving and metacognition and are common classroom contexts for peer collaboration (see page 353 in Chapter 9).

As children get older, they increasingly use the computer for schoolwork, mostly to search the Web for information and to prepare written assignments—activities linked to improved academic achievement (Attewell, 2001; Judge, Puckett, & Bell, 2006). In one study, the more low-SES middle-school students used home computers to access the Internet for information gathering (either for school or for personal interests), the better their subsequent reading achievement and school grades (Jackson et al., 2006). Perhaps those who use the Web to find information also devote more time to reading, given that many Web pages are heavily text-based. Nevertheless, a survey of a large, nationally representative sample of U.S. 8- to 18-year-olds revealed that on average, they used the computer only a half-hour a day for schoolwork compared with an hour a day for pleasure—surfing the Web, communicating by e-mail or instant messaging, and accessing music, video, and computer games (Roberts, Foehr, & Rideout, 2005).

■ At a classroom computer, fifth graders work together on interactive math activities. Schools must ensure that all children have rich opportunities to master the varied aspects of computer technology that enhance academic achievement. ■

The learning advantages of computers raise concerns about a "digital divide" between SES and gender groups. Poverty-stricken children are least likely to have home computers and Internet connections. And low-SES children who do have access devote less time to Internet use than their higher-SES counterparts (Jackson et al., 2006). By the end of elementary school, boys spend more time with computers than girls and use computers somewhat differently. Boys, for example, more often connect to the Internet to download games and music, trade and sell things, and create Web pages. Girls emphasize information gathering, area, and instant messaging (La Ferle, Edwards, & Lee, 2000; Jackson et al., 2008; Lenhart, Rainie, & Lewis, 2001). Furthermore, in a survey of a large, nationally representative sample of Canadian 15- and 16-year-olds, boys more often than girls engaged in writing computer programs, analyzing data, and using spreadsheets and graphics programs. And many more boys than girls rated their computer skills as "excellent" (Looker & Thiessen, 2003). Schools need to ensure that girls and low-SES students have many opportunities to benefit from the cognitively enriching aspects of computers—not just by equipping classrooms with more technology but also by providing the teacher guidance necessary to educate equitably and effectively (Attewell, 2001).

Most parents say they purchased a computer to enrich their child's education; about one-third of American school-age children and adolescents have a computer in their bedroom. At the same time, parents express great concern about the influence of violent computer games (see page 388 in Chapter 10) and the Internet. Yet only 30 percent of U.S. children and youths say their parents have rules about computer use and know what sites they visit on the Web (Rideout & Hamel, 2006; Roberts, Foehr, & Rideout, 2005). Not until ages 10 to 11 do children

Children's drawings of the Internet, reflecting increased understanding with age.
When elementary school children were asked to describe and draw a picture of the Internet, most children younger than age 10 had either a minimal understanding (viewed it as one computer) or a partial understanding (viewed it as a few connected computers). Most 10- and 11-year-olds had a sophisticated understanding of a networklike system in which computing centers link with many computers. *(From Z. Yan, 2006, "What Influences Children's and Adolescents' Understanding of the Complexity of the Internet?" Developmental Psychology, 42, p. 421. Copyright © 2006 by the American Psychological Association. Reprinted with permission of the American Psychological Association.)*

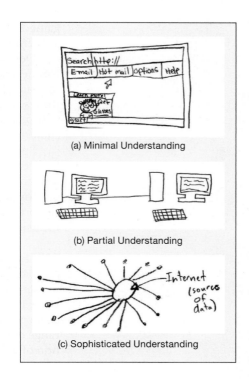

(a) Minimal Understanding

(b) Partial Understanding

(c) Sophisticated Understanding

acquire an adult-level understanding of the technical complexity of the Internet as a networklike system linking a computing center with many computers (see Figure 12.7) (Yan, 2006). This technical grasp precedes and probably contributes to sophisticated knowledge of the Internet's social risks (theft of personal information, virus attacks, exposure to unwanted content), which is attained around age 12 to 13.

Teaching Children with Special Needs

We have seen that effective teachers flexibly adjust their teaching strategies to accommodate students with a wide range of abilities and characteristics. But such adjustments are increasingly difficult at the very low and high ends of the ability distribution. How do schools serve children with special learning needs?

CHILDREN WITH LEARNING DIFFICULTIES U.S. legislation mandates that schools place children who require special supports for learning in the "least restrictive" (as close to normal as possible) environments that meet their educational needs. In **inclusive classrooms,** students with learning difficulties learn alongside typical students in the regular educational setting for part or all of the school day—a practice designed to prepare them for participation in society and to combat prejudices against individuals with disabilities (Kugelmass & Ainscow, 2004). Largely as the result of parental pressures, an increasing number of students experience *full inclusion*—full-time placement in regular classrooms.

Some students in inclusive classrooms have *mild mental retardation:* Their IQs fall between 55 and 70, and they also show problems in adaptive behavior, or skills of everyday living (American Psychiatric Association, 2000). But the largest number—5 to 10 percent of school-age children—have **learning disabilities,** great difficulty with one or more aspects of learning, usually reading. As a result, their achievement is considerably behind what would be expected on the basis of their IQ. Sometimes, deficits express themselves in other ways—for example, as severe inattention (see page 444), which depresses both IQ and achievement test scores. The problems of students with learning disabilities cannot be traced to any obvious physical or emotional difficulty or to environmental disadvantage. Instead, subtle deficits in brain functioning seem to be involved (Berninger, 2006). Some disorders run in families, and in certain cases, specific genes have been identified that contribute to the problem (Miller, Sanchez, & Hynd, 2003; Raskind et al., 2005). In many instances, the cause is unknown.

Although some students benefit academically from inclusion, many do not. Achievement gains depend on both the severity of the disability and the support services available (Klingner et al., 1998). Furthermore, children with disabilities often are rejected by regular-classroom peers. Students with mental retardation are overwhelmed by the social skills of their classmates; they cannot interact adeptly in a conversation or

■ In this inclusive second-grade classroom, a teacher encourages a special-needs child to listen to his classmate read a story. The child is likely to do well if he receives support from a special education teacher and if his classroom teacher minimizes comparisons and promotes cooperative learning. ■

game. And the processing deficits of some learning-disabled students lead to problems in social awareness and responsiveness (Kelly & Norwich, 2004; Sridhar & Vaughn, 2001).

Does this mean that students with special needs cannot be served in regular classrooms? Not necessarily. Often these children do best when they receive instruction in a resource room for part of the day and in the regular classroom for the remainder (Weiner & Tardif, 2004). In the resource room, a special education teacher works with students on an individual and small-group basis. Then, depending on their progress, children join regular classmates for different subjects and amounts of time.

Special steps must be taken to promote positive peer relations in inclusive classrooms. Cooperative learning and peer-tutoring experiences in which teachers guide children with learning difficulties and their classmates in working together lead to friendly interaction, improved peer acceptance, and achievement gains (Fuchs et al., 2002a, 2002b). Teachers also can prepare their class for the arrival of a student with special needs. Under these conditions, inclusion may foster emotional sensitivity and prosocial behavior among regular classmates.

GIFTED CHILDREN In Joey and Lizzie's school, some children were **gifted,** displaying exceptional intellectual strengths. One or two students in every grade have IQ scores above 130, the standard definition of giftedness based on intelligence test performance (Gardner, 1998). High-IQ children, as we have seen, have keen memories and an exceptional capacity to solve challenging academic problems. Yet recognition that intelligence tests do not sample the entire range of human mental skills, as noted earlier in this chapter, has led to an expanded conception of giftedness.

Creativity and Talent. **Creativity** is the ability to produce work that is *original* yet *appropriate*—something that others have not thought of that is useful in some way (Lubart, 2003; Sternberg, 2003). A child with high potential for creativity can be designated as gifted. Tests of creative capacity tap **divergent thinking**—the generation of multiple and unusual possibilities when faced with a task or problem. Divergent thinking contrasts sharply with **convergent thinking,** which involves arriving at a single correct answer and is emphasized on intelligence tests (Guilford, 1985).

Because highly creative children (like high-IQ children) are often better at some types of tasks than others, a variety of tests of divergent thinking are available (Runco, 1992; Torrance, 1988). A verbal measure might ask children to name uses for common objects (such as a newspaper). A figural measure might ask them to come up with drawings based on a circular motif (see Figure 12.8). A "real-world problem" measure requires students to suggest solutions to everyday problems. Responses can be scored for the number of ideas generated and their originality.

Yet critics point out that these measures are poor predictors of creative accomplishment in everyday life because they tap only one of the complex cognitive contributions to creativity. Also involved are defining new and important problems, evaluating divergent ideas, choosing the most promising, and calling on relevant knowledge to understand and solve problems (Sternberg, 2003b; Lubart, Georgsdottir, & Besançon, 2009).

Consider these ingredients, and you will see why people usually demonstrate expertise and creativity in only one or a few related areas. Even individuals designated as gifted by virtue of their high IQ often show uneven ability across academic subjects. Partly for this reason, definitions of giftedness have been extended to

FIGURE 12.8

Responses of an 8-year-old who scored high on a figural measure of divergent thinking. This child was asked to make as many pictures as she could from the circles on the page. The titles she gave her drawings, from left to right, are as follows: "Dracula," "one-eyed monster," "pumpkin," "Hula-Hoop," "poster," "wheelchair," "earth," "stop-light," "planet," "movie camera," "sad face," "picture," "beach ball," "the letter *O*," "car," "glasses." Tests of divergent thinking tap only one of the complex cognitive contributions to creativity.

include **talent**—outstanding performance in a specific field. Case studies reveal that excellence in such endeavors as creative writing, mathematics, science, music, visual arts, athletics, and leadership have roots in specialized skills that first appear in childhood (Moran & Gardner, 2006; Winner, 2003). Highly talented children are biologically prepared to master their domain of interest, and they display a passion for doing so.

But talent must be nurtured. Studies of the backgrounds of talented children and highly accomplished adults often reveal parents who are warm and sensitive, provide a stimulating home life, are devoted to developing their child's abilities, and provide models of hard work and high achievement. These parents are reasonably demanding but not driving or overambitious (Winner, 1996, 2000). They arrange for caring teachers while the child is young and for more rigorous master teachers as the child's talent develops.

Many gifted children and adolescents are socially isolated, partly because their highly driven, nonconforming, and independent styles leave them out of step with peers and partly because they enjoy solitude, which is necessary to develop their talents. Still, gifted children desire gratifying peer relationships, and some—more often girls than boys—try to become better-liked by hiding their abilities. Compared with their ordinary agemates, gifted youths, especially girls, report more emotional and social difficulties, including low self-esteem and depression (Reis, 2004; Winner, 2000).

■ These fourth graders collaborate in building a model lighthouse using modular construction materials. Challenging children to generate original solutions to problems helps nurture creativity. ■

Finally, whereas many talented youths become experts in their fields and solve problems in new ways, few become highly creative. Rapidly mastering an existing field and thinking flexibly within it require different skills than innovating in that field. Gifted individuals who are restless with the status quo and daring about changing it are rare. And before these individuals become creative masters, they typically spend a decade or more becoming proficient in their field of interest (Moran & Gardner, 2006; Simonton, 2009). The world, however, needs both experts and creators.

Educating the Gifted. Gifted children thrive in learning environments that permit them to choose topics for extended projects, take intellectual risks, reflect on ideas, and interact with like-minded peers. When not sufficiently challenged, they sometimes lose their drive to excel. And when parents and teachers push them too hard, by adolescence they are likely to ask, "Who am I doing this for?" If the answer is not "myself," they may decide not to pursue their gift (Winner, 1997, 2000, p. 166).

Although many schools offer programs for the gifted, debate about their effectiveness usually focuses on factors irrelevant to giftedness—whether to provide enrichment in regular classrooms, to pull children out for special instruction (the most common practice), or to advance brighter students to a higher grade. Overall, gifted children fare well within each of these models, as long as the special activities provided do not reinforce academic convergent thinking to the detriment of problem solving, critical thinking, and creativity (Guignard & Lubart, 2007).

When gifted students enter selective educational settings, interventions aimed at protecting their self-esteem are crucial. In a study of more than 100,000 students in 26 countries, the more selective the high school, the lower students' academic self-esteem (Marsh & Hau, 2003). A top student in elementary school who enters a selective secondary school may suddenly find herself average or below average, with potentially detrimental effects on motivation and achievement.

Gardner's theory of multiple intelligences has inspired several model programs that provide enrichment to all students in diverse subjects, so any child capable of high-level performance can manifest it. Meaningful activities, each tapping a specific intelligence or set of intelligences, serve as contexts for assessing strengths and weaknesses and, on that basis, teaching new knowledge and original thinking (Gardner, 1993, 2000). For example, linguistic intelligence might be fostered through storytelling or playwriting; spatial intelligence through

Country	Average Math Achievement Score
High-Performing Nations	
Taiwan	549
Finland	548
Hong Kong	547
Korea, Republic of	547
Netherlands	531
Switzerland	530
Canada	527
Macao, China	525
Japan	523
New Zealand	522
Belgium	520
Australia	520
Intermediate-Performing Nations	
Denmark	513
Czech Republic	510
Iceland	506
Austria	505
Germany	504
Sweden	502
Ireland	501
International Average = 498	
France	496
United Kingdom	495
Poland	495
Hungary	491
Luxembourg	491
Norway	490
Spain	480
United States	**474**
Low-Performing Nations	
Portugal	466
Italy	462
Greece	459
Turkey	424

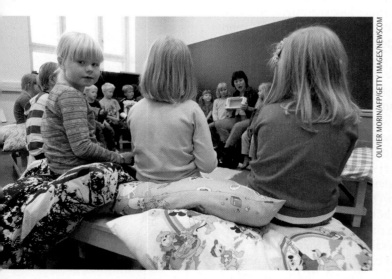

■ Finnish first graders get to know their teacher and classmates on the first day of school. They will benefit from a national education system designed to cultivate initiative, problem solving, and creativity. In international studies of academic achievement, Finland ranks among the best-performing nations. ■

OLIVIER MORIN/AFP/GETTY IMAGES/NEWSCOM

FIGURE 12.9

Average mathematics scores of 15-year-olds by country. The Programme for International Student Assessment measured achievement in many nations around the world. The United States performed below the international average in math. Outcomes were similar in science. U.S. performance in reading was at the international average. *(Adapted from Programme for International Student Assessment, 2006.)*

drawing, sculpting, or taking apart and reassembling objects; and kinesthetic intelligence through dance or pantomime.

Evidence is still needed on how effectively these programs nurture children's talents. But so far, they have succeeded in one way—by highlighting the strengths of some students who previously had been considered unexceptional or even at risk for school failure (Kornhaber, 2004). Consequently, they may be especially useful in identifying talented low-SES, ethnic minority children, who are often underrepresented in programs for the gifted (McBee, 2006).

How Well-Educated Are U.S. Children?

Our discussion of schooling has largely focused on how teachers can support the education of children. Yet we have also seen that many factors—both within and outside schools—affect children's learning. Societal values, school resources, quality of teaching, and parental encouragement all play important roles. Nowhere are these multiple influences more apparent than when schooling is examined in cross-cultural perspective.

In international studies of reading, mathematics, and science achievement, young people in Hong Kong, Korea, and Japan are consistently top performers. Among Western nations, Canada, Finland, the Netherlands, and Switzerland are also in the top tier. But U.S. students typically perform at the international average, and sometimes below it (see Figure 12.9) (Programme for International Student Assessment, 2003, 2006).

Why do U.S. children fall behind in academic accomplishments? According to international comparisons, instruction in the United States is less challenging, more focused on absorbing facts, and less focused on high-level reasoning and critical thinking than in other countries. According to a growing number of experts, the U.S. No Child Left Behind Act has contributed to these trends because it mandates severe sanctions for schools whose students do not meet targeted goals on achievement tests—initially, student transfers to higher-performing schools; and ultimately, staff firing, closure, state takeover, or other restructuring (Darling-Hammond, 2010; Noguera, 2010; Ravitch, 2010). Furthermore, compared with top-achieving countries, the United States is far less equitable in the quality of education it provides to its low-income and ethnic minority students. And U.S. teachers vary much more in training, salaries, and teaching conditions.

Finland is a case in point. In the 1980s, it abandoned a national testing system used to ability-group students and replaced it with curricula, teaching practices, and assessments aimed at cultivating initiative, problem solving, and creativity—vital abilities needed for success in the twenty-first century. Finnish teachers are highly trained: They must complete several years of graduate-level education at government expense (Sahlberg, 2010). And the Finnish education is grounded in equal opportunity for all—a policy that has nearly eliminated SES variations in achievement, despite an influx of immigrant students from low-income families into Finnish schools over the past decade.

In-depth research on learning environments in Asian nations, such as Japan, Korea, and Taiwan, also highlights social forces that foster strong student learning. Among these is cultural valuing of effort. Whereas American parents and teachers tend to regard native ability as the key to academic success, Japanese, Korean, and Taiwanese parents and teachers believe that all children can succeed academically as long as they try hard. Asian parents devote many more hours to helping their children with homework (Stevenson, Lee, & Mu, 2000). And Asian children, influenced by collectivist values, typically view striving to do well in school as a moral obligation—part of their responsibility to family and community.

As in Finland, all students in Japan, Korea, and Taiwan receive the same nationally mandated, high-quality instruction, delivered by teachers who are well-prepared, highly respected in their society, and far better paid than U.S. teachers (Kang & Hong, 2008; U.S. Department of Education, 2008). Academic lessons are particularly well-organized and presented in ways that capture children's attention and encourage high-level thinking (Grow-Maienza, Hahn, & Joo, 2001). And Japanese teachers are three times as likely as U.S. teachers to work outside class with students who need extra help (Woodward & Ono, 2004).

The Finnish and Asian examples underscore the need for American families, schools, and the larger society to work together to upgrade education. Over the past decade, U.S. international rankings in reading, math, and science achievement have declined. And following several decades of gains, from 1999 on the U.S. National Assessment of Educational Progress—in which challenging achievement tests are given to nationally representative samples of 9-, 13-, and 17-year-olds—showed only slight gains in reading and no improvement in math (U.S. Department of Education, 2008). These disappointing achievement outcomes underscore the need for "a broader, bolder approach to U.S. education." Recommended strategies, verified by research, include:

- providing intellectually challenging, relevant instruction with real-world applications
- strengthening teacher education
- supporting parents in creating stimulating home learning environments, monitoring their children's academic progress, and communicating often with teachers
- investing in high-quality preschool education, so every child arrives at school ready to learn
- vigorously pursuing school improvements that reduce the large inequities in quality of education between SES and ethnic groups (Economic Policy Institute, 2010).

ASK YOURSELF

◆ **REVIEW** List some teaching practices that foster children's academic achievement and some that undermine it. Provide a brief explanation of each practice.

◆ **APPLY** Sandy wonders why her daughter Mira's teacher often has students work on assignments in small, cooperative groups. Explain the benefits of this approach to Sandy. What must Mira's teacher do to ensure that cooperative learning succeeds?

◆ **CONNECT** Review research on child-rearing styles on pages 398–400 in Chapter 10. What style do gifted children who realize their potential typically experience? Explain.

◆ **REFLECT** What grouping practices were used in your elementary education—homogeneous, heterogeneous, or a combination? What impact do you think those practices had on your motivation and achievement?

Summary

Piaget's Theory: The Concrete Operational Stage

What are the major characteristics of concrete operational thought?

- In the **concrete operational stage,** children's thought becomes more logical, flexible, and organized. Mastery of conservation requires decentration and **reversibility** in thinking.

- School-age children are also better at hierarchical classification and **seriation,** including **transitive inference,** the ability to seriate mentally. Their spatial reasoning improves, as indicated by their understanding of **cognitive maps.**

Discuss follow-up research on concrete operational thought.

- Concrete operational children think logically only when dealing with concrete, tangible information, and mastery of concrete operational tasks occurs gradually. Specific cultural practices, especially those associated with schooling, promote mastery of Piagetian tasks.

- Some researchers attribute the gradual development of operational thought to gains in information-processing speed. Case's neo-Piagetian theory proposes that with practice, cognitive schemes demand less attention and become more automatic, freeing up space in working memory for combining old schemes and generating new ones. Eventually, children consolidate schemes into central conceptual structures and are increasingly able to coordinate and integrate multiple dimensions.

Information Processing

Cite basic changes in information processing, and describe the development of attention and memory in middle childhood.

- Brain development contributes to increases in processing speed and capacity and to gains in inhibition, facilitating many aspects of thinking.

- During middle childhood, attention becomes more sustained, selective, and adaptable. Attention (and memory) strategies develop in a four-step sequence: (1) **production deficiency** (failure to use the strategy); (2) **control deficiency** (failure to execute the strategy consistently); (3) **utilization deficiency** (consistent use of the strategy, but with little or no improvement in performance); and finally (4) **effective strategy use.**

- Children become better at planning, particularly when adults turn over responsibility to them and guide and support as needed.

- Deficits in executive processing and inhibition may underlie symptoms of **attention-deficit hyperactivity disorder (ADHD).** ADHD leads to serious academic and social problems.

- Memory strategies also improve. **Rehearsal** appears first, followed by **organization** and then **elaboration.** With age, children use several memory strategies at once.

- Development of the long-term knowledge base facilitates strategic memory processing. Children's motivation to use what they know also contributes. Memory strategies are not used by children in non-Western cultures who have no formal schooling.

Describe the school-age child's theory of mind and capacity to engage in self-regulation.

- Metacognition expands as school-age children view the mind as an active, constructive agent. Consequently, they better understand the process of thinking and factors that influence it. Awareness of the role of mental inferences enables mastery of second-order false belief. By the end of middle childhood, children grasp how interactions among variables—the learner's characteristics, use of strategies, and the task at hand—affect performance.

- **Cognitive self-regulation**—the ability to monitor progress toward a goal and redirect unsuccessful efforts— develops gradually. It improves with adult instruction in effective strategy use and predicts academic success.

Discuss current perspectives on teaching reading and mathematics to elementary school children.

- Skilled reading draws on all aspects of the information-processing system. A combination of **whole-language** and **phonics** is most effective for teaching beginning reading.

- Teaching that combines practice in basic skills with conceptual understanding also is best in mathematics. Students benefit from extensive opportunities to experiment with strategies and reason about number concepts.

Individual Differences in Mental Development

Describe major approaches to defining intelligence.

- During the school years, IQ becomes more stable and correlates moderately with academic achievement. Most intelligence tests yield an overall score as well as scores for separate intellectual factors. The *Stanford-Binet Intelligence Scales,* Fifth Edition, and the *Wechsler Intelligence Scale for Children–IV (WISC–IV)* are widely used individually administered intelligence tests.

- The componental approach to defining intelligence seeks to identify the inner, information- processing skills that contribute to mental test performance. Memory span, speed of thinking, and effective strategy use are positively related to IQ.

- Sternberg's **triarchic theory of successful intelligence** views intelligence as an interaction of analytical intelligence (information-processing skills), creative intelligence (ability to solve novel problems), and practical intelligence (application of intellectual skills in everyday situations).

- Gardner's **theory of multiple intelligences** identifies at least eight mental abilities, each with a distinct biological basis and course of development. It has been helpful in stimulating efforts to define, measure, and foster **emotional intelligence.**

Describe evidence indicating that both heredity and environment contribute to intelligence.

- Heritability estimates and adoption research reveal that intelligence is a product of both heredity and environment. Adoption studies indicate that the black–white IQ gap is substantially determined by environment. A dramatic generational increase in IQ also supports the role of environmental factors.

- IQ scores are affected by culturally influenced communication styles, knowledge, and by sheer amount of time spent in school. **Stereotype threat** can trigger anxiety that impairs children's test performance. **Dynamic assessment** helps many minority children perform more competently on mental tests.

Language Development

Describe changes in metalinguistic awareness, vocabulary, grammar, and pragmatics during middle childhood.

- Schooling, especially reading, contributes greatly to **metalinguistic awareness** and other complex language competencies. Vocabulary continues to grow rapidly, and children have a more precise and flexible understanding of word meanings. They also use more complex grammatical constructions and conversational strategies, and their narratives increase in organization, detail, and expressiveness.

What are the advantages of bilingualism in childhood?

- Children who learn two languages in early childhood acquire each according to a typical timetable. When school-age children acquire a second language, they typically take 5 to 7 years to attain the competence of native-speaking agemates.

- Bilingual children are advanced in cognitive development and metalinguistic awareness. They transfer their phonological awareness skills in one language to the other, which enhances reading achievement.

- In Canada, language immersion programs succeed in developing children who are proficient in both English and French. While current public opinion and educational practice favor English-only instruction in the United States, bilingual education that combines instruction in the native language and in English supports non-English-speaking minority children's academic learning.

Children's Learning in School

Describe the impact of class size and educational philosophies on children's motivation and academic achievement.

- As class size declines, academic achievement improves. Older students in **traditional classrooms** have a slight edge in academic achievement over those in **constructivist classrooms**, who gain in academic motivation, critical thinking, and social and moral maturity.

- Vygotsky-inspired **social-constructivist classrooms** use the rich social context of the classroom to promote learning, often employing such methods as **reciprocal teaching** and **communities of learners**. Students benefit from working collaboratively and from teaching adapted to each child's zone of proximal development.

Discuss the role of teacher–student interaction and grouping practices in academic achievement.

- Caring, helpful, and stimulating teaching fosters children's interest, involvement, and academic achievement. **Educational self-fulfilling prophecies** have a greater impact on low achievers and are most likely to occur in homogenous classrooms and ones that emphasize competition and public evaluation.

- The heterogeneous context of multigrade classrooms promotes academic achievement, self-esteem, and positive school attitudes. To benefit from collaboration with heterogeneous peers, children need extensive training in **cooperative learning**. Ethnically diverse magnet schools are also associated with higher achievement.

Describe educational benefits of computer use as well as concerns about computers.

- Using the computer for schoolwork, typically to search the Web for information and to prepare written assignments, is linked to improved academic achievement. However, low-SES children are disadvantaged in computer and Internet use, and boys tend to be more skilled at complex computer activities than girls.

Under what conditions is placement of mildly mentally retarded and learning disabled children in regular classrooms successful?

- Students with mild mental retardation and **learning disabilities** are often placed in **inclusive classrooms** where they learn alongside typical students. Success depends on meeting individual academic needs and promoting positive peer relations.

Describe the characteristics of gifted children and efforts to meet their educational needs.

- **Giftedness** includes high IQ, **creativity**, and **talent.** Tests of creativity that tap **divergent thinking** rather than **convergent thinking** focus on only one of the complex cognitive ingredients of creativity. Many gifted children, especially girls, report emotional and social difficulties.

- Gifted children have parents and teachers who nurture their extraordinary ability. They are best served by educational programs that build on their special strengths.

© JEFF MORGAN EDUCATION/ALAMY

How well-educated are U.S. children compared with children in other industrialized nations?

- In international studies, U.S. students typically display average or below-average performance. Compared with education in top-achieving countries, U.S. instruction is less focused on high-level reasoning and critical thinking. Whereas high-achieving nations emphasize equal opportunity for all, U.S. low-income and ethnic minority students typically attend inferior-quality schools.

IMPORTANT TERMS AND CONCEPTS

attention-deficit hyperactivity disorder (ADHD) (p. 444)
cognitive maps (p. 438)
cognitive self-regulation (p. 449)
communities of learners (p. 469)
concrete operational stage (p. 438)
constructivist classroom (p. 467)
control deficiency (p. 443)
convergent thinking (p. 474)
cooperative learning (p. 471)
creativity (p. 474)
divergent thinking (p. 474)
dynamic assessment (p. 461)

educational self-fulfilling prophecies (p. 470)
effective strategy use (p. 443)
elaboration (p. 446)
emotional intelligence (p. 457)
gifted (p. 474)
inclusive classrooms (p. 473)
learning disabilities (p. 473)
metalinguistic awareness (p. 462)
organization (p. 446)
phonics approach (p. 450)
production deficiency (p. 443)
reciprocal teaching (p. 468)

rehearsal (p. 446)
reversibility (p. 438)
seriation (p. 438)
social-constructivist classroom (p. 468)
stereotype threat (p. 460)
talent (p. 475)
theory of multiple intelligences (p. 456)
traditional classroom (p. 467)
transitive inference (p. 438)
triarchic theory of successful intelligence (p. 455)
utilization deficiency (p. 443)
whole-language approach (p. 450)

Untitled
Sarah Andreassen
12 years, Norway

As this artist's upbeat, imaginative portrayal suggests, school-age children become capable of viewing themselves and others from diverse perspectives—a change that contributes to an improved understanding of one's own and others' traits and competencies, a more flexible grasp of moral obligations, declining racial and ethnic prejudices, and deepening friendships.

Reprinted with permission from the International Museum of Children's Art, Oslo, Norway

Emotional and Social Development in Middle Childhood

*L*ate one afternoon, Rena heard her son Joey burst through the front door, run upstairs, and phone his best friend Terry. "Terry, gotta talk to you," Joey pleaded breathlessly. "Everything was going great until I got that word—*porcupine*," Joey went on, referring to the fifth-grade spelling bee at school that day. "Just my luck! *P-o-r-k,* that's how I spelled it! I can't believe it. Maybe I'm not so good at social studies," Joey confided, "but I *know* I'm better at spelling than that stuck-up Belinda Brown. I knocked myself out studying those spelling lists. Then *she* got all the easy words. If I *had* to lose, why couldn't it be to a nice person?"

Joey's conversation reflects new emotional and social capacities. By entering the spelling bee, he shows *industriousness,* the energetic pursuit of meaningful achievement in his culture—a major change of middle childhood. Joey's social understanding has also expanded. He can size up strengths, weaknesses, and personality characteristics. Furthermore, friendship means something different to Joey than it did earlier—he counts on his best friend, Terry, for understanding and emotional support.

For an overview of the personality changes of middle childhood, we return to Erikson's theory. Then we look at children's views of themselves and of others, their moral understanding, and their peer relationships. Each increases in complexity as children reason more effectively and spend more time in school and with agemates.

Despite changing parent–child relationships, the family remains powerfully influential in middle childhood. Today, family lifestyles are more diverse than ever before. Through Joey's and his younger sister Lizzie's experiences with parental divorce, we will see that family functioning is far more important than family structure in ensuring children's well-being. Finally, we look at some common emotional problems of middle childhood.

Erikson's Theory: Industry versus Inferiority

According to Erikson (1950), children whose previous experiences have been positive enter middle childhood prepared to redirect their energies from the make-believe of early childhood into realistic accomplishment. Erikson believed that the combination of adult expectations and children's drive toward mastery sets the stage for the psychological conflict of middle childhood: **industry versus inferiority,** which is resolved positively when experiences lead children to develop a sense of competence at useful skills and tasks.

In cultures everywhere, adults respond to children's improved physical and cognitive capacities by making new demands, and children are ready to benefit from those challenges. Among the Baka hunters and gatherers of Cameroon, 5- to 7-year-olds fetch and carry water, bathe and mind younger siblings, and accompany adults on food-gathering missions. In a miniature village behind the main camp, children practice hut building, spear shaping, and fire making (Avis & Harris, 1991). The Ngoni of Malawi, Central Africa, believe that when children shed their first teeth, they are mature enough for intensive skill training. Six and 7-year-old boys move out of family huts into dormitories, where they enter a system of male domination and instruction. All children of this age are expected to show independence and are held accountable for irresponsible and disrespectful behavior (Rogoff, 1996).

In industrialized nations, the beginning of formal schooling marks the transition to middle childhood. With it comes literacy training, which prepares children for a vast array of specialized careers. In school, children discover their own and others' unique capacities, learn the value of division of labor, and develop a sense of moral commitment and responsibility. The danger at this stage is *inferiority*, reflected in the pessimism of children who have little confidence in their ability to do things well. This sense of inadequacy can develop when family life has not prepared children for school life or when teachers and peers destroy children's feelings of competence and mastery with negative responses.

Erikson's sense of industry combines several developments of middle childhood: a positive but realistic self-concept, pride in accomplishment, moral responsibility, and cooperative participation with agemates. How do these aspects of self and social relationships change over the school years?

© IMAGES & STORIES/ALAMY

■ The industriousness of middle childhood involves mastery of useful skills and tasks. As they practice bow-hunting skills, these young members of the Pokot people of Kenya develop a sense of competence at an important adult activity in their culture. ■

Self-Understanding

In middle childhood, children become able to describe themselves in terms of psychological traits, to compare their own characteristics with those of their peers, and to speculate about the causes of their strengths and weaknesses. These transformations in self-understanding have a major impact on children's self-esteem.

Self-Concept

During the school years, children refine their self-concept, organizing their observations of behaviors and internal states into general dispositions. A major change takes place between ages 8 and 11, as the following self-description by an 11-year-old illustrates:

> My name is A. I'm a human being. I'm a girl. I'm a truthful person. I'm not pretty. I do so-so in my studies. I'm a very good cellist. I'm a very good pianist. I'm a little bit tall for my age. I like

several boys. I like several girls. I'm old-fashioned. I play tennis. I am a very good swimmer. I try to be helpful. I'm always ready to be friends with anybody. Mostly I'm good, but I lose my temper. I'm not well liked by some girls and boys. I don't know if I'm liked by boys or not. (Montemayor & Eisen, 1977, pp. 317–318)

Instead of specific behaviors, this child emphasizes competencies: "a very good cellist," "so-so in my studies" (Damon & Hart, 1988). She also describes her personality, mentioning both positive and negative traits: "truthful" but short-tempered. Older school-age children are far less likely than younger children to describe themselves in extreme, all-or-none ways (Harter, 2003, 2006).

These evaluative self-descriptions result from school-age children's frequent **social comparisons**—judgments of their appearance, abilities, and behavior in relation to those of others. For example, Joey observed that he was "better at spelling" than his peers but "not so good at social studies." Whereas 4- to 6-year-olds can compare their own performance to that of a single peer, older children can compare multiple individuals, including themselves (Butler, 1998; Harter, 2006).

Cognitive, Social, and Cultural Influences on Self-Concept

What factors account for these revisions in self-concept? Cognitive development affects the changing *structure* of the self. School-age children, as we saw in Chapter 12, can better coordinate several aspects of a situation in reasoning about their physical world. Similarly, in the social realm, they combine typical experiences and behaviors into stable psychological dispositions, blend positive and negative characteristics, and compare their own characteristics with those of many peers (Harter, 2003, 2006). In middle childhood, children also gain a clearer understanding that traits are linked to specific desires (a "generous" person *wants* to share) and, therefore, are causes of behavior (Yuill & Pearson, 1998).

The changing *content* of self-concept is a product of both cognitive capacities and feedback from others. Sociologist George Herbert Mead (1934) proposed that a well-organized, psychological self emerges when children adopt a view of the self that resembles others' attitudes toward the child. Mead's ideas indicate that *perspective-taking skills*—in particular, an improved ability to infer what other people are thinking—are crucial for developing a self-concept based on personality traits. School-age children become better at "reading" others' messages and internalizing their expectations. As they do so, they form an *ideal self* that they use to evaluate their real self. As we will see, a large discrepancy between the two can greatly undermine self-esteem, leading to sadness, hopelessness, and depression.

Parental support for self-development continues to be vitally important. School-age children with a history of elaborative parent–child conversations about past experiences construct a rich, positive narrative about the self and thus have more complex, favorable, and coherent self-concepts (Harter, 2006). In middle childhood, children also look to more people beyond the family for information about themselves as they enter a wider range of settings in school and community. And self-descriptions now include frequent reference to social groups: "I'm a Boy Scout, a paper boy, and a Prairie City soccer player," said Joey. As children move into adolescence, their sources of self-definition become more selective. Although parents and other adults remain influential, self-concept is increasingly vested in feedback from close friends (Oosterwegel & Openheimer, 1993).

But recall that the content of self-concept varies from culture to culture. In earlier chapters, we noted that Asian parents stress harmonious interdependence, whereas Western parents emphasize independence and self-assertion. When asked to recall personally significant past experiences (their last birthday, a time their parent scolded them), U.S. school-age children gave longer accounts including more personal preferences, interests, skills, and opinions. Chinese children, in contrast, more often referred to social interactions and to others rather than themselves. Similarly, in their self-descriptions, U.S. children listed more personal attributes ("I'm smart," "I like hockey"), Chinese children more attributes involving group membership and relationships with others ("I'm in second grade," "My friends are crazy about me") (Wang, 2004, 2006b).

LOOK AND LISTEN

◆◆

Ask several 8- to 11-year-old children to tell you about themselves. Do their self-descriptions include personality traits (both positive and negative), social comparisons, and references to social groups, as is typical in middle childhood?

Strong collectivist values also exist in many subcultures in Western nations. In one study, Puerto Rican children in a small fishing village described themselves as "polite," "respectful," and "obedient" more often than U.S. small-town children; they justified these social traits by noting others' positive reactions to them (Damon & Hart, 1988).

Self-Esteem

Recall that most preschoolers have extremely high self-esteem. But as children enter school and receive much more feedback about how well they perform compared with their peers, self-esteem differentiates and also adjusts to a more realistic level.

A HIERARCHICALLY STRUCTURED SELF-ESTEEM   Researchers have asked children to indicate the extent to which statements such as "I'm good at reading" or "I'm usually the one chosen for games" are true of themselves. By age 6 to 7, children in diverse Western cultures have formed at least four broad self-evaluations: academic competence, social competence, physical/athletic competence, and physical appearance. Within these are more refined categories that become increasingly distinct with age (Marsh, 1990; Marsh & Ayotte, 2003; Van den Bergh & De Rycke, 2003). Furthermore, the capacity to view the self in terms of stable dispositions permits school-age children to combine their separate self-evaluations into a general psychological image of themselves—an overall sense of self-esteem (Harter, 2003, 2006). As a result, self-esteem takes on the hierarchical structure shown in Figure 13.1.

Children attach greater importance to certain self-evaluations than to others, giving them more weight in the total picture. Although individual differences exist, during childhood and adolescence perceived physical appearance correlates more strongly with overall self-worth than does any other self-esteem factor (Klomsten, Skaalvik, & Espnes, 2004; Shapka & Keating, 2005). Emphasis on appearance—in the media, by parents and peers, and in society—has major implications for young people's overall satisfaction with themselves.

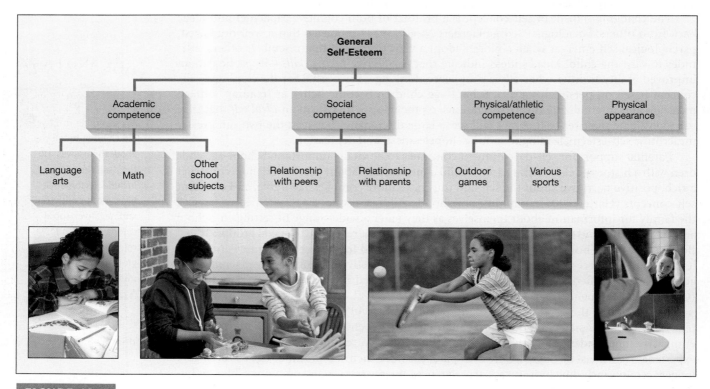

FIGURE 13.1

Hierarchical structure of self-esteem in the mid-elementary school years. From their experiences in different settings, children form at least four separate self-esteems: academic competence, social competence, physical/athletic competence, and physical appearance. These differentiate into additional self-evaluations and combine to form a general sense of self-esteem. *(Photos from left to right: © 2004 Laura Dwight Photography; © George Disario/Corbis; © Mitch Wojnarowicz/The Image Works; © Radius Images/Photolibrary.)*

CHANGES IN LEVEL OF SELF-ESTEEM   Self-esteem declines during the first few years of elementary school as children evaluate themselves in various areas (Marsh, Craven, & Debus, 1998; Wigfield et al., 1997). This decline occurs as children receive more competence-related feedback, as their performances are increasingly judged in relation to those of others, and as they become cognitively capable of social comparison.

To protect their self-worth, children eventually balance social comparisons with personal achievement goals (Ruble & Flett, 1988). Perhaps for this reason, the drop in self-esteem in the early school years usually is not harmful. Then, from fourth grade on, self-esteem rises for the majority of young people, who feel especially good about their peer relationships and athletic capabilities (Cole et al., 2001; Twenge & Campbell, 2001).

Influences on Self-Esteem

From middle childhood on, individual differences in self-esteem become increasingly stable (Trzesniewski, Donnellan, & Robins, 2003). And positive relationships among self-esteem, valuing of various activities, and success at those activities emerge and strengthen with age. Academic self-esteem predicts how important, useful, and enjoyable children judge school subjects to be, their willingness to try hard, and their achievement (Denissen, Zarrett, & Eccles, 2007; Valentine, DuBois, & Cooper, 2004). Children with high social self-esteem are consistently better-liked by classmates (Jacobs et al., 2002). And as we saw in Chapter 11, sense of athletic competence is positively associated with investment and performance in sports.

Furthermore, across age, sex, SES, and ethnic groups, individuals with favorable self-esteem tend to be well-adjusted, sociable, and conscientious. In contrast, a profile of low self-esteem in all areas is linked to anxiety, depression, and antisocial behavior (DuBois et al., 1999; Kim & Cicchetti, 2006; Robins et al., 2001).

CULTURE   Cultural forces profoundly affect self-esteem. An especially strong emphasis on social comparison in school may explain why Chinese and Japanese children, despite their higher academic achievement, score lower than U.S. children in self-esteem—a difference that widens with age (Harter, 2006; Hawkins, 1994; Twenge & Crocker, 2002). In Asian classrooms, competition is tough, and achievement pressure is high. At the same time, because their culture values modesty and social harmony, Asian children rely less on social comparisons to promote their own self-esteem. Rather, they tend to be reserved about judging themselves positively but generous in their praise of others (Falbo et al., 1997).

Gender-stereotyped beliefs also affect self-esteem. In one study, the more 5- to 8-year-old girls talked with friends about they way people look, watched TV shows focusing on physical appearance, and perceived their friends as valuing thinness, the greater their dissatisfaction with their physical self and the lower their overall self-esteem a year later (Dohnt & Tiggemann, 2006). By the end of middle childhood, girls feel less confident than boys about their physical appearance and athletic abilities. With respect to academic self-esteem, boys, again, are somewhat advantaged: Whereas girls score higher in language-arts self-esteem, boys have higher math and science self-esteem—even when children of equal skill levels are compared (Fredricks & Eccles, 2002; Jacobs et al., 2002; Kurtz-Costes et al., 2008). At the same time, girls exceed boys in self-esteem dimensions of close friendship and social acceptance.

Although only a slight difference exists between boys and girls in overall self-esteem, a widely held assumption is that boys' overall sense of self-worth is much higher than girls' (Cole et al., 2001; Marsh & Ayotte, 2003; Young & Mroczek, 2003). Girls may think less well of themselves because they internalize this negative cultural message.

Compared with their Caucasian agemates, African-American children tend to have slightly higher self-esteem, perhaps because of warm extended families and a stronger sense of ethnic pride (Gray-Little & Hafdahl, 2000). Finally, children and adolescents who attend schools or live in neighborhoods

■ An 11-year-old performs a traditional African dance at a community Kwanzaa celebration. A stronger sense of ethnic pride may be partly responsible for African-American children's higher self-esteem relative to their Caucasian agemates. ■

© SYRACUSE NEWSPAPERS/M. GREENLAR/THE IMAGE WORKS

where their SES and ethnic groups are well-represented feel a stronger sense of belonging and have fewer self-esteem problems (Gray-Little & Carels, 1997).

CHILD-REARING PRACTICES   Children whose parents use an *authoritative* child-rearing style (see Chapter 10) feel especially good about themselves (Carolson, Uppal, & Prosser, 2000; Rudy & Grusec, 2006; Wilkinson, 2004). Warm, positive parenting lets children know that they are accepted as competent and worthwhile. And firm but appropriate expectations, backed up with explanations, help them evaluate their own behavior against reasonable standards.

Controlling parents—those who too often help or make decisions for their child—communicate a sense of inadequacy to children. Having parents who are repeatedly disapproving and insulting is also linked to low self-esteem (Kernis, 2002; Pomerantz & Eaton, 2000). Children subjected to such parenting need constant reassurance, and many rely heavily on peers to affirm their self-worth—a risk factor for adjustment difficulties, including aggression and antisocial behavior (Donellan et al., 2005). In contrast, indulgent parenting is correlated with unrealistically high self-esteem, which also undermines development. These children tend to lash out at challenges to their overblown self-images and, as a result, are also likely to be hostile and aggressive (Hughes, Cavell, & Grossman, 1997; Thomaes, Stegge, & Olthof, 2007).

American cultural values have increasingly emphasized a focus on the self that may lead parents to indulge children and boost their self-esteem too much. The self-esteem of U.S. youths rose sharply from the 1970s to the 1990s—a period in which much popular parenting literature advised promoting children's self-esteem (Twenge & Campbell, 2001). Yet compared with previous generations, American youths are achieving less well and displaying more antisocial behavior and other adjustment problems (Berk, 2005). Research confirms that children do not benefit from compliments ("You're terrific") that have no basis in real accomplishment (Damon, 1995). Rather, the best way to foster a positive, secure self-image is to encourage children to strive for worthwhile goals. Over time, a bidirectional relationship emerges: Achievement fosters self-esteem, which contributes to further effort and gains in performance (Gest, Domitrovich, & Welsh, 2005; Marsh et al., 2005).

What can adults do to promote, and to avoid undermining, this mutually supportive relationship between motivation and self-esteem? Some answers come from research on the precise content of adults' messages to children in achievement situations. Let's look first at the meanings children assign to their successes and failures.

ACHIEVEMENT-RELATED ATTRIBUTIONS   *Attributions* are our common, everyday explanations for the causes of behavior—our answers to the question, "Why did I or another person do that?" Notice how Joey, in talking about the spelling bee at the beginning of this chapter, attributes his disappointing performance to *luck* (Belinda got all the easy words) and his usual success to *ability* (he *knows* he's a better speller than Belinda). Joey also appreciates that *effort* matters: "I knocked myself out studying those spelling lists."

The combination of improved reasoning skills and frequent evaluative feedback permits 10- to 12-year-olds to separate all these variables in explaining performance (Dweck, 2002). Those who are high in academic self-esteem and motivation make **mastery-oriented attributions,** crediting their successes to ability—a characteristic they can improve by trying hard and can count on when faced with new challenges. This *incremental view of ability*—that it can increase—influences the way mastery-oriented children interpret negative events. They attribute failure to factors that can be changed and controlled, such as insufficient effort or a difficult task (Heyman &

© LAURA DWIGHT PHOTOGRAPHY

■ Mastery-oriented children credit their successes to ability, and they seek information on how to increase their ability through effort. As a result, their performance improves over time. ■

Dweck, 1998). So whether these children succeed or fail, they take an industrious, persistent approach to learning.

In contrast, children who develop **learned helplessness** attribute their failures, not their successes, to ability. When they succeed, they are likely to conclude that external factors, such as luck, are responsible. Unlike their mastery-oriented counterparts, they hold a *fixed view of ability*—that it cannot be improved by trying hard (Cain & Dweck, 1995). When a task is difficult, these children experience an anxious loss of control—in Erikson's terms, a pervasive sense of inferiority. They give up without really trying.

Children's attributions affect their goals. Mastery-oriented children focus on *learning goals*—seeking information on how best to increase their ability through effort. Hence, their performance increases over time (Blackwell, Trzesniewski, & Dweck, 2007). In contrast, learned-helpless children focus on *performance goals*—obtaining positive and avoiding negative evaluations of their fragile sense of ability. Over time, their ability no longer predicts how well they do. In one study, the more fourth to sixth graders held self-critical attributions, the lower they rated their competence, the less they knew about effective study strategies, the more they avoided challenge, and the poorer their academic performance. These outcomes strengthened their fixed view of ability (Pomerantz & Saxon, 2001). Because learned-helpless children fail to connect effort with success, they do not develop the metacognitive and self-regulatory skills necessary for high achievement (see Chapter 12). Lack of effective learning strategies, reduced persistence, and a sense of loss of control sustain one another in a vicious cycle (Chan & Moore, 2006).

INFLUENCES ON ACHIEVEMENT-RELATED ATTRIBUTIONS What accounts for the different attributions of mastery-oriented and learned-helpless children? Adult communication plays a key role. When parents hold a fixed view of ability, their perceptions of children's academic competence tend to act as self-fulfilling prophecies (see page 470 in Chapter 12). Their children's self-evaluations and school grades conform more closely to parental ability judgments than do those of children whose parents deny that ability is fixed (Pomerantz & Dong, 2006). Parents who believe that little can be done to improve ability may ignore information that is inconsistent with their perceptions, giving their child little opportunity to counteract a negative parental evaluation.

Indeed, children with a learned-helpless style often have parents who believe that their child is not very capable and must work much harder than others to succeed. When the child fails, the parent might say, "You can't do that, can you? It's OK if you quit" (Hokoda & Fincham, 1995). When the child succeeds, the parent might offer feedback that evaluates the child's traits ("You're so smart"). Such trait statements—even when positive—encourage children to adopt a fixed view of ability, which leads them to question their competence in the face of setbacks and to retreat from challenge (Mueller & Dweck, 1998).

Teachers' messages also affect children's attributions. Teachers who are caring and helpful and who emphasize learning over getting good grades tend to have mastery-oriented students (Anderman et al., 2001). In a study of third to eighth graders, students who viewed their teachers as providing positive, supportive learning conditions worked harder and participated more in class—factors that predicted high achievement, which sustained children's belief in the role of effort. In contrast, students with unsupportive teachers regarded their performance as externally controlled (by their teachers or by luck). This attitude predicted withdrawal from learning activities and declining achievement—outcomes that led children to doubt their ability (Skinner, Zimmer-Gembeck, & Connell, 1998).

For some children, performance is especially likely to be undermined by adult feedback. Despite their higher achievement, girls more often than boys attribute poor performance to lack of ability. When girls do not do well, they tend to receive messages from teachers and parents that their ability is at fault, and negative stereotypes (for example, that girls are weak at math) undermine their interest and performance (Bleeker & Jacobs, 2004; Cole et al., 1999). And as Chapter 12 revealed, low-SES, ethnic-minority students often receive less favorable feedback from teachers, especially when assigned to homogeneous groups of poorly achieving students—conditions that result in a drop in academic self-esteem and achievement (Harris & Graham, 2007; Ogbu, 1997).

LOOK AND LISTEN

Observe a school-age child working on a challenging homework assignment under the guidance of a parent or other adult. What features of the adult's communication likely foster mastery-oriented attributions? How about learned helplessness? Explain.

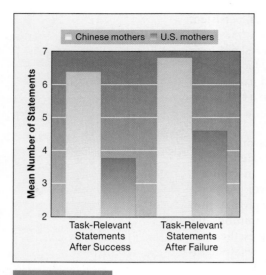

FIGURE 13.2

Chinese and U.S. mothers' task-relevant statements in response to their fourth-grade child's success or failure on puzzle tasks. Observations revealed that regardless of whether their child had just succeeded or failed, Chinese mothers were more likely than U.S. mothers to make task-relevant statements aimed at ensuring that the child exerted high effort. *(Adapted from Ng, Pomerantz, & Lam, 2007.)*

Finally, cultural values affect the likelihood that children will develop learned helplessness. Asian parents and teachers are more likely than their American counterparts to hold an incremental view of ability (see page 476 in Chapter 12). Because of the high value they place on effort and self-improvement, Asians attend more to failure than to success because failure indicates where corrective action is needed. Americans, in contrast, focus more on success because it enhances self-esteem. Observations of U.S. and Chinese mothers' responses to their fourth and fifth graders' puzzle solutions revealed that the U.S. mothers offered more praise after success, whereas the Chinese mothers more often pointed out the child's inadequate performance. And regardless of success or failure, Chinese mothers made more task-relevant statements aimed at ensuring that children exerted sufficient effort to do well ("You concentrated on it"; "You got only 6 out of 12") (see Figure 13.2). When children continued with the task after mothers left the room, the Chinese children showed greater gains in performance (Ng, Pomerantz, & Lam, 2007).

FOSTERING A MASTERY-ORIENTED APPROACH Attribution research suggests that well-intended messages from adults sometimes undermine children's competence. An intervention called **attribution retraining** encourages learned-helpless children to believe they can overcome failure by exerting more effort. Children are given tasks difficult enough that they will experience some failure, followed by repeated feedback that helps them revise their attributions: "You can do it if you try harder." After they succeed, children are given additional feedback—"You're really good at this" or "You really tried hard on that one"—so that they attribute their success to both ability and effort, not chance. Another approach is to encourage low-effort children to focus less on grades and more on mastering a task for its own sake (Hilt, 2004; Horner & Gaither, 2004). Instruction in effective strategies and self-regulation is also vital, to compensate for development lost in this area and to ensure that renewed effort pays off (Wigfield et al., 2006).

Attribution retraining is best begun in middle childhood, before children's views of themselves become hard to change. School-age children with low academic self-esteem whose parents regularly used mastery-oriented practices while helping with homework had gained in sense of academic competence, willingness to try hard on difficult tasks, and positive emotion six months later (Pomerantz, Ng, & Wang, 2006). An even better approach is to prevent learned helplessness, using strategies summarized in Applying What We Know on the following page.

ASK YOURSELF

◆ **REVIEW** How does level of self-esteem change in middle childhood, and what accounts for these changes?

◆ **APPLY** Should parents promote children's self-esteem by telling them they're "smart" or "wonderful"? Are children harmed if they do not feel good about everything they do? Why or why not?

◆ **CONNECT** What cognitive changes, described in Chapter 12 (page 441), support the transition to a self-concept emphasizing competencies, personality traits, and social comparisons?

◆ **REFLECT** Recall your own attributions for academic successes and failures when you were in elementary school. What are those attributions like now? What messages from others may have contributed to your attributions?

Applying What We Know

Fostering a Mastery-Oriented Approach to Learning

STRATEGY	DESCRIPTION
Provision of tasks	Select tasks that are meaningful, responsive to a diversity of student interests, and appropriately matched to current competence so that the child is challenged but not overwhelmed.
Parent and teacher encouragement	Communicate warmth, confidence in the child's abilities, the value of achievement, and the importance of effort in success.
	Model high effort in overcoming failure.
	(For teachers) Communicate often with parents, suggesting ways to foster children's effort and progress.
	(For parents) Monitor schoolwork; provide scaffolded assistance that promotes knowledge of effective strategies and self-regulation.
Performance evaluations	Make evaluations private; avoid publicizing success or failure through wall posters, stars, privileges to "smart" children, and prizes for "best" performance.
	Emphasize individual progress and self-improvement.
School environment	Offer small classes, which permit teachers to provide individualized support for mastery.
	Provide for cooperative learning (see page 470 in Chapter 12) and peer tutoring, in which children assist one another; avoid ability grouping, which makes evaluations of children's progress public.
	Accommodate individual and cultural differences in styles of learning.
	Create an atmosphere that sends a clear message that all pupils can learn.

Sources: Hilt, 2004; Wigfield et al., 2006.

Emotional Development

Greater self-awareness and social sensitivity support gains in emotional competence in middle childhood. Gains take place in experience of self-conscious emotions, emotional understanding, and emotional self-regulation.

Self-Conscious Emotions

As children integrate social expectations into their self-concepts, self-conscious emotions of pride and guilt become clearly governed by personal responsibility. Unlike preschoolers, school-age children experience pride in a new accomplishment and guilt over a transgression even when no adult is present (Harter & Whitesell, 1989). Also, children no longer report guilt for any mishap, as they did earlier, but only for intentional wrongdoing, such as ignoring responsibilities, cheating, or lying (Ferguson, Stegge, & Damhuis, 1991). These changes reflect the older child's more mature sense of morality, a topic addressed later in this chapter.

When school-age children feel pride or guilt, they view specific aspects of the self as leading to success or failure: "I tried hard on that difficult task, and it paid off" (pride) or "I made a mistake, and now I have to deal with it" (guilt). They tend to feel shame when their violation of a standard is not under their control (Lewis & Ramsay, 2002; Saarni et al., 2006). For example, Lizzie felt ashamed when she dropped a spoonful of spaghetti and had a large spot on her shirt for the rest of the school day. But as children develop an overall sense of self-esteem, they may also experience shame after a controllable breach of standards if someone blames them for it (Harter, 1999, 2006; Mascolo & Fischer, 1995). For example, the child who does poorly on a test and whose teacher or

© ELLEN B. SENISI PHOTOGRAPHY

■ If this child reacts with guilt to wrongdoing, he is likely to make amends. But adult blame and criticism may cause him to experience intense shame, leading to depression, anger, and a sharp drop in self-esteem. ■

parent reprimands him ("Everyone else can do it! Why can't you?") may hang his head in shame while repeating to himself, "I'm stupid! I'm a terrible kid!"

Pride motivates children to take on further challenges, whereas guilt prompts them to make amends and to strive for self-improvement. But profound feelings of shame (as noted in Chapter 10) are particularly destructive. A sharp, shame-induced drop in self-esteem can trigger withdrawal and depression or intense anger at those who participated in the shame-evoking situation (Lindsay-Hartz, de Rivera, & Mascolo, 1995; Mills, 2005).

Emotional Understanding

School-age children's understanding of mental activity means that, unlike preschoolers, they are likely to explain emotion by referring to internal states, such as happy or sad thoughts, rather than to external events (Flavell, Flavell, & Green, 2001). Also, between ages 6 and 12, children become more aware of circumstances likely to spark mixed emotions, each of which may be positive or negative and may differ in intensity, and they increasingly report experiencing more than one emotion at a time (Larsen, To, & Fireman, 2007; Pons et al., 2003). For example, recalling the birthday present he received from his grandmother, Joey reflected, "I was very happy I got something but a little sad that I didn't get just what I wanted."

Appreciating mixed emotions helps children realize that people's expressions may not reflect their true feelings (Misailidi, 2006; Saarni, 1999). It also fosters awareness of self-conscious emotions. For example, between ages 6 and 7, children improve sharply in ability to distinguish pride from happiness and surprise (Tracy, Robins, & Lagattuta, 2005). And 8- and 9-year-olds understand that pride combines two sources of happiness—joy in accomplishment and joy that a significant person recognized that accomplishment (Harter, 1999).

Furthermore, children of this age can reconcile contradictory facial and situational cues in figuring out another's feelings. And they can use information about "what might have happened" to predict how people will feel in a new situation—realizing, for example, that someone will feel a sense of relief when an actual outcome is more favorable than what might have occurred (Guttentag & Ferrell, 2004).

■ Detroit-area school-age children prepare meal packages for families in need. Gains in emotional understanding and perspective taking enable children to respond with empathy to people's general life condition. ■

As with self-understanding, gains in emotional understanding are supported by cognitive development and social experiences, especially adults' sensitivity to children's feelings and willingness to discuss emotions. Together, these factors contribute to a rise in empathy as well. As children move closer to adolescence, advances in perspective taking permit an empathic response not just to people's immediate distress but also to their general life condition (Hoffman, 2000). As at early ages, emotional understanding and empathy are linked to favorable social relationships and prosocial behavior (Schultz et al., 2001). As Joey and Lizzie imagined how people who are chronically ill or hungry feel and evoked those emotions in themselves, they gave part of their allowance to charity and joined in fundraising projects through school, community center, and scouting.

Emotional Self-Regulation

Rapid gains in emotional self-regulation occur in middle childhood. As children engage in social comparison and care more about peer approval, they must learn to manage negative emotion that threatens their self-esteem.

By age 10, most children shift adaptively between two general strategies for managing emotion. In **problem-centered coping,** they appraise the situation as changeable, identify the difficulty, and decide what to do about it. If problem solving does not work, they engage in **emotion-centered coping,** which is internal, private, and aimed at controlling distress when little can be done about an outcome (Kliewer, Fearnow, & Miller, 1996; Lazarus & Lazarus, 1994). For example, when faced with an anxiety-provoking test or an angry friend, older school-age children view problem solving and seeking social support as the best strategies. But when outcomes are beyond their control—for example, after receiving a bad grade—they opt for distraction or try to redefine the situation in ways that help them accept it: "Things could be worse. There'll be another test." School-age children's improved ability to appraise situations and reflect on thoughts and feelings means that, compared with preschoolers, they more often use these internal strategies to manage emotion (Brenner & Salovey, 1997).

Cognitive development and a wider range of social experiences permit children to flexibly vary their coping strategies. Furthermore, through interacting with parents, teachers, and peers, school-age children become more knowledgeable about socially approved ways to display negative emotion. With age, they increasingly prefer verbal strategies ("Please stop pushing and wait your turn") to crying, sulking, or aggression (Shipman et al., 2003). Young school-age children justify these more mature displays of emotion by mentioning avoidance of punishment or disapproval, but by third grade, they begin to emphasize concern for others' feelings. Children with this awareness are rated as especially helpful, cooperative, and socially responsive by teachers and as better-liked by peers (Garner, 1996; McDowell & Parke, 2000).

When emotional self-regulation has developed well, school-age children acquire a sense of *emotional self-efficacy*—a feeling of being in control of their emotional experience (Saarni, 2000). This fosters a favorable self-image and an optimistic outlook, which further help children face emotional challenges. As at younger ages, school-age children whose parents respond sensitively and helpfully when the child is distressed are emotionally well-regulated—generally upbeat in mood and also empathic and prosocial. In contrast, poorly regulated children often experience hostile, dismissive parental reactions to distress (Davidov & Grusec, 2006; Zeman, Shipman, & Suveg, 2002). These children are overwhelmed by negative emotion, a response that interferes with empathy and prosocial behavior.

Finally, culture influences emotional self-regulation. In a striking illustration, researchers studied children in two collectivist subcultures in rural Nepal. In response to stories about emotionally charged situations (such as peer aggression or unjust parental punishment), Hindu children more often said they would feel angry but would try to mask their feelings. Buddhist children, in contrast, interpreted the situation so that they felt just OK, rather than angry. "Why be angry?" they explained. "The event already happened." In line with this difference, Hindu mothers reported that they often teach their children how to control their emotional behavior, whereas Buddhist mothers pointed to the value their religion places on a calm, peaceful disposition (Cole & Tamang, 1998; Cole, Tamang, & Shrestha, 2006). Compared to both Nepalese groups, U.S. children preferred conveying anger verbally in these situations; for example, to an unjust punishment, they answered, "If I say I'm angry, he'll stop hurting me!" (Cole, Bruschi, & Tamang, 2002). Notice how this response fits with the Western individualistic emphasis on personal rights and self-expression.

Understanding Others: Perspective Taking

We have seen that middle childhood brings major advances in **perspective taking,** the capacity to imagine what other people may be thinking and feeling. These changes support self-concept and self-esteem, understanding of others, and a wide variety of social skills. Robert Selman's five-stage sequence describes changes in perspective-taking skill, based on children's and adolescents' responses to social dilemmas in which characters have differing information and opinions about an event.

As Table 13.1 on page 492 indicates, at first children have only a limited idea of others' thoughts and feelings. Over time, they become more aware that people can interpret the same event quite differently. Soon they can "step into another person's shoes" and reflect on how that person might regard their own thoughts, feelings, and behavior, as when they say something like, "I *thought you would think* I was just kidding when I said that." (Note the similarity between this

TABLE 13.1	Selman's Stages of Perspective Taking	

STAGE	APPROXIMATE AGE RANGE	DESCRIPTION
Level 0: Undifferentiated perspective taking	3–6	Children recognize that self and other can have different thoughts and feelings, but they frequently confuse the two.
Level 1: Social-informational perspective taking	4–9	Children understand that different perspectives may result because people have access to different information.
Level 2: Self-reflective perspective taking	7–12	Children can "step into another person's shoes" and view their own thoughts, feelings, and behavior from the other person's perspective. They also recognize that others can do the same.
Level 3: Third-party perspective taking	10–15	Children can step outside a two-person situation and imagine how the self and other are viewed from the point of view of an impartial third party.
Level 4: Societal perspective taking	14–adult	Individuals understand that third-party perspective taking can be influenced by one or more systems of broader societal values.

Sources: Selman, 1976; Selman & Byrne, 1974.

level of perspective taking and second-order false belief, described on page 448 in Chapter 12.) Finally, older children and adolescents can evaluate two people's perspectives simultaneously, at first from the vantage point of a disinterested spectator and later by referring to societal values (Gurucharri & Selman, 1982). The following explanation illustrates this ability: "I know why Joey hid the stray kitten in the basement, even though his mom was against keeping it. He believes in not hurting animals. If you put the kitten outside or give it to the pound, it might die."

Experiences in which adults and peers explain their viewpoints contribute greatly to children's perspective taking. Good perspective takers, in turn, are more likely to display empathy and sympathy and to handle difficult social situations effectively—among the reasons they are better-liked by peers (FitzGerald & White, 2003). Children with poor social skills, especially the angry, aggressive styles we discussed in Chapter 10, have great difficulty imagining others' thoughts and feelings. They often mistreat adults and peers without feeling the guilt and remorse prompted by awareness of another's viewpoint. Interventions that provide coaching and practice in perspective taking reduce antisocial behavior and increase empathy and prosocial responding (Chalmers & Townsend, 1990).

Moral Development

Recall from Chapter 10 that preschoolers pick up many morally relevant behaviors through modeling and reinforcement. By middle childhood, they have had time to internalize rules for good conduct: "It's good to help others in trouble" or "It's wrong to take something that doesn't belong to you." This change leads children to become considerably more independent and trustworthy.

In Chapter 10, we also saw that children do not just copy their morality from others. As the cognitive-developmental approach emphasizes, they actively think about right and wrong. An expanding social world, the capacity to consider more information when reasoning, and gains in perspective taking lead moral understanding to advance greatly in middle childhood.

Moral and Social-Conventional Understanding

During the school years, children construct a flexible appreciation of moral rules. By age 7 to 8, they no longer say truth telling is always good and lying is always bad but also consider prosocial and antisocial intentions. They evaluate very negatively certain types of truthfulness, such as bluntly telling a classmate that you don't like her drawing (Bussey, 1999). And although both Chinese and Canadian schoolchildren consider lying about antisocial acts "very naughty," Chinese children—influenced by collectivist values—more often rate lying favorably when the intention is modesty, as when a student who has thoughtfully picked up litter from the playground said, "I didn't do it" (Lee et al., 1997, 2001). Similarly, Chinese children are more likely to favor lying to support the group at the expense of the individual (claiming you're sick so, as a poor singer, you won't harm your class's chances of winning a singing competition). In contrast, Canadian children more often favor lying to support the individual at the expense of the group (asserting that a friend who is a poor speller is actually a good speller because the friend wants to participate in a spelling competition) (Fu et al., 2007).

As children construct more advanced ideas about justice, taking into account an increasing number of variables, they clarify and link moral imperatives and social conventions. School-age children, for example, distinguish social conventions with a clear *purpose* (not running in school hallways to prevent injuries) from ones with no obvious justification (crossing a "forbidden" line on the playground). They regard violations of purposeful conventions as closer to moral transgressions (Buchanan-Barrow & Barrett, 1998). With age, they also realize that people's *intentions* and the *context* of their actions affect the moral implications of violating a social convention. In one study, 8- to 10-year-olds judged that because of a flag's symbolic value, burning it to express disapproval of a country or to start a cooking fire is worse than burning it accidentally. They also stated that public flag burning is worse than private flag burning because it inflicts emotional harm on others. But they recognized that flag burning is a form of freedom of expression, and most agreed that it would be acceptable in a country that treated its citizens unfairly (Helwig & Prencipe, 1999).

In middle childhood, children also realize that people whose *knowledge* differs may not be equally responsible for moral transgressions. Many 7-year-olds tolerate a teacher's decision to give more snack to girls than to boys because she thinks (incorrectly) that girls need more food. But when a teacher gives girls more snack because she holds an *immoral belief* ("it's all right to be nicer to girls than boys"), almost all children judge her actions negatively (Wainryb & Ford, 1998).

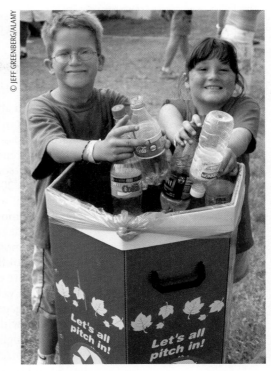

■ School-age children recognize that certain social conventions have a clear purpose—such as separating recyclables from trash to reduce waste. They regard violations of these types of conventions as closer to moral transgressions. ■

Understanding Individual Rights

When children challenge adult authority, they typically do so within the personal domain. As their grasp of moral imperatives and social conventions strengthens, so does their conviction that certain choices, such as hairstyle, friends, and leisure activities, are up to the individual (Nucci, 2005).

Notions of personal choice, in turn, enhance children's moral understanding. As early as age 6, children view freedom of speech and religion as individual rights, even if laws exist that deny those rights (Helwig, 2006). And they regard laws that discriminate against individuals—for example, denying certain people access to medical care or education—as wrong and worthy of violating (Helwig & Jasiobedzka, 2001). In justifying their responses, children appeal to personal privileges and, by the end of middle childhood, to the importance of individual rights for maintaining a fair society.

At the same time, older school-age children place limits on individual choice. Fourth graders faced with conflicting moral and personal concerns—such as whether or not to

■ This 10-year-old observes the social convention of respect for his country's flag. He also grasps individual rights such as free speech—for example, the right to destroy a flag in protest against a country that treats its citizens unfairly. ■

befriend a classmate of a different race or gender—typically decide in favor of kindness and fairness (Killen et al., 2002). Partly for this reason, prejudice generally declines in middle childhood.

Culture and Moral Understanding

Children and adolescents in diverse Western and non-Western cultures use similar criteria to reason about moral, social-conventional, and personal concerns (Neff & Helwig, 2002; Nucci, 2005, 2008). For example, Chinese young people, whose culture places a high value on respect for and deference to adult authority, nevertheless say that adults have no right to interfere in children's personal matters, such as how they spend free time (Hasebe, Nucci, & Nucci, 2004; Helwig et al., 2003). A Colombian child illustrated this passionate defense of personal control when asked if a teacher had the right to tell a student where to sit during circle time. In the absence of a moral reason from the teacher, the child declared, "She should be able to sit wherever she wants" (Ardila-Rey & Killen, 2001, p. 249).

Furthermore, American and Korean children alike claim that a child with no position of authority should be obeyed when she gives a directive that is fair and caring, such as telling others to share candy or to return lost money to its owner. And even in Korean culture, which places a high value on deference to authority, 7- to 11-year-olds evaluate negatively an adult's order to engage in immoral acts, such as stealing or refusing to share—a response that strengthens with age (Kim, 1998; Kim & Turiel, 1996). In sum, children everywhere seem to realize that higher principles, independent of rule and authority, must prevail when people's personal rights and welfare are at stake.

As children extend their grasp of moral imperatives, they also contemplate religious and spiritual concepts. Refer to the Cultural Influences box on the following page for current evidence on how children understand the existence of God, the core idea in the vast majority of the world's religions.

Understanding Diversity and Inequality

By the early school years, children associate power and privilege with white people and poverty and inferior status with people of color. They do not necessarily acquire these views directly from parents or friends. In one study, although white children assumed that parents' and friends' racial attitudes would resemble their own, no similarities in attitudes emerged (Aboud & Doyle, 1996). Perhaps many white parents are reluctant to discuss their racial and ethnic views with children, and friends also say little. Given limited or ambiguous information, children may fill in the gaps with information they encounter in the media and elsewhere in their environments and then use their own attitudes as the basis for inferring others'.

Consistent with this idea, research indicates that children pick up much information about group status from implicit messages in their surroundings. In another investigation, 7- to 12-year-olds attending a summer school were randomly assigned to social groups, identified by colored T-shirts (yellow or blue) that the children wore. The researchers hung posters in the classroom depicting yellow-group members as having higher status—for example, as having won more athletic and spelling competitions. When teachers used the groups as the basis for seating arrangements, assignments, and bulletin-board displays, the children in the high-status group evaluated their own group more favorably than the other group, and the children in the low-status group viewed their own group less favorably. But when teachers ignored the social groupings, no prejudice emerged (Bigler, Brown, & Markell, 2001).

These findings reveal that children do not necessarily form stereotypes even when some basis for them exists—in this instance, information on wall posters. But when an authority figure behaves in ways that endorse group status distinctions, children form biased attitudes.

IN-GROUP AND OUT-GROUP BIASES: DEVELOPMENT OF PREJUDICE Studies in diverse Western nations confirm that by age 5 to 7, white children generally evaluate their own racial group favorably and other racial groups less favorably or negatively (Aboud, 2003; Bennett et al., 2004; Nesdale et al., 2004). Many minority children of this age, in a reverse pat-

CULTURAL INFLUENCES

Children's Understanding of God

Here is how several 6- to 9-year-olds responded to the question: "What is God?"

- "You can pray anytime you feel like it, and they [Jesus and God] are sure to hear you because they got it worked out so one of them is on duty at all times."
- "God hears everything, not just prayers, so there must be an awful lot of noise in his ears, unless he has thought of a way to turn it off."
- "God is a spirit who can go anywhere." *What is a spirit?* "It's a ghost, like in the movies." (From Briggs, 2000; Gandy, 2004.)

Ideas about God differ radically from ideas about ordinary experiences because they violate real-world assumptions. Recall from Chapter 9 that between ages 4 and 8, children distinguish magical beings (such as Santa Claus and the Tooth Fairy) from reality (see page 342). At the same time, they embrace other beliefs that are part of their culturally transmitted religion. To avoid confusion, they must isolate their concepts of God from their grasp of human agents, placing God in a separate religious realm governed by superhuman rules (Woolley, 2000). This is a challenging task for preschool and school-age children.

Previous research, strongly influenced by Piaget's theory, led to a uniform conclusion: Children assign *anthropomorphic* (human) characteristics to God, whom they view as a parentlike figure residing in the sky. Not until adolescence does this concrete image of God as "big person" give way to an abstract, mystical view of God as formless, all-knowing (omniscient), all-powerful (omnipotent), and transcending the limits of time.

Consider the responses of children just given, which contain both concrete human images (God as being "on duty in the sky" or as overwhelmed by the "noise in his ears") and a variety of superhuman properties ("a spirit who can go anywhere"). Recent evidence reveals that even preschoolers are not limited to human, parental images of God. The procedures typically used to investigate children's religious knowledge—asking them to respond to open-ended questions—are so cognitively demanding that children often fall back on their highly detailed notions of humans to fill in for their sketchier thoughts about God.

When researchers make tasks less demanding, children recognize that God has supernatural powers not available to humans, such as seeing and hearing everything (Richert & Barrett, 2005). For example, in research in the United States and in a Mexican Mayan village, most 5- to 6-year-olds given a typical false-belief task indicated that their parents might hold a false belief, but God would not (Knight et al., 2004). Children of this age also say that God—but not a humanlike puppet—can see an object in a darkened box (Barrett, Richert, & Driesenga, 2001; Makris & Pnevmatikos, 2007). And with respect to God's omnipotence, even preschoolers state with certainty that God, but not humans, gives life to all natural things (animals, plants, and trees) (Petrovich, 1997).

Indeed, the most striking feature of children's concepts of God is their mix of tangible and intangible features. In this respect, their religious thinking is far more similar to adults' than previously thought. That children's representations of God are not restricted to a "big person" image suggests that religious education strongly influences their thinking.

Indeed, wide cultural variation in children's and adults' ideas exists (Barrett, 2002; Barrett & Van Orman, 1996). In studies in which school-age children drew pictures of God, Mormons, Lutherans, Mennonites, and Catholics, in line with the teachings of their denominations, more often represented God as humanlike than did Unitarians and Jews (Pitts, 1976; Tamminen, 1991). Furthermore, children say some things about God that seem strange or amusing because their culturally relevant knowledge is often incomplete. During the school years, they frequently ask thoughtful questions about God aimed at broadening their understanding: "Does God have parents?" or "Why doesn't God stop bad things from happening?"

Finally, some children are aware that visions of God can provide emotional comfort and guidance, as these comments reveal: "He comes down and helps you when you're sad or lonely or can't get to sleep at night." "In case you forget, he reminds you to act nice" (Berk, 2004). By adolescence, religiosity is linked to psychological well-being and to prosocial attitudes and behavior (Sherrod & Spiewak, 2008).

■ Cognitive development, religious education, and culture combine to influence children's understanding of God. Like adults, this young participant in an interfaith "blessing of the animals" ceremony probably views God as having both humanlike and supernatural powers. ■

tern, assign positive characteristics to the privileged white majority and negative characteristics to their own group (Averhart & Bigler, 1997; Corenblum, 2003).

But recall that with age, children pay more attention to inner traits. The capacity to classify the social world in multiple ways enables school-age children to understand that people can be both "the same" and "different"—those who look different need not think, feel, or act

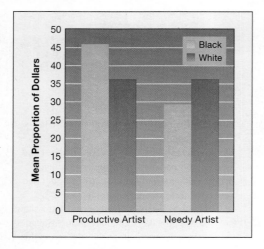

FIGURE 13.3

White fourth graders' racially biased distribution of money to child artists. When dividing money earned from selling children's art among three child artists—two white and one black—the fourth graders gave more money to a productive black artist (who countered a stereotype) than a productive white artist, and less money to a needy black artist (who conformed to a stereotype) than to a needy white artist. In both instances, the fourth graders seemed to engage in subtle, unintentional prejudice. *(From A. V. McGillicuddy-De Lisi, M. Daly, & A. Neal, 2006, "Children's Distributive Justice Judgments: Aversive Racism in Euro-American Children?" Child Development, 77, p. 1072. © The Society for Research in Child Development, Inc. Adapted by permission of Blackwell Publishing Ltd.)*

differently (Aboud & Amato, 2001). Consequently, voicing of negative attitudes toward minorities declines. After age 7 or 8, both majority and minority children express *in-group favoritism,* and white children's prejudice against *outgroup* members often weakens (Nesdale et al., 2005; Ruble et al., 2004). Most school-age children and adolescents are also quick to verbalize that it is wrong to exclude others from peer-group and learning activities on the basis of skin color—discrimination they evaluate as unfair (Killen et al., 2002).

Yet even in children aware of the injustice of discrimination, prejudice may operate unintentionally and without awareness—as it does in many adults (Dunham, Baron, & Banaji, 2006). Consider a study in which white second and fourth graders were asked to divide fairly among three child artists—two white and one black—money that had been earned from selling the children's art. In each version of the task, one artist was labeled as "productive" (making more artworks), one as "the oldest," and one as "poor and needing money for lunch." By age 8 to 9, most children recognize that special consideration should be given to those who either perform exceptionally or are at a disadvantage. But racial stereotypes interfered with fourth graders' evenhanded application of these principles. They gave more money to a productive black artist (who countered the racial stereotype of "low achiever") than to a productive white artist and less money to a needy black artist (who conformed to the racial stereotype of "poor") than to a needy white artist (see Figure 13.3) (McGillicuddy-De Lisi, Daly, & Neal, 2006).

Nevertheless, the extent to which children hold racial and ethnic biases varies, depending on the following personal and situational factors:

- *A fixed view of personality traits.* Children who believe that people's personality traits are fixed rather than changeable often judge others as either "good" or "bad." Ignoring motives and circumstances, they readily form prejudices on the basis of limited information. For example, they might infer that "a new child at school who tells a lie to get other kids to like her" is simply a bad person (Levy & Dweck, 1999).
- *Overly high self-esteem.* Children (and adults) with very high self-esteem are more likely to hold racial and ethnic prejudices (Baumeister et al., 2003; Bigler, Brown, & Markell, 2001). These individuals seem to belittle disadvantaged individuals or groups to justify their own extremely favorable self-evaluation. Children who say their own ethnicity makes them feel especially "good"—and thus perhaps socially superior—are more likely to display in-group favoritism and out-group prejudice (Pfeifer et al., 2007).
- *A social world in which people are sorted into groups.* The more adults highlight group distinctions for children and the less interracial contact children experience, the more likely white children are to display prejudice (Kowalski & Lo, 1999; McGlothlin & Killen, 2006).

REDUCING PREJUDICE Research confirms that an effective way to reduce prejudice is through intergroup contact, in which racially and ethnically different children work toward common goals and become personally acquainted (Tropp & Pettigrew, 2005). Children assigned to cooperative learning groups with peers of diverse backgrounds, for example, form more cross-race friendships. Sharing thoughts and feelings with close, cross-race friends, in turn, reduces even subtle, unintentional prejudices (Turner, Hewstone, & Voci, 2007). But the positive effects of cooperative learning seem not to generalize to out-group members who are not part of these learning teams.

Long-term contact and collaboration in neighborhoods, schools, and communities may be the best way to reduce prejudice. Classrooms that expose children to broad ethnic diversity, teach them to understand and value those differences, directly address the damage caused by prejudice, and encourage perspective taking and empathy both prevent children from forming negative biases and reduce already acquired biases (Pfeifer, Brown, & Juvonen, 2007).

Finally, inducing children to view others' traits as changeable, by discussing with them the many possible influences on those traits, is helpful. The more children believe that people can change their personalities, the more they report liking and perceiving themselves as similar to members of disadvantaged groups. Furthermore, children who believe that human attributes are changeable spend more time volunteering to help the needy—for example, by serving meals to the homeless or reading to poverty-stricken preschoolers (Karafantis & Levy, 2004). Volunteering, in turn, may promote changeable views of others by helping children take the perspective of the underprivileged and appreciate the social conditions that lead to disadvantage.

■ Fourth graders cooperate to figure out how many batteries they need to light a light bulb. Opportunities to work together toward common goals can reduce even subtle, unintentional prejudices as racially and ethnically different children get to know one another. ■

Ask Yourself

◆ **REVIEW** How does emotional self-regulation improve in middle childhood? What implications do these advances have for children's self-esteem?

◆ **APPLY** Ten-year-old Marla says her classmate Bernadette will never get good grades because she's lazy. Jane believes that Bernadette tries but can't concentrate because her parents are divorcing. Why is Marla more likely than Jane to develop prejudices?

◆ **CONNECT** Cite examples of how older children's capacity to take more information into account enhances their emotional understanding, perspective taking, and moral understanding.

◆ **REFLECT** Did you attend an integrated elementary school? Why is school integration vital for reducing racial and ethnic prejudice?

Peer Relations

In middle childhood, the society of peers becomes an increasingly important context for development. Peer contact, as we have seen, contributes to perspective taking and understanding of self and others. These developments, in turn, enhance peer interaction. Compared with preschoolers, school-age children resolve conflicts more effectively, using persuasion and compromise (Mayeux & Cillessen, 2003). Sharing, helping, and other prosocial acts also increase. In line with these changes, aggression declines. But the drop is greatest for physical attacks (Côte et al., 2007; Tremblay, 2000). As we will see, verbal and relational aggression continue as children form peer groups.

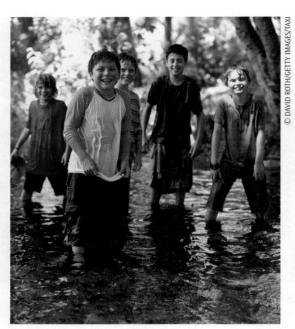

■ Peer groups first form in middle childhood. These boys have probably established a social structure of leaders and followers as they gather for joint activities. Their relaxed body language and similar way of dressing suggest a strong sense of group belonging. ■

Peer Groups

TAKE A MOMENT... Watch children in the schoolyard or neighborhood, and notice how they often gather in groups of three to a dozen or more. In what ways are members of the same group noticeably alike?

By the end of middle childhood, children display a strong desire for group belonging. They form **peer groups,** collectives that generate unique values and standards for behavior and a social structure of leaders and followers. Peer groups organize on the basis of proximity (being in the same classroom) and similarity in sex, ethnicity, academic achievement, popularity, and aggression (Rubin, Bukowski, & Parker, 2006). When groups are tracked for 3 to 6 weeks, membership changes very little. When they are followed for a year or longer, substantial change can occur, depending on whether children are reshuffled into different classrooms. For children who remain together, 50 to 70 percent of groups consist mostly of the same children from year to year (Cairns, Xie, & Leung, 1998).

The practices of these informal groups lead to a "peer culture" that typically involves a specialized vocabulary, dress code, and place to "hang out." Joey and three other boys formed a club whose "uniform" was T-shirts, jeans, and sneakers. They met at recess and on Saturdays in the tree house in Joey's backyard. Calling themselves "the pack," the boys devised a secret handshake and chose Joey as their leader. Their activities included improving the clubhouse, trading baseball cards, playing basketball and video games, and—just as important—keeping unwanted peers and adults out!

As children develop these exclusive associations, the codes of dress and behavior that grow out of them become more broadly influential. Peers who deviate—by "kissing up" to teachers, wearing the wrong clothes, or tattling on classmates—are often rebuffed, becoming targets of critical glances and comments. These customs bind peers together, creating a sense of group identity. Within the group, children acquire many social skills—cooperation, leadership, followership, and loyalty to collective goals. Through these experiences, children experiment with and learn about social organizations.

As with other aspects of social reasoning, children evaluate a group's decision to exclude a peer in complex ways. Most view exclusion as wrong, even when they see themselves as different from the excluded child. And with age, children are less likely to endorse excluding someone because of unconventional appearance or behavior. Girls, especially, regard exclusion as unjust, perhaps because they experience it more often than boys (Killen, Crystal, & Watanabe, 2002). But when a peer threatens group functioning, by acting disruptively or by lacking skills to participate in a valued group activity (such as sports), both boys and girls say that exclusion is justified—a perspective that strengthens with age (Killen & Stangor, 2001).

Despite these sophisticated understandings, children do exclude unjustly, often using relationally aggressive tactics. Peer groups—at the instigation of their leaders, who can be skillfully aggressive—frequently oust no longer "respected" children. Some of these cast-outs, whose own previous hostility toward outsiders reduces their chances of being included elsewhere, turn to other low-status peers with poor social skills (Werner & Crick, 2004). Socially anxious children, when ousted, often become increasingly peer-avoidant and thus more isolated (Gazelle & Rudolph, 2004). In either case, opportunities to acquire socially competent behavior diminish.

As excluded children's class participation declines, their academic achievement suffers (Buhs, Ladd, & Herald, 2006). And some aggressive children—especially popular boys—link up with popular, nonaggressive agemates (Bagwell et al., 2000; Farmer et al., 2002). In these groups, mild-mannered children may accept and even support the antisocial acts of their dominant, antisocial associates, who pick fights with other groups or bully weaker children. Consequently, teachers and counselors must target both antisocial and mixed peer groups to reduce peer aggression.

School-age children's desire for group belonging can also be satisfied through formal group ties such as scouting, 4-H, and religious youth groups. Adult involvement holds in check the negative behaviors associated with children's informal peer groups. And through working on joint projects and helping in their communities, children gain in social and moral maturity (Vandell & Shumow, 1999).

Friendships

Whereas peer groups provide children with insight into larger social structures, friendships contribute to the development of trust and sensitivity. During the school years, friendship becomes more complex and psychologically based. Consider the following 8-year-old's ideas:

> *Why is Shelly your best friend?* Because she helps me when I'm sad, and she shares. . . . *What makes Shelly so special?* I've known her longer, I sit next to her and got to know her better. . . . *How come you like Shelly better than anyone else?* She's done the most for me. She never disagrees, she never eats in front of me, she never walks away when I'm crying, and she helps me on my homework. . . . *How do you get someone to like you?* . . . If you're nice to [your friends], they'll be nice to you. (Damon, 1988, pp. 80–81)

As these responses show, friendship has become a mutually agreed-on relationship in which children like each other's personal qualities and respond to one another's needs and desires. And once a friendship forms, *trust* becomes its defining feature. School-age children state that a good friendship is based on acts of kindness, signifying that each person can be counted on to support the other (Hartup & Abecassis, 2004). Consequently, older children regard violations of trust, such as not helping when others need help, breaking promises, and gossiping behind the other's back, as serious breaches of friendship.

Because of these features, school-age children's friendships are more selective. Whereas preschoolers say they have lots of friends, by age 8 or 9, children name only a handful of good friends. Girls, who demand greater closeness than boys, are more exclusive in their friendships (Markovits, Benenson, & Dolensky, 2001). In addition, children tend to select friends similar to themselves in age, sex, race, ethnicity, and SES. Friends also resemble one another in personality (sociability, inattention/hyperactivity, aggression, depression), peer popularity, academic achievement, and prosocial behavior (Hartup, 2006; Mariano & Harton, 2005). But friendship opportunities offered by children's environments also affect their choices. As noted earlier, in integrated classrooms with mixed-race collaborative learning groups, students form more cross-race friendships.

Over middle childhood, high-quality friendships remain fairly stable, with about 50 to 70 percent enduring over a school year, and some for several years (Berndt, 2004). Through them, children learn the importance of emotional commitment. They come to realize that close relationships can survive disagreements if both parties are secure in their liking for one another (Rose & Asher, 1999). Friendship provides an important context in which children learn to tolerate criticism and resolve disputes in ways that meet both partners' needs.

Yet the impact of friendships on children's development depends on the nature of their friends. Children who bring kindness and compassion to their friendships strengthen each other's prosocial tendencies. But when aggressive children make friends, the relationship is often riddled with hostile interaction and is at risk for breakup, especially when just one member of the pair is aggressive (Ellis & Zarbatany, 2007). Aggressive girls' friendships are high in exchange of private feelings but also full of relational hostility, including jealousy, conflict, and betrayal (Werner & Crick, 2004).

LOOK AND LISTEN

Ask an 8- to 11-year-old to tell you what he or she looks for in a best friend. Is *trust* centrally important? Does the child mention personality traits, just as school-age children do in describing themselves (see page 483)?

■ School-age children tend to select friends similar to themselves in age, sex, race, ethnicity, and SES. However, in integrated classrooms with mixed-race collaborative learning groups, students form more cross-race friendships. ■

Aggressive boys' friendships involve frequent expressions of anger, coercive statements, physical attacks, and enticements to rule-breaking behavior, as well as relational aggression (Bagwell & Coie, 2004; Crick & Nelson, 2002; Dishion, Andrews, & Crosby, 1995). These findings indicate that the social problems of aggressive children operate within their closest peer ties. As we will see next, these children often acquire negative reputations in the wider world of peers.

Peer Acceptance

Peer acceptance refers to likability—the extent to which a child is viewed by a group of agemates, such as classmates, as a worthy social partner. Unlike friendship, likability is not a mutual relationship but a one-sided perspective, involving the group's view of an individual. Nevertheless, certain social skills that contribute to friendship also enhance peer acceptance. Better-accepted children tend to have more friends and more positive relationships with them (Lansford et al., 2006; Pedersen et al., 2007).

To assess peer acceptance, researchers usually use self-reports that measure *social preferences*—for example, asking children to identify classmates whom they "like very much" or "like very little" (Hymel et al., 2004). Another approach assesses *social prominence*—children's judgments of whom most of their classmates admire. Only moderate correspondence exists between the classmates children identify as prominent (looked up to by many others) and those they say they personally prefer (Prinstein & Cillessen, 2003).

Children's self-reports yield four general categories of peer acceptance:

- **Popular children,** who get many positive votes (are well-liked)
- **Rejected children,** who get many negative votes (are disliked)
- **Controversial children,** who receive many votes, both positive and negative (are both liked and disliked)
- **Neglected children,** who are seldom mentioned, either positively or negatively

About two-thirds of students in a typical elementary school classroom fit one of these categories (Coie, Dodge, & Coppotelli, 1982). The remaining one-third, who do not receive extreme scores, are *average* in peer acceptance.

Peer acceptance is a powerful predictor of current as well as later psychological adjustment. Rejected children, especially, are anxious, unhappy, disruptive, and low in self-esteem. Both teachers and parents rate them as having a wide range of emotional and social problems. Peer rejection in middle childhood is also strongly associated with poor school performance, absenteeism, dropping out, substance use, depression, antisocial behavior, and delinquency in adolescence and with criminality in adulthood (Laird et al., 2001; Parker et al., 1995; Rubin, Bukowski, & Parker, 2006).

However, earlier influences—children's characteristics combined with parenting practices—may largely explain the link between peer acceptance and adjustment. School-age children with peer-relationship problems are more likely to have preexisting, weak emotional self-regulation skills and to have experienced family stress due to low income, insensitive child rearing, and coercive discipline (Cowan & Cowan, 2004; Trentacosta & Shaw, 2009). Nevertheless, as we will see, rejected children evoke reactions from peers that contribute to their unfavorable development.

DETERMINANTS OF PEER ACCEPTANCE Why is one child liked while another is rejected? A wealth of research reveals that social behavior plays a powerful role.

Popular Children. The majority of **popular-prosocial children** combine academic and social competence. They perform well in school, communicate with peers in friendly and cooperative ways, and solve social problems constructively (Cillessen & Bellmore, 2004).

But other popular children are admired for their socially adept yet belligerent behavior. This smaller subtype, **popular-antisocial children,** includes "tough" boys—athletically skilled but poor students who cause trouble and defy adult authority—and relationally aggressive boys and girls who enhance their own status by ignoring, excluding, and spreading rumors about other children (Rodkin et al., 2000; Rose, Swenson, & Waller, 2004). Despite their aggressiveness, peers view these youths as "cool," perhaps because of their athletic ability and sophisticated but devious social skills. Although peer admiration gives these children some protection against lasting adjustment difficulties, their antisocial acts require intervention (Prinstein & La Greca, 2004; Rodkin et al., 2006). With age, peers like these high-status, aggressive youths less and less, a trend that is stronger for relationally aggressive girls. The more socially prominent and controlling these girls become, the more they engage in relational aggression (Cillessen & Mayeux, 2004). Eventually peers condemn their nasty tactics and reject them.

Rejected Children. Rejected children display a wide range of negative social behaviors. The largest subtype, **rejected-aggressive children,** show high rates of conflict, physical and relational aggression, and hyperactive, inattentive, and impulsive behavior. They are usually deficient in perspective taking, and they tend to misinterpret the innocent behaviors of peers as hostile and to blame others for their social difficulties (Crick, Casas, & Nelson, 2002; Dodge, Coie, & Lynam, 2006; Hoza et al., 2005). Compared with popular-aggressive children, they are more extremely antagonistic.

■ Schoolgirls in Beijing, China, gather around a popular classmate. Most popular children are *prosocial*—academically successful, socially sensitive, and cooperative. But some are *antisocial,* admired for their skill at controlling peer relationships through relational aggression. Over time, their popularity declines, and they may experience rejection. ■

In contrast, **rejected-withdrawn children** are passive and socially awkward. These timid children are overwhelmed by social anxiety, hold negative expectations for treatment by peers, and worry about being scorned and attacked. Like their aggressive counterparts, they typically feel like retaliating rather than compromising in conflicts with peers, although they less often act on those feelings (Hart et al., 2000; Ladd & Burgess, 1999; Troop-Gordon & Asher, 2005).

Rejected children are excluded by peers as early as kindergarten. Rejection, in turn, further impairs these children's biased social information processing, heightening their hostility (Dodge et al., 2003). Soon their classroom participation declines, their feelings of loneliness rise, their academic achievement falters, and they want to avoid school (Buhs & Ladd, 2001). Most have few friends, and some have none—a circumstance that compounds their adjustment difficulties (Ladd & Troop-Gordon, 2003; Pedersen et al., 2007).

Both types of rejected children are at risk for peer harassment. But as the Biology and Environment box on page 502 reveals, rejected-aggressive children also act as bullies, and rejected-withdrawn children are especially likely to be victimized (Putallaz et al., 2007; Sandstrom & Cillessen, 2003).

Controversial and Neglected Children. Consistent with the mixed peer opinion they engender, controversial children display a blend of positive and negative social behaviors. They are hostile and disruptive, but they also engage in positive, prosocial acts. Even though some peers dislike them, they have qualities that protect them from exclusion. They have as many friends as popular children and are happy with their peer relationships (Newcomb, Bukowski, & Pattee, 1993). But like their popular-antisocial counterparts, they often bully others and engage in calculated relational aggression to sustain their dominance (DeRosier & Thomas, 2003; Putallaz et al., 2007).

Perhaps the most surprising finding is that neglected children, once thought to be in need of treatment, are usually well-adjusted. Although they engage in low rates of interaction, most are just as socially skilled as average children. They do not report feeling unhappy about their social life, and when they want to, they can break away from their usual, preferred pattern of playing alone (Harrist et al., 1997; Ladd & Burgess, 1999). Largely for this reason, neglected status (like controversial status) is often temporary. Neglected, socially competent children remind us that an outgoing, gregarious personality style is not the only path to emotional well-being. Nevertheless, a few neglected children are socially anxious and poorly skilled and, thus, at risk for peer rejection.

BIOLOGY AND ENVIRONMENT

Bullies and Their Victims

Follow the activities of aggressive children over a school day, and you will see that they reserve their hostilities for certain peers. A particularly destructive form of interaction is **peer victimization,** in which certain children become targets of verbal and physical attacks or other forms of abuse. What sustains these repeated assault–retreat cycles between pairs of children?

About 10 to 20 percent of children are bullies, while 15 to 30 percent are repeatedly victimized. Most bullies are boys who use both physical and verbal attacks, but girls sometimes bombard a vulnerable classmate with verbal and relational hostility (Rigby, 2004). As bullies move into adolescence, many amplify their attacks through electronic means (Twyman et al., 2010). About 20 to 40 percent of youths have experienced "cyberbullying" through text messages, e-mail, chat rooms, or other electronic tools (Tokunaga, 2010). They often do not report it to parents or adults at school.

Some bullies are high-status youngsters who may be liked for their leadership or athletic abilities. But most are disliked, or become so, because of their cruelty (Vaillancourt, Hymel, & McDougall, 2003). Nevertheless, peers rarely intervene to help victims, and about 20 to 30 percent of onlookers actually encourage bullies, even joining in (Salmivalli & Voeten, 2004).

Chronic victims tend to be passive when active behavior is expected. On the playground, they hang around chatting or wander on their own. When bullied, they give in, cry, and assume defensive postures (Boulton, 1999). Biologically based traits—an inhibited temperament and a frail physical appearance—contribute to victimization. But victims also have histories of resistant attachment, overly controlling child rearing, and maternal overprotection—parenting that prompts anxiety, low self-esteem, and dependency, resulting in a fearful demeanor that marks these children

as vulnerable (Snyder et al., 2003). Victims' adjustment problems include depression, loneliness, poor school performance, disruptive behavior, and school avoidance (Paul & Cillessen, 2003).

Aggression and victimization are not polar opposites. One-third to one-half of victims are also aggressive, meeting out physical, relational, or cyber-hostilities. Occasionally, they retaliate against powerful bullies, who respond by abusing them again—a cycle that sustains their victim status (Kochenderfer-Ladd, 2003). Among rejected children, these bully/victims are the most despised. They often have histories of extremely maladaptive parenting, including child abuse. This combination of highly negative home and peer experiences places them at severe risk for maladjustment (Kowalski, Limber, & Agatston, 2008; Schwartz, Proctor, & Chien, 2001).

Interventions that change victimized children's negative opinions of themselves and that teach them to respond in nonreinforcing ways to their attackers are helpful. Another way to assist victimized children is to help them acquire the social skills needed to form and maintain a gratifying friendship. When children have a friend to whom they can turn for help, bullying episodes usually end quickly. Anxious, withdrawn children with a close friend have fewer adjustment problems than those with no friends (Fox & Boulton, 2006; Laursen et al., 2007).

Although modifying victimized children's behavior can help, this does not mean

they are to blame. The best way to reduce bullying is to change youth environments (including school, sports programs, recreation centers, and neighborhoods), promoting prosocial attitudes and behaviors. Effective approaches include developing school and community codes against both "traditional" and "cyber" bullying, teaching child bystanders to intervene, enlisting parents' assistance in changing bullies' behaviors, and (if necessary) moving socially prominent bullies to another class or school (Kiriakidis & Kavoura, 2010; Leadbeater & Hoglund, 2006).

The U.S. Department of Health and Human Services has launched a media campaign, Stop Bullying Now, *www.stopbullyingnow.hrsa.gov,* which raises awareness of the harmfulness of bullying through TV and radio public service announcements. It also provides parents, teachers, and students with information on prevention.

© PAUL BALDESARE/PHOTOFUSION

■ Some bullies are high-status youngsters, but most are disliked, or become so, because of their cruelty. And chronic victims are often easy targets—physically weak, passive, and rejected by peers. ■

HELPING REJECTED CHILDREN   A variety of interventions exist to improve the peer relations and psychological adjustment of rejected children. Most involve coaching, modeling, and reinforcing positive social skills, such as how to initiate interaction with a peer, cooperate in play, and respond to another child with friendly emotion and approval. Several of these programs have produced gains in social competence and peer acceptance still present from several weeks to a year later (Asher & Rose, 1997; DeRosier, 2007). Combining social-skills training with other treatments increases their effectiveness. Rejected children are often poor students, whose low academic self-esteem magnifies their negative reactions to teachers and classmates. Intensive academic tutoring improves both school achievement and social acceptance (O'Neil et al., 1997).

Still another approach focuses on training in perspective taking and social problem solving. But many rejected-aggressive children are unaware of their poor social skills and do not take responsibility for their social failures (Mrug, Hoza, & Gerdes, 2001). Rejected-withdrawn children, in contrast, are likely to develop a *learned-helpless* approach to peer acceptance—concluding, after repeated rebuffs, that they will never be liked (Wichmann, Coplan, & Daniels, 2004). Both types of rejected children need help attributing their peer difficulties to internal, changeable causes.

Finally, because rejected children's socially incompetent behaviors often originate in a poor fit between the child's temperament and parenting practices, interventions focusing on the child may not be sufficient (Bierman & Powers, 2009). As early as the preschool years, rejected children engage in similarly inept communication with parents and with peers (Black & Logan, 1995; Guralnick et al., 2007). Without interventions directed at improving the quality of parent–child interaction, rejected children will continue to practice poor interpersonal skills at home and, as a result, may soon return to their old behavior patterns.

LOOK AND LISTEN

Contact a nearby elementary school or a school district office to find out what practices are in place to prevent bullying. Inquire about a written antibullying policy, and request a copy.

Gender Typing

Children's understanding of gender roles broadens in middle childhood, and their gender identities (views of themselves as relatively masculine or feminine) change as well. We will see that development differs for boys and girls, and it can vary considerably across cultures.

Gender-Stereotyped Beliefs

By age 5, gender stereotyping of activities and occupations is well-established. During the school years, knowledge of stereotypes increases in the less obvious areas of personality traits and achievement.

PERSONALITY TRAITS   Research in many cultures reveals that stereotyping of personality traits increases steadily in middle childhood, becoming adultlike around age 11 (Best, 2001; Heyman & Legare, 2004). For example, children regard "tough," "aggressive," "rational," and "dominant" as masculine and "gentle," "affectionate," and "dependent" as feminine (Serbin, Powlishta, & Gulko, 1993).

Children derive these distinctions from observing sex differences in behavior as well as from adult treatment. When helping a child with a task, for example, parents (especially fathers) behave in a more mastery-oriented fashion with sons, setting higher standards, explaining concepts, and pointing out important features of tasks—particularly during gender-typed pursuits, such as science activities (Tenenbaum & Leaper, 2003; Tenenbaum et al., 2005). Furthermore, parents less often encourage girls to make their own decisions. And both parents and teachers more often praise boys for knowledge and accomplishment, girls for obedience (Good & Brophy, 2003; Leaper, Anderson, & Sanders, 1998; Pomerantz & Ruble, 1998).

ACHIEVEMENT AREAS   Shortly after entering elementary school, school-age children quickly figure out which academic subjects and skill areas are "masculine" and which are "feminine." They often regard reading, spelling, art, and music as more for girls and mathematics, athletics, and mechanical skills as more for boys (Eccles, Jacobs, & Harold, 1990; Jacobs & Weisz, 1994). These stereotypes—and the attitudes and behaviors of parents and teachers that promote them—influence children's preferences for and sense of competence at certain subjects. As we saw in our discussion of self-esteem, boys tend to feel more competent than girls

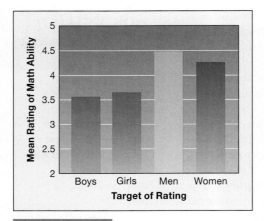

School-age girls' ratings of the math ability of children and adults. The girls regarded children of each gender as equally good at math. Their ratings of adults, however, reverted to the stereotype that men were better at math than women. *(Adapted from Steele, 2003.)*

at math, science, and athletics, and whereas girls feel more competent than boys at language arts (see page 485).

Adults' gender-typed judgments of children's competence can have lasting consequences. In one study, mothers' early perceptions of their children's competence at math continued to predict daughters' self-perceptions and also career choices in their mid-twenties. Young women whose mothers had regarded them as highly capable at math were far more likely to choose a physical science career (Bleeker & Jacobs, 2004). Yet mothers rarely made such optimistic judgments about girls.

Furthermore, girls often adopt a more general stereotype of males as smarter than females, which they apply to themselves. In a study of over 2,000 second to sixth graders from diverse cultures (Eastern and Western Europe, Japan, Russia, and the United States), girls consistently had higher school grades than boys. Yet despite awareness of their better performance, girls did not report stronger beliefs in their own ability but, compared with boys, discounted their talent (Stetsenko et al., 2000). Apparently, gender stereotyping of mental ability occurs in many parts of the world.

One encouraging sign is that some children's gender-stereotyped beliefs about achievement may be changing. In a recent investigation, U.S. elementary school girls from economically advantaged homes regarded children of each gender as equally good at math. But when asked about adults, the girls reverted to the stereotype, saying that men were better than women (see Figure 13.4). Boys, in contrast, held stereotyped views of math ability for both children and adults (Steele, 2003).

TOWARD GREATER FLEXIBILITY Although school-age children are aware of many gender stereotypes, they also develop a more flexible, open-minded view of what males and females *can do,* a trend that continues into adolescence. As they develop the capacity to integrate conflicting social cues, children realize that a person's sex is not a certain predictor of his or her personality traits, activities, and behaviors (Trautner et al., 2005). By the end of the school years, children regard gender typing as socially rather than biologically influenced (Taylor, 1996).

But acknowledging that people *can* cross gender lines does not mean that children always *approve* of doing so. In one longitudinal study, between ages 7 and 13, children generally became more open-minded about girls being offered the same opportunities as boys (Crouter et al., 2007). But the change was less pronounced for boys than girls, and for children whose parents held more traditional gender attitudes.

Furthermore, many school-age children take a harsh view of certain violations—boys playing with dolls and wearing girls' clothing, girls acting noisily and roughly. They are especially intolerant when boys engage in these "cross-gender" acts, which children regard as nearly as bad as moral transgressions (Blakemore, 2003; Levy, Taylor, & Gelman, 1995). When asked for open-ended descriptions of boys and girls, children most often mention girls' physical appearance ("is pretty," "wears dresses") and boys' activities and personality traits ("likes trucks," "is rough") (Miller et al., 2009). The salience of these stereotypes helps explain why, when children of the other sex display the behaviors just mentioned, they are likely to experience severe peer disapproval.

Nevertheless, school-age children do extend more flexible gender attitudes to the peer context to some degree. As with ethnicity, the majority regard excluding an agemate from peer group activities on the basis of gender as unfair. But between fourth and seventh grades, more young people—again, especially boys—say it is OK to exclude on the basis of gender than ethnicity (see Figure 13.5). When asked to explain, they point to concerns about group functioning related to sex differences in interests and communication styles—boys' preference for active pursuits and commanding forceful behavior, girls' preference for quiet activities, politeness, and compromise (Killen et al., 2002, p. 56). Indeed, sex-segregated peer associations strengthen during middle childhood and continue to contribute powerfully to gender typing (see Chapter 10, page 394).

FIGURE 13.5

Percentage of children and adolescents saying "It's OK" to exclude an agemate from a peer-group activity on the basis of gender and ethnicity. When asked about excluding an other-sex or other-ethnicity peer from a peer-group activity (a music club in which members trade CDs), many more young people said that it is OK to do so on the basis of gender than on the basis of ethnicity. Willingness to exclude on the basis of gender increased with age, with many participants justifying their decision by pointing to sex differences in interests and communication styles. *(Adapted from Killen et al., 2002.)*

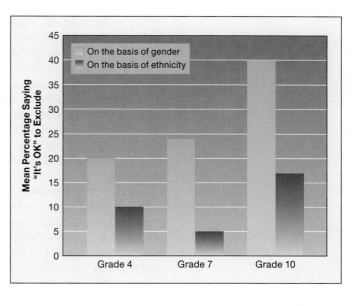

Gender Identity and Behavior

Children who were more strongly gender-typed relative to their agemates in early childhood usually remain so in middle childhood (Golombok et al., 2008). Nevertheless, overall changes do occur, with boys' and girls' gender identities following different paths.

From third to sixth grade, boys tend to strengthen their identification with "masculine" personality traits, whereas girls' identification with "feminine" traits declines. Girls often describe themselves as having some "other-gender" characteristics (Serbin, Powlishta, & Gulko, 1993). And whereas boys usually stick to "masculine" pursuits, many girls experiment with a wider range of options—from cooking and sewing to sports and science projects—and more often consider traditionally male future work roles, such as firefighter or astronomer (Liben & Bigler, 2002).

These changes reflect a mixture of cognitive and social forces. School-age children of both sexes are aware that society attaches greater prestige to "masculine" characteristics. For example, they rate "masculine" occupations as having higher status than "feminine" occupations (Liben, Bigler, & Krogh, 2001). Messages from adults and peers are also influential. In Chapter 10, we saw that parents (especially fathers) are far less tolerant when sons, as opposed to daughters, cross gender lines. Similarly, a tomboyish girl can make her way into boys' activities without losing the approval of her female peers, but a boy who hangs out with girls is likely to be ridiculed and rejected.

As school-age children characterize themselves in terms of general dispositions, their gender identity expands to include the following self-evaluations, which greatly affect their adjustment:

- *Gender typicality*—the degree to which the child feels similar to others of the same gender. Although children need not be highly gender typed to view themselves as gender-typical, their psychological well-being depends, to some degree, on feeling that they "fit in" with their same-sex peers.
- *Gender contentedness*—the degree to which the child feels comfortable with his or her gender assignment, which also promotes happiness.
- *Felt pressure to conform to gender roles*—the degree to which the child feels parents and peers disapprove of his or her gender-related traits. Because such pressure reduces the likelihood that children will explore options related to their interests and talents, children who feel strong gender-typed pressure are often distressed.

■ This 9-year-old girl enjoys karate lessons. Whereas school-age boys usually stick to "masculine" pursuits, girls experiment with a wider range of options. ■

In a longitudinal study of third through seventh graders, *gender-typical* and *gender-contented* children gained in self-esteem over the following year. In contrast, children who were *gender-atypical* and *gender-discontented* declined in self-worth. Furthermore, gender-atypical children who reported *intense pressure to conform to gender roles* experienced serious difficulties—withdrawal, sadness, disappointment, and anxiety (Yunger, Carver, & Perry, 2004).

Clearly, how children feel about themselves in relation to their gender group becomes vitally important in middle childhood and adolescence, and those who experience rejection because of their gender-atypical traits suffer profoundly. **TAKE A MOMENT...** Return to the case of David, the boy who was reared as a girl, on page 392 in Chapter 10. Note how David's dissatisfaction with his gender assignment joined with severe peer condemnation to impair his adjustment.

Currently, researchers and therapists are debating how best to help children who feel gender-atypical. Some favor providing these children with therapy that reinforces them for engaging in traditional gender-role activities, so they will feel more compatible with same-sex peers (Zucker, 2006). Others oppose this approach on grounds that it is likely to heighten felt pressure to conform (which predicts maladjustment) and—for children who fail to change—may result in parental rejection. These experts advocate intervening with parents and peers to help them become more accepting of children's gender-atypical interests and behaviors (Bigler, 2007; Conway, 2007; Crawford, 2003). **TAKE A MOMENT...** In view of what you have learned about the development of children's gender typing in Chapter 10 and this chapter, which approach to you think would be more successful, and why?

ASK YOURSELF

◆ **REVIEW** How does friendship change in middle childhood?

◆ **APPLY** What changes in parent–child relationships are probably necessary to help rejected children?

◆ **CONNECT** Return to page 395 in Chapter 10, and review the concept of androgyny. Which of the two sexes is more androgynous in middle childhood, and why?

◆ **REFLECT** As a school-age child, did you have classmates you would classify as popular-aggressive? What were they like, and why do you think peers admired them?

Family Influences

As children move into school, peer, and community contexts, the parent–child relationship changes. We will see that gradual lessening of direct control supports development as long as parental warmth and involvement are sustained. Our discussion will also reveal that families in industrialized nations have become more diverse. Today, there are fewer births per family unit, more lesbian and gay parents who are open about their sexual orientation, and more never-married parents. Further, high rates of divorce, remarriage, and maternal employment have reshaped the family system. **TAKE A MOMENT...** As you consider this array of family forms, note how children's well-being, in each instance, depends on the quality of family interaction, which is sustained by supportive ties to kin and community and by favorable public policies.

Parent–Child Relationships

In middle childhood, the amount of time children spend with parents declines dramatically. Children's growing independence means that parents must deal with new issues. "I've struggled with how many chores to assign, how much allowance to give, whether their friends are good influences, and what to do about problems at school," Rena remarked. "And then there's the challenge of keeping track of them when they're out—or even when they're home and I'm not there to see what's going on."

Despite these new concerns, child rearing becomes easier for parents who established an authoritative style during the early years. Reasoning is more effective with school-age children because of their greater capacity for logical thinking and their increased respect for parents' expert knowledge (Collins, Madsen, & Susman-Stillman, 2002). When parents communicate openly with children and engage in joint decision making when possible, children are more likely to listen to parents' perspectives in situations where compliance is vital (Kuczynski & Lollis, 2002; Russell, Mize, & Bissaker, 2004).

As children demonstrate that they can manage daily activities and responsibilities, effective parents gradually shift control from adult to child. They do not let go entirely but, rather, engage in **coregulation,** a form of supervision in which they exercise general oversight while letting children take charge of moment-by-moment decision making. Coregulation grows out of a warm, cooperative relationship between parent and child based on give-and-take and mutual respect. Parents must guide and monitor from a distance and effectively communicate expectations when they are with their children. And children must inform parents of their whereabouts, activities, and problems so parents can intervene when necessary (Maccoby, 1984). Coregulation supports and protects children while preparing them for adolescence, when they will make many important decisions themselves.

As at younger ages, mothers spend more time than fathers with school-age children and know more about children's everyday activities, although many fathers are highly involved (see pages 274–275 in Chapter 7). Both parents, however, tend to devote more time to children of their own sex (Crouter et al., 1999; Lamb & Lewis, 2004). In parents' separate activities with children, mothers are more concerned with caregiving and ensuring that children meet responsibilities for homework, after-school lessons, and chores. Fathers, especially those with sons, focus on achievement-related and recreational pursuits (Collins & Russell, 1991). But when both parents are present, fathers engage in as much caregiving as mothers.

Although children often press for greater independence, they also know how much they need their parents' support. In one study, fifth and sixth graders described parents as the most influential people in their lives, often turning to them for affection, advice, enhancement of self-worth, and assistance with everyday problems (Furman & Buhrmester, 1992). A strong sense of attachment security to both parents is positively related to school-age children's academic and social self-esteem (Diener et al., 2008). And in a longitudinal survey of more than 13,000 nationally representative U.S. parents, those who were warm and involved, monitored their child's activities, and avoided coercive discipline were more likely to have academically and socially competent children. Using these authoritative strategies in middle childhood predicted reduced engagement in antisocial behavior when children reached adolescence (Amato & Fowler, 2002).

Siblings

In addition to parents and friends, siblings continue to be important sources of support. Yet sibling rivalry tends to increase in middle childhood. As children participate in a wider range of activities, parents often compare siblings' traits and accomplishments. The child who gets less parental affection, more disapproval, or fewer material resources is likely to be resentful and show poorer adjustment over time (Dunn, 2004; Tamrouti-Makkink et al., 2004).

For same-sex siblings who are close in age, parental comparisons are more frequent, resulting in more quarreling and antagonism and in poorer adjustment. This effect is particularly strong when parents are under stress as a result of financial worries, marital conflict, single parenthood, or child negativity (Jenkins, Rasbash, & O'Connor, 2003). Parents whose energies are drained become less careful about being fair. Perhaps because fathers, overall, spend less time with children than mothers, children react especially intensely when fathers prefer one child (Brody, Stoneman, & McCoy, 1992).

To reduce this rivalry, siblings often strive to be different from one another. For example, two brothers I know deliberately selected different athletic pursuits and musical instruments. If the older one did especially well at an activity, the younger one did not want to try it. Parents can limit these effects by making an effort not to compare children, but some feedback about

© BRUCE LAURANCE/GETTY IMAGES/BLEND IMAGES

■ Although sibling rivalry tends to increase in middle childhood, siblings also provide each other with emotional support and, sometimes, patient help with difficult tasks. ■

their competencies is inevitable. As siblings attempt to win recognition for their own uniqueness, they shape important aspects of each other's development.

Although conflict rises, many siblings continue to rely on each other for companionship, assistance, and emotional support (Siebert & Kerns, 2009). When researchers asked siblings about shared daily activities, children mentioned that older siblings often helped younger siblings with academic and peer challenges. And both offered each other help with family issues (Tucker, McHale, & Crouter, 2001). But for siblings to reap these benefits, parental encouragement of warm, considerate sibling ties is vital. Providing parents with training in mediation—how to get siblings to lay down ground rules, clarify their points of disagreement and common ground, and discuss possible solutions—increases siblings' awareness of each other's perspectives and reduces animosity (Smith & Ross, 2007).

When siblings get along well, the older sibling's academic and social competence tends to "rub off on" the younger sibling, fostering more favorable achievement and peer relations (Brody & Murry, 2001; Lamarche et al., 2006). But older siblings with conflict-ridden peer relations tend to transmit their physically or relationally aggressive styles to their younger brothers and sisters (Ostrov, Crick, & Stauffacher, 2006).

Only Children

Although sibling relationships bring many benefits, they are not essential for normal development. Contrary to popular belief, only children are not spoiled, and, in some respects, they are advantaged. U.S. children growing up in one-child and multichild families do not differ in self-rated personality traits (Mottus, Indus, & Allik, 2008). And compared to children with siblings, only children are higher in self-esteem and achievement motivation, do better in school, and attain higher levels of education. One reason may be that only children have somewhat closer relationships with parents, who may exert more pressure for mastery and accomplishment (Falbo, 1992). Furthermore, only children have just as many close, high-quality friends as children with siblings. However, they tend to be less well-accepted in the peer group, perhaps because they have not had opportunities to learn effective conflict-resolution strategies through sibling interaction (Kitzmann, Cohen, & Lockwood, 2002).

Favorable development also characterizes only children in China, where a one-child family policy has been strictly enforced in urban areas for more than two decades to control population growth (Yang, 2008). Compared with agemates who have siblings, Chinese only children are advanced in cognitive development and academic achievement. They also feel more emotionally secure, perhaps because government disapproval promotes tension in families with more than one child (Falbo & Poston, 1993; Jiao, Ji, & Jing, 1996; Yang et al., 1995). Chinese mothers usually ensure that their children have regular contact with first cousins (who are considered siblings). Perhaps as a result, Chinese only children do not differ from agemates with siblings in social skills and peer acceptance (Hart, Newell, & Olsen, 2003). The next generation of Chinese only children, however, will have no first cousins.

Gay and Lesbian Families

Several million American gay men and lesbians are parents, most through previous heterosexual marriages, some through adoption, and a growing number through reproductive technologies (Ambert, 2005; Patterson, 2002). In the past, because of laws assuming that homosexuals could not be adequate parents, those who divorced a heterosexual partner lost custody of their children. Today, some U.S. states hold that sexual orientation in itself is irrelevant to custody. A few U.S. states, however, ban gay and lesbian couples from adopting children. Among other countries, gay and lesbian adoptions are legal in Argentina, Belgium, Canada, Mexico, the Netherlands, Norway, Spain, Sweden, the United Kingdom, and Uruguay.

Most research on homosexual parents and children is limited to volunteer samples. Findings of these investigations indicate that gay and lesbian parents are as committed to and effective at child rearing as heterosexual parents and sometimes more so (Bos, van Balen, & van den Boom, 2007; Tasker, 2005). Also, whether born to or adopted by their parents or conceived through donor insemination, children in gay and lesbian families did not differ from the children of heterosexuals in mental health, peer relations, or gender identity (Allen & Burrell, 1996; Farr, Forssell, & Patterson, 2010; Golombok & Tasker, 1996). Two additional studies, which surmounted the potential bias associated with volunteer samples by including all lesbian-mother families who had conceived children at a fertility clinic, also reported that children were developing favorably (Brewaeys et al., 1997; Chan, Raboy, & Patterson, 1998). Likewise, among participants drawn from a representative sample of British mothers and their 7-year-olds, children reared in lesbian-mother families did not differ from children reared in heterosexual families in adjustment and gender-role preferences (Golombok et al., 2003).

■ Gay and lesbian parents are as committed to and as effective at child rearing as heterosexual parents. Their children are well-adjusted, and the large majority develop a heterosexual orientation. ■

Furthermore, children of gay and lesbian parents do not differ from other children in sexual orientation: The large majority are heterosexual (Tasker, 2005). But some evidence suggests that more adolescents from homosexual families experiment for a time with partners of both sexes, perhaps as a result of being reared in families and communities highly tolerant of nonconformity and difference (Bos, van Balen, & van den Boom, 2004; Stacey & Biblarz, 2001).

A major concern of gay and lesbian parents is that their children will be stigmatized by their parents' sexual orientation. Most studies indicate that incidents of teasing or bullying are rare because parents and children carefully manage the information they reveal to others (Tasker, 2005). But in an Australian study, even though most third to tenth graders were guarded about discussing their parents' relationship with peers, nearly half reported harassment (Ray & Gregory, 2001). Overall, children of gay and lesbian parents can be distinguished from other children mainly by issues related to living in a nonsupportive society.

Never-Married Single-Parent Families

About 10 percent of U.S. children live with a single parent who has never married and does not have a partner. Of these parents, about 85 percent are mothers, 15 percent fathers (U.S. Census Bureau, 2010b). In recent years, more single women over age 30 in high-status occupations have become parents. But they are still few in number, and little is known about their children's development.

In the United States, African-American young women make up the largest group of never-married parents. About 64 percent of births to black mothers in their twenties are to women without a partner, compared with 28 percent of births to white women (U.S. Census Bureau, 2010b). African-American women postpone marriage more and childbirth less than women in other U.S. ethnic groups. Job loss, persisting unemployment, and consequent inability of many black men to support a family have contributed to the number of African-American never-married, single-mother families.

Never-married black mothers tap the extended family, especially their own mothers and sometimes male relatives, for help in rearing their children (Gasden, 1999; Jayakody & Kalil, 2002). For about one-third, marriage—not necessarily to the child's biological father—occurs within nine years after birth of the first child (Wu, Bumpass, & Musick, 2001). These couples function much like other first-marriage parents. Their children often are unaware that the father is a stepfather, and parents do not report the child-rearing difficulties typical of blended families (Ganong & Coleman, 1994).

Still, for low-SES women, never-married parenthood generally increases financial hardship. Nearly 50 percent of white mothers and 60 percent of black mothers have a second child while unmarried. And they are far less likely than divorced mothers to receive paternal child support payments, although child support enforcement both reduces financial stress and increases father involvement (Huang, 2006).

Children in single-mother homes display adjustment problems associated with economic hardship and living in run-down neighborhoods (Kotchick, Dorsey, & Heller, 2005). Furthermore, children of never-married mothers who lack a father's warmth and involvement achieve less well in school and engage in more antisocial behavior than children in low-SES, first-marriage families (Coley, 1998). But marriage to the child's biological father benefits children only when the father is a reliable source of economic and emotional support. When a mother pairs up with an antisocial father, her child is at far greater risk for conduct problems than if she had reared the child alone (Jaffee et al., 2003). Strengthening social support, education, and employment opportunities for low-SES parents would greatly enhance the well-being of unmarried mothers and their children.

Divorce

Children's interactions with parents and siblings are affected by other aspects of family life. Joey and Lizzie's relationship, Rena told me, had been particularly negative only a few years before. Joey pushed, hit, taunted, and called Lizzie names. Although she tried to retaliate, Lizzie was no match for Joey's larger size. The arguments usually ended with Lizzie running in tears to her mother. Joey and Lizzie's fighting coincided with their parents' growing marital unhappiness. When Joey was 8 and Lizzie 5, their father, Drake, moved out.

Between 1960 and 1985, divorce rates in Western nations rose dramatically before stabilizing in most countries. The United States has experienced a decline in divorces over the past decade, largely due to a rise in age at first marriage (couples marrying at older ages have a lower divorce rate) (Amato & Dorius, 2010). Nevertheless, the United States continues to have the highest divorce rate in the world (see Figure 13.6). Of the 45 percent of American marriages that end in divorce, half involve children. At any given time, one-fourth of U.S. children live in single-parent households. Although most reside with their mothers, the percentage in father-headed households has increased steadily, to about 12 percent (Federal Interagency Forum on Child and Family Statistics, 2008).

Children of divorce spend an average of five years in a single-parent home—almost a third of childhood. For many, divorce leads to new family relationships. About two-thirds of divorced parents marry again. Half their children eventually experience a third major change—the end of their parent's second marriage (Hetherington & Kelly, 2002).

These figures reveal that divorce is not a single event in the lives of parents and children. Instead, it is a transition that leads to a variety of new living arrangements, accompanied by changes in housing, income, and family roles and responsibilities. Since the 1960s, many studies have reported that marital breakup is stressful for children. But research also reveals great individual differences (Hetherington, 2003). How well children fare depends on many factors: the custodial parent's psychological health, the child's characteristics, and social supports within the family and surrounding community.

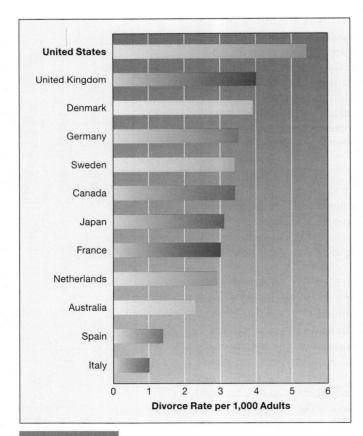

FIGURE 13.6

Divorce rates in 12 industrialized nations. The U.S. divorce rate is the highest in the world, far exceeding divorce rates in other countries. *(Adapted from U.S. Census Bureau, 2010b.)*

IMMEDIATE CONSEQUENCES "Things were worst during the period when Drake and I decided to separate," Rena reflected. "We fought over division of our belongings and the custody of the children, and the kids suffered. Sobbing, Lizzie told me she was 'sorry she made Daddy go away.' Joey kicked and threw things at home and didn't do his work at school. In the midst of everything, I could hardly deal with their problems. We had to sell the house; I couldn't afford it alone. And I needed a better-paying job."

Family conflict often rises in newly divorced households as parents try to settle disputes over children and possessions. Once one parent moves out, additional events threaten supportive inter- actions between parents and children. Mother-headed house- holds typically experience a sharp drop in income. In the United States, the majority of divorced mothers with young children live in poverty, getting less than the full amount of child support from the absent father or none at all (Children's Defense Fund, 2009). They often have to move to lower-cost housing, reducing sup- portive ties to neighbors and friends.

The transition from marriage to divorce typically leads to high maternal stress, depression, and anxiety and to a disorganized family situation. Declines in well-being are greatest for mothers of young children (Williams & Dunne-Bryant, 2006). "Meals and bedtimes were at all hours, the house didn't get cleaned, and I stopped taking Joey and Lizzie on weekend outings," said Rena. As children react with distress and anger to their less secure home lives, discipline may become harsh and inconsistent. Contact with noncustodial fathers often decreases over time (Hetherington & Kelly, 2002). Fathers who see their children only occasionally are inclined to be permissive and indulgent, making the mother's task of managing the child even more difficult.

The more parents argue and fail to provide children with warmth, involvement, and con- sistent guidance, the poorer children's adjustment. About 20 to 25 percent of children in divorced families display severe problems, compared with about 10 percent in nondivorced families (Lansford, 2009; Noller et al., 2008). At the same time, reactions vary with children's age, temperament, and sex.

■ When parents divorce, young children often blame themselves and respond with both fear and anger. This father's soothing words help his daughter understand that she is not responsible for the marital breakup. ■

Children's Age. Five-year-old Lizzie's fear that she had caused her father to leave home is not unusual. Preschool and young school-age children often blame themselves for a marital breakup and fear that both parents may abandon them (Lansford et al., 2006). Hence, they are more likely to display both anxious, fearful and angry, defiant reactions than older children and adolescents with the cognitive maturity to understand that they are not responsible for their parents' divorce.

Still, many school-age and adolescent youngsters also react strongly, experiencing depressed mood, declining in school performance, becoming unruly, and escaping into unde- sirable peer activities, such as running away, truancy, and early sexual activity, particularly when family conflict is high and parental supervision is low (D'Onofrio et al., 2006; Lansford et al., 2006). Some older children—especially the oldest child in the family—display more mature behavior, willingly taking on extra household tasks, care of younger siblings, and emo- tional support of a depressed, anxious mother. But if these demands are too great, these chil- dren may eventually become resentful, withdraw from the family, and engage in angry, acting-out behavior (Hetherington, 1999).

Children's Temperament and Sex. Exposure to stressful life events and inadequate parenting magnifies the problems of temperamentally difficult children (Lengua et al., 2000). In contrast, easy children are less often targets of parental anger and also cope more effectively with adversity.

These findings help explain sex differences in response to divorce. Girls sometimes respond as Lizzie did, with internalizing reactions such as crying, self-criticism, and with- drawal. More often, children of both sexes show demanding, attention-getting behavior. But in mother-custody families, boys are at slightly greater risk for serious adjustment problems

(Amato, 2001, 2010). Recall from Chapter 10 that boys are more active and noncompliant—behaviors that increase with exposure to parental conflict and inconsistent discipline. Research reveals that long before the marital breakup, sons of divorcing couples display higher rates of impulsivity, defiance, and aggression—behaviors that may have been caused by their parents' marital problems while also contributing to them (Hetherington, 1999; Shaw, Winslow, & Flanagan, 1999; Strohschein, 2005). As a result, more boys enter the period of turmoil surrounding divorce with reduced capacity to cope with family stress.

Perhaps because their behavior is more unruly, boys of divorcing parents receive less emotional support from mothers, teachers, and peers. And as Joey's behavior toward Lizzie illustrates, the coercive cycles of interaction between distressed children and their divorced mothers soon spread to sibling relations (Hetherington & Kelly, 2002; Sheehan et al., 2004). After divorce, children who are challenging to rear generally get worse.

LONG-TERM CONSEQUENCES   Rena eventually found better-paying work and gained control over the daily operation of the household. Her own feelings of anger and rejection also declined. And after several meetings with a counselor, Rena and Drake realized the harmful impact of their quarreling on Joey and Lizzie. Drake visited regularly and handled Joey's disruptiveness with firmness and consistency. Soon Joey's school performance improved, his behavior problems subsided, and both children seemed calmer and happier.

Most children show improved adjustment by two years after divorce. Yet overall, children and adolescents of divorced parents continue to score slightly lower than children of continuously married parents in academic achievement, self-esteem, social competence, and emotional and behavioral adjustment (Amato, 2001; Lansford, 2009). Children with difficult temperaments are more likely to drop out of school, to be depressed, and to engage in antisocial behavior in adolescence. And divorce is linked to problems with adolescent sexuality and development of intimate ties. Young people who experienced parental divorce—especially more than once—display higher rates of early sexual activity and adolescent parenthood (Wolfinger, 2000). Some experience other lasting difficulties—reduced educational attainment, troubled romantic relationships and marriages, divorce in adulthood, and unsatisfying parent–child relationships (Amato, 2006, 2010; Lansford, 2009). Thus, divorce can have consequences for subsequent generations.

The overriding factor in positive adjustment following divorce is effective parenting—how well the custodial parent handles stress and shields the child from family conflict, and the extent to which each parent uses authoritative child rearing (Leon, 2003; Wolchik et al., 2000). Where the custodial parent is the mother, regular contact with fathers is also important. In the United States, paternal contact has risen over the past three decades, with about one-third of children today experiencing at least weekly visits (Amato & Dorius, 2010).

The more paternal contact and the warmer the relationship, the less children react with defiance and aggression (Dunn et al., 2004). For girls, a good father–child relationship protects against early sexual activity and unhappy romantic involvements. For boys, it seems to affect overall psychological well-being. In fact, several studies report that outcomes for sons are better when the father is the custodial parent (Clarke-Stewart & Hayward, 1996; McLanahan, 1999). Fathers' greater economic security and image of authority seem to help them engage in effective parenting with sons. And boys in father-custody families may benefit from greater involvement of both parents because noncustodial mothers participate more in their children's lives than noncustodial fathers.

Although divorce is painful for children, remaining in an intact but high-conflict family is much worse than making the transition to a low-conflict, single-parent household (Greene et al., 2003; Strohschein, 2005). However, more parents today are divorcing because they are moderately (rather than extremely) dissatisfied with their relationship. Research suggests that children in these low-discord homes are especially puzzled and upset. Perhaps these youngsters' inability to understand the

■ Regular contact with fathers as well as mothers is an important factor in children's adjustment after divorce. In fact, some evidence indicates that sons do better when the father is the custodial parent. ■

marital breakup and grief over the loss of a seemingly happy home life explain why the adjustment problems of children of divorce have intensified over time (Amato, 2001; Lansford, 2009).

Regardless of the extent of their friction, parents who set aside their disagreements and engage in *coparenting* (see page 70 in Chapter 2), supporting each other in their child-rearing roles, greatly improve their children's chances of growing up competent, stable, and happy. Caring extended-family members, teachers, siblings, and friends also reduce the likelihood that divorce will result in long-term difficulties (Hetherington, 2003; Lussier et al., 2002).

DIVORCE MEDIATION, JOINT CUSTODY, AND CHILD SUPPORT   Awareness that divorce is highly stressful for children and families has led to community-based services aimed at helping them through this difficult time. One such service is **divorce mediation,** a series of meetings between divorcing adults and a trained professional aimed at reducing family conflict, including legal battles over property division and child custody. Research reveals that mediation increases out-of-court settlements, cooperation and involvement of both parents in child rearing, and parents' and children's feelings of well-being (Douglas, 2006; Emery, Sbarra, & Grover, 2005).

To further encourage parents to resolve their disputes, parent education programs are becoming common. During a series of weekly sessions over several months, professionals teach parents about the positive impact of constructive conflict resolution and of coparenting on children's well-being (Braver et al., 2005; Cookston et al., 2006; Wolchik et al., 2002). Because of the demonstrated impact of parent education on parental cooperation, courts in many U.S. states may require parents to attend a program.

Joint custody, which grants each parent an equal say in important decisions about the child's upbringing, is becoming increasingly common. Children usually reside with one parent and see the other on a fixed schedule, similar to the typical sole-custody situation. In other cases, parents share physical custody, and children move between homes and sometimes between schools and peer groups. These transitions can be especially hard on some children. Joint-custody parents usually report little conflict—fortunately so, since the success of the arrangement depends on coparenting. And their children, regardless of living arrangements, tend to be better-adjusted than children in sole-maternal-custody homes (Bauserman, 2002).

Finally, many single-parent families depend on child support from the absent parent to relieve financial strain. All U.S. states have procedures for withholding wages from parents who fail to make these payments. Although child support is usually not enough to lift a single-parent family out of poverty, it can ease its burdens substantially. Noncustodial fathers who have generous visitation schedules and who often see their children are more likely to pay child support regularly (Amato & Sobolewski, 2004). Applying What We Know on page 514 summarizes ways to help children adjust to their parents' divorce.

Blended Families

"If you get married to Wendell and Daddy gets married to Carol," Lizzie wondered aloud to Rena, "then I'll have two sisters and one more brother. And let's see, how many grandmothers and grandfathers? A lot!" exclaimed Lizzie.

About 60 percent of divorced parents remarry within a few years. Others *cohabit,* or share a sexual relationship and a residence with a partner outside of marriage. Parent, stepparent, and children form a new family structure called a **blended,** or **reconstituted, family.** For some children, this expanded family network is positive, bringing greater adult attention. But overall, they have more adjustment problems—including internalizing and externalizing symptoms and poor school performance—than children in stable, first-marriage families (Jeynes, 2007; Nicholson et al., 2008). Switching to stepparents' new rules and expectations can be stressful, and children often regard steprelatives as intruders. How well they adapt is, again, related to the quality of family functioning (Hetherington & Kelly, 2002). This depends on which parent forms a new relationship, the child's age and sex, and the complexity of blended-family relationships. As we will see, older children and girls seem to have the hardest time.

Applying What We Know

Helping Children Adjust to Their Parents' Divorce

SUGGESTION	EXPLANATION
Shield children from conflict.	Witnessing intense parental conflict is very damaging to children. If one parent insists on expressing hostility, children fare better if the other parent does not respond in kind.
Provide children with as much continuity, familiarity, and predictability as possible.	Children adjust better during the period surrounding divorce when their lives have some stability—for example, the same school, bedroom, babysitter, playmates, and daily schedule.
Explain the divorce and tell children what to expect.	Children are more likely to develop fears of abandonment if they are not prepared for their parents' separation. They should be told that their parents will not be living together anymore, which parent will be moving out, and when they will be able to see that parent. If possible, parents should explain the divorce together, providing a reason that the child can understand and assure the child that he is not to blame.
Emphasize the permanence of the divorce.	Fantasies of parents getting back together can prevent children from accepting the reality of their current life. Children should be told that the divorce is final and that they cannot change this fact.
Respond sympathetically to children's feelings.	Children need a supportive and understanding response to their feelings of sadness, fear, and anger. For children to adjust well, their painful emotions must be acknowledged, not denied or avoided.
Engage in authoritative parenting.	Parents who engage in authoritative parenting—providing affection and acceptance, reasonable demands for mature behavior, and consistent, rational discipline—greatly reduce their children's risk of maladjustment following divorce.
Promote a continuing relationship with both parents.	When parents disentangle their lingering hostility toward the former spouse from the child's need for a continuing relationship with the other parent, children adjust well. Grandparents and other extended-family members can help by not taking sides.

Source: Teyber, 2001.

MOTHER–STEPFATHER FAMILIES   Since mothers generally retain custody of children, the most common form of blended family is a mother–stepfather arrangement. Boys tend to adjust quickly, welcoming a stepfather who is warm, who refrains from exerting his authority too quickly, and who offers relief from coercive cycles of mother–son interaction. Mothers' friction with sons also declines as a result of greater economic security, another adult to share household tasks, and an end to loneliness (Visher, Visher, & Pasley, 2003). Stepfathers who marry rather than cohabit are more involved in parenting, perhaps because men who choose to marry a mother with children are more interested in and skilled at child rearing (Hofferth & Anderson, 2003). Girls, however, often have difficulty with their custodial mother's remarriage. Stepfathers disrupt the close ties many girls have established with their mothers, and girls often react with sulky, resistant behavior (Bray, 1999).

But age affects these findings. Older school-age children and adolescents of both sexes display more irresponsible, acting-out behavior than their peers not in stepfamilies (Hetherington & Stanley-Hagan, 2000; Robertson, 2008). If parents are warmer and more involved with their biological children than with their stepchildren, older children are more likely to notice and challenge unfair treatment. And adolescents often view the new stepparent as a threat to their freedom, especially if they experienced little parental monitoring in the single-parent family. But when teenagers have affectionate, cooperative relationships with their mothers, many eventually develop good relationships with their stepfathers—a circumstance linked to more favorable adolescent well-being (Yuan & Hamilton, 2006).

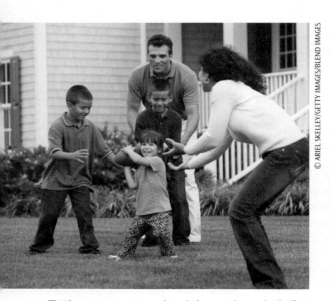

■ When stepparents move into their new roles gradually, first building warm relationships with stepchildren, they ease adjustment to life in a blended family. ■

© ARIEL SKELLEY/GETTY IMAGES/BLEND IMAGES

FATHER–STEPMOTHER FAMILIES Remarriage of noncustodial fathers often leads to reduced contact with their biological children, especially when fathers remarry quickly, before they have established post-divorce parent–child routines (Dunn, 2002; Juby et al., 2007). When fathers have custody, children typically react negatively to remarriage. One reason is that children living with fathers often start out with more problems. Perhaps the biological mother could no longer handle the difficult child (usually a boy), so the father and his new partner are faced with a youngster who has behavior problems. In other instances, the father has custody because of a very close relationship with the child, and his remarriage disrupts this bond (Buchanan, Maccoby, & Dornbusch, 1996).

Girls, especially, have a hard time getting along with their stepmothers, either because the remarriage threatens the girl's bond with her father or because she becomes entangled in loyalty conflicts between the two mother figures. But the longer children live in father–stepmother households, the closer they feel to their stepmothers and the more positive their interaction with them becomes (Hetherington & Jodl, 1994; King, 2007). With time and patience, children of both genders benefit from the support of a second mother figure.

SUPPORT FOR BLENDED FAMILIES Parenting education and couples counseling can help parents and children adapt to the complexities of blended families. Effective approaches encourage stepparents to move into their new roles gradually by first building a warm relationship with the child. Only when a warm bond has formed between stepparents and stepchildren is more active parenting possible (Nicholson et al., 2008). Counselors can offer couples guidance in coparenting to limit loyalty conflicts and provide consistency in child rearing. This allows children to benefit from the increased diversity that stepparent relationships bring to their lives.

Unfortunately, the divorce rate for second marriages is even higher than for first marriages. Parents with antisocial tendencies and poor child-rearing skills are particularly likely to have several divorces and remarriages. The more marital transitions children experience, the greater their adjustment difficulties (Amato, 2010). These families usually require prolonged, intensive therapy.

Maternal Employment and Dual-Earner Families

Today, U.S. single and married mothers are in the labor market in nearly equal proportions, and more than three-fourths of those with school-age children are employed (U.S. Census Bureau, 2010b). In Chapter 7, we saw that the impact of maternal employment on early development depends on the quality of child care and the continuing parent–child relationship. The same is true in middle childhood.

MATERNAL EMPLOYMENT AND CHILD DEVELOPMENT When mothers enjoy their work and remain committed to parenting, children show favorable adjustment—higher self-esteem, more positive family and peer relations, less gender-stereotyped beliefs, and better grades in school. Girls, especially, profit from the image of female competence. Regardless of SES, daughters of employed mothers perceive women's roles as involving more freedom of choice and satisfaction and are more achievement- and career-oriented (Hoffman, 2000).

Parenting practices contribute to these benefits. Employed mothers who value their parenting role are more likely to use authoritative child rearing and coregulation. Also, children in dual-earner households devote more daily hours to doing homework under parental guidance and participate more in household chores. And maternal employment leads fathers—especially those who believe in the importance of the paternal role and who feel successful at parenting—to take on greater child-rearing responsibilities, with a small but increasing number staying home full-time (Gottfried, Gottfried, & Bathurst, 2002; Jacobs & Kelley, 2006). Paternal involvement is associated with higher intelligence and achievement, more mature social behavior, and a flexible view of gender

© SIMON JARRATT/CORBIS

■ Employed mothers who enjoy their work while also valuing the parenting role tend to have children who show higher self-esteem, more positive family and peer relations, less gender-stereotyped beliefs, and better school performance. ■

roles in childhood and adolescence, and with generally better mental health in adulthood (Coltrane, 1996; Pleck & Masciadrelli, 2004).

But when employment places heavy demands on the mother's schedule or is stressful for other reasons, children are at risk for ineffective parenting. Working many hours or experiencing a negative workplace atmosphere is associated with reduced parental sensitivity, fewer joint parent–child activities, and poorer cognitive development throughout childhood and adolescence (Brooks-Gunn, Han, & Waldfogel, 2002; Bumpus, Crouter, & McHale, 2006; Strazdins et al., 2006). Negative consequences are magnified when low-SES mothers spend long days at low-paying, physically exhausting jobs—conditions linked to maternal depression and to harsh, inconsistent discipline (Raver, 2003). In contrast, part-time employment and flexible work schedules are associated with good child adjustment (Frederiksen-Goldsen & Sharlach, 2000; Hill et al., 2006). By preventing work–family life conflict, these arrangements help parents meet children's needs.

SUPPORT FOR EMPLOYED PARENTS AND THEIR FAMILIES   In dual-earner families, the father's willingness to share responsibilities is a crucial factor. If he helps little or not at all, the mother carries a double load, at home and at work, leading to fatigue, distress, and little time and energy for children. Fortunately, compared to three decades ago, today's U.S. fathers are far more involved in child care (see page 275 in Chapter 7). But their increased participation has resulted in a growing number of fathers who also report work–family life conflict (Galinsky, Aumann, & Bond, 2009).

Employed parents need assistance from work settings and communities in their child-rearing roles. Part-time employment, flexible schedules, job sharing, and paid leave when children are ill help parents juggle the demands of work and child rearing. Equal pay and employment opportunities for women are also important. Because these policies enhance financial status and morale, they improve the way mothers feel and behave when they arrive home at the end of the working day.

CHILD CARE FOR SCHOOL-AGE CHILDREN   High-quality child care is vital for parents' peace of mind and children's well-being, even during middle childhood. An estimated 7 million 5- to 13-year-olds in the United States are **self-care children,** who regularly look after themselves for some period of time during after-school hours (Durlak & Weissberg, 2007). Self-care increases with age and also with SES, perhaps because of the greater safety of higher-income neighborhoods. But when lower-SES parents lack alternatives to self-care, their children spend more hours on their own (Casper & Smith, 2002).

Some studies report that self-care children suffer from low self-esteem, antisocial behavior, poor academic achievement, and fearfulness. Others show no such effects. Children's maturity and the way they spend their time seem to explain these contradictions. Among younger school-age children, those who spend more hours alone have more adjustment difficulties (Vandell & Posner, 1999). As children become old enough to look after themselves, those who have a history of authoritative child rearing, are monitored by parental telephone calls, and have regular after-school chores appear responsible and well-adjusted. In contrast, children left to their own devices are more likely to bend to peer pressures and engage in antisocial behavior (Coley, Morris, & Hernandez, 2004; Vandell et al., 2006).

Before age 8 or 9, most children need supervision because they are not yet competent to handle emergencies (Galambos & Maggs, 1991). But throughout middle childhood and early adolescence, attending after-school programs with well-trained staffs, generous adult–child ratios, and skill-building activities is linked to good school performance and emotional and social adjustment (Durlak & Weissberg, 2007; Granger, 2008). Low-SES children who participate in "after-care" programs offering academic assistance and enrichment activities (scouting, music and art lessons, clubs) show special benefits. They exceed their

■ In this after-school program, children learn about fossils from an AmeriCorps volunteer. Attending high-quality after-school programs is linked to good school performance and emotional and social adjustment. ■

self-care counterparts in classroom work habits, academic achievement, and prosocial behavior and display fewer behavior problems (Lauer et al., 2006; Vandell et al., 2006).

Unfortunately, good after-care is in especially short supply in low-income neighborhoods, and children from the very poorest families are least likely to participate in enrichment activities (Afterschool Alliance, 2004; Dearing et al., 2009). A special need exists for well-planned programs in poverty-stricken areas—ones that provide safe environments, warm relationships with adults, and enjoyable, goal-oriented activities.

ASK YOURSELF

◆ REVIEW Describe and explain changes in sibling relationships during middle childhood.

◆ APPLY Steve and Marissa are in the midst of an acrimonious divorce. Their 9-year-old son Dennis has become hostile and defiant. How can Steve and Marissa help Dennis adjust?

◆ CONNECT How does each level in Bronfenbrenner's ecological systems theory—microsystem, mesosystem, exosystem, and macrosystem—contribute to the effects of maternal employment on children's development?

◆ REFLECT What after-school child-care arrangements did you experience in elementary school? How do you think they influenced your development?

Some Common Problems of Development

We have considered a variety of stressful experiences that place children at risk for future problems. Next, we address two more areas of concern: school-age children's fears and anxieties and the consequences of child sexual abuse. Finally, we sum up factors that help school-age children cope effectively with stress.

Fears and Anxieties

Although fears of the dark, thunder and lightning, and supernatural beings persist into middle childhood, older children's anxieties are also directed toward new concerns. As children begin to understand the realities of the wider world, the possibility of personal harm (being robbed, stabbed, or shot) and media events (war and disasters) often trouble them. Other common worries include academic failure, separation from parents, parents' health, physical injuries, the possibility of dying, and peer rejection (Muris et al., 2000; Weems & Costa, 2005). Because children often mull over frightening thoughts at bedtime, nighttime fears actually increase between ages 7 and 9 (Muris et al., 2001).

Children in Western nations mention exposure to negative information in the media as the most common source of their fears, followed by direct exposure to frightening events (Muris et al., 2001). Nevertheless, as we saw in Chapters 10 and 12, many parents have no rules about their children's TV viewing or computer use, including Internet access.

As long as fears are not too intense, most children handle them constructively, using the more sophisticated emotional self-regulation strategies that develop in middle childhood. Consequently, fears decline with age, especially for girls, who express more fears than boys throughout childhood and adolescence (Gullone, 2000). But about 5 percent of school-age children develop an intense, unmanageable fear, called a **phobia.** Children with inhibited temperaments are at high risk, displaying phobias five to six times as often as other children (Ollendick, King, & Muris, 2002).

For example, in *school phobia,* children feel severe apprehension about attending school, often accompanied by physical complaints (dizziness, nausea, stomachaches, and vomiting). About one-third of children with school phobia are 5- to 7-year-olds for whom the real fear is maternal separation. Family therapy helps these children, whose difficulty can often be traced to parental overprotection (Elliott, 1999).

CULTURAL INFLUENCES

Impact of Ethnic and Political Violence on Children

Around the world, many children live with armed conflict, terrorism, and other acts of violence stemming from ethnic and political tensions. Some children may participate in fighting, either because they are forced or because they want to please adults. Others are kidnapped, assaulted, and tortured. Those who are bystanders often come under direct fire and may be killed or physically maimed. And many watch in horror as family members, friends, and neighbors flee, are wounded, or die. In the past decade, wars have left 6 million children physically disabled, 20 million homeless, and more than 1 million separated from their parents (Ursano & Shaw, 2007; Wexler, Branski, & Kerem, 2006).

When war and social crises are temporary, most children can be comforted and do not show long-term emotional difficulties. But chronic danger requires children to make substantial adjustments that can seriously impair their psychological functioning. Many children of war lose their sense of safety, become desensitized to violence, are haunted by terrifying intrusive memories, are impaired in moral reasoning, and build a pessimistic view of the future. Anxiety and depression increase, as do aggression and antisocial behavior (Joshi et al., 2006; Klingman, 2006). These outcomes appear to be culturally universal, appearing among children from every war zone studied—from Bosnia, Angola, Rwanda, and the Sudan to the West Bank, Afghanistan, and Iraq (Barenbaum, Ruchkin, & Schwab-Stone, 2004).

Parental affection and reassurance are the best protection against lasting problems. When parents offer security, discuss traumatic experiences with children sympathetically, and serve as role models of calm emotional strength, most

children can withstand even extreme war-related violence (Gewirtz, Forgatch, & Wieling, 2008; Smith et al., 2001). Children who are separated from parents must rely on help from their communities. Orphans in Eritrea who were placed in residential settings where they could form close emotional ties with an adult showed less emotional stress five years later than orphans placed in impersonal settings (Wolff & Fesseha, 1999). Education and recreation programs are powerful safeguards, too, providing children with consistency in their lives along with teacher and peer supports.

With the September 11, 2001, terrorist attacks on the World Trade Center, some U.S. children experienced extreme wartime violence firsthand. Children in Public School 31 in Brooklyn, New York, for example, watched through classroom windows as the planes struck the towers and were engulfed in flames and as the towers crumbled. Many worried about the safety of family members, and some lost them. In the aftermath, most expressed intense fears—for example, that terrorists were infiltrating their neighborhoods and that planes flying overhead might smash into nearby buildings.

Unlike many war-traumatized children in the developing world, Public School 31 students

received immediate intervention—a "trauma curriculum" in which they expressed their emotions through writing, drawing, and discussion and participated in experiences aimed at restoring trust and tolerance (Lagnado, 2001). Older children learned about the feelings of their Muslim classmates, the dire condition of children in Afghanistan, and ways to help victims as a means of overcoming a sense of helplessness.

When wartime drains families and communities of resources, international organizations must step in and help children. Efforts to preserve children's physical, psychological, and educational well-being may be the best way to stop the transmission of violence to the next generation.

AP IMAGES/ANJA NIEDRINGHAUS

■ A trauma counselor comforts a child standing amid the rubble of her neighborhood in the Gaza Strip. Many children of war lose their sense of safety. Without special support from caring adults, they are likely to have lasting emotional problems. ■

Most cases of school phobia appear around age 11 to 13, in children who usually find a particular aspect of school frightening—an overcritical teacher, a school bully, or too much parental pressure to achieve. A change in school environment or parenting practices may be needed. Firm insistence that the child return to school, along with training in how to cope with difficult situations, is also helpful (Silverman & Pina, 2008).

Severe childhood anxieties may also arise from harsh living conditions. In inner-city ghettos and in war-torn areas of the world, many children live in the midst of constant danger, chaos, and deprivation. As the Cultural Influences box above reveals, they are at risk for long-term emotional distress and behavior problems. Finally, as we saw in our discussion of child abuse in Chapter 10, too often violence and other destructive acts become part of adult–child relationships. During middle childhood, child sexual abuse increases.

Child Sexual Abuse

Until recently, child sexual abuse was considered rare, and adults often dismissed children's claims of abuse. In the 1970s, efforts by professionals and media attention led to recognition of child sexual abuse as a serious and widespread problem. About 60,000 cases in the United States were confirmed in the most recently reported year (U.S. Department of Health and Human Services, 2009c). But this figure greatly underestimates the extent of sexual abuse, since most victims either delay disclosure for a long time or remain silent (London et al., 2005).

CHARACTERISTICS OF ABUSERS AND VICTIMS   Sexual abuse is committed against children of both sexes, but more often against girls. Most cases are reported in middle childhood, but for some victims, abuse begins early in life and continues for many years (Hoch-Espada, Ryan, & Deblinger, 2006; Trickett & Putnam, 1998).

Typically, the abuser is a male, either a parent or someone the parent knows well—a father, stepfather, or live-in boyfriend or, somewhat less often, an uncle or older brother. But in about 25 percent of cases, mothers are the offenders, more often with sons (Boroughs, 2004). If the abuser is a nonrelative, the person is usually someone the child has come to know and trust. However, the Internet and mobile phones have become avenues through which other adults commit sexual abuse—for example, by exposing children and adolescents to pornography and online sexual advances as a way of "grooming" them for sexual acts offline (Wolak et al., 2008).

Abusers make the child comply in a variety of distasteful ways, including deception, bribery, verbal intimidation, and physical force. You may wonder how any adult—especially a parent or close relative—could violate a child sexually. Many offenders deny their own responsibility, blaming the abuse on the willing participation of a seductive youngster. Yet children are not capable of making a deliberate, informed decision to enter into a sexual relationship! Even older children and adolescents are not free to say yes or no. Rather, the responsibility lies with abusers, who tend to have characteristics that predispose them toward sexual exploitation of children. They have great difficulty controlling their impulses and may suffer from psychological disorders, including alcohol and drug abuse. Often they pick out children who are unlikely to defend themselves or to be believed—those who are physically weak, emotionally deprived, socially isolated, or affected by disabilities (Bolen, 2001).

Reported cases of child sexual abuse are linked to poverty, marital instability, and resulting weakening of family ties. Children who live in homes with a constantly changing cast of characters—repeated marriages, separations, and new partners—are especially vulnerable. But children in economically advantaged, stable homes are also victims, although their abuse is more likely to escape detection (Putnam, 2003).

CONSEQUENCES OF SEXUAL ABUSE   The adjustment problems of child sexual abuse victims—including anxiety, depression, low self-esteem, mistrust of adults, and anger and hostility—are often severe and can persist for years after the abusive episodes. Younger children frequently react with sleep difficulties, loss of appetite, and generalized fearfulness. Adolescents may run away and show suicidal reactions, substance abuse, and delinquency. At all ages, persistent abuse accompanied by force, violence, and a close relationship to the perpetrator (incest) has a more severe impact (Feiring, Taska, & Lewis, 1999; Wolfe, 2006). And repeated sexual abuse, like physical abuse, is associated with central nervous system damage (Cichetti, 2007).

Sexually abused children frequently display precocious sexual knowledge and behavior. In adolescence, abused young people often become promiscuous, and as adults, they show increased arrest rates for sex crimes (mostly against children) and prostitution (Salter et al., 2003; Whipple, 2006). Furthermore,

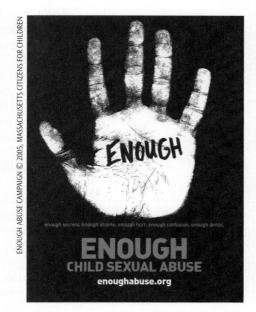

ENOUGH ABUSE CAMPAIGN © 2005, MASSACHUSETTS CITIZENS FOR CHILDREN

■ This public service announcement asks concerned adults to join in a "show of hands" to send a clear, simple message—"Enough"—about the reality of child sexual abuse and the urgent need for prevention. ■

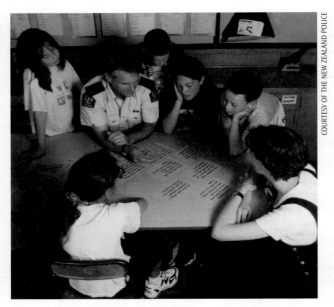

In Keeping Ourselves Safe, New Zealand's national, school-based child abuse prevention program, teachers and police officers collaborate in teaching children to recognize abusive adult behaviors so they can take steps to protect themselves. Parents are encouraged to support and extend these learning experiences at home. ■

women who were sexually abused are likely to choose partners who abuse them and their children. As mothers, they often engage in irresponsible and coercive parenting, including child abuse and neglect (Pianta, Egeland, & Erickson, 1989). In these ways, the harmful impact of sexual abuse is transmitted to the next generation.

PREVENTION AND TREATMENT Treating child sexual abuse is difficult. The reactions of family members—anxiety about harm to the child, anger toward the abuser, and sometimes hostility toward the victim for telling—can increase children's distress. Because sexual abuse typically appears in the midst of other serious family problems, long-term therapy with both children and parents is usually needed (Olafson & Boat, 2000). The best way to reduce the suffering of victims is to prevent sexual abuse from continuing. Today, courts are prosecuting abusers more vigorously and taking children's testimony more seriously (see the Social Issues: Health box on the following page).

Educational programs that teach children to recognize inappropriate sexual advances and whom to turn to for help reduce the risk of abuse (Hebert & Tourigny, 2004). Yet because of controversies over educating children about sexual abuse, few schools offer these interventions. New Zealand is the only country with a national, school-based prevention program targeting sexual abuse. In Keeping Ourselves Safe, children and adolescents learn that abusers are generally not strangers. Parent involvement ensures that home and school work together in teaching children self-protection skills. Evaluations reveal that virtually all New Zealand parents and children support the program and that it has helped many children avoid or report abuse (Sanders, 2006).

Fostering Resilience in Middle Childhood

Throughout middle childhood—and other periods of development—children are confronted with challenging and sometimes threatening situations that require them to cope with psychological stress. In this trio of chapters, we have considered such topics as chronic illness, learning disabilities, achievement expectations, divorce, harsh living conditions and wartime trauma, and sexual abuse. Each taxes children's coping resources, creating serious risks for development.

Nevertheless, only a modest relationship exists between stressful life experiences and psychological disturbance in childhood (Masten & Reed, 2002). In our discussion in Chapter 4 of the long-term consequences of birth complications, we noted that some children overcome the combined effects of birth trauma, poverty, and a troubled family life. The same is true for school difficulties, family transitions, children of war, and child maltreatment. Refer to Applying What We Know on page 522 for an overview of factors that promote *resilience*—the capacity to overcome adversity—during middle childhood.

Often just one or a few of these ingredients account for why one child is "stress-resilient" and another is not. Usually, however, personal and environmental factors are interconnected: Each resource favoring resilience strengthens others. For example, safe, stable neighborhoods with family-friendly community services reduce parents' daily hassles and stress, thereby promoting good parenting (Pinderhughes et al., 2001). In contrast, unfavorable home and neighborhood experiences increase the chances that children will act in ways that expose them to further hardship. And when negative conditions pile up, such as marital discord, poverty, crowded living conditions, neighborhood violence, and abuse and neglect, the rate of maladjustment multiplies (Wright & Masten, 2005).

Of great concern are children's violent acts. Violence committed in schools and communities by U.S. children and adolescents with troubled lives has at times reached the level of atrocities—maimings and murders of adults and peers. Because children spend a great deal of

SOCIAL ISSUES: HEALTH

Children's Eyewitness Testimony

*I*ncreasingly, children are being called on to testify in court cases involving child abuse and neglect, child custody, and other matters. The experience can be difficult and traumatic, requiring children to report on highly stressful events and sometimes to speak against a parent or other relative to whom they feel loyal. In some family disputes, they may fear punishment for telling the truth. In addition, child witnesses are faced with an unfamiliar situation—at the very least an interview in the judge's chambers and at most an open courtroom with judge, jury, spectators, and the possibility of unsympathetic cross-examination. Not surprisingly, these conditions can compromise the accuracy of children's recall.

Age Differences

Until recently, children younger than age 5 were rarely asked to testify, and not until age 10 were they assumed fully competent to do so. As a result of societal reactions to rising rates of child abuse and the difficulty of prosecuting perpetrators, legal requirements for child testimony have been relaxed in the United States (Sandler, 2006). Children as young as age 3 frequently serve as witnesses.

Compared with preschoolers, school-age children are better at giving accurate, detailed narrative accounts of past experiences and correctly inferring others' motives and intentions. Older children are also generally more resistant to misleading questions that attorneys may ask when probing for more information or, in cross-examination, trying to influence the child's response (Roebers & Schneider, 2001). Inhibition (ability to suppress impulses and focus on a competing goal), which improves from early to middle childhood, predicts children's resistance to suggestion (Melinder, Endestad, & Magnussen, 2006).

Nevertheless, when properly questioned, even 3-year-olds can recall recent events accurately (Peterson & Rideout, 1998). And in the face of biased interviewing, adolescents and adults often form elaborate, false memories of events (Ceci et al., 2007).

Suggestibility

Court testimony often involves repeated interviews. When adults lead witnesses by suggesting incorrect "facts," interrupt their denials, reinforce them for giving desired answers, or use a confrontational questioning style, they increase the likelihood of incorrect reporting by children and adolescents alike (Bruck & Ceci, 2004; Owen-Kostelnik, Reppucci, & Meyer, 2006).

In one study, 4- to 7-year-olds were asked to recall details about a visitor who had come to their classroom a week earlier. Half the children received a low-pressure interview containing leading questions that implied abuse ("He took your clothes off, didn't he?"). The other half receive a high-pressure interview in which an adult told the child that her friends had said "yes" to the leading questions, praised the child for agreeing ("You're doing great"), and, if the child did not agree, repeated the question. Children were far more likely to give false information—even to fabricate quite fantastic events—in the high-pressure condition (Finnilä et al., 2003).

By the time children appear in court, weeks, months, or even years have passed since the target events. When a long delay is combined with biased interviewing and with stereotyping of the accused ("He's in jail because he's been bad"), children can easily be misled into giving false information (Gilstrap & Ceci, 2005; Quas et al., 2007). The more distinctive and personally relevant an event is, the more likely children are to recall it accurately over time. For example, a year later, even when exposed to misleading information, children correctly reported details of an injury that required emergency room treatment (Peterson, Parsons, & Dean, 2004).

In many sexual abuse cases, anatomically correct dolls are used to prompt children's recall. Although this method helps older children provide more detail about experienced events, it increases the suggestibility of preschoolers, who report physical and sexual contact that never happened (Goodman & Melinder, 2007).

Interventions

Adults must prepare child witnesses so that they understand the courtroom process and know what to expect. In some places, "court schools" take children through the setting and give them an opportunity to role-play court activities. Practice interviews—in which children learn to provide the most accurate, detailed information possible and to admit not knowing rather than agreeing or guessing—are helpful (Saywitz, Goodman, & Lyon, 2002).

At the same time, legal professionals must use interviewing procedures that increase children's accurate reporting. Unbiased, open-ended questions that prompt children to disclose details—"Tell me what happened" or "You said there was a man; tell me about the man"—reduce suggestibility (Goodman & Melinder, 2007). Also, a warm, supportive interview tone fosters accurate recall, perhaps by easing children's anxiety so they feel freer to disagree with an interviewer's false suggestions (Ceci, Bruck, & Battin, 2000).

If children are likely to experience emotional trauma or later punishment (as in a family dispute), courtroom procedures can be adapted to protect them. For example, children can testify over closed-circuit TV so they do not have to face an abuser. When it is not wise for a child to participate directly, impartial expert witnesses can provide testimony that reports on the child's psychological condition and includes important elements of the child's story.

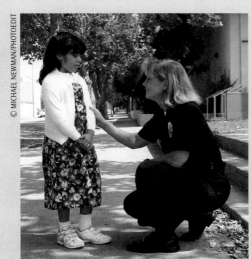

■ School-age eyewitnesses are better able than preschoolers to give accurate, detailed descriptions and correctly infer others' motives and intentions. This police officer can promote accurate recall by using a warm, supportive tone and avoiding leading questions. ■

Applying What We Know

Resources That Foster Resilience in Middle Childhood

TYPE OF RESOURCE	DESCRIPTION
Personal	• Easygoing, sociable temperament • Above-average intelligence • Favorable self-esteem • Persistence in the face of challenge and pleasure in mastery • Good emotional self-regulation and flexible coping strategies
Family	• Warm, trusting relationship with at least one parent • Authoritative child-rearing style • Positive discipline, avoidance of coercive tactics • Warm, supportive sibling relationships
School	• Teachers who are warm, helpful, and stimulating, who encourage students to collaborate, and who emphasize effort and self-improvement • Lessons in tolerance and respect and codes against bullying, which promote positive peer relationships and gratifying friendships • Extracurricular activities, including sports and social service pursuits, that strengthen physical, cognitive, and social skills • High-quality after-school programs that protect children's safety and offer stimulating, skill-building activities
Community	• High-quality after-school programs that protect children's safety and offer stimulating, skill-building activities • An adult—such as an extended-family member, teacher, or neighbor—who provides warmth and social support and is a positive coping model • Stability of neighborhood residents and services—safe outdoor play areas, community centers, and religious organizations—that relieve parental stress and encourage families and neighbors to share leisure time • Youth groups—scouting, clubs, religious youth groups, and other organized activities—that promote positive peer relationships and prosocial behavior

Note: One or a few resources may be sufficient to foster resilience, since each resource strengthens others.
Sources: Commission on Children at Risk, 2008; Wright & Masten, 2005.

© TONY FREEMAN/PHOTOEDIT

■ Personal and environmental factors work together to foster resilience. In the safe, stimulating environment of an after-school workshop in their community, these children acquire new skills, collaborate with peers, and develop gratifying friendships. ■

time in school, the quality of their relationships with teachers and classmates strongly influences their development, academically and socially (Elias, Parker, & Rosenblatt, 2005).

Several highly effective school-based *social and emotional learning programs* reduce violence (including bullying and gang involvement) and other antisocial acts and increase academic motivation by fostering social competence and supportive relationships. Among these is the Resolving Conflict Creatively Program (RCCP), used in more than 400 schools throughout the United States (Lantieri, 2003). RCCP provides children and adolescents with up to 51 hour-long lessons in emotional and social understanding and skills. Topics include expressing feelings, regulating anger, resolving social conflicts, cooperating, appreciating diversity, identifying and standing up against prejudice and bullying, and making decisions based on long- rather than short-term goals. In New York City, RCCP is integrated with language arts: High-quality children's literature, selected for relevance to program themes, complements each lesson. Discussion, writing, and role play of the stories deepen student's understanding of conflict, emotions, relationships, and community.

Compared with students receiving few or no lessons, second to sixth graders receiving substantial RCCP instruction less often misinterpreted others' acts as hostile, less often behaved aggressively, more often engaged in prosocial behavior, and more often gained in academic achievement. Two years of intervention, as opposed to just one, strengthened these outcomes (Brown et al., 2004; Jones, Brown, & Aber, 2008). In unsafe neighborhoods, the program transforms schools into places of safety and mutual respect, where learning can occur.

RCCP and other similar programs recognize that resilience is not a preexisting attribute but rather a capacity that *develops,* enabling children to use internal and external resources to cope with adversity (Dessel, 2010; Roberts & Masten, 2004). Throughout our discussion, we have seen how families, schools, communities, and society as a whole can enhance or undermine the school-age child's developing sense of competence. As the next three chapters reveal, young people whose childhood experiences helped them learn to control impulses, overcome obstacles, strive for self-direction, and respond considerately and sympathetically to others meet the challenges of the next period—adolescence—quite well.

ASK YOURSELF

◆ **REVIEW** When children must testify in court cases, what factors increase the chances of accurate reporting?

◆ **APPLY** Claire told her 6-year-old daughter to be very careful never to talk to or take candy from strangers. Why will Claire's warning not protect her daughter from sexual abuse?

◆ **CONNECT** Explain how factors that promote resilience, listed on the previous page, contribute to favorable adjustment following divorce.

◆ **REFLECT** Describe a challenging time during your childhood. What aspects of the experience increased stress? What resources helped you cope with adversity?

Summary

Erikson's Theory: Industry versus Inferiority

What personality changes take place during Erikson's stage of industry versus inferiority?

■ According to Erikson, children who successfully resolve the psychological conflict of **industry versus inferiority** develop a sense of competence at useful skills and tasks, learn the value of division of labor, and develop a sense of moral commitment and responsibility.

Self-Understanding

Describe school-age children's self-concept and self-esteem, and discuss factors that affect their achievement-related attributions.

■ During middle childhood, children's self-concepts include personality traits (both positive and negative), competencies, and **social comparisons.**

■ Self-esteem differentiates further and becomes hierarchically organized and more realistic, declining as children get more competence-related feedback and compare their performance to that of others. Cultural forces and child-rearing practices affect self-esteem. Warm extended families and strong ethnic pride may contribute to the slight self-esteem advantage of African-American over Caucasian children. The authoritative child-rearing style is linked to favorable self-esteem.

■ Children with **mastery-oriented attributions** hold an incremental view of ability, believing that it can be improved by trying hard, and attribute failure to insufficient effort. In contrast, children with **learned helplessness** attribute success to external factors, such as luck, and hold a fixed view of ability. They believe their failures are due to low ability, which cannot be modified.

■ Supportive parents and teachers and cultural valuing of effort increase the likelihood of a mastery-oriented approach. **Attribution retraining** encourages learned-helpless children to believe they can overcome failure by exerting more effort.

Emotional Development

Cite changes in the expression and understanding of emotion in middle childhood.

■ Self-conscious emotions of pride and guilt become clearly governed by personal responsibility. Intense shame can shatter self-esteem.

■ School-age children recognize that people can experience more than one emotion at a time and that emotional expressions may not reflect people's true feelings. They also reconcile contradictory cues in interpreting another's feelings. Empathy increases and includes sensitivity to both people's immediate distress and their general life condition.

- By age 10, most children can shift adaptively between **problem-centered** and **emotion-centered coping** in regulating emotion. Emotionally well-regulated children develop a sense of emotional self-efficacy and are optimistic, prosocial, and well-liked by peers.

Understanding Others: Perspective Taking

How does perspective taking change in middle childhood?

- As Selman's five-stage sequence indicates, **perspective taking**—the capacity to imagine others' thoughts and feelings—improves greatly, supported by cognitive maturity and experiences in which adults and peers explain their viewpoints. Good perspective takers show more empathy, sympathy, and positive social skills.

Moral Development

Describe changes in moral understanding during middle childhood, including children's understanding of diversity and inequality.

- By middle childhood, children have internalized rules for good conduct. They clarify and link moral imperatives and social conventions, considering the purpose of the rule; people's intentions, knowledge, and beliefs; and the context of their actions. They also better understand individual rights. But when moral and personal concerns conflict, older school-age children typically emphasize fairness. Children in diverse cultures use similar criteria to reason about moral, social-conventional, and personal concerns.

© SYRACUSE NEWSPAPERS/ J. BERRY/THE IMAGE WORKS

- Children of all races pick up prevailing societal attitudes about race and ethnicity. With age, school-age children understand that people who look different need not think, feel, or act differently, and prejudice typically declines. Children most likely to hold racial and ethnic biases are those who believe that personality traits are fixed, who have inflated self-esteem, and who live among adults who highlight group differences. Long-term, intergroup contact may be most effective at reducing prejudice.

Peer Relations

How do peer sociability and friendship change in middle childhood?

- Peer interaction becomes more prosocial, and physical aggression declines. By the end of middle childhood, children organize themselves into **peer groups.**
- Friendships develop into mutual relationships based on trust and become more selective. Children tend to select friends who resemble themselves in age, sex, race, ethnicity, SES, personality, popularity, academic achievement, and prosocial behavior. Girls form closer, more exclusive friendships than boys.

Describe major categories of peer acceptance and ways to help rejected children.

- On measures of **peer acceptance, popular children** are well-liked by many agemates; **rejected children** are actively disliked; **controversial children** are both liked and disliked; and **neglected children** arouse little reaction, positive or negative, but are usually well-adjusted.
- **Popular-prosocial children** are academically and socially competent, while **popular-antisocial children** are aggressive but admired, perhaps for their athletic ability and sophisticated but devious social skills. Rejected children also divide into two subtypes: **rejected-aggressive children,** who are especially high in conflict and hostility, and **rejected-withdrawn children,** who are passive, socially awkward, and frequent targets of **peer victimization.**
- Coaching in social skills, academic tutoring, and training in perspective taking and social problem solving have been used to help rejected youngsters. To produce lasting change, intervening in parent–child interaction is often necessary.

Gender Typing

What changes in gender-stereotyped beliefs and gender identity occur during middle childhood?

- School-age children extend their awareness of gender stereotypes to personality traits and academic subjects. But they also develop a more flexible, open-minded view of what males and females can do.

- Boys strengthen their identification with the masculine role, whereas girls feel free to experiment with "cross-gender" activities. Gender identity includes self-evaluations of gender typicality, contentedness, and felt pressure to conform to gender roles—each of which affects adjustment.

© PETER HVIZDAK/THE IMAGE WORKS

Family Influences

How do parent–child communication and sibling relationships change in middle childhood?

- Despite declines in time spent with parents, **coregulation** allows parents to exercise general oversight over children, who increasingly make their own decisions.
- Sibling rivalry tends to increase with greater participation in diverse activities and more frequent parental comparisons. Siblings often try to reduce this rivalry by striving to be different from one another. Only children do not differ from children with siblings in self-rated personality traits and are higher in self-esteem, school performance, and educational attainment.

How do children fare in gay and lesbian families and in single-parent, never-married families?

- Gay and lesbian parents are as committed to and effective at child rearing as heterosexuals. Their children do not differ from the children of heterosexual parents in adjustment and gender-role preferences.
- Never-married parenthood generally increases economic hardship for low-SES mothers and their children. Children of never-married mothers who lack a father's warmth and involvement achieve less well in school and engage in more antisocial behavior than children in low-SES, first-marriage families.

What factors influence children's adjustment to divorce and blended family arrangements?

■ Although marital breakup is often quite stressful for children, individual differences exist based on parental psychological health, child characteristics (age, temperament, and sex), and social supports. Children with difficult temperaments are at greater risk for adjustment problems. In both sexes, divorce is linked to early sexual activity, adolescent parenthood, and long-term relationship difficulties.

■ The overriding factor in positive adjustment following divorce is effective parenting. Positive father-child relationships have protective value, as do caring extended family members, teachers, siblings, and friends.

■ **Divorce mediation** and parent education programs can foster parental conflict resolution and cooperation in the period surrounding divorce. The success of joint custody depends on coparenting.

■ When divorced parents enter new relationships and form **blended, or reconstituted, families**, girls, older children, and children in father–stepmother families tend to have more adjustment problems. Stepparents who move into their roles gradually help children adjust.

How do maternal employment and life in dual-earner families affect children's development?

■ When employed mothers enjoy their work and remain committed to parenting, their children benefit from higher self-esteem, more positive family and peer relations, less gender-stereotyped beliefs, and better school grades. In dual-earner families, the father's willingness to share household responsibilities is linked to many positive child outcomes. Workplace supports help parents meet the demands of work and child rearing.

■ Authoritative child rearing, parental monitoring, and regular after-school chores lead **self-care children** to be responsible and well-adjusted. Good "after-care" programs also aid school performance and emotional and social adjustment, with low-SES children showing special benefits.

Some Common Problems of Development

Cite common fears and anxieties in middle childhood.

■ School-age children's fears are directed toward new concerns, including physical harm, media events, academic failure, parents' health, the possibility of dying, and peer rejection. Children with inhibited temperaments are at high risk for developing **phobias.** Harsh living conditions, presenting constant danger, chaos, and deprivation, can result in long-term emotional stress and behavior problems.

Discuss factors related to child sexual abuse, its consequences for children's development, and its prevention and treatment.

■ Child sexual abuse is generally committed by male family members, more often against girls than against boys. Abusers have characteristics that predispose them toward sexual exploitation of children. Reported cases are strongly associated with poverty and marital instability.

■ Abused children often have severe adjustment problems. Treatment typically requires long-term therapy with both children and parents. Educational programs that teach children to recognize inappropriate sexual advances and whom to turn to for help reduce the risk of sexual abuse.

Cite factors that foster resilience in middle childhood.

■ Overall, a modest relationship exists between stressful life experiences and psychological disturbance in childhood. Children's personal characteristics, a warm family life that includes authoritative parenting, and school and community resources predict resilience.

IMPORTANT TERMS AND CONCEPTS

attribution retraining (p. 488)
blended, or reconstituted, family (p. 513)
controversial children (p. 500)
coregulation (p. 507)
divorce mediation (p. 513)
emotion-centered coping (p. 490)
industry versus inferiority (p. 482)
learned helplessness (p. 487)

mastery-oriented attributions (p. 486)
neglected children (p. 500)
peer acceptance (p. 500)
peer groups (p. 498)
peer victimization (p. 502)
perspective taking (p. 491)
phobia (p. 517)
popular children (p. 500)

popular-antisocial children (p. 500)
popular-prosocial children (p. 500)
problem-centered coping (p. 490)
rejected children (p. 500)
rejected-aggressive children (p. 501)
rejected-withdrawn children (p. 501)
self-care children (p. 516)
social comparisons (p. 483)

Milestones

Development in Middle Childhood

6–8 years

PHYSICAL

- Slow gains in height and weight continue until adolescent growth spurt. (412)
- Permanent teeth gradually replace primary teeth. (414)
- Legibility of writing increases, preparing children to master cursive writing. (429)
- Drawings become more organized and detailed and include some depth cues. (429)
- Games with rules and rough-and-tumble play become common. (430, 431–432)

COGNITIVE

- Thought becomes more logical, as shown by the ability to pass Piagetian conservation, class inclusion, and seriation problems. (438)
- Attention becomes more selective, adaptable, and planful. (443–445)
- Uses memory strategies of rehearsal and then organization. (446)
- Views the mind as an active, constructive agent, capable of transforming information. (447)

- Awareness of memory strategies and the impact of psychological factors (such as focusing attention) on task performance improves. (448–449)
- Appreciates second-order false beliefs. (448)
- Uses informal knowledge of number concepts and counting to master more complex mathematical skills. (451–453)

LANGUAGE

- Vocabulary increases rapidly as children learn about 20 new words a day. (462)
- Word definitions are concrete, referring to functions and appearance. (463)
- Narratives increase in organization, detail, and expressiveness. (464)
- Transitions from "learning to read" to "reading to learn." (451)

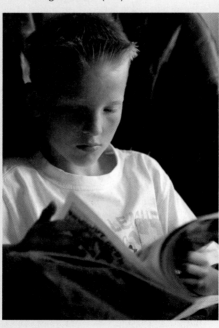

- Metalinguistic awareness improves. (462, 465)
- Conversational strategies become more refined. (464)

EMOTIONAL/SOCIAL

- Self-concept begins to include personality traits and social comparisons. (482–483)
- Self-esteem differentiates, is hierarchically organized, and declines to a more realistic level. (484–485)
- Self-conscious emotions of pride and guilt are governed by personal responsibility. (489–490)
- Understands that people may have different perspectives because they have access to different information. (493)
- Recognizes that people can experience more than one emotion at a time and that their expressions may not reflect their true feelings. (490)

- Empathy increases. (490)
- Attends to more cues (facial, situational, and past experiences) in interpreting another's feelings. (490)
- Becomes more independent and trustworthy. (492)
- Constructs a flexible appreciation of moral rules, taking prosocial and antisocial intentions into account. (492–493)
- Physical aggression declines; verbal and relational aggression continue. (497)

NOTE: Numbers in parentheses indicate the page or pages on which each milestone is discussed.

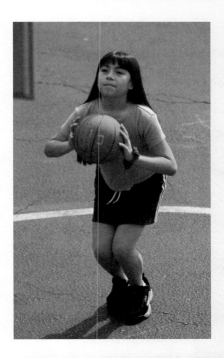

9–11 years

PHYSICAL

- Adolescent growth spurt begins two years earlier in girls than in boys. (412)
- Executes gross motor skills of running, jumping, throwing, catching, kicking, batting, and dribbling more quickly and with better coordination. (427–428)
- Steady gains in reaction time contribute to improved motor performance. (428)
- Representation of depth in drawings expands. (429)
- Dominance hierarchies become more stable, especially among boys. (432)

COGNITIVE

- Continues to master Piagetian tasks in a step-by-step fashion. (440)
- Spatial reasoning improves, as illustrated by more sophisticated map-reading and drawing skills, including an overall view of space and understanding of scale. (438–439)

- Selective attention and planning improve further. (443–445)
- Uses memory strategies of rehearsal and organization more effectively. (446)
- Applies several memory strategies simultaneously; begins to use elaboration. (446)
- Long-term knowledge base grows larger and becomes better organized. (446)
- Theory of mind becomes more elaborate and refined. (447)
- Cognitive self-regulation improves. (449)

LANGUAGE

- Thinks about and uses words more precisely; word definitions emphasize synonyms and categorical relations. (463)
- Grasps double meanings of words, as reflected in comprehension of metaphors and humor. (463)
- Continues to master complex grammatical constructions, such as passive voice and infinitive phrases. (463)
- Continues to refine conversational strategies. (464)
- Narratives lengthen and increase in organization, detail, and expressiveness. (464)

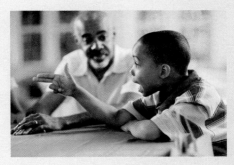

EMOTIONAL/SOCIAL

- Continues to refine self-concept to include competencies, positive and negative personality traits, and more sophisticated social comparisons. (483)
- Self-esteem tends to rise, as children balance social comparisons with personal achievement goals. (485)
- Distinguishes ability, effort, and luck in attributions for success and failure. (486–487)

- Empathic responding extends to general life conditions. (490)

- Shifts adaptively between problem-centered and emotion-centered strategies in regulating emotion. (490–491)
- Can "step into another's shoes" and view the self from that person's perspective; later, can view the relationship between self and other from the perspective of a third, impartial party. (491)
- Clarifies and links moral rules and social conventions. (493)
- Convictions about matters of personal choice strengthen, and understanding of individual rights expands. (493–494)
- Friendships become more selective and are based on mutual trust. (499)
- Peer groups emerge. (498)

- Becomes aware of more gender stereotypes, including personality traits and achievement, but has a flexible appreciation of what males and females can do. (503–504)
- Gender identity expands to include self-evaluations of typicality, contentedness, and pressure to conform. (504–505)
- Sibling rivalry tends to increase. (507–508)

"My Favorite Sport"
Gaith Hajeh
12 years, Syria

These basketball players seem
exhilarated by their growing
physical strength and competence.
But as Chapter 14 reveals,
adolescence can also be a time of
apprehension and social difficulty
as the body undergoes rapid
change.

Reprinted with permission from the
International Child Art Foundation,
Washington, D.C.

Physical Development in Adolescence

On Sabrina's eleventh birthday, her friend Joyce gave her a surprise party, but Sabrina seemed somber during the celebration. Although Sabrina and Joyce had been close friends since third grade, their relationship was faltering. Sabrina was a head taller and some 20 pounds heavier than most girls in her sixth-grade class. Her breasts were well-developed, her hips and thighs had broadened, and she had begun to menstruate. In contrast, Joyce still had the short, lean, flat-chested body of a school-age child.

Ducking into the bathroom while Joyce and the other girls put candles on the cake, Sabrina frowned at her image in the mirror. "I'm so big and heavy," she whispered. At church youth group on Sunday evenings, Sabrina broke away from Joyce and joined the eighth-grade girls. Around them, she didn't feel so large and awkward.

Once a month, parents gathered at Sabrina's and Joyce's school to discuss child-rearing concerns. Sabrina's parents, Franca and Antonio, attended whenever they could. "How you know they are becoming teenagers is this," volunteered Antonio. "The bedroom door is closed, and they want to be alone. Also, they contradict and disagree. I tell Sabrina, 'You have to go to Aunt Gina's on Saturday for dinner with the family.' The next thing I know, she's arguing with me."

Sabrina has entered **adolescence,** the transition between childhood and adulthood. In industrialized societies, the skills young people must master are so complex and the choices confronting them so diverse that adolescence is greatly extended. But around the world, the basic tasks of this period are much the same. Sabrina must accept her full-grown body, acquire adult ways of thinking, attain greater independence from her family, develop more mature ways of relating to peers of both sexes, and begin to construct an identity—a secure sense of who she is in terms of sexual, vocational, moral, ethnic, religious, and other life values and goals.

The beginning of adolescence is marked by **puberty,** a flood of biological events leading to an adult-sized body and sexual maturity. As Sabrina's reactions suggest, entry into adolescence can be an especially trying time for some young people. In this chapter, we trace the events of puberty and take up a variety of health concerns—physical exercise, nutrition, sexual activity, substance use and abuse, and other challenges that many teenagers encounter on the path to maturity. But first, let's consider how views of adolescence have changed over the past century.

Conceptions of Adolescence

Why is Sabrina self-conscious, argumentative, and in retreat from family activities? Historically, theorists explained the impact of puberty on psychological development by resorting to extremes—either a biological or a social explanation. Today, researchers realize that biological and social forces jointly contribute to adolescent psychological change.

The Biological Perspective

TAKE A MOMENT... Ask several parents of young children what they expect their sons and daughters to be like as teenagers. You will probably get answers like these: "Rebellious and irresponsible," "Full of rages and tempers" (Buchanan & Holmbeck, 1998). This widespread view can be traced back to the ideas of eighteenth-century philosopher Jean-Jacques Rousseau (see Chapter 1), who believed that the biological upheaval of puberty triggered heightened emotionality, conflict, and defiance of adults.

In the early twentieth century, major theorists picked up this storm-and-stress perspective. The most influential, G. Stanley Hall, based his ideas about development on Darwin's theory of evolution. Hall (1904) described adolescence as a cascade of instinctual passions, a period so turbulent that it resembled the era in which humans evolved from savages into civilized beings. Similarly, Anna Freud (1969), who expanded the focus on adolescence of her father Sigmund Freud's theory, viewed the teenage years as a biologically based, universal "developmental disturbance." In Freud's *genital stage,* sexual impulses reawaken, triggering psychological conflict and volatile behavior. As adolescents find intimate partners, inner forces gradually achieve a new, more mature harmony, and the stage concludes with marriage, birth, and child rearing. In this way, young people fulfill their biological destiny: sexual reproduction and survival of the species.

The Social Perspective

Contemporary research suggests that the storm-and-stress notion of adolescence is greatly exaggerated. Certain problems, such as eating disorders, depression, suicide, and lawbreaking, do occur more often than earlier (Farrington, 2004; Graber, 2004). But the overall rate of psychological disturbance rises only slightly (by about 3 percent) from childhood to adolescence, when it is nearly the same as in the adult population—about 15 percent (Roberts, Attkisson, & Rosenblatt, 1998). Although some teenagers encounter serious difficulties, emotional turbulence is not routine.

The first researcher to point out the wide variability in adolescent adjustment was anthropologist Margaret Mead (1928). She returned from the Pacific islands of Samoa with a startling conclusion: Because of the culture's relaxed social relationships and openness toward sexuality, adolescence "is perhaps the pleasantest time the Samoan girl (or boy) will ever know" (p. 308). In Mead's alternative view, the social environment is entirely responsible for the range of teenage experiences, from erratic and agitated to calm and stress-free. Later researchers found that Samoan adolescence was not as untroubled as Mead had assumed (Freeman, 1983). Still, she showed that to understand adolescent development, researchers must pay greater attention to social and cultural influences.

A Balanced Point of View

Today we know that biological, psychological, and social forces combine to influence adolescent development (Magnusson, 1999; Susman & Rogol, 2004). Biological changes are universal—found in all primates and all cultures. These internal stresses and the social expectations accompanying them—that the young person give up childish ways, develop new interpersonal relationships, and take on greater responsibility—are likely to prompt moments of uncertainty, self-doubt, and disappointment in all teenagers. Adolescents' prior and current experiences affect their success in surmounting these challenges.

At the same time, the length of adolescence and its demands and pressures vary substantially among cultures. Most tribal and village societies have only a brief intervening phase between childhood and full assumption of adult roles (Schlegel & Barry, 1991; Weisfeld, 1997). In industrialized nations, where successful participation in economic life requires many years of education, young people face prolonged dependence on parents and postponement of sexual gratification while they prepare for productive work roles. As a result, adolescence is greatly extended—so much so that researchers commonly divide it into three phases:

1. *Early adolescence* (11–12 to 14 years): This is a period of rapid pubertal change.
2. *Middle adolescence* (14 to 16 years): Pubertal changes are now nearly complete.
3. *Late adolescence* (16 to 18 years): The young person achieves full adult appearance and anticipates assumption of adult roles.

The more the social environment supports young people in achieving adult responsibilities, the better they adjust. For all the biological tensions and uncertainties about the future that teenagers feel, most negotiate this period successfully. With this in mind, let's look closely at puberty, the dawning of adolescent development.

Puberty: The Physical Transition to Adulthood

The changes of puberty are dramatic. Within a few years, the body of the school-age child is transformed into that of a full-grown adult. Genetically influenced hormonal processes regulate pubertal growth. Girls, who have been advanced in physical maturity since the prenatal period, reach puberty, on average, two years earlier than boys.

Hormonal Changes

The complex hormonal changes that underlie puberty occur gradually and are under way by age 8 or 9 (see Figure 14.1 on page 532). Recall from Chapter 8 that the *pituitary gland,* located at the base of the brain, releases *growth hormone (GH)* and stimulates other glands to produce hormones that act on body tissues, causing them to mature. Secretions of GH and *thyroxine* (a hormone released by the thyroid gland) increase, leading to tremendous gains in body size and to attainment of skeletal maturity.

Sexual maturation is controlled by the sex hormones. Although we think of *estrogens* as female hormones and *androgens* as male hormones, both types are present in each sex but in different amounts. The boy's testes release large quantities of the androgen *testosterone,* which leads to muscle growth, body and facial hair, and other male sex characteristics. Androgens (especially testosterone for boys) exert a GH-enhancing effect, contributing greatly to gains in body size. Because the testes secrete small amounts of estrogen as well, 50 percent of boys experience temporary breast enlargement.

■ Sex differences in pubertal growth are obvious among these middle school students. Although all are the same age, the girl is much taller and more mature looking than the boys. ■

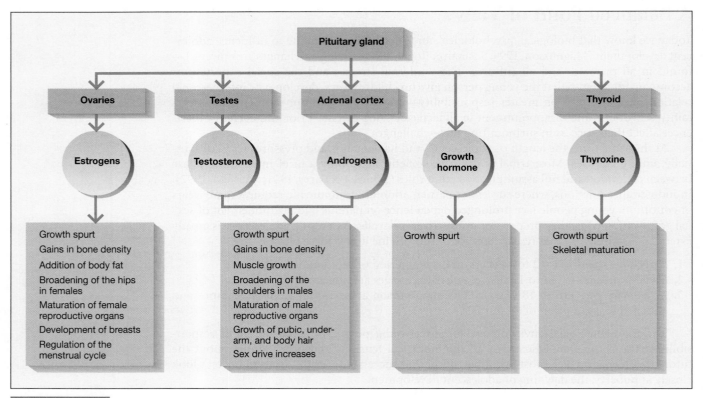

FIGURE 14.1

Hormonal influences on the body at puberty. The pituitary gland releases hormones that either induce growth directly or stimulate other endocrine glands to release growth-inducing hormones.

In both sexes, estrogens also increase GH secretion, adding to the growth spurt and, in combination with androgens, stimulating gains in bone density, which continue into early adulthood (Cooper, Sayer, & Dennison, 2006; Styne, 2003).

Estrogens released by girls' ovaries cause the breasts, uterus, and vagina to mature, the body to take on feminine proportions, and fat to accumulate. Estrogens also contribute to regulation of the menstrual cycle. *Adrenal androgens,* released from the adrenal glands on top of each kidney, influence girls' height spurt and stimulate growth of underarm and pubic hair. They have little impact on boys, whose physical characteristics are influenced mainly by androgen and estrogen secretions from the testes.

As you can see, pubertal changes are of two broad types: (1) overall body growth, and (2) maturation of sexual characteristics. We have seen that the hormones responsible for sexual maturity also affect body growth, making puberty the time of greatest sexual differentiation since prenatal life.

Body Growth

The first outward sign of puberty is the rapid gain in height and weight known as the **growth spurt.** On average, it is under way for North American and Western European girls shortly after age 10, for boys around age 12½. Because estrogens trigger and then restrain GH secretion more readily than androgens, the typical girl is taller and heavier during early adolescence (Archibald, Graber, & Brooks-Gunn, 2006; Bogin, 2001). At age 14, however, she is surpassed by the typical boy, whose adolescent growth spurt has now started, whereas hers is almost finished. Growth in body size is complete for most girls by age 16 and for boys by age 17½, when the epiphyses at the ends of the long bones close completely (see Chapter 8, page 290).

FIGURE 14.2

Body growth during adolescence. Because the pubertal growth spurt takes place earlier for girls than for boys, Amy reached her adult body size earlier than Andy. Rapid pubertal growth is accompanied by large sex differences in body proportions that were not present in middle childhood (see Chapter 11, page 412).

Altogether, adolescents add 10 to 11 inches in height and 50 to 75 pounds—nearly 50 percent of adult body weight. Even more striking is the swiftness of these changes. When growing at their peak, boys add more than 4 inches and 26 pounds in a single year, girls about 3.5 inches and 20 pounds (Rogol, Roemmich, & Clark, 2002). Figure 14.2 illustrates pubertal changes in general body growth.

BODY PROPORTIONS   During puberty, the cephalocaudal trend of infancy and childhood reverses. The hands, legs, and feet accelerate first, followed by the torso, which accounts for most of the adolescent height gain (Sheehy et al., 1999). This pattern helps explain why early adolescents often appear awkward and out of proportion—long-legged and with giant feet and hands.

Large sex differences in body proportions also appear, caused by the action of sex hormones on the skeleton. Boys' shoulders broaden relative to the hips, whereas girls' hips broaden relative to the shoulders and waist. Of course, boys also end up considerably larger than girls, and their legs are longer in relation to the rest of the body. The major reason is that boys have two extra years of preadolescent growth, when the legs are growing the fastest.

MUSCLE–FAT MAKEUP AND OTHER INTERNAL CHANGES   Sabrina worried about her weight because compared with her later-developing girlfriends, she had accumulated much more fat. Around age 8, girls start to add more fat than boys on their arms, legs, and trunk, a trend that accelerates between ages 11 and 16. In contrast, arm and leg fat decreases in adolescent boys. Although both sexes gain in muscle, this increase is 150 percent greater in boys, who develop larger skeletal muscles, hearts, and lung capacity (Rogol, Roemmich, &

LOOK AND LISTEN

◆◆

Observe 10- to 14-year-olds on school grounds or at another gathering place, noting changes in body size and proportions, along with sex differences in timing of the growth spurt.

Clark, 2002). Also, the number of red blood cells—and therefore the ability to carry oxygen from the lungs to the muscles—increases in boys but not in girls. Altogether, boys gain far more muscle strength than girls, a difference that contributes to boys' superior athletic performance during the teenage years (Ramos et al., 1998).

Motor Development and Physical Activity

Puberty brings steady improvement in gross-motor performance, but the pattern of change differs for boys and girls. Girls' gains are slow and gradual, leveling off by age 14. In contrast, boys show a dramatic spurt in strength, speed, and endurance that continues through the teenage years. The gender gap in physical skill widens with age. By mid-adolescence, few girls perform as well as the average boy in running speed, broad jump, or throwing distance. And practically no boys score as low as the average girl (Haywood & Getchell, 2005; Malina & Bouchard, 1991).

Because boys and girls are no longer well-matched physically, gender-segregated physical education usually begins in middle or junior high school. At the same time, athletic options for both sexes expand. Many new sports are added to the curriculum—track and field, wrestling, tackle football, weight lifting, floor hockey, archery, tennis, and golf, to name just a few.

Among adolescent boys, athletic competence is strongly related to peer admiration and self-esteem. Some adolescents become so obsessed with physical prowess that they turn to performance-enhancing drugs, with rates of use rising sharply with age. In recent large-scale surveys, about 8 percent of U.S. high school seniors, mostly boys, reported using creatine, an over-the-counter substance that enhances short-term muscle power but is associated with muscle cramping, intestinal discomfort, rashes, anxiety, fatigue, and (more seriously) muscle tissue disease, brain seizures, and heart irregularities (Castillo & Comstock, 2007). About 2 percent of seniors, again mostly boys, have taken anabolic steroids or a related substance, androstenedione—powerful prescription medications that boost muscle mass and strength

AP IMAGES/THE ALBUQUERQUE JOURNAL, MARIA BROSE

(Johnston et al., 2010). Teenagers usually obtain steroids illegally, ignoring side effects, which range from acne, excess body hair, and high blood pressure to mood swings, aggressive behavior, and damage to the liver, circulatory system, and reproductive organs (Casavant et al., 2007). Coaches and health professionals should inform teenagers of the dangers of performance-enhancing substances.

In 1972, the U.S. federal government required schools receiving public funds to provide equal opportunities for males and females in all educational programs, including athletics. Since then, high school girls' sports participation has increased, although it still falls far short of boys'. According to a recent survey of all 50 U.S. state high school athletic associations, 41 percent of sports participants are girls, 59 percent boys (National Federation of State High School Associations, 2009). In Chapter 11, we saw that girls get less encouragement and recognition for athletic achievement, a pattern that starts early and clearly persists into the teenage years (see page 430).

Furthermore, when researchers followed a large, representative sample of U.S. youths from ages 9 to 15, physical activity declined by about 40 minutes per day each year until, at age 15, fewer than one-third met the U.S. government recommendation of at least 60 minutes of moderate to strenuous physical activity per day (see Figure 14.3) (Nader et al., 2008). In high school, only 58 percent of U.S. boys and 55 percent of girls are enrolled in any physical education, with just one-third of all students experiencing a daily physical education class (U.S. Department of Health and Human Services, 2010g).

Besides improving motor performance, sports and exercise influence cognitive and social development. Interschool and intramural athletics provide important lessons in teamwork, problem

■ Although high school girls' participation in sports has increased, it still falls far short of boys'. Yet sports and exercise yield many benefits—not just gains in motor skills but also important lessons in teamwork, problem solving, assertiveness, and competition. ■

solving, assertiveness, and competition. And regular, sustained physical activity—which required physical education can ensure—is associated with lasting health benefits, including enhanced functioning of the immune system, cardiovascular health, better sleep quality, and improved psychological well-being (Brand et al., 2010).

Adolescents also gain in enjoyment of sports and exercise, which motivates continued involvement. In one study, participating in team or individual sports at age 14 at least once a week for girls and twice a week for boys predicted high physical activity rates at age 31. Endurance sports, such as running and cycling—activities that do not require expensive equipment or special facilities—were especially likely to continue into adulthood (Tammelin et al., 2003). And adolescent exertion during exercise, defined as sweating and breathing heavily, is one of the best predictors of adult physical exercise, perhaps because it fosters high *physical self-efficacy*—belief in one's ability to sustain an exercise program (Motl et al., 2002; Telama et al., 2005).

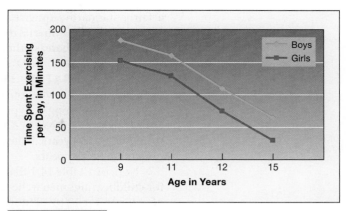

FIGURE 14.3

Decline in physical activity from ages 9 to 15 among U.S. boys and girls. In a large representative sample of youths followed over six years, time spent exercising dropped sharply until, at age 15, most youths did not meet government recommendations of at least 60 minutes of moderate to vigorous physical activity per day. At all ages, boys spent more time exercising than girls. *(Adapted from Nader et al., 2008.)*

Sexual Maturation

Accompanying rapid body growth are changes in physical features related to sexual functioning. Some, called **primary sexual characteristics,** involve the reproductive organs directly (ovaries, uterus, and vagina in females; penis, scrotum, and testes in males). Others, called **secondary sexual characteristics,** are visible on the outside of the body and serve as additional signs of sexual maturity (for example, breast development in females and the appearance of underarm and pubic hair in both sexes). As Table 14.1 shows, these characteristics develop in

TABLE 14.1   Pubertal Development in North American Girls and Boys

GIRLS	AVERAGE AGE ATTAINED	AGE RANGE	BOYS	AVERAGE AGE ATTAINED	AGE RANGE
Breasts begin to "bud"	10	8–13	Testes begin to enlarge	11.5	9.5–13.5
Height spurt begins	10	8–13	Pubic hair appears	12	10–15
Pubic hair appears	10.5	8–14	Penis begins to enlarge	12	10.5–14.5
Peak strength spurt	11.6	9.5–14	Height spurt begins	12.5	10.5–16
Peak height spurt	11.7	10–13.5	Spermarche (first ejaculation) occurs	13.5	12–16
Menarche (first menstruation) occurs	12.5	10.5–14	Peak height spurt	14	12.5–15.5
Peak weight spurt	12.7	10–14	Peak weight spurt	14	12.5–15.5
Adult stature reached	13	10–16	Facial hair begins to grow	14	12.5–15.5
Pubic hair growth completed	14.5	14–15	Voice begins to deepen	14	12.5–15.5
Breast growth completed	15	10–17	Penis and testes growth completed	14.5	12.5–16
			Peak strength spurt	15.3	13–17
			Adult stature reached	15.5	13.5–17.5
			Pubic hair growth completed	15.5	14–17

Sources: Chumlea et al., 2003; Herman-Giddens, 2006; Rogol, Roemmich, & Clark, 2002; Rubin et al., 2009; Wu, Mendola, & Buck, 2002.

Photos: (left) © David Young-Wolff/PhotoEdit; (right) © Rob Melnychuk/Getty Images/Taxi a fairly standard sequence, although the ages at which each begins and is completed vary greatly. Typically, pubertal development takes about four years, but some adolescents complete it in two years, whereas others take five to six years.

SEXUAL MATURATION IN GIRLS Female puberty usually begins with the budding of the breasts and the growth spurt. **Menarche,** or first menstruation (from the Greek word *arche,* meaning "beginning"), typically occurs relatively late in the sequence of pubertal events—around age 12½ for North American girls, 13 for Western Europeans. But the age range is wide, from 10½ to 15½ years. Following menarche, breast and pubic hair growth are completed, and underarm hair appears.

Notice in Table 14.1 that nature delays sexual maturity until the girl's body is large enough for childbearing; menarche takes place after the peak of the height spurt. As an extra measure of security, for 12 to 18 months following menarche, the menstrual cycle often occurs without the release of an ovum from the ovaries (Archibald, Graber, & Brooks-Gunn, 2006; Bogin, 2001). But this temporary period of sterility does not occur in all girls, and it cannot be counted on for protection against pregnancy.

SEXUAL MATURATION IN BOYS The first sign of puberty in boys is the enlargement of the testes (glands that manufacture sperm), accompanied by changes in the texture and color of the scrotum. Pubic hair emerges soon after, about the same time the penis begins to enlarge (Rogol, Roemmich, & Clark, 2002).

As Table 14.1 reveals, the growth spurt occurs much later in the sequence of pubertal events for boys than for girls. When it reaches its peak around age 14, enlargement of the testes and penis is nearly complete, and underarm hair appears. Facial and body hair also emerge just after the peak in body growth and increase gradually for several years. Another landmark of male physical maturity is the deepening of the voice as the larynx enlarges and the vocal cords lengthen. (Girls' voices also deepen slightly.) Voice change usually takes place at the peak of the male growth spurt and often is not complete until puberty is over (Archibald, Graber, & Brooks-Gunn, 2006). When it first occurs, boys' newly acquired baritone occasionally breaks into a high-pitched sound.

While the penis is growing, the prostate gland and seminal vesicles (which together produce semen, the fluid containing sperm) enlarge. Then, around age 13½, **spermarche,** or first ejaculation, occurs (Rogol, Roemmich, & Clark, 2002). For a while, the semen contains few living sperm. So, like girls, boys have an initial period of reduced fertility.

Individual Differences in Pubertal Growth

Heredity contributes substantially to the timing of pubertal changes. Identical twins are more similar than fraternal twins in attainment of most pubertal milestones, including growth spurt, menarche, breast development, body hair, and voice change (Eaves et al., 2004; Mustanski et al., 2004). Nutrition and exercise also make a difference. In females, a sharp rise in body weight and fat may trigger sexual maturation. Fat cells release a protein called *leptin,* which is believed to signal the brain that the girl's energy stores are sufficient for puberty—a likely reason that breast and pubic hair growth and menarche occur earlier for heavier and, especially, obese girls. In contrast, girls who begin rigorous athletic training at an early age or who eat very little (both of which reduce the percentage of body fat) usually experience later puberty (Kaplowitz, 2007; Lee et al., 2007; Rubin et al., 2009). Few studies, however, report a link between body fat and puberty in boys.

Variations in pubertal growth also exist between regions of the world and between SES and ethnic groups. Physical health plays a major role. In poverty-stricken regions where malnutrition and infectious disease are common, menarche is greatly delayed, occurring as late as age 14 to 16 in many parts of Africa. Within developing countries, girls from higher-income families typically reach menarche 6 to 18 months earlier than those living in economically disadvantaged homes (Parent et al., 2003).

But in industrialized nations where food is abundant, the joint roles of heredity and environment in pubertal growth are apparent. For example, breast and pubic hair growth begin, on average, around age 9 in African-American girls—a year earlier than in Caucasian-American girls. And African-American girls reach menarche about six months earlier, around age 12. Although widespread overweight and obesity in the black population contribute, a genetically influenced faster rate of physical maturation is also involved. Black girls usually reach menarche before white girls of the same age and body weight (Chumlea et al., 2003; Freedman et al., 2002; Herman-Giddens, 2006; Hillard, 2008).

Early family experiences may also affect pubertal timing. One theory suggests that humans have evolved to be sensitive to the emotional quality of their childhood environments. When children's safety and security are at risk, it is adaptive for them to reproduce early. Research indicates that girls and (less consistently) boys with a history of family conflict, harsh parenting, or parental separation tend to reach puberty early. In contrast, those with warm, stable family ties reach puberty relatively late (Belsky et al., 2007; Bogaert, 2005; Ellis, 2004; Ellis & Essex, 2007; Mustanski et al., 2004; Tremblay & Frigon, 2005). Critics offer an alternative explanation—that mothers who reached puberty early are more likely to bear children earlier, which increases the likelihood of marital conflict and separation (Mendle et al., 2006). But longitudinal evidence on a large, ethnically diverse sample of U.S. girls followed from birth through age 15 confirmed the former chain of influence: from harsh parenting in childhood to earlier menarche to increased sexual risk taking in adolescence (Belsky et al., 2010).

The Secular Trend

In Chapter 11 we saw that children in industrialized nations grow faster and larger than in past generations. Similarly, age of menarche declined steadily—by about 3 to 4 months per decade—from 1900 to 1970, a period in which nutrition, health care, sanitation, and control of infectious disease improved greatly (see Figure 14.4). Boys, too, have reached puberty earlier in recent decades (Karpati et al., 2002). This *secular trend* in pubertal timing lends added support to the role of physical well-being in adolescent growth.

As noted in Chapter 11, the secular gain in height has slowed. And the trend toward earlier menarche has stopped or undergone a slight reversal in most industrialized nations. But in the United States and a few European countries, soaring rates of overweight and obesity are responsible for a modest, continuing trend toward earlier menarche (Kaplowitz, 2006; Parent et al., 2003). A worrisome consequence is that girls who reach sexual maturity at age 10 or 11 will feel pressure to act much older than they are. As we will see shortly, early-maturing girls are at risk for unfavorable peer involvements, including sexual activity.

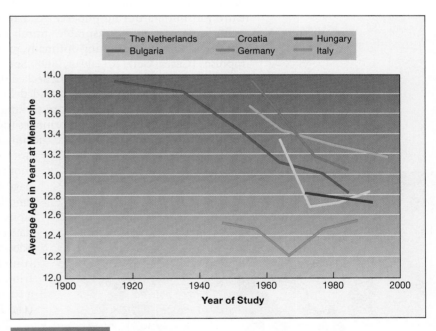

FIGURE 14.4

Secular trend in age at menarche in six industrialized nations. Age of menarche declined from 1900 to 1970. Thereafter, a few countries showed a modest, continuing decline due to rising rates of overweight and obesity. Others leveled off or underwent a slight reversal. *(From S. M. P. F. de Muinck Keizer-Schrama & D. Mul, 2001. "Trends in Pubertal Development in Europe," Human Reproduction Update, 7, p. 289. © European Society of Human Reproduction and Embryology. Reproduced by permission of Oxford University Press/Human Reproduction and S. M. P. F. de Muinck Keizer-Schrama.)*

Brain Development

The physical transformations of adolescence include major changes in the brain. In Chapter 11, we noted that during middle childhood and adolescence, *white matter* (myelinated nerve fibers) increases, especially in the prefrontal cortex, the parietal lobes, and the corpus callosum, while *gray matter* (neurons and supportive material) declines (see page 414 to review). Brain-imaging research reveals continued pruning of unused synapses in the cerebral cortex, especially in the prefrontal cortex—the "governor" of thought and action. In addition, growth and myelination of stimulated neural fibers accelerate, contributing to a slight increase in brain weight and strengthening connections among various brain regions. In particular, linkages between the two cerebral hemispheres through the corpus callosum, and between the prefrontal cortex and other areas in the cerebral cortex and the inner brain (including the amygdala), expand and attain rapid communication (Blakemore & Choudhury, 2006; Keating, 2004; Lenroot & Giedd, 2006). This sculpting of the adolescent brain supports diverse cognitive skills, including improved processing speed, inhibition, attention, memory, planning, and capacity to integrate information, along with gains in cognitive and emotional self-regulation.

But these advances in cognitive control occur gradually over the teenage years, continuing into the early twenties. fRMI evidence reveals that adolescents tend to recruit the prefrontal cortex's network of connections with other brain areas less effectively than adults do. Consequently, they perform less well on tasks requiring inhibition, planning, and future orientation (rejecting a smaller immediate reward in favor of a larger delayed reward) (Luna et al., 2001; McClure et al., 2004; Steinberg et al. 2009). The *prefrontal cognitive-control network* seems to require fine-tuning, including the more extensive interconnectivity attained at the end of the teenage years and into the twenties, to handle challenging self-regulation situations (Brown et al., 2005; Casey et al., 2005; Crone et al., 2006).

Compounding teenagers' self-regulation difficulties are changes in the brain's *emotional/social network*. In humans and other mammals, neurons become more responsive to excitatory neurotransmitters during puberty. As a result, adolescents react more strongly to stressful events and experience pleasurable stimuli more intensely. But because the cognitive-control network is not yet functioning optimally, most teenagers find it hard to control these powerful impulses (Casey, Getz, & Galvan, 2008; Spear, 2004, 2008; Steinberg et al., 2008). This imbalance contributes to adolescents' unchecked drive for novel experiences, including drug taking, reckless driving, unprotected sex, and delinquent activity, especially among those who are highly stressed and engage in reward seeking to counteract chronic emotional pain.

In addition, the surge in sex hormones (both androgens and estrogens) at puberty heightens sensitivity of the prefrontal cortex and inner-brain structures (such as the amygdala) to the hormone *oxytocin*. Recall from Chapter 4 that in new mothers, oxytocin promotes caregiving behavior (see page 143). In teenagers, it increases responsiveness to emotional and social stimuli, including facial expressions and feedback from others (Steinberg, 2008). Enhanced oxytocin sensitivity helps explain why young adolescents, as we will see in Chapter 15, are so self-conscious and sensitive to others' opinions. It also contributes to teenagers' receptiveness to peer influence—a strong predictor of adolescent risk-taking of all kinds (Gardner & Steinberg, 2005; Ranking et al., 2004).

In sum, changes in the brain's emotional/social network outpace development of the cognitive-control network in adolescence. Only over time are young people able to effectively manage their emotions and reward-seeking behavior (Steinberg et al., 2008; Yurgelun-Todd, 2007). Of course, not all teenagers manifest this rise in risk-taking in the form of careless, dangerous acts: Temperament, parenting, SES, and neighborhood resources, which are linked to encouragement and opportunities to take risks, make a difference. Nevertheless, transformations in the adolescent brain—much greater than previously thought—enhance our understanding of both the cognitive advances and the worrisome behaviors of this period, along with teenagers' need for adult patience, oversight, and guidance.

© JEFF GREENBERG/THE IMAGE WORKS

■ Because changes in the brain's emotional/social network outpace development of the cognitive-control network, adolescents experience pleasurable stimuli more intensely but do not yet have the capacity to control these powerful impulses. This imbalance contributes to teenagers' drive for novel experiences, receptiveness to peer influence, and risk-taking behavior. ■

Changing States of Arousal

At puberty, revisions occur in the way the brain regulates the timing of sleep, perhaps because of increased neural sensitivity to evening light. As a result, adolescents go to bed much later than they did as children. Yet they need almost as much sleep as they did in middle childhood—about nine hours. When the school day begins early, their sleep needs are not satisfied.

This sleep "phase delay" strengthens with pubertal growth. But today's teenager—with more evening social activities, part-time jobs, and bedrooms equipped with TVs, computers, and phones—get much less sleep than teenagers of previous generations (Carskadon, Acebo, & Jenni, 2004; Carskadon et al., 2002). Sleep-deprived adolescents perform especially poorly on cognitive tasks during morning hours. And they are more likely to achieve less well in school, suffer from depressed mood, and engage in high-risk behaviors (Dahl & Lewin, 2002; Hansen et al., 2005). Sleep rebound on weekends sustains the pattern by leading to difficulty falling asleep on subsequent evenings (Laberge et al., 2001). Later school start times ease but do not eliminate sleep loss. Educating teenagers about the importance of sleep is vital.

ASK YOURSELF

◆ REVIEW What changes in the brain contribute to cognitive advances during adolescence? What changes promote increased reward seeking along with high-risk behaviors?

◆ APPLY Jonah, age 16, routinely stays up until 2:00 A.M.—much later than he used to go to bed. He is often late for school and sometimes dozes in class. Why might Jonah's sleep habits have changed? What can his parents and his school do to help?

◆ CONNECT Historically, theorists believed that the rising sexual passions of puberty make adolescents rebellious, volatile, and uncontrollable. Where did this view originate? Why is it incorrect?

◆ REFLECT Do you currently engage in regular sports or exercise? If so, what activities do you enjoy, and why? How did your experiences during adolescence influence your current involvement in physical activity?

The Psychological Impact of Pubertal Events

TAKE A MOMENT... Think back to your late elementary and middle school days. As you reached puberty, how did your feelings about yourself and your relationships with others change? Research reveals that pubertal events affect the adolescent's self-image, mood, and interaction with parents and peers. Some outcomes are a response to dramatic physical change, whenever it occurs. Others have to do with pubertal timing.

Reactions to Pubertal Changes

Two generations ago, menarche was often traumatic. Today, girls commonly react with "surprise," undoubtedly due to the sudden onset of the event. Otherwise, they typically report a mixture of positive and negative emotions (DeRose & Brooks-Gunn, 2006). Yet wide individual differences exist that depend on prior knowledge and support from family members, which in turn are influenced by cultural attitudes toward puberty and sexuality.

For girls who have no advance information, menarche can be shocking and disturbing. In the 1950s, up to 50 percent received no prior warning, and of those who did, many were given negative, "grin-and-bear-it" messages (Costos, Ackerman, & Paradis, 2002; Shainess, 1961). Today, few girls are uninformed, a shift that is probably due to parents' greater willingness to

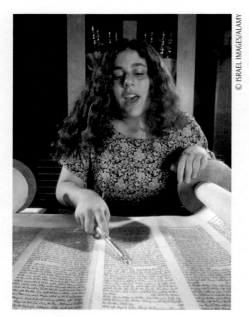

This 13-year-old's bat mitzvah ceremony is the culmination of several years of study and reflection. Although the event recognizes her as an adult with moral and religious responsibilities in the Jewish community, she will experience no change in status in the larger society. ■

discuss sexual matters and to the spread of health education classes (Omar, McElderry, & Zakharia, 2003). Almost all girls get some information from their mothers. And some evidence suggests that compared with Caucasian-American families, African-American families may better prepare girls for menarche, treat it as an important milestone, and express less conflict over girls reaching sexual maturity—factors that lead African-American girls to react more favorably (Martin, 1996).

Like girls' reactions to menarche, boys' responses to spermarche reflect mixed feelings. Virtually all boys know about ejaculation ahead of time, but many say that no one spoke to them prior to or during puberty about physical changes (Omar, McElderry, & Zakharia, 2003). Usually they get their information from reading material or websites. Even boys who had advance information often say that their first ejaculation occurred earlier than they expected and that they were unprepared for it. As with girls, boys who feel better prepared tend to react more positively (Stein & Reiser, 1994). But whereas almost all girls eventually tell a friend that they are menstruating, far fewer boys tell anyone about spermarche (DeRose & Brooks-Gunn, 2006; Downs & Fuller, 1991). Overall, boys get much less social support than girls for the changes of puberty. They might benefit, especially, from opportunities to ask questions and discuss feelings with a sympathetic parent or health professional.

Many tribal and village societies celebrate the onset of puberty with an *initiation ceremony,* a ritualized announcement to the community that marks an important change in privilege and responsibility. Consequently, young people know that reaching puberty is valued in their culture. In contrast, Western societies grant little formal recognition to movement from childhood to adolescence or from adolescence to adulthood. Ceremonies such as the Jewish bar or bat mitzvah and the *quinceañera* in Hispanic communities (celebrating a 15-year-old girl's sexual maturity and marriage availability) resemble initiation ceremonies, but only within the ethnic or religious subculture. They do not mark a significant change in social status in the larger society.

Instead, Western adolescents are granted partial adult status at many different ages—for example, an age for starting employment, for driving, for leaving high school, for voting, and for drinking. And in some contexts (at home and at school), they may still be regarded as children. The absence of a widely accepted marker of physical and social maturity makes the process of becoming an adult more confusing.

Pubertal Change, Emotion, and Social Behavior

A common belief is that puberty has something to do with adolescent moodiness and the desire for greater physical and psychological separation from parents. Let's see what research says about these relationships.

ADOLESCENT MOODINESS Higher pubertal hormone levels are linked to greater moodiness, but only modestly so (Buchanan, Eccles, & Becker, 1992; Graber, Brooks-Gunn, & Warren, 2006). What other factors might contribute? In several studies, the moods of children, adolescents, and adults were monitored by having them carry electronic pagers. Over a one-week period, they were beeped at random intervals and asked to write down what they were doing, whom they were with, and how they felt.

As expected, adolescents reported less favorable moods than school-age children and adults (Larson et al., 2002; Larson & Lampman-Petraitis, 1989). But negative moods were linked to a greater number of negative life events, such as difficulties with parents, disciplinary actions at school, and breaking up with a boyfriend or girlfriend. Negative events increased steadily from childhood to adolescence, and teenagers also seemed to react to them with greater emotion than children (Larson & Ham, 1993). (Recall that stress reactivity is heightened by changes in brain neurotransmitter activity during adolescence.)

Compared with the moods of older adolescents and adults, those of younger adolescents (ages 12 to 16) were less stable, often shifting from cheerful to sad and back again. These mood swings were strongly related to situational changes. High points of adolescents' days were times spent with friends and in self-chosen leisure activities. Low points tended to occur in adult-structured settings—class, job, and religious services. Furthermore, emotional highs coincided with Friday and Saturday evenings, especially in high school (see Figure 14.5). Going out with friends and romantic partners increases so dramatically during adolescence that it becomes a "cultural script" for what is *supposed* to happen. Consequently teenagers who spend weekend evenings at home often feel profoundly lonely (Larson & Richards, 1998).

Fortunately, frequent reports of negative mood level off in late adolescence, when teenagers' emotions also become more stable. After age 18, young people typically experience minor fluctuations around a mildly positive state (Holsen, Kraft, & Vittersø, 2000; Larson et al., 2002; Natsuaki, Biehl, & Ge, 2009). In sum, biological, psychological, and social forces combine to make adolescence a time of deeper valleys and higher peaks in emotional experience—a conclusion consistent with the balanced view presented earlier in this chapter.

FIGURE 14.5

Younger and older adolescents' emotional experiences across the week. Adolescents' reports revealed that emotional high points are on Fridays and Saturdays. Mood drops on Sunday, before returning to school, and during the week, as students spend much time in adult-structured settings in school. *(From R. Larson & M. Richards, 1998, "Waiting for the Weekend: Friday and Saturday Night as the Emotional Climax of the Week." In A. C. Crouter & R. Larson, eds., Temporal Rhythms in Adolescence: Clocks, Calendars, and the Coordination of Daily Life. San Francisco: Jossey-Bass, p. 41. Reprinted by permission from John Wiley & Sons, Inc.)*

PARENT–CHILD RELATIONSHIPS Sabrina's father noticed that as his children entered adolescence, they kept their bedroom doors closed, resisted spending time with the family, and became more argumentative. Sabrina and her mother squabbled over Sabrina's messy room ("It's *my* room, Mom. You don't have to live in it!"). And Sabrina resisted the family's regular weekend visits to Aunt Gina's ("Why do I have to go *every* week?"). Research in cultures as diverse as the United States and Turkey show that puberty is linked to a rise in intensity of parent–child conflict, which persists into middle adolescence (Gure, Ucanok, & Sayil, 2006; Laursen, Coy, & Collins, 1998; McGue et al., 2005).

Why should a youngster's more adultlike appearance trigger these disputes? From an evolutionary perspective, the association may have adaptive value. Among nonhuman primates, the young typically leave the family group around the time of puberty. The same is true in many nonindustrialized cultures (Caine, 1986; Schlegel & Barry, 1991). Departure of young people discourages sexual relations between close blood relatives. But adolescents in industrialized nations, who are still economically dependent on parents, cannot leave the family. Consequently, a modern substitute seems to have emerged: psychological distancing.

As children become physically mature, they demand to be treated in adultlike ways. And as we will see in later chapters, adolescents' new powers of reasoning may also contribute to a rise in family tensions. Parent–adolescent disagreements focus largely on everyday matters such as driving, dating partners, and curfews (Adams & Laursen, 2001). But beneath these disputes lie serious concerns: parental efforts to protect teenagers from substance use, auto accidents, and early sex. The larger the gap between parents' and adolescents' views of teenagers' readiness for new responsibilities, the more they quarrel (Deković, Noom, & Meeus, 1997).

Parent–daughter conflict tends to be more intense than conflict with sons, perhaps because girls reach puberty earlier and parents place more restrictions on

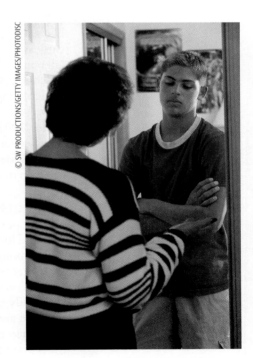

■ Puberty brings an increase in parent–child conflict—psychological distancing that may, in part, be a modern substitute for physical departure from the family. Unlike nonhuman primates and young people in many nonindustrialized cultures, adolescents in industrialized societies continue living with parents. ■

LOOK AND LISTEN

❖❖

Interview several parents and/or 12- to 14-year-olds about recent changes in parent–child relationships. Has conflict increased? Over what issues?

girls (Allison & Schultz, 2004). But most disputes are mild, and by late adolescence, only a small minority of families experience continuing friction. Parents and teenagers display both conflict and affection, and they usually agree on important values, such as honesty and the importance of education.

Although separation from parents is adaptive, both generations benefit from warm, protective family bonds throughout the lifespan. As the teenage years conclude, parent–adolescent interactions are less hierarchical, setting the stage for mutually supportive relationships in adulthood (Laursen & Collins, 2009).

Pubertal Timing

"All our children were early maturers," said Franca during the parents' discussion group. "The three boys were tall by age 12 or 13, but it was easier for them. They felt big and important. Sabrina was skinny as a little girl, but now she says she is too fat and needs to diet. She thinks about boys and doesn't concentrate on her schoolwork."

Findings of several studies match the experiences of Sabrina and her brothers. Both adults and peers viewed early-maturing boys as relaxed, independent, self-confident, and physically attractive. Popular with agemates, they tended to hold leadership positions in school and to be athletic stars. In contrast, late-maturing boys expressed more anxiety and depressed mood than their on-time counterparts (Brooks-Gunn, 1988; Huddleson & Ge, 2003). But early-maturing boys, though viewed as well-adjusted, reported more psychological stress, depressed mood, and problem behaviors (sexual activity, smoking, drinking, aggression, delinquency) than both their on-time and later-maturing agemates (Ge, Conger, & Elder, 2001; Natsuaki, Biehl, & Ge, 2009; Susman & Dorn, 2009).

In contrast, early-maturing girls were unpopular, withdrawn, lacking in self-confidence, anxious, and prone to depression, and they held few leadership positions (Ge, Conger, & Elder, 1996; Graber et al., 1997; Graber, Brooks-Gunn, & Warren, 2006; Jones & Mussen, 1958). And like early-maturing boys, they were more involved in deviant behavior (smoking, drinking, early sexual activity) (Caspi et al., 1993; Dick et al., 2000; Ge et al., 2006). In contrast, their later-maturing counterparts were regarded as physically attractive, lively, sociable, and leaders at school. In a one study of several hundred eighth graders, however, negative effects were not evident among early-maturing African-American girls, whose families—and perhaps friends as well—tend to be more unconditionally welcoming of menarche (see page 540) (Michael & Eccles, 2003).

Two factors largely account for these trends: (1) how closely the adolescent's body matches cultural ideals of physical attractiveness and (2) how well young people fit in physically with their agemates.

LOOK AND LISTEN

❖❖

Examine several magazines targeting teenage girls and several aimed at readers of diverse ages. What percentage of photos of females depict a thin body type?

THE ROLE OF PHYSICAL ATTRACTIVENESS **TAKE A MOMENT...** Flip through your favorite popular magazine. You will see evidence of our society's view of an attractive female as thin and long-legged and of a good-looking male as tall, broad-shouldered, and muscular. The female image is a girlish shape that favors the late developer. The male image fits the early-maturing boy.

Consistent with these preferences, early-maturing Caucasian girls tend to report a less positive **body image**—conception of and attitude toward their physical appearance—than their on-time and late-maturing agemates. Compared with African-American and Hispanic girls, Caucasian girls are more likely to have internalized the cultural ideal of female attractiveness. Most want to be thinner (Rosen, 2003; Stice, Presnell, & Bearman, 2001; Williams & Currie, 2000). Although boys are less consistent, early, rapid maturers are more likely to be satisfied with their physical characteristics (Alsaker, 1995; Sinkkonen, Anttila, & Siimes, 1998).

Body image is a strong predictor of young people's self-esteem (Harter, 2006). But the negative effects of pubertal timing on body image and—as we will see next—emotional adjustment are greatly amplified when accompanied by other stressors (Stice, 2003).

THE IMPORTANCE OF FITTING IN WITH PEERS

Physical status in relation to peers also explains differences in adjustment between early and late maturers. From this perspective, early-maturing girls and late-maturing boys have difficulty because they fall at the extremes of physical development and feel "out of place" when with their agemates. Not surprisingly, adolescents feel most comfortable with peers who match their own level of biological maturity (Stattin & Magnusson, 1990).

Because few agemates of the same pubertal status are available, early-maturing adolescents of both sexes seek out older companions, who often encourage them into activities they are not yet ready to handle. And hormonal influences on the brain's social/emotional network are stronger for early maturers, further magnifying their receptiveness to sexual activity, drug and alcohol use, and delinquent acts (Ge et al., 2002; Steinberg, 2008). For example, the eighth graders Sabrina met at church introduced her to several high school boys, who were unconcerned that she was only a sixth grader! And Sabrina welcomed their attentions, which gratified her desire to feel socially accepted and physically attractive. Perhaps because of involvements like these, early maturers of both sexes more often report feeling emotionally stressed and show declines in academic performance (Mendle, Turkheimer, & Emery, 2007; Natsuaki, Biehl, & Ge, 2009).

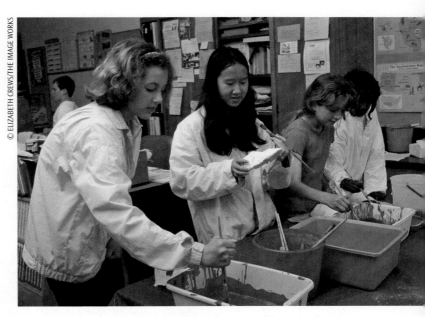

■ These 11-year-olds vary greatly in pubertal timing. Outside of school, early maturers often seek out older companions, who may encourage them into deviant activities. Early-maturing girls, especially, are at risk for lasting adjustment problems, including poor-quality relationships with family and friends and reduced educational attainment. ■

At the same time, the young person's context greatly increases the likelihood that early pubertal timing will lead to negative outcomes. Early maturers in economically disadvantaged neighborhoods are especially vulnerable to establishing ties with deviant peers, which heightens their defiant, hostile behavior (Obeidallah et al., 2004). And because families in such neighborhoods tend to be exposed to chronic, severe stressors and to have few social supports, these early maturers are also more likely to experience harsh, inconsistent parenting (see page 75 in Chapter 2). Parental coercion and inconsistency, in turn, predict both deviant peer associations and externalizing problems (Conger et al., 2002; Ge et al., 2002).

LONG-TERM CONSEQUENCES   Do the effects of pubertal timing persist? Follow-ups reveal that early-maturing girls, especially, are prone to lasting difficulties. In one study, depression subsided by age 13 in early-maturing boys but tended to persist in early-maturing girls (Ge et al., 2003). In another study, which followed young people from ages 14 to 24, early-maturing boys again showed good adjustment. But early-maturing girls reported poorer-quality relationships with family and friends, smaller social networks, and lower life satisfaction into early adulthood than did their on-time counterparts (Graber et al., 2004). Similarly, in a Swedish investigation, achievement and substance-use difficulties of early-maturing girls lingered, in the form of greater alcohol abuse and lower educational attainment than their agemates (Andersson & Magnusson, 1990; Stattin & Magnusson, 1990).

Recall that childhood family conflict and harsh parenting are linked to earlier pubertal timing, more so for girls than for boys (see page 537). Perhaps many early-maturing girls enter adolescence with emotional and social difficulties. As the stresses of puberty interfere with school performance and lead to unfavorable peer pressures, poor adjustment extends and deepens (Graber, 2003). Clearly, interventions that target at-risk early-maturing adolescents are needed. These include educating parents and teachers and providing adolescents with counseling and social supports so they will be better prepared to handle the emotional and social challenges of this transition.

ASK YOURSELF

◆ REVIEW Summarize the impact of pubertal timing on adolescent development.

◆ APPLY As a school-age child, Chloe enjoyed leisure activities with her parents. Now, at age 14, she spends hours in her room and resists going on weekend family excursions. Explain Chloe's behavior.

◆ CONNECT How might adolescent moodiness contribute to psychological distancing between parents and adolescents? (*Hint:* Think about bidirectional influences in parent–child relationships.)

◆ REFLECT Recall your own reactions to the physical changes of puberty. Are they consistent with research findings? Explain.

Health Issues

The arrival of puberty brings new health issues related to the young person's efforts to meet physical and psychological needs. As adolescents attain greater autonomy, their personal decision making becomes important, in health as well other areas. Yet none of the health concerns we are about to discuss can be traced to a single cause. Rather, biological, psychological, family, peer, and cultural factors jointly contribute.

Nutritional Needs

When their sons reached puberty, Franca and Antonio reported a "vacuum cleaner effect" in the kitchen as the boys routinely emptied the refrigerator. Rapid body growth leads to a dramatic rise in food intake. During the growth spurt, boys require about 2,700 calories a day and much more protein than they did earlier, girls about 2,200 calories but somewhat less protein than boys because of their smaller size and muscle mass (Cortese & Smith, 2003).

This increase in nutritional requirements comes at a time when the diets of many young people are the poorest. Of all age groups, adolescents are the most likely to skip breakfast (a practice linked to overweight and obesity), eat on the run, and consume empty calories rather than nutrient-rich fruits and vegetables (Ritchie et al., 2007; Striegel-Moore & Franko, 2006). Fast-food restaurants, where teenagers often gather, have begun to offer some healthy menu options. But adolescents need guidance in choosing these alternatives. Eating fast food and school purchases from snack bars and vending machines is strongly associated with consumption of high-fat foods and soft drinks, indicating that teenagers often make unhealthy food choices (Bowman et al., 2004; Kubik et al., 2003).

The most common nutritional problem of adolescence is iron deficiency. Iron requirements increase to a maximum during the growth spurt and remain high among girls because of iron loss during menstruation. A tired, irritable teenager may be suffering from anemia rather than unhappiness and should have a medical checkup. Most adolescents do not get enough calcium and are also deficient in riboflavin (vitamin B_2) and magnesium, both of which support metabolism (Cavadini, Siega-Riz, & Popkin, 2000). And contrary to what many parents believe, obese children rarely outgrow their weight problem as teenagers (Berkowitz & Stunkard, 2002).

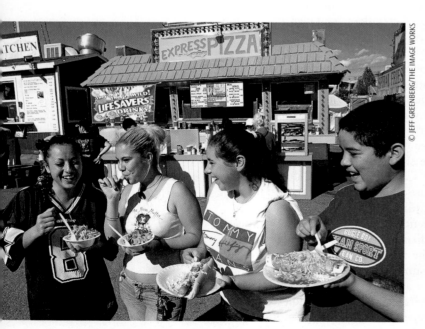

© JEFF GREENBERG/THE IMAGE WORKS

■ Of all age groups, teenagers are most likely to skip breakfast, eat on the run, and consume unhealthy fast foods—eating habits associated with vitamin and mineral deficiencies and with overweight and obesity. ■

Frequency of family meals is strongly associated with greater intake of fruits, vegetables, grains, and calcium-rich foods and reduced soft drink and fast-food consumption (Burgess-Champoux et al. 2009; Fiese & Schwartz, 2008). But compared to families with younger children, those with adolescents eat fewer meals together. In addition to their other benefits (see page 74 in Chapter 2 and page 464 in Chapter 12), family meals can greatly improve teenagers' diets.

Adolescents—especially girls concerned about their weight—tend to be attracted to fad diets. Unfortunately, most are too limited in nutrients and calories to be healthy for fast-growing, active teenagers (Donatelle, 2009). Adolescence is also a time when many young people choose to become vegetarians. As they formulate a philosophy of life, some find the killing of animals distasteful, while others claim that meats are sources of impurities and toxins. Vegetarian adolescents are far more likely than their nonvegetarian counterparts to have healthy eating habits (Perry et al., 2002). Still, because some vegetarian diets are deficient in certain nutrients, when a young person wants to try a special diet, parents should encourage consultation with a doctor or a dietitian.

Eating Disorders

Worried about her daughter's desire to lose weight, Franca explained to Sabrina that she was really quite average in build for an adolescent girl and reminded her that her Italian ancestors had considered a plump female body more beautiful than a thin one. Girls who reach puberty early, who are very dissatisfied with their body image, and who grow up in homes where concern with weight and thinness is high are at risk for eating problems. Severe dieting is the strongest predictor of the onset of an eating disorder in adolescence (Lock & Kirz, 2008). The two most serious are anorexia nervosa and bulimia.

ANOREXIA NERVOSA   **Anorexia nervosa** is a tragic eating disorder in which young people starve themselves because of a compulsive fear of getting fat. About 1 percent of North American and Western European teenage girls are affected. During the past half-century, cases have increased sharply, fueled by cultural admiration of female thinness. Anorexia nervosa is equally common in all SES groups, but Asian-American, Caucasian-American, and Hispanic girls are at greater risk than African-American girls, who tend to be more satisfied with their size and shape (Fairburn & Harrison, 2003; Granillo, Jones-Rodriguez, & Carvajal, 2005; Steinhausen, 2006). Boys account for 10 to 15 percent of anorexia cases; about half of these are homosexual or bisexual young people who are uncomfortable with a strong, muscular appearance (Raevuori et al., 2009; Robb & Dadson, 2002).

Individuals with anorexia have an extremely distorted body image. Even after they have become severely underweight, they see themselves as too heavy. Most go on self-imposed diets so strict that they struggle to avoid eating in response to hunger. To enhance weight loss, they exercise strenuously.

In their attempt to reach "perfect" slimness, individuals with anorexia lose between 25 and 50 percent of their body weight. Because a normal menstrual cycle requires about 15 percent body fat, either menarche does not occur or menstrual periods stop. Malnutrition causes pale skin, brittle discolored nails, fine dark hairs all over the body, and extreme sensitivity to cold. If it continues, the heart muscle can shrink, the kidneys can fail, and irreversible brain damage and loss of bone mass can occur. About 6 percent of individuals with anorexia die of the disorder, as a result of either physical complications or suicide (Katzman, 2005).

Forces within the person, the family, and the larger culture give rise to anorexia nervosa. Identical twins share the disorder more often than fraternal twins, indicating a genetic influence. Abnormalities in neurotransmitters in the brain,

■ Aiva, age 16, an anorexia nervosa patient, is shown at left on the day she entered treatment. She weighed just 77 pounds—69 percent of her normal body weight. At right, Aiva appears 10 weeks later, on her last day of treatment. Less than 50 percent of young people with anorexia recover fully. ■

linked to anxiety and impulse control, may make some individuals more susceptible (Kaye, 2008; Lock & Kirz, 2008). And problem eating behavior in early childhood—persistently refusing to eat or eating very little—is linked to anorexia in adolescence (Nicholls & Viner, 2009). Many young people with anorexia have unrealistically high standards for their own behavior and performance, are emotionally inhibited, and avoid intimate ties outside the family. Consequently, they are often excellent students who are responsible and well-behaved. But as we have also seen, the societal image of "thin is beautiful" contributes to the poor body image of many girls—especially early-maturing girls, who are at greatest risk for anorexia nervosa (Hogan & Strasburger, 2008).

In addition, parent–adolescent interactions reveal problems related to adolescent autonomy. Often the mothers of these girls have high expectations for physical appearance, achievement, and social acceptance and are overprotective and controlling. Fathers tend to be emotionally distant. These parental attitudes and behavior may contribute to affected girls' persistent anxiety and fierce pursuit of perfection in achievement, respectable behavior, and thinness (Kaye, 2008). Nevertheless, it remains unclear whether maladaptive parent–child relationships precede the disorder, emerge as a response to it, or both. In a longitudinal study in which 12- to 16-year-old girls were followed for four years, unhealthy eating behaviors led to conflict-ridden interactions with parents, not the reverse (Archibald et al., 2002).

Because individuals with anorexia commonly deny or minimize the seriousness of their disorder, treating it is difficult (Couturier & Lock, 2006). Hospitalization is often necessary to prevent life-threatening malnutrition. The most successful treatment is family therapy and medication to reduce anxiety and neurotransmitter imbalances (Fairburn, 2005; Treasure & Schmidt, 2005). As a supplementary approach, behavior modification—in which hospitalized patients are rewarded with praise, social contact, and opportunities for exercise when they eat and gain weight—is helpful.

Still, less than 50 percent of young people with anorexia recover fully. For many, eating problems continue in less extreme form. About 10 percent show signs of a less severe, but nevertheless debilitating, disorder: bulimia nervosa. And the chronic anxiety associated with both eating disorders increases girls' risk for major depression in both adolescence and adulthood (Godart et al., 2006).

BULIMIA NERVOSA   When Sabrina's 16-year-old brother, Louis, brought his girlfriend Cassie to the house, Sabrina admired her good figure. "What willpower!" Sabrina thought. "Cassie hardly touches food. But what's the matter with her teeth?"

Cassie's secret was not willpower. She actually had great difficulty controlling her appetite. Cassie suffered from **bulimia nervosa,** an eating disorder in which young people (again, mainly girls, but gay and bisexual boys are also vulnerable) engage in strict dieting and excessive exercise accompanied by binge eating, often followed by deliberate vomiting and purging with laxatives (Herzog, Eddy, & Beresin, 2006; Wichstrøm, 2006). When she was alone, Cassie often felt anxious and unhappy. She responded with eating rampages, consuming thousands of calories in an hour or two, followed by vomiting that eroded the enamel on her teeth. In some cases, bulimia can lead to life-threatening damage to the throat and stomach.

Bulimia is more common than anorexia nervosa, affecting about 2 to 4 percent of teenage girls, only 5 percent of whom previously suffered from anorexia. Twin studies show that bulimia, like anorexia, is influenced by heredity (Klump, Kaye, & Strober, 2001). Overweight and early menarche increase the risk. Some adolescents with bulimia, like those with anorexia, are perfectionists. But most are impulsive, sensation-seeking young people who lack self-control in many areas, engaging in petty shoplifting, alcohol abuse, and other risky behaviors (Kaye, 2008). And although girls with bulimia, like those with anorexia, are pathologically anxious about gaining weight, they may have experienced their parents as disengaged and emotionally unavailable rather than controlling (Fairburn & Harrison, 2003).

In contrast to young people with anorexia, those with bulimia usually feel depressed and guilty about their abnormal eating habits and desperately want help. As a result, bulimia is usually easier to treat than anorexia, through support groups, nutrition education, training in changing eating habits, and anti-anxiety, antidepressant, and appetite-control medication (Hay & Bacaltchuk, 2004).

Injuries

As noted in Chapter 11, the total rate of unintentional injuries increases during adolescence (see page 424), the result of risk taking fueled by sensation seeking and a tendency to act without forethought. Automobile accidents are the leading killer of U.S. teenagers, accounting for more than 40 percent of deaths between ages 15 and 19 (U.S. Department of Health and Human Services, 2010g). Many result from driving at high speeds, using alcohol, and not wearing seat belts. Parents must set firm limits on their teenagers' car use, particularly with respect to drinking and fastening seat belts. These efforts are more likely to succeed in families with a history of good parent–child communication—a powerful preventive of adolescent injury (Sleet & Mercy, 2003). Graduated licensing laws, aimed at keeping newly licensed teenagers from driving in high-risk situations—for example, by limiting the number of passengers, imposing a lower speed limit, and setting a curfew to be off the roads—reduce adolescent traffic fatalities by 6 to 11 percent (Dee, Grabowsky, & Morrisey, 2004). The more restrictive the regulations, the more lives saved.

In the United States, firearms cause the majority of other fatal injuries. Although violence-related behaviors among high school students have declined in the past decade, 14 percent report having carried a weapon within the past month—5 percent, a gun (U.S. Department of Health and Human Services, 2010g). The rate of disability and death resulting from firearms—mostly homicidal but occasionally accidental—is especially high in poverty-stricken inner-city neighborhoods. In response, many schools have installed metal detectors and security guards. But although these environmental changes increase teenagers' fear of crime, they have little impact on violence (Gagnon & Leone, 2002). School-based violence prevention programs (see Chapter 13, page 522) help reduce assaults. Banning handguns is an especially powerful tactic. In nations with strict gun registration, safety, and control policies, including prohibition of handguns, the firearm death rate among 15- to 19-year-olds is, on average, one-fourth the U.S. rate (see Figure 14.6).

A third type of adolescent injury is sports-related. More than one-fifth of students involved in sports experience injuries that require medical treatment (U.S. Department of Health and Human Services, 2010g). Most are muscle strains and bruises, but occasionally, severe injuries occur, generally from collision with others in basketball, football, ice hockey, and soccer and from physical fights between players (Cheng et al., 2000).

Teenagers who overestimate their sports ability are more likely to be reckless and, as a result, to be injured during games (Kontos, 2004). And coaches, in their drive to win, sometimes make unreasonable demands of players that can lead to injury. In one observational study, coaches of girls' softball tended to ignore players' complaints of pain from injury, encouraging them to "tough it out"—and highly committed players more often did so (Malcom, 2006). Young adolescents are especially vulnerable. Many coaches match competitors on the basis of age and weight without considering pubertal maturity, which yields massive gains in boys' muscle strength (Malina & Beunen, 1996). The safest athletic activities during the pubertal growth period are limited-contact team sports, such as basketball, softball, and volleyball, and individual sports, such as track, swimming, and tennis.

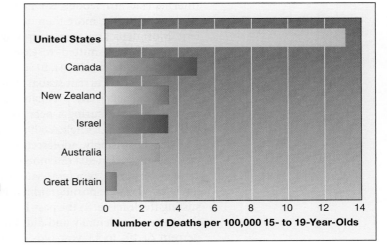

FIGURE 14.6

Firearm death rates among 15- to 19-year-olds in six industrialized nations. Death rates are far higher in the United States than in nations with strict gun control policies, including banning of handguns. *(From Fingerhut & Christoffel, 2002; U.S. Department of Health and Human Services, 2010g.)*

© JEFF GREENBERG/PHOTOEDIT

■ Adolescence is an especially important time for the development of sexuality. But American teenagers receive contradictory and confusing messages about their readiness for sex. ■

Sexual Activity

Louis and Cassie hadn't planned to have intercourse—it "just happened." But before and after, a lot of things passed through their minds. After they had been dating for three months, Cassie began to wonder, "Will Louis think I'm normal if I don't have sex with him? If he wants to and I say no, will I lose him?" Both young people knew their parents wouldn't approve. In fact, when Franca and Antonio noticed how attached Louis was to Cassie, they talked to him about the importance of waiting and the dangers of pregnancy. But that Friday evening, Louis and Cassie's feelings for each other seemed overwhelming. "If I don't make a move," Louis thought, "will she think I'm a wimp?"

With the arrival of puberty, hormonal changes—in particular, the production of androgens in young people of both sexes—lead to an increase in sex drive (Halpern, Udry, & Suchindran, 1997). In response, adolescents become very concerned about managing sexuality in social relationships. New cognitive capacities involving perspective taking and self-reflection affect their efforts to do so. Yet like the eating behaviors we have just discussed, adolescent sexuality is heavily influenced by the young person's social context.

THE IMPACT OF CULTURE **TAKE A MOMENT...** When did you first learn "the facts of life"—and how? Was sex discussed openly in your family, or was it treated with secrecy? Exposure to sex, education about it, and efforts to limit the sexual curiosity of children and adolescents vary widely around the world. At one extreme are a number of Middle Eastern peoples, who murder girls if they lose their virginity before marriage. At the other extreme are several Asian and Pacific Island groups with highly permissive sexual attitudes and practices. For example, among the Trobriand Islanders of Papua New Guinea, older companions provide children with instruction in sexual practices, and adolescents are expected to engage in sexual experimentation with a variety of partners (Weiner, 1988).

Despite the prevailing image of a sexually free adolescent, sexual attitudes in North America are relatively restrictive. Typically, parents provide little or no information about sex, discourage sex play, and rarely talk about sex in children's presence. When young people become interested in sex, only about half report getting information from parents about intercourse, pregnancy prevention, and sexually transmitted disease (see the Social Issues: Education box on pages 550–551).

Rather, the majority learn about sex from friends, books, magazines, movies, TV, and the Internet (Jaccard, Dodge, & Dittus, 2002; Sutton et al., 2002). On prime-time TV shows, which adolescents watch more than other TV offerings, 80 percent of programs contain sexual content. Most depict partners as spontaneous and passionate, taking no steps to avoid pregnancy or sexually transmitted disease, and experiencing no negative consequences (Roberts, Henriksen, & Foehr, 2004). In several studies, teenagers' media exposure to sexual content positively predicted current sexual activity, intentions to be sexually active in the future, and subsequent sexual activity, pregnancies, and sexual harassment behaviors (offensive name-calling or touching, pressuring a peer for a date), even after many other relevant factors were controlled (Brown & L'Engle, 2009; Chandra et al., 2008; Roberts, Henriksen, & Foehr, 2009).

Not surprisingly, adolescents who are prone to early sexual activity choose to consume more sexualized media (Steinberg & Monahan, 2010). Still, the Internet is a hazardous "sex educator." In a survey of a large sample of U.S. 10- to 17-year-old Web users, 42 percent said they had viewed online pornographic websites (images of naked people or people having sex) while surfing the Internet in the past 12 months. Of these, 66 percent indicated they had encountered the images accidentally and did not want to view them. Most were 13- to 17-year-olds, but 16 percent of 10- to 11-year-olds experienced these unwanted encounters. And youths who felt depressed, had been bullied by peers, or were involved in delinquent activities had more encounters with Internet pornography, which may have intensified their adjustment problems (Wolak, Mitchell, & Finkelhor, 2007).

Consider the contradictory messages delivered by these sources. On one hand, adults emphasize that sex at a young age and outside marriage is wrong. On the other hand, the social environment extols sexual excitement, experimentation, and promiscuousness. American teenagers are left bewildered, poorly informed about sexual facts, and with little sound advice on how to conduct their sex lives responsibly.

ADOLESCENT SEXUAL ATTITUDES AND BEHAVIOR

Although differences between subcultural groups exist, sexual attitudes of U.S. adolescents and adults have become more liberal over the past 40 years. Compared with a generation ago, more people approve of sexual intercourse before marriage, as long as two people are emotionally committed to each other (ABC News, 2004; Hoff, Greene, & Davis, 2003). During the past decade, adolescents have swung slightly back toward more conservative sexual beliefs, largely in response to the risk of sexually transmitted disease, especially AIDS, and to teenage sexual abstinence programs sponsored by schools and religious organizations (Ali & Scelfo, 2002; Cope-Farrar & Kunkel, 2002).

Trends in adolescents' sexual behavior are consistent with their attitudes. Rates of extramarital sex among U.S. young people rose for several decades but have recently declined (U.S. Department of Health and Human Services, 2010g). Nevertheless, as Figure 14.7 reveals, a substantial percentage of young people are sexually active quite early, by ninth grade (age 14 to 15).

Overall, teenage sexual activity rates are similar in the United States and other Western countries: Nearly half of adolescents have had intercourse. But quality of sexual experiences differs. U.S. youths become sexually active earlier than their Canadian and European counterparts (Boyce et al., 2006; U.S. Department of Health and Human Services, 2010g). And about 14 percent of adolescent boys in the United States—more than in other Western nations—have had sexual relations with three or more partners in the past year (Alan Guttmacher Institute, 2010). Most teenagers, however, have had only one or two sexual partners by the end of high school.

CHARACTERISTICS OF SEXUALLY ACTIVE ADOLESCENTS

Early and frequent teenage sexual activity is linked to personal, family, peer, and educational characteristics. These include childhood impulsivity, weak sense of personal control over life events, early pubertal timing, parental divorce, single-parent and stepfamily homes, large family size, little or no religious involvement, weak parental monitoring, disrupted parent–child communication, sexually active friends and older siblings, poor school performance, lower educational aspirations, and tendency to engage in norm-violating acts, including alcohol and drug use and delinquency (Coley, Votruba-Drzal, & Schindler, 2009; Crockett, Raffaelli, & Shen, 2006; Siebenbruner, Zimmer-Gembeck, & Egeland, 2007; Silver & Bauman, 2006).

Because many of these factors are associated with growing up in a low-income family, it is not surprising that early sexual activity is more common among young people from economically disadvantaged homes. Living in a neighborhood high in physical deterioration, crime, and violence also increases the likelihood that teenagers will be sexually active (Ge et al., 2002). In such neighborhoods, social ties are weak, adults exert little oversight and control over adolescents' activities, and negative peer influences are widespread. In fact, the high rate of sexual activity among African-American teenagers—65 percent report having had sexual intercourse, compared with 46 percent of all U.S. young people—is largely accounted for by widespread

FIGURE 14.7

U.S. adolescents who report ever having had sexual intercourse. Many young U.S. adolescents are sexually active—more than in other Western nations. Boys tend to have their first intercourse earlier than girls. In tenth and eleventh grades, rates of boys and girls having had sexual intercourse are similar. In twelfth grade, girls' rate exceeds boys'. *(From U.S. Department of Health and Human Services, 2010g.)*

SOCIAL ISSUES: EDUCATION

Parents and Teenagers (Don't) Talk About Sex

When a researcher asked a father of two girls and a boy to reflect on communication about sexual issues in his family, he replied,

I've never had to talk to my children . . . about these issues because . . . my wife's already done it. . . . I feel almost guilty for not partaking. The other thing, of course, is I don't know how—it's not an excuse, it's a fact. I don't know how comfortable they would be, me trying to talk to them about these topics. . . . So I guess it's a bit of a coward's way out, to save embarrassment by both parties. (Kirkman, Rosenthal, & Feldman, 2002, p. 60)

In families varying widely in SES and ethnicity, warm communication, in which parents provide information on sex and contraception and convey their values, is associated with teenagers' adoption of parents' views and with reduced sexual risk taking (Fasula & Miller, 2006; Jaccard, Dodge, & Dittus, 2003; Usher-Seriki, Bynum, & Callands, 2008). But many parents fail to discuss sex, birth control, and negative consequences of pregnancy with their teenagers. On average, only 50 percent of adolescents report such conversations (Jaccard, Dodge, & Dittus, 2002).

As this father's remarks suggest, parents steer clear of meaningful discussions with teenagers about sex out of fear of embarrassment and uncertainty about how to address sexual issues (Wilson et al., 2010). They also express concern that the adolescent will not take them seriously. And because teenagers frequently tell parents they already know everything they need to know, many parents conclude that talking about sex is unnecessary (Jaccard, Dittus, & Gordon, 2000). But adolescents' perceptions of their knowledge are only weakly related to their actual knowledge (Radecki & Jaccard, 1995).

When parents do initiate discussions, teenagers may be reluctant to participate. They complain that parents do not treat them as equals, know little about contemporary teenage lifestyles, and are not sufficiently open, supportive, and understanding. Perhaps because of their better communication skills, mothers talk to adolescents about sex and birth control more than fathers do. But mothers more often dominate conversations about sexual than about everyday matters, especially when talking to sons (Lefkowitz et al., 2002). When parents dominate, teenagers withdraw, reporting fewer sexual discussions and less knowledge (Lefkowitz, Sigman, & Au, 2000). Overall, balanced, mutual interaction and thorough consideration of sexual topics occur more often with daughters than with sons (Raffaelli & Green, 2003).

Cultural variations exist in parental communication about sex. For example, when Hispanic women who had grown up in U.S. Spanish-speaking families were asked to recall what their parents had told them about sex as teenagers, only a minority recalled talking about physical changes, intercourse, and pregnancy. Rather, parental messages usually took the form of strict limits on dating age, behavior, and place. Teresa, from a Mexican-American family, said, "You would be outside the house [where you could be observed] . . . your parents would tell you . . . no kissing or holding hands

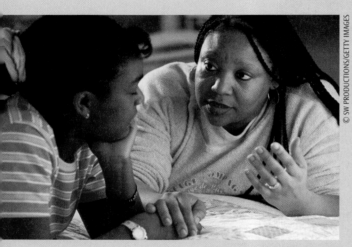

© SW PRODUCTIONS/GETTY IMAGES

■ By listening patiently and sympathetically, this mother encourages her daughter to ask questions and express opinions about sexual issues without feeling judged or uncomfortable. Warm communication about sexuality is associated with teenagers' adoption of parents' views and with reduced sexual risk taking. ■

poverty in the black population (Darroch, Frost, & Singh, 2001; U.S. Department of Health and Human Services, 2010g).

Early and prolonged father absence predicts higher rates of intercourse and pregnancy among adolescent girls, after many family background and personal characteristics are controlled (Ellis et al., 2003). Perhaps father absence exposes young people to the dating and sexual behaviors of their mothers, who serve as models for their physically maturing children. An alternative, evolutionary account proposes that fathers' investment in parenting encourages daughters to delay sexual activity in favor of seeking a similarly committed male partner to ensure their own and their offspring's well-being. Because father-absent girls view male commitment as uncertain, they may readily enter into casual sexual relationships.

CONTRACEPTIVE USE   Although adolescent contraceptive use has increased in recent years, about 20 percent of sexually active teenagers in the United States are at risk for unintended pregnancy because they do not use contraception consistently (see Figure 14.8 on page 552) (Alan Guttmacher Institute, 2002, 2005; Manlove, Ryan, & Franzetta, 2003). Why do so or nothing, actually it was just talking . . . until you decided whether you wanted to get married and then . . . the guy would have to . . . ask for your hand in marriage" (Raffaelli & Ontai, 2001, p. 301). The gap between parental expectations and U.S. cultural dating practices often became a source of conflict. Many women reported having engaged in "sneak dating," but they were ill-prepared to manage their own sexual behavior. Over half did not use birth control the first time they had sex, and nearly a third had an unplanned pregnancy.

In sum, parent-based sex education has many advantages. Parents can discuss topics in ways consistent with their own values and, unlike school classes, can tailor their delivery of information to the adolescent's personality and current life circumstances. But parents need help communicating effectively. In one study, mothers who received training in talking with teenagers about sex, compared with a no-training control group, engaged in more give-and-take, asked more open-ended questions, were less judgmental, and discussed dating and sexuality more extensively. And their teenagers reported increased comfort with conversations and more consideration of birth control (Lefkowitz, Sigman, & Au, 2000). Refer to Applying What We Know below for qualities of successful communication.

Applying What We Know

Communicating with Adolescents About Sexual Issues

STRATEGY	EXPLANATION
Foster open communication.	Let the teenager know you are a willing and trustworthy resource by stating that you are available when questions arise and will answer fully and accurately.
Use correct terms for body parts.	Correct vocabulary gives the young person a basis for future discussion and also indicates that sex is not a forbidden topic.
Use effective discussion techniques.	Listen, encourage the adolescent to participate, ask open-ended rather than yes/no questions, and give supportive responses. Avoid dominating and lecturing, which cause teenagers to withdraw.
Reflect before speaking.	When the adolescent asks questions or offers opinions about sex, remain nonjudgmental. If you differ with the teenager's views, convey your perspective in a nonthreatening manner, emphasizing that although you disagree, you are not attacking his or her character. Trying to dictate the young person's behavior generally results in alienation.
Keep conversations going.	Many parents think their job is finished once they have had the "big talk" in early adolescence. But young people are more likely to be influenced by an accumulation of smaller discussions. If open communication begins early and is sustained, the teenager is more likely to return with thoughts and questions.

Source: Berkowitz, 2004; Wilson et al., 2010.

many fail to take precautions? As we will see when we take up adolescent cognitive development in Chapter 15, although adolescents can consider many possibilities when faced with a problem, they often fail to apply this reasoning to everyday situations. When asked to explain why they did not use contraception, they are likely to say something like, "I was waiting until I had a steady boyfriend," or "I wasn't planning to have sex."

One reason for these responses is that, as noted earlier, young teenagers, especially, tend to be extremely concerned about others' opinion of them. Recall how Cassie and Louis each worried about what the other would think if they decided not to have sex. Furthermore, we have seen that in the midst of everyday peer pressures, self-regulation is difficult for adolescents, who often overlook the consequences of engaging in risky behaviors. And many teenagers—especially those from troubled, low-SES families—do not have realistic expectations about the impact of early parenthood on their current and future lives (Stevens-Simon, Sheeder, & Harter, 2005).

As these findings suggest, the social environment also contributes to adolescents' reluctance to use contraception. Those without the rewards of meaningful education and work are

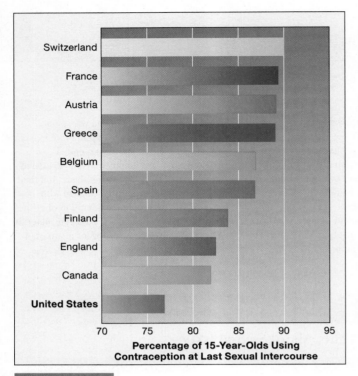

FIGURE 14.8

Contraceptive use by sexually active 15-year-olds in ten industrialized nations. Sexually active U.S. teenagers are less likely to use contraception (condom, contraceptive pill, or both) consistently than teenagers in other industrialized nations. *(Adapted from Godeau et al., 2008; U.S. Department of Health and Human Services, 2010g.)*

especially likely to engage in irresponsible sex, sometimes within relationships characterized by exploitation. About 11 percent of U.S. girls and 5 percent of boys say they were pressured to have intercourse when they were unwilling (U.S. Department of Health and Human Services, 2010g).

In contrast, teenagers who report good relationships with parents and who talk openly with them about sex and contraception are more likely to use birth control (Henrich et al., 2006; Kirby, 2002a). But few adolescents believe their parents would be understanding and supportive. School sex education classes, as well, often leave teenagers with incomplete or incorrect knowledge. Some young people do not know where to get birth control counseling and devices; those who do often worry that a doctor or family planning clinic might not keep their visits confidential. About 20 percent of adolescents using health services say that if their parents were notified, they would still have sex, but without contraception (Jones et al., 2005).

SEXUAL ORIENTATION   So far, we have focused only on heterosexual behavior. About 4 percent of U.S. 15- to 44-year-olds identify as lesbian, gay, or bisexual (Mosher, Chandra, & Jones, 2005). An unknown number experience same-sex attraction but have not come out to friends or family (see the Biology and Environment box on the following page). Adolescence is an equally crucial time for the sexual development of these individuals, and societal attitudes, once again, loom large in how well they fare.

Heredity makes an important contribution to homosexuality: Identical twins of both sexes are much more likely than fraternal twins to share a homosexual orientation; so are biological (as opposed to adoptive) relatives (Kendler et al., 2000; Kirk et al., 2000). Furthermore, male homosexuality tends to be more common on the maternal than on the paternal side of families, suggesting that it may be X-linked (see Chapter 2). Indeed, one gene-mapping study found that among 40 pairs of homosexual brothers, 33 (82 percent) had an identical segment of DNA on the X chromosome. One or several genes in that region might predispose males to become homosexual (Hamer et al., 1993).

How might heredity lead to homosexuality? According to some researchers, certain genes affect the level or impact of prenatal sex hormones, which modify brain structures in ways that induce homosexual feelings and behavior (Bailey et al., 1995; LeVay, 1993). In Chapter 10, we saw how prenatal androgen exposure influences children's gender-typical play behaviors (see page 391). Consistent with early hormonal influences, childhood gender nonconformity—boys' preference for quiet, "feminine" play and girls' preference for active, "masculine" pursuits—is strongly linked to homosexuality.

Keep in mind, however, that both genetic and environmental factors can alter prenatal hormones. Girls exposed prenatally to very high levels of androgens or estrogens—either because of a genetic defect or from drugs given to the mother to prevent miscarriage—are more likely to become homosexual or bisexual (Meyer-Bahlburg et al., 1995). Furthermore, homosexual men tend to be later in birth order and to have a higher-than-average number of older brothers (Blanchard & Bogaert, 2004). Perhaps mothers with several male children sometimes produce antibodies to androgens, which reduce the prenatal impact of male sex hormones on the brains of later-born boys.

Stereotypes and misconceptions about homosexuality and bisexuality continue to be widespread. For example, contrary to common belief, most homosexual adolescents and adults are not "gender-deviant" in dress or behavior. Also, attraction to members of the same sex is not limited to gay, lesbian, and bisexual teenagers. About 50 to 60 percent of adolescents who report having engaged in homosexual acts identify as heterosexual (Savin-Williams &

BIOLOGY AND ENVIRONMENT

Gay, Lesbian, and Bisexual Youths: Coming Out to Oneself and Others

Cultures vary as much in their acceptance of homosexuality as in their approval of extramarital sex. In the United States, homosexuals are stigmatized, as shown by the degrading language often used to describe them. This makes forming a sexual identity a much greater challenge for gay, lesbian, and bisexual youths than for their heterosexual counterparts.

Wide variations in sexual identity formation exist, depending on personal, family, and community factors. Yet interviews with gay and lesbian adolescents and adults reveal that many (though not all) move through a three-phase sequence in coming out to themselves and others.

Feeling Different

Many gay men and lesbians recall feeling different from other children when they were young. Typically, this first sense of their biologically determined sexual orientation appears between ages 6 and 12, in play interests more like those of the other gender (Rahman & Wilson, 2003). Boys may find that they are less interested in sports, more drawn to quieter activities, and more emotionally sensitive than other boys; girls that they are more athletic and active than other girls.

By age 10, many of these children start to engage in *sexual questioning*—wondering why the typical heterosexual orientation does not apply to them. Often, they experience their sense of being different as deeply distressing. Compared with children who are confident of their homosexuality, sexual-questioning children report greater anxiety about peer relationships and greater dissatisfaction with their biological gender over time (Carver, Egan, & Perry, 2004).

Confusion

With the arrival of puberty, feeling different clearly encompasses feeling sexually different. In research on ethnically diverse gay, lesbian, and bisexual youths, awareness of a same-sex physical attraction occurred, on average, between ages 11 and 12 for boys and 14 and 15 for girls, perhaps because adolescent social pressures toward heterosexuality are particularly intense for girls (D'Augelli, 2006; Diamond, 1998).

Realizing that homosexuality has personal relevance generally sparks additional confusion. A few adolescents resolve their discomfort by crystallizing a gay, lesbian, or bisexual identity quickly, with a flash of insight into their sense of

being different. But most experience an inner struggle and deep sense of isolation—outcomes intensified by lack of role models and social support (D'Augelli, 2002; Safren & Pantalone, 2006).

Some throw themselves into activities they associate with heterosexuality. Boys may go out for athletic teams; girls may drop softball and basketball in favor of dance. And many homosexual youths (more females than males) try heterosexual dating, sometimes to hide their sexual orientation and at other times to develop intimacy skills that they later apply to same-sex relationships (D'Augelli, 2006; Dubé, Savin-Williams, & Diamond, 2001). Those who are extremely troubled and guilt-ridden may escape into alcohol, drugs, and suicidal thinking. Suicide attempts are unusually high among gay, lesbian, and bisexual young people (McDaniel, Purcell, & D'Augelli, 2001; Morrow, 2006).

Self-Acceptance

By the end of adolescence, the majority of gay, lesbian, and bisexual teenagers accept their sexual identity. But they face another crossroad: whether to tell others. Powerful stigma against their sexual orientation leads some to decide that disclosure is impossible; while self-defining as gay, they otherwise "pass" as heterosexual (Savin-Williams, 2001). When homosexual youths do come out, they often face intense hostility. In a study of over 500 gay, lesbian, and bisexual youths in Canada, New Zealand, and the United States, 75 percent reported being verbally abused, and 15 percent physically attacked, because of their sexual orientation (D'Augelli, 2002). These experiences trigger intense emotional distress, depression, school truancy, and drug use in victims (Almeida et al., 2009; Birkett, Espelage, & Koenig, 2009).

Nevertheless, many young people eventually acknowledge their sexual orientation publicly, usually by telling trusted friends first. Once teenagers establish a same-sex sexual or romantic relationship, many come out to parents. Few parents respond with severe rejection; most are either positive or slightly negative and disbelieving (Savin-Williams & Ream, 2003). Parental understanding is

the strongest predictor of favorable adjustment—including reduced *internalized homophobia,* or societal prejudice turned against the self (D'Augelli, Grossman, & Starks, 2005, 2008).

When people react positively, coming out strengthens the young person's view of homosexuality as a valid, meaningful, and fulfilling identity. Contact with other gays and lesbians is important for reaching this phase, and changes in society permit many adolescents in urban areas to attain it earlier than their counterparts did a decade or two ago. Gay and lesbian communities exist in large cities, along with specialized interest groups, social clubs, religious groups, newspapers, and periodicals. But teenagers in small towns and rural areas may have difficulty meeting other gay and lesbian youths and finding a supportive environment. These adolescents have a special need for caring adults and peers who can help them find self- and social acceptance.

Gay, lesbian, and bisexual teenagers who succeed in coming out to themselves and others integrate their sexual orientation into a broader sense of identity, a process we will address in Chapter 16. As a result, they no longer need to focus so heavily on their homosexual self, and energy is freed for other aspects of psychological growth. In sum, coming out can foster many aspects of adolescent development, including self-esteem, psychological well-being, and relationships with family and friends.

■ Teenagers prepare to celebrate ALLY week, designed to encourage students to be allies against bullying and harassment of lesbians, gays, bisexuals, and transgender students in U.S. schools. When peers react with acceptance, coming out strengthens the young person's view of homosexuality as a valid and fulfilling identity. ■

Diamond, 2004). And a study of lesbian, bisexual, and "unlabeled" young women confirmed that bisexuality is not, as often assumed, a transient state (Diamond, 2008). Over a 10-year period, few bisexuals changed to a lesbian or heterosexual orientation, and most reported stable proportions of same-sex versus other-sex attractions over time.

The evidence to date suggests that genetic and prenatal biological influences are largely responsible for homosexuality; the origins of bisexuality are not yet known. In our evolutionary past, homosexuality may have served the adaptive function of reducing aggressive competition for other-sex mates, thereby promoting the survival of group members (Rahman & Wilson, 2003).

Sexually Transmitted Diseases

Sexually active adolescents, both homosexual and heterosexual, are at risk for sexually transmitted diseases (STDs) (see Table 14.2). Adolescents have the highest rates of STDs of all age groups. Despite a recent decline in STDs in the United States, one out of six sexually active teenagers contracts one of these illnesses each year—a rate three or more times higher than

TABLE 14.2 Most Common Sexually Transmitted Diseases of Adolescence

DISEASE	REPORTED U.S. CASES PER 100,000 15- TO 19-YEAR-OLDS	CAUSE	SYMPTOMS AND CONSEQUENCES	TREATMENT
AIDS	20[a]	Virus	Fever, weight loss, severe fatigue, swollen glands, and diarrhea. As the immune system weakens, severe pneumonias and cancers, especially on the skin, appear. Death due to other diseases usually occurs.	No cure; experimental drugs prolong life
Chlamydia	1,956	Bacteria	Discharge from the penis in males; painful itching, burning vaginal discharge, and dull pelvic pain in females. Often no symptoms. If left untreated, can lead to inflammation of the pelvic region, infertility, and sterility.	Antibiotic drugs
Cytomegalovirus	Unknown[b]	Virus of the herpes family	No symptoms in most cases. Sometimes a mild flulike reaction. In pregnant women, can spread to the embryo or fetus and cause miscarriage or serious birth defects (see page 111).	None; usually disappears on its own
Gonorrhea	453	Bacteria	Discharge from the penis or vagina, painful urination. Sometimes no symptoms. If left untreated, can spread to other regions of the body, resulting in such complications as infertility, sterility, blood poisoning, arthritis, and inflammation of the heart.	Antibiotic drugs
Herpes simplex 2 (genital herpes)	1,400	Virus	Fluid-filled blisters on the genitals, high fever, severe headache, and muscle aches and tenderness. No symptoms in a few people. In a pregnant woman, can spread to the embryo or fetus and cause miscarriage or serious birth defects (see page 111).	No cure; can be controlled with drug treatment
Human papillomavirus	15,000	Virus	Causes genital warts that typically grow near the vaginal opening in females, on the penis or scrotum in males, which may be accompanied by severe itching. Can cause cellular changes that lead to cervical, vaginal, anal, and less commonly penile and oral cancers. A vaccine that prevents the disease is recommended for adolescent girls and women age 11 to 26; its effectiveness for boys and men is not yet known.	Removal of warts, but virus persists
Syphilis	4.2	Bacteria	Painless chancre (sore) at site of entry of germ and swollen glands, followed by rash, patchy hair loss, and sore throat within 1 week to 6 months. These symptoms disappear without treatment. Latent syphilis varies from no symptoms to damage to the brain, heart, and other organs after 5 to 20 years. In pregnant women, can spread to the embryo and fetus and cause birth defects.	Antibiotic drugs

[a]This figure includes both adolescents and young adults. For most U.S. cases, the virus is contracted in adolescence, and symptoms appear in early adulthood.

[b]Cytomegalovirus is the most common STD. Because there are no symptoms in most cases, its precise rate of occurrence is unknown. Half of the population or more may have had the virus sometime during their lives.

Sources: U.S. Department of Health and Human Services, 2009h, 2010d, 2010f.

Applying What We Know

Preventing Sexually Transmitted Diseases

STRATEGY	EXPLANATION
Know your partner well.	Take time to get to know your partner. Find out whether your partner has had sex with many people or has used injectable drugs.
Maintain mutual faithfulness.	This strategy works only when neither partner has an STD at the start of the relationship.
Do not use drugs.	Using a needle, syringe, or drug liquid previously used by others can spread STDs. Alcohol, marijuana, or other illegal substances impair judgment, reducing your capacity to think clearly about the consequences of behavior.
Always use a latex condom and vaginal contraceptive when having sex with a nonmarital partner.	Latex condoms give good (but not perfect) protection against STDs by reducing the passage of bacteria and viruses. Vaginal contraceptives containing nonoxynol-9 can kill several kinds of STD microbes. They increase protection when combined with condom use.
Do not have sex with a person you know has an STD.	Even if you are protected by a condom, you still risk contracting STDs. If either partner has engaged in behavior that might have risked HIV infection, a blood test to detect infection must be administered and repeated at least six months after that behavior, to allow for the time the body takes to develop antibodies.
If you get an STD, inform all recent sexual partners.	Notifying people you may have exposed to an STD permits them to get treatment before spreading the disease to others.

that of Canada and Western Europe (Health Canada, 2008; U.S. Department of Health and Human Services, 2009). Teenagers at greatest risk are the same ones most likely to engage in irresponsible sexual behavior: poverty-stricken young people who feel a sense of hopelessness (Niccolai et al., 2004). Left untreated, STDs can lead to sterility and life-threatening complications.

By far the most serious STD is AIDS. In contrast to other Western nations, where the incidence of AIDS among people under age 30 is low, one-fifth of U.S. AIDS cases occur in young people between ages 20 and 29. Because AIDS symptoms typically do not emerge until 8 to 10 years after infection with the HIV virus, nearly all these cases originated in adolescence. Drug-abusing teenagers who share needles and male adolescents who have sex with HIV-positive same-sex partners account for most cases, but heterosexual spread of the disease remains high, especially among teenagers with more than one partner in the previous 18 months (U.S. Department of Health and Human Services, 2010a). It is at least twice as easy for a male to infect a female with any STD, including HIV, as for a female to infect a male. Currently, females account for about 37 percent of new U.S. cases among adolescents and young adults (Rangel et al., 2006).

As the result of school courses and media campaigns, about 60 percent of U.S. middle school students and 90 percent of high school students are aware of basic facts about AIDS. But most have limited understanding of other STDs and their consequences, underestimate their own susceptibility, and are poorly informed about how to protect themselves (Coholl et al., 2001; Ethier et al., 2003). Furthermore, high school students report engaging in oral sex much more often than intercourse, and with more partners. But few report consistently using STD protection during oral sex, which is a significant mode of transmission of several STDs, including chlamydia, gonorrhea, herpes, and perhaps AIDS (Prinstein, Meade, & Cohen, 2003). Concerted efforts are needed to educate young people about the full range of STDs and risky sexual behaviors. Applying What We Know above lists strategies for STD prevention.

Adolescent Pregnancy and Parenthood

Cassie didn't get pregnant after having sex with Louis, but some of her high school classmates were less fortunate. Cassie had heard about Veronica, who missed several periods, pretended nothing was wrong, and didn't go to a doctor until a month before she gave birth. Veronica

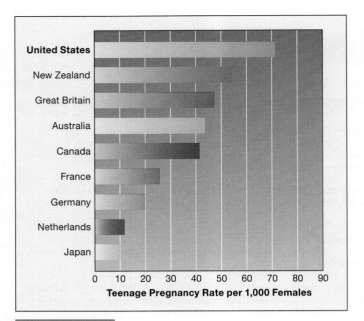

FIGURE 14.9

Pregnancy rates among 15- to 19-year-olds in nine industrialized nations. U.S. teenagers have the highest pregnancy rate. *(Adapted from Alan Guttmacher Institute, 2010; Alford & Hauser, 2009.)*

lived at home until she became pregnant a second time. When her parents told her they didn't have room for a second baby, Veronica dropped out of school and moved in with her 17-year-old boyfriend, Todd, who worked at a fast-food restaurant. A few months later, Todd—tired of being tied down with the babies—left Veronica, who had to apply for public aid to support herself and the two infants.

About 740,000 U.S. teenage girls (15,000 of them younger than age 15)—an estimated 20 percent of those who had sexual intercourse—became pregnant in the most recently reported year. Despite a steady decline since 1991, the U.S. adolescent pregnancy rate is much higher than that of any other industrialized country (see Figure 14.9). Three factors heighten the incidence of adolescent pregnancy: (1) Effective sex education reaches too few teenagers; (2) convenient, low-cost contraceptive services for adolescents are scarce; and (3) many families live in poverty, which encourages young people to take risks without considering the future implications of their behavior.

Because one-third of U.S. adolescent pregnancies end in abortion, the number of American teenage births is actually lower than it was 50 years ago (Alan Guttmacher Institute, 2010). But teenage parenthood is a much greater problem today because contemporary adolescents are far less likely to marry before childbirth. In 1960, only 15 percent of teenage births were to unmarried females, compared with 86 percent today (Child Trends, 2010). Increased social acceptance of single motherhood, along with the belief of many teenage girls that a baby might fill a void in their lives, means that very few girls give up their infants for adoption.

CORRELATES AND CONSEQUENCES OF ADOLESCENT PARENTHOOD Becoming a parent is especially challenging for adolescents, who have not yet established a clear sense of direction for their own lives. Life conditions and personal attributes jointly contribute to adolescent childbearing and also interfere with teenage mothers' capacity to parent effectively (Jaffee et al., 2001).

Teenage parents are far more likely to be poor than agemates who postpone parenthood. Their backgrounds often include low parental warmth and involvement, domestic violence and child abuse, repeated parental divorce and remarriage, adult models of unmarried parenthood, and residence in neighborhoods where other adolescents also display these risks. Girls at risk for early pregnancy also do poorly in school, engage in alcohol and drug use, have a childhood history of aggressive and antisocial behavior, associate with deviant peers, and experience high rates of depression (Elfenbein & Felice, 2003: Hillis et al., 2004; Luster & Haddow, 2005). A high percentage of out-of-wedlock births are to low-income ethnic minority teenagers. Many turn to early parenthood as a way to move into adulthood when educational and career avenues are unavailable.

The lives of expectant teenagers, already troubled in many ways, tend to worsen in several respects after the baby is born:

■ *Educational attainment.* Parenthood before age 18 reduces the likelihood of finishing high school. Only about 70 percent of U.S. adolescent mothers graduate, compared with 95 percent of girls who wait to become parents (National Women's Law Center, 2007). Lack of material resources—often due to living apart from one's own parents and not having access to child care—greatly reduces the likelihood of earning a high school diploma (Mollborn, 2007).

■ *Marital patterns.* Teenage motherhood reduces the chances of marriage and, for those who do marry, increases the likelihood of divorce compared with peers who delay childbearing

(Moore & Brooks-Gunn, 2002). Consequently, teenage mothers spend more of their parenting years as single parents. About 35 percent become pregnant again within two years. Of these, about half go on to deliver a second child (Child Trends, 2010).

■ *Economic circumstances.* Because of low educational attainment, marital instability, and poverty, many teenage mothers are unemployed and on welfare. If they are employed, their limited education restricts them to unsatisfying, low-paid jobs. Many adolescent fathers, too, are unemployed or work at unskilled jobs, usually earning too little to provide their children with basic necessities (Bunting & McAuley, 2004). An estimated 50 percent have committed illegal offenses resulting in imprisonment (Elfenbein & Felice, 2003). And for both mothers and fathers, reduced educational and occupational attainment often persists well into adulthood (Furstenburg, 2007; Taylor, 2009)

Because many pregnant teenage girls have inadequate diets, smoke, use alcohol and other drugs, and do not receive early prenatal care, their babies often experience prenatal and birth complications—especially low birth weight (Dell, 2001). And compared with adult mothers, adolescent mothers know less about child development, have unrealistically high expectations of their infants, perceive their babies as more difficult, interact less effectively with them, and more often engage in child abuse (Moore & Florsheim, 2001; Pomerleau, Scuccimarri, & Malcuit, 2003; Sieger & Renk, 2007). Their children tend to score low on intelligence tests, achieve poorly in school, and engage in disruptive social behavior.

Furthermore, teenage parents tend to pass on their personal attributes as well as create unfavorable child-rearing conditions. Consequently, their offspring are at risk for irresponsible sexual activity when they reach puberty. As the Social Issues: Health box on page 558 indicates, adolescent parenthood frequently is repeated in the next generation. Even when children born to teenage parents do not become early childbearers, their development is often compromised, in terms of likelihood of high school graduation, financial independence in adulthood, and long-term physical and mental health (Moore, Morrison, & Green, 1997; Pogarsky, Thornberry, & Lizotte, 2006).

Still, outcomes vary widely. If a teenage mother finishes high school, secures gainful employment, avoids additional births, and finds a stable partner, long-term disruptions in her own and her child's development will be less severe.

PREVENTION STRATEGIES   Preventing teenage pregnancy means addressing the many factors underlying early sexual activity and lack of contraceptive use. Too often, sex education courses are given late (after sexual activity has begun), last only a few sessions, and are limited to a catalog of facts about anatomy and reproduction. Sex education that goes beyond this minimum does not encourage early sex, as some opponents claim (Kirby, 2002c). It does improve awareness of sexual facts—knowledge that is necessary for responsible behavior.

Knowledge, however, is not enough. Sex education must also help teenagers build a bridge between what they know and what they do. Effective sex education programs combine several key elements:

■ They teach techniques for handling sexual situations—including refusal skills for avoiding risky sexual behaviors and communication skills for improving contraceptive use—through role-playing and other activities in which young people practice those behaviors.

■ They deliver clear, accurate messages that are appropriate in view of participating adolescents' culture and sexual experiences.

■ They last long enough to have an impact.

■ They provide specific information about contraceptives and ready access to them.

Many studies show that sex education that includes these components can delay the initiation of sexual activity, increase contraceptive use, change attitudes (for example, strengthen future orientation), and reduce pregnancy rates (Kirby, 2002b, 2008; Thomas & Dimitrov, 2007).

Proposals to increase access to contraceptives are the most controversial aspect of U.S. adolescent pregnancy prevention efforts. Many adults argue that placing birth control pills or

LOOK AND LISTEN

Contact a nearby public school district and ask for information about its sex education curriculum. Considering research findings, do you think it is likely to be effective in delaying initiation of sexual activity and reducing adolescent pregnancy rates?

SOCIAL ISSUES: HEALTH

Like Parent, Like Child: Intergenerational Continuity in Adolescent Parenthood

Does adolescent parenthood increase the chances of teenage childbearing in the next generation? To find out, researchers have conducted several unique studies of mothers (first generation)—some who gave birth as teenagers and some who postponed parenting—and their children (second generation), who were followed longitudinally (Barber, 2001b; Campa & Eckenrode, 2006; Hardy et al., 1998; Manlove, 1997; Mead, Kershaw, & Ickovics, 2008).

First-generation mothers' age at first childbirth strongly predicted the age at which second-generation young people—both daughters and sons—became parents. Yet becoming a second-generation teenage parent is not inevitable for individuals born to an adolescent mother. Rather, adolescent parenthood is linked to a set of related, unfavorable family conditions and personal characteristics, which negatively influence development over an extended time and, therefore, often transfer to the next generation:

- *Home environmental quality and parenting skills.* The long-term poverty and unstable marital patterns linked to adolescent parenthood reduce the quality of the home environment—in terms of organization, play and learning materials, and parental warmth, encouragement, verbal stimulation, and acceptance of the child (as opposed to punitiveness and abuse) (Mead, Kershaw, & Ickovics, 2008). Compared with daughters in other families, the daughters of unmarried

adolescent mothers live in families that obtain lower early childhood HOME scores (see page 347 in Chapter 9), even after mothers' prebirth SES is controlled (Campa & Eckenrode, 2006). Low HOME scores are associated with poorer language and IQ scores, which, in turn, contribute to the poor school performance and decision making associated with early sexual activity, laxity in use of contraceptives, and adolescent childbearing.

- *Intelligence and education.* Younger mothers' cognitive deficits and reduced educational attainment contribute to the likelihood their children will experience long-term, poor-quality home environments and, thus, in adolescence will engage in the maladaptive behaviors just mentioned (Barber, 2001a; Hardy et al., 1998).

- *Father absence.* In several studies, intergenerational continuity in adolescent parenthood—especially for daughters—was far greater when teenage mothers remained unmarried (Barber, 2001b; Campa & Eckenrode, 2006; Meade, Kershaw, & Ickovics, 2008). Marriage may limit the negative impact of teenage childbearing on development by strengthening parental financial resources

and involvement and reducing family stress. It may be particularly protective for girls because unmarried fathers are less likely to remain in regular contact with daughters than with sons. Recall from Chapter 13 that a warm, involved noncustodial father is linked to reduced early sexual activity in girls (see page 512).

In sum, a life course of adversity—poverty, depleted and disorganized home environments, poor parenting, father absence, intellectual deficits, poor academic performance, and limited educational opportunities—contribute to intergenerational continuity in adolescent pregnancy and parenthood.

■ Will the child of this teenage mother also become an adolescent parent? Negative family conditions and personal characteristics associated with early childbearing increase the likelihood that teenage parenthood will recur in the next generation. ■

---

condoms in the hands of teenagers is equivalent to approving of early sex. Yet sex education programs focusing on abstinence have little or no impact on delaying teenage sexual activity or on preventing pregnancy (Bennett & Assefi, 2005; Underhill, Montgomery, & Operario, 2007). In one study, teenagers who had not yet become sexually active and who had taken virginity pledges—a centerpiece of many abstinence programs—were just as likely to have sex as their nonpledging agemates. However, fewer pledgers than nonpledgers used birth control (Rosenbaum, 2009). And five years after the pledge, 82 percent of the pledgers denied having ever pledged.

In Canada and Western Europe, where community- and school-based clinics offer adolescents contraceptives and where universal health insurance helps pay for them, teenage sexual activity is no higher than in the United States—but pregnancy, childbirth, and abortion rates are much lower (Schalet, 2007). Radio and TV campaigns promoting contraceptive use—used widely in Africa, Europe, India, and South America—are associated with a reduction in early sexual activity and with an increase in teenagers' use of birth control (Keller & Brown, 2002).

Efforts to prevent adolescent pregnancy and parenthood must go beyond improving sex education and access to contraception to build academic and social competence (Allen, Seitz, & Apfel, 2007). In one study, researchers randomly assigned at-risk high school students to either a year-long community service class, called Teen Outreach, or to regular classroom experiences in health or social studies. In Teen Outreach, adolescents spent at least 20 hours per week in volunteer work tailored to their interests. They returned to school for discussions that focused on enhancing their community service skills and ability to cope with everyday challenges. At the end of the school year, pregnancy, school failure, and school suspension were substantially lower in the group enrolled in Teen Outreach, which fostered social skills, connection to community, and self-respect (Allen et al., 1997).

Finally, school involvement is linked to delayed initiation of sexual activity and to reduced teenage pregnancy, perhaps because it increases interaction with and attachment to adults who discourage risk taking, and it strengthens belief in a promising future (Harris, 2008). We will take up factors that promote adolescents' commitment to school in Chapter 15.

■ A young teenager involved in a Teen Outreach service project prepares a meal for cancer patients. Volunteer work and related class discussions aimed at skill-building promote self-respect and community connection while reducing adolescent pregnancy, school failure, and school suspension. ■

INTERVENING WITH ADOLESCENT PARENTS   The most difficult and costly way to deal with adolescent parenthood is to wait until it happens. Young parents need health care, encouragement to stay in school, job training, instruction in parenting and life-management skills, and high-quality, affordable child care. Schools that provide these services reduce the incidence of low-birth-weight babies, increase educational success, and prevent additional childbearing (Key et al., 2008; Seitz & Apfel, 2005).

Adolescent mothers also benefit from relationships with family members and other adults who are sensitive to their developmental needs. Older teenage mothers display more effective parenting when they establish their own residence with the help of relatives—an arrangement that offers a balance of autonomy and support (East & Felice, 1996). In one study, African-American teenage mothers who had a long-term "mentor" relationship—an aunt, neighbor, or teacher who provided emotional support and guidance—were far more likely than those without a mentor to stay in school and graduate (Klaw, Rhodes, & Fitzgerald, 2003).

Programs focusing on fathers attempt to increase their financial and emotional commitment to the baby. Although nearly half of young fathers visit their children during the first few years, contact usually diminishes. By the time the child starts school, fewer than one-fourth have regular paternal contact. As with teenage mothers, support from family members helps fathers say involved (Bunting & McAuley, 2004). Teenage mothers who receive financial and child-care assistance and emotional support from the child's father are less distressed and more likely to sustain a relationship with him (Cutrona et al., 1998; Gee & Rhodes, 2003). And infants with lasting ties to their teenage fathers receive warmer, more stimulating caregiving and show better long-term adjustment (Florsheim & Smith, 2005; Furstenberg & Harris, 1993).

Laws that enforce child support payments are aimed at increasing paternal responsibility. But unless these efforts are accompanied by assistance in finding adequate employment, teenage fathers may flee to evade arrest instead of becoming involved with their children. Fatherhood interventions that begin early, before the relationship with the adolescent mother withers or terminates, are more likely to succeed (McLanahan & Carlson, 2002).

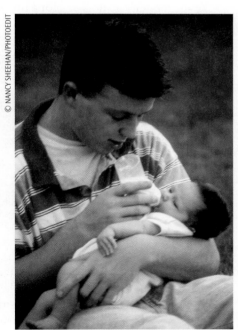

■ Early parenthood imposes lasting hardships on adolescent parents and their newborn babies. But the involvement of a caring father and a stable partnership between the parents can improve outcomes for young families. ■

Substance Use and Abuse

At age 14, Louis waited until he was alone at home, took some cigarettes from his uncle's pack, and smoked them. At an unchaperoned party, he and Cassie drank several cans of beer and lit up marijuana joints. Louis got little physical charge out of these experiences. A good student, who was well-liked by peers and got along well with his parents, he did not need drugs as an escape valve. But he knew of other teenagers who started with alcohol and cigarettes, moved on to harder substances, and eventually were hooked.

Teenage alcohol and drug use is pervasive in industrialized nations. According to the most recent, nationally representative survey of U.S. high school students, by tenth grade, 33 percent of U.S. young people have tried smoking, 59 percent drinking, and 38 percent at least one illegal drug (usually marijuana). At the end of high school, 15 percent smoke cigarettes regularly, and 16 percent have engaged in heavy drinking during the past month. About 24 percent have tried at least one highly addictive and toxic substance, such as amphetamines, cocaine, phencyclidine (PCP), Ecstasy (MDMA), inhalants, heroin, sedatives (including barbiturates), or OxyContin (a narcotic painkiller) (Johnston et al., 2010).

These figures represent a substantial decline since the mid-1990s, probably resulting from greater parent, school, and media focus on the hazards of drug taking. But use of some substances—marijuana, inhalants, sedatives, and OxyContin—has risen slightly in recent years (Johnson et al., 2010). Other drugs, such as LSD, PCP, and Ecstasy, have made a comeback as adolescents' knowledge of their risks faded.

In part, drug taking reflects the sensation seeking of the teenage years. But adolescents also live in drug-dependent cultural contexts. They see adults relying on caffeine to stay alert, alcohol and cigarettes to cope with daily hassles, and other remedies to relieve stress, depression, and physical discomfort. And compared to a decade or two ago, today doctors more often prescribe—and parents frequently seek—medication to treat children's problems (Brody, 2006). In adolescence, these young people may readily "self-medicate" when stressed. Furthermore, over 90 percent of teenagers are aware of cigarette and alcohol ads specifically targeting them, and most say these ads influence their behavior (Alcohol Concern, 2007).

The majority of teenagers who dabble in alcohol, tobacco, and marijuana are not headed for a life of decadence and addiction. These *minimal experimenters* are usually psychologically healthy, sociable, curious young people (Shedler & Block, 1990). As Figure 14.10 shows, tobacco and alcohol use is somewhat greater among European than among American adolescents, perhaps because European adults more often smoke and drink. But illegal drug use is far more prevalent among U.S. teenagers (Hibell, 2001). A greater percentage of American young people live in poverty, which is linked to family and peer contexts that promote illegal drug use. At the same time, use of diverse drugs is lower among African Americans than among Hispanic and Caucasian Americans; Native-American youths rank highest in drug taking (Johnston et al., 2010; Wallace et al., 2003). Researchers have yet to explain these variations.

Adolescent experimentation with any drug should not be taken lightly. Because most drugs impair perception and thought processes, a single heavy dose can lead to permanent injury or death. And a worrisome minority of teenagers move from substance *use* to *abuse*—taking drugs regularly, requiring increasing amounts to achieve the same effect, moving to harder substances, and using enough to impair their ability to meet daily responsibilities. Three percent of high school seniors are daily drinkers, and 5 percent have taken illegal drugs on a daily basis over the past month (Johnson et al., 2010).

Of all teenage drug habits, cigarette smoking has received the least attention because its short-term effects are

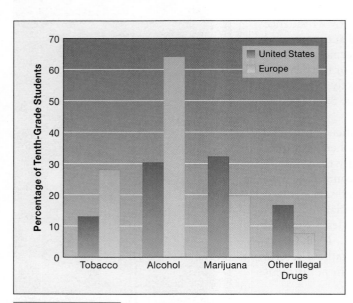

FIGURE 14.10

Tenth-grade students in the United States and Europe who have used various substances. Rates for tobacco and alcohol are based on any use in the past 30 days. Rates for marijuana and other illegal drugs are based on any lifetime use. Tobacco use and alcohol use are greater for European adolescents, whereas illegal drug use is greater for U.S. adolescents. *(Adapted from CAN, 2007; Johnson et al., 2010.)*

minimal. Yet in the long run, it is one of the deadliest substances—an established cause of heart and lung disease and cancer. Habitual cigarette use usually begins in early adolescence; 7 percent of U.S. eighth graders say they smoked in the last month, and 4 percent report doing so daily. Of the nearly 5 percent of twelfth graders who smoke half a pack or more a day, 50 percent indicate that they tried to quit but could not (Johnson et al., 2010).

CORRELATES AND CONSEQUENCES OF ADOLESCENT SUBSTANCE ABUSE   Unlike experimenters, drug abusers are seriously troubled young people. Longitudinal evidence reveals that their impulsive, disruptive, hostile style is often evident in early childhood, and they engage in other high-risk behaviors and are inclined to express their unhappiness through antisocial acts. Compared with other young people, their drug taking starts earlier and may have genetic roots (Dick, Prescott, & McGue, 2009; Ellickson et al., 2005; Tarter, Vanyukov, & Kirisci, 2008). But environmental factors also contribute. These include low SES, family mental health problems, parental and older sibling drug and alcohol abuse, lack of parental warmth and involvement, physical and sexual abuse, and poor school performance. Especially among teenagers with family difficulties, encouragement from friends who use and provide drugs increases substance abuse (Goldstein, Davis-Kean, & Eccles, 2005; Ohannessian & Hesselbrock, 2008; Prinstein, Boergers, & Spirito, 2001).

Adolescent substance abuse often has lifelong consequences. Teenagers who depend on alcohol and hard drugs to deal with daily stresses fail to learn responsible decision-making skills and alternative coping techniques. They show serious adjustment problems, including chronic anxiety, depression, and antisocial behavior, that are both cause and consequence of heavy drug taking (Kassel et al., 2005; Simons-Morton & Haynie, 2003). And they often enter into marriage, childbearing, and the work world prematurely and fail at these challenges—painful outcomes that further promote addictive behavior.

PREVENTION AND TREATMENT   School and community programs that reduce drug experimentation typically combine several features:

- They promote effective parenting, including monitoring of teenagers' activities.
- They teach skills for resisting peer pressure.
- They reduce the social acceptability of drug taking by emphasizing health and safety risks (Cuijpers, 2002; Stephens et al., 2009).

But some drug taking seems inevitable, so interventions that prevent teenagers from harming themselves and others when they do experiment are essential. Many communities offer weekend on-call transportation services that any young person can contact for a safe ride home, with no questions asked. Providing appealing substitute activities, such as drug-free dances and sports activities, is also helpful.

Because drug abuse has different roots than occasional use, different prevention strategies are required. One approach is to work with parents early, reducing family adversity and improving parenting skills, before children are old enough for drug involvement (Velleman, Templeton, & Copello, 2005). Programs that teach at-risk teenagers effective strategies for handling life stressors and that build competence through community service reduce alcohol and drug use, just as they reduce teenage pregnancy.

When an adolescent becomes a drug abuser, family and individual therapy are generally needed to treat maladaptive parent–child relationships, impulsivity, low self-esteem, anxiety, and depression. Academic and vocational training to improve life success also helps. But even comprehensive programs have alarmingly high relapse rates—from 35 to 85 percent (Brown & Ramo, 2005; Sussman, Skara, & Ames, 2008). One recommendation is to start treatment gradually, through support-group sessions that focus on reducing drug taking. Within the group, interveners can address drug-abusing teenagers' low motivation to change and

■ Teenagers enjoy a community party sponsored by Drug Free Youth in Town (DFYIT), a youth substance abuse prevention program. DFYIT trains high school students as peer educators, who teach middle school students life skills and strategies for resisting peer pressure. ■

resistance to adult referral, which they often view as an infringement on their personal freedom. Such brief interventions lessen drug taking in the short term (Myers et al., 2001). Modest improvement may boost the young person's sense of self-efficacy for behavior change and, as a result, increase motivation to make longer-lasting changes through intensive treatment.

ASK YOURSELF ◆◆

◆ REVIEW Compare risk factors for anorexia nervosa and bulimia nervosa. How do treatments and outcomes differ for the two disorders?

◆ APPLY Return to page 556 to review Veronica's life circumstances after she became a teenage mother. Why are Veronica and her children likely to experience long-term hardships?

◆ CONNECT What unfavorable life experiences do teenagers who engage in early and frequent sexual activity have in common with those who abuse drugs?

◆ REFLECT Describe your experiences with peer pressure to experiment with alcohol and drugs. What factors influenced your response?

Summary

Conceptions of Adolescence

How have conceptions of adolescence changed over the past century?

■ **Adolescence** is the transition between childhood and adulthood. Early theorists viewed adolescence as either a biologically determined period of storm and stress or entirely influenced by the social and cultural environment.

■ Contemporary research shows that adolescence is a joint product of biological, psychological, and social forces. In cultures that require many years of education for successful participation in work life, adolescence is greatly extended.

Puberty: The Physical Transition to Adulthood

Describe body growth, motor performance, and sexual maturation during puberty.

■ Hormonal changes under way in middle childhood initiate **puberty,** on average, two years earlier for girls than for boys. The first outward sign is the **growth spurt.** As the body enlarges, girls' hips and boys' shoulders broaden. Girls add more fat, boys more muscle.

MARY KATE DENNY/PHOTO EDIT

■ Puberty brings slow, gradual improvements in gross-motor performance for girls, dramatic gains for boys. Nevertheless, the number of U.S. adolescents participating in regular physical activity and physical education declines sharply with age.

■ At puberty, changes in **primary** and **secondary sexual characteristics** accompany rapid body growth. **Menarche** occurs late in the girl's sequence of pubertal events, after the growth spurt peaks. After menarche, growth of the breasts and of pubic and underarm hair are completed. In boys, as the sex organs and body enlarge and pubic and underarm hair appear, **spermarche** takes place. This is followed by growth of facial and body hair and deepening of the voice.

What factors influence the timing of puberty?

■ Heredity, nutrition, exercise, and overall health contribute to the timing of puberty. A secular trend toward earlier puberty has occurred in industrialized nations as physical well-being increased. In some countries, rising obesity rates have extended this trend.

■ Young people in conflict-ridden families tend to reach puberty earlier, whereas those with warm, stable family ties do so relatively late.

Describe brain development and changes in the organization of sleep and wakefulness during adolescence.

■ Pruning of unused synapses in the cerebral cortex continues during adolescence, and growth and myelination of stimulated neural fibers accelerate, supporting diverse cognitive skills. Because advances in cognitive control are gradual, teenagers tend to perform less well than adults on tasks requiring inhibition, planning, and future orientation.

■ Also, neurons become more responsive to excitatory neurotransmitters, contributing to teenagers' drive for novel experiences. Heightened sensitivity to oxytocin increases responsiveness to emotional and social stimuli, including peer influence. These changes in the brain's emotional/social network outpace development of the cognitive-control network, resulting in self-regulation difficulties.

© JEFF GREENBERG/THE IMAGE WORKS

■ Changes also occur in brain regulation of sleep timing, leading to a sleep "phase delay." Sleep deprivation increases, contributing to poorer achievement, depressed mood, and high-risk behaviors.

The Psychological Impact of Pubertal Events

Explain adolescents' reactions to the physical changes of puberty.

- Girls generally react to menarche with mixed emotions, although those who receive advance information and support from family members respond more positively. Boys also react to spermarche with mixed feelings but receive less social support for pubertal changes than girls.

- Besides higher hormone levels, negative life events and adult-structured situations are associated with adolescents' negative moods. In contrast, teenagers feel upbeat when with friends and in self-chosen leisure activities.

- Puberty is accompanied by psychological distancing between parent and child. The reaction may be a modern substitute for physical departure from the family, which typically occurs at sexual maturity in primate species. Parent–adolescent conflict also reflects parents' efforts to protect teenagers from such risks as substance use, auto accidents, and early sex.

Describe the impact of maturational timing on adolescent adjustment, noting sex differences.

- Early-maturing boys and late-maturing girls, whose appearance closely matches cultural standards of physical attractiveness, have a more positive **body image** and usually adjust well in adolescence. In contrast, early-maturing girls and late-maturing boys, who fit in least well physically with peers, tend to experience emotional and social difficulties, which—for girls—persist into early adulthood.

Health Issues

Describe nutritional needs, and cite factors related to eating disorders in adolescence.

- Nutritional requirements increase with rapid body growth. Poor eating habits lead to vitamin and mineral deficiencies in many adolescents. Frequency of family meals is associated with healthy eating.

- In girls who reach puberty early, who are dissatisfied with their body image, and who grow up in families where thinness is emphasized, genetic and environmental influences increase the risk of eating disorders. **Anorexia nervosa** typically affects girls with inhibited and perfectionist personalities, controlling mothers, and emotionally distant fathers. **Bulimia nervosa** is often associated with lack of self-control and disengaged parenting.

Cite common unintentional injuries in adolescence.

- In the United States, automobile accidents are the leading cause of adolescent injury and death, with firearms causing the majority of other fatal injuries. Sports-related injuries are also common.

Discuss social and cultural influences on adolescent sexual attitudes and behavior.

- U.S. attitudes toward adolescent sex remain relatively restrictive, and the social environment—parents, schools, and mass media—delivers contradictory messages. Sexual attitudes and behavior of adolescents have become more liberal, with a slight swing back recently toward more conservative beliefs.

- Early, frequent sexual activity is linked to a variety of factors associated with economic disadvantage. Many sexually active teenagers do not practice contraception consistently. Adolescent cognitive processes and weak social supports for responsible sexual behavior, including access to birth control, underlie this failure to take precautions against pregnancy.

Describe factors involved in the development of homosexuality.

- Biological factors, including heredity and prenatal hormone levels, play an important role in homosexuality. Gay and lesbian teenagers face special challenges in establishing a positive sexual identity.

Discuss factors related to sexually transmitted disease and to teenage pregnancy and parenthood.

- Early sexual activity, combined with inconsistent contraceptive use, results in high rates of sexually transmitted diseases (STDs) among U.S. teenagers.

- Adolescent pregnancy and parenthood rates are higher in the United States than in any other industrialized nation. Life conditions linked to economic disadvantage, along with personal attributes, contribute to adolescent childbearing. Teenage parenthood is associated with school dropout, reduced chances of marriage, greater likelihood of divorce, and poverty—circumstances that jeopardize the well-being of both adolescent and newborn child.

- Effective sex education, access to contraceptives, and programs that build academic and social competence help prevent early pregnancy. Adolescent parents need school programs that provide job training, instruction in life-management skills, and child care. Young mothers benefit from family relationships that are sensitive to their developmental needs. When teenage fathers stay involved, children develop more favorably.

What personal and social factors are related to adolescent substance use and abuse?

- Teenage alcohol and drug use is pervasive in industrialized nations, reflecting the sensation seeking of adolescence as well as drug-dependent cultural contexts. The minority who move to substance abuse tend to start drug-taking early and have serious personal, family, school, and peer problems. Effective prevention programs work with parents early to reduce family adversity, improve parenting skills, and build teenagers' competence.

IMPORTANT TERMS AND CONCEPTS

adolescence (p. 529)
anorexia nervosa (p. 545)
body image (p. 542)
bulimia nervosa (p. 546)

growth spurt (p. 532)
menarche (p. 536)
primary sexual characteristics (p. 535)

puberty (p. 530)
secondary sexual characteristics (p. 535)
spermarche (p. 536)

"Weaving Batik"
Sisylla Octavia Candra
16 years, Indonesia

As she masters the intricacies of weaving batik, this Indonesian adolescent takes on adult roles and responsibilities. Chapter 15 delves into the increasingly complex reasoning powers of this transitional period between childhood and adulthood.

Reprinted with permission from the World Awareness Children's Museum, Glens Falls, New York

Cognitive Development in Adolescence

*O*ne mid-December evening, a knock at the front door announced the arrival of Franca and Antonio's oldest son, Jules, home for vacation after the fall semester of his freshman year at college. The family gathered around the kitchen table. "How did it all go, Jules?" asked Antonio as he served pieces of apple pie.

"Well, physics and philosophy were awesome," Jules responded with enthusiasm. "The last few weeks, our physics prof introduced us to Einstein's theory of relativity. Boggles my mind, it's so incredibly counterintuitive."

"Counter-what?" asked 11-year-old Sabrina.

"Counterintuitive. Unlike what you'd normally expect," explained Jules. "Imagine you're on a train, going unbelievably fast, like 160,000 miles a second. The faster you go, approaching the speed of light, the slower time passes and the denser and heavier things get relative to on the ground. The theory revolutionized the way we think about time, space, matter—the entire universe."

Sabrina wrinkled her forehead, baffled at Jules's otherworldly reasoning. "Time slows down when I'm bored, like right now, not on a train when I'm going somewhere exciting. No speeding train ever made me heavier, but this apple pie will if I eat any more of it," Sabrina announced, leaving the table.

Sixteen-year-old Louis reacted differently. "Totally cool, Jules. If we could move at such extreme speeds, we'd age more slowly—imagine that! So what'd you do in philosophy?"

"It was a course in philosophy of technology. We studied the ethics of futuristic methods in human reproduction. For example, we argued the pros and cons of a world in which all embryos develop in artificial wombs."

"What do you mean?" asked Louis. "You order your kid at the lab?"

"That's right. I wrote my term paper on it. I had to evaluate it in terms of principles of justice and freedom. I can see some advantages but also lots of dangers. . . ."

As this conversation illustrates, adolescence brings with it vastly expanded powers of reasoning. At age 11, Sabrina finds it difficult to move beyond her own firsthand experiences to a world of possibilities. Over the next few years, her thinking will take on the complex qualities that characterize the cognition of her older brothers. Jules and Louis consider multiple variables simultaneously and think about situations that are not easily detected in the real world or that do not exist at all. As a result, they can grasp advanced scientific and mathematical principles, grapple with social and political issues, and delve deeply into the meaning of a poem or story. Compared with school-age children's thinking, adolescent thought is more enlightened, imaginative, and rational.

The first part of this chapter traces these extraordinary changes. Systematic research on adolescent cognitive development began with testing of Piaget's ideas (Keating, 2004; Kuhn, 2009). Recently, information-processing research has greatly enhanced our understanding. Next, we turn to research findings that have attracted a great deal of public attention: sex differences in mental abilities. We also discuss gains in language that reflect and also contribute to the advanced thinking of the teenage years. The middle portion of this chapter is devoted to the primary setting in which adolescent thought takes shape: the school. We conclude with a consideration of vocational development.

Piaget's Theory: The Formal Operational Stage

According to Piaget, around age 11 young people enter the **formal operational stage,** in which they develop the capacity for abstract, systematic, scientific thinking. Whereas concrete operational children can "operate on reality," formal operational adolescents can "operate on operations." In other words, they no longer require concrete things or events as objects of thought. Instead, they can come up with new, more general logical rules through internal reflection (Inhelder & Piaget, 1955/1958). Let's look at two major features of the formal operational stage.

Hypothetico-Deductive Reasoning

Piaget believed that at adolescence, young people first become capable of **hypothetico-deductive reasoning.** When faced with a problem, they start with a *hypothesis,* or prediction about variables that might affect an outcome, from which they *deduce* logical, testable inferences. Then they systematically isolate and combine variables to see which of these inferences are confirmed in the real world. Notice how this form of problem solving begins with possibility and proceeds to reality. In contrast, concrete operational children start with reality—with the most obvious predictions about a situation. When these are not confirmed, they usually cannot think of alternatives and fail to solve the problem.

Adolescents' performance on Piaget's famous *pendulum problem* illustrates their new approach. Suppose we present several school-age children and adolescents with strings of different lengths, objects of different weights to attach to the strings, and a bar from which to hang the strings (see Figure 15.1). Then we ask each of them to figure out what influences the speed with which a pendulum swings through its arc.

Formal operational adolescents hypothesize that four variables might be influential: (1) the length of the string,

FIGURE 15.1

Piaget's pendulum problem. Adolescents who engage in hypothetico-deductive reasoning think of variables that might possibly affect the speed with which a pendulum swings through its arc. Then they isolate and test each variable, as well as testing the variables in combination. Eventually they deduce that the weight of the object, the height from which it is released, and how forcefully it is pushed have no effect on the speed with which the pendulum swings through its arc. Only string length makes a difference.

(2) the weight of the object hung on it, (3) how high the object is raised before it is released, and (4) how forcefully the object is pushed. By varying one factor at a time while holding the other three constant, they test each variable separately and, if necessary, also in combination. Eventually they discover that only string length makes a difference.

In contrast, concrete operational children cannot separate the effects of each variable. They may test for the effect of string length without holding weight constant—comparing, for example, a short, light pendulum with a long, heavy one. Also, they typically fail to notice variables that are not immediately suggested by the concrete materials of the task—for example, how high the object is raised or how forcefully it is released.

Propositional Thought

A second important characteristic of Piaget's formal operational stage is **propositional thought**—adolescents' ability to evaluate the logic of propositions (verbal statements) without referring to real-world circumstances. In contrast, children can evaluate the logic of statements only by considering them against concrete evidence in the real world.

In a study of propositional reasoning, an adult showed children and adolescents a pile of poker chips and asked whether statements about the chips were true, false, or uncertain (Osherson & Markman, 1975). In one condition, the adult hid a chip in her hand and presented the following propositions:

> "*Either* the chip in my hand is green *or* it is not green."

> "The chip in my hand is green *and* it is not green."

In another condition, the adult made the same statements while holding either a red or a green chip in full view.

School-age children focused on the concrete properties of the poker chips. When the chip was hidden, they replied that they were uncertain about both statements. When it was visible, they judged both statements to be true if the chip was green and false if it was red. In contrast, adolescents analyzed the logic of the statements. They understood that the "either–or" statement is always true and the "and" statement is always false, regardless of the chip's color.

■ In Piaget's formal operational stage, adolescents engage in propositional thought. As these students discuss problems in a social studies class, they show that they can reason logically with symbols that do not necessarily represent objects in the real world. ■

Although Piaget did not view language as playing a central role in cognitive development (see Chapter 9), he acknowledged its importance in adolescence. Formal operations require language-based and other symbolic systems that do not stand for real things, such as those in higher mathematics. Secondary school students use such systems in algebra and geometry. Formal operational thought also involves verbal reasoning about abstract concepts. Jules was thinking in this way when he pondered relationships between time, space, and matter in physics and wondered about justice and freedom in philosophy.

Follow-Up Research on Formal Operational Thought

Research on formal operational thought poses questions similar to those we discussed with respect to Piaget's earlier stages: Does formal operational thinking appear earlier than Piaget expected? Do all individuals reach formal operations during their teenage years?

ARE CHILDREN CAPABLE OF HYPOTHETICO-DEDUCTIVE AND PROPOSITIONAL THINKING?   School-age children show the glimmerings of hypothetico-deductive reasoning, although they are less competent at it than adolescents. In simplified situations—ones involving no more than two possible causal variables—6-year-olds understand that hypotheses must be confirmed by appropriate evidence. They also realize that once a hypothesis is supported, it shapes predictions about what might happen in the future (Ruffman et al., 1993). But school-age children cannot sort out evidence that bears on three or more variables at once. And as we will see when we take up information-processing research on scientific reasoning, children have difficulty explaining why a pattern of observations supports a hypothesis, even when they recognize the connection between the two.

With respect to propositional thought, when a simple set of premises defies real-world knowledge ("All cats bark. Rex is a cat. Does Rex bark?"), 4- to 6-year-olds can reason logically in make-believe play. In justifying their answer, they are likely to say, "We can pretend cats bark!" (Dias & Harris, 1988, 1990). But in an entirely verbal mode, children have great difficulty reasoning from premises that contradict reality or their own beliefs.

Consider this set of statements: "If dogs are bigger than elephants, and elephants are bigger than mice, then dogs are bigger than mice." Children younger than 10 judge this reasoning to be false, since not all of the relations specified occur in real life (Moshman & Franks, 1986; Pillow, 2002). They automatically think of well-learned knowledge ("Elephants are larger than dogs") that casts doubt on the truthfulness of the premises. Children find it more difficult than adolescents to inhibit activation of such knowledge (Klaczynski, Schuneman, & Daniel, 2004; Simoneau & Markovits, 2003). Partly for this reason, they fail to grasp the **logical necessity** of propositional reasoning—that the accuracy of conclusions drawn from premises rests on the rules of logic, not on real-world confirmation.

Furthermore, in reasoning with propositions, school-age children rarely think carefully about the major premise and, therefore, violate the most basic rules of logic (Markovits, Schleifer, & Fortier, 1989). For example, when given the following problem, they almost always draw an incorrect conclusion:

Major premise: If Susan hits a tambourine, then she will make a noise.

Second premise: Suppose that Susan does not hit a tambourine.

Question: Did Susan make a noise?

Wrong conclusion: No, Susan did not make a noise.

Notice that the major premise did *not* state that Susan can make noise *if, and only if,* she hits a tambourine. Adolescents generally detect that Susan could make a noise in other ways, partly because they are better at searching their knowledge for examples that contradict wrong conclusions (Klaczynski, 2004; Markovits & Barrouillet, 2002).

As with hypothetico-deductive reasoning, in early adolescence, young people become better at analyzing the *logic* of a series of propositions, regardless of their *content*. And as they get older, they handle problems requiring increasingly complex sets of mental operations. Further, in justifying their reasoning, they move from giving a concrete example ("She could have hit a drum instead of a tambourine") to explaining the logical rules on which it is based ("We can be certain that Susan did not hit a tambourine. But we cannot be certain that Susan did not make a noise; she might have done so in many other ways") (Müller, Overton, & Reene, 2001; Venet & Markovits, 2001). Nevertheless, these capacities do not appear suddenly at puberty. Rather, gains occur gradually from childhood on—findings that call into question the emergence of a discrete new stage of cognitive development at adolescence (Keating, 2004; Kuhn, 2009; Moshman, 2005).

DO ALL INDIVIDUALS REACH THE FORMAL OPERATIONAL STAGE? TAKE A MOMENT... Try giving one or two of the formal operational tasks just described to your friends. How well do they do? Even many well-educated adults fail hypothetico-deductive tasks and have trouble reasoning with sets of propositions that contradict real-world facts (Kuhn, 2009; Markovits & Vachon, 1990)!

Why are so many adults not fully formal operational? One reason is that people are most likely to think abstractly and systematically on tasks in which they have had extensive guidance and practice in using such reasoning. This conclusion is supported by evidence that taking college courses leads to improvements in formal reasoning related to course content. Math and science prompt gains in propositional thought, social science in methodological and statistical reasoning (Lehman & Nisbett, 1990). Like concrete reasoning in children, formal operations do not emerge in all contexts at once but are specific to situation and task (Keating, 1990, 2004).

Individuals in tribal and village societies rarely do well on tasks typically used to assess formal operational reasoning (Cole, 1990). For example, people in nonliterate societies often refuse requests to engage in propositional thought. Take this hypothetical proposition: "In the North, where there is snow, all bears are white. Novaya Zemlya is in the Far North, and it always has snow. What color are the bears there?" In response, a Central Asian peasant explains that he must see the event to discern its logical implications. Yet the peasant uses propositions to defend his point of view: "*If* a man . . . had seen a white bear and had told about it, [*then*] he could be believed, *but* I've never seen one and *hence* I can't say" (Luria 1976, pp. 108–109). Although he rarely displays it in everyday life, the peasant is clearly capable of formal operational thought!

Piaget acknowledged that without the opportunity to solve hypothetical problems, people in some societies might not display formal operations. Still, these findings raise further questions about Piaget's stage sequence. Does the formal operational stage result largely from children's and adolescents' independent efforts to make sense of their world, as Piaget claimed? Or is it a culturally transmitted way of thinking that is specific to literate societies and taught in school? In an Israeli study of seventh to ninth graders, after controlling for participants' age, researchers found that years of schooling fully accounted for early adolescent gains in propositional thought (Artman, Cahan, & Avni-Babad, 2006). School tasks, the investigators speculated, provide crucial experience in setting aside the "if . . . then" logic of everyday conversations that is often used to convey intentions, promises, and threats ("If you don't do your chores, then you won't get your allowance") but that conflicts with the logic of academic reasoning. In school, then, adolescents encounter rich opportunities to realize their neurological potential to think more effectively.

These adolescents of Irian Jaya Province in Indonesia live in highland rainforests and have little contact with the outside world. Although they would probably have difficulty with Piaget's formal operational tasks, they deftly build a tree house, mentally coordinating multiple variables to ensure that the structure is stable and sturdy.

An Information-Processing View of Adolescent Cognitive Development

Information-processing theorists refer to a variety of specific mechanisms, supported by brain development and experience, that underlie cognitive change in adolescence. Each was discussed in previous chapters (Kuhn, 2009; Kuhn & Franklin, 2006; Luna et al., 2004). Now let's draw them together:

- *Attention* becomes more selective (focused on relevant information) and better-adapted to the changing demands of tasks.
- *Inhibition*—both of irrelevant stimuli and of well-learned responses in situations where they are inappropriate—improves, supporting gains in attention and reasoning.
- *Strategies* become more effective, improving storage, representation, and retrieval of information.
- *Knowledge* increases, easing strategy use.
- *Metacognition* (awareness of thought) expands, leading to new insights into effective strategies for acquiring information and solving problems.
- *Cognitive self-regulation* improves, yielding better moment-by-moment monitoring, evaluation, and redirection of thinking.
- *Speed of thinking* and *processing capacity* increase. As a result, more information can be held at once in working memory and combined into increasingly complex, efficient representations, "opening possibilities for growth" in the capacities just listed and also improving as a result of gains in those capacities (Case, 1998; Demetriou et al., 2002, p. 97).

As we look at influential findings from an information-processing perspective, we will see some of these mechanisms of change in action. And we will discover that researchers regard one of them—*metacognition*—as central to adolescent cognitive development.

Scientific Reasoning: Coordinating Theory with Evidence

During a free moment in physical education class, Sabrina wondered why more of her tennis serves and returns passed the net and dropped in her opponent's court when she used a particular brand of balls. "Is it something about their color or size?" she asked herself. "Hmm . . . or maybe it's their surface texture—that might affect their bounce."

The heart of scientific reasoning is coordinating theories with evidence. A scientist can clearly describe the theory he or she favors, knows what evidence is needed to support it and what would refute it, and can explain how pitting evidence against theories led to the acceptance of one theory as opposed to others. What evidence would Sabrina need to confirm her theory about the tennis balls?

Deanna Kuhn (2002) has conducted extensive research into the development of scientific reasoning, using problems that, like Piaget's tasks, involve several variables that might affect an outcome. In one series of studies, third, sixth, and ninth graders and adults were first given evidence—sometimes consistent and sometimes conflicting with theories—and then questioned about the accuracy of each theory.

For example, participants were given a problem much like Sabrina's: to theorize about which of several features of sports balls—size (large or small), color (light or dark), surface texture (rough or smooth), or presence or absence of ridges on the surface—influences the quality of a player's serve. Next, they were told about the theory of Mr. (or Ms.) S, who believes the ball's size is important, and the theory of Mr. (or Ms.) C, who thinks color matters. Finally, the interviewer presented evidence by placing balls with certain characteristics in two baskets labeled "good serve" and "bad serve" (see Figure 15.2).

Kuhn found that the capacity to reason like a scientist improved with age. The youngest participants often ignored conflicting evidence or distorted it in ways consistent with their theory. When one third grader, who judged that size was causal (that large balls produced good serves and small balls produced bad serves), was shown incomplete evidence (a single large, light-colored ball in the good-serve basket and no balls in the bad-serve basket), he insisted on the accuracy of Mr. S's theory (which was also his own). Asked to explain, he stated flatly, "Because this ball is big . . . the color doesn't really matter" (Kuhn, 1989, p. 677).

These findings, and others like them, reveal that instead of viewing evidence as separate from and bearing on a theory, children often blend the two into a single representation of "the way things are." They are especially likely to overlook evidence that does not match their prior beliefs when a causal variable is implausible (like color affecting the performance of a sports ball) and when task demands (number of variables to be evaluated) are high (Zimmerman, 2005, 2007). The ability to distinguish theory from evidence and to use logical rules to examine their relationship in complex, multivariable situations improves steadily from childhood through adolescence, continuing into adulthood (Kuhn & Dean, 2004; Kuhn & Pearsall, 2000).

How Scientific Reasoning Develops

What factors support adolescents' skill at coordinating theory with evidence? Greater working-memory capacity, permitting a theory and the effects of several variables to be compared at once, is vital. Adolescents also benefit from exposure to increasingly complex problems and instruction that highlights critical features of scientific reasoning—for example, why a scientist's expectations in a particular situation are inconsistent with everyday beliefs and experiences (Chinn & Malhotra, 2002). This explains why scientific reasoning is strongly influenced by years of schooling, whether individuals grapple with traditional scientific tasks (like the sports-ball problem or Piaget's pendulum task)

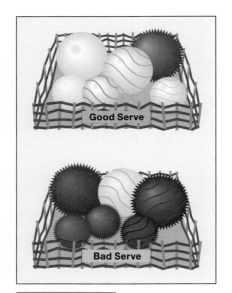

FIGURE 15.2

Which features of these sports balls— size, color, surface texture, or presence or absence of ridges—influence the quality of a player's serve? This set of evidence suggests that color might be important, since light-colored balls are largely in the good-serve basket and dark-colored balls in the bad-serve basket. But the same is true for texture! The good-serve basket has mostly smooth balls, the bad-serve basket rough balls. Since all light-colored balls are smooth and all dark-colored balls are rough, we cannot tell whether color or texture makes a difference. But we can conclude that size and presence or absence of ridges are not important, because these features are equally represented in the good-serve and bad-serve baskets. *(Adapted from Kuhn, Amsel, & O'Loughlin, 1988.)*

or engage in informal reasoning—for example, justifying a theory about what causes children to fail in school (Kuhn, 1993).

Researchers believe that sophisticated *metacognitive understanding* is vital for scientific reasoning (Kuhn, 2009; Kuhn & Pease, 2006). Microgenetic research (see Chapter 1, page 43) shows that when adolescents regularly pit theory against evidence over many weeks, they experiment with various strategies, reflect on and revise them, and gradually become aware of the nature of logic. Then they apply their appreciation of logic to an increasingly wide range of situations. The ability to *think about* theories, *deliberately isolate* variables, and *actively seek* disconfirming evidence is rarely present before adolescence (Kuhn, 2000b; Moshman, 1998).

But adolescents and adults vary widely in scientific reasoning skills. Many continue to show a self-serving bias, applying logic more effectively to ideas they doubt than to ideas they favor (Klaczynski, 1997; Klaczynski & Narasimham, 1998). Reasoning scientifically requires the metacognitive capacity to evaluate one's objectivity—to be fair-minded rather than self-serving (Moshman, 1999). As we will see in Chapter 16, this flexible, open-minded approach is not just a cognitive attainment but a personality trait—one that assists young people greatly in forming an identity and developing morally.

■ High school students attending an engineering summer camp at the University of Texas design a catapult for shooting water balloons. Extensive experience coordinating theory with evidence in complex problems results in gains in scientific reasoning as teenagers reflect on their strategies and revise them. ■

Adolescents develop scientific reasoning skills in a similar step-by-step fashion on different types of tasks. In a series of studies, 10- to 20-year olds were given sets of problems graded in difficulty. One set consisted of quantitative-relational tasks like the pendulum problem in Figure 15.1. Another set contained verbal propositional tasks like the tambourine problem on page 568. And in still another set were causal-experimental tasks like the sports ball problem in Figure 15.2 (Demetriou et al., 1993, 1996, 2002).

In each type of task, adolescents mastered component skills in sequential order by expanding their metacognitive awareness. For example, on causal-experimental tasks, they first became aware of the many variables that—separately and in combination—could influence an outcome. This enabled them to formulate and test hypotheses. Over time, adolescents combined separate skills into a smoothly functioning system, constructing a general model that they could apply to many instances of a given type of problem. In the researchers' words, young people seem to form a "hypercognitive system," or supersystem, that understands, organizes, and influences other aspects of cognition (Demetriou & Kazi, 2001).

TAKE A MOMENT... Return to Chapter 12, page 441, and review Robbie Case's information-processing view of development during Piaget's concrete operational stage. Does Case's concept of *central conceptual structures* remind you of the metacognitive advances just described? Piaget also underscored the role of metacognition in formal operational thought when he spoke of "operating on operations" (see page 566). But information-processing findings confirm that scientific reasoning does not result from an abrupt, stagewise change. Instead, it develops gradually out of many specific experiences that require children and adolescents to match theories against evidence and reflect on and evaluate their thinking.

LOOK AND LISTEN

❖

Describe one or more memorable experiences from your high school classes that helped you advance in scientific reasoning—pit theory against evidence and become receptive to disconfirming evidence, even for theories you favored.

Consequences of Adolescent Cognitive Changes

The development of increasingly complex, effective thinking leads to dramatic revisions in the way adolescents see themselves, others, and the world in general. But just as adolescents are occasionally awkward in the use of their transformed bodies, they initially falter in their abstract thinking. Teenagers' self-concern, idealism, criticism, and indecisiveness, though perplexing to adults, are usually beneficial in the long run. Applying What We Know on page 572 suggests ways to handle the everyday consequences of teenagers' newfound cognitive capacities.

◆ Applying What We Know

Handling Consequences of Teenagers' New Cognitive Capacities

ABSTRACT THOUGHT EXPRESSED AS . . .	SUGGESTION
Sensitivity to public criticism	Refrain from finding fault with the adolescent in front of others. If the matter is important, wait until you can speak to the teenager alone.
Exaggerated sense of personal uniqueness	Acknowledge the adolescent's unique characteristics. At opportune times, encourage a more balanced perspective by pointing out that you had similar feelings as a teenager.
Idealism and criticism	Respond patiently to the adolescent's grand expectations and critical remarks. Point out positive features of targets, helping the teenager see that all societies and people are blends of virtues and imperfections.
Difficulty making everyday decisions	Refrain from deciding for the adolescent. Model effective decision making, and offer diplomatic suggestions about the pros and cons of alternatives, the likelihood of various outcomes, and learning from poor choices.

Self-Consciousness and Self-Focusing

Adolescents' ability to reflect on their own thoughts, combined with physical and psychological changes, leads them to think more about themselves. Piaget believed that a new form of egocentrism arises, in which adolescents again have difficulty distinguishing their own and others' perspectives (Inhelder & Piaget, 1955/1958). Piaget's followers suggest that two distorted images of the relationship between self and other appear.

The first is called the **imaginary audience,** adolescents' belief that they are the focus of everyone else's attention and concern (Elkind & Bowen, 1979). As a result, they become extremely self-conscious, often going to great lengths to avoid embarrassment. When Sabrina woke up one Sunday morning with a large pimple on her chin, her first thought was, "I can't possibly go to church! Everyone will notice how ugly I look." The imaginary audience helps explain the long hours adolescents spend inspecting every detail of their appearance and why they are so sensitive to public criticism. To teenagers, who believe that everyone is monitoring their performance, a critical remark from a parent or teacher can be mortifying.

A second cognitive distortion is the **personal fable.** Certain that others are observing and thinking about them, teenagers develop an inflated opinion of their own importance—the feeling that they are special and unique. Many adolescents view themselves as reaching great heights of omnipotence and also sinking to unusual depths of despair—experiences that others could not possibly understand (Elkind, 1994). One teenager wrote in her diary, "My parents' lives are so ordinary, so stuck in a rut. Mine will be different. I'll realize my hopes and ambitions." Another, upset when a boyfriend failed to return her affections, rebuffed her mother's comforting words: "Mom, you don't know what it's like to be in love!"

Although imaginary-audience and personal-fable ideation is common in adolescence, these distorted visions of the self do not result from egocentrism, as Piaget suggested. Rather, they are partly an outgrowth of advances in perspective taking, which cause young teenagers to be more concerned with what others think (Vartanian & Powlishta, 1996).

In fact, certain aspects of the imaginary audience may serve positive, protective functions. When asked why they worry about the opinions of others, adolescents responded

© MICHAEL NEWMAN/PHOTOEDIT

■ Certain that others are observing them, teenagers develop a personal fable—an inflated opinion of their own importance. As long as the personal fable engenders a view of oneself as highly capable and influential, it may help young people cope with the challenges of adolescence. ■

that they do so because others' evaluations have important *real* consequences—for self-esteem, peer acceptance, and social support (Bell & Bromnick, 2003). The idea that others care about their appearance and behavior also has emotional value, helping teenagers hold onto important relationships as they struggle to separate from parents and establish an independent sense of self (Vartanian, 1997).

With respect to the personal fable, in a study of sixth through tenth graders, sense of omnipotence predicted self-esteem and overall positive adjustment. Viewing the self as highly capable and influential may help young people cope with challenges of adolescence. In contrast, sense of personal uniqueness was modestly associated with depression and suicidal thinking (Aalsma, Lapsley, & Flannery, 2006). Focusing on the distinctiveness of one's own experiences may interfere with forming close, rewarding relationships, which provide social support in stressful times. And when combined with a sensation-seeking personality, the personal fable seems to contribute to adolescent risk taking by reducing teenagers' sense of vulnerability. Young people with high personal-fable and sensation-seeking scores tend to take more sexual risks, more often use drugs, and commit more delinquent acts than their agemates (Greene et al., 2000).

Idealism and Criticism

Adolescents' capacity to think about possibilities opens up the world of the ideal. Teenagers can imagine alternative family, religious, political, and moral systems, and they want to explore them. They often construct grand visions of a world with no injustice, discrimination, or tasteless behavior. The disparity between teenagers' idealism and adults' greater realism creates tension between parent and child. Envisioning a perfect family against which their parents and siblings fall short, adolescents become fault-finding critics.

Overall, however, teenage idealism and criticism are advantageous. Once adolescents come to see other people as having both strengths and weaknesses, they have a much greater capacity to work constructively for social change and to form positive and lasting relationships (Elkind, 1994). Parents can help teenagers forge a better balance between the ideal and the real by tolerating their criticism while reminding them that all people are blends of virtues and imperfections.

Decision Making

Adolescents handle many cognitive tasks more effectively than they did when younger. But recall from Chapter 14 that changes in the brain's emotional/social network outpace development of the prefrontal cortex's cognitive control network. Consequently, teenagers perform less well than adults in planning and decision making, where they must inhibit emotion and impulses in favor of thinking rationally. Good decision making involves: (1) identifying pros and cons of each alternative, (2) assessing the likelihood of various outcomes, (3) evaluating one's choice in terms of whether one's goals were met, and, if not, (4) learning from the mistake and making a better future decision. When researchers modified a card game to trigger strong emotion by introducing immediate feedback about gains and losses after each choice, teenagers behaved more irrationally, taking far greater risks than adults in their twenties (Figner et al., 2009). In a second condition, in which players were merely asked what they would do at each step of the game but were not given feedback, adolescents and adults did not differ in quality of decision making.

Nevertheless, other research indicates that teenagers are less effective than adults at decision making even under "cool," unemotional conditions (Huizenga, Crone, & Jansen, 2007). In one study, participants were given challenging real-world dilemmas—whether to have cosmetic surgery, whether to participate in an experimental study of a new acne medication, which parent to live with after a divorce—and asked them to explain how they would decide. Adults outperformed adolescents, especially the younger ones, more often considering alternatives, weighing benefits and risks, and suggesting advice seeking, especially in areas (such as medical decisions) where they had little experience (Halpern-Felsher & Cauffman, 2001).

Furthermore, in making decisions, adolescents, more often than adults (who also have difficulty), fall back on well-learned intuitive judgments (Jacobs & Klaczynski, 2002). Consider a

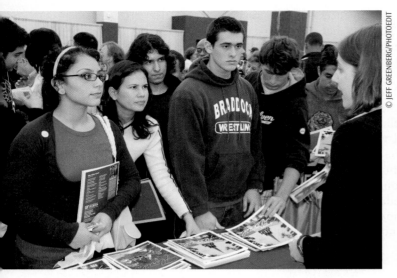

© JEFF GREENBERG/PHOTOEDIT

■ These high school students talking to a college recruiter will face many choices over the next few years. But in making decisions, teenagers are less effective than adults, who more often carefully weigh the pros and cons of each alternative. ■

hypothetical problem requiring a choice, on the basis of two arguments, between taking a traditional lecture class and taking a computer-based class. One argument contains large-sample information: course evaluations from 150 students, 85 percent of whom liked the computer class. The other argument contains small-sample personal reports: complaints of two honor-roll students who both hated the computer class and enjoyed the traditional class. Many adolescents, even those who knew that selecting the large-sample argument was "more intelligent," based their choice on the small-sample argument, which resembled the informal opinions they depend on in everyday life (Klaczynski, 2001).

In sum, in the heat of the moment, when making a good decision depends on inhibiting "feel-good" behavior and the possibility of immediate rewards, the brain's emotional/social network tends to prevail, and adolescents are far more likely than adults to emphasize short-term over long-term goals (Boyer, 2006; Reyna & Farley, 2006; Steinberg et al., 2009). In Chapter 14, we also noted that processing skills governed by the prefrontal cognitive-control system develop gradually, into the early twenties. Like other aspects of brain development, the cognitive-control system is affected by experience (Kuhn, 2009). As "first-timers" in many situations, adolescents do not have sufficient knowledge to consider pros and cons and predict potential outcomes. And after engaging in risky behavior without negative consequences, teenagers rate its benefits higher and its risks lower than peers who have not tried it (Halpern-Felsher et al., 2004).

Furthermore, when teenagers were younger, adults usually limited the decisions they had to make. As adolescents, they face an increasing number of decisions and often feel overwhelmed by their expanding range of options—abundant choices of school courses, extracurricular activities, and social events. As a result, their efforts to choose frequently break down, and they resort to habit, act on impulse, or postpone decision making. Louis, for example, procrastinated over his college plans. When Franca mentioned that he was about to miss the deadline for taking entrance tests, he agonized over the forms, unable to decide when to take the exam.

Over time, young people learn from their successes and failures and gather information from others about factors that affect decision making (Byrnes, 2003). School and community interventions that teach effective decision-making skills can help adolescents apply their capacity for metacognition, more often reflecting on and monitoring the decision process (Jacobs & Klaczynski, 2002). But because engaging in risk taking without experiencing harmful outcomes can heighten adolescents' sense of invulnerability, they also need supervision and protection from high-risk experiences until their decision making improves.

ASK YOURSELF

◆ REVIEW Describe research findings that challenge Piaget's notion of a new, discrete stage of cognitive development at adolescence.

◆ APPLY Clarissa, age 14, is convinced that no one appreciates how hurt she feels at not being invited to the homecoming dance. Meanwhile, 15-year-old Justine, alone in her room, pantomimes being sworn in as student body president with her awestruck parents looking on. Which aspect of the personal fable is each girl displaying? Which girl is more likely to be well-adjusted, which poorly adjusted? Explain.

◆ CONNECT How does evidence on adolescent decision making help us understand teenagers' risk taking in sexual activity and drug use?

◆ REFLECT Do you recall engaging in idealistic thinking or poor decision making as a teenager? Cite examples. How has your thinking changed?

Sex Differences in Mental Abilities

Sex differences in intellectual performance have sparked almost as much controversy as the ethnic and SES differences in IQ considered in Chapter 12. Although boys and girls do not differ in general intelligence, they do vary in specific mental abilities.

Verbal Abilities

Throughout the school years, girls attain higher scores in reading and writing achievement and account for a lower percentage of children referred for remedial reading instruction. Girls continue to score slightly higher on tests of verbal ability in middle childhood and adolescence in every country in which assessments have been conducted (Bussiére, Knighton, & Pennock, 2007; Mullis et al., 2007; Wai et al., 2010). And when verbal tests are heavily weighted with writing, girls' advantage is large (Halpern et al., 2007).

A special concern is that girls' advantage in reading and writing achievement increases in adolescence, with boys doing especially poorly in writing—trends evident in the United States and other industrialized nations (see Figure 15.3) (OECD, 2010; U.S. Department of Education, 2007, 2010b). These differences in literacy skills are believed to be major contributors to a widening gender gap in college enrollments. Thirty years ago, males accounted for 60 percent of U.S. undergraduate students; today, they are in the minority, at 42 percent (U.S. Department of Education, 2010).

Recall from Chapter 6 that girls have a biological advantage in earlier development of the left hemisphere of the cerebral cortex, where language is usually localized. And fMRI research indicates that in tackling language tasks (such as deciding whether two spoken or written words rhyme), 9- to 15-year-old girls show concentrated activity in language-specific brain areas. Boys, in contrast, display more widespread activation—in addition to language areas, considerable activity in auditory and visual areas, depending on how words are presented (Burman, Bitan, & Booth, 2007). This suggests that girls are more efficient language processors than boys, who rely heavily on sensory brain regions and process spoken and written words differently.

But girls also receive more verbal stimulation from the preschool years through adolescence, which may contribute to their more efficient processing (Peterson & Roberts, 2003). Furthermore, in Chapter 13 we noted that children view language arts as a "feminine" subject. And as a result of the high-stakes testing movement, students today spend more time at their desks being taught in a regimented way—an approach particularly at odds with boys' higher activity level, assertiveness, and incidence of learning problems.

Finally, high rates of divorce and out-of-wedlock births mean that more children today grow up without the continuous presence of a father who models and encourages good work habits and skill at reading and writing. Both maternal and paternal involvement influences the achievement and educational attainment of adolescents of both genders (Flouri & Buchanan, 2004). But some research suggests that high-achieving African-American boys are particularly likely to come from homes in which fathers are warm, verbally communicative, and demanding of achievement (Grief, Hrabowski, & Maton, 1998). Clearly, reversing boys' weakening literacy skills is a high priority, requiring a concerted effort by families, schools, and communities.

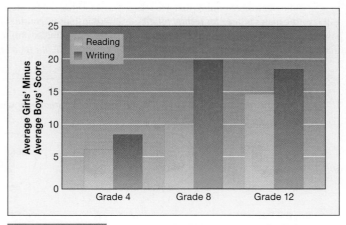

FIGURE 15.3

Reading and writing achievement gaps favoring girls at grades 4, 8, and 12. Findings are based on the U.S. National Assessment of Educational Progress. The bars represent the average girls' score minus the average boys' score. Thus, the height of the bar indicates the extent to which girls outperform boys, a difference that increases in adolescence. By grades 8 and 12, girls have an especially large advantage in writing skill. Similar trends are evident in other industrialized nations. *(Adapted from U.S. Department of Education, 2007, 2010b.)*

Mathematical Abilities

Studies of mathematical abilities in the early school grades are inconsistent. Some find no sex differences, others slight discrepancies depending on the skill assessed (Lachance & Mazzocco,

BIOLOGY AND ENVIRONMENT

Sex Differences in Spatial Abilities

Spatial skills are a key focus of researchers' efforts to explain sex differences in mathematical reasoning. The gender gap favoring males is large for *mental rotation tasks*, in which individuals must rotate a three-dimensional figure rapidly and accurately inside their heads (see Figure 15.4). Males also do considerably better on *spatial perception tasks*, in which people must determine spatial relationships by considering the orientation of the surrounding environment. Sex differences on *spatial visualization tasks*, involving analysis of complex visual forms, are weak or nonexistent. Because many strategies can be used to solve these tasks, both sexes may come up with effective procedures (Collaer & Hill, 2006; Voyer, Voyer, & Bryden, 1995).

Sex differences in spatial abilities are evident in early childhood, persist throughout the lifespan, and exist in many cultures (Levine et al., 1999; Silverman, Choi, & Peters, 2007). The pattern is consistent enough to suggest a biological explanation. One hypothesis is that heredity, perhaps through prenatal exposure to androgen hormones, enhances right-hemispheric functioning, giving males a spatial advantage. (Recall that for most people, spatial skills are housed in

Mental Rotation
Choose the responses that show the standard in a different orientation.

Standard   Responses

1   2   3   4

Spatial Perception
Pick the tilted bottle that has a horizontal water line.

1   2   3   4

Spatial Visualization
Find the figure embedded in this complex shape.

FIGURE 15.4

Types of spatial tasks. Large sex differences favoring males appear on mental rotation, and males do considerably better than females on spatial perception. In contrast, sex differences on spatial visualization are weak or nonexistent. *(From M. C. Linn & A. C. Petersen, 1985, "Emergence and Characterization of Sex Differences in Spatial Ability: A Meta-Analysis,"* Child Development, 56, pp. 1482, 1483, 1485. © The Society for Research in Child Development. Reprinted with permission.)

2006). Girls tend to be advantaged in arithmetic computation, perhaps because of their better verbal skills and more methodical approach to problem solving. But in early adolescence, when math concepts become more abstract and spatial, boys start to outperform girls. The difference is especially evident on tests of complex reasoning and geometry (Bielinski & Davison, 1998). In science achievement, too, boys' advantage increases as problems become more difficult (Penner, 2003).

This male advantage is evident in most countries where males and females have equal access to secondary education. But the gap is small, varies considerably across nations, and has diminished over the past 30 years (Bussière, Knighton, & Pennock, 2007; Halpern, Wai, & Saw, 2005; U.S. Department of Education, 2009b). Among the most capable, however, the gender gap is somewhat greater. In widely publicized research on more than 100,000 bright seventh and eighth graders invited to take the Scholastic Assessment Test (SAT), boys outscored girls on the mathematics subtest year after year. Yet even this disparity has been shrinking. A quarter-century ago, 13 times as many boys as girls scored over 700 (out of a possible 800) on the math portion of the SAT; today, the ratio is about 4 to 1 for seventh graders and 2 to 1 for high school students (Benbow & Stanley, 1983; Wai et al., 2010).

Some researchers believe that heredity contributes substantially to the gender gap in math, especially to the tendency for more boys to be extremely talented. Accumulating evidence indicates that boys' advantage originates in two skill areas: (1) their more rapid numerical the right hemisphere of the cerebral cortex.) In support of this idea, girls and women whose prenatal androgen levels were abnormally high show superior performance on spatial rotation tasks (Berenbaum, 2001; Halpern & Collaer, 2005). And in some studies, spatial performance varies with daily and annual androgen levels in both men and women (Temple & Carney, 1995; Van Goozen et al., 1995).

Why might a biologically based gender difference in spatial abilities exist? Evolutionary theorists point out that mental rotation skill predicts rapid, accurate map drawing and interpretation, areas in which boys and men do better than girls and women. Over the course of human evolution, the cognitive abilities of males became adapted for hunting, which required generating mental representations of large-scale spaces to find one's way (Jones, Braithwaite, & Healy, 2003). But this explanation is controversial. Critics point out that female gatherers also needed to travel long distances to find fruits and vegetables that ripened in different seasons (Newcombe, 2007).

Experience also contributes to males' superior spatial performance. Children who engage in manipulative activities, such as block play, model building, and carpentry, do better on spatial tasks (Baenninger & Newcombe, 1995). Furthermore, playing action video games enhances many cognitive processes important for spatial skills, including visual discrimination, speed of thinking, attention shifting, tracking of multiple objects, mental rotation, and wayfinding—gains that persist and generalize to diverse situations (Spence & Feng, 2010). Boys spend far more time than girls at these pursuits.

In studies of middle and high school students, *both* spatial ability and self-efficacy at doing math were related to performance on complex math problems, with spatial skills being the stronger predictor (Casey, Nuttal, & Pezaris, 1997, 2001). Boys are advantaged in both spatial abilities and math self-confidence.

Still, spatial skills respond readily to training, with improvements often larger than the sex differences themselves. But because boys and girls usually show similar training effects, sex differences typically persist (Liu et al., 2008; Newcombe & Huttenlocher, 2006). In one study of first graders, however, training in mental rotation strategies over several months—a more intensive approach than previously tried—led girls to reach the same performance level as boys (Tzuriel & Egozi, 2010). These findings suggest that the right kind of early intervention can override biologically based sex differences in spatial skills.

PHOTO COURTESY OF SIEMENS FOUNDATION

■ With encouragement and appropriate educational experiences, girls are capable of top-level achievement in math and science. In 2007, high school senior Isha Jain won first prize in the prestigious Siemens Competition in Math, Science, and Technology for her breakthrough discovery of a cellular mechanism underlying bone growth spurts. She aspires to lead a research lab focusing on biology and math. ■

memory, which permits them to devote more energy to complex mental operations; and (2) their superior spatial reasoning, which enhances their mathematical problem solving (Geary et al., 2000; Halpern et al., 2007). See the Biology and Environment box above for further consideration of this issue.

Social pressures are also influential. Long before sex differences in math achievement appear, many children view math as a "masculine" subject. Also, many parents think boys are better at it—an attitude that encourages girls to view themselves as having to work harder at math to do well, to blame their errors on lack of ability, and to consider math less useful for their future lives. These beliefs, in turn, reduce girls' confidence and interest in math, which undermines their performance and their willingness to consider math- or science-related careers (Bleeker & Jacobs, 2004; Ceci & Williams, 2010; Kenney-Benson et al., 2006). Furthermore, *stereotype threat*—fear of being judged on the basis of a negative stereotype (see page 460 in Chapter 12)—causes females to do worse than their abilities allow on difficult math problems (Ben-Zeev et al., 2005; Muzzatti & Agnoli, 2007). As a result of all these influences, even girls who are highly talented are less likely to develop effective math reasoning skills.

A positive sign is that today, boys and girls reach advanced levels of high school math and science study in equal proportions—a crucial factor in reducing sex differences in knowledge and skill (Gallagher & Kaufman, 2005). But, as noted in Chapter 12, boys spend more time than girls with computers, and they tend to use them differently. Whereas girls typically focus

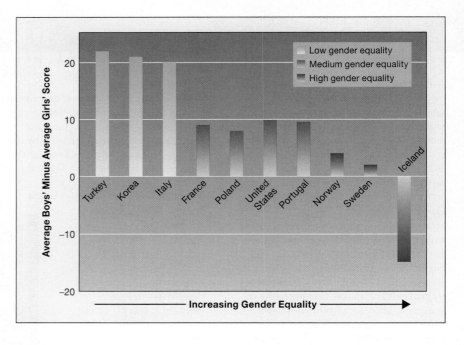

FIGURE 15.5

Math achievement gender gaps in ten industrial-ized nations, arranged in order of increasing gender equality. Math achievement scores are based on 15-year-olds' performance on an identical test in each country. Country gender equality is a composite measure that includes cultural attitudes toward women, women's participation in the labor force and in politics and government, and women's educational attainment and economic opportunities. As country gender equality increases, boys' advantage in math achievement declines; in Iceland, girls' math scores exceed boys'. *(Adapted from Guiso et al., 2008).*

on e-mail, instant messaging, gathering information for homework assignments, and social networking sites, boys more often write computer programs, analyze data, and use graphics programs. As a result, boys acquire more specialized computer knowledge (Freeman, 2004; Lenhart et al., 2010; Looker & Thiessen, 2003).

Clearly, extra steps must be taken to promote girls' interest in and confidence at math and science. As Figure 15.5 shows, in cultures that value gender equality, sex differences in math achievement are much smaller and, in one nation, reversed! Icelandic high school girls exceed boys in math scores (Guiso et al., 2008). And in an intervention in which students in seventh grade (about the time the gender gap emerges) were taught that mental abilities are not fixed but can be improved, both boys and girls improved in math grades relative to a control group, with girls gaining more and nearly closing the gender gap (Blackwell, Trzesniewski, & Dweck, 2007; Dweck, 2007).

Finally, a math curriculum beginning in kindergarten that teaches children how to apply effective spatial strategies—drawing diagrams, mentally manipulating visual images, searching for numerical patterns, and graphing—is vital (Nuttal, Casey, & Pezaris, 2005). Because girls are biased toward verbal processing, they may not attain their math and science potential unless they are specifically taught how to think spatially. Exposure to successful women as role models is likely to improve girls' belief in their own capacity to succeed.

Language Development

Although language development is largely complete by the end of childhood, subtle but important changes take place in adolescence. These gains are largely influenced by adolescents' improved capacity for reflective thought and abstraction, which enhances their *metalinguistic awareness,* or ability to think about language as a system.

Vocabulary and Grammar

Adolescents add a variety of abstract words to their vocabularies. In the conversation at the beginning of this chapter, note Jules's use of *counterintuitive, revolutionized, philosophy,* and *reproduction.* As a 9- or 10-year-old, he rarely used such words and had difficulty grasping their meaning. From high school to college, definitions of abstract words improve greatly in clarity and accuracy (Nippold, 1999). For example, in explaining the meaning of *burden,* Louis said, "It's like a heavy weight on your shoulders. You can also use it figuratively, to mean an unpleasant responsibility or a long-term problem."

Adolescents also master sarcasm and irony (Pexman & Glenwright, 2007; Winner, 1988). When Franca prepared a dish for dinner that Louis disliked, he quipped, "Oh boy, my favorite!" School-age children sometimes realize that a sarcastic remark is insincere if it is said in an exaggerated, mocking tone of voice. But adolescents and adults need only notice the discrepancy between the statement and its context to grasp the intended meaning (Capelli, Nakagawa, & Madden, 1990).

Similarly, grasp of figurative language improves greatly in adolescence. Proverbs—especially those that express subtle attitudes—are especially challenging. They can be used to comment ("Blood is thicker than water"), interpret ("His bark is worse than his bite"), advise ("Humility often gains more than pride"), warn ("Of idleness comes no goodness"), and encourage ("Every cloud has a silver lining") (Nippold, 2000). As with other aspects of semantic development, reading proficiency fosters understanding of proverbs (Nippold, Allen, & Kirsch, 2001). And a better grasp of figurative language enables teenagers to appreciate adult literary works.

Mastery of sarcasm and irony gives adolescents new ways to express themselves through language. Compared to school-age children, teenagers are better able to detect whether a remark is sarcastic or sincere.

Furthermore, adolescents use more elaborate grammatical constructions—longer sentences consisting of a greater number of subordinate clauses. Persuasive speaking and writing, which draw on adolescents' advanced perspective-taking skill, illustrate this change. With age, this challenging form of communication contains many more connecting words, such as "although," "moreover," and "on the other hand" (Crowhurst, 1990).

Finally, teenagers more effectively analyze and correct their grammar. In U.S. schools, overt grammar instruction—out of favor since the 1970s—is making a comeback, prompted by the mediocre writing skills of many adolescents. In the most recent national assessment of educational progress, only about one-fourth of U.S. high school seniors scored at a "proficient" level or above in writing achievement (U.S. Department of Education, 2007). But traditional grammar instruction (such as diagramming sentences) has no impact on students' writing skills (Andrews et al., 2006). Rather, grammatically accurate written expression is best learned in the context of writing. And writing improves when teachers show students how to write for different purposes, give them many opportunities to write, and help them critique and improve their compositions (Medina, 2006).

Pragmatics

One obvious gain in adolescents' communication skills is an improved capacity to adapt language style to social context—in part because teenagers have opportunities to enter many more situations. To succeed on the debate team, Louis had to speak in a persuasive, well-organized, rapid-fire manner. In theater class, he worked on reciting memorized lines as if they were natural. At work, his boss expected him to respond to customers cheerfully and courteously. Greater skill at reflecting on the features of language and engaging in cognitive self-regulation also supports effective use of language styles (Obler, 2008). Teenagers are far more likely than school-age children to practice what they want to say in an expected situation, review what they did say, and figure out how they could say it better.

TAKE A MOMENT... Listen to adolescents conversing, and note their use of slang—another illustration of their mastery of language styles. Adolescents' electronic communication—especially instant messaging, text messaging via cell phone, and, increasingly, interaction on social networking sites such as MySpace, Facebook, and Twitter—is also rich in slang. "Cyber slang," devised to facilitate communication while protecting its privacy, has become a familiar part of popular culture—for example, "gg" (gotta go), "mwah" (kiss), "lol" (laugh out loud), "brb" (be right back), "yt" (you there?"), "pos" (parents over shoulder). Teenagers use slang as a sign of group belonging and as a way to distinguish themselves from adults. Doing so is part of separating from parents and seeking a temporary self-definition in the peer group. We will discuss these developments in Chapter 16.

Learning in School

In complex societies, adolescence coincides with entry into secondary school. Most young people move into either a middle or a junior high school and then into a high school. With each change, academic achievement becomes more serious, affecting higher education options and job opportunities. In the following sections, we take up various aspects of secondary school life.

School Transitions

When Sabrina started middle school, she left a small, intimate, self-contained sixth-grade classroom for a much larger school. "I don't know most of the kids in my classes, and my teachers don't know me," Sabrina complained to her mother at the end of the first week. "Besides, there's too much homework. I get assignments in all my classes at once. I can't do all this!" she shouted, bursting into tears.

IMPACT OF SCHOOL TRANSITIONS   As Sabrina's reactions suggest, school transitions can create adjustment problems. With each school change—from elementary to middle or junior high and then to high school—adolescents' grades decline. The drop is partly due to tighter academic standards. At the same time, the transition to secondary school often means less personal attention, more whole-class instruction, and less chance to participate in classroom decision making (Seidman, Aber, & French, 2004).

In view of these changes, it is not surprising that students rate their middle- and high-school learning school experiences less favorably than their elementary school experiences. They also report that their teachers care less about them, are less friendly, offer less support, grade less fairly, and stress competition more. Consequently, many young people feel less academically competent, and their liking for school and motivation decline (Baker et al., 2001; Barber & Olsen, 2004; Gutman & Midgley, 2000; Otis, Grouzet, & Pelletier, 2005).

Inevitably, students must readjust their feelings of self-confidence and self-worth as they encounter revised academic expectations and a more complex social world. In several studies that followed students across the middle- and high-school transitions, grade point average declined and feelings of anonymity increased after each school change. Girls fared less well than boys. On entering middle school, girls' self-esteem dropped sharply, perhaps because the transition tended to coincide with other life changes: the onset of puberty and dating (Simmons & Blyth, 1987). And after starting high school, girls felt lonelier and more anxious than boys, and—although they were doing better academically—their grades declined more rapidly (Benner & Graham, 2009; Russell, Elder, & Conger, 1997).

Adolescents facing added strains at either transition—family disruption, poverty, low parental involvement, high parental conflict, or learned

© DWIGHT CENDROWSKI, WWW.CENDROWSKI.COM

■ This seventh grader hurries at his locker so he won't be late for class at his new middle school. Moving from a small, self-contained elementary school classroom to a large, impersonal secondary school is stressful for adolescents. ■

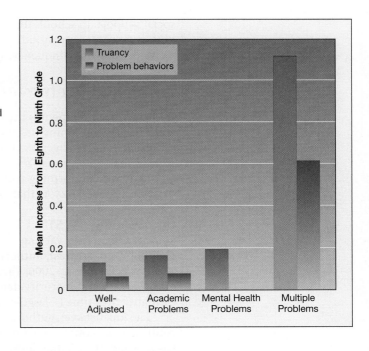

FIGURE 15.6

Increase in truancy and out-of-school problem behaviors across the transition to high school in four groups of students. Well-adjusted students, students with only academic problems, and students with only mental health problems showed little change. (Good students with mental health problems actually declined in problem behaviors, so no yellow bar is shown for them.) In contrast, multiple-problem students—with both academic and mental health difficulties—increased sharply in truancy and problem behaviors after changing schools from eighth to ninth grade. *(Adapted from Roeser, Eccles, & Freedman-Doan, 1999.)*

helplessness on academic tasks—are at greatest risk for self-esteem and academic difficulties (de Bruyn, 2005; Rudolph et al., 2001; Seidman et al., 2003). Furthermore, the high-school transition is particularly challenging for African-American and Hispanic students who move to a new school with substantially fewer same-ethnicity peers (Benner & Graham, 2009). Under these conditions, minority adolescents report decreased feelings of belonging and school liking, and they show steeper declines in grades.

Distressed youths whose school performance either remains low or drops sharply after school transition often show a persisting pattern of poor self-esteem, motivation, and achievement. In another study, researchers compared "multiple-problem" youths (those having both academic and mental health problems), youths having difficulties in just one area (either academic or mental health), and well-adjusted youths (those doing well in both areas) across the transition to high school. Although all groups declined in grade point average, well-adjusted students continued to get high marks and multiple-problem youths low marks, with the others falling in between. And as Figure 15.6 shows, the multiple-problem youths showed a far greater rise in truancy and out-of-school problem behaviors (Roeser, Eccles, & Freedman-Doan, 1999).

Adolescents with academic and emotional difficulties often turn to similarly alienated peers for the support they lack in other spheres of life (Rubin, Bukowski, & Parker, 2006). For these vulnerable youths, the transition to high school may initiate a downward spiral in school involvement and performance that eventually leads to failure and dropping out.

HELPING ADOLESCENTS ADJUST TO SCHOOL TRANSITIONS As these findings reveal, school transitions often lead to environmental changes that fit poorly with adolescents' developmental needs (Eccles, 2004). They disrupt close relationships with teachers at a time when adolescents need adult support. They emphasize competition during a period of heightened self-focusing. They reduce decision making and choice as the desire for autonomy is increasing. And they interfere with peer networks as young people become more concerned with peer acceptance.

Support from parents, teachers, and peers can ease these strains. Parental involvement, monitoring, gradual autonomy granting, and emphasis on mastery rather than merely good grades are associated with better adjustment (Grolnick et al., 2000; Gutman, 2006). Adolescents with close friends are more likely to sustain these friendships across the transition, which increases social integration and academic motivation in the new school (Aikins, Bierman, & Parker, 2005). Forming smaller units within large schools promotes closer relations with both teachers and peers along with greater extracurricular involvement (Seidman, Aber, & French, 2004). And a "critical mass" of same-ethnicity peers—according to one suggestion, at least 15 percent of the student body—helps teenagers feel socially accepted and reduces fear of out-group hostility (National Research Council, 2007).

Other less extensive changes are also effective. In the first year after a school transition, homerooms can be provided in which teachers offer academic and personal counseling and work closely with parents to promote favorable adjustment. Assigning students to classes with several familiar peers or a constant group of new peers strengthens emotional security and

LOOK AND LISTEN

❖❖

Ask several secondary school students to describe their experiences after school transition. What supports for easing the stress of transition did their teachers and school provide?

social support. In schools that took these steps, students were less likely to decline in academic performance or display other adjustment problems, including low self-esteem, depression, substance abuse, delinquency, and dropping out (Felner et al., 2002).

Academic Achievement

Adolescent achievement is the result of a long history of cumulative effects. Early on, positive educational environments, both family and school, lead to personal traits that support achievement—intelligence, confidence in one's own abilities, the desire to succeed, and high educational aspirations. Yet improving an unfavorable environment can foster resilience among poorly performing young people. See Applying What We Know below for a summary of environmental factors that enhance achievement during the teenage years.

CHILD-REARING STYLES Authoritative parenting is linked to higher grades in school among adolescents varying widely in SES, just as it predicts mastery-oriented behavior in childhood. In contrast, authoritarian and permissive styles are associated with lower grades (Collins & Steinberg, 2006; Vazsonyi, Hibbert, & Snider, 2003). Uninvolved parenting (low in both warmth and maturity demands) predicts the poorest grades and worsening school performance over time (Glasgow et al., 1997; Kaisa, Stattin, & Nurmi, 2000).

The link between authoritative parenting and adolescents' academic competence has been confirmed in countries with diverse value systems, including Argentina, Australia, China, Hong Kong, the Netherlands, Pakistan, and Scotland (de Bruyn, Deković, & Meijnen, 2003; Heaven & Ciarrochi, 2008; Steinberg, 2001). In Chapter 10, we noted that authoritative parents adjust their expectations to children's capacity to take responsibility for their own behavior. Adolescents whose parents engage in joint decision making, gradually permitting more autonomy with age, achieve especially well (Spera, 2005; Wang, Pomerantz, & Chen, 2007). Warmth, open discussion, firmness, and monitoring of adolescents' whereabouts and activities make young people feel cared about and valued, encourage reflective thinking and self-regulation, and increase awareness of the importance of doing well in school. These factors, in turn, are related to mastery-oriented attributions, effort, achievement, and high educational expectations (Aunola, Stattin, & Nurmi, 2000; Gregory & Weinstein, 2004; Trusty, 1999).

PARENT–SCHOOL PARTNERSHIPS High-achieving students typically have parents who keep tabs on their child's progress, communicate with teachers, and make sure their child is enrolled in challenging, well-taught classes. These efforts are just as important during middle

Applying What We Know

Supporting High Achievement in Adolescence

FACTOR	DESCRIPTION
Child-rearing practices	Authoritative parenting
	Joint parent–adolescent decision making
	Parent involvement in the adolescent's education
Peer influences	Peer valuing of and support for high achievement
School characteristics	Teachers who are warm and supportive, develop personal relationships with parents, and show them how to support their teenager's learning
	Learning activities that encourage high-level thinking
	Active student participation in learning activities and classroom decision making
Employment schedule	Job commitment limited to less than 15 hours per week
	High-quality vocational education for non-college-bound adolescents

and high school as they were earlier (Hill & Taylor, 2004). In a large, nationally representative sample of U.S. adolescents, parents' school involvement in eighth grade strongly predicted students' grade point average in tenth grade, beyond the influence of SES and previous academic achievement. This relationship held for each ethnic group included— black, white, Native American, and Asian (Keith et al., 1998). Parents who are in frequent contact with the school send a message to their child about the value of education, model constructive solutions to academic problems, and promote wise educational decisions—factors that induce in teenagers a sense of academic self-efficacy, of being able to handle academic challenges (Oyserman, 2007). Involved parents can also prevent school personnel from placing a bright student who is not working up to potential in unstimulating classes.

The daily stresses of living in low-income, high-risk neighborhoods reduce parents' energy for school involvement (Bowen, Bowen, & Ware, 2002). Yet stronger home–school links can relieve some of this stress. Schools can build parent–school partnerships by strengthening personal relationships between teachers and parents, building bridges between minority home cultures and the culture of the school, tapping parents' talents to improve the quality of school programs, and including parents in school governance so they remain invested in school goals.

By attending parent–teacher conferences and keeping tabs on her daughter's progress in school, this mother sends her child a message about the importance of education and also builds a bridge between the worlds of home and school. ■

PEER INFLUENCES Peers play an important role in adolescent achievement, in a way that relates to both family and school. Teenagers whose parents value achievement not only tend to be academically motivated but generally choose friends who share those values (Kiuru et al., 2009; Rubin, Bukowski, & Parker, 2006; Woolley, Kol, & Bowen, 2009). For example, when Sabrina began to make new friends in middle school, she often studied with her girlfriends. Each girl wanted to do well and reinforced this desire in the others. In an investigation that assessed a large sample of students at the beginning of seventh and again at the end of eighth grade, those with academically high-performing friends not only gained in school performance but were also more likely to avoid drugs, engage in responsible behavior, and participate in extracurricular activities (Cook, Deng, & Morgano, 2007). Of the diverse characteristics on which friends resemble each other, grade point average had the strongest association with future adjustment, predicting both academic and social outcomes.

Peer support for high achievement also depends on the overall climate of the peer culture, which, for ethnic minority youths, is powerfully affected by the surrounding social order. In one study, integration into the school peer network predicted higher grades among Caucasians and Hispanics but not among Asians and African Americans (Faircloth & Hamm, 2005). Asian cultural values stress respect for family and teacher expectations over close peer ties (Chao & Tseng, 2002; Chen, 2005). African-American minority adolescents may observe that their ethnic group is worse off than the white majority in educational attainment, jobs, income, and housing. And discriminatory treatment by teachers and peers, often resulting from stereotypes that they are "not intelligent," triggers anger, anxiety, self-doubts, declines in achievement, association with peers who are not interested in school, and increases in problem behaviors (Wong, Eccles, & Sameroff, 2003).

Yet not all economically disadvantaged African-American and other minority students respond this way. Case studies of inner-city, poverty-stricken African-American adolescents who were high-achieving and optimistic about their futures revealed that they were intensely aware of oppression but believed in striving to alter their social position (O'Connor, 1997). How did they develop this sense of agency? Parents, relatives, and teachers had convinced them through discussion and example that injustice should not be tolerated and that, together, African Americans could overcome it—a perspective that encouraged high academic motivation even in the face of peer pressures against excelling academically.

Schools that build close networks of support with teachers and other students are also powerful. One high school with a largely low-income ethnic minority student body (65 percent African American) reorganized into "career academies"—learning communities within the school, each offering a different career-related curriculum (for example, one focused on health, medicine, and life sciences, another on computer technology). The smaller-school climate and focus on a common theme helped create caring teacher–student relationships and a peer culture that fostered a sense of belonging, valuing of school engagement, mutual support, collaboration on projects, and academic success (Conchas, 2006). High school graduation and college enrollment rates rose from a small minority to over 90 percent.

Finally, teenagers' use of text messaging and e-mail to remain continuously in touch with peers—even during class and while working on homework—is an aspect of contemporary peer-group life that poses risks to achievement. Turn to the Social Issues: Education box on the following page to find out about the impact of "media multitasking" on attention and learning.

SCHOOL CHARACTERISTICS   Adolescents need school environments that are responsive to their expanding powers of reasoning and their emotional and social needs. Without appropriate learning experiences, their cognitive potential is unlikely to be realized.

Classroom Learning Experiences. As noted earlier, in large, departmentalized secondary schools, many adolescents report that their classes lack warmth and supportiveness—a circumstance that dampens their motivation. One study tracked changes in students' academic orientation in math classes from seventh to eighth grade. Those who entered classrooms high in teacher support, encouragement of student interaction about academic work, and promotion of mutual respect among classmates gained in academic motivation and cognitive self-regulation (reflected in whether they understood concepts and in their willingness to check their work). But in classrooms emphasizing competition and public comparison of students, declines in motivation and self-regulation occurred (Ryan & Patrick, 2001). In other investigations, adolescents who perceived their relationships with teachers as warm, trusting, and cooperative and who viewed classroom control as shared between teacher and students showed better attendance and achievement (Eshel & Kohavi, 2003; Schulte et al., 2003).

Of course, an important benefit of departmentalized teaching with separate classes in each subject is that adolescents can be taught by experts, who are more likely to encourage high-level thinking, teach effective learning strategies, and emphasize content relevant to students' experiences—factors that promote interest, effort, and achievement (Eccles, 2004). But many secondary school classrooms do not consistently provide interesting, challenging teaching. Because of the uneven quality of instruction, many seniors graduate from high school deficient in basic academic skills. Although the achievement gap separating African-American, Hispanic, and Native-American students from white students has declined since the 1970s, mastery of reading, writing, mathematics, and science by low-SES ethnic minority students remains disappointing (U.S. Department of Education, 2007, 2009b, 2010b). Too often these young people attend underfunded schools with rundown buildings, outdated equipment, and textbook shortages. In some, crime and discipline problems receive more attention than teaching and learning.

© ST. PETERSBURG TIMES/CHERIE DIEZ/THE IMAGE WORKS

■ This high school teacher's warm, supportive way of relating to students leads to gains in both academic motivation and cognitive self-regulation. ■

SOCIAL ISSUES: EDUCATION

Media Multitasking Disrupts Attention and Learning

"Mom, I'm going to study for my biology test now," called 16-year-old Ashley while shutting her bedroom door. Sitting down at her desk, she accessed a popular social-networking website on her laptop, donned headphones and began listening to a favorite song on her MP3 player, and laid her cell phone next to her elbow so she could hear it chime if any text messages arrived. Only then did she open her textbook and begin to read.

In a survey of a nationally representative sample of U.S. 8- to 18-year-olds, more than half reported engaging in two or more media activities at once, some or most of the time (Roberts, Foehr, & Rideout, 2005). Adolescents' most frequent type of media multitasking is listening to music while doing homework or communicating with friends, but many also report watching TV or using the Internet while studying (Jeong & Fishbein, 2007). The presence of a television or computer in the young person's bedroom is a strong predictor of this behavior (Foehr, 2006). And it extends into classrooms, where students can be seen text-messaging under their desks or surfing the Internet on cell phones.

Research confirms that media multitasking fragments the attention span, greatly reducing learning. In one experiment, participants were given two tasks: learning to predict the weather in two different cities using colored shapes as

cues and keeping a mental tally of how many high-pitched beeps they heard through headphones. Half the sample performed the tasks simultaneously, the other half separately. Both groups learned to predict the weather in the two-city situation, but the multitaskers were unable to apply their learning to new weather problems (Foerde, Knowlton, & Poldrack, 2006).

fMRI evidence revealed that the participants working only on the weather task activated the hippocampus, which plays a vital role in *explicit memory*—deliberate, strategic recall, which enables new information to be used flexibly and adaptively (see page 294 in Chapter 8). In contrast, the multitaskers activated brain areas involved in *implicit memory*—a superficial, automatic form of learning that takes place unconsciously.

As early as 1980, studies linked heavy media use with attention problems (Nunez-Smith et al., 2008). Frequent media multitaskers, who are accustomed to continuously shifting their attention from one task to another, have a harder time filtering out irrelevant stimuli when they are not multitasking (Ophir, Nass, & Wagner, 2009).

Beyond shallow preparation for her biology test, Ashley is likely to have difficulty concentrating after turning off her computer and MP3 player. Experienced teachers often remark that compared to students of a generation ago,

© BOB PARDUE—TEEN LIFESTYLE/ALAMY IMAGES

■ Media multitasking while doing homework fragments attention, yielding superficial learning. And frequent multitaskers are likely to have difficulty filtering out irrelevant stimuli even when they are not multitasking. ■

today's teenagers focus for shorter periods and are more easily distracted. One teacher reflected, "It's the way they've grown up—working short times on many different things at one time" (Clay, 2009, p. 40).

To upgrade the academic achievement of poorly performing students, a *high-stakes testing* movement has arisen, which makes progress through the school system contingent on passing achievement tests. But as the Social Issues: Education box on page 586 points out, high-stakes testing narrows the focus of classroom instruction to preparing for tests and, in some school districts, may widen group differences in educational attainment. Another source of educational inequity is the placement of many low-SES, minority students in low academic tracks, which compounds their learning difficulties.

Tracking. Ability grouping, as we saw in Chapter 12, is detrimental during the elementary school years. At least into middle school, mixed-ability classes are desirable. They effectively support the motivation and achievement of students who vary widely in academic progress (Gillies, 2003b; Gillies & Ashman, 1996).

By high school, some grouping is unavoidable because certain aspects of education must dovetail with the young person's future educational and vocational plans. In the United States,

LOOK AND LISTEN

Ask a long-time high school teacher for his or her views on the impact of high-stakes testing on quality of classroom teaching. How successful, in the teacher's view, are such tests in improving student achievement?

SOCIAL ISSUES: EDUCATION

High-Stakes Testing

To better hold schools accountable for educating students, during the past two decades many U.S. states have mandated that students pass exams for high school graduation. Currently, about two-thirds of public high school students take exit exams (Center on Education Policy, 2009). As these high-stakes achievement tests spread, schools stepped up their testing programs, extending them downward to elementary school. Some states and school districts also made grade promotion (in New York City, as early as the third grade) and secondary school academic course credits contingent on test scores (Gootman, 2005).

The U.S. No Child Left Behind Act broadens high-stakes testing to the identification of "passing" and "failing" schools. The law mandates that each state evaluate every public school's performance through annual achievement testing and publicize the results. Schools that consistently perform poorly (have a high percentage of failing students) must give parents options for upgrading their children's education, such as transfers to nearby, higher-performing schools or enrollment in remedial classes. Some states offer schoolwide rewards for high scores, including official praise and financial bonuses to school staff. Penalties imposed for low scores include withdrawal of accreditation, state takeover, and closure.

Proponents of high-stakes testing believe that it introduces greater rigor into classroom teaching, improves student motivation and achievement, and either turns around poor-performing schools or protects students from being trapped in them. But accumulating evidence indicates that high-stakes testing often undermines, rather than upgrades, the quality of education.

Research shows that high-stakes tests cause teachers to spend large amounts of time on activities that closely resemble test items—typically, drill-based exercises. Classroom experiences and assignments that require high level reasoning, including extended writing and research projects, are de-emphasized, as are subjects not covered on the tests (Jones & Egley, 2004; Linn, 2000). In a national survey of U.S. teachers, those in states with high-stakes tests reported that to "cover" the material likely to be tested, they felt pressured to move through the curriculum too quickly, yielding surface knowledge rather than in-depth understanding (Center on Education Policy, 2007).

Because the main goal of high-stakes testing is to upgrade the performance of poorly achieving students, low-income and ethnic minority students are especially likely to be exposed to narrowly focused, regimented teaching (Darling-Hammond, 2010). Simultaneously, the educational needs of gifted and talented students are neglected (Mondoza, 2006).

An additional concern is that high-stakes testing promotes fear—a poor motivator for upgrading teaching and learning. Principals and teachers worry about losing funding and their jobs if students do poorly—punishments that have sparked unprecedented levels of adult cheating and other educationally detrimental behaviors. These range from giving students answers, changing students' scores, and offering students rewards (including money and expensive toys) for earning high scores to suspending or expelling students likely to perform poorly just before test administration (Nichols & Berliner, 2007).

Furthermore, many students who get passing school grades, even high grades, fail exams because a time-limited test can tap only a small sampling of the skills covered in the classroom (Hursh, 2007). Students most likely to score poorly are minority youths living in poverty. When they are punished with course failure and grade retention, their self-esteem and motivation drop sharply. Research confirms that high-stakes testing requirements have contributed to the high U.S. dropout rates among inner-city minority youths (Balfanz et al., 2007).

The trend toward teaching to tests induced by high-stakes testing contrasts sharply with the emphasis on teaching for deeper understanding in countries that rank at the top in cross-cultural comparisons of academic achievement (see Chapter 12, pages 475–477). Even after hundreds of hours of class time devoted to test preparation, thousands of U.S. students fail school-exit exams and do not graduate. Although most retake these exams, some fail repeatedly, with potentially dire consequences for the course of their lives.

Clearly, serious issues remain for lawmakers and educators to resolve about the use of high-stakes tests. These include their questionable power to spark school reforms that make students better learners.

■ High-stakes testing often negatively affects educational quality and student learning. Pressure on teachers to "teach to the test" narrows the focus of the curriculum. And students who experience course failure or grade retention because of poor test performance are likely to decline in motivation and drop out of school. ■

high school students are counseled into college preparatory, vocational, or general education tracks. Unfortunately, low-SES minority students are assigned in large numbers to noncollege tracks, perpetuating educational inequalities of earlier years.

Longitudinal research following thousands of U.S. students from eighth to twelfth grade revealed that assignment to a college preparatory track accelerates academic progress, whereas assignment to a vocational or general education track decelerates it (Hallinan & Kubitschek, 1999). Even in secondary schools with no formal tracking program, low-SES minority students tend to be assigned to lower course levels in most or all of their academic subjects, resulting in *de facto* (unofficial) *tracking* (Lucas & Behrends, 2002).

Breaking out of a low academic track is difficult. Track or course enrollment is generally based on past performance, which is limited by placement history. Interviews with African-American students in one high school revealed that many thought their previous performance did not reflect their ability. Yet teachers and counselors, overburdened with other responsibilities, had little time to reconsider individual cases (Ogbu, 2003). And compared to students in higher tracks, students in low tracks exert substantially less effort—a difference due in part to less stimulating classroom experiences (Worthy, Hungerford-Kresser, & Hampton, 2009).

High school students are separated into academic and vocational tracks in virtually all industrialized nations. In China, Japan, and most Western European countries, students' placement is determined by their performance on a national exam. The outcome usually fixes the young person's future possibilities. In the United States, students who are not assigned to a college preparatory track or who achieve poorly in high school can still attend college. Ultimately, however, many young people do not benefit from the more open U.S. system. By adolescence, SES differences in quality of education and academic achievement are greater in the United States than in most other industrialized countries (Marks, Cresswell, & Ainley, 2006). And the United States has a higher percentage of young people who see themselves as educational failures and drop out of high school (see Figure 15.7).

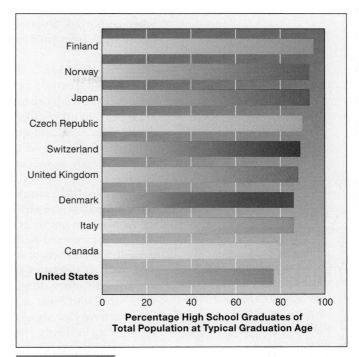

FIGURE 15.7

High school graduation rates in ten industrialized nations. The United States ranks below many other developed countries. *(OECD, 2010.)*

Dropping Out

Across the aisle from Louis in math class sat Norman, who daydreamed, crumpled his notes into his pocket after class, and rarely did his homework. On test days, he twirled a rabbit's foot for good luck but left most questions blank. Louis and Norman had been classmates since fourth grade, but they had little to do with each other. To Louis, who was quick at schoolwork, Norman seemed to live in another world. Once or twice each week, Norman cut class; then, one spring day, he stopped coming altogether.

Norman is one of about 8 percent of U.S. 16- to 24-year-olds who dropped out of high school and remain without a diploma or a GED (U.S. Department of Education, 2010). The dropout rate is higher among boys than girls and is particularly high among low-SES ethnic minority youths, especially Native-American and Hispanic teenagers (see Figure 15.8). The decision to leave school has dire consequences. Youths without upper secondary education have much lower literacy scores than high school graduates, and they lack the skills valued by employers in today's knowledge-based economy. Consequently, dropouts have much lower employment rates than high school graduates. Even

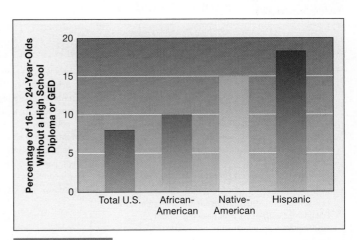

FIGURE 15.8

U.S. high school dropout rates by ethnicity. Because many African-American, Hispanic, and Native-American young people come from low-income and poverty-stricken families and attended underfunded, poor-quality schools, their dropout rates are above the national average. Rates for Native-American and Hispanic youths are especially high. *(From DeVoe & Darling-Churchill, 2008; U.S. Department of Education, 2010.)*

when employed, dropouts are far more likely to remain in menial, low-paid jobs and to be out of work from time to time.

FACTORS RELATED TO DROPPING OUT Table 15.1 lists diverse factors related to leaving school early. The more that are present, the greater the risk of dropping out. Many dropouts show a persistent pattern of disruptive behavior and poor achievement (Vitaro et al., 2001). But others, like Norman, have few behavior problems; they simply experience academic difficulties and quietly disengage from school (Janosz et al., 2000; Newcomb et al., 2002). The pathway to dropping out starts early. Risk factors in first grade predict later dropout nearly as well as risk factors in secondary school (Entwisle, Alexander, & Olson, 2005).

Norman had a long history of marginal-to-failing school grades and low academic self-esteem. Faced with a challenging task, he gave up, relying on luck—his rabbit's foot—to get by. As Norman got older, he attended class less regularly, paid little attention when he was there, and rarely did his homework. He didn't join school clubs or participate in sports. As a result, few teachers or students got to know him well. By the day he left, Norman felt alienated from all aspects of school life.

As with other dropouts, Norman's family background contributed to his problems. Compared with other students, even those with the same grade profile, dropouts are more likely to have parents who are uninvolved in their teenager's education and engage in little monitoring of their youngster's daily activities. Many parents are single, never finished high school themselves, and are unemployed (Englund, Egeland, & Collins, 2008; Pagani et al., 2008).

Academically marginal students who drop out often have school experiences that undermine their chances for success: grade retention, which marks them as academic failures; large, impersonal schools; and classes with unsupportive teachers and few opportunities for active participation (Brown & Rodriguez, 2009; Lee & Burkam, 2003). In such schools, rule breaking is common and often results in suspension, which—by excluding students from classes—contributes further to academic failure (Christie, Jolivette, & Nelson, 2007). Recent reports indicate that more than half of adolescents in some U.S. inner-city high schools do not graduate. Students in general education and vocational tracks, where teaching tends to be the least stimulating, are three times as likely to drop out as those in a college preparatory track (U.S. Department of Education, 2010).

LOOK AND LISTEN

Contact an adult education program that sponsors GED classes, and interview one or more teachers about their students' unique academic and social needs. What factors, in the teacher's view, distinguish students who succeed in earning a GED from those who fail to do so?

TABLE 15.1 Factors Related to Dropping Out of High School

STUDENT CHARACTERISTICS	FAMILY CHARACTERISTICS	SCHOOL AND COMMUNITY CHARACTERISTICS
Poor school attendance	Parents who do not support or emphasize achievement	Large, unstimulating classes
Inattentiveness in class	Parents who were high school dropouts	Lack of opportunity to form personal relationships with teachers
School discipline problems, especially aggressive behavior	Parents who are uninvolved in the adolescent's education	Curriculum irrelevant to student interests and needs
Inability to get along with teachers	Parents who react with anger and punishment to the adolescent's low grades	School authority structure that emphasizes the teacher and discourages student input
1 to 2 years behind in grade level	Single-parent household	Large student body
Low academic achievement	Low income	School located in low-SES racially or ethnically segregated neighborhood
A sharp drop in achievement after school transition	Frequent school changes	Availability of work that requires only on-the-job training
Dislike of school		
Enrollment in a general education or vocational track		
Low educational aspirations		
Low self-esteem, especially academic self-esteem		
Friendships with peers who have left school		
Low involvement in extracurricular activities		
Drug use		
Law-breaking behavior		
Adolescent parenthood		

Sources: Lee & Burkam, 2003; Stearns & Glennie, 2006.

The high dropout rates among urban minority teenagers are also influenced by young people's observations and experiences of discrimination, which strengthen their conviction that finishing school will not bring them greater vocational and financial rewards (Harwood et al., 2002; Valdés, 1997). When work requiring only on-the-job training becomes available in their communities, these teenagers (more often boys), despite being within a year or two of graduating, often choose employment over school attendance (Beekhoven & Dekkers, 2005; Stearns & Glennie, 2006). And young people in ethnic-minority families, especially girls, are more likely to be expected to take on family responsibilities, including care of elders and siblings, which may prompt school leaving.

PREVENTION STRATEGIES The most powerful way to prevent school dropout is to address the academic and social problems of at-risk students beginning in elementary school, and to involve their parents (Prevatt & Kelly, 2003). In addition, programs have been developed for adolescents. Among the diverse strategies available, several common themes are related to success:

- *Remedial instruction and counseling that offer personalized attention.* Most potential dropouts need intensive remedial instruction in small classes that permit warm, caring teacher–student relationships to form. To overcome the negative psychological effects of repeated school failure, academic assistance must be combined with social support (Christenson & Thurlow, 2004). In one successful approach, at-risk students are matched with retired adults, who serve as tutors, mentors, and role models in addressing academic and vocational needs (Prevatt, 2003).
- *High-quality vocational education.* For many marginal students, the real-life nature of vocational education is more comfortable and effective than purely academic work. To work well, vocational training must carefully integrate academic and job-related instruction so students can see the relevance of what happens in the classroom to their future goals (Harvey, 2001).
- *Efforts to address the many factors in students' lives related to leaving school early.* Programs that strengthen parent involvement, offer flexible work–study arrangements, and provide on-site child care for teenage mothers can make staying in school easier for at-risk adolescents.
- *Participation in extracurricular activities.* Another way of helping marginal students is to draw them into the community life of the school (Mahoney & Stattin, 2000). The most powerful influence on extracurricular involvement is small school size (Barker & Gump, 1964; Feldman & Matjasko, 2007). In high schools of 500 to 700 students or fewer, potential dropouts are far more likely to be needed to help staff and operate school activities. In large schools, creation of smaller "schools within schools" has the same effect.

    Participation focusing on the arts, community service, and vocational development promotes diverse aspects of adjustment, including improved academic performance, reduced antisocial behavior, more favorable self-esteem and initiative, and increased peer acceptance (Fredricks & Eccles, 2005, 2006; Mahoney, 2000). Adolescents with academic, emotional, and social problems are especially likely to benefit (Marsh & Kleitman, 2002).

■ St. Paul, Minnesota, police chief Thomas Smith warmly greets one of his student mentees following a high school fundraising event to benefit charitable organizations. Support from a caring adult and extracurricular involvement are effective ways to prevent school dropout. ■

As we conclude our discussion of academic achievement, let's place the school dropout problem in historical perspective. Over the second half of the twentieth century, the percentage of U.S. young people completing high school by age 24 increased steadily, from less than 50 percent to just over 90 percent. College attendance also rose during this same period: Today, nearly 40 percent of U.S. young people earn college degrees. Despite the worrisome decline in male college enrollment noted earlier, U.S. higher education rates continue to rank among the highest in the world (OECD, 2010; U.S. Department of Education, 2010).

Finally, although many dropouts get caught in a vicious cycle in which their lack of self-confidence and skills prevents them from seeking further education and training, about one-third return to finish their secondary education within a few years (U.S. Department of Education, 2010). And some extend their schooling further as they come to realize how essential education is for a rewarding job and a satisfying adult life.

ASK YOURSELF

◆ REVIEW List ways parents can promote their adolescent's academic achievement. Explain why each is effective.

◆ APPLY Tanisha is finishing sixth grade. She can either continue in her current school through eighth grade or switch to a much larger seventh- to ninth-grade middle school. What choice would you suggest, and why?

◆ CONNECT How are educational practices that prevent school dropout similar to those that improve learning for adolescents in general?

◆ REFLECT Describe your own experiences in making the transition to middle school and then to high school. What did you find stressful? What helped you adjust?

Vocational Development

As the end of adolescence approaches, young people face a major life decision: the choice of a suitable work role. As we will see in Chapters 16 and 17, selecting a vocation is central to the development of a solid, secure identity. This is not surprising, since economic independence and career progress are hallmarks of adulthood in industrialized societies.

Being a productive worker calls for many of the same qualities as being an active citizen and a nurturant family member—good judgment, responsibility, dedication, and cooperation. What influences young people's decisions about careers? What is the transition from school to work like, and what factors make it easy or difficult?

Selecting a Vocation

In societies with an abundance of career possibilities, occupational choice is a gradual process that begins long before adolescence and often extends into the mid-twenties. Major theorists view the young person as moving through several periods of vocational development (Gottfredson, 2005; Super, 1990, 1994):

1. The **fantasy period:** In early and middle childhood, children gain insight into career options by fantasizing about them. Their preferences, guided largely by familiarity, glamour, and excitement, usually bear little relation to the decisions they will eventually make.
2. The **tentative period:** Between ages 11 and 16, adolescents think about careers in more complex ways, at first in terms of their *interests,* and soon—as they become more aware of personal and educational requirements for different vocations—in terms of their *abilities* and *values.* "I like business and selling things," 16-year-old Louis said as he neared high

school graduation. "But I'm also good with people, and I'd like to do something to help others. So maybe counseling or social work would suit my needs."

3. The **realistic period:** By the late teens and early twenties, with the economic and practical realities of adulthood just around the corner, young people start to narrow their options. A first step is often further *exploration*—gathering more information about possibilities that blend with their personal characteristics. In the final phase, *crystallization,* they focus on a general vocational category and experiment for a time before settling on a single occupation. As a college freshman, Jules pursued his interest in science, but he is not sure whether he prefers chemistry, math, or physics. Within the next year, he is likely to choose a major. Then he will consider whether he wants to work for a company following graduation or study further to become a doctor or research scientist.

Factors Influencing Vocational Choice

Most, but not all, young people follow this pattern of vocational development. A few know from an early age just what they want to be and follow a direct path to a career goal. Some decide and later change their minds, and still others remain undecided for an extended period. College students are granted added time to explore various options. In contrast, the life conditions of many low-SES youths restrict their range of choices.

Making an occupational choice is not just a rational process in which young people weigh abilities, interests, and values against career options. Like other developmental milestones, it is the result of a dynamic interaction between person and environment (Gottfredson & Duffy, 2008). A great many influences feed into the decision, including personality, family, teachers, and gender stereotypes, among others.

PERSONALITY   People are attracted to occupations that complement their personalities. John Holland (1985, 1997) identified six personality types that affect vocational choice:

- The *investigative person,* who enjoys working with ideas, is likely to select a scientific occupation (for example, anthropologist, physicist, or engineer).
- The *social person,* who likes interacting with people, gravitates toward human services (counseling, social work, or teaching).
- The *realistic person,* who prefers real-world problems and work with objects, tends to choose a mechanical occupation (construction, plumbing, or surveying).
- The *artistic person,* who is emotional and high in need for individual expression, looks toward an artistic field (writing, music, or the visual arts).
- The *conventional person,* who likes well-structured tasks and values material possessions and social status, has traits well-suited to certain business fields (accounting, banking, or quality control).
- The *enterprising person,* who is adventurous, persuasive, and a strong leader, is drawn to sales and supervisory positions or to politics.

TAKE A MOMENT... Does one of these personality types describe you? Or do you have aspects of more than one type? Research confirms a relationship between personality and vocational choice in diverse cultures, but it is only moderate. Many people are blends of several personality types and can do well at more than one kind of occupation (Holland, 1997; Spokane & Cruza-Guet, 2005). Louis, for example, is both enterprising and social—dispositions that led him to consider both business and human services. Furthermore, career decisions are made in the context of family influences, educational opportunities, current life circumstances, and societal conditions.

FAMILY INFLUENCES   Young people's vocational aspirations correlate strongly with their parents' jobs. Teenagers from higher-SES homes are more likely to select high-status, white-collar occupations, such as doctor, lawyer, scientist, or engineer. In contrast, those with lower-SES backgrounds tend to choose less prestigious, blue-collar careers—for example, plumber, con-

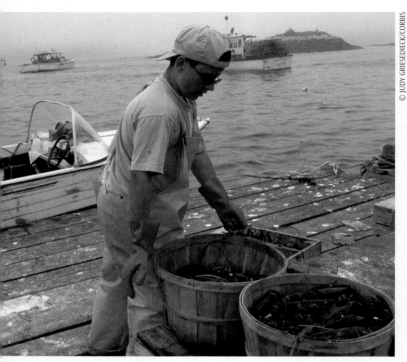

© JUDY GRIESEDIECK/CORBIS

■ A 13-year-old helps in his parents' business—a lobster fishery in Maine. Because of similarity in personality, intellectual abilities, and—especially—educational attainment, adolescents' vocational aspirations frequently resemble the jobs of their parents. ■

struction worker, food service employee, or office worker. Parent–child vocational similarity is partly a function of similarity in personality, intellectual abilities, and—especially—educational attainment (Ellis & Bonin, 2003; Schoon & Parsons, 2002). Number of years of schooling completed is a powerful predictor of occupational status.

Other factors also promote family resemblance in occupational choice. Higher-SES parents are more likely to give their children important information about the worlds of education and work and to have connections with people who can help the young person obtain a high-status position (Kalil, Levine, & Ziol-Guest, 2005). In a study of African-American mothers' influence on their adolescent daughters' academic and career goals, college-educated mothers engaged in a wider range of strategies to promote their daughters' progress, including gathering information on colleges and areas of study and identifying knowledgeable professionals who could help (Kerpelman, Shoffner, & Ross-Griffin, 2002). Parenting practices also shape work-related preferences. Recall from Chapter 2 (page 72) that higher-SES parents tend to promote curiosity and self-direction, which are required in many high-status careers. Lower-SES parents, in contrast, are more likely to emphasize conformity and obedience. Eventually, young people may choose careers that dovetail with these differences.

Still, parents can foster higher aspirations. Parental pressure to do well in school and encouragement toward high-status occupations predict vocational attainment beyond SES (Bryant, Zvonkovic, & Reynolds, 2006).

TEACHERS Jules regarded his high school chemistry teacher as the most important influence on his scientific career goal: "Mr. Garvin showed me how to think about chemistry—and science in general. If I hadn't taken his class my junior year, I probably wouldn't have considered a career in science." Young people preparing for or engaged in careers requiring extensive education often report that teachers influenced their choice (Bright et al., 2005; Reddin, 1997). High school students who say that most of their teachers are caring and accessible, interested in their future, and expect them to work hard feel more confident about choosing a personally suitable career and succeeding at it (Metheny, McWhirter, & O'Neil, 2008).

College-bound adolescents tend to have closer relationships with teachers than do other students—relationships that are especially likely to foster high career aspirations in young women (Wigfield et al., 2002). In contrast, students with academic and behavior problems generally have neither family nor teacher supports. Consequently, many feel discouraged about their career options, perceive barriers to attaining their goals, withdraw from making choices, and display large discrepancies between their vocational aspirations and their expectations (Rojewski & Hill, 1998). The power of teachers in offering encouragement and acting as role models can serve as an important source of resilience for these young people.

GENDER STEREOTYPES Over the past three decades, young women have expressed increasing interest in occupations largely held by men (Gottfredson, 2005). Changes in gender-role attitudes, along with a dramatic rise in numbers of employed mothers, who serve as career-oriented models for their daughters, are common explanations for girls' attraction to nontraditional careers.

But women's progress in entering and excelling at male-dominated professions has been slow. As Table 15.2 shows, although the percentage of women engineers, lawyers, doctors, and business executives in the United States has increased over the past quarter-century, it still falls far short of equal representation. Women remain concentrated in less-well-paid, traditionally feminine professions such as writing, social work, education, and nursing (U.S. Census Bureau, 2010b). In virtually all fields, women's achievements lag behind those of men, who write more books, make more discoveries, hold more positions of leadership, and produce more works of art.

Ability cannot account for these dramatic sex differences. As we have seen, girls are advantaged in reading and writing achievement, and the gender gap favoring boys in math is small. Rather, gender-stereotyped messages play a key role. Although girls earn higher grades than boys, they reach secondary school less confident of their abilities, more likely to underestimate their achievement, and less likely to express interest in math and science careers (Wigfield et al., 2002). In college, the career aspirations of many women decline further as they question their capacity and opportunities to succeed in male-dominated fields and worry about combining a highly demanding career with family responsibilities (Chhin, Bleeker, & Jacobs, 2008; Wigfield et al., 2006). Research indicates that many mathematically talented college women settle on nonscience majors. And those who remain in the sciences more often choose medicine or another health profession, and less often choose engineering or a math or physical science career, than their male counterparts (Benbow et al., 2000; Halpern et al., 2007).

These findings reveal a pressing need for programs that sensitize parents, teachers, and school counselors to the special problems girls face in developing and maintaining high career aspirations and selecting nontraditional careers. Girls' ambitions rise in response to parents' and teachers' confidence-building messages and career guidance that encourages students to set goals that match their abilities, interests, and values. Models of high-achieving women are also important (Wall, Covell, & MacIntyre, 1999; Zeldin & Pajares, 2000).

TABLE 15.2 Percentage of Women in Various Professions in the United States, 1983 and 2007		
PROFESSION	**1983**	**2007**
Engineer	5.8	10.5
Lawyer	15.8	32.6
Doctor	15.8	30.0
Business executive	32.4	37.5[a]
Author, artist, entertainer	42.7	47.1
Social worker	64.3	82.0
Elementary or middle school teacher	93.5	80.9
Secondary school teacher	62.2	56.9
College or university professor	36.3	46.2
Librarian	84.4	83.2
Registered nurse	95.8	91.7
Psychologist	57.1	64.4

Source: U.S. Census Bureau, 2010b.

[a]This percentage includes executives and managers at all levels. As of 2007, women made up only 25 percent of chief executive officers at large corporations, although that figure represents a sixfold increase over the past 25 years.

Vocational Preparation of Non-College-Bound Adolescents

Franca and Antonio's middle son, 18-year-old Martin—who is a year younger than Jules and two years older than Louis—graduated from high school in a vocational track. Like approximately one-third of U.S. young people with a high school diploma, he had no current plans to go to college. While in school, Martin held a part-time job selling candy at the local shopping mall. He hoped to work in data processing after graduation, but six months later he was still a part-time clerk at the candy store. Although Martin had filled out many job applications, he got no interviews or offers. He soon despaired of discovering any relationship between his schooling and a career.

Martin's inability to find a job other than the one he had held as a student is typical for U.S. non-college-bound high school graduates. Although they are more likely to find employment than youths who drop out, they have fewer work opportunities than high school graduates of several decades ago. About 20 percent of recent high school graduates who do not continue their education are unemployed (U.S. Department of Education, 2010). When they do find work, most hold low-paid, unskilled jobs. In addition, they have few alternatives for vocational counseling and job placement as they transition from school to work (Shanahan, Mortimer, & Krüger, 2002).

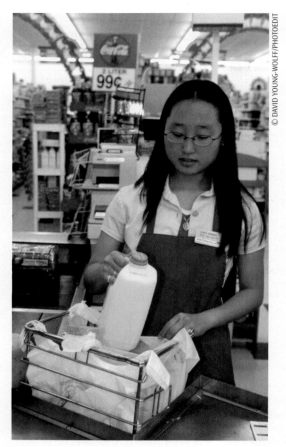

© DAVID YOUNG-WOLFF/PHOTOEDIT

■ Teenagers' employment opportunities are generally limited to menial tasks that do little to extend their knowledge or skills. Students with a heavy time commitment to such jobs are less likely to participate in extracurricular activities and more likely to drop out of school. ■

American employers regard recent high school graduates as poorly prepared for skilled business and industrial occupations and manual trades. And there is some truth to this impression. In high school, nearly half of U.S. adolescents are employed—a greater percentage than in other developed countries (Bowlby & McMullen, 2002; Children's Defense Fund, 2008). But most are middle-SES students in pursuit of spending money rather than vocational exploration and training. Low-income teenagers who need to contribute to family income or to support themselves find it harder to get jobs (U.S. Department of Education, 2010).

Adolescents typically hold jobs that involve low-level, repetitive tasks and provide little contact with adult supervisors. A heavy commitment to such jobs is harmful. The more hours students work, the poorer their school attendance, the lower their grades, the less likely they are to participate in extracurricular activities, and the more likely they are to drop out (Marsh & Kleitman, 2005). Students who spend many hours at such jobs also tend to feel more distant from their parents and report more drug and alcohol use and delinquent acts (Kouvonen & Kivivuori, 2001; Staff & Uggen, 2003).

In contrast, participation in work–study programs or other jobs that provide academic and vocational learning opportunities is related to positive school and work attitudes, improved achievement, and reduced delinquency (Hamilton & Hamilton, 2000; Staff & Uggen, 2003). Yet high-quality vocational preparation for non-college-bound U.S. adolescents is scarce. Unlike some European nations, the United States has no widespread training system to prepare youths for skilled business and industrial occupations and manual trades. Although U.S. federal and state governments support some job-training programs, most are too brief to make a difference and serve only a small minority of young people who need assistance.

In Germany, adolescents who do not go to a Gymnasium (college-preparatory high school) have access to one of the world's most successful work–study apprenticeship systems for entering business and industry. About two-thirds of German youths participate. After completing full-time schooling at age 15 or 16, they spend the remaining two years of compulsory education in the Berufsschule, combining part-time vocational courses with an apprenticeship that is jointly planned by educators and employers. Students train in work settings for more than 350 blue- and white-collar occupations (Deissinger, 2007). Apprentices who complete the program and pass a qualifying examination are certified as skilled workers and earn union-set wages. Businesses provide financial support because they know that the program guarantees a competent, dedicated work force (Heinz, 1999; Kerckhoff, 2002). Many apprentices are hired into well-paid jobs by the firms that trained them.

The success of the German system—and of similar systems in Austria, Denmark, Switzerland, and several Eastern European countries—suggests that a national apprenticeship program would improve the transition from high school to work for U.S. non-college-bound young people. The many benefits of bringing together the worlds of schooling and work include helping non-college-bound young people establish productive lives right after graduation, motivating at-risk youths to stay in school, and contributing to the nation's economic growth. Nevertheless, implementing an apprenticeship system poses major challenges: overcoming the reluctance of employers to assume part of the responsibility for vocational training, ensuring cooperation between schools and businesses, and preventing low-SES youths from being concentrated in the lowest-skilled apprenticeship placements, an obstacle that Germany itself has not yet fully overcome (Hamilton & Hamilton, 2000). Currently, small-scale school-to-work projects in the United States are attempting to solve these problems and build bridges between learning and working.

Although vocational development is a lifelong process, adolescence is a crucial period for defining occupational goals. Young people who are well-prepared for an economically and personally satisfying work life are much more likely to become productive citizens, devoted family members, and contented adults. The support of families, schools, businesses, communities, and society as a whole can contribute greatly to a positive outcome.

■ A baking and pastry student puts the finishing touches on a cake at a technical high school in Pennsylvania. High-quality vocational education, integrated with academic instruction, helps students at risk for dropping out see the relevance of school learning to their future goals. ■

◆ REVIEW What steps can schools take to help ensure that adolescents' occupational choices match their interests, personality dispositions, and abilities?

◆ APPLY Diane, a high school senior, knows that she wants to "work with people" but doesn't yet have a specific career in mind. Her father is a history professor, her mother a social worker. What can Diane's parents do to broaden her awareness of the world of work and help her focus on an occupational goal?

◆ CONNECT What have you learned in previous chapters about development of gender stereotypes that helps explain why women's progress in entering and excelling at male-dominated professions has been slow? (*Hint:* See Chapter 13, pages 503–504.)

◆ REFLECT Describe your progress in choosing a vocation. What personal and environmental factors have been influential?

Summary

Piaget's Theory: The Formal Operational Stage

What are the major characteristics of formal operational thought?

■ During Piaget's **formal operational stage,** adolescents become capable of **hypothetico-deductive reasoning:** When faced with a problem, they start with a hypothesis about variables that might affect an outcome; deduce logical, testable inferences; and systematically isolate and combine variables to see which inferences are confirmed.

■ **Propositional thought** also develops. Young people can evaluate the logic of verbal statements without referring to real-world circumstances.

Discuss follow-up research on formal operational thought and its implications for the accuracy of Piaget's formal operational stage.

■ School-age children display the beginnings of hypothetico-deductive reasoning but are less cognitively competent than adolescents. They cannot sort out evidence that bears on three or more variables at once, and they do not grasp the **logical necessity** of propositional reasoning. Also, adolescents are better than school-age children at representing major premises precisely and at thinking of examples that contradict wrong conclusions.

■ Adolescents and adults are most likely to think abstractly and systematically in situations in which they have had extensive guidance and practice in using such reasoning. Individuals in tribal and village societies rarely do well on tasks typically used to assess formal operational reasoning. Learning experiences in school provide adolescents with rich opportunities to acquire formal operations.

An Information-Processing View of Adolescent Cognitive Development

How do information-processing researchers account for cognitive changes in adolescence?

■ Information-processing researchers believe that a variety of specific mechanisms, supported by both brain development and experience, underlie adolescent cognitive development. These include gains in attention, inhibition, and knowledge; more effective strategies; expansion of metacognition; and increases in cognitive self-regulation, speed of thinking, and processing capacity.

■ Research on scientific reasoning reveals that the ability to coordinate theory with evidence improves as adolescents solve increasingly complex problems and reflect on their thinking, acquiring more sophisticated metacognitive understanding. Nevertheless, adolescents and adults continue to show a self-serving bias, applying logic more effectively to ideas they doubt than to ideas they favor.

■ Adolescents develop scientific reasoning skills in a similar, step-by-step fashion on different types of tasks. Gradually, they combine separate skills, constructing general models that they can apply to many instances of a given type of problem.

Consequences of Adolescent Cognitive Changes

Describe typical reactions of adolescents that result from their advancing cognition.

■ As adolescents reflect on their own thoughts, two distorted images of the relationship between self and other appear: the **imaginary audience** and the **personal fable.** Both are an outgrowth of gains in perspective taking and teenagers' concern with others' opinions of them.

■ Adolescents' capacity to think about possibilities prompts idealistic visions at odds with everyday reality, and they often become fault-finding critics.

■ Compared with adults, adolescents are less effective at decision making. In emotionally charged situations, they take greater risks, emphasizing short-term over long-term goals. Even under unemotional conditions, they less often consider alternatives and weigh benefits and risks, and more often fall back on intuitive judgments.

Sex Differences in Mental Abilities

What factors contribute to sex differences in mental abilities at adolescence?

■ Girls score slightly better than boys on tests of verbal ability, and their advantage in reading and writing achievement increases. Earlier development of the left hemisphere of the cerebral cortex, more efficient language processing, and greater verbal stimulation probably contribute to girls' better verbal performance. And gender stereotyping of language arts as "feminine" and regimented teaching may weaken boys' literacy skills.

■ In early adolescence, when math concepts become more abstract and spatial, boys start to outperform girls. Overall, the gender difference has declined over time and is small, but it is greater among the most capable students, though even this difference has been shrinking. Boys' biologically based superior spatial skills enhance their mathematical problem solving. Gender stereotyping of math as "masculine," self-confidence and interest in doing math, and specialized computer knowledge contribute to boys' spatial and math advantages.

Language Development

Describe changes in vocabulary, grammar, and pragmatics during adolescence.

■ Adolescents add many abstract words to their vocabulary and define these words with greater clarity and accuracy. They also master irony, sarcasm, and figurative language.

■ Adolescents use more elaborate grammatical constructions and more effectively analyze and correct their grammar. They also show an improved capacity to adapt language style to social context—a change supported by opportunities to enter more situations, the ability to reflect on the features of language, and gains in cognitive self-regulation.

Learning in School

Discuss the impact of school transitions on adolescent adjustment.

■ After middle- and high-school transitions, grades often decline and feelings of anonymity rise. Girls experience more adjustment difficulties than boys. Teenagers coping with added stresses, especially those with both academic and mental health difficulties, are at greatest risk for adjustment problems following school transition. Transitions are also particularly challenging for minority students who move to a new school with substantially fewer same-ethnicity peers.

Discuss family, peer, and school influences on academic achievement during adolescence.

■ Authoritative parenting and parents' school involvement promote high achievement. Teenagers whose parents value achievement are likely to choose friends who share those values.

■ Warm, supportive classroom environments that encourage student interaction about academic work, mutual respect among classmates, and high-level thinking enable adolescents to reach their academic potential.

■ By high school, separate educational tracks that dovetail with adolescents' future plans are necessary. But high school tracking in the United States usually extends the educational inequalities of earlier years. Low-SES students are at risk for unfair placement in noncollege tracks, less stimulating teaching, and resulting declines in school performance.

What factors increase the risk of high school dropout?

■ About 8 percent of U.S. young people, many of them low-SES minority youths, leave high school and remain without a diploma or a GED. Family and school risk factors include lack of parental support for achievement, a history of poor school performance, grade retention, large impersonal schools, unsupportive teachers, unstimulating classes, and minority students' experiences with discrimination.

Vocational Development

Trace the development of vocational choice, and cite factors that influence it.

■ Vocational development moves through a **fantasy period,** in which children explore career options by fantasizing about them; a **tentative period,** in which teenagers weigh careers against their interests, abilities, and values; and a **realistic period,** in which older adolescents and young adults settle on a vocational category and then a specific occupation.

■ Vocational choice is influenced by personality; parents' provision of educational opportunities, vocational information, and encouragement; and close relationships with teachers.

■ Women's progress in male-dominated professions has been slow, and their achievements lag behind those of men in virtually all fields. Gender-stereotyped messages play a key role. Girls' career aspirations rise in response to confidence-building messages from parents and teachers.

What problems do U.S. non-college-bound youths face in preparing for a vocation?

■ U.S. non-college-bound high school graduates are poorly prepared for skilled business and industrial occupations and manual trades. Most are limited to low-paid, unskilled jobs, and too many are unemployed. Youth apprenticeships, like those widely available in European countries, would address the need for vocational training and improve the transition from school to work for these young people.

IMPORTANT TERMS AND CONCEPTS

fantasy period (p. 590)
formal operational stage (p. 566)
hypothetico-deductive reasoning (p. 566)

imaginary audience (p. 572)
logical necessity (p. 568)
personal fable (p. 572)

propositional thought (p. 567)
realistic period (p. 591)
tentative period (p. 590)

Untitled
Mike Mubanga
15 years, Zambia

A Zambian artist depicts a celebration in his culture with energy and realism. As Chapter 16 reveals, for many adolescents a sense of ethnic group membership is central to the quest for identity.

Reprinted with permission from the International Museum of Children's Art, Oslo, Norway

Emotional and Social Development in Adolescence

*L*ouis sat on the grassy hillside overlooking the high school, waiting for his best friend, Darryl, to arrive from his fourth-period class. The two boys often had lunch together. Watching as hundreds of students poured onto the school grounds, Louis reflected on what he had learned in government class that day: "Suppose I *had* been born in the People's Republic of China. I'd be sitting here, speaking a different language, being called by a different name, and thinking about the world in different ways. Wow," Louis pondered. "I am who I am through some quirk of fate."

Louis awoke from his thoughts with a start to see Darryl standing in front of him. "Hey, dreamer! I've been shouting and waving from the bottom of the hill for five minutes. How come you're so spaced out lately, Louis?"

"Oh, just wondering about stuff—what I want, what I believe in. My older brother Jules—I envy him. He seems to know more about where he's going. I'm up in the air about it. You ever feel that way?"

"Yeah, a lot," Darryl admitted, looking at Louis seriously. "I wonder, what am I really like? Who will I become?"

Louis and Darryl's introspective remarks are signs of a major reorganization of the self at adolescence: the development of identity. Both young people are attempting to formulate who they are—their personal values and the directions they will pursue in life. The restructuring of the self that begins in adolescence is profound. Rapid physical changes prompt teenagers to reconsider what they are like as people. And the capacity to think hypothetically enables adolescents to project themselves into the distant future. They start to realize the significance of their choice of values, beliefs, and goals for their later lives.

We begin this chapter with Erikson's account of identity development and the research it has stimulated on teenagers' thoughts and feelings about themselves. The quest for identity extends to many aspects of development. We will see how a sense of cultural belonging, moral understanding, and masculine and feminine self-images are refined in adolescence. And as parent–child relationships are revised and young people become increasingly independent of the family, friendships and peer networks become crucial contexts for bridging the gap between childhood and adulthood. Our chapter concludes with a discussion of several serious adjustment problems of adolescence: depression, suicide, and delinquency.

Erikson's Theory: Identity versus Role Confusion

Erikson (1950, 1968) was the first to recognize **identity** as the major personality achievement of adolescence and as a crucial step toward becoming a productive, happy adult. Constructing an identity involves defining who you are, what you value, and the directions you choose to pursue in life. One expert described it as an explicit theory of oneself as a rational agent—one who acts on the basis of reason, takes responsibility for those actions, and can explain them (Moshman, 2005). This search for what is true and real about the self drives many choices—vocation, interpersonal relationships, community involvement, ethnic-group membership, and expression of one's sexual orientation, as well as moral, political, and religious ideals.

Although the seeds of identity formation are planted early, not until late adolescence and emerging adulthood do young people become absorbed in this task. According to Erikson, in complex societies, young people often experience an *identity crisis*—a temporary period of distress as they experiment with alternatives before settling on values and goals. They go

through a process of inner soul-searching, sifting through characteristics that defined the self in childhood and combining them with emerging traits, capacities, and commitments. Then they mold these into a solid inner core that provides a mature identity—a sense of self-continuity as they move through various roles in daily life. Once formed, identity continues to be refined in adulthood as people reevaluate earlier commitments and choices.

Erikson called the psychological conflict of adolescence **identity versus role confusion.** He believed that successful psychosocial outcomes of infancy and childhood pave the way toward a positive resolution. Adolescents with a weak sense of *trust* have trouble finding ideals to have faith in. Those with little *autonomy* or *initiative* do not engage in the active exploration required to choose among alternatives. And those who lack a sense of *industry* fail to select a vocation that matches their interests and skills. In addition, if society limits young people's choices to ones that do not match their abilities and desires, they are likely to appear shallow and directionless.

Current theorists agree with Erikson that questioning of values, plans, and priorities is necessary for a mature identity, but they no longer describe this process as a "crisis" (Grotevant, 1998; Kroger, 2005). In fact, Erikson himself did not believe that the adolescent's inner struggle need be severe to form a clear, unified identity (Côté, 2009). For most young people, identity development is not traumatic and disturbing but, rather, a process of *exploration* followed by *commitment*. As young people try out life possibilities, they gather important information about themselves and their environment and gradually move toward making enduring decisions. In doing so, they forge an organized self-structure (Arnett, 2000a, 2006; Moshman, 2005). In the following sections, we will see that young people go about the task of defining the self in ways that closely match Erikson's description.

■ Expressing individuality with an unconventional hairstyle grants this teenager a temporary identity, providing security as he explores alternatives and confronts a daunting array of life challenges. ■

© IMAGES-USA/ALAMY

Self-Understanding

During adolescence, the young person's vision of the self becomes more complex, well-organized, and consistent. Compared with younger children, adolescents have more or less positive feelings about an increasing variety of aspects of the self. Over time, they form a balanced, integrated representation of their strengths and limitations (Harter, 2003, 2006). Changes in self-concept and self-esteem set the stage for development of a unified personal identity.

Changes in Self-Concept

Recall from Chapter 13 that by the end of middle childhood, children can describe themselves in terms of personality traits. In early adolescence, the self differentiates further. Teenagers mention a wider array of traits, which vary with social context—for example, self with mother, father, close friends, romantic partner, and as student, athlete, and employee. As one young teenager commented:

> I'm an extrovert with my friends: I'm talkative, pretty rowdy, and funny. . . . With my parents, I'm more likely to be depressed. I feel sad as well as mad and also hopeless about ever pleasing them. . . . At school, I'm pretty intelligent. I know that because I'm smart when it comes to how I do in classes. I'm curious about learning new things, and I'm also creative when it comes to solving problems. . . . I can be a real introvert around people I don't know well. . . . I worry a lot about what others my age who are not my closest friends must think of me, probably that I'm a total dork. (Harter, 2006, p. 531)

Notice, also, that early adolescents unify separate traits ("smart," "talented") into more abstract descriptors ("intelligent"). But these generalizations about the self are not interconnected and are often contradictory. For example, 12- to 14-year-olds might mention opposing traits—"intelligent" and "dork," "extrovert" and "introvert." These disparities result from the expansion of adolescents' social world, which creates pressure to display different selves in different relationships. Over the teenage years, traits mentioned for different social contexts become increasingly dissimilar. As adolescents' awareness of these inconsistencies grows, they frequently agonize over "which is the real me" (Harter, 1998, 2003, 2006).

From middle to late adolescence, cognitive changes enable teenagers to combine their traits into an organized system. Their use of qualifiers ("I have a *fairly* quick temper," "I'm not *thoroughly* honest") reveals their awareness that psychological qualities can vary from one situation to the next. Older adolescents also add integrating principles that make sense of formerly troublesome contradictions. "I'm very adaptable," said one young person. "When I'm around my friends, who think what I say is important, I'm talkative; but around my family I'm quiet because they're never interested enough to really listen to me" (Damon, 1990, p. 88).

Compared with school-age children, teenagers place more emphasis on social virtues, such as being friendly, considerate, kind, and cooperative—traits that reflect adolescents' increasing concern with being viewed positively by others. Among older adolescents, personal and moral standards also appear as key themes. For example, here is how one 17-year-old described herself:

> I'm a pretty conscientious person. . . . Eventually I want to go to law school, so developing good study habits and getting top grades are both essential . . . I'd like to be an ethical person who treats other people fairly. That's the kind of lawyer I'd like to be, too. I don't always live up to that standard; that is, sometimes I do something that doesn't feel ethical. When that happens, I get a little depressed because I don't like myself as a person. But I tell myself that it's natural to make mistakes, so I don't really question the fact that deep down inside, the real me is a moral person. . . . While I am basically an introvert, especially on a date when I get pretty self-conscious, in the right social situation, like watching a ball game with my friends, I can be pretty extroverted. . . . I'm looking forward to leaving home and going to college, where I can be more independent, although I'm a little ambivalent. I love my parents, and really want to stay connected to them, plus, what they think about me is still important to how I feel about myself as a person. (Harter, 2006, pp. 545–546)

LOOK AND LISTEN

Pose the following question to a 12- to 14-year-old and a 16- to 18-year-old: "What are you like as a person?" Do differences in their self-descriptions match research findings on development of self-concept?

This well-integrated account of personal traits and values differs from the fragmented, list-like self-descriptions typical of children. As adolescents revise their views of themselves to include enduring beliefs and plans, they move toward the unity of self that is central to identity development.

Changes in Self-Esteem

Self-esteem, the evaluative side of self-concept, continues to differentiate in adolescence. Teenagers add several new dimensions of self-evaluation—close friendship, romantic appeal, and job competence—to those of middle childhood (see Chapter 13, page 484) (Harter, 1999, 2003, 2006).

Level of self-esteem also changes. Though some adolescents experience temporary or persisting declines after school transitions (see Chapter 15, page 580), self-esteem rises for most young people, who report feeling especially good about their peer relationships and athletic capabilities (Cole et al., 2001; Impett et al., 2008; Twenge & Campbell, 2001). Teenagers often assert that they have become more mature, capable, personable, and attractive than in the past.

In a study of adolescents in 13 industrialized nations, most were optimistic, felt a sense of control over their personal and vocational futures, and expressed confidence in their ability to cope with life's problems (Grob & Flammer, 1999).

At the same time, individual differences in self-esteem become increasingly stable in adolescence (Trzesniewski, Donnellan, & Robins, 2003). And positive relationships among self-esteem, valuing of various activities, and success at those activities strengthen. For example, academic self-esteem is a powerful predictor of teenagers' judgments of the importance and usefulness of school subjects, willingness to exert effort, achievement, and eventual career choice (Bleeker & Jacobs, 2004; Denissen, Zarrett, & Eccles, 2007; Valentine, DuBois, & Cooper, 2004; Whitesell et al., 2009).

Across SES and ethnic groups, adolescents with mostly favorable self-esteem profiles tend to be well-adjusted, sociable, and conscientious. In contrast, low self-esteem in all areas is linked to adjustment difficulties (DuBois et al., 1999; Robins et al., 2001). But certain self-esteem factors are more strongly related to adjustment. Teenagers who feel highly dissatisfied with parental relationships often are aggressive and antisocial. Those with poor academic self-esteem tend to be anxious and unfocused, and those with negative peer relationships are likely to be anxious and depressed (Marsh, Parada, & Ayotte, 2004; Rudolph, Caldwell, & Conley, 2005). And although virtually all teenagers become increasingly concerned about others' opinions, those who are overly dependent on social approval continually place their self-worth "on the line" and, as a result, report frequent self-esteem shifts—on average, about once a week (Harter & Whitesell, 2003). Let's take a closer look at factors that affect adolescents' self-esteem—both its level and its stability.

Photo credit: © BARRY AUSTIN/GETTY IMAGES/DIGITAL VISION

■ During adolescence, self-esteem rises for most young people, who feel especially good about their peer relationships and athletic capabilities. ■

Influences on Self-Esteem

In Chapters 14 and 15 we saw that adolescents who are off time in pubertal development, who are heavy drug users, and who fail in school feel poorly about themselves. And as in middle childhood, girls score lower than boys in overall sense of self-worth, though the difference remains slight (Birndorf et al., 2005; Shapka & Keating, 2005; Young & Mroczek, 2003). Nevertheless, of those young people whose self-esteem declines in adolescence, most are girls. Recall that teenage girls worry more than teenage boys about their physical appearance and feel more insecure about their abilities. At the same time, girls outscore boys on self-esteem dimensions of close friendship and social acceptance.

But the contexts in which young people find themselves can modify these group differences. In adolescence as in childhood, authoritative parenting—warmth, open communication, positive problem solving, and appropriate expectations for maturity—predicts stable, favorable self-esteem. Encouragement from teachers is associated with a positive self-image as well

(Carlson, Uppal, & Prosser, 2000; Lindsey et al., 2008; McKinney, Donnelly, & Renk, 2008; Wilkinson, 2004). In contrast, teenagers whose parents are critical and insulting tend to have highly unstable and generally low self-esteem (Kernis, 2002). Feedback that is negative, inconsistent, or not contingent on performance triggers, at best, uncertainty about the self's capacities and, at worst, a sense of being incompetent and unloved. As a result, these young people's self-worth fluctuates in response to every evaluative remark by an adult or peer. Adolescents who experience such parenting tend to rely heavily on peers rather than on adults to affirm their self-esteem—a risk factor for adjustment difficulties (DuBois et al., 1999, 2002a).

The larger social environment also influences self-esteem. Sustaining a middle-childhood trend, Caucasian-American adolescents' self-esteem is less positive than that of African-American and Hispanic teenagers, who benefit from warm, extended families and ethnic pride (Birndorf et al., 2005; Gray-Little & Hafdahl, 2000). And collectivist valuing of modesty and self-effacement leads Asians to score increasingly low in self-esteem relative to Caucasians as adolescence progresses (Twenge & Crocker, 2002). Finally, teenagers who attend schools or live in neighborhoods where their SES or ethnic group is well-represented have fewer self-esteem problems (Gray-Little & Carels, 1997). Schools and communities that accept the young person's cultural heritage support a positive sense of self-worth as well as a solid and secure personal identity.

Paths to Identity

Adolescents' well-organized self-descriptions and differentiated sense of self-esteem provide the cognitive foundation for forming an identity. Using a clinical interviewing procedure devised by James Marcia (1980) or briefer questionnaire measures, researchers evaluate progress in identity development on two key criteria derived from Erikson's theory: *exploration* and *commitment*. Their various combinations yield four *identity statuses:* **identity achievement,** commitment to values, beliefs, and goals following a period of exploration; **identity moratorium,** exploration without having reached commitment; **identity foreclosure,** commitment in the absence of exploration; and **identity diffusion,** an apathetic state characterized by lack of both exploration and commitment. Table 16.1 summarizes these identity statuses.

Identity development follows many paths. Some young people remain in one status, whereas others experience many status transitions. And the pattern often varies across *identity domains.* For example, in junior high school, Louis accepted his parents' religious beliefs (foreclosure)

TABLE 16.1 The Four Identity Statuses

IDENTITY STATUS	DESCRIPTION	EXAMPLE
Identity achievement	Having already explored alternatives, identity-achieved individuals are committed to a clearly formulated set of self-chosen values and goals. They feel a sense of psychological well-being, of sameness through time, and of knowing where they are going.	When asked how willing she would be to give up going into her chosen occupation if something better came along, Darla responded, "Well, I might, but I doubt it. I've thought long and hard about law as a career. I'm pretty certain it's for me."
Identity moratorium	*Moratorium* means "delay or holding pattern." These individuals have not yet made definite commitments. They are in the process of exploring—gathering information and trying out activities, with the desire to find values and goals to guide their lives.	When asked whether he had ever had doubts about his religious beliefs, Ramón said, "Yes, I guess I'm going through that right now. I just don't see how there can be a God and yet so much evil in the world."
Identity foreclosure	Identity-foreclosed individuals have committed themselves to values and goals without exploring alternatives. They accept a ready-made identity chosen for them by authority figures—usually parents but sometimes teachers, religious leaders, or romantic partners.	When asked if she had ever reconsidered her political beliefs, Hillary answered, "No, not really, our family is pretty much in agreement on these things."
Identity diffusion	Identity-diffused individuals lack clear direction. They are not committed to values and goals, nor are they actively trying to reach them. They may never have explored alternatives or may have found the task too threatening and overwhelming.	When asked about his attitude toward nontraditional gender roles, Joel responded, "Oh, I don't know. It doesn't make much difference to me. I can take it or leave it."

and gave little thought to a vocational direction (diffusion). In his last two years of high school, he began exploring these issues. Like Louis, most adolescents change from "lower" statuses (foreclosure or diffusion) to "higher" statuses (moratorium or achievement) between their mid-teens and mid-twenties, but some move in the reverse direction (Kroger, 2001, 2005; Meeus, 1996). And the number of domains explored and the intensity with which they are examined vary widely, depending on the contexts young people want to enter and the importance they attach to them. Almost all grapple with work, close relationships, and family. Others add political, religious, community, and leisure-time commitments, some of which are more central to their identity than others.

Because attending college provides many opportunities to explore career options and life-styles, college students make more identity progress than they did in high school (Montgomery & Côté, 2003b). After college, as we will see in Chapter 17, young people often sample a broad range of life experiences before choosing a life course. Those who go to work immediately after high school graduation often settle on a self-definition earlier. But if they encounter obstacles to realizing their occupational goals because of lack of training or vocational choices (see Chapter 15), they are at risk for long-term identity foreclosure or diffusion (Cohen et al., 2003; Eccles et al., 2003).

At one time, researchers thought that adolescent girls postponed establishing an identity and focused instead on Erikson's next stage, intimacy development. Some girls do show more sophisticated reasoning than boys in identity domains related to intimacy, such as sexuality and family versus career priorities. Otherwise, adolescents of both sexes typically make progress on identity concerns before experiencing genuine intimacy in relationships (Berman et al., 2006; Kroger, 2007).

Identity Status and Psychological Well-Being

According to identity theorists, individuals who move away from foreclosure and diffusion toward moratorium and achievement build a well-structured identity that integrates various domains. As a result, they experience a gratifying sense of personal continuity and social connection—of being the same person across time and contexts and a competent member of the adult community (Snarey & Bell, 2003; van Hoof & Raaijmakers, 2003). A wealth of research supports the conclusion that both identity achievement and moratorium are psychologically healthy routes to a mature self-definition, whereas long-term foreclosure and diffusion are maladaptive.

Although adolescents in moratorium are often anxious about the challenges they face, they resemble identity-achieved individuals in using an active, *information-gathering cognitive style* when making personal decisions and solving problems. They seek out relevant information, evaluate it carefully, and critically reflect on their views (Berzonsky, 2003; Berzonsky & Kuk, 2000). In Chapter 17, we will see that with age, the searching associated with moratorium becomes increasingly focused, involving in-depth consideration and reconsideration of potential commitments, which are often revised over time (Crocetti, Rubini, & Meeus, 2008).

Young people who are identity-achieved have higher self-esteem, feel more in control of their own lives, are more likely to view school and work as feasible avenues for realizing their aspirations, and are more advanced in moral reasoning (Adams & Marshall, 1996; Kroger, 2007; Serafini & Adams, 2002). When asked for a "turning point" narrative (an account of a past event that they view as important in understanding themselves), identity-achieved individuals tell stories with more sophisticated personal insights and in which negative life events are followed by good outcomes—personal renewal, improvement, and enlightenment (McLean & Pratt, 2006).

Adolescents stuck in either foreclosure or diffusion are passive in the face of identity concerns and have adjustment difficulties. Foreclosed individuals display a *dogmatic, inflexible cognitive style,* internalizing the values and beliefs of parents and others without deliberate evaluation and resisting information that might threaten their position (Berzonsky & Kuk, 2000). Most fear rejection by people on whom they depend for affection and self-esteem. A few foreclosed teenagers who are alienated from their families and society may join cults or other extremist groups, uncritically adopting a way of life different from their past.

Long-term diffused teenagers are the least mature in identity development. They typically use a *diffuse-avoidant cognitive style* in which they avoid dealing with personal decisions and problems and, instead, allow current situational pressures to dictate their reactions (Berzonsky & Kuk, 2000; Krettenauer, 2005). Taking an "I don't care" attitude, they entrust themselves to luck or fate and tend to go along with the crowd. As a result, they often experience time-management and academic difficulties and, of all young people, are the most likely to commit antisocial acts and to use and abuse drugs (Archer & Waterman, 1990; Schwartz et al., 2005). Often at the heart of their apathy and impulsiveness is a sense of hopelessness about the future. Many are at risk for serious depression and suicide—problems we will address in the final section of this chapter.

Factors Affecting Identity Development

Adolescent identity formation begins a lifelong dynamic process in which a change in either the individual or the context opens up the possibility of reformulating identity (Kunnen & Bosma, 2003). A wide variety of factors influence identity development.

PERSONALITY Identity status, as we saw in the previous section, is both cause and consequence of personality characteristics. Adolescents who assume that absolute truth is always attainable tend to be foreclosed, whereas those who doubt that they will ever feel certain about anything are more often identity-diffused. Young people who appreciate that they can use rational criteria to choose among alternatives are likely to be in a state of moratorium or identity achievement (Berzonsky & Kuk, 2000; Boyes & Chandler, 1992). This flexible, open-minded approach helps them greatly in identifying and pursuing educational, vocational, and other life goals.

FAMILY Recall from Chapter 7 that toddlers with a healthy sense of self have parents who provide both emotional support and freedom to explore. Similarly, teenagers' identity development is enhanced when their families serve as a "secure base" from which they can confidently move out into the wider world. In families of diverse ethnicities, adolescents who feel attached to their parents but also feel free to voice their own opinions tend to be in a state of moratorium or identity achievement (Berzonsky, 2004; Luyckx, Goossens, & Soenens, 2006; Schwartz et al., 2005). Foreclosed teenagers usually have close bonds with parents but lack opportunities for healthy separation. And diffused young people report the lowest levels of parental support and of warm, open communication (Reis & Youniss, 2004; Zimmerman & Becker-Stoll, 2002).

Recall that parents who engage in positive problem solving—who resolve conflicts by seeking their child's input and collaborating on a solution—foster high self-esteem. Notice, also, how this approach promotes the balance between family relatedness and autonomy that supports identity development (Deci & Ryan, 2002).

PEERS Interaction with diverse peers through school and community activities encourages adolescents' to explore values and role possibilities (Barber et al., 2005). And close friends, like parents, can act as a secure base, providing emotional support, assistance, and models of identity development. In one study, 15-year-olds with warm, trusting peer ties were more involved in exploring relationship issues—for example, thinking about what they valued in close friends and in a life partner (Meeus, Oosterwegel, & Vollebergh, 2002). In another study, college students' attachment to friends predicted progress in choosing a career (Felsman & Blustein, 1999).

SCHOOL, COMMUNITY, AND CULTURE Identity development also depends on schools and communities that offer rich and varied opportunities for exploration. Supportive experiences include classrooms that promote high-level thinking, teachers

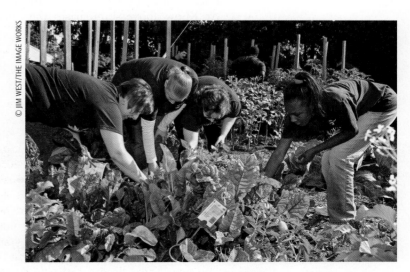

■ High school students harvest produce for a food bank. Opportunities to take on responsible community roles promote exploration and identity development. ■

Applying What We Know

Supporting Healthy Identity Development

STRATEGY	EXPLANATION
Engage in warm, open communication.	Provides both emotional support and freedom to explore values and goals.
Initiate discussions that promote high-level thinking at home and at school.	Encourages rational, deliberate selection among competing beliefs and values.
Provide opportunities to participate in extracurricular activities and vocational training programs.	Permits young people to explore the real world of adult work.
Provide opportunities to talk with adults and peers who have worked through identity questions.	Offers models of identity achievement and advice on how to resolve identity concerns.
Provide opportunities to explore ethnic heritage and learn about other cultures in an atmosphere of respect.	Fosters identity achievement in all areas as well as ethnic tolerance, which supports the identity explorations of others.

and counselors who encourage low-SES and ethnic minority students to go to college, extracurricular and community activities that offer teenagers responsible roles consistent with their interests and talents, and vocational training that immerses adolescents in the real world of adult work (Coatsworth et al., 2005; McIntosh, Metz, & Youniss, 2005).

Culture strongly influences an aspect of mature identity not captured by the identity-status approach: constructing a sense of self-continuity despite major personal changes. In one study, researchers asked Native Canadian and cultural-majority 12- to 20-year-olds to describe themselves in the past and in the present and then to justify why they regarded themselves as the same continuous person (Lalonde & Chandler, 2005). Both groups gave increasingly complex responses with age, but their strategies differed. Most cultural-majority adolescents used an individualistic approach: They described an *enduring personal essence,* a core self that remained the same despite change. In contrast, Native Canadian youths took an interdependent approach that emphasized a *constantly transforming self,* resulting from new roles and relationships. They typically constructed a *coherent narrative* in which they linked together various time slices of their life with a thread that explained how they had changed in meaningful ways.

Finally, societal forces are also responsible for the special challenges faced by gay, lesbian, and bisexual youths (see Chapter 14) and by ethnic minority adolescents in forming a secure identity (see the Cultural Influences box on the following page). Applying What We Know above summarizes ways that adults can support adolescents in their quest for identity.

ASK YOURSELF

◆ **REVIEW** List personal and contextual factors that promote identity development.

◆ **APPLY** Return to the conversation between Louis and Darryl in the opening of this chapter. Which identity status best characterizes each of the two boys, and why?

◆ **CONNECT** Explain the close link between adolescent identity development and cognitive processes.

◆ **REFLECT** Does your identity status vary across the domains of sexuality, close relationships, vocation, religious beliefs, and political values? Describe factors that may have influenced your identity development in an important domain.

CULTURAL INFLUENCES

Identity Development Among Ethnic Minority Adolescents

Most adolescents are aware of their cultural ancestry but relatively unconcerned about it. However, for teenagers who are members of minority groups, ethnic identity—a sense of ethnic group membership and attitudes and feelings associated with that membership—is central to the quest for identity. As they develop cognitively and become more sensitive to feedback from the social environment, minority youths become painfully aware that they are targets of prejudice and discrimination. This discovery complicates their efforts to develop a sense of cultural belonging and a set of personally meaningful goals.

Minority youths often feel caught between the standards of the larger society and the traditions of their culture of origin. In many immigrant families from collectivist cultures, adolescents' commitment to obeying their parents and fulfilling family obligations lessens the longer the family has been in the immigrant-receiving country—a circumstance that induces **acculturative stress,** psychological distress resulting from conflict between the minority and the host culture (Phinney, Ong, & Madden, 2000). When immigrant parents tightly restrict their teenagers through fear that assimilation into the larger society will undermine their cultural traditions, their youngsters often rebel, rejecting aspects of their ethnic background.

At the same time, discrimination can interfere with the formation of a positive ethnic identity. In one study, Mexican-American youths who had experienced more discrimination were less likely to explore their ethnicity and to report feeling good about it. Those with low ethnic pride showed a sharp drop in self-esteem in the face of discrimination (Romero & Roberts, 2003).

With age, some ethnic minority young people progress from ethnic-identity diffusion or foreclosure through moratorium to ethnic-identity achievement. But because the process of forging an ethnic identity can be painful and confusing, others show no change, and still others regress (Seaton, Scottham, & Sellers, 2006). Young people with parents of different ethnicities face extra challenges. In a large survey of high school students, part-black biracial teenagers reported as much discrimination as their monoracial black counterparts,

yet they felt less positively about their ethnicity. And compared with monoracial minorities, many biracials—including black–white, black–Asian, white–Asian, black–Hispanic, and white–Hispanic—regarded ethnicity as less central to their identities (Herman, 2004). Perhaps these adolescents encountered fewer opportunities in their homes and communities to forge a strong sense of belonging to either culture.

When family members encourage adolescents to disprove ethnic stereotypes of low achievement or antisocial behavior, young people typically surmount the threat that discrimination poses to a favorable ethnic identity. These young people manage experiences of unfair treatment effectively, by seeking social support and engaging in direct problem solving (Phinney & Chavira, 1995; Scott, 2003). Also, adolescents whose families taught them the history, traditions, values, and language of their ethnic group and who frequently interact with same-ethnicity peers are more likely to forge a favorable ethnic identity (Hughes et al., 2006; McHale et al., 2006).

How can society help minority adolescents resolve identity conflicts constructively? Here are some relevant approaches:

■ Promote effective parenting, in which children and adolescents benefit from family ethnic pride yet are encouraged to explore the meaning of ethnicity in their own lives.
■ Ensure that schools respect minority youths' native languages, unique learning styles, and right to a high-quality education.
■ Foster contact with peers of the same ethnicity, along with respect between ethnic groups (García Coll & Magnuson, 1997).

A strong, secure ethnic identity is associated with higher self-esteem, optimism, a sense of mastery over the environment, and more positive attitudes toward one's ethnicity (St. Louis & Liem, 2005; Umaña-Taylor & Updegraff, 2007; Worrell & Gardner-Kitt, 2006). For these

reasons, adolescents with a positive connection to their ethnic group are better-adjusted. They cope more effectively with stress, report higher levels of daily happiness, show better achievement in school, and have fewer emotional and behavior problems than agemates who identify only weakly with their ethnicity (Greene, Way, & Pahl, 2006; Kiang et al., 2006; Seaton, Scottham, & Sellers, 2006; Umaña-Taylor & Alfaro, 2006). In one study, Mexican-origin teenagers in a mostly non-Hispanic school expressed a stronger sense of ethnic identity than their agemates in an ethnically balanced environment (Umaña-Taylor, 2004). For teenagers faced with potential or actual adversity, ethnic identity is a powerful source of resilience.

Forming a **bicultural identity**—by exploring and adopting values from both the adolescent's subculture and the dominant culture—offers added benefits. Biculturally identified adolescents tend to be achieved in other areas of identity as well and to have especially favorable relations with members of other ethnic groups (Phinney, 2007; Phinney et al., 2001). In sum, achievement of ethnic identity enhances many aspects of emotional and social development.

© DAVID M. GROSSMAN/THE IMAGE WORKS

■ Stilt walkers celebrate their heritage at a Caribbean youth festival in New York. Minority youths whose cultural heritage is respected in their communities are more likely to incorporate ethnic values and customs into their identity. ■

Moral Development

Eleven-year-old Sabrina sat at the kitchen table reading the Sunday newspaper, her eyes wide with interest. "Look at this!" she said to 16-year-old Louis, who was munching cereal. Sabrina held up a page of large photos showing a 70-year-old woman standing in her home. The floor and furniture were piled with stacks of newspapers, cardboard boxes, tin cans, glass containers, food, and clothing. The accompanying article described crumbling plaster on the walls, frozen pipes, and nonfunctioning sinks, toilet, and furnace. The headline read: "Loretta Perry: My Life Is None of Their Business."

"Look what they're trying to do to this poor lady," exclaimed Sabrina. "They're throwing her out of her house and tearing it down! Those city inspectors must not care about anyone. Here it says, 'Mrs. Perry has devoted much of her life to doing favors for people.' Why doesn't someone help *her*?"

"Sabrina, you're missing the point," Louis responded. "Mrs. Perry is violating 30 building code standards. The law says you're supposed to keep your house clean and in good repair."

"But Louis, she's old, and she needs help. She says her life will be over if they destroy her home."

"The building inspectors aren't being mean, Sabrina. Mrs. Perry is stubborn. She's refusing to obey the law. And she's not just a threat to herself—she's a danger to her neighbors, too. Suppose her house caught on fire. You can't live around other people and say your life is nobody's business."

"You don't just knock someone's home down," Sabrina replied angrily. "Why aren't her friends and neighbors over there fixing up that house? You're just like those building inspectors, Louis. You've got no feelings!"

As Louis and Sabrina's disagreement over Mrs. Perry's plight illustrates, cognitive development and expanding social experiences permit adolescents to better understand larger social structures—societal institutions and law-making systems—that govern moral responsibilities in complex societies. As their grasp of social arrangements expands, adolescents construct new ideas about what ought to be done when the needs and desires of people conflict. As a result, they move toward increasingly just, fair, and balanced solutions to moral problems.

Kohlberg's Theory of Moral Development

Early work by Piaget (1932/1965) on the moral judgment of the child inspired Lawrence Kohlberg's more comprehensive theory of the development of moral understanding. Kohlberg used a clinical interviewing procedure in which he presented a sample of 10- to 16-year-old boys with hypothetical *moral dilemmas*—stories presenting a conflict between two moral values—and asked them what the main actor should do and why. Then he followed the participants longitudinally, reinterviewing them at 3- to 4-year intervals over the next 20 years. The best known of Kohlberg's dilemmas, the "Heinz dilemma," pits the value of obeying the law (not stealing) against the value of human life (saving a dying person):

> In Europe a woman was near death from cancer. There was one drug the doctors thought might save her. A druggist in the same town had discovered it, but he was charging ten times what the drug cost him to make. The sick woman's husband, Heinz, went to everyone he knew to borrow the money, but he could only get together half of what it cost. The druggist refused to sell the drug for less or let Heinz pay later. So Heinz got desperate and broke into the man's store to steal the drug for his wife. Should Heinz have done that? Why or why not? (paraphrased from Colby et al., 1983, p. 77)

Kohlberg emphasized that it is *the way an individual reasons* about the dilemma, not *the content of the response* (whether or not to steal), that determines moral maturity. Individuals who believe that Heinz should steal the drug and those who think he should not can be found at each of Kohlberg's first four stages. Only at the two highest stages do moral reasoning and content come together in a coherent ethical system (Kohlberg, Levine, & Hewer, 1983). Given a choice between obeying the law and preserving individual rights, the most advanced moral thinkers support individual rights (in the Heinz dilemma, stealing the drug to save a life). **TAKE A MOMENT...** Does this remind you of adolescents' effort to formulate a sound, well-organized set of personal values in constructing an identity? According to some theorists, the development of identity and moral understanding are part of the same process (Bergman, 2004; Blasi, 1994).

For more efficient gathering and scoring of moral reasoning, researchers have devised short-answer questionnaires. The most recent, the *Sociomoral Reflection Measure–Short Form* (SRM-SF), poses 11 questions that (like Kohlberg's clinical interview) ask individuals to evaluate the importance of moral values and to reason about them—for example: "Let's say a friend of yours needs help and may even die, and you're the only person who can save him or her. How important is it for a person (without losing his or her own life) to save the life of a friend?" For each question, participants rate the importance of the value it addresses (from "very important," to "not important") and write a brief explanation. Their explanations are coded according to a revised version of Kohlberg's stages. Scores on the SRM-SF correlate well with those obtained from Kohlberg's clinical interview but are far less time-consuming to obtain (Gibbs, Basinger, & Grime, 2003).

KOHLBERG'S STAGES OF MORAL UNDERSTANDING   Kohlberg organized moral development into three levels, each with two stages, yielding six stages in all. He believed that moral understanding is promoted by the same factors Piaget thought were important for cognitive development: (1) actively grappling with moral issues and noticing weaknesses in one's current reasoning and (2) gains in perspective taking, which permit individuals to resolve moral conflicts in more effective ways. Kohlberg's moral stages are related to Selman's perspective-taking stages, described on page 492 in Chapter 13. **TAKE A MOMENT...** As we examine Kohlberg's developmental sequence in light of possible responses to the Heinz dilemma, look for changes in perspective taking that each stage assumes.

The Preconventional Level.   At the **preconventional level,** morality is externally controlled: Children accept the rules of authority figures and judge actions by their consequences. Behaviors that result in punishment are viewed as bad, those that lead to rewards as good.

■ *Stage 1: The punishment and obedience orientation.* Children at this stage, while recognizing that others may have different thoughts and feelings, still find it difficult to consider two points of view in a moral dilemma. As a result, they overlook people's intentions. Instead, they focus on fear of authority and avoidance of punishment as reasons for behaving morally.

> *Prostealing:* "If you let your wife die, you will . . . be blamed for not spending the money to help her and there'll be an investigation of you and the druggist for your wife's death." (Kohlberg, 1969, p. 381)

> *Antistealing:* "You shouldn't steal the drug because you'll be caught and sent to jail if you do. If you do get away, [you'd be scared that] the police would catch up with you any minute." (Kohlberg, 1969, p. 381)

■ *Stage 2: The instrumental purpose orientation.* Children at this stage realize that people can have different perspectives in a moral dilemma, but at first this understanding is concrete. They view right action as flowing from self-interest and understand reciprocity as equal exchange of favors: "You do this for me, and I'll do that for you."

> *Prostealing:* "[I]f Heinz decides to risk jail to save his wife, it's his life he's risking; he can do what he wants with it. And the same goes for the druggist; it's up to him to decide what he wants to do." (Rest, 1979, p. 26)

> *Antistealing:* "[Heinz] is running more risk than it's worth [to save a wife who is near death]." (Rest, 1979, p. 27)

The Conventional Level.   At the **conventional level,** individuals continue to regard conformity to social rules as important, but not for reasons of self-interest. Rather, they believe that actively maintaining the current social system ensures positive human relationships and societal order.

■ If the 12-year-old on the right expects a favor in return for carrying her injured friend's backpack, she is at Kohlberg's preconventional level. If she is guided by ideal reciprocity— "Do unto others as you would have them do unto you"—she has advanced to the conventional level. ■

■ *Stage 3: The "good boy–good girl" orientation, or the morality of interpersonal cooperation.* The desire to obey rules because they promote social harmony first appears in the context of close personal ties. Stage 3 individuals want to maintain the affection and approval of friends and relatives by being a "good person"—trustworthy, loyal, respectful, helpful, and nice. The capacity to view a two-person relationship from the vantage point of an impartial, outside observer supports this new approach to morality. At this stage, individuals understand *ideal reciprocity:* They express the same concern for the welfare of another as they do for themselves—a standard of fairness summed up by the Golden Rule: "Do unto others as you would have them do unto you."

> *Prostealing:* "No one will think you're bad if you steal the drug, but your family will think you're an inhuman husband if you don't. If you let your wife die, you'll never be able to look anyone in the face again." (Kohlberg, 1969, p. 381)

> *Antistealing:* "It isn't just the druggist who will think you're a criminal, everyone else will too. . . . [Y]ou'll feel bad thinking how you've brought dishonor on your family and yourself." (Kohlberg, 1969, p. 381)

■ *Stage 4: The social-order-maintaining orientation.* At this stage, the individual takes into account a larger perspective—that of societal laws. Moral choices no longer depend on close ties to others. Instead, rules must be enforced in the same evenhanded fashion for everyone, and each member of society has a personal duty to uphold them. The Stage 4 individual believes that laws must be obeyed under all circumstances because they are vital for ensuring societal order and cooperation between people.

> *Prostealing:* "Heinz has a duty to protect his wife's life; it's a vow he took in marriage. But it's wrong to steal, so he would have to take the drug with the idea of paying the druggist for it and accepting the penalty for breaking the law later."

> *Antistealing:* "Even if his wife is dying, it's still [Heinz's] duty as a citizen to obey the law. . . . If everyone starts breaking the law in a jam, there'd be no civilization, just crime and violence." (Rest, 1979, p. 30)

The Postconventional or Principled Level. Individuals at the **postconventional level** move beyond unquestioning support for the laws and rules of their own society. They define morality in terms of abstract principles and values that apply to all situations and societies.

■ *Stage 5: The social contract orientation.* At Stage 5, individuals regard laws and rules as flexible instruments for furthering human purposes. They can imagine alternatives to their own social order, and they emphasize fair procedures for interpreting and changing the law. When laws are consistent with individual rights and the interests of the majority, each person follows them because of a *social contract orientation*—free and willing participation in the system because it brings about more good for people than if it did not exist.

> *Prostealing:* "Although there is a law against stealing, the law wasn't meant to violate a person's right to life. . . . If Heinz is prosecuted for stealing, the law needs to be reinterpreted to take into account situations in which it goes against people's natural right to keep on living."

> *Antistealing:* At this stage, there are no antistealing responses.

■ *Stage 6: The universal ethical principle orientation.* At this highest stage, right action is defined by self-chosen ethical principles of conscience that are valid for all humanity, regardless of law and social agreement. Stage 6 individuals typically mention such abstract principles as respect for the worth and dignity of each person.

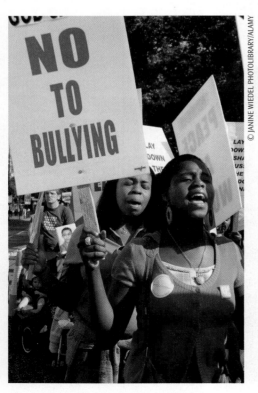

© JANINE WIEDEL PHOTOLIBRARY/ALAMY

■ Protestors in London march with families of teenage victims of extreme bullying. Young people make up a large part of public demonstrations over moral issues. In imagining an end to social ills, they convey a principled level of morality. ■

Prostealing: "It doesn't make sense to put respect for property above respect for life itself. [People] could live together without private property at all. Respect for human life and personality is absolute, and accordingly [people] have a mutual duty to save one another from dying." (Rest, 1979, p. 37)

Antistealing: At this stage, there are no antistealing responses.

RESEARCH ON KOHLBERG'S STAGE SEQUENCE Kohlberg's original research and other longitudinal studies provide the most convincing evidence for his stage sequence. With few exceptions, individuals move through the first four stages in the predicted order (Boom, Wouters, & Keller, 2007; Colby et al., 1983; Dawson, 2002; Walker & Taylor, 1991b). Moral development is slow and gradual: Reasoning at Stages 1 and 2 decreases in early adolescence, while Stage 3 reasoning increases through mid-adolescence and then declines. Stage 4 reasoning rises over the teenage years until, by early adulthood, it is the typical response.

Few people move beyond Stage 4. In fact, postconventional morality is so rare that no clear evidence exists that Kohlberg's Stage 6 actually follows Stage 5. This poses a key challenge to Kohlberg's theory: If people must reach Stages 5 and 6 to be considered truly morally mature, few individuals anywhere would measure up! According to one reexamination of Kohlberg's stages, moral maturity can be found in a revised understanding of Stages 3 and 4 (Gibbs, 1991, 2010). These stages are not "conventional"—based on social conformity—as Kohlberg assumed. Rather, they require profound moral constructions—an understanding of ideal reciprocity as the basis for relationships (Stage 3) and for widely accepted moral standards, set forth in rules and laws (Stage 4). In this view, "postconventional" morality is a highly reflective endeavor limited to a handful of people who have attained advanced education, usually in philosophy.

TAKE A MOMENT... Think of an actual moral dilemma you faced recently. How did you solve it? Did your reasoning fall at the same stage as your thinking about Heinz? Real-life conflicts, such as whether to continue helping a friend who is taking advantage of you, often elicit moral reasoning below a person's actual capacity because they involve practical considerations and mix cognition with intense emotion (Carpendale, 2000). Although adolescents and adults still mention reasoning as their most frequent strategy for resolving these dilemmas, they also refer to other strategies—talking through issues with others, relying on intuition, and calling on religious and spiritual ideas. And they report feeling drained, confused, and torn by temptation—an emotional side of moral judgment not tapped by hypothetical situations, which evoke the upper limits of moral thought because they allow reflection without the interference of personal risk (Walker, 2004).

The influence of situational factors on moral judgments indicates that, like Piaget's cognitive stages, Kohlberg's moral stages are loosely organized and overlapping. Rather than developing in a neat, stepwise fashion, people draw on a range of moral responses that vary with context. With age, this range shifts upward as less mature moral reasoning is gradually replaced by more advanced moral thought.

This girl takes great pleasure in helping her grandmother with everyday tasks. Adolescents of both sexes express themes of justice and caring in their moral responses. But females appear to place greater emphasis on care, especially when considering real-life dilemmas. ■

Are There Sex Differences in Moral Reasoning?

As we have seen, real-life moral dilemmas often highlight the role of emotion in moral judgment. In the discussion at the beginning of this section, notice how Sabrina's moral argument focuses on caring and commitment to others, while Louis's takes a more impersonal approach based on competing rights and justice.

Carol Gilligan (1982) is the best-known of those who have argued that Kohlberg's theory—originally formulated on the basis of interviews with males—does not adequately

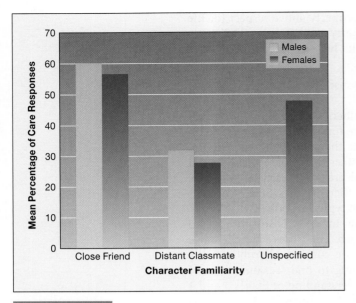

FIGURE 16.1

Relationship of familiarity of the main character in a moral dilemma to care responses. Australian university students were presented with one of three versions of a moral dilemma in which familiarity of the main character varied: close friend, distant classmate, and unspecified. Both male and female participants gave more care responses when considering a close friend than a distant classmate. Sex differences appeared only in the unspecified condition, where females may have assumed greater familiarity. *(From M. K. Ryan, B. David, & K. J. Reynolds, 2004, "Who Cares? The Effect of Gender and Context on the Self and Moral Reasoning,"* Psychology of Women Quarterly, 28, *246–255. Copyright © 2004 by the American Psychological Association. Reprinted by permission of the American Psychological Association.)*

represent the morality of girls and women. Gilligan believes that feminine morality emphasizes an "ethic of care" that Kohlberg's system devalues. Sabrina's reasoning falls at Stage 3 because it is based on mutual trust and affection, whereas Louis's is at Stage 4 because he emphasizes following the law to ensure societal order. According to Gilligan, a concern for others is a *different* but no less valid basis for moral judgment than a focus on impersonal rights.

Many studies have tested Gilligan's claim that Kohlberg's approach underestimates the moral maturity of females, and most do not support it (Turiel, 2006; Walker, 2006). On hypothetical dilemmas as well as everyday moral problems, adolescent and adult females display reasoning at the same stage as their male agemates and often at a higher stage. Themes of justice and caring appear in the responses of both sexes, and when girls do raise interpersonal concerns, they are not downgraded in Kohlberg's system (Jadack et al., 1995; Kahn, 1992; Walker, 1995). Rather, many studies report that girls shift from Stage 2 to Stage 3 reasoning earlier than boys (Gibbs et al., 2007). These findings suggest that although Kohlberg emphasized justice rather than caring as the highest moral ideal, his theory taps both sets of values.

Still, Gilligan makes a powerful claim that research on moral development has been limited by too much attention to rights and justice (a "masculine" ideal) and too little to caring and responsiveness (a "feminine" ideal). Some evidence shows that although the morality of males and females taps both orientations, females do tend to emphasize care, or empathic perspective taking, whereas males either stress justice or focus equally on justice and care (Jaffee & Hyde, 2000; Wark & Krebs, 1996; Weisz & Black, 2002). This difference in emphasis, which appears more often in real-life dilemmas than in hypothetical ones, may reflect women's greater involvement in daily activities involving care and concern for others.

Indeed, both cultural and situational contexts profoundly affect use of a care orientation. In one study, U.S. and Canadian 17- to 26-year-old females exceeded their male counterparts in complex reasoning about care issues. But Norwegian males were just as advanced as Norwegian females in care-based understanding (Skoe, 1998). Perhaps Norwegian culture, which explicitly endorses gender equality, induces boys and men to think deeply about interpersonal obligations. And in an Australian investigation, researchers presented 18- to 38-year-old university students with one of three versions of a moral dilemma, in which the main character varied in familiarity: (1) a close friend in class, (2) a person "known only vaguely" from class, or (3) a classmate whose relationship was unspecified (Ryan, David, & Reynolds, 2004). When asked whether they would permit the character, who was in danger of failing the course, to borrow a copy of their recently completed assignment despite risk of cheating, both males and females gave more care responses when considering a close friend than a socially distant classmate. As Figure 16.1 shows, gender differences emerged only in the unspecified condition, where women—who tend to forge closer relationships—may have assumed greater familiarity.

Coordinating Moral, Social-Conventional, and Personal Concerns

Adolescents' moral advances are also evident in their reasoning about situations that raise competing moral, social-conventional, and personal issues. In diverse Western and non-Western cultures, teenagers express great concern with matters of personal choice—a reflection of their quest for identity and strengthening independence (Neff & Helwig, 2002; Nucci, 2002).

More firmly than at younger ages, adolescents assert that dress, hairstyle, diary records, and friendships are the province of the individual and not subject to control by authority figures (such as parents) (Nucci, 2001, 2005). In countries varying widely in individualism versus collectivism—such as the United States and Japan—teenagers indicate that such matters should be theirs to decide alone. U.S. and Japanese adolescents whose parents frequently intrude into the personal domain report greater psychological stress (Hasebe, Nucci, & Nucci, 2004). In contrast, teenagers in both cultures believe that parents have a right to tell them what to do in moral and social-conventional situations and, when disagreements arise over these matters, are less likely to challenge parental authority (Smetana & Daddis, 2002).

As they enlarge the range of issues they regard as personal, adolescents think more intently about conflicts between personal choice and community obligations—whether, and under what conditions, it is permissible for laws to restrict speech, religion, marriage, childbearing, group membership, and other individual rights (Helwig, 1995; Wainryb, 1997). Teenagers display more subtle thinking than school-age children on such issues. For example, when asked if it is OK to exclude a child from a peer group on the basis of race or gender, fourth graders usually say exclusion is always unfair. But by tenth grade, young people, though increasingly mindful of fairness, indicate that under certain conditions—within friendship more often than peer groups, and on the basis of gender more often than race—exclusion is OK. In explaining, they mention the right to personal choice as well as concerns about effective group functioning. Justifying her opinion that members of an all-boys music club need not let a girl in, one tenth grader said, "It's not nice . . . but it's their club." Another commented, "[The girl and the boys] probably wouldn't relate on very many things" (Killen et al., 2002, p. 62; 2007).

As adolescents integrate personal rights with ideal reciprocity, they demand that the protections they want for themselves extend to others. For example, with age, adolescents are more likely to defend the government's right to limit the personal right to engage in risky health behaviors such as smoking and drinking, in the interest of the larger public good (Flanagan, Stout, & Gallay, 2008).

Similarly, they are increasingly mindful of the overlap between moral imperatives and social conventions. Eventually they realize that violating strongly held conventions—showing up at a wedding in a T-shirt, talking out of turn at a student council meeting—can harm others, either by inducing distress or by undermining fair treatment. Over time, as their grasp of fairness deepens, young people appreciate that many social conventions have moral implications: They are not just dictates of authority figures but vital for maintaining a just and peaceful society (Nucci, 2001). Notice how this understanding is central to Kohlberg's Stage 4, which is typically attained as adolescence draws to a close.

Influences on Moral Reasoning

Many factors affect the maturity of moral reasoning, including child-rearing practices, schooling, peer interaction, and culture. Growing evidence suggests that, as Kohlberg believed, these experiences work by presenting young people with cognitive challenges, which stimulate them to think about moral problems in more complex ways.

PERSONALITY　A flexible, open-minded approach to new information and experiences is linked to gains in moral reasoning, just as it is to identity development (Hart et al., 1998; Matsuba & Walker, 1998). Because open-minded young people are more socially skilled, they have more opportunities for social participation. A richer social life enhances exposure to others' perspectives, and open-mindedness helps adolescents derive moral insights from that exposure. In contrast, adolescents who have difficulty adapting to new experiences are less likely to be interested in others' moral ideas and justifications.

CHILD-REARING PRACTICES　As in childhood, parenting practices associated with moral maturity in adolescence combine warmth, exchange of ideas, and appropriate demands for maturity. Adolescents who gain most in moral understanding have parents who engage in moral discussions, encourage prosocial behavior, and create a supportive atmosphere by listening sensitively, asking clarifying questions, and presenting higher-level reasoning (Pratt, Skoe, & Arnold, 2004; Wyatt & Carlo, 2002). In one study, 11-year-olds were asked what they thought an adult would say to justify a moral rule, such as not lying, stealing, or breaking a promise. Those with warm, demanding, communicative parents were far more likely than their age-mates to point to the importance of ideal reciprocity: "You wouldn't like it if I did it to you" (Leman, 2005). In contrast, when parents lecture, use threats, or make sarcastic remarks, adolescents show little or no change in moral reasoning over time (Walker & Taylor, 1991a).

In sum, parents facilitate moral understanding by using an authoritative approach that is affectionate, rational, verbal, and respectful, and that promotes a cooperative style of family life. Notice that these are similar to the characteristics—discussed in Chapter 10—that promote moral internalization in young children.

SCHOOLING   Years of schooling is a powerful predictor of movement to Kohlberg's Stage 4 or higher (Dawson et al., 2003; Gibbs et al., 2007). Higher education introduces young people to social issues that extend beyond personal relationships to entire political or cultural groups. Consistent with this idea, college students who report more perspective-taking opportunities (for example, classes that emphasize open discussion of opinions, friendships with others of different cultural backgrounds) and who indicate that they have become more aware of social diversity tend to be advanced in moral reasoning (Comunian & Gielan, 2006; Mason & Gibbs, 1993a, 1993b).

PEER INTERACTION   Interaction among peers who present differing viewpoints promotes moral understanding. When young people negotiate and compromise with agemates, they realize that social life can be based on cooperation between equals (Killen & Nucci, 1995). Teenagers who report more close friendships and who more often participate in conversations with their friends are advanced in moral reasoning (Schonert-Reichl, 1999). The mutuality and intimacy of friendship, which foster decisions based on consensual agreement, may be particularly important for moral development. Furthermore, recall from Chapter 13 that intergroup contact—cross-race friendships and interactions in schools and communities—reduces racial and ethnic prejudice. It also affects young people morally, strengthening their conviction that race-based and other forms of peer exclusion are wrong (Crystal, Killen, & Ruck, 2008).

Peer discussions and role playing of moral problems have provided the basis for interventions aimed at improving high school and college students' progress through Kohlberg's stage sequence. For these discussions to be effective, young people must be highly engaged—confronting, critiquing, and attempting to clarify one another's viewpoints, as Sabrina and Louis did when they argued over Mrs. Perry's plight (Berkowitz & Gibbs, 1983; Comunian & Gielen, 2006). And because moral development occurs gradually, many peer interaction sessions over weeks or months typically are needed to produce moral change.

CULTURE   Individuals in industrialized nations move through Kohlberg's stages more quickly and advance to a higher level than individuals in village societies, who rarely move beyond Stage 3. One explanation of these cultural differences is that in village societies, moral cooperation is based on direct relations between people and does not allow for the development of advanced moral understanding (Stages 4 to 6), which depends on appreciating the role of larger social structures, such as laws and government institutions (Gibbs et al., 2007).

In support of this view, in cultures where young people participate in the institutions of their society at early ages, moral reasoning is advanced. For example, on *kibbutzim,* small but technologically complex agricultural settlements in Israel, children receive training in the governance of their community in middle childhood. By third grade, they mention more concerns about societal laws and rules when discussing moral conflicts than do Israeli city-reared or U.S. children (Fuchs et al., 1986). During adolescence and adulthood, a greater percentage of kibbutz than American individuals reach Kohlberg's Stages 4 and 5 (Snarey, Reimer, & Kohlberg, 1985).

© EARL & NAZIMA KOWALL/CORBIS

■ Growing up in a small village in the Pamir Mountains of China, these adolescents view moral cooperation as based on direct relations between people. Their moral reasoning is likely to emphasize a close connection between individual and group responsibility. ■

A second possible reason for cultural variation is that responses to moral dilemmas in collectivist cultures (including village societies) are often more other-directed than in Western Europe and North America (Miller, 2007). In both village and industrialized cultures that highly value interdependency, statements portraying the individual as vitally collected to the social group are common. In one study, both male and female Japanese adolescents, who almost always integrated care- and justice-based reasoning, placed greater weight on caring, which they regarded as a communal responsibility. As one boy remarked, *yasashii* (kindness/gentleness) and *omoiyari* (empathy) are "something 'normal' that everyone shows" (Shimizu, 2001). Similarly, in research conducted in India, even highly educated people (expected to have attained Kohlberg's Stages 4 and 5) viewed solutions to moral dilemmas as the responsibility of the entire society, not of a single person (Miller & Bersoff, 1995).

These findings raise the question of whether Kohlberg's highest level represents a culturally specific way of thinking—one limited to Western societies that emphasize individualism and an appeal to an inner, private conscience. At the same time, a review of over 100 studies confirmed an age-related trend consistent with Kohlberg's Stages 1 to 4 across diverse societies (Gibbs et al., 2007). A common justice morality is clearly evident in the dilemma responses of people from vastly different cultures.

Moral Reasoning and Behavior

A central assumption of the cognitive-developmental perspective is that moral understanding should affect moral action. According to Kohlberg, mature moral thinkers realize that behaving in line with their beliefs is vital for creating and maintaining a just social world (Gibbs, 2010). Consistent with this idea, higher-stage adolescents more often act prosocially by helping, sharing, and defending victims of injustice and by volunteering in their communities (Carlo et al., 1996; Comunian & Gielan, 2000, 2006). Also, they less often engage in cheating, aggression, and other antisocial behaviors (Gregg, Gibbs, & Fuller, 1994; Raaijmakers, Engels, & Van Hoof, 2005; Stams et al., 2006).

Yet the connection between more mature moral reasoning and action is only modest. As we saw in earlier chapters, moral behavior is influenced by many factors besides cognition, including the emotions of empathy, sympathy, and guilt; individual differences in temperament; and a long history of experiences that affect moral choice and decision making. **Moral self-relevance**— the degree to which morality is central to self-concept—also affects moral behavior (Walker, 2004). In a study of low-SES African-American and Hispanic teenagers, those who emphasized moral traits and goals in their self-descriptions displayed exceptional levels of community service (Hart & Fegley, 1995). But they did not differ from their agemates in moral reasoning.

Research has yet to identify the origins of a sense of moral self-relevance, or just how thought combines with other influences to foster moral commitment. Close relationships with parents, teachers, and friends may play vital roles by modeling prosocial behavior and fostering morally relevant emotions of empathy and guilt, which combine with moral cognition to powerfully motivate moral action (Arsenio, 2006; Hoffman, 2000). Another possibility is that *just educational environments*—in which teachers model and guide students in democratic decision making and rule setting, resolving disputes civilly and fairly, and taking responsibility for others' welfare—are influential (Atkins, Hart, & Donnelly, 2004). In one study, tenth graders who reported fair teacher treatment were more likely than those who had experienced unjust treatment (an unfair detention or a lower grade than they deserved) to regard excluding a peer on the basis of race as a moral transgression (Crystal, Killen, & Ruck, 2010).

Schools may also foster students' moral self-relevance by expanding opportunities for civic engagement. As the Social Issues: Education box on page 616 reveals, encouraging civic responsibility in young people can help them see the connection between their personal interests and the public interest—an insight that may foster all aspects of morality.

Religious Involvement and Moral Development

Recall that in resolving real-life moral dilemmas, many people express notions of religion and spirituality. Religion is especially important in U.S. family life. In recent national polls, nearly two-thirds of Americans reported being religious, compared with one-half of those in Canada,

LOOK AND LISTEN

❖❖❖

Would you characterize your high school as a *just educational environment?* Cite specific features and experiences that may have contributed to students' moral development and civic engagement.

SOCIAL ISSUES: EDUCATION

Development of Civic Responsibility

On Thanksgiving Day, Jules, Martin, Louis, and Sabrina joined their parents at a soup kitchen to serve a holiday dinner to poverty-stricken people. Throughout the year, Sabrina volunteered on Saturday mornings at a nursing home, conversing with bedridden elders. During a congressional election campaign, all four adolescents attended special youth meetings with candidates. At school, Louis and his girlfriend, Cassie, formed an organization devoted to promoting ethnic and racial tolerance.

These young people show a strong sense of *civic responsibility*—a complex combination of cognition, emotion, and behavior. Civic responsibility involves knowledge of political issues, a desire to make a difference in the community, and skills for achieving civic goals, such as how to resolve differing views fairly and conduct meetings so that all participants have a voice (Flanagan & Faison, 2001).

When young people engage in community service that exposes them to people in need or to public issues, they are especially likely to express a commitment to future service. And youth volunteers—who tend to be advanced in moral reasoning—gain further in moral maturity as a result of participation (Gibbs et al., 2007; Hart, Atkins, & Donnelly, 2006). Family, school, and community experiences contribute to adolescents' civic responsibility.

Family Influences

Teenagers whose parents encourage their children to form opinions about controversial issues are more knowledgeable about civic issues and better able to see them from more than one perspective (Santoloupo & Pratt, 1994). Also, adolescents whose parents engage in community service and stress compassion for the less fortunate tend to hold socially responsible values. When asked what causes unemployment or poverty, for example, these teenagers more often mention situational and societal factors (lack of education, government policies, or the state of the economy) than individual factors (low intelligence or personal problems). Youths who endorse situational and societal causes, in turn, have more altruistic life goals, such as working to eradicate poverty or to preserve the earth for future generations (Flanagan & Tucker, 1999). And they engage in more civic activities into early adulthood (Zaff, Malanchuk, & Eccles, 2008).

School and Community Influences

A democratic climate at school, in which teachers promote discussion of controversial social issues while insisting that students listen to and respect one another, fosters knowledge and critical analysis of political concerns and commitment to social causes (Torney-Purta, Barber, & Wilkenfeld, 2007). Furthermore, high school students who view their community as one in which adults care about youths and work to make the community better report higher levels of civic participation (Kahne & Sporte, 2008). Participation in nonsport extracurricular activities at school and in community youth organizations is also associated with civic commitment persisting into adulthood (Obradović & Masten, 2007).

Two aspects of these involvements seem to account for their lasting impact. First, they introduce adolescents to the vision and skills required for mature civic engagement. Within student government and other groups, young people see how their actions affect the wider school and community. They realize that collectively they can achieve results greater than any one person can achieve alone. And they learn to work together, balancing strong convictions with compromise (Atkins, Hart, & Donnelly, 2004; Kirshner, 2009). Second, while producing a weekly newspaper, participating in a dramatic production, or implementing a service project, young people explore political and moral ideals. Often they redefine their identities to include a responsibility to combat others' misfortunes (Wheeler, 2002).

The power of family, school, and community to promote civic responsibility may lie in discussions, educational practices, and activities that jointly foster moral thought, emotion, and behavior. In a comparison of nationally representative samples of 14-year-olds in 28 nations, U.S. young people excelled at community service, with more than 50 percent reporting membership in organizations devoted to volunteering (Torney-Purta, 2002).

Currently, 66 percent of U.S. public schools provide students with community service opportunities. Nearly half of these have *service-learning programs*, which integrate service activities into the academic curriculum, and about one-third of students enroll. High school students who are required to serve their communities express as strong a desire to remain engaged as do students who volunteer. And when they reach early adulthood, they are equally likely to vote and participate in community organizations (Hart et al., 2007; Metz & Youniss, 2005).

Still, most U.S. schools offering service learning do not have policies encouraging or mandating such programs (Scales & Roehlkepartain, 2004). Furthermore, low-SES, inner-city youths—although they express high interest in contributing to society—score substantially lower than higher-SES youths in civic knowledge and participation (Balsano, 2005). A broad societal commitment to fostering civic character must pay special attention to supportive school and community experiences for these young people, so their eagerness to make a difference can be realized.

■ Adolescents paint a mural on a wall once filled with graffiti in a low-income, inner-city neighborhood. Family, school, and community experiences contribute to their sense of civic responsibility. ■

one-third of those in Great Britain and Italy, and even fewer elsewhere in Europe (Gallup News Service, 2006; Jones, 2003). People who regularly attend religious services include many parents with children.

National survey findings reveal that the 81 percent of U.S. teenagers identify with one religion, and an additional 3 percent with two religions (Smith & Denton, 2005). Nevertheless, during adolescence, formal religious involvement declines—for U.S. youths, from 55 percent at ages 13 to 15 to 40 percent at ages 17 to 18 (Donahue & Benson, 1995; Kerestes & Youniss, 2003). The drop coincides with increased autonomy and efforts to construct a personally meaningful religious identity—a task usually not resolved until the late teens or twenties, as Chapter 17 will reveal (Hunsberger, Pratt, & Pancer, 2001).

But adolescents who remain part of a religious community are advantaged in moral values and behavior. Compared with nonaffiliated youths, they are more involved in community service activities aimed at helping the less fortunate (Kerestes, Youniss, & Metz, 2004). And religious involvement promotes responsible academic and social behavior and discourages misconduct (Dowling et al., 2004). It is associated with lower levels of drug and alcohol use, early sexual activity, and delinquency (Regnerus, Smith, & Fritsch, 2003).

A variety of factors probably contribute to these favorable outcomes. In a study of inner-city high school students, religiously involved young people were more likely to report trusting relationships with parents, other adults, and friends who hold similar worldviews. The more activities they shared with this network, the higher they scored in empathy and prosocial behavior (King & Furrow, 2004). Furthermore, religious education and youth activities directly teach concern for others and provide opportunities for moral discussions and civic engagement. And adolescents who feel connected to a higher being may develop certain inner strengths, including moral self-relevance and prosocial values, that help them translate their thinking into action (Hardy & Carlo, 2005; Sherrod & Spiewak, 2008).

Because most teenagers, regardless of formal affiliation, identify with a religious denomination and say they believe in a higher being, religious institutions may be uniquely suited to foster moral and prosocial commitments and discourage risky behaviors (Bridges & Moore, 2002). For youths in inner-city neighborhoods with few alternative sources of social support, outreach by religious institutions can lead to life-altering involvement (Jang & Johnson, 2001). An exception is seen in religious cults, where rigid indoctrination into the group's beliefs, suppression of individuality, and estrangement from society all work against moral maturity (Richmond, 2004).

■ Adolescents who are part of a religious community tend to be advantaged in moral values and behavior. The more activities they share with their religiously involved network of adults and peers, the higher they score in empathy and prosocial behavior. ■

Further Challenges to Kohlberg's Theory

Although much evidence is consistent with the cognitive-developmental approach to morality, Kohlberg's theory has faced major challenges. The most radical opposition comes from researchers who—referring to wide variability in moral reasoning across situations—claim that Kohlberg's stage sequence inadequately accounts for morality in everyday life (Krebs & Denton, 2005). These investigators favor abandoning Kohlberg's stages for a *pragmatic approach to morality*. They assert that each person makes moral judgments at varying levels of maturity, depending on the individual's current context and motivations: Conflict over a business deal is likely to evoke Stage 2 (instrumental purpose) reasoning, a friendship or romantic dispute Stage 3 (ideal reciprocity) reasoning, and a breach of contract Stage 4 (social-order-maintaining) reasoning (Krebs et al., 1991).

According to the pragmatic view, everyday moral judgments—rather than being efforts to arrive at just solutions—are practical tools that people use to achieve their goals. To benefit personally, they often must advocate cooperation with others. But people often act first and then invoke moral judgments to rationalize their actions, regardless of whether their behavior is self-centered or prosocial (Haidt, 2001). And sometimes people use moral judgments for immoral purposes—for example, to excuse their transgressions.

Is the pragmatic approach correct that people strive to resolve moral conflicts fairly only when they themselves have nothing to lose? Supporters of the cognitive-developmental perspective point out that people frequently rise above self-interest to defend others' rights. For example, moral leaders in business—rather than resorting to Stage 2 reasoning—endorse trust, integrity, good faith, and just laws and codes of conduct (Damon, 2004; Gibbs, 2006). Also, when presented with moral justifications varying in maturity, adolescents and adults are well aware of the greater adequacy of higher-stage thinking, which some people act on despite highly corrupt environments. Furthermore, individuals who engage in sudden altruistic action may have previously considered relevant moral issues so thoroughly that their moral judgment activates automatically, triggering an immediate response (Gibbs et al., 2009a; Pizzaro & Bloom, 2003). In these instances, people who appear to be engaging in after-the-fact moral justification are actually behaving with great forethought.

In sum, the cognitive-developmental approach to morality has done much to clarify our profound moral potential. And despite opposition, Kohlberg's central assumption—that with age, humans everywhere construct a deeper understanding of fairness and justice that guides moral action—remains powerfully influential.

Gender Typing

As Sabrina entered adolescence, she began to place more emphasis on excelling in literature, art, and music—traditionally feminine subjects. When with peers, she worried about walking, talking, eating, dressing, laughing, and competing in ways consistent with a feminine gender role.

Early adolescence is a period of **gender intensification**—increased gender stereotyping of attitudes and behavior, and movement toward a more traditional gender identity (Basow & Rubin, 1999; Galambos, Almeida, & Petersen, 1990). Both sexes experience gender intensification, but it is stronger for girls, who feel less free to experiment with "other-gender" activities and behavior than they did in middle childhood (Huston & Alvarez, 1990).

What accounts for gender intensification? Biological, social, and cognitive factors are involved. As puberty magnifies sex differences in appearance, teenagers spend more time thinking about themselves in gender-linked ways. Pubertal changes also prompt gender-typed pressures from others. Parents—especially those with traditional gender-role beliefs—may encourage "gender-appropriate" activities and behavior more than they did earlier (Crouter, Manke, & McHale, 1995; Shanahan et al., 2007). And when adolescents start to date, they often become more gender-typed as a way of increasing their attractiveness (Maccoby, 1998). Finally, cognitive changes—in particular, greater concern with what others think—make young teenagers more responsive to gender-role expectations.

Gender intensification declines by middle to late adolescence, but not all young people move beyond it to the same degree. Many adolescents, especially white, middle-SES girls, experience gender-typed pressures to act in ways inconsistent with their actual beliefs and desires. In one study, eighth-grade girls who compromised their authenticity—by withholding their true opinions and feelings to avoid parental or peer disapproval—were less likely than their more authentic agemates to display the typical adolescent rise in self-esteem (see page 602) (Impett et al., 2008). Teenagers who are encouraged to explore non-gender-typed options and to question the value of gender stereotypes for themselves and society are more likely to build an androgynous gender identity (see Chapter 10, page 395). Overall,

■ In early adolescence, young people, especially girls, move toward more traditional gender identities. By middle to late adolescence, gender intensification declines, especially among adolescents encouraged to explore non-gender-typed options. ■

© MICHAEL KRASOWITZ/GETTY IMAGES/PHOTOGRAPHER'S CHOICE

androgynous adolescents, particularly girls, tend to be psychologically healthier—more willing to speak their own mind, higher in self-confidence and self-esteem, better-liked by peers, and identity-achieved (Bronstein, 2006; Dusek, 1987; Harter, 2006).

ASK YOURSELF

◆ **REVIEW** How does an understanding of ideal reciprocity contribute to moral development? Why are Kohlberg's Stages 3 and 4 morally mature constructions?

◆ **APPLY** Tam grew up in a small village culture, Lydia in a large industrial city. At age 15, Tam reasons at Kohlberg's Stage 3, Lydia at Stage 4. What factors might account for the difference?

◆ **CONNECT** How might the exploration of values and goals associated with healthy identity development contribute to the eventual decline in adolescent gender intensification?

◆ **REFLECT** Do you favor a cognitive-developmental or a pragmatic approach to morality, or both? What research evidence and personal experiences influenced your viewpoint?

The Family

Franca and Antonio remember their son Louis's freshman year of high school as a difficult time. Because of a demanding project at work, Franca was away from home many evenings and weekends. In her absence, Antonio took over, but when business declined and he had to cut costs at his hardware store, he, too, had less time for the family. That year, Louis and two friends used their computer know-how to crack the code of a long-distance telephone service. From the family basement, they made calls around the country. Louis's grades fell, and he often left the house without saying where he was going. Franca and Antonio began to feel uncomfortable about the long hours Louis spent in the basement and their lack of contact with him. Finally, when the telephone company traced the illegal calls to their phone number, they knew they had cause for concern.

Development at adolescence involves striving for **autonomy**—a sense of oneself as a separate, self-governing individual. Autonomy first became a major issue in toddlerhood, but now it is revisited on a higher plane. Teenagers strive to rely more on themselves and less on parents for guidance and decision making (Collins & Laursen, 2004; Steinberg & Silk, 2002). Typically, they shift their attention away from family to peers, with whom they explore new courses of action. Nevertheless, parent–child relationships remain vital for helping adolescents become autonomous, responsible individuals.

Parent–Child Relationships

A variety of changes within the adolescent support autonomy. In Chapter 11, we saw that puberty triggers psychological distancing from parents. In addition, as young people look more mature, parents give them more freedom to think and decide for themselves, more opportunities to regulate their own activities, and more responsibility (McElhaney et al., 2009). Cognitive development also paves the way toward autonomy: Gradually, adolescents solve problems and make decisions more effectively. And an improved ability to reason about social relationships leads teenagers to *deidealize* their parents, viewing them as "just people." Consequently, they no longer bend as easily to parental authority as they did when younger. Yet as Franca and Antonio's episode with Louis reveals, teenagers still need guidance and, at times, protection from dangerous situations.

TAKE A MOMENT... Think back to what we said earlier about the type of parenting that fosters academic achievement (Chapter 15), identity formation, and moral maturity. You will find a common theme: Effective parenting of adolescents strikes a balance between *connection* and *separation*. In diverse ethnic groups, SES levels, nations, and family structures (including

Applying What We Know

Parenting Practices That Foster Adolescent Competence

PARENTING PRACTICE	ADOLESCENT OUTCOMES
Project warmth and acceptance.	Promotes high self-esteem, identity exploration and achievement, prosocial behavior, and more positive parent–adolescent communication.
Monitor activities.	Promotes high self-esteem and reduced likelihood of engaging in antisocial behavior. Most effective when parents have a cooperative relationship with the adolescent and modify their supervision to fit the young person's increasing competence.
Engage in democratic decision making and verbal give-and-take.	Promotes self-esteem and self-reliant, responsible behavior.
Establish firm control and consistent discipline.	When accompanied by warmth, explanations, and verbal give-and-take, promotes self-reliant, responsible behavior. (Firm control without explanations that clarify the legitimacy of parents' rules can undermine self-reliance and responsibility.)
Provide information and model effective skills.	Promotes competencies as diverse as academic achievement and conflict resolution; protects against high-risk behaviors, such as sex without contraception and substance use.

Sources: Collins & Steinberg, 2006; Steinberg & Silk, 2002.

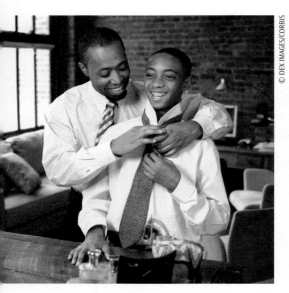

■ This teenager and father share an affectionate moment. Although adolescents may resist parental authority, most maintain close family ties, especially when parents make appropriate demands for maturity while gradually granting the young person increased freedom. ■

single-parent, two-parent, and stepparent), warm, supportive parent–adolescent ties that make appropriate demands for maturity while permitting young people to explore ideas and social roles foster autonomy—predicting high self-reliance, effortful control, academic motivation and achievement, work orientation, favorable self-esteem, and ease of separation in the transition to college (Bean, Barber, & Crane, 2007; Eisenberg et al., 2005; Supple et al., 2009; Vazsonyi, Hibbert, & Snider, 2003; Wang, Pomerantz, & Chen, 2007).

Note that these are features of the authoritative style. See Applying What We Know above for a summary of practices emanating from authoritative parenting that promote adolescent cognitive and social development.

Conversely, parents who are coercive or psychologically controlling interfere with the development of autonomy. These tactics are linked to low self-esteem, depression, drug and alcohol use, and antisocial behavior—outcomes that often persist into early adulthood (Barber, Stolz, & Olsen, 2005; Bronte-Tinkew, Moore, & Carrano, 2006; Wissink, Deković, & Meijer, 2006).

In Chapter 2, we described the family as a *system* that must adapt to changes in its members. The rapid physical and psychological changes of adolescence trigger conflicting expectations in parent–child relationships—a major reason that many parents find rearing teenagers to be stressful.

Earlier we noted that interest in making choices about personal matters strengthens in adolescence. Yet parents and teenagers—especially young teenagers—differ sharply on the appropriate age for granting certain privileges, such as control over clothing, school courses, going out with friends, and dating (Smetana, 2002). Consistent parental monitoring of the young person's daily activities, through a cooperative relationship in which the adolescent willingly discloses information, is linked to a variety of positive outcomes—prevention of delinquency, reduction in sexual activity, improved school performance, and positive psychological well-being (Crouter & Head, 2002; Jacobson & Crockett, 2000).

Parents' own development can also lead to friction with teenagers. While their children face a boundless future and a wide array of choices, middle-aged parents must accept the fact that their own possibilities are narrowing (Holmbeck, 1996). Often they can't understand why the adolescent wants to skip family activities to be with peers. And teenagers fail to appreciate that parents want the family to spend as much time together as possible because an important period in their adult life—child rearing—will soon end.

Immigrant parents from cultures that place a high value on family closeness and obedience to authority have greater difficulty adapting to their teenagers' push for autonomy, often reacting more strongly to adolescent disagreement (Phinney & Ong, 2001). And as adolescents acquire the host culture's language and are increasingly exposed to its individualistic values, immigrant parents may become even more critical, causing teenagers to rely less on the family network for social support. The resulting *acculturative stress* (see page 607) is associated with a decline in self-esteem and a rise in anxiety, depressive symptoms, and deviant behavior, including alcohol use and delinquency (Crane et al., 2005; Park, 2009; Suarez-Morales & Lopez, 2009; Warner et al., 2006).

Throughout adolescence, the quality of the parent–child relationship is the single most consistent predictor of mental health. In well-functioning families, teenagers remain attached to parents and seek their advice, but they do so in a context of greater freedom (Collins & Steinberg, 2006). The mild conflict that arises facilitates adolescent identity development and autonomy by helping family members express and tolerate disagreement. Conflicts also inform parents of teenagers' changing needs and expectations, signaling a need for adjustments in the parent–child relationship.

By middle to late adolescence, most parents and children achieve this mature, mutual relationship, and harmonious interaction is on the rise. The reduced time that Western teenagers spend with their families—for U.S. youths, a drop from 33 percent of waking hours in fifth grade to 14 percent in twelfth grade—has little to do with conflict (Larson et al., 1996). Rather, it results from the large amount of unstructured time available to teenagers in North America and Western Europe—on average, nearly half their waking hours (Larson, 2001). Young people tend to fill these free hours with activities that take them away from home—part-time jobs, a growing array of leisure and volunteer pursuits, and time with friends.

But this drop in family time is not universal. In one study, urban low- and middle-SES African-American youths showed no decline in hours spent at home with family—a pattern typical in cultures with collectivist values (Larson et al., 2001). Furthermore, teenagers living in risky neighborhoods tend to have more trusting relationships with parents and adjust more favorably when parents maintain tighter control and pressure them not to engage in worrisome behaviors (McElhaney & Allen, 2001). In harsh surroundings, young people seem to interpret more measured granting of autonomy as a sign of parental caring.

Family Circumstances

As Franca and Antonio's experience with Louis reminds us, adult life stresses can interfere with warm, involved parenting and, in turn, with children's adjustment at any phase of development. But parents who are financially secure, not overloaded with job pressures, and content with their marriages usually find it easier to grant teenagers appropriate autonomy and experience less conflict with them (Cowan & Cowan, 2002; Crouter & Bumpus, 2001). When Franca and Antonio's work stress eased and they recognized Louis's need for more involvement and guidance, his problems subsided.

Less than 10 percent of families with adolescents have seriously troubled relationships—chronic, escalating levels of conflict and repeated arguments over serious issues. Of these, most have difficulties that began in childhood (Collins & Laursen, 2004). Table 16.2 summarizes family conditions considered in earlier chapters that pose challenges for adolescents. Teenagers who develop well despite family stresses continue to benefit from factors that fostered resilience in

LOOK AND LISTEN

Ask an early adolescent and his or her parent for their views on when the young person is mature enough to spend unsupervised evenings with friends, begin dating, own a cell phone, create a MySpace or Facebook page, and be granted other privileges. Do adolescent and parent perspectives differ?

TABLE 16.2   Family Circumstances with Implications for Adolescent Adjustment

FAMILY CIRCUMSTANCE	TO REVIEW, TURN TO . . .
TYPE OF FAMILY	
Adoptive	Chapter 2, pages 65–68
Never-married, single parent	Chapter 13, pages 509–510
Divorced	Chapter 13, pages 510–513
Blended	Chapter 13, pages 513–515
Employed mother and dual-earner	Chapter 13, pages 515–517
Gay and lesbian	Chapter 13, pages 508–509
FAMILY CONDITIONS	
Economic hardship	Chapter 2, pages 72–74
Child maltreatment	Chapter 10, pages 401–405 Chapter 13, pages 519–520
Adolescent parenthood	Chapter 14, pages 555–557

earlier years: an appealing, easygoing disposition; a parent who combines warmth with high expectations; and (especially if parental supports are lacking) bonds with prosocial adults outside the family who care deeply about the adolescent's well-being (Masten, 2001; Masten & Shaffer, 2006).

Siblings

Like parent–child relationships, sibling interactions adapt to development at adolescence. As younger siblings become more self-sufficient, they accept less direction from their older brothers and sisters, and sibling influence declines. Also, as teenagers become more involved in friendships and romantic relationships, they invest less time and energy in their siblings, who are part of the family from which they are trying to establish autonomy. As a result, sibling relationships often become less intense, in both positive and negative feelings (Hetherington, Henderson, & Reiss, 1999; Kim et al., 2006).

Despite a drop in companionship, attachment between siblings, like closeness to parents, remains strong for most young people. Brothers and sisters who established a positive bond in early childhood continue to display greater affection and caring—an outcome linked to more favorable emotional and social adjustment (Branje et al., 2004; Kim et al., 2007). Culture also influences quality of sibling interaction. In one study, Mexican-American adolescents who expressed a strong Mexican cultural orientation resolved sibling conflicts more cooperatively—compromising rather than controlling or confronting—than did those more oriented toward U.S. individualistic values (Killoren, Thayer, & Updegraff, 2008). Older siblings with whom bonds are positive provide helpful advice as teenagers face challenges in romantic relationships, schoolwork, and decisions about the future.

Sibling interaction at adolescence continues to be affected by other relationships, and vice versa. As at earlier ages, teenagers whose parents are warm and supportive and who have a history of caring friendships have more positive sibling ties (Bussell et al., 1999; Kramer & Kowal, 2005). And in bidirectional fashion, warm adolescent sibling relationships contribute to more gratifying friendships (Yeh & Lempers, 2004). Finally, mild sibling differences in perceived parental affection no longer trigger jealousy but, instead, predict greater sibling warmth (Feinberg et al., 2003). Perhaps adolescents interpret a unique relationship with parents, as long as it is generally accepting, as a gratifying sign of their own individuality.

■■ Peer Relations

As adolescents spend less time with family members, peers become increasingly important. In industrialized societies, young people spend most of each weekday with agemates in school. Teenagers also spend much out-of-class time together, more in some cultures than others. For example, U.S. young people have about 50 hours of free time per week, Europeans about 45 hours, and East Asians about 33 hours (Larson, 2001). A shorter school year and less demanding academic standards, which lead American youths to devote much less time to schoolwork, account for this difference (see Figure 16.2).

In the following sections, we will see that adolescent peer relations can be both positive and negative. At their best, peers serve as crucial bridges between the family and adult social roles.

Friendships

Number of "best friends" declines from about four to six in early adolescence to one or two in adulthood (Hartup & Stevens, 1999). At the same time, the nature of the relationship changes.

CHARACTERISTICS OF ADOLESCENT FRIENDSHIPS   When asked about the meaning of friendship, teenagers stress three characteristics. The most important is *intimacy,* or psychological closeness, which is supported by *mutual understanding* of each other's values, beliefs, and

FIGURE 16.2

Weekly free time and time devoted to homework by adolescents in the United States, Europe, and East Asia. Figures are averages of those reported in many studies. American teenagers have more free time available to spend with peers than their European and, especially, Asian counterparts, a difference largely explained by American adolescents spending far less time doing homework. *(Adapted from Larson, 2001.)*

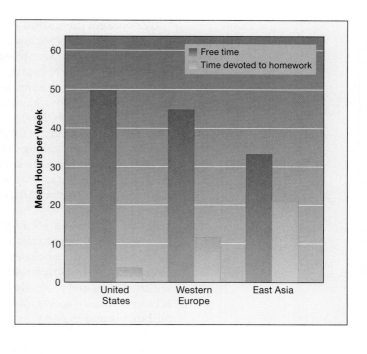

feelings. In addition, more than younger children, teenagers want their friends to be *loyal*—to stick up for them and not to leave them for somebody else (Collins & Madsen, 2006).

As frankness and faithfulness increase, *self-disclosure* (sharing of private thoughts and feelings) between friends rises steadily over the adolescent years (see Figure 16.3). As a result, teenagers get to know each other better as personalities. Cooperation, mutual affirmation, and feelings of companionship and caring between friends also increase—changes that reflect greater effort and skill at preserving the relationship and sensitivity to a friend's needs and desires (De Goede, Branje, & Meeus, 2009; Phillipsen, 1999). Adolescents also are less possessive of their friends than they were in childhood (Parker et al., 2005). Desiring a certain degree of autonomy for themselves, they recognize that friends need this, too.

In addition to the many characteristics that school-age friends share (see Chapter 13, page 499), adolescent friends tend to be alike in identity status, educational aspirations, political beliefs, and willingness to try drugs and engage in lawbreaking acts. Over time, they become more similar in these ways (Berndt & Murphy, 2002; Selfhout, Branje, & Meeus, 2008). Friendship similarity partly reflects the way adolescents' social world is organized. Most teenagers live in neighborhoods segregated by income, ethnicity, and belief systems. Through tracking, schools sort them further. Teenagers may also choose companions like themselves to increase the supportiveness of friendship. Occasionally, however, adolescents choose friends with differing attitudes and values, which permits them to explore new perspectives within the security of a compatible relationship.

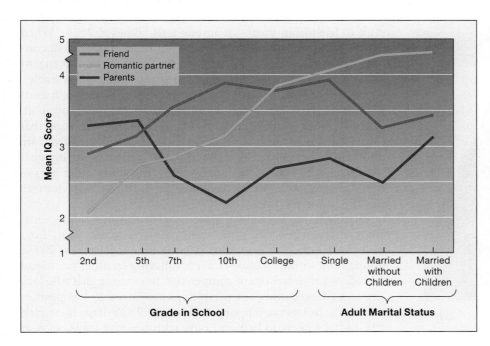

FIGURE 16.3

Age changes in reported self-disclosure to parents and peers, based on findings of several studies. Self-disclosure to friends increases steadily during adolescence, reflecting intimacy as a major basis of friendship. Self-disclosure to romantic partners also rises. However, not until the college years does it surpass intimacy with friends. Self-disclosure to parents declines in early adolescence, a time of mild parent–child conflict. As family relationships readjust to the young person's increasing autonomy, self-disclosure to parents rises. *(From D. Buhrmester, 1996, "Need Fulfillment, Interpersonal Competence, and the Developmental Contexts of Early Adolescent Friendship," in W. M. Bukowski, A. F. Newcomb, & W. W. Hartup, Eds.,* The Company They Keep: Friendship During Childhood and Adolescence, *New York: Cambridge University Press, p. 168. Reprinted with the permission of Cambridge University Press.)*

Adolescent friendships—especially, best friendships—are fairly stable and become more so with age (Degirmencioglu et al., 1998). Nevertheless, the transition to middle school brings changes in friendships as teenagers encounter new peers and become interested in romantic relationships (Chan & Poulin, 2007; Hardy, Bukowski, & Sippola, 2002). And for a time, young teenagers often sacrifice similarity for admiration of superficial features—whether a potential friend is popular, physically attractive, athletically skilled, or defiant and aggressive (Bukowski, Sippola, & Newcomb, 2000).

Over time, preference for friends who are prominent in the peer system subsides, and adolescents return to seeking friends whose traits, interests, and values resemble their own. Nevertheless, occasionally a friend's differing, positive traits have a favorable impact. In one study, low-achieving early adolescents who befriended a high-achieving classmate improved in academic performance (Altermatt & Pomerantz, 2005).

SEX DIFFERENCES IN FRIENDSHIP QUALITY   TAKE A MOMENT... Ask several adolescent girls and boys to describe their close friendships. You are likely to find a consistent sex difference. Emotional closeness is more common between girls (Markovits, Benenson, & Dolenszky, 2001). Girls frequently get together to "just talk," and their exchanges contain more self-disclosure and mutually supportive statements. In contrast, boys more often gather for an activity—usually sports and competitive games. Boys' discussions usually focus on accomplishments and mastery issues, such as attainments in sports and school, and involve more competition and conflict (Brendgen et al., 2001; Rubin, Bukowski, & Parker, 2006).

Because of gender-role expectations, girls' friendships typically focus on communal concerns, boys' on achievement and status. Boys do form close friendship ties, but the quality of their friendships is more variable. Gender identity plays a role: Androgynous boys are just as likely as girls to form intimate same-sex ties, whereas highly "masculine" boys are less likely to do so (Jones & Dembo, 1989).

Friendship closeness, though usually beneficial, can have costs. When focusing on deeper thoughts and feelings, adolescent friends tend to *coruminate,* or repeatedly mull over problems and negative emotions. Corumination, while contributing to high friendship quality, also triggers anxiety and depression—symptoms more common among girls than among boys (Hankin, Stone, & Wright, 2010; Rose, Carlson, & Waller, 2007). And when conflict arises between intimate friends, more potential exists for one party to harm the other through relational aggression—for example, by divulging sensitive personal information to outsiders.

Partly for this reason, girls' closest same-sex friendships tend to be of shorter duration than boys' (Benenson & Christakos, 2003). Also, whereas boys often resolve conflicts by minimizing their importance ("It's no big deal"), this strategy tends to result in friendship break-up among girls (Bowker, 2004). When friendships are emotionally intense, minimizing rather than confronting disagreement may restore superficial harmony but engender avoidance of self-disclosure, making the friendship less stable.

For adolescents of both genders, number of other-sex friends increases with age, though same-sex friends remain more common. Girls have more other-sex friends than boys, a difference that widens with age as teenage girls form friendships with boys who are somewhat older (Poulin & Pedersen, 2007). Early maturing girls have larger networks of other-sex friends, including older boys— relationships that can become contexts for antisocial behavior (see page 543 in Chapter 14).

Regardless of the gender make-up of friendships, adolescents report that girls provide more emotional support than boys (Kuttler, La Greca, & Prinstein, 1999; Poulin & Pedersen, 2007). Among boys without same-sex friends, having an other-sex friend is associated with feelings of competence. But among girls who lack same-sex friends, other-sex friendships are linked to less positive well-being (Bukowski, Sippola, & Hoza, 1999). Perhaps these girls are especially likely to befriend boys with negative traits, such as aggression.

© MYRLEEN FERGUSON CATE/PHOTOEDIT

■ Compared to boys, girls place a higher value on emotional closeness, engaging in more self-disclosure and mutually supportive statements with friends. ■

FRIENDSHIPS ON THE INTERNET   Teenagers frequently use the Internet to communicate with friends. Cell-phone texting and instant messaging—their preferred means of online interaction—seem to support friendship closeness (Lenhart, 2010). As amount of instant messaging between preexisting friends increases, so do young people's perceptions of intimacy in the relationship and feelings of well-being (Hu et al., 2004; Valkenburg & Peter, 2007a, 2007b).

Although mostly communicating with friends they know, adolescents are also drawn to meeting new people over the Internet. Social networking sites such as MySpace and Facebook, which are now used by nearly 75 percent of U.S. teenagers, along with blogs, message boards, and chat rooms, open up vast alternatives beyond their families, schools, and communities (Lenhart et al., 2010). Through these online ties, young people explore central adolescent concerns—sexuality, challenges in parent and peer relationships, and identity issues, including attitudes and values—in contexts that may feel less threatening than similar everyday conversations (Subrahmanyam, Smahel, & Greenfield, 2006). Online interactions with strangers also offer some teenagers vital social support. Young people suffering from eating disorders, depression, and other problems can access message boards where participants provide mutual assistance, including a sense of group belonging and acceptance (Whitlock, Powers, & Eckenrode, 2006).

But online communication also poses dangers. In unmonitored chat rooms, teenagers are likely to encounter degrading racial and ethnic slurs and sexually obscene and harassing remarks (Tynes, Reynolds, & Greenfield, 2004). And regardless of whether teen chat rooms are adult monitored, requests for romantic partners occur as frequently as two times per minute, with females initiating these slightly more often than males (Smahel & Subrahmanyam, 2007). In a survey of a nationally representative sample of U.S. 10- to 17-year-olds, 14 percent reported having formed online friendships or romances (Wolak, Mitchell, & Finkelhor, 2003). Although some of these youths were well-adjusted, many reported high levels of conflict with parents, peer victimization, depression, and delinquency and spent extensive time on the Internet (see Figure 16.4). They also more often had been asked by online friends for face-to-face meetings and had attended those meetings—without telling their parents.

The Internet's value for enabling convenient and satisfying communication among teenage friends must be weighed against its potential for facilitating harmful social experiences. Parents are wise to point out the risks of Internet communication, including harassment and exploitation, and to insist that teenagers follow Internet safety rules (see *www.safeteens.com*). Yet in a study of several hundred adolescent MySpace users and their parents, nearly half of the teenagers indicated that their page disclosed such personal information as their full name and e-mail address. More than one-third of the parents had never viewed their teenager's MySpace page, and over 70 percent placed no limits on MySpace use (Rosen, Cheever, & Carrier, 2008).

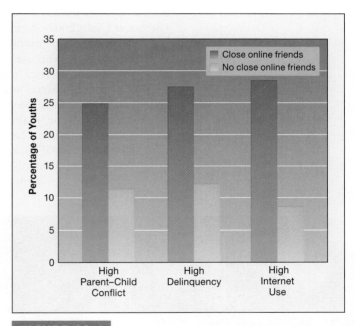

FIGURE 16.4

Association of close online friendships with parent–child conflict, delinquency, and high Internet use. In this survey of a nationally representative sample of 1,500 U.S. Internet-using 10- to 17-year-olds, those who reported that they had formed close online friendships or romances were more likely to be troubled youths who spent much time on the Internet. *(Adapted from Wolak, Mitchell, & Finkelhor, 2003.)*

FRIENDSHIP AND ADJUSTMENT   As long as adolescent friendships are high in trust, intimate sharing, and support and not characterized by relational aggression or attraction to antisocial behavior, they contribute to many aspects of psychological health and competence (Bukowski, 2001; Waldrip, 2008), for several reasons:

■ *Close friendships provide opportunities to explore the self and develop a deep understanding of another.* Through open, honest communication, friends become sensitive to each other's strengths and weaknesses, needs and desires—a process that supports the development of self-concept, perspective taking, and identity.

- *Close friendships provide a foundation for future intimate relationships.* Recall from Figure 16.3 that self-disclosure to friends precedes disclosure to romantic partners. Conversations with teenage friends about sexuality and romance, along with the intimacy of friendship itself, may help adolescents establish and work out problems in romantic partnerships (Connolly & Goldberg, 1999).
- *Close friendships help young people deal with the stresses of adolescence.* By enhancing sensitivity to and concern for another, supportive friendships promote empathy, sympathy, and prosocial behavior. As a result, they contribute to involvement in constructive youth activities, avoidance of antisocial acts, and psychological well-being (Lansford et al., 2003; Wentzel, Barry, & Caldwell, 2004).
- *Close friendships can improve adolescents' attitudes toward and involvement in school.* Close friendships promote good school adjustment, academically and socially, in both middle- and low-SES students (Berndt & Murphy, 2002; Wentzel, Barry, & Caldwell, 2004). When teenagers enjoy interacting with friends at school, they may begin to view all aspects of school life more positively.

Cliques and Crowds

In early adolescence, *peer groups* (see Chapter 13) become increasingly common and tightly knit. They are organized into **cliques**—groups of about five to eight members who are friends and, therefore, usually resemble one another in family background, attitudes, and values (Brown & Dietz, 2009). At first, cliques are limited to same-sex members. Among girls but not boys, being in a clique predicts academic and social competence. Clique membership is more important to girls, who use it as a context for expressing emotional closeness (Henrich et al., 2000). By midadolescence, mixed-sex cliques are common.

Often several cliques with similar values form a larger, more loosely organized group called a **crowd.** Unlike the more intimate clique, membership in a crowd is based on reputation and stereotype, granting the adolescent an identity within the larger social structure of the school. Prominent crowds in a typical high school might include "brains" (nonathletes who enjoy academics), "jocks" (who are very involved in sports), "populars" (class leaders who are highly social and involved in activities), "partyers" (who value socializing but care little about schoolwork), "nonconformists" (who like unconventional clothing and music), "burnouts" (who cut school and get into trouble), and "normals" (average to good students who get along with most other peers) (Kinney, 1999; Stone & Brown, 1999).

What influences the assortment of teenagers into cliques and crowds? Crowd affiliations are linked to strengths in adolescents' self-concepts, which reflect their abilities and interests (Prinstein & LaGreca, 2002). Ethnicity also plays a role. Minority teenagers who associate with an ethnically defined crowd, as opposed to a crowd reflecting their abilities and interests, sometimes are motivated by discrimination in their school or neighborhood. Alternatively, they may have joined the crowd as an expression of a strong ethnic orientation (Brown et al., 2008). Family factors are important, too. In a study of 8,000 ninth to twelfth graders, adolescents who described their parents as authoritative were members of "brain," "jock," and "popular" groups that accepted both adult and peer reward systems. In contrast, boys with permissive parents aligned themselves with "partyers" and "burnouts," suggesting lack of identification with adult reward systems (Durbin et al., 1993).

■ These high school drama club members form a crowd, establishing relationships on the basis of shared interests. Crowd membership grants them an identity within the larger social structure of the school. ■

© THE STAR-LEDGER/BILL PERLMAN/THE IMAGE WORKS

These findings indicate that many peer-group values are extensions of values acquired at home. Once adolescents join a clique or crowd, it can modify their beliefs and behavior. In research on crowd affiliation and health-risk behaviors, brains were the lowest risk takers, populars and jocks were intermediate, and nonconformists and burnouts were the highest, often engaging in unhealthy eating, substance use, and unprotected sex and agreeing that they would "do anything on a dare" (LaGreca, Prinstein, & Fetter, 2001; Mackey & La Greca, 2007). But the positive impact of having academically and socially skilled peers is greatest for teenagers whose own parents are authoritative. And the negative impact of having antisocial, drug-using friends is strongest for teenagers whose parents use less effective child-rearing styles (Mounts & Steinberg, 1995). In sum, family experiences affect the extent to which teenagers become like other group members over time.

As interest in dating increases, boys' and girls' cliques come together. Mixed-sex cliques provide boys and girls with models of how to interact and a chance to do so without having to be intimate (Connolly et al., 2004). Gradually, the larger group divides into couples, several of whom spend time going out together. By late adolescence, when boys and girls feel comfortable about approaching each other directly, the mixed-sex clique disappears (Connolly & Goldberg, 1999).

Crowds also decline in importance. As adolescents settle on personal values and goals, they no longer feel a need to broadcast, through dress, language, and preferred activities, who they are. From tenth to twelfth grade, about half of young people switch crowds, mostly in favorable directions (Strouse, 1999). "Brains" and "normal" crowds grow and deviant crowds lose members as teenagers focus more on their future.

Both cliques and crowds serve vital functions. The clique provides a context for acquiring social skills and experimenting with values and roles. The crowd offers the security of a temporary identity as adolescents separate from the family and construct a coherent sense of self (Newman & Newman, 2001).

Dating

The hormonal changes of puberty increase sexual interest (see Chapter 14), but cultural expectations determine when and how dating begins. Asian youths start dating later and have fewer dating partners than young people in Western societies, which tolerate and even encourage romantic involvements between teenagers from middle school on (see Figure 16.5). At age 12 to 14, these relationships are usually casual, lasting only briefly. By age 16, they have become steady relationships, continuing, on average, for nearly two years (Carver, Joyner, & Udry, 2003). Early adolescents tend to mention recreation and achieving peer status as reasons for dating. By late adolescence, as young people are ready for greater intimacy, they look for someone who offers companionship, affection, and social support (Collins & van Dulmen, 2006a; Meier & Allen, 2009).

The achievement of intimacy between dating partners typically lags behind that between friends. And positive relationships with parents and friends contribute to the development of warm romantic ties, whereas conflict-ridden parent–adolescent and peer relationships forecast hostile dating interactions (Connolly, Furman, & Konarski, 2000; Furman & Collins, 2009). Recall from Chapter 7 that according to ethological theory, early attachment bonds lead to an *internal working model,* or set of expectations about attachment figures, that guides later close relationships. Consistent with this idea, secure attachment to parents in infancy and childhood—together with recollections of that security in adolescence—predicts quality of teenagers' and young adults' friendships and romantic ties

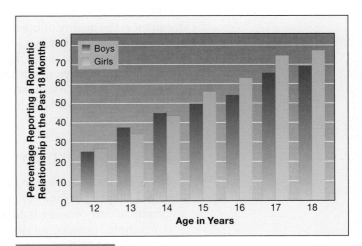

FIGURE 16.5

Increase in romantic relationships in adolescence. More than 16,000 U.S. youths responded to an interview in which they indicated whether they had been involved in a romantic relationship during the past 18 months. At age 12, about one-fourth of young people reported romantic involvement, a figure that rose to about three-fourths at age 18. *(Adapted from Carver, Joyner, & Udry, 2003.)*

© SPENCER GRANT/PHOTOEDIT

■ As long as dating does not begin too soon, it extends the benefits of adolescent friendships, promoting sensitivity, empathy, and identity development. ■

(Collins & van Dulmen, 2006b; Collins, Welsh, & Furman, 2009). In a study of high school seniors, secure models of attachment and supportive interactions with parents predicted secure models of friendship, which, in turn, were related to the security of romantic relationships (Furman et al., 2002).

Perhaps because early adolescent dating relationships are shallow and stereotyped, early dating is related to drug use, delinquency, and poor academic achievement (Eaton et al., 2007; Zimmer-Gembeck, Siebenbruner, & Collins, 2001). These factors, along with a history of uninvolved parenting and aggression in family and peer relationships, increase the likelihood of dating violence. About 10 to 20 percent of adolescents are physically or sexually abused by dating partners, with boys and girls equally likely to report being victims, and violence by one partner often returned by the other (Cyr, McDuff, & Wright, 2006; Williams et al., 2008). Mental health consequences are severe, including increased anxiety, depression, suicide attempts, risky sexual behavior, and—in girls—unhealthy weight control (vomiting and use of laxatives) (Carver, Joyner, & Udry, 2003; Silverman et al., 2001; Werkerle & Avgoustis, 2003). Furthermore, whereas early adolescent boys who date gain in status among same-sex peers, girls often experience conflict due to competition and jealousy of other girls. For all these reasons, sticking with group activities, such as parties and dances, before becoming involved with a steady boyfriend or girlfriend is best for young teenagers.

Gay and lesbian youths face special challenges in initiating and maintaining visible romances. Their first dating relationships seem to be short-lived and to involve little emotional commitment, but for reasons different from those of heterosexuals: They fear peer harassment and rejection (Diamond & Lucas, 2004). Recall from Chapter 14 that because of intense prejudice, homosexual adolescents often retreat into heterosexual dating. In addition, many have difficulty finding a same-sex partner because their homosexual peers have not yet come out. Often their first contacts with other sexual-minority youths occur in support groups, where they are free to date publicly and can discuss concerns about coming out (Diamond, 2003).

As long as it does not begin too soon, dating provides lessons in cooperation, etiquette, and dealing with people in a wide range of situations. Among older teenagers, close romantic ties promote sensitivity, empathy, self-esteem, social support, and identity development. In addition, teenagers' increasing capacity for interdependence and compromise within dating enhances the quality of other peer relationships (Collins, Welsh, & Furman, 2009).

Still, about half of first romances do not survive high school graduation, and those that do usually become less satisfying (Shaver, Furman, & Buhrmester, 1985). Because young people are still forming their identities, high school couples often find that they have little in common later. Nevertheless, warm, caring romantic ties in adolescence can have long-term implications. They are positively related to gratifying, committed relationships in early adulthood (Meier & Allen, 2009).

Peer Conformity

When Franca and Antonio discovered Louis's lawbreaking during his freshman year of high school, they began to worry about the negative side of adolescent peer networks. Although conformity to peer pressure is greater during adolescence than in childhood or early adulthood, it is a complex process, varying with the young person's age, current situation, need for social approval, and culture.

A study of several hundred U.S. youths revealed that adolescents felt greatest pressure to conform to the most obvious aspects of the peer culture—dress, grooming, and participation in social activities. Peer pressure to engage in proadult behavior, such as cooperating with parents and getting good grades, was also strong (Brown, Lohr, & McClenahan, 1986). Many teenagers said that their friends actively discouraged antisocial acts. In research conducted in Singapore, a culture that emphasizes family loyalty, outcomes were similar, except that peer pressure to meet family and school obligations exceeded pressure to join in peer-culture pursuits (Sim & Koh, 2003). As these findings reveal, peers and parents often act in concert, toward desirable ends!

Early adolescents are especially likely to give in to peer pressure to engage in drug taking and delinquent acts (Brown, Clasen, & Eicher, 1986; McIntosh, MacDonald, & McKeganey, 2006). Recall from Chapter 14 that changes in the brain at puberty contribute to both increased reward seeking and receptiveness to peer influence.

Resistance to peer pressure strengthens gradually with age, though wide individual differences exist (Steinberg & Monahan, 2007). Personal characteristics make a difference: Young people who feel competent and worthwhile, who score low in sensation-seeking, and who are more effective decision makers are less likely to fall in line with peer antisocial activity (Crocket, Raffaelli, & Shen, 2006; Steinberg, 2001). Authoritative child rearing is also influential. When parents are supportive and exert appropriate oversight, teenagers respect them—an attitude that acts as an antidote to unfavorable peer pressure (Dorius et al., 2004). In contrast, adolescents whose parents exert either too much or too little control tend to be highly peer-oriented (Allen, Porter, & McFarland, 2006). They more often rely on friends for advice about their personal lives and future plans and are more willing to break their parents' rules, ignore their schoolwork, and engage in other problem behaviors.

ASK YOURSELF

◆ REVIEW Describe the distinct positive functions of friendships, cliques, and crowds in adolescence. What factors lead some friendships and peer-group ties to be harmful?

◆ APPLY Thirteen-year-old Mattie's parents are warm, firm in their expectations, and consistent in monitoring her activities. At school, Mattie met some girls who want her to tell her parents she's going to a friend's house and then, instead, join them at the beach for a party. Is Mattie likely to comply? Explain.

◆ CONNECT How might gender intensification, discussed on page 618, contribute to the shallow quality of early adolescent dating relationships?

◆ REFLECT How did family experiences influence your crowd membership in high school? How did crowd membership influence your behavior?

Problems of Development

Most young people move through adolescence with little disturbance. But as we have seen, some encounter major disruptions in development, such as early parenthood, substance abuse, and school failure. In each instance, biological and psychological changes, families, schools, peers, communities, and culture combine to yield particular outcomes. Serious difficulties rarely occur in isolation but are usually interrelated—as is apparent in three additional problems of the teenage years: depression, suicide, and delinquency.

Depression

Depression—feeling sad, frustrated, and hopeless about life, accompanied by loss of pleasure in most activities and disturbances in sleep, appetite, concentration, and energy—is the most common psychological problem of adolescence. Among U.S. teenagers, 20 to 50 percent experience mild to moderate feelings of depression, bouncing back after a short time. More worrisome are the 15 to 20 percent who have had one or more major depressive episodes, a rate comparable to that of adults. From 2 to 8 percent are chronically depressed—gloomy and self-critical for many months and sometimes years (Graber & Sontag, 2009; Rushton, Forcier, & Schectman, 2002).

■ Depression in teenagers should not be dismissed as just a passing phase. Without treatment, it can persist, leading to long-term adjustment problems. ■

Serious depression affects only 1 to 2 percent of children, many of whom (especially girls) remain depressed in adolescence. In addition, depression increases sharply from ages 12 to 16 in industrialized nations, with many more girls than boys displaying adolescent onset of symptoms. Teenage girls are twice as likely as boys to report persistent depressed mood—a sex difference sustained throughout the lifespan (Dekker et al., 2007; Hankin & Abela, 2005; Nolen-Hoeksema, 2002).

If allowed to continue, depression seriously impairs social, academic, and vocational functioning. Unfortunately, the stereotypical view of adolescence as a period of storm and stress leads many adults to minimize the seriousness of adolescent depression, misinterpreting it as just a passing phase. As a result, the overwhelming majority of depressed teenagers do not receive treatment (Asarnow et al., 2005).

FACTORS RELATED TO ADOLESCENT DEPRESSION The precise combination of biological and environmental factors leading to depression varies from one individual to the next. Kinship studies reveal that heredity plays an important role (Glowinski et al., 2003). Genes can induce depression by affecting the balance of neurotransmitters in the brain, the development of brain regions involved in inhibiting negative emotion, or the body's hormonal response to stress (Kaufman & Charney, 2003).

But experience can also activate depression, promoting any of these biological changes. A high incidence of depression and other psychological disorders is seen in parents of depressed children and adolescents. Although a genetic risk may be passed from parent to child, in earlier chapters we saw that depressed or otherwise stressed parents often engage in maladaptive parenting. As a result, their child's emotional self-regulation, attachment, and self-esteem may be impaired, with serious consequences for many cognitive and social skills (Abela et al., 2005; Yap, Allen, & Ladouceur, 2008). Depressed youths usually display a learned-helpless attributional style (see Chapter 13), viewing positive academic and social outcomes as beyond their control (Graber, 2004). In a vulnerable young person, numerous negative life events can spark depression—for example, failing at something important, parental divorce, the end of a close friendship or romantic partnership, or the challenges of school transition.

SEX DIFFERENCES Why are girls more prone to depression than boys? Biological changes associated with puberty cannot be solely responsible because the gender difference is limited to industrialized nations. In developing countries, rates of depression are similar for males and females and occasionally higher in males (Culbertson, 1997). Even in nations where females exceed males in depression, the size of the difference varies.

Instead, stressful life events and gender-typed coping styles seem to be involved. Early-maturing girls are especially prone to depression (see Chapter 14). And the gender intensification of early adolescence often strengthens passivity, dependency, and tendency to ruminate on their anxieties and problems—maladaptive approaches to the tasks expected of teenagers in complex cultures. Consistent with this explanation, adolescents who identify strongly with "feminine" traits ruminate more and are more depressed, regardless of their sex (Broderick & Korteland, 2004; Papadakis et al., 2006). Girls who repeatedly feel overwhelmed develop an overly reactive physiological stress response and cope more poorly with future challenges (Hyde, Mezulis, & Abramson, 2008;

■ In China, depression is more common in boys than in girls—a reversal of the sex difference typically found in industrialized nations. Chinese boys report a higher level of stressful life events, including parental pressures and school performance expectations. ■

Nolen-Hoeksema, 2006). In this way, stressful experiences and stress reactivity feed on one another, sustaining depression.

An investigation of more than 17,000 youths from eight large cities in China underscores the contribution of both stressors and ineffective coping to depression. More Chinese boys than girls said they had felt depressed in the previous week. But boys also reported higher levels of stressful life events, resulting from parental pressures, school performance expectations, health problems, and romantic involvements (Sun et al., 2010). Adaptive coping was linked to reduced depression in both Chinese boys and girls.

Profound depression in adolescence predicts depression in adulthood and serious impairments in work, family life, and social life. And depression often leads to suicidal thoughts, which all too often are translated into action.

Suicide

Compared with his sister, who was an outstanding student, 17-year-old Brad couldn't measure up. With adulthood just around the corner, Brad's parents berated him for his lack of direction. "At your age, you oughta have a clue about where you're going!" Brad's father shouted. "Pick a college, get a trade—just stop sitting around!"

In high school, Brad had been a loner. He excelled in art class and spent hours in his room, sketching. But although Brad's parents worried that he seemed unhappy and didn't have many friends, they never showed much interest in his drawings, which were piled in a corner of his room. And they consoled themselves that at least he wasn't getting into trouble.

One day, Brad got up enough nerve to ask a girl out. His father, encouraged by Brad's interest in dating, gave him permission to use the family car. But when Brad arrived to pick up the girl, she wasn't home. Several hours later, Brad's parents got a call from the police. He had been picked up for speeding, "driving under the influence," and evading the police. The chase through city streets ended when Brad drove into a ditch. Although he wasn't injured, the car was totaled. A terrible argument followed between Brad and his parents.

Over the next two days, Brad was somber and withdrawn. Then, after dinner one night, he seemed resolved to make things better. "I've taken care of things. I won't cause any more problems," he told his parents. Handing several of his favorite drawings to his sister, he said, "Here, I want you to have these—for keeps, to think of me." Early the next morning, Brad's parents found him hanging from a rope in his room.

FACTORS RELATED TO ADOLESCENT SUICIDE The suicide rate increases from childhood to old age, but it jumps sharply at adolescence. Currently, suicide is the third-leading cause of death among American youths, after motor vehicle collisions and homicides. Perhaps because U.S. teenagers experience more stress and fewer supports than in the past, the adolescent suicide rate tripled between the mid-1960s and the mid-1990s, followed by a slight decline (Spirito & Esposito-Smythers, 2006; U.S. Census Bureau, 2010b). At the same time, rates of adolescent suicide vary widely among industrialized nations—low in Greece, Italy, the Netherlands, and Spain; intermediate in Australia, Canada, Japan, and the United States; and high in Finland, New Zealand, and Singapore (Bridge, Goldstein, & Brent, 2006). These international differences remain unexplained.

Striking sex differences in suicidal behavior exist. Despite girls' higher rates of depression, the number of boys who kill themselves exceeds the number of girls by a ratio of 3 or 4 to 1. Girls make more unsuccessful suicide attempts and use methods from which they are more likely to be revived, such as a sleeping pill overdose. In contrast, boys tend to choose techniques that lead to instant death, such as firearms or hanging. Gender-role expectations may contribute; less tolerance exists for feelings of helplessness and failed efforts in males than in females.

Perhaps because of greater extended-family support, African Americans and Hispanics have slightly lower suicide rates than Caucasian Americans. Recently, however, suicide has risen among Hispanic adolescents and African-American males, for whom the current rate approaches that of Caucasian-American males. And Native-American youths commit suicide at rates two to six times national averages (Balis & Postolache, 2008; U.S. Census Bureau, 2010b). High rates of profound family poverty, school failure, alcohol and drug use, and depression probably underlie these trends—factors that also make homeless, runaway, and imprisoned youths prone to suicide (Spirito & Esposito-Smythers, 2006).

Gay, lesbian, and bisexual youths also are at high risk, attempting suicide three times as often as other adolescents. Those who have tried to kill themselves report more family conflict over their gender-atypical behavior, inner turmoil about their sexuality, and peer victimization due to their sexual orientation (D'Augelli et al., 2005).

Suicide tends to occur in two types of young people. The first group includes adolescents much like Brad—highly intelligent but solitary, withdrawn, and unable to meet their own standards or those of important people in their lives. Members of the second, larger group show antisocial tendencies and express their unhappiness through bullying, fighting, stealing, increased risk taking, and drug abuse (Evans, Hawton, & Rodham, 2004). Besides being hostile and destructive toward others, they turn their anger and disappointment inward.

Suicidal adolescents often have a family history of emotional and antisocial disorders and suicide. In addition, they are likely to have experienced multiple stressful life events, including economic disadvantage, parental divorce, frequent parent–child conflict, and abuse and neglect. Stressors typically increase during the period preceding a suicide attempt or completion (Beautrais, 2003; Pfeffer, 2006). Triggering events include parental blaming of the teenager for family problems, the breakup of an important peer relationship, or the humiliation of having been caught engaging in antisocial acts.

Public policies resulting in cultural disintegration have amplified suicide rates among Native-American youths. From the late 1800s to the 1970s, Native-American families were forced to enroll their children in government-run residential boarding schools designed to erase tribal affiliations. In these repressive institutions, children were not allowed to "be Indian" in any way—culturally, linguistically, artistically, or spiritually (Goldston et al., 2008). The experience left many young people academically unprepared and emotionally scarred, contributing to family and community disorganization in current and succeeding generations. Consequently, youth crime and suicide rates escalated (Barnes, Josefowitz, & Cole, 2006; Howell & Yuille, 2004).

Why does suicide increase in adolescence? One factor seems to be teenagers' improved ability to plan ahead. Although some act impulsively, many young people, like Brad, take purposeful steps toward killing themselves. Furthermore, depressed youths' learned helplessness greatly increases the likelihood that, when faced with a stressful event, their despair, hopelessness, and isolation will deepen. Suicidal behavior often recurs, with about 10 percent of attempters trying again within 6 months and more than 40 percent within 21 months (Hawton, Zahl, & Weatherall, 2003).

PREVENTION AND TREATMENT To prevent suicides, parents and teachers must be trained to pick up on the signals that a troubled teenager sends (see Table 16.3). Schools and community settings, such as recreational and religious organizations, can help by strengthening adolescents' connections with their cultural heritage and providing knowledgeable, approachable, and sympathetic adults, peer support groups, and information about telephone hot lines (Goldston et al., 2008; Spirito et al., 2003). Once a teenager takes steps toward suicide, staying with the young person, listening, and expressing compassion and concern until professional help can be obtained are essential. Applying What We Know on the following page offers suggestions for how to respond to a young person who might be suicidal.

Treatments for depressed and suicidal adolescents range from antidepressant medication to individual,

TABLE 16.3 Warning Signs of Suicide

Efforts to put personal affairs in order—smoothing over troubled relationships, giving away treasured possessions
Verbal cues—saying goodbye to family members and friends, making direct or indirect references to suicide ("I won't have to worry about these problems much longer"; "I wish I were dead")
Feelings of sadness, despondency, "not caring" anymore
Extreme fatigue, lack of energy, boredom
No desire to socialize; withdrawal from friends
Easily frustrated
Emotional outbursts—spells of crying or laughing, bursts of energy
Inability to concentrate, distractibility
Decline in grades, absence from school, discipline problems
Neglect of personal appearance
Sleep change—loss of sleep or excessive sleepiness
Appetite change—eating more or less than usual
Physical complaints—stomachaches, backaches, headaches

Applying What We Know

Ways to Respond to a Young Person Who Might Be Suicidal

STRATEGY	DESCRIPTION
Be psychologically and physically available.	Grant the young person your full attention, indicate when and where you can be located, and emphasize that you are always willing to talk.
Communicate a caring, capable attitude.	With such statements as "I'm concerned. I care about you," encourage the adolescent to discuss feelings of despair. Conveying a capable attitude helps redirect the young person away from a world of confusion toward psychological order.
Assess the immediacy of risk.	Gently inquire into the young person's motives: "Do you want to harm yourself? Do you want to die or kill yourself?" If the answer is yes, ask about the adolescent's plan. If it is specific (involving a method and a time), the risk of suicide is high.
Empathize with the young person's feelings.	Express empathy through such statements as "I understand your confusion and pain." Empathy increases your persuasive power and defuses the adolescent's negative emotion.
Oppose the suicidal intent.	Communicate sensitively but firmly that suicide is not an acceptable solution and that you want to help the adolescent explore other options.
Offer a plan for help.	Offer to assist the young person in finding professional help and in telling others, such as parents and school officials, who need to know about the problem.
Obtain a commitment.	Ask the adolescent to agree to the plan. If the young person refuses, negotiate a promise to contact you or another supportive person if and when suicidal thoughts return.

Source: Kirk, 1993.

family, and group therapy. Sometimes hospitalization is necessary to ensure the teenager's safety. Until the adolescent improves, removing weapons, knives, razors, scissors, and drugs from the home is vital. Strengthening social supports and training young people in effective strategies for coping with stress and depressed mood promote resilience and can prevent repeated suicide attempts (Asarnow et al., 2005; Kalafat, 2005). On a broader scale, gun-control legislation that limits adolescents' access to the most frequent and deadly suicide method in the United States would greatly reduce both the number of suicides and the high teenage homicide rate (Commission on Adolescent Suicide Prevention, 2005).

After a suicide, family and peer survivors need support to help them cope with grief, anger, and guilt over not having been able to help the victim. Teenage suicides often occur in clusters, with one death increasing the likelihood of others among depressed peers who knew the young person or heard about the death through the media (Bearman & Moody, 2004; Feigelman & Gorman, 2008). In view of this trend, an especially watchful eye must be kept on vulnerable adolescents after a suicide happens. Restraint by journalists in publicizing teenage suicides also aids prevention.

■ Individual, family, and group therapy can prevent repeated suicide attempts by helping adolescents develop effective strategies to cope with stress and depressed mood. ■

Delinquency

Juvenile delinquents are children or adolescents who engage in illegal acts. Youth crime has declined in the United States since the mid-1990s. Nevertheless, 12- to 17-year-olds account for about 14 percent of police arrests, although they constitute only 8 percent of the population

Delinquency rises over early and middle adolescence, mostly involving petty stealing and disorderly conduct. But a small percentage of young people engage in repeated serious offenses and are at risk for a life of crime. ■

(U.S. Department of Justice, 2010). When asked directly and confidentially about lawbreaking, almost all teenagers admit to having committed some sort of offense—usually a minor crime, such as petty stealing or disorderly conduct (Flannery et al., 2003).

Both police arrests and self-reports show that delinquency rises over early and middle adolescence and then declines (Farrington, 2009; U.S. Department of Justice, 2010). Recall that antisocial behavior increases among teenagers as a result of heightened reward seeking and desire for peer approval. Over time, peers become less influential; decision making, emotional self-regulation, and moral reasoning improve; and young people enter social contexts (such as higher education, work, marriage, and career) that are less conducive to lawbreaking.

For most adolescents, a brush with the law does not forecast long-term antisocial behavior. But repeated arrests are cause for concern. Teenagers are responsible for 15 percent of violent offenses in the United States (U.S. Department of Justice, 2010). A small percentage become recurrent offenders, who commit most of these crimes, and some enter a life of crime. As the Biology and Environment box on pages 636–637 reveals, childhood-onset conduct problems are far more likely to persist than conduct problems that first appear in adolescence.

FACTORS RELATED TO DELINQUENCY In adolescence, the gender gap in physical aggression widens (Chesney-Lind, 2001). Although girls account for about one in five adolescent arrests for violence, their offenses are largely limited to simple assault (such as pushing and spitting), the least serious category. Once labeled status offenses (noncriminal behavior), today these acts are more likely to lead to arrests, especially in physical exchanges with parents, who may report the youth's behavior to the police (Chesney-Lind & Belknap, 2004). Serious violent crime is mostly the domain of boys (Dahlberg & Simon, 2006).

SES and ethnicity are strong predictors of arrests but only mildly related to teenagers' self-reports of antisocial acts. The difference is due to the tendency to arrest, charge, and punish low-SES ethnic minority youths more often than their higher-SES white and Asian counterparts (Farrington, 2004; U.S. Department of Justice, 2010). In isolation from other life circumstances, ethnicity tells us little about youths' propensity to engage in violence and other lawbreaking acts.

Difficult temperament, low intelligence, poor school performance, peer rejection in childhood, and association with antisocial peers are linked to chronic delinquency (Laird et al., 2005). How do these factors fit together? One of the most consistent findings about delinquent youths is that their families are low in warmth, high in conflict, and characterized by inconsistent discipline and low monitoring (Barnes et al., 2006; Capaldi et al., 2002). Because marital transitions often contribute to family discord and disrupted parenting, boys who experience parental separation and divorce are especially prone to delinquency (Farrington, 2004). And youth crime peaks on weekdays between 2:00 and 8:00 P.M., when many teenagers are unsupervised (U.S. Department of Justice, 2010).

Our discussion on page 387 in Chapter 10 explained how ineffective parenting can promote and sustain children's aggression, with boys—who are more active and impulsive— more often targets of parental anger, physical punishment, and inconsistency. When these child temperamental traits combine with emotionally negative, inept parenting, aggression rises sharply during childhood, leads to violent offenses in adolescence, and persists into adulthood (again, see the Biology and Environment box).

Disruptive, peer-rejected children and adolescents relieve their loneliness by seeking out antisocial friends, who facilitate one another's violent, antisocial behavior (Lacourse et al., 2003). Delinquent youths seem to stick with these friends to avoid social isolation and to bolster their fragile self-esteem. Indeed, many aggressive youths report overly high self-esteem.

When their arrogant, cocky behavior prompts others to challenge their inflated but vulnerable self-image, they lash out angrily (Costello & Dunaway, 2003; Orobio de Castro et al., 2007).

Teenagers commit more crimes in poverty-stricken neighborhoods with limited recreational and employment opportunities and high adult criminality (Hay et al., 2007; Kroneman, Loeber, & Hipwell, 2004). In such neighborhoods, adolescents have easy access to deviant peers, drugs, and firearms and are likely to be recruited into antisocial gangs, whose members commit the vast majority of violent delinquent acts. Furthermore, schools in these locales typically fail to meet students' developmental needs (Flannery et al., 2003). Large classes, weak instruction, and rigid rules with harsh consequences for infractions may increase teenagers' inclination toward defiance and aggression.

PREVENTION AND TREATMENT　Because delinquency has roots in childhood and results from events in several contexts, prevention must start early and take place at multiple levels (Frey et al., 2009). Positive family relationships, authoritative parenting, high-quality teaching in schools, well-designed work–study vocational education programs, and communities with healthy economic and social conditions go a long way toward reducing adolescent antisocial acts.

Lacking resources for effective prevention, many U.S. schools have implemented *zero tolerance policies,* which severely punish all disruptive and threatening behavior, major and minor, usually with suspension or expulsion. Yet often these policies are implemented inconsistently: Low-SES minority students are two to three times as likely to be punished, especially for minor misbehaviors (Goode & Goode, 2007; Skiba & Rausch, 2006). No evidence exists that zero tolerance achieves its objective of reducing youth aggression and other forms of misconduct (Stinchcomb, Bazemore, & Riestenberg, 2006). To the contrary, some studies find that by excluding students from school, zero tolerance heightens high school dropout and antisocial behavior.

Treating serious offenders requires an intensive, often lengthy approach that is also directed at the multiple determinants of delinquency. The most effective approaches include training parents in communication, monitoring, and discipline strategies and providing youths with experiences that improve cognitive and social skills, moral reasoning, anger management, and other aspects of emotional self-regulation (Gibbs et al., 2009b; Heilbrun, Lee, & Cottle, 2005).

Yet even these multidimensional treatments can fall short if adolescents remain embedded in hostile home lives, poor-quality schools, antisocial peer groups, and violent neighborhoods. In a program called *multisystemic therapy,* counselors combined family intervention with integrating violent youths into positive school, work, and leisure activities and disengaging them from deviant peers. Compared with conventional services or individual therapy, the intervention led to greater improvement in parent–adolescent relationships and school performance, a dramatic drop in number of arrests that persisted for at least four years after treatment, and—when participants did commit crimes—a reduction in their severity (Borduin, 2007; Henggeler et al., 2009). Efforts to create nonaggressive environments—at the family, community, and cultural levels—are needed to help delinquent youths and to foster healthy development of all young people.

ASK YOURSELF

◆ **REVIEW** Why are adolescent girls at greater risk for depression and adolescent boys at greater risk for suicide?

◆ **APPLY** Zeke had been well-behaved in elementary school, but at age 13 he started spending time with the "wrong crowd." At 16, he was arrested for property damage. Is Zeke likely to become a long-term offender? Why or why not?

◆ **CONNECT** Reread the sections on adolescent pregnancy and substance abuse in Chapter 14. What factors do these problems have in common with suicide and delinquency?

◆ **REFLECT** During adolescence, did you or your friends engage in any lawbreaking acts? If so, at what ages? Were you motivated by a desire for excitement and/or peer approval?

BIOLOGY AND ENVIRONMENT

Two Routes to Adolescent Delinquency

Persistent adolescent delinquency follows two paths of development, one involving a small number of youths with an onset of conduct problems in childhood, the second a larger number with an onset in adolescence. The early-onset type is far more likely to lead to a life-course pattern of aggression and criminality (Moffitt, 2006b). The late-onset type usually does not persist beyond the transition to early adulthood.

Both childhood-onset and adolescent-onset youths engage in serious offenses; associate with deviant peers; participate in substance abuse, unsafe sex, and dangerous driving; and spend time in correctional facilities. Why does antisocial activity more often continue and escalate into violence in the first group? Longitudinal studies yield similar answers to this question. Most research has focused on boys, but several investigations report that girls who were physically aggressive in childhood are also at risk for later problems—occasionally violent delinquency but more often other norm-violating behaviors and psychological disorders (Broidy et al., 2003; Chamberlain, 2003). Early relational aggression is linked to adolescent conduct problems as well.

Early-Onset Type

Early-onset youngsters seem to inherit traits that predispose them to aggressiveness (Pettit, 2004). For example, violence-prone boys are emotionally negative, restless, willful, and physically aggressive as early as age 2. They also show subtle deficits in cognitive functioning that seem to contribute to disruptions in the development of language, memory, and emotional self-regulation (Moffitt, 2006a; Shaw et al., 2003). Some have attention-deficit hyperactivity disorder (ADHD), which compounds their learning and self-control problems (see Chapter 12, page 444).

Yet these biological risks are not sufficient to sustain antisocial behavior: Most early-onset boys decline in aggression over time. Among those who follow the life-course path, inept parenting transforms their undercontrolled style into defiance and persistent aggression (Brame, Nagin, & Tremblay, 2001; Broidy et al., 2003). As they fail academically and are rejected by peers, they befriend other deviant youths, who facilitate one another's violent behavior while relieving loneliness (see Figure 16.6) (Lacourse et al., 2003). Limited cognitive and social skills result in high rates of school dropout and unemployment, contributing further to

antisocial involvements. Often these boys experience their first arrest before age 14—a good indicator that they will be chronic offenders by age 18 (Patterson & Yoerger, 2002).

Preschoolers high in relational aggression also tend to be hyperactive and frequently in conflict with peers and adults (Willoughby, Kupersmidt, & Bryant, 2001). As these behaviors trigger peer rejection, relationally aggressive girls befriend other girls high in relational hostility, and their relational aggression rises (Werner & Crick, 2004). Adolescents high in relational aggression are often angry, vengeful, and defiant of adult rules. Among teenagers who combine physical and relational hostility, these oppositional reactions intensify, increasing the likelihood of serious antisocial activity (Harachi et al., 2006; Prinstein, Boergers, & Vernberg, 2001).

Late-Onset Type

Other youths first display antisocial behavior around the time of puberty, gradually increasing their involvement. Their conduct problems arise from the peer context of early adolescence, not from biological deficits and a history of unfavorable development. For some, quality of parenting may decline for a time, perhaps

◼◻ At the Threshold

◼◻

The complex and rapid changes of development that occur during adolescence make teenagers vulnerable to certain problems. Most teenagers, however, do not show serious depression, suicidal tendencies, or persistent antisocial behavior. As we look back on the demands, expectations, dangers, and temptations of this period, the strength and vitality of young people are all the more remarkable. On a daily basis, adolescents must decide how vigorously to apply themselves in school, what kinds of friends to make, and whether to adopt risky behaviors. These short-term choices can profoundly affect the long-term paths they pursue.

Societies have good reason to treasure their youths as a rich national resource. Adolescents' ability to think seriously and deeply about possibilities, to commit themselves to idealistic causes, to be loyal to one another, and to experiment and take risks, while sometimes hazardous to themselves, energizes progress. But to realize their potential, teenagers must have family, school, and community environments that nurture personal strengths while limiting exposure to adversity. To factors that foster resilience considered in earlier chapters (see Chapter 13, page 522) we can add the following resources, which are particularly beneficial in adolescence:

FIGURE 16.6

Path to chronic delinquency for adolescents with childhood-onset antisocial behavior. Difficult temperament and cognitive deficits characterize many of these youths in early childhood; some have attention-deficit hyperactivity disorder. Inept parenting transforms biologically based self-control difficulties into hostility and defiance.

because of family stresses or the challenges of disciplining an unruly teenager (Moffitt, 2006a). When age brings gratifying adult privileges, these youths draw on prosocial skills mastered before adolescence and abandon their antisocial ways.

A few late-onset youths do continue to engage in antisocial acts. The seriousness of their adolescent offenses seems to trap them in situations that close off opportunities for responsible behavior. Being employed or in school and forming positive, close relationships predict an end to criminal offending by age 20 to 25 (Clingempeel & Henggeler, 2003; Stouthamer-Loeber et al., 2004). In contrast, the longer antisocial young people spend in prison, the more likely they are to sustain a life of crime.

These findings suggest a need for a fresh look at policies aimed at stopping youth crime. Keeping youth offenders locked up for many years disrupts their vocational lives and access to social support during a crucial period of development, condemning them to a bleak future.

- A balance between family connection and separation
- Effective family problem solving that models and encourages rational decision making
- Parental monitoring and school involvement
- Close, supportive friendships
- High-quality vocational education
- A culturally sensitive school and community that foster a secure ethnic or bicultural identity
- Affiliation with a religious organization
- Opportunities to participate in extracurricular activities, youth organizations, and community service

As we turn now to the conclusion of our developmental journey, we will see that many young people in industrialized nations face more complex choices today than even several decades ago. Consequently, researchers have begun to investigate a new period that stands between adolescence and young adulthood. The support provided during the first 18 years is crucial for preparing young people to embrace the challenges of this transition. At no other time of life will the scope of possibilities and the freedom to experiment and make independent decisions be greater.

Summary

Erikson's Theory: Identity versus Role Confusion

According to Erikson, what is the major personality achievement of adolescence?

- Erikson's theory regards **identity** as the major personality achievement of adolescence. Young people who successfully resolve the psychological conflict of **identity versus role confusion** construct a solid self-definition consisting of self-chosen values and goals.

Self-Understanding

Describe changes in self-concept and self-esteem during adolescence.

- Cognitive changes lead adolescents' self-descriptions to become more organized and consistent. They place more emphasis on social virtues, and personal and moral values appear as key themes.
- Self-esteem further differentiates, and for most adolescents, rises. At the same time, individual differences in self-esteem become more stable. Authoritative parenting and schools and neighborhoods that accept the young person's cultural heritage support positive self-esteem.

Describe the four identity statuses, along with factors that promote identity development.

- Researchers evaluate progress in identity development on two criteria: exploration of alternatives and commitment to self-chosen values and goals. **Identity achievement** (exploration followed by commitment) and **identity moratorium** (exploration without having reached commitment) are psychologically healthy identity statuses. Long-term **identity foreclosure** (commitment without exploration) and **identity diffusion** (lack of both exploration and commitment) are related to adjustment difficulties.

- An information-gathering cognitive style, parental attachment along with freedom to explore, interaction with diverse peers, close friendships, and schools and communities that provide rich and varied opportunities promote healthy identity development. Similarly, supportive parents, peers, and schools can foster a strong, secure **ethnic identity** among minority adolescents. A **bicultural identity** offers additional emotional and social benefits.

Moral Development

Describe Kohlberg's theory of moral development, and evaluate its accuracy.

- According to Kohlberg, moral reasoning gradually develops through three levels, each containing two stages: At the **preconventional level,** morality is externally controlled by rewards, punishments, and authority figures; at the **conventional level,** conformity to laws and rules preserves positive interpersonal relationships and societal order; and at the **postconventional level,** morality is defined by abstract, universal principles of justice.

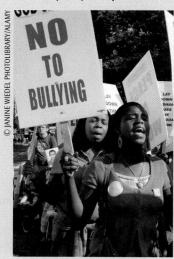

- A reexamination of Kohlberg's stages suggests that moral maturity can be found at Stages 3 and 4; few people move beyond to the postconventional level. The influence of situational factors on moral judgment suggests that Kohlberg's stages are best viewed as loosely organized and overlapping.

- Contrary to Gilligan's claim, Kohlberg's theory does not underestimate the moral reasoning of females but instead taps both justice and caring moralities.
- Compared with children, teenagers display more subtle reasoning about conflicts between personal choice and community obligations. They are also increasingly mindful of the moral implications of following social conventions.

Describe influences on moral reasoning and its relationship to moral behavior.

- Experiences contributing to moral maturity include warm, rational parenting, years of schooling, and peer discussions of moral issues. In village societies, where moral cooperation is based on direct relations between people, moral reasoning rarely moves beyond Kohlberg's Stage 3. In collectivist cultures, moral dilemma responses are more other-directed than in Western societies.
- Maturity of moral reasoning is only modestly related to moral behavior. Moral action is also influenced by the individual's empathy and guilt, temperament, history of morally relevant experiences, and **moral self-relevance.**
- Despite declines in formal religious involvement in adolescence, most religiously affiliated teenagers are advantaged in moral values and behavior.

Describe challenges to Kohlberg's theory.

- Critics favoring a pragmatic approach to morality assert that individuals make moral judgments at varying levels of maturity, depending on their current context and motivations. Supporters of the cognitive-developmental perspective believe people frequently rise above self-interest to defend others' rights.

Gender Typing

Why is early adolescence a period of gender intensification?

- Biological, social, and cognitive factors contribute to **gender intensification.** As pubertal changes occur and concern with what others think strengthens, teenagers focus on gender-linked attributes. Parents and dating partners also encourage gender-appropriate behavior. Androgynous adolescents tend to be psychologically healthier.

The Family

Discuss changes in parent–child and sibling relationships during adolescence.

- In their quest for **autonomy,** adolescents strive to rely more on themselves and less on parents for guidance and decision making. As teenagers deidealize their parents, they often question parental authority. During a time of major life transitions, adolescents and parents approach situations with conflicting expectations and from different perspectives. Warm, supportive parenting and consistent monitoring predict favorable adjustment, even in the face of reduced time spent with parents.

- Sibling relationships become less intense as adolescents separate from the family and turn toward peers. Still, attachment to siblings remains strong for most young people.

Peer Relations

Describe adolescent friendships, peer groups, and dating relationships and their consequences for development.

- Adolescent friendships are based on greater intimacy, mutual understanding, and loyalty and contain more self-disclosure. Girls' friendships place greater emphasis on emotional closeness, boys' on shared activities and accomplishments.

- Adolescents use the Internet to communicate with friends and to meet new people. Instant messaging and use of social networking sites are especially common and seem to support friendship closeness. But for some young people, online relationships pose risks of harmful social experiences, including harassment and exploitation.

- As long as they are not characterized by jealousy or aggression, adolescent friendships promote self-concept, identity, perspective taking, and the capacity for intimate relationships. They also help young people deal with stress and can foster improved attitudes toward and involvement in school.

- Adolescent peer groups are organized into more intimate **cliques,** particularly important to girls, and **crowds,** which grant teenagers an identity within the larger social structure of the school. Parenting styles influence the assortment of teenagers into cliques and crowds. With interest in dating, mixed-sex cliques grow in importance and then decline. Crowds also diminish as teenagers settle on personal values and goals.

© THE STAR-LEDGER/BILL PERLMAN/THE IMAGE WORKS

- Intimacy in dating relationships lags behind that of same-sex friendships. Positive relationships with parents and friends contribute to secure romantic ties, which enhance emotional and social development in older teenagers.

Discuss conformity to peer pressure in adolescence.

- Peer conformity is greater during adolescence than earlier or later. Young teenagers are especially likely to give in to peer pressure for antisocial behavior. Yet most peer pressure is not in conflict with important adult values. Authoritative parenting is related to resistance to unfavorable peer pressure.

Problems of Development

Describe factors related to adolescent depression and suicide.

- Depression is the most common psychological problem of the teenage years, with girls at greater risk in industrialized nations. Various combinations of biological and environmental factors are implicated—heredity, maladaptive parenting, a learned-helpless attributional style, and negative life events.

- The suicide rate increases sharply at adolescence. Boys account for most teenage deaths by suicide, while girls make more unsuccessful suicide attempts. Teenagers at risk for suicide may be solitary and withdrawn, but more often, they are antisocial. They often have a family history of emotional and antisocial disorders and suicide, economic disadvantage, and family conflict.

Discuss factors related to delinquency.

- Although almost all teenagers engage in some delinquent activity, only a few are serious repeat offenders. Most are boys with a childhood history of conduct problems. Difficult temperament, cognitive deficits, inept parenting, and peer rejection are linked to chronic, violent delinquency. Teenagers commit more crimes in poverty-stricken neighborhoods with high crime rates and ineffective schools.

At the Threshold

Review factors that foster resilience in adolescence.

- In addition to factors mentioned in earlier chapters, the following resources foster resilience in adolescence: a balance between family connection and separation, effective family problem solving, parental monitoring and school involvement, close friendships, high-quality vocational education, culturally sensitive schools and communities, religious affiliation, and opportunities to participate in extracurricular activities, youth organizations, and community service.

IMPORTANT TERMS AND CONCEPTS

acculturative stress (p. 607)
autonomy (p. 619)
bicultural identity (p. 607)
clique (p. 626)
conventional level (p. 609)
crowd (p. 626)

ethnic identity (p. 607)
gender intensification (p. 618)
identity (p. 600)
identity achievement (p. 603)
identity diffusion (p. 603)
identity foreclosure (p. 603)

identity moratorium (p. 603)
identity versus role confusion (p. 600)
moral self-relevance (p. 615)
postconventional level (p. 610)
preconventional level (p. 609)

Milestones

Development in Adolescence

Early adolescence 11–14

PHYSICAL

- If a girl, reaches peak of growth spurt. (532)
- If a girl, adds more body fat than muscle. (533)
- If a girl, starts to menstruate. (536)
- If a boy, begins growth spurt. (532)
- If a boy, starts to ejaculate seminal fluid. (536)
- Is likely to be aware of sexual orientation. (552–553)
- If a girl, motor performance increases gradually, leveling off by age 14. (534)
- Shows heightened stress response and novelty-seeking. (538)
- Sleep "phase delay" strengthens. (539)

COGNITIVE

- Shows gains in hypothetico-deductive reasoning and propositional thought. (566–567)
- Improves in scientific reasoning—coordinating theory with evidence—on complex, multivariable tasks. (570)
- Becomes more self-conscious and self-focused. (572–573)
- Becomes more idealistic and critical. (573)

- Improves in metacognition and self-regulation. (569)
- Evaluates vocational options in terms of interests. (590)

LANGUAGE

- Improves in metalinguistic awareness. (578)
- Vocabulary continues to increase as abstract words are added. (578–579)
- Grasps irony, sarcasm, and figurative language, such as proverbs. (579)
- Understanding and use of complex grammatical constructions improves further. (579)
- Capacity to adjust speech style, depending on the situation, improves. (579–580)

EMOTIONAL/SOCIAL

- Self-concept includes abstract descriptors unifying separate personality traits, but these are often contradictory and not interconnected. (601–602)
- Shows gender intensification—increased gender stereotyping of attitudes and behavior. (618)
- Moodiness and parent–child conflict tend to increase. (619–621)
- In striving for autonomy, spends less time with parents and siblings and more time with peers. (622)

- Friendships decline in number and are based on intimacy, mutual understanding, and loyalty. (622–623)
- Peer groups become organized around same-sex cliques. (626)
- Cliques with similar values form crowds. (626)
- Conformity in response to peer pressure increases. (628–629)

Middle adolescence 14–16

PHYSICAL

- If a girl, completes growth spurt. (532)
- If a boy, reaches peak of growth spurt. (532)
- If a boy, voice deepens. (536)
- If a boy, adds muscle while body fat declines. (533)
- If a boy, motor performance improves dramatically. (534)
- May have had sexual intercourse. (548–550)

COGNITIVE

- Continues to improve in hypothetico-deductive reasoning and propositional thought. (566–567)

NOTE: Numbers in parentheses indicate the page or pages on which each milestone is discussed.

- Continues to improve in scientific reasoning, following a similar sequential order on different types of tasks. (571)
- Evaluates vocational options in terms of interests, abilities, and values. (590–591)

LANGUAGE

- Can read and interpret adult literary works. (579)

- More effectively analyzes and corrects grammar. (579)

EMOTIONAL/SOCIAL

- Combines features of the self into an organized self-concept. (601–602)
- Self-esteem differentiates further and tends to rise. (602)
- In most cases, begins to move from "lower" to "higher" identity statuses. (603–604)
- Is likely to engage in societal perspective taking. (610)
- Increasingly emphasizes ideal reciprocity and societal laws as the basis for resolving moral dilemmas. (610)

- Engages in more subtle reasoning about conflicts between moral, social-conventional, and personal-choice issues. (612–613)
- Gender intensification declines. (618)
- Mixed-sex cliques become common. (626)

- Has probably started dating. (627–628)
- Conformity to peer pressure may decline. (629)

Late adolescence 16–18

PHYSICAL

- If a boy, completes growth spurt. (532)
- If a boy, gains in motor performance continue. (534)

COGNITIVE

- Becomes less self-conscious and self-focused. (572–573)
- Continues to improve in metacognition and self-regulation. (569)
- Improves in decision making. (574)
- Narrows vocational options through exploration. (591)

EMOTIONAL/SOCIAL

- Self-concept emphasizes personal and moral standards. (601)
- Continues to construct an identity, typically moving to higher identity statuses. (603–604)
- Continues to advance in maturity of moral reasoning. (608)
- Cliques and crowds decline in importance. (627)
- Seeks psychological intimacy in romantic ties, which last longer. (628)

c h a p t e r

17

"Three Figures"
Lucien
18 years, Haiti

This Haitian artist depicts a vibrant adult world that, at age 18, he has already entered. Most young people in developing countries do not experience the transitional period described in Chapter 17. As adolescence concludes, they move directly into adult roles.

Reprinted with permission from the International Collection of Child Art, Milner Library, Illinois State University, Normal, Illinois

Emerging Adulthood

*I*n their early twenties, David and Peter—my two grown sons— asked me how old I was when I got married, knew what I wanted to do for a career, and earnestly began to prepare for my life's work. To their surprise, I responded that I had attained all of these widely accepted markers of adulthood by age 22—and that nearly all my friends of several decades ago had done so as well.

My sons' experiences were vastly different. Throughout college and for several years beyond, they explored possibilities. David, for example, completed a bachelor's degree in chemistry and pursued a master's degree in public health. Then he made another about-face. After volunteering for several months in an elementary school, at age 24 he returned to graduate school to become a teacher. Peter also vacillated after college about a vocational direction. Following a "year off" that included an internship, he settled on law school. Both young men deferred romance while they launched their work lives.

Similarly, few of David's and Peter's friends made lasting career or romantic commitments in their late teens and early twenties. To the contrary, their experimentation became more varied and deliberate. After graduating from college, one traveled the world for eight months, explaining that she wanted "to experience as much as possible." Another accepted a Peace Corps assignment in a remote region of Peru, forged a romance with a Peruvian man that she ended at the conclusion of her tour of duty, then returned to school to prepare for a career in international education. Each of these young people received financial and other forms of support from parents and other family members, which made possible their extended explorations.

TAKE A MOMENT... Think about your own development. Do you consider yourself to have reached adulthood? When a large sample of American 18- to 25-year-olds was asked this question, the majority gave an ambiguous answer: "yes and no" (see Figure 17.1). Only after reaching their late twenties and early thirties did most feel that they were truly adult—findings evident in a wide range of industrialized nations, including Argentina, Austria, the Czech Republic, Finland,

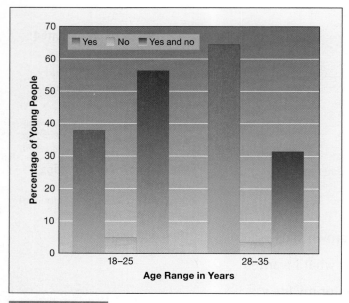

FIGURE 17.1

American young people's responses to the question, "Do you feel that you have reached adulthood?" Between ages 18 and 25, the majority answered "yes and no," reflecting their view that they had left adolescence but were not yet fully adult. Even in their late twenties and early thirties, about one-third of young people judged that they had not completed the transition to adulthood. *(Adapted from Arnett, 2001.)*

Germany, Italy, Spain, and Israel (Arnett, 2001, 2003, 2007b; Buhl & Lanz, 2007; Macek, Bejček, & Vaníčková, 2007; Sirsch et al., 2009). The life pursuits and subjective judgments of many contemporary youths indicate that the transition to adult roles has become so delayed and prolonged that it has spawned a new transitional period extending from the late teens to the mid-twenties, called **emerging adulthood.**

American psychologist Jeffrey Arnett (2006, 2007b) is the leader of a growing movement that regards emerging adulthood as a distinct period of life. As Arnett explains, emerging adults have left adolescence but are still a considerable distance from taking on adult responsibilities. Their parents agree: In a survey of parents of a large sample of ethnically and religiously diverse U.S. undergraduate and graduate students, most viewed their children as not yet fully adult (Nelson et al., 2007). Rather, young people who have the economic resources to do so explore alternatives in education, work, personal values, and love more intensely than they did as teenagers. Many are working on advanced degrees and credentials—accumulating experiences and mastering practical skills so that they can land a personally and financially rewarding job in an ever-more-complex labor market. Those who are less economically privileged, however, often struggle to acquire the skills needed for work that will provide a decent standard of living for the family they desire—or may have already begun (see the discussion of non-college-bound youths on pages 593–595 in Chapter 15).

A Period of Unprecedented Exploration

Emerging adulthood is a time of great challenge and uncertainty. During this period, many young people make frequent changes in educational paths, jobs, and love partners. Adult milestones—finishing school, living on one's own, launching a career, and building a lasting intimate partnership—are highly diverse in timing and order across individuals (Cohen et al., 2003). Consequently, it is harder to make general statements about development during emerging adulthood than for any other period.

Today, more college students than in past generations prolong their education, pursuing it in a nonlinear way. Only about half of U.S. young people who enroll in higher education have earned their bachelor's degree by age 25. Some take a few courses while working part-time. Others leave school temporarily to work full-time or travel. Most change their majors several times as they try out career options. After graduation, about one-third enter graduate school, taking even longer to settle into their desired career track (U.S. Department of Education, 2010).

Young people are postponing marriage, as well. In 1950, the average age of first marriage in the United States was about 20 for women and 23 for men. Currently, the comparable ages are 26 and 28 (U.S. Census Bureau, 2010b). Similar delays have occurred in other industrialized nations, allowing for a longer period of experimentation with sexuality and intimacy.

A half-century ago, Americans viewed marriage and parenthood as crucial markers of adult status. Today, the majority regard these milestones as personal choices and endorse individuals' right to alternative lifestyles (Furstenberg et al., 2004).

Together, extended education, delayed career entry, and later marriage lead to great residential instability. American 18- to 25-year-olds are "on the move," more than at any other time of life. About one-third move in and out of residence halls, fraternity and sorority houses, and apartments during college. And more than half move in with a romantic partner, choosing *cohabitation* as their preferred way of entering into a committed intimate partnership (Le Bourdais & Lapierre-Adamcyk, 2004; U.S. Census Bureau, 2010b).

Furthermore, nearly half of 18- to 25-year-olds return to their parents' home for brief periods after first leaving (Mitchell, 2006). Usually, role transitions, such as the end of college, bring young people back. For others, tight job markets, high housing costs, or failures in work or love prompt a temporary return home. As they encounter unexpected twists and turns on the road to adulthood, the parental home serves as a safety net and base of operations for launching adult life.

Economically well-off emerging adults are more likely to live independently than those from lower-SES and ethnic minority families. Among African-American, Hispanic, and Native-American groups, poverty and a cultural tradition of extended-family living lead to lower rates of leaving home, even among young people who are in college or working (Fussell & Furstenberg, 2005). Unmarried Asian emerging adults also tend to live with their parents, often exploring more hesitantly than their contemporaries as they reconcile their personal desires with the expectations of their parents, to whom they feel a strong sense of obligation (Fuligni, 2007). But the longer Asian families have lived in the United States, where they are exposed to individualistic values, the more likely young people are to move out earlier and explore vigorously. Whether or not they live at home, most emerging adults remain financially dependent on parents (Lindsay, Almey, & Normand, 2002; Mitchell, 2006). Indeed, without parents' economic support, including coresidence, few emerging adults would be able to advance their education, explore career possibilities, or regroup when they encounter difficulties (Aquilino, 2006).

In Chapter 16, we noted that college students make more progress than high school students in shaping their identities (see page 604). Notice how emerging adulthood greatly prolongs identity development. And changes in reasoning capacity permit emerging adults to revise, and sometimes replace, their political and religious perspectives. Then, as they continue their explorations, they modify these philosophies further.

What explains the recent appearance of this rich, complex bridge between adolescence and assumption of adult responsibilities? Rapid cultural change seems to be the answer: Research suggests that emerging adulthood is a *cultural construction*.

■ The U.S. couple of the 1950s on the top married and became parents in their early twenties. In contrast, the archaeology majors on the bottom, excavating a Mayan site in Belize, are not yet considering marriage or parenthood. Typical of young people in industrialized nations today, they are taking time to pursue higher education, travel, and explore career options. ■

Cultural Change, Cultural Variation, and Emerging Adulthood

As the economies of industrialized nations have become more technical and information based, the amount of education required to enter complex, well-paid careers has increased. In response, young people of the twenty-first century are pursuing higher education in record numbers. In 1950, only 14 percent of Americans enrolled in colleges and universities in the first year after graduating from high school; today, about two-thirds do so. And nearly half of the U.S. early-twenties population attend an educational institution full-time (U.S. Department of Education, 2010). This massive expansion of higher education has delayed financial independence and career commitment—trends that grant far more time for exploring options.

Dramatic gains in life expectancy in prosperous nations have also contributed to emerging adulthood. An American born in 1900 could expect to live to age 50. By 1950, life expectancy had increased to age 68. Today, it is 78 in the United States and even higher in most other industrialized countries (U.S. Census Bureau, 2010b). Nations with abundant wealth and longer-living populations have no pressing need for young people's labor, freeing 18- to 25-year-olds for the extended moratorium of emerging adulthood (Arnett, 2000a).

Recall from Chapter 14 that all societies, no matter how simple, have at least a brief period of adolescence. In contrast, emerging adulthood is limited to cultures that postpone entry into adult roles until the twenties. In developing nations such as Brazil, China, India, and Mexico, only a privileged few—usually those from wealthier families who are admitted to universities—experience emerging adulthood, often for a shorter time span than their Western counterparts (Badger, Nelson, & Barry, 2006; Nelson & Chen, 2007). Furthermore, the overwhelming majority of young people in traditional, non-Western countries—who have few economic resources or who remain in the rural regions where they grew up—have no emerging adulthood. With limited education, they typically enter marriage, parenthood, and lifelong work early (UNICEF, 2010b).

In industrialized countries, where many experience these transitional years, young people nevertheless vary in their beliefs about what it means to become an adult. Reflecting the self-searching of these years, respondents from diverse cultures, ethnicities, and religious backgrounds emphasize psychological qualities, especially self-sufficiency—accepting responsibility for one's actions, deciding on personal beliefs and values, establishing an equal relationship with parents, and becoming financially independent (Facio & Micocci, 2003; Mayseless & Sharf, 2003; Nelson et al., 2007).

Youths from collectivist cultures and subcultures also attach great importance to becoming more considerate of others, to attaining certain roles, and to self-control. For example, Asian, African-American, and Hispanic young people point to supporting and caring for a family as a major marker of adulthood (Badger, Nelson, & Barry, 2006; Galambos & Martinéz, 2007). Mormon college students believe that becoming less self-oriented and conducting oneself responsibly are as important as self-sufficiency, and they rate family commitments a close second (Nelson, 2003). And in a survey of Native Canadian and Métis (mixed Native-Canadian and European descent) students, those who identified strongly with their cultural heritage regarded "good control over emotions" and "capable of supporting parents financially" as more important than did those with less cultural identification. And both groups of students placed greater weight on financial self-sufficiency and on interdependent qualities (such as making lifelong commitments to others) than did Canadian white students (Cheah & Nelson, 2004).

Nevertheless, for low-SES young people in Western nations who are burdened by early parenthood, do not finish high school, are otherwise academically unprepared for college, or do not have access to vocational training, emerging adulthood is limited or nonexistent (see Chapters 14 and 15). Instead of excitement and personal expansion, these youths encounter a "floundering period" during which they alternate between unemployment and dead-end, low-paying jobs (Cohen et al., 2003; Eccles et al., 2003).

Because of its strong association with SES and higher education, some researchers reject the notion of emerging adulthood as a distinct period of development (see the Cultural Influences box on the following page). Others disagree, predicting that emerging adulthood will become increasingly common as *globalization*—the exchange of ideas, information, trade, and immigration among nations—accelerates. Contact between industrialized and developing countries fosters economic progress. It also heightens awareness of events, lifestyles, and practices in faraway places. As globalization proceeds, gains in financial security and higher education and the formation of a common "global identity" among young people may lead to the spread of emerging adulthood (Arnett, 2002, 2007b; Nelson & Chen, 2007). Eventually, proponents claim, this period may become a typical experience on the path to adult life around the world.

LOOK AND LISTEN

❖❖

Ask several 18- to 25-year-olds for their beliefs about what it means to become an adult. Are their responses consistent with research findings on emerging adulthood?

CULTURAL INFLUENCES

Is Emerging Adulthood Really a Distinct Period of Development?

Although broad consensus exists that cultural change has prolonged the transition to adult roles for many young people, disagreement exists over whether these years of "emergence" merit the creation of a new developmental period (Hendry & Kloep, 2007). Critics of the concept of emerging adulthood offer the following arguments.

First, burgeoning higher education enrollment, delayed career entry, and later marriage and parenthood are cultural trends that began as early as the 1970s in industrialized nations, only gradually becoming more conspicuous. At no time has adulthood in complex societies been attained at a distinct moment (Côté & Bynner, 2008). Rather, young people have in the past and continue today to reach adult status earlier in some domains, later in others. And they may reverse direction. For example, after finishing college or being laid off from a job, they might move back to the parental home to get their bearings (Cohen et al., 2003). Transitions occur during all periods of adult life, with societal conditions heavily influencing their timing, length, and complexity.

Second, emerging adulthood fails to describe the experiences of most of the world's youths (Galambos & Martínez, 2007). In most developing countries, young people—particularly women—are limited in education and marry and have children early (see page 73 in Chapter 2). According to one estimate, nearly 1.5 billion individuals—86 percent of the globe's young people—follow this traditional route to adulthood, with no prospect of alternatives (Lloyd, 2005). And as we have seen, many low-SES individuals in industrialized nations lack the academic preparation and financial resources to experience an emerging adulthood.

Third, research on emerging adulthood largely emphasizes its personal benefits. But the extended exploration that defines this period might be largely a coping mechanism on the part of young people who cannot find rewarding jobs, even after college graduation. If satisfying work enabling financial independence were plentiful, perhaps emerging adults would not choose to postpone these responsibilities (Côté & Bynner, 2008). Furthermore, an extended emerging adulthood could be risky for those who have not developed the capacity to make good choices and acquire adult skills (Levine, 2005). These young people may remain uncommitted for too long—an outcome that would impede the focused learning required for a successful work life. A favorable emerging adulthood, then, depends on whether it is used to acquire competencies essential for contemporary living.

Proponents of emerging adulthood as a distinct period respond that, though not universal, it applies to most young people in industrialized societies and is spreading in developing nations that play major roles in our global economy (Arnett, 2007a). Furthermore, the concept reminds us that the lives of many people in their twenties differ vastly from younger and older individuals, and of the need to clarify the contextual factors that contribute to their experiences.

But skeptics note that emerging adulthood is unlikely to become a prominent period of life in developing countries with high concentrations of poverty, or among poverty-stricken youths in industrialized countries (Côté & Bynner, 2008). They also point out that in developed nations, important milestones (such as marriage, career entry, parenthood, and retirement) have become less determined by age and more affected by social and economic conditions throughout contemporary adulthood (Hendry & Kloep, 2007). In their view, rather than being unique, emerging adults are part of a general trend toward blurring of age-related expectations, yielding multiple transitions and increased diversity in development across the adult years.

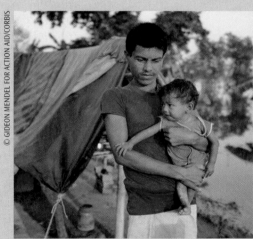

© GIDEON MENDEL FOR ACTION AID/CORBIS

■ Like the majority of young people in developing countries, this married man and father, who lives in rural India, has not experienced emerging adulthood. ■

■ ■ Development in Emerging Adulthood
■ ■

A wide array of demanding experiences and tasks await emerging adults. To make a successful transition to adulthood, they must acquire a wealth of new knowledge and skills.

Cognitive Changes

The cognitive gains of the late teens and early twenties are supported by further brain development, especially the prefrontal cortex and its connections with other brain regions (see pages 537–538 in Chapter 14). Pruning of synapses along with growth and myelination of stimulated neural fibers continue, though at a slower pace than in adolescence (Nelson, Thomas, &

De Haan, 2006). These changes are supported by experiences, including attaining higher education. fMRI evidence reveals that as young people become increasingly proficient in a chosen field of endeavor, regions of the cerebral cortex specialized for those activities undergo further *experience-dependent brain growth* (see page 172 in Chapter 5). In addition to functioning more efficiently, structural changes may occur as greater knowledge and refinement of skills results in more cortical tissue devoted to the task and, at times, reorganization of brain areas governing the activity (Hill & Schneider, 2006; Lenroot & Giedd, 2006).

Piaget (1967) recognized that important advances in thinking follow the attainment of formal operations. He observed that adolescents prefer an idealistic, internally consistent perspective on the world to one that is vague, contradictory, and adapted to particular circumstances (see page 573 in Chapter 15). Researchers who study **postformal thought**—cognitive development beyond Piaget's formal operational stage—have shown that college students make impressive strides in cognition. This is not surprising, since college serves as a "developmental testing ground," a time for devoting full attention to exploring alternative values, roles, and behaviors. To facilitate exploration, college exposes students to a form of culture shock—encounters with new ideas and beliefs, new freedoms and opportunities, and new academic and social demands. These experiences combine with personal effort to spark increasingly rational, flexible, and practical ways of thinking that accept uncertainties and vary across situations.

DEVELOPMENT OF EPISTEMIC COGNITION   The work of William Perry (1981, 1970/1998) provided the starting point for an expanding research literature on the development of *epistemic cognition. Epistemic* means "of or about knowledge," and **epistemic cognition** refers to our reflections on how we arrived at facts, beliefs, and ideas. When mature, rational thinkers reach conclusions that differ from those of others, they consider the justifiability of these conclusions. When they cannot justify their approach, they revise it, seeking a more balanced, adequate route to acquiring knowledge.

Perry wondered why students respond in dramatically different ways to the diversity of ideas they encounter in college. To find out, he interviewed Harvard University undergraduates at the end of each of their four years, asking "what stood out" during the previous year. Responses indicated that students' reflections on knowing changed as they experienced the complexities of university life and moved closer to adult roles—findings confirmed in many subsequent studies (King & Kitchener, 1994; Magolda, 2002; Moore, 2002).

Younger students regarded knowledge as made up of separate units (beliefs and propositions), whose truth can be determined by comparing them to objective standards—standards that exist apart from the thinking person and his or her situation. As a result, they engaged in **dualistic thinking,** dividing information, values, and authority into right and wrong, good and bad, we and they. As one college freshman put it, "When I went to my first lecture, what the man said was just like God's word. I believe everything he said because he is a professor . . . and this is a respected person" (Perry, 1981, p. 81). When asked, "If two people disagree on the interpretation of a poem, how would you decide which one is right?" a sophomore replied, "You'd have to ask the poet. It's his poem" (Clinchy, 2002, p. 67).

Older students, in contrast, had moved toward **relativistic thinking,** viewing all knowledge as embedded in a framework of thought. Aware of a diversity of opinions on many topics, they gave up the possibility of absolute truth in favor of multiple truths, each relative to its context. As a result, their thinking became more flexible and tolerant. As one college senior put it, "Just seeing how [famous philosophers] fell short of an all-encompassing answer, [you realize] that ideas are really individualized. And you begin to have respect for how great their thought could be, without its being absolute" (Perry, 1970/1998, p. 90). Relativistic thinking leads to the realization that one's own beliefs are often subjective, since several frameworks may satisfy the criterion of internal logical consistency (Moore, 2002; Sinnott, 2003). Thus, the relativistic thinker is acutely aware that each person, in arriving at a position, creates her own "truth."

Eventually, the most mature individuals progress to **commitment within relativistic thinking.** Instead of choosing between opposing views, they try to formulate a more satisfying perspective that synthesizes contradictions. When considering which of two theories studied in a college course is better or which of several movies most deserves an Oscar, the individual moves beyond the stance that everything is a matter of opinion and generates rational criteria against which options can be evaluated (Moshman, 2003, 2005). Few college students reach this extension of relativism. Those who do generally display a more sophisticated approach to learning, in which they actively seek differing perspectives to advance their knowledge and understanding. Attainment of commitment within relativism occurs more often among young people who pursue advanced graduate education (Greene, Torney-Purta, Azevedo, 2010; King & Kitchener, 2002).

IMPORTANCE OF PEER INTERACTION AND REFLECTION Advances in epistemic cognition depend on further gains in metacognition, which are likely to occur in situations that challenge young people's perspectives and induce them to consider the rationality of their thought processes (Moshman, 2005). In a study of the college learning experiences of seniors scoring low and high in epistemic cognition, high-scoring students frequently reported activities that encouraged them to struggle with realistic but ambiguous problems in a supportive environment, in which faculty offered encouragement and guidance. For example, an engineering major, describing an airplane-design project that required advanced epistemic cognition, noted his discovery that "you can design 30 different airplanes and each one's going to have its benefits and there's going to be problems with each one" (Marra & Palmer, 2004, p. 116). Low-scoring students rarely mentioned such experiences.

When students tackle challenging, ill-structured problems, interaction among individuals who are roughly equal in authority and knowledge is beneficial because it prevents acceptance of another's reasoning simply because of greater power or expertise. When college students were asked to devise the most effective solution to a difficult logical problem, only 3 out of 32 students (9 percent) in a "work-alone" condition succeeded. But in an "interactive" condition, 15 out of 20 small groups (75 percent) arrived at the best answer following extensive discussion (Moshman & Geil, 1998). Whereas few students working alone reflected on their solution strategies, most groups engaged in a process of "collective rationality" in which members challenged one another to justify their reasoning and collaborated in working out the most effective strategy.

■ University of Nevada students test a remotely controlled Mars Rover they designed. Collaboratively tackling challenging, ill-structured, real-world problems leads to gains in epistemic cognition. ■

Of course, reflection on one's own thinking can also occur individually. But peer interaction fosters the necessary type of individual reflection: arguing with oneself over competing ideas and strategies and coordinating opposing perspectives into a new, more effective structure. **TAKE A MOMENT...** Return to page 471 in Chapter 12 to review how peer collaboration fosters cognitive development in childhood. It remains a highly effective basis for education in emerging adulthood.

Emotional and Social Changes

During college, students' attitudes and values broaden. They express increased interest in literature, the performing arts, and philosophical and historical issues and greater tolerance for ethnic and cultural diversity. And as noted in Chapter 16, college leaves its mark on moral reasoning by fostering concern with individual rights and human welfare, sometimes expressed in political activism. Furthermore, exposure to multiple viewpoints encourages young people to look more closely at themselves. As a result, they develop a more complex self-concept that includes awareness of their own changing traits and values over time, along with enhanced self-esteem (Galambos, Barker, & Krahn, 2006; Labouvie-Vief, 2006; Montgomery & Côté, 2003a). Together, these developments contribute to advances in identity development.

In emerging adulthood, young people refine their approach to constructing an identity. Besides exploring *in breadth* (weighing multiple possibilities), they also explore *in*

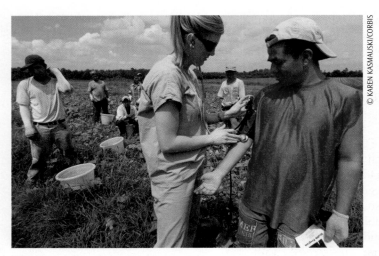

Students from Emory University School of Nursing provide free checkups for migrant workers. By exposing young people to multiple viewpoints, attending college encourages self-reflection and development of a more complex self-concept. ■

depth—evaluating existing commitments (Luyckx et al., 2006). For example, if you have not yet selected your major, you may be taking classes in a broad array of disciplines. Once you choose a major, you are likely to embark on an in-depth evaluation of your choice—reflecting on your interest, motivation, and performance and on your career prospects as you take additional classes in that field. Depending on the outcome of your evaluation, either your commitment to your major strengthens, or you return to a broad exploration of options.

In a longitudinal study extending over first two years of college, most students cycled between making commitments and evaluating commitments in various identity domains. Fluctuations in students' certainty about their commitments sparked movement between these two states (Luyckx, Goossens, & Soenens, 2006). **TAKE A MOMENT...** Think about your own identity progress. Does it fit this *dual-cycle model*, in which identity formation is a lengthy process of feedback loops? Notice how the model helps explain the movement between identity statuses displayed by many young people, described in Chapter 16. Emerging adults who move toward exploration in depth and certainty of commitment are higher in self-esteem and in academic and social adjustment. Those who spend much time exploring in breadth without making commitments tend to be poorly adjusted—anxious, depressed, and higher in drug use (Kunnen et al., 2008; Luyckx et al., 2006).

Many aspects of the life course that were once socially structured—marriage, parenthood, religious beliefs, career paths—are increasingly left to individuals to decide on their own. As a result, emerging adults are required to "individualize" their identities—a process that requires a sense of self-efficacy, purpose, confidence in overcoming obstacles and responsibility for outcomes (Côté & Schwartz, 2002). Among emerging adults of diverse ethnicities and SES levels, this set of qualities, termed *personal agency,* is positively related to an information-gathering cognitive style and identity exploration followed by commitment and negatively related to a diffuse-avoidant cognitive style and identity diffusion (Schwartz, Côté, & Arnett, 2005). Now let's turn to development in three main identity domains of this period: love, work, and worldview.

LOVE   Return to Chapter 1, pages 15–16, to review the description of Erikson's psychosocial theory, which identifies *intimacy* as a major task of these years. The increasing closeness of dating relationships in late adolescence extends further in emerging adulthood. With age, emerging adults' romantic ties last longer and involve greater trust, support, emotional closeness, and commitment. Frequently, they lead to cohabitation (Collins & van Dulmen, 2006b; Montgomery, 2005). Also, conceptions of close relationships become more complex, expressing a wider array of desired qualities from others and from oneself—a trend that reflects both a more differentiated self-concept and increased experience with close peer bonds (Waldinger et al., 2002). One emerging adult described this change: "Now you know what it means to support your partner, to be with him, to understand him. Today it is deeper, we discuss matters, we negotiate" (Shulman & Kipnis, 2001, p. 342). Whereas the adolescent asks, "With whom would I like to spend time now?" many emerging adults address a more serious question: "Whom do I want as a partner in life?" (Arnett, 2000a).

Emerging adults take their time about forging a committed relationship; many say they don't feel ready to make this choice and want to experience a variety of personal relationships before settling on one (Arnett, 2004). At the end of high school, about half of U.S. young people are sexually active, but by age 25 nearly all have become so, and the gender and SES differences in sexual activity that were apparent in adolescence (see page 549 in Chapter 14) have diminished. Although emerging adults have more sexual partners and engage in casual sex more often than adults over age 25, about 60 percent have had only one partner in the previous year (Lefkowitz & Gillen, 2006).

Finding a lifelong intimate partner is a major milestone, with profound consequences for psychological well-being. On average, married couples are physically and mentally healthier, are financially better-off, and have more frequent and satisfying sex than their single counterparts—including single emerging adults (Lansford et al., 2005; Marks, Bumpass, & Jun, 2004). Two interrelated factors increase the chances that an intimate bond forged in emerging adulthood will be mutually satisfying and last a lifetime: partner similarity and good communication.

Partner Similarity. Young people who establish happy, lasting intimate relationships rarely meet at bars or through personal ads. Instead, they meet in conventional ways: Family members or friends introduce them, or they get to know each other at work, school, or social events where people similar to themselves congregate (Schmeeckle & Sprecher, 2004). Sustaining an intimate tie is easier when couples share interests and values and when people they know approve of the match.

Over the past decade, the Internet has become an increasingly popular way to initiate relationships, with more than one-third of single adults going to dating websites or other online venues in search of romantic partners. Success rates, however, are much lower than with conventional strategies. In surveys of nationally representative samples of U.S. adult Internet users, only 3 percent reported meeting their spouse or current long-term partner through the Internet (Madden & Lenhart, 2006; Sprecher, 2009). Most said they met offline—at work, school, or a private social event.

Contrary to the popular belief that "opposites attract," lovers tend to resemble each other—in attitudes, personality, intelligence, educational plans, physical attractiveness, ethnicity, and (to a lesser extent) religious and political beliefs. The more alike two people are, the more satisfied they tend to be with their relationship, and the more likely they are to stay together (Blackwell & Lichter, 2004; Furnham, 2009; Lucas et al., 2004).

■ Romantic ties in emerging adulthood last longer than those in adolescence and involve a deeper sense of emotional closeness. Still, many emerging adults say they don't feel ready to settle on a life partner. ■

Good Communication. Lasting romantic relationships are based on good communication. Couples who sustain warm, tender expressions of intimacy and who decide to stay together, despite difficult moments, are more likely to express increased happiness over time. An important feature of their commitment is constructive conflict resolution—directly expressing wishes and needs, listening patiently, asking for clarification, compromising, accepting responsibility, and avoiding the escalation of negative emotion sparked by criticism, contempt, and defensiveness (Johnson et al., 2005; Schneewind & Gerhard, 2002).

As with best friendships and dating partners in adolescence (see page 627 in Chapter 16), a secure *internal working model* of attachment relationships fosters gratifying intimate ties in emerging adulthood. Young people who recall their attachment experiences with parents as warm and supportive tend to describe both their friendships and their romantic partnerships as trusting and happy (Cassidy, 2001; Collins & van Dulmen, 2006b). Their behaviors toward their partner are more supportive and their conflict resolution strategies more constructive than those of young people who describe their attachment histories as insecure. They are also more at ease in turning to their partner for comfort and assistance and report mutually initiated, enjoyable sexual activity (Collins et al., 2006; Creasey, 2002; Creasey & Ladd, 2004; Roisman et al., 2001)

However, memories of early attachments are only one of several influences on the quality of emerging adults' romantic relationships. Characteristics of the partner and current life conditions also make a difference. When one partner feels secure and behaves considerately, the other is likely to respond in kind (Cook, 2000). And young people who are content with progress in other aspects of their lives probably approach their love relationships with a more positive, relaxed state of mind.

Finally, although half of U.S. young couples cohabit, their relationships are more likely to break up within two years than those of Western European cohabiters (Jose, O'Leary, & Moyer, 2010; Kiernan, 2001). In the Netherlands, Norway, and Sweden, cohabitation is thoroughly integrated into society. Between 70 and 90 percent of young people live together before marriage, and cohabiting couples are nearly as committed to each other as married people (Fussell & Gauthier, 2005; Ramsøy, 1994). In the United Sates, societal attitudes toward cohabitation, though more tolerant than in the past, are not as positive as in Western Europe. Consequently, American emerging adults who cohabit prior to engagement tend to have less conventional values. They have had more sexual partners and are more politically liberal, less religious, and more androgynous. In addition, a larger number have parents who divorced (Axinn & Barber, 1997; Kurdek, 2006). Perhaps the nature of American cohabiting relationships—more open-ended than in Western Europe—reduces motivation to develop effective conflict-resolution skills. Consequently, these unions often dissolve when problems arise.

WORK   Recall from Chapter 15 that U.S. teenagers rarely have access to meaningful paid work activities. Most view their part-time work merely as a way to obtain spending money. In emerging adulthood, work experiences increasingly focus on preparation for adult work roles. Young people eagerly seek apprenticeships with experts and internships in companies and community agencies to resolve vocational identity issues. They ask, What kind of work am I good at, and what will I find personally rewarding? Their selection of college courses also addresses these questions. They try out various possibilities, often changing majors several times. And graduate school permits them to switch directions again.

Conducting in-depth interviews, Daniel Levinson (1978, 1996) asked middle-aged men and women to describe the challenges they had encountered in making the transition from adolescence to adulthood. Most reported that between ages 18 and 22, they constructed a *dream,* an image of themselves in the adult world that guided their decision making. For men, the dream usually emphasized becoming an independent achiever in a career role. In contrast, most career-oriented women displayed "split dreams," in which both marriage and career were prominent.

To help realize their dream, young people generally formed a relationship with a *mentor*—a person experienced in the career the young person wants to enter. Most of the time, professors and senior colleagues filled this role. Occasionally, knowledgeable friends or relatives provided mentoring. Mentors sometimes acted as teachers who enhanced the person's career-related skills. At other times, they served as guides who acquainted the person with the values and customs of the work setting.

Gender. Identity achievement in the vocational realm is more challenging for women than for men. As indicated in Chapter 15, during college, women's career ambitions are often eroded by unresolved questions about their abilities and concerns about combining work with parenthood. Many doubt whether they can succeed in male-dominated fields, which further limits their occupational choices. Recall that mathematically talented college women frequently choose nonscience majors or, if they remain in the sciences, enter one of the health professions rather than engineering, math, or physical science (see page 593).

Women who do pursue male-dominated careers usually have "masculine" traits—high achievement orientation, self-reliance, and a belief that their efforts will result in success. But even those with high self-efficacy are less certain than their male counterparts that they can overcome barriers to career success (Lindley, 2005). In fields dominated by men, women mentors are less available. And despite similarities in support offered in same-sex and other-sex mentoring relationships, women with female mentors tend to be more successful (Goldstein, 1979; O'Neill, Horton, & Crosby, 1999). Perhaps female mentors are more likely to be perceived as role models and to provide guidance on the unique educational and workplace challenges that women encounter.

Despite obstacles to success, most young women prefer to blend work and family. They seem to realize that a rewarding career will increase life satisfaction—an outcome confirmed by research (Burke, 2001). Those who continue to achieve usually have four experiences in common:

■ A college environment that values the accomplishments of women and that addresses women's historical and current experiences in its curriculum

■ Frequent interaction with faculty and professionals in their chosen fields

■ The opportunity to test their abilities in supportive extracurricular, internship, and work environments

■ Models of accomplished women who have successfully dealt with family–career role conflict (Swanson & Fouad, 1999; Zeldin & Pajares, 2000)

Ethnic Minorities. Many ethnic minority young people from low-SES families also arrive at emerging adulthood with past experiences that compromise their self-confidence and academic preparedness for college and career success (see, for example, Chapter 15, pages 585–587). Consequently, they are at increased risk of dropping out of college, with most dropouts leaving during the first year and many within the first six

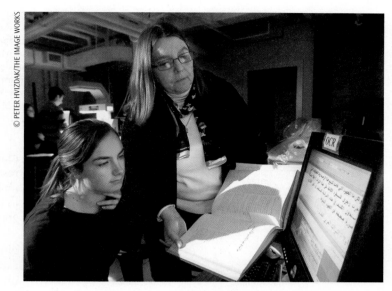

■ A Yale University digital archives specialist shows an apprentice librarian how to proofread a Persian text that has been scanned into digital files. Young women pursuing high career achievement often have mentors, especially accomplished women, who serve as role models and guides in overcoming challenges. ■

weeks (ACT, 2010; Montgomery & Côté, 2003a). Reflecting this trend, U.S. graduation rates after five years of study are 36 percent for African Americans, 42 percent for Hispanics, and 35 percent for Native Americans compared with 56 percent for Caucasians (U.S. Department of Education, 2010). Young people who leave college have few alternatives for successful entry into the work force. As a result, they often end in low-paid jobs or unemployed, with seriously compromised long-term work and earning prospects.

Preparing young people in childhood and adolescence with the necessary visions and skills can do much to improve college success. In a study that followed nearly 700 individuals from sixth grade until two years after high school graduation, a set of factors—grade point average, academic self-esteem, persistence in the face of challenge, parental SES and valuing of a college education, and the individual's plans to attend college—predicted college attendance at age 20 (Eccles, Vida, & Barber, 2004). Although parental SES is difficult to modify, improving parents' attitudes and behaviors and students' academic motivation and educational aspirations is within reach, through a wide array of strategies considered in Chapters 15 and 16.

Once emerging adults enroll in college, reaching out to them is crucial, especially in the early weeks and throughout the first year. Colleges that do little to help high-risk students, through developmental courses and other support services, have a higher percentage of dropouts (Moxley, Najor-Durack, & Dumbrigue, 2001). Programs that forge bonds between teachers and students and that provide academic support, on-campus part-time work opportunities, and meaningful extracurricular roles increase retention. Membership in campus-based social and religious organizations is especially helpful in strengthening minority students' sense of belonging (Fashola & Slavin, 1998; Kuh, Cruce, & Shoup, 2008). Young people who feel that they have entered a college community that is concerned about them as individuals are far more likely to graduate.

Despite laws guaranteeing equality of opportunity, racial bias in career opportunities remains strong (Smith, Brief, & Colella, 2010). In one study, researchers responded to more than 1,300 help-wanted newspaper ads with fictitious résumés, some containing higher qualifications and some lower qualifications. Half the résumés were assigned a white-sounding name ("Emily Walsh," "Brendan Baker") and half a black-sounding name ("Lakisha Washington," "Jamal Jones"). At all job levels, résumés with "white" names evoked 50 percent more callbacks than those with "black" names. And although whites with high-quality résumés received substantially more callbacks than those with low-quality résumés, having a high-quality résumé

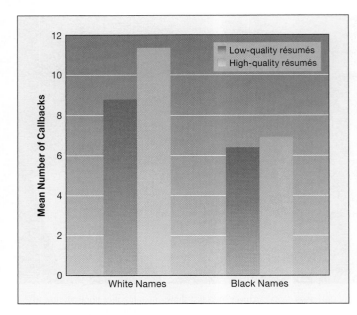

FIGURE 17.2

Relationship of ethnicity of job applicant's name to employer callbacks. Researchers responded to help-wanted newspaper ads with fictitious résumés, some having white-sounding names and others black-sounding names. Résumés with "white" names evoked many more callbacks than résumés with "black" names. When résumés were high in quality, callbacks to whites increased, but those to blacks showed little change. *(Adapted from Bertrand & Mullainathan, 2004.)*

made little difference for blacks (see Figure 17.2. As the researchers noted, "Discrimination appears to bite twice, making it harder for African Americans to find a job and to improve their employability" (Bertrand & Mullainathan, 2004, p. 4).

Ethnic minority women often must surmount combined gender and racial discrimination to realize their career potential. Those who succeed often develop an unusually high sense of self-efficacy, attacking problems head-on despite repeated obstacles to achievement (Byars & Hackett, 1998). In interviews with African-American women who had become leaders in diverse fields, all reported intense persistence, fueled by supportive relationships with other women, including teachers and peers. Many described their mothers as inspiring role models who had set high standards for them. Others mentioned support from their African-American communities, stating that a deep sense of connection to their people had empowered them (Richie et al., 1997).

WORLDVIEW Most emerging adults say that constructing a *worldview,* or set of beliefs and values to live by, is essential for attaining adult status—even more important than finishing their education and settling into a career and marriage (Arnett, 2001, 2006, 2007b). Do today's young people forge self-centered worldviews, as older adults who speak of the "me generation" believe they do?

This issue is the subject of heated controversy. Analyses of large, nationally representative samples of U.S. young people, collected repeatedly over several decades, suggest that compared to past generations, the Millennial generation reports greater narcissism (egotistical self-admiration) and valuing of money and leisure and reduced empathy for the less fortunate—signs that they are more arrogant and materialistic and less caring (Gentile, Twenge, & Campbell, 2010; O'Brien, Hsing, & Kornrath, 2010; Twenge et al., 2008, 2010).

But other researchers reject these conclusions, pointing out that generational changes in egotism and other traits are so small as not to be meaningful (Trzesniewski & Donnellan, 2009, 2010). Age-related gains in self-esteem extending from adolescence through emerging adulthood and into midlife, they emphasize, are far larger than any cohort differences (Galambos, Barker, & Krahn, 2006; Orth, Trzesniewski, & Robins, 2010). Over these years, adults make identity commitments, enter and succeed at their careers, have families, and become involved citizens in their communities—deriving a greater sense of competence from attaining these milestones.

Furthermore, when a sample of Americans in their twenties was asked directly, "What values do you think are most important to pass on to the next generation?" about one-third did give self-focused responses, referring to the importance of positive self-esteem, independence, and living life to the fullest. But two-thirds

■ Participation in community service promotes a broader worldview for members of the "millennial" generation. The experience of working with impoverished children in India helps this volunteer prepare for living in a diverse society. ■

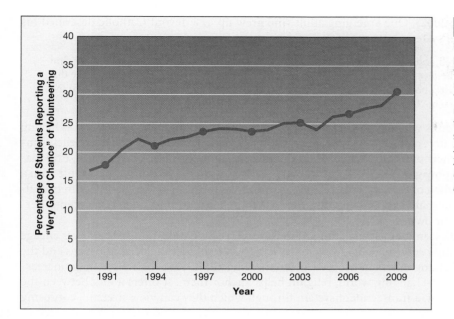

FIGURE 17.3

U.S. first-year college students' expectations of participating in community service from 1990 to 2009. Surveys of several hundred thousand freshman students revealed a steady increase in number who say there is a "very good chance" they will volunteer, with nearly twice as many with these intentions in 2009 as two decades ago. Most freshmen with high expectations of volunteering actually do so. *(From J. H. Pryor, S. Hurtado, L. DeAngelo, L. P. Blake, & S. Tran, 2009.* The American Freshman: National Norms Fall 2009, *p. 10. Los Angeles: Higher Education Research Institute, UCLA. © 2008 The Regents of the University of California. All Rights Reserved. Reprinted by permission.)*

either stressed communal values (commitments and responsibilities to others) or combined self and communal concerns (Arnett, Ramos, & Jensen, 2001).

Civic and Political Commitments. Additional evidence supports the view that many emerging adults want to improve their communities, nation, and world. In a survey of several hundred thousand first-year students enrolled in nearly 300 U.S. colleges and universities, a record number expected to participate in community service, with over 30 percent saying that there is "a very good chance" they will do so—nearly double the number two decades ago (see Figure 17.3) (Pryor et al., 2009). An additional 41 percent expressed "some chance" of participating, and only 6 percent said they had no intention of volunteering.

Among college students who expect to volunteer, the overwhelming majority actually do so within their first year (DeAngeleo, Hurtado, & Pryor, 2010). And compared to students not engaged in community service, those who volunteer have a stronger *pluralistic orientation*— disposition for living in a diverse society that includes respect for others with different beliefs, willingness to discuss and negotiate controversial issues, and openness to having one's own views challenged (Pryor et al., 2009).

But fewer U.S. young people than in previous generations vote or engage in political party activities, such as campaigning for candidates—a trend also evident in other Western nations (Flanagan et al., 1999; U.S. Census Bureau, 2010b). Many seem to lack faith in the conventional political process and in their own power to induce change in the broader society, perhaps because they see government as having made little progress on social problems that concern them (Snell, 2010). The 2008 U.S. national election was unusual, with 2 million more 18- to 29-year-olds having gone to the polls than in 2004. But they made up only a slightly greater percentage of voters—18 as opposed to 17 percent—because the turnout for all age groups had increased.

Religion and Spirituality. During the late teens and early twenties, attendance at religious services drops to its lowest level throughout the lifespan, as departure from home reduces parental pressure to attend and as young people continue to question the beliefs they acquired in their families (Lefkowitz, 2005; Smith, 2009). Still, about 30 percent of U.S. emerging adults sustain regular, formal religious activities (Bibby, 2000; Jones, 2003; Kerestes & Youniss, 2003). And whether or not they are involved in organized religion, many young people begin to construct their own individualized faith, often by weaving together beliefs and practices from a variety of sources, including Eastern and Western religious traditions, science, and popular culture. Often they struggle to reconcile religious or spiritual beliefs with scientific principles

LOOK AND LISTEN

Ask a class of college students to answer the following question: What would you do if you had one million dollars? How often do respondents mention prosocial as opposed to self-centered acts?

(Shipman et al., 2002). One emerging adult who grew up as a devout Catholic described his developing belief system:

> . . . all these religions, Mohammed and Buddha and Jesus, all the patterns there are very similar. . . . And I believe that there's a spirit, an energy. Not necessarily a guy or something like that, but maybe just a power force. Like in *Star Wars*—the Force . . . that makes it possible to live. (Arnett & Jensen, 2002, p. 460)

Emerging adults who feel securely attached to their parents and who view them as having used an authoritative child-rearing style are more likely to hold religious or spiritual beliefs similar to those of their parents (Okagaki, Hammond, & Seamon, 1999). The warmth, explanations, and autonomy granting of authoritative parenting seem to provide young people with a fuller understanding of their parents' religious ideology, as well as with greater freedom to evaluate it against alternatives. Consequently, they are more likely to integrate their parents' perspectives into their own worldview.

As with adolescents, emerging adults who view religion as important in their lives engage in more community service. Religion seems to serve as a reminder of social injustices and the importance of helping others in need. Also, as emerging adults seek their place in an increasingly complex, ever-changing world, religion helps anchor them. It offers a link between the past and the present, a transcendent system through which they can view stressful, confusing events, and an image of an ideal future toward which they can strive (Kerestes & Youniss, 2003).

Some young people regard their agemates who are religious as compliant and narrow-minded, but this is inaccurate. Rather, most are energetic, self-reliant individuals for whom religion is part of a broader approach to life (Youniss, McLellan, & Yates, 1999).

Risk and Resilience in Emerging Adulthood

In grappling with momentous choices, emerging adults play a more active role in their own development than at any earlier time. They must choose and coordinate demanding life roles and refine the skills necessary to succeed in those roles (Arnett, 2006; Eccles et al., 2003). As they experiment, they often encounter disappointments in love and work that require them to adjust, and sometimes radically change, their life path.

Emerging adults' vigorous explorations also extend earlier risks, including unprotected sexual activity, substance use, and hazardous driving behavior. And certain risks increase. For example, drug taking peaks between ages 19 and 22. Eager to try a wide range of experiences before settling down to the responsibilities of adulthood, young people of this age are more likely than younger or older individuals to smoke cigarettes, chew tobacco, engage in binge drinking, and experiment with prescription and illegal drugs, at times with tragic consequences (U.S. Department of Health and Human Services, 2010e).

Living on their own and making frequent moves, 18- to 24-year-olds spend more time by themselves than any other age group younger than 40. Consequently, feelings of loneliness peak during the late teens and early twenties (see Figure 17.4) (Rokach, 2001). As they move through school

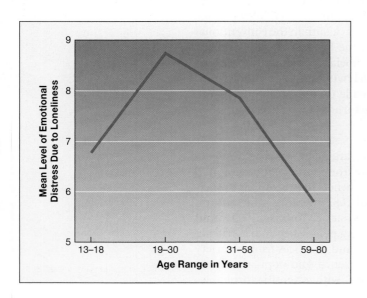

FIGURE 17.4

Changes in emotional distress due to loneliness over the lifespan.
More than 700 Canadian 13- to 80-year-olds responded to a questionnaire assessing the extent to which they experienced emotional distress due to loneliness. Loneliness rose sharply from the early teens to the late teens and early twenties, the period of emerging adulthood. *(Adapted from Rokach, 2001.)*

◆ Applying What We Know

Resources That Foster Resilience in Emerging Adulthood

TYPE OF RESOURCE	DESCRIPTION
Cognitive attributes	Effective planning and decision making
	Information-gathering cognitive style
	Good school performance
	Knowledge of vocational options and skills
Emotional and social attributes	Positive self-esteem
	Good emotional self-regulation and flexible coping strategies
	Good conflict-resolution skills
	Confidence in one's ability to reach one's goals
	Sense of personal responsibility for outcomes
	Persistence and good use of time
	Healthy identity development—movement toward exploration in depth and commitment certainty
	Strong moral character
	Sense of meaning and purpose in life, engendered by religion, spirituality, or other sources
	Desire to contribute meaningfully to one's community
Social supports	Positive relationships with parents, peers, teachers, and mentors
	Sense of connection to social institutions, such as school, church, workplace, and community center

Sources: Benson et al., 2006; Eccles and Gootman, 2002.

and employment settings, emerging adults must constantly separate from friends and develop new relationships. Extreme loneliness is associated with self-defeating attitudes and behavior, including low self-esteem and socially withdrawn and insensitive behaviors. But as long as loneliness is not overwhelming, it can motivate young people to reach out to others (Brehm, 2002; Rokach & Neto, 2006). It can also encourage them to find ways to be comfortably alone and to use this time to understand themselves better.

Longitudinal research shows that the personal attributes and social supports listed in Applying What We Know above foster successful passage through this period, as indicated by completing a college education, forging a warm, stable intimate relationship, finding and keeping a well-paying job, and volunteering in one's community (Benson et al., 2006; Eccles & Gootman, 2002). Notice how the factors in the table overlap with ones discussed in earlier chapters that promote development through *resilience,* the capacity to overcome challenge and adversity. Young people with more of these resources—and with resources in all three categories—probably make an especially smooth transition to adulthood. But many emerging adults with only a few resources also fare well.

As in childhood and adolescence, certain resources strengthen others. Relationships with parents have an especially wide-ranging influence. A secure, affectionate parent–emerging adult bond that extends the balance of connection and separation established in adolescence promotes many aspects of adaptive functioning: favorable self-esteem, identity progress, successful transition to college life, higher

© SW PRODUCTIONS/GETTY IMAGES/PHOTODISC

■ Warm relationships with parents promote resilience in emerging adulthood. As she moves out of her family's home to live on her own, this young woman knows she can still count on support and practical help from her family. ■

academic achievement, and more rewarding friendships and romantic ties. As one reviewer of research concluded, "What seems advantageous for emerging adults' achievement of independence is feeling connected, secure, understood, and loved in their families, and having the willingness to call on parental resources" (Aquilino, 2006, p. 201).

In contrast, parental overprotection, expressed through excessive contact and psychological control—including taking over when the young person encounters challenges—is linked to poor adjustment, including low self-esteem, inability to make commitments in identity formation, and increased anxiety, depression, and alcohol use (Luyckx et al., 2007; Patock-Peckam & Morgan-Lopez, 2009). And exposure to multiple negative life events—family conflict, abusive intimate relationships, repeated romantic breakups, academic or employment difficulties, and financial strain—undermines development, even in emerging adults whose childhood and adolescence prepared them well for this transition (Cui & Vaillant, 1996).

In sum, supportive family, school, and community environments are crucial, just as they were at earlier ages. The overwhelming majority of young people with access to these resources are optimistic about their future (Arnett, 2000b, 2006). Although they worry about grim aspects of their world, such as crime, war, and environmental destruction, they nevertheless are convinced that they will someday arrive at where they want to be in life: secure enough financially and happy in work and close relationships.

ASK YOURSELF

◆ REVIEW What cultural changes have led to the appearance of emerging adulthood?

◆ APPLY List supports that your college environment offers emerging adults in its health and counseling services, academic advising, residential living, and extracurricular activities. How does each help young people master the challenges of this period?

◆ CONNECT What family, school, and community experiences in adolescence increase the chances that emerging adults will engage in community service? (See Chapter 16, page 616.)

◆ REFLECT Give an example of how your thinking has become more relativistic. Which college experiences probably contributed to this change?

Summary

A Period of Unprecedented Exploration

What is emerging adulthood?

■ In **emerging adulthood,** young people have not yet taken on adult roles. Rather, from the late teens to the mid-twenties, they prolong identity development as they explore alternatives in education, work, personal values, and love.

Cultural Change, Cultural Variation, and Emerging Adulthood

How has cultural change contributed to the appearance of emerging adulthood?

■ Increased education required for entry-level positions in many fields, gains in economic prosperity and life expectancy, reduced need for young people's labor, and globalization have prompted the appearance and spread of emerging adulthood. Many low-SES and ethnic minority youths, however, do not have access to the benefits of this period.

Development in Emerging Adulthood

What cognitive, emotional, and social changes take place during emerging adulthood?

■ Cognitive gains of the late teens and early twenties are supported by further brain development, especially the prefrontal cortex and its connections with other brain regions.

- Studies of **postformal thought** reveal that as college students explore new ideas and beliefs, their reasoning becomes more rational, flexible, and practical. As **epistemic cognition** advances, they move away from **dualistic thinking,** dividing information into right and wrong, toward **relativistic thinking,** awareness of multiple truths. Eventually, the most mature individuals arrive at **commitment within relativistic thinking,** a perspective that synthesizes contradictions.

- Opportunities to tackle problems collaboratively with others who are equal in knowledge and authority promote reflection on one's own thinking and gains in epistemic cognition.

- College students' attitudes and values broaden, enhancing their self-understanding and self-esteem. They refine their approach to constructing an identity, exploring not just in breadth but also in depth, cycling between making commitments and evaluating commitments in various identity domains.

- Emerging adults' romantic ties last longer and are more emotionally intimate than adolescents' dating relationships. Partner similarity and good communication predict happy, lasting relationships, as does a secure internal working model of attachment.

- Emerging adults' work experiences increasingly focus on preparation for adult work roles. Most construct a dream, typically emphasizing career for men and marriage and career for women. Identity achievement in the vocational realm is more challenging for women, who often question their abilities and express concerns about combining work with child rearing. Ethnic minorities also face difficulties, as racial bias in career opportunities remains strong.

- Despite self-focused themes in their worldviews, many emerging adults also want to improve their communities, nation, and world and participate in community service. Whether or not they remain involved in formal religious activities, most young people begin to construct their own, individualized faith. Those who view religion as important in their lives engage in more community service.

Risk and Resilience in Emerging Adulthood

What risks do emerging adults face, and what factors foster a successful transition to adulthood?

- In trying out possibilities, emerging adults must adjust to disappointments in love and work, and their explorations also extend risky behaviors of adolescence. Also, loneliness peaks in emerging adulthood.

- During this time of great challenge, repeated exposure to negative life events can undermine well-being, even in well-adjusted young people. A wide array of personal attributes and social supports, especially secure, affectionate bonds with parents, foster resilience and successful passage into adulthood.

IMPORTANT TERMS AND CONCEPTS

commitment within relativistic thinking (p. 648)	emerging adulthood (p. 644)	postformal thought (p. 648)
dualistic thinking (p. 648)	epistemic cognition (p. 648)	relativistic thinking (p. 648)

GLOSSARY

A

academic programs Preschool and kindergarten programs in which teachers structure children's learning, teaching academic skills through formal lessons that often involve repetition and drill. Distinguished from *child-centered programs*. (p. 348)

accommodation In Piaget's theory, that part of adaptation in which new schemes are created and old ones adjusted to produce a better fit with the environment. Distinguished from *assimilation*. (p. 204)

acculturative stress Psychological distress resulting from conflict between an individual's minority culture and the host culture. (p. 607)

adaptation In Piaget's theory, the process of building schemes through direct interaction with the environment. Consists of two complementary activities: *assimilation* and *accommodation*. (p. 204)

adolescence The transition between childhood and adulthood that begins with puberty. It involves accepting one's full-grown body, acquiring adult ways of thinking, attaining greater independence from one's family, developing more mature ways of relating to peers of both sexes, and beginning to construct an identity. (p. 529)

affordances The action possibilities that a situation offers an organism with certain motor capabilities. Discovering affordances plays a major role in perceptual differentiation. (p. 199)

age of viability The age at which the fetus can first survive if born early. Occurs sometime between 22 and 26 weeks. (p. 100)

alcohol-related neurodevelopmental disorder (ARND) The least severe form of fetal alcohol spectrum disorder, involving brain injury but with typical physical growth and absence of facial abnormalities. Distinguished from *fetal alcohol syndrome (FAS)* and *partial fetal alcohol syndrome (p-FAS)*. (p. 109)

allele Each of two or more forms of a gene located at the same place on corresponding pairs of chromosomes. (p. 56)

amnion The inner membrane that forms a protective covering around the prenatal organism. (p. 98)

amniotic fluid The fluid that fills the amnion, which helps keep temperature constant and provides a cushion against jolts caused by the mother's movements. (p. 98)

amodal sensory properties Information that overlaps two or more sensory systems, such as common rate, rhythm, duration, and intensity in visual and auditory input. (p. 197)

amygdala An inner-brain structure that plays a central role in processing emotional information. (p. 295)

androgyny The gender identity held by individuals who score high on both traditionally masculine and traditionally feminine personality characteristics. (p. 395)

animistic thinking The belief that inanimate objects have lifelike qualities, such as thoughts, wishes, feelings, and intentions. (p. 321)

anorexia nervosa An eating disorder in which young people, mainly females, starve themselves because of a compulsive fear of getting fat and an extremely distorted body image. (p. 545)

A-not-B search error The error made by 8- to 12-month-olds who, after seeing an object moved from one hiding place (A) to another (B), still search for it only in the first hiding place (A). (p. 207)

anoxia Inadequate oxygen supply. (p. 135)

Apgar Scale A rating system used to assess the newborn baby's physical condition immediately after birth. (p. 128)

assimilation That part of adaptation in which the external world is interpreted in terms of current schemes. Distinguished from *accommodation*. (p. 204)

associative play A form of true social interaction in which children engage in separate activities but interact by exchanging toys and commenting on one another's behavior. Distinguished from *nonsocial activity, parallel play,* and *cooperative play*. (p. 372)

attachment The strong affectionate tie that humans have with special people in their lives, which leads them to feel pleasure when interacting with those people and to be comforted by their nearness in times of stress. (p. 264)

Attachment Q-Sort A method of assessing the quality of attachment in children between 1 and 4 years of age through home observations of a variety of attachment-related behaviors. (p. 267)

attention-deficit hyperactivity disorder A childhood disorder involving inattentiveness, impulsivity, and excessive motor activity, often leading to academic and social problems. (p. 444)

attribution retraining An intervention that encourages learned-helpless children to believe they can overcome failure by exerting more effort. (p. 488)

authoritarian child-rearing style A child-rearing style that is low in acceptance and involvement, high in coercive and psychological control, and low in autonomy granting. Distinguished from *authoritative, permissive,* and *uninvolved child-rearing styles*. (p. 399)

authoritative child-rearing style A child-rearing style that is high in acceptance and involvement, emphasizes adaptive control techniques, and includes gradual, appropriate autonomy granting. Distinguished from *authoritarian, permissive,* and *uninvolved child-rearing styles*. (p. 398)

autobiographical memory Long-lasting representations of personally meaningful one-time events from both the recent and the distant past. (p. 221)

autonomy At adolescence, a sense of oneself as a separate, self-governing individual. Involves relying more on oneself and less on parents for support and guidance and engaging in careful, well-reasoned decision making. (p. 619)

autonomy versus shame and doubt In Erikson's theory, the psychological conflict of toddlerhood, which is resolved favorably when parents provide young children with suitable guidance and reasonable choices. (p. 249)

autosomes The 22 matching chromosome pairs in each human cell. (p. 54)

avoidant attachment The attachment pattern characterizing infants who seem unresponsive to the parent when she is present, are usually not distressed by parental separation, and avoid or are slow to greet the parent when she returns. Distinguished from *secure, resistant,* and *disorganized/disoriented attachment*. (p. 267)

B

babbling Repetition of consonant–vowel combinations in long strings, beginning around 6 months of age. (p. 236)

basic emotions Emotions such as happiness, interest, surprise, fear, anger, sadness, and disgust that are universal in humans and other primates and have a long evolutionary history of promoting survival. (p. 250)

basic trust versus mistrust In Erikson's theory, the psychological conflict of infancy, which is resolved positively when the balance of care is sympathetic and loving. (p. 248)

behavioral genetics A field devoted to uncovering the contributions of nature and nurture to the diversity in human traits and abilities. (p. 82)

behaviorism An approach that regards directly observable events—stimuli and responses—as the appropriate focus of study and views the development of behavior as taking place through classical and operant conditioning. (p. 17)

behavior modification Procedures that combine conditioning and modeling to eliminate undesirable behaviors and increase desirable responses. (p. 18)

bicultural identity The identity constructed by individuals who explore and adopt values from both their family's subculture and the dominant culture. (p. 607)

blastocyst The zygote four days after fertilization, when the tiny mass of cells forms a hollow, fluid-filled ball. (p. 98)

blended, or **reconstituted, family** A family structure formed through cohabitation or remarriage that includes parent, child, and steprelatives. (p. 513)

body image Conception of and attitude toward one's physical appearance. (p. 542)

bonding Parents' feelings of affection and concern for the newborn baby. (p. 143)

brain plasticity The capacity of various parts of the cerebral cortex to take over functions of damaged regions. Declines as hemispheres of the cerebral cortex lateralize. (p. 168)

breech position A position of the baby in the uterus that would cause the buttocks or feet to be delivered first. (p. 134)

bulimia nervosa An eating disorder in which individuals, mainly females, engage in strict dieting and excessive exercise accompanied by binge eating, often followed by deliberate vomiting and purging with laxatives. (p. 546)

C

canalization The tendency of heredity to restrict the development of some characteristics to just one or a few outcomes. (p. 84)

cardinality The mathematical principle stating that the last number in a counting sequence indicates the quantity of items in the set. (p. 344)

carrier A heterozygous individual who can pass a recessive trait to his or her children. (p. 56)

central executive In information processing, the conscious part of working memory that directs the flow of information through the mental system by deciding what to attend to, coordinating incoming information with information already in the system, and selecting, applying, and monitoring strategies. (p. 218)

centration In Piaget's theory, the tendency of preoperational children to focus on one aspect of a situation while neglecting other important features. (p. 322)

cephalocaudal trend An organized pattern of physical growth in which the head develops more rapidly than the lower part of the body ("head to tail"). Distinguished from *proximodistal trend.* (p. 162)

cerebellum A structure at the rear and base of the brain that aids in balance and control of body movement. (p. 294)

cerebral cortex The largest, most complex structure of the human brain, containing the greatest number of neurons and synapses, which accounts for the highly developed intelligence of the human species. (p. 167)

cesarean delivery A surgical delivery in which the doctor makes an incision in the mother's abdomen and lifts the baby out of the uterus. (p. 134)

child-centered programs Preschool and kindergarten programs in which teachers provide a variety of activities from which children select, and much learning takes place through play. Distinguished from *academic programs.* (p. 348)

child development An area of study devoted to understanding constancy and change from conception through adolescence and emerging adulthood. (p. 4)

child-directed speech (CDS) A form of language adults use to speak to infants and toddlers, consisting of short sentences with high-pitched, exaggerated expression, clear pronunciation, distinct pauses between speech segments, clear gestures to support verbal meaning, and repetition of new words in a variety of contexts. (p. 241)

child-rearing styles Combinations of parenting behaviors that occur over a wide range of situations, creating an enduring child-rearing climate. (p. 398)

chorion The outer membrane that forms a protective covering around the prenatal organism. It sends out tiny hairlike villi, from which the placenta begins to develop. (p. 98)

chromosomes Rodlike structures in the cell nucleus that store and transmit genetic information. (p. 52)

chronosystem In ecological systems theory, temporal changes in environments, either externally imposed or arising from within the child, that produce new conditions affecting development. Distinguished from *microsystem, mesosystem, exosystem,* and *macrosystem.* (p. 27)

circular reaction In Piaget's theory, a means of building schemes in which infants try to repeat a chance event caused by their own motor activity. (p. 205)

classical conditioning A form of learning that involves associating a neutral stimulus with a stimulus that leads to a reflexive response. Once the nervous system makes the connection between the two stimuli, the neutral stimulus alone will produce the response. (p. 179)

clinical interview An interview method in which the researcher uses a flexible, conversational style to probe for the participant's point of view. Distinguished from *structured interview.* (p. 33)

clinical, or **case study, method** A research method in which the aim is to obtain as complete a picture as possible of one individual's psychological functioning by bringing together interview data, observations, and sometimes test scores. (p. 34)

clique A group of about five to eight members who are good friends and, therefore, usually resemble one another in family background, attitudes, values, and interests. (p. 626)

cognitive-developmental theory An approach introduced by Piaget that views children as actively constructing knowledge as they manipulate and explore their world, and in which cognitive development takes place in stages. (p. 19)

cognitive maps Mental representations of familiar large-scale spaces, such as neighborhood or school. (p. 438)

cognitive self-regulation The process of continuously monitoring progress toward a goal, checking outcomes, and redirecting unsuccessful efforts. (p. 449)

cohort effects The effects of cultural-historical change on the accuracy of longitudinal and cross-sectional research findings. Results based on one cohort—individuals developing in the same time period, who are influenced by particular historical and cultural conditions—may not apply to other cohorts. (p. 41)

collectivist societies Societies in which people define themselves as part of a group and stress group goals over individual goals. Distinguished from *individualistic societies.* (p. 78)

commitment within relativistic thinking The mature individual's formulation of a perspective that synthesizes contradictions between opposing views, rather than choosing between them. (p. 648)

communities of learners An educational approach inspired by Vygotsky's theory, in which teachers guide the overall process of learning, but otherwise, no distinction is made between adult and child contributors. All participate in joint endeavors, and students have the authority to define and resolve problems as they work toward project goals, which often address complex real-world issues.(p. 469)

compliance Voluntary obedience to requests and commands. (p. 282)

comprehension In language development, the words and word combinations that children understand. Distinguished from *production.* (p. 240)

concrete operational stage Piaget's third stage, extending from about 7 to 11 years of age, during which thought becomes logical, flexible, and organized in its application to concrete information, but the capacity for abstract thinking is not yet present. (p. 438)

conditioned response (CR) In classical conditioning, a new response produced by a conditioned stimulus (CS) that is similar to the unconditioned, or reflexive, response (UCR). (p. 179)

conditioned stimulus (CS) In classical conditioning, a neutral stimulus that, through pairing with an unconditioned stimulus (UCS), leads to a new, conditioned response (CR). Distinguished from *unconditioned stimulus.* (p. 179)

conservation The understanding that certain physical characteristics of objects remain the same, even when their outward appearance changes. (p. 321)

constructivist classroom A classroom grounded in Piaget's view of children as active learners who construct their own knowledge. Features include richly equipped learning centers, small groups and individuals solving self-chosen problems, a teacher who guides and supports in response to children's needs, and evaluation based on individual students' progress in relation to their own prior development. Distinguished from *traditional classroom* and *social-constructivist classroom.* (pp. 467–468)

contexts Unique combinations of personal and environmental circumstances that can result in different paths of development. (p. 8)

continuous development The view that development is a process of gradually adding more of the same types of skills that were there to begin with. Distinguished from *discontinuous development.* (p. 7)

contrast sensitivity A general principle accounting for early pattern preferences, which states that if babies can detect a difference in contrast between two patterns, they will prefer the pattern with more visual contrast. (p. 193)

control deficiency The inability to control, or execute, a mental strategy consistently. Distinguished from *production deficiency, utilization deficiency,* and *effective strategy use.* (p. 443)

controversial children Children who receive many votes, both positive and negative, on self-report measures of peer acceptance, indicating that they are both liked and disliked. Distinguished from *popular, rejected,* and *neglected children.* (p. 500)

conventional level Kohlberg's second level of moral development, in which moral understanding is based on conforming to social rules to ensure positive human relationships and maintain societal order. (p. 609)

convergent thinking The type of thinking emphasized on intelligence tests, which involves arriving at a single correct answer to a problem. Distinguished from *divergent thinking.* (p. 474)

cooing Pleasant vowel-like noises made by infants, beginning around 2 months of age. (p. 236)

cooperative learning Collaboration on a task by a small group of classmates who work toward common goals by resolving differences of opinion, sharing responsibilities, and providing one another with sufficient explanation to correct misunderstandings. (p. 471)

cooperative play A form of social interaction in which children orient toward a common goal, such as acting out a make-believe theme. Distinguished from *nonsocial activity, parallel play,* and *associative play.* (p. 372)

coparenting An approach in which parents mutually support each other's parenting behaviors. (p. 70)

coregulation A form of supervision in which parents exercise general oversight while permitting children to take charge of moment-by-moment decision making. (p. 507)

core knowledge perspective A perspective that states that infants are born with a set of innate knowledge systems, or core domains of thought, each of which permits a ready grasp of new, related information and therefore supports early, rapid development of certain aspects of cognition. (p. 214)

corpus callosum The large bundle of fibers connecting the two hemispheres of the cerebral cortex. (p. 295)

correlational design A research design in which the investigator gathers information on individuals without altering their experiences and then examines relationships between participants' characteristics and their behavior or development. Does not permit inferences about cause and effect. (p. 37)

correlation coefficient A number, ranging from +1.00 to −1.00, that describes the strength and direction of the relationship between two variables. (p. 37)

creativity The ability to produce work that is original yet appropriate—something others have not thought of that is useful in some way. (p. 474)

crossing over During meiosis, the exchange of genes between chromosomes next to each other. (p. 53)

cross-sectional design A research design in which groups of participants of different ages are studied at the same point in time. Distinguished from *longitudinal design.* (p. 41)

crowd A large, loosely organized social group consisting of several cliques with similar values. Membership is based on reputation and stereotype. (p. 626)

D

deferred imitation The ability to remember and copy the behavior of models who are not present. (p. 207)

delay of gratification The ability to wait for an appropriate time and place to engage in a tempting act. (p. 283)

deoxyribonucleic acid (DNA) Long, double-stranded molecules that make up chromosomes. (p. 52)

dependent variable The variable the investigator expects to be influenced by the independent variable in an experiment. Distinguished from *independent variable.* (p. 37)

developmental cognitive neuroscience An area of investigation that brings together researchers from psychology, biology, neuroscience, and medicine to study the relationship between changes in the brain and the developing child's cognitive processing and behavior patterns. (p. 23)

developmentally appropriate practice A set of standards devised by the National Association for the Education of Young Children, specifying program characteristics that meet the developmental and individual needs of young children of varying ages, based on current research and the consensus of experts. (p. 230)

developmental quotient (DQ) A score on an infant intelligence test, computed in the same manner as an IQ but labeled more conservatively because it does not tap the same dimensions of intelligence measured in older children. (p. 228)

developmental science An interdisciplinary field devoted to the study of all changes humans experience throughout the lifespan. (p. 4)

differentiation theory The view that perceptual development involves the detection of increasingly fine-grained, invariant features in the environment. (p. 198)

difficult child A child whose temperament is characterized by irregular daily routines, slow acceptance of new experiences, and a tendency to react negatively and intensely. Distinguished from *easy child* and *slow-to-warm-up child.* (p. 256)

dilation and effacement of the cervix Widening and thinning of the cervix during the first stage of labor. (p. 126)

discontinuous development A view of development as a process in which new ways of understanding and responding to the world emerge at specific times. Distinguished from *continuous development.* (p. 8)

disorganized/disoriented attachment The attachment pattern reflecting the greatest insecurity, characterizing infants who show confused, contradictory behaviors when reunited with the parent after a separation. Distinguished from secure, *avoidant,* and *resistant attachment.* (p. 267)

displaced reference The realization that words can be used to cue mental images of things that are not physically present. (p. 211)

divergent thinking The type of thinking associated with creativity, which involves generating multiple and unusual possibilities when faced with a task or problem. Distinguished from *convergent thinking.* (p. 474)

divorce mediation A series of meetings between divorcing adults and a trained professional that are aimed at reducing family conflict, including legal battles over property division and child custody. (p. 513)

dominance hierarchy A stable ordering of group members that predicts who will win when conflict arises. (p. 432)

dominant cerebral hemisphere The hemisphere of the cerebral cortex responsible for skilled motor action and other important abilities. In right-handed individuals, the left hemisphere is dominant; in left-handed individuals, motor and language skills are often shared between the hemispheres. (p. 293)

dominant–recessive inheritance A pattern of inheritance in which, under heterozygous conditions, the influence of only one allele is apparent. (p. 56)

dualistic thinking The cognitive approach typical of younger college students, who believe that knowledge is made up of separate beliefs and propositions, whose truth can be determined by comparing them with objective standards. As a result, they divide information, values, and authority into right and wrong, good and bad, we and they. Distinguished from *relativistic thinking*. (p. 648)

dual representation The ability to view a symbolic object as both an object in its own right and a symbol. (p. 320)

dynamic assessment An approach to testing consistent with Vygotsky's zone of proximal development, in which purposeful teaching is introduced into the testing situation to find out what the child can attain with social support. (p. 461)

dynamic systems perspective A view that regards the child's mind, body, and physical and social worlds as a dynamic, integrated system. A change in any part of the system leads the child to reorganize his or her behavior so the various components of the system work together again but in a more complex, effective way. (p. 28)

dynamic systems theory of motor development A theory that views new motor skills as reorganizations of previously mastered skills, which lead to more effective ways of exploring and controlling the environment. Each new skill is a joint product of central nervous system development, the body's movement possibilities, environmental supports for the skill, and the child's goals. (pp. 184–185)

E

easy child A child whose temperament is characterized by establishment of regular routines in infancy, general cheerfulness, and easy adaptation to new experiences. Distinguished from *difficult child* and *slow-to-warm-up child*. (p. 256)

ecological systems theory Bronfenbrenner's approach, which views the child as developing within a complex system of relationships affected by multiple levels of the surrounding environment, from immediate settings of family and school to broad cultural values, laws, customs, and resources. (pp. 25–26)

educational self-fulfilling prophecies Teachers' positive or negative views of individual children, who tend to adopt and start to live up to those views. (p. 470)

effective strategy use Consistent use of a mental strategy that leads to improvement in performance. Distinguished from *production deficiency, control deficiency,* and *utilization deficiency*. (p. 443)

effortful control The self-regulatory dimension of temperament, involving voluntary suppression of a dominant response in order to plan and execute a more adaptive response. (pp. 257–258)

egocentrism Failure to distinguish the symbolic viewpoints of others from one's own. (p. 321)

elaboration A memory strategy that involves creating a relationship, or shared meaning, between two or more items of information that are not members of the same category. (p. 446)

embryo The prenatal organism from 2 to 8 weeks after conception—the period when the groundwork for all body structures and internal organs is laid down. (p. 99)

embryonic disk A small cluster of cells on the inside of the blastocyst, from which the new organism will develop. (p. 98)

emergent literacy Children's active efforts to construct literacy knowledge through informal experiences. (p. 343)

emerging adulthood A new transitional period of development, extending from the late teens to the mid-twenties, during which young people have left adolescence but have not yet assumed adult responsibilities. Rather, they continue to explore alternatives in education, work, personal beliefs and values, and love. (p. 644)

emotional intelligence A set of emotional abilities that enable individuals to process and adapt to emotional information. Measured by tapping the emotional skills people use to manage their own emotions and interact competently with others. (p. 457)

emotional self-regulation Strategies for adjusting our emotional state to a comfortable level of intensity so we can accomplish our goals. (p. 254)

emotion-centered coping A strategy for managing emotion that is internal, private, and aimed at controlling distress when little can be done to change an outcome. Distinguished from *problem-centered coping*. (pp. 490–491)

empathy The ability to understand another's emotional state and to *feel with* that person, or respond emotionally in a similar way. (p. 282)

epigenesis Development resulting from ongoing, bidirectional exchanges between heredity and all levels of the environment. (p. 86)

epiphyses Growth centers at the ends of the long bones of the body, where new cartilage cells are produced and gradually harden. (p. 163)

episodic memory Memory for everyday experiences. (p. 336)

epistemic cognition Reflections on how one arrived at facts, beliefs, and ideas. (p. 648)

ethnic identity A sense of ethnic group membership and attitudes and feelings associated with that membership, as an enduring aspect of the self. (p. 607)

ethnography A research method in which an investigator attempts to understand the unique values and social processes of a culture or a distinct social group through participant observation—living with members of the cultural community and taking field notes over an extended period of time. (pp. 34–35)

ethological theory of attachment Bowlby's theory, the most widely accepted view of attachment, which regards the infant's emotional tie to the caregiver as an evolved response that promotes survival. (p. 265)

ethology An approach concerned with the adaptive, or survival, value of behavior and its evolutionary history. (p. 23)

evolutionary developmental psychology An approach that seeks to understand the adaptive value of species-wide cognitive, emotional, and social competencies as those competencies change with age. (p. 24)

exosystem In ecological systems theory, social settings that do not contain children but nevertheless affect children's experiences—for example, parents' workplaces, religious institutions, health and welfare services in the community, and parents' social networks. Distinguished from *microsystem, mesosystem, macrosystem,* and *chronosystem*. (p. 27)

expansions Adult responses that elaborate on children's speech, increasing its complexity. (p. 359)

experience-dependent brain growth Growth and refinement of established brain structures as a result of specific learning experiences that vary widely across individuals and cultures. Distinguished from *experience-expectant brain growth*. (p. 172)

experience-expectant brain growth The young brain's rapidly developing organization, which depends on ordinary experiences—opportunities to see and touch objects, to hear language and other sounds, and to move about and explore the environment. Distinguished from *experience-dependent brain growth*. (p. 172)

experimental design A research design in which the investigator randomly assigns participants to two or more treatment conditions and studies the effect that manipulating an independent variable has on a dependent variable. Permits inferences about cause and effect. (p. 37)

expressive style A style of early language learning in which toddlers use language mainly to talk about their own feelings and needs and those of others, with an initial vocabulary emphasizing social formulas and pronouns. Distinguished from *referential style*. (p. 240)

extended-family household A household in which parent and child live with one or more adult relatives. (p. 78)

F

fantasy period The period of vocational development in which children gain insight into career options by fantasizing about them. Distinguished from *tentative period* and *realistic period*. (p. 590)

fast mapping Children's ability to connect new words with their underlying concepts after only a brief encounter. (p. 354)

fetal alcohol spectrum disorder (FASD) A range of physical, mental, and behavioral outcomes caused by prenatal alcohol exposure, including *fetal alcohol syndrome (FAS), partial fetal alcohol syndrome (p-FAS),* and *alcohol-related neurodevelopmental disorder (ARND)*. (p. 108)

fetal alcohol syndrome (FAS) The most severe form of fetal alcohol spectrum disorder, distinguished by slow physical growth, facial abnormalities, and brain injury. Usually affects children whose mothers drank heavily during most or all of pregnancy. Distinguished from *partial fetal alcohol syndrome (p-FAS)* and *alcohol-related neurodevelopmental disorder (ARND).* (p. 108)

fetal monitors Electronic instruments that track the baby's heart rate during labor. (p. 132)

fetus The prenatal organism from the ninth week to the end of pregnancy—the period during which body structures are completed and dramatic growth in size occurs. (p. 100)

fontanels Six gaps, or "soft spots," separating the bones of the skull at birth. (p. 164)

formal operational stage Piaget's highest stage, beginning around 11 years of age, in which young people develop the capacity for abstract, systematic, scientific thinking. (p. 566)

fraternal, or dizygotic, twins Twins resulting from the release and fertilization of two ova. They are genetically no more alike than ordinary siblings. Distinguished from *identical,* or *monozygotic, twins.* (p. 55)

G

gametes Sex cells, or sperm and ova, which contain half as many chromosomes as regular body cells. (p. 53)

gender constancy A full understanding of the biologically based permanence of one's gender, including the realization that sex remains the same over time even if clothing, hairstyle, and play activities change. (p. 395)

gender identity An image of oneself as relatively masculine or feminine in characteristics. (p. 395)

gender intensification Increased gender stereotyping of attitudes and behavior and movement toward a more traditional gender identity, typical of early adolescence. (p. 618)

gender schema theory An information-processing approach to gender typing that explains how environmental pressures and children's cognitions work together to shape gender-role development. (p. 396)

gender typing Any association of objects, activities, roles, or traits with one sex or the other in ways that conform to cultural stereotypes. (p. 390)

gene A segment of a DNA molecule that contains instructions for production of various proteins that contribute to the body's growth and functioning. (p. 52)

genetic counseling A communication process designed to help couples assess their chances of giving birth to a baby with a hereditary disorder and choose the best course of action in view of risks and family goals. (p. 63)

genetic–environmental correlation The idea that heredity influences the environments to which individuals are exposed. (p. 85)

genomic imprinting A pattern of inheritance in which alleles are imprinted, or chemically marked, in such a way that one pair member is activated, regardless of its makeup. (p. 59)

genotype An individual's genetic makeup. Distinguished from *phenotype.* (p. 51)

gifted Displaying exceptional intellectual strengths, including high IQ, creativity, and specialized talent. (p. 474)

glial cells Cells that are responsible for myelination of neural fibers, improving the efficiency of message transfer and, in certain instances, also participate directly in neural communication. (p. 165)

goodness-of-fit model A model that describes how favorable adjustment depends on an effective match, or good fit, between a child's temperament and the child-rearing environment. (p. 262)

growth faltering Failure of an infant to grow normally, characterized by weight, height, and head circumference substantially below age-related norms and by withdrawn, apathetic behavior, with a disturbed parent–infant relationship often a contributing factor. (p. 178)

growth hormone (GH) A pituitary hormone that affects the development of all body tissues except the central nervous system and the genitals. (p. 297)

growth spurt Rapid gain in height and weight that is the first outward sign of puberty. (p. 532)

guided participation Shared endeavors between more expert and less expert participants, without specifying the precise features of communication, thereby allowing for variations across situations and cultures. A broader concept than *scaffolding.* (p. 331)

H

habituation A gradual reduction in the strength of a response due to repetitive stimulation. (pp. 180–181)

heritability estimate A measure of the extent to which individual differences in complex traits, such as intelligence or personality, in a specific population are due to genetic factors. (p. 82)

heterozygous Having two different alleles at the same place on a pair of chromosomes. Distinguished from *homozygous.* (p. 56)

hierarchical classification The organization of objects into classes and subclasses on the basis of similarities and differences between the groups. (p. 322)

hippocampus An inner-brain structure that plays a vital role in memory and in images of space we use to help us find our way. (p. 294)

Home Observation for Measurement of the Environment (HOME) A checklist for gathering information about the quality of children's home lives through observation and parental interview. (p. 229)

homozygous Having two identical alleles at the same place on a pair of chromosomes. Distinguished from *heterozygous.* (p. 56)

hypothetico-deductive reasoning A formal operational problem-solving strategy in which adolescents begin with a *hypothesis,* or prediction, about variables that might affect an outcome. From the hypothesis, they *deduce* logical, testable inferences. Then they systematically isolate and combine variables to see which of those inferences are confirmed in the real world. (p. 566)

I

identical, or monozygotic, twins Twins that result when a zygote, during early cell duplication, separates into two clusters of cells that have the same genetic makeup. Distinguished from *fraternal,* or *dizygotic, twins.* (p. 55)

identity A well-organized conception of the self that defines who one is, what one values, and what directions one wants to pursue in life. (p. 600)

identity achievement The identity status of individuals who, after a period of exploration, have committed themselves to a clearly formulated set of self-chosen values and goals. Distinguished from *identity moratorium, identity foreclosure,* and *identity diffusion.* (p. 603)

identity diffusion The identity status of individuals who do not engage in exploration and are not committed to a set of values and goals. Distinguished from *identity achievement, identity moratorium,* and *identity foreclosure.* (p. 603)

identity foreclosure The identity status of individuals who do not engage in exploration but, instead, are committed to ready-made values and goals chosen for them by authority figures. Distinguished from *identity achievement, identity moratorium,* and *identity diffusion.* (p. 603)

identity moratorium The identity status of individuals who are exploring but not yet committed to self-chosen values and goals. Distinguished from *identity achievement, identity foreclosure,* and *identity diffusion.* (p. 603)

identity versus role confusion In Erikson's theory, the psychological conflict of adolescence, which is resolved positively when adolescents achieve an identity after a period of exploration and inner soul-searching. (p. 600)

imaginary audience Adolescents' belief that they are the focus of everyone else's attention and concern. (p. 572)

imitation Learning by copying the behavior of another person. Also known as *modeling* or *observational learning.* (p. 181)

implantation Attachment of the blastocyst to the uterine lining, which occurs 7 to 9 days after fertilization. (p. 98)

inclusive classrooms Classrooms in which students with learning difficulties learn alongside typical students in a regular educational setting for part or all of the school day. (p. 473)

incomplete dominance A pattern of inheritance in which both alleles are expressed in the phenotype, resulting in a combined trait, or one that is intermediate between the two. (p. 57)

independent variable In an experiment, the variable the researcher expects to cause changes in another variable and that the researcher manipulates by randomly assigning participants to treatment conditions. Distinguished from *dependent variable.* (p. 37)

individualistic societies Societies in which people think of themselves as separate entities and are largely concerned with their own personal needs. Distinguished from *collectivist societies.* (p. 78)

induced labor A labor started artificially by breaking the amnion and giving the mother a hormone that stimulates contractions. (p. 134)

induction A type of discipline in which an adult helps the child notice feelings by pointing out the effects of the child's misbehavior on others. (p. 379)

industry versus inferiority In Erikson's theory, the psychological conflict of middle childhood, which is resolved positively when experiences lead children to develop a sense of competence at useful skills and tasks. (p. 482)

infantile amnesia The inability of most people to remember events that happened to them before age 3. (p. 221)

infant mortality The number of deaths in the first year of life per 1,000 live births. (p. 140)

information processing An approach that views the human mind as a symbol-manipulating system through which information flows and that regards cognitive development as a continuous process. (p. 21)

inhibited, or shy, child A child whose temperament is such that he or she displays negative reaction to and withdrawal from novel stimuli. Distinguished from *uninhibited, or sociable, child.* (p. 258)

initiative versus guilt In Erikson's theory, the psychological conflict of early childhood, which is resolved positively through play experiences that foster a healthy sense of purposefulness and through the development of a superego, or conscience, that is not overly strict or guilt-ridden. (p. 364)

intelligence quotient (IQ) A score that permits an individual's performance on an intelligence test to be compared to the performances of other individuals of the same age. (p. 227)

intentional, or goal-directed, behavior A sequence of actions in which schemes are deliberately coordinated to solve a problem. (p. 206)

interactional synchrony A form of communication in which the caregiver responds to infant signals in a well-timed, rhythmic, appropriate fashion and both partners match emotional states, especially positive ones. (p. 270)

intermodal perception Perception that combines information from more than one modality, or sensory system, resulting in an integrated whole. (p. 197)

internal working model A set of expectations derived from early caregiving experiences concerning the availability of attachment figures, their likelihood of providing support during times of stress, and the self's interaction with those figures. Becomes a model, or guide, for all future close relationships. (p. 266)

intersubjectivity The process by which two participants who begin a task with different understandings arrive at a shared understanding. (p. 331)

irreversibility The inability to mentally go through a series of steps in a problem and then reverse direction, returning to the starting point. Distinguished from *reversibility.* (p. 322)

J

joint attention A state in which the child and caregiver attend to the same object or event and the caregiver labels what the child sees. Supports language development. (p. 238)

K

kinship studies Studies comparing the characteristics of family members to determine the importance of heredity in complex human characteristics. (p. 82)

kwashiorkor A disease caused by an unbalanced diet very low in protein, which usually appears after weaning, between 1 and 3 years of age. Symptoms include an enlarged belly, swollen feet, hair loss, skin rash, and irritable, listless behavior. (p. 177)

L

language acquisition device (LAD) In Chomsky's theory, an innate system containing a universal grammar, or set of rules common to all languages, that enables children, no matter which language they hear, to understand and speak in a rule-oriented fashion as soon as they have learned enough words. (p. 234)

lanugo White, downy hair that covers the entire body of the fetus, helping the vernix stick to the skin. (p. 100)

lateralization Specialization of functions in the two hemispheres of the cerebral cortex. (p. 168)

learned helplessness Attribution of success to external factors such as luck, and failure to low ability, which cannot be improved through effort. Distinguished from *mastery-oriented attributions.* (p. 487)

learning disabilities Great difficulty with one or more aspects of learning, usually reading, resulting in achievement considerably behind what would be expected on the basis of a child's IQ. (p. 473)

logical necessity A basic property of propositional thought, which specifies that the accuracy of conclusions drawn from premises rests on the rules of logic, not on real-world confirmation. (p. 568)

longitudinal design A research design in which participants are studied repeatedly at different ages, and changes are noted as they get older. Distinguished from *cross-sectional design.* (p. 40)

long-term memory In information processing, the largest storage area in the mental system, containing our permanent knowledge base. (p. 218)

M

macrosystem In ecological systems theory, cultural values, laws, customs, and resources that influence experiences and interactions at inner levels of the environment. Distinguished from *microsystem, mesosystem, exosystem,* and *chronosystem.* (p. 27)

make-believe play A type of play in which children act out everyday and imaginary activities. (p. 207)

malocclusion A condition in which the upper and lower teeth do not meet properly. (p. 414)

marasmus A disease caused by a diet low in all essential nutrients that usually appears in the first year of life and leads to a wasted condition of the body. (p. 177)

mastery-oriented attributions Attributions that credit success to ability, which can be improved by trying hard, and failure to insufficient effort. Distinguished from *learned helplessness.* (p. 486)

matters of personal choice Concerns that do not violate the rights or welfare of others and, therefore, are up to each individual, such as choice of friends, hairstyle, and leisure activities. Distinguished from *moral imperatives* and *social conventions.* (p. 384)

maturation A genetically determined, naturally unfolding course of growth. (p. 13)

meiosis The process of cell division through which gametes are formed and in which the number of chromosomes in each cell is halved. (p. 53)

memory strategies Deliberate mental activities that improve the likelihood of remembering. (p. 336)

menarche First menstruation. (p. 536)

mental representation An internal depiction of information that the mind can manipulate. (p. 207)

mental strategies In information processing, procedures that operate on and transform information, thereby increasing the efficiency and flexibility of thinking and the chances that information will be retained. (p. 217)

mesosystem In ecological systems theory, connections between children's microsystems, or immediate settings. Distinguished from *microsystem, exosystem, macrosystem,* and *chronosystem.* (p. 26)

metacognition Thinking about thought; awareness of mental activities. (p. 338)

metalinguistic awareness The ability to think about language as a system. (p. 462)

microgenetic design A research design in which investigators present children with a novel task and follow their mastery over a series of closely spaced sessions. (p. 43)

microsystem In ecological systems theory, the innermost level of the environment, consisting of activities and interaction patterns in the child's immediate surroundings. Distinguished from *mesosystem, exosystem, macrosystem,* and *chronosystem.* (p. 26)

mirror neurons Specialized cells in many areas of the cerebral cortex in primates that underlie the ability to imitate by firing identically when a primate hears or sees an action and when it carries out that action on its own. (p. 182)

mitosis The process of cell duplication, in which each new cell receives an exact copy of the original chromosomes. (p. 53)

modifier genes Genes that enhance or dilute the effects of other genes. (p. 57)

moral imperatives Rules and standards that protect people's rights and welfare. Distinguished from *social conventions* and *matters of personal choice.* (p. 384)

moral self-relevance The degree to which morality is central to an individual's self-concept. (p. 615)

mutation A sudden but permanent change in a segment of DNA. (p. 60)

mutual exclusivity bias Early in vocabulary growth, children's assumption that words refer to entirely separate, nonoverlapping categories. (p. 355)

myelination The coating of neural fibers with *myelin,* an insulating fatty sheath that improves the efficiency of message transfer. (p. 165)

N

naturalistic observation A research method in which the researcher goes into the natural environment to observe the behavior of interest. Distinguished from *structured observation.* (p. 31)

natural, or **prepared, childbirth** A group of techniques designed to reduce pain and medical intervention and to make childbirth as rewarding an experience as possible. (p. 130)

nature–nurture controversy Debate among theorists about whether genetic or environmental factors are more important influences on development. (p. 9)

neglected children Children who are seldom mentioned, either positively or negatively, on self-report measures of peer acceptance. Distinguished from *popular, controversial,* and *rejected children.* (p. 500)

Neonatal Behavioral Assessment Scale (NBAS) A test developed to assess a newborn infant's behavior in terms of reflexes, muscle tone, state changes, and responsiveness to physical and social stimuli. (p. 152)

neonatal mortality The number of deaths in the first month of life per 1,000 live births. (p. 140)

neural tube During the period of the embryo, the primitive spinal cord that develops from the ectoderm, the top of which swells to form the brain. (p. 99).

neurons Nerve cells that store and transmit information. (p. 164)

neurotransmitters Chemicals released by neurons that cross the synapse to send messages to other neurons. (p. 164)

niche-picking A type of genetic–environmental correlation in which individuals actively choose environments that complement their heredity. (p. 85)

nocturnal enuresis Bedwetting during the night. (p. 422)

non-rapid-eye-movement (NREM) sleep A "regular" sleep state in which the body is almost motionless and heart rate, breathing, and brain-wave activity are slow and even. Distinguished from *rapid-eye-movement (REM) sleep.* (p. 146)

nonsocial activity Unoccupied, onlooker behavior and solitary play. Distinguished from *parallel play, associative play,* and *cooperative play.* (p. 372)

normal distribution The bell-shaped distribution that results when individual differences are measured in large samples. Most scores cluster around the mean, or average, with progressively fewer falling toward the extremes. (p. 228)

normative approach An approach to development in which measures of behavior are taken on large numbers of individuals and age-related averages are computed to represent typical development. (p. 13)

O

obesity A greater-than-20-percent increase over healthy weight, based on body mass index, a ratio of weight to height associated with body fat. (p. 416)

object permanence The understanding that objects continue to exist when they are out of sight. (p. 207)

operant conditioning A form of learning in which a spontaneous behavior is followed by a stimulus that influences the probability that the behavior will occur again. (p. 180)

ordinality The mathematical principle specifying order relationships (more than and less than) between quantities. (p. 344)

organization In Piaget's theory, the internal rearrangement and linking together of schemes so that they form a strongly interconnected cognitive system. In information processing, a memory strategy that involves grouping related items together to improve recall. (pp. 205, 446)

overextension An early vocabulary error in which a word is applied too broadly, to a wider collection of objects and events than is appropriate. Distinguished from *underextension.* (p. 239)

overlapping-waves theory A theory of problem solving, which states that when given challenging problems, children try out various strategies and gradually select those that are fastest and most accurate. (p. 338)

overregularization Extension of regular grammatical rules to words that are exceptions. (p. 357)

P

parallel play A form of limited social participation in which a child plays near other children with similar materials but does not interact with them. Distinguished from *nonsocial activity, associative play,* and *cooperative play.* (p. 372)

partial fetal alcohol syndrome (p-FAS) A form of fetal alcohol spectrum disorder characterized by facial abnormalities and brain injury, but less severe than fetal alcohol syndrome; usually seen in children whose mothers drank alcohol in smaller quantities during pregnancy. (p. 108)

peer acceptance Likability, or the extent to which a child is viewed by a group of agemates as a worthy social partner. (p. 500)

peer groups Collectives of peers who generate unique values and standards for behavior and a social structure of leaders and followers. (p. 498)

peer victimization A destructive form of peer interaction in which certain children become frequent targets of verbal and physical attacks or other forms of abuse. (p. 502)

permissive child-rearing style A child-rearing style that is high in acceptance but either overindulgent or inattentive, low in control, and inappropriately lenient in autonomy granting. Distinguished from *authoritative, authoritarian,* and *uninvolved child-rearing styles.* (p. 399)

personal fable Adolescents' inflated opinion of their own importance—the belief that they are special and unique and that others cannot possibly understand their thoughts and feelings. (p. 572)

perspective taking The capacity to imagine what other people may be thinking and feeling. (p. 491)

phenotype An individual's directly observable physical and behavioral characteristics, which are determined by both genetic and environmental factors. Distinguished from *genotype*. (p. 51)

phobia An intense, unmanageable fear that leads to persistent avoidance of the feared situation. (p. 517)

phonics approach An approach to beginning reading instruction that emphasizes coaching children on phonics—the basic rules for translating written symbols into sounds—before exposing them to complex reading material. Distinguished from *whole-language approach*. (p. 450)

phonological awareness The ability to reflect on and manipulate the sound structure of spoken language, as indicated by sensitivity to changes in sounds within words, to rhyming, and to incorrect pronunciation. A strong predictor of emergent literacy. (p. 343)

physical aggression A form of aggression that harms others through physical injury to themselves or their property. Distinguished from *verbal aggression* and *relational aggression*. (p. 385)

pincer grasp The well-coordinated grasp that emerges at the end of the first year, involving thumb and index finger opposition. (p. 188)

pituitary gland A gland located at the base of the brain that releases hormones affecting physical growth. (p. 297)

placenta The organ that permits exchange of nutrients and waste products between the bloodstreams of the mother and the embryo, while also preventing the mother's and embryo's blood from mixing directly. (p. 98)

planning Thinking out a sequence of acts ahead of time and allocating attention accordingly to reach a goal. (p. 335)

plasticity Openness of human development to change in response to influential experiences throughout life. (p. 9)

polygenic inheritance A pattern of inheritance in which many genes affect the characteristic in question. (p. 60)

popular-antisocial children A subtype of popular children who are admired for their socially adept yet belligerent behavior. Includes "tough" boys who are athletically skilled, aggressive, and poor students, as well as relationally aggressive boys and girls. Distinguished from *popular-prosocial children*. (p. 500)

popular children Children who receive many positive votes on self-report measures of peer acceptance, indicating they are well-liked. Distinguished from *rejected, controversial,* and *neglected children*. (p. 500)

popular-prosocial children A subtype of popular children who combine academic and social competence. Distinguished from *popular-antisocial children*. (p. 500)

postconventional level Kohlberg's highest level of moral development, in which individuals define morality in terms of abstract principles and values that apply to all situations and societies. (p. 610)

postformal thought Cognitive development beyond Piaget's formal operational stage. (p. 648)

pragmatics The practical, social side of language, concerned with how to engage in effective and appropriate communication. (p. 358)

preconventional level Kohlberg's first level of moral development, in which children accept the rules of authority figures and judge actions by their consequences, viewing behaviors that result in punishment as bad and those that lead to rewards as good. (p. 609)

prefrontal cortex The region of the cerebral cortex, lying in front of areas controlling body movement, that is responsible for thought—in particular, for consciousness, inhibition of impulses, integration of information, and use of memory, reasoning, planning, and problem-solving strategies. (p. 168)

prenatal diagnostic methods Medical procedures that permit detection of developmental problems before birth. (p. 63)

preoperational stage Piaget's second stage, extending from about 2 to 7 years of age, in which children undergo an extraordinary increase in representational, or symbolic, activity, although thought is not yet logical. (p. 318)

prereaching The poorly coordinated, primitive reaching movements of newborn babies. (p. 187)

preterm infants Infants born several weeks or more before their due date. (p. 137)

primary sexual characteristics Physical features of the reproductive organs—ovaries, uterus, and vagina in females; penis, scrotum, and testes in males. Distinguished from *secondary sexual characteristics*. (p. 535)

private speech Self-directed speech that children use to plan and guide their own behavior. (p. 330)

proactive aggression A type of aggression in which children act to fulfill a need or desire—to obtain an object, privilege, space, or social reward, such as adult attention—and unemotionally attack a person to achieve their goal. Also called *instrumental aggression*. Distinguished from *reactive aggression*. (p. 385)

problem-centered coping A strategy for managing emotion in which the individual appraises the situation as changeable, identifies the difficulty, and decides what to do about it. Distinguished from *emotion-centered coping*. (p. 490)

production In language development, the words and word combinations that children use. Distinguished from *comprehension*. (p. 240)

production deficiency The failure to produce a mental strategy when it could be helpful. Distinguished from *control deficiency, utilization deficiency,* and *effective strategy use*. (p. 443)

Project Head Start The most extensive federally funded preschool intervention program in the United States, which provides low-income children with a year or two of preschool education, along with nutritional and health services, and encourages parent involvement in children's learning and development. (p. 349)

propositional thought A type of formal operational reasoning involving the ability to evaluate the logic of propositions, or verbal statements, without referring to real-world circumstances. (p. 567)

prosocial, or altruistic, behavior Actions that benefit another person without any expected reward for the self. (p. 371)

proximodistal trend An organized pattern of physical growth that proceeds from the center of the body outward. Distinguished from *cephalocaudal trend*. (p. 162)

psychoanalytic perspective An approach to personality development introduced by Freud that assumes children move through a series of stages in which they confront conflicts between biological drives and social expectations. How these conflicts are resolved determines the person's ability to learn, to get along with others, and to cope with anxiety. (p. 15)

psychological control Parental behaviors that intrude on and manipulate children's verbal expression, individuality, and attachments to parents. (p. 399)

psychosexual theory Freud's theory, which emphasizes that how parents manage children's sexual and aggressive drives in the first few years of life is crucial for healthy personality development. (p. 15)

psychosocial dwarfism A growth disorder, usually appearing between 2 and 15 years of age, caused by extreme emotional deprivation. It is characterized by decreased GH secretion, very short stature, immature skeletal age, and serious adjustment problems, which help distinguish it from normal shortness. (p. 297)

psychosocial theory Erikson's theory, which emphasizes that at each Freudian stage, individuals not only develop a unique personality but also acquire attitudes and skills that help them become active, contributing members of their society. (p. 15)

puberty Biological changes that lead to an adult-sized body and sexual maturity. (p. 530)

public policies Laws and government programs designed to improve current conditions. (pp. 78–79)

punishment In operant conditioning, removal of a desirable stimulus or presentation of an unpleasant stimulus, either of which decreases the occurrence of a response. (p. 180)

R

random assignment An evenhanded procedure for assigning participants to treatment conditions in an experiment, such as drawing numbers out of a hat or flipping a coin. It increases the chances that participants' characteristics will be equally distributed across treatment groups. (p. 38)

range of reaction Each person's unique, genetically determined response to a range of environmental conditions. (p. 84)

rapid-eye-movement (REM) sleep An "irregular" sleep state in which brain-wave activity is similar to that of the waking state. Distinguished from *non-rapid-eye-movement (NREM) sleep*. (p. 146)

reactive aggression An angry, defensive response to provocation or a blocked goal that is intended to hurt another person. Also called *hostile aggression*. Distinguished from *proactive aggression*. (p. 385)

realistic period The period of vocational development in which older adolescents and young adults focus on a general vocational category and, within it, experiment for a time before settling on a single occupation. Distinguished from *fantasy period* and *tentative period*. (p. 591)

recall The form of memory that involves remembering something without perceptual support, by generating a mental image of a past experience. Distinguished from *recognition*. (p. 220)

recasts Adult responses that restructure children's grammatically inaccurate speech into correct form. (p. 359)

reciprocal teaching A teaching method in which a teacher and two to four students form a cooperative group and take turns leading dialogues, creating a zone of proximal development in which children scaffold one another's progress. (p. 468)

recognition The form of memory that involves noticing whether a new experience is identical or similar to a previous one. Distinguished from *recall*. (p. 220)

recovery Following habituation, an increase in responsiveness to a new stimulus. (p. 181)

referential style A style of early language learning in which toddlers use language mainly to label objects. Distinguished from *expressive style*. (p. 240)

reflex An inborn, automatic response to a particular form of stimulation. (p. 143)

rehearsal A memory strategy that involves repeating information to oneself to improve recall. (p. 446)

reinforcer In operant conditioning, a stimulus that increases the occurrence of a response. (p. 180)

rejected-aggressive children A subtype of rejected children who show high rates of conflict, physical and relational aggression, and hyperactive, inattentive, and impulsive behavior. Distinguished from *rejected-withdrawn children*. (p. 501)

rejected children Children who receive many negative votes on self-report measures of peer acceptance, indicating they are actively disliked. Distinguished from *popular, controversial,* and *neglected children*. (p. 500)

rejected-withdrawn children A subtype of rejected children who are passive, socially awkward, and overwhelmed by social anxiety. Distinguished from *rejected-aggressive children*. (p. 501)

relational aggression A form of aggression that damages another's peer relationships through social exclusion, malicious gossip, or friendship manipulation. Distinguished from *physical aggression* and *verbal aggression*. (p. 386)

relativistic thinking The cognitive approach typical of older college students, who view that all knowledge as embedded in a framework of thought and, therefore, give up the possibility of absolute truth in favor of multiple truths, each relative to its context. Distinguished from *dualistic thinking*. (p. 648)

resilience The ability to adapt effectively in the face of threats to development. (p. 10)

resistant attachment The attachment pattern characterizing infants who seek closeness to the parent before her departure, are usually distressed when she leaves, and combine clinginess with angry, resistive behavior when she returns. Distinguished from *secure, avoidant,* and *disorganized/disoriented attachment*. (p. 267)

reticular formation A structure in the brain stem that maintains alertness and consciousness. (p. 294)

reversibility The ability to think through a series of steps in a problem and then mentally reverse direction, returning to the starting point. Distinguished from *irreversibility*. (p. 438)

Rh factor incompatibility A condition that arises when the Rh protein is present in the fetus's blood but not in the mother's, causing the mother to build up antibodies. If these enter the fetus's system, they destroy red blood cells, reducing the oxygen supply to organs and tissues. (p. 115)

rooming in An arrangement in which the newborn baby stays in the mother's hospital room all or most of the time. (p. 143)

rough-and-tumble play A form of peer interaction involving friendly chasing and play-fighting that emerges in the preschool years and peaks in middle childhood. In our evolutionary past, it may have been important for the development of fighting skill. (p. 431)

S

scaffolding Adjusting the support offered during a teaching session to fit the child's current level of performance. As competence increases, the adult gradually and sensitively withdraws support, turning responsibility over to the child. (p. 331)

scale errors Toddlers' attempts to do things that their body size makes impossible, such as trying to put on dolls' clothes, fit themselves into a doll-sized chair, or walk through a door too narrow to pass through. Reflects a lack of objective understanding of one's own body dimensions. (p. 281)

scheme In Piaget's theory, a specific psychological structure, or organized way of making sense of experience, that changes with age. (p. 204)

scripts General descriptions of what occurs and when it occurs in a particular situation, used to organize, interpret, and predict everyday experiences. (p. 336)

secondary sexual characteristics Physical features visible on the outside of the body that serve as signs of sexual maturity but do not involve the reproductive organs—for example, breast development in females and the appearance of underarm and pubic hair in both sexes. Distinguished from *primary sexual characteristics*. (p. 535)

secular trends in physical growth Changes in body size from one generation to the next. (p. 413)

secure attachment The attachment pattern characterizing infants who use the parent as a secure base from which to explore and may be distressed by parental separation but actively seek contact and are easily comforted by the parent when she returns. Distinguished from *avoidant, resistant,* and *disorganized/disoriented attachment*. (p. 266)

secure base Role of the familiar caregiver as a point from which the infant explores, venturing into the environment and then returning for emotional support. (p. 252)

self-care children Children who are without adult supervision for some period of time after school. (p. 516)

self-concept The set of attributes, abilities, attitudes, and values that an individual believes defines who he or she is. (p. 365)

self-conscious emotions Emotions involving injury to or enhancement of the sense of self, such as guilt, shame, embarrassment, envy, and pride. (p. 253)

self-esteem An aspect of self-concept that involves judgments about one's own worth and the feelings associated with those judgments. (p. 366)

semantic bootstrapping Using semantics, or word meanings, to figure out grammatical rules. (p. 357)

sensitive caregiving Caregiving that involves responding promptly, consistently, and appropriately to infants and holding them tenderly and carefully. (p. 270)

sensitive period A time that is biologically optimal for certain capacities to emerge and in which the individual is especially responsive to environmental influences. (pp. 23–24)

sensorimotor stage Piaget's first stage, spanning the first two years of life, during which infants and toddlers "think" with their eyes, ears, hands, and other sensorimotor equipment. (p. 204)

sensory register In information processing, the part of the mental system in which sights and sounds are represented directly and stored briefly before they either decay or are transferred to working memory. (p. 217)

separation anxiety An infant's distressed reaction to the departure of the familiar caregiver. (p. 265)

sequential design A research design in which several similar cross-sectional or longitudinal studies (called sequences) are conducted at varying times. (p. 42)

seriation The ability to order items along a quantitative dimension, such as length or weight. (p. 438)

sex chromosomes The twenty-third pair of chromosomes—called XX in females, XY in males—which determines the sex of the individual. (p. 54)

shape constancy Perception of an object's shape as the same, despite changes in the shape projected on the retina. (p. 196)

size constancy Perception of an object's size as the same, despite changes in the size of its retinal image. (p. 196)

skeletal age An estimate of physical maturity based on development of the bones of the body. (p. 163)

slow-to-warm-up child A child whose temperament is characterized by inactivity; mild, low-key reactions to environmental stimuli; negative mood; and slow adjustment to new experiences. Distinguished from *easy child* and *difficult child*. (p. 257)

small-for-date infants Infants whose birth weight is below their expected weight considering the length of the pregnancy. (p. 137)

social comparisons Judgments of one's own appearance, abilities, and behavior in relation to those of others. (p. 483)

social-constructivist classroom A classroom grounded in Vygotsky's sociocultural theory, in which children participate in a wide range of challenging activities with teachers and peers, with whom they jointly construct understandings. Distinguished from *traditional classroom* and *constructivist classroom.* (p. 468)

social conventions Customs determined by consensus within a society, such as table manners and politeness rituals. Distinguished from *moral imperatives* and *matters of personal choice.* (p. 384)

social learning theory An approach that emphasizes the role of modeling, also known as imitation or observational learning, in the development of behavior. (p. 18)

social problem solving Generating and applying strategies that prevent or resolve disagreements, resulting in outcomes that are both acceptable to others and beneficial to the self. (p. 375)

social referencing Actively seeking emotional information from a trusted person in an uncertain situation. (p. 253)

social smile The infant's broad grin evoked by the parent's communication, first appearing between 6 and 10 weeks of age. (p. 251)

sociocultural theory Vygotsky's theory, in which children acquire the ways of thinking and behaving that make up a community's culture through social interaction, especially cooperative dialogues with more knowledgeable members of their society. (pp. 24–25)

sociodramatic play The make-believe play with others that is under way by the end of the second year and increases rapidly in complexity during early childhood. (p. 319)

socioeconomic status (SES) A measure of an individual's social position and economic well-being that combines three related variables: years of education, the prestige of one's job and the skill it requires, and income. (p. 71)

spermarche First ejaculation of seminal fluid. (p. 536)

stage A qualitative change in thinking, feeling, and behaving that characterizes a specific period of development. (p. 8)

standardization The practice of giving an intelligence test to a large, representative sample and using the results as the standard for interpreting individual scores. (p. 227)

states of arousal Degrees of sleep and wakefulness. (p. 145)

statistical learning capacity The capacity to analyze the speech stream for repeatedly occurring sequences of sounds, through which infants acquire a stock of speech structures for which they will later learn meanings. (p. 190)

stereotype threat The fear of being judged on the basis of a negative stereotype, which can trigger anxiety that interferes with performance. (p. 460)

stranger anxiety The infant's expression of fear in response to unfamiliar adults, which appears in many babies in the second half of the first year. (p. 252)

Strange Situation A laboratory procedure used to assess the quality of attachment between 1 and 2 years of age by observing the baby's responses to eight short episodes involving brief separations from and reunions with the caregiver in an unfamiliar playroom. (p. 266)

structured interview An interview method in which each participant is asked the same questions in the same way. Distinguished from *clinical interview.* (p. 33)

structured observation A research method in which the investigator sets up a laboratory situation that evokes the behavior of interest so that every participant has an equal opportunity to display the response. Distinguished from *naturalistic observation.* (pp. 31–32)

subculture A group of people with beliefs and customs that differ from those of the larger culture. (p. 78)

sudden infant death syndrome (SIDS) The unexpected death, usually during the night, of an infant under 1 year of age that remains unexplained after thorough investigation. (p. 147)

sympathy Feelings of concern or sorrow for another's plight. (p. 371)

synapses The gaps between neurons, across which chemical messages are sent. (p. 164)

synaptic pruning Loss of synapses by seldom-stimulated neurons, a process that returns them to an uncommitted state so they can support future development. (p. 165)

syntactic bootstrapping Figuring out word meanings by observing how words are used in syntax, or the structure of sentences. (p. 355)

T

talent Outstanding performance in a specific field. (p. 474)

telegraphic speech Toddlers' two-word utterances that, like a telegram, focus on high-content words while omitting smaller, less important ones. (p. 239)

temperament Early-appearing, stable individual differences in reactivity (quickness and intensity of emotional arousal, attention, and motor activity) and self-regulation (strategies that modify reactivity). (p. 256)

tentative period The period of vocational development in which adolescents begin to evaluate vocational options in terms of their interests, abilities, and values. Distinguished from *fantasy period* and *realistic period.* (p. 590)

teratogen Any environmental agent that causes damage during the prenatal period. (p. 102)

theory An orderly, integrated set of statements that describes, explains, and predicts behavior. (p. 7)

theory of multiple intelligences Gardner's theory, which proposes at least eight independent intelligences, defined in terms of distinct sets of processing operations that permit individuals to engage in a wide range of culturally valued activities. (p. 456)

thyroid-stimulating hormone (TSH) A pituitary hormone that stimulates the thyroid gland to release thyroxine, which is necessary for brain development and for growth hormone to have its full impact on body size. (p. 297)

time out A form of mild punishment in which children are removed from the immediate setting until they are ready to act appropriately. (p. 382)

traditional classroom A classroom in which the teacher is the sole authority for knowledge, rules, and decision making and students are relatively passive learners who are evaluated in relation to a uniform set of standards for their grade. Distinguished from *constructivist classroom* and *social-constructivist classroom.* (p. 467)

transition Climax of the first stage of labor, in which the frequency and strength of contractions are at their peak and the cervix opens completely. (p. 126)

transitive inference The ability to seriate, or order items along a quantitative dimension, mentally. (p. 438)

triarchic theory of successful intelligence Sternberg's theory, which identifies three broad, interacting intelligences—analytical, creative, and practical—that must be balanced to achieve success according to one's personal goals and the requirements of one's cultural community. (p. 455)

trimesters Three equal time periods, each lasting three months, into which prenatal development is divided. (p. 100)

trophoblast The thin outer ring of cells of the blastocyst, which will become the structures that provide protective covering and nourishment to the new organism. (p. 98)

U

ulnar grasp The clumsy grasp of the young infant, in which the fingers close against the palm. (p. 187)

umbilical cord The long cord connecting the prenatal organism to the placenta that delivers nutrients and removes waste products. (pp. 98–99)

unconditioned response (UCR) In classical conditioning, a reflexive response that is produced by an unconditioned stimulus (UCS). Distinguished from *conditioned response*. (p. 179)

unconditioned stimulus (UCS) In classical conditioning, a stimulus that leads to a reflexive response. Distinguished from *conditioned stimulus*. (p. 179)

underextension An early vocabulary error in which a word is applied too narrowly, to a smaller number of objects and events than is appropriate. Distinguished from *overextension*. (p. 239)

uninhibited, or **sociable, child** A child whose temperament is such that he or she displays positive emotion to and approaches novel stimuli. Distinguished from *inhibited,* or *shy, child*. (p. 258)

uninvolved child-rearing style A child-rearing style that combines low acceptance and involvement with little control and general indifference to issues of autonomy. Distinguished from *authoritative, authoritarian,* and *permissive child-rearing styles*. (p. 400)

utilization deficiency The inability to improve performance even with consistent use of a mental strategy. Distinguished from *control deficiency, production deficiency,* and *effective strategy use*. (p. 443)

V

verbal aggression A form of aggression that harms others through threats of physical aggression, name-calling, or hostile teasing. Distinguished from *physical* and *relational aggression*. (p. 385)

vernix A white, cheeselike substance that covers the fetus, protecting the skin from chapping due to constant exposure to amniotic fluid. (p. 100)

video deficit effect In toddlers, poorer performance on tasks after watching a video than a live demonstration. (p. 213)

violation-of-expectation method A method in which researchers show babies an expected event (one that is consistent with reality) and an unexpected event (a variation of the first event that violates reality). Heightened attention to the unexpected event suggests that the infant is "surprised" by a deviation from physical reality and, therefore, is aware of that aspect of the physical world. (p. 208)

visual acuity Fineness of visual discrimination. (p. 151)

W

whole-language approach An approach to beginning reading instruction in which, from the start, children are exposed to text in its complete form, using reading materials that are whole and meaningful to promote appreciation of the communicative function of written language. Distinguished from *phonics approach*. (p. 450)

working, or **short-term, memory** The part of the mental system where we actively "work" on a limited amount of information, actively applying mental strategies so the information will be retained and used effectively. (p. 217)

X

X-linked inheritance A pattern of inheritance in which a recessive gene is carried on the X chromosome, so that males are more likely than females to be affected. (p. 57)

Z

zone of proximal development In Vygotsky's theory, a range of tasks too difficult for a child to do alone but possible with the help of more skilled partners. (p. 224)

zygote The newly fertilized cell formed by the union of sperm and ovum at conception. (p. 53)

References

A

Aalsma, M., Lapsley, D. K., & Flannery, D. J. (2006). Personal fables, narcissism, and adolescent adjustment. *Psychology in the Schools, 43,* 481–491.

Aarnoudse-Moens, C. S., Weisglas-Kuperus, N., & van Goudoever, J. B. (2009). Meta-analysis of neurobehavioral outcomes in very preterm and/or very low birth weight children. *Pediatrics, 124,* 717–728.

ABC News. (2004). *The American Sex Survey: A peek beneath the sheets.* Retrieved from abcnews.go.com/images/Politics/959a1AmericanSexSurvey.pdf

Abela, J. R. Z., Hankin, B. L., Haigh, E. A. P., Adams, P., Vinokuroff, T., & Trayhern, L. (2005). Interpersonal vulnerability to depression in high-risk children: The role of insecure attachment and reassurance seeking. *Journal of Clinical Child and Adolescent Psychology, 34,* 182–192.

Aber, J. L., Jones, S. M., & Raver, C. C. (2007). Poverty and life development: New perspectives on a defining issue. In J. L. Aber, S. J. Bishop-Josef, S. M. Jones, K. T. McLearn, & D. A. Phillips (Eds.), *Child development and social policy: Knowledge for action* (pp. 149–166). Washington, DC: American Psychological Association.

Abikoff, H. B., Jensen, P. S., Arnold, L. L., Hoza, B., Hechtman, L., et al. (2002). Observed classroom behavior of children with ADHD: Relationship to gender and comorbidity. *Journal of Abnormal Child Psychology, 30,* 349–359.

Aboud, F. E. (2003). The formation of in-group favoritism and out-group prejudice in young children: Are they distinct attitudes? *Developmental Psychology, 39,* 48–60.

Aboud, F. E., & Amato, M. (2001). Developmental and socialization influences on intergroup bias. In R. Brown & S. Gaertner (Eds.), *Blackwell handbook of social psychology: Intergroup processes.* Oxford, UK: Blackwell.

Aboud, F. E., & Doyle, A. (1996). Parental and peer influences on children's racial attitudes. *International Journal of Intercultural Relations, 20,* 371–383.

Achenbach, T. M., Howell C. T., & Aoki, M. F. (1993). Nine-year outcome of the Vermont Intervention Program for low-birthweight infants, *Pediatrics, 91,* 45–55.

Acker, M. M., & O'Leary, S. G. (1996). Inconsistency of mothers' feedback and toddlers' misbehavior and negative affect. *Journal of Abnormal Child Psychology, 24,* 703–714.

ACT. (2010). *2010 retention/completion summary tables.* Retrieved from www.act.org/research/policymakers/pdf/10retain_trends.pdf

Adachi-Mejia, A. M., Longacre, M. R., Gibson, J. J., Beach, M. L., Titus-Ernstoff, L. T., & Dalton, M. A. (2007). Children with a TV in their bedroom at higher risk for being overweight. *International Journal of Obesity, 31,* 644–651

Adams, G. R., & Marshall, S. (1996). A developmental social psychology of identity: Understanding the person in context. *Journal of Adolescence, 19,* 429–442.

Adams, R., & Laursen, B. (2001). The organization and dynamics of adolescent conflict with parents and friends. *Journal of Marriage and the Family, 63,* 97–110.

Adams, R. J., & Courage, M. L. (1998). Human newborn color vision: Measurement with chromatic stimuli varying in excitation purity. *Journal of Experimental Child Psychology, 68,* 22–34.

Adamson, D. (2005). Regulation of assisted reproductive technologies in the United States. *Family Law Quarterly, 39,* 727–744.

Adolph, K. E. (2002). Learning to keep balance. In R. V. Kail (Ed.), *Advances in child development and behavior* (Vol. 30, pp. 1–40). Boston: Academic Press.

Adolph, K. E. (2008). Learning to move. *Current Directions in Psychological Science, 17,* 213–218.

Adolph, K. E., & Berger, S. E. (2006). Motor development. In D. Kuhn & R. Siegler (Eds.), *Handbook of child psychology: Vol. 2. Cognition, perception, and language* (6th ed., pp. 161–213). Hoboken, NJ: Wiley.

Adolph, K. E., & Joh, A. S. (2009). Multiple learning mechanisms in the development of action. In A. Woodward & A. Needham (Eds.), *Learning and the infant mind* (pp. 172–207). New York: Oxford University Press.

Adolph, K. E., Karasik, L. B., & Tamis-LeMonda, C. S. (2010). Motor skill. In M. H. Bornstein (Ed.), *Handbook of cultural developmental science* (pp. 61–88). New York: Psychology Press.

Adolph, K. E., Tamis-LeMonda, C. S., Ishak, S., Karasik, L. B., & Lobo, S. A. (2008). Locomotor experience and use of social information are posture specific. *Developmental Psychology, 44,* 1705–1714.

Adolph, K. E., Vereijken, B., & Shrout, P. E. (2003). What changes in infant walking and why. *Child Development, 74,* 475–497.

Afifi, T. O., Brownridge, D. A., Cox, B. J., & Sareen J. (2006). Physical punishment, childhood abuse and psychiatric disorders. *Child Abuse and Neglect, 30,* 1093–1103.

Afterschool Alliance. (2004). *America after 3 PM: A household survey on afterschool in America.* Retrieved from www.afterschoolalliance.org/researchFact Sheets.cfm

Aggarwal, R., Sentz, J., & Miller, M. A. (2007). Role of zinc administration in prevention of childhood diarrhea and respiratory illnesses: A meta-analysis. *Pediatrics, 119,* 1120–1130.

Aguiar, A., & Baillargeon, R. (2002). Developments in young infants' reasoning about occluded objects. *Cognitive Psychology, 45,* 267–336.

Ahlgren, M., Melbye, M., Wohlfahrt, J., & Sørensen, T. I. (2004). Growth patterns and the risk of breast cancer in women. *New England Journal of Medicine, 351,* 1619–1626

Aikins, J. W., Bierman, K. L., & Parker, J. G. (2005). Navigating the transition to junior high school: The influence of pre-transition friendship and self-system characteristics. *Social Development, 14,* 42–60.

Ainsworth, M. D. S., Blehar, M. C., Waters, E., & Wall, S. (1978). *Patterns of attachment.* Hillsdale, NJ: Erlbaum.

Akhtar, N., & Montague, L. (1999). Early lexical acquisition: The role of cross-situational learning. *First Language, 19,* 347–358.

Akimoto, S. A., & Sanbinmatsu, D. M. (1999). Differences in self-effacing behavior between European and Japanese Americans: Effect on competence evaluations. *Journal of Cross-Cultural Psychology, 30,* 159–177.

Akinbami, L. J., Moorman, J. E., Garbe, P. L., & Sondik, E. J. (2009). Status of childhood asthma in the United States, 1980–2007. *Pediatrics, 123,* S123–S145.

Aksan, N., & Kochanska, G. (2004). Heterogeneity of joy in infancy. *Infancy, 6,* 79–94.

Akshoomoff, N. A., Feroleto, C. C., Doyle, R. E., & Stiles, J. (2002). The impact of early unilateral brain injury on perceptual organization and visual memory. *Neuropsychologia, 40,* 539–561.

Alan Guttmacher Institute. (2002). Teen pregnancy: Trends and lessons learned. Retrieved from www.guttmacher.org/pubs/tgr/05/1/gr050107.html

Alan Guttmacher Institute. (2005). *Facts in brief: Contraceptive use.* Retrieved from www.guttmacher.org/pubs/fb_contr_use.html

Alan Guttmacher Institute. (2010). *Facts on American teens' sexual and reproductive health.* Retrieved from www.guttmacher.org/pubs/FB-ATSRH.html

Albers, C. A., & Grieve, A. J. (2007). Test review: Bayley, N. (2006). Bayley Scales of Infant and Toddler Development—Third Edition. San Antonio, TX: Harcourt Assessment. *Journal of Psychoeducational Assessment, 25,* 180–190.

Alcohol Concern. (2007). *Advertising alcohol.* Retrieved from www.alcoholconcern.org.uk

Aldridge, M. A., Stillman, R. D., & Bower, T. G. R. (2001). Newborn categorization of vowel-like sounds. *Developmental Science, 4,* 220–232.

Alexander, J. M., Fabricius, W. V., Fleming, V. M., Zwahr, M., & Brown, S. A. (2003). The development of metacognitive causal explanations. *Learning and Individual Differences, 13,* 227–238.

Alexandre-Bidon, D., & Lett, D. (1997). *Les enfants au Moyen Age, Ve–XVe siecles.* Paris: Hachette.

Alford, S., & Hauser, D. (2009). *Adolescent sexual health in Europe and the U.S.—why the difference?* Washington, DC: Advocates for Youth.

Alhusen, J. L. (2008). A literature update on maternal–fetal attachment. *Journal of Obstetric, Gynecologic, and Neonatal Nursing, 37,* 315–328.

Ali, L., & Scelfo, J. (2002, December 9). Choosing virginity. *Newsweek,* pp. 60–65.

Ali, U. A., & Norwitz, E. R. (2009). Vacuum-assisted vaginal delivery. *Reviews in Obstetrics and Gynecology, 2,* 5–17.

Alibali, M. W., Phillips, K. M. O., & Fischer, A. D. (2009). Learning new problem-solving strategies leads to changes in problem representation. *Cognitive Development, 24,* 89–101.

Aligne, C. A., Moss, M. E., Auinger, P., & Weitzman, M. (2003). Association of pediatric dental caries with passive smoking. *Journal of the American Medical Association, 289,* 1258–1264.

Alink, L. R. A., Mesman, J., van Zeijl, J., Stolk, M. N., Juffer, F., & Koot, H. M. (2006). The early childhood aggression curve: Development of physical aggression in 10- to 50-month-old children. *Child Development, 77,* 954–966.

Allen, J. P., Philliber, S., Herrling, S., & Kuperminc, G. P. (1997). Preventing teen pregnancy and academic failure: Experimental evaluation of a developmentally based approach. *Child Development, 64,* 729–742.

Allen, J. P., Porter, M. R., & McFarland, F. C. (2006). Leaders and followers in adolescent close friendships: Susceptibility to peer influence as a predictor of risky behavior, friendship instability, and depression. *Development and Psychopathology, 18,* 155–172.

Allen, J. P., Seitz, V., & Apfel, N. H. (2007). The sexually mature teen as a whole person. In J. L. Aber, S. J. Bishop-Josef, S. M. Jones, K. T. McLearn, & D. A. Phillips (Eds.), *New directions in prevention and intervention for teen pregnancy and parenthood* (pp. 185–199). Washington, DC: American Psychological Association.

Allen, M., & Burrell, N. (1996). Comparing the impact of homosexual and heterosexual parents on children: Meta-analysis of existing research. *Journal of Homosexuality, 32,* 19–35.

Allen, S. E. M., & Crago, M. B. (1996). Early passive acquisition in Inukitut. *Journal of Child Language, 23,* 129–156.

Allison, B. N., & Schultz, J. B. (2004). Parent–adolescent conflict in early adolescence. *Adolescence, 39,* 101–119.

Almeida, J., Johnson, R. M., Corliss, H. L., Molnar, B. E., & Azrael, D. (2009). Emotional distress among LGBT youth: The influence of perceived discrimination based on sexual orientation. *Journal of Youth and Adolescence, 38,* 1001–1014.

Al-Namlah, A. S., Fernyhough, C., & Meins, E. (2006). Sociocultural influences on the development of verbal mediation: Private speech and phonological recoding in Saudi Arabian and British samples. *Developmental Psychology, 42,* 117–131.

Alsaker, F. D. (1995). Timing of puberty and reactions to pubertal changes. In M. Rutter (Ed.), *Psychosocial disturbances in young people: Challenges for prevention* (pp. 37–82). New York: Cambridge University Press.

Alter, J. (2008, September 29). It's not just about the boys. Get girls into school. *Newsweek*, pp. 50–51.

Altermatt, E. R., & Pomerantz, E. M. (2005). The implications of having high-achieving versus low-achieving friends: A longitudinal analysis. *Social Development, 14*, 61–81.

Althaus, J., & Wax, J. (2005). Analgesia and anesthesia in labor. *Obstetrics and Gynecology Clinics of North America, 32*, 231–244.

Alwan, S., & Friedman, J. M. (2009). Safety of selective serotonin reuptake inhibitors in pregnancy. *CNS Drugs, 23*, 493–509.

Amato, P. R. (2001). Children of divorce in the 1990s: An update of the Amato and Keith (1991) meta-analysis. *Journal of Family Psychology, 15*, 355–370.

Amato, P. R. (2006). Marital discord, divorce, and children's well-being: Results from a 20-year longitudinal study of two generation. In A. Clarke-Stewart & J. Dunn (Eds.), *Families count: Effects on child and adolescent development* (pp. 179–202). New York: Cambridge University Press.

Amato, P. R. (2010). Research on divorce: Continuing trends and new developments. *Journal of Marriage and Family, 72*, 650–666.

Amato, P. R., & Dorius, C. (2010). Fathers, children, and divorce. In M. E. Lamb (Ed.), *The role of the father in child development* (5th ed., pp. 177–200). Hoboken, NJ: Wiley.

Amato, P. R., & Fowler, F. (2002). Parenting practices, child adjustment, and family diversity. *Journal of Marriage and the Family, 64*, 703–716.

Amato, P. R., Landale, N. S., Havasevich-Brooks, T. C., Booth, A., Eggebeen, D. J., Schoen, R., & McHale, S. M. (2008). Precursors of young women's family formation pathways. *Journal of Marriage and Family, 70*, 1271–1286.

Amato, P. R., & Sobolewski, J. M. (2004). The effects of divorce on fathers and children: Nonresidential fathers and stepfathers. In M. E. Lamb (Ed.), *The role of the father in child development* (4th ed., pp. 341–367). Hoboken, NJ: Wiley.

Ambert, A.-M. (2005). *Same-sex couples and same-sex parent families: Relationships, parenting, and issues of marriage.* Ontario: Vanier Institute of the Family. Retrieved from www.vifamily.ca/library/publications/samesexd.html

Ambert, A.-M. (2006). *One-parent families: Characteristics, causes, consequences, and issues.* Ontario, Canada: Vanier Institute of the Family.

American Academy of Pediatrics. (2001). Committee on Public Education: Children, adolescents, and television. *Pediatrics, 104*, 341–343.

American Academy of Pediatrics. (2005a). Breastfeeding and the use of human milk. *Pediatrics, 115*, 496–506.

American Academy of Pediatrics, Subcommittee on Attention-Deficit Hyperactivity Disorder. (2005b). Treatment of attention-deficit hyperactivity disorder. *Pediatrics, 115*, e749–e757.

American Academy of Pediatrics. (2006). Folic acid for the prevention of neural tube defects. *Pediatrics, 104*, 325–327.

American Diabetes Association. (2010). Diabetes statistics. Retrieved from www.diabetes.org/diabetes-basics/diabetes-statistics

American Psychiatric Association. (2000). *DSM-IV-TR: Diagnostic and statistical manual of mental disorders—Text revision* (4th ed.). Washington, DC: American Psychiatric Association.

American Psychological Association. (2002). Ethical principles of psychologists and code of conduct. *American Psychologist, 57*, 1060–1073.

Amso, D., & Johnson, S. P. (2006). Learning by selection: Visual search and object perception in young infants. *Developmental Psychology, 42*, 1236–1245.

Amsterlaw, J. (2006). Children's beliefs about everyday reasoning. *Child Development, 77*, 443–464.

Amsterlaw, J., & Wellman, H. M. (2006). Theories of mind in transition: A micro-genetic study of the development of false belief understanding. *Journal of Cognition and Development, 7*, 139–172.

Anand, S. S., Yusuf, S., Jacobs, R., Davis, A. D., Yi, Q., & Gerstein, H. (2001). Risk factors, arteriosclerosis, and cardiovascular disease among Aboriginal people in Canada: The study of health assessment and risk evaluation in Aboriginal peoples (SHARE-AP). *Lancet, 358*, 1147–1153.

Anderman, E. M., Eccles, J. S., Yoon, K. S., Roeser, R., Wigfield, A., & Blumenfeld, P. (2001). Learning to value mathematics and reading: Relations to mastery and performance-oriented instructional practices. *Contemporary Educational Psychology, 26*, 76–95.

Andersen, E. (2000). Exploring register knowledge: The value of "controlled improvisation." In L. Menn & N. B. Ratner (Eds.), *Methods for studying language production* (pp. 225–248). Mahwah, NJ: Erlbaum.

Anderson, C. A. (2004). An update on the effects of violent video games. *Journal of Adolescence, 27*, 113–122.

Anderson, C. A., Berkowitz, L., Donnerstein, E., Huesmann, R., Johnson, J. D., Linz, D., Malamuth, N. M., & Wartella, E. (2003). The influence of media violence on youth. *Psychological Science in the Public Interest, 4*(3), 81–106.

Anderson, C. A., Sakamoto, A., Gentile, D. A., Ihori, N., Shibuya, A., Yukawa, S., et al. (2008). Longitudinal effects of violent video games on aggression in Japan and the United States. *Pediatrics, 122*, e1067–e1072.

Anderson, D. M., Huston, A. C., Schmitt, K. L., Linebarger, D. L., & Wright, J. C. (2001). Early childhood television viewing and adolescent behavior. *Monographs of the Society for Research in Child Development, 66*(1, Serial No. 264).

Anderson, D. R. (2004). Watching children watch television and the creation of Blues Clues. In H. Hendershot (Ed.), *Nickelodeon nation: The history, politics, and economics of America's only TV channel for kids* (pp. 241–268). New York: New York University Press.

Anderson, L. L., Morgan, J. L., & White, K. S. (2003). A statistical basis for speech sound discrimination. *Language and Speech, 46*, 155–182.

Anderson, M. E., Johnson, D. C., & Batal, H. A. (2005). Sudden infant death syndrome and prenatal maternal smoking: Rising attributed risk in the Back to Sleep era. *BMC Medicine, 3*, 4.

Anderson, P. J., Wood, S. J., Francis, D. E., Coleman, L., Anderson, V., & Boneh, A. (2007). Are neuropsychological impairments in children with early-treated phenylketonuria (PKU) related to white matter abnormalities or elevated phenylalanine levels? *Developmental Neuropsychology, 32*, 645–668.

Anderson, V. A., Catroppa, C., Dudgeon, P., Morse, S. A., Haritou, F., & Rosenfeld, J. V. (2006). Understanding predictors of functional recovery and outcome 30 months following early childhood head injury. *Neuropsychology, 20*, 42–57.

Andersson, B.-E. (1989). Effects of public day care—A longitudinal study. *Child Development, 60*, 857–866.

Andersson, B.-E. (1992). Effects of day care on cognitive and socioemotional competence of thirteen-year-old Swedish schoolchildren. *Child Development, 63*, 20–36.

Andersson, T., & Magnusson, D. (1990). Biological maturation in adolescence and the development of drinking habits and alcohol abuse among young males: A prospective longitudinal study. *Journal of Youth and Adolescence, 19*, 33–41.

Andrews, G., & Halford, G. S. (1998). Children's ability to make transitive inferences: The importance of premise integration and structural complexity. *Cognitive Development, 13*, 479–513.

Andrews, G., & Halford, G. S. (2002). A cognitive complexity metric applied to cognitive development. *Cognitive Psychology, 45*, 475–506.

Andrews, R., Torgerson, C., Beverton, S., Locke, T., Low, G., Robinson, A., & Zhu, D. (2006). *The effect of grammar teaching (syntax) on 5 to 16 year olds' accuracy and quality in written composition.* York, UK: Department of Educational Studies. Retrieved from www.york.ac.ukdepts/educ/ResearchPaperSeries/English%20Grammar%20(Syntax).pdf

Anisfeld, M., Turkewitz, G., Rose, S. A., Rosenberg, F. R., Shelber, F. J., Couturier-Fagan, D. A., Ger, J. S., & Sommer I. (2001). No compelling evidence that newborns imitate oral gestures. *Infancy, 2*, 111–122.

Annett, M. (2002). *Handedness and brain asymmetry: The right shift theory.* Hove, UK: Psychology Press.

Apgar, V. (1953). A proposal for a new method of evaluation in the newborn infant. *Current Research in Anesthesia and Analgesia, 32*, 260–267.

Aquilino, W. S. (2006). Family relationships and support systems in emerging adulthood. In J. J. Arnett & J. L. Tanner (Eds.), *Emerging adults in America: Coming of age in the 21st century* (pp. 193–218). Washington, DC: American Psychological Association.

Aram, D., & Levin, I. (2001). Mother– child joint writing in low SES: Sociocultural factors, maternal mediation, and emergent literacy. *Cognitive Development, 16*, 831–852.

Aram, D., & Levin, I. (2002). Mother– child joint writing and storybook reading: Relations with literacy among low SES kindergartners. *Merrill-Palmer Quarterly, 48*, 202–224.

Archer, S. L., & Waterman, A. S. (1990). Varieties of identity diffusions and foreclosures: An exploration of subcategories of the identity statuses. *Journal of Adolescent Research, 5*, 96–111.

Archibald, A. B., Graber, J. A., & Brooks-Gunn, J. (2006). Pubertal processes and physiological growth in adolescence. In G. R. Adams & M. D. Berzonsky (Eds.), *Blackwell handbook of adolescence* (pp. 24–48). Malden, MA: Blackwell.

Archibald, A. B., Linver, M. R., Graber, J. A., & Brooks-Gunn, J. (2002). Parent–adolescent relationships and girls' unhealthy eating: testing reciprocal effects. *Journal of Research on Adolescence, 12*, 451–461.

Arcus, D., & Chambers, P. (2008). Childhood risks associated with adoption. In T. P. Gullotta & G. M. Blau (Eds.), *Family influences on childhood behavior and development* (pp. 117–142). New York: Routledge.

Ardila-Rey, A., & Killen, M. (2001). Middle-class Colombian children's evaluations of personal, moral, and social-conventional interactions in the classroom. *International Journal of Behavioral Development, 25*, 246–255.

Arija, V., Esparó, G., Fernández-Ballart, J., Murphy, M. M., Biarnés, E., & Canals, J. (2006). Nutritional status and performance in test of verbal and nonverbal intelligence in 6 year old children. *Intelligence, 34*, 141–149.

Arnett, J. J. (2000a). Emerging adulthood: A theory of development from the late teens through the twenties. *American Psychologist, 55*, 469–480.

Arnett, J. J. (2000b). High hopes in a grim world: Emerging adults' view of their futures and of "Generation X." *Youth and Society, 31*, 267–286.

Arnett, J. J. (2001). Conceptions of the transition to adulthood: Perspectives from adolescence to midlife. *Journal of Adult Development, 8*, 133–143.

Arnett, J. J. (2002). The psychology of globalization. *American Psychologist, 57*, 774–783.

Arnett, J. J. (2003). Conceptions of the transition to adulthood among emerging adults in American ethnic groups. In J. J. Arnett & N. L. Galambos (Eds.), *Exploring cultural conceptions of the transitions to adulthood (New directions for child and adolescent development,* No. 100, pp. 63–75). San Francisco: Jossey-Bass.

Arnett, J. J. (2004). *Emerging adulthood: The winding road from the late teens through the twenties.* New York: Oxford University Press.

Arnett, J. J. (2006). Emerging adulthood: Understanding the new way of coming of age. In J. J. Arnett & J. L. Tanner (Eds.), *Emerging adults in America: Coming of age in the 21st century* (pp. 3–19). Washington, DC: American Psychological Association.

Arnett, J. J. (2007a). Emerging adulthood, a 21st century theory: A rejoinder to Hendry and Kloep. *Child Development Perspectives, 1*, 80–82.

Arnett, J. J. (2007b). Emerging adulthood: What is it and what is it good for? *Child Development Perspectives, 1*, 68–73.

Arnett, J. J., & Jensen, L. A. (2002). A congregation of one: Individualized religious beliefs among emerging adults. *Journal of Adolescent Research, 17*, 451–467.

Arnett, J. J., Ramos, K. D., & Jensen, L. A. (2001). Ideological views in emerging adulthood: Balancing autonomy and community. *Journal of Adult Development, 8,* 69–79.

Arnett, J. J., & Tanner, J. L. (Eds.). (2006). *Emerging adults in America: Coming of age in the 21st century.* Washington, DC: American Psychological Association.

Arnold, D. H., McWilliams, L., & Harvey-Arnold, E. (1998). Teacher discipline and child misbehavior in daycare: Untangling causality with correlational data. *Developmental Psychology, 34,* 276–287.

Arnold, P. (1999). Emotional disorders in deaf children. In V. L. Schwean & D. H. Saklofske (Eds.), *Handbook of psychosocial characteristics of exceptional children* (pp. 493–522). New York: Kluwer.

Arnon, S., Shapsa, A., Forman, L., Regev, R., Bauer, S., & Litmanovitz, I. (2006). Live music is beneficial to preterm infants in the neonatal intensive care unit. *Birth, 33,* 131–136.

Aronson, A. A., & Henderson, S. O. (2006). Pediatrics, otitis media. *eMedicine Specialties, Pediatrics.* Retrieved from www.emedicine.com/emerg/topic393.htm

Arsenio, W. F. (2006). Happy victimizers and moral responsibility: Sociocultural and developmental considerations. In M. Schleifer & C. Martiny (Eds.), *Talking to children about responsibility and control of emotions* (pp. 49–69). Calgary, Canada: Detselig Enterprises.

Arsenio, W. F. (2010). Integrating emotion attributions, morality, and aggression: Research and theoretical foundations. In W. F. Arsenio & E. A. Lemerise (Eds.), *Emotions, aggression, and morality in children: Bridging development and psychopathology* (pp. 75–94). Washington, DC: American Psychological Association.

Arsenio, W. F., & Lemerise, E. A. (2001). Varieties of childhood bullying: Values, emotion processes, and social competence. *Social Development, 10,* 59–73.

Arterberry, M. E. (2008). Infants' sensitivity to the depth cue of height-in-the-picture-plane. *Infancy, 13,* 544–555.

Arterberry, M. E., Craton, L. G., & Yonas, A. (1993). Infants' sensitivity to motion-carried information for depth and object properties. In C. E. Granrud (Ed.), *Visual perception and cognition in infancy* (pp. 215– 234). Hillsdale, NJ: Erlbaum.

Artman, L., & Cahan, S. (1993). Schooling and the development of transitive inference. *Developmental Psychology, 29,* 753–759.

Artman, L., Cahan, S., & Avni-Babad, D. (2006). Age, schooling, and conditional reasoning. *Cognitive Development, 21,* 131–145.

Asakawa, K. (2001). Family socialization practices and their effects on the internationalization of educational values for Asian and white American adolescents. *Applied Developmental Science, 5,* 184–194.

Asarnow, J. R., Jaycox, L. H., Duan, N., LaBorde, A. P., Rea, M. M., & Murray, P. (2005). Effectiveness of a quality improvement intervention for adolescent depression in primary care clinics. *Journal of the American Medical Association, 293,* 311–319.

Asbjornsen, A. E., Obrzut, J. E., Boliek, C. A., Myking, E., Holmefjord, A., & Reisaeter, S. (2005). Impaired auditory attention skills following middle-ear infections. *Child Neuropsychology, 11,* 121–133.

Asher, S. R., & Rose, A. J. (1997). Promoting children's social-emotional adjustment with peers. In P. Salovey & D. J. Sluyter (Eds.), *Emotional development and emotional intelligence* (pp. 193–195). New York: Basic Books.

Aslin, R. N., Jusczyk, P. W., & Pisoni, D. B. (1998). Speech and auditory processing during infancy: Constraints on and precursors to language. In D. Kuhn & R. S. Siegler (Eds.), *Handbook of child psychology: Vol. 2. Cognition, perception, and language* (5th ed., pp. 147–198). New York: Wiley.

Aslin, R. N., & Newport, E. L. (2009). What statistical learning can and can't tell us about language acquisition. In J. Colombo, P. McCardle, & L. Freund (Eds.), *Infant pathways to language: Methods, models, and research directions* (pp. 15–29). New York: Psychology Press.

Astington, J. W., & Jenkins, J. M. (1995). Theory of mind development and social understanding. *Cognition and Emotion, 9,* 151–165.

Astington, J. W., & Pelletier, J. (2005). Theory of mind, language, and learning in the early years: Developmental origins of school readiness. In B. D. Homer & C. S. Tamis-LeMonda (Eds.), *The development of social cognition and communication* (pp. 205–230). Mahwah, NJ: Erlbaum.

Astington, J. W., Pelletier, J., & Homer, B. (2002). Theory of mind and epistemological development: The relation between children's second-order false belief understanding and their ability to reason about evidence. *New Ideas in Psychology, 20,* 131–144.

Atance, C. M., & Meltzoff, A. N. (2005). My future self: Young children's ability to anticipate and explain future states. *Cognitive Development, 20,* 341–361.

Atkins, R., Hart, D., & Donnelly, T. M. (2004). Moral identity development and school attachment. In D. Narvaez & D. Lapsley (Eds.), *Moral development, self, and identity* (pp. 65–82). Mahwah, NJ: Erlbaum.

Atkinson, R. C., & Shiffrin, R. M. (1968). Human memory: A proposed system and its control processes. In K. W. Spence & J. T. Spence (Eds.), *Advances in the psychology of learning and motivation* (Vol. 2, pp. 90–195). New York: Academic Press.

Attewell, P. (2001). The first and second digital divides. *Sociology of Education, 74,* 252–259.

Au, T. K., Sidle, A. L., & Rollins, K. B. (1993). Developing an intuitive understanding of conservation and contamination: Invisible particles as a plausible mechanism. *Developmental Psychology, 29,* 286–299.

Aunola, K., Stattin, H., & Nurmi, J.-E. (2000). Parenting styles and adolescents' achievement strategies. *Journal of Adolescence, 23,* 205–222.

Averhart, C. J., & Bigler, R. S. (1997). Shades of meaning: Skin tone, racial attitudes, and constructive memory in African-American children. *Journal of Experimental Child Psychology, 67,* 368–388.

Avis, J., & Harris, P. L. (1991). Belief–desire reasoning among Baka children: Evidence for a universal conception of mind. *Child Development, 62,* 460–467.

AWC (American Women's Club) Oslo. (2005). *Health care in Norway.* Retrieved from www.awcoslo.org/Sections/LivingInOslo/health_care_in_norway.htm

Axelin, A., Salantera, S., & Lehtonen, L. (2006). 'Facilitated tucking by parents' in pain management of preterm infants—a randomized crossover trial. *Early Human Development, 82,* 241–247.

Axinn, W. G., & Barber, J. S. (1997). Living arrangements and family formation attitudes in early adulthood. *Journal of Marriage and the Family, 59,* 595–611.

Azar, S. T., & Wolfe, D. A. (1998). Child physical abuse and neglect. In E. J. Mash & R. A. Barkley (Eds.), *Treatment of childhood disorders* (2nd ed., pp. 501–544). New York: Guilford.

Azurmendi, A., Braza, F., Garcia, A., Braza, P., Munoz, J. M., & Sanchez-Martin, J. R. (2006). Aggression, dominance, and affiliation: Their relationships with androgen levels and intelligence in 5-year-old children. *Hormones and Behavior, 50,* 132–140.

B

Bacallao, M. L., & Smokowski, P. R. (2007). The costs of getting ahead: Mexican family system changes after immigration. *Family Relations, 56,* 52–66.

Baddeley, A. (2000). Short-term and working memory. In E. Tulving & R. I. M. Craik (Eds.), *The Oxford handbook of memory* (pp. 77–92). New York: Oxford University Press.

Bader, A. P. (1995). Engrossment revisited: Fathers are still falling in love with their newborn babies. In J. L. Shapiro, M. J. Diamond, & M. Greenberg (Eds.), *Becoming a father* (pp 224–233). New York: Springer.

Bader, A. P., & Phillips, R. D. (2002). Fathers' recognition of their newborns by visual-facial and olfactory cues. *Psychology of Men and Masculinity, 3,* 79–84.

Badger, S., Nelson, L. J., & Barry, C. M. (2006). Perceptions of the transition to adulthood among Chinese and American emerging adults. *International Journal of Behavioral Development, 31,* 83–93.

Baenninger, M., & Newcombe, N. (1995). Environmental input to the development of sex-related differences in spatial and mathematical ability. *Learning and Individual Differences, 7,* 363–379.

Baer, J. (2002). Is family cohesion a risk or protective factor during adolescent development? *Journal of Marriage and Family, 64,* 668–675.

Bagwell, C. L., & Coie, J. D. (2004). The best friendships of aggressive boys: Relationship quality, conflict management, and rule-breaking behavior. *Journal of Experimental Child Psychology, 88,* 5–24.

Bagwell, C. L., Coie, J. D., Terry, R. A., & Lochman, J. E. (2000). Peer clique participation and social status in preadolescence. *Merrill-Palmer Quarterly, 46,* 280–305.

Bahrick, L. E., Gogate, L. J., & Ruiz, I. (2002). Attention and memory for faces and actions in infancy: The salience of actions over faces in dynamic events. *Child Development, 73,* 1629–1643.

Bahrick, L. E., Hernandez-Reif, M., & Flom, R. (2005). The development of infant learning about specific face–voice relations. *Developmental Psychology, 41,* 541–552.

Bahrick, L. E., Hernandez-Reif, M., & Pickens, J. N. (1997). The effect of retrieval cues on visual preferences and memory in infancy: Evidence for a four-phase attention function. *Journal of Experimental Child Psychology, 67,* 1–20.

Bahrick, L. E., Lickliter, R., & Flom, R. (2004). Intersensory redundancy guides the development of selective attention, perception, and cognition in infancy. *Current Directions in Psychological Science, 13,* 99–102.

Bahrick, L. E., Netto, D., & Hernandez-Reif, M. (1998). Intermodal perception of adult and child faces and voices by infants. *Child Development, 69,* 1263–1275.

Bahrick, L. E., & Pickens, J. N. (1995). Infant memory for object motion across a period of three months: Implications for a four-phase attention function. *Journal of Experimental Child Psychology, 59,* 343–371.

Bai, D. L., & Bertenthal, B. I. (1992). Locomotor status and the development of spatial search skills. *Child Development, 63,* 215–226.

Bailey, J. M., Bobrow, D., Wolfe, M., & Mikach, S. (1995). Sexual orientation of adult sons of gay fathers. *Developmental Psychology, 31,* 124–129.

Bailey, R. C. (1991). The comparative growth of Efe pygmies and African farmers from birth to age 5 years. *Annals of Human Biology, 18,* 113–120.

Baillargeon, R. (2004). Infants' reasoning about hidden objects: Evidence for event-general and event-specific expectations. *Developmental Science, 7,* 391–424.

Baillargeon, R., & DeVos, J. (1991). Object permanence in young infants: Further evidence. *Child Development, 62,* 1227–1246.

Baillargeon, R., Scott, R. M., & He, Z. (2010). False-belief understanding in infants. *Trends in Cognitive Sciences, 14,* 110–118.

Baillargeon, R. H., Zoccolillo, M., Keenan, K., Côté, S., Pérusse, D., Wu, H.-X., & Boivin, M. (2007). Gender differences in physical aggression: A prospective population-based survey of children before and after 2 years of age. *Developmental Psychology, 43,* 13–26.

Baker, J. A. (2006). Contributions of teacher–child relationships to positive school adjustment during elementary school. *Journal of School Psychology, 44,* 211–229.

Baker, J. A., Derrer, R. D., Davis, S. M., Dinklage-Travis, H. E., Linder, D. S., & Nicholson, M D. (2001). The flip side of the coin: Understanding the school's contribution to dropout and completion. *School Psychology Quarterly, 16,* 406–426.

Bakermans-Kranenberg, M. J., van IJzendoorn, M. H., Mesman, J., Alink, L. R. A., & Juffer, F. (2008a). Effects of an attachment-based intervention on daily cortisol moderated by dopamine receptor D4: A randomized control trial on 1-to 3-year-olds screened for externalizing behavior. *Development and Psychopathology, 20,* 805–820.

Bakermans-Kranenburg, M. J., van IJzendoorn, M. H., Pijlman, F. T. A., Mesman, J., & Juffer, F. (2008b).

Experimental evidence for differential sensitivity: Dopamine D4 receptor polymorphism (DRD4 VNTR) moderates intervention effects on toddlers' externalizing behavior in a randomized control trial. *Developmental Psychology, 44*, 293–300.

Baker-Sennett, J., Matusov, E., & Rogoff, B. (2008). Children's planning of classroom plays with adult or child direction. *Social Development, 17*, 998–1018.

Balaban, M. T., & Waxman, S. R. (1997). Do words facilitate object categorization in 9-month-old infants? *Journal of Experimental Child Psychology, 64*, 3–26.

Balfanz, R., Legters, N., West, T. C., & Weber, L. M. (2007). Are NCLB's measures, incentives, and improvement strategies the right ones for the nation's low-performing high schools? *American Educational Research Journal, 44*, 559–593.

Balis, T., & Postolache, T. T. (2008). Ethnic differences in adolescent suicide in the United States. *International Journal of Child Health and Human Development, 1*, 282–296.

Ball, H. (2006). Parent–infant bed-sharing behavior: Effects of feeding type and presence of father. *Human Nature, 17*, 301–318.

Balsano, A. B. (2005). Youth civic engagement in the United States: Understanding and addressing the impact of social impediments on positive youth and community development. *Applied Developmental Science, 9*, 188–201.

Baltes, P. B., Lindenberger, U., & Staudinger, U. M. (2006). Life span theory in developmental psychology. In R. M. Lerner & W. Damon (Eds.), *Handbook of child psychology: Vol. 1. Theoretical models of human development* (6th ed., pp. 569–664). Hoboken, N. J.: Wiley.

Band, G. P. H., van der Molen, M. W., Overtoom, C. C. E., & Verbaten, M. N. (2000). The ability to activate and inhibit speeded responses: Separate developmental trends. *Journal of Experimental Child Psychology, 75*, 263–290.

Bandura, A. (1977). *Social learning theory.* Englewood Cliffs, NJ: Prentice-Hall.

Bandura, A. (1992). Perceived self-efficacy in cognitive development and functioning. *Educational Psychologist, 28*, 117–118.

Bandura, A. (1999). Social cognitive theory of personality. In L. A. Pervin (Ed.), *Handbook of personality: Theory and research* (2nd ed., pp. 154–196). New York: Guilford.

Bandura, A. (2001). Social cognitive theory: An agentic perspective. *Annual Review of Psychology, 52*, 1–26.

Banish, M. T., & Heller, W. (1998). Evolving perspectives on lateralization of function. *Current Directions in Psychological Science, 7*, 1–2.

Banks, M. S. (1980). The development of visual accommodation during early infancy. *Child Development, 51*, 157–173.

Banks, M. S., & Ginsburg, A. P. (1985). Early visual preferences: A review and new theoretical treatment. In H. W. Reese (Ed.), *Advances in child development and behavior* (Vol. 19, pp. 207–246). New York: Academic Press.

Barber, B. K., & Olsen, J. A. (1997). Socialization in context: Connection, regulation, and autonomy in the family, school, and neighborhood, and with peers. *Journal of Adolescent Research, 12*, 287–315.

Barber, B. K., & Olsen, J. A. (2004). Assessing the transitions to middle and high school. *Journal of Adolescent Research, 19*, 3–30.

Barber, B. K., Stolz, H. E., & Olsen, J. A. (2005). Parental support, psychological control, and behavioral control: Assessing relevance across time, culture, and method. *Monographs of the Society for Research in Child Development, 70*(4, Serial No. 282).

Barber, B. L., Stone, M. R., Hunt, J. E., & Eccles, J. S. (2005). Benefits of activity participation: The roles of identity affirmation and peer group norm sharing. In J. L. Mahoney, R. W. Larson, & J. S. Eccles (Eds.), *Organized activities as contexts of development: Extracurricular activities, after-school and community programs* (pp. 185–210). Mahwah, NJ: Erlbaum.

Barber, J. S. (2001a). Ideational influences on the transition to parenthood: Attitudes toward childbearing and competing alternatives. *Social Psychology Quarterly, 64*, 101–127.

Barber, J. S. (2001b). The intergenerational transmission of age at first birth among married and unmarried men and women. *Social Sciences Research, 30*, 219–247.

Bard, K. A., Todd, B. K., Bernier, C., Love, J., & Leavens, D. A. (2006). Self-awareness in human and chimpanzee infants: What is measured and what is meant by the mark and mirror test? *Infancy, 9*, 191–219.

Barenbaum, J., Ruchkin, V., & Schwab-Stone, M. (2004). The psychosocial aspects of children exposed to war: Practice and policy initiatives. *Journal of Child Psychology and Psychiatry, 45*, 41–62.

Bar-Haim, Y., Ziv, T., Lamy, D., & Hodes, R. M. (2006). Nature and nurture in own-race face processing. *Psychological Science, 17*, 159–163.

Barker, D. J. (2008). Human growth and cardiovascular disease. *Nestlé Nutrition Workshop Series, 61*, 21–38.

Barker, D. J., Osmond, C., Thornburg, K. L., Kajantie, E., Forsen, T., & Eriksson, J. G. (2008). A possible link between the pubertal growth of girls and breast cancer in their daughters. *American Journal of Human Biology, 20*, 127–131.

Barker, R. G., & Gump, P. V. (1964). *Big school, small school: High school size and student behavior.* Stanford, CA: Stanford University Press.

Barkley, R. A. (2001). Executive functions and self-regulation: An evolutionary neuropsychological perspective. *Neuropsychology Review, 11*, 1–29.

Barkley, R. A. (2002a). Psychosocial treatments of attention-deficit/hyperactivity disorder in children. *Journal of Clinical Psychology, 63*(Suppl. 12), 36–43.

Barkley, R. A. (2002b). Major life activity and health outcomes associated with attention-deficit/hyperactivity disorder. *Journal of Clinical Psychiatry, 63*(Suppl. 12), 10–15.

Barkley, R. A. (2003). Attention-deficit/hyperactivity disorder. In E. J. Mash & R. A. Barkley (Eds.), *Child psychopathology* (2nd ed., pp. 75–143). New York: Guilford.

Barkley, R. A. (2006). Attention-deficit/hyperactivity disorder. In R. A. Barkley, D. A. Wolfe, & E. J. Mash (Eds.), *Behavioral and emotional disorders in adolescents: Nature, assessment, and treatment* (pp. 91–152). New York: Guilford.

Barnea-Goraly, N., Menon, V., Eckert, M., Tamm, L., Bammer, R., & Karchemskiy, A. (2005). White matter development during childhood and adolescence: A cross-sectional diffusion tensor imaging study. *Cerebral Cortex, 15*, 1848–1854.

Barnes, G. M., Hoffman, J. H., Welte, J. W., Farrell, M. P., & Dintcheff, B. A. (2006). Effects of parental monitoring and peer deviance on substance use and delinquency. *Journal of Marriage and Family, 68*, 1084–1104.

Barnes, G. M., Hoffman, J. H., Welte, J. W., Farrell, M. P., & Dintcheff, B. A. (2007). Adolescents' time use: Effects on substance use, delinquency and sexual activity. *Journal of Youth and Adolescence, 36*, 697–710.

Barnes, R., Josefowitz, N., & Cole, E. (2006). Residential schools: Impact on Aboriginal students' academic and cognitive development. *Canadian Journal of School Psychology, 21*, 18–32.

Barnes-Josiah, D., & Augustin, A. (1995). Secular trend in the age at menarche in Haiti. *American Journal of Human Biology, 7*, 357–362.

Barnett, D., & Vondra, J. I. (1999). Atypical patterns of early attachment: Theory, research, and current directions. In J. I. Vondra & D. Barnett (Eds.), *Atypical attachment in infancy and early childhood among children at developmental risk. Monographs of the Society for Research in Child Development, 64*(3, Serial No. 258), pp. 1–24.

Barnett, W. S. (2004). Does Head Start have lasting cognitive effects? The myth of fade-out. In E. Zigler & S. J. Styfco (Eds.), *The Head Start debates* (pp. 221–250). Baltimore: Brookes.

Baron-Cohen, S., Baldwin, D. A., & Crowson, M. (1997). Do children with autism use the speaker's direction of gaze strategy to crack the code of language? *Child Development, 68*, 48–57.

Baron-Cohen, S., & Belmonte, M. K. (2005). Autism: A window onto the development of the social and the analytic brain. *Annual Review of Neuroscience, 28*, 109–126.

Barr, H. M., Bookstein, F. L., O'Malley, K. D., Connor, P. D., Huggins, J. E., & Streissguth, A. P. (2006). Binge drinking during pregnancy as a predictor of psychiatric disorders on the structured clinical interview for DSM-IV in young adult offspring. *American Journal of Psychiatry, 163*, 1061–1065.

Barr, H. M., Streissguth, A. P., Darby, B. L., & Sampson, P. D. (1990). Prenatal exposure to alcohol, caffeine, tobacco, and aspirin: Effects on fine and gross motor performance in 4-year-old children. *Developmental Psychology, 26*, 339–348.

Barr, R., & Hayne, H. (2003). It's not what you know, it's who you know: Older siblings facilitate imitation during infancy. *International Journal of Early Years Education, 11*, 7–21.

Barr, R., Marrott, H., & Rovee-Collier, C. (2003). The role of sensory preconditioning in memory retrieval by preverbal infants. *Learning and Behavior, 31*, 111–123.

Barr, R., Muentener, P., & Garcia, A. (2007). Age-related changes in deferred imitation from television by 6- to 18-month-olds. *Developmental Science, 10*, 910–921.

Barr, R. G. (2001). "Colic" is something infants do, rather than a condition they "have": A developmental approach to crying phenomena patterns, pacification and (patho)genesis. In R. G. Barr, I. St James-Roberts, & M. R. Keefe (Eds.), *New evidence on unexplained infant crying* (pp. 87–104). St. Louis: Johnson & Johnson Pediatric Institute.

Barr, R. G., Paterson, J. A., MacMartin, L. M., & Lehtonen, L. (2005). Prolonged and unsoothable crying bouts in infants with and without colic. *Journal of Developmental and Behavioral Pediatrics, 26*, 14–23.

Barratt, M. S., Roach, M. A., & Leavitt, L. A. (1996). The impact of low-risk prematurity on maternal behaviour and toddler outcomes. *International Journal of Behavioral Development, 19*, 581–602.

Barrett, J. L. (2002). Do children experience God as adults do? In J. Andresen (Ed.), *Religion in mind* (pp. 173–190). New York: Cambridge University Press.

Barrett, J. L., Richert, R. A., & Driesenga, A. (2001). God's beliefs versus mother's: The development of nonhuman agent concepts. *Child Development, 72*, 50–65.

Barrett, J. L., & Van Orman, B. (1996). The effects of the use of images in worship on God concepts. *Journal of Psychology and Christianity, 15*, 38–45.

Barrett, K. C. (2005). The origins of social emotions and self-regulation in toddlerhood: New evidence. *Cognition and Emotion, 19*, 953–979.

Barrett, T. M., Traupman, E., & Needham, A. (2008). Infants' visual anticipation of object structure in grasp planning. *Infant Behavior and Development, 31*, 1–9.

Barros, R. M., Silver, E. J., & Stein, R. E. K. (2009). School recess and group classroom behavior. *Pediatrics, 123*, 431–436.

Bartgis, J., Lilly, A. R., & Thomas, D. G. (2003). Event-related potential and behavioral measures of attention in 5-, 7-, and 9-year-olds. *Journal of General Psychology, 130*, 311–335.

Bartocci, M., Berggvist, L. L., Lagercrantz, H., & Anand, K. J. (2006). Pain activates cortical areas in the preterm newborn brain. *Pain, 122*, 109–117.

Barton, M. E., & Strosberg, R. (1997). Conversational patterns of two-year-old twins in mother–twin–twin triads. *Journal of Child Language, 24*, 257–269.

Barton, M. E., & Tomasello, M. (1991). Joint attention and conversation in mother–infant–sibling triads. *Child Development, 62*, 517–529.

Bartrip, J., Morton, J., & de Schonen, S. (2001). Responses to mother's face in 3-week to 3-month-old infants. *British Journal of Developmental Psychology, 19*, 219–232.

Bartsch, K., & Wellman, H. M. (1995). *Children talk about the mind.* New York: Oxford University Press.

Basow, S. A., & Rubin, L. R. (1999). Gender influences on adolescent development. In N. G. Johnson & M. C. Roberts (Eds.), *Beyond appearance: A new look at adolescent girls* (pp. 25–52). Washington, DC: American Psychological Association.

Bass, J. L., Corwin, M., Gozal, D., Moore, C., Nishida, H., Parker, S., Schonwald, A., Wilker, R. E., Stehle, S., & Kinane, T. B. (2004). The effect of chronic or intermittent hypoxia on cognition in childhood: A review of the evidence. *Pediatrics, 114,* 805–816.

Batchelor, J. (2008). 'Failure to thrive' revisited. *Child Abuse Review, 17,* 147–159.

Bates, E. (2004). Explaining and interpreting deficits in language development across clinical groups: Where do we go from here? *Brain and Language, 88,* 248–253.

Bates, E., & MacWhinney, B. (1987). Competition, variation, and language learning. In B. MacWhinney (Ed.), *Mechanisms of language acquisition* (pp. 157–193). Hillsdale, NJ: Erlbaum.

Bates, E., Marchman, V., Thal, D., Fenson, L., Dale, P., Reznick, J. S., Reilly, J., & Hartung, J. (1994). Developmental and stylistic variation in the composition of early vocabulary. *Journal of Child Language, 21,* 85–123.

Bates, E., Wilson, S. M., Saygin, A. P., Dick, F., Sereno, M. I., Knight, R. T., & Dronkers, N. F. (2003). Voxel-based lesion-symptom mapping. *Nature Neuroscience, 6,* 448–450.

Bates, J. E., Wachs, T. D., & Emde, R. N. (1994). Toward practical uses for biological concepts. In J. E. Bates & T. D. Wachs (Eds.), *Temperament: Individual differences at the interface of biology and behavior* (pp. 275–306). Washington, DC: American Psychological Association.

Bauer, C. R., Langer, J. C., Shakaran, S., Bada, H. S., & Lester, B. (2005). Acute neonatal effects of cocaine exposure during pregnancy. *Archives of Pediatrics and Adolescent Medicine, 159,* 824–834.

Bauer, P. J. (2002). Early memory development. In U. Goswami (Ed.), *Blackwell handbook of child cognitive development* (pp. 127–150). Malden, MA: Blackwell.

Bauer, P. J. (2006). Event memory. In D. Kuhn & R. Siegler (Eds.), *Handbook of child psychology: Vol. 2. Cognition, perception, and language* (6th ed., pp. 373–425). Hoboken, NJ: Wiley.

Bauer, P. J. (2007). Recall in infancy: A neurodevelopmental account. *Current Directions in Psychological Science, 16,* 142–146.

Bauer, P. J. (2009). Learning and memory: Like a horse and carriage. In A. Woodward & A. Needham (Eds.), *Learning and the infant mind* (pp. 3–28). New York: Oxford University Press.

Bauer, P. J., Wiebe, S. A., Carver, L. J., Lukowski, A. F., Haight, J. C., Waters, J. M., & Nelson, C. A. (2006). Electrophysiological indexes of encoding and behavioral indexes of recall: Examining relations and developmental change late in the first year of life. *Developmental Neuropsychology, 29,* 293–320.

Baughman, F. D., & Cooper, R. P. (2006). Inhibition and young children's performance on the Tower of London task. In *Proceedings of the 7th International Conference on Cognitive Modeling* (pp. 26–31). Trieste, Italy.

Baumeister, R. F. (1998). Inducing guilt. In J. Bybee (Ed.), *Guilt and children* (pp. 185–213). San Diego: Academic Press.

Baumeister, R. F., Campbell, J. D., Krueger, J. I., & Vohs, K. D. (2003). Does high self-esteem cause better performance, interpersonal success, happiness, or healthier lifestyles? *Psychological Science in the Public Interest, 4*(1), 1–44.

Baumrind, D. (1971). Current patterns of parental authority. *Developmental Psychology Monograph, 4* (No. 1, Pt. 2).

Baumwell, L., Tamis-LeMonda, C. S., & Bornstein, M. H. (1997). Maternal verbal sensitivity and child language comprehension. *Infant Behavior and Development, 20,* 247–258.

Bauserman, R. (2002). Child adjustment in joint-custody versus sole-custody arrangements: A meta-analytic review. *Journal of Family Psychology, 16,* 91–102.

Baydar, N., Greek, A., & Brooks-Gunn, J. (1997). A longitudinal study of the effects of the birth of a sibling during the first 6 years of life. *Journal of Marriage and the Family, 59,* 939–956.

Bayless, S., & Stevenson, J. (2007). Executive functions in school-age children born very prematurely. *Early Human Development, 83,* 247–254.

Bayley, N. (1969). *Bayley Scales of Infant Development.* New York: Psychological Corporation.

Bayley, N. (1993). *Bayley Scales of Infant Development* (2nd ed.). New York: Psychological Corporation.

Bayley, N. (2005). *Bayley Scales of Infant and Toddler Development* (3rd ed.). (Bayley III). San Antonio, TX: Harcourt Assessment.

Baynes, K., & Gazzaniga, M. S. (1988). Right hemisphere language: Insights into normal language mechanisms. In F. Plum (Ed.), *Language, communication, and the brain* (pp. 117–126). New York: Raven.

Bean, R. A., Barber, B. K., & Crane, D. R. (2007). Parental support, behavioral control, and psychological control among African American youth: The relationships to academic grades, delinquency, and depression. *Journal of Family Issues, 27,* 1335–1355.

Bearman, P. S., & Moody, J. (2004). Suicide and friendships among American adolescents. *American Journal of Public Health, 94,* 89–95.

Beautrais, A. L. (2003). Life course factors associated with suicidal behaviors in young people. *American Behavioral Scientist, 46,* 1137–1156.

Becker, G., Beyene, Y., Newsome, E., & Mayen, N. (2003). Creating continuity through mutual assistance: Intergenerational reciprocity in four ethnic groups. *Journal of Gerontology, 38B,* S151–S159.

Becker, K., El-Faddagh, M., Schmidt, M. H., Esser, G., & Laucht, M. (2008). Interaction of dopamine transporter genotype with prenatal smoke exposure on ADHD symptoms. *Journal of Pediatrics, 152,* 263–269.

Beckett, C., Maughan, B., Rutter, M., Castle, J., Colvert, E., & Groothues, C. (2006). Do the effects of early severe deprivation on cognition persist into early adolescence? Findings from the English and Romanian adoptees study. *Child Development, 77,* 696–711.

Bedford, O. A. (2004). The individual experience of guilt and shame in Chinese culture. *Culture and Psychology, 10,* 29–52.

Beekhoven, S., & Dekkers, H. (2005). Early school leaving in the lower vocational track: Triangulation of qualitative and quantitative data. *Adolescence, 40,* 197–213.

Behnke, M., Eyler, F. D., Garvan, C. W., & Wobie, K. (2001). The search for congenital malformations in newborns with fetal cocaine exposure. *Pediatrics, 107,* e74.

Behnke, M., Eyler, F. D., Warner, T. D., Garvan, C. W., Hou, W., & Wobie, K. (2006). Outcome from a prospective, longitudinal study of prenatal cocaine use: Preschool development at 3 years of age. *Journal of Pediatric Psychology, 31,* 41–49.

Beilin, H. (1992). Piaget's enduring contribution to developmental psychology. *Developmental Psychology, 28,* 191–204.

Beitel, A. H., & Parke, R. D. (1998). Paternal involvement in infancy: The role of maternal and paternal attitudes. *Journal of Family Psychology, 12,* 268–288.

Bell, J. H., & Bromnick, R. D. (2003). The social reality of the imaginary audience: A grounded theory approach. *Adolescence, 38,* 205–219.

Bell, M. A. (1998). Frontal lobe function during infancy: Implications for the development of cognition and attention. In J. E. Richards (Ed.), *Cognitive neuroscience of attention: A developmental perspective* (pp. 327–362). Mahwah, NJ: Erlbaum.

Bell, M. A., & Fox, N. A. (1996). Crawling experience is related to changes in cortical organization during infancy: Evidence from EEG coherence. *Developmental Psychobiology, 29,* 551–561.

Bellagamba, F., Camaioni, L., & Colonnesi, C. (2006). Change in children's understanding of others' intentional actions. *Developmental Science, 9,* 182–188.

Bellamy, C. (2004). *The state of the world's children: 2004.* New York: UNICEF.

Bellinger, D. C. (2005). Teratogen update: Lead and pregnancy. *Birth Defects Research: Part A, Clinical and Molecular Teratology, 73,* 409–420.

Bellinger, D. C., Leviton, A., & Sloman, J. (1990). Antecedents and correlates of improved cognitive performance in children exposed in utero to low levels of lead. *Environmental Health Perspectives, 89,* 5–11.

Belsky, J. (2001). Emanuel Miller Lecture: Developmental risks (still) associated with early child care. *Journal of Child Psychology and Psychiatry, 42,* 845–859.

Belsky, J. (2005). Attachment theory and research in ecological perspective: Insights from the Pennsylvania Infant and Family Development Project and the NICHD Study of Early Child Care. In K. E. Grossmann, K. Grossmann, & E. Waters (Eds.), *Attachment from infancy to adulthood: The major longitudinal studies* (pp. 71–97). New York: Guilford.

Belsky, J. (2006). Early child care and early child development: Major findings of the NICHD Study of Early Child Care. *European Journal of Developmental Psychology, 3,* 95–110.

Belsky, J., Campbell, S. B., Cohn, J. F., & Moore, G. (1996). Instability of infant–parent attachment security. *Developmental Psychology, 32,* 921–924.

Belsky, J., & Fearon, R. M. P. (2002a). Early attachment security, subsequent maternal sensitivity, and later child development: Does continuity in development depend on caregiving? *Attachment and Human Development, 4,* 361–387.

Belsky, J., & Fearon, R. M. P. (2002b). Infant–mother attachment security, contextual risk, and early development: A moderational analysis. *Development and Pathology, 14,* 293–310.

Belsky, J., Steinberg, L. D., Houts, R. M., Friedman, S. L., DeHart, G., Cauffman, E., Roisman, G. I., & Halpern-Felsher, B. (2007). Family rearing antecedents of pubertal timing. *Child Development, 78,* 1302–1321.

Belsky, J., Steinberg, L., Houts, R. M., & Halpern-Felsher, B. L. (2010). The development of reproductive strategy in females: Early maternal harshness → earlier menarche → increased sexual risk taking. *Developmental Psychology, 46,* 120–128.

Belsky, J., Vandell, D. L., Burchinal, M., Clarke-Stewart, K. A., McCartney, K., & Owen, M. T. (2007). Are there long-term effects of early child care? *Child Development, 78,* 681–701.

Bemmels, H. R., Burt, A., Legrand, L. N., Iacono, W. G., & McGue, M. (2008). The heritability of life events: An adolescent twin and adoption study. *Twin Research and Human Genetics, 11,* 257–265.

Benarroch, F., Hirsch, H. J., Genstil, L., Landau, Y. E., & Gross-Tsur, V. (2007). Prader-Willi syndrome: Medical prevention and behavioral challenges. *Child and Adolescent Psychiatric Clinics of North America, 16,* 695–708.

Benbow, C. P., Lubinski, D., Shea, D. L., & Eftekhara-Sanjani, H. (2000). Sex differences in mathematical reasoning ability at age 13: Their status 20 years later. *Psychological Science, 11,* 474–480.

Benbow, C. P., & Stanley, J. C. (1983). Sex differences in mathematical reasoning: More facts. *Science, 222,* 1029–1031.

Bender, H. L., Allen, J. P., McElhaney, K. B., Antonishak, J., Moore, C. M., Kelly, H. L., & Davis, S. M. (2007). Use of harsh physical discipline and developmental outcomes in adolescence. *Development and Psychopathology, 19,* 227–242.

Benenson, J. F., & Christakos, A. (2003). The greater fragility of females' versus males' closest same-sex friendships. *Child Development, 74,* 1123–1129.

Bengtson, H. (2005). Children's cognitive appraisal of others' distressful and positive experiences.

International Journal of Behavioral Development, 29, 457–466.

Benner, A. D., & Graham, S. (2009). The transition to high school as a developmental process among multiethnic urban youth. *Child Development, 80,* 356–376.

Bennett, K. E., Haggard, M. P., Silva, P. A., & Stewart, I. A. (2001). Behaviour and developmental effects of otitis media with effusion into the teens. *Archives of Disease in Childhood, 85,* 91–95.

Bennett, M., Barrett, M., Karakozov, R., Kipiani, G., Lyons, E., Pavlenko, V., & Riazanova, T. (2004). Young children's evaluations of the ingroup and outgroups: A multinational study. *Social Development, 13,* 124–141.

Bennett, S. E., & Assefi, N. P. (2005). School-based teenage pregnancy prevention programs: A systematic review of randomized controlled trials. *Journal of Adolescent Health, 36,* 72–81.

Benson, P. L., Scales, P. C., Hamilton, S. F., & Sesma, A., Jr. (2006). Positive youth development: Theory, research, and applications. In R. M. Lerner (Ed.), *Handbook of child psychology: Vol. 1. Theoretical models of human development* (6th ed., pp. 894–941). Hoboken, NJ: Wiley.

Ben-Zeev, T., Carrasquillo, C. M., Ching, A. M. L., Patton, G. E., Stewart, T. D., & Stoddard, T. (2005). "Math is hard!" (Barbie™, 1994): Responses of threat vs. challenge-mediated arousal to stereotypes alleging intellectual inferiority. In A. M. Gallagher & J. C. Kaufman (Eds.), *Gender differences in mathematics: An integrative psychological approach* (pp. 189–206). New York: Cambridge University Press.

Berenbaum, S. A. (2001). Cognitive function in congenital adrenal hyperplasia. *Endocrinology and Metabolism Clinics of North America, 30,* 173–192.

Bergen, D., & Mauer, D. (2000). Symbolic play, phonological awareness, and literacy skills at three age levels. In K. A. Roskos & J. F. Christie (Eds.), *Play and literacy in early childhood: Research from multiple perspectives* (pp. 45–62). Mahwah, NJ: Erlbaum.

Berger, A., Tzur, G., & Posner, M. I. (2006). Infant brains detect arithmetic errors. *Proceedings of the National Academy of Sciences, 103,* 12649–12653.

Berger, L. M., Paxson, C., & Waldfogel, J. (2009). Income and child development. *Children and Youth Services Review, 31,* 978–989.

Berger, S. E., Theuring, C., & Adolph, K. E. (2007). How and when infants learn to climb stairs. *Infant Behavior and Development, 30,* 36–49.

Bergman, R. (2004). Identity as motivation. In D. K. Lapsley & D. Narvaez (Eds.), *Moral development, self, and identity* (pp. 21–46). Mahwah, NJ: Erlbaum.

Berk, L. E. (2001a). *Awakening children's minds: How parents and teachers can make a difference.* New York: Oxford University Press.

Berk, L. E. (2001b). Private speech and self-regulation in children with impulse-control difficulties: Implications for research and practice. *Journal of Cognitive Education and Psychology, 2*(1), 1–21.

Berk, L. E. (2004). *Conversations with children.* Normal, IL: Illinois State University.

Berk, L. E. (2005). Why parenting matters. In S. Olfman (Ed.), *Childhood lost: How American culture is failing our kids* (pp. 19–53). New York: Guilford.

Berk, L. E. (2006). Looking at kindergarten children. In D. Gullo (Ed.), *K today: Teaching and learning in the kindergarten year* (pp. 11–25). Washington, DC: National Association for the Education of Young Children.

Berk, L. E., & Harris, S. (2003). Vygotsky, Lev. In L. Nadel (Ed.), *Encyclopedia of cognitive science.* London: Macmillan.

Berk, L. E., Mann, T., & Ogan, A. (2006). Make-believe play: Wellspring for development of self-regulation. In D. Singer, K. Hirsh-Pasek, & R. Golinkoff (Eds.), *Play=learning* (pp. 74–100). New York: Oxford University Press.

Berk, L. E., & Spuhl, S. T. (1995). Maternal interaction, private speech, and task performance in preschool

children. *Early Childhood Research Quarterly, 10,* 145–169.

Berkowitz, C. M. (2004). *Talking to your kids about sex.* Somerville, NJ: Somerset Medical Center. Retrieved from www.somersetmedicalcenter.com/18417.cfm

Berkowitz, M. W., & Gibbs, J. C. (1983). Measuring the developmental features of moral discussion. *Merrill-Palmer Quarterly, 29,* 399–410.

Berkowitz, R. J., & Stunkard, A. J. (2002). Development of childhood obesity. In T. A. Wadden & A. J. Stunkard (Eds.), *Handbook of obesity treatment* (pp. 515–531). New York: Guilford.

Berkowitz, R. L., Roberts, J., & Minkoff, H. (2006). Challenging the strategy of maternal age-based prenatal genetic counseling. *Journal of the American Medical Association, 295,* 1446–1448.

Berlin, L. J., Ipsa, J. M., Fine, M. A., Malone, P. S., Brooks-Gunn, J., Brady-Smith, C., et al. (2009). Correlates and consequences of spanking and verbal punishment for low-income white, African-American, and Mexican-American toddlers. *Child Development, 80,* 1403–1420.

Berman, P. W. (1980). Are women more responsive than men to the young? A review of developmental and situational variables. *Psychological Bulletin, 88,* 668–695.

Berman, R. A. (2007). Developing linguistic knowledge and language use across adolescence. In K. Hirsh-Pasek & R. M. Golinkoff (Eds.), *Action meets word: How children learn verbs* (pp. 347–367). New York: Oxford University Press.

Berman, S. L., Weems, C. F., Rodriguez, E. T., & Zamora, I. J. (2006). The relation between identity status and romantic attachment style in middle and late adolescence. *Journal of Adolescence, 29,* 737–748.

Berndt, T. J. (2004). Children's friendships: Shifts over a half-century in perspectives on their development and effects. *Merrill-Palmer Quarterly, 50,* 206–223.

Berndt, T. J., & Murphy, L. M. (2002). Influences of friends and friendships: Myths, truths, and research recommendations. In R. V. Kail (Ed.), *Advances in child development and behavior* (Vol. 30, pp. 275–310). San Diego, CA: Academic Press.

Bernier, J. C., & Siegel, D. H. (1994). Attention-deficit hyperactivity disorder: A family ecological systems perspective. *Families in Society, 75,* 142–150.

Berninger, V. W. (2006). A developmental approach to learning disabilities. In K. A. Renninger & I. E. Sigel (Eds.), *Handbook of child psychology: Vol. 4. Child psychology in practice* (6th ed., pp. 420–452). Hoboken, NJ: Wiley.

Bertenthal, B. I., & Longo, M. R. (2007). Is there evidence of a mirror neuron system from birth? *Developmental Science, 10,* 513–523.

Bertenthal, B. I., Longo, M. R., & Kenny, S. (2007). Phenomenal permanence and the development of predictive tracking in infancy. *Child Development, 78,* 350–363.

Bertrand, M., & Mullainathan, S. (2004). *Are Emily and Brendan more employable than Lakisha and Jamal? A field experiment on labor market discrimination.* Unpublished manuscript, University of Chicago.

Berzonsky, M. D. (2003). Identity style and well-being: Does commitment matter? *Identity: An International Journal of Theory and Research, 3,* 131–142.

Berzonsky, M. D. (2004). Identity style, parental authority, and identity commitment. *Journal of Youth and Adolescence, 33,* 213–220.

Berzonsky, M. D., & Kuk, L. S. (2000). Identity status, identity processing style, and the transition to university. *Journal of Adolescent Research, 15,* 81–98.

Best, D. L. (2001). Gender concepts: Convergence in cross-cultural research and methodologies. *Cross-cultural Research: The Journal of Comparative Social Science, 35,* 23–43.

Betrán, A. P., Merialdi, M., Lauer, J. A., Bing-Shun, W., Thomas, J., et al. (2007). Rates of caesarean section: Analysis of global, regional, and national estimates. *Paediatric and Perinatal Epidemiology, 21,* 98–113.

Beyers, J. M., Bates, J. E., Pettit, G. S., & Dodge, K. A. (2003). Neighborhood structure, parenting processes, and the development of youths' externalizing behaviors: A multilevel analysis.

American Journal of Community Psychology, 31, 35–53.

Bhagavath, B., & Layman, L. C. (2007). The genetics of hypogonadotropic hypogonadism. *Seminars in Reproductive Medicine, 25,* 272–286.

Bhana, D. (2008). Beyond stigma? Young children's responses to HIV and AIDS. *Culture, Health and Sexuality, 10,* 725–738.

Bhat, A., Heathcock, J., & Galloway, J. C. (2005). Toy-oriented changes in hand and joint kinematics during the emergence of purposeful reaching. *Infant Behavior and Development, 28,* 445–465.

Bhatt, R. S., Rovee-Collier, C., & Weiner, S. (1994). Developmental changes in the interface between perception and memory retrieval. *Developmental Psychology, 30,* 151–162.

Bhatt, R. S., Wilk, A., Hill, D., & Rovee-Collier, C. (2004). Correlated attributes and categorization in the first half-year of life. *Developmental Psychobiology, 44,* 103–115.

Bialystok, E. (2001). *Bilingualism in development: Language, literacy, and cognition.* New York: Cambridge University Press.

Bialystok, E., & Martin, M. M. (2003). Notation to symbol: Development in children's understanding of print. *Journal of Experimental Child Psychology, 86,* 223–243.

Bialystok, E., & Martin, M. M. (2004). Attention and inhibition in bilingual children: Evidence from the dimensional change card sort task. *Developmental Science, 7,* 325–339.

Bialystok, E., McBride-Chang, C., & Luk, G. (2005). Bilingualism, language proficiency, and learning to read in two writing systems. *Journal of Educational Psychology, 97,* 580–590.

Bialystok, E., & Senman, L. (2004). Executive processes in appearance–reality tasks: The role of inhibition of attention and symbolic representation. *Child Development, 75,* 562–579.

Bianco, A., Stone, J., Lynch, L., Lapinski, R., Berkowitz, G., & Berkowitz, R. L. (1996). Pregnancy outcome at age 40 and older. *Obstetrics and Gynecology, 87,* 917–922.

Bibace, R., & Walsh, M. E. (1980). Development of children's concepts of illness. *Pediatrics, 66,* 912–917.

Bibby, R. W. (2000). *Restless gods: The renaissance of religion in Canada.* Toronto: Stoddart.

Biederman, J., Kwon, A., Aleardi, M., Chouinard, V.-A., Marino, T., & Cole, H. (2005). Absence of gender effects on attention-deficit hyperactivity disorder: Findings in nonreferred subjects. *American Journal of Psychiatry, 162,* 1083–1089.

Bielawska-Batorowicz, E., & Kossakowska-Petrycka, K. (2006). Depressive mood in men after the birth of their offspring in relation to a partner's depression, social support, fathers' personality and prenatal expectations. *Journal of Reproductive and Infant Psychology, 24,* 21–29.

Bielinski, J., & Davison, M. L. (1998). Gender differences by item difficulty interactions in multiple-choice mathematics items. *American Educational Research Journal, 35,* 455–476.

Bierman, K. L., Domitrovich, C. E., Nix, R. L., Gest, S. D., Welsh, J. A., Greenberg, M. T., et al. (2008). Promoting academic and social-emotional school readiness: The Head Start REDI program. *Child Development, 79,* 1802–1817.

Bierman, K. L., & Powers, C. J. (2009). Social skills training to improve peer relations. In K. H. Rubin, W. M. Bukowski, & B. Laursen (Eds.), *Handbook of peer interactions, relationships, and groups* (pp. 603–621). New York: Guilford.

Bifulco, R., Cobb, C. D., & Bell, C. (2009). Can interdistrict choice boost student achievement? The case of Connecticut's interdistrict magnet school program. *Educational Evaluation and Policy Analysis, 31,* 323–345.

Bigelow, A. E. (1992). Locomotion and search behavior in blind infants. *Infant Behavior and Development, 15,* 179–189.

Bigelow, A. E. (2003). The development of joint attention in blind infants. *Development and Psychopathology, 15,* 259–275.

Bigelow, A. E., MacLean, K., Proctor, J., Myatt, T., Gillis, R., & Power, M. (2010). Maternal sensitivity throughout infancy: Continuity and relation to attachment security. *Infant Behavior and Development, 33*, 50–60.

Bigler, R. S. (2007, June). Personal communication.

Bigler, R. S., Brown, C. S., & Markell, M. (2001). When groups are not created equal: Effects of group status on the formation of intergroup attitudes in children. *Child Development, 72*, 1151–1162.

Bimmel, N., Juffer, F., van IJzendoorn, M. H., & Bakermans-Kranenburg, M. J. (2003). Problem behavior of internationally adopted adolescents: A review and meta-analysis. *Harvard Review of Psychiatry, 11*, 64–77.

Bioethics Consultative Committee. (2003). *Comparison of ethics legislation in Europe*. Retrieved from www .synapse.net.mt/bioethics/euroleg1.htm

Birch, E. E. (1993). Stereopsis in infants and its developmental relation to visual acuity. In K. Simons (Ed.), *Early visual development: Normal and abnormal* (pp. 224–236). New York: Oxford University Press.

Birch, L. L. (1999). Development of food preferences. *Annual Review of Nutrition, 19*, 41–62.

Birch, L. L., & Fisher, J. A. (1995). Appetite and eating behavior in children. *Pediatric Clinics of North America, 42*, 931–953.

Birch, L. L., Fisher, J. O., & Davison, K. K. (2003). Learning to overeat: Maternal use of restrictive feeding practices promotes girls' eating in the absence of hunger. *American Journal of Clinical Nutrition, 78*, 215–220.

Birch, L. L., Zimmerman, S., & Hind, H. (1980). The influence of social-affective context on preschool children's food preferences. *Child Development, 51*, 856–861.

Birch, S. A. J., & Bloom, P. (2003). Children are cursed: An asymmetric bias in mental-state attribution. *Psychological Science, 14*, 283–285.

Birch, S. H., & Ladd, G. W. (1998). Children's interpersonal behaviors and the teacher–child relationship. *Developmental Psychology, 34*, 934–946.

Bird, A., & Reese, E. (2006). Emotional reminiscing and the development of an autobiographical self. *Developmental Psychology, 42*, 613–626.

Biringen, Z., Emde, R. N., Campos, J. J., & Appelbaum, M. I. (1995). Affective reorganization in the infant, the mother, and the dyad: The role of upright locomotion and its timing. *Child Development, 66*, 499–514.

Birken, C. S., Parkin, P. C., To, T., & Macarthur, C. (2006). Trends in rates of death from unintentional injury among Canadian children in urban areas: Influence of socioeconomic status. *Canadian Medical Association Journal, 175*, 867–868.

Birkett, M., Espelage, D. L., & Koenig, B. (2009). LGB and questioning students in schools: The moderating effects of homophobic bullying and school climate on negative outcomes. *Journal of Youth and Adolescence, 38*, 989–1000.

Birndorf, S., Ryan, S., Auinger, P., & Aten, M. (2005). High self-esteem among adolescents: Longitudinal trends, sex differences, and protective factors. *Journal of Adolescent Research, 37*, 194–201.

Birney, D. P., Citron-Pousty, J. H., Lutz, D. J., & Sternberg, R. J. (2005). The development of cognitive and intellectual abilities. In M. H. Bornstein & M. E. Lamb (Eds.), *Developmental science: An advanced textbook* (5th ed., pp. 327–358). Mahwah, NJ: Erlbaum.

Bjorklund, D. F. (2004). *Children's thinking* (4th ed.). Belmont, CA: Wadsworth.

Bjorklund, D. F., & Douglas, R. N. (1997). The development of memory strategies. In N. Cowan (Ed.), *The development of memory in childhood* (pp. 83–111). Hove, UK: Psychology Press.

Bjorklund, D. F., Schneider, W., Cassel, W. S., & Ashley, E. (1994). Training and extension of a memory strategy: Evidence for utilization deficiencies in high- and low-IQ children. *Child Development, 65*, 951–965.

Black, B., & Logan, A. (1995). Links between communication patterns in mother–child, father–child, and child–peer interactions and children's social status. *Child Development, 66*, 255–271.

Black, M. M. (2005). Failure to thrive. In M. C. Roberts (Ed.), *Handbook of pediatric psychology and psychiatry* (3rd ed., pp. 499–511). New York: Guilford.

Black, M. M., Dubowitz, H., Krishnakumar, A., & Starr, R. H., Jr. (2007). Early intervention and recovery among children with failure to thrive: Follow-up at age 8. *Pediatrics, 120*, 59–69.

Black, R. E., Williams, S. M., Jones, I. E., & Goulding, A. (2002). Children who avoid drinking cow milk have low dietary calcium intakes and poor bone health. *American Journal of Clinical Nutrition, 76*, 675–680.

Blackwell, D. L., & Lichter, D. T. (2004). Homogamy among dating, cohabiting, and married couples. *Sociological Quarterly, 45*, 719–737.

Blackwell, L. S., Trzesniewski, K. H., & Dweck, C. S. (2007). Implicit theories of intelligence predict achievement across an adolescent transition: A longitudinal study and an intervention. *Child Development, 78*, 246–263.

Blaga, O. M., & Colombo, J. (2006). Visual processing and infant ocular latencies in the overlap paradigm. *Developmental Psychology, 42*, 1069–1076.

Blair, C., & Razza, R. P. (2007). Relating effortful control, executive function, and false belief understanding to emerging math and literacy ability in kindergarten. *Developmental Psychology, 78*, 647–663.

Blakemore, J. E. O. (2003). Children's beliefs about violating gender norms: Boys shouldn't look like girls, and girls shouldn't act like boys. *Sex Roles, 48*, 411–419.

Blakemore, S.-J., & Choudhury, S. (2006). Development of the adolescent brain: Implications for executive function and social cognition. *Journal of Child Psychology and Psychiatry, 47*, 296–312.

Blanchard, R., & Bogaert, A. F. (2004). Proportion of homosexual men who owe their sexual orientation to fraternal birth order: An estimate based on two national probability samples. *American Journal of Human Biology, 16*, 151–157.

Blasi, A. (1994). Moral identity: Its role in moral functioning. In B. Puka (Ed.), *Fundamental research in moral development: A compendium* (Vol. 2, pp. 123–167). New York: Garland.

Blasi, C. H., & Bjorklund, D. F. (2003). Evolutionary developmental psychology: A new tool for better understanding human ontogeny. *Human Development, 46*, 259–281.

Blass, E. M., Ganchrow, J. R., & Steiner, J. E. (1984). Classical conditioning in newborn humans 2–48 hours of age. *Infant Behavior and Development, 7*, 223–235.

Blatchford, P., Bassett, P., & Brown, P. (2005). Teachers' and pupils' behavior in large and small classes: A systematic observation study of pupils aged 10 and 11 years. *Journal of Educational Psychology, 97*, 454–467.

Blatchford, P., Bassett, P., Goldstein, H., & Martin, C. (2003). Are class size differences related to pupils' educational progress and classroom processes? Findings from the Institute of Education Class Size Study of children aged 5–7 years. *British Educational Research Journal, 29*, 709–730.

Blatchford, P., Russell, A., Bassett, P., Brown, P., & Martin, C. (2007). The effect of class size on the teaching of pupils aged 7–11 years. *School Effectiveness and School Improvement, 18*, 147–172.

Bleeker, M. M., & Jacobs, J. E. (2004). Achievement in math and science: Do mothers' beliefs matter 12 years later? *Journal of Educational Psychology, 96*, 97–109.

Bloom, L. (1998). Language acquisition in its developmental context. In D. Kuhn & R. S. Siegler (Eds.), *Handbook of child psychology: Vol. 2. Cognition, perception, and language* (5th ed., pp. 309–370). New York: Wiley.

Bloom, L. (2000). The intentionality model of language development: How to learn a word, any word. In R. Golinkoff, K. Hirsh-Pasek, N. Akhtar, L. Bloom, G. Hollich, L. Smith, M. Tomasello, & A. Woodward (Eds.), *Becoming a word learner: A debate on lexical acquisition*. New York: Oxford University Press.

Bloom, P. (1999). The role of semantics in solving the bootstrapping problem. In R. Jackendoff & P. Bloom (Eds.), *Language, logic, and concepts* (pp. 285–309). Cambridge, MA: MIT Press.

Blumberg, M. S., & Lucas, D. E. (1996). A developmental and component analysis of active sleep. *Developmental Psychobiology, 29*, 1–22.

Blumenfeld, P. C., Marx, R. W., & Harris, C. J. (2006). Learning environments. In K. A. Renninger & I. E. Sigel (Eds.), *Handbook of child psychology: Vol. 4. Child psychology in practice* (6th ed., pp. 297–342). Hoboken, NJ: Wiley.

Boardman, J. D. (2004). Stress and physical health: The role of neighborhoods as mediating and moderating mechanisms. *Social Science and Medicine, 58*, 2473–2483.

Bodrova, E., & Leong, D. J. (2007). *Tools of the mind: The Vygotskian approach to early childhood education* (2nd ed.). Upper Saddle River, NJ: Merrill Prentice Hall.

Bogaert, A. F. (2005). Age at puberty and father absence in a national probability sample. *Journal of Adolescence, 28*, 541–546.

Bogartz, R. S., Shinskey, J. L., & Schilling, T. H. (2000). Object permanence in five-and-a-half-month-old infants. *Infancy, 1*, 403–428.

Bogin, B. (2001). *The growth of humanity*. New York: Wiley-Liss.

Bogin, B., Smith, P., Orden, A. B., Varela, S., & Loucky, J. (2002). Rapid change in height and body proportions of Maya American children. *American Journal of Human Biology, 14*, 753–761.

Bohannon, J. N., III, & Bonvillian, J. D. (2009). Theoretical approaches to language acquisition. In J. B. Gleason & B. Ratner (Ed.), *The development of language* (7th ed., pp. 227–284). Boston: Allyn and Bacon.

Bohannon, J. N., III, & Stanowicz, L. (1988). The issue of negative evidence: Adult responses to children's language errors. *Developmental Psychology, 24*, 684–689.

Boldizar, J. P. (1991). Assessing sex typing and androgyny in children: The children's sex role inventory. *Developmental Psychology, 27*, 505–515.

Bolen, R. M. (2001). *Child sexual abuse*. New York: Kluwer Academic.

Bolisetty, S., Bajuk, B., Me, A.-L., Vincent, T., Sutton, L., & Lui, K. (2006). Preterm outcome table (POT): A simple tool to aid counselling parents of very preterm infants. *Australian and New Zealand Journal of Obstetrics and Gynaecology, 46*, 189–192.

Bolzani, L. H., Messinger, D. S., Yale, M., & Dondi, M. (2002). Smiling in infancy. In M. H. Abel (Ed.), *An empirical reflection on the smile* (pp. 111–136). Lewiston, NY: Edwin Mellen Press.

Bonilla, S., Kehl, S., Kwong, K. Y., Morphew, T., Kachru, R., & Jones, C. A. (2005). School absenteeism in children with asthma in a Los Angeles inner-city school. *Journal of Pediatrics, 147*, 802–806.

Bono, M. A., & Stifter, C. A. (2003). Maternal attention-directing strategies and infant focused attention during problem solving. *Infancy, 4*, 235–250.

Boom, J., Wouters, H., & Keller, M. (2007). A cross-cultural validation of stage development: A Rasch re-analysis of longitudinal socio-moral reasoning data. *Cognitive Development, 22*, 213–229.

Borduin, C. M. (2007). Multisystemic treatment of violent youth and their families. In T. A. Cavell & K. T. Malcolm (Eds.), *Anger, aggression, and interventions for interpersonal violence* (pp. 239–265). Mahwah, NJ: Erlbaum.

Borke, H. (1975). Piaget's mountains revisited: Changes in the egocentric landscape. *Developmental Psychology, 11*, 240–243.

Bornstein, M. H. (1989). Sensitive periods in development: Structural characteristics and causal interpretations. *Psychological Bulletin, 105*, 179–197.

Bornstein, M. H. (2002). Parenting infants. In M. H. Bornstein (Ed.), *Handbook of parenting: Vol. 1* (2nd ed., pp. 3–44). Mahwah, NJ: Erlbaum.

Bornstein, M. H. (2006). Parenting science and practice. In K. Renninger & I. E. Sigel (Eds.), *Handbook of child psychology: Vol. 4. Child psychology in practice* (6th ed., pp. 893–949). Hoboken, NJ: Wiley.

Bornstein, M. H., & Arterberry, M. E. (1999). Perceptual development. In M. H. Bornstein & M. E. Lamb (Eds.), *Developmental psychology: An advanced textbook* (pp. 231–274). Mahwah, NJ: Erlbaum.

Bornstein, M. H., & Arterberry, M. E. (2003). Recognition, discrimination, and categorization of smiling by 5-month-old infants. *Developmental Science, 6*, 585–599.

Bornstein, M. H., Arterberry, M. E., & Mash, C. (2010). Infant object categorization transcends object–context relations. *Infant Behavior and Development, 33*, 7–15.

Bornstein, M. H., Haynes, O. M., Pascual, L., Painter, K. M., & Galperin, C. (1999a). Play in two societies: Pervasiveness of process, specificity of structure. *Child Development, 70*, 317–331.

Bornstein, M. H., Selmi, A. M., Haynes, O. M., Painter, K. M., & Marx, E. S. (1999b). Representational abilities and the hearing status of child/mother dyads. *Child Development, 70*, 833–852.

Bornstein, M. H., Vibbert, M., Tal, J., & O'Donnell, K. (1992). Toddler language and play in the second year: Stability, covariation, and influences of parenting. *First Language, 12*, 323–338.

Boroughs, D. S. (2004). Female sexual abusers of children. *Children and Youth Services Review, 26*, 481–487.

Borst, C. G. (1995). *Catching babies: The professionalization of childbirth, 1870–1920.* Cambridge, MA: Harvard University Press.

Bos, H. M. W., van Balen, F., & van den Boom, D. C. (2004). Experience of parenthood, couple relationship, social support, and child-rearing goals in planned lesbian mother families. *Journal of Child Psychology and Psychiatry, 25*, 755–764.

Bos, H. M. W., van Balen, F., & van den Boom, D. C. (2007). Child adjustment and parenting in planned lesbian-parent families. *American Journal of Orthopsychiatry, 77*, 38–48.

Bosacki, S. L., & Moore, C. (2004). Preschoolers' understanding of simple and complex emotions: Links with gender and language. *Sex Roles, 50*, 659–675.

Bost, K. K., Shin, N., McBride, B. A., Brown, G. L., Vaughn, B. E., & Coppola, G. (2006). Maternal secure base scripts, children's attachment security, and mother–child narrative styles. *Attachment and Human Development, 8*, 241–260.

Botton, J., Heude, B., Maccario, J., Ducimetiére, P., & Charles, M. A. (2008). Postnatal weight and height growth velocities at different ages between birth and 5y and body composition in adolescent boys and girls. *American Journal of Clinical Nutrition, 87*, 1760–1768

Bouchard, T. J., & Loehlin, J. C. (2001). Genes, evolution, and personality. *Behavior Genetics, 31*, 243–274.

Boucher, O., Muckle, G., & Bastien, C. H. (2009). Prenatal exposure to polychlorinated biphenyls: A neuropsychologic analysis. *Environmental Health Perspectives, 117*, 7–16.

Boukydis, C. F. Z., & Lester, B. M. (1998). Infant crying, risk status and social support in families of preterm and term infants. *Early Development and Parenting, 7*, 31–39.

Bouldin, P. (2006). An investigation of the fantasy predisposition and fantasy style of children with imaginary companions. *Journal of Genetic Psychology, 167*, 17–29.

Boulton, M. J. (1996). A comparison of 8- and 11-year-old girls' and boys' participation in specific types of rough-and-tumble play and aggressive fighting: Implications for functional hypotheses. *Aggressive Behavior, 22*, 271–287.

Boulton, M. J. (1999). Concurrent and longitudinal relations between children's playground behavior and social preference, victimization, and bullying. *Child Development, 70*, 944–954.

Bowen, N. K., Bowen, G. L., & Ware, W. B. (2002). Neighborhood social disorganization, families, and the educational behavior of adolescents. *Journal of Adolescent Research, 17*, 468–490.

Bower-Russa, M. E., Knutson, J. F., & Winebarger, A. (2001). Disciplinary history, adult disciplinary attitudes, and risk for abusive parenting. *Journal of Community Psychology, 29*, 219–240.

Bowker, A. (2004). Predicting friendship stability during early adolescence. *Journal of Early Adolescence, 24*, 85–112.

Bowlby, J. (1980). *Attachment and loss: Vol. 3. Loss.* New York: Basic Books.

Bowlby, J. W., & McMullen, K. (2002). *At a crossroads: First results for the 18- to 20-year-old cohort of the Youth in Transition Survey.* Ottawa, Canada: Human Resources Development Canada.

Bowman, S. A., Gortmaker, S. L., Ebbeling, C. B., Pereira, M. A., & Ludwig, D. S. (2004). Effects of fast-food consumption on energy intake and diet quality among children in a national household survey. *Pediatrics, 113*, 112–113.

Boyatzis, C. J. (2000). The artistic evolution of mommy: A longitudinal case study of symbolic and social processes. In C. J. Boyatzis & M. W. Watson (Eds.), *Symbolic and social constraints on the development of children's artistic style* (pp. 5–29). San Francisco: Jossey-Bass.

Boyce, W., Doherty-Poirier, M., MacKinnon, D., Fortin, C., Saab, H., King, M., & Gallupe, O. (2006). Sexual health of Canadian youth: Findings from the Canadian Youth, Sexual Health and HIV/AIDS Study. *Canadian Journal of Human Sexuality, 15*, 59–68.

Boyd-Franklin, N. (2006). *Black families in therapy* (2nd ed.). New York: Guilford.

Boyer, K., & Diamond, A. (1992). Development of memory for temporal order in infants and young children. In A. Diamond (Ed.), *Development and neural bases of higher cognitive function* (pp. 267–317). New York: New York Academy of Sciences.

Boyer, T. W. (2006). The development of risk-taking: A multi-perspective review. *Developmental Review, 26*, 291–345.

Boyes, M. C., & Chandler, M. (1992). Cognitive development, epistemic doubt, and identity formation in adolescence. *Journal of Youth and Adolescence, 21*, 277–304.

Boyle, M. H., & Lipman, E. L. (2002). Do places matter? Socioeconomic disadvantage and behavioral problems of children in Canada. *Journal of Consulting and Clinical Psychology, 70*, 378–389.

Boysson-Bardies, B. de, & Vihman, M. M. (1991). Adaptation to language: Evidence from babbling and first words in four languages. *Language, 67*, 297–319.

Bracci, R., Perrone, S., & Buonocore, G. (2006). The timing of neonatal brain damage. *Biology of the Neonate, 90*, 145–155.

Brackbill, Y., McManus, K., & Woodward, L. (1985). Medication in maternity: Infant exposure and maternal *information.* Ann Arbor: University of Michigan Press.

Bracken, B. A. (2000). *The psychoeducational assessment of preschool children.* Boston: Allyn and Bacon.

Brackett, M. A., Mayer, J. D., & Warner, R. M. (2004). Emotional intelligence and its relation to everyday behaviour. *Personality and Individual Differences, 36*, 1387–1402.

Bradford, K., Barber, B. K., Olsen, J. A., Maughan, S. L., Erickson, L. D., Ward, D., & Stolz, H. E. (2003). A multinational study of interparental conflict, parenting, and adolescent functioning: South Africa, Bangladesh, China, India, Bosnia, Germany, Palestine, Colombia, and the United States. *Marriage and Family Review, 35*, 107–137.

Bradley, P. J., & Bray, K. H. (1996). The Netherlands' Maternal-Child Health Program: Implications for the United States. *Journal of Obstetric, Gynecologic, and Neonatal Nursing, 25*, 471–475.

Bradley, R. H. (1994). The HOME Inventory: Review and reflections. In H. W. Reese (Ed.), *Advances in child development and behavior* (Vol. 25, pp. 241–288). San Diego: Academic Press.

Bradley, R. H., & Caldwell, B. M. (1982). The consistency of the home environment and its relation to child development. *International Journal of Behavioral Development, 5*, 445–465.

Bradley, R. H., & Corwyn, R. F. (2003). Age and ethnic variations in family process mediators of SES. In M. H. Bornstein & R. H. Bradley (Eds.), *Socioeconomic status, parenting, and child development* (pp. 161–188). Mahwah, NJ: Erlbaum.

Bradley, R. H., Corwyn, R. F., McAdoo, H. P., & García-Coll, C. (2001). The home environments of children in the United States. Part I: Variations by age, ethnicity, and poverty status. *Child Development, 72*, 1844–1867.

Bradley, R. H., Whiteside, L., Mundfrom, D. J., Casey, P. H., Kelleher, K. J., & Pope, S. K. (1994). Contribution of early intervention and early caregiving experiences to resilience in low-birthweight, premature children living in poverty. *Journal of Clinical Child Psychology, 23*, 425–434.

Braine, L. G., Schauble, L., Kugelmass, S., & Winter, A. (1993). Representation of depth by children: Spatial strategies and lateral biases. *Developmental Psychology, 29*, 466–479.

Braine, M. D. S. (1994). Is nativism sufficient? *Journal of Child Language, 21*, 1–23.

Brainerd, C. J. (2003). Jean Piaget, learning, research, and American education. In B. J. Zimmerman (Ed.), *Educational psychology: A century of contributions* (pp. 251–287). Mahwah, NJ: Erlbaum.

Brame, B., Nagin, D. S., & Tremblay, R. E. (2001). Developmental trajectories of physical aggression from school entry to late adolescence. *Journal of Child Psychology and Psychiatry, 42*, 503–512.

Branca, F., & Ferrari, M. (2002). Impact of micronutrient deficiencies on growth: The stunting syndrome. *Annals of Nutrition and Metabolism, 46*(Suppl. 1), 8–17.

Brand, S., Gerber, M., Beck, J., Hatzinger, M., Puhse, U., & Holsboer-Trachsler, E. (2010). High exercise levels are related to favorable sleep and psychological functioning in adolescence: A comparison of athletes and controls. *Journal of Adolescent Health, 46*, 133–141.

Brand, S. R., Engel, S. M., Canfield, R. L., & Yehuda, R. (2006). The effect of maternal PTSD following in utero trauma exposure on behavior and temperament in the 9-month-old infant. *Annals of the New York Academy of Sciences, 1071*, 454–458.

Branje, S. J. T., van Lieshout, C. F. M., van Aken, M. A. G., & Haselager, G. J. T. (2004). Perceived support in sibling relationships and adolescent adjustment. *Journal of Child Psychology and Psychiatry, 45*, 1385–1396.

Braswell, G. S. (2006). Sociocultural contexts for the early development of semiotic production. *Psychological Bulletin, 132*, 877–894.

Braswell, G. S., & Callanan, M. A. (2003). Learning to draw recognizable graphic representations during mother–child interactions. *Merrill-Palmer Quarterly, 49*, 471–494.

Bratt, R. G. (2002). Housing: The foundation of family life. In F. Jacobs, D. Wertlieb, & R. M. Lerner (Eds.), *Handbook of applied developmental science* (Vol. 2, pp. 445–468). Thousand Oaks, CA: Sage.

Braver, S. L., Griffin, W. A., Cookston, J. T., Sandler, I. N., & Williams, J. (2005). Promoting better fathering among divorced non-resident fathers. In W. M. Pinsof & J. Lebow (Eds.), *Family psychology: The art of the science* (pp. 295–325). New York: Oxford University Press.

Bray, G. A., Nielsen, J., & Popkin, B. M. (2004). Consumption of high-fructose corn syrup in beverages may play a role in the epidemic of obesity. *American Journal of Clinical Nutrition, 79*, 537–543.

Bray, J. H. (1999). From marriage to remarriage and beyond: Findings from the Developmental Issues in Stepfamilies Research Project. In E. M. Hetherington (Ed.), *Coping with divorce, single parenting, and remarriage: A risk and resiliency perspective* (pp. 295–319). Mahwah, NJ: Erlbaum.

Brazelton, T. B., Koslowski, B., & Tronick, E. (1976). Neonatal behavior among urban Zambians and

Americans. *Journal of the American Academy of Child Psychiatry, 15,* 97–107.

Brazelton, T. B., & Nugent, J. K. (1995). *Neonatal Behavioral Assessment Scale.* London: Mac Keith Press.

Brazelton, T. B., Nugent, J. K., & Lester, B. M. (1987). Neonatal Behavioral Assessment Scale. In J. D. Osofsky (Ed.), *Handbook of infant development* (2nd ed., pp. 780–817). New York: Wiley.

Brazelton, T. B., & Sparrow, J. D. (2004). Toilet learning: The child's role. In T. B. Brazelton (Ed.), *Toilet training the Brazelton way.* Cambridge, MA: Da Capo Press.

Brehm, S. S. (2002). *Intimate relationships* (3rd ed.). New York: McGraw-Hill.

Bremner, A. J., & Mareschal, D. (2004). Reasoning . . . what reasoning? *Developmental Science, 7,* 419–421.

Brendgen, M., Markiewicz, D., Doyle, A. B., & Bukowski, W. M. (2001). The relations between friendship quality, ranked-friendship preference, and adolescents' behavior with their friends. *Merrill-Palmer Quarterly, 47,* 395–415.

Brennan, W. M., Ames, E. W., & Moore, R. W. (1966). Age differences in infants' attention to patterns of different complexities. *Science, 151,* 354–356.

Brenner, E., & Salovey, P. (1997). Emotional regulation during childhood: Developmental, interpersonal, and individual considerations. In P. Salovey & D. Sluyter (Eds.), *Emotional literacy and emotional development* (pp. 168–192). New York: Basic Books.

Brenner, R. A., & Committee on Injury, Violence, and Poison Prevention. (2003). Prevention of drowning in infants, children, and adolescents. *Pediatrics, 112,* 440–445.

Bretherton, I., Fritz, J., Zahn-Waxler, C., & Ridgeway, D. (1986). Learning to talk about emotions: A functionalist perspective. *Child Development, 57,* 529–548.

Bretherton, I., & Munholland, K. A. (1999). Internal working models in attachment relationships: A construct revisited. In J. Cassidy & P. R. Shaver (Eds.), *Handbook of attachment* (pp. 89–111). New York: Guilford.

Breweays, A., Ponjaert, I., Van Hall, E. V., & Golombok, S. (1997). Donor insemination: Child development and family functioning in lesbian mother families. *Human Reproduction, 12,* 1349–1359.

Bridge, J. A., Goldstein, T. R., & Brent, D. A. (2006). Adolescent suicide and suicidal behavior. *Journal of Child Psychology and Psychiatry, 47,* 372–394.

Bridges, L. J., & Moore, K. A. (2002). Religious involvement and children's well-being: What research tells us (and what it doesn't). *Child Trends Research Brief.* Retrieved from http://www.childtrends.org

Bridgett, D. J., Gartstein, M. A., Putnam, S. P., McKay, T., Iddins, R., Robertson, C., et al. (2009). Maternal and contextual influences and the effect of temperament development during infancy on parenting in toddlerhood. *Infant Behavior and Development, 32,* 103–116.

Briefel, R. R., Reidy, K., Karwe, V., & Devaney, B. (2004). Feeding Infants and Toddlers study: Improvements needed in meeting infant feeding recommendations. *Journal of the American Dietetic Association, 104*(Suppl. 1), s31–s37.

Briggs, F. (2000). *Children's views of the world.* Magill, Australia: University of South Australia.

Bright, G. M., Mendoza, J. R., & Rosenfeld, R. G. (2009). Recombinant human insulin-like growth factor-1 treatment: Ready for primetime. *Endocrinology and Metabolism Clinics of North America, 38,* 625–638.

Bright, J. E. H., Pryor, R. G. L., Wilkenfeld, S., & Earl, J. (2005). The role of social context and serendipitous events in career decision making. *International Journal for Educational and Vocational Guidance, 5,* 19–36.

Broberg, A. G., Wessels, H., Lamb, M. E., & Hwang, C. P. (1997). Effects of day care on the development of cognitive abilities in 8-year-olds: A longitudinal study. *Developmental Psychology, 33,* 62–69.

Broderick, P. C., & Korteland, C. (2004). A prospective study of rumination and depression in early

adolescence. *Clinical Child Psychology and Psychiatry, 9,* 383–394.

Brody, G. H., & Flor, D. L. (1998). Maternal resources, parenting practices, and child competence in rural, single-parent African American families. *Child Development, 69,* 803–816.

Brody, G. H., Ge, X., Kim, S. Y., Murry, V. M., Simons, R. L., & Gibbons, F. X. (2003). Neighborhood disadvantage moderates associations of parenting and older sibling problem attitudes and behavior with conduct disorders in African American children. *Journal of Consulting and Clinical Psychology, 71,* 211–222.

Brody, G. H., & Murry, V. M. (2001). Sibling socialization of competence in rural, single-parent African American families. *Journal of Marriage and the Family, 63,* 996–1008.

Brody, G. H., Stoneman, Z., & McCoy, J. K. (1994). Forecasting sibling relationships in early adolescence from child temperament and family processes in middle childhood. *Child Development, 65,* 771–784.

Brody, L. (1999). *Gender, emotion, and the family.* Cambridge, MA: Harvard University Press.

Brody, M. (2006). Child psychiatry, drugs, and the corporation. In S. Olfman (Ed.), *No child left different* (pp. 89–105). Westport, CT: Praeger.

Brody, N. (1997). Intelligence, schooling, and society. *American Psychologist, 52,* 1046–1050.

Broidy, L. M., Nagin, D. S., Tremblay, R. E., Bates, J. E., Brame, B., Dodge, K. A., Fergusson, D., Horwood, J. L., Loeber, R., Laird, R., Lynam, D. R., Moffitt, T. E., Pettit, G. S., & Vitaro, F. (2003). Developmental trajectories of childhood disruptive behaviors and adolescent delinquency: A six-site, cross-national study. *Developmental Psychology, 39,* 222–245.

Bronfenbrenner, U. (Ed.). (2005). *Making human beings human.* Thousand Oaks, CA: Sage.

Bronfenbrenner, U., & Morris, P. A. (2006). The bioecological model of human development. In R. M. Lerner (Ed.), *Handbook of child psychology: Vol. 1. Theoretical models of human development* (6th ed., pp. 793–828). Hoboken, NJ: Wiley.

Bronson, G. W. (1994). Infant's transitions toward adult-like scanning. *Child Development, 65,* 1243–1261.

Bronstein, P. (2006). The family environment: Where gender role socialization begins. In J. Worell & C. D. Goodheart (Eds.), *Handbook of girls' and women's psychological health: Gender and well-being across the life span* (pp. 262–271). New York: Oxford University Press.

Bronte-Tinkew, J., Moore, K. A., & Carrano, J. (2006). The father–child relationship, parenting styles, and adolescent risk behaviors in intact families. *Journal of Family Issues, 27,* 850–881.

Brooks, K., Xu, X., Chen, W., Zhou, K., Neale, B., & Lowe, N. (2006). The analysis of 51 genes in DSM-IV combined type attention deficit hyperactivity disorder: Association signals in DRD4, DAT1, and 16 other genes. *Molecular Psychiatry, 11,* 935–953.

Brooks, P. J., Hanauere, J. B., Padowska, B., & Rosman, H. (2003). The role of selective attention in preschoolers' rule use in a novel dimensional card sort. *Cognitive Development, 18,* 195–215.

Brooks, R., & Meltzoff, A. N. (2002). The importance of eyes: How infants interpret looking behavior. *Developmental Psychology, 38,* 958–966.

Brooks, R., & Meltzoff, A. N. (2005). The development of gaze following and its relation to language. *Developmental Science, 8,* 535–543.

Brooks, R., & Meltzoff, A. N. (2008). Infant gaze following and pointing predict accelerated vocabulary growth through two years of age: A longitudinal, growth curve modeling study. *Journal of Child Language, 35,* 207–220.

Brooks-Gunn, J. (1988). Antecedents and consequences of variations in girls' maturational timing. *Journal of Adolescent Health Care, 9,* 365–373.

Brooks-Gunn, J. (2003). Do you believe in magic? What we can expect from early childhood intervention programs. *Social Policy Report of the Society for Research in Child Development, 27*(1).

Brooks-Gunn, J. (2004). Intervention and policy as change agents for young children. In P. L. Chase-Lansdale, K. Kiernan, & R. J. Friedman (Eds.), *Human development across lives and generations: The potential for change* (pp. 293–340). New York: Cambridge University Press.

Brooks-Gunn, J., Han, W.-J., & Waldfogel, J. (2002). Maternal employment and child cognitive outcomes in the first three years of life: The NICHD study of early child care. *Child Development, 73,* 1052–1072.

Brooks-Gunn, J., Klebanov, P. K., Smith, J., Duncan, G. J., & Lee, K. (2003). The black-white test score gap in young children. Contributions of test and family characteristics. *Applied Developmental Science, 7,* 239–252.

Brown, A. L. (1997). Transforming schools into communities of thinking and learning about serious matters. *American Psychologist, 52,* 399–413.

Brown, A. M., & Miracle, J. A. (2003). Early binocular vision in human infants: Limitations on the generality of the Superposition Hypothesis. *Vision Research, 43,* 1563–1574.

Brown, A. S. (2006). Prenatal infection as a risk factor for schizophrenia. *Schizophrenia Bulletin, 32,* 200–202.

Brown, B. B., Clasen, D., & Eicher, S. (1986). Perceptions of peer pressure, peer conformity dispositions, and self-reported behavior among adolescents. *Developmental Psychology, 22,* 521–530.

Brown, B. B., Herman, M., Hamm, J. V., & Heck, D. (2008). Ethnicity and image: Correlates of minority adolescents' affiliation with individual-based versus ethnically defined peer crowds. *Child Development, 79,* 529–546.

Brown, B. B., Lohr, M. J., & McClenahan, E. L. (1986). Early adolescents' perceptions of peer pressure. *Journal of Early Adolescence, 6,* 139–154.

Brown, C. S., & Bigler, R. S. (2004). Children's perceptions of gender discrimination. *Developmental Psychology, 40,* 714–726.

Brown, E. C., Catalano, R. F., Fleming, C. B., Haggerty, K. P., Abbott, R. D., Cortes, R. R., & Park, J. (2005). Mediator effects in the social development model: An examination of constituent theories. *Criminal Behavior and Mental Health, 15,* 221–235.

Brown, G. L., Mangelsdorf, S. C., Agathen, J. M., & Ho, M.-H. (2008). Young children's psychological selves: Convergence with maternal reports of child personality. *Social Development, 17,* 161–182.

Brown, G. L., Schoppe-Sullivan, S. J., Mangelsdorf, S. C., & Neff, C. (2010). Observed and reported supportive coparenting as predictors of infant–mother and infant–father attachment security. *Early Child Development and Care, 180,* 121–137.

Brown, J. D., & L'Engle, K. L. (2009). X-rated: Attitudes and behaviors associated with U.S. early adolescents' exposure to sexually explicit media. *Communication Research, 36,* 129–151.

Brown, J. L., Roderick, T., Lantieri, L., & Aber, J. L. (2004). The Resolving Conflict Creatively Program: A school-based social and emotional learning program. In J. E. Zins, R. P. Weissberg, M. C. Wang, & H. J. Walberg (Eds.), *Building academic success on social and emotional learning: What does the research say?* (pp. 151–169). New York: Teachers College Press.

Brown, J. R., Donelan-McCall, N., & Dunn, J. (1996). Why talk about mental states? The significance of children's conversations with friends, siblings, and mothers. *Child Development, 67,* 836–849.

Brown, J. R., & Dunn, J. (1996). Continuities in emotion understanding from 3 to 6 years. *Child Development, 67,* 789–802.

Brown, R. B., & Dietz, E. L. (2009). Informal peer groups in middle childhood and adolescence. In K. H. Rubin, W. M. Bukowski, & B. Larsen (Eds.), *Handbook of peer interactions, relationships, and groups* (pp. 361–376). New York: Guilford Press.

Brown, R. W. (1973). *A first language: The early stages.* Cambridge, MA: Harvard University Press.

Brown, T. E. (2005). *Attention deficit disorder: The unfocused mind in children and adults.* New Haven, CT: Yale University Press.

Brown, S. A., & Ramo, D. E. (2005). Clinical course of youth following treatment for alcohol and drug problems. In H. A. Liddle & C. L. Rowe (Eds.), *Adolescent substance abuse: Research and clinical advances* (pp. 79–103). Cambridge: Cambridge University Press.

Brown, T. E. (2006). Executive functions and attention deficit hyperactivity disorder: Implications of two conflicting views. *International Journal of Disability, Development and Education, 53*, 35–46.

Brown, T. M., & Rodriguez, L. F. (2009). School and the co-construction of dropout. *International Journal of Qualitative Studies in Education, 22*, 221–242.

Browne, C. A., & Woolley, J. D. (2004). Preschoolers' magical explanations for violations of physical, social, and mental laws. *Journal of Cognition and Development, 5*, 239–260.

Browne, J. V., & Talmi, A. (2005). Family-based intervention to enhance infant–parent relationships in the neonatal intensive care unit. *Journal of Pediatric Psychology, 30*, 667–677.

Brownell, C. A., & Kopp, C. B. (2007). Transitions in toddler socioemotional development: Behavior, understanding, relationships. In C. A. Brownell & C. B. Kopp (Eds.), *Socioemotional development in the toddler years: Transitions and transformations* (pp. 1–40). New York: Guilford.

Brownell, C. A., Zerwas, S., & Ramani, G. B. (2007). "So big": The development of body self-awareness in toddlers. *Child Development, 78*, 1426–1440.

Bruce, D., Dolan, A., & Phillips-Grant, K. (2000). On the transition from childhood amnesia to recall of personal memories. *Psychological Science, 11*, 360–364.

Bruck, M., & Ceci, S. J. (2004). Forensic developmental psychology: Unveiling four common misconceptions. *Current Directions in Psychological Science, 13*, 229–232.

Bruer, J. T. (1999). *The myth of the first three years.* New York: Free Press.

Bruschweiler-Stern, N. (2004). A multifocal neonatal intervention. In A. J. Sameroff, S. C. McDonough, & K. L. Rosenblum (Eds.), *Treating parent–infant relationship problems* (pp. 188–212). New York: Guilford.

Bruzzese, J., & Fisher, C. B. (2003). Assessing and enhancing the research consent capacity of children and youth. *Applied Developmental Science, 7*, 13–26.

Bryan, A. E., & Dix, T. (2009). Mothers' emotions and behavioral support during interactions with toddlers: The role of child temperament. *Social Development, 18*, 647–670.

Bryant, B. K., Zvonkovic, A. M., & Reynolds, P. (2006). Parenting in relation to child and adolescent vocational development. *Journal of Vocational Behavior, 69*, 149–175.

Bryant, P., & Nunes, T. (2002). Children's understanding of mathematics. In U. Goswami (Ed.), *Blackwell handbook of childhood cognitive development* (pp. 412–439). Malden, MA. Blackwell.

Buchanan, A. (1996). *Cycles of child maltreatment.* Chichester, UK: Wiley.

Buchanan, C. M., Eccles, J. S., & Becker, J. B. (1992). Are adolescents the victims of raging hormones? Evidence for activational effects of hormones on moods and behaviors at adolescence. *Psychological Bulletin, 111*, 62–107.

Buchanan, C. M., & Holmbeck, G. N. (1998). Measuring beliefs about adolescent personality and behavior. *Journal of Youth and Adolescence, 27*, 609–629.

Buchanan, C. M., Maccoby, E. E., & Dornbusch, S. M. (1996). *Adolescents after divorce.* Cambridge, MA: Harvard University Press.

Buchanan-Barrow, E., & Barrett, M. (1998). Children's rule discrimination within the context of the school. *British Journal of Developmental Psychology, 16*, 539–551.

Buckhalt, J. A., El-Sheikh, M., Keller, P. S., & Kelly, R. J. (2009). Concurrent and longitudinal relations between children's sleep and cognitive functioning: The moderating role of parent education. *Child Development, 80*, 875–892.

Buescher, E. S. (2001). Anti-inflammatory characteristics of human milk: How, where, why. *Advances in Experimental Medicine and Biology, 501*, 207–222.

Bugental, D. B., Ellerson, P. C., Lin, E. K., Rainey, B., & Kokotovic, A. (2002). A cognitive approach to child abuse prevention. *Journal of Family Psychology, 16*, 243–258.

Bugental, D. B., & Grusec, J. E. (2006). Socialization processes. In N. Eisenberg (Ed.), *Handbook of child psychology: Vol. 3. Social, emotional, and personality development* (6th ed., pp. 366–428). Hoboken, NJ: Wiley.

Bugental, D. B., & Happaney, K. (2004). Predicting infant maltreatment in low-income families: The interactive effects of maternal attributions and child status at birth. *Developmental Psychology, 40*, 234–243.

Buhl, H. M., & Lanz, M. (2007). Emerging adulthood in Europe: Common traits and variability across five European countries. *Journal of Adolescent Research, 22*, 439–443.

Buhrmester, D., & Furman, W. (1990). Perceptions of sibling relationships during middle childhood and adolescence. *Child Development, 61*, 1387–1398.

Buhs, E. S., & Ladd, G. W. (2001). Peer rejection as antecedent of young children's school adjustment: An examination of mediating processes. *Developmental Psychology, 37*, 550–560.

Buhs, E. S., Ladd, G. W., & Herald, S. L. (2006). Peer exclusion and victimization: Processes that mediate the relation between peer group rejection and children's classroom engagement and achievement. *Journal of Educational Psychology, 98*, 1–13.

Bukowski, W. M. (2001). Friendship and the worlds of childhood. In D. W. Nangle & C. A. Erdley (Eds.), *The role of friendship in psychological adjustment* (pp. 93–105). San Francisco: Jossey-Bass.

Bukowski, W. M., Sippola, L. K., & Hoza, B. (1999). Same and other: Interdependency between participation in same- and other-sex friendships. *Journal of Youth and Adolescence, 28*, 439–459.

Bukowski, W. M., Sippola, L. K., & Newcomb, A. F. (2000). Variations in patterns of attraction of same- and other-sex peers during early adolescence. *Developmental Psychology, 36*, 147–154.

Bullock, M., & Lutkenhaus, P. (1990). Who am I? The development of self-understanding in toddlers. *Merrill-Palmer Quarterly, 36*, 217–238.

Bumpus, M. F., Crouter, A. C., & McHale, S. M. (2006). Linkages between negative work-to-family spillover and mothers' and fathers' knowledge of their young adolescents' daily lives. *Journal of Early Adolescence, 26*, 36–59.

Bunge, S. A., & Wright, S. B. (2007). Neurodevelopmental changes in working memory and cognitive control. *Current Opinion in Neurobiology, 17*, 243–250.

Bunting, L., & McAuley, C. (2004). Teenage pregnancy and parenthood: The role of fathers. *Child and Family Social Work, 9*, 295–303.

Burden, M. J., Jacobson, S. W., & Jacobson, J. L. (2005). Relation of prenatal alcohol exposure to cognitive processing speed and efficiency in childhood. *Alcoholism: Clinical and Experimental Research, 29*, 1473–1483.

Burgess-Champoux, T. L., Larson, N., Neumark-Sztainer, D., Hannan, P. J., & Story, M. (2009). Are family meal patterns associated with overall diet quality during the transition from early to middle adolescence? *Journal of Nutrition Education and Behavior, 41*, 79–86.

Burhans, K. K., & Dweck, C. S. (1995). Helplessness in early childhood: The role of contingent worth. *Child Development, 66*, 1719–1738.

Burke, R. J. (2001). Organizational values, work experiences, and satisfactions among managerial and professional women. *Journal of Managerial Development, 20*, 346–354.

Burman, D. D., Bitan, T., & Booth, J. R. (2007). Sex differences in neural processing of language among some children. *Neuropsychologia, 46*, 1349–1362.

Burns, C. E. (2000). *Pediatric primary care: A handbook for nurse practitioners.* Philadelphia: Saunders.

Burts, D. C., Hart, C. H., Charlesworth, R., Fleege, P. O., Mosley, J., & Thomasson, R. H. (1992). Observed activities and stress behaviors of children in developmentally appropriate and inappropriate kindergarten classrooms. *Early Childhood Research Quarterly, 7*, 297–318.

Bush, K. R., & Peterson, G. W. (2008). Family influences on child development. In T. P. Gullotta & G. M. Blau (Eds.), *Handbook of child behavioral issues: Evidence-based approaches to prevention and treatment* (pp. 43–67). New York: Routledge.

Bushman, B. J., & Huesmann, L. R. (2001). Effects of televised violence of aggression. In D. G. Singer & J. L. Singer (Eds.), *Handbook of children and the media* (pp. 223–254). Thousand Oaks, CA: Sage.

Bushnell, E. W., & Boudreau, J. P. (1993). Motor development and the mind: The potential role of motor abilities as a determinant of aspects of perceptual development. *Child Development, 64*, 1005–1021.

Bussell, D. A., Neiderhiser, J. M., Pike, A., Plomin, R., Simmens, S., Howe, G. W., Hetherington, E. M., Carroll, E., & Reiss, D. (1999). Adolescents' relationships to siblings and mothers: A multivariate genetic analysis. *Developmental Psychology, 35*, 1248–1259.

Bussey, K. (1992). Lying and truthfulness: Children's definitions, standards, and evaluative reactions. *Child Development, 63*, 129–137.

Bussey, K. (1999). Children's categorization and evaluation of different types of lies and truths. *Child Development, 70*, 1338–1347.

Bussiére, P., Knighton, T., & Pennock, D. (2007). *Measuring up: Canadian results of the OECD PISA Study: The performance of Canada's youth in science, reading, and mathematics: 2006. First results for Canadians aged 15.* Catalogue No. 81-590XPE—No. 3. Ottawa: Human Resources and Social Development Canada, Council of Ministers of Education, Canada and Statistics Canada. Retrieved from www.statcan.ca/english/freepub/ 81-590-XIE/ 81-590-XIE2007001.htm

Buswell, S. D., & Spatz, D. L. (2007). Parent–infant co-sleeping and its relationship to breastfeeding. *Journal of Pediatric Health Care, 21*, 22–28.

Butler, M., & Meaney, J. (Eds.). (2005). *Genetics of developmental disabilities.* Boca Raton, FL: Taylor & Francis.

Butler, R. (1998). Age trends in the use of social and temporal comparison for self-evaluation: Examination of a novel developmental hypothesis. *Child Development, 69*, 1054–1073.

Butler, R. J., Golding, J., & Heron, J. (2005). Nocturnal enuresis: A survey of parental coping strategies at 7½ years. *Child: Care, Health and Development, 31*, 659–667.

Buttelmann, D., Carpenter, M., & Tomasello, M. (2009). Eighteen-month-old infants show false belief understanding in an active helping paradigm. *Cognition, 112*, 337–342.

Byars, A. M., & Hackett, G. (1998). Applications of social cognitive theory to the career development of women of color. *Applied and Preventive Psychology, 7*, 255–267.

Bybee, J., Merisca, R., & Velasco, R. (1998). The development of reactions to guilt-producing events. In J. Bybee (Ed.), *Guilt and children* (pp. 185–213). San Diego: Academic Press.

Byrnes, J. P. (2003). Cognitive development during adolescence. In G. R. Adams & M. D. Berzonsky (Eds.), *Blackwell handbook of adolescence* (pp. 227–246). Malden, MA: Blackwell.

C

Cabrera, N. J., Fitzgerald, H. E., Bradley, R. H., & Roggman, L. (2007). Modeling the dynamics of paternal influence on children over the life course. *Applied Developmental Science, 11*, 185–189.

Cabrera, N. J., & García-Coll, C. (2004). Latino fathers: Uncharted territory in need of much exploration. In M. E. Lamb (Ed.), *The role of the father in child development* (4th ed., pp. 98–120). Hoboken, NJ: Wiley.

Cabrera, N. J., Shannon, J. D., & Tamis-LeMonda, C. (2007). Fathers' influence on their children's cognitive and emotional development: From toddlers to pre-K. *Applied Developmental Science, 11,* 208–213.

Cabrera, N. J., Tamis-LeMonda, C. S., Bradley, R. H., Hoferth, S., & Lamb, M. E. (2000). Fatherhood in the twenty-first century. *Child Development, 71,* 127–136.

Cahill, A. G., & Macones, G. A. (2007). Vaginal birth after cesarean delivery: Evidence-based practice. *Clinical Obstetrics and Gynecology, 50,* 518–525.

Cain, K. M., & Dweck, C. S. (1995). The relation between motivational patterns and achievement cognitions through the elementary school years. *Merrill-Palmer Quarterly, 41,* 25–52.

Caine, N. (1986). Behavior during puberty and adolescence. In G. Mitchell & J. Erwin (Eds.), *Comparative primate biology: Vol. 2A. Behavior, conservation, and ecology* (pp. 327–361). New York: Liss.

Cairns, R. B., & Cairns, B. D. (2006). The making of developmental psychology. In R. M. Lerner (Ed.), *Handbook of child psychology: Vol. 1. Theoretical models of human development* (6th ed., pp. 89–165). Hoboken, NJ: Wiley.

Cairns, R. B., Xie, H., & Leung, M.-C. (1998). The popularity of friendship and the neglect of social networks: Toward a new balance. In W. M. Bukowski & A. H. Cillessen (Eds.), *Sociometry then and now: Building on six decades of measuring children's experiences with the peer group* (pp. 25–53). San Francisco: Jossey-Bass.

Caldera, Y. M., & Lindsey, E. W. (2006). Coparenting, mother–infant interaction, and infant–parent attachment relationships in two-parent families. *Journal of Family Psychology, 20,* 275–283.

Caldwell, B. M., & Bradley, R. H. (1994). Environmental issues in developmental follow-up research. In S. L. Friedman & H. C. Haywood (Eds.), *Developmental follow-up* (pp. 235–256). San Diego: Academic Press.

Callaghan, T. C. (1999). Early understanding and production of graphic symbols. *Child Development, 70,* 1314–1324.

Callaghan, T. C., & Rankin, M. P. (2002). Emergence of graphic symbol functioning and the question of domain specificity: A longitudinal training study. *Child Development, 73,* 359–376.

Callaghan, T., Rochat, P., Lillard, A., Claux, M. L., Odden, H., Itakura, S., Tapanya, S., & Singh, S. (2005). Synchrony in the onset of mental-state reasoning: Evidence from five cultures. *Psychological Science, 16,* 378–384.

Callanan, M. A., & Oakes, L. M. (1992). Preschoolers' questions and parents' explanations: Causal thinking in everyday activity. *Cognitive Development, 7,* 213–233.

Callanan, M. A., & Sabbagh, M. A. (2004). Multiple labels for objects in conversations with young children: Parents' language and children's developing expectations about word meanings. *Developmental Psychology, 40,* 746–763.

Callen, J., & Pinelli, J. (2005). A review of the literature examining the benefits and challenges, incidence and duration, and barriers to breastfeeding in preterm infants. *Advances in Neonatal Care, 5,* 72–88.

Calvert, S. L., Rideout, V. J., Woolard, J. L., Barr, R. F., & Strouse, G. A. (2005). Age, ethnicity, and socioeconomic patterns in early computer use. *American Behavioral Scientist, 48,* 590–607.

Calvert, S. L., Strong, B. L., & Gallagher, L. (2005). Control as an engagement feature for young children's attention to, and learning of, computer content. *American Behavioral Scientist, 48,* 578–589.

Cameron, C. A., & Lee, K. (1997). The development of children's telephone communication. *Journal of Applied Developmental Psychology, 18,* 55–70.

Cameron, P. A., & Gallup, G. G. (1988). Shadow recognition in human infants. *Infant Behavior and Development, 11,* 465–471.

Cameron-Faulkner, T., Lieven, E., & Tomasello, M. (2003). A construction based analysis of child directed speech. *Cognitive Science, 27,* 843–873.

Cammu, H., Martens, G., Ruyssinck, G., & Amy, J. J. (2002). Outcome after elective labor induction in nulliparous women: A matched cohort study. *American Journal of Obstetrics and Gynecology, 186,* 240–244.

Campa, M. I., & Eckenrode, J. J. (2006). Pathways to intergenerational adolescent childbearing in a high-risk sample. *Journal of Marriage and Family, 68,* 558–572.

Campbell, A., Shirley, L., & Candy, J. (2004). A longitudinal study of gender-related cognition and behaviour. *Developmental Science, 7,* 1–9.

Campbell, D. A., Lake, M. F., Falk, M., & Backstrand, J. R. (2006). A randomized control trial of continuous support in labor by a lay doula. *Journal of Obstetrics and Gynecology and Neonatal Nursing, 35,* 456–464.

Campbell, D., Scott, K. D., Klaus, M. H., & Falk, M. (2007). Female relatives or friends trained as labor doulas: Outcomes at 6 to 8 weeks postpartum. *Birth, 34,* 220–227.

Campbell, F. A., Pungello, E. P., Miller-Johnson, S., Burchinal, M., & Ramey, C. T. (2001). The development of cognitive and academic abilities: Growth curves from an early childhood educational experiment. *Developmental Psychology, 37,* 231–242.

Campbell, F. A., Ramey, C. T., Pungello, E., Sparling, J., & Miller-Johnson, S. (2002). Early childhood education: Young adult outcomes from the Abecedarian Project. *Applied Developmental Science, 6,* 42–57.

Campbell, S. B., Brownell, C. A., Hungerford, A., Spieker, S. J., Mohan, R., & Blessing, J. S. (2004). The course of maternal depressive symptoms and maternal sensitivity as predictors of attachment security at 36 months. *Development and Psychopathology, 16,* 231–252.

Campbell, S. B., Spieker, S., Burchinal, M., Poe, M. D., & the NICHD Early Child Care Research Network. (2006). Trajectories of aggression from toddlerhood to age 9 predict academic and social functioning through age 12. *Journal of Child Psychology and Psychiatry, 47,* 791–800.

Campos, J. J., Anderson, D. I., Barbu-Roth, M. A., Hubbard, E. M., Hertenstein, J. J., & Witherington, D. (2000). Travel broadens the mind. *Infancy, 1,* 149–219.

Campos, J. J., Frankel, C. B., & Camras, L. (2004). On the nature of emotion regulation. *Child Development, 75,* 377–394.

Campos, J. J., Witherington, D., Anderson, D. I., Frankel, C. I., Uchiyama, I., & Barbu-Roth, M. (2008). Rediscovering development in infancy. *Child Development, 79,* 1625–1632.

Campos, R. G. (1989). Soothing pain-elicited distress in infants with swaddling and pacifiers. *Child Development, 60,* 781–792.

Camras, L. A. (1992). Expressive development and basic emotions. *Cognition and Emotion, 6,* 267–283.

Camras, L. A., Oster, H., Campos, J. J., & Bakeman, R. (2003). Emotional facial expressions in European-American, Japanese, and Chinese infants. *Annals of the New York Academy of Sciences, 1000,* 1–17

Camras, L. A., Oster, H., Campos, J. J., Campos, R., Ujie, T., Miyake, K., Wang, L., & Meng, Z. (1998). Production of emotional and facial expressions in European-American, Japanese, and Chinese infants. *Developmental Psychology, 34,* 616–628.

Camras, L. A., Oster, H., Campos, J. J., Miyake, K., & Bradshaw, D. (1992). Japanese and American infants' responses to arm restraint. *Developmental Psychology, 28,* 578–583.

CAN (Swedish Council for Information on Alcohol and Other Drugs). (2007). *The European School Survey Project on Alcohol and Other Drugs: Key result generator, 2007.* Retrieved from www.espad.org/keyresult–generator

Canada Campaign 2000. (2009). 2009 Report Card on Child and Family Poverty in Canada: 1989–2009.

Retrieved from www.campaign2000.ca/reportcards.html

Canobi, K. H. (2004). Individual differences in children's addition and subtraction knowledge. *Cognitive Development, 19,* 81–93.

Canobi, K. H., Reeve, R. A., & Pattison, P. E. (2003). The role of conceptual understanding in children's addition problem solving. *Developmental Psychology, 39,* 521–534.

Capaldi, D., DeGarmo, D., Patterson, G. R., & Forgatch, M. (2002). Contextual risk across the early life span and association with antisocial behavior. In J. B. Reid, G. R. Patterson, & J. Snyder (Eds.), *Antisocial behavior in children and adolescents* (pp. 123–145). Washington, DC: American Psychological Association.

Capelli, C. A., Nakagawa, N., & Madden, C. M. (1990). How children understand sarcasm: The role of context and intonation. *Child Development, 61,* 1824–1841.

Capirci, O., Contaldo, A., Caselli, M. C., & Volterra, V. (2005). From action to language through gesture. *Gesture, 5,* 155–177.

Card, N. A., Stucky, B. D., Sawalani, G. M., & Little, T. D. (2008). Direct and indirect aggression during childhood and adolescence: A meta-analytic review of gender differences, intercorrelations, and relations to maladjustment. *Child Development, 79,* 1185–1229.

CARE Study Group. (2008). Maternal caffeine intake during pregnancy and risk of fetal growth restriction: A large prospective observational study. *British Medical Journal, 337,* a2337.

Carey, S. (1995). On the origins of causal understanding. In D. Sperber, D. Premack, & A. J. Premack (Eds.), *Causal cognition* (pp. 268–308). Oxford, UK: Clarendon Press.

Carey, S. (1999). Sources of conceptual change. In E. K. Scholnick, K. Nelson, S. A. Gelman, & P. H. Miller (Eds.), *Conceptual development: Piaget's legacy* (pp. 293–326). Mahwah, NJ: Erlbaum.

Carey, S., & Markman, E. M. (1999). Cognitive development. In B. M. Bly & D. E. Rumelhart (Eds.), *Cognitive science* (pp. 201–254). San Diego: Academic Press.

Carlo, G., Koller, S. H., Eisenberg, N., Da Silva, M., & Frohlich, C. (1996). A cross-national study on the relations among prosocial moral reasoning, gender role orientations, and prosocial behaviors. *Developmental Psychology, 32,* 231–240.

Carlson, C., Uppal, S., & Prosser, E. (2000). Ethnic differences in processes contributing to the self-esteem of early adolescent girls. *Journal of Early Adolescence, 20,* 44–67.

Carlson, M., & Earls, F. (1997). Psychological and neuroendocrinological sequelae of early social deprivation in institutionalized children in Romania. *Annals of the New York Academy of Sciences, 807,* 419–428.

Carlson, S. M., Moses, L. J., & Claxton, S. J. (2004). Individual differences in executive functioning and theory of mind: An investigation of inhibitory control and planning ability. *Journal of Experimental Child Psychology, 87,* 299–319.

Carlson, V. J., & Harwood, R. L. (2003). Attachment, culture, and the caregiving system: The cultural patterning of everyday experiences among Anglo and Puerto Rican mother–infant pairs. *Infant Mental Health Journal, 24,* 53–73.

Carmichael, S. L., & Shaw, G. M. (2000). Maternal life stress and congenital anomalies. *Epidemiology, 11,* 30–35.

Carolson, C., Uppal, S., & Prosser, E. C. (2000). Ethnic differences in processes contributing to the self-esteem of early adolescent girls. *Journal of Early Adolescence, 20,* 44–67.

Carpendale, J. I. M. (2000). Kohlberg and Piaget on stages and moral reasoning. *Developmental Review, 20,* 181–205.

Carpenter, M., Akhtar, N., & Tomasello, M. (1998). Fourteen- through eighteen-month-old infants differentially imitate intentional and accidental actions. *Infant Behavior and Development, 21,* 315–330.

Carpenter, M., Nagel, K., & Tomasello, M. (1998). Social cognition, joint attention, and communicative competence. *Monographs of the Society for Research in Child Development, 63*(4, Serial No. 255).

Carpenter, T. P., Fennema, E., Fuson, K., Hiebert, J., Human, P., & Murray, H. (1999). Learning basic number concepts and skills as problem solving. In E. Fennema & T. A. Romberg (Eds.), *Mathematics classrooms that promote understanding: Studies in mathematical thinking and learning series* (pp. 45–61). Mahwah, NJ: Erlbaum.

Carr, D., & Friedman, M. A. (2005). Is obesity stigmatizing? Body weight, perceived discrimination, and psychological well-being in the United States. *Journal of Health and Social Behavior, 46,* 244–256.

Carr, J. (2002). Down syndrome. In P. Howlin & O. Udwin (Eds.), *Outcomes in neurodevelopmental and genetic disorders* (pp. 169–197). New York: Cambridge University Press.

Carroll, J. B. (2005). The three-stratum theory of cognitive abilities. In D. P. Flanagan & P. L. Harrison (Eds.), *Contemporary intellectual assessment: Theories, tests, and issues* (2nd ed., pp. 69–76). New York: Guilford.

Carskadon, M. A., Acebo, C., & Jenni, O. G. (2004). Regulation of adolescent sleep: Implications for behavior. In R. E. Dahl & L. P. Spear (Eds.), *Adolescent brain development: Vulnerabilities and opportunities* (pp. 276–291). New York: New York Academy of Sciences.

Carskadon, M. A., Harvey, K., Duke, P., Anders, T. F., Litt, I. F., & Dement, W. C. (2002). Pubertal changes in daytime sleepiness. *Sleep, 25,* 525–605.

Carver, K., Joyner, K., & Udry, J. R. (2003). National estimates of adolescent romantic relationships. In P. Florsheim (Ed.), *Adolescent romantic relations and sexual behavior: Theory, research, and practical implications* (pp. 23–56). Mahwah, NJ: Erlbaum.

Carver, P. R., Egan, S. K., & Perry, D. G. (2004). Children who question their heterosexuality. *Developmental Psychology, 40,* 43–53.

Casalis, S., & Cole, P. (2009). On the relationship between morphological and phonological awareness: Effects of training in kindergarten and in first-grade reading. *First Language, 29,* 113–142.

Casasola, M., Bhagwat, J., & Burke, A. S. (2009). Learning to form a spatial category of tight-fit relations: How experience with a label can give a boost. *Developmental Psychology, 45,* 711–723.

Casasola, M., Cohen, L. B., & Chiarello, E. (2003). Six-month-old infants' categorization of containment spatial relations. *Child Development, 74,* 679–693.

Casavant, M. J., Blake, K., Griffith, J., Yates, A., & Copley, L. M. (2007). Consequences of use of anabolic androgenic steroids. *Pediatric Clinics of North America, 54,* 677–690.

Casby, M. W. (2001). Otitis media and language development: A meta-analysis. *American Journal of Speech-Language Pathology, 10,* 65–80.

Case, R. (1996). Introduction: Reconceptualizing the nature of children's conceptual structures and their development in middle childhood. In R. Case & Y. Okamoto (Eds.), The role of central conceptual structures in the development of children's thought. *Monographs of the Society for Research in Child Development, 246*(61, Serial No. 246), pp. 1–26.

Case, R. (1998). The development of conceptual structures. In D. Kuhn & R. S. Siegler (Eds.), *Handbook of child psychology: Vol. 2. Cognition, perception, and language* (pp. 745–800). New York: Wiley.

Case, R., & Okamoto, Y. (Eds.). (1996). The role of central conceptual structures in the development of children's thought. *Monographs of the Society for Research in Child Development, 61*(1–2, Serial No. 246).

Casey, B. J., Getz, S., & Galvan, A. (2008). The adolescent brain. *Developmental Review, 28,* 62–77.

Casey, B. J., Thomas, K. M., Davidson, M. C., Kunz, K., & Franzen, P. L. (2002). Dissociating striatal and hippocampal function developmentally with a stimulus-response compatibility task. *Journal of Cognitive Neuroscience, 22,* 8647–8652.

Casey, B. J., Tottenham, N., Liston, C., & Durston, S. (2005). Imaging the developing brain: What have we learned about cognitive development? *Trends in Cognitive Sciences, 9,* 104–110.

Casey, B. M. (1986). Individual differences in selective attention among prereaders: A key to mirror-image confusions. *Developmental Psychology, 22,* 824–831.

Casey, B. M., Nuttall, R. L., & Pezaris, E. (1997). Mediators of gender differences in mathematics college entrance test scores: A comparison of spatial skills with internalized beliefs and anxieties. *Developmental Psychology, 33,* 669–680.

Casey, B. M., Nuttall, R. L., & Pezaris, E. (2001). Spatial-mechanical reasoning skills versus mathematics self-confidence as mediators of gender differences on mathematics subtests using cross-national gender-based items. *Journal for Research in Mathematics Education, 32,* 28–57.

Cashon, C. H., & Cohen, L. B. (2000). Eight-month-old infants' perceptions of possible and impossible events. *Infancy, 1,* 429–446.

Casper, L. M., & Smith, K. E. (2002). Dispelling the myths: Self-care, class, and race. *Journal of Family Issues, 23,* 716–727.

Caspi, A. (2000). The child is father of the man: Personality continuities from childhood to adulthood. *Journal of Personality and Social Psychology, 78,* 158–172.

Caspi, A., Elder, G. H., Jr., & Bem, D. J. (1987). Moving against the world: Life-course patterns of explosive children. *Developmental Psychology, 23,* 308–313.

Caspi, A., Elder, G. H., Jr., & Bem, D. J. (1988). Moving away from the world: Life-course patterns of shy children. *Developmental Psychology, 24,* 824–831.

Caspi, A., Harrington, H., Milne, B., Amell, J. W., Theodore, R. F., & Moffitt, T. E. (2003). Children's behavioral styles at age 3 are linked to their adult personality traits at age 26. *Journal of Personality, 71,* 495–513.

Caspi, A., Lynam, D., Moffitt, T. E., & Silva, P. A. (1993). Unraveling girls' delinquency: Biological, dispositional, and contextual contributions to adolescent misbehavior. *Developmental Psychology, 29,* 19–30.

Caspi, A., McClay, J., Moffitt, T. E., Mill, J., Martin, J., & Craig, I. W. (2002). Role of genotype in the cycle of violence in maltreated children. *Science, 297,* 851–854.

Caspi, A., Moffitt, T. E., Morgan, J., Rutter, M., Taylor, A., Kim-Cohen, J., & Polo-Tomas, M. (2004). Maternal expressed emotion predicts children's antisocial behavior problems: Using monozygotic-twin differences to identify environmental effects on behavioral development. *Developmental Psychology, 40,* 149–161.

Caspi, A., & Roberts, B. W. (2001). Personality development across the life course: The argument for change and continuity. *Psychological Inquiry, 12,* 49–66.

Caspi, A., & Shiner, L. (2006). Personality development. In N. Eisenberg (Ed.), *Handbook of child psychology: Vol. 3. Social, emotional, and personality development* (6th ed., pp. 300–365). Hoboken, NJ: Wiley.

Cassia, V. M., Simion, F., & Umiltá, C. (2001). Face preference at birth: The role of an orienting mechanism. *Developmental Science, 4,* 101–108.

Cassia, V. M., Turati, C., & Simion, F. (2004). Can a nonspecific bias toward top-heavy patterns explain newborns' face preference? *Psychological Science, 15,* 379–383.

Cassidy, J. (2001). Adult romantic attachments: A developmental perspective on individual differences. *Review of General Psychology, 4,* 111–131.

Cassidy, J., & Berlin, L. J. (1994). The insecure/ambivalent pattern of attachment: Theory and research. *Child Development, 65,* 971–991.

Castillo, E. M., & Comstock, R. D. (2007). Prevalence of use of performance-enhancing substances among United States adolescents. *Pediatric Clinics of North America, 54,* 663–675.

Catalano, R. A. (2003). Sex ratios in the two Germanies: A test of the economic stress hypothesis. *Human Reproduction, 18,* 1972–1975.

Catalano, R., Ahern, J., Bruckner, T., Anderson, E., & Saxton, K. (2009). Gender-specific selection in utero among contemporary human birth cohorts. *Paediatric and Perinatal Epidemiology, 23,* 273–278.

Catalano, R., Bruckner, T., Anderson, E., & Gould, J. B. (2005). Fetal death sex ratios: A test of the economic stress hypothesis. *International Journal of Epidemiology, 34,* 944–948.

Caton, D., Corry, M. P., Frigoletto, F. D., Hopkins, D. P., Liberman, E., & Mayberry, L. (2002). The nature and management of labor pain: Executive summary. *American Journal of Obstetrics and Gynecology, 186,* S1–S15.

Caughey, R. W., & Michels, K. B. (2009). Birth weight and childhood leukemia: A meta-analysis and review of the current evidence. *International Journal of Cancer, 124,* 2658–2670.

Cavadini, C., Siega-Riz, A. M., & Popkin, B. M. (2000). U.S. adolescent food intake trends from 1965 to 1996. *Archives of Diseases in Childhood, 83,* 18–24.

Ceci, S. J. (1991). How much does schooling influence general intelligence and its cognitive components? A reassessment of the evidence. *Developmental Psychology, 27,* 703–722.

Ceci, S. J. (1999). Schooling and intelligence. In S. J. Ceci & W. M. Williams (Eds.), *The nature–nurture debate: The essential readings* (pp. 168–175). Oxford: Blackwell.

Ceci, S. J., Bruck, M., & Battin, D. (2000). The suggestibility of children's testimony. In Bjorklund, D. (Ed), *False-memory creation in children and adults* (pp. 169–201) Mahwah, NJ: Erlbaum.

Ceci, S. J., Kulkofsky, S., Klemfuss, J. Z., Sweeney, C. D., & Bruck, M. (2007). Unwarranted assumptions about children's testimonial accuracy. *Annual Review of Clinical Psychology, 3,* 311–328.

Ceci, S. J., & Roazzi, A. (1994). The effects of context on cognition: Postcards from Brazil. In R. J. Sternberg (Ed.), *Mind in context* (pp. 74–101). New York: Cambridge University Press.

Ceci, S. J., Rosenblum, T. B., & Kumpf, M. (1998). The shrinking gap between high- and low-scoring groups: Current trends and possible causes. In U. Neisser (Ed.), *The rising curve: Long-term gains in IQ and related measures* (pp. 287–302). Washington, DC: American Psychological Association.

Ceci, S. J., & Williams, W. M. (1997). Schooling, intelligence, and income. *American Psychologist, 52,* 1051–1058.

Ceci, S. J., & Williams, W. M. (2010). *The mathematics of sex: How biology and society conspire to limit talented women and girls.* New York: Oxford University Press.

Cecil, J. E., Watt, P., Murrie, I. S. L., Wrieden, W., Wallis, D. J., Hetherington, M. M., Bolton-Smith, C., & Palmer, C. N. A. (2005). Childhood obesity and socioeconomic status: A novel role for height growth limitation. *International Journal of Obesity, 29,* 1199–1203.

Center for Communication and Social Policy. (Ed.). (1998). *National Television Violence Study* (Vol. 2). Newbury Park, CA: Sage.

Center for Effective Discipline. (2005). *Worldwide bans on corporal punishment.* Retrieved from www.stophitting.com/disatschool/facts.php

Center on Education Policy. (2007). *State high school exit exams: Working to raise test scores.* Washington, D.C.: Author.

Center on Education Policy. (2009). *State high school exit exams: Trends in test programs, alternate pathways, and pass rates.* Washington, DC: Author.

Cernoch, J. M., & Porter, R. H. (1985). Recognition of maternal axillary odors by infants. *Child Development, 56,* 1593–1598.

Cervantes, C. A., & Callanan, M. A. (1998). Labels and explanations in mother–child emotion talk: Age and gender differentiation. *Developmental Psychology, 34,* 88–98.

Chall, J. S. (1983). *Stages of reading development.* New York: McGraw-Hill.

Chalmers, J. B., & Townsend, M. A. R. (1990). The effects of training in social perspective taking on socially maladjusted girls. *Child Development, 61,* 178–190.

Chamberlain, P. (2003). Antisocial behavior and delinquency in girls. In P. Chamberlain (Ed.), *Treating chronic juvenile offenders* (pp. 109–127). Washington, DC: American Psychological Association.

Champion, T. B. (2003a). "A matter of vocabulary": Performances of low-income African-American Head Start children on the Peabody Picture Vocabulary Test. *Communication Disorders Quarterly, 24,* 121–127.

Champion, T. B. (2003b). *Understanding storytelling among African-American children: A journey from Africa to America.* Mahwah, NJ: Erlbaum.

Chan, A., & Poulin, F. (2007). Monthly changes in the composition of friendship networks in early adolescence. *Merrill-Palmer Quarterly, 53,* 578–602.

Chan, L. K. S., & Moore, P. J. (2006). Development of attributional beliefs and strategic knowledge in years 5–9: A longitudinal analysis. *Educational Psychology, 26,* 161–185.

Chan, R. W., Raboy, B., & Patterson, C. J. (1998). Psychosocial adjustment among children conceived via donor insemination by lesbian and heterosexual mothers. *Child Development, 69,* 443–457.

Chandra, A., Martino, S. C., Collins, R. L., Elliott, M. N., Berry, S. H., Kanouse, D. E., & Miu, A. (2008). Does watching sex on television predict teen pregnancy? Findings from a national longitudinal survey of youth. *Pediatrics, 122,* 1047–1054.

Chandra, R. K. (1991). Interactions between early nutrition and the immune system. In *Ciba Foundation Symposium No. 156* (pp. 77– 92). Chichester, UK: Wiley.

Chang, F., Dell, G. S., & Bock, K. (2006). Becoming syntactic. *Psychological Review, 113,* 234–272.

Chang, L., Schwartz, D., Dodge, D. A., & McBride-Chang, C. (2003). Harsh parenting in relation to child emotion regulation and aggression. *Journal of Family Psychology, 17,* 598–606.

Chao, R. K. (1994). Beyond parental control and authoritarian parenting style: Understanding Chinese parenting through the cultural notion of training. *Child Development, 65,* 1111–1119.

Chao, R. K., & Tseng, V. (2002). Parenting of Asians. In M. H. Bornstein (Ed.), *Handbook of parenting: Vol. 4* (2nd ed., pp. 59–94). Mahwah, NJ: Erlbaum.

Chapman, R. S. (2000). Children's language learning: An interactionist perspective. *Journal of Child Psychology and Psychiatry, 41,* 33–54.

Chapman, R. S. (2006). Children's language learning: An interactionist perspective. In R. Paul (Ed.), *Language disorders from a developmental perspective* (pp. 1–53). Mahwah, NJ: Erlbaum.

Charchut, S. W., Allred, E. N., & Needleman, H. L. (2003). The effects of infant feeding patterns on the occlusion of the primary dentition. *Journal of Dentistry for Children, 70,* 197–203.

Charman, T., Baron-Cohen, S., Swettenham, J., Baird, G., Cox, A., & Drew, A. (2001). Testing joint attention, imitation, and play as infancy precursors to language and theory of mind. *Cognitive Development, 15,* 481–49.

Charpak, N., Ruiz-Peláez, J. G., & Figueroa, Z. (2005). Influence of feeding patterns and other factors on early somatic growth of healthy, preterm infants in home-based kangaroo mother care: A cohort study. *Journal of Pediatric Gastroenterology and Nutrition, 41,* 430–437.

Chase-Lansdale, P. L., Brooks-Gunn, J., & Zamsky, E. S. (1994). Young African-American multigenerational families in poverty: Quality of mothering and grandmothering. *Child Development, 65,* 373–393.

Chase-Lansdale, P. L., Gordon, R., Brooks-Gunn, J., & Klebanov, P. K. (1997). Neighborhood and family influences on the intellectual and behavioral competence of preschool and early school-age children. In J. Brooks-Gunn, G. Duncan, & J. L. Aber (Eds.), *Neighborhood poverty: Context and consequences for development* (pp. 79–118). New York: Russell Sage Foundation.

Chauhan, G. S., Shastri, J., & Mohite, P. (2005). Development of gender constancy in preschoolers. *Psychological Studies, 50,* 62–71.

Chavajay, P., & Rogoff, B. (1999). Cultural variation in management of attention by children and their caregivers. *Developmental Psychology, 35,* 1079–1090.

Chavajay, P., & Rogoff, B. (2002). Schooling and traditional collaborative social organization of problem solving by Mayan mothers and children. *Developmental Psychology, 38,* 55–66.

Chawarska, K., & Shic, F. (2009). Looking but not seeing: Atypical visual scanning and recognition of faces in 2- and 4-year-old children with autism spectrum disorder. *Journal of Autism and Developmental Disorders, 39,* 1663–1672.

Cheah, C. S. L., Leung, C. Y. Y., Tahseen, M., & Schultz, D. (2009). Authoritative parenting among immigrant Chinese mothers of preschoolers. *Journal of Family Psychology, 23,* 311–320.

Cheah, C. S. L., & Nelson, L. J. (2004). The role of acculturation in the emerging adulthood of aboriginal college students. *International Journal of Behavioral Development, 28,* 495–507.

Checkley, W., Epstein, L. D., Gilman, R. H., Cabrera, L., & Black, R. E. (2003). Effects of acute diarrhea on linear growth in Peruvian children. *American Journal of Epidemiology, 157,* 166–175.

Chen, D. W., Fein, G. G., Killen, M., & Tam, H.-P. (2001). Peer conflicts of preschool children: Issues, resolution, incidence, and age-related patterns. *Early Education and Development, 12,* 523–544.

Chen, J. J. (2005). Relation of academic support from parents, teachers, and peers to Hong Kong adolescents' academic achievement: The mediating role of academic engagement. *Genetic, Social, and General Psychology Monographs, 131,* 77–127.

Chen, L.-C., Metcalfe, J. S., Jeka, J. J., & Clark, J. E. (2007). Two steps forward and one back: Learning to walk affects infants' sitting posture. *Infant Behavior and Development, 30,* 16–25.

Chen, M. (2003). Wombs for rent: An examination of prohibitory and regulatory approaches to governing preconception arrangements. *Health Law in Canada, 23,* 33–50.

Chen, X., Cen, G., Li, D., & He, Y. (2005). Social functioning and adjustment in Chinese children: The imprint of historical time. *Child Development, 76,* 182–195.

Chen, X., DeSouza, A. T., Chen, H., & Wang, L. (2006). Reticent behavior and experiences in peer interactions in Chinese and Canadian children. *Developmental Psychology, 42,* 656–665.

Chen, X., & French, D. C. (2008). Children's social competence in cultural context. *Annual Review of Psychology, 59,* 591–616.

Chen, X., Hastings, P. D., Rubin, K. H., Chen, H., Cen, G., & Stewart, S. L. (1998). Child-rearing attitudes and behavioral inhibition in Chinese and Canadian toddlers: A cross-cultural study. *Developmental Psychology, 34,* 677–686.

Chen, X., Rubin, K. H., & Li, Z. (1995). Social functioning and adjustment in Chinese children: A longitudinal study. *Developmental Psychology, 31,* 531–539.

Chen, X., Wang, L., & DeSouza, A. (2006). Temperament, socioemotional functioning, and peer relationships in Chinese and North American children. In X. Chen, D. C. French, & B. H. Schneider (Eds.), *Peer relationships in cultural context* (pp. 123–147). New York: Cambridge University Press.

Chen, Y.-C., Yu, M.-L., Rogan, W., Gladen, B., & Hsu, C.-C. (1994). A 6-year follow-up of behavior and activity disorders in the Taiwan Yu-cheng children. *American Journal of Public Health, 84,* 415–421.

Chen, Y.-J., & Hsu, C.-C. (1994). Effects of prenatal exposure to PCBs on the neurological function of children: A neuropsychological and neuro-physiological study. *Developmental Medicine and Child Neurology, 36,* 312–320.

Chen, Z., Sanchez, R. P., & Campbell, T. (1997). From beyond to within their grasp: The rudiments of analogical problem solving in 10- to 13-month-olds. *Developmental Psychology, 33,* 790–801.

Chen, Z., & Siegler, R. S. (2000). Across the great divide: Bridging the gap between understanding of toddlers' and older children's thinking. *Monographs of the Society for Research in Child Development, 65*(2, Serial No. 261).

Cheng, T. L., Fields, C. B., Brenner, R. A., Wright, J. L., Lomax, T., Scheidt, P. C., & the District of Columbia Child/Adolescent Injury Research Network. (2000). Sports injuries: An important cause of morbidity in urban youth. *Pediatrics, 105,* e32.

Chesney-Lind, M. (2001). Girls, violence, and delinquency: Popular myths and persistent problems. In S. O. White (Ed.), *Handbook of youth and justice* (pp. 135–158). New York: Kluwer Academic.

Chesney-Lind, M., & Belknap, J. (2004). Trends in delinquent girls' aggression and violent behavior. In M. Putallaz & K. L. Bierman (Eds.), *Aggression, antisocial behavior, and violence among girls: A developmental perspective* (pp. 203–220). New York: Guilford.

Chess, S., & Thomas, A. (1984). *Origins and evolution of behavior disorders.* New York: Brunner/Mazel.

Chhin, C. S., Bleeker, M. M., & Jacobs, J. E. (2008). Gender-typed occupational choices: The long-term impact of parents' beliefs and expectations. In H. M. G. Watt & J. S. Eccles (Eds.), *Gender and occupational outcomes: Longitudinal assessments of individual, social, and cultural influences* (pp. 215–234). Washington, DC: American Psychological Association.

Child Trends. (2007). *Late or no prenatal care.* Retrieved from www.childtrendsdatabank.org/indicators/25PrenatalCare.cfm

Child Trends. (2010). *Teen births.* Retrieved from www.childtrendsdatabank.org/?q=node/311

Children's Defense Fund. (2008). *Annual Report 2007.* Washington, DC: Author.

Children's Defense Fund. (2009). *State of America's children: 2008.* Washington, DC: Author.

Chinn, C. A., & Malhotra, B. A. (2002). Children's responses to anomalous scientific data: How is conceptual change impeded? *Journal of Educational Psychology, 94,* 327–343.

Chisholm, K. (1998). Attachment security and indiscriminately friendly behavior in children adopted from Romanian orphanages. *Development and Psychopathology, 7,* 283–294.

Choby, B. A., & George, S. (2008). Toilet training. *American Family Physician, 78,* 1059–1064.

Choi, S., & Gopnik, A. (1995). Early acquisition of verbs in Korean: A cross-linguistic study. *Journal of Child Language, 22,* 497–529.

Choi, S., McDonough, L., Bowerman, M., & Mandler, J. M. (1999). Early sensitivity to language-specific spatial categories in English and Korean. *Cognitive Development, 14,* 241–268.

Chomsky, C. (1969). *The acquisition of syntax in children from five to ten.* Cambridge, MA: MIT Press.

Chomsky, N. (1957). *Syntactic structures.* The Hague: Mouton.

Chomtho, S., Wells, J. C., Williams, J. E., Davies, P. S., Lucas, A., & Fewtrell, M. S. (2008). Infant growth and later body composition: Evidence from the 4-component model. *American Journal of Clinical Nutrition, 87,* 1776–1784.

Chorzempa, B. F., & Graham, S. (2006). Primary-grade teachers' use of within-class ability grouping in reading. *Journal of Educational Psychology, 98,* 529–541.

Chouinard, M. M. (2007). Children's questions: A mechanism for cognitive development. *Monographs of the Society for Research in Child Development, 72*(1, Serial No. 286).

Chouinard, M. M., & Clark, E. V. (2003). Adult reformulations of child errors as negative evidence. *Journal of Child Language, 30,* 637–669.

Christ, S. E., Steiner, R. D., Grange, D. K., Abrams, R. A., & White, D. A. (2006). Inhibitory control in children with phenylketonuria. *Developmental Neuropsychology, 30,* 845–864.

Christakis, D. A., Zimmerman, F. J., DiGiuseppe, D. L., & McCarty, C. A. (2004). Early television exposure and subsequent attentional problems in children. *Pediatrics, 113,* 708–713.

Christenson, S. L., & Thurlow, M. L. (2004). School dropouts: Prevention considerations, interventions, and challenges. *Current Directions in Psychological Science, 13,* 36–39.

Christiansen, M. H., & Chater, N. (2008). Language as shaped by the brain. *Behavioral and Brain Sciences, 31,* 489–558.

Christie, C. A., Jolivette, K., & Nelson, M. (2007). School characteristics related to high school dropout rates. *Remedial and Special Education, 28,* 325–339.

Christophersen, E. R., & Mortweet, S. L. (2003). *Parenting that works: Building skills that last a lifetime.* Washington, DC: American Psychological Association.

Chudley, A. E., Conry, J., Cook, J. L., Loock, C., Rosales, T., & LeBlanc, N. (2005). Fetal alcohol spectrum disorder: Canadian guidelines for diagnosis. *Canadian Medical Association Journal, 172,* S1–S21.

Chumlea, W. C., Schubert, C. M., Roche, A. F., Kulin, H. E., Lee, P. A., Himes, J. H., & Sun, S. S. (2003). Age at menarche and racial comparisons in U.S. girls. *Pediatrics, 111,* 110–113.

Chung, H. H. (2006). Code switching as a communicative strategy: A case study of Korean–English bilinguals. *Bilingual Research Journal, 30,* 293–307.

Cicchetti, D. (2007). Intervention and policy implications of research on neurobiological functioning in maltreated children. In J. L. Aber, S. J. Bishop-Josef, S. M. Jones, K. T. McLearn, & D. A. Phillips (Eds.), *Child development and social policy* (pp. 167–184). Washington, DC: American Psychological Association.

Cicchetti, D., & Toth, S. L. (2006). Developmental psychopathology and preventive intervention. In K. A. Renninger & I. E. Sigel (Eds.), *Handbook of child psychology: Vol. 4. Child psychology in practice* (6th ed., pp. 497–547). Hoboken, NJ: Wiley.

Cillessen, A. H. N., & Bellmore, A. D. (2004). Social skills and interpersonal perception in early and middle childhood. In P. K. Smith & C. H. Hart (Eds.), *Blackwell handbook of childhood social development* (pp. 355–374). Malden, MA: Blackwell.

Cillessen, A. H. N., & Mayeux, L. (2004). From censure to reinforcement: Developmental changes in the association between aggression and social status. *Child Development, 75,* 147–163.

Clapp, J. F., III, Kim, H., Burciu, B., Schmidt, S., Petry, K., & Lopez, B. (2002). Continuing regular exercise during pregnancy: Effect of exercise volume on fetoplacental growth. *American Journal of Obstetrics and Gynecology, 186,* 142–147.

Clark, C. A., Woodward, L. J., Horwood, L. J., & Moor, S. (2008). Development of emotional and behavioral regulation in children born extremely preterm and very preterm: Biological and social influences. *Child Development, 79,* 1444–1462.

Clark, E. V. (1990). On the pragmatics of contrast. *Journal of Child Language, 17,* 417–431.

Clark, E. V. (2007). Young children's uptake of new words in conversation. *Language in Society, 36,* 157–182.

Clark, K. E., & Ladd, G. W. (2000). Connectedness and autonomy support in parent–child relationships: Links to children's socioemotional orientation and peer relationships. *Developmental Psychology, 36,* 485–498.

Clark, S. L., Miller, D. D., Belfort, M. A., Dildy, G. A., Frye, D. K., & Meyers, J. A. (2009). Neonatal and maternal outcomes associated with elective term delivery. *American Journal of Obstetrics and Gynecology, 200,* 156.e1–e4.

Clark, S. M., Ghulmiyyah, L. M., & Hankins, G. D. (2008). Antenatal antecedents and the impact of obstetric care in the etiology of cerebral palsy. *Clinical Obstetrics and Gynecology, 51,* 775–786.

Clarke-Stewart, K. A. (1998). Historical shifts and underlying themes in ideas about rearing young children in the United States: Where have we been? Where are we going? *Early Development and Parenting, 7,* 101–117.

Clarke-Stewart, K. A., Allhusen, V., & Goossens, F. (2001). Day care and the Strange Situation. In A. Göncü & E. L., Klein (Eds.), *Children in play, story, and school* (pp. 241–266). New York: Guilford.

Clarke-Stewart, K. A., & Hayward, C. (1996). Advantages of father custody and contact for the psychological well-being of school-age children. *Journal of Applied Developmental Psychology, 17,* 239–270.

Clarkson, T. W., Magos, L., & Myers, G. J. (2003). The toxicology of mercury—current exposures and clinical manifestations. *New England Journal of Medicine, 349,* 1731–1737.

Claxton, L. J., Keen, R., & McCarty, M. E. (2003). Evidence of motor planning in infant reaching behavior. *Psychological Science, 14,* 354–356.

Clay, R. A. (2009, Feb.). Mini-multitaskers. *Monitor on Psychology, 40*(2), 38–40.

Clearfield, M. W., & Nelson, N. M. (2006). Sex differences in mothers' speech and play behavior with 6-, 9-, and 14-month-old infants. *Sex Roles, 54,* 127–137.

Clearfield, M. W., Osborn, C. N., & Mullen, M. (2008). Learning by looking: Infants' social looking behavior across the transition from crawling to walking. *Journal of Experimental Child Psychology, 100,* 297–307.

Clements, D. H., & Sarama, J. (2003). Young children and technology: What does the research say? *Young Children, 58*(6), 34–40.

Clements, D. H., & Sarama, J. (2008). Experimental evaluation of the effects of a research-based preschool mathematics curriculum. *American Educational Research Journal, 45,* 443–494.

Cleveland, E. S., & Reese, E. (2005). Maternal structure and autonomy support in conversations about the past: Contributions to children's autobiographical memory. *Developmental Psychology, 41,* 376–388.

Clifford, R. M., Barbarin, O., Chang, F., Early, D., Bryant, D., Howes, C., Burchinal, M., & Pianta, R. (2005). What is pre-kindergarten? Characteristics of public pre-kindergarten programs. *Applied Developmental Science, 9,* 126–143.

Clifton, R. K., Rochat, P., Robin, D. J., & Berthier, N. E. (1994). Multimodal perception in the control of infant reaching. *Journal of Experimental Psychology: Human Perception and Performance, 20,* 876–886.

Clinchy, B. M. (2002). Revisiting women's ways of knowing. In B. K. Hofer & P. R. Pintrich (Eds.), *Personal epistemology: The psychological beliefs about knowledge and knowing* (pp. 63–87). Mahwah, NJ: Erlbaum.

Clingempeel, W. G., & Henggeler, S. W. (2003). Aggressive juvenile offenders transitioning into emerging adulthood: Factors discriminating persistors and desistors. *American Journal of Orthopsychiatry, 73,* 310–323.

Cluett, E. R., & Burns, E. (2009). Immersion in water in labour and birth. *Cochrane Database of Systematic Reviews,* Issue 2. Art. No. CD000111.

Cnattingius, S., Lundberg, F., Sandin, S., Grönberg, H., & Iliadou, A. (2009). Birth characteristics and risk of prostate cancer: The contribution of genetic factors. *Cancer Epidemiology, 18,* 2422–2466.

Coatsworth, J. D., Sharp, E. H., Palen, L., Darling, N., Cumsille, P., & Marta, M. (2005). Exploring adolescent self-defining leisure activities and identity experiences across three countries. *International Journal of Behavioral Development, 29,* 361–370.

Cohen, L. B. (2003). Commentary on Part I: Unresolved issues in infant categorization. In D. H. Rakison & L. M. Oakes (Eds.), *Early category and concept development: Making sense of the blooming, buzzing confusion* (pp. 193–209). New York: Oxford University Press.

Cohen, L. B. (2009). The evolution of infant cognition: A personal account. *Infancy, 14,* 403–413.

Cohen, L. B. (2010). A bottom-up approach to infant perception and cognition: A summary of evidence and discussion of issues. In S. P. Johnson (Ed.), *Neoconstructivism: The new science of cognitive development* (pp. 335–346). New York: Oxford University Press.

Cohen, L. B., & Brunt, J. (2009). Early word learning and categorization: Methodological issues and recent empirical evidence. In J. Colombo, P. McCardle, & L. Freund (Eds.), *Infant pathways to language: Methods, models, and research disorders* (pp. 245–266). New York: Psychology Press.

Cohen, L. B., & Cashon, C. H. (2001). Infant object segregation implies information integration. *Journal of Experimental Child Psychology, 78,* 75–83.

Cohen, L. B., & Cashon, C. H. (2006). Infant cognition. In D. Kuhn & R. Siegler (Eds.), *Handbook of child psychology: Vol. 2. Cognition, perception, and language* (6th ed., pp. 214–251). Hoboken, NJ: Wiley.

Cohen, L. B., & Marks, K. S. (2002). How infants process addition and subtraction events. *Developmental Science, 5,* 186–201.

Cohen, P., Kasen, S., Chen, H., Hartmark, C., & Gordon, K. (2003). Variations in patterns of developmental transitions in the emerging adulthood period. *Developmental Psychology, 39,* 657–669.

Cohen, S., & Herbert, T. B. (1996). Health psychology: Psychological factors and physical disease from the perspective of human psychoneuroimmunology. *Annual Review of Psychology, 47,* 113–142.

Cohen-Bendahan, C. C. C., van de Beek, C., & Berenbaum, S. A. (2005). Prenatal sex hormones effects on child and adult sex-typed behavior: Methods and findings. *Neuroscience and Biobehavioral Reviews, 29,* 353–384.

Coholl, A., Kassotis, J., Parks, R., Vaughan, R., Bannister, H., & Northridge, M. (2001). Adolescents in the age of AIDS: Myths, misconceptions, and misunderstandings regarding sexually transmitted diseases. *Journal of the National Medical Association, 93,* 64–69.

Coie, J. D., Dodge, K. A., & Coppotelli, H. (1982). Dimensions and types of social status: A cross-age perspective. *Developmental Psychology, 18,* 557–570.

Colapinto, J. (2001). *As nature made him: The boy who was raised as a girl.* New York: Perennial.

Colby, A., Kohlberg, L., Gibbs, J., & Lieberman, M. (1983). A longitudinal study of moral judgment. *Monographs of the Society for Research in Child Development, 48*(1–2, Serial No. 200).

Cole, D. A., Martin, J. M., Peeke, L. A., Seroczynski, A. D., & Fier, J. (1999). Children's over- and underestimation of academic competence: A longitudinal study of gender differences, depression, and anxiety. *Child Development, 70,* 459–473.

Cole, D. A., Maxwell, S. E., Martin, J. M., Peeke, L. G., Seroczynski, A. D., & Tram, J. M. (2001). The development of multiple domains of child and adolescent self-concept: A cohort sequential longitudinal design. *Child Development, 72,* 1723–1746.

Cole, M. (1990). Cognitive development and formal schooling: The evidence from cross-cultural research. In L. C. Moll (Ed.), *Vygotsky and education* (pp. 89–110). New York: Cambridge University Press.

Cole, M. (2006). Culture and cognitive development in phylogenetic, historical, and ontogenetic perspective. In D. Kuhn & R. S. Siegler (Eds.), *Handbook of child psychology: Vol. 2. Cognition, perception, and language* (6th ed., pp. 636–685). Hoboken, NJ: Wiley.

Cole, P. M., Armstrong, L. M., & Pemberton, C. K. (2010). The role of language in the development of emotion regulation. In S. D. Calkins & M. A. Bell (Eds.), *Child development at the intersection of emotion and cognition* (pp. 59–77). Washington, DC: American Psychological Association.

Cole, P. M., Bruschi, C. J., & Tamang, B. L. (2002). Cultural differences in children's emotional reactions to difficult situations. *Child Development, 73,* 983–996.

Cole, P. M., & Tamang, B. L. (1998). Nepali children's ideas about emotional displays in hypothetical challenges. *Developmental Psychology, 34,* 640–648.

Cole, P. M., Tamang, B. L., & Shrestha, S. (2006). Cultural variations in the socialization of young children's anger and shame. *Child Development, 77,* 1237–1251.

Cole, S. A. (2006). Building secure relationships: Attachment in kin and unrelated foster caregiver–infant relationships. *Families in Society, 87,* 497–508.

Cole, T. J. (2000). Secular trends in growth. *Proceedings of the Nutrition Society, 59,* 317–324.

Coley, R. L. (1998). Children's socialization experiences and functioning in single-mother households: The importance of fathers and other men. *Child Development, 69,* 219–230.

Coley, R. L., Morris, J. E., & Hernandez, D. (2004). Out-of-school care and problem behavior trajectories among low-income adolescents: Individual, family, and neighborhood characteristics as added risks. *Child Development, 75,* 948–965.

Coley, R. L., Votruba-Drzal, E., & Schindler, H. S. (2009). Fathers' and mothers' parenting predicting and responding to adolescent sexual risk behaviors. *Child Development, 80,* 808–827.

Collaer, M. L., & Hill, E. M. (2006). Large sex difference in adolescents on a timed line judgment task: Attentional contributors and task relationship to mathematics. *Perception, 35,* 561–572.

Collins, N. L., Guichard, A. C., Ford, M. B., & Feeney, B. C. (2006). Responding to need in intimate relationships: Normative processes and individual differences. In M. Mikulincer & G. S. Goodman (Eds.), *Dynamics of romantic love* (pp. 149–189). New York: Guilford.

Collins, W. A., & Laursen, B. (2004). Parent–adolescent relationships and influences. In R. M. Lerner & L. Steinberg (Eds.), *Handbook of adolescent psychology* (2nd ed., pp. 331–361). New York: Wiley.

Collins, W. A., Maccoby, E. E., Steinberg, L., Hetherington, E. M., & Bornstein, M. H. (2000). Contemporary research on parenting: The case for nature and nurture. *American Psychologist, 52,* 218–232.

Collins, W. A., & Madsen, S. D. (2006). Personal relationships in adolescence and early adulthood. In A. L. Vangelisti & D. Perlman (Eds.), *Cambridge handbook of personal relationships* (pp. 191–209). New York: Cambridge University Press.

Collins, W. A., Madsen, S. D., & Susman-Stillman, A. (2002). Parenting during middle childhood. In M. H. Bornstein (Ed.), *Handbook of parenting: Vol. 1. Children and parenting* (2nd ed., pp. 73–101). Mahwah, NJ: Erlbaum.

Collins, W. A., & Russell, G. (1991). Mother–child and father–child interactions in middle childhood and adolescence. *Developmental Review, 11,* 99–136.

Collins, W. A., & Steinberg, L. (2006). Adolescent development in interpersonal context. In N. Eisenberg (Ed.), *Handbook of child psychology: Vol. 3. Social, emotional, and personality development* (6th ed., pp. 1003–1067). Hoboken, NJ: Wiley.

Collins, W. A., & van Dulmen, M. (2006a). Friendships and romantic relationships in emerging adulthood: Continuities and discontinuities. In J. J. Arnett & J. Tanner (Eds.), *Emerging adults in America: Coming of age in the 21st century* (pp. 219–234). Washington, DC: American Psychological Association.

Collins, W. A., & van Dulmen, M. (2006b). "The course of true love(s) . . .": Origins and pathways in the development of romantic relationships. In A. Booth & A. Crouter (Eds.), *Romance and sex in adolescence and emerging adulthood: Risks and opportunities* (pp. 63–86). Mahwah, NJ: Erlbaum.

Collins, W. A., Welsh, D. P., & Furman W. (2009). Adolescent romantic relationships. *Annual Review of Psychology, 60,* 631–652.

Colman, L. L., & Colman, A. D. (1991). *Pregnancy: The psychological experience.* Noonday Press.

Colman, R. A., Hardy, S. A., Albert, M., Raffaelli, M., & Crockett, L. (2006). Early predictors of self-regulation in middle childhood. *Infant and Child Development, 15,* 421–437.

Colombo, J. (1995). On the neural mechanisms underlying developmental and individual differences in visual fixation in infancy. *Developmental Review, 15,* 97–135.

Colombo, J. (2002). Infant attention grows up: The emergence of a developmental cognitive neuroscience perspective. *Current Directions in Psychological Science, 11,* 196–199.

Coltrane, S. (1996). *Family man.* New York: Oxford University Press.

Commission on Adolescent Suicide Prevention. (2005). Targeted youth suicide prevention programs. In D. L. Evans, E. B. Foa, R. E. Gur, H. Hending, & C. P. O'Brien (Eds.), *Treating and preventing adolescent mental health disorders: What we know and what we don't know* (pp. 463–469). New York: Oxford University Press.

Commission on Children at Risk. (2008). Hardwired to connect: The new scientific case for authoritative communities. In K. K. Kline (Ed.), *Authoritative communities: The scientific case for nurturing the whole child* (pp. 3–68). New York: Springer.

Comstock, G., & Scharrer, E. (2006). Media and popular culture. In K. A. Renninger & I. E. Sigel (Eds.), *Handbook of child psychology: Vol. 4. Child psychology in practice* (6th ed., pp. 817–863). Hoboken, NJ: Wiley.

Comunian, A. L., & Gielen, U. P. (2006). Promotion of moral judgment maturity through stimulation of social role-taking and social reflection: An Italian intervention study. *Journal of Moral Education, 35,* 51–69.

Conboy, B. T., & Thal, D. J. (2006). Ties between the lexicon and grammar: Cross-sectional and longitudinal studies of bilingual toddlers. *Child Development, 77,* 712–735.

Conchas, G. Q. (2006). *The color of success: Race and high-achieving urban youth.* New York: Teachers College Press.

Condron, D. J. (2007). Stratification and educational sorting: Explaining ascriptive inequalities in early childhood reading group placement. *Social Problems, 54,* 139–160.

Conger, R., Wallace, L., Sun, Y., Simons, L., McLoyd, V., & Brody, G. (2002). Economic pressure in African American families: A replication and extension of the family stress model. *Developmental Psychology, 38,* 179–193.

Conger, R. D., & Conger, K. J. (2002). Resilience in Midwestern families: Selected findings from the first decade of a prospective, longitudinal study. *Journal of Marriage and the Family, 64,* 361–373.

Conger, R. D., & Donnellan, M. B. (2007). An interactionist perspective on the socioeconomic context of human development. *Annual Review of Psychology, 58,* 175–199.

Connell, M. W., Sheridan, K., & Gardner, H. (2003). On abilities and domains. In R. J. Sternberg & E. Grigorenko (Eds.), *Perspectives on the psychology of abilities, competencies, and expertise* (pp. 126–155). New York: Cambridge University Press.

Conner, D. B., & Cross, D. R. (2003). Longitudinal analysis of the presence, efficacy, and stability of maternal scaffolding during informal problem-solving interactions. *British Journal of Developmental Psychology, 21,* 315–334.

Connolly, J., Craig, W., Goldberg, A., & Pepler, D. (2004). Mixed-gender groups, dating, and romantic relationships in early adolescence. *Journal of Research on Adolescence, 14,* 185–207.

Connolly, J., Furman, W., & Konarski, R. (2000). The role of peers in the emergence of romantic relationships in adolescence. *Child Development, 71,* 1395–1408.

Connolly, J., & Goldberg, A. (1999). Romantic relationships in adolescence: The role of friends and peers in their emergence and development. In W. Furman, B. B. Brown, & C. Feiring (Eds.), *The development of romantic relationships in adolescence* (pp. 266–290). New York: Cambridge University Press.

Connolly, J. A., & Doyle, A. B. (1984). Relations of social fantasy play to social competence in preschoolers. *Developmental Psychology, 20,* 797–806.

Connor, J. M. (2003). Physical activity and well-being. In M. H. Bornstein, L. Davidson, C. L. M. Keyes, K. A. Moore, & the Center for Child Well-Being (Eds.), *Well-being: Positive development across the life course* (pp. 65–79). Mahwah, NJ: Erlbaum.

Conti-Ramsden, G., & Pérez-Pereira, M. (1999). Conversational interactions between mothers and their infants who are congenitally blind, have low vision, or are sighted. *Journal of Visual Impairment and Blindness, 93,* 691–703.

Conway, L. (2007, April 5). Drop the Barbie: Ken Zucker's reparatist treatment of gender-variant children. *Trans News Updates.* Retrieved from ai.eecs.umich.edu/people/conway/TS/News/Drop%20the%20Barbie.htm

Conyers, C., Miltenberger, R., Maki, A., Barenz, R., Jurgens, M., Sailer, A., Haugen, M., & Kopp, B. (2004). A comparison of response cost and differential reinforcement of other behaviors to reduce disruptive behavior in a preschool classroom. *Journal of Applied Behavior Analysis, 37,* 411–415.

Cook, T. D., Deng, Y., & Morgano, E. (2007). Friendship influences during early adolescence: The special role of friends' grade point average. *Journal of Research in Adolescence, 17,* 325–356.

Cook, W. L. (2000). Understanding attachment security in family context. *Journal of Personality and Social Psychology, 78,* 285–294.

Cookston, J. T., Braver, S. L., Griffin, W. A., De Lusé, S. R., & Miles, J. C. (2006). Effects of the Dads for Life intervention on interparental conflict and coparenting in the two years after divorce. *Family Process, 46,* 123–137.

Cooper, C., Sayer, A. A., & Dennison, E. M. (2006). The developmental environment: Clinical perspectives on effects on the musculoskeletal system. In P. Gluckman & M. Hanson (Eds.), *Developmental origins of health and disease* (pp. 392–405). Cambridge, UK: Cambridge University Press.

Cooper, R., & Huh, C. R. (2008). Improving academic possibilities of students of color during the middle school to high school transition: Conceptual and strategic considerations in a U.S. context. In J. K. Asamen, M. L. Ellis, & G. L. Berry (Eds.), *Sage handbook of child development, multiculturalism, and media* (pp. 143–162). Thousand Oaks, CA: Sage.

Cope-Farrar, K. M., & Kunkel, D. (2002). Sexual messages in teens' favorite prime-time television programs. In J. D. Brown, J. R. Steele, & K. Walsh-Childers (Eds.), *Sexual teens, sexual media* (pp. 59–78). Mahwah, NJ: Erlbaum.

Coplan, R. J., & Arbeau, K. A. (2008). The stresses of a "brave new world": Shyness and school adjustment in kindergarten. *Journal of Research in Childhood Education, 22,* 377–389.

Coplan, R. J., & Armer, M. (2007). A "multitude" of solitude: A closer look at social withdrawal and nonsocial play in early childhood. *Child Development Perspectives, 1,* 26–32.

Coplan, R. J., Gavinsky-Molina, M. H., Lagace-Seguin, D., & Wichmann, C. (2001). When girls versus boys play alone: Nonsocial play and adjustment in kindergarten. *Developmental Psychology, 37,* 464–474.

Coplan, R. J., Prakash, K., O'Neil, K., & Armer, M. (2004). Do you "want" to play? Distinguishing between conflicted shyness and social disinterest in early childhood. *Developmental Psychology, 40,* 244–258.

Copple, C., & Bredekamp, S. (2009). *Developmentally appropriate practice in early childhood programs* (3rd ed.). Washington, DC: National Association for the Education of Young Children.

Corapci, F., Radan, A. E., & Lozoff, B. (2006). Iron deficiency in infancy and mother–child interaction at 5 years. *Journal of Developmental and Behavioral Pediatrics, 27,* 371–378.

Corenblum, B. (2003). What children remember about ingroup and outgroup peers: Effects of stereotypes on children's processing of information about group members. *Journal of Experimental Child Psychology, 86,* 32–66.

Cornish, A. M., McMahon, C. A., Ungerer, J. A., Barnett, B., Kowalenko, N., & Tennant, C. (2005). Postnatal depression and infant cognitive and motor development in the second postnatal year: The impact of depression chronicity and infant gender. *Infant Behavior and Development, 28,* 407–417.

Cornwell, A. C., & Feigenbaum, P. (2006). Sleep biological rhythms in normal infants and those at high risk for SIDS. *Chronobiology International, 23,* 935–961.

Correa-Chavez, M., Rogoff, B., & Arauz, R. M. (2005). Cultural patterns in attending to two events at once. *Child Development, 76,* 664–678.

Cortese, D. A., & Smith, H. C. (2003). *Mayo Clinic family health book* (3rd ed.). New York: HarperCollins.

Cosden, M., Peerson, S., & Elliott, K. (1997). Effects of prenatal drug exposure on birth outcomes and early child development. *Journal of Drug Issues, 27,* 525–539.

Costello, B. J., & Dunaway, R. G. (2003). Egotism and delinquent behavior. *Journal of Interpersonal Violence, 18,* 572–590.

Costos, D., Ackerman, R., & Paradis, L. (2002). Recollections of menarche: Communication between mothers and daughters regarding menstruation. *Sex Roles, 46,* 49–59.

Côté, J. E. (2009). Identity formation and self-development in adolescence. In R. M. Lerner & L. Steinberg (Eds.), *Handbook of adolescent psychology: Vol. 1. Individual bases of adolescent development* (3rd ed., pp. 266–304). Hoboken, NJ: Wiley.

Côté, J. E., & Bynner, J. M. (2008). Changes in the transition to adulthood in the UK and Canada: The role of structure and agency in emerging adulthood. *Journal of Youth Studies, 11,* 251–268.

Côté, J. E., & Schwartz, S. J. (2002). Comparing psychological and sociological approaches to identity: Identity status, identity capital, and the individualization process. *Journal of Adolescence, 25,* 571–586.

Côté, S. M., Vaillancourt, T., Barker, E. D., Nagin, D., & Tremblay, R. E. (2007). The joint development of physical and indirect aggression: Predictors of continuity and change during childhood. *Development and Psychopathology, 19,* 37–55.

Coulton, C. J., Crampton, D. S., Irwin, M., Spilsbury, J. C., & Korbin, J. E. (2007). How neighborhoods influence child maltreatment: A review of the literature and alternative pathways. *Child Abuse and Neglect, 31,* 1117–1142.

Courage, M. L., & Howe, M. L. (1998). The ebb and flow of infant attentional preferences: Evidence for long-term recognition memory in 3-month-olds. *Journal of Experimental Child Psychology, 18,* 98–106.

Courage, M. L., & Howe, M. L. (2002). From infant to child: The dynamics of cognitive change in the second year of life. *Psychological Bulletin, 128,* 250–277.

Courchesne, E., Carper, R., & Akshoomoff, N. (2003). Evidence of brain overgrowth in the first year of life in autism. *Journal of the American Medical Association, 290,* 337–344.

Couturier, J. L., & Lock, J. (2006). Denial and minimization in adolescents with anorexia nervosa. *International Journal of Eating Disorders, 39,* 212–216.

Covington, C. Y., Nordstrom-Klee, B., Ager, J., Sokol, R., & Delaney-Black, V. (2002). Birth to age 7 growth of children prenatally exposed to drugs: A prospective cohort study. *Neurotoxicology and Teratology, 24,* 489–496.

Cowan, C. P., & Cowan, P. A. (1997). Working with couples during stressful transitions. In S. Dreman (Ed.), *The family on the threshold of the 21st century* (pp. 17–47). Mahwah, NJ: Erlbaum.

Cowan, C. P., & Cowan, P. A. (2000). *When partners become parents.* Mahwah, NJ: Erlbaum.

Cowan, P. A., & Cowan, C. P. (2002). Interventions as tests of family systems theories: Marital and family relationships in children's development and psychopathology. *Development and Psychopathology, 14,* 731–759.

Cowan, P. A., & Cowan, C. P. (2004). From family relationships to peer rejection to antisocial behavior in middle childhood. In J. B. Kupersmidt & K. A. Dodge (Eds.), *Children's peer relations: From development to intervention* (pp. 159–177). Washington, DC: American Psychological Association.

Cox, M., & Littlejohn, K. (1995). Children's use of converging obliques in their perspective drawings. *Educational Psychology, 15,* 127–139.

Cox, M. J., Owen, M. T., Henderson, V. K., & Margand, N. A. (1992). Prediction of infant–father and infant–mother attachment. *Developmental Psychology, 28,* 474–483.

Cox, S. M., Hopkins, J., & Hans, S. L. (2000). Attachment in preterm infants and their mothers: Neonatal risk status and maternal representations. *Infant Mental Health Journal, 21,* 464–480.

Coyle, T. R., & Bjorklund, D. F. (1997). Age differences in, and consequences of, multiple- and variable-strategy use on a multitrial sort-recall task. *Developmental Psychology, 33,* 372–380.

Crago, M. B., Annahatak, B., & Ningiuruvik, L. (1993). Changing patterns of language socialization in Inuit homes. *Anthropology and Education Quarterly, 24,* 205–223.

Craig, C. M., & Lee, D. N. (1999). Neonatal control of sucking pressure: Evidence for an intrinsic τ-guide. *Experimental Brain Research, 124,* 371–382.

Craig, W. M., Pepler, D., & Atlas, R. (2000). Observations of bullying in the playground and in the classroom. *School Psychology International, 21,* 22–36.

Crain, W. (2005). *Theories of development* (5th ed.). Upper Saddle River, NJ: Prentice-Hall.

Crair, M. C., Gillespie, D. C., & Stryker, M. P. (1998). The role of visual experience in the development of columns in the cat visual cortex. *Science, 279,* 566–570.

Crane, D. R., Ngai, S. W., Larson, J. H., & Hafen, M., Jr. (2005). The influence of family functioning and parent–adolescent acculturation on North American Chinese adolescent outcomes. *Family Relations, 54,* 400–410.

Cratty, B. J. (1986). *Perceptual and motor development in infants and children* (3rd ed.). Englewood Cliffs, NJ: Prentice-Hall.

Crawford, N. (2003, September). Understanding children's atypical gender behavior. *APA Monitor,* p. 40.

Creasey, G. (2002). Associations between working models of attachment and conflict management behavior in romantic couples. *Journal of Counseling Psychology, 49,* 365–375.

Creasey, G., & Ladd, A. (2004). Negative mood regulation expectancies and conflict behaviors in late adolescent college student romantic relationships: The moderating role of generalized attachment representations. *Journal of Research on Adolescence, 14,* 235–255.

Creasey, G. L., Jarvis, P. A., & Berk, L. E. (1998). Play and social competence. In O. N. Saracho & B. Spodek (Eds.), *Multiple perspectives on play in early childhood education* (pp. 116–143). Albany: State University of New York Press.

Crick, N. R., Casas, J. F., & Nelson, D. A. (2002). Toward a more comprehensive understanding of peer maltreatment: Studies of relational victimization. *Current Directions in Psychological Science, 11,* 98–101.

Crick, N. R., & Dodge, K. A. (1994). A review and reformulation of social information-processing mechanisms in children's social adjustment. *Psychological Bulletin, 115,* 74–101.

Crick, N. R., & Nelson, D. A. (2002). Relational and physical victimization within friendships: Nobody told me there'd be friends like these. *Journal of Abnormal Child Psychology, 30,* 599–607.

Crick, N. R., Ostrov, J. M., Appleyard, K., Jansen, E., & Casas, J. F. (2004). Relational aggression in early childhood: You can't come to my birthday party unless. . . . In M. Putallaz & K. Bierman (Eds.), *Duke series in child development and public policy: Aggressive antisocial behavior and violence among girls: A developmental perspective* (Vol. 1, pp. 71–89). New York: Guilford.

Crick, N. R., Ostrov, J. M., & Werner, N. E. (2006). A longitudinal study of relational aggression, physical aggression, and social-psychological adjustment. *Journal of Abnormal Child Psychology, 34,* 131–142.

Critser, G. (2003). *Fat land.* Boston: Houghton Mifflin.

Crocetti, E., Rubini, M., & Meeus, W. (2008). Capturing the dynamics of identity formation in various ethnic groups: Development and validation of a three-dimensional model. *Journal of Adolescence, 31,* 207–222.

Crockenberg, S., & Leerkes, E. M. (2000). Infant social and emotional development in family context. In C. H. Zeanah, Jr. (Ed.), *Handbook of infant mental health* (2nd ed., pp. 60–90). New York: Guilford.

Crockenberg, S., & Leerkes, E. M. (2003a). Infant negative emotionality, caregiving, and family relationships. In A. C. Crouter & A. Booth (Eds.), *Children's influence on family dynamics* (pp. 57–78). Mahwah, NJ: Erlbaum.

Crockenberg. S. C., & Leerkes, E. M. (2003b). Parental acceptance, postpartum depression, and maternal sensitivity: Mediating and moderating processes. *Journal of Family Psychology, 17,* 80–93.

Crockenberg, S. C., & Leerkes, E. M. (2004). Infant and maternal behaviors regulate infant reactivity to novelty at 6 months. *Developmental Psychology, 40,* 1123–1132.

Crockett, L. J., Raffaelli, M., & Shen, Y.-L. (2006). Linking self-regulation and risk-proneness to risky sexual behavior: Pathways through peer pressure and early substance use. *Journal of Research on Adolescence, 16,* 503–525.

Crone, E. A., Riek, J. M., Somsen, K. Z., & van der Molen, M. W. (2006). A heart rate analysis of developmental change in feedback processing and rule shifting from childhood to early adulthood. *Journal of Experimental Child Psychology, 95,* 99–116.

Crosby, B., LeBourgeois, M. K., & Harsh, J. (2005). Racial differences in reported napping and nocturnal sleep in 2- to 8-year-old children. *Pediatrics, 115,* 225–232.

Crosno, R., Kirkpatrick, M., & Elder, G. H., Jr. (2004). Intergenerational bonding in school: The behavioral and contextual correlates of student–teacher relationships. *Sociology of Education, 77,* 60–81.

Crouch, J. L., Skowronski, J. J., Milner, J. S., & Harris, B. (2008). Parental responses to infant crying: The influence of child physical abuse risk and hostile priming. *Child Abuse and Neglect, 32,* 702–710.

Crouter, A. C., & Bumpus, M. F. (2001). Linking parents' work stress to children's and adolescents' psychological adjustment. *Current Directions in Psychological Science, 10,* 156–159.

Crouter, A. C., & Head, M. R. (2002). Parental monitoring and knowledge of children. In M. H. Bornstein (Ed.), *Handbook of parenting: Vol. 3. Being and becoming a parent* (2nd ed., pp. 461–483). Mahwah, NJ: Erlbaum.

Crouter, A. C., Helms-Erikson, H., Updegraff, K., & McHale, S. M. (1999). Conditions underlying parents' knowledge about children's daily lives in middle childhood: Between- and within-family comparisons. *Child Development, 70,* 246–259.

Crouter, A. C., Manke, B. A., & McHale, S. M. (1995). The family context of gender intensification in early adolescence. *Child Development, 66,* 317–329.

Crouter, A. C., Whiteman, S. D., McHale, S. M., & Osgood, D. W. (2007). Development of gender attitude traditionality across middle childhood and adolescence. *Child Development, 78,* 911–926.

Crowhurst, M. (1990). Teaching and learning the writing of persuasive/argumentative discourse. *Canadian Journal of Education, 15,* 348–359.

Crystal, D. S., Killen, M., & Ruck, M. D. (2008). It is who you know that counts: Intergroup contact and judgments about race-based exclusion. *British Journal of Developmental Psychology, 26,* 51–70.

Crystal, D. S., Killen, M., & Ruck, M. D. (2010). Fair treatment by authorities is related to children's and adolescents' evaluations of interracial exclusion. *Applied Developmental Science, 14,* 125–136.

Cui, X., & Vaillant, G. E. (1996). Antecedents and consequences of negative life events in adulthood: A longitudinal study. *American Journal of Psychiatry, 153,* 21–26.

Cuijpers, P. (2002). Effective ingredients of school-based drug prevention programs: A systematic review. *Addictive Behaviors, 27,* 1009–1023.

Culbertson, F. M. (1997). Depression and gender: An international review. *American Psychologist, 52,* 25–51.

Culnane, M., Fowler, M. G., Lee, S. S., McSherry, G., Brady, M., & O'Donnell, K. (1999). Lack of long-term effects of in utero exposure to zidovudine among uninfected children born to HIV-infected women. *Journal of the American Medical Association, 281,* 151–157.

Cummings, E. M., Goeke-Morey, M. C., & Papp, L. M. (2004). Everyday marital conflict and child aggression. *Journal of Abnormal Child Psychology, 32,* 191–202.

Cummings, E. M., & Merrilees, C. E. (2010). Identifying the dynamic processes underlying links between marital conflict and child adjustment. In M. S. Schulz, M. K. Pruett, P. K. Kerig, & R. D. Parke (Eds.), *Strengthening couple relationships for optimal child development* (pp. 27–40). Washington, DC: American Psychological Association.

Cunningham, A. E., & Stanovich, K. E. (1998). What reading does for the mind. *American Educator,* Spring/Summer, 8–15.

Curby, T. W., LoCasale-Crouch, J., Konold, T. R., Pianta, R. C., Howes, C., Burchinal, M., et al. (2009). The relations of observed pre-K classroom quality profiles to children's achievement and social competence. *Early Education and Development, 20,* 346–372.

Curran, M., Hazen, N., Jacobvitz, D., & Feldman, A. (2005). Representations of early family relationships predict marital maintenance during the transition to parenthood. *Journal of Family Psychology, 19,* 189–197.

Cutrona, C. E., Hessling, R. M., Bacon, P. L., & Russell, D. W. (1998). Predictors and correlates of continuing involvement with the baby's father among adolescent mothers. *Journal of Family Psychology, 12,* 369–387.

Cutter, W. J., Daly, E. M., Robertson, D. M. W., Chitnis, X. A., van Amelsvoort, T. A. M. J., Simmons, A., et al. (2006). Influence of X chromosome and hormones on human brain development: A magnetic resonance imaging and proton magnetic resonance spectroscopy study of Turner syndrome. *Biological Psychiatry, 59,* 273–283.

Cyr, M., McDuff, P., & Wright, J. (2006). Prevalence and predictors of dating violence among adolescent female victims of child sexual abuse. *Journal of Interpersonal Violence, 21,* 1000–1017.

D

Dabrowska, E. (2000). From formula to schema: The acquisition of English questions. *Cognitive Linguistics, 11,* 1–20.

Dahl, R. E., & Lewin, D. S. (2002). Pathways to adolescent health: Sleep regulation and behavior, *Journal of Adolescent Health, 31*(6 Suppl.), 175–184.

Dahl, R. E., Scher, M. S., Williamson, D. E., Robles, N., & Day, N. (1995). A longitudinal study of prenatal marijuana use: Effects on sleep and arousal at age 3 years. *Archives of Pediatric and Adolescent Medicine, 149,* 145–150.

Dahlberg, L. L., & Simon, T. R. (2006). Predicting and preventing youth violence: Developmental pathways and risk. In L. L. Dahlberg & T. R. Simon (Eds.), *Preventing violence: Research and evidence-based intervention strategies* (pp. 97–124). Washington, DC: American Psychological Association.

Dal Santo, J. A., Goodman, R. M., Glik, D., & Jackson, K. (2004). Childhood unintentional injuries: Factors predicting injury risk among preschoolers. *Journal of Pediatric Psychology, 29,* 273–283.

Dales, L., Hammer, S. J., & Smith, N. J. (2001). Time trends in autism and MMR immunization coverage in California. *Journal of the American Medical Association, 285,* 1183–1185.

Damashek, A., & Peterson, L. (2002). Unintentional injury prevention efforts for young children: Levels, methods, types, and targets. *Developmental and Behavioral Pediatrics, 23,* 443–455.

Damon, W. (1988). *The moral child.* New York: Free Press.

Damon, W. (1990). Self-concept, adolescent. In R. M. Lerner, A. C. Petersen, & J. Brooks-Gunn (Eds.), *The encyclopedia of adolescence* (Vol. 2, pp. 87–91). New York: Garland.

Damon, W. (1995). *Greater expectations: Overcoming the culture of indulgence in America's homes and schools.* New York: Free Press.

Damon, W. (2004). *The moral advantage: How to succeed in business by doing the right thing.* San Francisco: Berrett-Koehler.

Damon, W., & Hart, D. (1988). *Self-understanding in childhood and adolescence.* New York: Cambridge University Press.

Daniels, E., & Leaper, C. (2006). A longitudinal investigation of sport participation, peer acceptance, and self-esteem among adolescent girls and boys. *Sex Roles, 55,* 875–880.

Daniels, P., Noe, G. F, & Mayberry, R. (2006). Barriers to prenatal care among Black women of low socioeconomic status. *American Journal of Health Behavior, 30,*:188–198.

Dannemiller, J. L., & Stephens, B. R. (1988). A critical test of infant pattern preference models. *Child Development, 59,* 210–216.

Dapretto, M., & Bjork, E. L. (2000). The development of word retrieval abilities in the second year and its relation to early vocabulary growth. *Child Development, 71,* 635–648.

Darling, N., & Steinberg, L. (1997). Community influences on adolescent achievement and deviance. In J. Brooks-Gunn, G. Duncan, & L. Aber (Eds.), *Neighborhood poverty: Context and consequences for children: Conceptual, ethological, and policy approaches to studying neighborhoods* (Vol. 2, pp. 120–131). New York: Russell Sage Foundation.

Darling-Hammond, L. (2010). *The flat world and education: How America's commitment to equity will determine our future.* New York: Teachers College Press.

Darroch, J. E., Frost, J. J., & Singh, S. (2001). *Teenage sexual and reproductive behavior in developed countries: Can more progress be made?* New York: Alan Guttmacher Institute.

Das, D. A., Grimmer, D. A., Sparnon, A. L., McRae, S. E., & Thomas, B. H. (2005). The efficacy of playing a virtual reality game in modulating pain for children with acute burn injuries: A randomized controlled trial. *BMC Pediatrics, 5*(1), 1–10.

D'Augelli, A. R. (2002). Mental health problems among lesbian, gay, and bisexual youths ages 14 to 21. *Clinical Child Psychology and Psychiatry, 7,* 433–456.

D'Augelli, A. R. (2006). Developmental and contextual factors and mental health among lesbian, gay, and bisexual youths. In A. M. Omoto & H. S. Howard (Eds.), *Sexual orientation and mental health: Examining identity and development in lesbian, gay, and bisexual people* (pp. 37–53). Washington, DC: American Psychological Association.

D'Augelli, A. R., Grossman, A. H., Salter, N. P., Vasey, J. J., Starks, M. T., & Sinclair, K. O. (2005). Predicting the suicide attempts of lesbian, gay, and bisexual youth. *Suicide and Life-Threatening Behavior, 35,* 646–660.

D'Augelli, A. R., Grossman, A. H., & Starks, M. T. (2005). Parents' awareness of lesbian, gay, and bisexual youths' sexual orientation. *Journal of Marriage and Family, 67,* 474–482.

D'Augelli, A. R., Grossman, A. H., & Starks, M. T. (2008). Families of gay, lesbian, and bisexual youth: What do parents and siblings know and how do they react? *Journal of GLBT Family Studies, 4,* 95–115.

Davidov, M., & Grusec, J. E. (2006). Untangling the links of parental responsiveness to distress and warmth to child outcomes. *Child Development, 77,* 44–58.

Davidson, R. J. (1994). Asymmetric brain function, affective style, and psychopathology: The role of early experience and plasticity. *Development and Psychopathology, 6,* 741–758.

Davies, P. T., & Lindsay, L. L. (2004). Interparental conflict and adolescent adjustment: Why does gender moderate early adolescent vulnerability? *Journal of Family Psychology, 18,* 160–170.

Davis, K. F., Parker, K. P., & Montgomery, G. L. (2004). Sleep in infants and young children. Part 1: Normal sleep. *Journal of Pediatric Health Care, 18,* 65–71.

Dawley, K., Loch, J., & Bindrich, I. (2007). The Nurse–Family Partnership. *American Journal of Nursing, 107,* 60–67.

Dawson, G., Ashman, S. B., Panagiotides, H., Hessl, D., Self, J., Yamada, E., & Embry, L. (2003). Preschool outcomes of children of depressed mothers: Role of maternal behavior, contextual risk, and children's brain activity. *Child Development, 74,* 1158–1175.

Dawson, T. L. (2002). New tools, new insights: Kohlberg's moral judgment stages revisited. *International Journal of Behavioral Development, 26,* 154–166.

de Bruyn, E. H. (2005). Role strain, engagement and academic achievement in early adolescence. *Educational Studies, 31,* 15–27.

de Bruyn, E. H., Deković, M., & Meijnen, G. W. (2003). Parenting, goal orientations, classroom behavior, and school success in early adolescence. *Journal of Applied Developmental Psychology, 24,* 393–412.

De Corte, E., & Verschaffel, L. (2006). Mathematical thinking and learning. In K. A. Renninger & I. E. Sigel (Eds.), *Handbook of child psychology: Vol. 4. Child psychology in practice* (6th ed., pp. 103–152). Hoboken, NJ: Wiley.

De Goede, I. H. A., Branje, S. J. T., & Meeus, W. H. J. (2009). Developmental changes and gender differences in adolescents' perceptions of friendships. *Journal of Adolescence, 32,* 1105–1123.

de Haan, M., & Johnson, M. H. (2003). Mechanisms and theories of brain development. In M. de Haan & M. H. Johnson (Eds.), *The cognitive neuroscience of development* (pp. 1–18). Hove, UK: Psychology Press.

de Haan, M., & Matheson, A. (2009). The development and neural bases of processing emotion in faces and voices. In M. de Haan & M. R. Gunnar (Eds.), *Handbook of developmental social science* (pp. 107–121). New York: Guilford.

De Lisi, R., & Gallagher, A. M. (1991). Understanding gender stability and constancy in Argentinian children. *Merrill-Palmer Quarterly, 37,* 483–502.

de Pree-Geerlings, B., de Pree, I. M., & Bulk-Bunschoten, A. M. (2001). 1901–2001: 100 years of physicians of infant and toddler welfare centers in the Netherlands. *Netherlands Tijdschrift Voor Geneeskunde, 145,* 2461–2465.

de Ribaupierre, A., & Lecerf, T. (2006). Relationships between working memory and intelligence from a developmental perspective: Convergent evidence from a neo-Piagetian and a psychometric approach. *European Journal of Cognitive Psychology, 18,* 109–137.

de Rosnay, M., & Hughes, C. (2006). Conversation and theory of mind: Do children talk their way to socio-cognitive understanding? *British Journal of Developmental Psychology, 24,* 7–37.

De Schipper, J. C., Tavecchio, L. W. C., van IJzendoorn, M. H., & van Zeijl, J. (2004). Goodness-of-fit in center day care: Relations of temperament, stability, and quality of care with the child's adjustment. *Early Childhood Research Quarterly, 19,* 257–272.

De Schipper, J. C., van IJzendoorn, M. H., & Tavecchio, L. W. C. (2004). Stability in center day care: Relations with children's well-being and problem behavior in day care. *Social Development, 13,* 531–550.

De Souza, E., Alberman, E., & Morris, J. K. (2009). Down syndrome and paternal age, a new analysis of case-control data collected in the 1960s. *American Journal of Medical Genetics, 149A,* 1205–1208.

de Villiers, J. G., & de Villiers, P. A. (1973). A cross-sectional study of the acquisition of grammatical morphemes in child speech. *Journal of Psycholinguistic Research, 2,* 267–278.

de Villiers, J. G., & de Villiers, P. A. (2000). Linguistic determinism and the understanding of false beliefs. In P. Mitchell & K. J. Riggs (Eds.), *Children's reasoning and the mind* (pp. 87–99). Hove, UK: Psychology Press.

de Waal, F. B. M. (1993). Sex differences in chimpanzee (and human) behavior: A matter of social values? In M. Hechter, L. Nadel, & R. E. Michod (Eds.), *The origin of values* (pp. 285–303). New York: Aldine de Gruyter.

de Waal, F. B. M. (2001). *Tree of origin.* Cambridge, MA: Harvard University Press.

de Weerd, A. W., & van den Bossche, A. S. (2003). The development of sleep during the first months of life. *Sleep Medicine Reviews, 7,* 179–191.

de Weerth, C., & Buitelaar, J. K. (2005). Physiological stress reactivity in human pregnancy—a review. *Neuroscience and Biobehavioral Reviews, 29,* 295–312.

de Winter, M., Balledux, M., & de Mare, J. (1997). A critical evaluation of Dutch preventive child health care. *Child: Care, Health and Development, 23,* 437–446.

De Wolff, M. S., & van IJzendoorn, M. H. (1997). Sensitivity and attachment: A meta-analysis on parental antecedents of infant attachment. *Child Development, 68,* 571–591.

Deafness Research Foundation. (2010). *Hearing statistics.* Retrieved from www.drf.org/statistics

Deák, G. O. (2000). Hunting the fox of word learning: Why "constraints" fail to capture it. *Developmental Review, 20,* 29–80.

Deák, G. O., Ray, S. D., & Brenneman, K. (2003). Children's perseverative appearance–reality errors are related to emerging language skills. *Child Development, 74,* 944–964.

Deák, G. O., Yen, L., & Pettit, J. (2001). By any other name: When will preschoolers produce several labels for a reference? *Journal of Child Language, 28,* 787–804.

DeAngeleo, L., Hurtado, S., & Pryor, J. H. (2010). *Your first college year: National norms for the 2008 YFCY survey.* Los Angeles: Higher Education Research Institute, UCLA.

Dearing, E. (2008). The psychological costs of growing up poor. *Annals of the New York Academy of Sciences, 1136,* 324–332.

Dearing, E., Wimer, C., Simpkins, S. D., Lund, T., Bouffard, S. M., Caronongan, P., & Kreider, H. (2009). Do neighborhood and home contexts help explain why low-income children miss opportunities to participate in activities outside of school? *Developmental Psychology, 45,* 1545–1562.

Deary, I. J. (2001). g and cognitive elements of information progressing: An agnostic view. In R. J. Sternberg & E. L. Grigorenko (Eds.), *The general factor of intelligence: How general is it?* (pp. 447–479). Mahwah, NJ: Erlbaum.

Deary, I. J., Strand, S., Smith, P., & Fernandes, C. (2007). Intelligence and educational achievement. *Intelligence, 35,* 13–21.

Deater-Deckard, K., Lansford, J. E., Dodge, K. A., Pettit, G. S., & Bates, J. E. (2003). The development of attitudes about physical punishment: An 8-year longitudinal study. *Journal of Family Psychology, 17,* 351–360.

Deater-Deckard, K., Pike, A., Petrill, S. A., Cutting, A. L., Hughes, C., & O'Connor, T. G. (2001). Nonshared environmental processes in social-emotional development: An observational study of identical twin differences in the preschool period. *Developmental Science, 4,* F1–F6.

Deater-Deckard, K., Scarr, S., McCartney, K., & Eisenberg, M. (1994). Paternal separation anxiety: Relationships with parenting stress, child-rearing attitudes, and maternal anxieties. *Psychological Science, 5,* 341–346.

DeBerry, K. M., Scarr, S., & Weinberg, R. (1996). Family racial socialization and ecological competence: Longitudinal assessments of African-American transracial adoptees. *Child Development, 67,* 2375–2399.

DeBoer, T., Scott, L. S., & Nelson, C. A. (2007). Methods for acquiring and analyzing infant event-related

potentials. In M. de Haan (Ed.), *Infant EEG and event-related potentials* (pp. 5–37). New York: Psychology Press.

DeCasper, A. J., & Spence, M. J. (1986). Prenatal maternal speech influences newborns' perception of speech sounds. *Infant Behavior and Development, 9,* 133–150.

DeCasper, A. J., & Spence, M. J. (1988). Prenatal maternal speech influences newborns' perception of speech sounds. In S. Chess, A. Thomas, & M. Hertzig (Eds.), *Annual progress in child psychiatry and child development, 1987* (pp. 5–25). Philadelphia: Brunner/Mazel.

Deci, E. L., & Ryan, R. M. (2002). Self-determination research: Reflections and future directions. In E. L. Deci & R. M. Ryan (Eds.), *Handbook of self-determination research* (pp. 431–441). Rochester, NY: University of Rochester Press.

Dee, Y. S., Grabowski, D. C., & Morrisey, M. A. (2005). Graduated driver licensing and teen traffic fatalities. *Journal of Health Economics, 24,* 571–589.

Degirmencioglu, S. M., Urberg, K. A., Tolson, J. M., & Richard, P. (1998). Adolescent friendship networks: Continuity and change over the school year. *Merrill-Palmer Quarterly, 44,* 313–337.

Deissinger, T. (2007). "Making schools practical": Practice firms and their function in the full-time vocational school system in Germany. *Education + Training, 49,* 364–378.

Dekker, M. C., Ferdinand, R. F., van Lang, D. J., Bongers, I. L., van der Ende, J., & Verhulst, F. C. (2007). Developmental trajectories of depressive symptoms from early childhood to late adolescence: Gender differences and adult outcome. *Journal of Child Psychology and Psychiatry, 48,* 657–666.

Deković, M., & Buist, K. L. (2005). Multiple perspectives within the family: Family relationship patterns. *Journal of Family Issues, 26,* 467–490.

Deković, M., Noom, M. J., & Meeus, W. (1997). Expectations regarding development during adolescence: Parent and adolescent perceptions. *Journal of Youth and Adolescence, 26,* 253–271.

Delahunty, K. M., McKay, D. W., Noseworthy, D. E., & Storey, A. E. (2007). Prolactin responses to infant cues in men and women: Effects of parental experience and recent infant contact. *Hormones and Behavior, 51,* 213–220.

Delgado-Gaitan, C. (1994). Socializing young children in Mexican-American families: An intergenerational perspective. In P. Greenfield & R. Cocking (Eds.), *Cross-cultural roots of minority child development* (pp. 55–86). Hillsdale, NJ: Erlbaum.

Dell, D. L. (2001). Adolescent pregnancy. In N. L. Stotland & D. E. Stewart (Eds.), *Psychological aspects of women's health care* (pp. 95–116). Washington, DC: American Psychiatric Association.

DeLoache, J. S. (1987). Rapid change in symbolic functioning of very young children. *Science, 238,* 1556–1557.

DeLoache, J. S. (2000). Dual representation and children's use of scale models. *Child Development, 71,* 329–338.

DeLoache, J. S. (2002). The symbol-mindedness of young children. In W. Hartup & R. A. Weinberg (Eds.), *Minnesota symposia on child psychology* (Vol. 32, pp. 73–101). Mahwah, NJ: Erlbaum.

DeLoache, J. S., & Ganea, P. A. (2009). Symbol-based learning in infancy. In A. Woodward & A. Needham (Eds.), *Learning and the infant mind* (pp. 263–285). New York: Oxford University Press.

DeLoache, J. S., Pierroutsakos, S. L., Uttal, D. H., Rosengren, K. S., & Gottlieb, A. (1998). Grasping the nature of pictures. *Psychological Science, 9,* 205–210.

DeLoache, J. S., & Todd, C. M. (1988). Young children's use of spatial categorization as a mnemonic strategy. *Journal of Experimental Child Psychology, 46,* 1–20.

DeLoache, J. S., Uttal, D., & Rosengren, K. (2004). Scale errors offer evidence for a perception–action dissociation early in life. *Science, 304,* 1027–1029.

Delobel-Ayoub, M., Arnaud, C., White-Koning, M., Casper, C., Pierrat, V., Garel, M., et al. (2009). Behavioral problems and cognitive performance at 5

years of age after very preterm birth: The EPIPAGE Study. *Pediatrics, 123,* 1485–1492.

Deltondo, J., Por, I., Hu, W., Merchenthaler, I., Semeniken, K., Jojart, J., & Dudas, B. (2008). Associations between the human growth hormone-releasing hormone and neuropeptide-Y-immunoreactive systems in the human diencephalons: A possible morphological substrate of the impact of stress on growth. *Neuroscience, 153,* 1146–1152.

DeMarie, D., Miller, P. H., Ferron, J., & Cunningham, W. R. (2004). Path analysis tests of theoretical models of children's memory performance. *Journal of Cognition and Development, 5,* 461–492.

Demetriou, A., Christou, C., Spanoudis, G., & Platsidou, M. (2002). The development of mental processing: Efficiency, working memory, and thinking. *Monographs of the Society for Research in Child Development, 67*(1, Serial No. 268).

Demetriou, A., Efklides, A., Papadaki, M., Papantoniou, G., & Economou, A. (1993). Structure and development of causal–experimental thought: From early adolescence to youth. *Developmental Psychology, 29,* 480–497.

Demetriou, A., & Kazi, S. (2001). *Unity and modularity in the mind and the self: Studies on the relationships between self-awareness, personality, and intellectual development from childhood to adolescence.* London: Routledge.

Demetriou, A., Pachaury, A., Metallidou, Y., & Kazi, S. (1996). Universals and specificities in the structure and development of quantitative-relational thought: A cross-cultural study in Greece and India. *International Journal of Behavioral Development, 19,* 255–290.

Dempster, F. N., & Corkill, A. J. (1999). Interference and inhibition in cognition and behavior: Unifying themes for educational psychology. *Educational Psychology Review, 11,* 1–88.

Denham, S. (1998). *Emotional development in young children.* New York: Guilford.

Denham, S. A. (2005). Emotional competence counts: Assessment as support for school readiness. In K. Hirsh-Pasek, A. Kochanoff, N. S. Newcombe, & J. de Villiers (Eds.), Using scientific knowledge to inform preschool assessment. *Social Policy Report of the Society for Research in Child Development, 19*(No.1), 12.

Denham, S. A. (2006). Emotional competence: Implications for social functioning. In J. L. Luby (Ed.), *Handbook of preschool mental health: Development, disorders, and treatment* (pp. 23–44). New York: Guilford.

Denham, S. A., & Burton, R. (2003). *Social and emotional prevention and intervention programming for preschoolers.* New York: Kluwer-Plenum.

Denham, S. A., & Kochanoff, A. T. (2002). Parental contributions to preschoolers' understanding of emotion. *Marriage and Family Review, 34,* 311–343.

Denissen, J. J. A., Zarrett, N. R., & Eccles, J. S. (2007). I like to do it, I'm able, and I know I am: Longitudinal couplings between domain-specific achievement, self-concept, and interest. *Child Development, 78,* 430–447.

Dennis, T., Bendersky, M., Ramsay, D., & Lewis, M. (2006). Reactivity and regulation in children prenatally exposed to cocaine. *Developmental Psychology, 42,* 688–697.

Dennis, W. (1960). Causes of retardation among institutionalized children: Iran. *Journal of Genetic Psychology, 96,* 47–59.

Deocampo, J. A. (2003, April). *Tools on TV: A new paradigm for testing dual representational understanding.* Poster presented at the biennial meeting of the Society for Research in Child Development, Tampa, FL.

Der, G., Batty, G. D., & Deary, I. J. (2006). Effect of breastfeeding on intelligence in children: Prospective study, sibling pairs analysis, and meta-analysis. *British Medical Journal, 333,* 945.

deRegnier, R. A. (2005). Neurophysiologic evaluation of early cognitive development in high-risk infants and toddlers. *Mental Retardation and Developmental Disabilities, 11,* 317–324.

deRegnier, R. A., Long, J. D., Georgieff, M. K., & Nelson, C. A. (2007). Using event-related potentials and brain development in infants of diabetic mothers. *Developmental Neuropsychology, 31,* 379–396.

DeRoche, K., & Welsh, M. (2008). Twenty-five years of research on neurocognitive outcomes in early-treated phenylketonuria: Intelligence and executive function. *Developmental Neuropsychology, 33,* 474–504.

Derom, C., Thiery, E., Vlietinck, R., Loos, R., & Derom, R. (1996). Handedness in twins according to zygosity and chorion type: A preliminary report. *Behavior Genetics, 26,* 407–408.

DeRose, L. M., & Brooks-Gunn, J. (2006). Transition into adolescence: The role of pubertal processes. In L. Balter & C. S. Tamis-LeMonda (Eds.), *Child psychology: A handbook of contemporary issues* (2nd ed., pp. 385–414). New York: Psychology Press.

DeRosier, M. E. (2007). Peer-rejected and bullied children: A safe schools initiative for elementary school students. In J. E. Zins, M. J. Elias, & C. A. Maher (Eds.), *Bullying, victimization, and peer harassment* (pp. 257–276). New York: Haworth.

DeRosier, M. E., & Thomas, J. M. (2003). Strengthening sociometric prediction: Scientific advances in the assessment of children's peer relations. *Child Development, 75,* 1379–1392.

Desrochers, S. (2008). From Piaget to specific Genevan developmental models. *Child Development Perspectives, 2,* 7–12.

Dessel, A. (2010). Prejudice in schools: Promotion of an inclusive culture and climate. *Education and Urban Society, 42,* 407–429.

deUngria, M., Rao, R., Wobken, J. D., Luciana, M., & Georgieff, M. K. (2000). Neurophysiologic evaluation of auditory recognition memory in healthy newborn infants and infants of diabetic mothers. *Journal of Pediatrics, 137,* 777–784.

Deutsch, F. M., Ruble, D. N., Fleming, A., Brooks-Gunn, J., & Stangor, C. (1988). Information-seeking and maternal self-definition during the transition to motherhood. *Journal of Personality and Social Psychology, 55,* 420–431.

Deutsch, W., & Pechmann, T. (1982). Social interaction and the development of definite descriptions. *Cognition, 11,* 159–184.

Devi, N. P. G., Shenbagvalli, R., Ramesh, K., & Rathinam, S. N. (2009). Rapid progression of HIV infection in infancy. *Indian Pediatrics, 46,* 53–56.

DeVoe, J. F., & Darling-Churchill, K. E. (2008). *Status and trends in the education of American Indians and Alaska Natives: 2008* (NCES 2008–84). Washington, DC: U.S. Department of Education.

DeVries, R. (2001). Constructivist education in preschool and elementary school: The sociomoral atmosphere as the first educational goal. In S. L. Golbeck (Ed.), *Psychological perspectives on early childhood education* (pp. 153–180). Mahwah, NJ: Erlbaum.

Deynoot-Schaub, M. J. G., & Riksen-Walraven, J. M. (2006a). Peer contacts of 15-month-olds in childcare: Links with child temperament, parent–child interaction and quality of childcare. *Social Development 15,* 709–729.

Deynoot-Schaub, M. J. G., & Riksen-Walraven, J. M. (2006b). Peer interaction in child care centres at 15 and 23 months: Stability and links with children's socioemotional adjustment. *Infant Behavior and Development, 29,* 276–288.

Diamond, A. (2000). Close interrelation of motor development and cognitive development and of the cerebellum and prefrontal cortex. *Child Development, 71,* 44–56.

Diamond, A. (2004). Normal development of prefrontal cortex from birth to young adulthood: Cognitive functions, anatomy, and biochemistry. In D. T. Stuss & R. T. Knight (Eds.), *Principles of frontal lobe function* (pp. 466–503). New York: Oxford University Press.

Diamond, A. (2009). The interplay of biology and the environment broadly defined. *Developmental Psychology, 45,* 1–8.

Diamond, A., Barnett, W. S., Thomas, J., & Munro, S. (2007). Preschool program improves cognitive control. *Science, 318,* 1387–1388.

Diamond, A., Cruttenden, L., & Neiderman, D. (1994). AB with multiple wells: 1. Why are multiple wells sometimes easier than two wells? 2. Memory or memory + inhibition. *Developmental Psychology, 30,* 192–205.

Diamond, L. M. (1998). Development of sexual orientation among adolescent and young adult women. *Developmental Psychology, 34,* 1085–1095.

Diamond, L. M. (2003). Love matters: Romantic relationships among sexual-minority adolescents. In P. Florsheim (Ed.), *Adolescent romantic relations and sexual behavior* (pp. 85–108). Mahwah, NJ: Erlbaum.

Diamond, L. M. (2008). Female bisexuality from adolescence to adulthood: Results from a 10-year longitudinal study. *Developmental Psychology, 44,* 5–14.

Diamond, L. M., & Lucas, S. (2004). Sexual-minority and heterosexual youths' peer relationships: Experiences, expectations, and implications for well-being. *Journal of Research on Adolescence, 14,* 313–340.

Diamond, M., & Sigmundson, H. K. (1999). Sex reassignment at birth. In S. J. Ceci & W. M. Williams (Eds.), *The nature–nurture debate* (pp. 55–75). Malden, MA: Blackwell.

Dias, M. G., & Harris, P. (1988). The effect of make-believe play on deductive reasoning. *British Journal of Developmental Psychology, 6,* 207–221.

Dias, M. G., & Harris, P. (1990). The influence of the imagination on reasoning by young children. *British Journal of Developmental Psychology, 8,* 305–318.

Dick, D. M., Prescott, C., & McGue, M. (2008). The genetics of substance use and substance use disorders. In Y.-K. Kim (Ed.), *Handbook of behavior genetics* (pp. 433–453). New York: Springer.

Dick, D. M., Rose, R. J., Viken, R. J., & Kaprio, J. (2000). Pubertal timing and substance use: Associations between and within families across late adolescence. *Developmental Psychology, 36,* 180–189.

Dick, F., Dronkers, N. F., Pizzamiglio, L., Saygin, A. P., Small, S. L., Wilson, S. (2004). Language and the brain. In M. Tomasello & D. I Slobin (Eds.), *Beyond nature–nurture: Essays in honor of Elizabeth Bates* (pp. 237–260). Mahwah, NJ: Erlbaum.

Dickinson, D. K., & McCabe, A. (2001). Bringing it all together: The multiple origins, skills, and environmental supports of early literacy. *Learning Disabilities Research and Practice, 16,* 186–202.

Dickinson, D. K., McCabe, A., Anastasopoulos, L., Peisner-Feinberg, E. S., & Poe, M. D. (2003). The comprehensive language approach to early literacy: The interrelationships among vocabulary, phonological sensitivity, and print knowledge among preschool-age children. *Journal of Educational Psychology, 95,* 465–481.

Dickinson, D. K., & Sprague, K. E. (2001). The nature and impact of early childhood care environments on the language and early literacy development of children from low-income families. In S. B. Neuman & D. K. Dickinson (Eds.), *Handbook of early literacy research.* New York: Guilford.

Dick-Read, G. (1959). *Childbirth without fear.* New York: Harper & Brothers.

Dickson, K. L., Fogel, A., & Messinger, D. (1998). The development of emotion from a social process view. In M. F. Mascolo (Ed.), *What develops in emotional development?* (pp. 253–271). New York: Plenum.

Diehr, S. (2003). How effective is desmopressin for primary nocturnal enuresis? *Journal of Family Practice, 52,* 568–569.

Diener, M. L., Isabella, R., Behunin, M. G., & Wong, M. S. (2008). Attachment to mothers and fathers during middle childhood: Associations with child gender, grade, and competence. *Social Development, 17,* 84–101.

Dietrich, K. N., Ware, J. H., Salganik, M., Radcliffe, J., Rogan, W. J., & Rhoads, G. C. (2004). Effect of chelation therapy on the neuropsychological and behavioral development of lead-exposed children after school entry. *Pediatrics, 114,* 19–26.

Dietrich, K. N., Ris, M. D., Succop, P. A., Berger, O. G., & Bornschein, R. L. (2001). Early exposure to lead and juvenile delinquency. *Neurotoxicology and Teratology, 23,* 511–518.

Dildy, G. A., Jackson, G. M., Fowers, G. K., Oshiro, B. T., Varner, M. W., & Clark, S. L. (1996). Very advanced maternal age: Pregnancy after age 45. *American Journal of Obstetrics and Gynecology, 175,* 668–674.

DiMatteo, M. R., & Kahn, K. L. (1997). Psychosocial aspects of childbirth. In S. J. Gallant, G. P. Keita, & R. Royak-Schaler (Eds.), *Health care for women: Psychological, social, and behavioral influences* (pp. 175–186). Washington, DC: American Psychological Association.

Ding, Z. Y. (2008). National epidemiological survey on childhood obesity, 2006. *Chinese Journal of Pediatrics, 46,* 179–184.

DiPietro, J. A., Bornstein, M. H., Costigan, K. A., Pressman, E. K., Hahn, C.-S., & Painter, K. (2002). What does fetal movement predict about behavior during the first two years of life? *Developmental Psychobiology, 40,* 358–371.

DiPietro, J. A., Hodgson, D. M., Costigan, K. A., & Hilton, S. C. (1996). Fetal neurobehavioral development. *Child Development, 67,* 2553–2567.

DiPietro, J. A., Novak, M. F. S. X., Costigan, K. A., Atella, L. D., & Reusing, S. P. (2006). Maternal psychological distress during pregnancy in relation to child development at age two. *Child Development, 77,* 573–587.

Dirix, C. E. H., Nijhuis, J. G., Jongsma, H. W., & Hornstra, G. (2009). Aspects of fetal learning and memory. *Child Development, 80,* 1251–1258.

Dirks, J. (1982). The effect of a commercial game on children's Block Design scores on the WISC–R test. *Intelligence, 6,* 109–123.

Dishion, T. J., Andrews, D. W., & Crosby, L. (1995). Antisocial boys and their friends in early adolescence: Relationship characteristics, quality, and interactional processes. *Child Development, 66,* 139–151.

Dishion, T. J., Shaw, D., Connell, A., Gardner, F., Weaver, C., & Wilson, M. (2008). The family check-up with high-risk indigent families: Preventing problem behavior by increasing parents' positive behavior support in early childhood. *Child Development, 79,* 1395–1414.

Dix, T., Stewart, A. D., Gershoff, E. T., & Day, W. H. (2007). Atutonomy and children's reactions to being controlled: Evidence that both compliance and defiance may be positive markers in early development. *Child Development, 78,* 1204–1221.

Dmitrieva, J., Steinberg, L., & Belsky, J. (2007). Child-care history, classroom composition and children's functioning in kindergarten. *Psychological Science, 18,* 1032–1039

Dodd, V. L. (2005). Implications of kangaroo care for growth and development in preterm infants. *JOGNN, 34,* 218–232.

Dodge, K. A., Coie, J. D., & Lynam, D. (2006). Aggression and antisocial behavior in youth. In N. Eisenberg (Ed.), *Handbook of child psychology: Vol. 3. Social, emotional, and personality development* (6th ed., pp. 719–788). Hoboken, NJ: Wiley.

Dodge, K. A., Lansford, J. E., Burks, V. S., Bates, J. E., Pettit, G. S., Fontaine, R., & Price, J. M. (2003). Peer rejection and social information-processing factors in the development of aggressive behavior problems in children. *Child Development, 74,* 374–393.

Dodge, K. A., Lochman, J. E., Harnish, J. D., Bates, J. E., & Pettit, G. S. (1997). Reactive and proactive aggression in school children and psychiatrically impaired chronically assaultive youth. *Journal of Abnormal Psychology, 106,* 37–51.

Dodge, K. A., McLoyd, V. C., & Lansford, J. E. (2006). The cultural context of physically disciplining children. In V. C. McLoyd, N. E. Hill, & K A. Dodge (Eds.), *African-American family life: Ecological and cultural diversity* (pp. 245–263). New York: Guilford.

Dodge, K. A., Pettit, G. S., McClaskey, C. L., & Brown, M. M. (1986). Social competence in children. *Monographs of the Society for Research in Child Development, 51*(2, Serial No. 213).

Doherty, N. N., & Hepper, P. G. (2000). Habituation in fetuses of diabetic mothers. *Early Human Development, 59,* 85–93.

Dohnt, H., & Tiggemann, M. (2006). The contribution of peer and media influences to the development of body satisfaction and self-esteem in young girls: A prospective study. *Developmental Psychology, 42,* 929–936.

Dombrowski, K. J., Lantz, P. M., & Freed, G. L. (2004). Risk factors for delay in age-appropriate vaccination. *Public Health Reports, 119,* 144–155.

Dombrowski, S. C., Noonan, K., & Martin, R. P. (2007). Low birth weight and cognitive outcomes: Evidence for a gradient relationship in an urban, poor, African American birth cohort. *School Psychology Quarterly, 22,* 26–43.

Domitrovich, C. E., Cortes, R. C., & Greenberg, M. T. (2007). Improving young children's social and emotional competence: A randomized trial of the preschool "PATHS" curriculum. *The Journal of Primary Prevention, 28,* 67–91.

Donahue, M. J., & Benson, P. L. (1995). Religion and the well-being of adolescents. *Journal of Social Issues, 51,* 145–160.

Donatelle, R. J. (2009). *Health: The basics* (8th ed.). San Francisco: Benjamin Cummings.

Dondi, M., Simion, F., & Caltran, G. (1999). Can newborns discriminate between their own cry and the cry of another newborn infant? *Developmental Psychology, 35,* 418–426.

Donnellan, M. B., Trzesniewski, K. H., Robins, R. W., Moffitt, T. E., & Caspi, A. (2005). Low self-esteem is related to aggression, antisocial behavior, and delinquency. *Psychological Science, 16,* 328–335.

Donnerstein, E., Slaby, R. G., & Eron, L. D. (1994). The mass media and youth aggression. In L. D. Eron, J. H. Gentry, & P. Schlegel (Eds.), *Reason to hope: A psychosocial perspective on violence and youth* (pp. 219–250). Washington, DC: American Psychological Association.

D'Onofrio, B. M., Turkheimer, E., Emery, R. E., Slutske, W. S., Heath, A. C., Madden, P. A., & Martin, N. G. (2006). A genetically informed study of the processes underlying the association between parental marital instability and offspring adjustment. *Developmental Psychology, 42,* 486–499.

Dorius, C. J., Bahr, S. J., Hoffman, J. P., & Harmon, E. L. (2004). Parenting practices as moderators of the relationship between peers and adolescent marijuana use. *Journal of Marriage and Family, 66,* 163–178.

Dorris, M. (1989). *The broken cord.* New York: Harper & Row.

dos Santos Silva, I., De Stavola, B. L., Hardy, R. J., Kuh, D. J., McCormack, V. A., & Wadsworth, M. E. J. (2004). Is the association of birth weight with premenopausal breast cancer risk mediated through childhood growth? *British Journal of Cancer, 91,* 519–524.

Doss, B. D., Rhoades, G. K., & Stanley, S. M. (2009). The effect of the transition to parenthood on relationship quality: An 8-year prospective study. *Journal of Personality and Social Psychology, 96,* 601–619.

Douglas, E. M. (2006). *Mending broken families: Social policies for divorced families.* Lanham, MD: Rowman & Littlefield.

Dowker, A. (2003). Younger children's estimates for addition: The zone of partial knowledge and understanding. In A. J. Baroody & A. Dowker (Eds.), *The development of arithmetic concepts and skills: Constructing adaptive expertise* (pp. 243–265). Mahwah, NJ: Erlbaum.

Dowling, E. M., Gestsdottir, S., Anderson, P. M., von Eye, A., Almerigi, J., & Lerner, R. M. (2004). Structural relations among spirituality, religiosity, and thriving in adolescence. *Applied Developmental Psychology, 8,* 7–16.

Downe, S., Finlayson, K., Walsh, D., & Lavender, T. (2009). "Weighing up and balancing out": A meta-synthesis of barriers to antenatal care for marginalized women in high-income countries. *BJOG, 116,* 518–529.

Downs, A. C., & Fuller, M. J. (1991). Recollections of spermarche: An exploratory investigation. *Current Psychology: Research and Reviews, 10,* 93–102.

Dozier, M., Stovall, K. C., Albus, K. E., & Bates, B. (2001). Attachment for infants in foster care: The role of caregiver state of mind. *Child Development, 72,* 1467–1477.

Drabman, R. S., Cordua, G. D., Hammer, D., Jarvie, G. J., & Horton, W. (1979). Developmental trends in eating rates of normal and overweight preschool children. *Child Development, 50,* 211–216.

Drewett, R. F., Corbett, S. S., & Wright, C. M. (2006). Physical and emotional development, appetite and body image in adolescents who failed to thrive as infants. *Journal of Child Psychology and Psychiatry, 47,* 524–531.

Driscoll, M. C. (2007). Sickle cell disease. *Pediatrics in Review, 28,* 259–268.

Drotar, D., Witherspoon, D. O., Zebracki, K., & Peterson, C. C. (2006). *Psychological interventions in childhood chronic illness.* Washington, DC: American Psychological Association.

Dubé, E. M., Savin-Williams, R. C., & Diamond, L. M. (2001). Intimacy development, gender, and ethnicity among sexual-minority youths. In A. R. D'Augelli & C. J. Patterson (Eds.), *Lesbian, gay, and bisexual identities and youth* (pp. 129–152). New York: Oxford University Press.

DuBois, D. L., Burk-Braxton, C., Swenson, L. P., Tevendale, H. D., Lockerd, E. M., & Moran, B. L. (2002). Getting by with a little help from self and others: Self-esteem and social support as resources during early adolescence. *Developmental Psychology, 38,* 822–939.

DuBois, D. L., Felner, R. D., Brand, S., & George, G. R. (1999). Profiles of self-esteem in early adolescence: Identification and investigation of adaptive correlates. *American Journal of Community Psychology, 27,* 899–932.

Duckworth, A. L., & Seligman, M. E. P. (2005). Self-discipline outdoes IQ in predicting academic performance of adolescents. *Psychological Science, 12,* 939–944.

Dueker, G. L., Modi, A., & Needham, A. (2003). 4.5-month-old infants' learning, retention and use of object boundary information. *Infant Behavior and Development, 26,* 588–605.

Duggan, A., McFarlane, E., Fuddy, L., Burrell, L., Higman, S. M., Windham, A., & Sia, C. (2004). Randomized trial of a statewide home visiting program: Impact in preventing child abuse and neglect. *Child Abuse and Neglect, 28,* 597–622.

Duncan, G. J., & Magnuson, K. A. (2003). Off with Hollingshead: Socioeconomic resources, parenting, and child development. In M. H. Bornstein & R. H. Bradley (Eds.), *Socioeconomic status, parenting, and child development* (pp. 83–106). Mahwah, NJ: Erlbaum.

Duncan, G. J., Dowsett, C. J., Claessens, A., Magnuson, K., Huston, A. C., Klebanov, P., et al. (2007). School readiness and later achievement. *Developmental Psychology, 43,* 1428–1446.

Duncan, S. R., Paterson, D. S., Hoffman, J. M., Mokler, D. J., et al. (2010). Brainstem serotonergic deficiency in sudden infant death syndrome. *Journal of the American Medical Association, 303,* 430-437.

Dundek, L. H. (2006) Establishment of a Somali doula program at a large metropolitan hospital. *Journal of Perinatal and Neonatal Nursing, 20,* 128–137.

Dunham, Y., Baron, A. S., & Banaji, M. R. (2006). From American city to Japanese village: A cross-cultural investigation of implicit race attitudes. *Child Development, 77,* 1129–1520.

Dunifon, R., Kalil, A., & Danziger, S. K. (2003). Maternal work behavior under welfare reform: How does the transition from welfare to work affect child development? *Children and Youth Services Review, 25,* 55–82.

Dunn, J. (1989). Siblings and the development of social understanding in early childhood. In P. G. Zukow (Ed.), *Sibling interaction across cultures* (pp. 106–116). New York: Springer-Verlag.

Dunn, J. (1994). Temperament, siblings, and the development of relationships. In W. B. Carey & S. C. McDevitt (Eds.), *Prevention and early intervention* (pp. 50–58). New York: Brunner/Mazel.

Dunn, J. (2002). The adjustment of children in stepfamilies: Lessons from community studies. *Child and Adolescent Mental Health, 7,* 154–161.

Dunn, J. (2004). Sibling relationships. In P. K. Smith & C. H. Hart (Eds.), *Handbook of childhood social development* (pp. 223–237). Malden, MA: Blackwell.

Dunn, J. (2005). Moral development in early childhood and social interaction in the family. In M. Killen & J. G. Smetana (Eds.), *Handbook of moral development* (pp. 331–350). Mahwah, NJ: Erlbaum.

Dunn, J., Brown, J. R., & Maguire, M. (1995). The development of children's moral sensibility: Individual differences and emotion understanding. *Developmental Psychology, 31,* 649–659.

Dunn, J., Cheng, H., O'Connor, T. G., & Bridges, L. (2004). Children's perspectives on their relationships with their nonresident fathers: Influences, outcomes and implications. *Journal of Child Psychology and Psychiatry, 45,* 553–566.

Dunn, J. R., Schaefer-McDaniel, N. J., & Ramsay, J. T. (2010). Neighborhood chaos and children's development: Question and contradictions. In G. W. Evans & T. D. Wachs (Eds.), *Chaos and its influence on children's development: An ecological perspective,* (pp. 173–189.). Washington, DC: American Psychological Association.

Dunphy-Lelii, S., & Wellman, H. M. (2004). Infants' understanding of occlusion of others' line of sight: Implications for an emerging theory of mind. *European Journal of Developmental Psychology, 1,* 49–66.

Durbin, D. L., Darling, N., Steinberg, L., & Brown, B. B. (1993). Parenting style and peer group membership among European-American adolescents. *Journal of Research on Adolescence, 3,* 87–100.

Durkin, M. S., Laraque, D., Lubman, I., & Barlow, B. (1999). Epidemiology and prevention of traffic injuries to urban children and adolescents. *Pediatrics, 103,* e74.

Durlach, J. (2004). New data on the importance of gestational Mg deficiency. *Journal of the American College of Nutrition, 23,* 694S-700S.

Durlak, J. A., & Weissberg, R. P. (2007). *The impact of after-school programs that promote personal and social skills.* Chicago: Collaborative for Academic, Social, and Emotional Learning.

Durston, S., & Conrad, K. (2007). Integrating genetic, psychopharmacological and neuroimaging studies: A converging methods approach to understanding the neurobiology of ADHD. *Developmental Review, 27,* 374–395.

Durston, S., & Casey, B. J. (2006). What have we learned about cognitive development from neuroimaging? *Neuropsychologia, 44,* 2149–2157.

Dusek, J. B. (1987). Sex roles and adjustment. In D. B. Carter (Ed.), *Current conceptions of sex roles and sex typing* (pp. 211–222). New York: Praeger.

Duszak, R. S. (2009). Congenital rubella syndrome—major review. *Optometry, 80,* 36–43.

Dweck, C. (2007). Is math a gift? Beliefs that put females at risk. In S. J. Ceci & W. M. Williams (Eds.), *Why aren't more women in science? Top researchers debate the evidence* (pp. 47–55). Washington, DC: American Psychological Association.

Dweck, C. S. (2002). Messages that motivate: How praise molds students' beliefs, motivation, and performance (in surprising ways). In J. Aronson (Ed.), *Improving academic achievement: Impact of psychological factors on education* (pp. 37–60). San Diego, CA: Academic Press.

Dynarski, M., James-Burdumy, S., Moore, M., Rosenberg, L., Deke, J., & Mansfield, W. (2004). *When schools stay open late: The national evaluation of the 21st Century Community Learning Centers Program: New findings.* Washington DC: U.S. Department of Education.

Dzurova, D., & Pikhart, H. (2005). Down syndrome, paternal age and education: Comparison of California and the Czech Republic. *BMC Public Health, 5,* 69.

E

East, P. L., & Felice, M. E. (1996). *Adolescent pregnancy and parenting: Findings from a racially diverse sample.* Mahwah, NJ: Erlbaum.

Eaton, D. K., Davis, K. S., Barrios, L., Brener, N. D., & Noonan, R. K. (2007). Associations of dating violence victimization with lifetime participation, co-occurrence, and early initiation of risk behaviors among U.S. high school students. *Journal of Interpersonal Violence, 22,* 585–602.

Eaves, L., Silberg, J., Foley, D., Bulik, C., Maes, H., & Erkanli, A. (2004). Genetic and environmental influences on the relative timing of pubertal change. *Twin Research, 7,* 471–481.

Ebeling, K. S., & Gelman, S. A. (1994). Children's use of context in interpreting "big" and "little." *Child Development, 65,* 1178–1192.

Eberhard, J., Stein, S., & Geissbuehler, V. (2005). Experience of pain and analgesia with water and land births. *Journal of Psychosomatic Obstetrics and Gynecology, 26,* 127–133.

Eccles, J. S. (2004). Schools, academic motivation, and stage–environment fit. In R. M. Lerner & L. Steinberg (Eds.), *Handbook of adolescent psychology* (2nd ed., pp. 125–154). Hoboken, NJ: Wiley.

Eccles, J. S., & Gootman, J. (Eds.). (2002). *Community programs to promote youth development.* Washington, DC: National Academy Press.

Eccles, J. S., Jacobs, J., & Harold, R. D. (1990). Gender-role stereotypes, expectancy effects, and parents' role in the socialization of gender differences in self-perceptions and skill acquisition. *Journal of Social Issues, 46,* 183–201.

Eccles, J. S., Templeton, J., Barber, B., & Stone, M. (2003). Adolescence and emerging adulthood: The critical passage ways to adulthood. In M. H. Bornstein, L. Davidson, C. L. M. Keyes, K. A. Moore, & the Center for Child Well-Being (Eds.), *Well-being: Positive development across the life course* (pp. 383–406). Mahwah, NJ: Erlbaum.

Eccles, J. S., Vida, M. N., & Barber, B. (2004). The relation of early adolescents' college plans and both academic ability and task-value beliefs to subsequent college enrollment. *Journal of Early Adolescence, 24,* 63–77.

Eckerman, C. O., & Peterman, K. (2001). Peers and infant social/communicative development. In G. Bremner & A. Fogel (Eds.), *Blackwell handbook of infant development* (pp. 326–350). Malden, MA: Blackwell.

Eckerman, C. O., & Whitehead, H. (1999). How toddler peers generate coordinated action: A cross-cultural exploration. *Early Education and Development, 10,* 241–266.

Economic Policy Institute. (2010). *A broader, bolder approach to education.* Retrieved from www.boldapproach.org

Eder, R. A., & Mangelsdorf, S. C. (1997). The emotional basis of early personality development: Implications for the emergent self-concept. In R. Hogan, J. Johnson, & S. Briggs (Eds.), *Handbook of personality psychology* (pp. 209–240). San Diego, CA: Academic Press.

Edmondson, P. (2006). Deaf children's understanding of other people's thought processes. *Educational Psychology in Practice, 22,* 159–169.

Edwards, O. W., & Oakland, T. D. (2006). Factorial invariance of Woodcock-Johnson III scores for African Americans and Caucasian Americans. *Journal of Psychoeducational Assessment, 24,* 358–366.

Egeland, B., Jacobvitz, D., & Sroufe, L. A. (1988). Breaking the cycle of abuse. *Child Development, 59,* 1080–1088.

Ehri, L. C., & Roberts, T. (2006). The roots of learning to read and write: Acquisition of letters and phonemic awareness. In D. K. Dickinson & S. B. Neuman (Eds.),

Handbook of early literacy research (Vol. 2, pp. 113–131). New York: Guilford.

Eichstedt, J. A., Serbin, L. A., Poulin-Dubois, D., & Sen, M. G. (2002). Of bears and men: Infants' knowledge of conventional and metaphorical gender stereotypes. *Infant Behavior and Development, 25,* 296–310.

Einspieler, C., Marschik, P. B., & Prechtl, H. F. R. (2008). Human motor behavior: Prenatal origin and early postnatal development. *Zeitschrift für Psychologie, 216,* 147–153.

Eisbach, A. O. (2004). Children's developing awareness of diversity in people's trains of thought. *Child Development, 75,* 1694–1707.

Eisenberg, N. (2003). Prosocial behavior, empathy, and sympathy. In M. H. Bornstein & L. Davidson (Eds.), *Well-being: Positive development across the life course* (pp. 253–265). Mahwah, NJ: Erlbaum.

Eisenberg, N. (2010). Empathy-related responding: Links with self-regulation, moral judgment, and moral behavior. In M. Mikulincer & P. R. Shaver (Eds.), *Prosocial motives, emotions, and behavior: The better angels of our nature* (pp. 129-148). Washington, D. C.: American Psychological Association.

Eisenberg, N., Eggum, N. D., & Edwards, A. (2010). Empathy-related responding and moral development. In W. F. Arsenio & E. A. Lemerise (Eds.), *Emotions, aggression, and morality in children: Bridging development and psychopathology* (pp. 115–135). Washington, DC: American Psychological Association.

Eisenberg, N., Fabes, R. A., Shepard, S. A., Murphy, B. C., Jones, S., & Guthrie, I. K. (1998). Contemporaneous and longitudinal prediction of children's sympathy from dispositional regulation and emotionality. *Developmental Psychology, 34,* 910–924.

Eisenberg, N., Fabes, R. A., & Spinrad, T. L. (2006). Prosocial development. In N. Eisenberg (Ed.), *Handbook of child psychology: Vol. 3. Social, emotional, and personality development* (6th ed., pp. 646–718). Hoboken, NJ: Wiley.

Eisenberg, N., Sadovsky, A., Spinrad, T. L., Fabes, R. A., Losoya, S., & Valiente, C. (2005). The relations of problem behavior status to children's negative emotionality, effortful control, and impulsivity: Concurrent relations and prediction of change. *Developmental Psychology, 41,* 193–211.

Eisenberg, N., Smith, C. L., Sadovsky, A., & Spinrad, T. L. (2004a). Effortful control: Relations with emotion regulation, adjustment, and socialization in childhood. In R. Baumeister & K. D. Vohs (Eds.), *Handbook of self-regulation: Research, theory, and applications* (pp. 259–282). New York: Guilford.

Eisenberg, N., & Spinrad, T. L. (2004). Emotion-related regulation: Sharpening the definition. *Child Development, 75,* 334–339.

Eisenberg, N., Spinrad, T., Fabes, R., Reiser, M., Cumberland, A., & Shepard, S. (2004b). The relations of effortful control and impulsivity to children's resiliency and adjustment. *Child Development, 75,* 25–46.

Eisenberg, N., Zhou, Q., Spinrad, T. L., Valiente, C., Fabes, R. A., & Liew, J. (2005). Relations among positive parenting, children's effortful control, and externalizing problems: A three-wave longitudinal study. *Child Development, 76,* 1055–1071.

Ekeus, C., Christensson, K., & Hjern, A. (2003). Unintentional and violent injuries among preschool children of teenage mothers in Sweden: A national cohort study. *Journal of Epidemiology and Community Health, 58,* 680–685.

Ekman, P. (2003). *Emotions revealed.* New York: Times Books.

Ekman, P., & Friesen, W. (1972). Constants across culture in the face and emotion. *Journal of Personality and Social Psychology, 17,* 124–129.

Elfenbein, D. S., & Felice, M. E. (2003). Adolescent pregnancy. *Pediatric Clinics of North America, 50,* 781–800.

Eliakim, A., Friedland, O., Kowen, G., Wolach, B., & Nemet, D. (2004). Parental obesity and higher pre-intervention BMI reduce the likelihood of a

multidisciplinary childhood obesity program to succeed: A clinical observation. *Journal of Pediatric Endocrinology and Metabolism, 17,* 1055–1061.

Elias, C. L., & Berk, L. E. (2002). Self-regulation in young children: Is there a role for sociodramatic play? *Early Childhood Research Quarterly, 17,* 1–17.

Elias, M. J., Parker, S., & Rosenblatt, J. L. (2005). Building educational opportunity. In S. Goldstein & R. B. Brooks (Eds.), *Handbook of resilience in children* (pp. 315–336). New York: Kluwer Academic.

Elicker, J., Englund, M., & Sroufe, L. A. (1992). Predicting peer competence and peer relationships in childhood from early parent–child relationships. In R. D. Parke & G. W. Ladd (Eds.), *Family–peer relationships: Modes of linkage* (pp. 77–106). Hillsdale, NJ: Erlbaum.

Elkind, D. (1994). *A sympathetic understanding of the child: Birth to sixteen* (3rd ed.). Boston: Allyn and Bacon.

Elkind, D., & Bowen, R. (1979). Imaginary audience behavior in children and adolescents. *Developmental Psychology, 15,* 33–44.

Ellickson, P. L., D'Amico, E. J., Collins, R. L., & Klein, D. J. (2005). Marijuana use and later problems: When frequency of recent use explains age of initiation effects. *Substance Use and Misuse, 40,* 343–359.

Elliott, J. G. (1999). School refusal: Issues of conceptualization, assessment, and treatment. *Journal of Child Psychology and Psychiatry and Allied Disciplines, 40,* 1001–1012.

Ellis, A. E., & Oakes, L. M. (2006). Infants flexibly use different dimensions to categorize objects. *Developmental Psychology, 42,* 1000–1011.

Ellis, B. J. (2004). Timing of pubertal maturation in girls: An integrated life history approach. *Psychological Bulletin, 130,* 920–958.

Ellis, B. J., Bates, J. E., Dodge, K. A., Fergusson, D. M., Horwood, L. J., Pettit, G. S., & Woodward, L. (2003). Does father absence place daughters at special risk for early sexual activity and teenage pregnancy? *Child Development, 74,* 801–821.

Ellis, B. J., & Essex, M. J. (2007). Family environments, adrenarche, and sexual maturation: A longitudinal test of a life history model. *Child Development, 78,* 1799–1817.

Ellis, L., & Bonin, S. L. (2003). Genetics and occupation-related preferences: Evidence from adoptive and non-adoptive families. *Personality and Individual Differences, 35,* 929–937.

Ellis, W. E., & Zarbatany, L. (2007). Explaining friendship formation and friendship stability: The role of children's and friends' aggression and victimization. *Merrill-Palmer Quarterly, 53,* 79–104.

Elman, J. L. (2001). Connectionism and language acquisition. In M. Tomasello & E. Bates (Eds.), *Language development* (pp. 295–306). Oxford, UK: Blackwell.

Else-Quest, N. M., Hyde, J. S., Goldsmith, H. H., & Van Hulle, C. A. (2006). Gender differences in temperament: A meta-analysis. *Psychological Bulletin, 132,* 33–72.

El-Sheikh, M., Cummings, E. M., & Reiter, S. (1996). Preschoolers' responses to ongoing interadult conflict: The role of prior exposure to resolved versus unresolved arguments. *Journal of Abnormal Child Psychology, 24,* 665–679.

Eltzschig, H. K., Lieberman, E. S., & Camann, W. R. (2003). Regional anesthesia and analgesia for labor and delivery. *New England Journal of Medicine, 384,* 319–332.

Eluvathingal, T. J., Chugani, H. T., Behen, M. E., Juhasz, C., Muzik, O., Maqbook, M., et al. (2006). Abnormal brain connectivity in children after early severe socioemotional deprivation: A diffusion tensor imaging study. *Pediatrics, 117,* 2093–2100.

Emery, R. E., Sbarra, D., & Grover, T. (2005). Divorce mediation: Research and reflections. *Family Court Review, 43,* 22–37.

Emory, E. K., Schlackman, L. J., & Fiano, K. (1996). Drug–hormone interactions on neurobehavioral responses in human neonates. *Infant Behavior and Development, 19,* 213–220.

Englund, M. E., Egeland, B., & Collins, W. A. (2008). Exceptions to high school dropout predictions in a low-income sample: Do adults make a difference? *Journal of Social Issues, 64,* 77–93.

Ennemoser, M., & Schneider, W. (2007). Relations of television viewing and reading: Findings from a 4-year longitudinal study. *Journal of Educational Psychology, 99,* 349–368.

Entwisle, D. R., Alexander, K. L., & Olson, L. S. (2005). First grade and educational attainment by age 22: A new story. *American Journal of Sociology, 110,* 1458–1502.

Epstein, L. H., Roemmich, J. N., & Raynor, H. A. (2001). Behavioral therapy in the treatment of pediatric obesity. *Pediatric Clinics of North America, 48,* 981–983.

Epstein, L. H., Saelens, B. E., Myers, M. D., & Vito, D. (1997). Effects of decreasing sedentary behaviors on activity choice in obese children. *Health Psychology, 16,* 107–113.

Epstein, L. H., Saelens, B. E., & O'Brien, J. G. (1995). Effects of reinforcing increases in active versus decreases in sedentary behavior for obese children. *International Journal of Behavioral Medicine, 2,* 41–50.

Erath, S. A., Bierman, K. L., & the Conduct Problems Prevention Research Group. (2006). Aggressive marital conflict, maternal harsh punishment, and child aggressive-disruptive behavior: Evidence for direct and mediate relations. *Journal of Family Psychology, 20,* 217–226.

Erden, F., & Wolfgang, C. H. (2004). An exploration of the differences in prekindergarten, kindergarten, and first-grade teachers' beliefs related to discipline when dealing with male and female students. *Early Child Development and Care, 174,* 3–11.

Erickson, J. D., Patterson, J. M., Wall, M., & Neumark-Sztainer, D. (2005). Risk behaviors and emotional well-being in youth with chronic health conditions. *Children's Health Care, 34,* 181–192.

Erikson, E. H. (1950). *Childhood and society.* New York: Norton.

Erikson, E. H. (1968). *Identity, youth, and crisis.* New York: Norton.

Ernst, M., Moolchan, E. T., & Robinson, M. L. (2001). Behavioral and neural consequences of prenatal exposure to nicotine. *Journal of the American Academy of Child and Adolescent Psychiatry, 40,* 630–641.

Eshel, Y., & Kohavi, R. (2003). Perceived classroom control, self-regulated learning strategies, and academic achievement. *Educational Psychology, 23,* 249–260.

Espy, K. A., Molfese, V. J., & DiLalla, L. F. (2001). Effects of environmental measures on intelligence in young children: Growth curve modeling of longitudinal data. *Merrill-Palmer Quarterly, 47,* 42–73.

Estourgie-van Burk, G. F., Bartels, M., van Beijsterveldt, T. C., Delemarre-van de Waal, H. A., & Boomsma, D. I. (2006). Body size in five-year-old twins: Heritability and comparison to singleton standards. *Twin Research and Human Genetics, 9,* 646–655.

Ethier, K. A., Kershaw, T., Niccolai, L., Lewis, J. B., & Ickovics, J. R. (2003). Adolescent women underestimate their susceptibility to sexually transmitted infections. *Sexually Transmitted Infections, 79,* 408–411.

Evanoo, G. (2007). Infant crying: A clinical conundrum. *Journal of Pediatric Health Care, 21,* 333–338.

Evans, A. M. (2008). Growing pains: Contemporary knowledge and recommended practice. *Journal of Foot and Ankle Research, 1,* 4.

Evans, E., Hawton, K., & Rodham, K. (2004). Factors associated with suicidal phenomena in adolescents: A systematic review of population-based studies. *Clinical Psychology Review, 24,* 957–979.

Evans, G. W. (2006). Child development and the physical environment. *Annual Review of Psychology, 57,* 424–451.

Evans, G. W., Maxwell, L. E., & Hart, B. (1999). Parental language and verbal responsiveness to children in crowded homes. *Developmental Psychology, 35,* 1020–1023.

Everman, D. B., & Cassidy, S. B. (2000). Genetics of childhood disorders: XII. Genomic imprinting: Breaking the rules. *Journal of the American Academy of Child and Adolescent Psychiatry, 38,* 386–389.

F

Fabes, R. A., Eisenberg, N., Hanish, L. D., & Spinrad, T. L. (2001). Preschoolers' spontaneous emotion vocabulary: Relations to likability. *Early Education and Development, 12,* 11–27.

Fabes, R. A., Eisenberg, N., McCormick, S. E., & Wilson, M. S. (1988). Preschoolers' attributions of the situational determinants of others' naturally occurring emotions. *Developmental Psychology, 24,* 376–385.

Fabes, R. A., Martin, C. L., & Hanish, L. D. (2003). Young children's play qualities in same-, other-, and mixed-sex peer groups. *Child Development, 74,* 921–932.

Facio, A., & Micocci, F. (2003). Emerging adulthood in Argentina. *New Directions for Child and Adolescent Development, 100,* 21–31.

Fagan, J. F., & Holland, C. R. (2007). Racial equality in intelligence: Predictions from a theory of intelligence as processing. *Intelligence, 35,* 319–334.

Fagan, J. F., Holland, C. R., & Wheeler, K. (2007). The prediction, from infancy, of adult IQ and achievement. *Intelligence, 35,* 225–231.

Fagan, J. F., III. (1973). Infants' delayed recognition memory and forgetting. *Journal of Experimental Child Psychology, 16,* 424–450.

Fagard, J., & Pezé, A. (1997). Age changes in interlimb coupling and the development of bimanual coordination. *Journal of Motor Behavior, 29,* 199–208.

Fagard, J., Spelke, E., & von Hofsten, C. (2009). Reaching and grasping a moving object in 6-, 8-, and 10-month-old infants: Laterality and performance. *Infant Behavior and Development, 32,* 137–146.

Fagot, B. I. (1984). The child's expectations of differences in adult male and female interactions. *Sex Roles, 11,* 593–600.

Fagot, B. I. (1985). Changes in thinking about early sex role development. *Developmental Review, 5,* 83–98.

Fagot, B. I., & Hagan, R. I. (1991). Observations of parent reactions to sex-stereotyped behaviors: Age and sex effects. *Child Development, 62,* 617–628.

Fagot, B. I., & Leinbach, M. D. (1989). The young child's gender schema: Environmental input, internal organization. *Child Development, 60,* 663–672.

Fahrmeier, E. D. (1978). The development of concrete operations among the Hausa. *Journal of Cross-Cultural Psychology, 9,* 23–44.

Fairburn, C. G. (2005). Evidence-based treatment of anorexia nervosa. *International Journal of Eating Disorders, 37,* S26–S30.

Fairburn, C. G., & Harrison, P. J. (2003). Eating disorders. *Lancet, 361,* 407–416.

Faircloth, B. S., & Hamm, J. V. (2005). Sense of belonging among high school students representing four ethnic groups. *Journal of Youth and Adolescence, 34,* 293–309.

Falbo, T. (1992). Social norms and the one-child family: Clinical and policy implications. In F. Boer & J. Dunn (Eds.), *Children's sibling relationships* (pp. 71–82). Hillsdale, NJ: Erlbaum.

Falbo, T., & Poston, D. L., Jr. (1993). The academic, personality, and physical outcomes of only children in China. *Child Development, 64,* 18–35.

Falbo, T., Poston, D. L., Jr., Triscari, R. S., & Zhang, X. (1997). Self-enhancing illusions among Chinese schoolchildren. *Journal of Cross-Cultural Psychology, 28,* 172–191.

Falk, D. (2005). Brain lateralization in primates and its evolution in hominids. *American Journal of Physical Anthropology, 30,* 107–125.

Fantz, R. L. (1961, May). The origin of form perception. *Scientific American, 204*(5), 66–72.

Faraone, S. V. (2008). Statistical and molecular genetic approaches to developmental psychopathology: The pathway forward. In J. J. Hudziak (Ed.), *Developmental psychology and wellness: Genetic and environmental influences* (pp. 245–265). Washington, DC: American Psychiatric Publishing.

Faraone, S. V., & Mick, E. (2010). Molecular genetics of attention deficit hyperactivity disorder. *Psychiatric Clinics of North America, 33,* 159–180.

Farmer, T. W., Leung, M., Pearl, R., Rodkin, P. C., Cadwallader, T. W., & Van Acker, R. (2002). Deviant or diverse peer groups? The peer affiliations of aggressive elementary students. *Journal of Educational Psychology, 94,* 611–620.

Farr, R. H., Forssell, S. L., & Patterson, C. J. (2010). Parenting and child development in adoptive families: Does parental sexual orientation matter? *Applied Developmental Science, 14,* 164–178.

Farrant, K., & Reese, E. (2000). Maternal style and children's participation in reminiscing: Stepping stones in children's autobiographical memory development. *Journal of Cognition and Development, 1,* 193–225.

Farrington, D. P. (2004). Conduct disorder, aggression, and delinquency. In R. M. Lerner & L. Steinberg (Eds.), *Handbook of adolescent psychology* (2nd ed., pp. 627–664). New York: Wiley.

Farrington, D. P. (2009). Conduct disorder, aggression, and delinquency. In R. M. Lerner & L. Steinberg (Eds.), *Handbook of adolescent psychology: Vol. 1. Individual bases of adolescent development* (3rd ed., pp. 683–722). Hoboken, NJ: Wiley.

Farroni, T., Csibra, G., Simion, F., & Johnson, M. H. (2002). Eye contact detection in humans from birth. *Proceedings of the National Academy of Sciences, 99,* 9602–9605.

Farroni, T., Massaccesi, S., Menon, E., & Johnson, M. H. (2007). Direct gaze modulates face recognition in young infants. *Cognition, 102,* 396–404.

Farver, J. M., & Branstetter, W. H. (1994). Preschoolers' prosocial responses to their peers' distress. *Developmental Psychology, 30,* 334–341.

Farver, J. M., Kim, Y. K., & Lee, Y. (1995). Cultural differences in Korean- and Anglo-American preschoolers' social interaction and play behaviors. *Child Development, 66,* 1099–1099.

Farver, J. M., & Wimbarti, S. (1995). Indonesian children's play with their mothers and older siblings. *Child Development, 66,* 1493–1503.

Fashola, O. S., & Slavin, R. E. (1998). Effective dropout prevention and college attendance programs for students placed at risk. *Journal of Education for Students Placed at Risk, 3,* 159–183.

Fasolo, M., Majorano, M., & D'Odorico, L. (2008). Babbling and first words in children with slow expressive development. *Clinical Linguistics and Phonetics, 22,* 83–94.

Fasula, A. M., & Miller, K. S. (2006). African-American and Hispanic adolescents' intentions to delay first intercourse: Parental communication as a buffer for sexually active peers. *Journal of Adolescent Health, 38,* 193–200.

Fattibene, P., Mazzei, F., Nuccetelli, C., & Risica, S. (1999). Prenatal exposure to ionizing radiation: Sources, effects, and regulatory aspects. *Acta Paediatrica, 88,* 693–702.

Fearon, R. P., Bakermans-Kranenburg, M. J., Lapsley, A., & Roisman, G. I. (2010). The significance of insecure attachment and disorganization in the development of children's externalizing behavior: A meta-analytic study. *Child Development, 81,* 435–456.

Federal Interagency Forum on Child and Family Statistics. (2008). *America's children: Key national indicators of well-being, 2008.* Retrieved from www.childstats.gov/americaschildren/tables.asp

Federal Interagency Forum on Child and Family Statistics. (2009). *America's children: Key national indicators of well-being, 2009.* Washington, DC: U.S. Government Printing Office.

Federico, M. J., & Liu, A. H. (2003). Overcoming childhood asthma disparities of the inner-city poor. *Pediatric Clinics of North America, 50,* 655–675.

Feeney, J. A., Hohaus, L., Noller, P., & Alexander, R. P. (2001). *Becoming parents: Exploring the bonds between mothers, fathers, and their infants.* New York: Cambridge University Press.

Feigelman, W., & Gorman, B. S. (2008). Assessing the effects of peer suicide on youth suicide. *Suicide and Life-Threatening Behavior, 38,* 181–194.

Feinberg, M. E., McHale, S. M., Crouter, A. C., & Cumsille, P. (2003). Sibling differentiation: Sibling and parent relationship trajectories in adolescence. *Child Development, 74,* 1261–1274.

Feiring, C., Taska, L., & Lewis, M. (1999). Age and gender differences in children's and adolescents' adaptation to sexual abuse. *Child Abuse and Neglect, 23,* 115–128.

Feldkámper, M., & Schaeffel, F. (2003). Interactions of genes and environment in myopia. *Developmental Ophthalmology, 37,* 34–49.

Feldman, A. F., & Matjasko, J. L. (2007). Profiles and portfolios of adolescent school-based extracurricular activity participation. *Journal of Adolescence, 30,* 313–332.

Feldman, D. H. (2004). Piaget's stages: The unfinished symphony of cognitive development. *New Ideas in Psychology, 3,* 175–231.

Feldman, R. (2003). Infant–mother and infant–father synchrony: The coregulation of positive arousal. *Infant Mental Health Journal, 24,* 1–23.

Feldman, R. (2006). From biological rhythms to social rhythms: Physiological precursors of mother–infant synchrony. *Developmental Psychology, 42,* 175–188.

Feldman, R. (2007a). Maternal–infant contact and child development: Insights from the kangaroo intervention. In L. L'Abate (Ed.), *Low-cost approaches to promote physical and mental health: Theory, research, and practice* (pp. 323–351). New York: Springer.

Feldman, R. (2007b). Maternal versus child risk and the development of parent–child and family relationships in five high-risk populations. *Development and Psychopathology, 19,* 293–312.

Feldman, R., & Eidelman, A. I. (2003). Skin-to-skin contact (kangaroo care) accelerates autonomic and neurobehavioral maturation in preterm infants. *Developmental Medicine and Child Neurology, 45,* 274–281.

Feldman, R., Eidelman, A. I., & Rotenberg, N. (2004). Parenting stress, infant emotion regulation, maternal sensitivity, and the cognitive development of triplets: A model for parent and child influences in a unique ecology. *Child Development, 75,* 1774–1791.

Feldman, R., Eidelman, A., Sirota, L., & Weller, A. (2002). Comparison of skin-to-skin (kangaroo) and traditional care: Parenting outcomes and preterm infant development. *Pediatrics, 110,* 16–26.

Feldman, R., Greenbaum, C. W., & Yirmiya, N. (1999). Mother–infant affect synchrony as an antecedent of the emergence of self-control. *Developmental Psychology, 35,* 223–231.

Feldman, R., & Klein, P. S. (2003). Toddlers' self-regulated compliance to mothers, caregivers, and fathers: Implications for theories of socialization. *Developmental Psychology, 39,* 680–692.

Feldman, R., Sussman, A. L., & Zigler, E. (2004). Parental leave and work adaptation at the transition to parenthood: Individual, marital, and social correlates. *Journal of Applied Developmental Psychology, 25,* 459–479.

Feldman, R., Weller, A., Sirota, L., & Eidelman, A. I. (2003). Testing a family intervention hypothesis: The contribution of mother–infant skin-to-skin contact (kangaroo care) to family interaction, proximity, and touch. *Journal of Family Psychology, 17,* 94–107.

Felner, R. D., Favazza, A., Shim, M., Brand, S., Gu, K., & Noonan, N. (2002). Whole school improvement and restructuring as prevention and promotion: Lessons from STEP and the Project on High Performance Learning Communities. *Journal of School Psychology, 39,* 177–202.

Felsman, D. E., & Blustein, D. L. (1999). The role of peer relatedness in late adolescent career development. *Journal of Vocational Behavior, 54,* 279–295.

Feng, Q. (2005). Postnatal consequences of prenatal cocaine exposure and myocardial apoptosis: Does cocaine in utero imperil the adult heart? *British Journal of Pharmacology, 144,* 887–888.

Fenson, L., Dale, P. S., Reznick, J. S., Bates, E., Thal, D. J., & Pethick, S. J. (1994). Variability in early communicative development. *Monographs of the Society for Research in Child Development, 59*(5, Serial No. 242).

Ferguson, T. J., Stegge, H., & Damhuis, I. (1991). Children's understanding of guilt and shame. *Child Development, 62,* 827–839.

Fergusson, D. M., & Horwood, J. (2003). Resilience to childhood adversity: Results of a 21-year study. In S. S. Luthar (Ed.), *Resilience and vulnerability* (pp. 130–155). New York: Cambridge University Press.

Fergusson, D. M., & Woodward, L. J. (1999). Breast-feeding and later psychosocial adjustment. *Paediatric and Perinatal Epidemiology, 13,* 144–157.

Fernald, A., & Morikawa, H. (1993). Common themes and cultural variations in Japanese and American mothers' speech to infants. *Child Development, 64,* 637–656.

Fernald, A., Perfors, A., & Marchman, V. A. (2006). Picking up speed in understanding: Speech processing efficiency and vocabulary growth across the 2nd year. *Developmental Psychology, 42,* 98–116.

Fernald, A., Taeschner, T., Dunn, J., Papousek, M., Boysson-Bardies, B., & Fukui, I. (1989). A cross-language study of prosodic modifications in mothers' and fathers' speech to preverbal infants. *Journal of Child Language, 16,* 477–502.

Fernald, L. C., & Grantham-McGregor, S. M. (1998). Stress response in school-age children who have been growth-retarded since early childhood. *American Journal of Clinical Nutrition, 68,* 691–698.

Fernyhough, C., & Fradley, E. (2005). Private speech on an executive task: Relations with task difficulty and task performance. *Cognitive Development, 20,* 103–120.

Ficca, G., Fagioli, I., Giganti, F., & Salzarulo, P. (1999). Spontaneous awakenings from sleep in the first year of life. *Early Human Development, 55,* 219–228.

Field, T. M. (1998). Massage therapy effects. *American Psychologist, 53,* 1270–1281.

Field, T. (2001). Massage therapy facilitates weight gain in preterm infants. *Current Directions in Psychological Science, 10,* 51–54.

Field, T., Diego, M., Hernandez-Reif, M., Figueiredo, B., Schanberg, S., & Kuhn, C. (2007). Sleep disturbances in depressed pregnant women and their newborns. *Infant Behavior and Development, 30,* 127–133.

Field, T., Hernandez-Reif, M., Feijo, L., & Freedman, J. (2006). Prenatal, perinatal and neonatal stimulation: A survey of neonatal nurseries. *Infant Behavior and Development, 29,* 24–31.

Field, T., Hernandez-Reif, M., & Freedman, J. (2004) Stimulation programs for preterm infants. *Social Policy Report of the Society for Research in Child Development, 18*(1).

Fiese, B. H., & Schwartz, M. (2008). Reclaiming the family table: Mealtimes and child health and wellbeing. *Social Policy Report of the Society for Research in Child Development, 22*(4), 3–18.

Figner, B., Mackinlay, R. J., Wilkening, F., & Weber, E. U. (2009). Affective and deliberative processes in risky choice: Age differences in risk taking in the Columbia Card Task. *Journal of Experimental Psychology: Learning, Memory, and Cognition, 35,* 709–770.

Findlay, L. C., & Coplan, R. J. (2008). Come out and play: Shyness in childhood and the benefits of organized sports participation. *Canadian Journal of Behavioural Science, 40,* 153–161.

Finger, B., Hans, S. L., Bernstein, V. J., & Cox, S. M. (2009). Parent relationship quality and infant–mother attachment. *Attachment and Human Development, 11,* 285–306.

Fingerhut, L. A., & Christoffel, K. K. (2002). Firearm-related death and injury among children and adolescents. *Future of Children, 12,* 25–37.

Finkelstein, E. A., Trogdon, J. G., Cohen, J. W., & Dietz, W. (2009). Annual medical spending attributable to obesity: Payer- and service-specific estimates. *Health Affairs, 28,* w822–w831.

Finn, J. D., Gerber, S. B., & Boyd-Zaharias, J. (2005). Small classes in the early grades, academic achievement, and graduating from high school. *Journal of Educational Psychology, 97,* 214–233.

Finnilä, K., Mahlberga, N., Santtilia, P., & Niemib, P. (2003). Validity of a test of children's suggestibility for predicting responses to two interview situations differing in degree of suggestiveness. *Journal of Experimental Child Psychology, 85,* 32–49.

Fischer, K. W., & Bidell, T. (1991). Constraining nativisit inferences about cognitive capacities. In S. Carey & R. Gelman (Eds.), *The epigenesis of mind: Essays on biology and cognition* (pp. 199–235). Hillsdale, NJ: Erlbaum.

Fischer, K. W., & Bidell, T. R. (2006). Dynamic development of action and thought. In R. M. Lerner (Ed.), *Handbook of child psychology: Vol. 1. Theoretical models of human development* (6th ed., pp. 313–399). Hoboken, NJ: Wiley.

Fischman, M. G., Moore, J. B., & Steele, K. H. (1992). Children's one-hand catching as a function of age, gender, and ball location. *Research Quarterly for Exercise and Sport, 63,* 349–355.

Fish, M. (2004). Attachment in infancy and preschool in low socioeconomic status rural Appalachian children: Stability and change and relations to preschool and kindergarten competence. *Development and Psychopathology, 16,* 293–312.

Fisher, C. B. (1993, Winter). Integrating science and ethics in research with high-risk children and youth. *Social Policy Report of the Society for Research in Child Development, 4*(4).

Fisher, C. B., Hoagwood, K., Boyce, C., Duster, T., Frank, D. A., & Grisso, T. (2002). Research ethics for mental health science involving ethnic minority children and youths. *American Psychologist, 57,* 1024–1040.

Fisher, J. O., & Birch, L. L. (1999). Restricting access to palatable foods affects children's behavioral response, food selection, and intake. *American Journal of Clinical Nutrition, 69,* 1264–1272.

Fisher, J. O., Mitchell, D. S., Smiciklas-Wright, H., & Birch, L. L. (2001). Maternal milk consumption predicts the tradeoff between milk and soft drinks in young girls' diets. *Journal of Nutrition, 131,* 246–250.

Fisher, J. O., Rolls, B. J., & Birch, L. L. (2003). Children's bite size and intake of an entrée are greater with large portions than with age-appropriate or self-selected portions. *American Journal of Clinical Nutrition, 77,* 1164–1170.

Fisher, L., Ames, E. W., Chisholm, K., & Savoie, L. (1997). Problems reported by parents of Romanian orphans adopted to British Columbia. *International Journal of Behavioral Development, 20,* 67–82.

Fisher, S. E., Francks, C., McCracken, J. T., McGough, J. J., Marlow, A. J., & MacPhie, I. L. (2002). A genomewide scan for loci involved in attention-deficit/hyperactivity disorder. *American Journal of Human Genetics, 70,* 1183–1196.

Fite, P. J., Stauffacher, K., Ostrov, J. M., & Colder, C. R. (2008). Replication and extension of Little et al.'s (2003) forms and functions of aggression measure. *International Journal of Behavioral Development, 32,* 238–242.

FitzGerald, D. P., & White, K. J. (2003). Linking children's social worlds: Perspective-taking in parent–child and peer contexts. *Social Behavior and Personality, 31,* 509–522.

Fivush, R. (2001). Owning experience: Developing subjective perspective in autobiographical narratives. In C. Moore & K. Lemmon (Eds.), *The self in time: Developmental perspectives* (pp. 35–52). Mahwah, NJ: Erlbaum.

Fivush, R., & Haden, C. A. (2005). Parent–child reminiscing and the construction of a subjective self. In B. D. Homer & C. S. Tamis-LeMonda (Eds.), *The development of social cognition and communication* (pp. 315–336). Mahwah, NJ: Erlbaum.

Fivush, R., & Wang, Q. (2005). Emotion talk in mother–child conversations of the shared past: The effects of culture, gender, and event valence. *Journal of Cognition and Development, 6,* 489–506.

Flanagan, C. A., & Faison, N. (2001). Youth civic development: Implications of research for social policy and programs. *Social Policy Report of the Society for Research in Child Development, 15*(1).

Flanagan, C. A., Jonsson, B., Botcheva, L., Csapo, B., Bowes, J., Macek, P., Averina, I., & Sheblanova, E.

(1999). Adolescents and the social contract: Developmental roots of citizenship in seven countries. In M. Yates & J. Youniss (Eds.), *Roots of civic identity: International perspectives on community service and activism in youth* (pp. 135–155). New York: Cambridge University Press.

Flanagan, C. A., Stout, M., & Gallay, L. S. (2008). It's my body and none of your business: Developmental changes in adolescents' perceptions of rights concerning health. *Journal of Social Issues, 64,* 815–834.

Flanagan, C. A., & Tucker, C. J. (1999). Adolescents' explanations for political issues: Concordance with their views of self and society. *Developmental Psychology, 35,* 1198–1209.

Flannery, D. J., Hussey, D. L., Biebelhausen, L., & Wester, K. L. (2003). Crime, delinquency, and youth gangs. In G. R. Adams & M. D. Berzonsky (Eds.), *Blackwell handbook of adolescence* (pp. 502–522). Malden, MA: Blackwell.

Flannery, K. A., & Liederman, J. (1995). Is there really a syndrome involving the co-occurrence of neurodevelopmental disorder, talent, non-right handedness and immune disorder among children? *Cortex, 31,* 503–515.

Flavell, J. H. (2000). Development of children's knowledge about the mental world. *International Journal of Behavioral Development, 24,* 15–23.

Flavell, J. H., Flavell, E. R., & Green, F. L. (2001). Development of children's understanding of connections between thinking and feeling. *Psychological Science, 12,* 430–432.

Flavell, J. H., Green, F. L., & Flavell, E. R. (1987). Development of knowledge about the appearance–reality distinction. *Monographs of the Society for Research in Child Development, 51*(1, Serial No. 212).

Flavell, J. H., Green, F. L., & Flavell, E. R. (1993). Children's understanding of the stream of consciousness. *Child Development, 64,* 387–398.

Flavell, J. H., Green, F. L., & Flavell, E. R. (1995). Young children's knowledge about thinking. *Monographs of the Society for Research in Child Development, 60*(1, Serial No. 243).

Flavell, J. H., Green, F. L., Flavell, E. R., & Grossman, J. B. (1997). The development of children's knowledge about inner speech. *Child Development, 68,* 39–47.

Flegal, K. M., Carroll, M. D., Ogden, C. L., & Curtin, L. R. (2010). Prevalence and trends in obesity among U.S. adults, 1999–2008. *Journal of the American Medical Association, 303,* 235–241.

Flegal, K. M., Graubard, B. I., Williamson, D. F., & Gail, M. H. (2007). Cause-specific excess deaths associated with underweight, overweight, and obesity. *Journal of the American Medical Association, 299,* 1260–1261.

Fletcher, A. C., Nickerson, P., & Wright, K. L. (2003). Structured leisure activities in middle childhood: Links to well-being. *Journal of Community Psychology, 31,* 641–659.

Floccia, C., Christophe, A., & Bertoncini, J. (1997). High-amplitude sucking and newborns: The quest for underlying mechanisms. *Journal of Experimental Child Psychology, 64,* 175–198.

Flom, R., & Pick, A. D. (2003). Verbal encouragement and joint attention in 18-month-old infants. *Infant Behavior and Development, 26,* 121–134.

Florsheim, P., & Smith, A. (2005). Expectant adolescent couples' relations and subsequent parenting behavior. *Infant Mental Health Journal, 26,* 533–548.

Flouri, E., & Buchanan, A. (2004). Early father's and mother's involvement and child's later educational outcomes. *British Journal of Educational Psychology, 74,* 141–153.

Flynn, E. (2006). A microgenetic investigation of stability and continuity in theory of mind development. *British Journal of Developmental Psychology, 24,* 631–654.

Flynn, E., & Siegler, R. (2007). Measuring change: Current trends and future directions in microgenetic research. *Infant and Child Development, 16,* 135–149.

Flynn, J. R. (1999). Searching for justice: The discovery of IQ gains over time. *American Psychologist, 54,* 5–20.

Flynn, J. R. (2003). Movies about intelligence: The limitations of *g. Current Directions in Psychological Science, 12,* 95–99.

Flynn, J. R. (2007). *What is intelligence? Beyond the Flynn effect.* New York: Cambridge University Press.

Foehr, U. G. (2006). *Media multitasking among American youth: Prevalence, predictors, and pairings.* Menlo Park: Kaiser Family Foundation.

Foerde, K., Knowlton, B. J., & Poldrack, R. A. (2006). Modulation of competing memory systems by distraction. *Proceedings of the National Academy of Sciences, 103,* 11778–11783.

Fogel, A. (1993). *Developing through relationships: Origins of communication, self and culture.* New York: Harvester Wheatsheaf.

Fogel, A., & Garvey, A. (2007). Alive communication. *Infant Behavior and Development, 30,* 251–257.

Fomon, S. J., & Nelson, S. E. (2002). Body composition of the male and female reference infants. *Annual Review of Nutrition, 22,* 1–17.

Fordham, K., & Stevenson-Hinde, J. (1999). Shyness, friendship quality, and adjustment during middle childhood. *Journal of Child Psychology and Psychiatry, 40,* 757–768.

Forman, D. R., Aksan, N., & Kochanska, G. (2004). Toddlers' responsive imitation predicts preschool-age conscience. *Psychological Science, 15,* 699–704.

Forman, D. R., O'Hara, M. W., Stuart, S., Gorman, L. L., Larsen, K. E., & Coy, K. C. (2007). Effective treatment for postpartum depression is not sufficient to improve the developing mother–child relationship. *Development and Psychopathology, 19,* 585–602.

Foster, J. A., Gore, S. A., & West, D. S. (2006). Altering TV viewing habits: An unexplored strategy for adult obesity intervention? *American Journal of Health Behavior, 30,* 3–14.

Foster, M. A., Lambert, R., Abbott-Shim, M., McCarty, F., & Franze, S. (2005). A model of home learning environment and social risk factors in relation to children's emergent literacy and social outcomes. *Early Childhood Research Quarterly, 20,* 13–36.

Foster, W. A., & Miller, M. (2007). Development of the literacy achievement gap: A longitudinal study of kindergarten through third grade. *Language, Speech, and Hearing Services in Schools, 38,* 173–181.

Fox, C. L., & Boulton, M. J. (2006). Friendship as a moderator of the relationship between social skills problems and peer victimization. *Aggressive Behavior, 32,* 110–121.

Fox, N. A. (1991). If it's not left, it's right: Electroencephalograph asymmetry and the development of emotion. *American Psychologist, 46,* 863–872.

Fox, N. A., & Calkins, S. D. (2003). The development of self-control of emotion: Intrinsic and extrinsic influences. *Motivation and Emotion, 27,* 7–26.

Fox, N. A., & Davidson, R. J. (1986). Taste-elicited changes in facial signs of emotion and the asymmetry of brain electrical activity in newborn infants. *Neuropsychologia, 24,* 417–422.

Foy, J. G., & Mann, V. (2003). Home literacy environment and phonological awareness in preschool children: Differential effects for rhyme and phoneme awareness. *Applied Psycholinguistics, 24,* 59–88.

Fraiberg, S. (1971). *Insights from the blind.* New York: Basic Books.

Franco, P., Danias, A. P., Akamine, E. H., Kawamoto, E. M., Fortes, Z. B., Scavone, C., & Tostes, R. C. (2002). Enhanced oxidative stress as a potential mechanism underlying the programming of hypertension in utero. *Journal of Cardiovascular Pharmacology, 40,* 501–509.

Frank, D. A., Rose-Jacobs, R., Beeghly, M., Wilbur, M., Bellinger, D., & Cabral, H. (2005). Level of prenatal cocaine exposure and 48-month IQ: Importance of preschool enrichment. *Neurotoxicology and Teratology, 27,* 15–28.

Frank, J. B., Jarit, G. J., Bravman, J. T., & Rosen, J. E. (2007). Lower extremity injuries in the skeletally immature athlete. *Journal of the American Academy of Orthopaedic Surgeons, 15,* 356–366.

Frankenburg, E., & Orfield, G. (2007). *Lessons in integration: Realizing the promise of racial diversity in American schools.* Charlottesville, VA: University of Virginia Press.

Frederiksen-Goldsen, K. I., & Sharlach, A. E. (2000). *Families and work: New directions in the twenty-first century.* New York: Oxford University Press.

Fredricks, J. A., & Eccles, J. S. (2002). Children's competence and value beliefs from childhood through adolescence: Growth trajectories in two male-sex-typed domains. *Developmental Psychology, 38,* 519–533.

Fredricks, J. A., & Eccles, J. S. (2005). Developmental benefits of extracurricular involvement: Do peer characteristics mediate the link between activities and youth outcomes? *Journal of Youth and Adolescence, 34,* 507–520.

Fredricks, J. A., & Eccles, J. S. (2006). Is extracurricular participation associated with beneficial outcomes? Concurrent and longitudinal relations. *Developmental Psychology, 42,* 698–713.

Freedman, D. S., Khan, L. K., Serdula, M. K., Dietz, W. H., Srinivasan, S. R., & Berenson, G. S. (2002). Relation of age at menarche to race, time period, and anthropometric dimensions: The Bogalusa Heart Study. *Pediatrics, 110,* e43–e49.

Freeman, C. E. (2004). *Trends in educational equity of girls and women: 2004.* U.S. Department of Education, National Center for Education Statistics. Washington, DC: U.S. Government Printing Office.

Freeman, D. (1983). *Margaret Mead and Samoa: The making and unmaking of an anthropological myth.* Cambridge, MA: Harvard University Press.

Freeman, H., & Newland, L. A. (2010). New directions in father attachment. *Early Child Development and Care, 180,* 1–8.

Freitag, C. M., Rohde, L. A., Lempp, T., & Romanos, M. (2010). Phenotypic and measurement influences on heritability estimates in childhood ADHD. *European Child and Adolescent Psychiatry, 19,* 311–323.

Freud, A. (1969). Adolescence as a developmental disturbance. In G. Caplan & S. Lebovici (Eds.), *Adolescence* (pp. 5–10). New York: Basic Books.

Freud, S. (1973). *An outline of psychoanalysis.* London: Hogarth. (Original work published 1938)

Freud, S. (1974). *The ego and the id.* London: Hogarth. (Original work published 1923)

Frey, A., Ruchkin, V., Martin, A., & Schwab-Stone, M. (2009). Adolescents in transition: School and family characteristics in the development of violent behaviors entering high school. *Child Psychiatry and Human Development, 40,* 1–13.

Fried, P. A. (1993). Prenatal exposure to tobacco and marijuana: Effects during preganancy, infancy, and early childhood. *Clinical Obstetrics and Gynecology, 36,* 319–337.

Friedman, S. L., & Scholnick, E. K. (1997). An evolving "blueprint" for planning: Psychological requirements, task characteristics, and social–cultural influences. In S. L. Friedman & E. K. Scholnick (Eds.), *The developmental psychology of planning: Why, how, and when do we plan?* (pp. 3–22). Mahwah, NJ: Erlbaum.

Fries, A. B. W., & Pollak, S. D. (2004). Emotion understanding in postinstitutionalized Eastern European children. *Development and Psychopathology, 16,* 355–369.

Fries, A. B. W., Ziegler, T. E., Kurian, J. R., Jacoris, S., & Pollak, S. D. (2005). Early experience in humans is associated with changes in neuropeptides critical for regulating social behavior. *Proceedings of the National Academy of Sciences, 102,* 17237–17240.

Frith, L. (2001). Gamete donation and anonymity: The ethical and legal debate. *Human Reproduction, 16,* 818–824.

Frith, U. (2003). *Autism: Explaining the enigma* (2nd ed.). Malden, MA: Blackwell.

Fryer, S. L., Crocker, N. A., & Mattson, S. N. (2008). Exposure to teratogenic agents as a risk factor for psychopathology. In T. P. Beauchaine & S. P. Hinshaw (Eds.), *Child and adolescent psychopathology* (pp. 180–207). Hoboken, NJ: Wiley.

Fu, G., Xu, F., Cameron, C. A., Heyman, G., & Lee, K. (2007). Cross-cultural differences in children's choices, categorizations, and evaluations of truths and lies. *Developmental Psychology, 43,* 278–293.

Fuchs, D., Fuchs, L. S., Mathes, P. G., & Martinez, E. A. (2002a). Preliminary evidence on the standing of students with learning disabilities in PALS and No-PALS classrooms. *Learning Disabilities Research and Practice, 17,* 205–215.

Fuchs, I., Eisenberg, N., Hertz-Lazarowitz, R., & Sharabany, R. (1986). Kibbutz, Israeli city, and American children's moral reasoning about prosocial moral conflicts. *Merrill-Palmer Quarterly, 32,* 37–50.

Fuchs, L. S., Fuchs, D., Yazdian, L., & Powell, S. R. (2002b). Enhancing first-grade children's mathematical development with peer-assisted learning strategies. *School Psychology Review, 31,* 569–583.

Fuligni, A. J. (1998). Authority, autonomy, and parent–adolescent conflict and cohesion: A study of adolescents from Mexican, Chinese, Filipino, and European backgrounds. *Developmental Psychology, 34,* 782–792.

Fuligni, A. J. (2004). The adaptation and acculturation of children from immigrant families. In U. P. Gielen & J. Roopnarine (Eds.), *Childhood and adolescence: Cross-cultural perspectives* (pp. 297–318). Westport, CT: Praeger.

Fuligni, A. J. (2007). Family obligation, college enrollment, and emerging adulthood in Asian and Latin American families. *Child Development Perspectives, 1,* 96–100.

Fuligni, A. J., Yip, T., & Tseng, V. (2002). The impact of family obligation on the daily activities and psychological well-being of Chinese-American adolescents. *Child Development, 73,* 302–314.

Fuligni, A. J., & Yoshikawa, H. (2003). Socioeconomic resources, parenting, and child development among immigrant families. In M. H. Bornstein & R. H. Bradley (Eds.), *Socioeconomic status, parenting, and child development* (pp. 107–124). Mahwah, NJ: Erlbaum.

Fuligni, A. S., Han, W.-J., & Brooks-Gunn, J. (2004). The Infant-Toddler HOME in the 2nd and 3rd years of life. *Parenting: Science and Practice, 4,* 139–159.

Fuller, C., Keller, L., Olson, J., Plymale, A., & Gottesman, M. (2005). Helping preschoolers become healthy eaters. *Journal of Pediatric Health Care, 19,* 178–182.

Fuller-Thomson, E., & Minkler, M. (2005). Native American grandparents raising grandchildren: Findings from the Census 2000 Supplementary Survey and implications for social work practice. *Social Work, 50,* 131–139.

Fuller-Thomson, E., & Minkler, M. (2007). Mexican American grandparents raising grandchildren: Findings from the Census 2000 American Community Survey. *Families in Society, 88,* 567–574.

Fullerton, J. T., Navarro, A. M., & Young, S. H. (2007). Outcomes of planned home birth: An integrative review. *Journal of Midwifery and Women's Health, 52,* 323–333.

Furman, W., & Buhrmester, D. (1992). Age and sex differences in perceptions of networks of personal relationships. *Child Development, 63,* 103–115.

Furman, W., & Collins, W. A. (2009). Adolescent romantic relationships and experiences. In K. Rubin, W. M. Bukowski, & B. Laursen (Eds.), *Handbook of peer interactions, relationships, and groups* (pp. 341–360). New York: Guilford.

Furman, W., Simon, V. A., Shaffer, L., & Bouchey, H. A. (2002). Adolescents' working models and styles for relationships with parents, friends, and romantic partners. *Child Development, 73,* 241–255.

Furnham, A. (2009). Sex differences in mate selection preferences. *Personality and Individual Differences, 47,* 262–267.

Furstenberg, F. F. (2007). *Destinies of the disadvantaged.* New York: Russell Sage Foundation.

Furstenberg, F. F., Jr., & Harris, K. M. (1993). When and why fathers matter: Impact of father involvement on children of adolescent mothers. In R. I. Lerman &

T. J. Ooms (Eds.), *Young unwed fathers* (pp. 117–138). Philadelphia: Temple University Press.

Furstenberg, F. F., Jr., Kennedy, S., McLoyd, V. C., Rumbaut, R. G., & Settersten, R. A., Jr. (2004). Growing up is harder to do. *Contexts, 3*(3), 33–41.

Furusawa, T., Naka, I., Yamauchi, T., Natsuhara, K., Kimura, R., Nakazawa, M., et al. (2010). The Q223r polymorphism in LEPR is associated with obesity in Pacific Islanders. *Human Genetics, 127,* 287–294.

Fuson, K. C. (2009). Avoiding misinterpretations of Piaget and Vygotsky: Mathematical teaching without learning, learning without teaching, or helpful learning-path teaching? *Cognitive Development, 24,* 343–361.

Fuson, K. C., & Burghard, B. H. (2003). Multidigit addition and subtraction methods invented in small groups and teacher support of problem solving and reflection. In A. J. Baroody & A. Dowker (Eds.), *The development of arithmetic concepts and skills* (pp. 267–304). Mahwah, NJ: Erlbaum.

Fussell, E., & Furstenberg, F. F., Jr. (2005). The transition to adulthood during the twentieth century. In R. A. Settersten, Jr., F. F. Furstenberg, Jr., & R. G. Rumbaut (Eds.), *On the frontier of adulthood* (pp. 29–75). Chicago: University of Chicago Press.

Fussell, E., & Gauthier, A. H. (2005). American women's transition to adulthood in comparative perspective. In R. A. Settersten, Jr., F. F. Furstenberg, Jr., & R. G. Rumbaut (Eds.), *On the frontier of adulthood: Theory, research, and public policy* (pp. 76–109). Chicago: University of Chicago Press.

G

Gagnon, J. C., & Leone, P. E. (2002). Alternative strategies for school violence prevention. In R. J. Skiba & G. G. Noam (Eds.), *Zero tolerance: Can suspension and expulsion keep school safe?* (pp. 101–125). San Francisco: Jossey-Bass.

Galambos, N. L., & Martínez, M. L. (2007). Poised for emerging adulthood in Latin America: A pleasure for the privileged. *Child Development Perspectives, 1,* 109–114.

Galambos, N. L., Almeida, D. M., & Petersen, A. C. (1990). Masculinity, femininity, and sex role attitudes in early adolescence: Exploring gender intensification. *Child Development, 61,* 1905–1914.

Galambos, N. L., Barker, E. T., & Krahn, H. J. (2006). Depression, anger, and self-esteem in emerging adulthood: Seven-year trajectories. *Developmental Psychology, 42,* 350–365.

Galambos, S. J., & Maggs, J. L. (1991). Children in self-care: Figures, facts and fiction. In J. V. Lerner & N. L. Galambos (Eds.), *Employed mothers and their children* (pp. 131–157). New York: Garland.

Galinsky, E., Aumann, K., & Bond, J. T. (2009). *Times are changing: Gender and generation at work and at home.* New York: Families and Work Institute.

Gallagher, A. M., & Kaufman, J. C. (2005). Gender differences in mathematics: What we know and what we need to know. In A. M. Gallagher & J. C. Kaufman (Eds.), *Gender differences in mathematics: An integrative psychological approach* (pp. 316–331). New York: Cambridge University Press.

Galler, J. R., Ramsey, C. F., Morley, D. S., Archer, E., & Salt, P. (1990). The long-term effects of early kwashiorkor compared with marasmus. IV. Performance on the National High School Entrance Examination. *Pediatric Research, 28,* 235–239.

Galloway, J. C., & Thelen, E. (2004). Feet first. Object exploration in young infants. *Infant Behavior and Development, 27,* 107-112

Gallup News Service. (2006). *Religion most important to blacks, women, and older Americans.* Retrieved from www.gallup.com/poll/25585/Religion-Most-Important-Blacks-Women-Older-Americans .aspx?version=print

Gandy, J. (2004). *Children explain God.* Retrieved from http://www.geocities.com/jonathangandy.geo/ chilrendescribeGod.html

Ganea, P. A., Allen, M. L., Butler, L., Carey, S., & DeLoache, J. S. (2009). Toddlers' referential understanding of pictures. *Journal of Experimental Child Psychology, 104,* 283–295.

Ganea, P. A., & Harris, P. A. (2010). Not doing what you are told: Early perseverative errors in updating mental representations via language. *Child Development, 81,* 457–463.

Ganea, P. A., Pickard, M. B., & DeLoache, J. S. (2008). Transfer between picture books and the real world by very young children. *Journal of Cognition and Development, 9,* 46–66.

Ganea, P. A., Shutts, K., Spelke, E., & DeLoache, J. S. (2007). Thinking of things unseen: Infants' use of language to update object representations. *Psychological Science, 8,* 734–739.

Ganger, J., & Brent, M. R. (2004). Reexamining the vocabulary spurt. *Developmental Psychology, 40,* 621–632.

Ganji, V., Hampl, J. S., & Betts, N. M. (2003). Race-, gender-, and age-specific differences in dietary micronutrient intakes of U.S. children. *International Journal of Food Sciences and Nutrition, 54,* 485–490.

Ganong, L. H., & Coleman, M. (1994). *Remarried family relationships.* Thousand Oaks, CA: Sage.

Garces, E., Thomas, D., & Currie, J. (2002). Longer-term effects of Head Start. *American Economic Review, 92,* 999–1012.

Garcia, M. M., Shaw, D. S., Winslow, E. B., & Yaggi, K. E. (2000). Destructive sibling conflict and the development of conduct problems in young boys. *Developmental Psychology, 36,* 44–53.

Garcia-Bournissen, F., Tsur, L., Goldstein, L. H., Staroselsky, A., Avner, M., & Asrar, F. (2008). Fetal exposure to isotretinoin—an international problem. *Reproductive Toxicology, 25,* 124–128.

García Coll, C., & Magnuson, K. (1997). The psychological experience of immigration: A developmental perspective. In A. Booth, A. C. Crouter, & N. Landale (Eds.), *Immigration and the family* (pp. 91–131). Mahwah, NJ: Erlbaum.

Gardner, H. (1983). *Frames of mind: The theory of multiple intelligences.* New York: Basic Books.

Gardner, H. (1993). *Multiple intelligences: The theory in practice.* New York: Basic Books.

Gardner, H. (1998). Extraordinary cognitive achievements (ECA): A symbol systems approach. In R. M. Learner (Ed.), *Handbook of child psychology: Vol. 1. Theoretical models of human development* (5th ed., pp. 415–466). New York: Wiley.

Gardner, H. (2000). *Intelligence reframed: Multiple intelligences for the twenty-first century.* New York: Basic Books.

Gardner, M., & Steinberg, L. (2005). Peer influence on risk taking, risk preference, and risky decision making in adolescence and adulthood: An experimental study. *Developmental Psychology, 41,* 625–635.

Garner, P. W. (1996). The relations of emotional role taking, affective/moral attributions, and emotional display rule knowledge to low-income school-age children's social competence. *Journal of Applied Developmental Psychology, 17,* 19–36.

Garner, P. W. (2003). Child and family correlates of toddlers' emotional and behavioral responses to a mishap. *Infant Mental Health Journal, 24,* 580–596.

Garner, P. W., & Estep, K. (2001). Emotional competence, emotion socialization, and young children's peer-related social competence. *Early Education and Development, 12,* 29–48.

Garrison, M. M., & Christakis, D. A. (2005). *A teacher in the living room? Educational media for babies, toddlers, and preschoolers.* Menlo Park, CA: Henry J. Kaiser Family Foundation.

Gartstein, M. A., & Rothbart, M. K. (2003). Studying infant temperament via the revised infant behavior questionnaire. *Infant Behavior and Development, 26,* 64–86.

Gartstein, M. A., Slobodskaya, H. R., & Kinsht, I. A. (2003). Cross-cultural differences in temperament in the first year of life: United States of America (U.S.) and Russia. *International Journal of Behavioral Development, 27,* 316–328.

Gasden, V. (1999). Black families in intergenerational and cultural perspective. In M. E. Lamb (Ed.), *Parenting and child development in "nontraditional" families* (pp. 221– 246). Mahwah, NJ: Erlbaum.

Gaskins, S. (1999). Children's daily lives in a Mayan village: A case study of culturally constructed roles and activities. In R. Göncü (Ed.), *Children's engagement in the world: Sociocultural perspectives* (pp. 25– 61). Cambridge, UK: Cambridge University Press.

Gaskins, S. (2000). Children's daily activities in a Mayan village: A culturally grounded description. *Cross-Cultural Research, 34,* 375–389.

Gaskins, S., Haight, W., & Lancy, D. F. (2007). The cultural construction of play. In A. Göncü & S. Gaskins (Eds.), *Play and development: Evolutionary, sociocultural, and functional perspectives* (pp. 179–202). Mahwah, NJ: Erlbaum.

Gathercole, S. E., Adams, A.-M., & Hitch, G. (1994). Do young children rehearse? An individual-differences analysis. *Memory and Cognition, 22,* 201–207.

Gathercole, V., Sebastián, E., & Soto, P. (1999). The early acquisition of Spanish verbal morphology: Across-the-board or piecemeal knowledge? *International Journal of Bilingualism, 3,* 133–182.

Gauvain, M. (2004). Bringing culture into relief: Cultural contributions to the development of children's planning skills. In R. V. Kail (Ed.), *Advances in child development and behavior* (pp. 39–71). San Diego, CA: Elsevier.

Gauvain, M., de la Ossa, J. L., & Hurtado-Ortiz, M. T. (2001). Parental guidance as children learn to use cultural tools: The case of pictorial plans. *Cognitive Development, 16,* 551–575.

Gauvain, M., & Rogoff, B. (1989a). Collaborative problem solving and children's planning skills. *Developmental Psychology, 25,* 139–151.

Gauvain, M., & Rogoff, B. (1989b). Ways of speaking about space: The development of children's skill in communicating spatial knowledge. *Cognitive Development, 4,* 295–307.

Gawlitzek-Maiwald, I., & Tracy, R. (1996). Bilingual bootstrapping. *Linguistics, 34,* 901–926.

Gaylor, E. E., Burnham, M. M., Goodlin-Jones, B. L., & Anders, T. (2005). A longitudinal follow-up study of young children's sleep patterns using a developmental classification system. *Behavioral Sleep Medicine, 3,* 44–61.

Gazelle, H., & Rudolph, K. D. (2004). Moving toward and away from the world: Social approach and avoidance trajectories in anxious and solitary youth. *Child Development, 75,* 829–849.

Ge, X., Brody, G. H., Conger, R. D., Simons, R. L., & Murry, V. (2002). Contextual amplification of the effects of pubertal transition on African American children's deviant peer affiliation and externalized behavioral problems. *Developmental Psychology, 38,* 42–54.

Ge, X., Conger, R. D., & Elder, G. H., Jr. (1996). Coming of age too early: Pubertal influences on girls' vulnerability to psychological distress. *Child Development, 67,* 3386–3400.

Ge, X., Conger, R. D., & Elder, G. H., Jr. (2001). The relation between puberty and psychological distress in adolescent boys. *Journal of Research on Adolescence, 11,* 49–70.

Ge, X., Jin, R., Natsuaki, M. N., Frederick, X., Brody, G. H., Cutrona, C. E., & Simons, R. L. (2006). Pubertal maturation and early substance use risks among African American children. *Psychology of Addictive Behaviors, 20,* 404–414.

Ge, X., Kim, I. J., Brody, G. H., Conger, R. D., & Simons, R. L. (2003). It's about timing and change: pubertal transition effects on symptoms of major depression among African American youths. *Developmental Psychology, 39,* 430–439.

Geary, D. C. (1999). Evolution and developmental sex differences. *Current Directions in Psychological Science, 8,* 115–120.

Geary, D. C. (2006a). Development of mathematical understanding. In D. Kuhn & R. Siegler (Eds.), *Handbook of child psychology: Vol. 2. Cognition, perception, and language* (6th ed., pp. 777–810). Hoboken, NJ: Wiley.

Geary, D. C. (2006b). Evolutionary developmental psychology: Current status and future directions. *Developmental Review, 26,* 113–119.

Geary, D. C., Saults, J. S., Liu, F., & Hoard, M. K. (2000). Sex differences in spatial cognition, computational fluency, and arithmetic reasoning. *Journal of Experimental Child Psychology, 77,* 337–353.

Gee, C. B., & Rhodes, J. E. (2003). Adolescent mothers' relationship with their children's biological fathers: Social support, social strain, and relationship continuity. *Journal of Family Psychology, 17,* 370–383.

Geerts, M., Steyaert, J., & Fryns, J. P. (2003). The XYY syndrome: A follow-up study on 38 boys. *Genetic Counseling, 14,* 267–279.

Gelman, R. (1972). Logical capacity of very young children: Number invariance rules. *Child Development, 43,* 75–90.

Gelman, R., & Shatz, M. (1978). Appropriate speech adjustments: The operation of conversational constraints on talk to two-year-olds. In M. Lewis & L. A. Rosenblum (Eds.), *Interaction, conversation, and the development of language* (pp. 27–61). New York: Wiley.

Gelman, S. A. (2003). *The essential child.* New York: Oxford University Press.

Gelman, S. A. (2006). Early conceptual development. In K. McCartney & D. Phillips (Eds.), *Blackwell handbook of early childhood development* (pp. 149–166). Malden, MA: Blackwell.

Gelman, S. A., & Kalish, C. W. (2006). Conceptual development. In D. Kuhn & R. Siegler (Eds.), *Handbook of child psychology: Vol. 2. Cognition, perception, and language* (6th ed., 687–733). New York: Wiley.

Gelman, S. A., & Koenig, M. A. (2003). Theory-based categorization in early childhood. In D. H. Rakison & L. M. Oakes (Ed.), *Early category and concept development* (pp. 330–359). New York: Oxford University Press.

Gelman, S. A., Taylor, M. G., & Nguyen, S. P. (2004). Mother–child conversations about gender. *Monographs of the Society for Research in Child Development, 69*(1, Serial No. 275), pp. 1–127.

Gendler, M. N., Witherington, D. C., & Edwards, A. (2008). The development of affect specificity in infants' use of emotion cues. *Infancy, 13,* 456–468.

Genesee, F. (2001). Portrait of the bilingual child. In V. Cook (Ed.), *Portraits of the second language user* (pp. 170–196). Clevedon, UK: Multilingual Matters.

Genesee, F., & Nicoladis, E. (2007). Bilingual first language acquisition. In E. Hoff & M. Shatz (Eds.), *Blackwell handbook of language development* (pp. 324–342). Malden, MA: Blackwell.

Gennetian, L. A., & Morris, P. A. (2003). The effects of time limits and make-work-pay strategies on the well-being of children: Experimental evidence from two welfare reform programs. *Children and Youth Services Review, 25,* 17–54.

Gentile, B., Twenge, J. M., & Campbell, W. K. (2010). Birth cohort differences in self-esteem, 1988–2008: A cross-temporal meta-analysis. *Review of General Psychology, 14,* 261–268.

Gentner, D., & Namy, L. L. (2004). The role of comparison in children's early word learning. In D. G. Hall & S. R. Waxman (Eds.), *Weaving a lexicon* (pp. 533–568). Cambridge, MA: MIT Press.

Gerardi-Caulton, G. (2000). Sensitivity to spatial conflict and the development of self-regulation in children 24–36 months of age. *Developmental Science, 3,* 397–404.

Gergely, G., & Watson, J. (1996). The social biofeedback theory of parental affect-mirroring: The development of emotional self-awareness and self-control in infancy. *International Journal of Psychoanalysis, 77,* 1181–1212.

Gergely, G., & Watson, J. (1999). Early socio-emotional development: Contingency perception and the social-biofeedback model. In P. Rochat (Ed.), *Early social cognition: Understanding others in the first months of life* (pp. 101–136). Mahwah, NJ: Erlbaum.

Gershoff, E. T. (2002). Corporal punishment, physical abuse, and the burden of proof: Reply to Baumrind, Larzelere, and Cowan (2002), Holden (2002), and Parke (2002). *Psychological Bulletin, 128,* 602–611.

Gershoff, E. T., & Aber, J. L. (2006). Neighborhoods and schools: Contexts and consequences for the mental health and risk behaviors of children and youth. In L. Balter & C. S. Tamis-LeMonda (Eds.), *Child psychology: A handbook of contemporary issues* (2nd ed., pp. 611–645). New York: Psychology Press.

Gershoff-Stowe, L., & Hahn, E. R. (2007). Fast mapping skills in the developing lexicon. *Journal of Speech, Language, and Hearing Research, 50,* 682–697.

Gerson, S., & Woodward, A. L. (2010). Building intentional action knowledge with one's hands. In S. P. Johnson (Ed.), *Neoconstructivism: The new science of cognitive development* (pp. 295–313). New York: Oxford University Press.

Gesell, A. (1933). Maturation and patterning of behavior. In C. Murchison (Ed.), *A handbook of child psychology.* Worcester, MA: Clark University Press.

Gest, S. D., Domitrovich, C. E., & Welsh, J. A. (2005). Peer academic reputation in elementary school: Associations with changes in self-concept and academic skills. *Journal of Educational Psychology, 97,* 337–346.

Gewirtz, A., & Edleson, J. L. (2004). Young children's exposure to adult domestic violence: Toward a developmental risk and resilience framework for research and intervention. In S. Schechter (Ed.), *Early childhood, domestic violence, and poverty: Helping young children and their families,* Series Paper 6. Iowa City: University of Iowa School of Social Work.

Gewirtz, A., Forgatch, M., & Weiling, E. (2008). Parenting practices as potential mechanisms for child adjustment following mass trauma. *Journal of Marital and Family Therapy, 34,* 177–192.

Ghim, H. R. (1990). Evidence for perceptual organization in infants: Perception of subjective contours by young infants. *Infant Behavior and Development, 13,* 221–248.

Gibbons, A. (1998). Which of our genes make us human? *Science, 281,* 1432–1434

Gibbons, R., Dugaiczyk, L. J., Girke, T., Duistermars, B., Zielinski, R., & Dugaiczyk, A. (2004). Distinguishing humans from great apes with AluYb8 repeats. *Journal of Molecular Biology, 339,* 721–729.

Gibbs, J. C. (1991). Toward an integration of Kohlberg's and Hoffman's theories of morality. In W. M. Kurtines & J. L. Gewirtz (Eds.), *Handbook of moral behavior and development* (Vol. 1, pp. 183–222). Hillsdale, NJ: Erlbaum.

Gibbs, J. C. (2006). Should Kohlberg's cognitive developmental approach to morality be replaced with a more pragmatic approach? Comment on Krebs and Denton (2005). *Psychological Review, 113,* 666–671.

Gibbs, J. C. (2010). Beyond the conventionally moral. *Journal of Applied Developmental Psychology, 31,* 106–108.

Gibbs, J. C. (2010b). *Moral development and reality: Beyond the theories of Kohlberg and Hoffman* (2nd ed.). Boston: Pearson Allyn & Bacon.

Gibbs, J. C., Basinger, K. S., & Grime, R. L. (2003). Moral judgment maturity: From clinical to standard measures. In S. J. Lopez & C. R. Snyder (Eds.), *Handbook of positive psychological assessment* (pp. 361–373). Washington, DC: American Psychological Association.

Gibbs, J. C., Basinger, K. S., Grime, R. L., & Snarey, J. R. (2007). Moral judgment development across cultures: Revisiting Kohlberg's universality claims. *Developmental Review, 24,* 443–500.

Gibbs, J. C., Moshman, D., Berkowitz, M. W., Basinger, K. S., & Grime, R. L. (2009a). Taking development seriously: Critique of the 2008 JME special issue on moral functioning. *Journal of Moral Education, 38,* 271–282.

Gibbs, J. C., Potter, G. B., DiBiase, A.-M., & Devlin, R. (2009b). The EQUIP program: Social perspective-taking for responsible thought and behavior. In B. Glick (Ed.), *Cognitive behavioral interventions for at-risk youth* (2nd ed.). Kingston, NJ: Civic Research Institute.

Gibson, E. J. (1970). The development of perception as an adaptive process. *American Scientist, 58,* 98–107.

Gibson, E. J. (2000). Perceptual learning in development: Some basic concepts. *Ecological Psychology, 12,* 295–302.

Gibson, E. J. (2003). The world is so full of a number of things: On specification and perceptual learning. *Ecological Psychology, 15,* 283–287.

Gibson, E. J., & Walk, R. D. (1960). The "visual cliff." *Scientific American, 202,* 64–71.

Gibson, J. J. (1979). *The ecological approach to visual perception.* Boston: Houghton Mifflin.

Giedd, J. N., Blumenthal, J., Jeffries, N. O., Rajapakse, J. C., et al. (1999). Development of the human corpus callosum during childhood and adolescence: A longitudinal MRI study. *Progress in Neuro-Psychology and Biological Psychiatry, 23,* 571-588.

Giles, J. W., & Heyman, G. D. (2005). Young children's beliefs about the relationship between gender and aggressive behavior. *Child Development, 76,* 107–121.

Giles-Sims, J., Straus, M. A., & Sugarman, D. B. (1995). Child, maternal, and family characteristics associated with spanking. *Family Relations, 44,* 170–176.

Gill, M., Daly, G., Heron, S., Hawi, Z., & Fitzgerald, M. (1997). Confirmation of association between attention deficit hyperactivity disorder and a dopamine transporter polymorphism. *Molecular Psychiatry, 2,* 311–313.

Gillet, J.-P., Macadangdang, B., Rathke, R. L., Gottesman, M. M., & Kimchi-Sarfaty, C. (2009). The development of gene therapy: From monogenic recessive disorders to complex diseases such as cancer. *Methods in Molecular Biology, 542,* 5–54.

Gillies, R. M. (2002). The residual effects of cooperative-learning experiences: A two-year follow-up. *Journal of Educational Research, 96,* 15–20.

Gillies, R. M. (2003). Structuring co-operative learning experiences in primary school. In R. M. Gillies & A. F. Ashman (Eds.), *Co-operative learning: The social and intellectual outcomes of learning in groups* (pp. 36–53). New York: Routledge.

Gillies, R. M. (2003b). The behaviors, interactions, and perceptions of junior high school students during small-group learning. *Journal of Educational Psychology, 95,* 137–147.

Gillies, R. M., & Ashman, A. F. (1996). Teaching collaborative skills to primary school children in classroom-based workgroups. *Learning and Instruction, 6,* 187–200.

Gilligan, C. F. (1982). *In a different voice.* Cambridge, MA: Harvard University Press.

Gilliom, M., Shaw, D. S., Beck, J. E., Schonberg, M. A., & Lukon, J. L. (2002). Anger regulation in disadvantaged preschool boys: Strategies, antecedents, and the development of self-control. *Developmental Psychology, 38,* 222–235.

Gilstrap, L. L., & Ceci, S. J. (2005). Reconceptualizing children's suggestibility: Bidirectional and temporal properties. *Child Development, 76,* 40–53.

Ginsburg, H. P., Lee, J. S., & Boyd, J. S. (2008). Mathematics education for young children: What it is and how to promote it. *Social Policy Report of the Society for Research in Child Development, 12*(1).

Ginsburg-Block, M. D., Rohrbeck, C. A., & Fantuzzo, J. W. (2006). A meta-analytic review of social, self-concept, and behavioral outcomes of peer-assisted learning. *Journal of Educational Psychology, 98,* 732–749.

Giuliani, A., Schöll, W. M., Basver, A., & Tasmussino, K. F. (2002). Mode of delivery and outcome of 699 term singleton breech deliveries at a single center. *American Journal of Obstetrics and Gynaecology, 187,* 1694–1698.

Glade, A. C., Bean, R. A., & Vira, R. (2005). A prime time for marital/relational intervention: A review of the transition to parenthood literature with treatment recommendations. *American Journal of Family Therapy, 33,* 319–336.

Gladstone, I. M., & Katz, V. L. (2004). The morbidity of the 34- to 35-week gestation: Should we reexamine the paradigm? *American Journal of Perinatology, 21,* 9–13.

Gladwell, M. (1998, February 2). The Pima paradox. *The New Yorker,* pp. 44–57.

Glasgow, K. L., Dornbusch, S. M., Troyer, L., Steinberg, L., & Ritter, P. L. (1997). Parenting styles, adolescents' attributions, and educational outcomes

in nine heterogeneous high schools. *Child Development, 68,* 507–523.

Gleason, J. B. (2009). The development of language. In J. B. Gleason (Ed.), *The development of language* (7th ed., pp. 1–33). Boston: Allyn and Bacon.

Gleason, T. R. (2002). Social provisions of real and imaginary relationships in early childhood. *Developmental Psychology, 38,* 979–992.

Gleason, T. R., & Hohmann, L. M. (2006). Concepts of real and imaginary friendships in early childhood. *Social Development, 15,* 128–144.

Gleason, T. R., Sebanc, A. M., & Hartup, W. W. (2000). Imaginary companions of preschool children. *Developmental Psychology, 36,* 419–428.

Gleitman, L. R., Cassidy, K., Nappa, R., Papfragou, A., & Trueswell, J. C. (2005). Hard words. *Language Learning and Development, 1,* 23–64.

Gleitman, L. R., & Newport, E. (1996). *The invention of language by children.* Cambridge, MA: MIT Press.

Glover, V., Bergman, K., & O'Connor, T. G. (2008). The effects of maternal stress, anxiety, and depression during pregnancy on the neurodevelopment of the child. In S. D. Stone & A. E. Menken (Eds.), *Perinatal and postpartum mood disorders: Perspectives and treatment guide for the health care practitioner* (pp. 3–15). New York: Springer.

Glowinski, A. L., Madden, P. A. F., Bucholz, K. K., Lynskey, M. T., & Heath, A. C. (2003). Genetic epidemiology of self-reported lifetime DSM-IV major depressive disorder in a population-based twin sample of female adolescents. *Journal of Child Psychology and Psychiatry and Allied Disciplines, 44,* 988–996.

Gluckman, P. D., Sizonenko, S. V., & Bassett, N. S. (1999). The transition from fetus to neonate—an endocrine perspective. *Acta Paediatrica Supplement, 88*(428), 7–11.

Gnepp, J. (1983). Children's social sensitivity: Inferring emotions from conflicting cues. *Developmental Psychology, 19,* 805–814.

Godart, N. T., Perdereau, F., Curt, F., Rein, Z., Lang, F., & Venisse, J. L. (2006). Is major depressive episode related to anxiety disorders in anorexics and bulimics? *Comprehensive Psychiatry, 47,* 91–98.

Godeau, E., Nic Gabhainn, S., Vignes, C., Ross, J., Boyce, W., & Todd, J. (2008). Contraceptive use by 15-year-old students at their last sexual intercourse. *Archives of Pediatric and Adolescent Medicine, 162,* 66–73.

Godfrey, K. M., & Barker, D. J. (2000). Fetal nutrition and adult disease. *American Journal of Clinical Nutrition, 71,* 1344S–1352S.

Goering, J. (Ed.). (2003). Choosing a better life? *How public housing tenants selected a HUD experiment to improve their lives and those of their children: The Moving to Opportunity Demonstration Program.* Washington, DC: Urban Institute Press.

Goetz, T., Frenzel, A. C., Pekrun, R., & Hall, N. (2005). Emotional intelligence in the context of learning and achievement. In R. Schulze & R. D. Roberts (Eds.), *Emotional intelligence: An international handbook* (pp. 233–253). Göttingen, Germany: Hogrefe & Huber.

Gogate, L. J., & Bahrick, L. E. (1998). Intersensory redundancy facilitates learning of arbitrary relations between vowel sounds and objects in seven-month-old infants. *Journal of Experimental Child Psychology, 69,* 133–149.

Gogate, L. J., & Bahrick, L. E. (2001). Intersensory redundancy and 7-month-old infants' memory for arbitrary syllable–object relations. *Infancy, 2,* 219–231.

Goh, Y. I., & Koren, G. (2008). Folic acid in pregnancy and fetal outcomes. *Journal of Obstetrics and Gynaecology, 28,* 3–13.

Goldberg, A. E., & Perry-Jenkins, M. (2003). Division of labor and working-class women's well-being across the transition to parenthood. *Journal of Family Psychology, 18,* 225–236.

Goldenberg, C., Gallimore, R., Reese, L., & Garnier, H. (2001). Cause or effect? Immigrant Latino parents' aspirations and expectations, and their children's

school performance. *American Educational Research Journal, 38,* 547–582.

Goldfield, B. A. (1987). Contributions of child and caregiver to referential and expressive language. *Applied Psycholinguistics, 8,* 267–280.

Goldin-Meadow, S., & Butcher, S. (2003). Pointing toward two-word speech in young children. In S. Kita (Ed.), *Pointing: Where language, culture, and cognition meet* (pp. 85–107). Mahwah, NJ: Erlbaum.

Goldschmidt, L., Richardson, G. A., Cornelius, M. D., & Day, N. L. (2004). Prenatal marijuana and alcohol exposure and academic achievement at age 10. *Neurotoxicology and Teratology, 26,* 521–532.

Goldstein, E. (1979). Effect of same-sex and cross-sex role models on the subsequent academic productivity of scholars. *American Psychologist, 34,* 407–410.

Goldstein, M. H., & Schwade, J. A. (2008). Social feedback to infants' babbling facilitates rapid phonological learning. *Psychological Science, 19,* 515–523.

Goldstein, S. E., Davis-Kean, P. E., & Eccles, J. S. (2005). Parents, peers, and problem behavior: A longitudinal investigation of the impact of relationship perceptions and characteristics on the development of adolescent problem behavior. *Developmental Psychology, 41,* 401–413.

Goldstein, S. E., & Tisak, M. S. (2004). Adolescents' outcome expectancies about relational aggression within acquaintanceships, friendships, and dating relationships. *Journal of Adolescence, 27,* 283–302.

Goldston, D. B., Molock, S. D., Whitbeck, L. B., Murakami, J. L., Zayas, L. H., & Hall, G. C. N. (2008). Cultural considerations in adolescent suicide prevention and psychosocial treatment. *American Psychologist, 63,* 14–31.

Goleman, D. (1995). *Emotional intelligence.* New York: Bantam.

Goleman, D. (1998). *Working with emotional intelligence.* New York: Bantam.

Golfier, F., Vaudoyer, F., Ecochard, R., Champion, F., Audra, P., & Raudrant, D. (2001). Planned vaginal delivery versus elective caesarean section in singleton term breech presentation: A study of 1116 cases. *European Journal of Obstetrics and Gyncecology, 98,* 186–192.

Golinkoff, R. M., & Hirsh-Pasek, K. (2006). Baby wordsmith: From associationist to social sophisticate. *Current Directions in Psychological Science, 15,* 30–33.

Golinkoff, R. M., & Hirsh-Pasek, K. (2008). How toddlers begin to learn verbs. *Trends in Cognitive Sciences, 12,* 397–403.

Golomb, C. (2004). *The child's creation of a pictorial world* (2nd ed.). Mahwah, NJ: Erlbaum.

Golombok, S., Lycett, E., MacCallum, F., Jadva, V., Murray, C., Rust, J., Abdalla, H., Jenkins, J., & Margar, R. (2004). Parenting of infants conceived by gamete donation. *Journal of Family Psychology, 18,* 443–452.

Golombok, S., Perry, B., Burston, A., Murray, C., Mooney-Somers, J., Stevens, M., & Golding, J. (2003). Children with lesbian parents: A community study. *Developmental Psychology, 39,* 20–33.

Golombok, S., Rust, J., Zervoulis, K., Croudace, T., Golding, J., & Hines, M. (2008). Developmental trajectories of sex-typed behavior in boys and girls: A longitudinal general population study of children aged 2.5–8 years. *Child Development, 79,* 1583–1593.

Golombok, S., & Tasker, F. L. (1996). Do parents influence the sexual orientation of their children? Findings from a longitudinal study of lesbian families. *Developmental Psychology, 32,* 3–11.

Gomez-Perez, E., & Ostrosky-Solis, F. (2006). Attention and memory evaluation across the life span: Heterogeneous effects of age and education. *Journal of Clinical and Experimental Neuropsychology, 28,* 477–494.

Göncü, A., Patt, M. B., & Kouba E. (2004). Understanding young children's pretend play in context. In P. K. Smith & C. H. Hart (Eds.), *Blackwell handbook of childhood social development* (pp. 418–437). Malden, MA: Blackwell.

Gonzales, N. A., Cauce, A. M., Friedman, R. J., & Mason, C. A. (1996). Family, peer, and neighborhood influences on academic achievement among African-American adolescents: One-year prospective effects. *American Journal of Community Psychology, 24,* 365–387.

Gonzalez, A.-L., & Wolters, C. A. (2006). The relation between perceived parenting practices and achievement motivation in mathematics. *Journal of Research in Childhood Education, 21,* 203–217.

Gonzalez-Rivera, M., & Bauermeister, J. A. (2007). Children's attitudes toward people with AIDS in Puerto Rico: Exploring stigma through drawings and stories. *Qualitative Health Research, 17,* 250–263.

Good, T. L., & Brophy, J. (2003). *Looking in classrooms* (9th ed.). Boston: Allyn and Bacon.

Goode, V., & Goode, J. D. (2007). De facto zero tolerance: An exploratory study of race and safe school violations. In J. L. Kincheloe & K. Hayes (Eds.), *Teaching city kids: Understanding and appreciating them* (pp. 85–96). New York: Peter Lang.

Goodlin-Jones, B. L., Burnham, M. M., & Anders, T. F. (2000). Sleep and sleep disturbances: Regulatory processes in infancy. In A. J. Sameroff, M. Lewis, & S. M. Miller (Eds.), *Handbook of developmental psychology* (2nd ed., pp. 309–325). New York: Kluwer.

Goodman, G. S., & Melinder, A. (2007). Child witness research and forensic interviews of young children: A review. *Legal and Criminological Psychology, 12,* 1–19.

Goodman, S. H., Gravitt, G. W., Jr., & Kaslow, N. J. (1995). Social problem solving: A moderator of the relation between negative life stress and depression symptoms in children. *Journal of Abnormal Child Psychology, 23,* 473–485.

Goodnow, J. J. (2010). Culture. In M. H. Bornstein (Ed.), *Handbook of cultural developmental science* (pp. 3–20). New York: Psychology Press.

Goodvin, R., Meyer, S., Thompson, R. A., & Hayes, R. (2008). Self-understanding in early childhood: Associations with child attachment security and maternal negative affect. *Attachment and Human Development, 10,* 433–450.

Goodwin, M. H. (1998). Games of stance: Conflict and footing in hopscotch. In S. Hoyle & C. T. Adger (Eds.), *Language practices of older children* (pp. 23–46). New York: Oxford University Press.

Gootman, E. (2005, January 16). New York City: the politics of promotion. *New York Times.* Retrieved from www.nytimes.com/2005/01/16/education/edlife/EDGOOT.html

Gopnik, A., & Choi, S. (1990). Do linguistic differences lead to cognitive differences? A cross-linguistic study of semantic and cognitive development. *First Language, 11,* 199–215.

Gopnik, A., & Nazzi, T. (2003). Words, kinds, and causal powers: A theory theory perspective on early naming and categorization. In D. H. Rakison & L. M. Oakes (Eds.), *Early category and concept development* (pp. 303– 329). New York: Oxford University Press.

Gordon, R. A., Chase-Lansdale, P. L., & Brooks-Gunn, J. (2004). Extended households and the life course of young mothers: Understanding the associations using a sample of mothers with premature, low-birth-weight babies. *Child Development, 75,* 1013–1038.

Gormally, S., Barr, R. G., Wertheim, L., Alkawaf, R., Calinoiu, N., & Young, S. N. (2001). Contact and nutrient caregiving effects on newborn infant pain responses. *Developmental Medicine and Child Neurology, 43,* 28–38.

Goswami, U. (1996). Analogical reasoning and cognitive development. In H. Reese (Ed.), *Advances in child development and behavior* (Vol. 26, pp. 91–138). New York: Academic Press.

Gottesman, I. I. (1963). Genetic aspects of intelligent behavior. In N. Ellis (Ed.), *Handbook of mental deficiency* (pp. 253– 296). New York: McGraw-Hill.

Gottfredson, G. D., & Duffy, R. D. (2008). Using a theory of vocational personalities and work environments to explore subjective well-being. *Journal of Career Assessment, 16,* 44–59.

Gottfredson, L. S. (2005). Applying Gottfredson's theory of circumscription and compromise in career

guidance and counseling. In S. D. Brown & R. W. Lent (Eds.), *Career development and counseling* (pp. 71–100). Hoboken, NJ: Wiley.

Gottfried, A. E., Gottfried, A. W., & Bathurst, K. (2002). Maternal and dual-earner employment status and parenting. In M. H. Bornstein (Ed.), *Handbook of parenting: Vol. 3. Being and becoming a parent* (2nd ed., pp. 207–230). Mahwah, NJ: Erlbaum.

Gottlieb, G. (1998). Normally occurring environmental and behavioral influences on gene activity: From central dogma to probabilistic epigenesis. *Psychological Review, 105,* 792–802.

Gottlieb, G. (2003). On making behavioral genetics truly developmental. *Human Development, 46,* 337–355.

Gottlieb, G. (2007). Probabilistic epigenesis. *Developmental Science, 10,* 1–11.

Gottlieb, G., Wahlsten, D., & Lickliter, R. (2006). The significance of biology for human development: A developmental psychobiological systems of view. In R. M. Lerner (Ed.), *Handbook of child psychology: Vol. 1. Theoretical models of human development* (6th ed., pp. 210–257). Hoboken, NJ: Wiley.

Gould, J. L., & Keeton, W. T. (1996). *Biological science* (6th ed.). New York: Norton.

Govaerts, P. J., De Beukelaer, C., Daemers, K., De Ceulaer, G., Yperman, M., Somers, T., Schatteman, I., & Offeciers, F. E. (2002). Outcome of cochlear implantation at different ages from 0 to 6 years. *Otology and Neurotology, 23,* 885–890.

Graber, J. A. (2003). Puberty in context. In C. Hayward (Ed.), *Gender differences at puberty* (pp. 307–325). New York: Cambridge University Press.

Graber, J. A. (2004). Internalizing problems during adolescence. In R. M. Lerner & L. Steinberg (Eds.), *Handbook of adolescent psychology* (2nd ed., pp. 587–626). Hoboken, NJ: Wiley.

Graber, J. A., Brooks-Gunn, J., & Warren, M. P. (2006). Pubertal effects on adjustment in girls: Moving from demonstrating effects to identifying pathways. *Journal of Youth and Adolescence, 35,* 413–423.

Graber, J. A., Lewinsohn, P. M., Seeley, J. R., & Brooks-Gunn, J. (1997). Is psychopathology associated with the timing of pubertal development? *Journal of the American Academy of Child and Adolescent Psychiatry, 36,* 1768–1776.

Graber, J. A., Nichols, T., Lynne, S. D., Brooks-Gunn, J., & Botwin, G. J. (2006). A longitudinal examination of family, friend, and media influences on competent versus problem behaviors among urban minority youth. *Applied Developmental Science, 10,* 75–85.

Graber, J. A., Seeley, J. R., Brooks-Gunn, J., & Lewinsohn, P. M. (2004). Is pubertal timing associated with psychopathology in young adulthood? *Journal of the American Academy of Child and Adolescent Psychiatry, 43,* 718–726.

Graber, J. A., & Sontag, L. M. (2009). Internalizing problems during adolescence. In R. M. Lerner & L. Steinberg (Eds.), *Handbook of adolescent psychology: Vol. 1. Individual bases of adolescent development* (3rd ed., pp. 642–682). Hoboken, NJ: Wiley.

Gralinski, J. H., & Kopp, C. B. (1993). Everyday rules for behavior: Mothers' requests to young children. *Developmental Psychology, 29,* 573–584.

Granger, R. C. (2008). After-school programs and academics: Implications for policy, practice, and research. *Social Policy Report of the Society for Research in Child Development, 22*(2), 3–11.

Granic, I., Hollenstein, T., Dishion, T. J., & Patterson, G. R. (2003). Longitudinal analysis of flexibility and reorganization in early adolescence: A dynamic systems study of family interactions. *Developmental Psychology, 39,* 606–617.

Granier-Deferre, C., Bassereau, S., Ribeiro, A., Jacquet, A. Y., & Lecanuet, J.-P. (2003). *Cardiac "orienting" response in fetuses and babies following an in utero melody-learning.* Paper presented at the 11th European Conference on Developmental Psychology, Milan, Italy.

Granillo, T., Jones-Rodriguez, G., & Carvajal, S. C. (2005). Prevalence of eating disorders in Latina adolescents: Associations with substance use and

other correlates. *Journal of Adolescent Health, 36,* 214–220.

Grant, K. B., & Ray, J. A. (2010). *Home, school, and community collaboration: Culturally responsive family involvement.* Thousand Oaks, CA: Sage Publications.

Grant, K. E., O'Koon, J., Davis, T., Roache, N., Poindexter, L., & Armstrong, M. (2000). Protective factors affecting low-income urban African American youth exposed to stress. *Journal of Early Adolescence, 20,* 388–418.

Grantham-McGregor, S., & Ani, C. (2001). A review of studies on the effect of iron deficiency on cognitive development in children. *Journal of Nutrition, 131,* 649S–668S.

Grantham-McGregor, S., Powell, C., Walker, S., Chang, S., & Fletcher, P. (1994). The long-term follow-up of severely malnourished children who participated in an intervention program. *Child Development, 65,* 428–439.

Grantham-McGregor, S., Schofield, W., & Powell, C. (1987). Development of severely malnourished children who received psychosocial stimulation: Six-year follow-up. *Pediatrics, 79,* 247–254.

Grantham-McGregor, S., Walker, S. P., & Chang, S. (2000). Nutritional deficiencies and later behavioral development. *Proceedings of the Nutrition Society, 59,* 47–54.

Grattan, M. P., De Vos, E., Levy, J., & McClintock, M. K. (1992). Asymmetric action in the human newborn: Sex differences in patterns of organization. *Child Development, 63,* 273–289.

Gray, K. A., Day, N. L., Leech, S., & Richardson, G. A. (2005). Prenatal marijuana exposure: Effect on child depressive symptoms at ten years of age. *Neurotoxicology and Teratology, 27,* 439–448.

Gray, M. R., & Steinberg, L. (1999). Unpacking authoritative parenting: Reassessing a multidimensional construct. *Journal of Marriage and the Family, 61,* 574–587.

Gray-Little, B., & Carels, R. (1997). The effects of racial and socioeconomic consonance on self-esteem and achievement in elementary, junior high, and high school students. *Journal of Research on Adolescence, 7,* 109–131.

Gray-Little, B., & Hafdahl, A. R. (2000). Factors influencing racial comparisons of self-esteem: A quantitative review. *Psychological Bulletin, 126,* 26–54.

Green, G. E., Irwin, J. R., & Gustafson, G. E. (2000). Acoustic cry analysis, neonatal status and long-term developmental outcomes. In R. G. Barr, B. Hopkins, & J. A. Green (Eds.), *Crying as a sign, a symptom, and a signal* (pp. 137–156). Cambridge, UK: Cambridge University Press.

Greenberg, D., Hoffman, S., Leibovitz, E., & Dagan, R. (2008). Acute otitis media in children: Association with day care centers—Antibacterial resistance, treatment, and prevention. *Pediatric Drugs, 10,* 75–83.

Greenberger, E., O'Neil, R., & Nagel, S. K. (1994). Linking workplace and homeplace: Relations between the nature of adults' work and their parenting behaviors. *Developmental Psychology, 30,* 990–1002.

Greendorfer, S. L., Lewko, J. H., & Rosengren, K. S. (1996). Family and gender-based socialization of children and adolescents. In F. L. Smoll & R. E. Smith (Eds.), *Children and youth in sport: A biopsychological perspective* (pp. 89–111). Dubuque, IA: Brown & Benchmark.

Greene, J. A., Torney-Purta, J., & Azevedo, R. (2010). Empirical evidence regarding relations among a model of epistemic and ontological cognition, academic performance, and educational level. *Journal of Educational Psychology, 102,* 234–255.

Greene, K., Krcmar, M., Walters, L. H., Rubin, D. L., Hale, J., & Hale, L. (2000). Targeting adolescent risk-taking behaviors: The contributions of egocentrism and sensationseeking. *Journal of Adolescence, 23,* 439–461.

Greene, M. L., Way, N., & Pahl, K. (2006). Trajectories of perceived adult and peer discrimination among Black, Latino, and Asian American adolescents:

Patterns and psychological correlates. *Developmental Psychology, 42,* 218–238.

Greene, S. M., Anderson, E., Hetherington, E. M., Forgath, M. S., & DeGarmo, D. S. (2003). Risk and resilience after divorce. In R. Walsh (Ed.), *Normal family processes* (pp. 96–120). New York: Guilford.

Greenfield, P. M. (1992, June). *Notes and references for developmental psychology.* Conference on Making Basic Texts in Psychology More Culture-Inclusive and Culture-Sensitive, Western Washington University, Bellingham, WA.

Greenfield, P. M. (2004). *Weaving generations together: Evolving creativity in the Maya of Chiapas.* Santa Fe, NM: School of American Research.

Greenfield, P. M., Keller, H., Fuligni, A., & Maynard, A. (2003). Cultural pathways through universal development. *Annual Review of Psychology, 54,* 461–490.

Greenfield, P. M., Maynard, A. E., & Childs, C. P. (2000). History, culture, learning, and development. *Cross-Cultural Research, 34,* 351–374.

Greenfield, P. M., Suzuki, L. K., & Rothstein-Fish, C. (2006). Cultural pathways through human development. In K. A. Renninger & I. E. Sigel (Eds.), *Handbook of child psychology: Vol. 4. Child psychology in practice* (6th ed., pp. 655–699). Hoboken, NJ: Wiley.

Greenhill, L. L., Halperin, J. M., & Abikoff, H. (1999). Stimulant medications. *Journal of the American Academy of Child and Adolescent Psychiatry, 38,* 503–512.

Greenough, W. T., & Black, J. E. (1992). Induction of brain structure by experience: Substrates for cognitive development. In M. Gunnar & C. A. Nelson (Eds.), *Minnesota symposia on child psychology* (pp. 155–200). Hillsdale, NJ: Erlbaum.

Greer, T., & Lockman, J. J. (1998). Using writing instruments: Invariances in young children and adults. *Child Development, 69,* 888–902.

Gregg, V., Gibbs, J. C., & Fuller, D. (1994). Patterns of developmental delay in moral judgment by male and female delinquents. *Merrill-Palmer Quarterly, 40,* 538–553.

Gregory, A., & Weinstein, R. S. (2004). Connection and regulation at home and in school: predicting growth in achievement for adolescents. *Journal of Adolescent Research, 19,* 405–427.

Gregory, A. M., Eley, T. C., O'Connor, T. G., & Plomin, R. (2004). Etiologies of associations between childhood sleep and behavioral problems in a large twin sample. *Journal of the American Academy of Child and Adolescent Psychiatry, 43,* 744–751.

Grief, G. L., Hrabowski, F. A., & Maton, K. I. (1998). African-American fathers of high-achieving sons: Using outstanding members of an at-risk population to guide intervention. *Families in Society, 79,* 45–52.

Grigorenko, E. L. (2000). Heritability and intelligence. In R. J. Sternberg (Ed.), *Handbook of intelligence* (pp. 53–91). Cambridge, UK: Cambridge University Press.

Grigorenko, E. L., & Sternberg, R. J. (1998). Dynamic testing. *Psychological Bulletin, 124,* 75–111.

Grob, A., & Flammer, A. (1999). Macrosocial context and adolescents' perceived control. In F. D. Alsaker & A. Flammer (Eds.), *The adolescent experience* (pp. 99–114). Mahwah, NJ: Erlbaum.

Grolnick, W. S., Kurowski, C. O., Dunlap, K. G., & Hevey, C. (2000). Parental resources and the transition to junior high. *Journal of Research on Adolescence, 10,* 466–488.

Groome, L. J., Swiber, M. J., Holland, S. B., Bentz, L. S., Atterbury, J. L., & Trimm, R. F., III. (1999). Spontaneous motor activity in the perinatal infant before and after birth: Stability in individual differences. *Developmental Psychobiology, 35,* 15–24.

Grossmann, K., Grossmann, K. E., Fremmer-Bombik, E., Kindler, H., Scheuerer-Englisch, H., & Zimmermann, P. (2002). The uniqueness of the child–father attachment relationship: Fathers' sensitive and challenging play as a pivotal variable in a 16-year longitudinal study. *Social Development, 11,* 307–331.

Grossmann, K., Grossmann, K. E., Kindler, H., & Zimmermann, P. (2008). A wider view of attachment and exploration: The influence of mothers and fathers on the development of psychological security from infancy to young adulthood. In J. Cassidy & P. R. Shaver (Eds.), *Handbook of attachment: Theory, research, and clinical applications* (2nd ed., pp. 880–905). New York: Guilford.

Grossmann, K., Grossmann, K. E., Spangler, G., Suess, G., & Unzner, L. (1985). Maternal sensitivity and newborns' orientation responses as related to quality of attachment in Northern Germany. In I. Bretherton & E. Waters (Eds.), Growing points of attachment theory and research. *Monographs of the Society for Research in Child Development, 50*(1–2, Serial No. 209).

Grossmann, T., Striano, T., & Friederici, A. D. (2007). Developmental changes in infants' processing of happy and angry facial expressions: A neurobehavioral study. *Brain and Cognition, 64,* 30–41.

Grotevant, H. D. (1998). Adolescent development in family contexts. In N. Eisenberg (Ed.), *Handbook of child psychology: Vol. 3. Social, emotional, and personality development* (5th ed., pp. 1097–1149). New York: Wiley.

Grotuss, J., Bjorklund, D. F., & Csinady, A. (2007). Evolutionary developmental psychology: Developing human nature. *Acta Psychologica Sinica, 39,* 439–453.

Grow-Maienza, J., Hahn, D.-D., & Joo, C.-A. (2001). Mathematics instruction in Korean primary schools: Structures, processes, and a linguistic analysis of questioning. *Journal of Educational Psychology, 93,* 363–376.

Gruendel, J., & Aber, J. L. (2007). Bridging the gap between research and child policy change: The role of strategic communications in policy advocacy. In J. L. Aber, S. J. Bishop-Josef, S. M. Jones, K. T. McLearn, & D. A. Phillips (Eds.), *Child development and social policy: Knowledge for action* (pp. 43–58). Washington, DC: American Psychological Association.

Grusec, J. E. (1988). *Social development: History, theory, and research.* New York: Springer-Verlag.

Grusec, J. E. (2006). The development of moral behavior and conscience from a socialization perspective. In M. Killen & J. Smetana (Eds.), *Handbook of moral development* (pp. 243–265). Philadelphia: Erlbaum.

Grusec, J. E., & Goodnow, J. J. (1994). Impact of parental discipline methods on the child's internalization of values: A reconceptualization of current points of view. *Developmental Psychology, 30,* 4–19.

Grych, J. H., & Clark, R. (1999). Maternal employment and development of the father–infant relationship in the first year. *Developmental Psychology, 35,* 893–903.

Guignard, J.-H., & Lubart, T. I. (2007). A comparative study of convergent and divergent thinking in intellectually gifted children. *Gifted and Talented International, 22*(1), 9–15.

Guilford, J. P. (1985). The structure-of-intellect model. In B. B. Wolman (Ed.), *Handbook of intelligence* (pp. 225–266). New York: Wiley.

Guilleminault, C., Palombini, L., Pelayo, R., & Chervin, R. D. (2003). Sleepwalking and sleep terrors in prepubertal children: What triggers them? *Pediatrics, 111,* e17–e25.

Guiso, L., Mont, F., Sapienza, P., & Zingales, L. (2008). Culture, gender, and math. *Science, 320,* 1164–1165.

Gullone, E. (2000). The development of normal fear: A century of research. *Clinical Psychology Review, 20,* 429–451.

Gulotta, T. P. (2008). How theory influences treatment and prevention practice within the family. In T. P. Gulotta (Ed.), *Family influences on child behavior and development: Evidence-based prevention and treatment approaches* (pp. 1–20). New York: Routledge.

Gunnar, M. R., & Cheatham, C. L. (2003). Brain and behavior interfaces: Stress and the developing brain. *Infant Mental Health Journal, 24,* 195–211.

Gunnar, M. R., Morison, S. J., Chisholm, K., & Schuder, M. (2001). Salivary cortisol levels in children adopted from Romanian orphanages. *Development and Psychopathology, 13,* 611–628.

Gunnar, M. R., & Vasquez, D. M. (2001). Low cortisol and a flattening of expected daytime rhythm: Potential indices of risk in human development. *Development and Psychopathology, 13,* 515–538.

Gunnarsdottir, I., Schack-Nielsen, L., Michaelson, K. F., Sørensen, T. I., & Thorsdottir, I. (2010). Infant weight gain, duration of exclusive breast-feeding, and childhood BMI—two similar follow-up cohorts. *Public Health Nutrition, 13,* 201–207.

Gunnoe, M. L., & Mariner, C. L. (1997). Toward a developmental-contextual model of the effects of parental spanking on children's aggression. *Archives of Pediatrics and Adolescent Medicine, 151,* 768–775.

Gunstad, J., Spitznagel, M. B., Luyster, F., Cohen, R. A., & Paul, R. H. (2007). Handedness and cognition across the healthy lifespan. *International Journal of Neuroscience, 117,* 477–485.

Guo, G., & VanWey, L. K. (1999). Sibship size and intellectual development: Is the relationship causal? *American Sociological Review, 64,* 169–187.

Guralnick, M. J., Neville, B., Hammond, M. A., & Connor, R. T. (2007). Linkages between delayed children's social interactions with mothers and peers. *Child Development, 78,* 459–473.

Gure, A., Ucanok, Z., & Sayil, M. (2006). The associations among perceived pubertal timing, parental relations and self-perception in Turkish adolescents. *Journal of Youth and Adolescence, 35,* 541–550.

Gurucharri, C., & Selman, R. L. (1982). The development of interpersonal understanding during childhood, preadolescence, and adolescence: A longitudinal follow-up study. *Child Development, 53,* 924–927.

Gustafson, G. E., Green, J. A., & Cleland, J. W. (1994). Robustness of individual identity in the cries of human infants. *Developmental Psychobiology, 27,* 1–9.

Gustafson, G. E., Wood, R. M., & Green, J. A. (2000). Can we hear the causes of infants' crying? In R. G. Barr & B. Hopkins (Eds.), *Crying as a sign, a symptom, and a signal: Clinical, emotional, and developmental aspects of infant and toddler crying* (pp. 8–22). New York: Cambridge University Press.

Gutman, L. M. (2006). How student and parent goal orientations and classroom goal structures influence the math achievement of African Americans during the high school transition. *Contemporary Educational Psychology, 31,* 44–63.

Gutman, L. M., & Midgley, C. (2000). The role of protective factors in supporting the academic achievement of poor African-American students during the middle school transition. *Journal of Youth and Adolescence, 29,* 223–248.

Gutman, L. M., Sameroff, A. J., & Cole, R. (2003). Academic growth curve trajectories from 1st grade to 12th grade: Effects of multiple social risk factors and preschool child factors. *Developmental Psychology, 39,* 777–790.

Gutteling, B. M., de Weerth, C., Zandbelt, N., Mulder, E. J. H., Visser, G. H. A., & Buitelaar, J. K. (2006). Does maternal prenatal stress adversely affect the child's learning and memory at age six? *Journal of Abnormal Child Psychology, 34,* 789–798.

Guttentag, R., & Ferrell, J. (2004). Reality compared with its alternatives: Age differences in judgments of regret and relief. *Developmental Psychology, 40,* 764–775.

Gwiazda, J., & Birch, E. E. (2001). Perceptual development: Vision. In E. B. Goldstein (Ed.), *Blackwell handbook of perception* (pp. 636–668). Oxford, UK: Blackwell.

H

Hack, M., & Klein, N. (2006). Young adult attainments of preterm infants. *Journal of the American Medical Association, 295,* 695–696.

Hagerman, R. J., Berry-Kravis, E., Kaufmann, W. E., Ono, M. Y., Tartaglia, N., & Lachiewicz, A. (2009). Advances in the treatment of fragile X syndrome. *Pediatrics, 123,* 378–390.

Hahn, S., & Chitty, L. S. (2008). Noninvasive prenatal diagnosis: Current practice and future perspectives. *Current Opinion in Obstetrics and Gynecology, 20,* 146–151.

Haidt, J. (2001). The emotional dog and its rational tail: A social intuitionist approach to moral judgment. *Psychological Review, 108,* 814–834.

Haight, W. L., & Miller, P. J. (1993). *Pretending at home: Early development in a sociocultural context.* Albany: State University of New York Press.

Hainline, L. (1998). The development of basic visual abilities. In A. Slater (Ed.), *Perceptual development: Visual, auditory, and speech perception in infancy* (pp. 37–44). Hove, U.K: Psychology Press.

Hakuta, K., Bialystok, E., & Wiley, E. (2003). Critical evidence: A test of the critical period hypothesis for second-language acquisition. *Psychological Science, 14,* 31–38.

Halberstadt, A. G., Denham, S. A., & Dunsmore, J. C. (2001). Affective social competence. *Social Development, 10,* 79–119.

Hale, C. M., & Tager-Flusberg, H. (2003). The influence of language on theory of mind: A training study. *Developmental Science, 6,* 346–359.

Hales, V. N., & Ozanne, S. E. (2003). The dangerous road of catch-up growth. *Journal of Physiology, 547,* 5–10.

Halfon, N., & McLearn, K. T. (2002). Families with children under 3: What we know and implications for results and policy. In N. Halfon & K. T. McLearn (Eds.), *Child rearing in America: Challenges facing parents with young children* (pp. 367–412). New York: Cambridge University Press.

Halford, G. S. (2002). Information-processing models of cognitive development. In U. Goswami (Ed.), *Blackwell handbook of childhood cognitive development* (pp. 555–574). Malden, MA: Blackwell.

Halford, G. S. (2005). Development of thinking. In K. J. Holyoak & R. G. Morrison (Eds.), *The Cambridge handbook of thinking and reasoning* (pp. 529–558). New York: Cambridge University Press.

Halford, G. S., & Andrews, G. (2006). Reasoning and problem solving. In D. Kuhn & R. Siegler (Eds.), *Handbook of child psychology: Vol. 2. Cognition, perception, and language* (6th ed., pp. 557–608). Hoboken, NJ: Wiley.

Halford, G. S., Wilson, W. H., Phillips, S. (1998). Processing capacity defined by relational complexity: Implications for comparative, developmental, and cognitive psychology. *Behavioral and Brain Sciences, 21,* 803–864.

Hall, D. G., & Graham, S. A. (1999). Lexical form class information guides word-to-object mapping in preschoolers. *Child Development, 70,* 78–91.

Hall, D. G., Burns, T., & Pawluski, J. (2003). Input and word learning: Caregivers' sensitivity to lexical category distinctions. *Journal of Child Language, 30,* 711–729.

Hall, G. S. (1904). *Adolescence.* New York: Appleton-Century-Crofts.

Hall, J. G. (2003). Twinning. *Lancet, 362,* 735–743.

Halle, T. G. (2003). Emotional development and well-being. In M. H. Bornstein, L. Davidson, C. L. M. Keyes, K. A. Moore, & the Center for Child Well-Being (Eds.), *Well-being: Positive development across the life course* (pp. 125–138). Mahwah, NJ: Erlbaum.

Haller, J. (2005). Vitamins and brain function. In H. R. Lieberman, R. B. Kanarek, & C. Prasad (2005). *Nutritional neuroscience* (pp. 207–233). Philadelphia: Taylor & Francis.

Hallinan, M. T., & Kubitschek, W. N. (1999). Curriculum differentiation and high school achievement. *Social Psychology of Education, 3,* 41–62.

Halpern, C. T., Udry, J. R., & Suchindran, C. (1997). Testosterone predicts initiation of coitus in adolescent females. *Psychosomatic Medicine, 59,* 161–171.

Halpern, D. F., Benbow, C. P., Geary, D. C., Gur, R. C., Hyde, J. S., & Gernsbacher, M. A. (2007). The science of sex differences in science and mathematics. *Psychological Science in the Public Interest, 8,* 1–51.

Halpern, D. F., & Collaer, M. L. (2005). Sex differences in visuospatial abilities: More than meets the eye.

In P. Shah & A. Miyake (Eds.), *Handbook of visuospatial thinking* (pp. 170–212). New York: Cambridge University Press.

Halpern, D. F., Wai, J., & Saw, A. (2005). A psychobiosocial model: Why females are sometimes greater than and sometimes less than males in math achievement. In D. F. Halpern, J. Wai, & A. Saw (Eds.), *Gender differences in mathematics: An integrative psychological approach* (pp. 48–72). New York: Cambridge University Press.

Halpern-Felsher, B. L., Biehl, M., Kropp, R. Y., & Rubinstein, M. L. (2004). Perceived risks and benefits of smoking: Differences among adolescents with different smoking experiences and intentions. *Preventive Medicine, 39,* 559–567.

Halpern-Felsher, B. L., & Cauffman, E. (2001). Costs and benefits of a decision: Decision-making competence in adolescents and adults. *Journal of Applied Developmental Psychology, 22,* 257–273.

Hamer, D. H., Hu, S., Magnuson, V. L., Hu, N., & Pattatucci, A. M. L. (1993). A linkage between DNA markers on the X chromosome and male sexual orientation. *Science, 261,* 321–327.

Hamilton, H. A. (2005). Extended families and adolescent well-being. *Journal of Adolescent Health, 36,* 260–266.

Hamilton, S. F., & Hamilton, M. A. (2000). Research, intervention, and social change: Improving adolescents' career opportunities. In L. J. Crockett & R. K. Silbereisen (Eds.), *Negotiating adolescence in times of social change* (pp. 267–283). New York: Cambridge University Press.

Hamlin, J. K., Wynn, K., & Bloom, P. (2007). Social evaluation by preverbal infants. *Nature, 450,* 557–559.

Hammes, B., & Laitman, C. J. (2003). Diethylstilbestrol (DES) update: Recommendations for the identification and management of DES-exposed individuals. *Journal of Midwifery and Women's Health, 48,* 19–29.

Hanawalt, B. A. (1993). *Growing up in medieval London: The experience of childhood in history.* New York: Oxford University Press.

Hanawalt, B. A. (2003). The child in the Middle Ages and the Renaissance. In W. Koops & M. Zuckerman (Eds.), *Beyond the century of childhood: Cultural history and developmental psychology.* Philadelphia: University of Pennsylvania Press.

Hane, A. A., Cheah, C., Rubin, K. H., & Fox, N. A. (2008). The role of maternal behavior in the relation between shyness and social reticence in early childhood and social withdrawal in middle childhood. *Social Development, 17,* 795–811.

Hanke, W., Sobala, W., & Kalinka, J. (2004). Environmental tobacco smoke exposure among pregnant women: Impact on fetal biometry at 20–24 weeks of gestation and newborn child's birth weight. *International Archives of Occupational and Environmental Health, 77,* 47–52.

Hankin, B. L., & Abela, J. R. Z. (2005). Depression from childhood through adolescence and adulthood.: A developmental vulnerability and stress perspective. In B. L. Hankin & J. R. Z. Abela (Eds.), *Development of psychopathology: A vulnerability-stress perspective* (pp. 245–288). Thousand Oaks, CA: Sage.

Hankin, B. L., Stone, L., & Wright, P. A. (2010). Corumination, interpersonal stress generation, and internalizing symptoms: Accumulating effects and transactional influences in a multiwave study of adolescents. *Development and Psychopathology, 22,* 217–235.

Hannon, E. E., & Johnson, S. P. (2004). Infants use meter to categorize rhythms and melodies: Implications for musical structure learning. *Cognitive Psychology, 50,* 354–377.

Hannon, E. E., & Trehub, S. E. (2005a). Metrical categories in infancy and adulthood. *Psychological Science, 16,* 48–55.

Hannon, E. E., & Trehub, S. E. (2005b). Tuning in to musical rhythms: Infants learn more readily than adults. *Proceedings of the National Academy of Sciences, 102,* 12639–12643.

Hannon, T. S., Rao, G., & Arslanian, S. A. (2005). Childhood obesity and type 2 diabetes mellitus. *Pediatrics, 116,* 473–480.

Hans, S. L., & Jeremy, R. J. (2001). Postneonatal mental and motor development of infants exposed in utero to opiate drugs. *Infant Mental Health Journal, 22,* 300–315.

Hansen, M., Janssen, I., Schiff, A., Zee, P. C., & Dubocovich, M. L. (2005). The impact of school daily schedule on adolescent sleep. *Pediatrics, 115,* 1555–1561.

Hansen, M. B., & Markman, E. M. (2009). Children's use of mutual exclusivity to learn labels for parts of objects. *Developmental Psychology, 45,* 592–596.

Happé, F., & Frith, U. (2006). The weak coherence account: Detail-focused cognitive style in autism spectrum disorders. *Journal of Autism and Developmental Disorders, 1,* 1–21.

Harachi, T. W., Fleming, C. B., White, H. R., Ensminger, M. E., Abbott, R. D., Catalano, R. F., & Haggerty, K. P. (2006). Aggressive behavior among girls and boys during middle childhood: Predictors and sequelae of trajectory group membership. *Aggressive Behavior, 32,* 279–293.

Harari, M. D., & Moulden, A. (2000). Nocturnal enuresis: What is happening? *Journal of Paediatrics and Child Health, 36,* 78–81.

Hardy, C. L., Bukowski, W. M., & Sippola, L. K. (2002). Stability and change in peer relationships during the transition to middle-level school. *Journal of Early Adolescence, 22,* 117–142.

Hardy, J. B., Astone, N. M., Brooks-Gunn, J., Shapiro, S., & Miller, T. L. (1998). Like mother, like child: Intergenerational patterns of age at first birth and associations with childhood and adolescent characteristics and adult outcomes in the second generation. *Developmental Psychology, 34,* 1220–1232.

Hardy, S. A., & Carlo, G. (2005). Religiosity and prosocial behaviours in adolescence: The mediating role of prosocial values. *Journal of Moral Education, 34,* 231–249.

Harley, B., & Jean, G. (1999). Vocabulary skills of French immersion students in their second language. *Zeitschrift für Interkulturellen Fremdsprachenunterricht, 4*(2). Retrieved from www.ualberta.ca

Harley, K., & Reese, E. (1999). Origins of autobio-graphical memory. *Developmental Psychology, 35,* 1338–1348.

Harlow, H. F., & Zimmerman, R. (1959). Affectional responses in the infant monkey. *Science, 130,* 421–432.

Harris, G. (1997). Development of taste perception and appetite regulation. In G. Bremner, A. Slater, & G. Butterworth (Eds.), *Infant development: Recent advances* (pp. 9–30). East Sussex, UK: Erlbaum.

Harris, M. B. (2008). Primary prevention of pregnancy: Effective school-based programs. In C. Franklin, M. B. Harris, & P. Allen-Meares (Eds.), *The school practitioner's concise companion to preventing dropout and attendance problems* (pp. 89–100). New York: Oxford University Press.

Harris, P. L., Brown, E., Marriott, C., Whitall, S., & Harmer, S. (1991). Monsters, ghosts and witches: Testing the limits of the fantasy–reality distinction in young children. *British Journal of Developmental Psychology, 9,* 105–123.

Harris, R. C., Robinson, J. B., Chang, F., & Burns, B. M. (2007). Characterizing preschool children's attention regulation in parent–child interactions: The roles of effortful control and motivation. *Journal of Applied Developmental Psychology, 28,* 25–39.

Harris, S., & Berk, L. E. (March, 2011). *Impact of individualized, supplementary preschool intervention on literacy, school readiness, and socioemotional skills.* Poster presented at the biennial meeting of the Society for Research in Child Development, Montreal, Canada.

Harris, Y. R., & Graham, J. A. (2007). *The African American child: Development and challenges.* New York: Springer.

Harrison, A. O., Wilson, M. N., Pine, C. J., Chan, S. Q., & Buriel, R. (1994). Family ecologies of ethnic minority children. In G. Handel & G. G. Whitchurch (Eds.),

The psychosocial interior of the family (pp. 187–210). New York: Aldine De Gruyter.

Harrison, Y. (2004). The relationship between daytime exposure to light and night-time sleep in 6–12-week-old infants. *Journal of Sleep Research, 13,* 345–352.

Harrist, A. W., Zaia, A. F., Bates, J. E., Dodge, K. A., & Pettit, G. S. (1997). Subtypes of social withdrawal in early childhood: Sociometric status and social-cognitive differences across four years. *Child Development, 68,* 278–294.

Hart, B. (2004). What toddlers talk about. *First Language, 24,* 91–106.

Hart, B., & Risley, T. R. (1995). *Meaningful differences in the everyday experience of young American children.* Baltimore: Paul H. Brookes.

Hart, C. H., Burts, D. C., Durland, M. A., Charlesworth, R., DeWolf, M., & Fleege, P. O. (1998). Stress behaviors and activity type participation of preschoolers in more and less developmentally appropriate classrooms: SES and sex differences. *Journal of Research in Childhood Education, 13.*

Hart, C. H., Newell, L. D., & Olsen, S. F. (2003). Parenting skills and social–communicative competence in childhood. In J. O. Greene & B. R. Burleson (Eds.), *Handbook of communication and social interaction skills* (pp. 753–797). Mahwah, NJ: Erlbaum.

Hart, C. H., Yang, C., Charlesworth, R., & Burts, D. C. (2003, April). *Kindergarten teaching practices: Associations with later child academic and social/emotional adjustment to school.* Paper presented at the biennial meeting of the Society for Research in Child Development, Tampa, FL.

Hart, C. H., Yang, C., Nelson, L. J., Robinson, C. C., Olsen, J. A., Nelson, D. A., et al. (2000). Peer acceptance in early childhood and subtypes of socially withdrawn behavior in China, Russia and the United States. *International Journal of Behavioral Development, 24,* 73–81.

Hart, D., Atkins, R., & Donnelly, T. M. (2006). Community service and moral development. In M. Killen & J. G. Smetana (Eds.), *Handbook of moral development* (pp. 633–656). Philadelphia: Erlbaum.

Hart, D., Atkins, R., & Matsuba, M. K. (2008). The association of neighborhood poverty with personality change in childhood. *Journal of Personality and Social Psychology, 94,* 1048–1061.

Hart, D., Donnelly, T. M., Youniss, J., & Atkins, R. (2007). High school community service as a predictor of adult voting and volunteering. *American Educational Research Journal, 44,* 197–219.

Hart, D., & Fegley, S. (1995). Prosocial behavior and caring in adolescence: Relations to self-understanding and social judgment. *Child Development, 66,* 1346–1359.

Harter, S. (1998). The development of self-representations. In N. Eisenberg (Ed.), *Handbook of child psychology: Vol. 3. Social, emotional, and personality development* (5th ed., pp. 553–618). New York: Wiley.

Harter, S. (1999). *The construction of self: A developmental perspective.* New York: Guilford.

Harter, S. (2003). The development of self-representations during childhood and adolescence. In M. R. Leary & J. P. Tangney (Eds.), *Handbook of self and identity* (pp. 610–642). New York: Guilford.

Harter, S. (2006). The self. In N. Eisenberg (Ed.), *Handbook of child psychology: Vol. 3. Social, emotional, and personality development* (6th ed., pp. 505–570). Hoboken, NJ: Wiley.

Harter, S., & Whitesell, N. (1989). Developmental changes in children's understanding of simple, multiple, and blended emotion concepts. In C. Saarni & P. Harris (Eds.), *Children's understanding of emotion* (pp. 81–116). Cambridge, UK: Cambridge University Press.

Harter, S., & Whitesell, N. R. (2003). Beyond the debate: Why some adolescents report stable self-worth over time and situation, whereas others report changes in self-worth. *Journal of Personality, 71,* 1027–1058.

Hartshorn, K. (2003). Reinstatement maintains a memory in human infants for 1½ years. *Developmental Psychobiology, 42,* 269–282.

Hartshorn, K., Rovee-Collier, C., Gerhardstein, P., Bhatt, R. S., Klein, P. J., Aaron, F., Wondoloski, T. L., & Wurtzel, N. (1998a). Developmental changes in the specificity of memory over the first year of life. *Developmental Psychology, 33,* 61–78.

Hartshorn, K., Rovee-Collier, C., Gerhardstein, P., Bhatt, R. S., Wondoloski, T. L., Klein, P., Gilch, J., Wurtzel, N., & Campos-deCarvalho, M. (1998b). The ontogeny of long-term memory over the first year-and-a-half of life. *Developmental Psychobiology, 32,* 69–89.

Hartup, W. W. (1999). Peer experience and its developmental significance. In M. Bennett (Ed.), *Developmental psychology: Achievements and prospects* (pp. 106–125). Philadelphia, PA: Psychology Press.

Hartup, W. W. (2006). Relationships in early and middle childhood. In A. L. Vangelisti & D. Perlman (Eds.), *Cambridge handbook of personal relationships* (pp. 177–190). New York: Cambridge University Press.

Hartup, W. W., & Abecassis, M. (2004). Friends and enemies. In P. K. Smith & C. H. Hart (Eds.), *Blackwell handbook of childhood social development* (pp. 285–306). Malden, MA: Blackwell.

Hartup, W. W., & Stevens, N. (1999). Friendships and adaptation across the life span. *Current Directions in Psychological Science, 8,* 76–79.

Harvey, M. W. (2001). Vocational-technical education: A logical approach to dropout prevention for secondary special education. *Preventing School Failure, 45,* 108–113.

Harwood, M. D., & Farrar, M. J. (2006). Conflicting emotions: The connection between affective perspective taking and theory of mind. *British Journal of Developmental Psychology, 24,* 401–418.

Harwood, R., Leyendecker, B., Carlson, V., Asencio, M., & Miller, A. (2002). Parenting among Latino families in the U.S. In M. H. Bornstein (Ed.), *Handbook of Parenting: Vol. 4. Social conditions and applied parenting* (2nd ed., pp. 21–46). Mahwah, NJ: Lawrence Erlbaum Associates.

Hasebe, Y., Nucci, L., & Nucci, M. S. (2004). Parental control of the personal domain and adolescent symptoms of psychopathology: A cross-national study in the United States and Japan. *Child Development, 75,* 815–828.

Hatton, D. D., Bailey, D. B., Jr., Burchinal, M. R., & Ferrell, K. A. (1997). Developmental growth curves of preschool children with vision impairments. *Child Development, 68,* 788–806.

Hausenblas, H. A., & Downs, D. S. (2005). Prospective examination of leisure-time exercise behavior during pregnancy. *Journal of Applied Psychology, 17,* 240–246.

Hauser-Cram, P., Warfield, M. E., Stadler, J., & Sirin, S. R. (2006). School environments and the diverging pathways of students living in poverty. In A. C. Huston & M. N. Ripke (Eds.), *Developmental contexts in middle childhood* (pp. 198–216). New York: Cambridge University Press.

Hausfather, A., Toharia, A., LaRoche, C., & Engelsmann, F. (1997). Effects of age of entry, day-care quality, and family characteristics on preschool behavior. *Journal of Child Psychology and Psychiatry, 38,* 441–448.

Hawke, S., & Knox, D. (1978). The one-child family: A new life-style. *The Family Coordinator, 27,* 215–219.

Hawkins, J. N. (1994). Issues of motivation in Asian education. In H. F. O'Neil, Jr., & M. Drillings (Eds.), *Motivation: Theory and research* (pp. 101–115). Hillsdale, NJ: Erlbaum.

Haws, R. A., Yakoob, M. Y., Soomro, T., Menezes, E. V., Darmstadt, G. L., & Bhutta, Z. A. (2009). Reducing stillbirths: Screening and monitoring during pregnancy and labour. *BMC Pregnancy and Childbirth, 9*(Suppl. S1).

Hawton, K., Zahl, D., & Weatherall, R. (2003). Suicide following deliberate self-harm: Long-term follow-up of patients who presented to a general hospital. *British Journal of Psychiatry, 182,* 537–542.

Hay, C., Fortson, E. N., Hollist, D. R., Altheimer, I., & Schaible, L. M. (2007). Compounded risk: The implications for delinquency of coming from a poor family that lives in a poor community. *Journal of Youth and Adolescence, 36,* 593–605.

Hay, D. F., Pawlby, S., Waters, C. S., Perra, O., & Sharp, D. (2010). Mothers' antenatal depression and their children's antisocial outcomes. *Child Development, 81,* 149–165.

Hay, D. F., Payne, A., & Chadwick, A. (2004). Peer relations in childhood. *Journal of Child Psychology and Psychiatry, 45,* 84–108.

Hay, P., & Bacaltchuk, J. (2004). Bulimia nervosa. *Clinical Evidence, 12,* 1326–1347.

Hayne, H. (2002). Thoughts from the crib: Meltzoff and Moore (1994) alter our views of mental representation during infancy. *Infant Behavior and Development, 25,* 62–64.

Hayne, H. (2004). Infant memory development: Implications for childhood amnesia. *Developmental Review, 24,* 33–73.

Hayne, H., Boniface, J., & Barr, R. (2000). The development of declarative memory in human infants: Age-related changes in deferred imitation. *Behavioral Neuroscience, 114,* 77–83.

Hayne, H., Herbert, J., & Simcock, G. (2003). Imitation from television by 24- and 30-month-olds. *Developmental Science, 6,* 254–261.

Hayne, H., & Rovee-Collier, C. K. (1995). The organization of reactivated memory in infancy. *Child Development, 66,* 893–906.

Hayne, H., Rovee-Collier, C., & Perris, E. E. (1987). Categorization and memory retrieval by three-month-olds. *Child Development, 58,* 750–767.

Hayslip, B., Emick, M. A., Henderson, C. E., & Elias, K. (2002). Temporal variations in the experiences of custodial grandparenting: A short-term longitudinal study. *Journal of Applied Gerontology, 21,* 139–156.

Haywood, H. C., & Lidz, C. (2007). *Dynamic assessment in practice.* New York: Cambridge University Press.

Haywood, K. M., & Getchell, N. (2005). *Life span motor development* (4th ed.). Champaign, IL: Human Kinetics.

Hazen, N. L., McFarland, L., Jacobvitz, D., & Boyd-Soisson, E. (2010). Fathers' frightening behaviours and sensitivity with infants: Relations with fathers' attachment representations, father–infant attachment, and children's later outcomes. *Early Child Development and Care, 180,* 51–69.

Head Start Bureau. (2008) *Head Start fact sheet.* Retrieved from www.acf.hhs.gov/programs/ohs/about/fy2008.html

Health Canada. (2008). *Report on sexually transmitted infections in Canada.* Retrieved from www.phac-aspc.gc.ca/ std-mts/report/ sti-its2008/ index-eng.php

Heath, S. B. (1990). The children of Trackton's children: Spoken and written language in social change. In J. Stigler, G. Herdt, & R. A. Shweder (Eds.), *Cultural psychology: Essays on comparative human development* (pp. 496–519). New York: Cambridge University Press.

Heaven, P. C. L., & Ciarrochi, J. (2008). Parental styles, conscientiousness, and academic performance in high school: A three-wave longitudinal study. *Personality and Social Psychology Bulletin, 34,* 451–461.

Hebert, M., & Tourigny, M. (2004). Child sexual abuse prevention: A review of evaluative studies and recommendations for program development. In S. P. Serge (Eds.), *Advances in psychology research* (Vol. 29, pp. 123–155). Hauppauge, NY: Nova Science Publishers.

Heckman, J. J., & Masterov, D. V. (2004). *The productivity argument for investing in young children.* Working Paper 5, Invest in Kids Working Group, Committee for Economic Development. Retrieved from jenni.uchicago.edu/Invest

Hediger, M. L., Overpeck, M. D., Ruan, W. J., & Troendle, J. F. (2002). Birthweight and gestational age effects on motor and social development. *Paediatric and Perinatal Epidemiology, 16,* 33–46.

Heilbrun, K., Lee, R., & Cottle, C. C. (2005). Risk factors and intervention outcomes: Meta-analyses of juvenile offending. In K. Heilbrun, N. E. S. Goldstein, & R. E. Redding (Eds.), *Juvenile delinquency: Prevention, assessment, and intervention* (pp. 111–133). New York: Oxford University Press.

Heinz, W. R. (1999). Job-entry patterns in a life-course perspective. In W. R. Heinz (Ed.), *From education to work: Cross-national perspectives* (pp. 214–231). New York: Cambridge University Press.

Helburn, S. W. (Ed.). (1995). *Cost, quality and child outcomes in child care centers.* Denver: University of Colorado.

Helwig, C. C. (2006). Rights, civil liberties, and democracy across cultures. In M. Killen & J. G. Smetana (Eds.), *Handbook of moral development* (pp. 185–210). Philadelphia: Erlbaum.

Helwig, C. C., Arnold, M. L., Tan, D., & Boyd, D. (2003). Chinese adolescents' reasoning about democratic and authority-based decision making in peer, family, and school contexts. *Child Development, 74,* 783–800.

Helwig, C. C., & Jasiobedzka, U. (2001). The relation between law and morality: Children's reasoning about socially beneficial and unjust laws. *Child Development, 72,* 1382–1393.

Helwig, C. C., & Prencipe, A. (1999). Children's judgments of flags and flag-burning. *Child Development, 70,* 132–143.

Helwig, C. C., & Turiel, E. (2004). Children's social and moral reasoning. In P. K. Smith & C. H. Hart (Eds.), *Blackwell handbook of childhood social development* (pp. 476–490). Malden, MA: Blackwell.

Helwig, C. C., Zelazo, P. D., & Wilson, M. (2001). Children's judgments of psychological harm in normal and canonical situations. *Child Development, 72,* 66–81.

Henderson, H. A., Marshall, P. J., Fox, N. A., & Rubin, K. H. (2004). Psychophysiological and behavioral evidence for varying forms and functions of nonsocial behavior in preschoolers. *Child Development, 75,* 251–263.

Hendry, L. B., & Kloep, M. (2007). Conceptualizing emerging adulthood: Inspecting the emperor's new clothes? *Child Development Perspectives, 1,* 74–79.

Henggeler, S. W., Schoenwald, S. K., Borduin, C. M., Rowland, M. D., & Cunningham, P. B. (2009). *Multisystemic therapy for antisocial behavior in children and adolescents* (2nd ed.). New York: Guilford.

Henrich, C. C., Brookmeyer, K. A., Shrier, L. A., & Shahar, G. (2006). Supportive relationships and sexual risk behavior in adolescence: An ecological–transactional approach. *Journal of Pediatric Psychology, 31,* 286–297.

Henrich, C. C., Kuperminc, G. P., Sack, A., Blatt, S. J., & Leadbeater, B. J. (2000). Characteristics and homogeneity of early adolescent friendship groups: A comparison of male and female clique and nonclique members. *Applied Developmental Science, 4,* 15–26.

Henricsson, L., & Rydell, A.-M. (2004). Elementary school children with behavior problems: Teacher–child relations and self-perception. A prospective study. *Merrill-Palmer Quarterly, 50,* 111–138.

Hepper, P. G., McCartney, G. R., & Shannon, E. A. (1998). Lateralised behaviour in first trimester human foetuses. *Neuropsychologia, 43,* 313–315.

Heraghty, J. L., Hilliard, T. N., Henderson, A. J., & Fleming, P. J. (2008). The physiology of sleep in infants. *Archives of Disease in Childhood, 93,* 982–985.

Herbert, J., & Hayne, H. (2000). The ontogeny of long-term retention during the second year of life. *Developmental Science, 3,* 50–56.

Herman, M. (2004). Forced to choose: Some determinants of racial identification in multiracial adolescents. *Child Development, 75,* 730–748.

Herman-Giddens, M. E. (2006). Recent data on pubertal milestones in United States children: The secular trend toward earlier development. *International Journal of Andrology, 29,* 241–246.

Hernandez, D. J., Denton, N. A., & Macartney, S. E. (2008). Children in immigrant families: Looking to America's future. *Social Policy Report of the Society for Research in Child Development, 12*(11).

Herrera, E., Reissland, N., & Shepherd, J. (2004). Maternal touch and maternal child-directed speech:

Effects of depressed mood in the postnatal period. *Journal of Affective Disorders, 81,* 29–39.

Herrnstein, R. J., & Murray, C. (1994). *The bell curve.* New York: Free Press.

Hertenstein, M. J., & Campos, J. J. (2004). The retention effects of an adult's emotional displays on infant behavior. *Child Development, 75,* 595–613.

Herzog, D. B., Eddy, K. T., & Beresin, E. V. (2006). Anorexia and bulimia nervosa. In M. K. Dulcan & J. M. Wiener (Eds.), *Essentials of child and adolescent psychiatry* (pp. 527–560). Washington, DC: American Psychiatric Publishing.

Hesketh, K., Ball, K., Crawford, D., Campbell, K., & Salmon, J. (2007). Mediators of the relationship between maternal education and children's TV viewing. *American Journal of Preventive Medicine, 33,* 41–47.

Hespos, S. J., & Baillargeon, R. (2001). Reasoning about containment events in very young infants. *Cognition, 78,* 207–245.

Hespos, S. J., Ferry, A. L., Cannistraci, C. J., Gore, J., & Park, S. (2010). Using optical imaging to investigate functional cortical activity in human infants. In A. W. Roe (Ed.), *Imaging the brain with optical methods* (pp. 159–176). New York: Springer Science + Business Media.

Hesse, E., & Main, M. (2000). Disorganized infant, child, and adult attachment: Collapse in behavioral and attentional strategies. *Journal of the American Psychoanalytic Association, 48,* 1097–1127.

Hetherington, E. M. (1999). Should we stay together for the sake of the children? In E. M. Hetherington (Ed.), *Coping with divorce, single parenting, and remarriage: A risk and resiliency perspective* (pp. 93–116). Hillsdale, NJ: Erlbaum.

Hetherington, E. M. (2003). Social support and the adjustment of children in divorced and remarried families. *Childhood, 10,* 237–254

Hetherington, E. M., Henderson, S. H., & Reiss, D. (1999). Adolescent siblings in stepfamilies: Family functioning and adolescent adjustment. *Monographs of the Society for Research in Child Development, 64*(4, Serial No. 259).

Hetherington, E. M., & Jodl, K. M. (1994). Stepfamilies as settings for child development. In A. Booth & J. Dunn (Eds.), *Stepfamilies: Who benefits? Who does not?* (pp. 55–79). Hillsdale, NJ: Erlbaum.

Hetherington, E. M., & Kelly, J. (2002). *For better or for worse: Divorce reconsidered.* New York: Norton.

Hetherington, E. M., & Stanley-Hagan, M. (2000). Diversity among stepfamilies. In D. H. Demo, K. R. Allen, & M. A. Fine (Eds.), *Handbook of family diversity* (pp. 173–196). New York: Oxford University Press.

Hewlett, B. S. (1992). Husband–wife reciprocity and the father–infant relationship among Aka pygmies. In B. S. Hewlett (Ed.), *Father–child relations: Cultural and biosocial contexts* (pp. 153– 176). New York: Aldine De Gruyter.

Hewlett, B. S. (2004). Fathers in forager, farmer, and pastoral cultures. In M. E. Lamb (Ed.), *The role of the father in child development* (4th ed., pp. 182–195). Hoboken, NJ: Wiley.

Hewlett, S. (2003). *Creating a life.* New York: Miramax.

Heyes, C. (2005). Imitation by association. In S. Hurley & N. Chater (Eds.), *Perspectives on imitation: From neuroscience to social science: Vol. 1. Mechanisms of imitation and imitation in animals* (pp. 157–177). Cambridge, MA: MIT Press.

Heyman, G. D., & Dweck, C. S. (1998). Children's thinking about traits: Implications for judgments of the self and others. *Child Development, 69,* 391–403.

Heyman, G. D., Dweck, C. S., & Cain, K. M. (1992). Young children's vulnerability to self-blame and helplessness: Relationship to beliefs about goodness. *Child Development, 63,* 401–415.

Heyman, G. D., & Gelman, S. A. (1999). The use of trait labels in making psychological inferences. *Child Development, 70,* 604–619.

Heyman, G. D., & Gelman, S. A. (2000). Preschool children's use of trait labels to make inductive inferences. *Journal of Experimental Child Psychology, 77,* 1–19.

Heyman, G. D., & Legare, C. H. (2004). Children's beliefs about gender differences in the academic and social domains. *Sex Roles, 50,* 227–239.

Hibell, B. (2001). *European School Survey Project on Alcohol and Drugs.* Stockholm: Swedish Council for Information on Alcohol and Other Drugs.

Hickling, A. K., & Wellman, H. M. (2001). The emergence of children's causal explanations and theories: Evidence from everyday conversation. *Developmental Psychology, 37,* 668–683.

Hicks, J. H., & Goedereis, E. A. (2009). The importance of context and the gain-loss dynamic for understanding grandparent caregivers. In K. Shifren (Ed.), *How caregiving affects development: Psychological implications for child, adolescent, and adult caregivers* (pp. 169–190). Washington, DC: American Psychological Association.

Higginbottom, G. M. A. (2006). 'Pressure of life': Ethnicity as a mediating factor in mid-life and older peoples' experience of high blood pressure. *Sociology of Health and Illness, 28,* 583–610.

Higgins, C., & Duxbury, L. (2002). *The 2001 National Work-Life Conflict Study: Report One.* Retrieved from www. phac-aspc.gc.ca/publicat/worktravail/report1/index.html

High, P. C., LaGasse, L., Becker, S., Ahlgren, I., & Gardner, A. (2000). Literacy promotion in primary care pediatrics: Can we make a difference? *Pediatrics, 105,* 927–934.

Hildreth, K., & Rovee-Collier, C. (2002). Forgetting functions of reactivated memories over the first year of life. *Developmental Psychology, 41,* 277–288.

Hildreth, K., Sweeney, B., & Rovee-Collier, C. (2003). Differential memory-preserving effects of reminders at 6 months. *Journal of Experimental Child Psychology, 84,* 41–62.

Hilgers, K. K., Akridge, M., Scheetz, J. P., & Kinance, D. E. (2006). Childhood obesity and dental development. *Pediatric Dentistry, 28,* 18–22.

Hill, A. L., Degnan, K. A., Calkins, S. D., & Keane, S. P. (2006). Profiles of externalizing behavior problems for boys and girls across preschool: The roles of emotion regulation and inattention. *Developmental Psychology, 42,* 913–928.

Hill, E. J., Mead, N. T., Dean, L. R., Hafen, D. M., Gadd, R., Palmer, A. A., & Ferris, M. S. (2006). Researching the 60-hour dual-earner workweek: An alternative to the "opt-out revolution." *American Behavioral Scientist, 49,* 1184–1203.

Hill, J. L., Brooks-Gunn, J., & Waldfogel, J. (2003). Sustained effects of high participation in an early intervention for low-birth-weight premature infants. *Developmental Psychology, 39,* 730–744.

Hill, N. E., & Taylor, I. C. (2004). Parental school involvement and children's academic achievement: Pragmatics and issues. *Current Directions in Psychological Science, 13,* 161–164.

Hill, N. M., & Schneider, W. (2006). Brain changes in the development of expertise: Neuroanatomical and neurophysiological evidence about skill-based adaptations. In K. A. Ericsson, N. Charness, P. J. Feltovich, & R. R. Hoffman (Eds.), *The Cambridge handbook of expertise and expert performance* (pp. 653–682). New York: Cambridge University Press.

Hillard, P. J. A. (2008). Menstruation in adolescents: What's normal, what's not. *Annals of the New York Academy of Sciences, 1135,* 29–35.

Hillis, S. D., Anda, R. F., Dube, S. R., Felitti, V. J., Marchbanks, P. A., & Marks, J. S. (2004). The association between adverse childhood experiences and adolescent pregnancy, long-term psychosocial consequences, and fetal death. *Pediatrics, 113,* 320–327.

Hilt, L. M. (2004). Attribution retraining for therapeutic change: Theory, practice, and future directions. *Imagination, Cognition, and Personality, 23,* 289–307.

Hinojosa, T., Sheu, C.-F., & Michael, G. F. (2003). Infant hand-use preference for grasping objects contributes to the development of a hand-use preference for manipulating objects. *Developmental Psychobiology, 43,* 328–334.

Hirsh-Pasek, K., & Burchinal, M. (2006). Mother and caregiver sensitivity over time: Predicting language and academic outcomes with variable- and person-centered approaches. *Merill-Palmer Quarterly, 52,* 449-485.

Hirsh-Pasek, K., & Golinkoff, R. M. (2003). *Einstein never used flash cards.* New York: Rodale.

Hirsh-Pasek, K., Golinkoff, R. M., Berk, L. E., & Singer, D. G. (2009). *A mandate for playful learning in preschool: Presenting the evidence.* New York: Oxford University Press.

Hjälmäs, K. (1998). Nocturnal enuresis: Basic facts and new horizons. *European Urology, 33*(Suppl. 3), 53–57.

Hoch-Espada, A., Ryan, E., & Deblinger, E. (2006). Child sexual abuse. In J. E. Fisher & W. T. O'Donohue (Eds.), *Practitioner's guide to evidence-based psychotherapy* (pp. 177–188). New York: Springer.

Hock, H. S., Park, C. L., & Bjorklund, D. F. (1998). Temporal organization in children's strategy formation. *Journal of Experimental Child Psychology, 70,* 187–206.

Hodges, J., & Tizard, B. (1989). Social and family relationships of ex-institutional adolescents. *Journal of Child Psychology and Psychiatry, 30,* 77–97.

Hodges, R. M., & French, L. A. (1988). The effect of class and collection labels on cardinality, class-inclusion, and number conservation tasks. *Child Development, 59,* 1387–1396.

Hodnett, E. D., Gates, S., Hofmeyr, G. J., & Sakala, C. (2003). Continuous support for women during childbirth. *Cochrane Database of Systematic Reviews, 3,* CD003766.

Hoehn, T., Hansmann, G., Bührer, C., Simbruner, G., Gunn, A. J., Yager, J., et al. (2008). Therapeutic hypothermia in neonates: Review of current clinical data, ILCOR recommendations and suggestions for implementation in neonatal intensive care units. *Resuscitation, 78,* 7–12.

Hoekstra, R. A., Bartels, M., Hudziak, J. J., Van Beijsterveldt, T. C., & Boomsma, D. I. (2008). Genetic and environmental influences on the stability of withdrawn behavior in children: A longitudinal, multi-informant twin study. *Behavior Genetics, 38,* 447–461.

Hoff, E. (2003). The specificity of environmental influence: Socioeconomic status affects early vocabulary development via maternal speech. *Child Development, 74,* 1368–1378.

Hoff, E. (2006). How social contexts support and shape language development. *Developmental Review, 26,* 55–88.

Hoff, E., Laursen, B., & Tardif, T. (2002). Socioeconomic status and parenting. In M. H. Bornstein (Ed.), *Handbook of parenting: Vol. 2. Biology and ecology of parenting* (pp. 231–252). Mahwah, NJ: Erlbaum.

Hoff, E. V. (2005). A friend living inside me: The forms and functions of imaginary companions. *Imagination, Cognition and Personality, 24,* 151–189.

Hoff, T., Greene, L., & Davis, J. (2003). *National survey of adolescents and young adults: Sexual health knowledge, attitudes and experiences.* Menlo Park, CA: Henry J. Kaiser Family Foundation.

Hofferth, S. L., & Anderson, K. G. (2003). Are all dads equal? Biology versus marriage as a basis for paternal investment. *Journal of Marriage and the Family, 65,* 213–232.

Hoffman, L. W. (2000). Maternal employment: Effects of social context. In R. D. Taylor & M. C. Wang (Eds.), *Resilience across contexts: Family, work, culture, and community* (pp. 147–176). Mahwah, NJ: Erlbaum.

Hoffman, M. K., Vahratian, A., Sciscione, A. C., Troendle, J. F., & Zhang, J. (2006). Comparison of labor progression between induced and noninduced multiparous women. *Obstetrics and Gynecology, 107,* 1029–1034.

Hoffman, M. L. (2000). *Empathy and moral development.* New York: Cambridge University Press.

Hoffmann, W. (2001). Fallout from the Chernobyl nuclear disaster and congenital malformations in Europe. *Archives of Environmental Health, 56,* 478–483.

Hoffner, C., & Badzinski, D. M. (1989). Children's integration of facial and situational cues to emotion. *Child Development, 60,* 411–422.

Hogan, M. J., & Strasburger, V. C. (2008). Body image, eating disorders, and the media. *Adolescent Medicine, 19,* 521–546.

Hokoda, A., & Fincham, F. D. (1995). Origins of children's helpless and mastery achievement patterns in the family. *Journal of Educational Psychology, 87,* 375–385.

Holden, G. W., Coleman, S. M., & Schmidt, K. L. (1995). Why 3-year-old children get spanked: Determinants as reported by college-educated mothers. *Merrill-Palmer Quarterly, 41,* 431–452.

Holditch-Davis, D., Belyea, M., & Edwards, L. J. (2005). Prediction of 3-year developmental outcomes from sleep development over the preterm period. *Infant Behavior and Development, 79,* 49–58.

Holland, A. L. (2004). Plasticity and development. *Brain and Language, 88,* 254–255.

Holland, J. L. (1985). *Making vocational choices: A theory of vocational personalities and work environments.* Englewood Cliffs, NJ; Prentice-Hall.

Holland, J. L. (1997). *Making vocational choices: A theory of vocational personalities and work environments* (3rd ed.). Odessa, FL: Psychological Assessment Resources.

Hollich, G. J., Hirsh-Pasek, K., & Golinkoff, R. M. (2000). Breaking the language barrier: An emergentist coalition model for the origins of word learning. *Monographs of the Society for Research in Child Development, 65*(3, Serial No. 262).

Holmbeck, G. N. (1996). A model of family relational transformations during the transition to adolescence: Parent–adolescent conflict and adaptation. In J. A. Graber, J. Brooks-Gunn, & A. C. Petersen (Eds.), *Transitions through adolescence* (pp. 167–199). Mahwah, NJ: Erlbaum.

Holobow, N., Genesee, F., & Lambert, W. (1991). The effectiveness of a foreign language immersion program for children from different ethnic and social class backgrounds: Report 2. *Applied Psycholinguistics, 12,* 179–198.

Holowka, S., Brosseau-Lapré, F., & Petitto, L. A. (2002). Semantic and conceptual knowledge underlying bilingual babies' first signs and words. *Language Learning, 52,* 205–262.

Holsen, I., Kraft, P., & Vittersø, J. (2000). Stability in depressed mood in adolescence: Results from a 6-year longitudinal study. *Journal of Youth and Adolescence, 29,* 61–78.

Honein, M. A., Paulozzi, L. J., & Erickson, J. D. (2001). Continued occurrence of Accutane-exposed pregnancies. *Teratology, 64,* 142–147.

Hood, B. M. (2004). Is looking good enough or does it beggar belief? *Developmental Science, 7,* 415–417.

Hood, M., Conlon, E., & Andrews, G. (2008). Preschool home literacy practices and children's literacy development: A longitudinal analysis. *Journal of Educational Psychology, 100,* 252–271.

Hopkins, B., & Westra, T. (1988). Maternal handling and motor development: An intracultural study. *Genetic, Social and General Psychology Monographs, 14,* 377–420.

Hopkins-Golightly, T., Raz, S., & Sander, C. J. (2003). Influence of slight to moderate risk for birth hypoxia on acquisition of cognitive and language function in the preterm infant: A cross-sectional comparison with preterm-birth controls. *Neuropsychology, 17,* 3–13.

Horgan, D. (1978). The development of the full passive. *Journal of Child Language, 5,* 65–80.

Horner, S. L., & Gaither, S. M. (2004). Attribution retraining instruction with a second-grade class. *Early Childhood Education Journal, 31,* 165–170.

Horner, T. M. (1980). Two methods of studying stranger reactivity in infants: A review. *Journal of Child Psychology and Psychiatry, 21,* 203–219.

Horst, J. S., Oakes, L. M., & Madole, K. L. (2005). What does it look like and what can it do? Category structure influences how infants categorize. *Child Development, 76,* 614–631.

Houlihan, J., Kropp. T. Wiles, R., Gray, S., & Campbell, C. (2005). *Body burden: The pollution in newborns.* Washington, DC: Environmental Working Group.

Houts, A. C. (2003). Behavioral treatment for enuresis. In A. E. Kazdin (Ed.), *Evidence-based psychotherapies for children and adolescents* (pp. 389–406). New York: Guilford.

Hoven, C. W., Duarte, C. S., Lucas, C. P., Wu, P., Mandell, D. J., Goodwin, R. D., et al. (2005). Psychopathology among New York City public school children 6 months after September 11. *Archives of General Psychiatry, 62,* 545–552.

Howard, B. J., & Wong, J. (2001). Sleep disorders. *Pediatrics in Review, 22,* 327–342.

Howard, K. S., & Brooks-Gunn, J. (2009). The role of home-visiting programs in preventing child abuse and neglect. *Future of Children, 19,* 119–146.

Howell, K. K., Coles, C. D., & Kable, J. A. (2008). The medical and developmental consequences of prenatal drug exposure. In J. Brick (Ed.), *Handbook of the medical consequences of alcohol and drug abuse* (2nd ed., pp. 219–249). New York: Haworth Press.

Howell, K. K., Lynch, M. E., Platzman, K. A., Smith, G. H., & Coles, C. D. (2006). Prenatal alcohol exposure and ability, academic achievement, and school functioning in adolescence: A longitudinal follow-up. *Journal of Pediatric Psychology, 31,* 116–126.

Howell, T. M., & Yuille, J. C. (2004). Healing and treatment of Aboriginal offenders: A Canadian example. *American Journal of Forensic Psychology, 22,* 53–76.

Howes, C., & Matheson, C. C. (1992). Sequences in the development of competent play with peers: Social and social pretend play. *Developmental Psychology, 28,* 961–974.

Hoza, B., Gerdes, A. C., Hinshaw, S. P., Bukowski, W. M., Gold, J. A., Kraemer, H. C., Pelham, W. E., Jr., Wigal, T., & Arnold, L. E. (2005). What aspects of peer relationships are impaired in children with attention-deficit/hyperactivity disorder? *Journal of Consulting and Clinical Psychology, 73,* 411–423.

Huang, C.-C. (2006). Child support enforcement and father involvement for children in never-married mother families. *Fathering, 4,* 97–111.

Hubbs-Tait, L., Nation, J. R., Krebs, N. F., & Bellinger, D. C. (2005). Neurotoxicants, micronutrients, and social environments: Individual and combined effects on children's development. *Psychological Science in the Public Interest, 6,* 57–121.

Huddleston, J., & Ge, X. (2003). Boys at puberty: Psychosocial implications. In C. Hayward (Ed.), *Gender differences at puberty* (pp. 113–134). New York: Cambridge University Press.

Hudson, J. A., Fivush, R., & Kuebli, J. (1992). Scripts and episodes: The development of event memory. *Applied Cognitive Psychology, 6,* 483–505.

Hudson, J. A., Sosa, B. B., & Shapiro, L. R. (1997). Scripts and plans: The development of preschool children's event knowledge and event planning. In S. L. Friedman & E. K. Scholnick (Eds.), *The developmental psychology of planning* (pp. 77–102). Mahwah, NJ: Erlbaum.

Hudziak, J. J., & Rettew, D. C. (2009). Genetics of ADHD. In T. E. Brown (Ed.), *ADHD comorbidties: Handbook for ADHD complications in children and adults* (pp. 23–36). Arlington, VA: American Psychiatric Publishing.

Huesmann, L. R. (1986). Psychological processes promoting the relation between exposure to media violence and aggressive behavior by the viewer. *Journal of Social Issues, 42,* 125–139.

Huesmann, L. R., Moise-Titus, J., Podolski, C., & Eron, L. D. (2003). Longitudinal relations between children's exposure to TV violence and their aggressive and violent behavior in young adulthood: 1977–1992. *Developmental Psychology, 39,* 201–221.

Hughes, C. (1998). Finding your marbles: Does preschoolers' strategic behavior predict later understanding of mind? *Developmental Psychology, 34,* 1326–1339.

Hughes, C., & Dunn, J. (1998). Understanding mind and emotion: Longitudinal associations with mental-state talk between young friends. *Developmental Psychology, 34,* 1026–1037.

Hughes, D., Rodriguez, J., Smith, E. P., Johnson, D. J., Stevenson, H. C., & Spicer, P. (2006). Parents' ethnic-racial socialization practices: A review of research and directions for future study. *Developmental Psychology, 42,* 747–770.

Hughes, D. C., & Ng, S. (2003). Reducing health disparities among children. *Future of Children, 13,* 153–167.

Hughes, J. N., Cavell, T. A., & Grossman, P. B. (1997). A positive view of self: Risk or protection for aggressive children? *Development and Psychopathology, 9,* 75–94.

Hughes, J. N., & Kwok, O. (2006). Classroom engagement mediates the effect of teacher–student support on elementary students' peer acceptance. *Journal of School Psychology, 43,* 465–480.

Hughes, J. N., & Kwok, O. (2007). Influence of student–teacher and parent–teacher relationships on lower achieving readers' engagement and achievement in the primary grades. *Journal of Educational Psychology, 99,* 39–51.

Hughes, J. N., Zhang, D., & Hill, C. R. (2006). Peer assessments of normative and individual teacher–student support predict social acceptance and engagement among low-achieving children. *Journal of School Psychology, 43,* 447–463.

Huizenga, H., Crone, E. A., & Jansen, B. (2007). Decision making in healthy children and adults explained by the use of increased complex proportional reasoning rules. *Developmental Science, 10,* 814–825.

Huizink, A. C., & Mulder, E. J. H. (2006). Maternal smoking, drinking or cannabis use during pregnancy and neurobehavioral and cognitive functioning in human offspring. *Neuroscience and Biobehavioral Reviews, 30,* 24–41.

Huizink, A. C., Mulder, E. J. H., & Buitelaar, J. K. (2004). Prenatal stress and risk for psychopathology: Specific effects or induction of general susceptibility. *Psychological Bulletin, 130,* 115–142.

Human Genome Program. (2008). *How many genes are in the human genome?* Retrieved from www.ornl.gov/sci/techresources/Human_Genome/faq/genenumber.shtml

Humphrey, T. (1978). Function of the nervous system during prenatal life. In U. Stave (Ed.), *Perinatal physiology* (pp. 651– 683). New York: Plenum.

Hunnius, S., & Geuze, R. H. (2004a). Developmental changes in visual scanning of dynamic faces and abstract stimuli in infants: A longitudinal study. *Infancy, 6,* 231–255.

Hunnius, S., & Geuze, R. H. (2004b). Gaze shifting in infancy: A longitudinal study using dynamic faces and abstract stimuli. *Infant Behavior and Development, 27,* 397–416.

Hunt, C. E., & Hauck, F. R. (2006). Sudden infant death syndrome. *Canadian Medical Association Journal, 174,* 1861–1869.

Hunsberger, B., Pratt, M., & Pancer, S. M. (2001). Adolescent identity formation: Religious exploration and commitment. *Identity, 1,* 365–386.

Huotilainen, M., Kujala, A., Hotakainen, M., Parkkonen, L., Taulu, S., & Simola, J. (2005). Short-term memory functions of the human fetus recorded with magnetoencephalography. *Neuroreport, 16,* 81–84.

Hurewitz, F., Brown-Schmidt, S., Thorpe, K., Gleitman, L. R., & Trueswell, J. C. (2000). One frog, two frog, red frog, blue frog: Factors affecting children's syntactic choices in production and comprehension. *Journal of Psycholinguistic Research, 29,* 597–626.

Hursh, D. (2007). Assessing No Child Left Behind and the rise of neoliberal education policies. *American Educational Research Journal, 44,* 493–518.

Hursti, U.-K. (1999). Factors influencing children's food choice. *Annals of Medicine, 31,* 26–32.

Hurt, H., Brodsky, N. L., Roth, H., Malmud, E., & Giannetta, J. M. (2005). School performance of children with gestational cocaine exposure. *Neurotoxicology and Teratology, 27,* 203–211.

Huston, A. C., & Alvarez, M. M. (1990). The socialization context of gender role development in early adolescence. In R. Montemayor, G. R. Adams, & T. P. Gullotta (Eds.), *From childhood to adolescence: A transitional period?* (pp. 156– 179). Newbury Park, CA: Sage.

Huston, A. C., Wright, J. C., Marquis, J., & Green, S. B. (1999). How young children spend their time: Television and other activities. *Developmental Psychology, 35,* 912–925.

Hutinger, P. L., Bell, C., Beard, M., Bond, J., Johanson, J., & Terry, C. (1998). *The early childhood emergent literacy technology research study: Final report.* Macomb, IL: Western Illinois University. ERIC ED 418545.

Huttenlocher, P. R. (2002). *Neural plasticity: The effects of environment on the development of the cerebral cortex.* Cambridge, MA: Harvard University Press.

Huyck, M. H. (1996). Continuities and discontinuities in gender identity in midlife. In V. L. Bengtson (Ed.), *Adulthood and aging* (pp. 98–121). New York: Springer-Verlag.

Hyde, J. S., Essex, M. J., Clark, R., & Klein, M. H. (2001). Maternity leave, women's employment, and marital incompatibility. *Journal of Family Psychology, 15,* 476–491.

Hyde, J. S., Mezulis, A. H., & Abramson, L. Y. (2008). The ABCs of depression: Integrating affective, biological, and cognitive models to explain the emergence of the gender difference in depression. *Psychological Review, 115,* 291–313.

Hymel, S., Vaillancourt, T., McDougall, P., & Renshaw, P. D. (2004). Peer acceptance and rejection in childhood. In P. K. Smith & C. H. Hart (Eds.), *Blackwell handbook of childhood social development* (pp. 265–284). Malden, MA: Blackwell.

Hyppönen, E., Power, C., & Smith, G. D. (2003). Prenatal growth, BMI, and risk of type 2 diabetes by early midlife. *Diabetes Care, 26,* 2512–2517.

I

Iglowstein, I., Jenni, O. G., Molinari, L., & Largo, R. H. (2003). Sleep duration from infancy to adolescence: Reference values and generational trends. *Pediatrics, 111,* 302–307.

Imai, M., & Haryu, E. (2004). The nature of word-learning biases and their roles for lexical development: From a cross-linguistic perspective. In D. G. Hall & S. R. Waxman (Eds.), *Weaving a lexicon* (pp. 411–444). Cambridge, MA: MIT Press.

Imai, M., Li, L., Haryu, E., Okada, H., Hirsh-Pasek, K., Golinkoff, R. M., & Shigematsu, J. (2008). Novel noun and verb learning in Chinese-, English-, and Japanese-speaking children. *Child Development, 79,* 979–1000.

Impett, E. A., Sorsoli, L., Schooler, D., Henson, J. M., & Tolman, D. L. (2008). Girls' relationship authenticity and self-esteem across adolescence. *Developmental Psychology, 44,* 722–733.

Inhelder, B., & Piaget, J. (1958). *The growth of logical thinking from childhood to adolescence: An essay on the construction of formal operational structures.* New York: Basic Books. (Original work published 1955)

Iocaboni, M., Molnar-Szakacs, I., Gallese, V., Buccino, G., & Mazziotta, J. C. (2005). Grasping the intentions of others with one's own mirror neuron system. *Public Library of Science: Biology, 3*(3), e79.

Isabella, R. (1993). Origins of attachment: Maternal interactive behavior across the first year. *Child Development, 64,* 605–621.

Isabella, R., & Belsky, J. (1991). Interactional synchrony and the origins of infant–mother attachment: A replication study. *Child Development, 62,* 373–384.

Isasi, R. M., Nguyen, T. M., & Knoppers, B. M. (2006) *National regulatory frameworks regarding human genetic modification technologies (somatic and germline modification).* Montréal, Québec: Centre de Recherche en Droit Public (CRDP), Université de Montréal.

Ishihara, K., Warita, K., Tanida, T., Sugawara, T., Kitagawa, H., & Hoshi, N. (2007). Does paternal exposure to 2,3,7, 8-tetrachlorodibenzo-p-dioxin (TCDD) affect the sex ratio of offspring? *Journal of Veterinary Medical Science, 69,* 347–352.

Israel, M. Johnson, C., & Brooks, P. J. (2000). From states to events: The acquisition of English passive participles. *Cognitive Linguistics, 11,* 103–129.

Itti, E., Gaw, G. I. T., Pawlikowska-Haddal, A., Boone, K. B., Mlikotic, A., & Itti, L. (2006). The structural brain correlates of cognitive deficits in adults with Klinefelter's syndrome. *Journal of Clinical Endocrinology and Metabolism, 91,* 1423–1427.

Izard, C. E., & Ackerman, B. P. (2000). Motivational, organizational, and regulatory functions of discrete emotions. In M. Lewis & J. M. Haviland-Jones (Eds.), *Handbook of emotions* (2nd ed., pp. 253–264). New York: Guilford.

Izard, C. E., Trentacosta, C. J., King, K. A., & Mostow, A. J. (2004). An emotion-based prevention program for Head Start children. *Early Education and Development, 15,* 407–422.

J

Jaakkola, J. J., & Gissler, M. (2004). Maternal smoking in pregnancy, fetal development, and childhood asthma. *American Journal of Public Health, 94,* 136–140.

Jaccard, J., Dittus, P., & Gordon, V. V. (2000). Parent–adolescent congruency in reports of adolescent sexual behavior and in communications about sexual behavior. *Child Development, 69,* 247–261.

Jaccard, J., Dodge, T., & Dittus, P. (2002). Parent–adolescent communication about sex and birth control: A conceptual framework. In S. S. Feldman & D. A. Rosenthal (Eds.), *Talking sexuality: Parent–adolescent communication* (pp. 9–41). San Francisco: Jossey-Bass.

Jaccard, J., Dodge, T., & Dittus, P. (2003). Maternal discussions about pregnancy and adolescents' attitudes toward pregnancy. *Journal of Adolescent Health, 33,* 84–87.

Jackson, A. P., Bentler, P. M., & Franke, T. M. (2006). Employment and parenting among current and former welfare recipients. *Journal of Social Service Research, 33,* 13–25.

Jackson, L. A., von Eye, A., Biocca, F. A., Barbatsis, G., Zhao, Y., & Fitzgerald, H. E. (2006). Does home Internet use influence the academic performance of low-income children? *Developmental Psychology, 42,* 429–435.

Jackson, L. A., Zhao, Y., Kolenic, A., III, Fitzgerald, H. E., Harold, R., & von Eye, A. (2008). Race, gender, and information technology use: The new digital divide. *CyberPsychology and Behavior, 11,* 437–442.

Jackson, R. A., Gibson, K. A., & Wu, Y. W. (2004). Perinatal outcomes in singletons following in vitro fertilization: A meta-analysis. *Obstetrics and Gynecology, 103,* 551–563.

Jacobs, J. A., & Gerson, K. (2004). *The time divide: Work, family, and gender inequality.* Cambridge, MA: Harvard University Press.

Jacobs, J. E., & Klaczynski, P. A. (2002). The development of judgment and decision making during childhood and adolescence. *Current Directions in Psychological Science, 11,* 145–149.

Jacobs, J. E., Lanza, S., Osgood, D. W., Eccles, J. S., & Wigfield, A. (2002). Changes in children's self-competence and values: Gender and domain differences across grades one through twelve. *Child Development, 73,* 509–527.

Jacobs, J. E., & Weisz, V. (1994). Gender stereotypes: Implications for gifted education. *Roeper Review, 16,* 152–155.

Jacobs, J. N., & Kelley, M. L. (2006). Predictors of paternal involvement in childcare in dual-earner families with young children. *Fathering, 4,* 23–47.

Jacobson, J. L., & Jacobson, S. W. (2003). Prenatal exposure to polychlorinated biphenyls and attention at school age. *Journal of Pediatrics, 143,* 780–788.

Jacobson, K. C., & Crockett, L. J. (2000). Parental monitoring and adolescent adjustment: An ecological perspective. *Journal of Research on Adolescence, 10,* 65–97.

Jacobson, S. W., Jacobson, J. L., Sokol, R. J., Chiodo, L. M., & Corobana, R. (2004). Maternal age, alcohol abuse history, and quality of parenting as moderators of the effects of prenatal alcohol exposure on 7.5-year intellectual function. *Alcoholism, Clinical and Experimental Research, 28,* 1732–1745.

Jacquet, P. (2004). Sensitivity of germ cells and embryos to ionizing radiation. *Journal of Biological Regulators and Homeostatic Agents, 18,* 106–114.

Jadack, R. A., Hyde, J. S., Moore, C. F., & Keller, M. L. (1995). Moral reasoning about sexually transmitted diseases. *Child Development, 66,* 167–177.

Jaffe, J., Beebe, B., Feldstein, S., Crown, C. L., & Jasnow, M. D. (2001). Rhythms of dialogue in infancy. *Monographs of the Society for Research in Child Development, 66*(2, Serial No. 265).

Jaffee, S. R., Caspi, A., Moffitt, T. E., Belsky, J., & Silva, P. (2001). Why are children born to teen mothers at risk for adverse outcomes in young adulthood? *Development and Psychopathology, 13,* 377–397.

Jaffee, S. R., & Hyde, J. S. (2000). Gender differences in moral orientation: A meta-analysis. *Psychological Bulletin, 126,* 703–706.

Jaffee, S. R., Moffitt, T. E., Caspi, A., & Taylor, A. (2003). Life with (or without) father: The benefits of living with two biological parents depend on the father's antisocial behavior. *Child Development, 74,* 109–126.

Jambunathan, S., Burts, D. C., & Pierce, S. (2000). Comparisons of parenting attitudes among five ethnic groups in the United States. *Journal of Comparative Family Studies, 31,* 395–406.

Jamieson, J. R. (1995). Interactions between mothers and children who are deaf. *Journal of Early Intervention, 19,* 108–117.

Jang, S. J., & Johnson, B. R. (2001). Neighborhood disorder, individual religiosity, and adolescent use of illicit drugs: A test of multilevel hypotheses. *Criminology, 39,* 109–143.

Janosz, M., Le Blanc, M., Boulerice, B., & Tremblay, R. E. (2000). Predicting different types of school dropouts: A typological approach with two longitudinal samples. *Journal of Educational Psychology, 92,* 171–190.

Jansen, A., Theunissen, N., Slechten, K., Nederkoorn, C., Boon, B., Mulkens, S., & Roefs, A. (2003). Overweight children overeat after exposure to food cues. *Eating Behaviors, 4,* 197–209.

Jansen, J., de Weerth, C., & Riksen-Walraven, J. M. (2008). Breastfeeding and the mother–infant relationship. *Developmental Review, 28,* 503–521.

Janssens, J. M. A. M., & Deković, M. (1997). Child rearing, prosocial moral reasoning, and prosocial behavior. *International Journal of Behavioral Development, 20,* 509–527.

Janz, K. F., Dawson, J. D., & Mahoney, L. T. (2000). Tracking physical fitness and physical activity from childhood to adolescence: The Muscatine study. *Medicine and Science in Sports and Exercise, 32,* 1250–1257.

Jaudes, P. K., & Mackey-Bilaver, L. (2008). Do chronic conditions increase young children's risk of being maltreated? *Child Abuse and Neglect, 32,* 671–681.

Jayakody, R., & Kalil, A. (2002). Social fathering in low-income, African-American families with preschool children. *Journal of Marriage and the Family, 64,* 504–516.

Jeffrey, J. (2004, November). Parents often blind to their kids' weight. *British Medical Journal Online.* Retrieved from content.health.msn.com/content/article/97/104292.htm

Jenkins, J. M., Rasbash, J., & O'Connor, T. G. (2003). The role of the shared family context in differential parenting. *Developmental Psychology, 39,* 99–113.

Jenkins, J. M., Turrell, S. L., Kogushi, Y., Lollis, S., & Ross, H. S. (2003). A longitudinal investigation of the dynamics of mental state talk in families. *Child Development, 74,* 905–920.

Jenni, O. G., Molinari, L., Caflisch, J. A., & Largo, R. H. (2007). Sleep duration from ages 1 to 10 years: Variability and stability in comparison with growth. *Pediatrics, 120,* e769–e776.

Jenni, O. G., & O'Connor, B. B. (2005). Children's sleep: An interplay between culture and biology. *Pediatrics, 115,* 204–216.

Jensen, A. R. (1969). How much can we boost IQ and scholastic achievement? *Harvard Educational Review, 39,* 1–123.

Jensen, A. R. (1998). *The g factor: The science of mental ability.* New York: Praeger.

Jensen, A. R. (2001). Spearman's hypothesis. In J. M. Collis & S. Messick (Eds.), *Intelligence and personality: Bridging the gap in theory and measurement* (pp. 3–24). Mahwah, NJ: Erlbaum.

Jensen, A. R. (2002). Galton's legacy to research on intelligence. *Journal of Biosocial Science, 34,* 145–172.

Jeong, S.-H. & Fishbein, M. (2007). Predictors of multitasking with media: Media factors and audience factors. *Media Psychology, 10,* 364–384.

Jerome, E. M., Hamre, B. K., & Pianta, R. C. (2009). Teacher-child relationships from kindergarten to sixth grade: Early childhood predictors of teacher-perceived conflict and closeness. *Social Development, 18,* 915–945.

Jeynes, W. H. (2005). A meta-analysis of the relation of parental involvement to urban elementary school student academic achievement. *Urban Education, 40,* 237–269.

Jeynes, W. H. (2007). The impact of parental remarriage on children: A meta-analysis. *Marriage and Family Review, 40,* 75–102.

Ji, C. Y., & Cheng, T. O. (2008). Prevalence and geographic distribution of childhood obesity in China in 2005. *International Journal of Cardiology, 131,* 1–8.

Jiao, S., Ji, G., & Jing, Q. (1996). Cognitive development of Chinese urban only children and children with siblings. *Child Development, 67,* 387–395.

Jipson, J. L., & Gelman, S. A. (2007). Robots and rodents: Children's inferences about living and nonliving kinds. *Child Development, 78,* 1675–1688.

Joh, A. S., & Adolph, K. E. (2006). Learning from falling. *Child Development, 77,* 89–102.

Johnson, D. E. (2000). Medical and developmental sequelae of early childhood institutionalization in Eastern European adoptees. In C. A. Nelson (Ed.), *Minnesota symposia on child psychology* (Vol. 31, pp. 113–162). Mahwah, NJ: Erlbaum.

Johnson, E. K., & Seidl, A. (2008). Clause segmentation by 6-month-old infants: A crosslinguistic perspective. *Infancy, 13,* 440–455.

Johnson, J., Im-Bolter, N., & Pascual-Leone, J. (2003). Development of mental attention in gifted and mainstream children: The role of mental capacity, inhibition, and speed of processing. *Child Development, 74,* 1594–1614.

Johnson, J. G., Cohen, P., Smailes, E. M., Kasen, S., & Brook, J. S. (2002). Television viewing and aggressive behavior during adolescence and adulthood. *Science, 295,* 2468–2471.

Johnson, K. C., & Daviss, B.-A. (2005). Outcomes of planned home births with certified professional midwives: Large prospective study in North America. *British Medical Journal, 330,* 1416.

Johnson, M. D., Cohan, C. L., Davilla, J., Lawrence, E., Rogge, R. D., Karney, B. R., et al. (2005). Problem-solving skills and affective expressions as predictors of change in marital satisfaction. *Journal of Consulting and Clinical Psychology, 73,* 15–27.

Johnson, M. H. (1999). Ontogenetic constraints on neural and behavioral plasticity: Evidence from imprinting and face processing. *Canadian Journal of Experimental Psychology, 55,* 77–90.

Johnson, M. H. (2001a). The development and neural basis of face recognition: Comment and speculation. *Infant and Child Development, 10,* 31–33.

Johnson, M. H. (2001b). Infants' initial "knowledge" of the world: A cognitive neuroscience perspective. In F. Lacerda, C. von Hofsten, & M. Heimann (Eds.), *Emerging cognitive abilities in early infancy* (pp. 53–72). Mahwah, NJ: Erlbaum.

Johnson, M. H. (2005). Developmental neuroscience, psychophysiology, and genetics. In M. H. Bornstein & M. E. Lamb (Eds.), *Developmental science: An advanced textbook* (5th ed., pp. 187–222). Mahwah, NJ: Erlbaum.

Johnson, S. C., Dweck, C. S., & Chen, F. S. (2007). Evidence for infants' internal working models of attachment. *Psychological Science, 18,* 501–502.

Johnson, S. P. (1997). Young infants' perception of object unity: Implications for development of attentional and cognitive skills. *Current Directions in Psychological Science, 6,* 5–11.

Johnson, S. P. (2009). Developmental origins of object perception. In A. Woodward & A. Needham (Eds.), *Learning and the infant mind* (pp. 47–65). New York: Oxford University Press.

Johnson, S. P., Bremner, J. G., Slater, A., Mason, U., Foster, K., & Cheshire, A. (2003). Infants' perception of object trajectories. *Child Development, 74,* 94–108.

Johnson, S. P., Slemmer, J. A., & Amso, D. (2004). Where infants look determines how they see: Eye movements and object perception performance in 3-month-olds. *Infancy, 6,* 185–201.

Johnston, L. D., O'Malley, P. M., Bachman, J. G., & Schulenberg, J. E. (2010). *Monitoring the future: National results on adolescent drug use: Overview of key findings, 2009.* Bethesda, MD: National Institute on Drug Abuse.

Johnston, M. V., Nishimura, A., Harum, K., Pekar, J., & Blue, M. E. (2001). Sculpting the developing brain. *Advances in Pediatrics, 48,* 1–38.

Jones, B. D., & Egley, R. J. (2004). Voices from the frontlines: Teachers' perceptions of high-stakes testing. *Education Policy Analysis Archives, 12*(39). Retrieved from epaa.asu.edu/epaa/v12n39

Jones, C. M., Braithwaite, V. A., & Healy, S. D. (2003). The evolution of sex differences in spatial ability. *Behavioral Neuroscience, 117,* 403–411.

Jones, E. F., & Thompson, N. R. (2001). Action perception and outcome valence: Effects on children's inferences of intentionality and moral and liking judgments. *Journal of Genetic Psychology, 162,* 154–166.

Jones, F. (2003). Religious commitment in Canada, 1997 and 2000. *Religious Commitment Monograph No. 3.* Ottawa: Christian Commitment Research Institute.

Jones, G. P., & Dembo, M. H. (1989). Age and sex role differences in intimate friendships during childhood and adolescence. *Merrill-Palmer Quarterly, 35,* 445–462.

Jones, H. E. (2006). Drug addiction during pregnancy: Advances in maternal treatment and understanding child outcomes. *Current Directions in Psychological Science, 15,* 126–130.

Jones, J., Lopez, A., & Wilson, M. (2003). Congenital toxoplasmosis. *American Family Physician, 67,* 2131–2137.

Jones, M. C., & Mussen, P. H. (1958). Self-conceptions, motivations, and interpersonal attitudes of early- and late-maturing girls. *Child Development, 29,* 491–501.

Jones, N. A., Field, T., & Davalos, M. (2000). Right frontal EEG asymmetry and lack of empathy in preschool children of depressed mothers. *Child Psychiatry and Human Development, 30,* 189–204.

Jones, R. K., Purcell, A., Singh, S., & Finer, L. B. (2005). Adolescents' reports of parental knowledge of adolescents' use of sexual health services and their reactions to mandated parental notification for prescription contraceptives. *Journal of the American Medical Association, 293,* 340–348.

Jones, R. L., Homa, D. M., Meyer, P. A., Brody, D. J., Caldwell, K. L., Pirkle J. L., et al. (2009). Trends in blood lead levels and blood lead testing among U.S. children aged 1 to 5 years: 1998–2004. *Pediatrics, 123,* e376–385.

Jones, S. M., Brown, J. L., & Aber, J. L. (2008). Classroom settings as targets of intervention and research. In M. Shinn & H. Yoshikawa (Eds.), *Toward positive youth development: Transforming schools and community programs* (pp. 58–77). New York: Oxford University Press.

Jones, S. S. (2006). Exploration or imitation? The effect of music on 4-week-old infants' tongue protrusions. *Infant Behavior and Development, 29,* 126–130.

Jongbloet, P. H., Zielhuis, G. A., Groenewoud, H. M., & Pasker-De Jong, P. C. (2001). The secular trends in male:female ratio at birth in postwar industrialized countries. *Environmental Health Perspectives, 109,* 749–752.

Jordan, B. (1993). *Birth in four cultures.* Prospect Heights, IL: Waveland.

Jose, A., O'Leary, D., & Moyer, A. (2010). Does premarital cohabitation predict subsequent marital stability and marital quality? A meta-analysis. *Journal of Marriage and Family, 72,* 105–116.

Joseph, R. M., & Tager-Flusberg, H. (2004). The relationship of theory of mind and executive functions to symptom type and severity in children with autism. *Development and Psychopathology, 16,* 137–155.

Joshi, P. T., O'Donnell, D. A., Cullins, L. M., & Lewin, S. (2006). Children exposed to war and terrorism. In M. M. Feerick & G. B. Silverman (Eds.), *Children exposed to violence* (pp. 53–84). Baltimore: Paul H. Brookes.

Juby, H., Billette, J.-M., Laplante, B., & Le Bourdais, C. (2007). Nonresident fathers and children: Parents' new unions and frequency of contact. *Journal of Family Issues, 28,* 1220–1245.

Judge, S., Puckett, K., & Bell, S. M. (2006). Closing the digital divide: Update from the Early Childhood Longitudinal Study. *Journal of Educational Research, 100,* 52–60.

Jumpstart Evaluation Team. (2008, April). *Influence of Jumpstart implementation quality on child outcomes.* Paper presented at the annual meeting of the American Educational Research Association, New York.

Jürgensen, M., Hiort, O., Holterhus, P.-M., & Thyen, U. (2007). Gender role behavior in children with XY karyotype and disorders of sex development. *Hormones and Behavior, 51,* 443–453.

Jusczyk, P. W. (2001). In the beginning was the word . . . In F. Lacerda & C. von Hofsten (Eds.), *Emerging cognitive abilities in early infancy* (pp. 173–192). Mahwah, NJ: Erlbaum.

Jusczyk, P. W. (2002). Some critical developments in acquiring native language sound organization. *Annals of Otology, Rhinology and Laryngology, 189,* 11–15.

Jusczyk, P. W., & Hohne, E. A. (1997). Infants' memory for spoken words. *Science, 277,* 1984–1986.

Jusczyk, P. W., Johnson, S. P., Spelke, E. S., & Kennedy, L. J. (1999). Synchronous change and perception of object unity: Evidence from adults and infants. *Cognition, 71,* 257–288.

Jusczyk, P. W., & Luce, P. A. (2002). Speech perception. In H. Pashler & S. Yantis (Eds.), *Steven's handbook of experimental psychology: Vol. 1. Sensation and perception* (3rd ed., pp. 493–536). New York: Wiley.

Justice, E. M. (1986). Developmental changes in judgments of relative strategy effectiveness. *British Journal of Developmental Psychology, 4,* 75–81.

K

Kagan, J. (1998). Biology and the child. In N. Eisenberg (Ed.), *Handbook of child psychology: Vol. 3. Social, emotional, and personality development* (5th ed., pp. 177–236). New York: Wiley.

Kagan, J. (2003). Behavioral inhibition as a temperamental category. In R. J. Davidson, K. R. Scherer, & H. H. Goldsmith (Eds.), *Handbook of affective sciences* (pp. 320–331). New York: Oxford University Press.

Kagan, J. (2008). Behavioral inhibition as a risk factor for psychopathology. In T. P. Beauchaine & S. P. Hinshaw (Eds.), *Child and adolescent psychopathology* (pp. 157–179). Hoboken, NJ: Wiley.

Kagan, J. (2010). Emotions and temperament. In M. H. Bornstein (Ed.), *Handbook of cultural developmental science* (pp, 175–194). New York: Psychology Press.

Kagan, J., Arcus, D., Snidman, N., Feng, W. Y., Hendler, J., & Greene, S. (1994). Reactivity in infants: A cross-national comparison. *Developmental Psychology, 30,* 342–345.

Kagan, J., & Fox, N. A. (2006). Biology, culture, and temperamental biases. In N. Eisenberg (Ed.), *Handbook of child psychology: Vol. 3. Social, emotional, and personality development* (6th ed., pp. 167–225). Hoboken, NJ: Wiley.

Kagan, J., & Saudino, K. J. (2001). Behavioral inhibition and related temperaments. In R. N. Emde & J. K. Hewitt (Eds.), *Infancy to early childhood: Genetic and environmental influences on developmental change* (pp. 111–119). New York: Oxford University Press.

Kagan, J., & Snidman, N. (2004). *The long shadow of temperament.* Cambridge, MA: Belknap Press.

Kagan, J., Snidman, N., Kahn, V., & Towsley, S. (2007). The preservation of two infant temperaments into adolescence. *Monographs of the Society for Research in Child Development, 72*(2, Serial No. 287).

Kagan, J., Snidman, N., Zentner, M., & Peterson, E. (1999). Infant temperament and anxious symptoms in school-age children. *Development and Psychopathology, 11,* 209–224.

Kahn, P. H., Jr. (1992). Children's obligatory and discretionary moral judgments. *Child Development, 63,* 416–430.

Kahn, R. S., Khoury, J., Nichols, W. C., & Lanphear, B. M. (2003). Role of dopamine transporter genotype and maternal prenatal smoking in childhood hyperactive–impulsive, inattentive, and oppositional behaviors. *Journal of Pediatrics, 143,* 104–110.

Kahne, J. E., & Sporte, S. E. (2008). Developing citizens: The impact of civic learning opportunities on students' commitments to civic participation. *American Educational Research Journal, 45,* 738–766.

Kaijser, M., Bonamy, A. K., Akre, O., Cnattingius, S., Granath, F., Norman, M., et al. (2009). Perinatal risk factors for diabetes in later life. *Diabetes, 58,* 523–526.

Kail, R., & Park, Y. (1992). Global developmental change in processing time. *Merrill-Palmer Quarterly, 38,* 525–541.

Kail, R., & Park, Y. (1994). Processing time, articulation time, and memory span. *Journal of Experimental Child Psychology, 57,* 281–291.

Kail, R. V. (2003). Information processing and memory. In M. H. Bornstein, L. Davidson, C. L. M. Keyes, K. A. Moore, and the Center for Child Well-Being (Eds.), *Well-being: Positive development across the life course* (pp. 269–280). Mahwah, NJ: Erlbaum.

Kaisa, A., Stattin, H., & Nurmi, J. (2000). Parenting styles and adolescents' achievement strategies. *Journal of Adolescence, 23,* 205–222.

Kaiser Commission on Medicaid and the Uninsured. (2009). *Children's Health Insurance Program Reauthorization Act of 2009.* Washington, DC: Henry J. Kaiser Family Foundation.

Kaitz, M., Good, A., Rokem, A. M., & Eidelman, A. I. (1987). Mothers' recognition of their newborns by olfactory cues. *Developmental Psychobiology, 20,* 587–591.

Kaitz, M., Good, A., Rokem, A. M., & Eidelman, A. I. (1988). Mothers' and fathers' recognition of their newborns' photographs during the postpartum period. *Journal of Developmental and Behavioral Pediatrics, 9,* 223–226.

Kaitz, M., Meirov, H., Landman, I., & Eidelman, A. I. (1993a). Infant recognition by tactile cues. *Infant Behavior and Development, 16,* 333–341.

Kaitz, M., Shiri, S., Danziger, S., Hershko, Z., & Eidelman, A. I. (1993b). Fathers can also recognize their newborns by touch. *Infant Behavior and Development, 17,* 205–207.

Kalafat, J. (2005). Suicide. In T. P. Gullotta & G. R. Adams (Eds.), *Handbook of adolescent behavioral problems: Evidence-based approaches to prevention and treatment* (pp. 231–254). New York: Springer.

Kalil, A., Levine, J. A., & Ziol-Guest, K. M. (2005). Following in their parents' footsteps: How characteristics of parental work predict adolescents' interest in parents' jobs. In B. Schneider & L. J. Waite (Eds.), *Being together, working apart: Dual-career families and the work-life balance* (pp. 422–442). New York: Cambridge University Press.

Kaller, C. P., Rahm, B., Spreer, J., Mader, I., & Unterrainer, J. M. (2008). Thinking around the corner: The development of planning abilities. *Brain and Cognition, 67,* 360–370.

Kalra, L., & Ratan, R. (2007). Recent advances in stroke rehabilitation. *Stroke, 38,* 235–237.

Kane, C. M. (2000). African-American family dynamics as perceived by family members. *Journal of Black Studies, 30,* 691–702.

Kane, P., & Garber, J. (2004). The relations among depression in fathers, children's psychopathology, and father–child conflict: A meta-analysis. *Clinical Psychology Review, 24,* 339–360.

Kang, N. H., & Hong, M. (2008). Achieving excellence in teacher workforce and equity in learning opportunities in South Korea. *Educational Researcher, 37,* 200–207.

Kaplowitz, P. (2006). Pubertal development in girls: Secular trends. *Current Opinion in Obstetrics and Gynecology, 18,* 487–491.

Kaplowitz, P. B. (2007). Link between body fat and the timing of puberty. *Pediatrics, 121,* S208–S217.

Karafantis, D. M., & Levy, S. R. (2004). The role of children's lay theories about the malleability of human attributes in beliefs about and volunteering for disadvantaged groups. *Child Development, 75,* 236–250.

Karpati, A. M., Rubin, C. H., Kieszak, S. M., Marcus, M., & Troiano, R. P. (2002). Stature and pubertal stage assessment in American boys: The 1988–1994 Third National Health and Nutrition Examination Survey. *Journal of Adolescent Health, 30,* 205–212.

Karrass, J., & Braungart-Rieker, J. M. (2005). Effects of shared parent–infant book reading on early language acquisition. *Applied Developmental Psychology, 26,* 133–148.

Kassel, J. D., Weinstein, S., Skitch, S. A., Veilleux, J., & Mermelstein, R. (2005). The development of substance abuse in adolescence: Correlates, causes, and consequences. In J. D. Kassel, S. Weinstein, S. A. Skitch, J. Veilleux, & R. Mermelstein (Eds.), *Development of psychopathology: A vulnerability-stress perspective* (pp. 355–384). Thousand Oaks, CA: Sage.

Kastens, K. A., & Liben, L. S. (2007). Eliciting self-explanations improves children's performance on a field-based map skills task. *Cognition and Instruction, 25,* 45–74.

Kato, I., Franco, P., Groswasser, J., Scaillet, S., Kelmanson, I., Togari, H., & Kahn, A. (2003). Incomplete arousal processes in infants who were victims of sudden death. *American Journal of Respiratory and Critical Care, 168,* 1298–1303.

Katz, L. F., & Windecker-Nelson, B. (2004). Parental meta-emotion philosophy in families with conduct-problem children: Links with peer relations. *Journal of Abnormal Child Psychology, 32,* 385–398.

Katzman, D. K. (2005). Medical complications in adolescents with anorexia nervosa: A review of the literature. *International Journal of Eating Disorders, 37,* S52–S59.

Katzmarzyk, P. T., & Leonard, W. R. (1998). Climatic influences on human body size and proportions: Ecological adaptations and secular trends. *American Journal of Physical Anthropology, 106,* 483–500.

Kaufman, J., & Charney, D. (2003). The neurobiology of child and adolescent depression: Current knowledge and future directions. In D. Cicchetti & E. Walker (Eds.), *Neurodevelopmental mechanisms in psychopathology* (pp. 461–490). New York: Cambridge University Press.

Kaufman, J., Csibra, G., & Johnson, M. H. (2005). Oscillatory activity in the infant brain reflects object maintenance. *Proceedings of the National Academy of Sciences, 102,* 15271–15274.

Kavanaugh, R. D. (2006a). Pretend play. In B. Spodek & O. N. Saracho (Eds.), *Handbook of research on the education of young children* (2nd ed., pp. 269–278). Mahwah, NJ: Erlbaum.

Kavanaugh, R. D. (2006b). Pretend play and theory of mind. In L. Balter & C. S. Tamis-LeMonda (Eds.), *Child psychology: A handbook of contemporary issues* (2nd ed., pp. 153–166). New York: Psychology Press.

Kavsek, M. (2004). Predicting later IQ from infant visual habituation and dishabituation: A meta-analysis. *Journal of Applied Developmental Psychology, 25,* 369–393.

Kaye, K., & Marcus, J. (1981). Infant imitation: The sensory-motor agenda. *Developmental Psychology, 17,* 258–265.

Kaye, W. (2008). Neurobiology of anorexia and bulimia nervosa. *Physiology and Behavior, 94,* 121–135.

Kazdin, A. E. (2003). Problem-solving skills training and parent management training for conduct disorder. In A. E. Kazdin & J. R. Weisz (Eds.), *Evidence-based psychotherapies for children and adolescents* (pp. 241–262). New York: Guilford.

Kazdin, A. E., & Whitley, M. E. (2003). Treatment of parental stress to enhance therapeutic change among children referred for aggressive and antisocial behavior. *Journal of Consulting and Clinical Psychology, 71,* 504–515.

Keating, D. P. (1990). Adolescent thinking. In S. S. Feldman & G. R. Elliott (Eds.), *At the threshold* (pp. 54–89). Cambridge, MA: Harvard University Press.

Keating, D. P. (2004). Cognitive and brain development. In R. M. Lerner & L. Steinberg (Eds.), *Handbook of adolescent psychology* (2nd ed., pp. 45–84). Hoboken, NJ: Wiley.

Keating-Lefler, R., Hudson, D. B., Campbell-Grossman, C., Fleck, M. O., & Westfall, J. (2004). Needs, concerns, and social support of single, low-income mothers. *Issues in Mental Health Nursing, 25,* 381–401.

Keefe, M. R., Barbosa, G. A., Froese-Fretz, A., Kotzer, A. M., & Lobo, M. (2005). An intervention program for families with irritable infants. *American Journal of Maternal/Child Nursing, 30,* 230–236.

Keil, F. C. (1986). Conceptual domains and the acquisition of metaphor. *Cognitive Development, 1,* 72–96.

Keil, F. C., & Lockhart, K. L. (1999). Explanatory understanding in conceptual development. In E. K. Scholnick, K. Nelson, S. A. Gelman, & P. H. Miller (Eds.), *Conceptual development: Piaget's legacy* (pp. 103–130). Mahwah, NJ: Erlbaum.

Keith, T. Z., Keith, P. B., Quirk, K. J., Sperduto, J., Santillo, S., & Killings, S. (1998). Longitudinal effects of parent involvement on high school grades: Similarities and differences across gender and ethnic groups. *Journal of School Psychology, 36,* 335–363.

Keller, H., Borke, Y. J., Kärtner, J., Jensen, H., & Papaligoura, Z. (2004). Developmental consequences of early parenting experiences: Self-recognition and self-regulation in three cultural communities. *Child Development, 75,* 1745–1760.

Keller, H., Kärtner, J., Borke, J., Yovsi, R., & Kleis, A. (2005). Parenting styles and the development of the categorical self: A longitudinal study on mirror self-recognition in Cameroonian Nso and German families. *International Journal of Behavioral Development, 29,* 496–504.

Keller, S. N., & Brown, J. D. (2002). Media interventions to promote responsible sexual behavior. *Journal of Sex Research, 39,* 67–72.

Keller, S. S., Crow, T., Foundas, A., Amunts, K., & Roberts, N. (2009). Broca's area: Nomenclature, anatomy, typology and symmetry. *Brain and Language, 109,* 29–48.

Kelley, S. A., Brownell, C. A., & Campbell, S. B. (2000). Mastery motivation and self-evaluative affect in toddlers: Longitudinal relations with maternal behavior. *Child Development, 71,* 1061–1071.

Kellman, P. J., & Arterberry, M. E. (2006). Infant visual perception. In D. Kuhn & R. Siegler (Eds.), *Handbook of child psychology: Vol. 2. Cognition, perception, and language* (6th ed., pp. 109–160). Hoboken, NJ: Wiley.

Kelly, D. J., Liu, S., Ge, L., Quinn, P. C., Slater, A. M., Lee, K., et al. (2007a). Cross-race preferences for same-race faces extend beyond the African versus Caucasian contrast in 3-month-old infants. *Infancy, 11,* 87–95.

Kelly, D. J., Quinn, P. C., Slater, A. M., Lee, K., Ge, L., & Pascalis, O. (2007b). The other-race effect develops during infancy: Evidence of perceptual narrowing. *Psychological Science, 18,* 1084–1089.

Kelly, N., & Norwich, B. (2004). Pupils' perceptions of self and of labels: Moderate learning difficulties in mainstream and special schools. *British Journal of Educational Psychology, 74,* 411–435.

Kemeny, M. E. (2003). The psychobiology of stress. *Current Directions in Psychological Science, 12,* 124–129.

Kempe, C. H., Silverman, B. F., Steele, P. W., Droegemueller, P. W., & Silver, H. K. (1962). The battered-child syndrome. *Journal of the American Medical Association, 181,* 17–24.

Kendall, G., & Peebles, D. (2005). Acute fetal hypoxia: The modulating effect of infection. *Early Human Development, 81,* 27–34.

Kendler, K. S., Thornton, L. M., Gilman, S. E., & Kessler, R. C. (2000). Sexual orientation in a U.S. national sample of twin and non-twin sibling pairs. *American Journal of Psychiatry, 157,* 1843–1846.

Kendrick, D., Barlow, J., Hampshire, A., Stewart-Brown, S., & Polnay, L. (2008). Parenting interventions and the prevention of unintentional injuries in childhood: Systematic review and meta-analysis. *Child: Care, Health and Development, 34,* 682–695.

Kennedy, A. M., & Gust, D. A. (2008). Measles outbreak associated with a church congregation: A study of immunization attitudes of congregation members. *Public Health Reports, 123,* 126–134.

Kennell, J. H., Klaus, M., McGrath, S., Robertson, S., & Hinkley, C. (1991). Continuous emotional support during labor in a U.S. hospital. *Journal of the American Medical Association, 265,* 2197–2201.

Kenney, G. M., Lunch, V., & Cook, A. (2010). Who and where are the children yet to enroll in Medicaid and the Children's Health Insurance Program? *Health Affairs, 29,* 1920–1929.

Kenney-Benson, G. A., Pomerantz, E. M., Ryan, A. M., & Patrick, H. (2006). Sex differences in math performance: The role of children's approach to schoolwork. *Developmental Psychology, 42,* 11–26.

Kerckhoff, A. C. (2002). The transition from school to work. In J. T. Mortimer & R. Larson (Eds.), *The changing adolescent experience* (pp. 52–87). New York: Cambridge University Press.

Keren, M., Feldman, R., Namdari-Weinbaum, I., Spitzer, S., & Tyano, S. (2005). Relations between parents' interactive style in dyadic and triadic play and toddlers' symbolic capacity. *American Journal of Orthopsychiatry, 75,* 599–607.

Kerestes, M., & Youniss, J. E. (2003). Rediscovering the importance of religion in adolescent development. In R. M. Lerner, F. Jacobs, & D. Wertlieb (Eds.), *Handbook of applied developmental science* (Vol. 1, pp. 165–184). Thousand Oaks, CA: Sage.

Kerestes, M., Youniss, J., & Metz, E. (2004). Longitudinal patterns of religious perspective and civic integration. *Applied Developmental Science, 8,* 39–46.

Kern, S. (2007). Lexicon development in French-speaking infants. *First Language, 27,* 227–250.

Kernis, M. H. (2002). Self-esteem as a multifaceted construct. In T. M. Brinthaupt & R. P. Lipka (Eds.), *Understanding early adolescent self and identity* (pp. 57–88). Albany, NY: State University of New York Press.

Kerpelman, J. L., Shoffner, M. F., & Ross-Griffin, S. (2002). African American mothers' and daughters' beliefs about possible selves and their strategies for reaching the adolescents' future academic and career goals. *Journal of Youth and Adolescence, 31,* 289–302.

Kerr, D. C. R., Lopez, N. L., Olson, S. L., & Sameroff, A. J. (2004). Parental discipline and externalizing behavior problems in early childhood: The roles of moral regulation and child gender. *Journal of Abnormal Child Psychology, 32,* 369–383.

Kesler, S. R. (2007). Turner syndrome. *Child and Adolescent Psychiatric Clinics of North America, 16,* 709–722.

Kessen, W. (1967). Sucking and looking: Two organized congenital patterns of behavior in the human newborn. In H. W. Stevenson, E. H. Hess, & H. L. Rheingold (Eds.), *Early behavior: Comparative and developmental approaches* (pp. 147–179). New York: Wiley.

Kessler, R. C., Adler, L. A., Barkley, R., Biederman, J., Conners, C. K., & Demler, O. (2006). The prevalence and correlates of adult ADHD in the United States: Results from the National Comorbidity Survey Replication. *American Journal of Psychiatry, 163,* 716–723.

Kessler, R. C., Adler, L. A., Barkley, R., Biederman, J., Conners, C. K., & Faraone, S. V. (2005). Patterns and predictors of attention-deficit/hyperactivity disorder persistence into adulthood: Results from the National Comorbidity Survey Replication. *Biological Psychiatry, 57,* 1442–1451.

Key, J. D., Gebregziabher, M. G., Marsh, L. D., & O'Rourke, K. M. (2008). Effectiveness of an intensive, school-based intervention for teen mothers. *Journal of Adolescent Health, 42,* 394–400.

Kiang, L., Yip, T., Gonzales-Backen, M., Witkow, M, & Fuligni, A. J. (2006). Ethnic identity and the daily psychological well-being of adolescents from Mexican and Chinese backgrounds. *Child Development, 77,* 1338–1350.

Kieffer, M. J. (2008). Catching up or falling behind? Initial English proficiency, concentrated poverty, and the reading growth of language minority learners in the United States. *Journal of Educational Psychology, 100,* 851–868.

Kieras, J. E., Tobin, R. M., Graziano, W. G., & Rothbart, M. K. (2005). You can't always get what you want: Effortful control and children's responses to undesirable gifts. *Psychological Science, 16,* 391–396.

Kiernan, K. (2001). European perspectives on nonmarital childbearing. In L. L. Wu & B. Wolfe (Eds.), *Out of wedlock: Causes and consequences of nonmarital fertility* (pp. 77–108). New York: Russell Sage Foundation.

Killen, M., Crystal, D., & Watanabe, H. (2002). The individual and the group: Japanese and American children's evaluations of peer exclusion, tolerance of difference, and prescriptions for conformity. *Child Development, 73,* 1788–1802.

Killen, M., Henning, A., Kelly, M. C., Crystal, D., & Ruck, M. (2007). Evaluations of interracial peer encounters by majority and minority U.S. children and adolescents. *International Journal of Behavioral Development, 31,* 491–500.

Killen, M., Lee-Kim, J., McGlothlin, H., & Stangor, C. (2002). How children and adolescents evaluate gender and racial exclusion. *Monographs of the Society for Research in Child Development, 67*(4, Serial No. 271).

Killen, M., Margie, N. G., & Sinno, S. (2006). Morality in the context of intergroup relationships. In M. Killen & J. G. Smetana (Eds.), *Handbook of moral development* (pp. 155–183). Mahwah, NJ: Erlbaum.

Killen, M., & Stangor, M. (2001). Children's social reasoning about inclusion and exclusion in gender and race peer group contexts. *Child Development, 72,* 174–186.

Killoren, S. E., Thayer, S. M., & Updegraff, K. A. (2008). Conflict resolution between Mexican origin adolescent siblings. *Journal of Marriage and Family, 70,* 1200–1212.

Kilpatrick, S. W., & Sanders, D. M. (1978). Body image stereotypes: A developmental comparison. *Journal of Genetic Psychology, 132,* 87–95.

Kim, J., & Cicchetti, D. (2006). Longitudinal trajectories of self-system processes and depressive symptoms among maltreated and nonmaltreated children. *Child Development, 77,* 624–639.

Kim, J., McHale, S. M., Osgood, D. W., & Crouter, A. C. (2006). Longitudinal course and family correlates of sibling relationships from childhood through adolescence. *Child Development, 77,* 1746–1761.

Kim, J. M. (1998). Korean children's concepts of adult and peer authority and moral reasoning. *Developmental Psychology, 34,* 947–955.

Kim, J. M., & Turiel, E. (1996). Korean children's concepts of adult and peer authority. *Social Development, 5,* 310–329.

Kim, J.-Y., McHale, S. M., Crouter, A. C., & Osgood, D. W. (2007). Longitudinal linkages between sibling relationships and adjustment from middle childhood through adolescence. *Developmental Psychology, 43,* 960–973.

Kim, J.-Y., McHale, S. M., Osgood, D. W., & Crouter, A. C. (2006). Longitudinal course and family correlates of sibling relationships from childhood through adolescence. *Child Development, 77,* 1746–1761.

Kim, M., McGregor, K. K., & Thompson, C. K. (2000). Early lexical development in English- and Korean-speaking children: Language-general and language-specific patterns. *Journal of Child Language, 27,* 225–254.

Kimbro, R. T. (2006). On-the-job moms: Work and breastfeeding initiation and duration for a sample of low-income women. *Maternal and Child Health Journal, 10,* 19–26.

King, E. M., & Mason, A. D. (2001). *Engendering development: Through gender equality in rights, resources, and voice.* Washington, DC: UNICEF.

King, P. E., & Furrow, J. L. (2004). Religion as a resource for positive youth development: Religion, social capital, and moral outcomes. *Developmental Psychology, 40,* 703–713.

King, P. M., & Kitchener, K. S. (1994). *Developing reflective judgment: Understanding and promoting intellectual growth and critical thinking in adolescents and adults.* San Francisco: Jossey-Bass.

King, P. M., & Kitchener, K. S. (2002). The reflective judgment model: Twenty years of research on epistemic cognition. In B. K. Hofer & P. R. Pintrich (Eds.), *Personal epistemology: The psychological beliefs about knowledge and knowing* (pp. 37–61). Mahwah, NJ: Erlbaum.

King, V. (2007). When children have two mothers: Relationships with nonresident mothers, stepmothers, and fathers. *Journal of Marriage and Family, 69,* 1178–1193.

Kinney, D. (1999). From "headbangers" to "hippies": Delineating adolescents' active attempts to form an alternative peer culture. In J. A. McLellan & M. J. V. Pugh (Eds.), *The role of peer groups in adolescent social identity: Exploring the importance of stability and change* (pp. 21–35). San Francisco: Jossey-Bass.

Kinney, H. C. (2009). Brainstem mechanisms underlying the sudden infant death syndrome: Evidence from human pathologic studies. *Developmental Psychobiology, 51,* 223–233.

Kinnunen, M.-L., Pietilainen, K., & Rissanen, A. (2006). Body size and overweight from birth to adulthood. In L. Pulkkinen & J. Kaprio (Eds.), *Socioemotional development and health from adolescence to adulthood* (pp. 95–107). New York: Cambridge University Press.

Kirby, D. (2002a). Antecedents of adolescent initiation of sex, contraceptive use, and pregnancy. *American Journal of Health Behavior, 26,* 473–485.

Kirby, D. (2002b). Effective approaches to reducing adolescent unprotected sex, pregnancy, and childbearing. *Journal of Sex Research, 39,* 51–57.

Kirby, D. (2002c). The impact of schools and school programs upon adolescent sexual behavior. *Journal of Sex Research, 39,* 27–33.

Kirby, D. B. (2008). The impact of abstinence and comprehensive sex and STD/HIV education programs on adolescent sexual behavior. *Sexuality Research and Social Policy, 5,* 18–27.

Kirchner, G. (2000). *Children's games from around the world.* Boston: Allyn and Bacon.

Kiriakidis, S. P., & Kavoura, A. (2010). Cyberbullying: A review of the literature on harassment through the Internet and other electronic means. *Family and Community Health, 33,* 82–93.

Kirk, K. M., Bailey, J. M., Dunne, M. P., & Martin, N. G. (2000). Measurement models for sexual orientation in a community twin sample. *Behavior Genetics, 30,* 345–356.

Kirk, W. G. (1993). *Adolescent suicide.* Champaign, IL: Research Press.

Kirkham, N. Z., Cruess, L., & Diamond, A. (2003). Helping children apply their knowledge to their behavior on a dimension-switching task. *Developmental Science, 6,* 449–476.

Kirkman, M., Rosenthal, D. A., & Feldman, S. S. (2002). Talking to a tiger: Fathers reveal their difficulties in communicating about sexuality with adolescents. In S. S. Feldman & D. A. Rosenthal (Eds.), *Talking sexuality: Parent–adolescent communication* (pp. 57–74). San Francisco: Jossey-Bass.

Kirshner, B. (2009). "Power in numbers:" Youth organizing as a context for exploring civic identity. *Journal of Research on Adolescence, 19,* 414–440.

Kisilevsky, B. S., Hains, S. M. J., Lee, K., Muir, D. W., Xu, F., Fu, G., Zhao, Z. Y., & Yang, R. L. (1998). The still-face effect in Chinese and Canadian 3- to 6-month-old infants. *Developmental Psychology, 34,* 629–639.

Kisilevsky, B. S., Hains, S. M. J., Lee, K., Xie, X., Huang, H., Ye, H. H., Zhang, K., & Wang, Z. (2003). Effects of experience on fetal voice recognition. *Psychological Science, 14,* 220–224.

Kisilevsky, B. S., Hains, S. M. J., Brown, C. A., Lee, C. T., Cowperthwaite, B., & Stutzman, S. S. (2009). Fetal sensitivity to properties of maternal speech and language. *Infant Behavior and Development, 32,* 59–71.

Kisilevsky, B. S., & Low, J. A. (1998). Human fetal behavior: 100 years of study. *Developmental Review, 18,* 1–29.

Kitzmann, K. M., Cohen, R., & Lockwood, R. L. (2002). Are only children missing out? Comparison of the peer-related social competence of only children and siblings. *Journal of Social and Personal Relationships, 19,* 299–316.

Kitzmann, K. M., Gaylord, N. K., Holt, A. R., & Kenny, E. D. (2003). Child witnesses to domestic violence: A meta-analytic review. *Journal of Consulting and Clinical Psychology, 71,* 339–352.

Kiuru, N., Aunola, K., Vuori, J., & Nurmi, J.-E. (2009). The role of peer groups in adolescents' educational expectations and adjustment. *Journal of Youth and Adolescence, 36,* 995–1009.

Kjønniksen, L., Torsheim, T., & Wold, B. (2008). Tracking of leisure-time physical activity during adolescence and young adulthood: A 10-year longitudinal study. *International Journal of Behavioral Nutrition and Physical Activity, 5,* 69.

Klaczynski, P. A. (1997). Bias in adolescents' everyday reasoning and its relationships with intellectual ability, personal theories, and self-serving motivation. *Developmental Psychology, 33,* 273–283.

Klaczynski, P. A. (2001). Analytic and heuristic processing influences on adolescent reasoning and decision-making. *Child Development, 72,* 844–861.

Klaczynski, P. A. (2004). A dual-process model of adolescent development: Implications for decision making, reasoning, and identity. In R. Kail (Ed.), *Advances in child development and behavior* (Vol. 31, pp. 73–123). San Diego, CA: Academic Press.

Klaczynski, P. A., & Narasimham, G. (1998). Development of scientific reasoning biases: Cognitive versus ego-protective explanations. *Developmental Psychology, 34,* 175–187.

Klaczynski, P. A., Schuneman, M. J., & Daniel, D. B. (2004). Theories of conditional reasoning: A developmental examination of competing hypotheses. *Developmental Psychology, 40,* 559–571.

Klahr, D., & MacWhinney, B. (1998). Information processing. In D. Kuhn & R. S. Siegler (Eds.), *Handbook of child psychology: Vol. 2. Cognition, perception, and language* (5th ed., pp. 631–678). New York: Wiley.

Klahr, D., & Nigam, M. (2004). The equivalence of learning paths in early science instruction: Effects of direct instruction and discovery learning. *Psychological Science, 15,* 661–667.

Klaus, M. H., & Kennell, J. H. (1982). *Parent–infant bonding.* St. Louis: Mosby.

Klaw, E. L., Rhodes, J. E., & Fitzgerald, L. F. (2003). Natural mentors in the lives of African-American adolescent mothers: Tracking relationships over time. *Journal of Youth and Adolescence, 32,* 223–232.

Klebanov, P. K., Brooks-Gunn, J., McCarton, C., & McCormick, M. C. (1998). The contribution of neighborhood and family income to developmental test scores over the first three years of life. *Child Development, 69,* 1420–1436.

Klein, M. C. (2006). Does epidural analgesia increase rate of cesarean section? *Canadian Family Physician, 52,* 419–421.

Klein, P. J., & Meltzoff, A. N. (1999). Long-term memory, forgetting, and deferred imitation in 12-month-old infants. *Developmental Science, 2,* 102–113.

Klenberg, L., Korkman, M., & Lahti-Nuuttila, P. (2001). Differential development of attention and executive functions in 3- to 12-year-old Finnish children. *Developmental Neuropsychology, 20,* 407–428.

Klesges, L. M., Johnson, K. C., Ward, K. D., & Barnard, M. (2001). Smoking cessation in pregnant women. *Obstetrics and Gynecology Clinics of North America, 28,* 269–282.

Klibanoff, R. S., Levine, S. C., Huttenlocher, J., Vasilyeva, M., & Hedges, L. V. (2006). Preschool children's mathematical knowledge: The effect of teacher "math talk." *Developmental Psychology, 42,* 59–69.

Kliegman, R. M., Behrman, R. E., Jenson, H. B., & Stanton, B. F. (Eds.). (2008). *Nelson textbook of pediatrics e-dition* (18th ed. text with continually updated online references.) Philadelphia: Saunders.

Kliewer, W., Fearnow, M. D., & Miller, P. A. (1996). Coping socialization in middle childhood: Tests of maternal and paternal influences. *Child Development, 67,* 2339–2357.

Klimes-Dougan, B., & Kistner, J. (1990). Physically abused preschoolers' responses to peers' distress. *Developmental Psychology, 26,* 599–602.

Klingman, A. (2006). Children and war trauma. In K. A. Renninger & I. E. Sigel (Eds.), *Handbook of child psychology: Vol. 4. Child psychology in practice* (6th ed., pp. 619–652). Hoboken, NJ: Wiley.

Klingner, J. K., Vaughn, S., Hughes, M. T., Schumm, J. S., & Elbaum, B. (1998). Outcomes for students with and without learning disabilities in inclusive classrooms. *Learning Disabilities Research and Practice, 13,* 153–161.

Klitzing, K. von, Simoni, H., Amsler, F., & Buergin, D. (1999). The role of the father in early family interactions. *Infant Mental Health Journal, 20,* 222–237.

Klomsten, A. T., Skaalvik, E. M., & Espnes, G. A. (2004). Physical self-concept and sports: Do gender differences exist? *Sex Roles, 50,* 119–127.

Klump, K. L., Kaye, W. H., & Strober, M. (2001). The evolving genetic foundations of eating disorders. *Psychiatric Clinics of North America, 24,* 215–225.

Knafo, A., & Plomin, R. (2006). Parental discipline and affection and children's prosocial behavior: Genetic and environmental links. *Journal of Personality and Social Psychology, 90,* 147–164.

Knickmeyer, R. C., Gouttard, S., Kang, C., Evans, D., Wilber, K., Smith, J. K., et al. (2008). A structural MRI study of human brain development from birth to 2 years. *Journal of Neuroscience, 28,* 12176–12182.

Knight, N., Sousa, P., Barrett, J. L., & Atran, S. (2004). Children's attributions of beliefs to humans and God: Cross-cultural evidence. *Cognitive Science, 28,* 117–126.

Knobloch, H., & Pasamanick, B. (Eds.). (1974). *Gesell and Amatruda's Developmental Diagnosis.* Hagerstown, MD: Harper & Row.

Knopf, M., Kraus, U., & Kressley-Mba, R. A. (2006). Relational information processing of novel unrelated actions by infants. *Infant Behavior and Development, 29,* 44–53.

Kobayashi, T., Hiraki, K., & Hasegawa, T. (2005). Auditory-visual intermodal matching of small numerosities in 6-month-old infants. *Developmental Science, 8,* 409–419.

Kobayashi, T., Kazuo, H., Ryoko, M., & Hasegawa, T. (2004). Baby arithmetic: One object plus one tone. *Cognition, 91,* B23–B34.

Kobayashi, Y. (1994). Conceptual acquisition and change through social interaction. *Human Development, 37,* 233–241.

Kochanska, G. (1991). Socialization and temperament in the development of guilt and conscience. *Child Development, 62,* 1379–1392.

Kochanska, G., & Aksan, N. (2006). Children's conscience and self-regulation. *Journal of Personality, 74,* 1587–1617.

Kochanska, G., Aksan, N., & Carlson, J. J. (2005). Temperament, relationships, and young children's receptive cooperation with their parents. *Developmental Psychology, 41,* 648–660.

Kochanska, G., Aksan, N., & Joy, M. E. (2007). Children's fearfulness as a moderator of parenting in early socialization: Two longitudinal studies. *Developmental Psychology, 43,* 222–237.

Kochanska, G., Aksan, N., & Nichols, K. E. (2003). Maternal power assertion in discipline and moral discourse contexts: Commonalities, differences, and implications for children's moral conduct and cognition. *Developmental Psychology, 39,* 949–963.

Kochanska, G., Aksan, N., Prisco, T. R., & Adams, E. E. (2008). Mother–child and father–child mutually responsive orientation in the first 2 years and children's outcomes at preschool age: Mechanisms of influence. *Child Development, 79,* 30–44.

Kochanska, G., Casey, R. J., & Fukumoto, A. (1995). Toddlers' sensitivity to standard violations. *Child Development, 66,* 643–656.

Kochanska, G., Forman, D. R., Aksan, N., & Dunbar, S. B. (2005). Pathways to conscience: Early mother–child mutually responsive orientation and children's moral emotion, conduct, and cognition. *Journal of Child Psychology and Psychiatry, 46,* 19–34.

Kochanska, G., Gross, J. N., Lin, M.-H., & Nichols, K. E. (2002). Guilt in young children: Development, determinants, and relations with broader system standards. *Child Development, 73,* 461–482.

Kochanska, G., & Knaack, A. (2003). Effortful control as a personality characteristic of young children: Antecedents, correlates, and consequences. *Journal of Personality, 71,* 1087–1112.

Kochanska, G., Murray, K. T., & Harlan, E. T. (2000). Effortful control in early childhood: Continuity and change, antecedents, and implications for social development. *Developmental Psychology, 36,* 220–232.

Kochenderfer-Ladd, B. (2003). Identification of aggressive and asocial victims and the stability of their peer victimization. *Merrill-Palmer Quarterly, 49,* 401–425.

Koelsch, S., Gunter, T., von Cramon, D., Zysset, S., Lohmann, G., & Friederici, A. (2002). Bach speaks: A cortical "language-network" serves the processing of music. *NeuroImage, 17,* 956–966.

Koestner, R., Franz, C., & Weinberger, J. (1990). The family origins of empathic concern: A 26-year longitudinal study. *Journal of Personality and Social Psychology, 58,* 709–717.

Kohen, D. E., Leventhal, T., Dahinten, V. S., & McIntosh, C. N. (2008). Neighborhood disadvantage: Pathways of effects for young children. *Child Development, 79,* 156–169.

Kohlberg, L. (1966). A cognitive-developmental analysis of children's sex-role concepts and attitudes. In E. E. Maccoby (Ed.), *The development of sex differences* (pp. 82–173). Stanford, CA: Stanford University Press.

Kohlberg, L. (1969). Stage and sequence: The cognitive-developmental approach to socialization. In D. A. Goslin (Ed.), *Handbook of socialization theory and research* (pp. 347–480). Chicago: Rand McNally.

Kohlberg, L., Levine, C., & Hewer, A. (1983). *Moral stages: A current formulation and a response to critics.* Basel, Switzerland: Karger.

Kolomer, S. R., & McCallion, P. (2005). Depression and caregiver mastery in grandfathers caring for their grandchildren. *International Journal of Aging and Human Development, 60,* 283–294.

Komsi, N., Räikkönen, K., Pesonen, A.-K., Heinonen, K., Keskivaara, P., Järvenpää, A.-L., & Strandberg, T. E. (2006). Continuity of temperament from infancy to middle childhood. *Infant Behavior and Development, 29,* 494–508.

Konner, M. J. (1977). Infancy among the Kalahari Desert San. In P. H. Leiderman, S. R. Tulkin, & A. Rosenfield (Eds.), *Culture and infancy: Variations in the human experience* (pp. 287–328). New York: Academic Press.

Konold, T. R., & Pianta, R. C. (2005). Empirically-derived, person-oriented patterns of school readiness in typically developing children: Description and prediction to first-grade achievement. *Applied Developmental Science, 9,* 174–187.

Kontic-Vucinic, O., Sulovic, N., & Radunovic, N. (2006). Micronutrients in women's reproductive health: II. Minerals and trace elements. *International Journal of Fertility and Women's Medicine, 51,* 116–124.

Kontos, A. P. (2004). Perceived risk, risk taking, estimation of ability and injury among adolescent sport participants. *Journal of Pediatric Psychology, 29,* 447–455.

Kooijman, V., Hagoort, P., & Cutler, A. (2009). Prosodic structure in early word segmentation: ERP evidence from Dutch ten-month-olds. *Infancy, 14,* 591–612.

Kopp, C. B., & Neufeld, S. J. (2003). Emotional development during infancy. In R. Davidson, K. R. Scherer, & H. H. Goldsmith (Eds.), *Handbook of affective sciences* (pp. 347–374). Oxford, UK: Oxford University Press.

Korkman, M., Kettunen, S., & Autti-Raemoe, I. (2003). Neurocognitive impairment in early adolescence following prenatal alcohol exposure of varying duration. *Child Neurology, 9,* 117–128.

Kornhaber, M. L. (2004). Using multiple intelligences to overcome cultural barriers to identification for gifted education. In D. Boothe & J. C. Stanley (Eds.), *In the eyes of the beholder: Critical issues for diversity in gifted education* (pp. 215–225). Waco, TX: Prufrock Press.

Kotchick, B. A., Dorsey, S., & Heller, L. (2005). Predictors of parenting among African-American single mothers: Personal and contextual factors. *Journal of Marriage and Family, 67,* 448–460.

Kouvonen, A., & Kivivuori, J. (2001). Part-time jobs, delinquency, and victimization among Finnish adolescents. *Journal of Scandinavian Studies in Criminology and Crime Prevention, 2,* 191–212.

Kowalski, K., & Lo, Y. (1999, April). *The influence of perceptual features and sociocultural information on the development of ethnic/racial bias in young children.* Paper presented at the biennial meeting of the Society for Research in Child Development, Albuquerque, NM.

Kowalski, R. M., Limber, S. P., & Agatston, P. W. (2008). *Cyber bullying: Bullying in the digital age.* Malden, MA: Blackwell.

Kozer, E., Costei, A. M., Boskovic, R., Nulman, I., Nikfar, S., & Koren, G. (2003). Effects of aspirin consumption during pregnancy on pregnancy outcomes: Meta-analysis. *Birth Defects Research: Part B, Developmental and Reproductive Toxicology, 68,* 70–84.

Kozol, J. (2005). *The shame of the nation: The restoration of apartheid schooling in America.* New York: Three Rivers Press.

Kozulin, A. (Ed.). (2003). *Vygotsky's educational theory in cultural context.* Cambridge, UK: Cambridge University Press.

Krafft, K., & Berk, L. E. (1998). Private speech in two preschools: Significance of open-ended activities and make-believe play for verbal self-regulation. *Early Childhood Research Quarterly, 13,* 637–658.

Kramer, L., & Kowal, A. K. (2005). Sibling relationship quality from birth to adolescence: The enduring contributions of friends. *Journal of Family Psychology, 19,* 503–511.

Krascum, R. M., & Andrews, S. (1998). The effects of theories on children's acquisition of family-resemblance categories. *Child Development, 69,* 333–346.

Krcmar, M., Grela, B., & Linn, K. (2007). Can toddlers learn vocabulary from television? An experimental approach. *Media Psychology, 10,* 41–63.

Krebs, D. L., & Denton, K. (2005). Toward a more pragmatic approach to morality: A critical evaluation of Kohlberg's model. *Psychological Review, 112,* 629–649.

Krebs, D. L., Vermeulen, S. C., Carpendale, J. I., & Denton, K. (1991). Structural and situational influences on moral judgment: The interaction between stage and dilemma. In W. Kurtines & J. Gewirtz (Eds.), *Handbook of moral behavior and development: Theory, research, and application* (pp. 139–169). Hillsdale, NJ: Erlbaum.

Kreppner, J., Kumsta, R., Rutter, M., Beckett, C., Castle, J., Stevens, S., et al. (2010). Developmental course of deprivation-specific psychological patterns: Early manifestations, persistence to age 15, and clinical features. *Monographs of the Society for Research in Child Development, 75*(1, Serial No. 295), 79–101.

Kreppner, J., Rutter, M., Beckett, C., Castle, J., Colvert, E., Groothues, C., et al. (2007). Normality and impairment following profound early institutional deprivation: A longitudinal follow-up into early adolescence. *Developmental Psychology, 43,* 931–946.

Krettenauer, T. (2005). The role of epistemic cognition in adolescent identity formation: Further evidence. *Journal of Youth and Adolescence, 34,* 185–198.

Krevans, J., & Gibbs, J. C. (1996). Parents' use of inductive discipline: Relations to children's empathy and prosocial behavior. *Child Development, 67,* 3263–3277.

Krieg, D. B. (2007). Does motherhood get easier the second-time around? Examining parenting stress and marital quality among mothers having their first or second child. *Parenting: Science and Practice, 7,* 149–175.

Krishnamoorthy, J. S., Hart, C., & Jelalian, E. (2006). The epidemic of childhood obesity: Review of research and implications for public policy. *Social Policy Report of the Society for Research in Child Development, 9*(2).

Kroger, J. (2001). What transits in an identity status transition: A rejoinder to commentaries. *Identity, 3,* 291–304.

Kroger, J. (2005). *Identity in adolescence: The balance between self and other.* New York: Routledge.

Kroger, J. (2007). *Identity development: Adolescence through adulthood* (2nd ed.). Thousand Oaks, CA: Sage.

Kroneman, L., Loeber, R., & Hipwell, A. E. (2004). Is neighborhood context differently related to externalizing problems and delinquency for girls compared with boys? *Clinical Child and Family Psychology Review, 7,* 109–122.

Krumhansl, C. L., & Jusczyk, P. W. (1990). Infants' perception of phrase structure in music. *Psychological Science, 1,* 70–73.

Kubik, M. Y., Lytle, L. A., Hannan, P. J., Perry, C. L., & Story, M. (2003). The association of the school food environment with dietary behaviors of young adolescents. *American Journal of Public Health, 93,* 1168–1173.

Kuchner, J. (1989). *Chinese-American and European-American mothers and infants: Cultural influences in the first three months of life.* Paper presented at the biennial meeting of the Society for Research in Child Development, Kansas City, MO.

Kuczynski, L. (1984). Socialization goals and mother–child interaction: Strategies for long-term and short-term compliance. *Developmental Psychology, 20,* 1061–1073.

Kuczynski, L. (2003). Beyond bidirectionality. In L. Kuczynski (Ed.), *Handbook of dynamics in parent–child relations* (pp. 3–24). Thousand Oaks, CA: Sage.

Kuczynski, L., & Lollis, S. (2002). Four foundations for a dynamic model of parenting. In J. R. M. Gerris (Ed.), *Dynamics of parenting.* Hillsdale, NJ: Erlbaum.

Kuebli, J., Butler, S., & Fivush, R. (1995). Mother–child talk about past emotions: Relations of maternal language and child gender over time. *Cognition and Emotion, 9,* 265–283.

Kugelmass, J., & Ainscow, M. (2004). Leadership for inclusion: A comparison of international practices. *Journal of Research in Special Educational Needs, 4,* 133–141.

Kuh, G. D., Cruce, T. M., & Shoup, R. (2008). Unmasking the effects of student engagement on first-year college grades and persistence. *Journal of Higher Education, 79,* 540–553.

Kuhl, P. K., Tsao, F.-M., & Liu, H.-M. (2003). Foreign-language experience in infancy: Effects of short-term exposure and social interaction on phonetic learning. *Proceedings of the National Academy of Sciences, 100,* 9096–9101.

Kuhn, D. (1989). Children and adults as intuitive scientists. *Psychological Review, 96,* 674–689.

Kuhn, D. (1993). Connecting scientific and informal reasoning. *Merrill-Palmer Quarterly, 39,* 74–103.

Kuhn, D. (1995). Microgenetic study of change: What has it told us? *Psychological Science, 6,* 133–139.

Kuhn, D. (2000). Theory of mind, metacognition, and reasoning: A life-span perspective. In P. Mitchell & K. J. Riggs (Eds.), *Children's reasoning and the mind* (pp. 301–326). Hove, UK: Psychology Press.

Kuhn, D. (2000b). Why development does (and does not) occur: Evidence from the domain of inductive reasoning. In R. Siegler & J. McClelland (Eds.), *Mechanisms of cognitive development* (pp. 221–249). Mahwah, NJ: Erlbaum.

Kuhn, D. (2002). What is scientific thinking, and how does it develop? In U. Goswami (Ed.), *Blackwell handbook of childhood cognitive development* (pp. 371–393). Malden, MA: Blackwell.

Kuhn, D. (2008). Formal operations from a twenty-first century perspective. *Human Development, 51,* 48–55.

Kuhn, D. (2009). Adolescent thinking. In R. M. Lerner & L. Steinberg (Eds.), *Handbook of adolescent psychology* (3rd ed., pp. 152–186). Hoboken, NJ: Wiley.

Kuhn, D., Amsel, E., & O'Loughlin, M. (1988). *The development of scientific thinking skills.* Orlando, FL: Academic Press.

Kuhn, D., & Dean, D. (2004). Connecting scientific reasoning and causal inference. *Journal of Cognition and Development, 5,* 261–288.

Kuhn, D., & Franklin, S. (2006). The second decade: What develops (and how)? In D. Kuhn & R. S. Siegler (Eds.), *Handbook of child psychology: Vol. 2. Cognition, perception, and language* (6th ed., pp. 953–994). Hoboken, NJ: Wiley.

Kuhn, D., & Pearsall, S. (2000). Developmental origins of scientific thinking. *Journal of Cognition and Development, 1,* 113–129.

Kuhn, D., & Pease, M. (2006). Do children and adults learn differently? *Journal of Cognition and Development, 7,* 279–293.

Kuklinski, M. R., & Weinstein, R. S. (2001). Classroom and developmental differences in a path model of teacher expectancy effects. *Child Development, 72,* 1554–1578.

Kumar, S., & O'Brien, A. (2004). Recent developments in fetal medicine. *British Medical Journal, 328,* 1002–1006.

Kunisaki, S. M., & Jennings, R. W. (2008). Fetal surgery. *Journal of Intensive Care Medicine, 23,* 33–51.

Kunnen, E. S., & Bosma, H. A. (2003). Fischer's skill theory applied to identity development: A response to Kroger. *Identity, 3,* 247–270.

Kunnen, E. S., Sappa, V., van Geert, P. L. C., & Bonica, L. (2008). The shapes of commitment development in emerging adulthood. *Journal of Adult Development, 15,* 113–131.

Kunzinger, E. L., III. (1985). A short-term longitudinal study of memorial development during early grade school. *Developmental Psychology, 21,* 642–646.

Kuppens, S., Grietens, H., Onghena, P., & Michiels, D. (2009). Associations between parental control and children's overt and relational aggression. *British Journal of Developmental Psychology, 27,* 607–623.

Kurdek, L. A. (2006). Differences between partners from heterosexual, gay, and lesbian cohabiting couples. *Journal of Marriage and Family, 68,* 509–528.

Kurdek, L. A., & Fine, M. A. (1994). Family acceptance and family control as predictors of adjustment in young adolescents: Linear, curvilinear, or interactive effects? *Child Development, 65,* 1137–1146.

Kurtz-Costes, B., Rowley, S. J., Harris-Britt, A., & Woods, T. A. (2008). Gender stereotypes about mathematics and science and self-perceptions of ability in late childhood and early adolescence. *Merrill-Palmer Quarterly, 54,* 386–409.

Kuttler, A. M., La Greca, A. M., & Prinstein, M. J. (1999). Friendship qualities and social-emotional functioning of adolescents with close, cross-sex friendships. *Journal of Research on Adolescence, 9,* 339–366.

Kyratzis, A., & Guo, J. (2001). Preschool girls' and boys' verbal conflict strategies in the United States and China. *Research on Language and Social Interaction, 34,* 45–74.

L

La Ferle, C., Edwards, S. M., & Lee, W. N. (2000). Teens' use of traditional media and the Internet. *Journal of Advertising Research, 40,* 55–65.

Laberge, L., Petit, D., Simard, C., Vitaro, F., & Tremblay, R. E. (2001). Development of sleep patterns in early adolescence. *Journal of Sleep Research, 10,* 59–67.

Labouvie-Vief, G. (2006). Emerging structures of adult thought. In J. J. Arnett & J. L. Tanner (Eds.), *Emerging adults in America: Coming of age in the 21st century* (pp. 59–84). Washington, DC: American Psychological Association.

Lachance, J. A., & Mazzocco, M. M. M. (2006). A longitudinal analysis of sex differences in math and spatial skills in primary school age children. *Learning and Individual Differences, 16,* 195–216.

Lacourse, E., Nagin, D., Tremblay, R. E., Vitaro, F., & Claes, M. (2003). Developmental trajectories of boys' delinquent group membership and facilitation of violent behaviors during adolescence. *Development and Psychopathology, 15,* 183–197.

Ladd, G. W., Birch, S. H., & Buhs, E. S. (1999). Children's social and scholastic lives in kindergarten: Related spheres of influence? *Child Development, 70,* 1373–1400.

Ladd, G. W., Buhs, E. S., & Seid, M. (2000). Children's initial sentiments about kindergarten: Is school liking an antecedent of early classroom participation and achievement? *Merrill-Palmer Quarterly, 46,* 255–279.

Ladd, G. W., & Burgess, K. B. (1999). Charting the relationship trajectories of aggressive, withdrawn, and aggressive/withdrawn children during early grade school. *Child Development, 70,* 910–929.

Ladd, G. W., Herald, S. L., & Kochel, K. P. (2006). School readiness: Are there social prerequisites? *Early Education and Development, 17,* 115–150.

Ladd, G. W., LeSieur, K., & Profilet, S. M. (1993). Direct parental influences on young children's peer relations. In S. Duck (Ed.), *Learning about relationships* (Vol. 2, pp. 152–183). London: Sage.

Ladd, G. W., & Pettit, G. S. (2002). Parenting and the development of children's peer relationships. In M. Bornstein (Ed.), *Handbook of parenting: Vol. 5. Practical issues in parenting* (2nd ed., pp. 269–309). Mahwah, NJ: Erlbaum.

Ladd, G. W., & Price, J. M. (1987). Predicting children's social and school adjustment following the transition from preschool to kindergarten. *Child Development, 58,* 1168–1189.

Ladd, G. W., & Troop-Gordon, W. (2003). The role of chronic peer difficulties in the development of children's psychological adjustment problems. *Child Development, 74,* 1344–1367.

Lagattuta, K. H., Wellman, H. M., & Flavell, J. H. (1997). Preschoolers' understanding of the link between thinking and feeling: Cognitive cuing and emotional change. *Child Development, 68,* 1081–1104.

Lagnado, L. (2001, November 2). Kids confront Trade Center trauma. *Wall Street Journal,* pp. B1, B6.

LaGreca, A. M., Prinstein, M. J., & Fetter, M. D. (2001). Adolescent peer crowd affiliation: Linkages with health-risk behaviors and close friendships. *Journal of Pediatric Psychology, 26,* 131–143.

Laible, D. (2004). Mother–child discourse in two contexts: Links with child temperament, attachment security, and socioemotional competence. *Developmental Psychology, 40,* 979–992.

Laible, D. (2007). Attachment with parents and peers in late adolescence: Links with emotional competence and social behavior. *Personality and Individual Differences, 43,* 1185–1197.

Laible, D., & Song, J. (2006). Constructing emotional and relational understanding: The role of affect and mother–child discourse. *Merrill-Palmer Quarterly, 52,* 44–69.

Laible, D., & Thompson, R. A. (2002). Mother–child conflict in the toddler years: Lessons in emotion, morality, and relationships. *Child Development, 73,* 1187–1203.

Laird, R. D., Jordan, K. Y., Dodge, K. A., Pettit, G. S., & Bates, J. E. (2001). Peer rejection in childhood, involvement with antisocial peers in early adolescence, and the development of externalizing behavior problems. *Development and Psychopathology, 13,* 337–354.

Laird, R. D., Pettit, G. S., Mize, J., & Lindsey, E. (1994). Mother–child conversations about peers: Contributions to competence. *Family Relations, 43,* 425–432.

Lalonde, C., & Chandler, M. (2005). Culture, selves, and time: Theories of personal persistence in native and non-native youth. In C. Lightfoot, C. Lalonde, & M. Chandler (Eds.), *Changing conceptions of psychological life* (pp. 207–229). Mahwah, NJ: Erlbaum.

Lalonde, C. E., & Chandler, M. J. (1995). False-belief understanding goes to school: On the social-emotional consequences of coming early or late to a first theory of mind. *Cognition and Emotion, 9,* 167–185.

Lamarche, V., Brendgen, M., Boivin, M., Vitaro, F., Perusse, D., & Dionne, G. (2006). Do friendships and sibling relationships provide protection against peer victimization in a similar way? *Social Development, 15,* 373–393.

Lamaze, F. (1958). *Painless childbirth.* London: Burke.

Lamb, M. (1994). Infant care practices and the application of knowledge. In C. B. Fisher & R. M. Lerner (Eds.), *Applied developmental psychology* (pp. 23–45). New York: McGraw-Hill.

Lamb, M. E., & Ahnert, L. (2006). Nonparental child care: Context, concepts, correlates, and consequences. In K. A. Renninger & I. E. Sigel (Eds.), *Handbook of child psychology: Vol. 4. Child psychology in practice* (6th ed., pp. 700–778). Hoboken, NJ: Wiley.

Lamb, M. E., & Lewis, C. (2004). The development and significance of father–child relationships in two-parent families. In M. E. Lamb (Ed.), *The role of the father in child development* (4th ed., pp. 272–306). Hoboken, NJ: Wiley.

Lamb, M. E., & Oppenheim, D. (1989). Fatherhood and father–child relationships: Five years of research. In S. H. Cath, A. Gurwitt, & L. Gunsberg (Eds.), *Fathers and their families* (pp. 11–26). Hillsdale, NJ: Erlbaum.

Lamb, M. E., Sternberg, K. J., & Prodromidis, M. (1992). Nonmaternal care and the security of infant–mother attachment: A reanalysis of the data. *Infant Behavior and Development, 15,* 71–83.

Lamb, M. E., Thompson, R. A., Gardner, W., Charnov, E. L., & Connell, J. P. (1985). Infant–mother attachment: The origins and developmental significance of individual differences in the Strange Situation: Its study and biological interpretation. *Behavioral and Brain Sciences, 7,* 127–147.

Lambert, S. M., Masson, P., & Fisch, H. (2006). The male biological clock. *World Journal of Urology, 24,* 611–617.

Lamphear, B. P., Hornung, R., Khoury, J., Yolton, K., Baghurst, P., & Bellinger, D. C. (2005). Low-level environmental lead exposure and children's intellectual function: An international pooled analysis. *Environmental Health Perspectives, 113,* 894–899.

Lampl, M. (1993). Evidence of saltatory growth in infancy. *American Journal of Human Biology, 5,* 641–652.

Lampl, M., Veldhuis, J. D., & Johnson, M. L. (1992). Saltation and stasis: A model of human growth. *Science, 258,* 801–803.

Landry, S. H., Smith, K. E., Swank, P. R., & Miller-Loncar, C. L. (2000). Early maternal and child influences on children's later independent cognitive and social functioning. *Child Development, 71,* 358–375.

Langdridge, D., Connolly, K., & Sheeran, P. (2000). Reasons for wanting a child: A network analytic study. *Journal of Reproductive and Infant Psychology, 18,* 321–338.

Langer, J., Gillette, P., & Arriaga, R. I. (2003). Toddlers' cognition of adding and subtracting objects in action and in perception. *Cognitive Development, 18,* 233–246.

Lansford, J. E. (2009). Parental divorce and children's adjustment. *Perspectives on Psychological Science, 4,* 140–152.

Lansford, J. E., Antonucci, T. C., Akiyama, H., & Takahashi, K. (2005). A quantitative and qualitative approach to social relationships and well-being in the United States and Japan. *Journal of Comparative Family Studies, 36,* 1–22.

Lansford, J. E., Criss, M. M., Dodge, K. A., Shaw, D. S., Pettit, G. S., & Bates, J. E. (2009). Trajectories of physical discipline: Early childhood antecedents and developmental outcomes. *Child Development, 80,* 1385–1402.

Lansford, J. E., Criss, M. M., Pettit, G. S., Dodge, K. A., & Bates, J. E. (2003). Friendship quality, peer group affiliation, and peer antisocial behavior as moderators of the link between negative parenting and adolescent externalizing behavior. *Journal of Research on Adolescence, 13,* 161–184.

Lansford, J. E., Deater-Deckard, K., Dodge, K. A., Bates, J. E., & Pettit, G. S. (2004a). Ethnic differences in the link between physical discipline and later adolescent externalizing behaviors. *Journal of Child Psychology and Psychiatry, 45,* 801–812.

Lansford, J. E., Deater-Deckard, K., Dodge, K. A., Bates, J. E., & Pettit, G. S. (2004b). Ethnic differences in the link between physical punishment by parents: An updated literature review. *Clinical Child and Family Psychology Review, 3,* 199–221.

Lansford, J. E., Malone, P. S., Castellino, D. R., Dodge, K. A., Pettit, G., & Bates, J. E. (2006). Trajectories of internalizing, externalizing, and grades for children who have and have not experienced their parents' divorce or separation. *Journal of Family Psychology, 20,* 292–301.

Lantieri, L. (2003). Waging peace in our schools: The Resolving Conflict Creatively Program. In M. J. Elias & H. Arnold (Eds.), *EQ + IQ = best leadership practices for caring and successful schools* (pp. 76–88). Thousand Oaks, CA: Corwin.

Largo, R. H., Caflisch, J. A., Hug, F., Muggli, K., Molnar, A. A., & Molinari, L. (2001). Neuromotor development from 5 to 18 years. Part 1: Timed performance. *Developmental Medicine and Child Neurology, 43,* 436–443.

Larroque, B., Ancel, P.-Y., Marret, S., Marchand, L., André, M., Arnaud, C., et al. (2008). Neurodevelopmental disabilities and special care of 5-year-old children born before 33 weeks of gestation (the EPIPAGE study): A longitudinal cohort study. *Lancet, 371,* 813–820.

Larsen, J. A., & Nippold, M. A. (2007). Morphological analysis in school-age children: Dynamic assessment of a word learning strategy. *Language, Speech, and Hearing Services in Schools, 38,* 201–212.

Larsen, J. T., To, Y. M., & Fireman, G. (2007). Children's understanding and experience of mixed emotions. *Psychological Science, 18,* 186–191.

Larson, R., & Ham, M. (1993). Stress and "storm and stress" in early adolescence: The relationship of negative events with dysphoric affect. *Developmental Psychology, 29,* 130–140.

Larson, R., & Lampman-Petraitis, C. (1989). Daily emotional states as reported by children and adolescents. *Child Development, 60,* 1250–1260.

Larson, R. W. (2001). How U.S. children and adolescents spend time: What it does (and doesn't) tell us about their development. *Current Directions in Psychological Science, 10,* 160–164.

Larson, R. W., Moneta, G., Richards, M. H., & Wilson, S. (2002). Continuity, stability, and change in daily emotional experience across adolescence. *Child Development, 73,* 1151–1165.

Larson, R. W., & Richards, M. H. (1991). Daily companionship in late childhood and early adolescence: Changing developmental contexts. *Child Development, 62,* 284–300.

Larson, R. W., Richards, M. H., Moneta, G., Holmbeck, G., & Duckett, E. (1996). Changes in

adolescents' daily interactions with their families from ages 10 to 18: Disengagement and transformation. *Developmental Psychology, 32,* 744–754.

Larzelere, R. E., Schneider, W. N., Larson, D. B., & Pike, P. L. (1996). The effects of discipline responses in delaying toddler misbehavior recurrences. *Child and Family Behavior Therapy, 18,* 35–7.

Lashley, F. R. (2007). *Essentials of clinical genetics in nursing practice.* New York: Springer.

Latz, S., Wolf, A. W., & Lozoff, B. (1999). Sleep practices and problems in young children in Japan and the United States. *Archives of Pediatric and Adolescent Medicine, 153,* 339–346.

Laucht, M., Esser, G., & Schmidt, M. H. (1997). Developmental outcome of infants born with biological and psychosocial risks. *Journal of Child Psychology and Psychiatry, 38,* 843–853.

Lauer, J. A., Betrán, A. P., Victora, C. G., de Onís, M., & Barros, A. J. D. (2004). Breastfeeding patterns and exposure to suboptimal breastfeeding among children in developing countries: Review and analysis of nationally representative surveys. *BMC Medicine, 2,* 26.

Lauer, P. A., Akiba, M., Wilkerson, S. B., Apthorp, H. S., Snow, D., & Martin-Glenn, M. (2006). Out-of-school time programs: A meta-analysis of effects for at-risk students. *Review of Educational Research, 76,* 275–313.

Laurent, H., Kim, H., & Capaldi, D. (2008). Prospective effects of interparental conflict on child attachment security and the moderating role of parents' romantic attachment. *Journal of Family Psychology, 22,* 377–388.

Laursen, B., Bukowski, W. M., Aunola, K., & Nurmi, J.-E. (2007). Friendship moderates prospective associations between social isolation and adjustment problems in young children. *Child Development, 78,* 1395–1404.

Laursen, B., & Collins, W. A. (2009). Parent–child relationships during adolescence. In R. M. Lerner (Ed.), *Handbook of adolescent psychology: Vol. 2. Contextual influences on adolescent development* (3rd ed., pp. 3–42). Hoboken, NJ: Wiley.

Laursen, B., Coy, K., & Collins, W. A. (1998). Reconsidering changes in parent–child conflict across adolescence: A meta-analysis. *Child Development, 69,* 817–832.

Lavelli, M., & Fogel, A. (2005). Developmental changes in the relationship between the infant's attention and emotion during early face-to-face communication: The 2-month transition. *Developmental Psychology, 41,* 265–280.

Lavigne, J. V., Arend, R., Rosenbaum, D., Smith, A., Weissbluth, M., Binns, H. J., et al. (1999). Sleep and behavior problems among preschoolers. *Journal of Developmental and Behavioral Pediatrics, 20,* 164–169.

Law, K. L., Stroud, L. R., Niaura, R., LaGasse, L. L., Liu, J., & Lester, B. M. (2003). Smoking during pregnancy and newborn neurobehavior. *Pediatrics, 111,* 1318–1323.

Lawrence, K., Kuntsi, J., Coleman, M., Campbell, R., & Skuse, D. (2003). Face and emotion recognition deficits in Turner syndrome: A possible role for X-linked genes in amygdala development. *Neuropsychology, 17,* 39–49.

Lawson, K. R., & Ruff, H. A. (2004). Early attention and negative emotionality predict later cognitive and behavioral function. *International Journal of Behavioral Development, 28,* 157–165.

Lazar, I., & Darlington, R. (1982). Lasting effects of early education: a report from the Consortium for Longitudinal Studies. *Monographs of the Society for Research in Child Development, 47*(2–3, Serial No. 195).

Lazarus, R. S., & Lazarus, B. N. (1994). *Passion and reason.* New York: Oxford University Press.

Lazinski, M. J., Shea, A. K., & Steiner, M. (2008). Effects of maternal prenatal stress on offspring development: A commentary. *Archives of Women's Mental Health, 11,* 363–375.

Le Bourdais, C., & Lapierre-Adamcyk, E. (2004). Changes in conjugal life in Canada: Is cohabitation progressively replacing marriage? *Journal of Marriage and Family, 66,* 929–942.

Le Grand, R., Mondloch, C. J., Maurer, D., & Brent, H. P. (2001). Early visual experience and face processing. *Nature, 410,* 890.

Le Grand, R., Mondloch, C. J., Maurer, D., & Brent, H. P. (2003). Expert face processing requires input to the right hemisphere during infancy. *Nature Neuroscience, 6,* 1108–1112.

Leadbeater, B., & Hoglund, W. (2006). Changing the social texts of peer victimization. *Journal of the Canadian Academy of Child and Adolescent Psychiatry, 15,* 21–26.

Leaper, C. (1994). Exploring the correlates and consequences of gender segregation: Social relationships in childhood, adolescence, and adulthood. In C. Leaper (Ed.), *New directions for child development* (No. 65, pp. 67–86). San Francisco: Jossey-Bass.

Leaper, C. (2000). Gender, affiliation, assertion, and the interactive context of parent–child play. *Developmental Psychology, 36,* 381–393.

Leaper, C., Anderson, K. J., & Sanders, P. (1998). Moderators of gender effects on parents' talk to their children: A meta-analysis. *Developmental Psychology, 34,* 3–27.

Leaper, C., & Friedman, C. K. (2007). The socialization of gender. In J. E. Grusec & P. D. Hastings (Eds.), *Handbook of socialization: Theory and research* (pp. 561–587). New York: Guilford.

Leaper, C., Leve, L., Strasser, T., & Schwartz, R. (1995). Mother–child communication sequences: Play activity, child gender, and marital status effects. *Merrill-Palmer Quarterly, 41,* 307–327.

Leaper, C., Tenenbaum, H. R., & Shaffer, T. G. (1999). Communication patterns of African-American girls and boys from low-income, urban backgrounds. *Child Development, 70,* 1489–1503.

LeBlanc, L. A., Goldsmith, T., & Patel, D. R. (2003). Behavioral aspects of chronic illness in children and adolescents. *Pediatric Clinics of North America, 50,* 859–878.

Lecanuet, J.-P., Granier-Deferre, C., & DeCasper, A. (2005). Are we expecting too much from prenatal sensory experiences? In B. Hopkins & S. P. Johnson (Eds.), *Prenatal development of postnatal functions* (pp. 31–49). Westport, CT: Praeger.

Lecanuet, J.-P., Granier-Deferre, C., Jacquet, A.-Y., Capponi, I., & Ledru, L. (1993). Prenatal discrimination of a male and female voice uttering the same sentence. *Early Development and Parenting, 2,* 217–228.

Lecuyer, E., & Houck, G. M. (2006). Maternal limit-setting in toddlerhood: Socialization strategies for the development of self-regulation. *Infant Mental Health Journal, 27,* 344–370.

Lee, C.-Y. S., & Doherty, W. J. (2007). Marital satisfaction and father involvement during the transition to parenthood. *Fathering, 5,* 75–96.

Lee, E. A., Torrance, N., & Olson, D. R. (2001). Young children and the say/mean distinction: Verbatim and paraphrase recognition in narrative and nursery rhyme contexts. *Journal of Child Language, 28,* 531–543.

Lee, J. M., Appulgiese, D., Kaciroti, N., Corwyn, R. F., Bradley, R. H., & Lumeng, J. C. (2007). Weight status in young girls and the onset of puberty. *Pediatrics, 119,* e624–e630.

Lee, K., Cameron, C., Xu, F., Fu, G., & Board, J. (1997). Chinese and Canadian children's evaluations of lying and truth telling: Similarities and differences in the context of pro- and antisocial behaviors. *Child Development, 68,* 924–934.

Lee, K., Xu, F., Fu, G., Cameron, C. A., & Chen, S. (2001). Taiwan and Mainland Chinese and Canadian children's categorization and evaluation of lie- and truth-telling: A modesty effect. *British Journal of Developmental Psychology, 19,* 525–542.

Lee, S. (2001). More than "model minorities" or "delinquents": A look at Hmong American high school students. *Harvard Educational Review, 71,* 505–528.

Lee, S. J., Ralston, H. J., Partridge, J. C., & Rosen, M. A. (2005). Fetal pain: A systematic multidisciplinary review of the evidence. *Journal of the American Medical Association, 294,* 947–954.

Lee, S. M., Burgeson, C. R., Fulton, J. E., & Spain, C. G. (2007). Physical education and physical activity: Results from the School Health Policies and Programs Study, 2006. *Journal of School Health, 77,* 435–463.

Lee, V. E., & Burkam, D. T. (2002). *Inequality at the starting gate.* Washington, DC: Economic Policy Institute.

Lee, V. E., & Burkam, D. T. (2003). Dropping out of high school: The role of school organization and structure. *American Educational Research Journal, 40,* 353–393.

Leet, T., & Flick, L. (2003). Effect of exercise on birth weight. *Clinical Obstetrics and Gynecology, 46,* 423–431.

Lefkowitz, E. S. (2005). "Things have gotten better": Developmental changes among emerging adults after the transition to university. *Journal of Adolescent Research, 20,* 40–63.

Lefkowitz, E. S., Boone, T. L., Sigman, M., & Au, T. K. (2002). He said, she said: Gender differences in mother–adolescent conversations about sexuality. *Journal of Research on Adolescence, 12,* 217–242.

Lefkowitz, E. S., & Gillen, M. M. (2006)."Sex is just a normal part of life": Sexuality in emerging adulthood. In J. J. Arnett & J. L. Tanner (Eds.), *Emerging adults in America* (pp. 235–256). Washington, DC: American Psychological Association.

Lefkowitz, E. S., Sigman, M., & Au, T. K. (2000). Helping mothers discuss sexuality and AIDS with adolescents. *Child Development, 71,* 1383–1394.

Lehman, D. R., & Nisbett, R. E. (1990). A longitudinal study of the effects of undergraduate training on reasoning. *Developmental Psychology, 26,* 952–960.

Lehr, V. T., Zeskind, P. S., Ofenstein, J. P., Cepeda, E., Warrier, I., & Aranda, J. V. (2007). Neonatal facial coding system scores and spectral characteristics of infant crying during newborn circumcision. *Clinical Journal of Pain, 23,* 417–424.

Leiferman, J. A., & Evenson, K. R. (2003). The effect of regular physical activity on birth outcomes. *Maternal and Child Health Journal, 7,* 59–64.

Leman, P. J. (2005). Authority and moral reasons: Parenting style and children's perceptions of adult rule justifications. *International Journal of Behavioral Development, 29,* 265–270.

Lemche, E., Lennertz, I., Orthmann, C., Ari, A., Grote, K., Hafker, J., & Klann-Delius, G. (2003). Emotion-regulatory process in evoked play narratives: Their relation with mental representations and family interactions. *Praxis der Kinderpsychologie und Kinderpsychiatrie, 52,* 156–171.

Lempert, H. (1989). Animacy constraints on preschoolers' acquisition of syntax. *Child Development, 60,* 237–245.

Lempert, H. (1990). Acquisition of passives: The role of patient animacy, salience, and lexical accessibility. *Journal of Child Language, 17,* 677–696.

Lengua, L. J., Wolchik, S., Sandler, I. N., & West, S. G. (2000). The additive and interactive effects of parenting and temperament in predicting problems of children of divorce. *Journal of Clinical Psychology, 29,* 232–244.

Lenhart, A. (2010). *Teens, cell phones and texting.* Washington, DC: Pew Internet and American Life Project. Retrieved from pewresearch.org/pubs/1572/teens-cell-phones-text-messages

Lenhart, A., Purcell, K, Smith, A., & Zickuhr, K. (2010). *Social media & mobile internet use among teens and young adults.* Washington, DC: Pew Research Center.

Lenhart, A., Rainie, L., & Lewis, O. (2001). *Teenage life online: The rise of the instant-message generation and the Internet's impact on friendships and family relationships.* Washington, DC: Pew Internet & American Life Project. Retrieved from www .pewinternet.org/reports/toc?aspReport=36

Lenroot, R. K., & Giedd, J. N. (2006). Brain development in children and adolescents: Insights from anatomical magnetic resonance imaging. *Neuroscience and Biobehavioral Reviews, 30,* 718–729.

Leon, K. (2003). Risk and protective factors in young children's adjustment to parental divorce: A review of the research. *Family Relations, 52,* 258–270.

Lepage, J.-F., & Théoret, H. (2007). The mirror neuron system: Grasping others' actions from birth? *Developmental Science, 10,* 513–523.

Lerner, R. M. (2006). Developmental science, developmental systems, and contemporary theories of human development. In R. M. Lerner (Ed.), *Handbook of child psychology: Vol. 1. Theoretical models of human development* (6th ed., pp. 1–17). Hoboken, NJ: Wiley.

Lerner, R. M., & Overton, W. F. (2008). Exemplifying the integrations of the relational developmental system. *Journal of Adolescent Research, 23,* 245–255.

Lerner, R. M., Rothbaum, F., Boulos, S., & Castellino, D. R. (2002). Developmental systems perspective on parenting. In M. H. Bornstein (Ed.), *Handbook of parenting: Vol. 2. Biology and ecology of parenting* (2nd ed., pp. 315–344). Mahwah, NJ: Erlbaum.

Leslie, A. M. (2004). Who's for learning? *Developmental Science, 7,* 417–419.

Lester, B. M. (1985). Introduction: There's more to crying than meets the ear. In B. M. Lester & C. F. Z. Boukydis (Eds.), *Infant crying* (pp. 1–27). New York: Plenum.

Lester, B. M., LaGasse, L., Seifer, R., Tronick, E. Z., Bauer, C., & Shankaran, S. (2003). The maternal lifestyle study (MLS): Effects of prenatal cocaine and/or opiate exposure on auditory brain response at one month. *Journal of Pediatrics, 142,* 279–285.

Lester, B. M., Masten, A. S., & McEwen, B. (2006). Resilience in children. *Annals of the New York Academy of Sciences, 1094.*

Lester, B. M., & Tronick, E. Z. (2004). *NICU Network Neurobehavioral Scale (NNNS).* Baltimore, MD: Brookes.

Lett, D. (1997). *L'enfant des miracles: Enfance et société au Moyen Age (XIIe–XIIIe siecle).* Paris: Aubier.

LeVay, S. (1993). *The sexual brain.* Cambridge, MA: MIT Press.

Leventhal, T., & Brooks-Gunn, J. (2003). Children and youth in neighborhood contexts. *Current Directions in Psychological Science, 12,* 27–31.

Levi, J., Vinter, S., Richardson, L., St. Laurent, R., & Segal, L. M. (2009). *F as in fat: How obesity policies are failing in America.* Washington, DC: Trust for America's Health.

Levin, I., & Bus, A. G. (2003). How is emergent writing based on drawing? Analyses of children's products and their sorting by children and mothers. *Developmental Psychology, 39,* 891–905.

Levine, L. J. (1995). Young children's understanding of the causes of anger and sadness. *Child Development, 66,* 697–709.

Levine, L. (2005). *Ready or not, here life comes.* New York: Simon & Schuster.

LeVine, R. A., Dixon, S., LeVine, S., Richman, A., Leiderman, P. H., Keefer, C. H., & Brazelton, T. B. (1994). *Child care and culture: Lessons from Africa.* New York: Cambridge University Press.

LeVine, R. A., LeVine, S., Richman, A., Tapia Uribe, M. R., Sunderland Correa, C., & Miller, P. (1991). Women's schooling and child care in the demographic transition: A Mexican case study. *Population and Development Review, 17,* 459–496.

LeVine, R. A., LeVine, S. E., Rowe, M. L., & Schnell-Anzola, B. (2004). Maternal literacy and health behavior: A Nepalese case study. *Social Science and Medicine, 58,* 863–877.

LeVine, R. A., LeVine, S. E., & Schnell, B. (2001)."Improve the women": Mass schooling, female literacy, and worldwide social change. *Harvard Educational Review, 71,* 1–50.

Levine, S. C., Huttenlocher, J., Taylor, A., & Langrock, A. (1999). Early sex differences in spatial skill. *Developmental Psychology, 35,* 940–949.

Levinson, D. J. (1978). *The seasons of a man's life.* New York: Knopf.

Levinson, D. J. (1996). *The seasons of a woman's life.* New York: Knopf.

Levtzion-Korach, O., Tennenbaum, A., Schnitzer, R., & Ornoy, A. (2000). Early motor development of blind children. *Journal of Paediatric and Child Health, 36,* 226–229.

Levy, G. D., Taylor, M. G., & Gelman, S. A. (1995). Traditional and evaluative aspects of flexibility in gender roles, social conventions, moral rules, and physical laws. *Child Development, 66,* 515–531.

Levy, S. R., & Dweck, C. S. (1999). The impact of children's static vs. dynamic conceptions of people on stereotype information. *Child Development, 70,* 1163–1180.

Levy-Shiff, R., & Israelashvili, R. (1988). Antecedents of fathering: Some further exploration. *Developmental Psychology, 24,* 434–440.

Lewis, C., Freeman, N. H., Kyriadidou, C., Maridakikassotaki, K., & Berridge, D. M. (1996). Social influences on false belief access—specific sibling influences or general apprenticeship? *Child Development, 67,* 2930–2947.

Lewis, M. (1992). *Shame: The exposed self.* New York: Free Press.

Lewis, M. (1995). Embarrassment: The emotion of self-exposure and evaluation. In J. P. Tangney & K. W. Fischer (Eds.), *Self-conscious emotions* (pp. 198–218). New York: Guilford.

Lewis, M. (1998). Emotional competence and development. In D. Pushkar, W. M. Bukowski, A. E. Schwartzman, E. M. Stack, & D. R. White (Eds.), *Improving competence across the lifespan* (pp. 27–36). New York: Plenum.

Lewis, M., & Brooks-Gunn, J. (1979). *Social cognition and the acquisition of self.* New York: Plenum.

Lewis, M., & Ramsay, D. (2002). Cortisol response to embarrassment and shame. *Child Development, 73,* 1034–1045.

Lewis, M., & Ramsay, D. (2004). Development of self-recognition, personal pronoun use, and pretend play during the 2nd year. *Child Development, 75,* 1821–1831.

Lewis, M., Ramsay, D. S., & Kawakami, K. (1993). Differences between Japanese infants and Caucasian American infants in behavioral and cortisol response to inoculation. *Child Development, 64,* 1722–1731.

Lewis, M., Sullivan, M. W., Stanger, C., & Weiss, M. (1989). Self development and self-conscious emotions. *Child Development, 60,* 146–156.

Lewis, M. D. (2000). The promise of dynamic systems approaches for an integrated account of human development. *Child Development, 71,* 36–43.

Lewis, M. D. (2008). Emotional habits in brain and behavior: A window on personality development. In A. Fogel, B. J. King, & S. G. Shanker (Eds.), *Human development in the twenty-first century* (pp. 72–80). New York: Cambridge University Press.

Lewis, T. L., & Maurer, D. (2005). Multiple sensitive periods in human visual development: Evidence from visually deprived children. *Developmental Psychobiology, 46,* 163–183.

Li, D.-K., Willinger, M., Petitti, D. B., Odouli, R., Liu, L., & Hoffman, H. J. (2006). Use of a dummy (pacifier) during sleep and risk of sudden infant death syndrome (SIDS): Population based case-control study. *British Medical Journal, 332,* 18–21.

Li, S.-C., Lindenberger, U., Hommel, B., Aschersleben, G., Prinz, W., & Baltes, P. B. (2004). Transformation in the couplings among intellectual abilities and constituent cognitive processes across the life span. *Psychological Science, 15,* 155–163.

Liben, L. S. (2006). Education for spatial thinking. In K. A. Renninger & I. E. Sigel (Eds.), *Handbook of child psychology: Vol. 4. Child psychology in practice* (6th ed., pp. 197–247). Hoboken, NJ: Wiley.

Liben, L. S. (2009). The road to understanding maps. *Current Directions in Psychological Science, 18,* 310–315.

Liben, L. S., & Bigler, R. S. (2002). The developmental course of gender differentiation: Conceptualizing, measuring, and evaluating constructs and pathways. *Monographs of the Society for Research in Child Development, 67*(2, Serial No. 269).

Liben, L. S., Bigler, R. S., & Krogh, H. R. (2001). Pink and blue collar jobs: Children's judgments of job status and job aspirations in relation to sex of worker. *Journal of Experimental Child Psychology, 79,* 346–363.

Liben, L. S., & Downs, R. M. (1993). Understanding person-space-map relations: Cartographic and developmental perspectives. *Developmental Psychology, 29,* 739–752.

Liben, L. S., Kastens, K. A., & Stevenson, L. M. (2002). Real-world knowledge through real-world maps: A developmental guide for navigating the educational terrain. *Developmental Review, 22,* 267–322.

Liben, L. S., & Signorella, M. L. (1993). Gender-schematic processing in children: The role of initial interpretations of stimuli. *Developmental Psychology, 29,* 141–149.

Lickliter, R., & Bahrick, L. E. (2000). The development of infant intersensory perception: Advantages of a comparative convergent-operations approach. *Psychological Bulletin, 126,* 260–280.

Lidz, C. S. (2001). Multicultural issues and dynamic assessment. In L. A. Suzuki & J. G. Ponterotto (Eds.), *Handbook of multicultural assessment: Clinical, psychological, and educational applications* (2nd ed., pp. 523–539). San Francisco: Jossey-Bass.

Lidz, J. (2007). The abstract nature of syntactic representations. In E. Hoff & M. Shatz (Eds.), *Blackwell handbook of language development* (pp. 277–303). Malden, MA: Blackwell.

Lidz, J., Gleitman, H., & Gleitman, L. (2004). Kidz in the 'hood: Syntactic bootstrapping and the mental lexicon. In D. G. Hall & S. R. Waxman (Eds.), *Weaving a lexicon* (pp. 603–636). Cambridge, MA: MIT Press.

Lieven, E., Pine, J., & Baldwin, G. (1997). Lexically based learning and early grammatical development. *Journal of Child Language, 24,* 187–220.

Li-Grining, C. P. (2007). Effortful control among low-income preschoolers in three cities: Stability, change, and individual differences. *Developmental Psychology, 43,* 208–221.

Lillard, A. S. (2003). Pretend play and cognitive development. In U. Goswami (Ed.), *Blackwell handbook of childhood cognitive development* (pp. 189–205). Malden, MA: Blackwell.

Lillard, A. (2007). *Montessori: The science behind the genius.* New York: Oxford University Press.

Lillard, A., & Else-Quest, N. (2006). Evaluating Montessori education. *Science, 313,* 1893–1894.

Lillard, A. S., Nishida, T., Massaro, D., Vaish, A., Ma, L., & McRoberts, G. (2007). Signs of pretense across age and scenario. *Infancy, 11,* 130.

Lillard, A. S., & Witherington, D. (2004). Mothers' behavior modifications during pretense snacks and their possible signal value for toddlers. *Developmental Psychology, 40,* 95–113.

Lin, Z. L., Yu, H. M., Chen, S. Q., Liang, Z. Q., & Zhang, Z. Y. (2006). Mild hypothermia via selective head cooling as neuroprotective therapy in term neonates with perinatal asphyxia: An experience from a single neonatal intensive care unit. *Journal of Perinatology, 26,* 180–184.

Linares, T. J., Singer, L. T., Kirchner, H., Lester, H., Short, E. J., & Minn, M. O. (2006). Mental health outcomes of cocaine-exposed children at 6 years of age. *Journal of Pediatric Psychology, 31,* 85–97.

Lincove, J. A., & Painter, G. (2006). Does the age that children start kindergarten matter? Evidence of long-term educational and social outcomes. *Educational Evaluation and Policy Analysis, 28,* 153–179.

Lindley, L. D. (2005). Perceived barriers to career development in the context of social-cognitive career theory. *Journal of Career Assessment, 13,* 271–287.

Lindsay, C., Almay, M., & Normand, J. (2002). *Youth in Canada.* Retrieved from www.statcan.ca/english/IPS/Data/ 85-511-XPE.htm

Lindsay-Hartz, J., de Rivera, J., & Mascolo, M. F. (1995). Differentiating guilt and shame and their effects on motivation. In J. P. Tangney & K. W. Fischer (Eds.), *Self-conscious emotions* (pp. 274–300). New York: Guilford.

Lindsey, E. W., & Colwell, M. J. (2003). Preschoolers' emotional competence: Links to pretend and physical play. *Child Study Journal, 33,* 39–52.

Lindsey, E. W., Colwel, M. J., Frabutt, J. M., Chambers, J. C., & MacKinnon-Lewis, C. (2008). Mother–child dyadic synchrony in European-American and African-American families during early adolescence: Relations with self-esteem and prosocial behavior. *Merrill-Palmer Quarterly, 54,* 289–315.

Lindsey, E. W., & Mize, J. (2000). Parent–child physical and pretense play: Links to children's social competence. *Merrill-Palmer Quarterly, 46,* 565–591.

Linebarger, D. L., Kosanic, A. Z., Greenwood, C. R., & Doku, N. S. (2004). Effects of viewing the television program *Between the Lions* on the emergent literacy skills of young children. *Journal of Educational Psychology, 96,* 297–308.

Linn, R. L. (2000). Assessments and accountability. *Educational Researcher, 29*(2), 4–16.

Linn, R. L., & Welner, K. G. (2007). *Race-conscious policies for assigning students to schools: Social science research and the Supreme Court cases.* Washington, DC: National Academy Press.

Lino, M., & Carlson, A. (2009). *Expenditures on children by families, 2008.* Miscellaneous Publication Number 1528–2008. Washington, DC: U.S. Department of Agriculture.

Linscheid, T. R., Budd, K. S., & Rasnake, L. K. (2005). Pediatric feeding problems. In M. C. Roberts (Ed.), *Handbook of pediatric psychology and psychiatry* (3rd ed., pp. 481–488). New York: Guilford.

Linver, M. R., Martin, A., & Brooks-Gunn, J. (2004). Measuring infants' home environment: The IT-HOME for infants between birth and 12 months in four national data sets. *Parenting: Science and Practice, 4,* 115–137.

Lipsitt, L. P. (2003). Crib death: A biobehavioral phenomenon? *Psychological Science, 12,* 164–170.

Lipton, J. S., & Spelke, E. S. (2003). Origins of number sense: Large-number discrimination in human infants. *Psychological Science, 14,* 396–401.

Liszkowski, U., Carpenter, M., & Tomasello, M. (2007). Pointing out new news, old news, and absent referents at 12 months of age. *Developmental Science, 10,* F1–F7.

Liszkowski, U., Carpenter, M., & Tomasello, M. (2008). Twelve-month-olds communicate helpfully and appropriately for knowledgeable and ignorant partners. *Cognition, 108,* 732–739.

Litovsky, R. Y., & Ashmead, D. H. (1997). Development of binaural and spatial hearing in infants and children. In R. H. Gilkey & T. R. Anderson (Eds.), *Binaural and spatial hearing in real and virtual environments* (pp. 571–592). Mahwah, NJ: Erlbaum.

Little, C., & Carter, A. S. (2005). Negative emotional reactivity and regulation in 12-month-olds following emotional challenge: Contributions of maternal–infant emotional availability in a low-income sample, *Infant Mental Health Journal, 26,* 354–368.

Little, T. D., Jones, S. M., Henrich, C. C., & Hawley, P. H. (2003). Disentangling the "whys" from the "whats" of aggressive behavior. *International Journal of Behavioral Development, 27,* 122–133.

Liu, D., Sabbagh, M. A., Gehring, W. J., & Wellman, H. M. (2009). Neural correlates of children's theory of mind development. *Child Development, 80,* 318–326.

Liu, J., Raine, A., Venables, P. H., Dalais, C., & Mednick, S. A. (2003). Malnutrition at age 3 years and lower cognitive ability at age 11 years. *Archives of Paediatric and Adolescent Medicine, 157,* 593–600.

Liu, J., Raine, A., Venables, P. H., & Mednick, S. A. (2004). Malnutrition at age 3 years and externalizing behavior problems at ages 8, 11, and 17 years. *American Journal of Psychiatry, 161,* 2005–2013.

Liu, L. L., Uttal, D. H., Marulis, L. M., & Newcombe, N. S. (2008). Training spatial skills: What works, for whom, why and for how long? Poster presented at the annual meeting of the Association for Psychological Science, Chicago.

Lloyd, C. B. (2005). *The changing transitions to adulthood in developing countries: Selected studies.* Washington: National Academies Press.

Lloyd, L. (1999). Multi-age classes and high ability students. *Review of Educational Research, 69,* 187–212.

Lochman, J. E., & Dodge, K. A. (1998). Distorted perceptions in dyadic interactions of aggressive and nonaggressive boys: Effects of prior expectations, context, and boys' age. *Development and Psychopathology, 10,* 495–512.

Lock, J., & Kirz, N. (2008). Eating disorders: Anorexia nervosa. In W. E. Craighead, D. J. Miklowitz, & L. W. Craighead (Eds.), *Psychopathology: History, diagnosis, and empirical foundations* (pp. 467–494). Hoboken, NJ: Wiley.

Locke, J. (1892). Some thoughts concerning education. In R. H. Quick (Ed.), *Locke on education* (pp. 1– 236). Cambridge, UK: Cambridge University Press. (Original work published 1690).

Lockhart, R. S., & Craik, F. I. M. (1990). Levels of processing: A retrospective commentary on a framework for memory research. *Canadian Journal of Psychology, 44,* 87–112.

Loeb, S., Fuller, B., Kagan, S. L., & Carrol, B. (2004). Child care in poor communities: Early learning effects of type, quality, and stability. *Child Development, 75,* 47–65.

Loehlin, J. C., & Martin, N. G. (2001). Age changes in personality traits and their heritabilities during the adult years: Evidence from Australian twin registry samples *Personality and Individual Differences, 30,* 1147–1160.

Loehlin, J. C., Horn, J. M., & Willerman, L. (1997). Heredity, environment, and IQ in the Texas Adoption Project. In R. J. Sternberg & E. L. Grigorenko (Eds.), *Intelligence, heredity, and environment* (pp. 105–125). New York: Cambridge University Press.

Loganovskaja, T. K., & Loganovsky, K. N. (1999). EEG, cognitive and psychopathological abnormalities in children irradiated in utero. *International Journal of Psychophysiology, 34,* 213–224.

Loganovsky, K. N., Loganovskaja, T. K., Nechayev, S. Y., Antipchuk, Y. Y., & Bomko, M. A. (2008). Disrupted development of the dominant hemisphere following prenatal irradiation. *The Journal of Neuropsychiatry and Clinical Neurosciences, 20,* 274–291.

Lohman, D. F. (2000). Measures of intelligence: Cognitive theories. In A. E. Kazdin (Ed.), *Encyclopedia of psychology: Vol. 5* (pp. 147–150). Washington, DC: American Psychological Association.

London, K., Bruck, M., Ceci, S. J., & Shuman, D. (2005). Disclosure of child sexual abuse: What does the research tell us about the ways that children tell? *Psychology and Public Policy Law, 11,* 194–226.

Longstaffe, S., Moffatt, M. E., & Whalen, J. C. (2000). Behavioral and self-concept changes after six months of enuresis treatment: A randomized, controlled trial. *Pediatrics, 105,* 935–940.

Loock, C., Conry, J., Cook, J. L., Chudley, A. E., & Rosales, T. (2005). Identifying fetal alcohol spectrum disorder in primary care. *Canadian Medical Association Journal, 172,* 628–630.

Looker, D., & Thiessen, V. (2003). *The digital divide in Canadian schools: Factors affecting student access to and use of information technology.* Ottawa: Canadian Education Statistics Council.

Loots, G., & Devise, I. (2003). The use of visual-tactile communication strategies by deaf and hearing fathers and mothers of deaf infants. *Journal of Deaf Studies and Deaf Education, 8,* 31–42.

Lorenz, K. Z. (1952). *King Solomon's ring.* New York: Crowell.

LoTurco, J. J. (2000). Neural circuits in the 21st century: Synaptic networks of neurons and glia. *Proceedings of the National Academy of Sciences, 97,* 8196–8197.

Louie, V. (2001). Parents' aspirations and investment: The role of social class in the educational experiences of 1. 5- and second-generation Chinese Americans. *Harvard Educational Review, 71,* 438–474.

Louis, J., Cannard, C., Bastuji, H., & Challamel, M.-J. (1997). Sleep ontogenesis revisited: A longitudinal

24-hour home polygraphic study on 15 normal infants during the first two years of life. *Sleep, 20,* 323–333.

Lourenco, O. (2003). Making sense of Turiel's dispute with Kohlberg: The case of the child's moral competence. *New Ideas in Psychology, 21,* 43–68.

Love, J. M., Chazan-Cohen, R., & Raikes, H. (2007). Forty years of research knowledge and use: From Head Start to Early Head Start and beyond. In. J. L. Aber, S. J. Bishop-Josef, S. M. Jones, K. T. McLearn, & D. Phillips (Eds.), *Child development and social policy: Knowledge for action* (pp. 79–95). Washington, DC: American Psychological Association.

Love, J. M., Harrison, L., Sagi-Schwartz, A., van IJzendoorn, M. H., Ross, C., & Ungerer, J. A. (2003). Child care quality matters: How conclusions may vary with context. *Child Development, 74,* 1021–1033.

Love, J. M., Kisker, E. E., Ross, C., Raikes, H., Constantine, J., Boller, K., & Brooks-Gunn, J. (2005). The effectiveness of early Head Start for 3-year-old children and their parents: Lessons for policy and programs. *Developmental Psychology, 41,* 885–901.

Love, J. M., Tarullo, L. B., Raikes, H., & Chazan-Cohen, R. (2006). Head Start: What do we know about its effectiveness? What do we need to know? In K. McCartney & D. Phillips (Eds.), *Blackwell handbook of early childhood development* (pp. 550–575). Malden, MA: Blackwell.

Lubart, T. I. (2003). In search of creative intelligence. In R. J. Sternberg, J. Lautrey, & T. I. Lubart (Eds.), *Models of intelligence: International perspectives* (pp. 279–292). Washington, DC: American Psychological Association.

Lubart, T. I., Georgsdottir, A., & Besançon, M. (2009). The nature of creative giftedness and talent. In T. Balchin, B. Hymer, & D. J. Matthews (Eds.), *The Routledge international companion to gifted education* (pp. 42–49). New York: Routledge.

Luby, J., Belden, A., Sullivan, J., Hayen, R., McCadney, A., & Spitznagel, E. (2009). Shame and guilt in preschool depression: Evidence for elevations in self-conscious emotions in depression as early as age 3. *Journal of Child Psychology and Psychiatry, 50,* 1156–1166.

Lucas, S. R., & Behrends, M. (2002). Sociodemographic diversity, correlated achievement, and de facto tracking. *Sociology of Education, 75,* 328–348.

Lucas, T. W., Wendorf, C. A., Imamoglu, E. O., Shen, J., Parkhill, M. R., Weisfeld, C. C., & Weisfeld, G. E. (2004). Marital satisfaction in four cultures as a function of homogamy, male dominance, and female attractiveness. *Sexualities, Evolution & Gender, 6,* 97–130.

Lucas-Thompson, R., & Clarke-Stewart, K. A. (2007). Forecasting friendship: How marital quality, maternal mood, and attachment security are linked to children's peer relationships. *Journal of Applied Developmental Psychology, 28,* 499–514.

Luciana, M. (2007). Special issue: Developmental cognitive neuroscience. *Developmental Review, 27,* 277–282.

Ludemann, P. M. (1991). Generalized discrimination of positive facial expressions by seven- and ten-month-old infants. *Child Development, 62,* 55–67.

Luna, B., Garver, K. E., Urban, T. A., Lazar, N. A., & Sweeney, J. A. (2004). Maturation of cognitive processes from late childhood to adulthood. *Child Development, 75,* 1357–1372.

Luna, B., Thulborn, K. R., Monoz, D. P., Merriam, E. P., Garver, K. E., Minshew, N. J., Keshavan, M. S., Genovese, C. R., Eddy, W. F., & Sweeney, J. A. (2001). Maturation of widely distributed brain function subserves cognitive development. *Neuroimage, 13,* 786–793.

Lund, N., Pedersen, L. H., & Henriksen, T. B. (2009). Selective serotonin reuptake inhibitor exposure in utero and pregnancy outcomes. *Archives of Pediatrics and Adolescent Medicine, 163,* 949–954.

Lundy, B. L. (2002). Paternal socio-psychological factors and infant attachment: The mediating role of synchrony in father–infant interactions. *Infant Behavior and Development, 25,* 221–236.

Lundy, B. L. (2003). Father– and mother–infant face-to-face interactions: Differences in mind-related comments and infant attachment? *Infant Behavior and Development, 26,* 200–212.

Luo, Y., & Baillargeon, R. (2005). When the ordinary seems unexpected: Evidence for incremental physical knowledge in young infants. *Cognition, 95,* 297–328.

Luria, A. R. (1976). *Cognitive development: Its cultural and social foundations.* Cambridge, MA: Harvard University Press.

Lussier, G., Deater-Deckard, K., Dunn, J., & Davies, L. (2002). Support across two generations: Children's closeness to grandparents following parental divorce and remarriage. *Journal of Family Psychology, 16,* 363–376.

Luster, T., & Haddow, J. L. (2005). Adolescent mothers and their children: An ecological perspective. In T. Luster & J. L. Haddow (Eds.), *Parenting: An ecological perspective* (2nd ed., pp. 73–101). Mahwah, NJ: Erlbaum.

Luthar, S. S., & Becker, B. E. (2002). Privileged but pressured: A study of affluent youth. *Child Development, 73,* 1593–1610.

Luthar, S. S., & Goldstein, A. S. (2008). Substance use and related behaviors among suburban late adolescents: The importance of perceived parent containment. *Development and Psychopathology, 20,* 591–614.

Luthar, S. S., & Latendresse, S. J. (2005a). Children of the affluent: Challenges to well-being. *Current Directions in Psychological Science, 14,* 49–53.

Luthar, S. S., & Latendresse, S. J. (2005b). Comparable "risks" at the socioeconomic status extremes: Preadolescents' perceptions of parenting. *Development and Psychopathology, 17,* 207–230.

Luthar, S. S., & Sexton, C. (2004). The high price of affluence. In R. V. Kail (Ed.), *Advances in child development* (Vol. 32, pp. 126–162). San Diego, CA: Academic Press.

Luyckx, K., Goossens, L., & Soenens, B. (2006). A developmental contextual perspective on identity construction in emerging adulthood: Change dynamics in commitment formation and commitment evaluation. *Developmental Psychology, 42,* 366–380.

Luyckx, K., Goossens, L., Soenens, B., & Beyers, W. (2006). Unpacking commitment and exploration: Preliminary validation of an integrative model of late adolescent identity formation. *Journal of Adolescence, 29,* 361–378.

Luyckx, K., Soenens, B., Vansteenkiste, M., Goossens, L., & Berzonsky, M. D. (2007). Parental psychological control and dimensions of identity formation in emerging adulthood. *Journal of Family Psychology, 21,* 546–550.

Lynch, S. K., Turkheimer, E., D'Onofrio, B. M., Mendle, J., Emery, R. E., Slutske, W. S., & Martin, N. G. (2006). A genetically informed study of the association between harsh punishment and offspring behavioral problems. *Journal of Family Psychology, 20,* 190–198.

Lyon, T. D., & Flavell, J. H. (1994). Young children's understanding of "remember" and "forget." *Child Development, 65,* 1357–1371.

Lyons-Ruth, K. (1996). Attachment relationships among children with aggressive behavior problems: The role of disorganized early attachment patterns. *Journal of Consulting and Clinical Psychology, 64,* 64–73.

Lyons-Ruth, K., Bronfman, E., & Parsons, E. (1999). Maternal frightened, frightening, or ayptical behavior and disorganized infant attachment patterns. *Monographs of the Society for Research in Child Development, 64*(3, Serial No. 258), 67–96.

Lyons-Ruth, K., Easterbrooks, A., & Cibelli, C. (1997). Infant attachment strategies, infant mental lag, and maternal depressive symptoms: Predictors of internalizing and externalizing problems at age 7. *Developmental Psychology, 33,* 681–692.

Lytton, H., & Gallagher, L. (2002). Parenting twins and the genetics of parenting. In M. H. Bornstein (Ed.), *Handbook of parenting: Vol. 1. Children and parenting* (pp. 227–253). Mahwah, NJ: Erlbaum.

M

Ma, L., & Lillard, A. S. (2006). Where is the real cheese? Young children's ability to discriminate between real and pretend acts. *Child Development, 77,* 1762–1777.

Ma, W., Golinkoff, R. M., Hirsh-Pasek, K., McDonough, C., & Tardif, T. (2009). Imageability predicts the age of acquisition of verbs in Chinese children. *Journal of Child Language, 36,* 405–423.

Maas, F. K. (2008). Children's understanding of promising, lying, and false belief. *Journal of General Psychology, 13,* 301–321.

Maas, F. K., & Abbeduto, L. J. (2001). Children's judgments about intentionally and unintentionally broken promises. *Journal of Child Language, 28,* 517–529.

Maccoby, E. E. (1984). Middle childhood in the context of the family. In W. A. Collins (Ed.), *Development during middle childhood* (pp. 184– 239). Washington, DC: National Academy Press.

Maccoby, E. E. (1998). *The two sexes: Growing up apart, coming together.* Cambridge, MA: Belknap/Harvard University Press.

Maccoby, E. E. (2002). Gender and group process: A developmental perspective. *Current Directions in Psychological Science, 11,* 54–58.

Macek, P., Bejček, J., & Vaníčková, J. (2007). Contemporary Czech emerging adults: Generation growing up in the period of social changes. *Journal of Adolescent Research, 22,* 444–475.

Machin, G. A. (2005). Multiple birth. In H. W. Taeusch, R. A. Ballard, & C. A. Gleason (Eds.), *Avery's diseases of the newborn* (8th ed., pp. 57–62). Philadelphia: Saunders.

Mackey, E. R., & La Greca, A. M. (2007). Adolescents' eating, exercise, and weight control behaviors: Does peer crowd affiliation play a role? *Journal of Pediatric Psychology, 32,* 13–23.

Mackey, K., Arnold, M. L., & Pratt, M. W. (2001). Adolescents' stories of decision making in more and less authoritative families: Representing the voices of parents in narrative. *Journal of Adolescent Research, 16,* 243–268.

Mackie, S., Show, P., Lenroot, R., Pierson, R., Greenstein, D. K., & Nugent, T. F., III. (2007). Cerebellar development and clinical outcome in attention deficit hyperactivity disorder. *American Journal of Psychiatry, 164,* 647–655.

Macpherson, A., & Spinks, A. (2007). Bicycle helmet legislation for the uptake of helmet use and prevention of head injuries. *Cochrane Database of Systematic Reviews,* Issue 3. Chichester, UK: Wiley.

MacWhinney, B. (2005). Language development. In M. H. Bornstein & M. E. Lamb (Eds.), *Developmental science: An advanced textbook* (5th ed., pp. 359–387). Mahwah, NJ: Erlbaum.

Madden, M., & Lenhart, A. (2006). *Online dating.* Washington, DC: Report for the Pew Internet and American Life Project. Retrieved from www.pewinternet.org

Madigan, S., Moran, G., & Pederson, D. R. (2006). Unresolved states of mind, disorganized attachment relationships, and disrupted interactions of adolescent mothers and their infants. *Developmental Psychology, 42,* 293–304.

Madom, S., Jussim, L., & Eccles, J. (1997). In search of the powerful self-fulfilling prophecy. *Journal of Personality and Social Psychology, 72,* 791–809.

Madsen, S. A., & Juhl, T. (2007). Paternal depression in the postnatal period assessed with traditional and male depression scales. *Journal of Men's Health and Gender, 4,* 26–31.

Magnusson, D. (1999). Holistic interactionism: A perspective for research on personality development. In L. A. Pervin & O. P. John (Eds.), *Handbook of personality: Theory and research* (2nd ed., pp. 219–247). New York: Guilford.

Magolda, M. B. B. (2002). Epistemological reflection: The evolution of epistemological assumptions from age 18 to 30. In B. K. Hofer & P. R. Pintrich (Eds.), *Personal epistemology* (pp. 89–102). Mahwah, NJ: Erlbaum.

Mahoney, J. L. (2000). Participation in school extracurricular activities as a moderator in the development of antisocial patterns. *Child Development, 71*, 502–516.

Mahoney, J. L., & Stattin, H. (2000). Leisure activities and antisocial behavior: The role of structure and social context. *Journal of Adolescence, 23*, 113–127.

Main, M. (2000). The organized categories of infant, child, and adult attachment: Flexible vs. inflexible attention under attachment-related stress. *Journal of the American Psychoanalytic Association, 48*, 1055–1096.

Main, M., & Goldwyn, R. (1998). *Adult attachment classification system.* London: University College.

Main, M., & Solomon, J. (1990). Procedures for identifying infants as disorganized/disoriented during the Ainsworth Strange Situation. In M. Greenberg, D. Cicchetti, & M. Cummings (Eds.), *Attachment in the preschool years: Theory, research, and intervention* (pp. 121–160). Chicago: University of Chicago Press.

Majdandžić, M., & van den Boom, D. C. (2007). Multimethod longitudinal assessment of temperament in early childhood. *Journal of Personality, 75*, 121–167.

Majnemer, A., & Barr, R. G. (2005). Influence of supine sleep positioning on early motor milestone acquisition. *Developmental Medicine and Child Neurology, 47*, 370–376.

Major, B., Spencer, S., Schmader, T., Wolfe, C., & Crocker, J. (1998). Coping with negative stereotypes about intellectual performance: The role of psychological disengagement. *Personality and Social Psychology Bulletin, 24*, 34–50.

Makin, J. E., Fried, P. A., & Watkinson, B. (1991). A comparison of active and passive smoking during pregnancy: Long-term effects. *Neurotoxicology and Teratology, 13*, 5–12.

Makris, N., & Pnevmatikos, D. (2007). Children's understanding of human and super-natural mind. *Cognitive Development, 22*, 365–375.

Malatesta, C. Z., Grigoryev, P., Lamb, C., Albin, M., & Culver, C. (1986). Emotion socialization and expressive development in preterm and full-term infants. *Child Development, 57*, 316–330.

Malcom, N. L. (2006). "Shaking it off" and "toughing it out": Socialization to pain and injury in girls' softball. *Journal of Contemporary Ethnography, 35*, 495–525.

Malina, R. M., & Beunen, G. (1996). Matching of opponents in youth sports. In O. Bar-Or (Ed.), *The child and adolescent athlete* (pp. 202–213). Oxford: Blackwell.

Malina, R. M., & Bouchard, C. (1991). *Growth, maturation, and physical activity.* Champaign, IL: Human Kinetics.

Mandara, J., Varner, F., Greene, N., & Richman, S. (2009). Intergenerational family predictors of the black–white achievement gap. *Journal of Educational Psychology, 101*, 867–878.

Mandler, J. M. (2004). Thought before language. *Trends in Cognitive Sciences, 8*, 508–513.

Mandler, J. M., & McDonough, L. (1998). On developing a knowledge base in infancy. *Developmental Psychology, 34*, 1274–1288.

Mangelsdorf, S. C., Schoppe, S. J., & Buur, H. (2000). The meaning of parental reports: A contextual approach to the study of temperament and behavior problems. In V. J. Molfese & D. L. Molfese (Eds.), *Temperament and personality across the life span* (pp. 121–140). Mahwah, NJ: Erlbaum.

Manlove, J. (1997). Early motherhood in an intergenerational perspective: The experiences of a British cohort. *Journal of Marriage and the Family, 59*, 263–279.

Manlove, J., Ryan, S., & Franzetta, K. (2003). Patterns of contraceptive use within teenagers' first sexual relationships. *Perspectives on Sexual and Reproductive Health, 35*, 246–255.

Mao, A., Burnham, M. M., Goodlin-Jones, B. L., Gaylor, E. E., & Anders, T. F. (2004). A comparison of the sleep–wake patterns of cosleeping and solitary-sleeping infants. *Child Psychiatry and Human Development, 35*, 95–105.

Maratsos, M. (2000). More overregularizations after all: New data and discussion on Marcus, Pinker, Ullman, Hollander, Rosen, & Xu. *Journal of Child Language, 27*, 183–212.

Marchman, V. A., & Thal, D. J. (2005). Words and grammar. In M. Tomasello & D. I. Slobin (Eds.), *Beyond nature–nurture: Essays in honor of Elizabeth Bates* (pp. 141–164). Mahwah, NJ: Erlbaum.

Marcia, J. E. (1980). Identity in adolescence. In J. Adelson (Ed.), *Handbook of adolescent psychology* (pp. 159–187). New York: Wiley.

Marcon, R. A. (1999a). Differential impact of preschool models on development and early learning of inner-city children: A three-cohort study. *Developmental Psychology, 35*, 358–375.

Marcon, R. A. (1999b). Positive relationships between parent–school involvement and public school inner-city preschoolers' development and academic performance. *School Psychology Review, 28*, 395–412.

Marcus, G. F. (1995). Children's overregularization of English plurals: A quantitative analysis. *Journal of Child Language, 22*, 447–459.

Marcus, G. F., Fernandes, K. J., & Johnson, S. P. (2007). Infant rule learning facilitated by speech. *Psychological Science, 18*, pp. 387–391.

Marcus, G. F., Vijayan, S., Rao, S. B., & Vishton, P. M. (1999). Rule learning by seven-month-old infants. *Science, 283*, 77–80.

Mardh, P. A. (2002). Influence of infection with *Chlamydia trachomatis* on pregnancy outcome, infant health and life-long sequelae in infected offspring. *Best Practices in Clinical Obstetrics and Gynaecology, 16*, 847–964.

Marian, V., Neisser, U., & Rochat, P. (1996). *Can 2-month-old infants distinguish live from videotaped interactions with their mothers* (Emory Cognition Project, Report #33). Atlanta, GA: Emory University.

Mariano, K. A., & Harton, H. C. (2005). Similarities in aggression, inattention/hyperactivity, depression, and anxiety in middle childhood friendships. *Journal of Social and Clinical Psychology, 24*, 471–496.

Markman, E. M. (1992). Constraints on word learning: Speculations about their nature, origins, and domain specificity. In M. R. Gunnar & M. P. Maratsos (Eds.), *Minnesota Symposia on Child Psychology* (Vol. 25, pp. 59–101). Hillsdale, NJ: Erlbaum.

Markova, G., & Legerstee, M. (2006). Contingency, imitation, and affect sharing: Foundations of infants' social awareness. *Developmental Psychology, 42*, 132–141.

Markovits, H., & Barrouillet, P. (2002). The development of conditional reasoning: A Piagetian reformulation of mental models theory. *Merrill-Palmer Quarterly, 39*, 131–158.

Markovits, H., Benenson, J., & Dolenszky, E. (2001). Evidence that children and adolescents have internal models of peer interactions that are gender differentiated. *Child Development, 72*, 879–886.

Markovits, H., Schleifer, M., & Fortier, L. (1989). Development of elementary deductive reasoning in young children. *Developmental Psychology, 25*, 787–793.

Markovits, H., & Vachon, R. (1990). Conditional reasoning, representation, and level of abstraction. *Developmental Psychology, 26*, 942–951.

Marks, G. N., Cresswell, J., & Ainley, J. (2006). Explaining socioeconomic inequalities in student achievement: The role of home and school factors. *Educational Research and Evaluation, 12*, 105–128.

Marks, N. F., Bumpass, L. L., & Jun, H. (2004). Family roles and well-being during the middle life course. In O. G. Brim, C. D. Ryff, & R. C. Kessler (Eds.), *How healthy are we? A national study of well-being at midlife* (pp. 514–549). Chicago: University of Chicago Press.

Marlier, L., & Schaal, B. (2005). Human newborns prefer human milk: Conspecific milk odor is attractive without postnatal exposure. *Child Development, 76*, 155–168.

Marra, R., & Palmer, B. (2004). Encouraging intellectual growth: Senior college student profiles. *Journal of Adult Development, 11*, 111–122.

Marsee, M. A., & Frick, P. J. (2010). Callous-unemotional traits and aggression in youth. In W. F. Arsenio & E. A. Lemerise (Eds.), *Emotions, aggression, and morality in children: Bridging development and psychopathology* (pp. 137–156). Washington, D. C.: American Psychological Association.

Marsh, H. W. (1990). The structure of academic self-concept: The Marsh/Shavelson model. *Journal of Educational Psychology, 82*, 623–636.

Marsh, H. W., & Ayotte, V. (2003). Do multiple dimensions of self-concept become more differentiated with age? The differential distinctiveness hypothesis. *Journal of Educational Psychology, 95*, 687–706.

Marsh, H. W., Craven, R., & Debus, R. (1998). Structure, stability, and development of young children's self-concepts: A multicohort–multioccasion study. *Child Development, 69*, 1030–1053.

Marsh, H. W., Ellis, L. A., & Craven, R. G. (2002). How do preschool children feel about themselves? Unraveling measurement and multidimensional self-concept structure. *Developmental Psychology, 38*, 376–393.

Marsh, H. W., Gerlach, E., Trautwein, U., Lüdtke, O., & Brettschneider, W.-D. (2007). Longitudinal study of predadolescent sport self-concept and performance: Reciprocal effects and causal ordering. *Child Development, 78*, 1640–1656.

Marsh, H. W., & Hau, K.-T. (2003). Big-fish–little-pond effect on academic self-concept: A cross-cultural (26-country) test of the negative effects of academically selective schools. *American Psychologist, 58*, 364–376.

Marsh, H. W., & Kleitman, S. (2002). Extracurricular school activities: The good, the bad, and the non-linear. *Harvard Educational Review, 72*, 464–514.

Marsh, H. W., & Kleitman, S. (2005). Consequences of employment during high school: Character building, subversion of academic goals, or a threshold? *American Educational Research Journal, 42*, 331–369.

Marsh, H. W., Parada, R. H., & Ayotte, V. (2004). A multidimensional perspective of relations between self-concept (Self Description Questionnaire II) and adolescent mental health (Youth Self Report). *Psychological Assessment, 16*, 27–41

Marsh, H. W., Trautwein, U., Lüdtke, O., Koller, O., & Baumert, J. (2005). Academic self-concept, interest, grades, and standardized test scores: Reciprocal effects models of causal ordering. *Child Development, 76*, 397–416.

Marshall-Baker, A., Lickliter, R., & Cooper, R. P. (1998). Prolonged exposure to a visual pattern may promote behavioral organization in preterm infants. *Journal of Perinatal and Neonatal Nursing, 12*, 50–62.

Martin, C. L., Eisenbud, L., & Rose, H. (1995). Children's gender-based reasoning about toys. *Child Development, 66*, 1453–1471.

Martin, C. L., & Fabes, R. A. (2001). The stability and consequences of young children's same-sex peer interactions. *Developmental Psychology, 37*, 431–446.

Martin, C. L., Fabes, R. A., Evans, S. M., & Wyman, H. (1999). Social cognition on the playground: Children's beliefs about playing with girls versus boys and their relations to sex segregated play. *Journal of Social and Personal Relationships, 16*, 751–771.

Martin, C. L., & Halverson, C. F. (1987). The role of cognition in sex role acquisition. In D. B. Carter (Ed.), *Current conceptions of sex roles and sex typing: Theory and research* (pp. 123–137). New York: Praeger.

Martin, C. L., & Ruble, D. (2004). Children's search for gender cues: Cognitive perspectives on gender development. *Current Directions in Psychological Science, 13*, 67–70.

Martin, C. L., Ruble, D. N., & Szkrybalo, J. (2002). Cognitive theories of early gender development. *Psychological Bulletin, 128*, 903–933.

Martin, G. L., & Pear, J. (2007). *Behavior modification: What it is and how to do it* (8th ed.). Upper Saddle River, NJ: Prentice-Hall.

Martin, K. A. (1996). *Puberty, sexuality and the self: Girls and boys at adolescence.* New York: Routledge.

Martin, R. (2008). Meiotic errors in human oogenesis and spermatogenesis. *Reproductive Biomedicine Online, 16,* 523–531.

Martinez-Frias, M. L., Bermejo, E., Rodríguez-Pinilla, E., & Frías, J. L. (2004). Risk for congenital anomalies associated with different sporadic and daily doses of alcohol consumption during pregnancy: A case-control study. *Birth Defects Research, Part A, Clinical and Molecular Teratology, 70,* 194–200.

Martlew, M., & Connolly, K. J. (1996). Human figure drawings by schooled and unschooled children in Papua New Guinea. *Child Development, 67,* 2743–2762.

Martyn, C. N., Barker, D. J. P., & Osmond, C. (1996). Mothers' pelvic size, fetal growth, and death from stroke and coronary heart disease in men in the UK. *Lancet, 348,* 1264–1268.

Marzolf, D. P., & DeLoache, J. S. (1994). Transfer in young children's understanding of spatial representations. *Child Development, 65,* 1–15.

Masataka, N. (1996). Perception of motherese in a signed language by 6-month-old deaf infants. *Developmental Psychology, 32,* 874–879.

Mascolo, M. F., & Fischer, K. W. (1995). Developmental transformations in appraisals for pride, shame, and guilt. In J. P. Tangney & K. W. Fischer (Eds.), *Self-conscious emotions* (pp. 114–139). New York: Guilford.

Mascolo, M. F., & Fischer, K. W. (2007). The codevelopment of self and sociomoral emotions during the toddler years. In C. A. Brownell & C. B. Kopp (Eds.), *Socioemotional development in the toddler years: Transitions and transformations* (pp. 66–99). New York: Guilford.

Mashburn, A. J. (2008). Quality of social and physical environments in preschools and children's development of academic, language, and literacy skills. *Applied Developmental Science, 12,* 113–127.

Mashburn, A. J., Pianta, R. C., Hamre, B. K., Downer, J. T., Barbarin, O. A., Bryant, D., et al. (2008). Measures of classroom quality in prekindergarten and children's development of academic, language, and social skills. *Child Development, 79,* 732–749.

Mason, M. G., & Gibbs, J. C. (1993a). Role-taking opportunities and the transition to advanced moral judgment. *Moral Education Forum, 18,* 1–12.

Mason, M. G., & Gibbs, J. C. (1993b). Social perspective taking and moral judgment among college students. *Journal of Adolescent Research, 8,* 109–123.

Massey, Z., Rising, S. S., & Ickovics, J. (2006). CenteringPregnancy group prenatal care: Promoting relationship-centered care. *JOGNN, 35,* 286–294.

Masten, A. S. (2001). Ordinary magic: Resilience processes in development. *American Psychologist, 56,* 227–238.

Masten, A. S., Coatsworth, J. D., Neemann, J., Gest, S. D., Tellegen, A., & Garmezy, N. (1995). The structure and coherence of competence from childhood through adolescence. *Child Development, 66,* 1635–1659.

Masten, A. S., & Gewirtz, A. H. (2006). Vulnerability and resilience in early child development. In K. McCartney & D. Phillips (Eds.), *Blackwell handbook of early childhood development* (pp. 22–43). Malden, MA: Blackwell.

Masten, A. S., & Powell, J. L. (2003). A resilience framework for research, policy, and practice. In S. S. Luthar (Ed.), *Resilience and vulnerability* (pp. 1–25). New York: Cambridge University Press.

Masten, A. S., & Reed, M. J. (2002). Resilience in development. In C. R. Snyder & S. J. Lopez (Eds.), *Handbook of positive psychology* (pp. 74–88). New York: Oxford University Press.

Masten, A. S., & Shaffer, A. (2006). How families matter in child development: Reflections from research on risk and resilience. In A. S. Masten & A. Shaffer (Eds.), *Families count: Effects on child and adolescent development* (pp. 5–25). New York: Cambridge University Press.

Mastropieri, D., & Turkewitz, G. (1999). Prenatal experience and neonatal responsiveness to vocal expressions of emotion. *Developmental Psychobiology, 35,* 204–214.

Masur, E. F., McIntyre, C. W., & Flavell, J. H. (1973). Developmental changes in apportionment of study time among items in a multi-trial free recall task. *Journal of Experimental Child Psychology, 15,* 237–246.

Masur, E. F., & Rodemaker, J. E. (1999). Mothers' and infants' spontaneous vocal, verbal, and action imitation during the second year. *Merrill-Palmer Quarterly, 45,* 392–412.

Mathews, F., Yudkin, P., & Neil, A. (1999). Influence of maternal nutrition on outcome of pregnancy: Prospective cohort study. *British Medical Journal, 319,* 339–343.

Mathews, T. J., & MacDorman, M. F. (2006, May). Infant mortality statistics from the 2003 period linked birth/infant death data set. *National Vital Statistics Reports, 54*(16), 1–29.

Mathews, T. J., & MacDorman, M. F. (2008). Infant mortality statistics from the 2005 period linked birth/infant death data set. *National Vital Statistics Reports from the Centers for Disease Control and Prevention, 57,* 1–32.

Mathiesen, K. S., & Prior, M. (2006). The impact of temperament factors and family functioning on resilience processes from infancy to school age. *European Journal of Developmental Psychology, 3,* 357–387.

Matsuba, M. K., & Walker, L. J. (1998). Moral reasoning in the context of ego functioning. *Merrill-Palmer Quarterly, 44,* 464–483.

Mattson, S. N., Calarco, K. E., & Lang, A. R. (2006). Focused and shifting attention in children with heavy prenatal alcohol exposure. *Neuropsychology, 20,* 361–369.

Maupin, R., Lyman, R., Fatsis, J., Prystowiski, E., Nguyen, A., & Wright, C. (2004). Characteristics of women who deliver with no prenatal care. *Journal of Maternal-Fetal and Neonatal Medicine, 16,* 45–50.

Maurer, D., Lewis, T. L., Brent, H. P., & Levin, A. V. (1999). Rapid improvement in the acuity of infants after visual input. *Science, 286,* 108–110.

Mavroveli, S., Petrides, K. V., Rieffe, C., & Bakker, F. (2007). Trait emotional intelligence, psychological well-being and peer-rated social competence in adolescence. *British Journal of Developmental Psychology, 25,* 263–275.

Mayberry, R. I. (1994). The importance of childhood to language acquisition: Evidence from American Sign Language. In J. C. Goodman & H. C. Nusbaum (Eds.), *The development of speech perception: The transition from speech sounds to spoken words* (pp. 57–90). Cambridge, MA: MIT Press.

Mayeiux, L., & Cillessen, A. H. N. (2003). Development of social problem solving in early childhood: Stability, change, and associations with social competence. *Journal of Genetic Psychology, 164,* 153–173.

Mayer, J. D., Roberts, R. D., & Barsade, S. G. (2008). Human abilities: Emotional intelligence. *Annual Review of Psychology, 59,* 507–536.

Mayer, J. D., Salovey, P., & Caruso, D. R. (2003). *Mayer–Salovey–Caruso Emotional Intelligence Test (MSCEIT): User's manual.* Toronto, Ontario: Multi-Health Systems.

Mayer, J. D., Salovey, P., & Caruso, D. R. (2008). Emotional intelligence: New ability or eclectic traits? *American Psychologist, 63,* 503–517.

Mayes, L. C. (1999). Reconsidering the concept of vulnerability in children using the model of prenatal cocaine exposure. In T. B. Cohen & E. M. Hossein (Eds.), *The vulnerable child* (Vol. 3, pp. 35–54). Madison, CT: International Universities Press.

Mayes, L. C., & Zigler, E. (1992). An observational study of the affective concomitants of mastery in infants. *Journal of Child Psychology and Psychiatry, 33,* 659–667.

Mayes, R., Bagwell, C., & Erkulwater, J. (2008). ADHD and the rise in stimulant use among children. *Harvard Review of Psychiatry, 16,* 151–166.

Maynard, A. E. (2002). Cultural teaching: The development of teaching skills in Maya sibling interactions. *Child Development, 73,* 969–982.

Maynard, A. E., & Greenfield, P. M. (2003). Implicit cognitive development in cultural tools and children: Lessons from Maya Mexico. *Cognitive Development, 18,* 489–510.

Maynard, A. E., Subrahmanyam, K., & Greenfield, P. M. (2005). Technology and the development of intelligence: From the loom to the computer. In R. J. Sternberg & D. D. Preiss (Eds.), *Intelligence and technology: The impact of tools on the nature and development of human abilities* (pp. 29–53). Mahwah, NJ: Erlbaum.

Mayseless, O., & Sharf, M. (2003). What does it mean to be an adult? The Israeli experience. *New Directions for Child and Adolescent Development, 100,* 33–49.

McAlister, A., & Peterson, C. C. (2006). Mental playmates: Siblings, executive functioning and theory of mind. *British Journal of Developmental Psychology, 24,* 733–751.

McAlister, A., & Peterson, C. C. (2007). A longitudinal study of child siblings and theory of mind development. *Cognitive Development, 22,* 258–270.

McBee, M. T. (2006). A descriptive analysis of referral sources for gifted identification screening by race and socioeconomic status. *Journal of Secondary Gifted Education, 17,* 103–111.

McBride-Chang, C., & Kail, R. V. (2002). Cross-cultural similarities in the predictors of reading acquisition. *Child Development, 73,* 1392–1407.

McCabe, A. (1997). Developmental and cross-cultural aspects of children's narration. In M. Bamberg (Ed.), *Narrative development: Six approaches* (pp. 137–174). Mahwah, NJ: Erlbaum.

McCall, R. B. (1993). Developmental functions for general mental performance. In D. K. Detterman (Ed.), *Current topics in human intelligence* (Vol. 3, pp. 3–29). Norwood, NJ: Ablex.

McCall, R. B., & Carriger, M. S. (1993). A meta-analysis of infant habituation and recognition memory performance as predictors of later IQ. *Child Development, 64,* 57–79.

McCartney, K., Dearing, E., Taylor, B., & Bub, K. (2007). Quality child care supports the achievement of low-income children: Direct and indirect pathways through caregiving and the home environment. *Journal of Applied Developmental Psychology, 28,* 411–426.

McCartney, K., Harris, M. J., & Bernieri, F. (1990). Growing up and growing apart: A developmental meta-analysis of twin studies. *Psychological Bulletin, 107,* 226–237.

McCartney, K., Owen, M., Booth, C., Clarke-Stewart, A., & Vandell, D. (2004). Testing a maternal attachment model of behavior problems in early childhood. *Journal of Child Psychology and Psychiatry, 45,* 765–778.

McCarton, C. (1998). Behavioral outcomes in low birth weight infants. *Pediatrics, 102,* 1293–1297.

McCarty, M. E., & Ashmead, D. H. (1999). Visual control of reaching and grasping in infants. *Developmental Psychology, 35,* 620–631.

McCarty, M. E., & Keen, R. (2005). Facilitating problem-solving performance among 9- and 12-month-old infants. *Journal of Cognition and Development, 6,* 209–228.

McClelland, M. M., Cameron, C. E., Wanless, S. B., & Murray, A. (2007). Executive function, behavioral self-regulation, and social-emotional competence: Links to school readiness. In O. Saracho & B. Spodek (Eds.), *Contemporary perspectives on social learning in early childhood education* (pp. 83–107). Charlotte, NC: Information Age Publishing.

McClure, S., Laibson, D., Loewenstein, G., & Cohen, J. (2004). Separate neural systems value immediate and delayed monetary rewards. *Science, 306,* 503–507.

McColgan, K. L., & McCormack, T. (2008). Searching and planning: Young children's reasoning about past and future event sequences. *Child Development, 79,* 1477–1479.

McCormack, V. A., dos Santos Silva, I., Koupil, I., Leon, D. A., & Lithell, H. O. (2005). Birth characteristics and adult cancer incidence: Swedish cohort of over 11,000 men and women. *International Journal of Cancer, 115,* 611–617.

McCormick, M. C., Brooks-Gunn, J., Buka, S. L., Goldman, J., Yu, J., Salganik, M., Scott, D. T., et al. (2006). Early intervention in low birth weight premature infants: Results at 18 years of age for the Infant Health and Development Program. *Pediatrics, 117*, 771–780.

McCune, L. (1993). The development of play as the development of consciousness. In M. H. Bornstein & A. O'Reilly (Eds.), *New directions for child development* (No. 59, pp. 67– 79). San Francisco: Jossey-Bass.

McDaniel, J., Purcell, D., & D'Augelli, A. R. (2001). The relationship between sexual orientation and risk for suicide: Research findings and future directions for research and prevention. *Suicide and Life-Threatening Behavior, 31*, 84–105.

McDonagh, M. S., Osterweil, P., & Guise, J. M. (2005). The benefits and risks of inducing labour in patients with prior cesarean delivery: A systematic review. *BJOG, 112*, 1007–1015.

McDonough, L. (1999). Early declarative memory for location. *British Journal of Developmental Psychology, 17*, 381–402.

McDowell, D. J., & Parke, R. D. (2000). Differential knowledge of display rules for positive and negative emotions: Influences from parents, influences on peers. *Social Development, 9*, 415–432.

McElhaney, K. B., & Allen, J. P. (2001). Autonomy and adolescent social functioning: The moderating effect of risk. *Child Development, 72*, 220–235.

McElhaney, K. B., Allen, J. P., Stephenson, J. C., & Hare, A. L. (2009). Attachment and autonomy during adolescence. In R. M. Lerner & L. Steinberg (Eds.), *Handbook of adolescent psychology: Vol. 1. Individual bases of adolescent development* (3rd ed., pp. 358–403). Hoboken, NJ: Wiley.

McElwain, N. L., & Booth-LaForce, C. (2006). Maternal sensitivity to infant distress and nondistress as predictors of infant–mother attachment security. *Journal of Family Psychology, 20*, 247–255.

McGee, G. (1997). Legislating gestation. *Human Reproduction, 12*, 407–408.

McGee, L. M., & Richgels, D. J. (2008). *Literacy's beginnings: Supporting young readers and writers* (5th ed.). Boston: Allyn and Bacon.

McGillicuddy-De Lisi, A. V., Daly, M. & Neal, A. (2006). Children's distributive justice judgments: Aversive racism in Euro-American children? *Child Development, 77*, 1063–1080.

McGlothlin, H., & Killen, M. (2006). Intergroup attitudes of European American children attending ethnically homogeneous schools. *Child Development, 77*, 1375–1386.

McGrath, S. K., & Kennell, J. H. (2008). A randomized controlled trial of continuous labor support for middle-class couples: Effect on cesarean delivery rates. *Birth: Issues in Perinatal Care, 35*, 9–97.

McGue, M., Elkins, I., Walden, B., & Iacono, W. G. (2005). Perceptions of the parent–adolescent relationship: A longitudinal investigation. *Developmental Psychology, 41*, 971–984.

McHale, J. P., Kazali, C., Rotman, T., Talbot, J., Carleton, M., & Lieberson, R. (2004). The transition to coparenting: Parents' prebirth expectations and early coparental adjustment at 3 months postpartum. *Development and Psychopathology, 16*, 711–733.

McHale, J. P., Lauretti, A., Talbot, J., & Pouquette, C. (2002). Retrospect and prospect in the psychological study of coparenting and family group process. In J. P. McHale & W. S. Grolnick (Eds.), *Retrospect and prospect in the psychological study of families* (pp. 127–165). Mahwah, NJ: Erlbaum.

McHale, J. P., & Rotman, T. (2007). Is seeing believing? Expectant parents' outlooks on coparenting and later coparenting solidarity. *Infant Behavior and Development, 30*, 63–81.

McHale, J. P., Vinden, P. G., Bush, L., Richer, D., Shaw, D., & Smith, B. (2005). Patterns of personal and social adjustment among sport-involved and noninvolved urban middle-school children. *Sociology of Sport Journal, 22*, 119–136.

McHale, S. M., Crouter, A. C., Kim, J.-Y., Burton, L. M., Davis, K. D., Dotterer, A. M., & Swanson, D. P. (2006). Mothers' and fathers' racial socialization in African-American families: Implications for youth. *Child Development, 77*, 1387–1402.

McHale, S. M., Updegraff, K. A., Helms-Erikson, H., & Crouter, A. C. (2001). Sibling influences on gender development in middle childhood and early adolescence: A longitudinal study. *Developmental Psychology, 37*, 115–125.

McIntosh, H., Metz, E., & Youniss, J. (2005). Community service and identity formation in adolescents. In J. S. Mahoney, R. W. Larson, & J. S. Eccles (Eds.), *Organized activities as contexts of development: Extracurricular activities, after-school and community programs* (pp. 331–351). Mahwah, NJ: Erlbaum.

McIntosh, J., MacDonald, F., & McKeganey, N. (2006). Why do children experiment with illegal drugs? The declining role of peer pressure with increasing age. *Addiction Research and Theory, 14*, 275–287.

McKelvie, P., & Low, J. (2002). Listening to Mozart does not improve children's spatial ability: Final curtains for the Mozart effect. *British Journal of Developmental Psychology, 20*, 241–258.

McKenna, J. J. (2001). Why we never ask "Is it safe for infants to sleep alone?" *Academy of Breast Feeding Medicine News and Views, 7*(4), 32, 38.

McKenna, J. J. (2002, September/October). Breastfeeding and bedsharing still useful (and important) after all these years. *Mothering, 114*. Retrieved from www.mothering.com/articles/ new_baby/sleep/mckenna.html

McKenna, J. J., & McDade, T. (2005). Why babies should never sleep alone: A review of the co-sleeping controversy in relation to SIDS, bedsharing, and breastfeeding. *Paediatric Respiratory Reviews, 6*, 134–152.

McKenna, J. J., & Volpe, L. E. (2007). Sleeping with baby: An Internet-based sampling of parental experiences, choices, perceptions, and interpretations in a Western industrialized context. *Infant and Child Development, 16*, 359–385.

McKinney, C., Donnelly, R., & Renk, K. (2008). Perceived parenting, positive and negative perceptions of parents, and late adolescent emotional adjustment. *Child and Adolescent Mental health, 13*, 66–73.

McKown, C., & Strambler, M. J. (2009). Developmental antecedents and social and academic consequences of stereotype-consciousness in middle childhood. *Child Development, 80*, 1643–1659.

McKown, C., & Weinstein, R. S. (2003). The development and consequences of stereotype consciousness in middle childhood. *Child Development, 74*, 498–515.

McKown, C., & Weinstein, R. S. (2008). Teacher expectations, classroom context, and the achievement gap. *Journal of School Psychology, 46*, 235–261.

McKusick, V. A. (2007). *Online Mendelian inheritance in man.* Retrieved from www.ncbi.nlm.nih.gov/ sites/entrez?db=omim

McLanahan, S. (1999). Father absence and the welfare of children. In E. M. Hetherington (Ed.), *Coping with divorce, single parenting, and remarriage: A risk and resiliency perspective* (pp. 117–145). Mahwah, NJ: Erlbaum.

McLanahan, S. S., & Carlson, M. J. (2002). Welfare reform, fertility, and father involvement. *Future of Children, 12*, 111–115.

McLean, K. C., & Pratt, M. W. (2006). Life's little (and big) lessons: identity statuses and meaning-making in the turning point narratives of emerging adults. *Developmental Psychology, 42*, 714–722.

McLoyd, V. C., Aikens, N. L., & Burton, L. M. (2006). Childhood poverty, policy, and practice. In K. A. Renninger & I. E. Sigel (Eds.), *Handbook of child psychology: Vol. 4. Child psychology in practice* (6th ed., pp. 700–778). Hoboken, NJ: Wiley.

McLoyd, V. C., Kaplan, R., Hardaway, C. R., & Wood, D. (2007). Does endorsement of physical discipline matter? Assessing moderating influences on the maternal and child psychological correlates of physical discipline in African-American families. *Journal of Family Psychology, 21*, 165–175.

McLoyd, V. C., & Smith, J. (2002). Physical discipline and behavior problems in African-American, European-American, and Hispanic children: Emotional support as a moderator. *Journal of Marriage and the Family, 64*, 40–53.

McMahon, C. A., Barnett, B., Kowalenko, N. M., & Tennant, C. C. (2006). Maternal attachment state of mind moderates the impact of postnatal depression on infant attachment. *Journal of Child Psychology and Psychiatry and Allied Disciplines, 47*, 660–669.

McManus, I. C., Sik, G., Cole, D. R., Mellon, A. F., Wong, J., & Kloss, J. (1988). The development of handedness in children. *British Journal of Developmental Psychology, 6*, 257–273.

MCR Vitamin Study Research Group. (1991). Prevention of neural tube defects: Results of the Medical Research Council Vitamin Study. *Lancet, 338*, 131–137.

Mead, G. H. (1934). *Mind, self, and society.* Chicago: University of Chicago Press.

Mead, M. (1928). *Coming of age in Samoa.* Ann Arbor, MI: Morrow.

Mead, M., & Newton, N. (1967). Cultural patterning of perinatal behavior. In S. Richardson & A. Guttmacher (Eds.), *Childbearing: Its social and psychological aspects* (pp. 142–244). Baltimore: Williams & Wilkins.

Meade, C. S., Kershaw, T. S., & Ickovics, J. R. (2008). The intergenerational cycle of teenage motherhood: An ecological approach. *Health Psychology, 27*, 419–429.

Mechelli, A., Crinion, J. T., Noppeney, U., O'Doherty, J., Ashburner, J., Frackowiak, R. S., & Price, C. J. (2004). Structural plasticity in the bilingual brain: Proficiency in a second language and age at acquisition affect grey-matter density. *Nature, 431*, 757.

Medina, A. L. (2006). The parallel bar: Writing assessment and instruction. In J. S. Schumm (Ed.), *Reading assessment and instruction for all learners* (pp. 381–430). New York: Guilford Press.

Meek, J. (2002). Basic principles of optical imaging and application to the study of infant development. *Developmental Science, 5*, 371–380.

Meeus, W. (1996). Studies on identity development in adolescence: An overview of research and some new data. *Journal of Youth and Adolescence, 25*, 569–598.

Meeus, W., Oosterwegel, A., & Vollebergh, W. (2002). Parental and peer attachment and identity development in adolescence. *Journal of Adolescence, 25*, 93–106.

Mehlmadrona, L., & Madrona, M. M. (1997). Physician- and midwife-attended home births—effects of breech, twin, and post-dates outcome data on mortality rates. *Journal of Nurse-Midwifery, 42*, 91–98.

Meier, A., & Allen, G. (2009). Romantic relationships from adolescence to young adulthood: Evidence from the National Longitudinal Study of Adolescent Health. *Sociological Quarterly, 50*, 308–335.

Meins, E., Fernyhough, C., Russell, J., & Clark-Carter, D. (1998). Security of attachment as a predictor of symbolic and mentalizing abilities: A longitudinal study. *Social Development, 7*, 1–24.

Meins, E., Fernyhough, C., Wainwright, R., Clark-Carter, D., Gupta, M. D., Fradley, E., & Tucker, M. (2003). Pathways to understanding mind: Construct validity and predictive validity of maternal mind-mindedness. *Child Development, 74*, 1194–1211.

Melby, J. N., Conger, R. D., Fang, S., Wichrama, K. A. S., & Conger, K. J. (2008). Adolescent family experiences and educational attainment during early adulthood. *Developmental Psychology, 44*, 1519-1536.

Melinder, A., Endestad, T., & Magnussen, S. (2006). Relations between episodic memory, suggestibility, theory of mind, and cognitive inhibition in the preschool child. *Scandinavian Journal of Psychology, 47*, 485–495.

Melton, G. B. (2005). Treating children like people: A framework for research and advocacy. *Journal of Clinical Child and Adolescent Psychology, 34*, 646–657.

Meltzoff, A. N. (1995). Understanding the intentions of others: Reenactment of intended acts by 18-month-old children. *Developmental Psychology, 31,* 838–850.

Meltzoff, A. N. (2007). 'Like me': A foundation for social cognition. *Developmental Science, 10,* 126–134.

Meltzoff, A. N., & Kuhl, P. K. (1994). Faces and speech: Intermodal processing of biologically relevant signals in infants and adults. In D. J. Lewkowicz & R. Lickliter (Eds.), *The development of intersensory perception: Comparative perspectives* (pp. 335–369). Hillsdale, NJ: Erlbaum.

Meltzoff, A. N., & Moore, M. K. (1977). Imitation of facial and manual gestures by human neonates. *Science, 198,* 75–78.

Meltzoff, A. N., & Moore, M. K. (1994). Imitation, memory, and the representation of persons. *Infant Behavior and Development, 17,* 83–99.

Meltzoff, A. N., & Moore, M. K. (1999). Persons and representation: Why infant imitation is important for theories of human development. In J. Nadel & G. Butterworth (Eds.), *Imitation in infancy* (pp. 9–35). Cambridge, UK: Cambridge University Press.

Melzi, G., & Ely, R. (2009). Language development in the school years. In J. B. Gleason & N. B. Ratner (Eds.), *Development of language* (7th ed., pp. 391–435). Boston: Allyn and Bacon.

Mendle, J., Turkheimer, E., D'Onofrio, B. M., Lynch, S., Emery, R. E., & Slutske, W. S. (2006). Family structure and age at menarche: A children-of-twins approach. *Developmental Psychology, 42,* 533–542.

Mendle, J., Turkheimer, E., & Emery, R. E. (2007). Detrimental psychological outcomes associated with early pubertal timing in adolescent girls. *Developmental Review, 27,* 151–171.

Mennella, J. A., & Beauchamp, G. K. (1998). Early flavor experiences: Research update. *Nutrition Reviews, 56,* 205–211.

Ment, L. R., Vohr, B., Allan, W., Katz, K. H., Schneider, K. C., Westerveld, M., Cuncan, C. C., & Makuch, R. W. (2003). Change in cognitive function over time in very-low-birth-weight infants. *Journal of the American Medical Association, 289,* 705–711.

Menyuk, P., Liebergott, J. W., & Schultz, M. C. (1995). *Early language development in full-term and premature infants.* Hillsdale, NJ: Erlbaum.

Meredith, N. V. (1978). *Human body growth in the first ten years of life.* Columbia, SC: State Printing.

Mervis, C. B., Pani, J. R., & Pani, A. M. (2003). Transaction of child cognitive-linguistic abilities and adult input in the acquisition of lexical categories at the basic and subordinate levels. In D. H. Rakison & L. M. Oakes (Ed.), *Early category and concept development* (pp. 242–274). New York: Oxford University Press.

Metheny, J., McWhirter, E. H., & O'Neil, M. E. (2008). Measuring perceived teacher support and its influence on adolescent career development. *Journal of Career Assessment, 16,* 218–237.

Metz, E. C., & Youniss, J. (2005). Longitudinal gains in civic development through school-based required service. *Political Psychology, 26,* 413–437.

Meyer, P. A., Pivetz, T., Dignam, T. A., Hma, D. M., Schoonover, J., & Brody, D. (2003). Surveillance for elevated blood lead levels among children—United States, 1997–2001. *Morbidity and Mortality Weekly Report, 52*(No. SS-10), 1–21.

Meyer, R. (2009). Infant feeding in the first year. 1: Feeding practices in the first six months of life. *Journal of Family Health Care, 19,* 13–16.

Meyer-Bahlburg, H. F. L., Ehrhardt, A. A., Rosen, L. R., Gruen, R. S., Veridiano, N. P., Vann, F. H., & Neuwalder, H. F. (1995). Prenatal estrogens and the development of homosexual orientation. *Developmental Psychology, 31,* 12–21.

Mezulis, A. H., Hyde, J. S., & Clark, R. (2004). Father involvement moderates the effect of maternal depression during a child's infancy on child behavior problems in kindergarten. *Journal of Family Psychology, 18,* 575–588.

Miccio, A. W., Yont, K. M., Clemons, H. L., & Vernon-Feagans, L. (2002). Otitis media and the acquisition of consonants. In F. Windsor & M. L. Kelly (Eds.), *Investigations in clinical phonetics and linguistics* (pp. 429– 235). Mahwah, NJ: Erlbaum.

Miceli, P. J., Whitman, T. L., Borkowski, J. G., Braungart-Riekder, J., & Mitchell, D. W. (1998). Individual differences in infant information processing: The role of temperamental and maternal factors. *Infant Behavior and Development, 21,* 119–136.

Michael, A., & Eccles, J. S. (2003). When coming of age means coming undone: Links between puberty and psychosocial adjustment among European American and African American girls. In C. Hayward (Ed.), *Gender differences at puberty* (pp. 277–303). New York: Cambridge University Press.

Michalik, N. M., Eisenberg, N., Spinrad, T. L., Ladd, B., Thompson, M., & Valiente, C. (2007). Longitudinal relations among parental emotional expressivity and sympathy and prosocial behavior in adolescence. *Social Development, 16,* 286–309.

Michels, K. B., Willett, W. C., Graubard, B. I., Vaidya, R. L., Cantwell, M. M., Sansbury, L. B., & Forman, M. R. (2007). A longitudinal study of infant feeding and obesity throughout the life course. *International Journal of Obesity, 31,* 1078–1085.

Michiels, D., Grietens, H., Onghena, P., & Kuppens, S. (2010). Perceptions of maternal and paternal attachment security in middle childhood: Links with positive parental affection and psychological adjustment. *Early Child Development and Care, 180,* 211–225.

Midlin, M., Jenkins, R., & Law, C. (2009). Maternal employment and indicators of child health: A systematic review in pre-school children in OECD countries. *Journal of Epidemiology and Community Health, 63,* 340–350.

Milan, S., Snow, S., & Belay, S. (2007). The context of preschool children's sleep: Racial/ethnic differences in sleep locations, routines, and concerns. *Journal of Family Psychology, 21,* 20–28.

Milevsky, A., Schlechter, M., Netter, S., & Keehn, D. (2007). Maternal and paternal parenting styles in adolescents: Associations with self-esteem, depression, and life satisfaction. *Journal of Child and Family Studies, 16,* 39–47.

Miller, C. F., Lurye, L. E., Zosuls, K. M., & Ruble, D. N. (2009). Accessibility of gender stereotype domains: Developmental and gender differences in children. *Sex Roles, 60,* 870–881.

Miller, C. J., Sanchez, J., & Hynd, G. W. (2003). Neurological correlates of reading disabilities. In H. L. Swanson, K. R. Harris, & S. Graham (Eds.), *Handbook of learning disabilities* (pp. 242–255). New York: Guilford.

Miller, J. G. (2007). Cultural psychology of moral development. In S. Kitayama (Ed.), *Handbook of cultural psychology* (pp. 477–499). New York: Guilford.

Miller, J. G., & Bersoff, D. M. (1995). Development in the context of everyday family relationships: Culture, interpersonal morality, and adaptation. In M. Killen & D. Hart (Eds.), *Morality in everyday life: Developmental perspectives* (pp. 259–282). Cambridge, U.K.: Cambridge University Press.

Miller, L. T., & Vernon, P. A. (1992). The general factor in short-term memory, intelligence, and reaction time. *Intelligence, 16,* 5–29.

Miller, P. H. (2000). How to best utilize a deficiency. *Child Development, 71,* 1013–1017.

Miller, P. H. (2009). *Theories of developmental psychology* (5th ed.) New York: Worth.

Miller, P. H., & Bigi, L. (1979). The development of children's understanding of attention. *Merrill-Palmer Quarterly, 25,* 235–250.

Miller, P. J., Fung, H., & Koven, M. (2007). Narrative reverberations: How participation in narrative practices co-creates persons and cultures. In S. Kitayama & D. Cohen (Eds.), *Handbook of cultural psychology* (pp. 595–614). New York: Guilford.

Miller, P. J., Fung, H., & Mintz, J. (1996). Self-construction through narrative practices: A Chinese and American comparison of early socialization. *Ethos, 24,* 1–44.

Miller, P. J., Hengst, J. A., & Wang, S. (2003). Ethnographic methods: Applications from developmental cultural psychology. In P. M. Camic & J. E. Rhodes (Eds.), *Qualitative research in psychology* (pp. 219– 242). Washington, DC: American Psychological Association.

Miller, P. J., Wang, S., Sandel, T., & Cho, G. E. (2002). Self-esteem as folk theory: A comparison of European American and Taiwanese mothers' beliefs. *Parenting: Science and Practice, 2,* 209–239.

Miller, P. J., Wiley, A. R., Fung, H., & Liang, C.-H. (1997). Personal storytelling as a medium of socialization in Chinese and American families. *Child Development, 68,* 557–568.

Miller, S. A. (2009). Children's understanding of second-order mental states. *Psychological Bulletin, 135,* 749–773.

Miller, S. A., Hardin, C. A., & Montgomery, D. E. (2003). Young children's understanding of the conditions for knowledge acquisition. *Journal of Cognition and Development, 4,* 325–356.

Milligan, K., Astington, J. W., & Dack, L. A. (2007). Language and theory of mind: Meta-analysis of the relation between language ability and false-belief understanding. *Child Development, 78,* 622–646.

Mills, D., & Conboy, B. T. (2005). Do changes in brain organization reflect shifts in symbolic functioning? In L. Namy (Ed.), *Symbol use and symbolic representation* (pp. 123–153). Mahwah, NJ: Erlbaum.

Mills, D., Plunkett, K., Prat, C., & Schafer, G. (2005). Watching the infant brain learn words: Effects of language and experience. *Cognitive Development, 20,* 19–31.

Mills, R. S. L. (2005). Taking stock of the developmental literature on shame. *Developmental Review, 25,* 26–63.

Mills, R. S. L., & Grusec, J. E. (1989). Cognitive, affective, and behavioral consequences of praising altruism. *Merrill-Palmer Quarterly, 35,* 299–326.

Mills, T. L., Gomez-Smith, Z., & De Leon, J. M. (2005). Skipped generation families: Sources of psychological distress among grandmothers of grandchildren who live in homes where neither parent is present. *Marriage and Family Review, 37,* 191–212.

Mindell, J. A. (2005). *Sleeping through the night.* New York: HarperResource.

Minkler, M., & Fuller-Thomson, E. (2005). African American grandparents raising grandchildren: A national study using the Census 2000 American Community Survey. *Journal of Gerontology, 60B,* S82–S92.

Misailidi, P. (2006). Young children's display rule knowledge: Understanding the distinction between apparent and real emotions and the motives underlying the use of display rules. *Social Behavior and Personality, 34,* 1285–1296.

Mischel, W., & Liebert, R. M. (1966). Effects of discrepancies between observed and imposed reward criteria on their acquisition and transmission. *Journal of Personality and Social Psychology, 3,* 45–53.

Mishna, F., Antle, B. J., & Regehr, C. (2004). Tapping the perspectives of children. *Qualitative Social Work, 3,* 449–468.

Mistry, R. S., Biesanz, J. C., Chien, N., Howes, C., & Benner, A. D. (2008). Socioeconomic status, parental investments, and the cognitive and behavioral outcomes of low-income children from immigrant and native households. *Early Childhood Research Quarterly, 23,* 193–212.

Mitchell, A., & Boss, B. J. (2002). Adverse effects of pain on the nervous systems of newborns and young children: A review of the literature. *Journal of Neuroscience Nursing, 34,* 228–235.

Mitchell, B. A. (2006). Changing courses: The pendulum of family transitions in comparative perspective. *Journal of Comparative Family Studies, 37,* 325–343.

Miura, I. T., & Okamoto, Y. (2003). Language supports for mathematics understanding and performance. In A. J. Baroody & A. Dowker (Eds.), *The development of arithmetic concepts and skills* (pp. 229–242). Mahwah, NJ: Erlbaum.

Mize, J., & Pettit, G. S. (1997). Mothers' social coaching, mother–child relationship style, and children's peer competence: Is the medium the message? *Child Development, 68,* 312–332.

Mocarelli, P., Gerthoux, P., Ferrari, E., Patterson, D. G., Jr., Kieszak, S. M., & Brambilla, P. (2000). Paternal concentrations of dioxin and sex ratio of offspring. *Lancet, 355*, 1858–1862.

Moens, E., Braet, C., & Soetens, B. (2007). Observation of family functioning at mealtime: A comparison between families of children with and without overweight. *Journal of Pediatric Psychology, 32*, 52–63.

Moerk, E. L. (2000). *The guided acquisition of first language skills*. Westport, CT: Ablex.

Moffitt, T. E. (2006a). Life-course-persistent versus adolescence-limited antisocial behavior. In D. Cicchetti & D. J. Cohen (Eds.), *Developmental psychopathology: Vol. 3. Risk, disorder, and adaptation* (2nd ed., pp. 570–598). Hoboken, NJ: Wiley.

Moffitt, T. E. (2006b). A review of research on the taxonomy of life-course persistent versus adolescence-limited antisocial behavior. In F. T. Cullen, J. P. Wright, & K. Blevins (Eds.), *Taking stock: The status of criminological theory* (pp. 277–311). New Brunswick, NJ: Transaction Publishers.

Moll, H., & Tomasello, M. (2006). Level I perspective-taking at 24 months of age. *British Journal of Developmental Psychology, 24*, 603–613.

Moll, I. (1994). Reclaiming the natural line in Vygotsky's theory of cognitive development. *Human Development, 37*, 333–342.

Mollborn, S. (2007). Making the best of a bad situation: Material resources and teenage parenthood. *Journal of Marriage and Family, 69*, 92–104.

Moller, K., Hwang, C. P., & Wickberg, B. (2008). Couple relationship and transition to parenthood: Does workload at home matter? *Journal of Reproductive and Infant Psychology, 26*, 57–68.

Möller, O., & Krawinkel, M. (2005). Malnutrition and health in developing countries. *Canadian Medical Association Journal, 173*, 279–286.

Mondloch, C. J., Lewis, T., Budreau, D. R., Maurer, D., Dannemiller, J. L., Stephens, B. R., & Kleiner-Gathercoal, K. A. (1999). Face perception during early infancy. *Psychological Science, 10*, 419–422.

Mondoza, C. (2006). Inside today's classrooms: Teacher voices on No Child Left Behind and the education of gifted children. *Roeper Review, 29*, 28–31.

Monk, C., Fifer, W. P., Myers, M. M., Sloan, R. P., Trien, L., & Hurtado, A. (2000). Maternal stress responses and anxiety during pregnancy: Effects on fetal heart rate. *Developmental Psychobiology, 36*, 67–77.

Monk, C., Sloan, R., Myers, M. M., Ellman, L., Werner, E., Jeon, J., Tager, F., & Fifer, W. P. (2004). Fetal heart rate reactivity differs by women's psychiatric status: An early marker for developmental risk? *Journal of the American Academy of Child and Adolescent Psychiatry, 43*, 283–290.

Monk, C. S., Weng, S.-J., Wiggins, J. L., Kurapati, N., Louro, H. M. C., Carrasco, M., et al. (2010). Neural circuitry of emotional face processing in autism spectrum disorders. *Journal of Psychiatry and Neuroscience, 35*, 105–114.

Montague, D. P. F., & Walker-Andrews, A. S. (2001). Peekaboo: A new look at infants' perception of emotion expressions. *Developmental Psychology, 37*, 826–838.

Montemayor, R., & Eisen, M. (1977). The development of self-conceptions from childhood to adolescence. *Developmental Psychology, 13*, 314–319.

Montgomery, M. J. (2005). Psychosocial intimacy and identity: From early adolescence to emerging adulthood. *Journal of Adolescent Research, 20*, 346–374.

Montgomery, M. J., & Côté, J. E. (2003a). College as a transition to adulthood. In G. R. Adams & M. D. Berzonsky (Eds.), *Blackwell handbook of adolescence* (pp. 150–172). Malden, MA: Blackwell.

Montgomery, M. J., & Côté, J. E. (2003b). The transition to college: Adjustment, development, and outcomes. In G. R. Adams & M. D. Berzonsky (Eds.), *Blackwell handbook of adolescence* (pp. 179–194). Malden, MA: Blackwell.

Moon, C., Cooper, R. P., & Fifer, W. P. (1993). Two-day-old infants prefer their native language. *Infant Behavior and Development, 16*, 495–500.

Moon, R. Y., Horne, R. S. C., & Hauck, F. R.(2007). Sudden infant death syndrome. *The Lancet, 370*, 1578–1587.

Moonie, D. A., Sterling, D. A., Figgs, L., & Castro, M. (2006). Asthma status and severity affects missed school days. *Journal of School Health, 76*, 18–24.

Moore, C., Mealiea, J., Garon, N., & Povinelli, D. (2007). The development of body self-awareness. *Infancy, 11*, 157–174.

Moore, D. R., & Florsheim, P. (2001). Interpersonal processes and psychopathology among expectant and nonexpectant adolescent couples. *Journal of Consulting and Clinical Psychology, 69*, 101–113.

Moore, E. G. J. (1986). Family socialization and the IQ test performance of traditionally and transracially adopted black children. *Developmental Psychology, 22*, 317–326.

Moore, G. A., Cohn, J. E., & Campbell, S. B. (2001). Infant affective responses to mother's still face at 6 months differentially predict externalizing and internalizing behaviors at 18 months. *Developmental Psychology, 37*, 706–714.

Moore, K. A., Morrison, D. R., & Green, A. D. (1997). Effects on the children born to adolescent mothers. In R. A. Maynard (Ed.), *Kids having kids* (pp. 145–180). Washington, DC: Urban Institute.

Moore, K. L., & Persaud, T. V. N. (2008). *Before we are born* (7th ed.). Philadelphia: Saunders.

Moore, M. K., & Meltzoff, A. N. (1999). New findings on object permanence: A developmental difference between two types of occlusion. *British Journal of Developmental Psychology, 17*, 563–584.

Moore, M. K., & Meltzoff, A. N. (2004). Object permanence after a 24-hr delay and leaving the locale of disappearance: The role of memory, space, and identity. *Developmental Psychology, 40*, 606–620.

Moore, M. K., & Meltzoff, A. N. (2008). Factors affecting infants' manual search for occluded objects and the genesis of object permanence. *Infant Behavior and Development, 31*, 168–180.

Moore, M. R., & Brooks-Gunn, J. (2002). Adolescent parenthood. In M. H. Bornstein (Ed.), *Handbook of parenting: Vol. 3* (2nd ed., pp. 173–214). Mahwah, NJ: Erlbaum.

Moore, W. S. (2002). Understanding learning in a postmodern world: Reconsidering the Perry scheme of ethical and intellectual development. In B. K. Hofer & P. R. Pintrich (Eds.), *Personal epistemology* (pp. 17–36). Mahwah, NJ: Erlbaum.

Moran, G., Forbes, L., Evans, E., Tarabulsy, G. M., & Madigan, S. (2008). Both maternal sensitivity and atypical maternal behavior independently predict attachment security and disorganization in adolescent mother–infant relationships. *Infant Behavior and Development, 31*, 321–325.

Moran, G. F., & Vinovskis, M. A. (1986). The great care of godly parents: Early childhood in Puritan New England. *Monographs of the Society for Research in Child Development, 50*(4–5, Serial No. 211).

Moran, S., & Gardner, H. (2006). Extraordinary achievements: A developmental and systems analysis. In J. Kuhn & R. S. Siegler (Eds.), *Handbook of child psychology: Vol. 2. Cognition, perception, and language* (6th ed., pp. 905–949). Hoboken, NJ: Wiley.

Morelli, G. A., Rogoff, B., & Angelillo, C. (2003). Cultural variation in young children's access to work or involvement in specialized child-focused activities. *International Journal of Behavioral Development, 27*, 264–274.

Morelli, G. A., Rogoff, B., Oppenheim, D., & Goldsmith, D. (1992). Cultural variation in infants' sleeping arrangements: Questions of independence. *Developmental Psychology, 28*, 604–613.

Moreno, A. J., Klute, M. M., & Robinson, J. L. (2008). Relational and individual resources as predictors of empathy in early childhood. *Social Development, 17*, 613–637.

Morgan, B., Maybery, M., & Durkin, K. (2003). Weak central coherence, poor joint attention, and low verbal ability: Independent deficits in early autism. *Developmental Psychology, 39*, 646–656.

Morgan, P. L., Farkas, G., Hillemeier, M. M., & Maczuga, S. (2009). Risk factors for learning-related

behavior problems at 24 months of age: Population-based estimates. *Journal of Abnormal Child Psychology, 37*, 401-413.

Morgane, P. J., Austin-LaFrance, R., Bronzino, J., Tonkiss, J., Diaz-Cintra, S., Cintra, L., Kemper, T., & Galler, J. R. (1993). Prenatal malnutrition and development of the brain. *Neuroscience and Biobehavioral Reviews, 17*, 91–128.

Mori, L., & Peterson, L. (1995). Knowledge of safety of high and low active–impulsive boys: Implications for child injury prevention. *Journal of Clinical Child Psychology, 24*, 370–376.

Morris, G., & Baker-Ward, L. (2007). Fragile but real: Children's capacity to use newly acquired words to convey preverbal memories. *Child Development, 78*, 448–458.

Morrongiello, B. A., Fenwick, K. D., & Chance, G. (1998). Crossmodal learning in newborn infants: Inferences about properties of auditory-visual events. *Infant Behavior and Development, 21*, 543–554.

Morrongiello, B. A., & Kiriakou, S. (2004). Mothers' home-safety practices for preventing six types of childhood injuries: What do they do, and why? *Journal of Pediatric Psychology, 29*, 285–297.

Morrongiello, B. A., Midgett, C., & Shields, R. (2001). Don't run with scissors: Young children's knowledge of home safety rules. *Journal of Pediatric Psychology, 26*, 105–115.

Morrongiello, B. A., Ondejko, L., & Littlejohn, A. (2004). Understanding toddlers' in-home injuries: I. Context, correlates, and determinants. *Journal of Pediatric Psychology, 29*, 415–431.

Morrongiello, B. A., & Rennie, H. (1998). Why do boys engage in more risk taking than girls? The role of attributions, beliefs, and risk appraisals. *Journal of Pediatric Psychology, 23*, 33–43.

Morrow, D. F. (2006). Gay, lesbian, and transgender adolescents. In D. F. Morrow & L. Messinger (Eds.), *Sexual orientation and gender expression in social work practice* (pp. 177–195). New York: Columbia University Press.

Morse, S. B., Zheng, H., Tang, Y., & Roth, J., (2009). Early school-age outcomes of late preterm infants. *Pediatrics, 123*, e622–e629.

Mosby, L., Rawls, A. W., Meehan, A. J., Mays, E., & Pettinari, C. J. (1999). Troubles in interracial talk about discipline: An examination of African American child rearing narratives. *Journal of Comparative Family Studies, 30*, 489–521.

Mosely-Howard, G. S., & Evans, C. B. (2000). Relationships and contemporary experiences of the African-American family: An ethnographic case study. *Journal of Black Studies, 30*, 428–451.

Moses, L. J., Baldwin, D. A., Rosicky, J. G., & Tidball, G. (2001). Evidence for referential understanding in the emotions domain at twelve and eighteen months. *Child Development, 72*, 718–735.

Mosher, W. D., Chandra, A., & Jones, J. (2005). *Sexual behavior and selected health measures: Men and women 15–44 years of age, United States, 2002*. (Advance data from Vital and Health Statistics, No. 362). Hyattsville, MD: National Center for Health Statistics.

Moshman, D. (1998). Cognitive development beyond childhood. In D. Kuhn & R. S. Siegler (Eds.), *Handbook of child psychology: Vol. 2. Cognition, perception, and language* (5th ed., pp. 947– 978). New York: Wiley.

Moshman, D. (1999). *Adolescent psychological development: Rationality, morality, and identity*. Mahwah, NJ: Erlbaum.

Moshman, D. (2003). Developmental change in adulthood. In J. Demick & C. Andreoletti (Eds.), *Handbook of adult development* (pp. 43–61). New York: Plenum.

Moshman, D. (2005). *Adolescent psychological development: Rationality, morality, and identity* (2nd ed.). Mahwah, NJ: Erlbaum.

Moshman, D., & Franks, B. A. (1986). Development of the concept of inferential validity. *Child Development, 57*, 153–165.

Moshman, D., & Geil, M. (1998). Collaborative reasoning: Evidence for collective rationality. *Thinking and Reasoning, 4,* 231–248.

Moss, E., Cyr, C., Bureau, J.-F., Tarabulsy, G. M., & Dubois-Comtois, K. (2005). Stability of attachment during the preschool period. *Developmental Psychology, 41,* 773–783.

Moss, E., Cyr, C., & Dubois-Comtois, K. (2004). Attachment at early school age and developmental risk: Examining family contexts and behavior problems of controlling-caregiving, controlling-punitive, and behaviorally disorganized children. *Developmental Psychology, 40,* 519–532.

Moss, E., Smolla, N., Guerra, I., Mazzarello, T., Chayer, D., & Berthiaume, C. (2006). Attachment and self-reported internalizing and externalizing behavior problems in a school period. *Canadian Journal of Behavioural Science, 38,* 142–157.

Mosteller, F. (1995). The Tennessee Study of Class Size in the Early School Grades. *Future of Children, 5*(2), 113–127.

Mota, J., Silva, P., Santos, M. P., Ribeiro, J. C., Oliveira, J., & Duarte, J. A. (2005). Physical activity and school recess time: Differences between the sexes and the relationship between children's playground physical activity and habitual physical activity. *Journal of Sports Sciences, 23,* 269–275.

Motl, R. W., Dishman, R. K., Saunders, R. P., Dowda, M., Felton, G., Ward, D. S., & Pate, R. R. (2002). Examining social–cognitive determinants of intention and physical activity among black and white adolescent girls using structural equation modeling. *Health Psychology, 21,* 459–467.

Mottus, R., Indus, K., & Allik, J. (2008). Accuracy of only children stereotype. *Journal of Research in Personality, 42,* 1047–1052.

Mounts, N. S., & Steinberg, L. (1995). An ecological analysis of peer influence on adolescent grade point average and drug use. *Developmental Psychology, 31,* 915–922.

Mounts, N. S., Valentiner, D. P., Anderson, K. L., & Boswell, M. K. (2006). Shyness, sociability, and parental support for the college transition: Relation to adolescents' adjustment. *Journal of Youth and Adolescence, 35,* 71–80.

Moxley, D. P., Najor-Durack, A., & Dumbrigue, C. (2001). *Keeping students in higher education.* London: Kogan Page.

Mrug, S., Hoza, B., & Gerdes, A. C. (2001). Children with attention-deficit/hyperactivity disorder: Peer relationships and peer-oriented interventions. In D. W. Nangle & C. A. Erdley (Eds.), *The role of friendship in psychological adjustment* (pp. 51–77). San Francisco: Jossey-Bass.

Mueller, C. M., & Dweck, C. S. (1998). Intelligence praise can undermine motivation and performance. *Journal of Personality and Social Psychology, 75,* 33–52.

Muenchow, S., & Marsland, K. W. (2007). Beyond baby steps: Promoting the growth and development of U.S. child-care policy. In J. L. Aber, S. J. Bishop-Josef, S. M. Jones, K. T. McLearn, & D. Phillips (Eds.), *Child development and social policy: Knowledge for action* (pp. 97–112). Washington, DC: American Psychological Association.

Müller, U., Overton, W. F., & Reene, K. (2001). Development of conditional reasoning: A longitudinal study. *Journal of Cognition and Development, 2,* 27–49.

Mullett-Hume, E., Anshel, D., Guevara, V., & Cloitre, M. (2008). Cumulative trauma and posttraumatic stress disorder among children exposed to the 9/11 World Trade Center attack. *American Journal of Orthopsychiatry, 78,* 103–108.

Mullis, I. V. S., Martin, M. O., Kennedy, A. M., & Foy, P. (2007). *PIRLS 2006 international report: IEA's Progress in International Reading Literacy Study.* Boston: TIMSS & PIRLS International Study Center.

Mulvaney, M. K., McCartney, K., Bub, K. L., & Marshall, N. L. (2006). Determinants of dyadic scaffolding and cognitive outcomes in first graders. *Parenting: Science and Practice, 6,* 297–310.

Mulvaney, M. K., & Mebert, C. J. (2007). Parental corporal punishment predicts behavior problems in early childhood. *Journal of Family Psychology, 21,* 389–397.

Mumme, D. L., Bushnell, E. W., DiCorcia, J. A., & Lariviere, L. A. (2007). Infants' use of gaze cues to interpret others' actions and emotional reactions. In R. Flom, K. Lee, & D. Muir (Eds.), *Gaze-following: Its development and significance* (pp. 143–170). Mahwah, NJ: Erlbaum.

Munakata, Y. (2001). Task-dependency in infant behavior: Toward an understanding of the processes underlying cognitive development. In F. Lacerda, C. von Hofsten, & M. Heimann (Eds.), *Emerging cognitive abilities in early infancy* (pp. 29–52). Mahwah, NJ: Erlbaum.

Munakata, Y. (2006). Information processing approaches to development. In D. Kuhn & R. S. Siegler (Eds.), *Handbook of child psychology: Vol. 2. Cognition, perception, and language* (6th ed., pp. 426–463). Hoboken, NJ: Wiley.

Munakata, Y., & Stedron, J. M. (2002). Modeling infants' perception of object unity: What have we learned? *Developmental Science, 5,* 176.

Mundy, P., & Stella, J. (2000). Joint attention, social orienting, and nonverbal communication in autism. In A. M. Wetherby & B. M. Prizant (Eds.), *Autism spectrum disorders* (Vol. 9, pp. 55–77). Baltimore, MD: Paul H. Brookes.

Munroe, R. L., & Romney, A. K. (2006). Gender and age differences in same-sex aggregation and social behavior. *Journal of Cross-Cultural Psychology, 37,* 3–19.

Muret-Wagstaff, S., & Moore, S. G. (1989). The Hmong in America: Infant behavior and rearing practices. In J. K. Nugent, B. M. Lester, & T. B. Brazelton (Eds.), *Biology, culture, and development* (Vol. 1, pp. 319–339). Norwood, NJ: Ablex.

Muris, P., Merckelbach, H., Gadet, B., & Moulaert, V. (2000). Fears, worries, and scary dreams in 4- to 12-year-old children: Their content, developmental pattern, and origins. *Journal of Clinical Child Psychology, 29,* 43–52.

Muris, P., Merckelbach, H., Ollendick, T. H., King, N. J., & Bogie, N. (2001). Children's nighttime fears: Parent–child ratings of frequency, content, origins, coping behaviors and severity. *Behaviour Research and Therapy, 39,* 13–28.

Murphy, T. H., & Corbett, D. (2009). Plasticity during recovery: From synapse to behaviour. *Nature Reviews Neuroscience, 10,* 861–872.

Murray, A. D. (1985). Aversiveness is in the mind of the beholder. In B. M. Lester & C. F. Z. Boukydis (Eds.), *Infant crying* (pp. 217–239). New York: Plenum.

Mussen, P., & Eisenberg-Berg, N. (1977). *Roots of caring, sharing, and helping.* San Francisco: Freeman.

Mustanski, B. S., Viken, R. J., Kaprio, J., Pulkkinen, L., & Rose, R. J. (2004). Genetic and environmental influences on pubertal development: Longitudinal data from Finnish twins at ages 11 and 14. *Developmental Psychology, 40,* 1188–1198.

Mutti, D. O., Mitchell, G. L., Moeschberger, M. L., Jones, L. A., & Zadnik, K. (2002). Parental myopia, near work, school achievement, and children's refractive error. *Investigative Ophthalmology and Visual Science, 43,* 3633–3640.

Muzzatti, B., & Agnoli, F. (2007). Gender and mathematics: Attitudes and stereotype threat susceptibility in Italian children. *Developmental Psychology, 43,* 747–759.

Myant, K. A., & Williams, J. M. (2005). Children's concepts of health and illness: Understanding of contagious illnesses, noncontagious illnesses and injuries. *Journal of Health Psychology, 10,* 805–819.

Myers, L. J., & Liben, L. S. (2008). The role of intentionality and iconicity in children's developing comprehension and production of cartographic symbols. *Child Development, 79,* 668–684.

Myers, M. G., Brown, S. A., Tate, S., Abrantes, A., & Tomlinson, K. (2001). *Adolescents, alcohol, and substance abuse* (pp. 275–296). New York: Guilford.

Myowa-Yamakoshi, M., Tomonaga, M., Tanaka, M., & Matsuzawa, T. (2004). Imitation in neonatal chimpanzees (Pan troglodytes). *Developmental Science, 7,* 437–442.

N

Nadel, J., Prepin, K., & Okanda, M. (2005). Experiencing contingency and agency: First step toward self-understanding in making a mind? *Interaction Studies, 6,* 447–462.

Nader, P. R., Bradley, R. H., Houts, R. M., McRitchie, S. L., & O'Brien, M. (2008). Moderate-to-vigorous physical activity from ages 9 to 15 years. *Journal of the American Medical Association, 16,* 295–305.

Nader, P. R., O'Brien, M., Houts, R., Bradley, R., Belsky, J., Crosnoe, R., et al. (2006). Identifying risk for obesity in early childhood. *Pediatrics, 118,* e594–e601.

Nafstad, P., Hagen, J. A., Öie, L., Magnus, P., & Jaakkola, J. J. K. (1999). Day care centers and respiratory health. *Pediatrics, 103,* 753–758.

Nagy, E., Compagne, H., Orvos, H., Pal, A., Molnar, P., & Janszky, I. (2005). Index finger movement imitation by human neonates: Motivation, learning, and left-hand preference. *Pediatric Research, 58,* 749–753.

Nagy, W. E., & Scott, J. A. (2000). Vocabulary processes. In M. L. Kamil & P. B. Mosenthal (Eds.), *Handbook of reading research* (Vol. 3, pp. 269–284). Mahwah, NJ: Erlbaum.

Naigles, L. R., & Swenson, L. D. (2007). Syntactic supports for word learning. In E. Hoff & M. Shatz (Eds.), *Blackwell handbook of language development* (pp. 212–231). Malden, MA: Blackwell.

Naito, M., & Seki, Y. (2009). The relationship between second-order false belief and display rules reasoning: Integration of cognitive and affective social understanding. *Developmental Science, 12,* 150–164.

Nánez, J., Sr., & Yonas, A. (1994). Effects of luminance and texture motion on infant defensive reactions to optical collision. *Infant Behavior and Development, 17,* 165–174.

Narr, K. L., Woods, R. P., Lin, J., Kim, J., Phillips, O. R., Del'Homme, M., et al. (2009). Widespread cortical thinning is a robust anatomical marker for attention-deficit/hyperactivity disorder. *Journal of the American Academy of Child and Adolescent Psychiatry, 48,* 1014–1022.

Nastasi, B. K., & Clements, D. H. (1994). Effectance motivation, perceived scholastic competence, and higher-order thinking in two cooperative computer environments. *Journal of Educational Computing Research, 10,* 249–275.

Natale, R., & Dodman, N. (2003). Birth can be a hazardous journey: Electronic fetal monitoring does not help. *JOGC, 25,* 1007–1009.

National Association for Sport and Physical Education. (2009). *Active start: A statement of physical activity guidelines for children from birth to age 5* (2nd ed.). Reston, VA: Author.

National Center for Biotechnology Information, National Institutes of Health. (2007). *Genes and disease: Sickle cell anemia.* Retrieved from www.ncbi.nlm.nih.gov/bookshelf/br.fcgi?book=gnd&part=anemiasicklecell

National Coalition for the Homeless. (2008). *Homeless families with children.* Washington, DC: Author.

National Council of Youth Sports. (2008). Report on trends and participation in organized youth sports. Stuart, FL: Author.

National Early Literacy Panel. (2008). *Developing early literacy: A scientific synthesis of early literacy development and implications for intervention.* Jessup, MD: National Institute for Literacy.

National Federation of State High School Associations. (2009). *2007–08 High School Athletics Participation Survey.* Retrieved from www.nfhs.org/Participation/HistoricalSearch.aspx

National Institutes of Health. (2008). *Genes and disease.* Retrieved from www.ncbi.nlm.nih.gov/books/bv.fcgi?rid=gnd.TOC&depth=2

National Research Council. (2007). *Race conscious policies for assigning students to schools: Social science research and the Supreme Court cases.* Washington, DC: National Academy Press.

National Women's Law Center. (2007). *When girls don't graduate we all fail*. Washington, DC: Author.

Natsuaki, M. N., Biehl, M. C., & Ge, X. (2009). Trajectories of depressed mood from early adolescence to young adulthood: The effects of pubertal timing and adolescent dating. *Journal of Research on Adolescence, 19*, 47–74.

Navarrete, C., Martinez, I., & Salamanca, F. (1994). Paternal line of transmission in chorea of Huntington with very early onset. *Genetic Counseling, 5*, 175–178.

Needham, A. (2001). Object recognition in 4.5-month-old infants. *Journal of Experimental Child Psychology, 78*, 3–24.

Needleman, H. L., MacFarland, C., Ness, R. B., Reinberg, S., & Tobin, M. J. (2002). Bone lead levels in adjudicated delinquents: A case control study. *Neurotoxicology and Teratology, 24*, 711–717.

Neff, K. D., & Helwig, C. C. (2002). A constructivist approach to understanding the development of reasoning about rights and authority within cultural contexts. *Cognitive Development, 17*, 1429–1450.

Neitzel, C., & Stright, A. D. (2003). Mothers' scaffolding of children's problem solving: Establishing a foundation of academic self-regulatory competence. *Journal of Family Psychology, 17*, 147–159.

Nelson, C. A. (2002). Neural development and lifelong plasticity. In R. M. Lerner, F. Jacobs, & D. Wertlieb (Eds.), *Handbook of applied developmental science* (Vol. 1, pp. 31–60). Thousand Oaks, CA: Sage.

Nelson, C. A. (2007a). A developmental cognitive neuroscience approach to the study of atypical development: A model system involving infants of diabetic mothers. In D. Coch, G. Dawson, & K. W. Fischer (Eds.), *Human behavior, learning, and the developing brain: Atypical development* (2nd ed., pp. 37–59). New York: Guilford.

Nelson, C. A. (2007b). A neurobiological perspective on early human deprivation. *Child Development Perspectives, 1*, 13–18.

Nelson, C. A., & Bosquet, M. (2000). Neurobiology of fetal and infant development: Implications for infant mental health. In C. H. Zeanah, Jr. (Ed.), *Handbook of infant mental health* (2nd ed., pp. 37–59). New York: Guilford.

Nelson, C. A., Thomas, K. M., & de Haan, M. (2006). Neural bases of cognitive development. In D. Kuhn & R. Siegler (Eds.), *Handbook of child psychology: Vol. 2. Cognition, perception, and language* (6th ed., pp. 3–57). Hoboken, NJ: Wiley.

Nelson, C. A., Wewerka, S., Borscheid, A. J., deRegnier, R., & Georgieff, M. K. (2003). Electrophysiologic evidence of impaired cross-modal recognition memory in 8-month-old infants of diabetic mothers. *Journal of Pediatrics, 142*, 575–582.

Nelson, C. A., Wewerka, S., Thomas, K. M., Tribby-Walbridge, S., deRegnier, R., & Georgieff, M. K. (2000). Neurocognitive sequelae of infants of diabetic mothers. *Behavioral Neuroscience, 114*, 950–956.

Nelson, D. A., & Coyne, S. M. (2009). Children's intent attributions and feelings of distress: Associations with maternal and paternal parenting practices. *Journal of Abnormal Child Psychology, 37*, 223–237.

Nelson, D. A., Hart, C. H., Yang, C., Olsen, J. A., & Jin, S. (2006). Aversive parenting in China: Associations with child physical and relational aggression. *Child Development, 77*, 554–572.

Nelson, D. A., Nelson, L. J., Hart, C. H., Yang, C., & Jin, S. (2005). Parenting and peer-group behavior in cultural context. In X. Chen, B. Schneider, & D. French (Eds.), *Peer relations in cultural context*. New York Cambridge University Press.

Nelson, D. A., Robinson, C. C., & Hart, C. H. (2005). Relational and physical aggression of preschool-age children: Peer status linkages across informants. *Early Education and Development, 16*, 115–139.

Nelson, J. (1996). *Positive discipline*. New York: Ballantine.

Nelson, K. (1973). Structure and strategy in learning to talk. *Monographs of the Society for Research in Child Development, 38*(1–2, Serial No. 149).

Nelson, K. (2001). Language and the self: From the "experiencing I" to the "continuing me." In C. Moore & K. Lemmon (Eds.), *The self in time* (pp. 15–33). Mahwah NJ: Erlbaum.

Nelson, K. (2003). Narrative and the emergence of a consciousness of self. In G. D. Fireman & T. E. McVay, Jr. (Eds.), *Narrative and consciousness: Literature, psychology, and the brain* (pp. 17–36). London: Oxford University Press.

Nelson, K. (2007). *Young minds in social worlds: Experience, meaning, and memory*. Cambridge, MA: Harvard University Press.

Nelson, K., & Fivush, R. (2004). The emergence of autobiographical memory: A social cultural developmental theory. *Developmental Review, 111*, 486–511.

Nelson, L. J. (2003). Rites of passage in emerging adulthood: Perspectives of young Mormons. In J. J. Arnett & N. L. Galambos (Eds.), *Exploring cultural conceptions of the transitions to adulthood* (*New directions for child and adolescent development*, No. 100, pp. 33–49). San Francisco: Jossey-Bass.

Nelson, L. J., & Chen, X. (2007). Emerging adulthood in China: The role of social and cultural factors. *Child Development Perspectives, 1*, 86–91.

Nelson, L. J., Padilla-Walker, L. M., Carroll, J. S., Madsen, S. D., Barry, C. M., & Badger, S. (2007). "If you want me to treat you like an adult, start acting like one!" Comparing the criteria that emerging adults and their parents have for adulthood. *Journal of Family Psychology, 21*, 665–674.

Nemet, D., Barkan, S., Epstein, Y., Friedland, O., Kowen, G., & Eliakim, A. (2005). Short- and long-term beneficial effects of a combined dietary–behavioral–physical activity intervention for the treatment of childhood obesity. *Pediatrics, 115*, e443–e449.

Nepomnyaschy, L., & Waldfogel, J. (2007). Paternity leave and fathers' involvement with their young children. *Community, Work and Family, 10*, 427–453.

Neri, Q., Takeuchi, T., & Palermo, G. D. (2008). An update of assisted reproductive technologies in the United States. *Annals of the New York Academy of Sciences, 1127*, 41–48.

Nesdale, D., Durkin, K., Maas, A., & Griffiths, J. (2004). Group status, outgroup ethnicity, and children's ethnic attitudes. *Applied Developmental Psychology, 25*, 237–251.

Nesdale, D., Durkin, K., Maas, A., & Griffiths, J. (2005). Threat, group identification, and children's ethnic prejudice. *Social Development, 14*, 189–205.

Nettelbeck, T., & Burns, N. R. (2010). Processing speed, working memory and reasoning ability from childhood to old age. *Personality and Individual Differences, 48*, 379–384.

Neuman, S. B. (1999). Books make a difference: A study of access to literacy. *Reading Research Quarterly, 34*, 286–311.

Neuman, S. B. (2003). From rhetoric to reality: The case for high-quality compensatory prekindergarten programs. *Phi Delta Kappan, 85*(4), 286–291.

Neuman, S. B. (2006). The knowledge gap: Implications for early education. In D. K. Dickinson & S. B. Neuman (Eds.), *Handbook of early literacy research* (Vol. 2, pp. 29–40). New York: Guilford.

Neuman, S. B., & Celano, D. (2001). Access to print in middle- and low-income communities: An ecological study of four neighborhoods. *Reading Research Quarterly, 36*, 8–26.

Neumark-Sztainer, D., Hannan, P. J., Story, M., Croll, J., & Perry, C. (2003). Family meal patterns: Associations with sociodemographic characteristics and improved dietary intake among adolescents. *Journal of the American Dietetic Association, 103*, 317–322.

Neville, H. J., & Bavelier, D. (2002). Human brain plasticity: Evidence from sensory deprivation and altered language experience. In M. A. Hofman, G. J. Boer, A. J. G. D. Holtmaat, E. J. W. van Someren, J. Berhaagen, & D. F. Swaab (Eds.), *Plasticity in the adult brain: From genes to neurotherapy* (pp. 177–188). Amsterdam: Elsevier Science.

Neville, H. J., & Bruer, J. T. (2001). Language processing: How experience affects brain organization. In D. B. Bailey, Jr., J. T. Bruer, F. J. Symons, & J. W. Lichtman (Eds.), *Critical thinking about critical periods* (pp. 151–172). Baltimore: Paul H. Brookes.

Nevin, R. (2000). How lead exposure relates to temporal changes in IQ, violent crime, and unwed pregnancy. *Environmental Research, 83*, 1–22.

Newachek, P., Hung, Y.-Y., Hochstein, M., & Halfon, N. (2002). Access to health care for disadvantaged young children. *Journal of Early Intervention, 25*, 1–11.

Newcomb, A. F., Bukowski, W. M., & Pattee, L. (1993). Children's peer relations: A meta-analytic review of popular, rejected, neglected, controversial, and average sociometric status. *Psychological Bulletin, 113*, 99–128.

Newcomb, M. D., Abbott, R. D., Catalano, R. F., Hawkins, J. D., Battin-Pearson, S., & Hill, K. (2002). Mediational and deviance theories of late high school failure: Process roles of structural strains, academic competence, and general versus specific problem behavior. *Journal of Counseling Psychology, 49*, 172–186.

Newcombe, N. S. (2007). Taking science seriously: Straight thinking about spatial sex differences. In S. J. Ceci & W. M. Williams (Eds.), *Why aren't more women in science?* (pp. 69–77). Washington, DC: American Psychological Association.

Newcombe, N. S., & Huttenlocher, J. (1992). Children's early ability to solve perspective-taking problems. *Developmental Psychology, 28*, 635–643.

Newcombe, N. S., & Huttenlocher, J. (2006). Development of spatial cognition. In D. Kuhn & R. Siegler (Eds.), *Handbook of child psychology: Vol. 2. Cognition, perception, and language* (6th ed., pp. 734–776). Hoboken, NJ: Wiley.

Newcombe, N. S., Sluzenski, J., & Huttenlocher, J. (2005). Preexisting knowledge versus on-line learning: What do young infants really know about spatial location? *Psychological Science, 16*, 222–227.

Newland, L. A., Coyl, D. D., & Freeman, H. (2008). Predicting preschoolers' attachment security from fathers' involvement, internal working models, and use of social support. *Early Child Development and Care, 178*, 785–801.

Newman, A. J., Bavelier, D., Corina, D., Jezzard, P., & Neville, H. J. (2002). A critical period for right hemisphere recruitment in American sign language processing. *Nature Neuroscience, 5*, 76–80.

Newman, B. M., & Newman, P. R. (2001). Group identity and alienation: Giving the we its due. *Journal of Youth and Adolescence, 30*, 515–538.

Newnham, C. A., Milgrom, J., & Skouteris, H. (2009). Effectiveness of a modified mother–infant transaction program on outcomes for preterm infants from 3 to 24 months of age. *Infant Behavior and Development, 32*, 17–26.

Newport, E. L. (1991). Contrasting conceptions of the critical period for language. In S. Carey & R. Gelman (Eds.), *The epigenesis of mind: Essays on biology and cognition* (pp. 111–130). Hillsdale, NJ: Erlbaum.

Newport, E. L., & Aslin, R. N. (2000). Innately constrained learning: Blending old and new approaches to language acquisition. In S. C. Howell, S. A. Fish, & T. Keith-Lucas (Eds.), *Proceedings of the 24th Annual Boston University Conference on Language Development* (pp. 1–21). Somerville, MA: Cascadilla Press.

Newson, J., & Newson, E. (1975). Intersubjectivity and the transmission of culture: On the social origins of symbolic functioning. *Bulletin of the British Psychological Society, 28*, 437–446.

Ng, F. F., Pomerantz, E. M., & Lam, S. (2007). European-American and Chinese parents' responses to children's success and failure: Implications for children's responses. *Developmental Psychology, 43*, 1239–1255.

Ni, Y. (1998). Cognitive structure, content knowledge, and classificatory reasoning. *Journal of Genetic Psychology, 159*, 280–296.

NICHD (National Institute for Child Health and Human Development) Early Child Care Research Network. (1997). The effects of infant child care on infant–mother attachment security: Results of the NICHD Study of Early Child Care. *Child Development, 68,* 860–879.

NICHD (National Institute for Child Health and Human Development) Early Child Care Research Network. (1999). Child care and mother–child interaction in the first 3 years of life. *Developmental Psychology, 35,* 1399–1413.

NICHD (National Institute of Child Health and Human Development) Early Child Care Research Network. (2000a). Characteristics and quality of child care for toddlers and preschoolers. *Applied Developmental Science, 4,* 116–135.

NICHD (National Institute of Child Health and Human Development) Early Child Care Research Network. (2000b). The relation of child care to cognitive and language development. *Child Development, 71,* 960–980.

NICHD (National Institute of Child Health and Human Development) Early Child Care Research Network. (2001). Before Head Start: Income and ethnicity, family characteristics, child care experiences, and child development. *Early Education and Development, 12,* 545–575.

NICHD (National Institute of Child Health and Human Development) Early Child Care Research Network. (2002a). Child-care structure → process → outcome: Direct and indirect effects of child-care quality on young children's development. *Psychological Science, 13,* 199–206.

NICHD (National Institute of Child Health and Human Development) Early Child Care Research Network. (2002b). The interaction of child care and family risk in relation to child development at 24 and 36 months. *Applied Developmental Science, 6,* 144–156.

NICHD (National Institute of Child Health and Human Development) Early Child Care Research Network. (2003a). Does amount of time spent in child care predict socioemotional adjustment during the transition to kindergarten? *Child Development, 74,* 976–1005.

NICHD (National Institute of Child Health and Human Development) Early Child Care Research Network. (2003b). Does quality of child care affect child outcomes at age *Developmental Psychology, 39,* 451–469.

NICHD (National Institute of Child Health and Human Development) Early Child Care Research Network. (2004). Type of child care and children's development at 54 months. *Early Childhood Research Quarterly, 19,* 203–230.

NICHD (National Institute of Child Health and Human Development) Early Child Care Research Network. (2006). Child-care effect sizes for the NICHD Study of Early Child Care and Youth Development. *American Psychologist, 61,* 99–116.

Niccolai, L. M., Ethier, K. A., Kershaw, T. S., Lewis, J. B., Meade, C. S., & Ickovics, J. R. (2004). New sex partner acquisition and sexually transmitted disease risk among adolescent females. *Journal of Adolescent Health, 34,* 216–223.

Nicholls, A. L., & Kennedy, J. M. (1992). Drawing development: From similarity of features to direction. *Child Development, 63,* 227–241.

Nicholls, D. E., & Viner, R. M. (2009). Childhood risk factors for lifetime anorexia nervosa by age 30 in a national birth cohort. *Journal of the American Academy of Child and Adolescent Psychiatry, 48,* 791–799.

Nichols, K. E., Fox, N., & Mundy, P. (2005). Joint attention, self-recognition, and neurocognitive function in toddlers. *Infancy, 7,* 35–51.

Nichols, S. L., & Berliner, D. C. (2007). The pressure to cheat in a high-stakes testing environment. In E. M. Anderman & T. B. Murdock (Eds.), *Psychology of academic cheating* (pp. 289–311). San Francisco: Jossey-Bass.

Nicholson, C. (2006, September). Thinking it over: fMRI and psychological science. *APS Observer,* pp. 21–25.

Nicholson, J. M., Sanders, M. R., Halford, W. K., Phillips, M., & Whitton, S. W. (2008). The prevention and treatment of children's adjustment problems in stepfamilies. In J. Pryor (Ed.), *International handbook of stepfamilies: Policy and practice in legal, research, and clinical environments* (pp. 485–521). Hoboken, NJ: Wiley.

Nickman, S. L., Rosenfeld, A. A., & Fine, P. (2005). Children in adoptive families: Overview and update. *Journal of the American Academy of Child and Adolescent Psychiatry, 44,* 987–995.

Nickman, S. L., Rosenfeld, A. A., Fine, P., MacIntyre, J. C., Pilowsky, D. J., & Howe, R.-A. (2005). Children in adoptive families: Overview and update. *Journal of the American Academy of Child and Adolescent Psychiatry, 44,* 987–995.

Niehaus, M. D., Moore, S. R., Patrick, P. D., Derr, L. L., Lorntz, B., Lima, A. A., & Gurerrant, R. L. (2002). Early childhood diarrhea is associated with diminished cognitive function 4 to 7 years later in children in a northeast Brazilian shantytown. *American Journal of Tropical Medicine and Hygiene, 66,* 590–593.

Nielsen Company. (2008). *An overview of home Internet access in the U.S.* Retrieved from blog.nielsen.com/ nielsenwire/online_mobile/ home-internet-access-continuing-to-grow-but-big-differences-among-demographics/

Nielsen, M., & Christie, T. (2008). Adult modeling facilitates young children's generation of novel pretend acts. *Infant and Child Development, 17,* 151–162.

Nielsen, S. J., & Popkin, B. M. (2003). Patterns and trends in food portion sizes. *Journal of the American Medical Association, 289,* 450–453.

Nievar, M. A., & Becker, B. J. (2008). Sensitivity as a privileged predictor of attachment: A second perspective on De Wolff & van IJzendoorn's meta-analysis. *Social Development, 17,* 102–114.

Nigg, J. T. & Breslau, N. (2007). Prenatal smoking exposure, low birth weight, and disruptive behavior disorders. *Journal of the American Academy of Child and Adolescent Psychiatry, 46,* 362–369.

Nippold, M. A. (1999). Word definition in adolescents as a function of reading proficiency: A research note. *Child Language Teaching and Therapy, 15,* 171–176.

Nippold, M. A. (2000). Language development during the adolescent years: Aspects of pragmatics, syntax, and semantics. *Topics in Language Disorders, 20,* 15–28.

Nippold, M. A., Allen, M. M., & Kirsch, D. I. (2001). Proverb comprehension as a function of reading proficiency in preadolescents. *Language, Speech and Hearing Services in the Schools, 32,* 90–100.

Nippold, M. A., Taylor, C. L., & Baker, J. M. (1996). Idiom understanding in Australian youth: A cross-cultural comparison. *Journal of Speech and Hearing Research, 39,* 442–447.

Nisbett, R. E. (2009). *Intelligence and how to get it.* New York: Norton.

Nishitani, S., Miyamura, T., Tagawa, M., Sumi, M., Takase, R., Doi, H., Moriuchi, H., & Shinohara, K. (2009). The calming effect of a maternal breast milk odor on the human newborn infant. *Neuroscience Research, 63,* 66–71.

Nix, R. L., Pinderhughes, E. E., Dodge, K. A., Bates, J. E., Pettit, G. S., & McFadyen-Ketchum, S. A. (1999). The relation between mothers' hostile attribution tendencies and children's externalizing behavior problems: The mediating role of mothers' harsh discipline practices. *Child Development, 70,* 896–909.

Noguera, P. (2010, June 14). A new vision for school reform. *The Nation,* pp. 11–14.

Noland, J. S., Singer, L. T., Short, E. J., Minnes, S., Arendt, R. E., & Krichner, H. L. (2005). Prenatal drug exposure and selective attention in preschoolers. *Neurotoxicology and Teratology, 27,* 429–438.

Nolen-Hoeksema, S. (2002). Gender differences in depression. In I. H. Gotlib & C. L. Hammen (Eds.), *Handbook of depression* (pp. 492–509). New York: Guilford.

Nolen-Hoeksema, S. (2006). The etiology of gender differences in depression. In C. M. Mazure, G. P. Keita, & G. Puryear (Eds.), *Understanding depression in women: Applying empirical research to practice and policy* (pp. 9–43). Washington, DC: American Psychological Association.

Noller, P., Feeney, J. A., Sheehan, G., Darlington, Y., & Rogers, C. (2008). Conflict in divorcing and continuously married families: A study of marital, parent–child and sibling relationships. *Journal of Divorce and Remarriage, 49,* 1–24.

Noonan, C. W., Kathman, S. J., Sarasua, S. M., & White, M. C. (2003). Influence of environmental zinc on the association between environmental and biological measures of lead in children. *Journal of Exposure Analysis and Environmental Epidemiology, 13,* 318–323.

Nord, M., Andrews, M., & Carlson, S. (2009). *Household food security in the United States, 2008.* Washington, DC: U.S. Department of Agriculture.

Norwitz, E. R. (2009). A blood test to predict preterm birth: Don't mess with maternal–fetal stress. *Journal of Clinical Endocrinology and Metabolism, 94,* 1886–1889.

Noterdaeme, M., Mildenberger, K., Minow, F., & Amorosa, H. (2002). Evaluation of neuromotor deficits in children with autism and children with a specific speech and language disorder. *European Child and Adolescent Psychiatry, 11,* 219–225.

Nucci, L. (2001). *Education in the moral domain.* New York: Cambridge University Press.

Nucci, L. (2005). Culture, context, and the psychological sources of human rights concepts. In W. Edelstein & G. Nunner-Winkler (Eds.), *Morality in context* (pp. 365–394). Amsterdam: Elsevier.

Nucci, L. (2008). *Nice is not enough: Facilitating moral development.* Upper Saddle River, NY: Prentice Hall.

Nucci, L. P. (1996). Morality and the personal sphere of action. In E. Reed, E. Turiel, & T. Brown (Eds.), *Values and knowledge* (pp. 41–60). Hillsdale, NJ: Erlbaum.

Nucci, L. P. (2002). The development of moral reasoning. In U. Goswami (Ed.), *Blackwell handbook of childhood cognitive development* (pp. 303–325). Malden, MA: Blackwell.

Nunez-Smith, M., Wolf, E., Huang, H. M., Chen, P. G., Lee, L., Emanuel, E. J., et al. (2008). *The impact of media on child and adolescent health.* Retrieved from www.commonsensemedia.org.

Nuttal, R. L., Casey, M. B., & Pezaris, E. (2005). Spatial ability as a mediator of gender differences on mathematics tests: A biological–environmental framework. In A. M. Gallagher & C. J. Kaufman (Eds.), *Gender differences in mathematics: An integrated psychological approach* (pp. 121–142). New York: Cambridge University Press.

Nye, B., Hedges, L. V., & Konstantopoulos, S. (2001). Are effects of small classes cumulative? Evidence from a Tennessee experiment. *Journal of Educational Research, 94,* 336–345.

O

Oakes, L. M., Coppage, D. J., & Dingel, A. (1997). By land or by sea: The role of perceptual similarity in infants' categorization of animals. *Developmental Psychology, 33,* 396–407.

Oakes, L. M., Horst, J. S., & Kovack-Lesh, K. A. (2009). How infants learn categories. In A. Woodward & A. Needham (Eds.), *Learning and the infant mind* (pp. 144–171). New York: Oxford University Press.

Oakes, L. M., & Madole, K. L. (2003). Principles of developmental change in infants' category formation. In D. H. Rakison & L. M. Oakes (Eds.), *Early category and concept development: Making sense of the blooming, buzzing confusion* (pp. 132–158). New York: Oxford University Press.

Obeidallah, D., Brennan, R. T., Brooks-Gunn, J., & Earls, F. (2004). Links between pubertal timing and neighborhood contexts: Implications for girls' violent behavior. *Journal of the American Academy of Child and Adolescent Psychiatry, 43,* 1460–1468.

Oberecker, R., & Friederici, A. D. (2006). Syntactic event-related potential components in 24-month-olds' sentence comprehension. *NeuroReport, 17,* 1017–1021.

Oberecker, R., Friedrich, M., & Friederici, A. D. (2005). Neural correlates of syntactic processing in two-year-olds. *Journal of Cognitive Neuroscience, 17,* 1667–1678.

Oberlander, T. F., Warburton, W., Misri, S., Aghajanian, J., & Hertzman, C. (2006). Neonatal outcomes after prenatal exposure to selective serotonin reuptake inhibitor antidepressants and maternal depression using population-based linked health data. *Archives of General Psychiatry, 63,* 898–906.

Obler, L. K. (2008). Developments in the adult years. In J. B. Gleason & B. Ratner (Eds.), *The development of language* (7th ed., pp. 436–464). Boston: Allyn and Bacon.

Obradović, J., Long, J. D., Cutuli, J. J., Chan, C.-K., Hinz, E., Heistad, D., & Masten, A. S. (2009). Academic achievement of homeless and highly mobile children in an urban school district: Longitudinal evidence on risk, growth, and resilience. *Development and Psychopathology, 21,* 493–518.

Obradović, J., & Masten, A. S. (2007). Developmental antecedents of young adult civic engagement. *Applied Developmental Science, 11,* 2–19.

O'Brien, E. H., Hsing, C., & Kornrath, S. (2010, May). *Empathy is declining in American college students.* Poster presented at the annual meeting of the Association for Psychological Science, Boston.

O'Brien, M. A., Prosser, L. A., Paradise, J., Ray, G. T., et al. (2009). New vaccines against otitis media: Projected benefits and cost-effectiveness. *Pediatrics, 123,* 1452–1463.

O'Callaghan, M. J., Burn, Y. R., Mohay, H. A., Rogers, Y., & Tudehope, D. I. (1993). The prevalence and origins of left hand preference in high risk infants, and its implications for intellectual, motor, and behavioral performance at four and six years. *Cortex, 29,* 617–627.

O'Connor, A. R., Stephenson, T., Johnson, A., Tobin, M. J., Ratib, S., Ng, Y., & Fielder, A. R. (2002). Long-term ophthalmic outcome of low birth weight children with and without retinopathy of prematurity. *Pediatrics, 109,* 12–18.

O'Connor, C. (1997). Dispositions toward (collective) struggle and educational resilience in the inner city: A case analysis of six African-American high school students. *American Educational Research Journal, 34,* 593–629.

O'Connor, E., & McCartney, K. (2007). Examining teacher–child relationships and achievement as part of an ecological model of development. *American Educational Research Journal, 44,* 340–369.

O'Connor, T. G., & Croft, C. M. (2001). A twin study of attachment in preschool children. *Child Development, 72,* 1501–1511.

O'Connor, T. G., Marvin, R. S., Rutter, M., Olrich, J. T., Britner, P. A., & the English and Romanian Adoptees Study Team. (2003). Child–parent attachment following early institutional deprivation. *Development and Psychopathology, 15,* 19–38.

O'Connor, T. G., Rutter, M., Beckett, C., Keaveney, L., Dreppner, J. M., & the English and Romanian Adoptees Study Team. (2000). The effects of global severe privation on cognitive competence: Extension and longitudinal follow-up. *Child Development, 71,* 376–390.

O'Dea, J. A. (2003). Why do kids eat healthful food? Perceived benefits of and barriers to healthful eating and physical activity among children and adolescents. *Journal of the American Dietetic Association, 103,* 497–501.

OECD (Organisation for Economic Cooperation and Development). (2006). *Starting strong II: Early childhood education and care.* Paris: OECD Publishing. Retrieved from www.sourceoecd.org/education/9264035451

OECD (Organisation for Economic Cooperation and Development). (2008a). *Education at a glance 2008: OECD indicators.* Paris: Author. Retrieved from www.oecd.org/infobycountry/0,3380,en_2649_33715_1_1_1_1_1,00.html

OECD (Organisation for Economic Cooperation and Development). (2008b). OECD Health data: 2008.

Retrieved from secure.cihi.ca/cihiweb/dispPage.jsp?cw_page=media_26jun2008_e

OECD (Organisation for Economic Cooperation and Development). (2010). *Education at a glance 2010: OECD indicators.* Paris: Author.

Ogan, A., & Berk, L. E. (2009, April). *Effects of two approaches to make-believe play training on self-regulation in Head Start children.* Paper presented at the biennial meeting of the Society for Research in Child Development, Denver, CO.

Ogbu, J. U. (1997). Understanding the school performance of urban blacks: Some essential background knowledge. In H. J. Walberg, O. Reyes, & R. P. Weissberg (Eds.), *Children and youth: Interdisciplinary perspectives* (pp. 190–222). Thousand Oaks, CA: Sage.

Ogbu, J. U. (2003). *Black American students in an affluent suburb: A study of academic disengagement.* Mahwah, NJ: Erlbaum.

Ogden, C. L., Carroll, M. D., Curtin, L. R., Lamb, M. M., & Flegal, K. M. (2010). Prevalence of high body mass index in U.S. children and adolescents, 2007–2008. *Journal of the American Medical Association, 303,* 242–249.

Ohannessian, C. M., & Hesselbrock, V. M. (2008). Paternal alcoholim and youth substance abuse: The indirect effects of negative affect, conduct problems, and risk taking. *Journal of Adolescent Health, 42,* 198–200.

Ohgi, S., Arisawa, K., Takahashi, T., Kusumoto, T., Goto, Y., Akiyama, T., & Saito, H. (2003a). Neonatal behavioral assessment scale as a predictor of later developmental disabilities of low-birth-weight and/or premature infants. *Brain and Development, 25,* 313–321.

Ohgi, S., Takahashi, T., Nugent, J. K., Arisawa, K., & Akiyama, T. (2003b). Neonatal behavioral characteristics and later behavioral problems. *Clinical Pediatrics, 42,* 679–686.

Ohlsson, G., Buchhave, P., Leandersson, U., Nordstrom, L., Rydhstrom, H., & Sjolin, I. (2001). Warm tub bathing during labor: Maternal and neonatal effects. *Acta Obstetricia et Gynecologica Scandinavica, 80,* 311–314.

Okagaki, L., Hammond, K. A., & Seamon, L. (1999). Socialization of religious beliefs. *Journal of Applied Developmental Psychology, 20,* 273–294.

Okagaki, L., & Sternberg, R. J. (1993). Parental beliefs and children's school performance. *Child Development, 64,* 36–56.

Okami, P., Weisner, T., & Olmstead, R. (2002). Outcome correlates of parent–child bedsharing: An eighteen-year longitudinal study. *Developmental and Behavioral Pediatrics, 23,* 244–253.

O'Keefe, M. J., O'Callaghan, M., Williams, G. M., Najman, J. M., & Bor, W. (2003). Learning, cognitive, and attentional problems in adolescents born small for gestational age. *Pediatrics, 112,* 301–307.

Olafson, E., & Boat, B. W. (2000). Long-term management of the sexually abused child: Considerations and challenges. In R. M. Reece (Ed.), *Treatment of child abuse: Common ground for mental health, medical, and legal practitioners* (pp. 14–35). Baltimore: Johns Hopkins University Press.

O'Laughlin, E. M., & Anderson, V. N. (2001). Perceptions of parenthood among young adults: Implications for career and family planning. *American Journal of Family Therapy, 29,* 95–108.

Olds, D. L., Kitzman, H., Cole, R., Robinson, J., Sidora, K., Luckey, D. W., et al. (2004). Effects of nurse home–visiting on maternal life course and child development: Age 6 follow-up results of a randomized trial. *Pediatrics, 114,* 1550–1559.

Olds, D. L., Kitzman, H., Hanks, C., Cole, R., Anson, E., Sidora-Arcoleo, K., et al. (2007). Effects of nurse home visiting on maternal and child functioning: Age-9 follow-up of a randomized trial. *Pediatrics, 120,* e832–e845.

Olds, D. L., Robinson, J., O'Brien, R., Luckey, D. W., Pettitt, L. M., Henderson, C. R., Jr., et al. (2002). Home visiting by paraprofessionals and by nurses: A randomized, controlled trial. *Pediatrics, 110,* 486–496.

Olineck, K. M., & Poulin-Dubois, D. (2007). Imitation of intentional actions and internal state language in infancy predict preschool theory of mind skills. *European Journal of Developmental Psychology, 4,* 14–30.

Olineck, K. M., & Poulin-Dubois, D. (2009). Infants' understanding of intention from 10 to 14 months: Interrelations among violation of expectancy and imitation tasks. *Infant Behavior and Development, 32,* 404–415.

Ollendick, T. H., King, N. J., & Muris, P. (2002). Fears and phobias in children: Phenomenology, epidemiology, and aetiology. *Child and Adolescent Mental Health, 7,* 98–106.

Oller, D. K. (2000). *The emergence of the speech capacity.* Mahwah, NJ: Erlbaum.

Olson, D., Sikka, R. S., Hayman, J., Novak, M., & Stavig, C. (2009). Exercise in pregnancy. *Current Sports Medicine Reports, 8,* 147–153.

Olson, S. L., Bates, J. E., Sandy, J. M., & Lantheir, R. (2000). Early development precursors of externalizing behavior in middle childhood and adolescence. *Journal of Abnormal Child Psychology, 28,* 119–133.

Omar, H., McElderry, D., & Zakharia, R. (2003). Educating adolescents about puberty: What are we missing? *International Journal of Adolescent Medicine and Health, 15,* 79–83.

Ondrusek, N., Abramovitch, R., Pencharz, P., & Koren, G. (1998). Empirical examination of the ability of children to consent to clinical research. *Journal of Medical Ethics, 24,* 158–165.

O'Neil, R., Welsh, M., Parke, R. D., Wang, S., & Strand, C. (1997). A longitudinal assessment of the academic correlates of early peer acceptance and rejection. *Journal of Clinical Child Psychology, 26,* 290–303.

O'Neill, M., Bard, K. A., Kinnell, M., & Fluck, M. (2005). Maternal gestures with 20-month-old infants in two contexts. *Developmental Science, 8,* 352–359.

O'Neill, R. M., Horton, S. S., & Crosby, F. J. (1999). Gender issues in developmental relationships. In A. J. Murrell, F. J. Crosby, & R. J. Ely (Eds.), *Mentoring dilemmas* (pp. 63–80). Mahwah, NJ: Erlbaum.

Ong, K. K., Ahmed, M. L., & Dunger, D. B. (2006). Lessons from large population studies on timing and tempo of puberty (secular trends and relation to body size): the European trend. *Molecular and Cellular Endocrinology, 254–255,* 8–12.

Ong, W., Allison, J., & Haladyna, T. M. (2000). Student achievement of third graders in comparable single-age and multiage classrooms. *Journal of Research in Childhood Education, 14,* 205–215.

Ontai, L. L., & Thompson, R. A. (2008). Attachment, parent–child discourse and theory-of-mind development. *Social Development, 17,* 47–60.

Oosterwegel, A., & Openheimer, L. (1993). *The self-system: Developmental changes between and within self-concepts.* Hillsdale, NJ: Erlbaum.

Ophir, E., Nass, C., & Wagner, A. D. (2009). Cognitive control in media multitaskers. *Proceedings of the National Academy of Sciences, 106,* 15583–15587.

O'Rahilly, R., & Müller, F. (2001). *Human embryology and teratology.* New York: Wiley-Liss.

Ordonana, J. R., Caspi, A., & Moffitt, T. E. (2008). Unintentional injuries in a twin study of preschool children: Environmental, not genetic risk factors. *Journal of Pediatric Psychology, 33,* 185–194.

O'Reilly, A. W. (1995). Using representations: Comprehension and production of actions with imagined objects. *Child Development, 66,* 999–1010.

Orobio de Castro, B., Brendgen, M., Van Boxtel, H., Vitaro, F., & Schaepers, L. (2007). "Accept me, or else . . .": Disputed overestimation of social competence predicts increases in proactive aggression. *Journal of Abnormal Child Psychology, 35,* 165–178.

Orobio de Castro, B., Veerman, J. W., Koops, W., Bosch, J. D., & Monshouwer, H. J. (2002). Hostile attribution of intent and aggressive behavior: A meta-analysis. *Child Development, 73,* 916–934.

Orth, U., Trzesniewski, K. H., & Robins, R. W. (2010). Self-esteem development from young adulthood to old age: A cohort-sequential longitudinal study.

Journal of Personality and Social Psychology, 98, 645–658.

Osherson, D. N., & Markman, E. M. (1975). Language and the ability to evaluate contradictions and tautologies. *Cognition, 2,* 213–226.

Oshima-Takane, Y., & Robbins, M. (2003). Linguistic environment of secondborn children. *First Language, 23,* 21–40.

Ostad, S. A., & Sorensen, P. M. (2007). Private speech and strategy-use patterns: Bidirectional comparisons of children with and without mathematical difficulties in a developmental perspective. *Journal of Learning Disabilities, 40,* 2–14.

Ostrov, J. M., Crick, N. R., & Stauffacher, K. (2006). Relational aggression in sibling and peer relationships during early childhood. *Applied Developmental Psychology, 27,* 241–253.

Ostrov, J. M., Gentile, D. A., & Crick, N. R. (2006). Media exposure, aggression, and prosocial behavior during early childhood: A longitudinal study. *Social Development, 15,* 612–627.

Otis, N., Grouzet, F. M. E., & Pelletier, L. G. (2005). Latent motivational change in an academic setting: A three-year longitudinal study. *Journal of Educational Psychology, 97,* 170–183.

Oude, L. H., Baur, L., Jansen, H., Shrewsbury, V. A., O'Malley, C., Stolk, R. P., & Summerbell, C. D. (2009). Interventions for treating obesity in children. *Cochrane Database of Systematic Reviews,* Issue 4. Chichester, UK: Wiley.

Ouko, L. A., Shantikumar, K., Knezovich, J., Haycock, P., Schnugh, D. J., & Ramsay, M. (2009). Effect of alcohol consumption on CpG methylation in the differentially methylated regions of H19 and IG-DMR in male gametes: Implications for fetal alcohol spectrum disorders. *Alcoholism, Clinical and Experimental Research, 33,* 1615–1627.

Ovando, C. J., & Collier, V. P. (1998). *Bilingual and ESL classrooms: Teaching in multicultural contexts.* Boston: McGraw-Hill.

Ovelese, Y., & Ananth, C. V. (2006). Placental abruption. *Obstetrics and Gynecology, 108,* 1005–1016.

Ovelese, Y., & Smulian, J. C. (2006). Placenta previa, placenta accreta, and vasa previa. *Obstetrics and Gynecology, 107,* 927–941.

Owen, C. G., Whincup, P. H., Kaye, S. J., Martin, R. M., Smith, G. D., Cook, D. G., et al. (2008). Does initial breastfeeding lead to lower blood cholesterol in adult life? A quantitative review of the evidence. *American Journal of Clinical Nutrition, 88,* 305–314.

Owen-Kostelnik, J., Reppucci, N. D., & Meyer, J. R. (2006). Testimony and interrogation of minors: Assumptions about maturity and morality. *American Psychologist, 61,* 286–304.

Owens, R. E. (2008). *Language development: An introduction.* Boston: Allyn and Bacon.

Oyserman, D. (2007). Social identity and self-regulation. In A. Kruglanski & E. T. Higgins (Eds.), *Handbook of social psychology: Basic principles* (2nd ed., pp. 432–453). New York: Guilford.

Oyserman, D., Bybee, D., Mowbray, C., & Hart-Johnson, T. (2005). When mothers have serious mental health problems: Parenting as a proximal mediator. *Journal of Adolescence, 28,* 443–463.

Ozçaliskan, S., & Goldin-Meadow, S. (2005). Gesture is at the cutting edge of early language development. *Cognition, 96,* B101–B113.

P

Pacella, R., McLellan, M., Grice, K., Del Bono, E. A., Wiggs, J. L., & Gwiazda, J. E. (1999). Role of genetic factors in the etiology of juvenile-onset myopia based on a longitudinal study of refractive error. *Optometry and Vision Science, 76,* 381–386.

Pagani, L. S., Japel, C., Vitaro, F., Tremblay, R. E., Larose, S., & McDuff, P. (2008). When predictions fail: The case of unexpected pathways toward high school dropout. *Journal of Social Issues, 64,* 175–193.

Paladino, J. (2006). *Private speech in children with autism: Developmental course and functional utility.* Unpublished doctoral dissertation, Illinois State University.

Palincsar, A. S. (2003). Advancing a theoretical model of learning and instruction. In B. J. Zimmerman (Ed.), *Educational psychology: A century of contributions* (pp. 459–475). Mahwah, NJ: Erlbaum.

Palincsar, A. S., & Herrenkohl, L. R. (1999). Designing collaborative contexts: Lessons from three research programs. In A. M. O'Donnell & A. King (Eds.), *Cognitive perspectives on peer learning. The Rutgers Invitational Symposium on Education Series* (pp. 151–177). Mahwah, NJ: Erlbaum.

Palmer, J. R., Hatch, E. E., Rao, R. S., Kaufman, R. H., Herbst, A. L., & Noller, K. L. (2001). Infertility among women exposed prenatally to diethylstilbestrol. *American Journal of Epidemiology, 154,* 316–321.

Pan, B. A., & Snow, C. E. (1999). The development of conversation and discourse skills. In M. Barrett (Ed.), *The development of language* (pp. 229–249). Hove, UK: Psychology Press.

Pan, H. W. (1994). Children's play in Taiwan. In J. L. Roopnarine, J. E. Johnson, & F. H. Hooper (Eds.), *Children's play in diverse cultures* (pp. 31–50). Albany, NY: SUNY Press.

Papadakis, A. A., Prince, R. P., Jones, N. P., & Strauman, T. J. (2006). Self-regulation, rumination, and vulnerability to depression in adolescent girls. *Development and Psychopathology, 18,* 815–829.

Papousek, M. (2007). Communication in early infancy: An arena of intersubjective learning. *Infant Behavior and Development, 30,* 258–266.

Paquette, D. (2004). Theorizing the father–child relationship: Mechanisms and developmental outcomes. *Human Development, 47,* 193–219.

Paradis, J. (2007). Second language acquisition in childhood. In E. Hoff & M. Shatz (Eds.), *Blackwell handbook of language development* (pp. 387–405). Malden, MA: Blackwell.

Paradise, R., & Rogoff, B. (2009). Side by side: Learning by observing and pitching in. *Ethos, 27,* 102–138.

Parameswaran, G. (2003). Experimenter instructions as a mediator in the effects of culture on mapping one's neighborhood. *Journal of Environmental Psychology, 23,* 409–417.

Parent, A., Teilmann, G., Juul, A., Skakkebaek, N. E., Toppari, J., & Bourguignon, J. (2003). The timing of normal puberty and the age limits of sexual precocity: Variations around the world, secular trends, and changes after migration. *Endocrine Reviews, 24,* 668–693.

Paris, S. G., & Paris, A. G. (2006). Assessments of early reading. In K. A. Renninger & I. E. Sigel (Eds.), *Handbook of child psychology: Vol. 4. Child psychology in practice* (6th ed., pp. 48–74). Hoboken, NJ: Wiley.

Park, W. (2009). Acculturative stress and mental health among Korean adolescents in the United States. *Journal of Human Behavior in the Social Environment, 19,* 626–634.

Parke, R. D. (2002). Fathers and families. In M. H. Bornstein (Ed.), *Handbook of parenting: Vol. 3* (2nd ed., pp. 27–73). Mahwah, NJ: Erlbaum.

Parke, R. D., & Buriel, R. (2006). Socialization in the family: Ethnic and ecological perspectives. In N. Eisenberg (Ed.), *Handbook of child psychology: Vol. 3. Social, emotional, and personality development* (6th ed., pp. 429–504). Hoboken, NJ: Wiley.

Parke, R. D., Coltrane, S., Fabricius, W., Powers, J., & Adams, M. (2004). Assessing father involvement in Mexican-American families. In R. Day & M. E. Lamb (Eds.), *Conceptualizing and measuring paternal involvement* (pp. 17–38). Mahwah, NJ: Erlbaum.

Parke, R. D., Simpkins, S. D., McDowell, D. J., Kim, M., Killian, C., Dennis, J., Flyr, M. L., Wild, M., & Rah, Y. (2004). Relative contributions of families and peers to children's social development. In P. K. Smith & C. H. Hart (Eds.), *Blackwell handbook of childhood social development* (pp. 156–177). Malden, MA: Blackwell.

Parke, R. D., & Tinsley, B. R. (1981). The father's role in infancy: Determinants of involvement in caregiving and play. In M. E. Lamb (Ed.), *The role of the father in child development* (pp. 429–458). New York: Wiley.

Parker, F. L., Boak, A. Y., Griffin, K. W., Ripple, C., & Peay, L. (1999). Parent–child relationship, home learning environment, and school readiness. *School Psychology Review, 28,* 413–425.

Parker, J. G., Low, C. M., Walker, A. R., & Gamm, B. K. (2005). Friendship jealousy in young adolescents: Individual differences and links to sex, self-esteem, aggression, and social adjustment.

Parker, J. G., Rubin, K. H., Price, J., & DeRosier, M. E. (1995). Peer relationships, child development, and adjustment: A developmental psychopathology perspective. In D. Cicchetti & D. Cohen (Eds.), *Developmental psychopathology: Vol. 2. Risk, disorder, and adaptation* (pp. 96–161). New York: Wiley.

Parker, S. W., Nelson, C. A., & the Bucharest Early Intervention Project Core Group. (2005). The impact of early institutional rearing on the ability to discriminate facial expressions of emotion: An event-related potential study. *Child Development, 76,* 54–72.

Parten, M. (1932). Social participation among preschool children. *Journal of Abnormal and Social Psychology, 27,* 243–269.

Pascalis, O., de Haan, M., & Nelson, C. A. (1998). Long-term recognition memory for faces assessed by visual paired comparison in 3- and 6-month-old infants. *Journal of Experimental Psychology: Learning, Memory, and Cognition, 24,* 249–260.

Pascalis, O., de Haan, M., & Nelson, C. A. (2002). Is face processing species-specific during the first year of life? *Science, 296,* 1321–1323.

Pasterski, V. L., Geffner, M. E., Brain, C., Hindmarsh, P., Brook, C., & Hines, M. (2005). Prenatal hormones and postnatal socialization by parents as determinants of male-typical toy play in girls with congenital adrenal hyperplasia. *Child Development, 76,* 264–278.

Paterson, D. S., Trachtenberg, F. L., Thompson, E. G., Belliveau, R. A., Beggs, A. H., & Darnall, R. (2006). Multiple serotonergic brainstem abnormalities in sudden infant death syndrome. *Journal of the American Medical Association, 296,* 2124–2132.

Patock-Peckham, J. A., & Morgan-Lopez, A. A. (2009). Mediational links among parenting styles, perceptions of parental confidence, self-esteem, and depression on alcohol-related problems in emerging adulthood. *Journal of Studies on Alcohol and Drugs, 70,* 215–226.

Pattenden, S., Antova, T., Neuberger, M., Nikiforov, B., De Sario, M., Grize, L., & Heinrich, J. (2006). Parental smoking and children's respiratory health: Independent effects of prenatal and postnatal exposure. *Tobacco Control, 15,* 294–301.

Patterson, C. J. (2002). Lesbian and gay parenthood. In M. H. Bornstein (Ed.), *Handbook of parenting: Vol. 3. Being and becoming a parent* (2nd ed., pp. 317–338).

Patterson, G. R., & Fisher, P. A. (2002). Recent developments in our understanding of parenting: Bidirectional effects, causal models, and the search for parsimony. In M. H. Bornstein (Ed.), *Handbook of parenting* (Vol. 5, pp. 59–88). Mahwah, NJ: Erlbaum.

Patterson, G. R., & Yoerger, K. (2002). A developmental model for early- and late-onset delinquency. In J. B. Reid & G. R. Patterson (Eds.), *Antisocial behavior in children and adolescents* (pp. 147–172). Washington, DC: American Psychological Association.

Paul, J. J., & Cillessen, A. H. N. (2003). Dynamics of peer victimization in early adolescence: Results from a four-year longitudinal study. *Journal of Applied School Psychology, 19,* 25–43.

Pauli, S. A., Berga, S. L., Shang, W., & Session, D. R. (2009). Current status of the approach to assisted reproduction. *Pediatric Clinics of North America, 56,* 467–488.

Paulussen-Hoogeboom, M. C., Stams, G. J. J. M., Hermanns, J. M. A., & Peetsma, T. T. D. (2007). Child negative emotionality and parenting from infancy to preschool: A meta-analytic review. *Developmental Psychology, 43,* 438–453.

PCA America. (2009). Healthy Families America FAQ. Retrieved from www.healthyfamiliesamerica.org/about_us/findex.shtml

Pearl, P. L., Capp, P. K., Novotny, E. J., & Gibson, K. M. (2005). Inherited disorders of neurotransmitters in children and adults. *Clinical Biochemistry, 38,* 1051–1058.

Pearlman, D. N., Zierler, S., Meersman, S., Kim, H. K., Viner-Brown, & Caron, C. (2006). Race disparities in childhood asthma: Does where you live matter? *Journal of the National Medical Association, 98,* 239–247.

Pedersen, S., Vitaro, F., Barker, E. D., & Anne, I. H. (2007). The timing of middle-childhood peer rejection and friendship: Linking early behavior to early adolescent adjustment. *Child Development, 78,* 1037–1051.

Pederson, D. R., & Moran, G. (1996). Expressions of the attachment relationship outside of the Strange Situation. *Child Development, 67,* 915–927.

Peirano, P., Algarin, C., & Uauy, R. (2003). Sleep–wake states and their regulatory mechanisms throughout early human development. *Journal of Pediatrics, 143,* S70–S79.

Pellegrini, A. D. (1992). Kindergarten children's social cognitive status as a predictor of first grade success. *Early Childhood Research Quarterly, 7,* 565–577.

Pellegrini, A. D. (2003). Perceptions and functions of play and real fighting in early adolescence. *Child Development, 74,* 1522–1533.

Pellegrini, A. D. (2004). Rough-and-tumble play from childhood through adolescence: Development and possible functions. In P. K. Smith & C. H. Hart (Eds.), *Blackwell handbook of childhood social development* (pp. 438–453). Malden, MA: Blackwell.

Pellegrini, A. D. (2005). *Recess: Its role in development and education.* Mahwah, NJ: Erlbaum.

Pellegrini, A. D., & Holmes, R. M. (2006). The role of recess in primary school. In D. G. Singer, R. M. Golinkoff, & K. Hirsh-Pasek (Eds.), *Play=learning* (pp. 36–53). New York: Oxford University Press.

Pellegrini, A. D., Huberty, P. D., & Jones, I. (1995). The effects of recess timing on children's playground and classroom behaviors. *American Educational Research Journal, 32,* 845–864.

Pellegrini, A. D., Kato, K., Blatchford, P., & Baines, E. (2002). A short-term longitudinal study of children's playground games across the first year of school: Implications for social competence and adjustment to school. *American Educational Research Journal, 39,* 991–1015.

Pellegrini, A. D., & Smith, P. K. (1998). Physical activity play: The nature and function of a neglected aspect of play. *Child Development, 69,* 577–598.

Pellicano, E., Maybery, M., Durkin, K., & Maley, A. (2006). Multiple cognitive capabilities/deficits in children with an autism spectrum disorder: "Weak" central coherence and its relationship to theory of mind and executive control. *Development and Psychopathology, 18,* 77–98.

Peña, R., Wall, S., & Person, L. (2000). The effect of poverty, social inequality, and maternal education on infant mortality in Nicaragua, 1988–1993. *American Journal of Public Health, 90,* 64–69.

Penner, A. M. (2003). International gender item difficulty interactions in mathematics and science achievement tests. *Journal of Educational Psychology, 95,* 650–655.

Pennington, B. F., Snyder, K. A., & Roberts, R. J., Jr. (2007). Developmental cognitive neuroscience: Origins, issues, and prospects. *Developmental Review, 27,* 428–441.

Penny, H., & Haddock, G. (2007). Anti-fat prejudice among children: The 'mere proximity' effect in 5–10 year olds. *Journal of Experimental Social Psychology, 43,* 678–683.

Peralta de Mendoza, O. A., & Salsa, A. M. (2003). Instruction in early comprehension and use of a symbol–referent relation. *Cognitive Development, 18,* 269–284.

Perelle, I. B., & Ehrman, L. (2009). Handedness: A behavioral laterality manifestation. In Y.-K. Kim (Ed.), *Handbook of behavior genetics* (pp. 331–342). New York: Springer Science + Business Media.

Perlman, M., & Ross, H. S. (1997). The benefits of parent intervention in children's disputes: An examination of concurrent changes in children's fighting styles. *Child Development, 64,* 690–700.

Perlmutter, M. (1984). Continuities and discontinuities in early human memory: Paradigms, processes, and performances. In R. V. Kail, Jr., & N. R. Spear (Eds.), *Comparative perspectives on the development of memory* (pp. 253–287). Hillsdale, NJ: Erlbaum.

Perren, S., von Wyl, A., Burgin, D., Simoni, H., & von Klitzing, K. (2005). Intergenerational transmission of marital quality across the transition to parenthood. *Family Process, 44,* 441–459.

Perry, C. L., McGuire, M. T., Neumark-Sztainer, D., & Story, M. (2002). Adolescent vegetarians: How well do their dietary patterns meet the Healthy People 2010 objectives? *Archives of Pediatric and Adolescent Medicine, 156,* 431–437.

Perry, G. H., & Dominy, N. J. (2009). Evolution of the human pygmy phenotype. *Trends in Ecology and Evolution, 24,* 218–225.

Perry, W. G. (1998). *Forms of intellectual and ethical development in the college years: A scheme.* San Francisco: Jossey-Bass. (Originally published 1970.)

Perry, W. G., Jr. (1981). Cognitive and ethical growth. In A. Chickering (Ed.), *The modern American college* (pp. 76–116). San Francisco: Jossey-Bass.

Peshkin, A. (1994). *Growing up American: Schooling and the survival of community.* Prospect Heights, IL: Waveland Press.

Peshkin, A. (1997). *Places of memory: Whiteman's schools and Native American communities.* Mahwah, NJ: Erlbaum.

Pesonen, A.-K., Räikkönen, K., Heinonen, K., & Komsi, N. (2008). A transactional model of temperament development: Evidence of a relationship between child temperament and maternal stress over five years. *Social Development, 17,* 326–340.

Petch, J., & Halford, W. K. (2008). Psycho-education to enhance couples' transition to parenthood. *Clinical Psychology Review, 28,* 1125–1137.

Peters, R. D. (2005). A community-based approach to promoting resilience in young children, their families, and their neighborhoods. In R. D. Peters, B. Leadbeater, & R. J. McMahon (Eds.), *Resilience in children, families, and communities: Linking context to practice and policy* (pp. 157–176). New York: Kluwer Academic.

Peters, R. D., Petrunka, K., & Arnold, R. (2003). The Better Beginnings, Better Futures Project: A universal, comprehensive, community-based prevention approach for primary school children and their families. *Journal of Clinical Child and Adolescent Psychology, 32,* 215–227.

Peterson, C., Parsons, T., & Dean, M. (2004). Providing misleading and reinstatement information a year after it happened: Effects on long-term memory. *Memory, 12,* 1–13.

Peterson, C., & Rideout, R. (1998). Memory for medical emergencies experienced by 1- and 2-year-olds. *Developmental Psychology, 34,* 1059–1072.

Peterson, C., & Roberts, C. (2003). Like mother, like daughter: Similarities in narrative style. *Developmental Psychology, 39,* 551–562.

Petinou, K. C., Schwartz, R. G., Gravel, J. S., & Raphael, L. J. (2001). A preliminary account of phonological and morphological perception in young children with and without otitis media. *International Journal of Language and Communication Disorders, 36,* 21–42.

Petitto, L. A., Holowka, S., Sergio, L. E., Levy, B., & Ostry, D. J. (2004). Baby hands that move to the rhythm of language: Hearing babies acquiring sign languages babble silently on the hands. *Cognition, 93,* 43–73.

Petitto, L. A., Holowka, S., Sergio, L. E., & Ostry, D. (2001). Language rhythms in babies' hand movements. *Nature, 413,* 35–36.

Petitto, L. A., & Marentette, P. F. (1991). Babbling in the manual mode: Evidence for the ontogeny of language. *Science, 251,* 1493–1496.

Petrides, K. V., Sangareau, Y., Furnham, A., & Fredrickson, N. (2006). Trait emotional intelligence and children's peer relations at school. *Social Development, 15,* 537–547.

Petrill, S. A., & Deater-Deckard, K. (2004). The heritability of general cognitive ability: A within-family adoption design. *Intelligence, 32,* 403–409.

Petrovich, O. (1997). Understanding non-natural causality in children and adults: The case against artificialism. *Psyche en Geloof, 8,* 151–165.

Pettit, G. S. (2004). Violent children in developmental perspective. *Current Directions in Psychological Science, 13,* 194–197.

Pettit, G. S., Brown, E. G., Mize, J., & Lindsey, E. (1998). Mothers' and fathers' socializing behaviors in three contexts: Links with children's peer competence. *Merrill-Palmer Quarterly, 44,* 173–193.

Pexman, P. M., & Glenwright, M. (2007). How do typically developing children grasp the meaning of verbal irony? *Journal of Neurolinguistics, 20,* 178–196.

Pfeffer, C. R. (2006). Suicide and suicidality. In M. K. Dulcan & J. M. Wiener (Eds.), *Essentials of child and adolescent psychiatry* (pp. 621–632). Washington, DC: American Psychiatric Publishing.

Pfeffer, C. R., Altemus, M., Heo, M., & Jiang, H. (2007). Salivary cortisol and psychopathology in children bereaved by the September 11, 2001 terror attacks. *Biological Psychiatry, 61,* 957–965.

Pfeifer, J. H., Brown, C. S., & Juvonen, J. (2007). Fifty years since Brown vs. Board of Education: Lessons learned about the development and reduction of children's prejudice. *Social Policy Report 21*(2), 3–23.

Pfeifer, J. H., Ruble, D. N., Bachman, M. A., Alvarez, J. M., Cameron, J. A., & Fuligni, A. J. (2007). Social identities and intergroup bias in immigrant and nonimmigrant children. *Developmental Psychology, 43,* 496–507.

Philips, S. U. (1983). *The invisible culture: Communication in classroom and community on the Warm Springs Indian Reservation.* Prospect Heights, IL: Waveland.

Phillips, M. (1997). What makes schools effective? A comparison of the relationships of communitarian climate and academic climate to mathematics achievement and attendance during middle school. *American Educational Research Journal, 34,* 633–662.

Phillipsen, L. C. (1999). Associations between age, gender, and group acceptance and three components of friendship quality. *Journal of Early Adolescence, 19,* 438–464.

Phinney, J. S. (2007). Ethnic identity exploration in emerging adulthood. In J. J. Arnett & J. L. Tanner (Eds.), *Emerging adults in America: Coming of age in the 21st century* (pp. 117–134). Washington, DC: American Psychological Association.

Phinney, J. S., & Chavira, V. (1995). Parental ethnic socialization and adolescent outcomes in ethnic minority families. *Journal of Research on Adolescence, 5,* 31–53.

Phinney, J. S., Horenczyk, G., Liebkind, K., & Vedder, P. (2001). Ethnic identity, immigration, and well-being: An interactional perspective. *Journal of Social Issues, 57,* 493–510.

Phinney, J. S., & Ong, A. (2001). Family obligations and life satisfaction among adolescents from immigrant and non-immigrant families: Direct and moderated effects. Unpublished manuscript, California State University, Los Angeles.

Phinney, J. S., Ong, A., & Madden, T. (2000). Cultural values and intergenerational value discrepancies in immigrant and non-immigrant families. *Child Development, 71,* 528–539.

Piaget, J. (1926). *The language and thought of the child.* New York: Harcourt, Brace & World. (Original work published 1923.)

Piaget, J. (1930). *The child's conception of the world.* New York: Harcourt, Brace, & World. (Original work published 1926.)

Piaget, J. (1951). *Play, dreams, and imitation in childhood.* New York: Norton. (Original work published 1945.)

Piaget, J. (1952). *The origins of intelligence in children.* New York: International Universities Press. (Original work published 1936.)

Piaget, J. (1965). *The moral judgment of the child.* New York: Free Press. (Original work published 1932.)

Piaget, J. (1967). *Six psychological studies.* New York: Vintage.

Piaget, J. (1971). *Biology and knowledge.* Chicago: University of Chicago Press.

Pianta, R., Egeland, B., & Erickson, M. F. (1989). The antecedents of maltreatment: Results of the Mother–Child Interaction Research Project. In D. Cicchetti & V. Carlson (Eds.), *Child maltreatment* (pp. 203–253). New York: Cambridge University Press.

Pianta, R. C., Hamre, B., & Stuhlman, M. (2003). Relationships between teachers and children. In W. M. Reynolds & G. E. Miller (Eds.), *Handbook of psychology: Educational psychology* (Vol. 7, pp. 199–234). New York: Wiley.

Pianta, R. C., Howes, C., Burchinal, M., Bryant, D., Clifford, R., Early, D., & Barbarin, O. (2005). Features of prekindergarten programs, classrooms, and teachers: Do they predict observed classroom quality and child–teacher interactions? *Applied Developmental Science, 9*, 144–159.

Pickens, J., Field, T., & Nawrocki, T. (2001). Frontal EEG asymmetry in response to emotional vignettes in preschool age children. *International Journal of Behavioral Development, 25*, 105–112.

Pickett, K. E., Luo, Y., & Lauderdale, D. S. (2005). Widening social inequalities in risk for sudden infant death syndrome. *American Journal of Public Health, 95*, 1976–1981.

Pierce, S. H., & Lange, G. (2000). Relationships among metamemory, motivation and memory performance in young school-age children. *British Journal of Developmental Psychology, 18*, 121–135.

Pierroutsakos, S. L., & Troseth, G. L. (2003). Video verite: Infants' manual investigation of objects on video. *Infant Behavior and Development, 26*, 183–199.

Pierson, L. (1996). Hazards of noise exposure on fetal hearing. *Seminars in Perinatology, 20*, 21–29.

Pietz, J., Peter, J., Graf, R., Rauterberg, R. I., Rupp, A., & Sontheimer, D. (2004). Physical growth and neurodevelopmental outcome of nonhandicapped low-risk children born preterm. *Early Human Development, 79*, 131–143.

Piirto, J. (2007). *Talented children and adults* (3rd ed.). Waco, TX: Prufrock Press.

Pillow, B. (2002). Children's and adults' evaluation of the certainty of deductive inferences, inductive inferences, and guesses. *Child Development, 73*, 779–792.

Pinderhughes, E. E., Dodge, K. A., Bates, J. E., Pettit, G. S., & Zelli, A. (2000). Discipline responses: Influences of parents' socioeconomic status, ethnicity, beliefs about parenting, stress, and cognitive-emotional processes. *Journal of Family Psychology, 14*, 380–400.

Pinderhughes, E. E., Nix, R., Foster, E. M., Jones, D., & the Conduct Problems Prevention Research Group. (2001). Parenting in context: Impact of neighborhood poverty, residential stability, public services, social networks, and danger on parental behaviors. *Journal of Marriage and the Family, 63*, 941–953.

Pine, J. M. (1995). Variation in vocabulary development as a function of birth order. *Child Development, 66*, 272–281.

Ping, R. M., & Goldin-Meadow, S. (2008). Hands in the air: Using ungrounded iconic gestures to teach children conservation of quantity. *Developmental Psychology, 44*, 1277–1287.

Pinker, S. (1989). *Learnability and cognition.* Cambridge, MA: MIT Press.

Pinker, S. (1999). *Words and rules: The ingredients of language.* New York: Basic Books.

Pinker, S., Lebeaux, D. S., & Frost, L. A. (1987). Productivity and constraints in the acquisition of the passive. *Cognition, 26*, 195–267.

Pipp, S., Easterbrooks, M. A., & Brown, S. R. (1993). Attachment status and complexity of infants' self- and other-knowledge when tested with mother and father. *Social Development, 2*, 1–14.

Pipp, S., Easterbrooks, M. A., & Harmon, R. J. (1992). The relation between attachment and complexity of self and mother in one-year-old infants to three-year-old infants. *Child Development, 63*, 738–750.

Pitts, V. P. (1976). Drawing the invisible: Children's conceptualization of God. *Character Potential, 8*, 12–24.

Pizarro, D. A., & Bloom, P. (2003). The intelligence of the moral intuitions: Comment on Haidt (2001). *Psychological Review, 110*, 193–196.

Pleck, J. H., & Masciadrelli, B. P. (2004). Paternal involvement by U.S. residential fathers: Levels, sources, and consequences. In M. E. Lamb (Ed.), *The role of the father in child development* (4th ed., pp. 222–271). Hoboken, NJ: Wiley.

Plomin, R. (1994). *Genetics and experience: The interplay between nature and nurture.* Thousand Oaks, CA: Sage.

Plomin, R. (2003). General cognitive ability. In R. Plomin & J. C. DeFries (Eds.), *Behavioral genetics in the postgenomic era* (pp. 183–201). Washington, DC: American Psychological Association.

Plomin, R. (2005). *Finding genes in child psychology and psychiatry: When are we going to be there?* Unpublished manuscript. London: King's College.

Plomin, R. (2009). The nature of nurture. In K. McCartney & R. A. Weinberg (Eds.), *Experience and development: A festschrift in honor of Sandra Wood Scarr* (pp. 61–80). New York: Psychology Press.

Plomin, R., & Davis, O. S. P. (2009). The future of genetics in psychology and psychiatry: Microarrays, genome-wide association, and non-coding RNA. *Journal of Child Psychology and Psychiatry, 50*, 63–71.

Plomin, R., DeFries, J. C., McClearn, G. E., & McGuffin, P. (2001). *Behavioral genetics* (4th ed.). New York: Worth.

Plomin, R., & Spinath, F. M. (2004). Intelligence: Genetics, genes, and genomics. *Journal of Personality and Social Psychology, 86*, 112–129.

Poehlmann, J. (2003). An attachment perspective on grandparents raising their very young grandchildren: Implications for intervention and research. *Infant Mental Health Journal, 24*, 149–173.

Poehlmann, J., & Fiese, B. H. (2001). The interaction of maternal and infant vulnerabilities on developing attachment relationships. *Development and Psychopathology, 13*, 1–11.

Pogarsky, G., Thornberry, T. P., & Lizotte, A. J. (2006). Developmental outcomes for children of young mothers. *Journal of Marriage and Family, 68*, 332–344.

Pohl, R. (2002). *Poverty in Canada.* Ottawa: Innercity Ministries.

Polka, L., & Rvachew, S. (2005). The impact of otitis media with effusion on infant phonetic perception. *Infancy, 8*, 101–117.

Polka, L., & Werker, J. F. (1994). Developmental changes in perception of non-native vowel contrasts. *Journal of Experimental Psychology: Human Perception and Performance, 20*, 421–435.

Pollitt, E. (1996). A reconceptualization of the effects of undernutrition on children's biological, psychosocial, and behavioral development. *Social Policy Report of the Society for Research in Child Development, 10*(5).

Pollitt, E. (2001). The developmental and probabilistic nature of the functional consequences of iron-deficiency anemia in children. *Journal of Nutrition, 131*(Suppl. 2), 669S–675S.

Polman, H., Orobio de Castro, B., Koops, W., van Boxtel, H. W., & Merk, W. W. (2007). A meta-analysis of the distinction between reactive and proactive aggression in children and adolescents. *Journal of Abnormal Child Psychology, 35*, 522–535.

Pomerantz, E. M., & Dong, W. (2006). Effects of mothers' perceptions of children's competence: The moderating role of mothers' theories of competence. *Developmental Psychology, 42*, 950–961.

Pomerantz, E. M., & Eaton, M. M. (2000). Developmental differences in children's conceptions of parental control: "They love me, but they make me feel incompetent." *Merrill-Palmer Quarterly, 46*, 140–167.

Pomerantz, E. M., Ng, F. F., & Wang, Q. (2006). Mothers' mastery-oriented involvement in children's homework: Implications for the well-being of children with negative perceptions of competence. *Journal of Educational Psychology, 98*, 99–111.

Pomerantz, E. M., & Saxon, J. L. (2001). Conceptions of ability as stable and self-evaluative processes: A longitudinal examination. *Child Development, 72*, 152–173.

Pomerleau, A., Scuccimarri, C., & Malcuit, G. (2003). Mother–infant behavioral interactions in teenage and adult mothers during the first six months postpartum: Relations with infant development. *Infant Mental Health Journal, 24*, 495–509.

Pong, S., Johnston, J., & Chen, V. (2010). Authoritative parenting and Asian adolescent school performance. *International Journal of Behavioral Development, 34*, 62–72.

Pons, F., Lawson, J., Harris, P. L., & de Rosnay, M. (2003). Individual differences in children's emotion understanding: Effects of age and language. *Scandinavian Journal of Psychology, 44*, 347–353.

Portes, A., & Rumbaut, R. G. (2005). Introduction: The second generation and the Children of Immigrants Longitudinal Study. *Ethnic and Racial Studies, 28*, 983–999.

Posada, G., Carbonell, O. A., Alzate, G., & Plata, S. J. (2004). Through Colombian lenses: Ethnographic and conventional analyses of maternal care and their associations with secure base behavior. *Developmental Psychology, 40*, 508–518.

Posada, G., Jacobs, A., Richmond, M. K., Carbonell, O. A., Alzate, G., Bustamante, M. R., & Quiceno, J. (2002). Maternal caregiving and infant security in two cultures. *Developmental Psychology, 38*, 67–78.

Posner, M. I., & Rothbart, M. K. (2007a). *Educating the human brain.* Washington, DC: American Psychological Association.

Posner, M. I., & Rothbart, M. K. (2007b). Temperament and learning. In M. I. Posner & M. K. Rothbart (Eds.), *Educating the human brain* (pp. 121–146). Washington, DC: American Psychological Association.

Poulin, F., & Pedersen, S. (2007). Developmental changes in gender composition of friendship networks in adolescent girls and boys. *Developmental Psychology, 43*, 1484–1496.

Poulin-Dubois, D., Brooker, I., & Chow, V. (2009). The developmental origins of naïve psychology in infancy. *Advances in Child Development and Behavior, 37*, 55–104.

Poulin-Dubois, D., Serbin, L. A., Eichstedt, J. A., Sen, M. G., & Beissel, C. F. (2002). Men don't put on make-up: Toddlers' knowledge of the gender stereotyping of household activities. *Social Development, 11*, 166–181.

Povinelli, D. J. (2001). The self—Elevated in consciousness and extended in time. In C. Moore & K. Lemmon (Eds.), *The self in time: Developmental perspectives* (pp. 75–95). Mahwah, NJ: Erlbaum.

Power, T. G. (2000). *Play and exploration in children and animals.* Mahwah, NJ: Erlbaum.

Powlishta, K. K., Serbin, L. A., & Moller, L. C. (1993). The stability of individual differences in gender typing: Implications for understanding gender segregation. *Sex Roles, 29*, 723–737.

Powls, A., Botting, N., Cooke, R. W. I., & Marlow, N. (1996). Handedness in very-low-birthweight (VLBW) children at 12 years of age: Relation to perinatal and outcome variables. *Developmental Medicine and Child Neurology, 38*, 594–602.

Pratt, M. W., Skoe, E. E., & Arnold, M. L. (2004). Care reasoning development and family socialization patterns in later adolescence: A longitudinal analysis. *International Journal of Behavioral Development, 28*, 139–147.

Prechtl, H. F. R. (1958). Problems of behavioral studies in the newborn infant. In D. S. Lehrmann, R. A. Hinde, & E. Shaw (Eds.), *Advances in the study of behavior* (Vol. 1, pp. 75–98). New York: Academic Press.

Prechtl, H. F. R., & Beintema, D. (1965). *The neurological examination of the full-term newborn infant.* London: Heinemann Medical.

Preisler, G. M. (1991). Early patterns of interaction between blind infants and their sighted mothers. *Child: Care, Health and Development, 17*, 65–90.

Preisler, G. M. (1993). A descriptive study of blind children in nurseries with sighted children. *Child: Care, Health and Development, 19*, 295–315.

Preissler, M. A., & Carey, S. (2004). Do both pictures and words function as symbols for 18- and 24-month-old children? *Journal of Cognition and Development, 5*, 185–212.

Pressley, M., & Hilden, D. (2006). Cognitive strategies. In D. Kuhn & R. Siegler (Eds.), *Handbook of child psychology: Vol. 2. Cognition, perception, and language* (6th ed., pp. 511–556). Hoboken, NJ: Wiley.

Pressley, M., Wharton-McDonald, R., Raphael, L. M., Bogner, K., & Roehrig, A. (2002). Exemplary first-grade teaching. In B. M. Taylor & P. D. Pearson (Eds.), *Teaching reading: Effective schools, accomplished teachers* (pp. 73–88). Mahwah, NJ: Erlbaum.

Prevatt, F. (2003). Dropping out of school: A review of intervention programs. *Journal of School Psychology, 41*, 377–399.

Prevatt, F., & Kelly, F. D. (2003). Dropping out of school: A review of intervention programs. *Journal of School Psychology, 41*, 377–395.

Previc, F. H. (1991). A general theory concerning the prenatal origins of cerebral lateralization. *Psychological Review, 98*, 299–334.

Prinstein, M. J., Boergers, J., & Spirito, A. (2001). Adolescents' and their friends' health-risk behavior: Factors that alter or add to peer influence. *Journal of Pediatric Psychology, 26*, 287–298.

Prinstein, M. J., Boergers, J., & Vernberg, E. M. (2001). Overt and relational aggression in adolescents: Social–psychological adjustment of aggressors and victims. *Journal of Clinical Child Psychology, 30*, 479–491.

Prinstein, M. J., & Cillessen, A. H. N. (2003). Forms and functions of adolescent peer aggression associated with high levels of peer status. *Merrill-Palmer Quarterly, 49*, 310–342.

Prinstein, M. J., & La Greca, A. M. (2002). Peer crowd affiliation and internalizing distress in childhood and adolescence: A longitudinal follow-back study. *Journal of Research on Adolescence, 12*, 325–351.

Prinstein, M. J., & La Greca, A. (2004). Childhood peer rejection and aggression as predictors of adolescent girls' externalizing and health risk behaviors: A 6-year longitudinal study. *Journal of Consulting and Clinical Psychology, 72*, 103–112.

Prinstein, M. J., Meade, C. S., & Cohen, G. L. (2003). Adolescent oral sex, peer popularity, and perceptions of best friends' sexual behavior. *Journal of Pediatric Psychology, 28*, 243–249.

Proctor, M. H., Moore, L. L. Gao, D., Cupples, L. A., Bradlee, M. L., Hood, M. Y., & Ellison, R. C. (2003). Television viewing and change in body fat from preschool to early adolescence: The Framingham Children's Study. *International Journal of Obesity, 27*, 827–833.

Proffitt, D. R., & Bertenthal, B. I. (1990). Converging operations revisited: Assessing what infants perceive using discrimination measures. *Perception and Psychophysics, 47*, 1–11.

Programme for International Student Assessment. (2003). Learning for tomorrow's world: First results from Programme for International Student Assessment 2003. Retrieved from www.pisa.oecd.org

Programme for International Student Assessment. (2006). PISA 2006: Science competencies for tomorrow's world. Retrieved from www.oecd.org

Provins, K. A. (1997). Handedness and speech: A critical reappraisal of the role of genetic and environmental factors in the cerebral lateralization of function. *Psychological Review, 104*, 554–571.

Pruden, S. M., Hirsh-Pasek, K., Golinkoff, R. M., & Hennon, E. A. (2006). The birth of words: Ten-month-olds learn words through perceptual salience. *Child Development, 77*, 266–280.

Pryor, J. H., Hurtado, S., DeAngelo, L., Blake, L. P., & Tran, S. (2009). *The American freshman: National norms for fall 2009*. Los Angeles: Higher Education Research Institute, UCLA.

Prysak, M., Lorenz, R. P., & Kisly, A. (1995). Pregnancy outcome in nulliparous women 35 years and older. *Obstetrics and Gynecology, 85*, 65–70.

Puhl, R. M., & Latner, J. D. (2007). Stigma, obesity, and the health of the nation's children. *Psychological Bulletin, 133*, 557–580.

Pujol, J., Soriano-Mas, C., Ortiz, H., Sebastián-Gallés, N., Losilla, J. M., & Deus, J. (2006). Myelination of language-related areas in the developing brain. *Neurology, 66*, 339–343.

Punamaki, R. L. (2006). Ante- and perinatal factors and child characteristics predicting parenting experience among formerly infertile couples during the child's first year: A controlled study. *Journal of Family Psychology, 20*, 670–679.

Purcell-Gates, V. (1996). Stories, coupons, and the TV guide: Relationships between home literacy experiences and emergent literacy knowledge. *Reading Research Quarterly, 31*, 406–428.

Putallaz, M., Grimes, C. L., Foster, K. J., Kupersmidt, J. B., Coie, J. D., & Dearing, K. (2007). Overt and relational aggression and victimization: Multiple perspectives within the school setting. *Journal of School Psychology, 45*, 523–547.

Putnam, F. W. (2003). Ten-year research update review: Child sexual abuse. *Journal of the American Academy of Child and Adolescent Psychiatry, 42*, 269–278.

Putnam, S. P., Samson, A. V., & Rothbart, M. K. (2000). Child temperament and parenting. In V. J. Molfese & D. L. Molfese (Eds.), *Temperament and personality across the life span* (pp. 255–277). Mahwah, NJ: Erlbaum.

Q

Quas, J. A., Malloy, L. C., Melinder, A., Goodman, G. S., & D'Mello, M. (2007). Developmental differences in the effects of repeated interviews and interviewer bias on young children's event memory and false reports. *Developmental Psychology, 43*, 823–837.

Quinn, P. C. (2008). In defense of core competencies, quantitative change, and continuity. *Child Development, 79*, 1633–1638.

Quinn, P. C., & Intraub, H. (2007). Perceiving "outside the box" occurs early in development: Evidence for boundary extension in three- to seven-month-old infants. *Child Development, 78*, 324–334.

Quinn, P. C., Yahr, J., Kuhn, A., Slater, A. M., & Pascalis, O. (2002). Representation of the gender of human faces by infants: A preference for female. *Perception, 31*, 1109–1121.

Quinn, T. C., & Overbaugh, J. (2005). HIV/AIDS in women: An expanding epidemic. *Science, 308*, 1582–1583.

R

Raaijmakers, Q. A. W., Engels, R. C. M. E., & Van Hoof, A. (2005). Delinquency and moral reasoning in adolescence and young adulthood. *International Journal of Behavioral Development, 29*, 247–258.

Radecki, C. M., & Jaccard, J. (1995). Perceptions of knowledge, actual knowledge, and information search behavior. *Journal of Experimental Social Psychology, 31*, 107–138.

Radelet, M. A., Lephart, S. M., Rubinstein, E. N., & Myers, J. B. (2002). Survey of the injury rate for children in community sports. *Pediatrics, 110*, e28.

Radziszewska, B., & Rogoff, B. (1988). Influence of adult and peer collaboration on the development of children's planning skills. *Developmental Psychology, 24*, 840–848.

Raevuori, A., Hoek, H. W., Susser, E., Kaprio, J., Rissanen, A., & Keski-Rahkonen, A. (2009). Epidemiology of anorexia nervosa in men: A nationwide study of Finnish twins. *PLoS ONE, 4*, e4402.

Raffaeli, M., & Green, S. (2003). Parent–adolescent communication about sex: Retrospective reports by Latino college students. *Journal of Marriage and Family, 65*, 474–481.

Raffaelli, M., & Ontai, L. L. (2001). 'She's 16 years old and there's boys calling over to the house': An exploratory study of sexual socialization in Latino families. *Culture, Health and Sexuality, 3*, 295–310.

Rahman, Q., & Wilson, G. D. (2003). Born gay? The psychobiology of human sexual orientation. *Personality and Individual Differences, 34*, 1337–1382.

Raikes, H. A., & Thompson, R. A. (2005). Links between risk and attachment security: Models of influence. *Journal of Applied Developmental Psychology, 26*, 440–455.

Raikes, H. A., & Thompson, R. A. (2006). Family emotional climate, attachment security, and young children's emotion knowledge in a high-risk sample. *British Journal of Developmental Psychology, 24*, 89–104.

Raikes, H. A., Robinson, J. L., Bradley, R. H., Raikes, H. H., & Ayoub, C. C. (2007). Developmental trends in self-regulation among low-income toddlers. *Social Development, 16*, 128–149.

Rakison, D. H. (2005). Developing knowledge of objects' motion properties in infancy. *Cognition, 96*, 183–214.

Rakison, D. H. (2006). Make the first move: How infants learn about self-propelled objects. *Developmental Psychology, 42*, 900–912.

Rakison, D. H., & Lupyan, G. (2008). Developing object concepts in infancy: An associative learning perspective. *Monographs of the Society for Research in Child Development, 73*(1, Serial No. 289).

Rakoczy, H., Tomasello, M., & Striano, T. (2004). Young children know that trying is not pretending: A test of the " behaving-as-if " construal of children's early concept of pretense. *Developmental Psychology, 40*, 388–399.

Rakoczy, H., Tomasello, M., & Striano, T. (2005). How children turn objects into symbols: A cultural learning account. In L. Namy (Ed.), *Symbol use and symbol representation* (pp. 67–97). New York: Erlbaum.

Raman, L., & Gelman, S. A. (2004). A cross-cultural developmental analysis of children's and adults' understanding of illness in South Asia (India) and the United States. *Journal of Cognition and Culture, 4*, 293–317.

Ramchandani, P. G., Stein, A., O'Connor, T. G., Heron, J., Murray, L., & Evans, J. (2008). Depression in men in the postnatal period and later child psychopathology: A population cohort study. *Journal of the American Academy of Child and Adolescent Psychiatry, 47*, 390–398.

Ramey, C. T., Ramey, S. L., & Lanzi, R. G. (2006). Children's health and education. In K. A. Renninger & I. E. Sigel (Eds.), *Handbook of child psychology: Vol. 4. Child psychology in practice* (6th ed., pp. 864–892). Hoboken, NJ: Wiley.

Ramey, S. L., & Ramey, C. T. (1999). Early experience and early intervention for children "at risk" for developmental delay and mental retardation. *Mental Retardation and Developmental Disabilities, 5*, 1–10.

Ramos, E., Frontera, W. R., Llopart, A., & Feliciano, D. (1998). Muscle strength and hormonal levels in adolescents: Gender related differences. *International Journal of Sports Medicine, 19*, 526–531.

Ramos, M. C., Guerin, D. W., Gottfried, A. W., Bathurst, K., & Oliver, P. H. (2005). Family conflict and children's behavior problems: The moderating role of child temperament. *Structural Equation Modeling, 12*, 278–298.

Ramsøy, N. R. (1994). Non-marital cohabitation and change in norms: The case of Norway. *Acta Sociologica, 37*, 23–37.

Ramus, F. (2002). Language discrimination by newborns: Teasing apart phonotactic, rhythmic, and intonational cues. *Annual Review of Language Acquisition, 2*, 85–115.

Rangel, M. C., Gavin, L., Reed, C., Fowler, M. G., & Lee, L. M. (2006). Epidemiology of HIV and AIDS among adolescents and young adults in the United States. *Journal of Adolescent Health, 39*, 156–163.

Ranking, J., Lane, D., Gibbons, F., & Gerrard, M. (2004). Adolescent self-consciousness: Longitudinal age changes and gender differences in two cohorts. *Journal of Research on Adolescence, 14*, 1–12.

Raskind, W. H., Igo, R. P. Jr., Chapman, N. H., Berninger, V. W., Thomson, J. B., Matsushita, M., & Brkanac, Z. (2005). A genome scan in multigenerational families with dyslexia: Identification of a novel locus on chromosome 2q that contributes to phonological decoding efficiency. *Molecular Psychiatry, 10*, 699–711.

Rasmussen, C., Ho, E., & Bisanz, J. (2003). Use of the mathematical principle of inversion in young children. *Journal of Experimental Child Psychology, 85*, 89–102.

Rasmussen, C., Neuman, R. J., Heath, A. C., Levy, F., Hay, D. A., & Todd, R. D. (2004). Familial clustering of latent class and DSM-IV defined attention-deficit hyperactivity disorder (ADHD) subtypes. *Journal of Child Psychology and Psychiatry, 45*, 589–598.

Rathunde, K., & Csikszentmihalyi, M. (2005). The social context of middle school: Teachers, friends, and activities in Montessori and traditional school environments. *Elementary School Journal, 106*, 59–79.

Rauber, M. (2006, May 18). Parents aren't sitting still as recess disappears. *Parents in Action.* Retrieved from www.parentsaction.org/news/ parents-in-action/ index.cfm?i=410

Rauscher, F. H., Shaw, G. L., & Ky, K. N. (1993). Music and spatial task performance. *Nature, 365*, 611.

Raver, C. C. (2003). Does work pay psychologically as well as economically? The role of employment in predicting depressive symptoms and parenting among low-income families. *Child Development, 74*, 1720–1736.

Ravid, D., & Tolchinsky, L. (2002). Developing linguistic literacy: A comprehensive model. *Journal of Child Language, 29*, 417–447.

Ravitch, D. (2010). *The death and life of the great American school system: How testing and choice are undermining education.* New York: Basic Books.

Ray, N., & Gregory, R. (2001). School experiences of the children of lesbian and gay parents. *Family Matters, 59*, 28–35.

Rayner, K., & Pollatsek, A. (1989). *The psychology of reading.* Englewood Cliffs, NJ: Prentice Hall.

Rayner, K., Pollatsek, A., & Starr, M. S. (2003). Reading. In A. F. Healy & R. W. Proctor (Eds.). (2003). *Handbook of psychology: Experimental psychology* (Vol. 4, pp. 549–574). New York: Wiley.

Raz, S., Shah, F., & Sander, C. J. (1996). Differential effects of perinatal hypoxic risk on early developmental outcome: A twin study. *Neuropsychology, 10*, 429–436.

Reddin, J. (1997). High-achieving women: Career development patterns. In H. S. Farmer (Ed.), *Diversity and women's career development* (pp. 95–126). Thousand Oaks, CA: Sage.

Reed, R. K. (2005). *Birthing fathers.* New Brunswick, NJ: Rutgers University Press.

Reese, E., & Newcombe, R. (2007). Training mothers in elaborative reminiscing enhances children's autobiographical memory and narrative. *Child Development, 78*, 1153–1170.

Reese, E., Newcombe, R., & Bird, G. M. (2006). The emergence of autobiographical memory: Cognitive, social, and emotional factors. In C. M. Flinn-Fletcher & G. M. Haberman (Eds.), *Cognition and language: Perspectives from New Zealand* (pp. 177–189). Bowen Hills, Australia: Australian Academic Press.

Regnerus, M., Smith, C., & Fritsch, M. (2003). *Religion in the lives of American adolescents: A review of the literature.* Chapel Hill, NC: National Study of Youth and Religion.

Reilly, J. S., Bates, E. A., & Marchman, V. A. (1998). Narrative discourse in children with early focal brain injury. *Brain and Language, 61*, 335–375.

Reilly, J., Losh, M., Bellugi, U., & Wulfeck, B. (2004). "Frog, where are you?" Narratives in children with specific language impairment, early focal brain injury, and Williams syndrome. *Brain and Language, 88*, 229–247.

Reis, O., & Youniss, J. (2004). Patterns in identity change and development in relationships with mothers and friends. *Journal of Adolescent Research, 19*, 31–44.

Reis, S. M. (2004). We can't change what we don't recognize: Understanding the special needs of gifted females. In S. Baum (Ed.), *Twice-exceptional and special populations of gifted students* (pp. 67–80). Thousand Oaks, CA: Corwin Press.

Reisman, J. E. (1987). Touch, motion, and proprioception. In P. Salapatek & L. Cohen (Eds.), *Handbook of infant perception: Vol. 1. From sensation to perception* (pp. 265–303). Orlando, FL: Academic Press.

Reiss, D. (2003). Child effects on family systems: Behavioral genetic strategies. In A. C. Crouter & A. Booth (Eds.), *Children's influence on family dynamics* (pp. 3–36). Mahwah, NJ: Erlbaum.

Renninger, K. A. (1998). Developmental psychology and instruction: Issues from and for practice. In I. Sigel & K. A. Renninger (Eds.), *Handbook of child psychology: Vol. 4. Child psychology and practice* (pp. 211–274). New York: Wiley.

Repacholi, B. M. (1998). Infants' use of attentional cues to identify the referent of another person's emotional expression. *Developmental Psychology, 34*, 1017–1025.

Repacholi, B. M., & Gopnik, A. (1997). Early reasoning about desires: Evidence from 14- and 18-month-olds. *Developmental Psychology, 33*, 12–21.

Repacholi, B. M., & Meltzoff, A. N. (2007). Emotional eavesdropping: Infants selectively respond to indirect emotional signals. *Child Development, 78*, 503–521.

Reschly, A. L., & Christenson, S. L. (2009). Parents as essential partners for fostering students' learning outcomes. In R. Gilman & E. Scott Huebner (Eds.), *Handbook of positive psychology in schools* (pp. 257–272). New York: Routledge.

Resnick, M., & Silverman, B. (2005). *Some reflections on designing construction kits for kids.* Proceedings of the Conference on Interaction Design and Children, Boulder, CO.

Resnick, M. B., Gueorguieva, R. V., Carter, R. L., Ariet, M., Sun, Y., Roth, J., Bucciarelli, R. L., Curran, J. S., & Mahan, C. S. (1999). The impact of low birth weight, perinatal conditions, and sociodemographic factors on educational outcome in kindergarten. *Pediatrics, 104*, e74.

Rest, J. R. (1979). *Development in judging moral issues.* Minneapolis: University of Minnesota Press.

Resta, R., Biesecker, B. B., Bennett, R. L., Blum, S., Hahn, S. E., Strecker, M. N., & Williams, J. L. (2006). A new definition of genetic counseling: National Society of Genetic Counselors' Task Force Report. *Journal of Genetic Counseling, 15*, 77–83.

RESULTS. (2006). *The abolition of public school fees.* Retrieved from www.results.org/website/article. asp?id=1718

Reyna, V. F., & Farley, F. (2006). Risk and rationality in adolescent decision making: Implications for theory, practice, and public policy. *Psychological Science in the Public Interest, 7*, 1–44.

Reynolds, A. J., & Temple, J. A. (1998). Extended early childhood intervention and school achievement: Age thirteen findings from the Chicago Longitudinal Study. *Child Development, 69*, 231–246.

Rhoades, B. L., Greenberg, M. T., & Domitrovich, C. E. (2009). The contribution of inhibitory control to preschoolers' social-emotional competence. *Journal of Applied Developmental Psychology, 30*, 310–320.

Richardson, H. L., Walker, A. M., & Horne, R. S. C. (2008) Sleep position alters arousal processes maximally at the high-risk age for sudden infant death syndrome. *Journal of Sleep Research, 17*, 450–457.

Richert, R. A., & Barrett, J. L. (2005). Do you see what I see? Young children's assumptions about God's perceptual abilities. *International Journal for the Psychology of Religion, 15*, 283–295.

Richie, B. S., Fassinger, R. E., Linn, S. G., Johnson, J., Prosser, J., & Robinson, S. (1997). Persistence, connection, and passion: A qualitative study of the career development of highly achieving African American black and white women. *Journal of Counseling Psychology, 44*, 133–148.

Richler, J., Luyster, R., Risi, S., Hsu, W.-L., Dawson, G., & Bernier, R. (2006). Is there a 'regressive phenotype' of autism spectrum disorder associated with the measles-mumps-rubella vaccine? A CPEA study. *Journal of Autism and Developmental Disorders, 36*, 299–316.

Richmond, J., Colombo, M., & Hayne, H. (2007). Interpreting visual preferences in the visual paired-comparison task. *Journal of Experimental Psychology: Learning, Memory, and Cognition, 33*, 823–831.

Richmond, L. J. (2004). When spirituality goes awry: Students in cults. *Professional School Counseling, 7*, 367–375.

Ridenour, T. A. (2000). Genetic epidemiology of antisocial behavior. In D. H. Fishbein (Ed.), *The science, treatment, and prevention of antisocial behaviors: Application to the criminal justice system* (pp. 7.1–7.24). Kingston, NJ: Civic Research Institute.

Rideout, V., & Hamel, E. (2006). *The media family: Electronic media in the lives of infants, toddlers, preschoolers and their parents.* Menlo Park, CA: Henry J. Kaiser Family Foundation.

Rideout, V. J., Vandewater, E. A., & Wartella, E. A. (2003). *Zero to six: Electronic media in the lives of infants, toddlers and preschoolers.* Menlo Park, CA: Henry J. Kaiser Family Foundation.

Rigby, K. (2004). Bullying in childhood. In P. K. Smith & C. H. Hart (Eds.), *Blackwell handbook of childhood social development* (pp. 549–568). Malden, MA: Blackwell.

Riggs, K. J., & Peterson, D. M. (2000). Counterfactual thinking in preschool children: Mental state and causal inferences. In P. Mitchell & K. J. Riggs (Eds.), *Children's reasoning and the mind* (pp. 87–99). Hove, UK: Psychology Press.

Rijsdijk, F. V., & Boomsma, D. I. (1997). Genetic mediation of the correlation between peripheral nerve conduction velocity and IQ. *Behavior Genetics, 27*, 87–98.

Riley, E. P., McGee, C. L., & Sowell, E. R. (2004). Teratogenic effects of alcohol: A decade of brain imaging. *American Journal of Medical Genetics: Part C, Seminars in Medical Genetics, 127*, 35–41.

Riordan, J., Gross, A., Angeron, J., Drumwiede, B., & Melin, J. (2000). The effect of labor pain relief medication on neonatal suckling and breastfeeding duration. *Journal of Human Lactation, 16*, 7–12.

Ripple, C. H., & Zigler, E. (2003). Research, policy, and the federal role in prevention initiatives for children. *American Psychologist, 58*, 482–490.

Ris, M. D., Dietrich, K. N., Succop, P. A., Berger, O. G., & Bornschein, R. L. (2004). Early exposure to lead and neuropsychological outcome in adolescence. *Journal of the International Neuropsychological Society, 10*, 261–270.

Ritchie, L. D., Spector, P., Stevens, M. J., Schmidt, M. M., Schreiber, G. B., Striegel-Moore, R. H., et al. (2007) Dietary patterns in adolescence are related to adiposity in young adulthood in black and white females. *Journal of Nutrition, 137*, 399–406.

Riva, D., & Giorgi, C. (2000). The cerebellum contributes to higher functions during development: Evidence from a series of children surgically treated for posterior fossa tumors. *Brain, 123*, 1051–1061.

Rivera, S. M., Wakeley, A., & Langer, J. (1999). The drawbridge phenomenon: Representational reasoning or perceptual preference? *Developmental Psychology, 35*, 427–435.

Rivkees, S. A. (2003). Developing circadian rhythmicity in infants. *Pediatrics, 112*, 373–381.

Rizzo, T. A., Metzger, B. E., Dooley, S. L., & Cho, N. H. (1997). Early malnutrition and child neurobehavioral development: Insights from the study of children of diabetic mothers. *Child Development, 68*, 26–38.

Rizzolatti, G., & Craighero, L. (2004). The mirror-neuron system. *Annual Review of Neuroscience, 27*, 169–192.

Robb, S., & Dadson, M. J. (2002). Eating disorders in males. *Child and Adolescent Psychiatric Clinics of North America, 11*, 399–418.

Roberts, B. W., & DelVecchio, W. F. (2000). The rank-order consistency of personality traits from childhood to old age: A quantitative review of longitudinal studies. *Psychological Bulletin, 126*, 3–25.

Roberts, D. F., Foehr, U. G., & Rideout, V. (2005). *Generation M: Media in the lives of 8–18 year olds.* Menlo Park, CA: Henry J. Kaiser Family Foundation.

Roberts, D. F., Henriksen, L., & Foehr, U. G. (2004). Adolescents and media. In R. M. Lerner & L. Steinberg (Eds.), *Handbook of adolescent psychology* (2nd ed., pp. 627–664). Hoboken, NJ: Wiley.

Roberts, D. F., Henriksen, L., & Foehr, U. G. (2009). Adolescence, adolescents, and media. In R. M. Lerner & L. Steinberg (Eds.), *Handbook of adolescent psychology: Vol. 2. Contextual influences on adolescent development* (3rd ed., pp. 314–344). Hoboken, NJ: Wiley

Roberts, J. E., Burchinal, M. R., & Durham, M. (1999). Parents' report of vocabulary and grammatical development of American preschoolers: Child and environment associations. *Child Development, 70,* 92–106.

Roberts, J. E., Burchinal, M. R., Zeisel, S. A., Neebe, E. C., Hooper, S. R., Roush, J., Bryant, D., Mundy, M., & Henderson, F. W. (1998). Otitis media, the caregiving environment, and language and cognitive outcomes at 2 years. *Pediatrics, 102,* 346–354.

Roberts, J. M., & Masten, A. S. (2004). Resilience in context. In R. D. Peters, R. McMahon, & B. Leadbeater (Eds.), *Resilience in children, families, and communities: Linking context to practice and policy* (pp. 13–25). New York: Kluwer Academic.

Roberts, R. E., Attkisson, C. C., & Rosenblatt, A. (1998). Prevalence of psychopathology among children and adolescents. *American Journal of Psychiatry, 155,* 715–725.

Robertson, J. (2008). Stepfathers in families. In J. Pryor (Ed.), *International handbook of stepfamilies: Policy and practice in legal, research, and clinical environments* (pp. 125–150). Hoboken, NJ: Wiley.

Robin, D. J., Berthier, N. E., & Clifton, R. K. (1996). Infants' predictive reaching for moving objects in the dark. *Developmental Psychology, 32,* 824–835.

Robins, R. W., Tracy, J. L., Trzesniewski, K., Potter, J., & Gosling, S. D. (2001). Personality correlates of self-esteem. *Journal of Research in Personality, 35,* 463–482.

Robinson, C. C., Anderson, G. T., Porter, C. L., Hart, C. H., & Wouden-Miller, M. (2003). Sequential transition patterns of preschoolers' social interactions during child-initiated play: Is parallel-aware play a bidirectional bridge to other play states? *Early Childhood Research Quarterly, 18,* 3–21.

Robinson, J. L., Lee, B. E., Preiksaitis, J. K., Plitt, S., & Tipplies, G. A. (2006). Prevention of congenital rubella syndrome—What makes sense in 2006? *Epidemiologic Reviews, 28,* 81–87.

Robinson, S., Goddard, L., Dritschel, B., Wisley, M., & Howlin, P. (2009). Executive functions in children with autism spectrum disorders. *Brain and Cognition, 71,* 362–368.

Rochat, P. (1989). Object manipulation and exploration in 2- to 5-month-old infants. *Developmental Psychology, 25,* 871–884.

Rochat, P. (1998). Self-perception and action in infancy. *Experimental Brain Research, 123,* 102–109.

Rochat, P. (2001). *The infant's world.* Cambridge, MA: Harvard University Press.

Rochat, P. (2003). Five levels of self-awareness as they unfold early in life. *Consciousness and Cognition, 12,* 717–731.

Rochat, P., & Goubet, N. (1995). Development of sitting and reaching in 5- to 6-month-old infants. *Infant Behavior and Development, 18,* 53–68.

Rochat, P., & Hespos, S. J. (1997). Differential rooting responses by neonates: Evidence for an early sense of self. *Early Development and Parenting, 6,* 105–112.

Rochat, P., Querido, J. G., & Striano, T. (1999). Emerging sensitivity to the timing and structure of protoconversation. *Developmental Psychology, 35,* 950–957.

Rochat, P., & Striano, T. (2002). Who's in the mirror? Self–other discrimination in specular images by four- and nine-month-old infants. *Child Development, 73,* 35–46.

Rochat, P., Striano, T., & Blatt, L. (2002). Differential effects of happy, neutral, and sad still-faces on 2-, 4-, and 6-month-old infants. *Infant and Child Development, 11,* 289–303.

Rodgers, J. L., Cleveland, H. H., van den Oord, E., & Rowe, D. C. (2000). Resolving the debate over birth order, family size, and intelligence. *American Psychologist, 55,* 599–612.

Rodgers, J. L., & Wänström, L. (2007). Identification of a Flynn effect in the NLSY: Moving from the center to the boundaries. *Intelligence, 35,* 187–196.

Rodkin, P. C., Farmer, T. W., Pearl, R., & Van Acker, R. (2000). Heterogeneity of popular boys: Antisocial and prosocial configurations. *Developmental Psychology, 36,* 14–24.

Rodkin, P. C., Farmer, T. W., Pearl, R., & Van Acker, R. (2006). They're cool: Social status and peer group supports for aggressive boys and girls. *Social Development, 15,* 175–204.

Rodriguez, A., & Waldenström, U. (2008). Fetal origins of child non-right-handedness and mental health. *Child Psychology and Psychiatry, 49,* 967–976.

Roebers, C. M., & Schneider, W. (2001). Individual differences in children's eyewitness recall: The influence of intelligence and shyness. *Applied Developmental Science, 5,* 9–20.

Roelfsema, N. M., Hop, W. C., Boito, S. M., & Wladimiroff, J. W. (2004). Three-dimensional sonographic measurement of normal fetal brain volume during the second half of pregnancy. *American Journal of Obstetrics and Gynecology, 190,* 275–280.

Roeser, R. W., Eccles, J. S., & Freedman-Doan, C. (1999). Academic functioning and mental health in adolescence: Patterns, progressions, and routes from childhood. *Journal of Adolescent Research, 14,* 135–174.

Rogan, W. J., Dietrich, K. N., Ware, J. H., Dockery, D. W., Salganik, M., & Radcliffe, J. (2001). The effect of chelation therapy with succimer on neuropsychological development in children exposed to lead. *New England Journal of Medicine, 344,* 1421–1426.

Rogers, J. M. (2009). Tobacco and pregnancy. *Reproductive Toxicology, 28,* 152–160.

Rogge, M. M., Greenwald, M., & Golden, A. (2004). Obesity, stigma, and civilized oppression. *Advances in Nursing Science, 27,* 301–315.

Roggman, L. A., Langlois, J. H., Hubbs-Tait, L., & Rieser-Danner, L. A. (1994). Infant day-care, attachment, and the "file drawer problem." *Child Development, 65,* 1429–1443.

Rogoff, B. (1996). Developmental transitions in children's participation in sociocultural activities. In A. J. Sameroff & M. M. Haith (Eds.), *The five to seven year shift: The age of reason and responsibility* (pp. 273–294). Chicago: University of Chicago Press.

Rogoff, B. (1998). Cognition as a collaborative process. In D. Kuhn & R. S. Siegler (Eds.), *Handbook of child psychology: Vol. 2. Cognition, perception, and language* (5th ed., pp. 679–744). New York: Wiley.

Rogoff, B. (2003). *The cultural nature of human development.* New York: Oxford University Press.

Rogoff, B., & Chavajay, P. (1995). What's become of research on the cultural basis of cognitive development? *American Psychologist, 50,* 859–877.

Rogoff, B., Malkin, C., & Gilbride, K. (1984). Interaction with babies as guidance in development. In B. Rogoff & J. V. Wertsch (Eds.), *Children's learning in the "zone of proximal development"* (New directions for child development, No. 23, pp. 31–44). San Francisco: Jossey-Bass.

Rogoff, B., Paradise, R., Arauz, R. M., Correa-Chávez, M., & Angelillo, C. (2003). Firsthand learning through intent participation. *Annual Review of Psychology, 54,* 175–203.

Rogoff, B., & Waddell, K. J. (1982). Memory for information organized in a scene by children from two cultures. *Child Development, 53,* 1224–1228.

Rogol, A. D., Roemmich, J. N., & Clark, P. A. (2002). Growth at puberty. *Journal of Adolescent Health, 31,* 192–200.

Rohner, R. P., & Veneziano, R. A. (2001). The importance of father love: History and contemporary evidence. *Review of General Psychology, 5,* 382–405.

Roid, G. (2003). *The Stanford-Binet Intelligence Scales, Fifth Edition, interpretive manual.* Itasca, IL: Riverside Publishing.

Roisman, G. I., Madsen, S. D., Hennighausen, K. H., Sroufe, L. A., & Collins, W. A. (2001). The coherence of dyadic behavior across parent–child and romantic relationships as mediated by the internalized representation of experience. *Attachment and Human Development, 3,* 156–172.

Roisman, R., & Fraley, C. (2006). The limits of genetic influence: A behavior-genetic analysis of infant–caregiver relationship quality and temperament. *Child Development, 77,* 1656–1667.

Rojewski, J. W., & Hill, R. B. (1998). Influence of gender and academic risk behavior on career decision making and occupational choice in early adolescence. *Journal of Education for Students Placed at Risk, 3,* 265–287.

Rokach, A. (2001). Perceived causes of loneliness in adulthood. *Journal of Social Behavior and Personality, 15,* 67–84.

Rokach, A., & Neto, F. (2006). Age, culture, and coping with loneliness. *Psychology and Education, 43,* 1–21.

Romano, A. M., & Lothian, J. A. (2008). Promoting, protecting, and supporting normal birth: A look at the evidence. *Journal of Obstetric, Gynecologic, and Neonatal Nursing, 37,* 94–104.

Rome-Flanders, T., & Cronk, C. (1995). A longitudinal study of infant vocalizations during mother–infant games. *Journal of Child Language, 22,* 259–274.

Romero, A. J., & Roberts, R. E. (2003). The impact of multiple dimensions of ethnic identity on discrimination and adolescents' self-esteem. *Journal of Applied Social Psychology, 33,* 2288–2305.

Rönnqvist, L., & Domellof, E. (2006). Quantitative assessment of right and left reaching movements in infants: A longitudinal study from 6 to 36 months. *Developmental Psychobiology, 48,* 444–459.

Rönnqvist, L., & Hopkins, B. (1998). Head position preference in the human newborn: A new look. *Child Development, 69,* 13–23.

Roopnarine, J. L., & Evans, M. E. (2007). Family structural organization, mother–child and father–child relationships and psychological outcomes in English-speaking African Caribbean and Indo Caribbean families. In M. Sutherland (Ed.), *Psychology of development in the Caribbean.* Kingston, Jamaica: Ian Randle.

Roopnarine, J. L., Hossain, Z., Gill, P., & Brophy, H. (1994). Play in the East Indian context. In J. L. Roopnarine, J. E. Johnson, & F. H. Hooper (Eds.), *Children's play in diverse cultures* (pp. 9–30). Albany, NY: SUNY Press.

Roopnarine, J. L., Krishnakumar, A., Metindogan, A., & Evans, M. (2006). Links between parenting styles, parent–child academic interaction, parent–school interaction, and early academic skills and social behaviors in young children of English-speaking Caribbean immigrants. *Early Childhood Research Quarterly, 21,* 238–252.

Roopnarine, J. L., Talukder, E., Jain, D., Joshi, P., & Srivastav, P. (1990). Characteristics of holding, patterns of play, and social behaviors between parents and infants in New Delhi, India. *Developmental Psychology, 26,* 667–673.

Rosander, K., & von Hofsten, C. (2002). Development of gaze tracking of small and large objects. *Experimental Brain Research, 146,* 257–264.

Rosander, K., & von Hofsten, C. (2004). Infants' emerging ability to represent occluded object motion. *Cognition, 91,* 1–22.

Rose, A. J., & Asher, S. R. (1999). Children's goals and strategies in response to conflicts within a friendship. *Developmental Psychology, 35,* 69–79.

Rose, A. J., Carlson, W., & Waller, E. M. (2007). Prospective associations of co-rumination with friendship and emotional adjustment: Considering the socioemotional trade-offs of co-rumination. *Developmental Psychology, 43,* 1019–1031.

Rose, A. J., Swenson, L. P., & Waller, E. M. (2004). Overt and relational aggression and perceived popularity: Developmental differences in concurrent and prospective relations. *Developmental Psychology, 40,* 378–387.

Rose, L. (2000). Fathers of full-term infants. In N. Tracey (Ed.), *Parents of premature infants: Their emotional world* (pp. 105–116). London: Whurr.

Rose, S. A., & Feldman, J. F. (1997). Memory and speed: Their role in the relation of infant information processing to later IQ. *Child Development, 68,* 610–620.

Rose, S. A., Feldman, J. F., & Jankowski, J. J. (2001). Attention and recognition memory in the 1st year of life: A longitudinal study of preterm and full-term infants. *Developmental Psychology, 37,* 135–151.

Rose, S. A., Feldman, J. F., & Wallace, I. F. (1992). Infant information processing in relation to six-year cognitive outcomes. *Child Development, 63,* 1126–1141.

Rose, S. A., Jankowski, J. J., & Senior, G. J. (1997). Infants' recognition of contour-deleted figures. *Journal of Experimental Psychology: Human Perception and Performance, 23,* 1206–1216.

Rosen, A. B., & Rozin, P. (1993). Now you see it, now you don't: The preschool child's conception of invisible particles in the context of dissolving. *Developmental Psychology, 29,* 300–311.

Rosen, D. (2003). Eating disorders in children and young adolescents: Etiology, classification, clinical features, and treatment. *Adolescent Medicine: State of the Art Reviews, 14,* 49–59.

Rosen, L. D., Cheever, N. A., & Carrier, L. M. (2008). The association of parenting style and child age with parental limit setting and adolescent MySpace behavior. *Journal of Applied Developmental Psychology, 29,* 459–471.

Rosenbaum, J. E. (2009). Patient teenagers? A comparison of the sexual behavior of virginity pledgers and matched nonpledgers. *Pediatrics, 123,* e110–e120.

Rosenberger, L. R., Zeck, J., Berl, M. M., Moore, E. N., Ritzl, E. K., Shamim, S., et al. (2009). Interhemispheric and intrahemispheric language reorganization in complex partial epilepsy. *Neurology, 72,* 1830–1836.

Rosenbloom, A. L. (2009). Idiopathic short stature: Conundrums of definition and treatment. *International Journal of Pediatric Endocrinology,* Article ID 470378.

Rosengren, K. S., & Hickling, A. K. (2000). The development of children's thinking about possible events and plausible mechanisms. In K. S. Rosengren, C. N. Johnson, & P. L. Harris (Eds.), *Imagining the impossible* (pp. 75–98). Cambridge, UK: Cambridge University Press.

Rosenshine, B., & Meister, C. (1994). Reciprocal teaching: A review of nineteen experimental studies. *Review of Educational Research, 64,* 479–530.

Roseth, C. J., Pellegrini, A. D., Bohn, C. M., van Ryzin, M., & Vance, N. (2007). Preschoolers' aggression, affiliation, and social dominance relationships: An observational, longitudinal study. *Journal of School Psychology, 45,* 479–497.

Rosetta, L., & Baldi, A. (2008). On the role of breastfeeding in health promotion and the prevention of allergic diseases. *Advances in Experimental Medicine and Biology, 606,* 467–483.

Ross, H. S., Conant, C., Cheyne, J. A., & Alevizos, E. (1992). Relationships and alliances in the social interactions of kibbutz toddlers. *Social Development, 1,* 1–17.

Rothbart, M. K. (2003). Temperament and the pursuit of an integrated developmental psychology. *Merrill-Palmer Quarterly, 50,* 492–505.

Rothbart, M. K., Ahadi, S. A., & Evans, D. E. (2000). Temperament and personality: Origins and outcome. *Journal of Personality and Social Psychology, 78,* 122–135.

Rothbart, M. K., & Bates, J. E. (2006). Temperament. In N. Eisenberg (Ed.), *Handbook of child psychology: Vol. 3. Social, emotional, and personality development* (6th ed., pp. 99–166). Hoboken, NJ: Wiley.

Rothbart, M. K., & Mauro, J. A. (1990). Questionnaire approaches to the study of infant temperament. In J. W. Fagen & J. Colombo (Eds.), *Individual differences in infancy: Reliability, stability and prediction* (pp. 411–429). Hillsdale, NJ: Erlbaum.

Rothbart, M. K., Posner, M. I., & Kieras, J. (2006). Temperament, attention, and the development of self-regulation. In K. McCartney & D. Phillips (Eds.), *Blackwell handbook of early childhood development* (pp. 338–357). Malden, MA: Blackwell.

Rothbaum, F., Kakinuma, M., Nagaoka, R., & Azuma, H. (2007). Attachment and *amae:* Parent–child closeness in the United States and Japan. *Journal of Cross-Cultural Psychology, 38,* 465–486.

Rothbaum, F., Pott, M., Azuma, H., Miyake, K., & Weisz, J. (2000a). The development of close relationships in Japan and the United States: Paths of symbiotic harmony and generative tension. *Child Development, 71,* 1121–1142.

Rothbaum, F., Weisz, J., Pott, M., Miyake, K., & Morelli, G. (2000b). Attachment and culture: Security in the United States and Japan. *American Psychologist, 55,* 1093–1104.

Rouselle, L., Palmers, E., & Noël, M.-P. (2004). Magnitude comparison in preschoolers: What counts? Influence of perceptual variables. *Journal of Experimental Child Psychology, 87,* 57–84.

Rovee-Collier, C. (1999). The development of infant memory. *Current Directions in Psychological Science, 8,* 80–85.

Rovee-Collier, C., & Barr, R. (2001). Infant learning and memory. In G. Bremner & A. Fogel (Eds.), *Blackwell handbook of infant development* (pp. 139–168). Oxford, UK: Blackwell.

Rovee-Collier, C., & Bhatt, R. S. (1993). Evidence of long-term memory in infancy. *Annals of Child Development, 9,* 1–45.

Rovee-Collier, C., & Cuevas, K. (2009). Multiple memory systems are unnecessary to account for infant memory development: An ecological model. *Developmental Psychology, 45,* 160–174.

Rovers, M. M., Numans, M. E., Langenbach, E., Grobbee, D. E., et al. (2008). Is pacifier use a risk factor for acute otitis media? A dynamic cohort study. *Family Practice, 25,* 233–236.

Rowe, D. (1994). *The limits of family influence: Genes, experience, and behavior.* New York: Guilford.

Rowe, M. L. (2008). Child-directed speech: Relation to socioeconomic status, knowledge of child development and child vocabulary skill. *Journal of Child Language, 35,* 185–205.

Rowe, R., Maughan, B., & Goodman, R. (2004). Childhood psychiatric disorder and unintentional injury: Findings from a national cohort study. *Journal of Pediatric Psychology, 29,* 119–130.

Rowland, C. F. (2007). Explaining errors in children's questions. *Cognition, 104,* 106–134.

Rowland, C. F., & Pine, J. M. (2000). Subject-auxiliary inversion errors and wh-question acquisition: "What children do know?" *Journal of Child Language, 27,* 157–181.

Rubin, C., Maisonet, M., Kieszak, S., Monteilh, C., Holmes A., Flanders, D., et al. (2009). Timing of maturation and predictors of menarche in girls enrolled in a contemporary British cohort. *Paediatric and Perinatal Epidemiology, 23,* 492–504.

Rubin, K. H., Bukowski, W. M., & Parker, J. G. (2006). Peer interactions, relationships, and groups. In N. Eisenberg (Ed.), *Handbook of child psychology: Vol. 3. Social, emotional, and personality development* (6th ed., pp. 571–645). Hoboken, NJ: Wiley.

Rubin, K. H., & Burgess, K. (2002). Parents of aggressive and withdrawn children. In M. Bornstein (Ed.), *Handbook of parenting* (2nd ed., pp. 383–418). Hillsdale, NJ: Erlbaum.

Rubin, K. H., Burgess, K. B., & Coplan, R. (2002). Social withdrawal and shyness. In P. K. Smith & C. H. Hart (Eds.), *Blackwell handbook of child social development* (pp. 329–352). Oxford: Blackwell.

Rubin, K. H., Burgess, K. B., Dwyer, K. M., & Hastings, P. D. (2003). Predicting preschoolers' externalizing behaviors from toddler temperament, conflict, and maternal negativity. *Developmental Psychology, 39,* 164–176.

Rubin, K. H., Burgess, K. B., & Hastings, P. D. (2002). Stability and social-behavioral consequences of toddlers' inhibited temperament and parenting behaviors. *Child Development, 73,* 483–495.

Rubin, K. H., Coplan, R. J., Chen, X., Buskirk, A. A., & Wojslawowicz, J. C. (2005). Peer relationships in childhood. In M. H. Bornstein & M. E. Lamb (Eds.), *Developmental science: An advanced textbook* (pp. 469–512). Mahwah, NJ: Erlbaum.

Rubin, K. H., Fein, G. G., & Vandenberg, B. (1983). Play. In E. M. Hetherington (Ed.), *Handbook of child psychology: Vol. 4. Socialization, personality, and social development* (4th ed., pp. 693–744). New York: Wiley.

Rubin, K. H., Stewart, S. L., & Coplan, R. J. (1995). Social withdrawal in childhood: Conceptual and empirical perspectives. In T. H. Ollendick & R. J. Prinz (Eds.), *Advances in clinical child psychology* (Vol. 17, pp. 157–196). New York: Plenum.

Rubin, K. H., Watson, K. S., & Jambor, T. W. (1978). Free-play behaviors in preschool and kindergarten children. *Child Development, 49,* 539–536.

Ruble, D. N., Alvarez, J., Bachman, M., Cameron, J., Fuligni, A., Garcia Coll, C. T., & Rhee, E. (2004). The development of a sense of "we": The emergence and implications of children's collective identity. In M. Bennett & F. Sani (Eds.), *The development of the social self* (pp. 29–76). Hove, UK: Psychology Press.

Ruble, D. N., & Flett, G. L. (1988). Conflicting goals in self-evaluative information seeking: Developmental and ability level analyses. *Child Development, 59,* 97–106.

Ruble, D. N., Martin, C. L., & Berenbaum, S. A. (2006). Gender development. In N. Eisenberg (Ed.), *Handbook of child psychology: Vol. 3. Social, emotional, and personality development* (6th ed., pp. 858–932). Hoboken, NJ: Wiley.

Ruble, D. N., Taylor, L. J., Cyphers, L., Greulich, F. K., Lurye, L. E., & Shrout, P. E. (2007). The role of gender constancy in early gender development. *Child Development, 78,* 1121–1136.

Rudolph, K. D., Caldwell, M. S., & Conley, C. S. (2005). Need for approval and children's well-being. *Child Development, 76,* 309–323.

Rudolph, K. D., & Heller, T. L. (1997). Interpersonal problem solving, externalizing behavior, and social competence in preschoolers: A knowledge-performance discrepancy? *Journal of Applied Developmental Psychology, 18,* 107–117.

Rudolph, K. D., Lambert, S. F., Clark, A. G., & Kurlakowsky, K. D. (2001). Negotiating the transition to middle school: The role of self-regulatory processes. *Child Development, 72,* 929–946.

Rudy, D., & Grusec, J. E. (2006). Authoritarian parenting in individualist and collectivist groups: Associations with maternal emotion and cognition and children's self-esteem. *Journal of Family Psychology, 20,* 68–78.

Ruff, C. (2002). Variation in human body size and shape. *Annual Review of Anthropology, 31,* 211–232.

Ruff, H. A., & Capozzoli, M. C. (2003). Development of attention and distractibility in the first 4 years of life. *Developmental Psychology, 39,* 877–890.

Ruff, H. A., & Rothbart, M. K. (1996). *Attention in early development.* New York: Oxford University Press.

Ruffman, J., & Perner, T. (2005). Do infants really understand false belief? *Trends in Cognitive Sciences, 9,* 462–463.

Ruffman, T. (1999). Children's understanding of logical inconsistency. *Child Development, 70,* 872–886.

Ruffman, T., & Langman, L. (2002). Infants' reaching in a multi-well A not B task. *Infant Behavior and Development, 25,* 237–246.

Ruffman, T., Perner, J., Olson, D. R., & Doherty, M. (1993). Reflecting on scientific thinking: Children's understanding of the hypothesis–evidence relation. *Child Development, 64,* 1617–1636.

Ruffman, T., Slade, L., Devitt, K., & Crowe, E. (2006). What mothers say and what they do: The relation between parenting, theory of mind, language, and conflict/cooperation. *British Journal of Developmental Psychology, 24,* 105–124.

Runco, M. A. (1992). Children's divergent thinking and creative ideation. *Developmental Review, 12,* 233–264.

Rushton, J. L., Forcier, M., & Schectman, R. M. (2002). Epidemiology of depressive symptoms in the National Longitudinal Study of Adolescent Health. *Journal of the American Academy of Child and Adolescent Psychiatry, 41,* 199–205.

Rushton, J. P., & Jensen, A. R. (2005). Thirty years of research on race differences in cognitive ability. *Psychology, Public Policy, and Law, 11,* 235–294.

Rushton, J. P., & Jensen, A. R. (2006). The totality of available evidence shows the race IQ gap still remains. *Psychological Science, 17*, 921–922.

Rushton, J. P., & Jensen, A. R. (2010). The rise and fall of the Flynn effect as a reason to expect a narrowing of the black–white IQ gap. *Intelligence, 38*, 213–219.

Russell, A., Mize, J., & Bissaker, K. (2004). Parent–child relationships. In P. K. Smith & C. H. Hart (Eds.), *Blackwell handbook of childhood social development* (pp. 204–222). Malden, MA: Blackwell.

Russell, J. A. (1990). The preschooler's understanding of the causes and consequences of emotion. *Child Development, 61*, 1872–1881.

Russell, J. A., Douglas, A. J., & Ingram, C. D. (2001). Brain preparations for maternity—Adaptive changes in behavioral and neuroendocrine systems during pregnancy and lactation: An overview. *Progress in Brain Research, 133*, 1–38.

Russell, R. B., Petrini, J. R., Damus, K., Mattison, D. R., & Schwarz, R. H. (2003). The changing epidemiology of multiple births in the United States. *Obstetrics and Gynecology, 101*, 129–135.

Russell, S. T., Elder, G. H., & Conger, R. D. (1997). *School transitions and academic achievement*. Paper presented at the annual meeting of the American Sociological Association, Toronto, Canada.

Rust, J., Golombok, S., Hines, M., Johnston, K., Golding, J., & the ALSPAC Study Team. (2000). The role of brothers and sisters in the gender development of preschool children. *Journal of Experimental Child Psychology, 77*, 292–303.

Rutter, M. (1996). Maternal deprivation. In M. H. Bornstein (Ed.), *Handbook of parenting: Vol. 4. Applied and practical parenting* (pp. 3–31). Mahwah, NJ: Erlbaum.

Rutter, M. (2002). Nature, nurture, and development: From evangelism through science toward policy and practice. *Child Development, 73*, 1–21.

Rutter, M. (2007a). Gene–environment interdependence. *Developmental Science, 10*, 12–18.

Rutter, M. (2007b). Proceeding from observed correlation to causal inference: The use of natural experiments. *Perspectives on Psychological Science, 2*, 377–395.

Rutter, M., Colvert, E., Kreppner, J., Beckett, C., Castle, J., & Groothues, C. (2007). Early adolescent outcomes for institutionally deprived and non-deprived adoptees. I: Disinhibited attachment. *Journal of Child Psychology and Psychiatry, 48*, 17–30.

Rutter, M., & the English and Romanian Adoptees Study Team. (1998). Developmental catch-up, and deficit, following adoption after severe global early privation. *Journal of Child Psychology and Psychiatry, 39*, 465–476.

Rutter, M., O'Connor, T. G., and the English and Romanian Adoptees Study Team. (2004). Are there biological programming effects for psychological development? Findings from a study of Romanian adoptees. *Developmental Psychology, 40*, 81–94.

Rutter, M., Pickles, A., Murray, R., & Eaves, L. (2001). Testing hypotheses on specific environmental causal effects on behavior. *Psychological Bulletin, 127*, 291–324.

Rutter, M., Sonuga-Barke, E. J, Beckett, C., Castle, J., Kreppner, J., Kumsta, R., et al. (2010). Deprivation-specific psychological patterns: Effects of institutional deprivation. *Monographs of the Society for Research in Child Development, 75*(1, Serial No. 295).

Ryan, A. M., & Patrick, H. (2001). The classroom social environment and changes in adolescents' motivation and engagement during middle school. *American Educational Research Journal, 38*, 437–460.

Ryan, M. K., David, B., & Reynolds, K. J. (2004). Who cares? The effect of gender and context on the self and moral reasoning. *Psychology of Women Quarterly, 28*, 246–255.

Ryan, R. M., Fauth, R. C., & Brooks-Gunn, J. (2006). Childhood poverty: Implications for school readiness and early childhood education In B. Spodek & O. N. Saracho (Eds.), *Handbook of research on the education of young children* (2nd ed., pp. 323–346). Mahwah, NJ: Erlbaum.

Ryding, M., Konradsson, K., Kalm, O., & Prellner, K. (2002). Auditory consequences of recurrent acute purulent otitis media. *Annals of Otology, Rhinology, and Laryngology, 111*(3, Pt. 1), 261–266.

S

Saarni, C. (1999). *The development of emotional competence*. New York: Guilford.

Saarni, C. (2000). Emotional competence: A developmental perspective. In R. Bar-On & J. D. A. Parker (Eds.), *Handbook of emotional intelligence* (pp. 68–91). San Francisco: Jossey-Bass.

Saarni, C., Campos, J. J., Camras, L. A., & Witherington, D. (2006). Emotional development: Action, communication, and understanding. In N. Eisenberg (Ed.), *Handbook of child psychology: Vol. 3. Social, emotional, and personality development* (6th ed., pp. 226–299). Hoboken, NJ: Wiley.

Sabbagh, M. A., & Baldwin, D. A. (2001). Learning words from knowledgeable versus ignorant speakers: Links between preschoolers' theory of mind and semantic development. *Child Development, 72*, 1054–1070.

Sabbagh, M. A., Xu, F., Carlson, S. M., Moses, L. J., & Lee, K. (2006). The development of executive functioning and theory of mind: A comparison of Chinese and U.S. preschoolers. *Psychological Science, 17*, 74–81.

Sacks, P. (2005). "No child left": What are schools for in a democratic society? In S. Olfman (Ed.), *Childhood lost: How American culture is failing our kids* (pp. 185–202). Westport, CT: Praeger.

Sadeh, A. (1997). Sleep and melatonin in infants: A preliminary study. *Sleep, 20*, 185–191.

Sadeh, A. (2007). Consequences of sleep loss or sleep disruption in children. *Sleep Medicine Reviews, 2*, 513–520.

Sadeh, A., Flint-Ofir, E., Tirosh, T., & Tikotzky, L. (2007). Infant sleep and parental sleep-related cognitions. *Journal of Family Psychology, 21*, 74–87.

Sadler, T. W. (2009). *Langman's medical embryology* (11th ed.). Baltimore: Lippincott Williams & Wilkins.

Saenger, P. (2003). Dose effects of growth hormone during puberty. *Hormone Research, 60*(Suppl. 1), 52–57.

Safe Kids USA. (2007). *Car seats, booster seats and seat belts*. Retrieved from usa.safekids.org

Safe Kids USA. (2008). *Report to the nation: Trends in unintentional childhood injury mortality and parental views on child safety*. Retrieved from usa.safekids.org

Saffran, J. R. (2009). What can statistical learning tell us about infant learning? In A. Woodward & A. Needham (Eds.), *Learning and the infant mind* (pp. 29–48). New York: Oxford University Press.

Saffran, J. R., Aslin, R. N., & Newport, E. L. (1996). Statistical learning by 8-month-old infants. *Science, 27*, 1926–1928.

Saffran, J. R., & Thiessen, E. D. (2003). Pattern induction by infant language learners. *Developmental Psychology, 39*, 484–494.

Saffran, J. R., Werker, J. F., & Werner, L. A. (2006). The infant's auditory world: Hearing, speech, and the beginnings of language. In D. Kuhn & R. Siegler (Eds.), *Handbook of child psychology: Vol. 2. Cognition, perception, and language* (6th ed., pp. 58–108). Hoboken, NJ: Wiley.

Safren, S. A., & Pantalone, D. W. (2006). Social anxiety and barriers to resilience among lesbian, gay, and bisexual adolescents. In A. M. Omoto & H. S. Kurtzman (Eds.), *Sexual orientation and mental health: Examining identity and development in lesbian, gay, and bisexual young people* (pp. 55–71). Washington, DC: American Psychological Association.

Sagi, A., van IJzendoorn, M. H., Aviezer, O., Donnell, F., Koren-Karie, N., Joels, T., & Harel, Y. (1995). Attachments in a multiple-caregiver and multiple-infant environment: The case of the Israeli kibbutzim. In E. Waters, B. E. Vaughn, G. Posada, & K. Kondo-Ikemura (Eds.), Caregiving, cultural, and cognitive perspectives on secure-base behavior and working models: New growing points in attachment theory and research. *Monographs of the Society for Research in Child Development, 60*(1, Serial No. 244), 71–91.

Sahlberg, P. (2010). Educational change in Finland. In A. Hargreaves, M. Fullan, A. Lieberman, & D. Hopkins (Eds.), *Second International handbook of educational change*. New York: Springer.

Saigal, S., Stoskopf, B., Streiner, D., Boyle, M., Pinelli, J., & Paneth, N. (2006). Transition of extremely low-birthweight infants from adolescence to young adulthood. *Journal of the American Medical Association, 295*, 667–675.

Saitta, S. C., & Zackai, E. H. (2005). Specific chromosome disorders in newborns. In H. W. Taeusch, R. A. Ballard, & C. A. Gleason (Eds.), *Avery's diseases of the newborn* (8th ed., pp. 204–215). Philadelphia: Saunders.

Salbe, A. D., Weyer, C., Lindsay, R. S., Ravussin, E., & Tataranni, P. A. (2002). Assessing risk factors for obesity between childhood and adolescence: I. Birth weight, childhood adiposity, parental obesity, insulin, and leptin. *Pediatrics, 110*, 299–306.

Salerno, M., Micillo, M., Di Maio, S., Capalbo, D., Ferri, P., & Lettiero, T. (2001). Longitudinal growth, sexual maturation and final height in patients with congenital hypothyroidism detected by neonatal screening. *European Journal of Endocrinology, 145*, 377–383.

Salihu, H. M., Shumpert, M. N., Slay, M., Kirby, R. S., & Alexander, G. R. (2003). Childbearing beyond maternal age 50 and fetal outcomes in the United States. *Obstetrics and Gynecology, 102*, 1006–1014.

Salley, B. J., & Dixon, W. E., Jr. (2007). Temperamental and joint attentional predictors of language development. *Merrill-Palmer Quarterly, 53*, 131–154.

Salmela-Aro, K., Nurmi, J.-E., Saisto, T., & Halmesmaki, E. (2000). Women's and men's personal goals during the transition to parenthood. *Journal of Family Psychology, 14*, 171–186.

Salmivalli, C., & Voeten, M. (2004). Connections between attitudes, group norms, and behaviour in bullying situations. *International Journal of Behavioral Development, 28*, 246–258.

Salovey, P., & Pizzaro, D. A. (2003). The value of emotional intelligence. In R. J. Sternberg, J. Lautrey, & T. I. Lubart (Eds.), *Models of intelligence: International perspectives* (pp. 263–278). Washington, DC: American Psychological Association.

Salter, D., McMillan, D., Richards, M., Talbot, T., Hodges, J., Bentovim, A., & Hastings, R. (2003). Development of sexually abusive behavior in sexually victimized males: A longitudinal study. *Lancet, 361*, 471–476.

Sameroff, A. (2006). Identifying risk and protective factors for healthy child development. In A. Clarke-Stewart & J. Dunn (Eds.), *Families count: Effects on child and adolescent development* (pp. 53–76). New York: Cambridge University Press.

Samuels, M. (2003). Viruses and sudden infant death. *Peaediatric Respiratory Review, 4*, 178–183.

Sanchez, M. M., & Pollak, S. D. (2009). Socioemotional development following early abuse and neglect: Challenges and insight from translational research. In M. de Haan & M. R. Gunnar (Eds.), *Handbook of developmental social neuroscience* (pp. 497–520). New York: Guilford.

Sandberg, D. E., & Voss, L. D. (2002). The psychosocial consequences of short stature: A review of the evidence. *Best Practice and Research in Clinical Endocrinology and Metabolism, 16*, 449–463.

Sanders, O. (2006). Evaluating the Keeping Ourselves Safe Programme. Wellington, NZ: Youth Education Service, New Zealand Police. Retrieved from www.nzfvc.org.nz/accan/papers-presentations/abstract11v.shtml

Sanderson, J. A., & Siegal, M. (1988). Conceptions of moral and social rules in rejected and nonrejected preschoolers. *Journal of Clinical Child Psychology, 17*, 66–72.

Sandler, J. C. (2006). Alternative methods of child testimony: A review of law and research. In C. R. Bartol & A. M. Bartol (Eds.), *Current perspectives in forensic psychology and criminal justice* (pp. 203–212). Thousand Oaks, CA: Sage.

Sandnabba, N. K., & Ahlberg, C. (1999). Parents' attitudes and expectations about children's cross-gender behavior. *Sex Roles, 40,* 249–263.

Sandstrom, M. J., & Cillessen, A. H. N. (2003). Sociometric status and children's peer experiences: Use of the daily diary method. *Merrill-Palmer Quarterly, 49,* 427–452.

Sangrigoli, S., Pallier, C., Argenti, A. M., Ventureyra, V. A. G., & de Schonen, S. (2005). Reversibility of the other-race effect in face recognition during childhood. *Psychological Science, 16,* 440–444.

Sann, C., & Streri, A. (2007). Perception of object shape and texture in human newborns: Evidence from cross-modal transfer tasks. *Developmental Science, 10,* 399–410.

Sann, C., & Streri, A. (2008). The limits of newborn's grasping to detect texture in a cross-modal transfer task. *Infant Behavior and Development, 31,* 523–531.

Sansavini, A., Bertoncini, J., & Giovanelli, G. (1997). Newborns discriminate the rhythm of multisyllabic stressed words. *Developmental Psychology, 33,* 3–11.

Santoloupo, S., & Pratt, M. (1994). Age, gender, and parenting style variations in mother–adolescent dialogues and adolescent reasoning about political issues. *Journal of Adolescent Research, 9,* 241–261.

Sapp, F., Lee, K., & Muir, D. (2000). Three-year-olds' difficulty with the appearance–reality distinction: Is it real or is it apparent? *Developmental Psychology, 36,* 547–560.

Sarnecka, B. W., & Gelman, S. A. (2004). Six does not just mean a lot: Preschoolers see number words as specific. *Cognition, 92,* 329–352.

Sato, T., Matsumoto, T., Kawano, H., Watanabe, T., Uematsu, Y., & Semine, K. (2004). Brain masculinization requires androgen receptor function. *Proceedings of the National Academy of Sciences, 101,* 1673–1678.

Saucier, J. F., Sylvestre, R., Doucet, H., Lambert, J., Frappier, J. Y., Charbonneau, L., & Malus, M. (2002). Cultural identity and adaptation to adolescence in Montreal. In F. J. C. Azima & N. Grizenko (Eds.), *Immigrant and refugee children and their families: Clinical, research, and training issues* (pp. 133–154). Madison, WI: International Universities Press.

Saudino, K. J. (2003). Parent ratings of infant temperament: Lessons from twin studies. *Infant Behavior and Development, 26,* 100–107.

Saudino, K. J., & Cherny, S. S. (2001). Sources of continuity and change in observed temperament. In R. N. Emde & J. K. Hewitt (Eds.), *Infancy to early childhood: Genetic and environmental influences on developmental change* (pp. 89–110). New York: Oxford University Press.

Saudino, K. J., & Plomin, R. (1997). Cognitive and temperamental mediators of genetic contributions to the home environment during infancy. *Merrill-Palmer Quarterly, 43,* 1–23.

Savin-Williams, R. C. (2001). A critique of research on sexual-minority youths. *Journal of Adolescence, 24,* 5–13.

Savin-Williams, R. C., & Diamond, L. M. (2004). Sex. In R. M. Lerner & L. Steinberg (Eds.), *Handbook of adolescent development* (2nd ed., pp. 189–231). Hoboken, NJ: Wiley.

Savin-Williams, R. C., & Ream, G. L. (2003). Sex variations in the disclosure to parents of same-sex attractions. *Journal of Family Psychology, 17,* 429–438.

Saw, S. M., Carkeet, A., Chia, K. S., Stone, R. A., & Tan, D. T. (2002). Component dependent risk factors for ocular parameters in Singapore Chinese children. *Ophthalmology, 109,* 2065–2071.

Saxe, G. B. (1988, August–September). Candy selling and math learning. *Educational Researcher, 17*(6), 14–21.

Saxe, R. R., Whitfield-Gabrieli, S., Scholz, J., & Pelphrey, K. A. (2009). Brain regions for perceiving and reasoning about other people in school-aged children. *Child Development, 80,* 1197–1209.

Saxton, M., Backley, P., & Gallaway, C. (2005). Negative input for grammatical errors: Effects after a lag of 12 weeks. *Journal of Child Language, 32,* 643–672.

Saygin, A. P., Wilson, S. M., Dronkers, N. F., & Bates, E. (2004). Action comprehension in aphasia: Linguistic and non-linguistic deficits and their lesion correlates. *Neuropsychologia, 42,* 1788–1804.

Saylor, M. M. (2004). Twelve- and 16-month-old infants recognize properties of mentioned absent things. *Developmental Science, 7,* 599–611.

Saylor, M. M., Baldwin, D. A., & Sabbagh, M. A. (2005). Word learning: A complex product. In G. Hall & S. Waxman (Eds.), *Weaving a lexicon.* Cambridge, MA: MIT Press.

Saylor, M. M., Sabbagh, M. A., & Baldwin, D. A. (2002). Children use whole–part juxtaposition as a pragmatic cue to word meaning. *Developmental Psychology, 38,* 993–1003.

Saylor, M. M., & Troseth, G. L. (2006). Preschoolers use information about speakers' desires to learn new words. *Cognitive Development, 21,* 214–231.

Saywitz, K. J., Goodman, G. S., & Lyon, T. D. (2002). Interviewing children in and out of court: Current research and practice implications. In J. E. B. Myers & L. Berliner (Eds.), *The APSAC handbook on child maltreatment* (2nd ed., pp. 349–377). Thousand Oaks, CA: Sage.

Scales, P. C., & Roehlkepartain, E. C. (2004). *Community service and service learning in U.S. public schools, 2004. Findings from a national survey.* St. Paul, MN: National Youth Leadership Council.

Scarr, S., & McCartney, K. (1983). How people make their own environments: A theory of genotype–environment effects. *Child Development, 54,* 424–435.

Scarr, S., & Weinberg, R. A. (1983). The Minnesota adoption studies: Genetic differences and malleability. *Child Development, 54,* 260–267.

Schaal, B., Marlier, L., & Soussignan, R. (2000). Human fetuses learn odours from their pregnant mother's diet. *Chemical Senses, 25,* 729–737.

Schacht, P. M., Cummings, E. M., & Davies, P. T. (2009). Fathering in family context and child adjustment: A longitudinal analysis. *Journal of Family Psychology, 23,* 790–797.

Schalet, A. (2007). Adolescent sexuality viewed through two different cultural lenses. In M. S. Tepper & A. F. Owens (Eds.), *Sexual health: Vol. 3. Moral and cultural foundations* (pp. 365–387). Westport, CT: Praeger.

Scharrer, E., & Comstock, G. (2003). Entertainment televisual media: Content patterns and themes. In E. L. Palmer & B. M. Young (Eds.), *The faces of televisual media: Teaching violence, selling to children* (pp. 161–193). Mahwah, NJ: Erlbaum.

Schauwers, K., Gillis, S., Daemers, K., De Beukelaer, C., De Ceulaer, G., Yperman, M., & Govaerts, P. J. (2004). Normal hearing and language development in a deaf-born child. *Otology and Neurotology, 25,* 924–929.

Schellenberg, E. G. (2004). Music lessons enhance IQ. *Psychological Science, 15,* 511–514.

Schellenberg, E. G., Nakata, T., Hunter, P. G., & Tamoto, S. (2007). Exposure to music and cognitive performance: Tests of children and adults. *Psychology of Music, 35,* 5–19.

Scher, A., Epstein, R., & Tirosh, E. (2004). Stability and changes in sleep regulation: A longitudinal study from 3 months to 3 years. *International Journal of Behavioral Development, 28,* 268–274.

Scher, A., Tirosh, E., Jaffe, M., Rubin, L., Sadeh, A., & Lavie, P. (1995). Sleep patterns of infants and young children in Israel. *International Journal of Behavioral Development, 18,* 701–711.

Schlaggar, B. L., & McCandliss, B. D. (2007). Development of neural systems for reading. *Annual Review of Neuroscience, 30,* 475–503.

Schlagmüller, M., & Schneider, W. (2002). The development of organizational strategies in children: Evidence from a microgenetic longitudinal study. *Journal of Experimental Child Psychology, 81,* 298–319.

Schlegel, A., & Barry, H., III. (1991). *Adolescence: An anthropological inquiry.* New York: Free Press.

Schmeeckle, M., & Sprecher, S. (2004). Extended family and social networks. In A. Vangelisti (Ed.), *Handbook of family communication* (pp. 349–375). Mahwah, NJ: Erlbaum.

Schmid, R. G., Tirsch, W. S., & Scherb, H. (2002). Correlation between spectral EEG parameters and intelligence test variables in school-age children. *Clinical Neurophysiology, 113,* 1647–1656.

Schmidt, L. A., Fox, N. A., Rubin, K. H., Sternberg, E. M., Gold, P. W., & Smith, C. C. (1997). Behavioral and neuroendocrine responses in shy children. *Developmental Psychobiology, 35,* 119–135.

Schmidt, L. A., Fox, N. A., Schulkin, J., & Gold, P. W. (1999). Behavioral and psychophysiological correlates of self-presentation in temperamentally shy children. *Developmental Psychobiology, 30,* 127–140.

Schmidt, L. A., Santesso, D. L., Schulkin, J., & Segalowitz, S. J. (2007). Shyness is a necessary but not sufficient condition for high salivary cortisol in typically developing 10-year-old children. *Personality and Individual Differences, 43,* 1541–1551.

Schmidt, M. E., Crawley-Davis, A. M., & Anderson, D. R. (2007). Two-year-olds' object retrieval based on television: Testing a perceptual account. *Media Psychology, 9,* 389–409.

Schmitz, S., Fulker, D. W., Plomin, R., Zahn-Waxler, C., Emde, R. N., & DeFries, J. C. (1999). Temperament and problem behaviour during early childhood. *International Journal of Behavioral Development, 23,* 333–355.

Schneewind, K. A., & Gerhard, A. (2002). Relationship personality, conflict resolution, and marital satisfaction in the first 5 years of marriage. *Family Relations, 51,* 63–71.

Schneider, B. H., Atkinson, L., & Tardif, C. (2001). Child–parent attachment and children's peer relations: A quantitative review. *Developmental Psychology, 37,* 86–100.

Schneider, W. (1986). The role of conceptual knowledge and metamemory in the development of organizational processes in memory. *Journal of Experimental Child Psychology, 42,* 218–236.

Schneider, W. (2002). Memory development in childhood. In U. Goswami (Ed.), *Blackwell handbook of childhood cognitive development* (pp. 236–256). Malden, MA: Blackwell.

Schneider, W., & Bjorklund, D. F. (1992). Expertise, aptitude, and strategic remembering. *Child Development, 63,* 461–473.

Schneider, W., & Bjorklund, D. F. (1998). Memory. In D. Kuhn & R. S. Siegler (Eds.), *Handbook of child psychology: Vol. 2. Cognition, perception, and language* (5th ed., pp. 467–521). New York: Wiley.

Schneider, W., & Bjorklund, D. F. (2003). Memory and knowledge development. In J. Valsiner & K. Connolly (Eds.), *Handbook of developmental psychology.* London: Sage.

Schneider, W., & Pressley, M. (1997). *Memory development between two and twenty* (2nd ed.). Mahwah, NJ: Erlbaum.

Scholl, B. J., & Leslie, A. M. (2000). Minds, modules, and meta-analysis. *Child Development, 72,* 696–701.

Scholl, T. O., Hediger, M. L., & Belsky, D. (1996). Prenatal care and maternal health during adolescent pregnancy: A review and meta-analysis. *Journal of Adolescent Health, 15,* 444–456.

Schonberg, R. L., & Tifft, C. J. (2007). Birth defects and prenatal diagnosis. In M. L. Batshaw, L. Pellegrino, & N. J. Roizen (Eds.), *Children with disabilities* (6th ed., pp. 83–96). Baltimore: Paul H. Brookes.

Schonert-Reichl, K. A. (1999). Relations of peer acceptance, friendship adjustment, and social behavior to moral reasoning during early adolescence. *Journal of Early Adolescence, 19,* 249–279.

Schoon, I., & Parsons, S. (2002). Teenage aspirations for future careers and occupational outcomes. *Journal of Vocational Behavior, 60,* 262–288.

Schoppe-Sullivan, S. J., Brown, G. L., Cannon, E. A., Mangelsdorf, S. C., & Sokolowski, M. S. (2008). Maternal gatekeeping, coparenting quality, and fathering behavior in families with infants. *Journal of Family Psychology, 22,* 389–398.

Schoppe-Sullivan, S. J., Mangelsdorf, S. C., Brown, G. L., & Sokolowski, M. S. (2007). Goodness-of-fit in family context: Infant temperament, marital quality, and early coparenting behavior. *Infant Behavior and Development, 30,* 82–96.

Schor, J. B. (2002). Time crunch among American parents. In S. A. Hewlett, N. Rankin, & C. West (Eds.), *Taking parenting public* (pp. 83–102). Boston: Rowman & Littlefield.

Schott, J. M., & Rossor, M. N. (2003). The grasp and other primitive reflexes. *Journal of Neurological and Neurosurgical Psychiatry, 74,* 558–560.

Schuetze, P., & Eiden, R. D. (2006). The association between maternal cocaine use during pregnancy and physiological regulation in 4- to 8-week-old infants: An examination of possible mediators and moderators. *Journal of Pediatric Psychology, 31,* 15–26,

Schull, W. J. (2003). The children of atomic bomb survivors: A synopsis. *Journal of Radiological Protection, 23,* 369–394.

Schulte, L. E., Shanahan, S., Anderson, T. D., & Sides, J. (2003). Student and teacher perceptions of their middle and high schools' sense of community. *School Community Journal, 13,* 7–33.

Schulte-Ruther, M., Markowitsch, H. J., Fink, G. R., & Piefke, M. (2007). Mirror neuron and theory of mind mechanisms involved in face-to-face interactions: A functional magnetic resonance imaging approach to empathy. *Journal of Cognitive Neuroscience, 19,* 1354–1372.

Schultz, D., Izar, C. E., Ackerman, B. P., & Youngstrom, E. A. (2001). Emotion knowledge in economically disadvantaged children: Self-regulatory antecedents and relations to social difficulties and withdrawal. *Development and Psychopathology, 13,* 53–67.

Schulz, M. S., Cowan, C. P., & Cowan, P. A. (2006). Promoting healthy beginnings: A randomized controlled trial of a preventive intervention to preserve marital quality during the transition to parenthood. *Journal of Consulting and Clinical Psychology, 74,* 20–31.

Schumann, C. M., & Amaral, D. G. (2010). The human amygdala in autism. In P. J. Whalen & E. A. Phelps (Eds.), *The human amygdala* (pp. 362–381). New York: Guilford.

Schumann, C. M., Barnes, C. C., Lord, C., & Courchesne, E. (2009). Amygdala enlargement in toddlers with autism related to severity of social and communication impairments. *Biological Psychiatry, 66,* 942–949.

Schunk, D. H., & Pajares, F. (2005). Competence perceptions and academic functioning. In A. J. Andrew & C. S. Dweck (Eds.), *Handbook of competence and motivation* (pp. 85–104). New York: Guilford.

Schwanenflugel, P. J., Henderson, R. L., & Fabricius, W. V. (1998). Developing organization of mental verbs and theory of mind in middle childhood: Evidence from extensions. *Developmental Psychology, 34,* 512–524.

Schwarte, A. R. (2008). Fragile X syndrome. *School Psychology Quarterly, 23,* 290–300.

Schwartz, C. E., Wright, C. I., Shin, L. M., Kagan, J., & Rauch, S. L. (2003). Inhibited and uninhibited infants "grown up": Adult amygdalar response to novelty. *Science, 300,* 1952–1953.

Schwartz, D., Proctor, L. J., & Chien, D. H. (2001). The aggressive victim of bullying: Emotional and behavioral dysregulation as a pathway to victimization by peers. In J. Juonen & S. Graham (Eds.), *Peer harassment in school: The plight of the vulnerable and victimized* (pp. 147–174). New York: Guilford.

Schwartz, S. J., Côté, J. E., & Arnett, J. J. (2005). Identity and agency in emerging adulthood: Two developmental routes in the individualization process. *Youth and Society, 37,* 201–229.

Schwarz, N. (1999). Self-reports: How the questions shape the answers. *American Psychologist, 54,* 93–105.

Schwebel, D. C., & Bounds, M. L. (2003). The role of parents and temperament on children's estimation of physical ability: Links to unintentional injury prevention. *Journal of Pediatric Psychology, 28,* 505–516.

Schwebel, D. C., & Brezausek, C. M. (2007). Father transitions in the household and young children's injury risk. *Psychology of Men and Masculinity, 8,* 173–184.

Schwebel, D. C., & Gaines, J. (2007). Pediatric unintentional injury: Behavioral risk factors and implications for prevention. *Journal of Developmental and Behavioral Pediatrics, 28,* 245–254.

Schwebel, D. C., Brezausek, C. M., Ramey, S. L., & Ramey, C. T. (2004). Interactions between child behavior patterns and parenting: Implications for children's unintentional injury risk. *Journal of Pediatric Psychology, 29,* 93–104.

Schwebel, D. C., Hodgens, J. B., & Sterling, S. (2006). How mothers parent their children with behavior disorders: Implications for unintentional injury risk. *Journal of Safety Research, 37,* 167–173.

Schweiger, W. K., & O'Brien, M. (2005). Special needs adoption: An ecological systems approach. *Family Relations, 54,* 512–522.

Schweinhart, L. J., Montie, J., Xiang, Z., Barnett, W. S., Belfield, C. R., & Nores, M. (2005). *Lifetime effects: The High/Scope Perry Preschool Study through age 40.* Ypsilanti, MI: High/Scope Press.

Schweizer, K., Moosbrugger, H., & Goldhammer, F. (2006). The structure of the relationship between attention and intelligence. *Intelligence, 33,* 589–611.

Schwier, C., van Maanen, C., Carpenter, M., & Tomasello, M. (2006). Rational imitation in 12-month-old infants. *Infancy, 10,* 303–311.

Schwimmer, J. B., Burwinkle, T. M., & Varni, J. W. (2003). Health-related quality of life of severely obese children and adolescents. *Journal of the American Medical Association, 289,* 1813–1819.

Scott, K. D., Berkowitz, G., & Klaus, M. (1999). A comparison of intermittent and continuous support during labor: A meta-analysis. *American Journal of Obstetrics and Gynecology, 180,* 1054–1059.

Scott, L. D. (2003). The relation of racial identity and racial socialization to coping with discrimination among African Americans. *Journal of Black Studies, 20,* 520–538.

Scott, L. S. (2009). *Two is enough.* Berkeley, CA: Seal Press.

Scrutton, D. (2005). Influence of supine sleeping positioning on early motor milestone acquisition. *Developmental Medicine and Child Neurology, 47,* 364.

Seaton, E. K., Scottham, K. M., & Sellers, R. M. (2006). The status model of racial identity development in African American adolescents: Evidence of structure, trajectories, and well-being. *Child Development, 77,* 1416–1426.

Seibert, A. C., & Kerns, K. A. (2009). Attachment figures in middle childhood. *International Journal of Behavioral Development, 33,* 347–355.

Seidman, E., Aber, J. L., & French, S. E. (2004). Assessing the transitions to middle and high school. *Journal of Adolescent Research, 19,* 3–30.

Seidman, E., Lambert, L. E., Allen, L., & Aber, J. L. (2003). Urban adolescents' transition to junior high school and protective family transactions. *Journal of Early Adolescence, 23,* 166–193.

Seifer, R., & Schiller, M. (1995). The role of parenting sensitivity, infant temperament, and dyadic interaction in attachment theory and assessment. In E. Waters, B. E. Vaughn, G. Posada, & K. Kondo-Ikemura (Eds.), *Caregiving, cultural, and cognitive perspectives on secure-base behavior and working models: New growing points of attachment theory and research. Monographs of the Society for Research in Child Development, 60*(2–3, Serial No. 244).

Seitz, V., & Apfel, N. H. (2005). Creating effective school-based interventions for pregnant teenagers. In R. DeV. Peters, B. Leadbeater, & R. J. McMahon (Eds.), *Resilience in children, families, and communities: Linking context to practice and policy* (pp. 65–82). New York: Kluwer Academic.

Sekido, R., & Lovell-Badge, R. (2009). Sex determination and SRY: Down to a wink and a nudge? *Trends in Genetics, 25,* 19–29.

Selfhout, M. H. W., Branje, S. J. T., & Meeus, W. H. J. (2008). The development of delinquency and perceived friendship quality in adolescent best friendship dyads. *Journal of Abnormal Child Psychology, 36,* 471–485.

Selman, R. L. (1976). Social-cognitive understanding: A guide to educational and clinical practice. In T. Lickona (Ed.), *Moral development and behavior: Theory, research, and social issues* (pp. 299–316). New York: Holt, Rinehart, & Winston.

Selman, R. L., & Byrne, D. F. (1974). A structural-developmental analysis of levels of role taking in middle childhood. *Child Development, 45,* 803–806.

Sen, M. G., Yonas, A., & Knill, D. C. (2001). Development of infants' sensitivity to surface contour information for spatial layout. *Perception, 30,* 167–176.

Senechal, M., & LeFevre, J. (2002). Parental involvement in the development of children's reading skill: A five-year longitudinal study. *Child Development, 73,* 445–460.

Senju, A., Csibra, G., & Johnson, M. H. (2008). Understanding the referential nature of looking: Infants' preference for object-directed gaze. *Cognition, 108,* 303–319.

Serafini, T. E., & Adams, G. R. (2002). Functions of identity: Scale construction and validation. *Identity: An International Journal of Theory and Research, 2,* 361–389.

Serbin, L. A., Powlishta, K. K., & Gulko, J. (1993). The development of sex typing in middle childhood. *Monographs of the Society for Research in Child Development, 58*(2, Serial No. 232).

Sermon, K., Van Steirteghem, A., & Liebaers, I. (2004). Preimplantation genetic diagnosis. *Lancet, 363,* 1633–1641.

Sesame Workshop. (2008). *Sesame Street season 37 press kit.* Retrieved from www.sesameworkshop.org/aboutus/pressroom/presskits/season37/sesame_street.php

Sevigny, P. R., & Loutzenhiser, L. (2010). Predictors of parenting self-efficacy in mothers and fathers of toddlers. *Child Care, Health and Development, 36,* 179–189.

Seymour, S. C. (1999). *Women, family, and child care in India.* Cambridge, UK: Cambridge University Press.

Shafer, V. L., & Garrido-Nag, K. (2007). The neurodevelopmental bases of language. In E. Hoff & M. Shatz (Eds.), *Blackwell handbook of language development* (pp. 21–45). Malden, MA: Blackwell.

Shah, T., Sullivan, K., & Carter, J. (2006). Sudden infant death syndrome and reported maternal smoking during pregnancy. *American Journal of Public Health, 96,* 1757–1759.

Shahar, S. (1990). *Childhood in the Middle Ages.* London: Routledge & Kegan Paul.

Shainess, N. (1961). A re-evaluation of some aspects of femininity through a study of menstruation: A preliminary report. *Comparative Psychiatry, 2,* 20–26.

Shanahan, L., McHale, S. M., Crouter, A. C., & Osgood, D. W. (2007). Warmth with mothers and fathers from middle childhood to late adolescence: Within- and between-families comparisions. *Developmental Psychology, 43,* 551–563.

Shanahan, M. J., Mortimer, J. T., & Krüger, H. (2002). Adolescence and adult work in the twenty-first century. *Journal of Research on Adolescence, 12,* 99–120.

Shankaran, S., Laptook, A. R., Ehrenkranz, R. A., Tyson, J. E., McDonald, S. A., & Donovan, E. F. (2005). Whole-body hypothermia for neonates with hypoxic–ischemic encephalopathy. *New England Journal of Medicine, 353,* 1574–1584.

Shapiro, A. E., Gottman, J. M., & Carrere, S. (2000). The baby and the marriage: Identifying factors that buffer against decline in marital satisfaction after the first baby arrives. *Journal of Family Psychology, 14,* 59–70.

Shapka, J. D., & Keating, D. P. (2005). Structure and change in self-concept during adolescence. *Canadian Journal of Behavioural Science, 37,* 83–96.

Shatz, M. (2007). On the development of the field. In E. Hoff & M. Shatz (Eds.), *Blackwell handbook of language development* (pp. 1–20). Malden, MA: Blackwell.

Shaver, P., Furman, W., & Buhrmester, D. (1985). Transition to college: Network changes, social skills, and loneliness. In S. Duck & D. Perlman (Eds.), *Understanding personal relationships: An interdisciplinary approach* (pp. 193–219). London: Sage.

Shaw, D. S., Gilliom, M., Ingoldsby, E. M., & Nagin, D. S. (2003). Trajectories leading to school-age conduct problems. *Developmental Psychology, 39,* 189–200.

Shaw, D. S., Lacourse, E., & Nagin, D. S. (2005). Developmental trajectories of conduct problems and hyperactivity from ages 2 to 10. *Journal of Child Psychology and Psychiatry, 46,* 931–942.

Shaw, D. S., Winslow, E. B., & Flanagan, C. (1999). A prospective study of the effects of marital status and family relations on young children's adjustment among African-American and European-American families. *Child Development, 70,* 742–755.

Shaw, P., Brierley, B., & David, A. S. (2005). A critical period for the impact of amygdala damage on the emotional enhancement of memory? *Neurology, 65,* 326–328.

Shaw, P., Eckstrand, K., Sharp, W., Blumenthal, J., Lerch, J. P., & Greenstein, D. (2007, November 16). Attention-deficit/hyperactivity disorder is characterized by a delay in cortical maturation. *Proceedings of the National Academy of Sciences Online.* Retrieved from www.pnas.org/cgi/content/abstract/0707741104v1

Shedler, J., & Block, J. (1990). Adolescent drug use and psychological health: A longitudinal inquiry. *American Psychologist, 45,* 612–630.

Sheehan, G., Darlington, Y., Noller, P., & Feeney, J. (2004). Children's perceptions of their sibling relationships during parental separation and divorce. *Journal of Divorce and Remarriage, 41,* 69–94.

Sheehy, A., Gasser, T., Molinari, L., & Largo, R. H. (1999). An analysis of variance of the pubertal and midgrowth spurts for length and width. *Annals of Human Biology, 26,* 309–331.

Sheldon, J. P. (2004). Gender stereotypes in educational software for young children. *Sex Roles, 51,* 433–444.

Shenkin, J. D., Broffitt, B., Levy, S. M., & Warren, J. J. (2004). The association between environmental tobacco smoke and primary tooth caries. *Journal of Public Health Dentistry, 64,* 184–186.

Sherman, S. L., Allen, E. G., Bean, L. H., & Freeman, S. B. (2007). Epidemiology of Down syndrome. *Mental Retardation and Developmental Disabilities Research Reviews, 13,* 221–227.

Sherman, S. L., Freeman, S. B., Allen, E. G., & Lamb, N. E. (2005). Risk factors for nondisjunction of trisomy 21. *Cytogenetic Genome Research, 111,* 273–280.

Sherrod, L. R., & Spiewak, G. S. (2008). Possible interrelationships between civic engagement, positive youth development, and spirituality/religiosity. In R. M. Lerner, R. W. Roeser, & E. Phelps (Eds.), *Positive youth development and spirituality: From theory to research* (pp. 322–338). West Conshohocken, PA: Templeton Foundation Press.

Sherry, B., McDivitt, J., Brich, L. L., Cook, F. H., Sanders, S., Prish, J. L., Francis, L. A., & Scanlon, K. S. (2004). Attitudes, practices, and concerns about child feeding and child weight status among socioeconomically diverse white, Hispanic, and African-American mothers. *Journal of the American Dietetic Association, 104,* 215–221.

Shimada, S., & Hiraki, K. (2006). Infant's brain responses to live and televised action. *NeuroImage, 32,* 930–939.

Shimizu, H. (2001). Japanese adolescent boys' senses of empathy (omoiyari) and Carol Gilligan's perspectives on the morality of care: A phenomenological approach. *Culture and Psychology, 7,* 453–475.

Shinn, M., Schteingart, J. S., Williams, N. C., Carlin-Mathis, J., Bialo-Karagis, N., Becker-Klein, R., & Weitzman, B. C. (2008). Long-term associations of homelessness with children's well-being. *American Behavioral Scientist, 51,* 789–809.

Shipman, H. L., Brickhouse, N. W., Dagher, Z., & Letts, W. J., IV. (2002). Changes in student views of religion and science in a college astronomy course. *Science Education, 86,* 526–547.

Shipman, K. L., Zeman, J., Nesin, A. E., & Fitzgerald, M. (2003). Children's strategies for displaying anger and sadness: What works with whom? *Merrill-Palmer Quarterly, 49,* 100–122.

Shonkoff, J., & Phillips, D. (Eds.). (2001). *Neurons to neighborhoods: The science of early childhood development.* Washington, DC: National Academy Press.

Shulman, S., & Kipnis, O. (2001). Adolescent romantic relationships: A look from the future. *Journal of Adolescence, 24,* 337–351.

Shwalb, D. W., Nakawaza, J., Yamamoto, T., & Hyun, J.-H. (2004). Fathering in Japanese, Chinese, and Korean cultures: A review of the research literature. In M. E. Lamb (Ed.), *The role of the father in child development* (4th ed., pp. 146–181). Hoboken, NJ: Wiley.

Shweder, R. A., Goodnow, J. J., Hatano, G., LeVine, R. A., Markus, H. R., & Miller, P. J. (2006). The cultural psychology of development: One mind, many mentalities. In R. M. Lerner (Ed.), *Handbook of child psychology: Vol. 1. Theoretical models of human development* (6th ed., pp. 716–792). Hoboken, NJ: Wiley.

Sidappa, A., Georgieff, M. K., Wewerka, S., Worwa, C., Nelson, C. A., & deRegnier, R. (2004). Iron deficiency alters auditory recognition memory in newborn infants of diabetic mothers. *Pediatric Research, 55,* 1034–1041.

Sidebotham, P., Heron, J., & the ALSPAC Study Team. (2003). Child maltreatment in the "children of the nineties": The role of the child. *Child Abuse and Neglect, 27,* 337–352.

Siebenbruner, J., Zimmer-Gembeck, M. J., & Egeland, B. (2007). Sexual partners and contraceptive use: A 16-year prospective study predicting abstinence and risk behavior. *Journal of Research on Adolescence, 17,* 179–206.

Siebert, A. C., & Kerns, K. A. (2009). Attachment figures in middle childhood. *International Journal of Behavioral Development, 33,* 347–355.

Siegal, M., Iozzi, L., & Surian, L. (2009). Bilingualism and conversational understanding in young children. *Cognition, 110,* 115–122.

Sieger, K., & Renk, K. (2007). Pregnant and parenting adolescents: A study of ethnic identity, emotional and behavioral functioning, child characteristics, and social support. *Journal of Youth and Adolescence, 36,* 567–581.

Siegler, R. S. (1996). *Emerging minds: The process of change in children's thinking.* New York: Oxford University Press.

Siegler, R. S. (2002). Microgenetic studies of self-explanation. In N. Granott & J. Parziale (Eds.), *Microdevelopment: Transition processes in development and learning* (pp. 31–58). New York: Cambridge University Press.

Siegler, R. S. (2006). Microgenetic analyses of learning. In D. Kuhn & R. Siegler (Eds.), *Handbook of child psychology: Vol. 2. Cognition, perception, and language* (6th ed., pp. 464–510). Hoboken, NJ: Wiley.

Siegler, R. S. (2007). Cognitive variability. *Developmental Science, 10,* 104–109.

Siegler, R. S. (2009). Improving preschoolers' number sense using information-processing theory. In O. A. Barbarin & B. H. Wasik (Eds.), *Handbook of child development and early education: Research to practice* (pp. 429–454). New York: Guilford.

Siegler, R. S., & Alibali, M. W. (2005). *Children's thinking* (4th ed.). Upper Saddle River, NJ: Prentice-Hall.

Siegler, R. S., & Booth, J. L. (2004). Development of numerical estimation in young children. *Child Development, 75,* 428–444.

Siegler, R. S., & Crowley, K. (1991). The microgenetic method: A direct means for studying cognitive development. *American Psychologist, 46,* 606–620.

Siegler, R. S., & Jenkins, E. A. (1989). *How children discover new strategies.* Hillsdale, NJ: Erlbaum.

Siegler, R. S., & Mu, Y. (2008). Chinese children excel on novel mathematics problems even before elementary school. *Psychological Science, 19,* 759–763.

Siegler, R. S., & Svetina, M. (2006). What leads children to adopt new strategies? A microgenetic/cross-sectional study of class inclusion. *Child Development, 77,* 997–1015.

Siervogel, R. M., Maynard, L. M., Wisemandle, W. A., Roche, A. F., Guo, S. S., Chumlea, W. C., & Towne, B. (2000). Annual changes in total body fat and fat-free mass in children from 8 to 18 years in relation to changes in body mass index: The Fels Longitudinal Study. *Annals of the New York Academy of Sciences, 904,* 420–423.

Sigman, M. (1995). Nutrition and child development: More food for thought. *Current Directions in Psychological Science, 4,* 52–55.

Signorielli, N. (2001). Television's gender-role images and contribution to stereotyping. In D. G. Singer & J. L. Singer (Eds.), *Handbook of children and the media* (pp. 341–358). Thousand Oaks, CA: Sage.

Silk, J. S., Morris, A. S., Kanaya, T., & Steinberg, L. D. (2003). Psychological control and autonomy granting: Opposite ends of a continuum or distinct constructs? *Journal of Research on Adolescence, 13,* 113–128.

Silk, J. S., Sessa, F. M., Morris, A. S., Steinberg, L., & Avenevoli, S. (2004). Neighborhood cohesion as a buffer against hostile maternal parenting. *Journal of Family Psychology, 18,* 135–146.

Silvén, M. (2001). Attention in very young infants predicts learning of first words. *Infant Behavior and Development, 24,* 229–237.

Silver, E. J., & Bauman, L. J. (2006). The association of sexual experience with attitudes, beliefs, and risk behaviors of inner-city adolescents. *Journal of Research on Adolescence, 16,* 29–45.

Silverman, I., Choi, J., & Peters, M. (2007). The hunter-gatherer theory of sex differences in spatial abilities. *Archives of Sexual Behavior, 36,* 261–268.

Silverman, J. G., Raj, A., Mucci, L. A., & Hathaway, J. E. (2001). Dating violence against adolescent girls and associated substance use, unhealthy weight control, sexual risk behavior, pregnancy, and suicidality. *Journal of the American Medical Association, 286,* 572–579.

Silverman, W. K., & Pina, A. A. (2008). Psychosocial treatments for phobic and anxiety disorders in youth. In R. G. Steele, T. D. Elkin, & M. Roberts (Eds.), *Handbook of evidence-based therapies for children and adolescents: Bridging science and practice* (pp. 65–82). New York: Springer.

Sim, T. N., & Koh, S. F. (2003). A domain conceptualization of adolescent susceptibility to peer pressure. *Journal of Research on Adolescence, 13,* 57–80.

Simcock, G., & DeLoache, J. (2006). Get the picture? The effects of iconicity on toddlers' reenactment from picture books. *Developmental Psychology, 42,* 1352–1357.

Simcock, G., & Hayne, H. (2002). Breaking the barrier? Children fail to translate their preverbal memories into language. *Psychological Science, 13,* 225–231.

Simcock, G., & Hayne, H. (2003). Age-related changes in verbal and nonverbal memory during early childhood. *Developmental Psychology, 39,* 805–814.

Simion, F., Cassia, V. M., Turati, C., & Valenza, E. (2001). The origins of face perception: Specific versus non-specific mechanisms. *Infant and Child Development, 10,* 59–65.

Simmons, R. G., & Blyth, D. A. (1987). *Moving into adolescence.* New York: Aldine De Gruyter.

Simoneau, M., & Markovits, H. (2003). Reasoning with premises that are not empirically true: Evidence for the role of inhibition and retrieval. *Developmental Psychology, 39,* 964–975.

Simons, L. G., Chen, Y. F., Simons, R. L., Brody, G., & Cutrona, C. (2006). Parenting practices and child adjustment in different types of households: A study of African-American families. *Journal of Family Issues, 27,* 803–825.

Simons, R. L., Whitbeck, L. B., Conger, R. D., & Chyi-In, W. (1991). Intergenerational transmission of harsh parenting. *Developmental Psychology, 27,* 159–171.

Simons-Morton, B. G., & Haynie, D. L. (2003). Growing up drug free: A developmental challenge. In M. H. Bornstein, L. Davidson, C. L. M. Keyes, K. A. Moore, & the Center for Child Well-Being (Eds.), *Well-being: Positive development across the life course* (pp. 109–122). Mahwah, NJ: Erlbaum.

Simonton, D. K. (2009). Giftedness: The gift that keeps on giving. In T. Balchin, B. Hymer, & D. J. Matthews (Eds.), *The Routledge international companion to gifted education* (pp. 26–31). New York: Routledge.

Simpson, J. A., Rholes, W. S., Campbell, L., Tran, S., & Wilson, C. L. (2003). Adult attachment, the transition to parenthood, and depressive symptoms. *Journal of Personality and Social Psychology, 84,* 1172–1187.

Simpson, J. L., de la Cruz, F., Swerdloff, R. S., Samango-Sprouse, C., Skakkebaek, N. E., & Graham, J. M., Jr. (2003). Klinefelter syndrome: Expanding the phenotype and identifying new research directions. *Genetic Medicine, 5,* 460–468.

Singer, D. G., & Singer, J. L. (2005). *Imagination and play in the electronic age.* Cambridge, MA: Harvard University Press.

Singer, L. T., Minnes, S., Short, E., Arendt, R., Farkas, K., Lewis, B., & Klein, N. (2004). Cognitive outcomes of preschool children with prenatal cocaine exposure. *Journal of the American Medical Association, 291,* 2448–2456.

Singleton, J. L., & Newport, E. L. (2004). When learners surpass their models: The acquisition of American Sign Language from inconsistent input. *Cognitive Psychology, 49,* 370–407.

Sinkkonen, J., Anttila, R., & Siimes, M. A. (1998). Pubertal maturation and changes in self-image in early adolescent Finnish boys. *Journal of Youth and Adolescence, 27,* 209–218.

Sinnott, J. D. (2003). Postformal thought and adult development: Living in balance. In J. Demic & C. Andreoletti (Eds.), *Handbook of adult development* (pp. 221–238). New York: Kluwer Academic.

Sirios, S., & Jackson, I. (2007). Social cognition in infancy: A critical review of research on higher-order abilities. *European Journal of Developmental Psychology, 4,* 46–64.

Sirsch, U., Erher, E., Mayr, E., & Willinger, U. (2009). What does it take to be an adult in Austria? *Journal of Adolescent Research, 24,* 275–292.

Skiba, R. J., & Rausch, M. K. (2006). Zero tolerance, suspension, and expulsion: Questions of equity and effectiveness. In C. M. Evertson & C. S. Weinstein (Eds.), *Handbook of classroom management: Research, practice, and contemporary issues* (pp. 1063–1089). Mahwah, NJ: Erlbaum.

Skoe, E. S. A. (1998). The ethic of care: Issues in moral development. In E. E. A. Skoe & A. L. von der Lippe (Eds.), *Personality development in adolescence* (pp. 143–171). London: Routledge.

Skinner, B. F. (1957). *Verbal behavior.* New York: Appleton-Century-Crofts.

Skinner, E. A., Zimmer-Gembeck, M. J., & Connell, J. P. (1998). Individual differences and the development of perceived control. *Monographs of the Society for Research in Child Development, 63*(2–3, Serial No. 254).

Slack, K. S., & Yoo, J. (2005). Food hardship and child behavior problems among low-income children. *Social Service Review, 79,* 511–536.

Slade, A., Belsky, J., Aber, J. L., & Phelps, J. L. (1999). Mothers' representations of their relationships with their toddlers: Links to adult attachment and observed mothering. *Developmental Psychology, 35,* 611–619.

Slater, A. (2001). Visual perception. In G. Bremner & A. Fogel (Eds.), *Blackwell handbook of infant development* (pp. 5–34). Malden, MA: Blackwell.

Slater, A., Bremner, G., Johnson, S. P., Sherwood, P., Hayes, R., & Brown, E. (2000). Newborn infants' preference for attractive faces: The role of internal and external facial features. *Infancy, 1,* 265–274.

Slater, A., Brown, E., Mattock, A., & Bornstein, M. H. (1996). Continuity and change in habituation in the first 4 months from birth. *Journal of Reproductive and Infant Psychology, 14,* 187–194.

Slater, A., & Johnson, S. P. (1999). Visual sensory and perceptual abilities of the newborn: Beyond the blooming, buzzing confusion. In A. Slater & S. P. Johnson (Eds.), *The development of sensory, motor and cognitive capacities in early infancy* (pp. 121–141). Hove, UK: Sussex Press.

Slater, A., & Quinn, P. C. (2001). Face recognition in the newborn infant. *Infant and Child Development, 10,* 21–24.

Sleet, D. A., & Mercy, J. A. (2003). Promotion of safety, security, and well-being. In M. H. Bornstein, L. Davidson, C. M. M. Keyes, K. A. Moore, & the Center for Child Well-Being (Eds.), *Well-being: Positive development across the life course* (pp. 81–97). Mahwah, NJ: Erlbaum.

Sloan, S., Gildea, A., Stewart, M., Sneddon, H., & Iwaniec, D. (2008). Early weaning is related to weight and rate of weight gain in infancy. *Child: Care, Health and Development, 34,* 59–64.

Slobin, D. I. (1985). Cross-linguistic evidence for language-making capacity. In D. I. Slobin (Ed.), *The cross-linguistic study of language acquisition: Vol. 2. Theoretical issues* (pp. 1157–1256). Hillsdale, NJ: Erlbaum.

Slobin, D. I. (1997). On the origin of grammaticalizable notions: Beyond the individual mind. In D. I. Slobin (Ed.), *The cross-linguistic study of language acquisition: Vol. 5* (pp. 265–324). Hillsdale, NJ: Erlbaum.

Slonims, V., & McConachie, H. (2006). Analysis of mother–infant interaction in infants with Down syndrome and typically developing infants. *American Journal of Mental Retardation, 111,* 273–289.

Sluzenski, J., Newcombe, N. S., & Kovacs, S. L. (2006). Binding, relational memory, and recall of naturalistic events: A developmental perspective. *Journal of Experimental Psychology: Learning, Memory, and Cognition, 32,* 89–100.

Smahel, D., & Subrahmanyam, K. (2007). "Any girls want to chat press 911": Partner selection in monitored and unmonitored teen chat rooms. *CyberPsychology and Behavior, 10,* 346–353.

Small, M. (1998). *Our babies, ourselves.* New York: Anchor.

Smart, J., & Hiscock, H. (2007). Early infant crying and sleeping problems: A pilot study of impact on parental well-being and parent-endorsed strategies for management. *Journal of Paediatrics and Child Health, 43,* 284–290.

Smetana, J. G. (2002). Culture, autonomy, and personal jurisdiction in adolescent–parent relationships. In R. V. Kail & H. W. Reese (Eds.), *Advances in child development and behavior* (Vol. 29, pp. 51–87). San Diego, CA: Academic Press.

Smetana, J. G. (2006). Social-cognitive domain theory: Consistencies and variations in children's moral and social judgments. In M. Killen & J. G. Smetana (Eds.), *Handbook of moral development* (pp. 119–154). Mahwah, NJ: Erlbaum.

Smetana, J. G., & Daddis, C. (2002). Domain-specific antecedents of parental psychological control and monitoring: The role of parenting beliefs and practices. *Child Development, 73,* 563–580.

Smith, A. N., Brief, A. P., & Colella, A. (2010). Bias in organizations. In J. F. Dovidio, M. Hewstone, P. Glick, & V. M. Esses (Eds.), *Sage handbook of prejudice, stereotyping, and discrimination* (pp. 441–456). Thousand Oaks, CA: Sage.

Smith, B. H., Barkley, R. A., & Shapiro, C. J. (2006). Attention-deficit/hyperactivity disorder. In E. J. Mash & R. A. Barkley (Eds.), *Treatment of childhood disorders* (3rd ed., pp. 65–136). New York: Guilford.

Smith, C. (2009). *Souls in transition: The religious and spiritual lives of emerging adults.* New York: Oxford University Press.

Smith, C., & Denton, M. L. (2005). *Soul searching: The religious and spiritual lives of American teenagers.* Oxford, UK: Oxford University Press.

Smith, C. L., Calkins, S. D., Keane, S. P., Anastopoulos, A. D., & Shelton, T. L. (2004). Predicting stability and change in toddler behavior problems: Contributions of maternal behavior and child gender. *Developmental Psychology, 40,* 29–42.

Smith, J. R., Brooks-Gunn, J., Kohen, D., & McCarton, C. (2001). Transitions on and off AFDC: Implications for parenting and children's cognitive development. *Child Development, 72,* 1512–1533.

Smith, J., & Ross, H. (2007). Training parents to mediate sibling disputes affects children's negotiation and conflict understanding. *Child Development, 78,* 790–805.

Smith, L. B., Jones, S. S., Landau, B., Gershkoff-Stowe, L., & Samuelson, L. (2002). Object name learning provides on-the-job training for attention. *Psychological Science, 13,* 13–19.

Smith, P. K. (2003). Play and peer relations. In A. Slater & G. Bremner (Eds.), *An introduction to developmental psychology* (pp. 311–333). Malden, MA: Blackwell.

Smith, P., Perrin, S., Yule, W., & Rabe-Hesketh, S. (2001). War exposure and maternal reactions in the psychological adjustment of children from Bosnia-Hercegovina. *Journal of Child Psychology and Psychiatry and Allied Disciplines, 42,* 395–404.

Smith, R. (2007). Parturition. *New England Journal of Medicine, 356,* 271–283.

Smith, R., Smith, J. I., Shen, X., Engel, P. J., Bowman, M. E., McGrath, S. A., et al. (2009). Patterns of plasma corticotrophin-releasing hormone, progesterone, estradiol and estriol change and the onset of human lablor. *Journal of Clinical Endocrinology and Metabolism, 94,* 2066–2074.

Snarey, J. R., & Bell, D. (2003). Distinguishing structural and functional models of human development: A response to "what transits in an identity status transition?" *Identity, 3,* 221–230.

Snarey, J. R., Reimer, J., & Kohlberg, L. (1985). The development of social–moral reasoning among kibbutz adolescents: A longitudinal cross-cultural study. *Developmental Psychology, 21,* 3–17.

Snell, E. K., Adam, E. K., & Duncan, G. J. (2007). Sleep and the body mass index and overweight status of children and adolescents. *Child Development, 78,* 309–323.

Snell, P. (2010). Emerging adult civic and political disengagement: A longitudinal analysis of lack of involvement with politics. *Journal of Adolescent Research, 25,* 258–287.

Snidman, N., Kagan, J., Riordan, L., & Shannon, D. C. (1995). Cardiac function and behavioral reactivity. *Psychophysiology, 32,* 199–207.

Snow, C. E., & Beals, D. E. (2006). Mealtime talk that supports literacy development. In R. W. Larson, A. R. Wiley, & K. R. Branscomb (Eds.), *Family mealtime as a context of development and socialization* (pp. 51–66). San Francisco: Jossey-Bass.

Snow, C. E., & Kang, J. Y. (2006). Becoming bilingual, biliterate, and bicultural. In K. A. Renninger & I. E. Sigel (Eds.), *Handbook of child psychology: Vol. 4. Child psychology in practice* (6th ed., pp. 75–102). Hoboken, NJ: Wiley.

Snow, C. E., Pan, B. A., Imbens-Bailey, A., & Herman, J. (1996). Learning how to say what one means: A longitudinal study of children's speech act use. *Social Development, 5,* 56–84.

Snyder, J., Brooker, M., Patrick, M. R., Snyder, A., Schrepferman, L., & Stoolmiller, M. (2003). Observed peer victimization during early elementary school: Continuity, growth, and relation to risk for child antisocial and depressive behavior. *Child Development, 74,* 1881–1898.

Sobel, D. M. (2006). How fantasy benefits young children's understanding of pretense. *Developmental Science, 9,* 63–75.

Society for Research in Child Development. (2007). *SRCD ethical standards for research with children.* Retrieved from www.srcd.org/index.php?option= com_content&task=view&id=68&Itemid=110

Society of Obstetricians and Gynaecologists. (2008). *Record high caesarean rate raising concerns among Canada's obstetricians.* Retrieved from www.sogcorg/media/pdf/articles/artcaesareanrate080625.pdf

Soderstrom, M., Seidl, A., Nelson, D. G. K., & Jusczyk, P. W. (2003). The prosodic bootstrapping of phrases: Evidence from prelinguistic infants. *Journal of Memory and Language, 49,* 249–267.

Solomon, G. B., & Bredemeier, B. J. L. (1999). Children's moral conceptions of gender stratification in sport. *International Journal of Sport Psychology, 30,* 350–368.

Solomon, G. E. A., & Johnson, S. C. (2000). Conceptual change in the classroom: Teaching young children to understand biological inheritance. *British Journal of Development Psychology, 18,* 81–96.

Sondergaard, C., Henriksen, T. B., Obel, C., & Wisborg, K. (2002). Smoking during pregnancy and infantile colic. *Journal of the American Academy of Child and Adolescent Psychiatry, 41,* 147.

Sonuga-Barke, E. J, Schlotz, W., & Kreppner, J. (2010). Differentiating developmental trajectories for conduct, emotion, and peer problems following early deprivation. *Monographs of the Society for Research in Child Development, 75*(1, Serial No. 295),102–124.

Sophian, C. (1995). Representation and reasoning in early numerical development: Counting, conservation, and comparisons between sets. *Child Development, 66,* 559–577.

Sosa, R., Kennell, J., Klaus, M., Robertson, S., & Urrutia, J. (1980). The effect of a supportive companion on perinatal problems, length of labor, and mother–infant interaction. *New England Journal of Medicine, 303,* 597–600.

South African Department of Health. (2009). *2008 National Antenatal Sentinel HIV and Syphilis Prevalence Survey.* Retrieved from www.doh.gov.za/docs/nassps-f.html

Sowell, E. R., Thompson, P. M., Welcome, S. E., Henkenius, A. L., Toga, A. W., & Peterson, B. S. (2003). Cortical abnormalities in children and adolescents with attention-deficit hyperactivity disorder. *Lancet, 362,* 1699–1707.

Sowell, E. R., Trauner, D. A., Camst, A., & Jernigan, T. (2002). Development of cortical and subcortical brain structures in childhood and adolescence: A structural MRI study. *Developmental Medicine and Child Neurology, 44,* 4–16.

Spadoni, A. D., McGee, C. L., Fryer, S. L., & Riley, E. P. (2007). Neuroimaging and fetal alcohol spectrum disorders. *Neuroscience and Biobehavioral Reviews, 31,* 239–245.

Spangler, G., Fremmer-Bomik, E., & Grossmann, K. (1996). Social and individual determinants of attachment security and disorganization during the first year. *Infant Mental Health Journal, 17,* 127–139.

Spear, L. P. (2008). The psychobiology of adolescence. In K. K. Kline (Ed.), *Authoritative communities: The scientific case for nurturing the whole child* (pp. 263–280). New York: Springer Science + Business Media.

Spector, A. Z. (2006). Fatherhood and depression: A review of risks, effects, and clinical application. *Issues in Mental Health Nursing, 27,* 867–883.

Speece, D. L., Ritchey, K. D., Cooper, D. H., Roth, F. P., & Schatschneider, C. (2004). Growth in early reading skills from kindergarten to third grade. *Contemporary Educational Psychology, 29,* 312–332.

Spelke, E. (2000). Core knowledge. *American Psychologist, 55,* 1233–1242.

Spelke, E. S. (2004). Core knowledge. In N. Kanwisher & J. Duncan (Eds.), *Attention and Performance* (Vol. 20, pp. 29–56). Oxford, UK: Oxford University Press.

Spelke, E. S., & Hermer, L. (1996). Early cognitive development: Objects and space. In R. Gelman & T. K. Au (Eds.), *Perceptual and cognitive development* (pp. 71–114). San Diego: Academic Press.

Spelke, E. S., & Kinzler, K. D. (2007). Core knowledge. *Developmental Science, 10,* 89–96.

Spelke, E. S., Phillips, A., & Woodward, A. L. (1995). Infants' knowledge of object motion and human action. In D. Sperber, D. Premack, & A. J. Premack (Eds.), *Causal cognition: A multidisciplinary debate* (pp. 44–78). New York: Oxford University Press.

Spence, I., & Feng, J. (2010). Video games and spatial cognition. *Review of General Psychology, 14,* 92–104.

Spence, M. J., & DeCasper, A. J. (1987). Prenatal experience with low-frequency maternal voice sounds influences neonatal perception of maternal voice samples. *Infant Behavior and Development, 10,* 133–142.

Spencer, J. P., & Perone, S. (2008). Defending qualitative change: The view from dynamical systems theory. *Child Development, 79,* 1639–1647.

Spencer, J. P., & Schöner, G. (2003). Bridging the representational gap in the dynamic systems approach to development. *Developmental Science, 6,* 392–412.

Spencer, J. P., Verejiken, B., Diedrich, F. J., & Thelen, E. (2000). Posture and the emergence of manual skills. *Developmental Science, 3,* 216–233.

Spencer, P. E. (2000). Looking without listening: Is audition a prerequisite for normal development of visual attention in infancy? *Journal of Deaf Studies and Education, 5,* 291–302.

Spencer, P. E., & Lederberg, A. (1997). Different modes, different models: Communication and language of young deaf children and their mothers. In L. B. Adamson & M. Romski (Eds.), *Communication and language acquisition: Discoveries from atypical development* (pp. 203–230). Baltimore: Paul H. Brookes.

Spencer, P. E., & Meadow-Orlans, K. P. (1996). Play, language, and maternal responsiveness: A longitudinal study of deaf and hearing infants. *Child Development, 67,* 3176–3191.

Spera, C. (2005). A review of the relationship among parenting practices, parenting styles, and adolescent school achievement. *Educational Psychology Review, 17,* 125–146.

Spere, K. A., Schmidt, L. A., Theall-Honey, L. A., & Martin-Chang, S. (2004). Expressive and receptive language skills of temperamentally shy preschoolers. *Infant and Child Development, 13,* 123–133.

Spirito, A., & Esposito-Smythers, C. (2006). Attempted and completed suicide. *Annual Review of Clinical Psychology, 2,* 237–266.

Spirito, A., Valeri, S., Boergers, J., & Donaldson, D. (2003). Predictors of continued suicidal behavior in adolescents following a suicide attempt. *Journal of Clinical Child and Adolescent Psychology, 32,* 284–289.

Spitz, R. A. (1946). Anaclitic depression. *Psychoanalytic Study of the Child, 2,* 313–342.

Spock, B., & Needlman, R. (2004). *Dr. Spock's baby and child care* (8th ed.). New York: Pocket.

Spokane, A. R., & Cruza-Guet, M. C. (2005). Holland's theory of vocational personalities in work environments. In S. D. Brown & R. W. Lent (Eds.), *Career development and counseling* (pp. 24–41). Hoboken, NJ: Wiley.

Sporer, N., Brunstein, J. C., & Kieschke, U. (2009). Improving students' reading comprehension skills: Effects of strategy instruction and reciprocal teaching. *Learning and Instruction, 19,* 272–286.

Sprecher, S. (2009). Relationship initiation and formation on the Internet. *Marriage & Family Review, 45,* 761–782.

Spruijt-Metz, D., Lindquist, C. H., Birch, L. L., Fisher, J. O., & Goran, M. I. (2002). Relation between mothers' child-feeding practices and children's adiposity. *American Journal of Clinical Nutrition, 75,* 581–586.

Sridhar, D., & Vaughn, S. (2001). Social functioning of students with learning disabilities. In D. P. Hallahan & B. K. Keogh (Eds.), *Research and global perspectives in learning disabilities* (pp. 65–91). Mahwah, NJ: Erlbaum.

Sroufe, L. A. (2002). From infant attachment to promotion of adolescent autonomy: Prospective, longitudinal data on the role of parents in development. In J. G. Borkowski & S. L. Ramey (Eds.), *Parenting and the child's world* (pp. 187–202). Mahwah, NJ: Erlbaum.

Sroufe, L. A. (2005). Attachment and development: A prospective, longitudinal study from birth to adulthood. *Attachment and Human Development, 7,* 349–367.

Sroufe, L. A., Egeland, B., Carlson, E., & Collins, W. (2005). *Minnesota Study of Risk and Adaptation from birth to maturity: The development of the person.* New York: Guilford.

Sroufe, L. A., & Waters, E. (1976). The ontogenesis of smiling and laughter: A perspective on the organization of development in infancy. *Psychological Review, 83,* 173–189.

Sroufe, L. A., & Wunsch, J. P. (1972). The development of laughter in the first year of life. *Child Development, 43,* 1324–1344.

St James-Roberts, I. (2007). Infant crying and sleeping: Helping parents to prevent and manage problems. *Sleep Medicine Clinics, 2,* 363–375.

St James-Roberts, I., Alvarez, M., Csipke, E., Abramsky, T., Goodwin, J., & Sorgenfrei, E. (2006). Infant crying and sleeping in London, Copenhagen and when parents adopt a "proximal" form of care. *Pediatrics, 117,* e1146–e1155.

St. Louis, G. R., & Liem, J. H. (2005). Ego identity, ethnic identity, and the psychosocial well-being of ethnic minority and majority college students. *Identity, 5,* 227–246.

Stacey, J., & Biblarz, T. (2001). (How) Does the sexual orientation of parents matter? *American Sociological Review, 66,* 159–183.

Staff, J., & Uggen, C. (2003). The fruits of good work: Early work experiences and adolescent deviance. *Journal of Research in Crime and Delinquency, 40,* 263–290.

Stahl, S. A., & Miller, P. D. (2006). Whole language and language experience approaches for beginning reading: A quantitative research synthesis. In K. A. Dougherty Stahl & M. C. McKenna (Eds.), *Reading research at work: Foundations of effective practice* (pp. 9–35). New York: Guilford.

Stams, G. J. M., Brugman, D., Deković, M., van Rosmalen, L., van der Laan, P., & Gibbs, J. C. (2006). The moral judgment of juvenile delinquents: A meta-analysis. *Journal of Abnormal Child Psychology, 34,* 697–713.

Stams, G. J. M., Juffer, F., & van IJzendoorn, M. H. (2002). Maternal sensitivity, infant attachment, and temperament in early childhood predict adjustment in middle childhood: The case of adopted children and their biologically unrelated parents. *Developmental Psychology, 38,* 806–821.

Standley, J. M. (1998). The effect of music and multimodal stimulation on responses of premature infants in neonatal intensive care. *Pediatric Nursing, 24,* 532–538.

Stanley, C., Murray, L., & Stein, A. (2004). The effect of postnatal depression on mother–infant interaction, infant response to the still-face perturbation, and performance on an instrumental learning task. *Development and Psychopathology, 16,* 1–18.

Stanovich, K. E. (2007). *How to think straight about psychology* (8th ed.). Boston: Allyn and Bacon.

Stattin, H., & Magnusson, D. (1990). *Pubertal maturation in female development.* Hillsdale, NJ: Erlbaum.

Staub, F. C., & Stern, E. (2002). The nature of teachers' pedagogical content beliefs matters for students' achievement gains: Quasi-experimental evidence from elementary mathematics. *Journal of Educational Psychology, 94,* 344–355.

Stearns, E., & Glennie, E. J. (2006). When and why dropouts leave high school. *Youth and Society, 38,* 29–57.

Steele, C. M. (1997). A threat in the air: How stereotypes shape intellectual identity and performance. *American Psychologist, 52,* 613–629.

Steele, J. (2003). Children's gender stereotypes about math: The role of stereotype stratification. *Journal of Applied Social Psychology, 33,* 2587–2606.

Steele, S., Joseph, R. M., & Tager-Flusberg, H. (2003). Developmental change in theory of mind abilities in children with autism. *Journal of Austism and Developmental Disorders, 33,* 461–467.

Steenhuis, I. H., & Vermeer, W. M. (2009). Portion size: Review and framework for interventions. *International Journal of Behavioral Nutrition and Physical Activity, 6,* 58.

Stehr-Green, P., Tull, P., Stellfeld, M., Mortenson, P. B., & Simpson, D. (2003). Autism and thimerosal-containing vaccines: Lack of consistent evidence for an association. *American Journal of Preventive Medicine, 25,* 101–106.

Stein, J. H., & Reiser, L. W. (1994). A study of white middle-class adolescent boys' responses to "semenarche" (the first ejaculation). *Journal of Youth and Adolescence, 23,* 373–384.

Stein, N., & Levine, L. J. (1999). The early emergence of emotional understanding and appraisal: Implications for theories of development. In T. Dalgleish & M. J. Power (Eds.), *Handbook of cognition and emotion* (pp. 383–408). Chichester, UK: Wiley.

Stein, Z., Susser, M., Saenger, G., & Marolla, F. (1975). *Famine and human development: The Dutch hunger winter of 1944–1945.* New York: Oxford.

Steinberg, L. (2001). We know some things: Parent–adolescent relationships in retrospect and prospect. *Journal of Research on Adolescence, 11,* 1–19.

Steinberg, L. (2008). A social neuroscience perspective on adolescent risk-taking. *Developmental Review, 28,* 78–106.

Steinberg, L., Albert, D., Cauffman, E., Banich, M., & Graham, S. (2008). Age differences in sensation seeking and impulsivity as indexed by behavior and self-report: Evidence for a dual systems model. *Developmental Psychology, 44,* 1764–1778.

Steinberg, L., Blatt-Eisengart, I., & Cauffman, E. (2006). Patterns of competence and adjustment among adolescents from authoritative, authoritarian, indulgent, and neglectful homes: A replication in a sample of serious juvenile offenders. *Journal of Research on Adolescence, 16,* 47–58.

Steinberg, L., Darling, N. E., & Fletcher, A. C. (1995). Authoritative parenting and adolescent development: An ecological journey. In P. Moen, G. H. Elder, Jr., & K. Luscher (Eds.), *Examining lives in context* (pp. 423–466). Washington, DC: American Psychological Association.

Steinberg, L., Graham, S., O'Brien, L., Woolard, J., Cauffman, E., & Banich, M. (2009). Age differences in future orientation and delay discounting. *Child Development, 80,* 28–44.

Steinberg, L., & Monahan, K. C. (2007). Age differences in resistance to peer influence. *Developmental Psychology, 43,* 1531–1543.

Steinberg, L., & Monahan, K. C. (2010). Adolescents' exposure to sexy media does not hasten the initiation of sexual intercourse. *Developmental Psychology, 46* [in press]. Retrieved from www.temple.edu/ psychology/lds/documents/Exposure_to_Sexy _Media_proof.pdf

Steinberg, L., & Silk, J. S. (2002). Parenting adolescents. In M. H. Bornstein (Ed.), *Handbook of parenting: Vol. 1. Children and parenting* (pp. 103–134). Mahwah, NJ: Erlbaum.

Steiner, J. E. (1979). Human facial expression in response to taste and smell stimulation. In H. W. Reese & L. P. Lipsitt (Eds.), *Advances in child development and behavior* (Vol. 13, pp. 257–295). New York: Academic Press.

Steiner, J. E., Glaser, D., Hawilo, M. E., & Berridge, D. C. (2001). Comparative expression of hedonic impact: Affective reactions to taste by human infants and other primates. *Neuroscience and Biobehavioral Reviews, 25,* 53–74.

Steinhausen, C. (2006). Eating disorders: Anorexia nervosa and bulimia nervosa. In C. Gillberg, R. Harrington, & H. Steinhausen (Eds.), *A clinician's handbook of child and adolescent psychiatry* (pp. 272–303). New York: Cambridge University Press.

Stenberg, C. R., & Campos, J. J. (1990). The development of anger expressions in infancy. In N. Stein, B. Leventhal, & T. Trabasso (Eds.), *Psychological and biological approaches to emotion* (pp. 247–282). Hillsdale, NJ: Erlbaum.

Stenberg, G. (2003). Effects of maternal inattentiveness on infant social referencing. *Infant and Child Development, 12,* 399–419.

Stephens, B. E., & Vohr, B. R. (2009). Neurodevelopmental outcome of the premature infant. *Pediatric Clinics of North America, 56,* 631–646.

Stephens, P. C., Sloboda, Z., Stephens, R. C., Teasdale, B., Grey, S. F., Hawthorne, R. D., & Williams, J. (2009). Universal school-based substance abuse prevention programs: Modeling targeted mediators and outcomes for adolescent cigarette, alcohol, and marijuana use. *Drug and Alcohol Dependence, 102,* 19–29.

Stern, D. (1985). *The interpersonal world of the infant.* New York: Basic Books.

Stern, M., & Karraker, K. H. (1989). Sex stereotyping of infants: A review of gender labeling studies. *Sex Roles, 20,* 501–522.

Sternberg, R. J. (2001). Beyond g: The theory of successful intelligence. In R. J. Sternberg & E. L. Grigorenko (Eds.), *The general factor of intelligence: How general is it?* (pp. 447–479). Mahwah, NJ: Erlbaum.

Sternberg, R. J. (2003). The development of creativity as a decision-making process. In R. K. Sawyer, V. John-Steiner, S. Moran, R. J. Sternberg, D. H. Feldman, J. Nakamura, & M. Csikszentmihalyi (Eds.), *Creativity and development* (pp. 91–138). New York: Oxford University Press.

Sternberg, R. J. (2005). The triarchic theory of successful intelligence. In D. P. Flanagan & P. L. Harrison (Eds.), *Contemporary intellectual assessment: Theories, tests, and issues* (pp. 103–119). New York: Guilford.

Sternberg, R. J. (2008). The triarchic theory of successful intelligence. In N. Salkind (Ed.), *Encyclopedia of educational psychology* (Vol. 2, pp. 988–994). Thousand Oaks, CA: Sage.

Sternberg, R. J., Forsythe, G. B., Hedlund, J., Horvath, J. A., Wagner, R. K., Williams, W. M., Snook, S. A., & Grigorenko, E. L. (2000). *Practical intelligence in everyday life.* Cambridge, UK: Cambridge University Press.

Sternberg, R. J., & Grigorenko, E. L. (2002). *Dynamic testing.* New York: Cambridge University Press.

Sternberg, R. J., & Jarvin, L. (2003). Alfred Binet's contributions as a paradigm for impact in psychology. In R. J. Sternberg (Ed.), *The anatomy of impact: What makes the great works of psychology great* (pp. 89–107). Washington, DC: American Psychological Association.

Stetsenko, A., Little, T. D., Gordeeva, T., Grasshof, M., & Oettingen, G. (2000). Gender effects in children's beliefs about school performance. *Child Development, 21,* 517–527.

Stevens-Simon, C., Sheeder, J., & Harter, S. (2005). Teen contraceptive decisions: Childbearing intentions are the tip of the iceberg. *Women and Health, 42,* 55–73.

Stevenson, H. W., Lee, S., & Mu, X. (2000). Successful achievement in mathematics: China and the United States. In C. F. M. van Lieshout & P. G. Heymans (Eds.), *Developing talent across the lifespan* (pp. 167–183). Philadelphia: Psychology Press.

Stevenson, R., & Pollitt, C. (1987). The acquisition of temporal terms. *Journal of Child Language, 14,* 533–545.

Stewart, P. W., Lonky, E., Reihman, J., Pagano, J., Gump, B. B., & Darvill, T. (2008). The relationship between prenatal PCB exposure and intelligence (IQ). *Environmental Health Perspectives, 116,* 1416–1422.

Stewart, R. B., Jr. (1990). *The second child: Family transition and adjustment.* Newbury Park, CA: Sage.

Stewart-Brown, S., & Edmunds, L. (2007). Assessing emotional intelligence in children: A review of existing measures of emotional and social competence. In R. Bar-On, J. M. Elias, & J. G. Maree (Eds.), *Educating people to be emotionally intelligent* (pp. 241–257). Westport, CT: Praeger.

Stice, E. (2003). Puberty and body image. In C. Hayward (Ed.), *Gender differences at puberty* (pp. 61–76). New York: Cambridge University Press.

Stice, E., Presnell, K., & Bearman, S. K. (2001). Relation of early menarche to depression, eating disorders, substance abuse, and comorbid psychopathology among adolescent girls. *Developmental Psychology, 37,* 608–619.

Stiles, J. (2001a). Neural plasticity in cognitive development. *Developmental Neuropsychology, 18,* 237–272.

Stiles, J. (2001b). Spatial cognitive development. In C. A. Nelson & M. Luciana (Eds.), *Handbook of developmental cognitive neuroscience* (pp. 399–414). Cambridge, MA: MIT Press.

Stiles, J. (2008). *Fundamentals of brain development.* Cambridge, MA: Harvard University Press.

Stiles, J., Bates, E. A., Thal, D., Trauner, D. A., & Reilly, J. (2002). Linguistic and spatial cognitive development in children with pre- and perinatal focal brain injury: A ten-year overview from the San Diego longitudinal project. In M. H. Johnson & Y. Munakata (Eds.), *Brain development and cognition: A reader* (2nd ed., pp. 272–291). Malden, MA: Blackwell.

Stiles, J., Moses, P., Roe, K., Akshoomoff, N. A., Trauner, D., & Hesselink, J. (2003). Alternative brain organization after prenatal cerebral injury: Convergent fMRI and cognitive data. *Journal of the International Neuropsychological Society, 9,* 604–622.

Stiles, J., Reilly, J., Paul, B., & Moses, P. (2005). Cognitive development following early brain injury: Evidence for neural adaptation. *Trends in Cognitive Sciences, 9,* 136–143.

Stiles, J., Stern, C., Appelbaum, M., & Nass, R. (2008). Effects of early focal brain injury on memory for visuospatial patterns: Selective deficits of global–local processing. *Neuropsychology, 22,* 61–73.

Stilson, S. R., & Harding, C. G. (1997). Early social context as it relates to symbolic play: A longitudinal investigation. *Merrill-Palmer Quarterly, 43,* 682–693.

Stinchcomb, J. B., Bazemore, G., & Riestenberg, N. (2006). Beyond zero tolerance: Restoring justice in secondary schools. *Youth Violence and Juvenile Justice, 4,* 123–147.

Stipek, D. (2002). At what age should children enter kindergarten? A question for policy makers and parents. *Social Policy Report of the Society for Research in Child Development, 16*(3).

Stipek, D. (2004). Teaching practices in kindergarten and first grade: Different strokes for different folks. *Early Childhood Research Quarterly, 19,* 548–568.

Stipek, D. J., & Byler, P. (1997). Early childhood education teachers: Do they practice what they preach? *Early Childhood Research Quarterly, 12,* 305–326.

Stipek, D. J., & Byler, P. (2001). Academic achievement and social behaviors associated with age of entry into kindergarten. *Journal of Applied Developmental Psychology, 22,* 175–189.

Stipek, D. J., Feiler, R., Daniels, D., & Milburn, S. (1995). Effects of different instructional approaches on young children's achievement and motivation. *Child Development, 66,* 209–223.

Stipek, D. J., Gralinski, J. H., & Kopp, C. B. (1990). Self-concept development in the toddler years. *Developmental Psychology, 26,* 972–977.

Stoch, M. B., Smythe, P. M., Moodie, A. D., & Bradshaw, D. (1982). Psychosocial outcome and CT findings after growth undernourishment during infancy: A 20-year developmental study. *Developmental Medicine and Child Neurology, 24,* 419–436.

Stocker, C. J., Arch, J. R., & Cawthorne, M. A. (2005). Fetal origins of insulin resistance and obesity. *Proceedings of the Nutrition Society, 64,* 143–151.

Stone, M. R., & Brown, B. B. (1999). Identity claims and projections: Descriptions of self and crowds in secondary school. In J. A. McLellan & M. J. V. Pugh (Eds.), *The role of peer groups in adolescent social identity: Exploring the importance of stability and change* (pp. 7–20). San Francisco: Jossey-Bass.

Stone, R. (2005). *Best classroom management practices for reaching all learners: What award-winning classroom teachers do.* Thousand Oaks, CA: Corwin Press.

Storch, S. A., & Whitehurst, G. J. (2001). The role of family and home in the literacy development of children from low-income backgrounds. In P. R. Britto & J. Brooks-Gunn (Eds.), *The role of family literacy environments in promoting young children's emerging literacy skills (New directions for child and adolescent development,* No. 92, pp. 53–71). San Francisco: Jossey-Bass.

Storey, A. E., Walsh, C. J., Quinton, R. L., & Wynn-Edwards, K. E. (2000). Hormonal correlates of paternal responsiveness in new and expectant fathers. *Evolution and Human Behavior, 21,* 79–95.

Stormshak, E. A., Bierman, K. L., McMahon, R. J., Lengua, L. J., & the Conduct Problems Prevention

Research Group. (2000). Parenting practices and child disruptive behavior problems in early elementary school. *Journal of Clinical Child Psychology, 29,* 17–29.

Story, R. (2007). Asthma and obesity in children. *Current Opinion in Pediatrics, 19,* 680–684.

Stouthamer-Loeber, M., Wei, E., Loeber, R., & Masten, A. S. (2004). Desistance from persistent serious delinquency in the transition to adulthood. *Development and Psychopathology, 16,* 897–918.

Strapp, C. M., & Federico, A. (2000). Imitations and repetitions: What do children say following recasts? *First Language, 20,* 273–290.

Straus, M. A., & Stewart, J. H. (1999). Corporal punishment by American parents: National data on prevalence, chronicity, severity, and duration, in relation to child and family characteristics. *Clinical Child and Family Psychology Review, 2,* 55–70.

Strayer, L., & Roberts, W. (2004). Children's anger, emotional expressiveness, and empathy: Relations with parents' empathy, emotional expressiveness, and parenting practices. *Social Development, 13,* 229–254.

Strazdins, L., Clements, M. S., Korda, R. J., Broom, D. H., & D'Souza, R. M. (2006). Unsociable work? Nonstandard work schedules, family relationships, and children's well-being. *Journal of Marriage and the Family, 68,* 394–410.

Streissguth, A. P., Bookstein, F. L., Barr, H. M., Sampson, P. D., O'Malley, K., & Young, J. K. (2004). Risk factors for adverse life outcomes in fetal alcohol syndrome and fetal alcohol effects. *Journal of Developmental and Behavioral Pediatrics, 25,* 228–238.

Streissguth, A. P., Treder, R., Barr, H. M., Shepard, T., Bleyer, W. A., Sampson, P. D., & Martin, D. (1987). Aspirin and acetaminophen use by pregnant women and subsequent child IQ and attention decrements. *Teratology, 35,* 211–219.

Streri, A. (2005). Touching for knowing in infancy: The development of manual abilities in very young infants. *European Journal of Developmental Psychology, 2,* 325–343.

Streri, A., Lhote, M., & Dutilleul, S. (2000). Haptic perception in newborns. *Developmental Science, 3,* 319–327.

Stretesky, P. B., & Lynch, M. J. (2001). The relationship between lead exposure and homicide. *Archives of Pediatrics and Adolescent Medicine, 155,* 579–582.

Striano, T., & Rochat, P. (2000). Emergence of selective social referencing in infancy. *Infancy, 1,* 253–264.

Striano, T., Tomasello, M., & Rochat, P. (2001). Social and object support for early symbolic play. *Developmental Science, 4,* 442–455.

Striegel-Moore, R. H., & Franko, D. L. (2006). Adolescent eating disorders. In R. H. Striegel-Moore & D. L. Franko (Eds.), *Child and adolescent psychopathology: Theoretical and clinical implications* (pp. 160–183). New York: Routledge.

Stright, A. D., Neitzel, C., Sears, K. G., & Hoke-Sinex, L. (2002). Instruction begins in the home: Relations between parental instruction and children's self-regulation in the classroom. *Journal of Educational Psychology, 93,* 456–466.

Strohschein, L. (2005). Parental divorce and child mental health trajectories. *Journal of Marriage and Family, 67,* 1286–1300.

Strohschein, L., Gauthier, A. H., Campbell, R., & Kleparchuk, C. (2008). Parenting as a dynamic process: A test of the resource dilution hypothesis. *Journal of Marriage and Family, 70,* 670–683.

Stromquist, N. P. (2007). Gender equity education globally. In S. S. Klein, B. Richardson, D. A. Grayson, L. H. Fox, & C. Kramarae (Eds.), *Handbook for achieving gender equity through education* (2nd ed., pp. 33–42). Mahwah, NJ: Erlbaum.

Stromswold, K. (2000). The cognitive neuroscience of language acquisition. In M. S. Gazzaniga (Ed.), *The new cognitive neurosciences* (pp. 909–932). Boston: MIT Press.

Strouse, D. L. (1999). Adolescent crowd orientations: A social and temporal analysis. In J. A. McLellan & M. J. V. Pugh (Eds.), *The role of peer groups in adolescent social identity: Exploring the importance of*

stability and change (pp. 37–54). San Francisco: Jossey-Bass.

Stryer, B. K., Tofler, I. R., & Lapchick, R. (1998). A developmental overview of child and youth sports in society. *Child and Adolescent Psychiatric Clinics of North America, 7,* 697–719.

Sturge-Apple, M. L., Davies, P. T., Winter, M. A., Cummings, E. M., & Schermerhorn, A. (2008). Interparental conflict and children's school adjustment: The explanatory role of children's internal representations of interparental and parent–child relationships. *Developmental Psychology, 44,* 1678–1690.

Styne, D. M. (2003). The regulation of pubertal growth. *Hormone Research, 60*(Suppl.1), 22–26.

Suarez-Morales, L., & Lopez, B. (2009). The impact of acculturative stress and daily hassles on pre-adolescent psychological adjustment: Examining anxiety symptoms. *Journal of Primary Prevention, 30,* 335–349.

Suárez-Orozco, C., Todorova, I., & Qin, D. B. (2006). The well-being of immigrant adolescents: A longitudinal perspective on risk and protective factors. In F. A. Villarruel & T. Luster (Eds.), *The crisis in youth mental health: Critical issues and effective programs: Vol. 2. Disorders in adolescence* (pp. 53–83). Westport, CT: Praeger.

Subbotsky, E. (2004). Magical thinking in judgments of causation: Can anomalous phenomena affect ontological causal beliefs in children and adults? *British Journal of Developmental Psychology, 22,* 123–152.

Subrahmanyam, K., Gelman, R., & Lafosse, A. (2002). Animate and other separably moveable things. In G. Humphreys (Ed.), *Category-specificity in brain and mind* (pp. 341–371). London: Psychology Press.

Subrahmanyam, K., Smahel, D., & Greenfield, P. (2006). Connecting developmental constructions to the Internet: Identity presentation and sexual exploration in online teen chat rooms. *Developmental Psychology, 42,* 395–406.

Suddendorf, T., Simcock, G., & Nielsen, M. (2007). Visual self-recognition in mirrors and live videos: Evidence for a developmental asynchrony. *Cognitive Development, 22,* 185–196.

Sullivan, M. C., McGrath, M. M. Hawes, K., & Lester, B. M. (2008). Growth trajectories of preterm infants: Birth to 12 years. *Journal of Pediatric Health Care, 22,* 83–93.

Sullivan, M. W., & Lewis, M. (2003). Contextual determinants of anger and other negative expressions in young infants. *Developmental Psychology, 39,* 693–705.

Sullivan, S., & Glanz, J. (2006). *Building effective learning communities: Strategies for leadership, learning, and collaboration.* Thousand Oaks, CA: Corwin Press.

Sullivan, S. A., & Birch, L. L. (1990). Pass the sugar, pass the salt: Experience dictates preference. *Developmental Psychology, 26,* 546–551.

Sun, Y., Tao, F., Hao, J., & Wan, Y. (2010). The mediating effects of stress and coping on depression among adolescents in China. *Journal of Child and Adolescent Psychiatric Nursing, 23,* 173–180.

Super, C. M. (1981). Behavioral development in infancy. In R. H. Monroe, R. L. Monroe, & B. B. Whiting (Eds.), *Handbook of cross-cultural human development* (pp. 181–270). New York: Garland.

Super, D. E. (1990). A life span, life space approach to career development. In D. Brown & L. Brooks (Eds.), *Career choice and development* (2nd ed., pp. 197–261). San Francisco: Jossey-Bass.

Super, D. E. (1994). A life span, life space perspective on convergence. In M. L. Savikas & R. W. Lent (Eds.), *Convergence in career development theories* (pp. 62–71). Palo Alto, CA: Consulting Psychologists Press.

Supple, A. J., Ghazarian, S. R., Peterson, G. W., & Bush, K. R. (2009). Assessing the cross-cultural validity of a parental autonomy granting measure: Comparing adolescents in the United States, China, Mexico, and India. *Journal of Cross-Cultural Psychology, 40,* 816–833.

Supple, A. J., & Small, S. A. (2006). The influence of parental support, knowledge, and authoritative parenting on Hmong and European American adolescent development. *Journal of Family Issues, 27,* 1214–1232.

Survey USA. (2005). *Disciplining a child.* Retrieved from www.surveyusa.com/ 50StateDisciplineChild0805 SortedbyTeacher.htm

Susman, E. J., & Dorn, L. D. (2009). Puberty: Its role in development. In R. M. Lerner (Ed.), *Handbook of adolescent psychology: Vol. 1. Individual bases of adolescent development* (3rd ed., pp. 116–151). Hoboken, NJ: Wiley.

Susman, E. J., & Rogol, A. (2004). Puberty and psychological development. In R. M. Lerner & L. Steinberg (Eds.), *Handbook of adolescent psychology* (2nd ed., pp.15–44). Hoboken, NJ: Wiley.

Sussman, S., Skara, S., & Ames, S. L. (2008). Substance abuse among adolescents. *Substance Use and Misuse, 43,* 1802–1828.

Sutton, M. J., Brown, J. D., Wilson, K. M., & Klein, J. D. (2002). Shaking the tree of forbidden fruit: Where adolescents learn about sexuality and contraception. In J. D. Brown, J. R. Steele, & K. Walsh-Childers (Eds.), *Sexual teens, sexual media* (pp. 25–55). Mahwah, NJ: Erlbaum.

Svensson, A. (2000). Computers in school: Socially isolating or a tool to promote collaboration? *Journal of Educational Computing Research, 22,* 437–453.

Svirsky, M. A., Teoh, S. W., & Neuburger, H. (2004). Development of language and speech perception in congenitally profoundly deaf children as a function of age at cochlear implantation. *Audiology and Neuro-Otology, 9,* 224–233.

Swanson, J. L., & Fouad, N. A. (1999). Applying theories of person–environment fit: The transition from school to work. *Career Development Quarterly, 47,* 337–347.

Sweet, M. A., & Appelbaum, M. L. (2004). Is home visiting an effective strategy? A meta-analytic review of home visiting programs for families with young children. *Child Development, 75,* 1435–1456.

Swingley, D. (2005). Statistical clustering and the contents of the infant vocabulary. *Cognitive Psychology, 50,* 86–132.

Symons, D. K. (2001). A dyad-oriented approach to distress and mother–child relationship outcomes in the first 24 months. *Parenting: Science and Practice, 1,* 101–122.

Szepkouski, G. M., Gauvain, M., & Carberry, M. (1994). The development of planning skills in children with and without mental retardation. *Journal of Applied Developmental Psychology, 15,* 187–206.

Szkrybalo, J., & Ruble, D. N. (1999). "God made me a girl": Sex-category constancy judgments and explanations revisited. *Developmental Psychology, 35,* 392–402.

Szlemko, W. J., Wood, J. W., & Thurman, P. J. (2006). Native Americans and alcohol: Past, present, and future. *Journal of General Psychology, 133,* 435–451.

T

Tabibi, Z., & Pfeffer, K. (2007). Finding a safe place to cross the road: The effect of distractors and the role of attention in children's identification of safe and dangerous road-crossing sites. *Infant and Child Development, 16,* 193–206.

Tacon, A., & Caldera, Y. (2001). Attachment and parental correlates in late adolescent Mexican American women. *Hispanic Journal of Behavioral Sciences, 23,* 71–88.

Tager-Flusberg, H., & Zukowski, A. (2009). Putting words together: Morphology and syntax in the preschool years. In J. B. Gleason & B. Ratner (Ed.), *The development of language* (7th ed., pp. 139–191). Boston: Allyn and Bacon.

Takahashi, K. (1990). Are the key assumptions of the "Strange Situation" procedure universal? A view from Japanese research. *Human Development, 33,* 23–30.

Takala, M. (2006). The effects of reciprocal teaching on reading comprehension in mainstream and special (SLI) education. *Scandinavian Journal of Educational Research, 50,* 559–576.

Tamis-LeMonda, C. S., & Bornstein, M. H. (1989). Habituation and maternal encouragement of attention in infancy as predictors of toddler language, play, and representational competence. *Child Development, 60,* 738–751.

Tamis-LeMonda, C. S., Shannon, J. D., Cabrera, N. J., & Lamb, M. E. (2004). Fathers and mothers at play with their 2- and 3-year-olds: Contributions to language and cognitive development. *Child Development, 75,* 1806–1820.

Tamis-LeMonda, C. S., Way, N., Hughes, D., Yoshikawa, H., Kalman, R. K., & Niwa, E. Y. (2008). Parents' goals for children: The dynamic coexistence of individualism and collectivism in cultures and individuals. *Social Development, 17,* 183–209.

Tammelin, T., Näyhä, S., Hills, A. P., & Järvelin, M. (2003). Adolescent participation in sports and adult physical activity. *American Journal of Preventive Medicine, 24,* 22–28.

Tamminen, K. (1991). *Religious development in childhood and youth.* Helsinki, Finland: Gummerus Kirjapaino Oy.

Tamrouti-Makkink, I. D., Dubas, J. S., Gerris, J. R. M., & van Aken, A. G. (2004). The relation between the absolute level of parenting and differential parental treatment with adolescent siblings' adjustment. *Journal of Child Psychology and Psychiatry, 45,* 1397–1406.

Tangney, J. P., Stuewig, J., & Mashek, D. J. (2007). Moral emotions and moral behavior. *Annual Review of Psychology, 58,* 345–372.

Tanimura, M., Takahashi, K., Kataoka, N., Tomita, K., Tanabe, I., Yasuda, M., et al. (2004). Proposal: Heavy television and video viewing poses a risk for infants and young children. *Nippon Shonika Gakkai Zasshi, 108,* 709–712 (in Japanese).

Tanner, J. M., Healy, M., & Cameron, N. (2001*). Assessment of skeletal maturity and prediction of adult height* (3rd ed.). Philadelphia: Saunders.

Tardif, T. (2006). But are they really verbs? Chinese words for action. In K. Hirsh-Pasek & R. M. Golinkoff (Eds.), *Action meets word: How children learn verbs* (pp. 477–498). New York: Oxford University Press.

Tardif, T., Fletcher, P., Liang, W., Zhang, Z., Kaciroti, N., & Marchman, V. A. (2008). Baby's first 10 words. *Developmental Psychology, 44,* 929–938.

Tardif, T., Gelman, S. A., & Xu, F. (1999). Putting the "noun bias" in context: A comparison of English and Mandarin. *Child Development, 70,* 620–635.

Tardif, T., Wellman, H. M., & Cheung, K. M. (2004). False belief understanding in Cantonese-speaking children. *Journal of Child Language, 31,* 779–800.

Tarren-Sweeney, M. (2006). Patterns of aberrant eating among preadolescent children in foster care. *Journal of Abnormal Child Psychology, 34,* 623–634.

Tarter, R. E., Vanyukov, M., & Kirisci, L. (2008). Etiology of substance use disorder: Developmental perspective. In Y. Kaminer & O. G. Bukstein (Eds.), *Adolescent substance abuse: Psychiatric comorbidity and high-risk behaviors* (pp. 5–27). New York: Routledge.

Tarullo, A. R., & Gunnar, M. R. (2006). Child maltreatment and the developing HPA axis. *Hormones and Behavior, 50,* 632–639.

Tasker, F. (2005). Lesbian mothers, gay fathers, and their children: A review. *Developmental and Behavioral Pediatrics, 26,* 224–240.

Taumoepeau, M., & Ruffman, T. (2006). Mother and infant talk about mental states relates to desire language and emotion understanding. *Child Development, 77,* 465–481.

Taylor, C. A., Manganello, J. A., Lee, S. J., & Rice, J. C. (2010). Mothers' spanking of 3-year-old children and subsequent risk of children's aggressive behavior. *Pediatrics, 125,* e1057–e1065.

Taylor, E. (2004). ADHD is best understood as a cultural construct. *British Journal of Psychiatry, 184,* 8–9.

Taylor, J. L. (2009). Midlife impacts of adolescent parenthood. *Journal of Family Issues, 30,* 484–510.

Taylor, J. S. (2002). Caregiver support for women during childbirth: Does the presence of a labor-support person affect maternal–child outcomes? *American Family Physician, 66,* 1205–1206.

Taylor, M., & Carlson, S. M. (1997). The relation between individual differences in fantasy and theory of mind. *Child Development, 68,* 436–455.

Taylor, M., & Carlson, S. M. (2000). The influence of religious beliefs on parental attitudes about children's fantasy behavior. In K. S. Rosengren, C. N. Johnson, & P. L. Harris (Eds.), *Imagining the impossible* (pp. 247–268). New York: Cambridge University Press.

Taylor, M., Carlson, S. M., Maring, B. L., Gerow, L., & Charley, C. M. (2004). The characteristics and correlates of fantasy in school-age children: Imaginary companions, impersonation, and social understanding. *Developmental Psychology, 40,* 1173–1187.

Taylor, M., Esbensen, B. M., & Bennett, R. T. (1994). Children's understanding of knowledge acquisition: The tendency for children to report that they have always known what they have just learned. *Child Development, 65,* 1581–1604.

Taylor, M. C., & Hall, J. A. (1982). Psychological androgyny: Theories, methods, and conclusions. *Psychological Bulletin, 92,* 347–366.

Taylor, M. G. (1996). The development of children's beliefs about the social and biological aspects of gender differences. *Child Development, 67,* 1555–1571.

Taylor, R. L. (2000). Diversity within African-American families. In D. H. Demo & K. R. Allen (Eds.), *Handbook of family diversity* (pp. 232–251). New York: Oxford University Press.

Teicher, M. H., Dumont, N. L., Ito, Y., Vaituzis, C., Giedd, J., & Andersen, S. L. (2004). Childhood neglect is associated with reduced corpus callosum area. *Biological Psychiatry, 56,* 80–85.

Telama, R., Yang, X., Viikari, J., Valimaki, I., Wanne, O., & Raitakari, O. (2005). Physical activity from childhood to adulthood: A 21-year tracking study. *American Journal of Preventive Medicine, 28,* 267–273.

Tellings, A. (1999). Psychoanalytical and genetic-structuralistic approaches of moral development: Incompatible views? *Psychoanalytic Review, 86,* 903–914.

Temple, C. M., & Carney, R. A. (1995). Patterns of spatial functioning in Turner's syndrome. *Cortex, 31,* 109–118.

Temple, J. A., & Reynolds, A. J. (2006). Economic returns of investments in preschool education. In E. Zigler & S. Jones (Eds.), *A vision for universal prekindergarten* (pp. 37–68). New York: Cambridge University Press.

Temple, J. L., Giacomelli, A. M., Roemmich, J. N., & Epstein, L. H. (2007). Overweight children habituate slower than nonoverweight children to food. *Physiology and Behavior, 9,* 250–254.

ten Tusscher, G. W., & Koppe, J. G. (2004). Perinatal dioxin exposure and later effects—A review. *Chemosphere, 54,* 1329–1336.

Tenenbaum, H. R., & Leaper, C. (2002). Are parents' gender schemas related to their children's gender-related cognitions? A meta-analysis. *Developmental Psychology, 38,* 615–630.

Tenenbaum, H. R., & Leaper, C. (2003). Parent–child conversations about science: The socialization of gender inequities? *Developmental Psychology, 39,* 34–57.

Tenenbaum, H. R., Snow, C. E., Roach, K. A., & Kurland, B. (2005). Talking and reading science: Longitudinal data on sex differences in mother–child conversations in low-income families. *Journal of Applied Developmental Psychology, 26,* 1–19.

Terwel, J., Gillies, R. M., van den Eeden, P., & Hoek, D. (2001). Cooperative learning processes of students: A longitudinal multilevel perspective. *British Journal of Educational Psychology, 71,* 619–645.

Tessier, R., Cristo, M., Velez, S., Giron, M., Nadeau, L., & Figueroa, Z. (2003). Kangaroo mother care: A method of protecting high-risk premature infants against developmental delay. *Infant Behavior and Development, 26,* 384–397.

Teti, D. M., Gelfand, D. M., Messinger, D. S., & Isabella, R. (1995). Maternal depression and the quality of early attachment: An examination of infants, preschoolers, and their mothers. *Developmental Psychology, 31,* 364–376.

Teyber, E. (2001). *Helping children cope with divorce* (rev. ed.). San Francisco: Jossey-Bass.

Thacker, S. B., & Stroup, D. F. (2003). Revisiting the use of the electronic fetal monitor. *Lancet, 361,* 445–446.

Tharpe, A. M., & Ashmead, D. H. (2001). A longitudinal investigation of infant auditory sensitivity. *American Journal of Audiology, 10,* 104–112.

Thatcher, R. W., Walker, R. A., & Giudice, S. (1987). Human cerebral hemispheres develop at different rates and ages. *Science, 236,* 1110–1113.

Theil, S. (2006, September 4). Beyond babies. *Newsweek: International Edition.* Retrieved from www.msnbc .msn.com/id/14535863/site/newsweek

Thelen, E. (1989). The (re)discovery of motor development: Learning new things from an old field. *Developmental Psychology, 25,* 946–949.

Thelen, E., & Adolph, K. E. (1992). Arnold Gesell: The paradox of nature and nurture. *Developmental Psychology, 28,* 368–380.

Thelen, E., & Corbetta, D. (2002). Microdevelopment and dynamic systems: Applications to infant motor development. In N. Granott & J. Parziale (Eds.), *Microdevelopment: Transition processes in development and learning* (pp. 59–79). New York: Cambridge University Press.

Thelen, E., Fisher, D. M., & Ridley-Johnson, R. (1984). The relationship between physical growth and a newborn reflex. *Infant Behavior and Development, 7,* 479–493.

Thelen, E., Schöner, G., Scheier, C., & Smith, L. B. (2001). The dynamics of embodiment: A field theory of infant perseverative reaching. *Behavioral and Brain Sciences, 24,* 1–34.

Thelen, E., & Smith, L. B. (1994). *A dynamic systems approach to the development of cognition and action.* Cambridge, MA: Cambridge University Press.

Thelen, E., & Smith, L. B. (2006). Dynamic systems theories. In R. M. Lerner (Ed.), *Handbook of child psychology: Vol. 1. Theoretical models of human development* (6th ed., pp. 258–312). Hoboken, NJ: Wiley.

Théoret, H., Halligan, E., Kobayashi, M., Fregni, F., Tager-Flusberg, H., & Pascual-Leone, A. (2005). Impaired motor facilitation during action observation in individuals with autism spectrum disorder, *Current Biology, 15,* R84–R85.

Thiedke, C. C. (2001). Sleep disorders and sleep problems in childhood. *American Family Physician, 63,* 277–284.

Thiedke, C. C. (2003). Nocturnal enuresis. *American Family Physician, 67,* 1499–1506.

Thiessen, E. D., & Saffran, J. R. (2007). Learning to learn: Infants' acquisition of stress-based strategies for word segmentation. *Language Learning and Development, 3,* 75–102.

Thomaes, S., Stegge, H., & Olthof, T. (2007). Externalizing shame responses in children: The role of fragile-positive self-esteem. *British Journal of Developmental Psychology, 25,* 559–577.

Thoman, E., & Ingersoll, E. W. (1993). Learning in premature infants. *Developmental Psychology, 29,* 692–700.

Thomas, A., & Chess, S. (1977). *Temperament and development.* New York: Brunner/Mazel.

Thomas, A., Chess, S., & Birch, H. G. (1968). *Temperament and behavior disorders in children.* New York: New York University Press.

Thomas, C. L., & Dimitrov, D. M. (2007). Effects of a teen pregnancy prevention program on teens' attitudes toward sexuality: A latent trait modeling approach. *Developmental Psychology, 43,* 173–185.

Thomas, K. A., & Tessler, R. C. (2007). Bicultural socialization among adoptive families: Where there is a will, there is a way. *Journal of Family Issues, 28,* 1189–1219.

Thomas, R. M. (2005). *Comparing theories of child development* (6th ed.). New York: New York University Press.

Thompson, A., Hollis, C., & Richards, D. (2003). Authoritarian parenting attitudes as a risk for conduct problems: Results of a British national cohort study. *European Child and Adolescent Psychiatry, 12,* 84–91.

Thompson, L. A., Goodman, D. C., & Little, G. A. (2002). Is more neonatal intensive care always better? Insights from a cross-national comparison of reproductive care. *Pediatrics, 109,* 1036–1043.

Thompson, P. M., Giedd, J. N., Woods, R. P., MacDonald, D., Evans, A. C., & Toga, A. W. (2000). Growth patterns in the developing brain detected by using continuum mechanical tensor maps. *Nature, 404,* 190–192.

Thompson, R. A. (1990). Vulnerability in research: A developmental perspective on research risk. *Child Development, 61,* 1–16.

Thompson, R. A. (2000). The legacy of early attachments. *Child Development, 71,* 145–152.

Thompson, R. A. (2006). The development of the person: Social understanding, relationships, conscience, self. In N. Eisenberg (Ed.), *Handbook of child psychology: Vol. 3. Social, emotional, and personality development* (6th ed., pp. 24–98). Hoboken, NJ: Wiley.

Thompson, R. A. (2009). Early foundations: Conscience and the development of moral character. In D. Narvaez & D. K. Lapsley (Eds.), *Personality, identity, and character: Explorations in moral psychology* (pp. 159–184). New York: Cambridge University Press.

Thompson, R. A., Easterbrooks, M. A., & Padilla-Walker, L. M. (2003). Social and emotional development in infancy. In R. M. Lerner & M. A. Easterbrooks (Eds.), *Social and emotional development in infancy* (pp. 91–112). New York: Wiley.

Thompson, R. A., & Goodvin, R. (2007). Taming the tempest in the teapot. In C. A. Brownell & C. B. Kopp (Eds.), *Socioemotional development in the toddler years: Transitions and transformations* (pp. 320–341). New York: Guilford.

Thompson, R. A., & Meyer, S. (2007). Socialization of emotion regulation in the family. In J. J. Gross (Ed.), *Handbook of emotion regulation* (pp. 249–268). New York: Guilford.

Thompson, R. A., Meyer, S., & McGinley, M. (2006). Understanding values in relationships: The development of conscience. In M. Killen & J. G. Smetana (Eds.), *Handbook of moral development* (pp. 267–298). Mahwah, NJ: Erlbaum.

Thompson, R. A., & Nelson, C. A. (2001). Developmental science and the media. *American Psychologist, 56,* 5–15.

Thompson, R. A., & Raikes, H. A. (2007). The social and emotional foundations of school readiness. In D. F. Perry, R. K. Kaufmann, & J. Knitzer (Eds.), *Social and emotional health in early childhood: Building bridges between services and systems* (pp. 13–35). Baltimore, MD: Paul H. Brookes.

Thompson, W. W., Price, C., Goodson, B., Shay, D. K., Benson, P., Hinrichsen, V. L., et al. (2007). Early thimerosal exposure and neuropsychological outcomes at 7 to 10 years. *New England Journal of Medicine, 357,* 1281–1292.

Thornton, S. (1999). Creating conditions for cognitive change: The interaction between task structures and specific strategies. *Child Development, 70,* 588–603.

Thorpy, M. J., & Yager, J. (2001). *Encyclopedia of sleep and sleep disorders.* New York: Facts on File.

Tienari, P., Wahlberg, K. E., & Wynne, L. C. (2006). Finnish adoption study of schizophrenia: Implications for family interventions. *Families, Systems, and Health, 24,* 442–451.

Tienari, P., Wynne, L. C., Laksy, K., Moring, J., Nieminen, P., Sorri, A., et al. (2003). Genetic boundaries of the schizophrenia spectrum: Evidence from the Finnish adoptive family study of schizophrenia. *The American Journal of Psychiatry, 160,* 1587–1594.

Tiggemann, M., & Anesbury, T. (2000). Negative stereotyping of obesity in children: The role of controllability beliefs. *Journal of Applied Social Psychology, 30,* 1977–1993.

Tincoff, R., & Jusczyk, P. W. (1999). Some beginnings of word comprehension in 6-month-olds. *Psychological Science, 10,* 172–175.

Tinsley, B. J. (2003). *How children learn to be healthy.* Cambridge, UK: Cambridge University Press.

Tizard, B., & Rees, J. (1975). The effect of early institutional rearing on the behaviour problems and affectional relationships of four-year-old children. *Journal of Child Psychology and Psychiatry, 16,* 61–73.

Tofler, I. R., Knapp, P. K., & Drell, M. J. (1998). The achievement by proxy spectrum in youth sports: Historical perspective and clinical approach to pressured and high-achieving children and adolescents. *Child and Adolescent Psychiatric Clinics of North America, 7,* 803–820.

Tokunaga, R. S. (2010). Following you home from school: A critical review and synthesis of research on cyberbullying victimization. *Computers in Human Behavior, 26,* 277–287.

Tomasello, M. (1992). *First verbs: A case study of early grammatical development.* New York: Cambridge University Press.

Tomasello, M. (1999). Having intentions, understanding intentions, and understanding communicative intentions. In P. D. Zelazo, J. W. Astington, & J. Wilde (Eds.), *Developing theories of intention: Social understanding and self-control* (pp. 63–75). Mahwah, NJ: Erlbaum.

Tomasello, M. (2000). Do young children have adult syntactic competence? *Cognition, 74,* 209–253.

Tomasello, M. (2003). *Constructing a language: A usage-based theory of language acquisition.* Cambridge, MA: Harvard University Press.

Tomasello, M. (2005). Beyond formalities: The case of language acquisition. *Linguistic Review, 22,* 183–197.

Tomasello, M. (2006). Acquiring linguistic constructions. In D. Kuhn & R. Siegler (Eds.), *Handbook of child psychology: Vol. 2: Cognition, perception, and language* (6th ed., pp. 255–298). Hoboken, NJ: Wiley.

Tomasello, M., & Akhtar, N. (1995). Two-year-olds use pragmatic cues to differentiate reference to objects and actions. *Cognitive Development, 10,* 201–224.

Tomasello, M., Akhtar, N., Dodson, K., & Rekau, L. (1997). Differential productivity in young children's use of nouns and verbs. *Journal of Child Language, 24,* 373–387.

Tomasello, M., & Brandt, S. (2009). Flexibility in the semantics and syntax of children's early verb use. *Monographs of the Society for Research in Child Development, 74*(2, Serial No. 293), 113–126.

Tomasello, M., Call, J., & Hare, B. (2003). Chimpanzees understand psychological states—the question is which ones and to what extent. *Trends in Cognitive Sciences, 7,* 153–156.

Tomasello, M., Carpenter, M., & Liszkowski, U. (2007). A new look at infant pointing. *Child Development, 78,* 705–722.

Tong, S., Baghurst, P., Vimpani, G., & McMichael, A. (2007). Socioeconomic position, maternal IQ, home environment, and cognitive development. *Journal of Pediatrics, 151,* 284–288.

Tong, S., McMichael, A. J., & Baghurst, P. A. (2000). Interactions between environmental lead exposure and sociodemographic factors on cognitive development. *Archives of Environmental Health, 55,* 330–335.

Tong, V. T., Jones, J. R., Dietz, P. M., D'Angelo, D., & Bombard, J. M. (2009, May 29). Trends in smoking before, during, and after pregnancy—Pregnancy Risk Assessment Monitoring System (PRAMS), United States, 31 Sites, 2000–2005. *Morbidity and Mortality Weekly Report, 58* (No. SS-4).

Toomela, A. (1999). Drawing development: Stages in the representation of a cube and a cylinder. *Child Development, 70,* 1141–1150.

Toomela, A. (2002). Drawing as a verbally mediated activity: A study of relationships between verbal, motor, visuospatial skills and drawing in children. *International Journal of Behavioral Development, 26,* 234–247.

Torney-Purta, J. (2002). The school's role in developing civic engagement: A study of adolescents in twenty-eight countries. *Applied Developmental Science, 6,* 203–212.

Torney-Purta, J., Barber, C. H., & Wilkenfeld, B. (2007). Latino adolescents' civic development in the United States: Research results from the IEA Civic Education Study. *Journal of Youth and Adolescence, 36,* 111–125.

Torrance, E. P. (1988). The nature of creativity as manifest in its testing. In R. J. Sternberg (Ed.), *The nature of creativity: Contemporary psychological perspectives* (pp. 43–75). New York: Cambridge University Press.

Tottenham, N., Hare, T. A., & Casey, B. J. (2009). A developmental perspective on human amygdala function. In P. J. Whalen & E. A. Phelps (Eds.), *The human amygdala* (pp. 107–117). New York: Guilford Press.

Tough, S., Tofflemire, K., Benzies, K., Fraser-Lee, N., & Newburn-Cook, C. (2007). Factors influencing childbearing decisions and knowledge of preinatal risks among Canadian men and women. *Maternal and Child Health Journal, 11,* 189–198.

Townsend, D. A., & Rovee-Collier, C. (2007). *The transitivity of 6-month-olds' preconditioned memories in deferred imitation.* Paper presented at the annual meeting of the Eastern Psychological Association, Philadelphia.

Toyamo, N. (2000). "What are food and air like inside our bodies?" Children's thinking about digestion and respiration. *International Journal of Behavioral Development, 24,* 222–230.

Tracy, J. L., Robins, R. W., & Lagattuta, K. H. (2005). Can children recognize pride? *Emotion, 5,* 251–257.

Traurig, M., Mack, J., Hanson, R. L., Ghoussaini, M., Meyre, D., Knowler, W., et al. (2009). Common variation in SIM1 is reproducibly associated with BMI in Pima Indians. *Diabetes, 58,* 1682–1689.

Trautner, H. M., Gervai, J., & Nemeth, R. (2003). Appearance–reality distinction and development of gender constancy understanding in children. *International Journal of Behavioral Development, 27,* 275–283.

Trautner, H. M., Ruble, D. N., Cyphers, L., Kirsten, B., Behrendt, R., & Hartman, P. (2005). Rigidity and flexibility of gender stereotypes in childhood: Developmental or differential? *Infant and Child Development, 14,* 365–381.

Trautwein, U., Ludtke, O., Marsh, H. W., Koller, O., & Baumert, J. (2006). Tracking, grading, and student motivation: Using group composition and status to predict self-concept and interest in ninth-grade mathematics. *Journal of Educational Psychology, 98,* 788–806.

Treasure, J., & Schmidt, U. (2004). Anorexia nervosa. *Clinical Evidence, 13,* 1148–1157.

Trehub, S. E. (2001). Musical predispositions in infancy. *Annals of the New York Academy of Sciences, 930,* 1–16.

Tremblay, L., & Frigon, J.-Y. (2005). Precocious puberty in adolescent girls: A biomarker of later psychosocial adjustment problems. *Child Psychiatry and Human Development, 36,* 73–94.

Tremblay, R. E. (2000). The development of aggressive behavior during childhood: What have we learned in the past century? *International Journal of Behavioral Development, 24,* 129–141.

Tremblay, R. E. (2004). Decade of Behavior Distinguished Lecture: Development of physical aggression during infancy. *Infant Mental Health Journal, 25,* 399–407.

Tremblay, R. E., Japel, C., Perusse, D., Voivin, M., Zoccolillo, M., Montplaisir, J., & McDuff, P. (1999). The search for the age of "onset" of physical aggression: Rousseau and Bandura revisited. *Criminal Behavior and Mental Health, 9,* 8–23.

Trent, K., & Harlan, S. L. (1994). Teenage mothers in nuclear and extended households. *Journal of Family Issues, 15,* 309–337.

Trentacosta, C. J., & Shaw, D. S. (2009). Emotional self-regulation, peer rejection, and antisocial behavior: Developmental associations from early childhood to early adolescence. *Journal of Applied Developmental Psychology, 30,* 356–365.

Trevarthen, C. (2003). Infant psychology is an evolving culture. *Human Development, 46,* 233–246.

Triandis, H. C. (1995). *Individualism and collectivism.* Boulder, CO: Westview Press.

Triandis, H. C. (2005). Issues in individualism and collectivism research. In R. M. Sorrentino, D. Cohen, J. M. Olson, & M. P. Zanna (Eds.), *Culture and social behavior: The Ontario Symposium* (Vol. 10, pp. 207–225). Mahwah, NJ: Erlbaum.

Triandis, H. C. (2007). Culture and psychology: A history of their relationship. In S. Kitahama (Ed.), *Handbook of cultural psychology* (pp. 59–76). New York: Guilford Press.

Trickett, P. K., & Putnam, F. W. (1998). Developmental consequences of child sexual abuse. In P. K. Trickett & C. J. Schellenbach (Eds.), *Violence against children in the family and community* (pp. 39–56). Washington, DC: American Psychological Association.

Trocmé, N., & Wolfe, D. (2002). *Child maltreatment in Canada: The Canadian Incidence Study of Reported Child Abuse and Neglect.* Retrieved from http://www.hcsc.gc.ca/pphb-dgspsp/cm-vee

Troiano, R. P., Berrigan, D., Dodd, K. W., Màsse, L. C., Tillert, T., & McDowell, M. (2007). Physical activity in the United States measured by accelerometer. *Medicine and Science in Sports and Exercise, 40,* 181–188.

Tronick, E. Z., Morelli, G., & Ivey, P. (1992). The Efe forager infant and toddler's pattern of social relationships: Multiple and simultaneous. *Developmental Psychology, 28,* 568–577.

Tronick, E. Z., Thomas, R. B., & Daltabuit, M. (1994). The Quechua manta pouch: A caretaking practice for buffering the Peruvian infant against the multiple stressors of high altitude. *Child Development, 65,* 1005–1013.

Troop-Gordon, W., & Asher, S. R. (2005). Modifications in children's goals when encountering obstacles to conflict resolution. *Child Development, 76,* 568–582.

Tropp, L. R., & Pettigrew, T. F. (2005). Relationships between intergroup contact and prejudice among minority and majority status groups. *Psychological Science, 16,* 951–957.

Troseth, G. L. (2003). Getting a clear picture: Young children's understanding of a televised image. *Developmental Science, 6,* 247–253.

Troseth, G. L., & DeLoache, J. S. (1998). The medium can obscure the message: Young children's understanding of video. *Child Development, 69,* 950–965.

Troseth, G. L., Saylor, M. M., & Archer, A. H. (2006). Young children's use of video as a source of socially relevant information. *Child Development, 77,* 786–799.

True, M. M., Pisani, L., & Oumar, F. (2001). Infant–mother attachment among the Dogon of Mali. *Child Development, 72,* 1451–1466.

Trusty, J. (1999). Effects of eighth-grade parental involvement on late adolescents' educational expectations. *Journal of Research and Development in Education, 32,* 224–233.

Trzesniewski, K. H., & Donnellan, M. B. (2009). Reevaluating the evidence for increasingly positive self-views among high school students: More evidence for consistency across generations. *Psychological Science, 20,* 920–922.

Trzesniewski, K. H., & Donnellan, M. B. (2010). Rethinking "Generation Me": A study of cohort effects from 1976–2006. *Perspectives on Psychological Science, 5,* 58–75.

Trzesniewski, K. H., Donnellan, M. B., & Robins, R. W. (2003). Stability of self-esteem across the life span. *Journal of Personality and Social Psychology, 84,* 205–220.

Tsujimoto, S. (2008). The prefrontal cortex: Functional neural development during early childhood. *Neuroscientist, 14,* 345–358.

Tuchfarber, B. S., Zins, J. E., & Jason, L. A. (1997). Prevention and control of injuries. In R. Weissberg, T. P. Gullotta, R. L. Hampton, B. A. Ryan, & G. R. Adams (Eds.), *Enhancing children's wellness* (pp. 250–277). Thousand Oaks, CA: Sage.

Tucker, C. J., McHale, S. M., & Crouter, A. C. (2001). Conditions of sibling support in adolescence. *Journal of Family Psychology, 15,* 254–271.

Tudge, J. R. H. (1992). Processes and consequences of peer collaboration: A Vygotskian analysis. *Child Development, 63,* 1364–1397.

Tudge, J. R. H., Hogan, D. M., Snezhkova, I. A., Kulakova, N. N., & Etz, K. E. (2000). Parents' child-rearing values and beliefs in the United States and Russia: The impact of culture and social class. *Infant and Child Development, 9,* 105–121.

Turati, C., Cassia, V. M., Simion, F., & Leo, I. (2006). Newborns' face recognition: Role of inner and outer facial features. *Child Development, 77,* 297–311.

Turiel, E. (2006). The development of morality. In N. Eisenberg (Ed.), *Handbook of child psychology: Vol. 3. Social, emotional, and personality development* (6th ed., pp. 789–857). Hoboken, NJ: Wiley.

Turiel, E., & Killen, M. (2010). Taking emotions seriously: The role of emotions in moral development. In W. F. Arsenio & E. A. Lemerise (Eds.), *Emotions, aggression, and morality in children: Bridging development and psychopathology* (pp. 33–52). Washington, DC: American Psychological Association.

Turkheimer, E., Haley, A., Waldron, M., D'Onofrio, B., & Gottesman, I. I. (2003). Socioeconomic status modifies heritability of IQ in young children. *Psychological Science, 14,* 623–628.

Turnbull, K. P., Anthony, A. B., Justice, L., & Bowles, R. (2009). Preschoolers' exposure to language stimulation in classrooms serving at-risk children: The contribution of group size and activity context. *Early Education and Development, 20,* 53–79.

Turnbull, M., Hart, D., & Lapkin, S. (2003). Grade 6 French immersion students' performance on large-scale reading, writing, and mathematics tests: Building explanations. *Alberta Journal of Educational Research, 49,* 6–23.

Turner, P. J., & Gervai, J. (1995). A multidimensional study of gender typing in preschool children and their parents: Personality, attitudes, preferences, behavior, and cultural differences. *Developmental Psychology, 31,* 759–772.

Turner, R. N., Hewstone, M., & Voci, A. (2007). Reducing explicit and implicit outgroup prejudice via direct and extended contact: The mediating role of self-disclosure and intergroup anxiety. *Journal of Personality and Social Psychology, 93,* 369–388.

Tuyen, J. M., & Bisgard, K. (2003). *Community setting: Pertussis outbreak.* Atlanta, GA: U.S. Centers for Disease Control and Prevention. Retrieved from www.cdc.gov/nip/publications/pertussis/chapter10.pdf

Twenge, J. M., & Campbell, W. K. (2001). Age and birth cohort differences in self-esteem: A cross-temporal meta-analysis. *Personality and Social Psychology Review, 5,* 321–344.

Twenge, J. M., & Crocker, J. (2002). Race and self-esteem: Meta-analyses comparing whites, blacks, Hispanics, Asians, and American Indians and comment on Gray-Little and Hafdahl (2000). *Psychological Bulletin, 128,* 371–408.

Twenge, J. M., Konrath, S., Foster, J. D., Campbell, W. K., & Bushman, B. J. (2008). Egos inflating over time: A cross-temporal meta-analysis of the Narcissistic Personality Inventory. *Journal of Personality, 76,* 875–902.

Twenge, J. M., Konrath, S., Foster, J. D., Campbell, W. K., Bushman, B. J., Trzesniewski, K. H., et al. (2010). Are today's youth more self-centered than previous generations? In B. Slife (Ed.), *Taking sides: Clashing views on psychological issues* (16th ed., pp. 175–195). New York: McGraw-Hall.

Twyman, K., Saylor, C., Taylor, L. A., & Comeaux, D. (2010). Comparing children and adolescents engaged in cyberbullying to matched peers. *Cyberpsychology, Behavior, and Social Networking, 13,* 195–199.

Tynes, B., Reynolds, L., & Greenfield, P. M. (2004). Adolescence, race and ethnicity on the Internet: A comparison of discourse in monitored vs. unmonitored chat rooms. *Journal of Applied Developmental Psychology, 25,* 667–684.

Tzuriel, D. (2001). *Dynamic assessment of young children.* New York: Kluwer Academic.

Tzuriel, D., & Egozi, G. (2010). Gender differences in spatial ability of young children: The effects of training and processing strategies. *Child Development, 81,* 1417–1430.

Tzuriel, D., & Kaufman, R. (1999). Mediated learning and cognitive modifiability: Dynamic assessment of young Ethiopian immigrant children to Israel. *Journal of Cross-Cultural Psychology, 30,* 359–380.

U

Uauy, R., Kain, J., Mericq, V., Rojas, J., & Corvalán, C. (2008). Nutrition, child growth, and chronic disease prevention. *Annals of Medicine, 40,* 11–20.

Ukrainetz, T. A., Justice, L. M., Kaderavek, J. N., Eisenberg, S. L., Gillam, R., & Harm, H. M. (2005). The development of expressive elaboration in fictional narratives. *Journal of Speech, Language, and Hearing Research, 48,* 1363–1377.

Ullrich-French, S., & Smith, A. L. (2006). Perceptions of relationships with parents and peers in youth sport: Independent and combined prediction of motivational outcomes. *Psychology of Sport and Exercise, 7,* 193–214.

Umaña-Taylor, A. J. (2004). Ethnic identity and self-esteem: Examining the role of social context. *Journal of Adolescence, 27,* 139–146.

Umaña-Taylor, A. J., & Alfaro, E. C. (2006). Ethnic identity among U.S. Latino adolescents: Measurement and implications for well-being. In F. A. Villarruel & T. Luster (Eds.), *The crisis in youth mental health: Critical issues and effective programs: Vol. 2. Disorders in adolescence* (pp. 195–211). Westport, CT: Praeger.

Umaña-Taylor, A. J., & Updegraff, K. A. (2007). Latino adolescents' mental health: Exploring the interrelations among discrimination, ethnic identity, cultural orientation, self-esteem, and depressive symptoms. *Journal of Adolescence, 30,* 549–567.

Underhill, K., Montgomery, P., & Operario, D. (2007). Sexual abstinence only programmes to prevent HIV infection in high-income countries: Systematic review. *British Medical Journal, 335,* 248.

Underwood, M. K. (2003). *Social aggression in girls.* New York: Guilford.

UNICEF (United Nations Children's Fund). (2006). *Immunization summary 2006.* Geneva, Switzerland: World Health Organization.

UNICEF (United Nations Children's Fund). (2007). *An overview of child well-being in rich countries, Innocenti Report Card 7.* Florence, Italy: UNICEF Innocenti Research Centre.

UNICEF (United Nations Children's Fund). (2008). *Immunization summary: A statistical reference containing data through 2006.* Geneva, Switzerland: World Health Organization.

UNICEF (United Nations Children's Fund). (2009a). *All children everywhere: A strategy for basic education and gender equality.* New York: Author.

UNICEF (United Nations Children's Fund). (2009b). *Children and AIDS: Fourth stocktaking report, 2009.* New York: United Nations.

UNICEF (United Nations Children's Fund). (2010). *Young champions for education: A progress review.* Retrieved from www.ungei.org/resources/1612_2341.html

UNICEF (United Nations Children's Fund). (2010b). *The state of the world's children* (special edition). New York: Author.

United Nations. (2006). *World population prospects: The 2006 revision. Population database.* Retrieved from esa.un.org/unpp/index.asp?panel=2

U.S. Census Bureau. (2010a). *International data base.* Retrieved from www.census.gov/ipc/www/idb

U.S. Census Bureau. (2010b). *Statistical abstract of the United States* (129th ed.). Washington, DC: U.S. Government Printing Office.

U.S. Centers for Disease Control. (2009). Breastfeeding Report Card, United States: Outcome indicators. Retrieved from www.cdc.gov/breastfeeding/data/report_card2.htm

U.S. Department of Agriculture. (2009). Frequently asked questions about WIC. Retrieved from www.fns.usda.gov/wic/FAQs/faq.htm#3

U.S. Department of Education. (2006). *Calories in, calories, out: Food and exercise in public elementary schools, 2005.* Retrieved from nces.ed.gov/Pubs2006/nutrition

U.S. Department of Education. (2007). *The Nation's Report Card: Writing 2007.* Retrieved from nces.ed.gov/pubsearch/pubsinfo.asp?pubid=2008468

U.S. Department of Education. (2008). *The condition of education.* Retrieved from nces.ed.gov/programs/coe/list/i4.asp

U.S. Department of Education. (2009). *Digest of education statistics, 2008.* Washington, DC: U.S. Government Printing Office.

U.S. Department of Education. (2009b). *The Nation's Report Card: Mathematics 2009.* Retrieved from nces.ed.gov/nationsreportcard/mathematics/

U.S. Department of Education. (2010). *Digest of education statistics, 2009.* Washington, DC: U.S. Government Printing Office.

U.S. Department of Education. (2010b). *The Nation's Report Card: Reading 2010.* Retrieved from nces.ed.gov/pubsearch/pubsinfo.asp?pubid=2010458

U.S. Department of Health and Human Services. (2007a). *Prenatal care.* Retrieved from wwww.cdc.gov/nchs/fastats/prenatal.htm

U.S. Department of Health and Human Services. (2007b). *The Surgeon General's call to action to prevent and decrease overweight and obesity: Overweight children and adolescents.* Retrieved from www.surgeongeneral.gov/topics/obesity/calltoaction/fact_adolescents.htm

U.S. Department of Health and Human Services. (2007c, April). Trends in oral health status: United States, 1988–1994 and 1999–2004. *Vital and Health Statistics, 11*(No. 248).

U.S. Department of Health and Human Services. (2008a). CDC childhood injury report: Patterns of unintentional injuries among 0–19 year olds in the United States, 2000–2006. Atlanta, GA: National Center for Injury Control and Prevention.

U.S. Department of Health and Human Services. (2008b). *Child maltreatment 2006.* Retrieved from www.acf.hhs.gov/programs/cb/pubs/cm06/index.htm

U.S. Department of Health and Human Services. (2009a). *Benefits of breastfeeding.* Retrieved from www.womenshealth.gov/breastfeeding/benefits

U.S. Department of Health and Human Services. (2009b, January 7). Births: Final data for 2006. *National Vital Statistics Report, 57*(7).

U.S. Department of Health and Human Services. (2009c). *Child maltreatment 2007: Summary of key findings.* Retrieved from www.childwelfare.gov/pubs/factsheets/canstats.pdf

U.S. Department of Health and Human Services. (2009d). *Down syndrome.* Retrieved from www.cdc.gov/ncbddd/birthdefects/DownSyndrome.htm

U.S. Department of Health and Human Services. (2009e). *Key statistics from the National Survey of Family Growth.* Retrieved from www.cdc.gov/nchs/nsfg/abc_list_i.htm#impaired

U.S. Department of Health and Human Services. (2009f). National, state, and local vaccination coverage among children aged 19–35 months—United States, 2008. *Morbidity and Mortality Weekly Report, 58*, 921–926.

U.S. Department of Health and Human Services. (2009g). U.S. obesity trends 1985–2007. Retrieved from www.cdc.gov/obesity/data.trends.html

U.S. Department of Health and Human Services. (2009h). *Sexually transmitted disease surveillance, 2008.* Atlanta, GA: Author.

U.S. Department of Health and Human Services. (2010a). *Child maltreatment 2010.* Retrieved from www.acf.hhs.gov/programs/cb/stats_research/index.htm#can

U.S. Department of Health and Human Services. (2010b). *Head Start Impact Study: Final report.* Washington, DC: U.S Government Printing Office.

U.S. Department of Health and Human Services. (2010c). *Vital statistics—mortality.* Retrieved from www.cdc.gov/nchs/data_access/vitalstats/VitalStats_Mortality.htm

U.S. Department of Health and Human Services. (2010d). Diagnoses of HIV infection and AIDS in the United States and Dependent Areas, 2008. *HIV Surveillance Report, Vol. 20.* Retrieved from www.cdc.gov/hiv/surveillance/resources/reports/2008report/index.htm

U.S. Department of Health and Human Services. (2010e). *Results from the 2009 National Survey on Drug Use and Health: Volume I. Summary of national findings.* Rockville, MD: Substance Abuse and Mental Health Services Administration.

U.S. Department of Health and Human Services. (2010f). Seroprevalence of herpes simplex virus type 2 among persons aged 14–49 years—United States, 2005–2008. *Morbidity and Mortality Weekly Report, 59*, 456–459.

U.S. Department of Health and Human Services. (2010g). Youth Risk Behavior Surveillance—United States, 2009. *Morbidity and Mortality Weekly Report, 59*(SS-5), 1–142.

U.S. Department of Justice. (2010). *Crime in the United States, 2009.* Retrieved from www.fbi.gov/ucr/09cius.htm

Ursano, R. J., & Shaw, J. A. (2007). Children of war and opportunities for peace. *Journal of the American Medical Association, 298*, 567.

Usher-Seriki, K. K., Bynum, M. S., & Callands, T. A. (2008). Mother–daughter communication about sex and sexual intercourse among middle-to upper-class African American girls. *Journal of Family Issues, 29*, 901–917.

Usta, I. M., & Nassar, A. H. (2008). Advanced maternal age. Part I: Obstetric complications. *American Journal of Perinatology, 25*, 521–534.

V

Vaillancourt, T., Hymel, S., & McDougall, P. (2003). Bullying is power: Implications for school-based intervention strategies. *Journal of Applied Social Psychology, 19*, 157–176.

Vaish, A., & Striano, T. (2004). Is visual reference necessary? Contributions of facial versus vocal cues in 12-month-olds' social referencing behavior. *Developmental Science, 7*, 261–269.

Vakil, E., Blachstein, H., Sheinman, M., & Greenstein, Y. (2009). Developmental changes in attention tests norms: Implications for the structure of attention. *Child Neuropsychology, 15*, 21–39.

Valdés, G. (1997). Dual-language immersion programs: A cautionary note concerning the education of language-minority students. *Harvard Educational Review, 67*, 391–429.

Valdés, G. (1998). The world outside and inside schools: Language and immigrant children. *Educational Researcher, 27*(6), 4–18.

Valentine, J. C., DuBois, D. L., & Cooper, H. (2004). The relation between self-beliefs and academic achievement: A meta-analytic review. *Educational Psychologist, 39*, 111–133.

Valian, V. (1999). Input and language acquisition. In W. C. Ritchie & T. K. Bhatia (Eds.), *Handbook of child language acquisition* (pp. 497–530). San Diego: Academic Press.

Valiente, C., Eisenberg, N., Fabes, R. A., Shepard, S. A., Cumberland, A., & Losoya, S. H. (2004). Prediction of children's empathy-related responding from their effortful control and parents' expressivity. *Developmental Psychology, 40*, 911–926.

Valiente, C., Lemery-Chalfant, K., Swanson, J., & Reiser, M. (2008). Prediction of children's academic competence from their effortful control, relationships, and classroom participation. *Journal of Educational Psychology, 100*, 67–77.

Valkenburg, P. M., & Peter, J. (2007a). Internet communication and its relation to well-being: Identifying some underlying mechanisms. *Media Psychology, 9*, 43–58.

Valkenburg, P. M., & Peter, J. (2007b). Preadolescents' and adolescents' online communication and their closeness to friends. *Developmental Psychology, 43*, 267–277.

van Aken, C., Junger, M., Verhoeven, M., van Aken, M. A. G., & Deković, M. (2007). The interactive effects of temperament and maternal parenting on toddlers' externalizing behaviours. *Infant and Child Development, 16*, 553–572.

Van Cleave, J., Gortmaker, S. L., & Perrin, J. M. (2010). Dynamics of obesity and chronic health conditions among children and youth. *Journal of the American Medical Association, 303*, 623–630.

Van de Vijver, P. J. R., Hofer, J., & Chasiotis, A. (2010). Methodology. In M. H. Bornstein (Ed.), *Handbook of cultural developmental science* (pp. 21–37). New York: Psychology Press.

Van den Bergh, B. R. H. (2004). High antenatal maternal anxiety is related to ADHD symptoms, externalizing problems, and anxiety in 8- and 9-year-olds. *Child Development, 75*, 1085–1097.

Van den Bergh, B. R. H., & De Rycke, L. (2003). Measuring the multidimensional self-concept and global self-worth of 6- to 8-year-olds. *Journal of Genetic Psychology, 164*, 201–225.

van den Boom, D. C., & Hoeksma, J. B. (1994). The effect of infant irritability on mother–infant interaction: A growth-curve analysis. *Developmental Psychology, 30*, 581–590.

van den Dries, L., Juffer, F., van IJzendoorn, M. H., & Bakermans-Kranenburg, M. J. (2009). Fostering security? A meta-analysis of attachment in adopted children. *Children and Youth Services Review, 31*, 410–421.

van der Meer, A. L. (1997). Keeping the arm in the limelight: Advanced visual control of arm movements in neonates. *European Journal of Paediatric Neurology, 4*, 103–108.

van der Wal, M. F., van Eijsden, M., & Bonsel, G. J. (2007). Stress and emotional problems during pregnancy and excessive infant crying. *Developmental and Behavioral Pediatrics, 28*, 431–437.

Van Eyk, J., & Dunn, M. J. (Eds.). (2008). *Clinical proteomics.* Weinheim, Germany: Wiley-VCH.

Van Goozen, S. H. M., Cohen-Kettenis, P. T., Gooren, I. J. G., Frijda, N. H., & Van De Poll, N. E. (1995). Gender differences in behaviour: Activating effects of cross-sex hormones. *Psychoneuroendocrinology, 20*, 171–177.

van Hoof, A., & Raaijmakers, Q. A. W. (2003). The search for the structure of identity formation. *Identity, 3*, 271–289.

van IJzendoorn, M. H. (1995). Adult attachment representations, parental responsiveness, and infant attachment: A meta-analysis on the predictive validity of the Adult Attachment Interview. *Psychological Bulletin, 117*, 387–403.

van IJzendoorn, M. H., & Bakermans-Kranenburg, M. J. (2006). DRD4 7-repeat polymorphism moderates the association between maternal unresolved loss or trauma and infant disorganization. *Attachment and Human Development, 8*, 291–307.

van IJzendoorn, M. H., & Kroonenberg, P. M. (1988). Cross-cultural patterns of attachment: A meta-analysis of the Strange Situation. *Child Development, 59*, 147–156.

van IJzendoorn, M. H., & Sagi, A. (1999). Cross-cultural patterns of attachment. In J. Cassidy & P. R. Shaver (Eds.), *Handbook of attachment: Theory, research, and clinical applications* (pp. 713–734). New York: Guilford.

van IJzendoorn, M. H., Juffer, F., & Poelhuis, C. W. K. (2005). Adoption and cognitive development: A meta-analytic comparison of adopted and nonadopted children's IQ and school performance. *Psychological Bulletin, 131*, 301–316.

van IJzendoorn, M. H., Schuengel, C., & Bakermans-Kranenburg, M. J. (1999). Disorganized attachment in early childhood: Meta-analysis of precursors, concomitants, and sequelae. *Development and Psychopathology, 11*, 225–249.

van IJzendoorn, M. H., Vereijken, C. M. J. L., Bakermans-Kranenburg, M. J., & Riksen-Walraven, J. M. (2004). Assessing attachment security with the Attachment Q Sort: Meta-analytic evidence for the validity of the Observer AQS. *Child Development, 75,* 1188–1213.

Van Keer, H. (2004). Fostering reading comprehension in fifth grade by explicit instruction in reading strategies and peer tutoring. *British Journal of Educational Psychology, 74,* 37–70.

Vandell, D. L., & Mueller, E. C. (1995). Peer play and friendships during the first two years. In H. C. Foot, A. J. Chapman, & J. R. Smith (Eds.), *Friendship and social relations in children* (pp. 181–208). New Brunswick, NJ: Transaction.

Vandell, D. L., & Posner, J. K. (1999). Conceptualization and measurement of children's after-school environments. In S. L. Friedman & T. D. Wachs (Eds.), *Measuring environment across the life span* (pp. 167–196). Washington, DC: American Psychological Association.

Vandell, D. L., & Shumow, L. (1999). After-school child care programs. *Future of Children, 9*(2), 64–80.

Vandell, D. L., Reisner, E. R., & Pierce, K. M. (2007). *Outcomes linked to high-quality after-school programs: Longitudinal findings from the Study of Promising After-School Programs.* Retrieved from www.gse.uci. edu/childcare/pdf/afterschool/PP%20Longitudinal %20Findings%20Final%20Report.pdf

Vandell, D. L., Reisner, E. R., Pierce, K. M., Brown, B. B., Lee, D., Bolt, D., & Pechman, E. M. (2006). *The study of promising after-school programs: Examination of longer term outcomes after two years of program experiences.* Madison, WI: University of Wisconsin. Retrieved from www.wcer.wisc.edu/childcare/ statements.html

Vanderbilt-Adriance, E., & Shaw, D. S. (2008). Protective factors and the development of resilience in the context of neighborhood disadvantage. *Journal of Abnormal Child Psychology, 36,* 887–901.

Vandewater, E. A., & Bickham, D. S. (2004). The impact of educational television on young children's reading in the context of family stress. *Applied Developmental Psychology, 25,* 717–728.

Vandewater, E. A., Bickham, D. S., Lee, J. H., Cummings, H. M., Wartella, E. A., & Rideout, V. J. (2005). When the television is always on: Heavy television exposure and young children's development. *American Behavioral Scientist, 48,* 562–577.

Varela-Silva, M. I., Frisancho, A. R., Bogin, B., Chatkoff, D., Smith, P. K., Dickinson, F., & Winham, D. (2007). Behavioral, environmental, metabolic, and intergenerational components of early life undernutrition leading to later obesity in developing nations and in minority groups in the U.S.A. *Collegium Antropologicum, 31,* 39–46.

Varendi, H., & Porter, R. H. (2001). Breast odour as the only maternal stimulus elicits crawling toward the odour source. *Acta Paediactrica, 90,* 372–375.

Varnhagen, C. (2007). Children and the Internet. In J. Gackenbach (Ed.), *Psychology and the Internet* (2nd ed., pp. 37–54). Amsterdam: Elsevier.

Vartanian, L. R. (1997). Separation–individuation, social support, and adolescent egocentrism: An exploratory study. *Journal of Early Adolescence, 17,* 245–270.

Vartanian, L. R., & Powlishta, K. K. (1996). A longitudinal examination of the social-cognitive foundations of adolescent egocentrism. *Journal of Early Adolescence, 16,* 157–178.

Vaughn, B. E., & Bost, K. K. (1999). Attachment and temperament: Redundant, independent, or interacting influences on interpersonal adaptation and personality development? In J. Cassidy & P. Shaver (Eds.), *Handbook of attachment: Theory, research, and clinical applications* (pp. 265–286). New York: Guilford.

Vaughn, B. E., Colvin, T. N., Azria, M. R., Caya, L., & Krzysik, L. (2001). Dyadic analyses of friendship in a sample of preschool-age children attending Head Start: Correspondence between measures and implications for social competence. *Child Development, 72,* 862–878.

Vaughn, B. E., Kopp, C. B., & Krakow, J. B. (1984). The emergence and consolidation of self-control from eighteen to thirty months of age: Normative trends and individual differences. *Child Development, 55,* 990–1004.

Vaughn, B. E., Vollenweider, M., Bost, K. K., Azria-Evans, M. R., & Snider, J. B. (2003). Negative interactions and social competence for preschool children in two samples: Reconsidering the interpretation of aggressive behavior for young children. *Merrill-Palmer Quarterly, 49,* 245–278.

Vazsonyi, A. T., Hibbert, J. R., & Snider, J. B. (2003). Exotic enterprise no more? Adolescent reports of family and parenting processes from youth in four countries. *Journal of Research on Adolescence, 13,* 129–160.

Velderman, M. K., Bakermans-Kranenburg, M. J., Juffer, F., & van IJzendoorn, M. H. (2006). Effects of attachment-based interventions on maternal sensitivity and infant attachment: Differential susceptibility of highly reactive infants. *Journal of Family Psychology, 20,* 266–274.

Velleman, R. D. B., Templeton, L. J., & Copello, A. G. (2005). The role of the family in preventing and intervening with substance use and misuse: A comprehensive review of family interventions, with a focus on young people. *Drug and Alcohol Review, 24,* 93–109.

Venet, M., & Markovits, H. (2001). Understanding uncertainty with abstract conditional premises. *Merrill-Palmer Quarterly, 47,* 74–99.

Venezia, M., Messinger, D. S., Thorp, D., & Mundy, P. (2004). The development of anticipatory smiling. *Infancy, 6,* 397–406.

Veneziano, R. A. (2003). The importance of paternal warmth. *Cross-Cultural Research, 37,* 265–281.

Vereijken, B., & Adolph, K. E. (1999). Transitions in the development of locomotion. In G. J. P. Savelsbergh, H. L. J. van der Maas, & P. C. L. van Geert (Eds.), *Non-linear analyses of developmental processes* (pp. 137–149). Amsterdam: Elsevier.

Verhulst, F. C. (2008). International adoption and mental health: Long-term behavioral outcome. In M. E. Garralda & J.-P. Raynaud (Eds.), *Culture and conflict in adolescent mental health* (pp. 83–105). Lanham, MD: Jason Aronson.

Verissimo, M., & Salvaterra, F. (2006). Maternal secure-base scripts and children's attachment security in an adopted sample. *Attachment and Human Development, 8,* 261–273.

Vernon-Feagans, L., Hurley, M., & Yont, K. (2002). The effect of otitis media and daycare quality on mother/child bookreading and language use at 48 months of age. *Journal of Applied Developmental Psychology, 23,* 113–133.

Vernon-Feagans, L., Pancsofar, N., Willoughby, M., Odom, E., Quade, A., & Cox, M. (2008). Predictors of maternal language to infants during a picture book task in the home: Family SES, child characteristics and the parenting environment. *Journal of Applied Developmental Psychology, 29,* 213–226.

Vidaeff, A. C., Carroll, M. A., & Ramin, S. M. (2005). Acute hypertensive emergencies in pregnancy. *Critical Care Medicine, 33,* S307–S312.

Vinden, P. G. (1996). Jun'n Quechua children's understanding of mind. *Child Development, 67,* 1707–1716.

Vinden, P. G. (2002). Understanding minds and evidence for belief: A study of Mofu children in Cameroon. *International Journal of Behavioral Development, 26,* 445–452.

Visher, E. B., Visher, J. S., & Pasley, K. (2003). Remarriage families and stepparenting. In F. Walsh (Ed.), *Normal family processes: Growing diversity and complexity* (pp. 153–175). New York: Guilford.

Vitaro, F., Larocque, D., Janosz, M., & Tremblay, R. E. (2001). Negative social experiences and dropping out of school. *Educational Psychology, 21,* 401–415.

Vivanti, G., Nadig, A., Ozonoff, S., & Rogers, S. J. (2008). What do children with autism attend to during imitation tasks? *Journal of Experimental Psychology, 101,* 186–205.

Vogel, D. A., Lake, M. A., Evans, S., & Karraker, H. (1991). Children's and adults' sex-stereotyped perceptions of infants. *Sex Roles, 24,* 605–616.

Vohr, B., Jodoin-Krauzyk, J., Tucker, R., Johnson, M. J., Topol, D., & Ahlgren, M. (2008). Early language outcomes of early-identified infants with permanent hearing loss at 12 to 16 months of age. *Pediatrics, 122,* 535–544.

Volling, B. L. (2001). Early attachment relationships as predictors of preschool children's emotion regulation with a distressed sibling. *Early Education and Development, 12,* 185–207.

Volling, B. L., & Belsky, J. (1992). Contribution of mother–child and father–child relationships to the quality of sibling interaction: A longitudinal study. *Child Development, 63,* 1209–1222.

Volling, B. L., Mahoney, A., & Rauer, A. J. (2009). Sanctification of parenting, moral socialization, and young children's conscience development. *Psychology of Religion and Spirituality, 1,* 53–68.

Volling, B. L., McElwain, N. L., & Miller, A. L. (2002). Emotion regulation in context: The jealousy complex between young siblings and its relations with child and family characteristics. *Child Development, 73,* 581–600.

von Hofsten, C. (1993). Prospective control: A basic aspect of action development. *Human Development, 36,* 253–270.

von Hofsten, C. (2004). An action perspective on motor development. *Trends in Cognitive Sciences, 8,* 266–272.

von Hofsten, C., & Rosander, K. (1998). The establishment of gaze control in early infancy. In S. Simion & G. Butterworth (Eds.), *The development of sensory, motor and cognitive capacities in early infancy* (pp. 49–66). Hove, UK: Psychology Press.

Vondra, J. I., Hommerding, K. D., & Shaw, D. S. (1999). Stability and change in infant attachment in a low-income sample. In J. I Vondra & D. Barnett (Eds.), *Atypical attachment in infancy and early childhood among children at developmental risk. Monographs of the Society for Research in Child Development, 64*(3, Serial No. 258), pp. 119–144.

Vondra, J. I., Shaw, D. S., Searingen, L., Cohen, M., & Owens, E. B. (2001). Attachment stability and emotional and behavioral regulation from infancy to preschool age. *Development and Psychopathology, 13,* 13–33.

Vouloumanos, A., & Werker, J. F. (2004). Tuned to the signal: The privileged status of speech for young infants. *Developmental Science, 7,* 270–276.

Voyer, D., Voyer, S., & Bryden, M. P. (1995). Magnitude of sex differences in spatial abilities: A meta-analysis and consideration of critical variables. *Psychological Bulletin, 117,* 250–270.

Vuoksimaa, E., Koskenvuo, M., Rose, R. J., & Kaprio, J. (2009). Origins of handedness: A nationwide study of 30,1671 adults. *Neuropsychologia, 47,* 1294–1301.

Vurpillot, E. (1968). The development of scanning strategies and their relation to visual differentiation. *Journal of Experimental Psychology, 6,* 632–650.

Vygotsky, L. S. (1978). *Mind in society: The development of higher psychological processes.* Cambridge, MA: Harvard University Press. (Original works published 1930, 1933, and 1935)

Vygotsky, L. S. (1987). Thinking and speech. In R. W. Rieber, A. S. Carton (Eds.), & N. Minick (Trans.), *The collected works of L. S. Vygotsky: Vol. 1. Problems of general psychology* (pp. 37–285). New York: Plenum. (Original work published 1934)

W

Wachs, T. D., & Bates, J. E. (2001). Temperament. In G. Bremner & A. Fogel (Eds.), *Blackwell handbook of infant development* (pp. 465–501). Oxford, UK: Blackwell.

Waddington, C. H. (1957). *The strategy of the genes.* London: Allen & Unwin.

Wadsworth, M. E., & Santiago, C. D. (2008). Risk and resiliency processes in ethnically diverse families in poverty. *Journal of Family Psychology, 22,* 399–410.

Wagenaar, K., Huisman, J., Cohen-Kettenis, P. T., & Delemarre-van de Waal, H. A. (2008). An overview of studies on early development, cognition, and psychosocial well-being in children born after in vitro fertilization. *Journal of Developmental and Behavioral Pediatrics, 29,* 219–230.

Wahlsten, D. (1994). The intelligence of heritability. *Canadian Psychology, 35,* 244–259.

Wai, J., Cacchio, M., Putallaz, M., & Makel, M. C. (2010). Sex differences in the right tail of cognitive abilities: A 30-year examination. *Intelligence, 38,* 412–423.

Wainryb, C. (1997). The mismeasure of diversity: Reflections on the study of cross-cultural differences. In H. D. Saltzstein (Ed.), *New directions for child development* (No. 76, pp. 51–65). San Francisco: Jossey-Bass.

Wainryb, C., & Ford, S. (1998). Young children's evaluations of acts based on beliefs different from their own. *Merrill-Palmer Quarterly, 44,* 484–503.

Wakeley, A., Rivera, S., & Langer, J. (2000). Can young infants add and subtract? *Child Development, 71,* 1477–1720.

Walberg, H. J. (1986). Synthesis of research on teaching. In M. C. Wittrock (Ed.), *Handbook of research on teaching* (3rd ed., pp. 214–229). New York: Macmillan.

Waldenström, U. (1999). Experience of labor and birth in 1111 women. *Journal of Psychosomatic Research, 47,* 471–482.

Waldfogel, J. (2001). International policies toward parental leave and child care. *Future of Children 11,* 52–61.

Waldinger, R. J., Diguer, L., Guastella, F., Lefebvre, R., Allen, J. P., & Luborsky, L. (2002). The same old song? Stability and change in relationship schemas from adolescence to young adulthood. *Journal of Youth and Adolescence, 31,* 17–44.

Waldman, I. D., Rowe, D. C., Abramowitz, A., Kozel, S. T., Mohr, J. H., & Sherman, S. L. (1998). Association and linkage of the dopamine transporter gene and attention-deficit hyperactivity disorder in children: Heterogeneity owing to diagnostic subtype and severity. *American Journal of Human Genetics, 63,* 1767–1776.

Waldrip, A. M. (2008). With a little help from your friends: The importance of high-quality friendships on early adolescent adjustment. *Social Development, 17,* 832–852.

Walenski, M., Tager-Flusberg, H., & Ullman, M. T. (2006). Language in autism. In S. O. Moldin & J. L. R. Rubenstein (Eds.), *Understanding autism: From basic neuroscience to treatment* (pp. 175–203). Boca Raton, FL: CRC Press.

Walker, L. J. (1995). Sexism in Kohlberg's moral psychology? In W. M. Kurtines & J. L. Gewirtz (Eds.), *Moral development: An introduction* (pp. 83–107). Boston: Allyn and Bacon.

Walker, L. J. (2004). Progress and prospects in the psychology of moral development. *Merrill-Palmer Quarterly, 50,* 546–557.

Walker, L. J. (2006). Gender and morality. In M. Killen & J. G. Smetana (Eds.), *Handbook of moral development* (pp. 93–118). Philadelphia: Erlbaum.

Walker, L. J., & Taylor, J. H. (1991). Family interactions and the development of moral reasoning. *Child Development, 62,* 264–283.

Walker, L. J., & Taylor, J. H. (1991b). Stage transitions in moral reasoning: A longitudinal study of developmental processes. *Developmental Psychology, 27,* 330–337.

Walker-Andrews, A. S. (1997). Infants' perception of expressive behaviors: Differentiation of multimodal information. *Psychological Bulletin, 121,* 437–456.

Wall, J., Covell, K., & MacIntyre, P. D. (1999). Implications of social supports for adolescents' education and career aspirations. *Canadian Journal of Behavioural Science, 31,* 63–71.

Wall, M., & Côté, J. (2007). Developmental activities that lead to dropout and investment in sport. *Physical Education and Sport Pedagogy, 12,* 77–87.

Wallace, J. M., Jr., Bachman, J. G., O'Malley, P. M., Schulenberg, J. E., Cooper, S. M., & Johnston, L. D. (2003). Gender and ethnic differences in smoking, drinking, and illicit drug use among American 8th, 10th, and 12th grade students, 1976–2000. *Addiction, 98,* 225–234.

Walton, G. E., Armstrong, E. S., & Bower, T. G. R. (1998). Newborns learn to identify a face in eight-tenths of a second? *Developmental Science, 1,* 79–84.

Wang, Q. (2004). The emergence of cultural self-constructs: Autobiographical memory and self-description in European American and Chinese children. *Developmental Psychology, 40,* 3–15.

Wang, Q. (2006a). Earliest recollections of self and others in European American and Taiwanese young adults. *Psychological Science, 17,* 708–714.

Wang, Q. (2006b). Relations of maternal style and child self-concept to autobiographical memories in Chinese, Chinese immigrant, and European American 3-year-olds. *Child Development, 77,* 1794–1809.

Wang, Q., Pomerantz, E. M., & Chen, H. (2007). The role of parents' control in early adolescents' psychological functioning: A longitudinal investigation in the United States and China. *Child Development, 78,* 1592–1610.

Wang, S., Baillargeon, R., & Paterson, S. (2005). Detecting continuity violations in infancy: A new account and new evidence from covering and tube effects. *Cognition, 95,* 129–173.

Wark, G. R., & Krebs, D. L. (1996). Gender and dilemma differences in real-life moral judgment. *Developmental Psychology, 32,* 220–230.

Warner, L. A., Valdez, A., Vega, W. A., de la Rosa, M., Turner, R. J., & Canino, G. (2006). Hispanic drug abuse in an evolving cultural context: An agenda for research. *Drug and Alcohol Dependence, 84*(Suppl. 1), S8–S16.

Warnock, F., & Sandrin, D. (2004). Comprehensive description of newborn distress behavior in response to acute pain (newborn male circumcision). *Pain, 107,* 242–255.

Warren, A. R., & Tate, C. S. (1992). Egocentrism in children's telephone conversations. In R. M. Diaz & L. E. Berk (Eds.), *Private speech: From social interaction to self-regulation* (pp. 245–264). Hillsdale, NJ: Erlbaum.

Warren, D. H. (1994). *Blindness and children: An individual difference approach.* New York: Cambridge University Press.

Warren, S. L., & Simmens, S. J. (2005). Predicting toddler anxiety/depressive symptoms: Effects of caregiver sensitivity on temperamentally vulnerable children. *Infant Mental Health Journal, 26,* 40–55.

Wasik, B. A., & Bond, M. A. (2001). Beyond the pages of a book: Interactive book reading and language development in preschool classrooms. *Journal of Educational Psychology, 93,* 243–250.

Wasserman, E. A., & Rovee-Collier, C. (2001). Pick the flowers and mind your As and 2s! Categorization by pigeons and infants. In M. E. Carroll & J. B. Overmier (Eds.), *Animal research and human health: Advancing human welfare through behavioral science* (pp. 263–279). Washington, DC: American Psychological Association.

Watamura, S. E., Donzella, B., Alwin, J., & Gunnar, M. R. (2003). Morning-to-afternoon increases in cortisol concentrations for infants and toddlers at child care: Age differences and behavioral correlates. *Child Development, 74,* 1006–1020.

Waters, E., & Cummings, E. M. (2000). A secure base from which to explore close relationships. *Child Development, 71,* 164–172.

Waters, E., Merrick, S., Treboux, D., Crowell, J., & Albersheim, L. (2000). Attachment security in infancy and early adulthood: A twenty-year longitudinal study. *Child Development, 71,* 684–689.

Waters, E., Vaughn, B. E., Posada, G., & Kondo-Ikemura, K. (Eds.). (1995). Caregiving, cultural, and cognitive perspectives on secure-base behavior and working models: New growing points of attachment theory and research. *Monographs of the Society for Research in Child Development, 60*(2–3, Serial No. 244).

Watkins, W. E., & Pollitt, E. (1998). Iron deficiency and cognition among school-age children. In S. G. McGregor (Ed.), *Recent advances in research on the effects of health and nutrition on children's development and school achievement in the Third World.* Washington, DC: Pan American Health Organization.

Watson, A. C., Nixon, C. L., Wilson, A., & Capage, L. (1999). Social interaction skills and theory of mind in young children. *Developmental Psychology, 35,* 386–391.

Watson, D. J. (1989). Defining and describing whole language. *Elementary School Journal, 90,* 129–141.

Watson, J. B., & Raynor, R. (1920). Conditioned emotional reactions. *Journal of Experimental Psychology, 3,* 1–14.

Watson, M. (1990). Aspects of self development as reflected in children's role playing. In D. Cicchetti & M. Beeghly (Eds.), *The self in transition: Infancy to childhood* (pp. 281–307). Chicago: University of Chicago Press.

Watts-English, T., Fortson, B. L., Gibler, N., Hooper, S. R., & De Bellis, M. D. (2006). The psychobiology of maltreatment in childhood. *Journal of Social Issues, 62,* 717–736.

Waxman, S. R. (2003). Links between object categorization and naming: Origins and emergence in human infants. In D. H. Rakison & L. M. Oakes (Eds.), *Early category and concept development: Making sense of the blooming, buzzing confusion* (pp. 193–209). New York: Oxford University Press.

Waxman, S. R., & Lidz, J. L. (2006). Early word learning. In D. Kuhn & R. Siegler (Eds.), *Handbook of child psychology: Vol. 2. Cognition, perception, and language* (6th ed., pp. 464–510). Hoboken, NJ: Wiley.

Waxman, S. R., & Senghas, A. (1992). Relations among word meanings in early lexical development. *Developmental Psychology, 28,* 862–873.

Weaver, A., & Dobson, P. (2007). Nocturnal enuresis in children. *Journal of Family Health Care, 17,* 159–161.

Webb, N. M., Franke, M. L., Ing, M., Chan, A., De, T., Freund, D., & Battey, D. (2008). The role of teacher instructional practices in student collaboration. *Contemporary Educational Psychology, 33,* 360–381.

Webb, N. M., Nemer, K. M., & Chizhik, A. W. (1998). Equity issues in collaborative group assessment: Group composition and performance. *American Educational Research Journal, 35,* 607–651.

Webb, S. J., Monk, C. S., & Nelson, C. A. (2001). Mechanisms of postnatal neurobiological development: Implications for human development. *Developmental Neuropsychology, 19,* 147–171.

Weber, C., Hahne, A., Friedrich, M., & Friederici, A. (2004). Discrimination of word stress in early infant perception: Electrophysiological evidence. *Cognitive Brain Research, 18,* 149–161.

Wechsler, D. (2002). *WPPSI-III: Wechsler Preschool and Primary Scale of Intelligence* (3rd ed.). San Antonio, TX: Psychological Corporation.

Wechsler, D. (2003). *WISC-IV: Wechsler Intelligence Scale for Children* (4th ed.). San Antonio, TX: Psychological Corporation.

Weems, C. F., & Costa, N. M. (2005). Developmental differences in the expression of childhood anxiety symptoms and fears. *Journal of the American Academy of Child and Adolescent Psychiatry, 44,* 656–663.

Wehren, A., DeLisi, R., & Arnold, M. (1981). The development of noun definition. *Journal of Child Language, 8,* 165–175.

Weikart, D. P. (1998). Changing early childhood development through educational intervention. *Preventive Medicine, 27,* 233–237.

Weinberg, M. K., & Tronick, E. Z. (1994). Beyond the face: An empirical study of infant affective configurations of facial, vocal, gestural, and regulatory behaviors. *Child Development, 65,* 1503–1515.

Weiner, A. (1988). *The Trobrianders of Papua New Guinea.* New York: Holt.

Weiner, J., & Tardif, C. (2004). Social and emotional functioning of children with learning disabilities: Does special education placement make a difference? *Learning Disabilities Research and Practice, 19,* 20–32.

Weinert, F. E., & Hany, E. A. (2003). The stability of individual differences in intellectual development: Empirical evidence, theoretical problems, and new research questions. In R. J. Sternberg & J. Lautrey (Eds.), *Models of intelligence: International perspectives* (pp. 169–181). Washington, DC: American Psychological Association.

Weinert, F. E., & Schneider, W. (Eds.). (1999). *Individual development from 3 to 12: Findings from the Munich Longitudinal Study.* Cambridge, UK: Cambridge University Press.

Weinfield, N. S., Sroufe, L. A., & Egeland, B. (2000). Attachment from infancy to early adulthood in a high-risk sample: Continuity, discontinuity, and their correlates. *Child Development, 71,* 695–702.

Weinfield, N. S., Whaley, G. J. L., & Egeland, B. (2004). Continuity, discontinuity, and coherence in attachment from infancy to late adolescence: Sequelae of organization and disorganization. *Attachment and Human Development, 6,* 73–97.

Weinstein, R. S. (2002). *Reaching higher: the power of expectations in schooling.* Cambridge, MA: Harvard University Press.

Weinstock, M. (2008). The long-term behavioural consequences of prenatal stress. *Neuroscience and Biobehavioral Reviews, 32,* 1073–1086.

Weisfield, G. (1997). Puberty rites as clues to the nature of human adolescence. *Cross-Cultural Research, 31,* 27–54.

Weisner, T. S., & Wilson-Mitchell, J. E. (1990). Nonconventional family life-styles and sex typing in six-year-olds. *Child Development, 61,* 1915–1933.

Weiss, K. M. (2005). Cryptic causation of human disease: Reading between the germ lines. *Trends in Genetics, 21,* 82–88.

Weisz, A. N., & Black, B. M. (2002). Gender and moral reasoning: African American youths respond to dating dilemmas. *Journal of Human Behavior in the Social Environment, 6,* 17–34.

Weizman, Z. O., & Snow, C. E. (2001). Lexical output as related to children's vocabulary acquisition: Effects of sophisticated exposure and support for meaning. *Developmental Psychology, 37,* 265–279.

Wekerle, C., Wall, A.-M., Leung, E., & Trocmé, N. (2007). Cumulative stress and substantiated maltreatment: The importance of caregiver vulnerability and adult partner violence. *Child Abuse and Neglect, 31,* 427–443.

Wekerle, C., & Wolfe, D. A. (2003). Child maltreatment. In E. J. Mash & R. A. Barkley (Eds.), *Child psychopathology* (2nd ed., pp. 632–684). New York: Guilford.

Weller, E. B., Kloos, A. L., & Weller, R. A. (2006). Mood disorders. M. K. Dulcan & J. M. Wiener (Eds.), *Essentials of child and adolescent psychiatry* (pp. 267–320). Washington, DC: American Psychiatric Association.

Wellman, H. M. (1990). *The child's theory of mind.* Cambridge, MA: MIT Press.

Wellman, H. M. (2002). Understanding the psychological world: Developing a theory of mind. In U. Goswami (Ed.), *Blackwell handbook of child cognitive development* (pp. 167–187). Malden, MA: Blackwell.

Wellman, H. M., & Hickling, A. K. (1994). The mind's "I": Children's conception of the mind as an active agent. *Child Development, 65,* 1564–1580.

Wellman, H. M., Lopez-Duran, S., LaBounty, J., & Hamilton, B. (2008). Infant attention to intentional action predicts preschool theory of mind. *Developmental Psychology, 44,* 618–623.

Weng, X., Odouli, R., & Li, D.-K. (2008). Maternal caffeine consumption during pregnancy and the risk of miscarriage: A prospective cohort study. *American Journal of Obstetrics and Gynecology, 198,* 279e1–279e8.

Wentworth, N., Benson, J. B., & Haith, M. M. (2000). The development of infants' reaches for stationary and moving targets. *Child Development, 71,* 576–601.

Wentworth, N., & Haith, M. M. (1998). Infants' acquisition of spatiotemporal expectations. *Developmental Psychology, 24,* 247–257.

Wentzel, K. R., Barry, C. M., & Caldwell, K. A. (2004). Friendships in middle school: Influences on motivation and school adjustment. *Journal of Educational Psychology, 96,* 195–203.

Werkele, C., & Avgoustis, E. (2003). Child maltreatment, adolescent dating, and adolescent

dating violence. In P. Florsheim (Ed.), *Adolescent romantic relations and sexual behavior: Theory, research, and practical implications* (pp. 213–242). Mahwah, NJ: Erlbaum.

Werner, E. E. (1989, April). Children of the garden island. *Scientific American, 260(4),* 106–111.

Werner, E. E. (2001). *Journeys from childhood to midlife: Risk, resilience, and recovery.* Ithaca, NY: Cornell University Press.

Werner, E. E., & Smith, R. S. (1982). *Vulnerable but invincible: A study of resilient children.* New York: McGraw-Hill.

Werner, E. E., & Smith, R. S. (1992). *Overcoming the odds: High risk children from birth to adulthood.* Ithaca, NY: Cornell University Press.

Werner, E. E., & Smith, R. S. (2001). *Journeys from childhood to midlife: Risk, resilience, and recovery.* Ithaca, NY: Cornell University Press.

Werner, N. E., & Crick, N. R. (2004). Maladaptive peer relationships and the development of relational and physical aggression during middle childhood. *Social Development, 13,* 495–514.

Wesson, D. E., Stephens, D., Lam, K., Parsons, D., Spence, L., & Parkin, P. C. (2008). Trends in pediatric and adult bicycling deaths before and after passage of a bicycle helmet law. *Pediatrics, 122,* 605–610.

Westermann, G., Mareschal, D., Johnson, M. H., Sirois, S., Spratling, M. W., & Michael, S. C. (2007). Neuroconstructivism. *Developmental Science, 10,* 75-83.

Wexler, I. D., Branski, D., & Kerem, E. (2006). War and children. *Journal of the American Medical Association, 296,* 579–581.

Weyermann, M., Rothenbacher, D., & Brenner, H. (2006). Duration of breast-feeding and risk of overweight in childhood: A prospective birth cohort study from Germany. *International Journal of Obesity, 30,* 1281–1287.

Whalen, P. J., Davis, F. C., Oler, J. A., Kim, H., Kim, M. J., & Neta, M., (2009). Human amygdala responses to facial expressions of emotion. In P. J. Whalen & E. A. Phelps (Eds.), *The human amygdala* (pp. 265–288). New York: Guilford.

Wheeler, W. (2002). Youth leadership for development: civic activism as a component of youth development programming and a strategy for strengthening civil society. In R. M. Lerner, F. Jacobs, & D. Wertlieb (Eds.), *Handbook of applied developmental science: Vol. 2* (pp. 491–506). Thousand Oaks, CA: Sage.

Whincup, P. H., Kaye, S. G., Owen, C. G., Huxley, R., Cook, D. G., Anazawa, S., et al. (2008). Birth weight and risk of type 2 diabetes: A systematic review. *Journal of the American Medical Association, 24,* 2886–2897.

Whipple, E. E. (2006). Child abuse and neglect: Consequences of physical, sexual, and emotional abuse of children. In H. E. Fitzgerald, B. M. Lester, & B. Zuckerman (Eds.), *The crisis in youth mental health: Vol 1. Childhood disorders* (pp. 205–229). Westport, CT: Praeger.

White, B., & Held, R. (1966). Plasticity of sensorimotor development in the human infant. In J. F. Rosenblith & W. Allinsmith (Eds.), *The causes of behavior* (pp. 60–70). Boston: Allyn and Bacon.

White, M. A., Wilson, M. E., Elander, G., & Persson, B. (1999). The Swedish family: Transition to parenthood. *Scandinavian Journal of Caring Sciences, 13,* 171–176.

Whitehurst, G. J., & Lonigan, C. J. (1998). Child development and emergent literacy. *Child Development, 69,* 848–872.

Whiteman, S. D., & Loken, E. (2006). Comparing analytic techniques to classify dyadic relationships: An example using siblings. *Journal of Marriage and Family, 68,* 1370–1382.

Whitesell, N. R., Mitchell, C. M., Spicer, P., and the Voices of Indian Teens Project Team. (2009). A longitudinal study of self-esteem, cultural identity, and academic success among American Indian adolescents. *Cultural Diversity and Ethnic Minority Psychology, 15,* 38–50.

Whiteside-Mansell, L., Bradley, R. H., Owen, M. T., Randolph, S. M., & Cauce, A. M. (2003). Parenting

and children's behavior at 36 months: Equivalence between African-American and European-American mother–child dyads. *Parenting: Science and Practice, 3,* 197–234.

Whiting, B., & Edwards, C. P. (1988). *Children in different worlds.* Cambridge, MA: Harvard University Press.

Whitington, V., & Ward, C. (1999). Intersubjectivity in caregiver–child communication. In L. E. Berk (Ed.), *Landscapes of development* (pp. 109– 120). Belmont, CA: Wadsworth.

Whitlock, J. L., Powers, J. L., & Eckenrode, J. (2006). The virtual cutting edge: The Internet and adolescent self-injury. *Developmental Psychology, 42,* 407–417.

Wichmann, C., Coplan, R. J., & Daniels, T. (2004). The social cognitions of socially withdrawn children. *Social Development, 13,* 377–392.

Wichstrøm, L. (2006). Sexual orientation as a risk factor for bulimic symptoms. *International Journal of Eating Disorders, 39,* 448–453.

Wigfield, A., Battle, A., Keller, L. B., & Eccles, J. S. (2002). Sex differences in motivation, self-concept, career aspiration, and career choice: Implications for cognitive development. In A. McGillicudy-De Lisi & R. De Lisi (Eds.), *Biology, society, and behavior: The development of sex differences in cognition* (pp. 93–124). Westport, CT: Ablex.

Wigfield, A., Eccles, J. S., Schiefele, U., Roeser, R. W., & Davis-Kean, P. (2006). Development of achievement motivation. In N. Eisenberg (Ed.), *Handbook of child psychology: Vol. 3. Social, emotional, and personality development* (6th ed., pp. 933–1002). Hoboken, NJ: Wiley.

Wigfield, A., Eccles, J. S., Yoon, K. S., Harold, R. D., Arbreton, A. J., Freedman-Doan, C., & Blumenfeld, P. C. (1997). Changes in children's competence beliefs and subjective task values across the elementary school years: A three-year study. *Journal of Educational Psychology, 89,* 451–469.

Wilcox, A. J., Weinberg, C. R., & Baird, D. D. (1995). Timing of sexual intercourse in relation to ovulation: Effects on the probability of conception, survival of the pregnancy, and sex of the baby. *New England Journal of Medicine, 333,* 1517–1519.

Wilcox, T., & Woods, R. (2009). Experience primes infants to individuate objects. In A. Woodward & A. Needham (Eds.), *Learning and the infant mind* (pp. 117–143). New York: Oxford University Press.

Wilkinson, K., Ross, E., & Diamond, A. (2003). Fast mapping of multiple words: Insights into when "the information provided" does and does not equal "the information perceived." *Applied Developmental Psychology, 24,* 739–762.

Wilkinson, R. B. (2004). The role of parental and peer attachment in the psychological health and self-esteem of adolescents. *Journal of Youth and Adolescence, 33,* 479–493.

Willatts, P. (1999). Development of means–end behavior in young infants: Pulling a support to retrieve a distant object. *Developmental Psychology, 35,* 651–667.

Williams, C. (2006). Dilemmas in fetal medicine: Premature application of technology or responding to women's choice? *Sociology of Health and Illness, 28,* 1–20.

Williams, G. R. (2008). Neurodevelopmental and neurophysiological actions of thyroid hormone. *Journal of Neuroendocrinology, 20,* 784–794.

Williams, J. M., & Currie, C. (2000). Self-esteem and physical development in early adolescence: Pubertal timing and body image. *Journal of Early Adolescence, 20,* 129–149.

Williams, K., & Dunne-Bryant, A. (2006). Divorce and adult psychological well-being: Clarifying the role of gender and age. *Journal of Marriage and Family, 68,* 1178–1196.

Williams, K., Haywood, K. I., & Painter, M. (1996). Environmental versus biological influences on gender differences in the overarm throw for force: Dominant and nondominant arm throws. *Women in Sport and Physical Activity Journal, 5,* 29–48.

Williams, P. E., Weiss, L. G., & Rolfhus, E. (2003). *WISC-IV: Theoretical model and test blueprint*. San Antonio, TX: Psychological Corporation.

Williams, T. S., Connolly, J., Pepler, D., Craig, W., & Laporte, L. (2008). Risk models of dating aggression across different adolescent relationships: A developmental psychopathology approach. *Journal of Consulting and Clinical Psychology, 76*, 622–632.

Williamson, J., Softas-Nall, B., & Miller, J. (2003). Grandmothers raising grandchildren: An exploration of their experiences and emotions. *Counseling and Therapy for Couples with Families, 11*, 23–32.

Willinger, M., Ko, C. W., Hoffman, H. J., Kessler, R. C., & Corwin, M. J. (2003). Trends in infant bed sharing in the United States, 1993–2000: The National Infant Sleep Position Study. *Archives of Pediatric and Adolescent Medicine, 157*, 43–49.

Willoughby, J., Kupersmidt, J. B., & Bryant, D. (2001). Overt and covert dimensions of antisocial behavior. *Journal of Abnormal Child Psychology, 29*, 177–187.

Wilson, E. K., Dalberth, B. T., Koo, H. P., & Gard, J. C. (2010). Parents' perspectives on talking to preteenage children about sex. *Perspectives on Sexual and Reproductive Health, 42*, 56–63.

Winkler, I., Háden, G. P., Ladinig, O., Sziller, I., & Honing, H. (2009). Newborn infants detect the beat in music. *Proceedings of the National Academy of Sciences, 106*, 2468–2471.

Winner, E. (1986, August). Where pelicans kiss seals. *Psychology Today, 20*(8), 25–35.

Winner, E. (1988). *The point of words: Children's understanding of metaphor and irony*. Cambridge, MA: Harvard University Press.

Winner, E. (1996). *Gifted children: Myths and realities*. New York: Basic Books.

Winner, E. (1997). Exceptionally high intelligence and schooling. *American Psychologist, 52*, 1070–1081.

Winner, E. (2000). The origins and ends of giftedness. *American Psychologist, 55*, 159–169.

Winner, E. (2003). Creativity and talent. In M. H. Bornstein, L. Davidson, C. L. M. Keyes, K. A. Moore, & the Center for Child Well-Being, (Eds.), *Well-being: Positive development across the life course* (pp. 371–380). Mahwah, NJ: Erlbaum.

Winsler, A. (2009). Still talking to ourselves after all these years: A review of current research on private speech. In A. Winsler, C. Fernyhough, & I. Montero (Eds.), *Private speech, executive functioning, and the development of self-regulation*. New York: Cambridge University Press.

Winsler, A., Abar, B., Feder, M. A., Rubio, D. A., & Schunn, C. D. (2007). Private speech and executive functioning among high functioning children with autism spectrum disorders. *Journal of Autism and Developmental Disorders, Online First™*.

Winsler, A., Fernyhough, C., & Montero, I. (2009). *Private speech, executive functioning, and the development of verbal self-regulation*. New York: Cambridge University Press.

Winsler, A., Naglieri, J., & Manfra, L. (2006). Children's search strategies and accompanying verbal and motor strategic behavior: Developmental trends and relations with task performance among children age 5 to 17. *Cognitive Development, 21*, 232–248.

Wiseman, F. K., Alford, K. A., Tybulewicz, V. L. J., & Fisher, E. M. C. (2009). Down syndrome—recent progress and future prospects. *Human Molecular Genetics, 18*, R75–R83.

Wissink, I. B., Deković, M., & Meijer, A. M. (2006). Parenting behavior, quality of the parent–adolescent relationship, and adolescent functioning in four ethnic groups. *Journal of Early Adolescence, 26*, 133–159.

Witherington, D. C. (2005). The development of prospective grasping control between 5 and 7 months: A longitudinal study. *Infancy, 7*, 143–161.

Witherington, D. C., Campos, J. J., & Hertenstein, M. J. (2001). Principles of emotion and its development in infancy. In G. Bremner & A. Fogel (Eds.), *Blackwell handbook of infant development* (pp. 427–464). Malden, MA: Blackwell.

Wolak, J., Finkelhor, D., Mitchell, K. J., & Ybarra, M. L. (2008). Online "predators" and their victims: Myths, realities, and implications for prevention and treatment. *American Psychologist, 63*, 111–128.

Wolak, J., Mitchell, K. J., & Finkelhor, D. (2003). Escaping or connecting? Characteristics of youth who form close online relationships. *Journal of Adolescence, 26*, 105–119.

Wolchik, S. A., Sandler, I. N., Millsap, R. E., Plummer, B. A., Greene, S. M., Anderson, E. R., et al. (2002). Six-year follow-up of preventive interventions for children of divorce: A randomized controlled trial. *Journal of the American Medical Association, 288*, 1874–1881.

Wolchik, S. A., Wilcox, K. L., Tein, J.-Y., & Sandler, I. N. (2000). Maternal acceptance and consistency of discipline as buffers of divorce stressors on children's psychological adjustment problems. *Journal of Abnormal Child Psychology, 28*, 87–102.

Wolf, A. W., Jimenez, E., & Lozoff, B. (2003). Effects of iron therapy on infant blood lead levels. *Journal of Pediatrics, 143*, 789–795.

Wolfe, D. A. (2005). *Child abuse* (2nd ed.) Thousand Oaks, CA: Sage.

Wolfe, D. A., Scott, K., Wekerle, C., & Pittman, A. (2001). Child maltreatment: Risk of adjustment problems and dating violence in adolescence. *Journal of the American Academy of Child and Adolescent Psychiatry, 40*, 282–289.

Wolfe, V. V. (2006). Child sexual abuse. In E. J. Mash & R. A. Barkley (Eds.), *Treatment of childhood disorders* (3rd ed., pp. 647–727). New York: Guilford.

Wolff, P. H. (1966). The causes, controls and organization of behavior in the neonate. *Psychological Issues, 5*(1, Serial No. 17).

Wolff, P. H., & Fesseha, G. (1999). The orphans of Eritrea: A five-year follow-up study. *Journal of Child Psychology and Psychiatry and Allied Disciplines, 40*, 1231–1237.

Wolfinger, N. H. (2000). Beyond the intergenerational transmission of divorce: Do people replicate the patterns of marital instability they grew up with? *Journal of Family Issues, 21*, 1061–1086.

Wong, C. A., Eccles, J. S., & Sameroff, A. (2003). The influence of ethnic discrimination and ethnic identification on African American adolescents' school and socioemotional adjustment. *Journal of Personality, 71*, 1197–1232.

Wong, M. M., Nigg, J. T., Zucker, R. A., Puttler, L. I., Fitzgerald, H. E., Jester, J. M., Glass, J. M., & Adams, K. (2006). Behavioral control and resiliency in the onset of alcohol and illicit drug use: A prospective study from preschool to adolescence. *Child Development, 77*, 1016–1033.

Wood, E., Desmarais, S., & Gugula, S. (2002). The impact of parenting experience on gender stereotyped toy play of children. *Sex Roles, 47*, 39–49.

Wood, J. J., Emmerson, N. A., & Cowan, P. A. (2004). Is early attachment security carried forward into relationships with preschool peers? *British Journal of Developmental Psychology, 22*, 245–253.

Woodward, A. (2009). Infants' grasp of others' intentions. *Current Directions in Psychological Science, 18*, 53–57.

Woodward, A. L., & Markman, E. M. (1998). Early word learning. In D. Kuhn & R. S. Siegler (Eds.), *Handbook of child psychology: Vol. 2. Cognition, perception, and language* (5th ed., pp. 371–420). New York: Wiley.

Woodward, J., & Ono, Y. (2004). Mathematics and academic diversity in Japan. *Journal of Learning Disabilities, 37*, 74–82.

Woody-Dorning, J., & Miller, P. H. (2001). Children's individual differences in capacity: Effects on strategy production and utilization. *British Journal of Developmental Psychology, 19*, 543–571.

Woolley, J. D. (1997). Thinking about fantasy: Are children fundamentally different thinkers and believers from adults? *Child Development, 68*, 991–1011.

Woolley, J. D. (2000). The development of beliefs about direct mental–physical causality in imagination, magic, and religion. In K. S. Rosengren, C. N. Johnson, & P. L. Harris (Eds.), *Imagining the impossible* (pp. 99–129). New York: Cambridge University Press.

Woolley, J. D., Browne, C. A., & Boerger, E. A. (2006). Constraints on children's judgments of magical causality. *Journal of Cognition and Development, 7*, 253–277.

Woolley, J. D., & Cox, V. (2007). Development of beliefs about storybook reality. *Developmental Science, 10*, 681–693.

Woolley, M. E., Kol, K. L., & Bowen, G. L. (2009). The social context of school success for Latino middle school students: Direct and indirect influences of teachers, family, and friends. *Journal of Early Adolescence, 29*, 43–70.

World Cancer Research Fund/American Institute for Cancer Research. (2007). *Food, nutrition, physical activity, and the prevention of cancer: A global perspective*. Washington, DC: American Institute for Cancer Research.

World Health Organization. (2008a). *The global burden of disease: 2004*. Geneva, Switzerland: Author.

World Health Organization. (2008b). *World report on child injury prevention*. Geneva, Switzerland: Author.

World Health Organization. (2009a). *Obesity and overweight*. Retrieved from www.who.int/dietphysicalactivity/publications/facts/obesity/en/

World Health Organization. (2009b). *World health statistics, 2009*. Retrieved from www.who.int/whosis/whostat/2009/en/index.html

World Health Organization. (2010a). *Population-based prevention strategies for childhood obesity*. Geneva, Switzerland: Author.

World Health Organization. (2010b). *The World Health Organization's infant feeding recommendation*. Retrieved from www.who.int/nutrition/topics/infantfeeding_recommendation/en/index.html

Worrell, F. C., & Gardner-Kitt, D. L. (2006). The relationship between racial and ethnic identity in black adolescents: The cross-racial identity scale and the multigroup ethnic identity measure. *Identity, 6*, 293–315.

Worthy, J., Hungerford-Kresser, H., & Hampton, A. (2009). Tracking and ability grouping. In L. Christenbury, R. Bomer, & P. Smargorinsky (Eds.), *Handbook of adolescent literacy research* (pp. 220–235). New York: Guilford.

Wright, B. C. (2006). On the emergence of the discriminative mode for transitive inference. *European Journal of Cognitive Psychology, 18*, 776–800.

Wright, J. C., Huston, A. C., Murphy, K. C., St. Peters, M., Pinon, M., Scantlin, R., & Kotler, J. (2001). The relations of early television viewing to school readiness and vocabulary of children from low-income families: The Early Window Project. *Child Development, 72*, 1347–1366.

Wright, M. J., Gillespie, N. A., Luciano, M., Zhu, G., & Martin, N. G. (2008). Genetics of personality and cognition in adolescents. In J. J. Hudziak (Eds.), *Developmental psychology and wellness: Genetic and environmental influences* (pp. 85–107). Washington, DC: American Psychiatric Publishing.

Wright, M. O., & Masten, A. S. (2005). Resilience processes in development. In S. Goldstein & R. B. Brooks (Eds.), *Handbook of resilience in children* (pp. 17–37). New York: Springer.

Wright, R. O., Tsaih, S. W., Schwartz, J., Wright, R. J., & Hu, H. (2003). Associations between iron deficiency and blood lead level in a longitudinal analysis of children followed in an urban primary care clinic. *Journal of Pediatrics, 142*, 9–14.

Wrotniak, B. H., Epstein, L. H., Raluch, R. A., & Roemmich, J. N. (2004). Parent weight change as a predictor of child weight change in family-based behavioral obesity treatment. *Archives of Pediatric and Adolescent Medicine, 158*, 342–347.

Wu, G., Bazer, F. W., Cudd, T. A., Meininger, C. J., & Spencer, T. E. (2004). Maternal nutrition and fetal development. *Journal of Nutrition, 134*, 2169–2172.

Wu, L. L., Bumpass, L. L., & Musick, K. (2001). Historical and life course trajectories of nonmarital childbearing. In L. L. Wu & B. Wolfe (Eds.), *Out of wedlock: Causes and consequences of nonmarital fertility* (pp. 3–48). New York: Russell Sage Foundation.

Wu, P., Robinson, C. C., Yang, C., Hart, C. H., Olsen, S. F., Porter, C. L., Jin, S., Wo, J., & Wu, X. (2002). Similarities and differences in mothers' parenting of preschoolers in China and the United States. *International Journal of Behavioral Development, 26*, 481–491.

Wu, T., Mendola, P., & Buck, G. M. (2002). Ethnic differences in the presence of secondary sex characteristics and menarche among U.S. girls: The Third National Health and Nutrition Examination Survey, 1988–1994. *Pediatrics, 110*, 752–757.

Wulczyn, F. (2009). Epidemiological perspectives on maltreatment prevention. *Future of Children, 19*, 39–66.

Wust, S., Entringer, S., Federenko, I. S., Schlotz, W., Helhammer, D. H. (2005). Birth weight is associated with salivary cortisol responses to psychosocial stress in adult life. *Psychoneuroendocrinology, 30*, 591–598.

Wyatt, J. M., & Carlo, G. (2002). What will my parents think? Relations among adolescents' expected parental reactions, prosocial moral reasoning and prosocial and antisocial behaviors. *Journal of Adolescent Research, 17*, 646–666.

Wynn, K. (1992). Addition and subtraction by human infants. *Nature, 358*, 749–750.

Wynn, K., Bloom, P., & Chiang, W.-C. (2002). Enumeration of collective entities by 5-month-old infants. *Cognition, 83*, B55–B62.

Wynne-Edwards, K. E. (2001). Hormonal changes in mammalian fathers. *Hormones and Behavior, 40*, 139–145.

X

Xu, F., Spelke, E., & Goddard, S. (2005). Number sense in human infants. *Developmental Science, 8*, 88–101.

Xue, Y., & Meisels, S. J. (2004). Early literacy instruction and learning in kindergarten: Evidence from the Early Childhood Longitudinal Study—kindergarten classes of 1998–1999. *American Educational Research Journal, 41*, 191–229.

Y

Yale, M. E., Messinger, D. S., Cobo-Lewis, A. B., Oller, D. K., & Eilers, R. E. (1999). An event-based analysis of the coordination of early infant vocalizations and facial actions. *Developmental Psychology, 35*, 505–513.

Yan, Z. (2006). What influences children's and adolescents' understanding of the complexity of the Internet? *Developmental Psychology, 42*, 418–428.

Yang, B., Ollendick, T. H., Dong, Q., Xia, Y., & Lin, L. (1995). Only children and children with siblings in the People's Republic of China: Levels of fear, anxiety, and depression. *Child Development, 66*, 1301–1311.

Yang, C. (2008, April). *The influence of one-child policy on child rearing, family, and society in post-Mao China.* Invited address, Illinois State University.

Yang, C., Hart, C. H., Nelson, D. A., Porter, C. L., Olsen, S. F., Robinson, C. C., & Jin, S. (2003). Fathering in a Beijing Chinese sample: Associations with boys' and girls' negative emotionality and aggression. In R. D. Day & M. E. Lamb (Eds.), *Conceptualizing and measuring father involvement* (pp. 185–215). Mahwah, NJ: Erlbaum.

Yang, C.-K., & Hahn, H.-M. (2002). Cosleeping in young Korean children. *Developmental and Behavioral Pediatrics, 23*, 151–157.

Yap, M. B. H., Allen, N. B., & Ladouceur, C. D. (2008). Maternal socialization of positive affect: The impact of invalidation on adolescent emotion regulation and depressive symptomatology. *Child Development, 79*, 1415–1431.

Yarrow, M. R., Scott, P. M., & Waxler, C. Z. (1973). Learning concern for others. *Developmental Psychology, 8*, 240–260.

Yeates, K. O., Schultz, L. H., & Selman, R. L. (1991). The development of interpersonal negotiation strategies in thought and action: A social-cognitive link to behavioral adjustment and social status. *Merrill-Palmer Quarterly, 37*, 369–405.

Yeh, C. J., Kim, A. B., Pituc, S. T., & Atkins, M. (2008). Poverty, loss, and resilience: The story of Chinese immigrant youth. *Journal of Counseling Psychology, 55*, 34–48.

Yeh, H.-C., & Lempers, J. D. (2004). Perceived sibling relationships and adolescent development. *Journal of Youth and Adolescence, 33*, 133–147.

Yehuda, R., Engel, S. M., Brand, S. R., Seckl, J., Marcus, S. M., & Berkowitz, G. S. (2005). Transgenerational effects of posttraumatic stress disorder in babies of mothers exposed to the World Trade Center attacks during pregnancy. *Journal of Clinical Endocrinology and Metabolism, 90*, 4115–4118.

Yip, R., Scanlon, K., & Trowbridge, F. (1993). Trends and patterns in height and weight status of low-income U.S. children. *Critical Reviews in Food Science and Nutrition, 33*, 409–421.

Yirmiya, N., Erel, O., Shaked, M., & Solomonica-Levi, D. (1998). Meta-analyses comparing theory of mind abilities of individuals with autism, individuals with mental retardation, and normally developing individuals. *Psychological Bulletin, 124*, 283–307.

Yonas, A., Elieff, C., & Aterberry, M. E. (2002). Emergence of sensitivity to pictorial depth cues: Charting development in individual infants. *Infant Behavior and Development, 25*, 295–514.

Yonas, A., & Granrud, C. E. (2006). Infants' perception of depth from cast shadows. *Perception and Psychophysics, 68*, 154–160.

Yoshida, H., & Smith, L. B. (2003). Known and novel noun extensions: Attention at two levels of abstraction. *Child Development, 74*, 564–577.

Yoshinaga-Itano, C. (2003). Early intervention after universal neonatal hearing screening: Impact on outcomes. *Mental Retardation and Developmental Disabilities Research and Reviews, 9*, 252–266.

Young, J. F., & Mroczek, D. K. (2003). Predicting intraindividual self-concept trajectories during adolescence. *Journal of Adolescence, 26*, 589–603.

Youngblade, L. M., & Dunn, J. (1995). Individual differences in young children's pretend play with mother and sibling: Links to relationships and understanding of other people's feelings and beliefs. *Child Development, 66*, 1472–1492.

Young-Hyman, D., Tanofsky-Kraff, M., Yanovski, S. Z., Keil, M., Cohen, M. L., & Peyrot, M. (2006). Psychological status and weight-related distress in overweight or at-risk-for-overweight children. *Obesity, 14*, 2249–2258.

Youngstrom, E., Wolpaw, J. M., Kogos, J. L., Schoff, K., Ackerman, B., & Izard, C. (2000). Interpersonal problem solving in preschool and first grade: Developmental change and ecological validity. *Journal of Clinical Child Psychology, 29*, 589–602.

Youniss, J., McLellan, J., & Yates, M. (1999). Religion, community service, and identity in American youth. *Journal of Adolescence, 22*, 243–253.

Yu, R. (2002). On the reform of elementary school education in China. *Educational Exploration, 129*, 56–57.

Yuan, A. S. V., & Hamilton, H. A. (2006). Stepfather involvement and adolescent well-being: Do mothers and nonresidential fathers matter? *Journal of Family Issues, 27*, 1191–1213.

Yuill, N., & Pearson, A. (1998). The developmental bases for trait attribution: Children's understanding of traits as causal mechanisms based on desire. *Developmental Psychology, 34*, 574–586.

Yumoto, C., Jacobson, S. W., & Jacobson, J. L. (2008). Fetal substance exposure and cumulative environmental risk in an African-American cohort. *Child Development, 79*, 1761–1776.

Yunger, J. L., Carver, P. R., & Perry, D. G. (2004). Does gender identity influence children's psychological well-being? *Developmental Psychology, 40*, 572–582.

Yurgelun-Todd, D. (2007). Emotional and cognitive changes during adolescence. *Current Opinion in Neurobiology, 17*, 251–257.

Z

Zafeiriou, D. I. (2000). Plantar grasp reflex in high-risk infants during the first year of life. *Pediatric Neurology, 22*, 75–76.

Zaff, J. F., Malanchuk, O., & Eccles, J. S. (2008). Predicting positive citizenship from adolescence to young adulthood: The effects of a civic context. *Applied Developmental Science, 12*, 38–53.

Zahn-Waxler, C., Kochanska, G., Krupnick, J., & McKnew, D. (1990). Patterns of guilt in children of depressed and well mothers. *Developmental Psychology, 26*, 51–59.

Zahn-Waxler, C., Radke-Yarrow, M., & King, R. M. (1979). Child-rearing and children's prosocial initiations toward victims of distress. *Child Development, 50*, 319–330.

Zahn-Waxler, C., & Robinson, J. (1995). Empathy and guilt: Early origins of feelings of responsibility. In J. P. Tangney & K. W. Fischer (Eds.), *Self-conscious emotions* (pp. 143–173). New York: Guilford.

Zahn-Waxler, C., Schiro, K., Robinson, J. L., Emde, R. N., & Schmitz, S. (2001). Empathy and prosocial patterns in young MZ and DZ twins: Development and genetic and environmental influences. In R. N. Emde & J. K. Hewitt (Eds.), *Infancy to early childhood: Genetic and environmental influences on developmental change* (pp. 141–162). New York: Oxford University Press.

Zanetti-Daellenbach, R. A., Tschudin, S., Zhong, X. Y., Holzgreve, W., Lapaire, O., & Hösli, I. (2007). Maternal and neonatal infections and obstetrical outcome in water birth. *European Journal of Obstetrics and Gynecology and Reproductive Biology, 134*, 37–43.

Zaslow, M. J., Weinfield, N. S., Gallagher, M., Hair, E. C., Ogawa, J. R., Egeland, B., Tabors, P. O., & De Temple, J. M. (2006). Longitudinal prediction of child outcomes from differing measures of parenting in a low-income sample. *Developmental Psychology, 42*, 27–37.

Zeanah, C. H. (2000). Disturbances of attachment in young children adopted from institutions. *Journal of Developmental and Behavioral Pediatrics, 21*, 230–236.

Zelazo, N. A., Zelazo, P. R., Cohen, K. M., & Zelazo, P. D. (1993). Specificity of practice effects on elementary neuromotor patterns. *Developmental Psychology, 29*, 686–691.

Zelazo, P. D., Frye, D., & Rapus, T. (1996). An age-related dissociation between knowing rules and using them. *Cognitive Development, 11*, 37–63.

Zelazo, P. D., Muller, U., Frye, D., & Marcovitch, S. (2003). The development of executive function: Cognitive complexity and control—revised. *Monographs of the Society for Research in Child Development, 68*(3), 93–119.

Zeldin, A. L. & Pajares, F. (2000). Against the odds: Self-efficacy beliefs of women in mathematical, scientific, and technological careers. *American Educational Research Journal, 37*, 215–246.

Zeller, M. H., & Modi, A. C. (2006). Predictors of health-related quality of life in obese youth. *Obesity Research, 14*, 122–130.

Zeman, J., Shipman, K., & Suveg, C. (2002). Anger and sadness regulation: Predictions to internalizing and externalizing symptoms in children. *Journal of Clinical Child and Adolescent Psychology, 31*, 393–398.

Zeskind, P. S., & Barr, R. G. (1997). Acoustic characteristics of naturally occurring cries of infants with "colic." *Child Development, 68*, 394–403.

Zeskind, P. S., & Lester, B. M. (2001). Analysis of infant crying. In L. T. Singer & P. S. Zeskind (Eds.), *Biobehavioral assessment of the infant* (pp. 149–166). New York: Guilford.

Zhang, T.-Y., & Meaney, M. J. (2010). Epigenetics and the environmental regulation of the genome and its function. *Annual Review of Psychology, 61*, 439–466.

Zhou, M., & Bankston, C. L. (1998). *Growing up American: How Vietnamese children adapt to life in the United States.* New York: Russell Sage Foundation.

Zhou, M., & Xiong, S. (2005). The multifaceted American experiences of the children of Asian immigrants: Lessons for segmented assimilation. *Ethnic and Racial Studies, 28*, 1119–1152.

Zhou, Q., Lengua, L. J., & Wang, Y. (2009). The relations of temperament reactivity and effortful control to children's adjustment problems in China and the United States. *Developmental Psychology, 45*, 724–739.

Zhou, X., Huang, J., Wang, Z., Wang, B., Zhao, Z., Yang, L., & Zheng-zheng, Y. (2006). Parent–child interaction and children's number learning. *Early Child Development and Care, 176,* 763–775.

Zhu, L., & Liu, G. (2007). Preschool children's understanding of illness. *Acta Psychologica Sinica, 39,* 96–103.

Zielinski, D. S., & Bradshaw, C. P. (2006). Ecological influences on the sequelae of child maltreatment: A review of the literature. *Child Maltreatment, 11,* 49–62.

Zimmer-Gembeck, M. J., Siebenbruner, J., & Collins, W. A. (2001). Diverse aspects of dating: Associations with psychosocial functioning from early to middle adolescence. *Journal of Adolescence, 24,* 313–336.

Zimmerman, B. J., & Cleary, T. J. (2009). Motives to self-regulate learning: A social cognitive account. In K. R. Wenzel & A. Wigfield (Eds.), *Handbook of motivation at school* (pp. 247–264). New York: Routledge.

Zimmerman, C. (2005). *The development of scientific reasoning skills: What psychologists contribute to an understanding of elementary science learning.* Report to the National Research Council, Committee on Science Learning Kindergarten through Eighth Grade. Normal, IL: Illinois State University.

Zimmerman, C. (2007). The development of scientific thinking skills in elementary and middle school. *Developmental Review, 27,* 172–223.

Zimmerman, F. J., & Christakis, D. A. (2005). Children's television viewing and cognitive outcomes. *Archives of Pediatrics and Adolescent Medicine, 159,* 619–625.

Zimmerman, F. J., Christakis, D. A., & Meltzoff, A. N. (2007). Television and DVD/video viewing in children younger than 2 years. *Archives of Pediatrics and Adolescent Medicine, 161,* 473–479.

Zimmerman, L. K., & Stansbury, K. (2004). The influence of emotion regulation, level of shyness, and habituation on the neuroendocrine response of three-year-old children. *Psychoneuroendocrinology, 29,* 973–982.

Zimmerman, P., & Becker-Stoll, F. (2002). Stability of attachment representations during adolescence: The influence of ego-identity status. *Journal of Adolescence, 25,* 107–124.

Zins, J. E., Garcia, V. F., Tuchfarber, B. S., Clark, K. M., & Laurence, S. C. (1994). Preventing injury in children and adolescents. In R. J. Simeonsson (Ed.), *Risk, resilience, and prevention: Promoting the well-being of all children* (pp. 183–202). Baltimore: Paul H. Brookes.

Zosuls, K. M., Ruble, D. N., Tamis-LeMonda, C. S., Shrout, P. E., Bornstein, M. H., & Greulich, F. K. (2009). The acquisition of gender labels in infancy: Implications for gender-typed play. *Developmental Psychology, 45,* 688–701.

Zucker, K. J. (2006). "I'm half-boy, half-girl": Play psychotherapy and parent counseling for gender identity disorder. In R. L. Spitzer, M. B. First, J. B. W. Williams, & M. Gibbon (Eds.), *DSM-IVTR Casebook: Vol. 2. Experts tell how they treated their own patients* (pp. 322–334). Washington, DC: American Psychiatric Publishing.

Zukow-Goldring, P. (2002). Sibling caregiving. In M. H. Bornstein (Ed.), *Handbook of parenting: Vol. 3* (2nd ed., pp. 253–286). Hillsdale, NJ: Erlbaum.

Zur, O., & Gelman, R. (2004). Young children can add and subtract by predicting and checking. *Early Childhood Research Quarterly, 19,* 121–137.

Zwart, M. (2007). The Dutch system of perinatal care. *Midwifery Today with International Midwife, 81*(Spring), 46.

Italic "*n*" following page number indicates caption or note accompanying figure, illustration, or table.

Figures and tables are indicated by f and t following page numbers.